JOSEPH CONRAD

Translation of text by
HALINA CARROLL-NAJDER

J·O·S·E·P·H
C·O·N·R·A·D

A CHRONICLE   *By Zdzisław Najder*

RUTGERS UNIVERSITY PRESS

NEW BRUNSWICK, NEW JERSEY

SECOND PRINTING, 1984

Library of Congress Cataloging in Publication Data
Najder, Zdzisław.
Joseph Conrad, a chronicle.
Translation of: Życie Conrada-Korzeniowskiego.
Bibliography: p.
Includes indexes.
1. Conrad, Joseph, 1857–1924.   2. Authors, English—
20th century—Biography.   I. Title.
PR6005.04Z7844313 1983   823'.912   82-10193
ISBN 0-8135-0944-0
ISBN 0-8135-0945-9 (pbk.)

Contents

Preface

BIOGRAPHIES of writers are read for two main reasons. First, the lives of exceptional men, distinguished by their achievement, experience, and unusual personalities have always held a fascination for others. Second, readers familiar with the books of a writer want to obtain, through knowledge of his life, additional perspectives on and even keys to his work. They feel they know it as it were from the outside and hope to get an inside view of it, an intimate access to its secrets.

There are biographers who wish to satisfy primarily the latter demand, and do it not only with zest but with a consciousness of performing an important, even necessary, mission. I should say at once that I do not share their attitude. I believe the knowledge of an author's life is only rarely and rather marginally important for understanding and appreciating his work. I emphasize this general belief because I think that in fact Conrad's work is one that, to be adequately understood and appreciated, requires an inordinately large amount of background information. Exceptionally large—but cautiously applied.

In general, however, biography provides critics, scholars, students, and also (and particularly!) "ordinary" readers—and "specialists" ought not to differ too much from them in their attitudes—only with supplementary material. It lays ground for and substantiates statements and hypotheses that concern influences, participation in given trends and groups and in the intellectual and artistic life of the time, and transformation of personal experience into literary texts. In cases of "atypical" writers, who defy the prevailing artistic and intellectual pattern of their time, a biographer performs something of the function of a lexicographer. He establishes the meaning of signs used by the given author by pointing not only at his intentions but, much more important, at his cultural background and resources. The biographer's textual function does not essentially consist in explaining private allusions or subconsciously used codes but in identifying the scope within which we can define the meanings of words, images, and conventions employed.

Joseph Conrad was an English writer who grew up in other linguistic environments. His work can be seen as located in the borderland of auto-translation. This fact poses peculiar problems of interpretation. Conrad's biographer has to step in as an exegete of the text: to explain certain cultural and intellectual categories to the English-speaking reader who, while understanding the language, is not always able to decipher the implicit meanings; and to Poles who are apt to see in Conrad a Polish Romantic writer and forget about his later life, his original artistic aims, and his complex attitude toward his Polish background.

vii

Such a role of biographer as lexicographer was the main psychological stimulus in my work on this book. The project was born out of a concrete scholarly demand, not of personal predilections and interests, which are, I have to confess, quite distant from biography. The original demand was for a biography that would deal fairly extensively with the Polish aspects of Conrad's life, break away from the traditional treatment of his memories and "autobiographical" pieces as reports on what actually happened, and also analyze his opinions—philosophical, social, political, and aesthetic—as expressed outside his fiction. Such was the situation in 1957. Jocelyn Baines, author of the best biography of Conrad so far (1960), performed the second task to a large extent; the first only partly (relying on my chapter about Conrad's Polish years, published three years earlier); the third he carried out only occasionally, without differentiating between opinions expressed discursively and those embodied in the content of Conrad's works.

Both Baines's biography and the life of Conrad by Jean-Aubry (1947), valuable as a pioneer work but hardly dependable in view of its author's naiveté and lack of precision, were in their time described as "definitive." I do not wish to claim this epithet. I am conscious of several blank spots left, and there are certainly more of them than I am aware of. Psychological hypotheses proffered here will perhaps be replaced by other and more adequate theories. I know also that my methodological attitude is—quite independently of my ability to implement it—only one of many possible.

The description of this attitude (or at least the conscious part of it) can be combined with answering the question, To whom is this book addressed? I did not take the fact that Joseph Conrad had been a great writer as the "key" to his life, for the "essence" of the reconstructed events. Of course, this fact has determined the writing of my book; it constitutes the source of our curiosity about the man born as Konrad Korzeniowski. However, without trying to separate—unreasonably—"writer" from "man," I wanted to tell as much as possible about the man who had written books. One has, and one ought, to get acquainted with these books in their own right. Reading a biography should increase and enlighten our interest, but not force our understanding. Konrad Korzeniowski was an exceptional person not only (although primarily) because he was a writer. What is perhaps more important, he is, among other writers, a man particularly fascinating on account of his unusual life. It is well known that this difficult writer finds admirers among most diverse readers; in this respect he is quite exceptional in our century. The interest aroused by his personality deserves, I believe, a documented and critical response. This is why this book is addressed to all sufficiently patient readers of Conrad—and to specialists, students of literature, as well. It is supposed to provide them with "scholarly assistance" in the form of a chronicle of the writer's life and thought, marginally touching his fiction, with which they can cope themselves. Of course, while writing this biography I remembered the content of Conrad's works, their artistic structure and style. Many years of close contact with them, lecturing about them and editing them, must have influenced my thinking even if unconsciously—but I have tried not to take over the job of critics or historians of literature, only to help them.

I have also tried, even at the risk of monotonous pedantry and endless repetition of words like "it seems," "perhaps," "probably," "apparently," and so forth, to separate factual statements from guesses and commentaries.

Time for another confession. I have read few biographies and cannot say that I have taken any one as my model. Not because I am so sure of myself. True, I disagree with many of them with regard to their methods of handling facts and hypotheses. But when reading the best, classical "lives" I was always conscious that I could not, as they did, render the "atmosphere of the time," reconstruct the hero's physical environment, re-create the mood of his relationships with other people. My mind, long ago programmed by logical empiricists, is too angular for that. I haven't even tried.

In self-justification I have, however, to point out that the character of knowledge we possess about Conrad's life precludes certain kinds of biography. He lived sixty-seven years; for the first thirty-seven factual sources are meager, frequently for whole years almost nothing. To "re-create" the texture and atmosphere of his life during those periods would amount to giving free reign to fantasy. And this is not a result of the present state of research, but the final, unchangeable outcome of our hero's wanderings, and, even more important, a consequence of the fact that wars and revolutions have destroyed most of the documents relating to his early years and Polish connections. Such a loss as the burning of letters written by Konrad Korzeniowski to his uncle Tadeusz Bobrowski between 1869 and 1894—two hundred would be, I think, a very cautious estimate of their number—can never in any way be made up for. And later, in his "literary" three decades, there are obscure spots. Conrad did not live within a community. He was not a member of a group or a coterie; he stayed in the country, led an almost isolated and atypical life, without a stable social environment until his last years. Discreet about himself, he did not keep a diary, destroyed all his notes and most letters to himself, and in his autobiographical statements carefully (albeit not consistently) framed his own past. Leon Edel, author of the monumental biography of Henry James, complains about difficulties in learning about his subject. But in comparison to Joseph Conrad, Henry James is an open book: a man about whom his family and friends left numerous and extensive memories, a writer well established within the cultural milieu of his time, a sociable man of the world. Compared to him, Conrad is a foundling from an unknown country, a hermit, a unique specimen.

Numerous quotations, woven by me into the text, are intended to be a partial substitute for re-creating the atmosphere and environment. I tried to use them not so much as illustrations or arguments for my statements but as immediate, visual presentations of pieces of reality. They are supposed to give the reader a feeling of authenticity, a chance for individual insight into the subject of biographical narration.

For the instruction and amusement of those particularly who may think that I correct Conrad's statements about himself too frequently or, conversely, that too little is said here about his auto-mythologizing, I present here Conrad's original vita, penned by himself in 1900. The first nine chapters of this book may be read as an extensive commentary on that autobiographical sketch.

Conrad went to sea in 1874 in a small collier between Lowestoft and the Tyne. On board that vessel he acquired the rudiments of the English language from East Coast sailors.

Later on he sailed in so-called deep-water ships between London and Australian ports. In 1880 he passed his first Board of Trade examination for mate in London. Four years later he passed his examination for Master. At the same time he obtained his naturalization papers as British subject, and took steps to get himself formally released from his allegiance to Russia. His sojourns on shore between the voyages were rather long—during which he would meet various surviving members of his family on the Continent.

He never attached himself to any firm or line of ships; seeking variety in the pursuit of his profession. After 1885 he found his work in the Eastern seas and in the Pacific. He commanded both in steam and sail. In 1890 he came home—to London—for a long stay and then visited the part of Poland where he had been born after more than twenty years absence. In that year also he began to write tentatively his first novel, Almayers Folly of which some chapters were written in London, some in Poland, and a couple in Africa—in the Belgian Congo—where he went in 1891 to command a river steamer but really prompted by curiosity and nothing else. This curiosity was fully satisfied. He returned very ill. This was the newest experience of all, he not having had a day of simple indisposition since the age of sixteen.

His health was seriously and as it turned out permanently affected. After two more years at sea he concluded that in common honesty to his employers—whoever they may be—he must leave the sea. He judged himself no longer to be physically fit for the life of his choice, where he can remember many hard days but not a single day of bitterness.

He spent some months in Switzerland undergoing a cure. It was on his return to England while staying with some friends in the country and uncertain as to his future that he finished at last "Almayers Folly" practically rewriting it. It was published by [Unwin].

Shortly afterwards he lost all his money in the South African slump after an exciting experience which except for the obvious inconvenience of the thing he does not regret. He was then writing the *Outcast of the Islands*. With no money and in uncertain health the position seemed desperate. Mr. Conrad married a woman who was not afraid to face it with him. This was the most dangerous the most reckless and the most fortunate adventure he had in his life.

This instructive and amusing piece cannot be passed over without a more general reflection. The vision of Conrad's own life contained in this vita is not the only attempt at shaping his own past. He made several, and all his "auto-biographical" writings are subservient to such shaping a posteriori. Conrad cherished various self-images, sometimes contradicting not only the facts, but each other. But it would not do to accuse him of "lying." It is one thing to give false answers to a personal questionnaire (this, incidentally, also was done by Conrad)—and another to transform one's own past into a piece of literature, even if described as "authentic." A writer is a double-personality creature. He is a Mr. X, born on a certain day, living in a given place, and so on—and also the author of works that are read because they communicate something about subjects that would interest us even if Mr. X had never existed. He is an author understood by his readers thanks to the fact that he uses a language not invented by himself, and conventions which he may have enriched but which existed before his birth. He is an element in the great chain and wide field of literature that feeds itself on deep, immemorial layers of tradition. We cannot put an equation mark, nor any other sign of strict correlation, between the personal and the cultural, transcendental "I." And probably every writer is aware (Conrad certainly was) that his private-personal I presents for his public-cultural I an exploitable raw material analogous to the so-called external reality.

Therefore, when in the course of my narration I point out discrepancies between facts of Konrad Korzeniowski's life and what in his works—and also in his letters, an intermediate, half- or three-quarters-private, genre—the writer Joseph Conrad would tell, this should not be understood as unmasking falsehoods. And when I tender the hypothesis that literary creativity was for Conrad also a compensative activity, a making-up for the insufficiencies of his own life and character, that among other functions it was psychotherapeutic—this refers solely to Conrad's private personality and has nothing to do with an assessment of his novels and stories.

This book was begun in 1957 and completed in 1977; its English version was brought up to date and supplemented in early 1983. Twelve out of fifteen chapters were published separately before 1977. The long delay that intervened between then and the appearance of this volume makes it necessary to clarify the principles that have guided me in referring to the work of other scholars. I have tried to be as meticulous and fair as possible in acknowledging what I owe to others: I must, however, explain that, as regards the findings that other scholars made in the period between the completion of my manuscript and the final publication of this book, I make acknowledgment only in cases when I had not already made the finding independently myself; the curious are invited to verify this by referring to the original versions which I published between 1957 and 1977, and which are listed in the Bibliographical Note.

This explanation particularly applies to the last major biography of Joseph Conrad, Frederick R. Karl's *Joseph Conrad: The Three Lives*, published in 1979, that is, two years after the completion of this book. Though I cooperated with Professor Karl for several years on the edition of Conrad's letters, I was completely unaware that he was engaged on a large-scale biography.

In October 1981 my old college in Oxford, St. Antony's, kindly made it possible for me to come to England to complete the updating of the English version of this book. Thus, almost accidentally, I found myself abroad when martial law was introduced in Poland on 13 December 1981. I decided to remain abroad, and quite unexpectedly have become, like Conrad, an exile.

Acknowledgments

MANY PERSONS, and in many ways, have assisted me in collecting material for this book and in writing it. One Conrad biographer, Jocelyn Baines, whom I met in 1957, remained a good friend of mine for many years—until his untimely death. After he had completed his book, he let me use his sources in my work on mine.

Among those who have offered their help I should mention in the first place both sons of Joseph Conrad: Borys and John. From the time I met them in 1957 and as long as they lived they remained most loyal and helpful friends to me. I learned much from talks also with other persons who had known Joseph Conrad personally: David Garnett, Teodor Kosch, Józef H. Retinger, Otolia Retinger, and Cecil Roberts.

From among fellow Conradian scholars I owe a particular gratitude to Ian Watt, who read the text in manuscript and offered numerous valuable suggestions, and to Hans van Marle, who indefatigably and meticulously conducted research in many archives in England, France, Belgium, the Netherlands, and West Germany, unstintingly sharing with me the results of his investigations and alerting me to many an oversight.

With Dr. Robert F. Hobson, eminent psychiatrist, I spent many hours discussing Conrad's depression. Maria Janion, reviewing the Polish manuscript of the book, acutely discerned many points in need of clarification and elaboration.

Many other friends, acquaintances, and also correspondents whom I have never met in person, helped to find and collect documents and data, and offered advice about the text itself when it was being published in separate chapters. I am afraid I may not remember them all, but I wish to mention at least the following: Conrad's cousins Maria Kołodziejczyk and Stanisław Bobrowski; the patient and hospitable Mme Françoise Meykiechel, who among other things let me read and quote the diary of her mother, Emilie Briquel, also Laetitia Cerio, Maria Danilewicz-Zielińska, Monika Gronkiewicz, Jadwiga Kosicka, Danuta Kossowska, Lola Szladits, Julian Vinogradov, Irena de Virion, Joanna Więckowska, and Marjorie Wynne. And Roman Aftanazy, Andrzej Biernacki, Viktor Borisov, Włodzimierz Borys, Tadeusz Chrzanowski, Mario Curreli, Zbigniew Folejewski, Tadeusz Garczyński, Karol Górski, Zbigniew Herbert, Jerzy Illg, Jarosław Iwaszkiewicz, George T. Keating, Stefan Kieniewicz, Magnus J. Krynski, Thomas C. Moser, Ugo Mursia, Valentin Panov, John Pomian, Bertrand Russell, John H. Stape, F. J. Temple, Claude Thomas, Cedric Watts, and Stefan Zabierowski. I thank them all cordially and apologize if the use to which I have put their assistance does not equal their generosity.

Last but not least, I wish to thank my wife, who while working on the translation suggested many improvements; her help throughout has been invaluable. She in turn wishes to express her gratitude to Mrs. Catherine Mannings and to Mr. Nicholas Carroll for their patient help.

I am very grateful to the Trustees of the Joseph Conrad Estate for their permission to quote so extensively from Conrad's letters. Due thanks are also given to the following collections, which have kindly permitted me to quote from unpublished manuscripts in their possession: The Bienecke Rare Book and Manuscript Library, Yale University; the Henry W. and Albert A. Berg Collection, The New York Public Library, Astor, Lenox and Tilden Foundations; The British Library; the Brotherton Collection, Leeds University; Colgate University Library; Cornell University Library; Dartmouth College Library; The Houghton Library, Harvard University; the Humanities Research Center, The University of Texas at Austin; The Lilly Library, Indiana University; the J. Pierpont Morgan Library, New York; The New York Public Library, Manuscript Division; the William T. Perkins Library, Duke University; the Princeton University Library; The Philip H. and A. S. W. Rosenbach Foundation, Philadelphia; the University of Birmingham Library; the University of Virginia Library.

Maps

Note on Geographical Names

With the exception of those which possess established English versions (Cracow, Warsaw, and so forth), all geographical names within the territory of the prepartition Polish Commonwealth are given in their standard Polish form. I have followed the spelling as given in *Słownik geograficzny Królestwa Polskiego i innych ziem słowiańskich* [Geographical dictionary of the Polish Kingdom and other Slavonic territories], volumes 1–16 (Warsaw, 1880–1914). In the Ukraine several of these names have repeatedly changed since Conrad's time, and many exist in three forms: Polish, Ukrainian, and Russian. However, in most sources important to Conrad scholars, these names appear in their Polish form, which I therefore kept throughout for the sake of simplicity. Current versions are given in the index as cross-references.

Genealogies

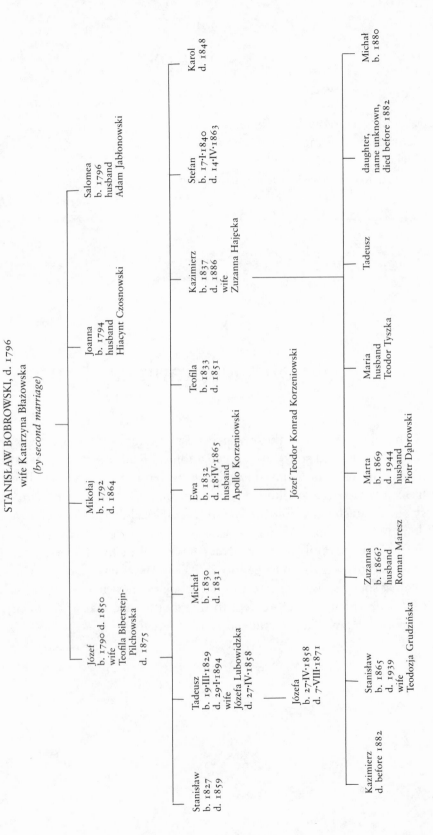

STANISŁAW BOBROWSKI, d. 1796
wife Katarzyna Błażowska
(by second marriage)

Józef
b. 1790 d. 1850
wife
Teofila Biberstein-
Pilchowska
d. 1875

Mikołaj
b. 1792
d. 1864

Joanna
b. 1794
husband
Hiacynt Czosnowski

Salomea
b. 1796
husband
Adam Jabłonowski

Michał
b. 1830
d. 1831

Tadeusz
b. 19·III·1829
d. 29·I·1894
wife
Józefa Lubowidzka
d. 27·IV·1858

Ewa
b. 1832
d. 18·IV·1865
husband
Apollo Korzeniowski

Teofila
b. 1833
d. 1851

Kazimierz
b. 1837
d. 1886
wife
Zuzanna Hajęcka

Stefan
b. 17·I·1840
d. 14·IV·1863

Karol
d. 1848

Stanisław
b. 1827
d. 1859

Józefa
b. 27·IV·1858
d. 7·VIII·1871

Józef Teodor Konrad Korzeniowski

Stanisław
b. 1865
d. 1939
wife
Teodozja Grudzińska

Zuzanna
b. 1866?
husband
Roman Maresz

Marta
b. 1869
d. 1944
husband
Piotr Dąbrowski

Maria
husband
Teodor Tyszka

Tadeusz

daughter,
name unknown,
died before 1882

Michał
b. 1880

Kazimierz
d. before 1882

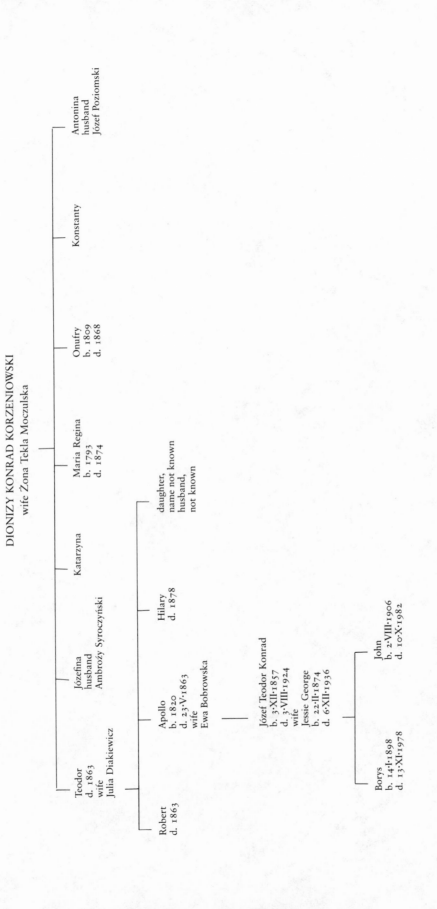

DIONIZY KONRAD KORZENIOWSKI
wife Żona Tekla Moczulska

Chronology

3 December 1857	Józef Teodor Konrad Korzeniowski born in Berdyczów in the Ukraine, son of Apollo Korzeniowski and Ewa (née Bobrowska).
21 October 1861	Apollo Korzeniowski imprisoned in Warsaw by Russian police for his underground patriotic activities.
9 May 1862	The Korzeniowskis are sentenced to exile and sent under escort to northern Russia.
18 April 1865	Ewa Korzeniowska dies of tuberculosis.
January 1868	Apollo Korzeniowski, seriously ill, is reprieved and leaves Russia with his son.
23 May 1869	Apollo Korzeniowski dies in Cracow.
26 September 1874	Konrad Korzeniowski leaves Poland for Marseilles.
11 July 1878	Joins his first British ship, the *Skimmer of the Sea*.
19 August 1886	Becomes a British subject.
10 November 1886	Passes his examination for Ordinary Master of the British merchant marine.
12 June– 4 December 1890	Works in the Belgian Congo.
17 January 1894	Leaves his last position as a seaman.
24 April 1894	Finishes the draft of *Almayer's Folly*.
29 April 1895	*Almayer's Folly—A Story of an Eastern River* published in London. Korzeniowski adopts "Joseph Conrad" as his pen name.
4 March 1896	*An Outcast of the Islands* published.
24 March 1896	Conrad marries Miss Jessie George, born 22 February 1873.
2 December 1897	*The Nigger of the "Narcissus"—A Tale of the Sea* published.

26 March 1898	*Tales of Unrest* ("Karain," "The Idiots," "An Outpost of Progress," "The Return," "The Lagoon") published.
6 February 1899	Conrad finishes writing "Heart of Darkness."
15 October 1900	*Lord Jim—A Tale* published.
26 June 1901	*The Inheritors—An Extravagant Story*, a novel Conrad wrote in collaboration with Ford Madox Hueffer (later Ford Madox Ford), published.
13 November 1902	*Youth and Two Other Stories* published.
22 April 1903	*Typhoon and Other Stories* published.
16 October 1903	*Romance—A Novel*, written in collaboration with F. M. Hueffer, published.
14 October 1904	*Nostromo—A Tale of the Seaboard* published.
23 April 1905	Conrad finishes "Autocracy and War."
4 October 1906	*The Mirror of the Sea—Memories and Impressions* published.
12 September 1907	*The Secret Agent—A Simple Tale* published.
6 August 1908	*A Set of Six* published.
5 October 1911	*Under Western Eyes* published.
19 January 1912	*Some Reminiscences* (later renamed *A Personal Record*) published.
14 October 1912	*'Twixt Land and Sea—Tales* published.
18 September 1913	*Chance—A Tale in Two Parts* published.
25 July– 3 November 1914	Conrad travels to Poland with his family.
24 February 1915	*Within the Tides—Tales* published.
27 March 1915	*Victory—An Island Tale* published.
19 March 1917	*The Shadow Line—A Confession* published.
12 December 1918	Conrad finishes "The Crime of Partition."
6 August 1919	*The Arrow of Gold—A Story Between Two Notes* published.

21 May 1920	*The Rescue—A Romance of the Shallows*, novel begun by Conrad in 1896, published.
25 March 1921	*Notes on Life and Letters* published.
June 1921	Conrad translates from Polish Bruno Winawer's *Księga Hioba: The Book of Job*.
1 May–2 June 1923	Conrad travels to the United States.
1 December 1923	*The Rover* published.
3 August 1924	Conrad dies of heart attack at his home near Canterbury.

JOSEPH CONRAD

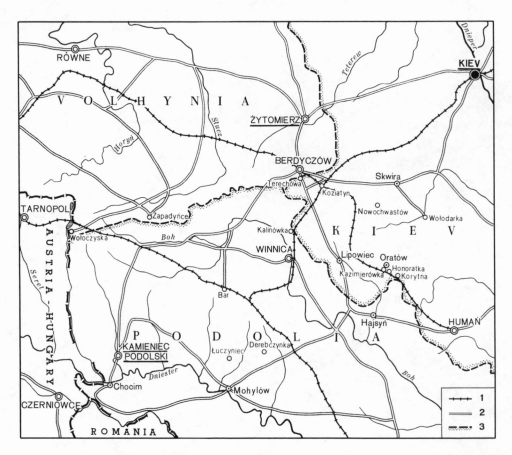

KONRAD KORZENIOWSKI'S HOMELAND

1. railways till 1893
2. main roads
3. provincial boundaries

I

IN THE SHADOW OF ALIEN GHOSTS

1857–1874

IN 1795, POLAND was divided among three neighboring powers and disappeared from the political map of Europe for 123 years. It had been a peculiar state. Though a kingdom, it was called a republic because its kings were elected, and their power was severely limited by the Polish parliament, the "Sejm," established in 1493. Poland was also a commonwealth of two nations, Polish and Lithuanian, bound together by the unions of Krewo (1385) and Lublin (1569). The commonwealth's territory was inhabited by peoples of many languages, including Polish, Ukrainian (or Ruthenian, as it was then called), Byelorussian, Lithuanian, Latvian, and Yiddish. The ruling class, the *szlachta*,* all spoke Polish, whatever their original ethnic background. This reflected not only Polish cultural superiority but the fact that their many privileges were an extension of those originally won by Poles. By European standards the szlachta was unusually large, forming something like 10 percent of the whole population, and therefore several times larger proportionally than the gentry and nobility combined in England or France. Only the szlachta had political power, and the scope of this power was extensive. On the other hand, members of the szlachta were passionately attached to their liberties and prided themselves on never having tolerated autocracy: absolute monarchy was for Poles a thing unknown.

To defend his country and participate in its political affairs were considered duties of every member of the szlachta. At the same time, the szlachta was virtually the sole culturally active social class. Soldierly and chivalric values were dominant, and, at least theoretically, whoever pursued material gain had to do so more or less surreptitiously. The more enlightened members of the szlachta also cherished the traditions of religious and racial tolerance for which Poland had been famous when wars of religion ravaged western Europe in the sixteenth

---

* The term cannot be adequately rendered in English; in Poland there was no distinction between nobility and gentry. Every member of the szlachta was legally equal to any other; members addressed each other as "brothers"; no titles, such as lord or count, were allowed; any *szlachcic* could become a member of the Sejm or even, at least in theory, be elected king. Only members of the szlachta were permitted to carry arms. Membership in this class was marked by possession of a coat of arms; the same coat of arms was often shared by several families, but unrelated people of the same family name could have different coats of arms.

and seventeenth centuries. There was no lack of obscurantism and class selfish-ness among the szlachta, but the constitution, proclaimed by the Sejm in 1791, was impressively liberal, apart from being the first codified constitution in Europe since antiquity. This liberalism alarmed Poland's autocratic neighbors and precipitated its partition in 1795. The central and eastern Polish territories, in-cluding the Ukraine, Byelorussia, and Lithuania, were directly annexed by Rus-sia; the western part of these territories became the so-called Kingdom of Po-land, with the tsar as its titular king at least until 1830, when the tsars stopped using the title; southern Poland was incorporated into the Austrian empire, and western Poland given to Prussia.

The long years of foreign occupation which followed 1795 were broken at least once in every generation by an insurrection, directed mainly against the most severe oppressor, Russia. The Polish tradition of patriotic conspiracies was almost uninterrupted, and it strengthened the social and cultural role of the heroic virtues of duty, fidelity, and honor. Polish literature took over the func-tions of suppressed national institutions, and volumes of forbidden poems and dramas were widely circulated, often in handwritten copies, continually re-minding their readers of Poland's past glory and their duty to restore the coun-try's independence. In the first half of the nineteenth century many Polish lead-ers, virtually all of them of szlachta origin, coupled demands for national independence with advocacy of democratic political reforms. And as the exhor-tations to do one's patriotic duty were addressed not only to the traditional arms-bearing class of the szlachta but to all inhabitants of the former common-wealth, there followed a peculiar "democratization" of chivalric ideals: the honor of serving one's country was no longer restricted to the privileged.

Such was the Polish socio-political scene in the mid-nineteenth century, when Joseph Conrad's father was born.*

Apollo Korzeniowski—coat of arms Nałęcz, as he was wont to add—came from a szlachta family of moderate means, which had moved a long time before from central Poland to the Ukraine.[1] His father, Teodor, was a landowner and soldier. From 1807 to 1812, having sneaked across the frontiers of partitioned Poland, Teodor served as a lieutenant in the army of the Duchy of Warsaw and fought the Austrians in the battle of Raszyn. During the 1830 insurrection against Russia, he formed his own cavalry squadron, was promoted to the rank of colonel, and won a medal for valor. He had four children by his wife Julia (née Dyakiewicz): three sons, Robert, Apollo, and Hilary, and one daughter, whose name is unknown.[2] Apollo was born on 21 February 1820, in the village of Honoratka, in the Lipowiec district. He was eleven when his father's estate

* The different ways the hero of this book is referred to in its text reflect changes in what he called himself and how he was addressed by others. In his official documents and to his Polish family he remained Konrad Korzeniowski until the end of his life. In the familial context I refer to him as Konrad. Whenever he is men-tioned as an author, his pen name, Joseph Conrad, is used.

was confiscated by the Russian authorities in reprisal for his participation in the 1830 uprising. Teodor took the post of estate manager at Korytna in the Hajsyń district. Tadeusz Bobrowski, about whom we will hear more later, characterized Teodor Korzeniowski in his memoirs as a kind-hearted braggart, a competent and hard-working farmer, and an irresponsible dreamer. It seems, however, that the main manifestation of his "irresponsible dreams" consisted of being always ready "to mount his horse and chase the enemy out of the country . . . without consulting his head."[3]

It is difficult to tell to what extent Bobrowski, an appeaser and "rationalist," was prejudiced in this portrayal, or in his appraisals of Teodor's children, Robert and Hilary. He pictured Robert as a gambler and drunkard, and accused Hilary of being lightheaded and tending to futile daydreaming.[4] From other sources we know only that Robert was killed in 1863 during an insurrection, and that Hilary, who dabbled in poetry and worked to establish an agricultural school near Żytomierz, was arrested before the uprising, and died in 1878, exiled in Tomsk.[5]

Apollo's education took him to various towns in Poland, and it was in Żytomierz that he finished the local gymnasium course. His friend and biographer, Stefan Buszczyński wrote, "The prolific intellect, warm heart, and personal integrity of the young man won him the affection of colleagues but resulted in several changes of schools. Moscow educational authorities harrassed him continually for his free-thinking."[6] In 1840 he left the Ukraine for St. Petersburg University, where he spent a year reading Oriental languages and five years reading law and literature. It is not known whether he graduated, and if so, in what field.* At all events he read widely and cultivated his interest in literature and theater, interests which had already revealed themselves in his childhood.

In 1846 Apollo returned to his home province and spent several years helping his father manage successive leaseholds, although following an undistinguished poetic début in 1844 and the translation of Victor Hugo's *Les Burgraves* in 1846, he devoted more and more time to literary work. Later he added courtship to his occupations; probably in 1847 he met Ewelina (such was at the time the fashionable version of the name Ewa) Bobrowska, the adolescent sister of Tadeusz Bobrowski, an acquaintance from Żytomierz. Ewelina was already known for her beauty, and Apollo fell in love immediately. However, he faced strong opposition from her family, not so much because of the difference in age, hardly unusual at that time, but because of a basic difference in outlook between the two families.

---

* Bobrowski claims in *Pamiętniki*, 1:426, not to know what Apollo studied at the university but says that he did not get a degree. Conrad in his letter of 20 January 1900 to Garnett writes that his father was in the department of oriental studies and philology. From other sources we know that Apollo also read law. R. Blüth points out that Korzeniowski, when applying for a release from his enforced exile, claimed to possess a degree. "Dwie rodziny kresowe" [Two borderland families], *Ateneum*, no. 1, (1939).

While Teodor Korzeniowski wasted his health and money fighting for Poland, Józef Bobrowski, Ewa's father, augmented his wealth by holding himself aloof from all freedom movements. He referred to the 1830 uprising as "noble madness" and was not loath to accept the favors of his cousins, the Poradowskis, who served in the tsar's army as generals. Józef Bobrowski tried to inculcate in his eight children practical and "sensible" attitudes. His sons were Stanisław (b. 1827), Tadeusz (1829), Michał (1830–1832), Kazimierz (1837), Stefan (1840), and Karol (died 1848 in infancy), and his daughters Ewa (1831) and Teofila (1833).* Józef Bobrowski was not altogether successful in his attempt. His eldest son, Stanisław, became a respected officer in the hussars of the Tsar's Guard, and if it were not for his untimely death in 1859 might have attained high rank, but he would probably have resigned from the service at the outbreak of the 1863 rising. This is what his brother, Kazimierz, an officer of the Sappers, did. Both soldiers cared little for their careers. Probably the Bobrowski children were under the stronger influence of their patriotic mother, Teofila, born Biberstejn-Pilchowska. Only Tadeusz turned out according to his father's wishes. Intelligent and hard-working, judicious and "realistic"—in effect, an appeaser—he dreamed in his youth about a civil service career and for it even gave up his excellent academic prospects.**

Apollo had first met Tadeusz at the Żytomierz Gymnasium, but nine years difference in age was too much for them to become more closely acquainted. Later they met at the university, and while Apollo regarded Tadeusz as his friend and Tadeusz confessed that Apollo was the only person he then liked, Tadeusz Bobrowski's attitude remained critical throughout. This reserve may have begun merely as a reflection of his father's negative opinion, but it increased later as a result of psychological and political differences, possibly exacerbated by jealousy of Apollo's popularity and renown.

At any rate, in 1849 the main opponent of the marriage was Ewelina's father. He took Apollo on a round of visits to country houses in the neighborhood, a scheme to get him married off to someone else, but, as Tadeusz wrote with sneering regret, "he [Apollo] was always clever enough to evoke disapproval from either the girl or her parents." Apollo was sociable; his lively mind made him a welcome guest, but he also inspired a certain amount of apprehension. According to Bobrowski, "He had the reputation of being very ugly and sarcastic. In fact he was not beautiful, nor even handsome, but his eyes had a very kind expression and his sarcasm was only verbal, of the drawing-room type; for I have never detected any of it in his feelings or in his actions."[7] From Korze-

* In *Pamiętniki*, Bobrowski maintained that Ewa was nearly four years younger than he; apparently he confused her with Teofila (1:12). Ewa's year of birth is in 2:4.
** In February 1850 he turned down an offer of the chair of international law in Kazań. He was striving at that time for a high post in the ministry of justice. In spite of strong backing his efforts failed on account of his Polish origin and Catholic faith (Bobrowski, *Pamiętniki*, 1:437–442).

niowski's writings we can easily guess the objects of his mordant tongue. Extremely courteous toward women, highly emotional, and with a tendency to be carried away by his enthusiasms, he hated hypocrisy and vanity, and felt only contempt for rich people or social upstarts. According to Bobrowski, this contempt was characteristic of the szlachta attitude towards the moneyed class. There may be a grain of truth in this, but even Tadeusz, who prudently reserved his own biting remarks for his posthumous *Memoirs*, admits that the targets of Apollo's spite were well chosen.

The long and effusive letter Apollo wrote to Tadeusz soon after meeting his sister, testifies to his wit and the sharpness of his tongue. Typically romantic passages of lofty exaltation accompany passages of self-criticism and attempts at genuine intellectual honesty. The letter ends with an appeal to his younger correspondent in which he hopes that "in spite of our different characters you will remember that we share the same feelings on human dignity, and you will not deny me your friendship." *

In any case, Korzeniowski showed no signs of becoming a sedate country squire. As Bobrowski wrote, "While supposed to help his father to run the estate, he read, wrote and traveled around more than he worked." [8] Obviously Tadeusz Bobrowski did not regard writing as work. In fact, Apollo does not seem to have done much writing at that time, but one could hardly take him for an idler, considering that he mastered four languages (English, French, German, and Russian) and that his surviving original works and translations fill several sizable volumes. It is clear, however, that Apollo's conception of his duties in life was very different from those held by Józef and Tadeusz Bobrowski.

Apollo's first work of any significance, *Czyścowe pieśni* [Purgatorial songs] (1849–1855), consisted of semireligious, semipatriotic poems. Since censorship prevented their publication, they circulated in the Ukraine in handwritten copies. The work reveals two characteristics of Korzeniowski's writings: the conventional derivativeness of his poetic imagination, and a lively, often original, social and political perception. As an artist Apollo was an epigone of romanticism; as a man of action he was very brave in word and deed. Both traits are borne out by his earliest play, *Komedia* (1854). The first half is based on a well-known comedy by A. S. Griboedov, *Wit Works Woe* (1824); the other,

---

* Korzeniowski to Bobrowski, 11 May. And here is a fragment of the description of the family from which Apollo's father leased the estate Popowice, in Berdyczów district:

Then I fall into the clutches of his son who reeks of the stable, for he is perpetually with his horse, harness and riding-whip. Were this last to have been used against him, he might have grown to be somebody. Wiszniewski's fame as the author of *Polish Literature* is dimmed by the education of that confident boor. . . . If I stay here a bit longer methinks I shall grow a mane and a tail, stand on all fours and buck like a well-fed jade. . . . There are also two maiden ladies: one is the aunt who has lived half a century in spinsterhood, the other is the daughter whose fate would be the same if everybody shared my taste. If you know what a spinster is—you may commiserate with me; if you do not—pray accept my most sincere wishes to remain ignorant. It is impossible that God created old maids.

original, half, though less skillful theatrically, is astonishingly sharp in its presentation of social problems.* The author rails at the hypocrisy and egoism of the newly enriched landowners, and contrasts them with the idealism of the protagonist, Henryk, who had been exiled, probably for his participation in the movement begun by Szymon Konarski in 1838 for the enfranchisement of peasants. Significantly, an educated plebeian sides with Henryk in the conflict, and the play thus presents a nucleus of the social programme that was to be advocated by the Polish "Reds" in the sixties. *Komedia* caused a certain scandal, and Korzeniowski earned the reputation of being a radical.

Meanwhile, he inclined more and more toward active politics. During the Crimean War (September 1854–February 1856), a belligerent section of the Polish szlachta in the Ukraine conceived a plan for organized insurgent action in cooperation with the allied armies. The insurgents were to cut the Russian supply lines. A special emissary was sent to Paris for talks with the French government, but owing to the indifference of England and France the plan fell through. Apollo Korzeniowski was one of the most fervent supporters of the insurrection, which he wanted to be founded on a peasant revolt. The idea is revealed in *Przedgrom* [Before the thunderstorm], his best work from that period:

> You have everything! . . . God's will,
> Long suffering to avenge
> And People's debt to repay!
> Forward Brothers! With morn! With dawn!
> With People, in People your power . . .
> With People, in People your salvation . . .
> Poland must belong to the People
> To live for ever![9]

Apollo was soon to express still more radical views. In the spring of 1855 a peasant rebellion against the state administration started in the Skwira district in the Ukraine. According to Korzeniowski's diary, the peasants called on the Polish szlachta for help in organizing detachments and leading the movement: "All we've got is our hands—but no head. On, gentlemen! Give us the head!"[10] Apollo hurried to the scene of rebellion but was too late. Most landowners, terrified by the memory of the eighteenth-century Cossack massacres, took shelter in the towns and called on the authorities for help. The Russian forces

---

* The population of the Ukraine was mixed. Nearly all peasants spoke Ukrainian; most of them were Orthodox, although some, especially farther west, were Uniate (Greek Catholic) and thus independent of St. Petersburg in matters of religion. In the western and central Ukraine, in the territories that had belonged to the Polish Commonwealth before its partitioning, almost all landowners were Poles. About half the inhabitants of towns were Jewish, and the rest Poles, Russians, and Ukrainians. Unlike Apollo, most of Polish szlachta were wary of all major social change, because of their mistrust of and contempt for the Ukrainian "mob."

had no difficulty in breaking up the disorganized and defenseless peasant groups. The incident shook Korzeniowski to the core, and he burst forth with stanzas of exceptional power:

> In the Ukraine cannons roar,
> Women weep over the pall.
> For masters-informers—victory!
> Serfs back to work, back to factory!
> Peasant rising: noble and clean,
> Crucified by lords infamous and mean.
> The Tsar laughs like a demon,
> The bier is ready . . ."[11]

In 1852 Korzeniowski took over the administration of Madame Sobańska's estate, Łuczyniec, in Podolia. Although Józef Bobrowski had been dead for over two years and although Ewa from the beginning had looked favorably upon Apollo, her family was still opposed to their marriage. Tadeusz had become the head of the Bobrowski family in 1850. He was obliged to abandon his studies (during which he had won a silver medal for his 1848 dissertation "On the redemption of family estates"), and his hope of pursuing a legal and administrative career. It was he who at last, in July 1855, granted permission for Ewa's engagement to Apollo.[12] The concession was brought about partly by Ewa's long-lasting depression which affected her health, and partly by the mediation of her uncle, Adolf Pilchowski. The engagement lasted nearly a year; meanwhile Korzeniowski won Tadeusz Bobrowski's gratitude by helping him in his own matrimonial endeavors, which were directed at the richly dowered Józefa Lubowidzka.

On 4 May 1856 at Oratów, the family estate of the Bobrowskis, the marriage of Ewa Bobrowska and Apollo Korzeniowski was celebrated. The event was not free from complications, however: it was only with difficulty that the bride's paternal uncle was persuaded to participate in the ceremony, and one aunt failed to turn up. Apparently there was also an argument between Apollo and the priest who, presumably out of suspicion at the pagan sound of his name, insisted on calling him Apolinary.[13]

The young couple spent their first year at Łuczyniec. From that period dates what is probably Korzeniowski's best translation, Vigny's *Chatterton*. The drama contains the tirade based on a comparison of England to a ship; we may detect its echo in Joseph Conrad's *The Nigger of the "Narcissus."*

In 1857, having received Ewa's dowry of nine thousand rubles in silver, Apollo took on lease one of the Sobańskis' farms, Derebczynka, in Podolia.[14] Probably toward the end of Ewa's pregnancy the couple moved to Terechowa, where Ewa's mother was living. Their only son was born on 3 December 1857 at nearby Berdyczów.* There must have been some anxiety about his life, for a private baptism with water took place two days later. The baby boy was given three names: Józef Teodor Konrad. First came the names of both grandfathers, then the name of the hero of Mickiewicz's dramatic poem *Dziady* [The Fore-

* Regarding Conrad's birthplace there is a certain confusion for which he himself is partly responsible. He used to put down Żytomierz, probably because that was where his birth certificate had been issued. Mercantile Marine documents; naturalization file; Conrad to Jasieński, 25 April 1905, *CPB*, p. 244. In the first posthumous edition of Conrad's works, the so-called Medallion Edition, 1925, in the volume of *Victory* there is a photograph captioned, "The house where Joseph Conrad was born on the 6th [sic] December 1857, in the Ukraine, Poland." The same photograph was included by Jessie Conrad in her *Joseph Conrad and His Circle* (London, 1935), with a caption, "Berdiczew. The house where 'Joseph Conrad' was born." The picture, however, represents a neo-Gothic pavilion, nonexistent today, erected in Nowochwastów at the beginning of the nineteenth century by the Lubowidzki family (identified with the assistance of Roman Aftanazy). The drawing of the building, made by Napoleon Orda, is in the Czapski Collection in the National Museum, Cracow. Quite apart from other reasons, Nowochwastów is too far from Berdyczów for Conrad to have been born there. The caption under the photograph—which apparently dates from Konrad's visits to Tadeusz Bobrowski in the years 1863 to 1868—must be a result of misunderstanding or mystification.

The matter has been complicated further by Baines, who located the Derebczynka estate, leased by Apollo Korzeniowski, "near Berdichev" (in fact, the distance is about 110 miles), maintaining that Derebczynka Manor was Conrad's place of birth (*Joseph Conrad: A Critical Biography* [London, 1960], p. 7). Dmitrij Urnov, a Russian journalist, set out following the trail which brought him to Iwańkowce, about 5 miles from Berdyczów, where he found a manor house, once the property of the Żukowski family, with a small tower slightly reminiscent of the one on the Nowochwastów pavilion. Urnov published (*Vokrug Sveta*, no. 2 [1972]) a drawing of the house, clearly executed on the basis of the photograph in Jessie's book, with a claim that it was the "discovered" place of Conrad's birth. He also advanced the unfounded supposition that Iwańkowce and Derebczynka are, in fact, one and the same place. Urnov's article was also the basis of Ugo Mursia's paper, presented at the International Conrad Conference at Canterbury, in July 1974, and published in the collected essays *Joseph Conrad: A Commemoration*, edited by Norman Sherry (London, 1976), which supported the theory of Conrad's birth at Iwańkowce. On the other hand, Sherry, in *Conrad and His World* (London, 1973), labeled that same photograph, "Joseph Conrad's birthplace, Derebczynka Manor, near Berdyczów, in the Ukraine." Lastly, Barbara Koc in *Conrad—opowieść biograficzna* [Conrad—a biographical tale] (Warsaw, 1977) captioned that same photograph, "The house at Iwańkowce near Berdyczów, Konrad Korzeniowski's birthplace." And finally, to make the confusion still more confounding, Frederick Karl, in *Joseph Conrad: The Three Lives* (New York, 1979), not only repeated Sherry's erroneous caption under the same much used photograph, but to all earlier mistakes added a new one in claiming that Conrad was born on Derebczynka Manor, near Berdyczów, in Podolia (p. 38). As any map shows, Berdyczów is not in Podolia.

The documents, however, reveal the following: Bobrowski, "Document," gives the date and place of birth as 21 November (old style) 1857, at Berdyczów, at which place the child was christened with water. See also his letter to Korzeniowski, 3 January 1889, *CPB*, p. 128. Conrad himself used to give the date as 3 December; both that date and the fact of the previously performed private baptism are confirmed by an extract from the Żytomierz parish register, preserved in the Jagiellonian Library (MS 6391). The formal baptism took place at Żytomierz in 1862. The certificate gives the date of birth as 1856, which is probably due to a mistake by the copyist. "A Song for the Day of Christening," a poem written by Apollo for his son, bears the date 23 November (obviously also old style) 1857, Berdyczów.

Clearly, Konrad could not have been born at Derebczynka and within two days find himself at Berdyczów. Also, there does not seem to be the slightest reason why Bobrowski should give wrong information. Terechowa, the Bobrowski family estate, was five miles from Berdyczów, but in a different parish; had Konrad been born there, his uncle, sensitive on the subject of his family, is sure to have recorded the fact. Perhaps there were medical reasons for the delivery to take place in town.

Anyway, soon afterwards, the family moved to Terechowa. Writing to J. I. Kraszewski on 5 December 1857 to ask him for a blessing for his newly born son, Apollo gives the date of birth as 21 November and his return address as "Terechowa via Berdyczów." MS 6468, Jagiellonian Library.

fathers' Eve] (1832).* Thus, three traditions were united as guardian presences for the child: those of the two families, at once so different from each other, and the great tradition of Polish romantic poetry.

The last tradition was evoked by Apollo Korzeniowski in his poem, "To My Son Born in the 85th Year of Muscovite Oppression, A Song For the Day of His Christening." There is nothing in the poem about the warmth of the family hearth, only about the bitterness of captivity; nothing about happiness, only about the ability to bear suffering; and nothing about education or work, only about unrelenting fidelity and struggle.

> Baby son, sleep in peace.
> Alien ghosts cast their shadows,
> Two hearts are all you have,
> And your only armour—*the cross.*
> But such treasures do not perish,
> The World's rust will not destroy the cross,
> The hearts are faithful. Close your eyes,
> Hushaby, my baby son!
> [. . .]
> Baby son, sleep . . . let Holy Water flow
> On your soul, on your forehead;
> *Heaven* and *Godliness* surround you . . .
> Bless you, my little son:
> Be a *Pole*! Though foes
> May spread before you
> A web of happiness,
> Renounce it—love your poverty.
> Hushaby, my baby son!
> [. . .]
> Baby son, tell yourself
> You are without land, without love,

---

* At the beginning of this powerful drama, the hero bears the name Gustaw and is a typical young romantic poet, self-centered, lonely, desperately in love, immersed in fantasies. Then, under the impact of the political persecution by Russian authorities to which he and his friends are exposed, his personality and his poetry undergo a radical transformation. He changes his name to Konrad and becomes a romantic patriot, a poetic spokesman for his oppressed people. For the significance of Conrad's Polish background for his work, and for Polish socio-cultural and political traditions which influenced his outlook generally, see the introduction to my *Conrad's Polish Background* (Oxford, 1964).

A note about dates: The difference between the new style (Gregorian) calendar and old style (Julian) calendar was twelve days at that time. In Poland the new style was introduced in 1583, but in Russia the old style was in compulsory use. In the Congress Kingdom of Poland, the Russian authorities permitted both styles, but in the Ukraine only the old style. Most letters and documents written in the Ukraine and in Russia referred to in this book were dated in both styles, but sometimes only in one. In a few cases it is impossible to tell which style was used. I have preserved original datings in references, but have used only the new style in the narrative.

> Without country, without people,
> While *Poland—your Mother* is entombed.
> [. . .]
> The time will come, the days will pass,
> This thought will make your courage grow,
> Give Her—and yourself—Immortality.
>   Hushaby, my baby son![15]

The mood was not unusual either for its author or his contemporaries. A year and a half later Apollo wrote a poem to his wife:

> In our Motherland life is hard and sad,
> For her breast is crushed by tombstones,
> [. . .]
> All around ruins and graves,
> Sunless days and starless nights,
> Into an abyss our eyes gaze,
> For nowhere, nowhere can Poland be seen![16]

And he continued about two hearts joined together by the love of motherland and about the patriotic duties of a family. His attitude may appear unusually exalted, even morbid, but looking at the diaries and letters written during this period one sees that such sentiments were far from uncommon. Thousands of Apollo's contemporaries were guided in life primarily by thoughts of freedom and patriotism.

At the beginning of 1859, having sunk most of their money into the tenancy of Derebczynka, the Korzeniowskis moved to Żytomierz.[17] Later that unsuccessful business venture was frequently attacked by Bobrowski, but it is also to him that we owe a possible explanation that does not seem to incriminate Korzeniowski. Bobrowski gives the following description of his brother-in-law: "Open-hearted and passionate in his feelings, he had a sincere love of people; in his deeds he was impractical, often even helpless. Uncompromising in speech and writing, in everyday life he was frequently over-tolerant—evidently for the sake of balance, as I pointed out to him many a time; he also had two sets of measures: one for the weak and ignorant, the other for the mighty of this world." Elsewhere he ascribes the loss of money on the tenancy to "unfavorable circumstances and a little to Korzeniowski's want of prudence."[18] Resourcefulness was certainly not one of Apollo's strong points, but Bobrowski's mention of his special tolerance for "the weak and ignorant"—primarily for peasants—when set side by side with Korzeniowski's views, suggests that his "want of prudence" consisted of taking upon himself the material consequences of bad harvests. After all, in his poem written for the occasion of his brother-in-law's wedding, he wrote:

For your happiness God must be repayed . . .
In your home—think of the homeless . . .
Eating bread—think of the hungry . . .

and he appealed to the newlyweds to direct their happy gaze

. . . Down to earth—at the peasants, at their
tears, poverty and work,
which fill the lives of our brotherly tribe![19]

In Żytomierz, Korzeniowski not only wrote and translated extensively but also participated actively in the cultural life of the Volhynia's capital. He became a shareholder and secretary of a publishing company, devoted primarily to educational books, which was soon closed down by the authorities. Once again he lost money for "want of prudence." His satirical comedy, *Dla miłego grosza* [For the love of money], attacking nouveau riche landowners and opportunists, was successfully staged in Żytomierz, Wilno, Kiev, and Lublin. He began sending regular contributions to Warsaw's *Gazeta codzienna* and other papers. His political and social articles became more dynamic and his poetic output declined; he even expressed doubts about being a poet.[20] He translated his favorite author, Victor Hugo. But politics soon prevailed over literature. The entire country resounded with the echo of Warsaw's patriotic demonstrations: in November 1860, for which Korzeniowski wrote a grandiloquent poem in February 1861, and of the so-called April massacre, when about one hundred peaceful demonstrators were killed by Russian soldiers in the center of Warsaw.

The increasing restlessness among Poles living under Russian rule was caused by several factors. Thirty years had passed since the last major insurrection, and a new generation was finding that within the tsarist system all possibilities of shaping the affairs of their native country were barred. Expectations of liberalizing reforms, raised by the new Tsar Alexander II after the battering Russia had suffered in the Crimean War, were fulfilled to such a small degree that in the end they caused more frustration than good will. The tsar's words, *"point de rêveries, messieurs"* ("no dreaming, gentlemen"), spoken in Warsaw in 1856, dashed all hopes for national self-government. Poles were bitterly conscious of the breakup of their ancient unity and of the growing divergence of developments, economic, social and political, in the three zones of partition. Also, a modicum of autonomy in matters of education, enjoyed by Poles in the Congress Kingdom of Poland (Russia's westernmost provinces), brought out in sharper relief the policy of thorough Russification of peoples in other territories of the Polish Commonwealth. There was little doubt, in fact, that Russification of all subjects was the ultimate goal of tsarist policy.

Korzeniowski had been one of the most active patriots in the Ukraine. Then, in 1861, he moved to Warsaw, ostensibly to establish a new fortnightly, *Dwuty-godnik*, modeled on the Parisian *Revue des Deux Mondes*, but in fact to participate through the spoken and written word in the resistance movement. His wife sent him letters from Terechowa and Żytomierz, entrusting the more important missives to friends and acquaintances rather than the mail, since both she and Apollo were involved in many clandestine activities. She described at length the persecutions that followed the patriotic demonstrations. "Mourning is generally observed to the extent that colored dresses can be seen only occasionally. Konradek still wears our three favorite colors [blue, white and red, the colors of the French revolution]; but he has a mourning frock which I always make him put on for church."[21]

The black color, mourning clothes, funereal phraseology, and visions of death and graves characterized the outward expression of patriotism at the time. Originally they were supposed to bring to mind the "entombed" motherland, but from 26 February 1861 on, mourning was worn in Warsaw as a sign of protest against the suppression by the Cossacks of a freedom demonstration.[22] On the next day, during another demonstration, five people were killed, and then memorial services became the most popular form of displaying patriotic feelings for the entire territory of the old Poland. Requiems were suitable rituals for expressing the idea of independence, entwined with images of sacrifice by death and a "victory through resurrection." Konrad was not yet four when symbolic mourning became real mourning, soon after the outbreak of the 1863 insurrection.

Ewa's letters to her husband abound in enthusiastic references to their son. "Konradek is a good boy: it is amazing how God lets him win people's hearts. Everyone loves him . . . he mentions you every day, asks that we go to you." Ewa's mother echoed her words: "No pen can catch and render all the shades of goodness that child has in him . . . I suspect that our dear Konradzio will grow into an exceptional man."[23]

Among politically active Poles of the time, three factions may be distinguished. The first, and smallest, consisted of the appeasers, who wanted to preserve and even strengthen Polish national identity within the scope of the Russian Empire. The second and largest group was the often vacillating "Whites," who wanted to restore the prepartition Commonwealth without very radical changes in its socio-political structure; they based their hopes on foreign, mainly French, support of the Polish cause. Third were the "Reds" of various shades, who were the most active and enterprising if not always clear-headed; they linked the struggle for national independence with programs for broad social reforms, particularly the liberation of peasants, and they counted mainly on the success of an armed uprising.

Tadeusz Bobrowski was apparently of the opinion that his brother-in-law "affected Redness in order to prove to himself and to others that he was not a mediocrity."[24] This estimate was true to the extent that for Apollo Korzeniowski the whole meaning of life rested on belief in national and social ideals. Bobrowski claimed that he could never fathom "Apollo's political and social convictions," and he attributed this to Korzeniowski's somewhat amorphous opinions. Apollo was allegedly even hesitant on the subject of the abolition of serfdom, but this statement is belied by solid evidence.[25] His poems are explicitly radical. His excessive enthusiasm for the peasantry may have been naive, and his outbursts of feelings certainly dominated any rationally devised political program, but his beliefs, although occasionally lacking cohesion, were always sincere and unwavering. Korzeniowski introduced Tadeusz's brother, Stefan, later called "the brain and heart of the Reds," to conspiratorial work. We also learn by implication from Tadeusz Bobrowski himself why he was unable to comprehend his brother-in-law's views: he admits to refraining from political discussions even with his own brother, Stefan, because of their differences in outlook.[26]

Korzeniowski was in the forefront of the most active and versatile Red activists: he was the leader of the youth at the Arts School and at the Realschule, the organizer of the celebrations commemorating the anniversary of the Lublin Union of Poland and Lithuania (in 1569); he continued his political agitation and published political pamphlets. *Dwutygodnik* was to be the organ of a clandestine national organization. The launching of the fortnightly was announced by the other papers, and Korzeniowski, its founder and editor-in-chief, put out an informational leaflet, gathered material, and looked for contributors.

As a political activist he had the reputation of being a democrat, friend of the peasants, and leader of "the most revolutionary and radical party."[27] His "revolutionism," shown by his advocacy of armed rebellion and a national uprising combined with the abolition of serfdom, went side by side with a deep traditionalism. He wrote to one of *Dwutygodnik*'s correspondents, "Over and above everything I implore you that your articles be fresh—lively—democratic, based on our traditional 'szlachta' democracy."[28] "Traditional szlachta democracy" meant the heritage of citizens' personal liberties and responsibility for the community; here it implied extending those liberties and responsibilities to other groups of society. This kind of traditionalism ought not to be confused with conservatism. Similarly, the call for a united action on the part of the Congress Kingdom, Lithuania, and Ruthenia cannot be interpreted in terms of Polish national expansion. The Reds were aware of the aspirations of other nations who lived in the territory of the old Polish republic, and they strove for the liberation that might lead to coexistence within the framework of one state.[29]

In early October 1861, shortly before a state of emergency was declared in the Kingdom, Ewa Korzeniowska and her son moved to Warsaw. On 17 October the underground Committee of the Movement—the kernel of the future Central Committee and National Government—was formed in the Korzeniowskis' flat at Nowy Świat 45.[30] Many years later, Conrad recalled that "its first meetings were held in our Warsaw house, of which all I remember distinctly is one room, white and crimson, probably the drawing-room. In one of its walls there was the loftiest of all archways. Where it led to remains a mystery; but to this day I cannot get rid of the belief that all this was of enormous proportions, and that the people appearing and disappearing in that immense space were beyond the usual stature of mankind as I got to know it in later life."[31]

Three days later, Apollo Korzeniowski found himself within the walls of the Pavillion X of the Warsaw Citadel.[32] The shadows of alien ghosts thickened into brutal force.

Korzeniowski spent over six months in prison, suffering from rheumatism and scurvy. But he was allowed to read and sometimes even to translate; it was then that he translated Hugo's *Le roi s'amuse*.[33] The records of the investigation and court proceedings were destroyed by fire in 1944, but a summary of the Permanent Investigating Commission has survived. According to it, Apollo Korzeniowski was arrested on four counts: for his participation, together with students, in the "Mierosławski's Reds'" committee opposing the elections to the Warsaw Municipal Council; for inciting disturbances at Wedel's confectionery shop in Miodowa Street; for being the author of the memorial demanding a union of Poland and Lithuania and of the unlawful pamphlet *Narodzie! Baczność!* [Nation! Attention!]; for organizing, with his wife's help, mass prayers in Żytomierz for "those killed in Warsaw by the Russians."[34] Obviously the authorities were not well acquainted with Korzeniowski's real activities, since he was not entirely opposed to elections, could not belong to the nonexistent "committee," nor was he the author of *Nation! Attention!* The police were unaware of his most important conspiratorial work and, instead, tried to ascribe to him the stirring up of ordinary brawls.

The defendant pleaded not guilty. The authorities, however, intending their action to be retaliatory and preventive, "proved" the offence by means of his wife's letters from Żytomierz found during the search. On 9 May the military tribunal sentenced both Korzeniowskis "to exile, under strict police supervision, to the Perm province."[35]

The governor of the province, General Lashkarev, was Korzeniowski's former schoolmate. On learning about the sentence, he asked higher authorities to send the condemned man elsewhere. And so the Korzeniowskis were diverted to Vologda, known for its unhealthy climate. The journey under escort was most disagreeable, and the hardships suffered by the exiles were only occasionally alleviated by accidental meetings with regular army officers, friends of the late Stanisław Bobrowski. On 12 June they reached their destination. From Vologda, Korzeniowski wrote a long letter to his cousins Gabriela and Jan Zagórski.

My beloved Gabrynia and Jaś! This is our sixteenth day at Vologda. We are in good health if you do not count my homesickness. . . . You simply cannot imagine the intolerable conditions of my travel. While we were still on home territory and at every station in the presence of scores of people, the Blue Men [the Russian gendarmes wore blue uniforms] were immensely, despicably polite. But as soon as we left the Mohyleva province and there was nobody around, they became despicably impolite. *Evidently*, over there they were afraid, here they *evidently* turned into heroes. . . . In the White-Stony city [Moscow] our boy gets pneumonia; the doctor applies leeches and gives him calomel; so far so good.[36] But suddenly they harness the horses. Naturally I object to leaving, especially as the doctor makes it clear that this may mean death to the child. My passive resistance delays the journey but prompts my guardian to make his way to the local oracle. The civilized oracle, having listened to the report, confirms the order for immediate departure, since children are born to die [sic]. And so we move on and all I gained by my passive resistance was about a dozen hours. . . . Ewusia fell ill in Nizhny [Nov]gorod. While telegrams enquiring if she could be treated started going to and fro a few days passed and, although permission for treatment was refused, thanks to this delay we learned about a change of our destination. . . . What is Vologda? . . . Vologda is a huge quagmire stretching over three *versts*, cut up with parallel and intersecting lines of wooded footbridges, all rotten and shaky under one's feet: this is the only means of communication for the local people. . . . A year here has two seasons: white winter and green winter. The white winter lasts nine and a half months, the green winter two and a half. Now is the beginning of the green winter: it has been raining continually for 21 days and it will do so till the end. . . . Apart from us there are men from 1830, 1846 and 1848 . . . for them our arrival was like a few drops of water fallen on quick-lime. . . . Anyway we do not regard exile as a punishment but as a new way of serving our country. There can be no punishment for us since we are innocent. . . . Our serene faces, proud bearing and defiant eye cause great wonder here. . . . So do not pity us and do not think of us as martyrs.[37]

There is no despondency in this letter; on the contrary, it is even high spirited in places.

Soon the Korzeniowskis' quarters became a weekly meeting place for Polish and Ukrainian political exiles. All they were served was tea and rusks. As one of the exiles remembered later, "Our hosts could not afford anything else but thanks to their warm hospitality our spiritual needs were amply satisfied, considering our general position at that time." Apollo was respected by the exiles and before long became their natural leader. On his initiative a set of rules was drawn up. While manifesting their Polishness they were, at the same time, expected to give the Russians an example of "how to strive for constitutional freedom"; their behavior should be beyond reproach, and they ought to keep their word even if it were given to a policeman; they should not be ashamed of any work done in order to earn a living.[38] Longin Panteleyev, a future member of the Land and Freedom organization, who visited Vologda at that time and even spoke with the "proud" Apollo, full of optimism about Poland's chances of regaining independence, recalls that all Poles at Vologda "were remarkably patriotic (particularly the women), which contrasted with the absolute passivity of the local population."[39]

Korzeniowski was under constant, although secret, police surveillance.[40] Vologda's governor, Stanisław Chomiński, a Pole, tried to make the exiles' lives a little easier, but after a few months the climate began to undermine the Korzeniowskis' health. Apollo wrote to the Zagórskis, his relatives in Poland, "We are bitterly cold here. For the last couple of days we had plenty of snow. Firewood is as expensive as in Warsaw and the number of stoves equals that of the windows, so we must heat furiously but even when the stoves are red-hot, after several days of frost a white moss appears in the corners of the warmest rooms. We shall turn into excellent preserves. Did I write to you that a couple of weeks ago, on 2nd October, the governor gave permission to move us to Chernikhov but it is impossible on account of our health and the state of local roads."[41] But in spite of everything Korzeniowski kept his spirits up.

For the new year 1863, Konrad received from Uncle Tadeusz a beautiful book on the lives of outstanding and virtuous people, *Les Anges de la terre*, by M. A. E. de Saintes; it bore the inscription, "May it remind you of the year which began in exile, far from your relatives, together with your dear parents—and which, with God's help, will not end in exile."[42] A little later, the boy wrote on his photograph: "To my dear Granny who helped me send pastries to my poor Daddy in prison—grandson, Pole-Catholic and szlachcic, Konrad."[43]

In January 1863 the Korzeniowskis were transferred to Chernikhov in the northeast Ukraine.[44] The conditions and climate were much better, but a new blow fell upon the exiles as news reached them of the outbreak of the insurrection and of the first defeats. "All life within us has come to an end, we are stunned by despair," wrote Apollo.[45] His brother Hilary had been under arrest since 23 January; his father died toward the end of April; Robert was killed in May.[46] Stefan Bobrowski was killed on 12 April in a duel provoked by his right-wing opponents. His brother Kazimierz was put in prison. And while both families were suffering heavy losses, Korzeniowski felt helpless. He knew that the date of the outbreak of the insurrection had been imposed on the conspirators by the occupying power—the Russians had forced the hand of Poles by ordering compulsory conscription. He saw the great plans for national organized action crumble. His health was visibly deteriorating, and Ewa's condition was daily growing more serious.

In the summer of 1863, thanks to Tadeusz Bobrowski's endeavors and the assistance of Stanisław's old friends, Ewa and her son were granted a three-month "leave of absence" for medical treatment and for visiting her relatives at Nowochwastów, the estate of Tadeusz's parents-in-law. Tadeusz was looked upon with a certain respect by a colonel of the Kiev gendarmerie, Ivensen, and had never been suspected of siding with the insurgents (a fact he recorded with some gratification in his memoirs). Nevertheless, at the end of three months, the governor of Kiev Province, Alexandr Bezak, ordered Ewa, at that moment ill, to leave immediately for Chernikhov: he would place her in a prison hospital should she plead bad health. It was only thanks to the assistance of a district police inspector that this threat was not carried out.

"I did not understand the tragic significance of it all at the time," wrote Conrad in *A Personal Record*, "though indeed I remember that doctors also came. There were no signs of invalidism about her—but I think that already they had pronounced her doom unless perhaps the change to a southern climate could re-establish her declining strength. . . . Over all this hung the oppressive shadow of the great Russian Empire—the shadow lowering with the darkness of a new-born national hatred fostered by the Moscow school of journalists against the Poles after the ill-omened rising of 1863."[47]

Strong echoes of the anti-Polish campaign of Mikhail Katkov in *Moskovskie Viedomosti* and of the raging Tsarist terror reverberate in the memoirs, *Poland and Muscovy*, written by Apollo Korzeniowski at Chernikhov. This embittered disquisition deals with Russo-Polish relations from the time of the first partition of Poland. Korzeniowski argued that the history of mankind consists of a struggle between barbarism and civilization; he considered Tsarist Russia a contemporary embodiment of Asiatic, Tartar, and Byzantine barbarism.[48]

In Chernikhov, Korzeniowski also completed a number of translations: Dickens's *Hard Times*, Hugo's *Les travailleurs de la mer*, Shakespeare's *Comedy of Errors*.[49] He was obliged to work hard for his living since he had lost all his savings, together with *Dwutygodnik*, and the two thousand rubles he received in 1862 from Kazimierz Bobrowski could not last long.

Ewa Korzeniowska's health steadily deteriorated after her return to exile. She faded slowly, racked with consumption and deprived of proper medical care; the climate was noxious, and she was tormented by the collapse of the insurrection and the harrassment of patriots. Her brother Tadeusz wrote later in his "Document for the information of my beloved Nephew": "After her return to Chernikhov in the autumn of 1863 she continued to pay no attention to her bad state of health, which was steadily deteriorating and in spite of the insistence of her Mother, who came to you in the summer of 1863, she refused to undergo treatment. On my arrival at your parents' home for the New Year of 1865, I became alarmed at your Mother's condition and I extorted from her a promise to seek the advice of Mr. Romański, whom I brought from Żytomierz and who at first expressed some hope of saving her. Subsequently he visited her once again, in February, only to inform us of the inevitable loss of this most beloved sister." Bobrowski, who consistently concealed the fact that his sister had been convicted and therefore deprived of freedom of movement, gave a one-sided account of the situation. We get a fuller picture from Apollo Korzeniowski's letters to his friend in Warsaw, Kazimierz Kaszewski.

> Despair like rust has been slowly eating into the physical constitution of my wife. For eighteen months the poor girl has been putting everything down to nerves; the local doctors—are they doctors?—kept saying "nothing, nothing, it will pass." I, anxious—never having done anything for my own benefit—cringed, pleaded, begged for a year to change our place of exile. . . . Constantly let down and deferred, I lost hope. And a couple of months ago a sudden consuming fever, a lung condition and an internal tumor requiring removal caused by an irregular blood flow. An old friend—a doctor—from Żytomierz . . . having accidentally heard about my wife's illness, came to us —he has come for the third time, this kindest of men. He sees the operation as indispensable but cannot perform it owing to her lack of strength; he wants to increase her strength—the lung disease becomes more menacing; her strength is greater—haemorrhages take it away. . . . We are very miserable and unhappy today—but even had we been fully aware of the fate which awaited us, we would have acted in the same way. We are very miserable and unhappy—but we praise God for letting us carry our destiny together. . . . And all this has resulted from unity—not of ideas but of principles; from unity—not of tastes but of a sense of duty. [28 February 1865]

> My poor wife, who these two years has been destroyed by despair and by the repeated blows that fall on the members of our joined families, for the last four months terribly—gravely—ill, has barely the strength to look at me, to speak with a hollow voice. This state has been caused by the lack of everything for the body and the soul—no doctors, no medicaments. Today she is allowed to go for treatment to Kiev but her lack of strength makes it impossible. May God be with us for now people cannot help us much. For several months I have been everything in the house—master and servant. I am not complaining about this burden but about how often I am unable to satisfy, help or console my poor patient. Konradek is of course neglected. [26 February 1865]

Ten days later in a letter written jointly by the couple, Apollo announced that their request to move to Odessa had again been refused. Ewa did not want to go alone to Kiev for the operation, the more so as she would not be allowed to follow it with treatment elsewhere. Apollo appealed to Dr. Józef Mianowski to intervene with General Berg, the kingdom's governor general, for permission to leave Chernikhov, and asked him to telegraph his reply.[50] But again his efforts failed.

Ewa Korzeniowska died on 18 April 1865.[51] She was the only person in Konrad Korzeniowski's whole family about whom there are no conflicting reports. All the evidence points to her exceptional qualities. She had intended to become a teacher—quite an extraordinary idea in those days for a young lady from a well-to-do home—but she had to give up the plan for family reasons.[52] For many years she kept her faith in the man she loved, even when his hope was waning, and her unshakable decision to participate in all his activities testifies to her strong character. Ewa's letters to her husband are moving proof of her inquiring mind and affection for him. Tadeusz, fond of pointing out everybody's defects, wrote about his sister: "My elder sister possessed beauty and worldly deportment; her education was above that of our contemporary women; she had a lively imagination and a warm heart. . . . In later years, united with the man she loved, her unusual qualities of intelligence, feelings, mind, and heart blossomed. Amidst the greatest hardships of personal life, beset by all possible social and national misfortunes, she always chose, and with fortitude adhered to, her duties of wife, mother, and citizen, winning the respect of friends and strangers, sharing her husband's exile, and representing Polish womankind with dignity."[53]

After his wife's death, Apollo broke down. He was himself gravely ill with tuberculosis. He wrote to Kaszewski:

My deepest beliefs are shaken; doubts consume all my thoughts. When she is not here, when all I dream about is to see her again—this creature without a blemish, who constituted the entire delight of my existence—doubts overwhelm me and call out: and if my faith is but deluded imagination? . . . If death does end everything? . . . When in the sadness of our parting, gazing at our tiny one, Konradek, you said: if you were not to return for a long time, send him to me and I shall look after him as I do after my Bronek [addressee's son]. Well, she will never return, and perhaps I shall never return either; and Konradek is growing up at my side and by the time he is grown up I shall not be here. Please fulfill your promise.

Poor child: he does not know what a contemporary playmate is; he looks at the decrepitude of my sadness, and who knows if that sight does not make his young heart wrinkled or his awakening soul grizzled. These are important reasons forcing me to tear this poor child away from my dejected heart.[54]

The separation of father and son occurred in the following school year. It is significant that Korzeniowski did not want to leave his son in the care of his family, preferring a friend whose ideas were closer to his own. Meanwhile, Kaszewski was sending schoolbooks and educational advice. What did the seven-year-old boy study in Chernikhov? He had been able to read and write since he was five. Apollo asked for school programs, but it remains unclear which of them he followed. In his correspondence with Kaszewski we read about "classical books," a geometry manual, and Konrad's excellent progress in French. It is rather unlikely that Apollo, given to fits of melancholy, was a versatile and stimulating teacher. According to his own estimate, however, he was a demanding one. He confided to his friend, "Your observation went straight to my heart: indeed we are both without any points of comparison; I teach and demand too much and the little one sees nobody except me, and burrows too deeply into books."[55] There can be no doubt that the boy read extensively and he apparently never saw a children's book.[56] His early reading introduced him to the two elements that later dominated the two major stages of his own life. In *Les travailleurs de la mer* he encountered the sphere of activity to which he was to devote the best years of his youth; in reading Shakespeare, whose loyal disciple he remained for the rest of his life, he was brought into the orbit of English literature. Most of all, however, he must have been reading Polish romantic poetry. Fifty years later he explained, "The Polishness in my works comes from Mickiewicz and Słowacki. My father read [Mickiewicz's] *Pan Tadeusz* aloud to me and made me read it aloud. Not just once or twice. I used to prefer *Konrad Wallenrod, Grażyna*. Later I preferred Słowacki. You know why Słowacki? Il est l'âme de toute la Pologne, lui [He is the soul of all Poland]."[57]

For his name day, 26 November, in 1865, Konrad received a magnificent present from a relative, Regina Korzeniowska: one thousand rubles "to buy shoes, galoshes and a fur coat."[58] Regina, an editor of historical atlases, was known mainly for her eccentricity. In the Korzeniowski family she and her sister Katarzyna were the only ones whose estates had not been confiscated as the result of the insurrection. Hilary, sentenced to settlement in Tomsk, "started on a sixteen-month walk," wrote Apollo. "Any day now my sister will begin her walk—perhaps not exactly along the same road, but one just as long. This has caused the loss of everything we have which was kept undivided, since we loved each other; and two beggars have joined in my wealth."[59] The gift of money could be very useful—not only for the purchase of warm clothes. Konrad's father was in constant financial difficulties. Translations did not bring much money, and he had no other source of income.[60]

One of the most frequent motifs in Apollo's letters is his anxiety about Konrad. "My health has been declining badly and my dear little mite takes care of me—only the two of us left on this earth. I need never be ashamed on account of his heart; he inherited his gifts from his mother but his head is not to be envied—it is mine." "My little one is in good health and we carry on with our work—although we are both throttled by many, many hands. Ah! If I could describe those hands it would make an interesting article. Following your advice I have released the poor child from some of his tasks. My God, my God—how I miss a kind word of mitigation from someone close."[61]

The atmosphere in the Korzeniowski home at Chernikhov must have been quite strange. Father and son led a lonely life; Apollo worked a lot but went through periods of numbness and prostration. He lived in a state of continual emotional stress that must have been aggravated by his lung disease. For this self-sacrificing man full of fighting spirit, now condemned to inactivity, only the great fundamental issues were important. He looked at the world and his own life in terms of struggling ideologies, of a clash between freedom and oppression, sacrifice and anarchy. Much of this was beyond Konrad's grasp, but he felt and remembered the general atmosphere; only later, when his father was no more, and Uncle Tadeusz was explaining everything his own way, only then could Konrad attempt to understand his father's attitude.

A most moving document is Apollo's letter written at New Year's 1866 to his cousins, the Zagórskis:

If there is a smile anywhere in our country, may it light up your life; may tears not scorch your hearts but bring relief to your tormented souls. . . . I have survived those hard, terrible days of my most sacred memories, I have lived through them with God given strength, not my own. . . . By looking continually at the Cross I kept fortifying my enfeebled soul, my confused thoughts. And thus the holy days of torture had passed and I, feeling slightly broken but still alive and breathing, rose to meet my everyday existence. The little orphan keeps clinging to me and it is impossible not to be constantly worrying about him. And so, my beloved, I continue living and loving—whatever is left to love, as strongly as before, except that in the past I could give something, sacrifice something, to the objects of my love—and today I cannot. . . . When bitter misery chokes me and a kind of godly sadness—not proud despair—descends upon me, I read your dear letter again and again; tears stream down—thoughts flow away—and slightly calmer I begin once again to tackle my life, which is, at present, confined solely to Konradek. I teach him all I know myself—alas it is not much; I guard him against the influence of the local atmosphere, and the little mite is growing up as though, in a cloister; the grave of our Unforgettable is our *memento mori* and every letter from the East, West, South or North brings us fastings, cilice, and flogging. We tremble with cold, die of hunger, struggle in abject poverty of our brothers; and in our prayers, God knows it, we put only a couple of words about ourselves. I am here as though by a bolted door behind which a beloved being is dying and we cannot as much as wipe the mortal sweat off her forehead; on the other side there is a wide open door through which we cannot enter but are permitted to look at something that Dante had not described, for his soul, stricken with countless horrors but nonetheless Christian, could not have inhuman visions. That is our life.[62]

In May 1866, Apollo sent Konrad for the summer to his grandmother, Teofila Bobrowska, in Nowochwastów. In August the boy became ill, and in the autumn his grandmother took him back to Chernikhov—not for long though, since medical treatment in Kiev was necessary.[63] Lessons had to be interrupted and sending Konrad to Warsaw was postponed. On 22 November, Korzeniowski wrote to Kaszewski: "I am lonely. Konradek is with his granny; his first month away was at Kiev visiting the doctors, then, on their advice, he went to his uncle in the country. We both suffer equally: just imagine, the boy is so foolish that he misses his loneliness where all he saw was my clouded face and where the only diversion of his nine-year-old life was arduous lessons; he misses me in the clean country air, amidst amusements with his first cousin, his contemporary, under the caressing wings of his granny, with his indulgent uncle who has transferred all his love for his sister on to her son. . . . And the boy pines away—he must be foolish and I fear will remain so all his life. He has grown, his little face has altered, he begins to look very much like his mother."

Konrad's stay with his uncle at Nowochwastów did not last long, and he remained in Kiev until the following spring, undergoing medical treatment. On his return to the country he came down with German measles and had to be sent away again for treatment, this time to Żytomierz.[64] In the summer of 1867 his Uncle Tadeusz took him to Odessa, where he saw the sea for the first time.[65] Conrad's recollection of a hero of the 1830 insurrection, Prince Roman Sanguszko, to whom he was to devote his story "Prince Roman," dates from this period.

What was the cause of Konrad's persistent ill health? Apollo's mention of kidney trouble in one of his later letters is somewhat vague. And from several independent sources we learn that epileptic attacks were among the boy's symptoms.[66] We do not know when the first one occurred and, not possessing detailed medical diagnosis, we may only assume that his epilepsy was psychosomatic, brought on by his painful experiences. The character of his illness explains, as we shall see, a number of puzzling aspects of Konrad Korzeniowski's young life.

In December 1867, as the result of his family's sustained efforts, the Russian Ministry of Internal Affairs issued Apollo Korzeniowski a permit to leave with his son for Algiers and Madeira. On 17 January the permission was confirmed by the chancellery of Chernikhov's governor, Prince Golitsyn.[67] The mortally sick man had neither the money nor the desire to go to Madeira, but for his son's sake he decided to go abroad, to the Austrian part of Poland, which for the last two years had been enjoying considerable internal freedom and a degree of self-government. Father and son met at Nowochwastów, whence, at the end of February, they left for Lwów.[68]

For Apollo, the last stage of his exile must have been the hardest since his wife's death. When the time came for him to leave, he expected to be able to breathe freely among his countrymen in the Austrian Empire, where life was incomparably less constrained. But the joy of being allowed to publish patriotic works and to correspond openly with friends, such as Buszczyński, was soon marred by disappointment with Galician inactivity and sycophancy, with quarrels between Poles, with their neglect of national affairs and the squandering of money on festivities, and, finally, with the Germanization of the Polish language. Korzeniowski's entire political activity had hitherto been confined to the underground, and he was therefore unable to understand the different conditions of life in Galicia. His reactions were extreme, triggered by exaggerated expectations based on the high principles of a man who had always done his utmost for the cause. What was more, even now he was still reproaching himself for having "deserted his post" and abandoned his exiled countrymen.[69] He felt like a prisoner who, on being released, realizes that people around him are leading ordinary, quiet lives, using freedom for their own private ends, without giving a thought to the cause for which he has suffered. His own infirmity and declining strength added to his general frustration. The indignation of an idealist and the resignation of dying are closely intertwined in his letters.

The two Korzeniowskis spent the first two months in Lwów. Apollo published several poems, among them *Morze-Lud* [The sea—the people], a paraphrase of *Au peuple* from Hugo's *Flogging*. It ends with this eloquent stanza:

> The Sea, like you People, foams and bursts forth;
> But it never fails. He, who from afar
> Wistfully looks out, waiting
> for the incoming tide . . . shall see it come![70]

Apart from politics his two main preoccupations were his son's upbringing and concern for his failing health. He wrote to Buszczyński, "My second, if not my first, object is to bring up Konradek not as a democrat, aristocrat, demagogue, republican, monarchist, nor as a servant and a flunky of those parties— but only as a Pole."[71]

In April and May father and son spent some time on the estate belonging to the Mniszek family in Kruhel Wielki on the outskirts of Przemyśl. Apollo was then carrying on discussions and correspondence with Prince Adam Sapieha about his co-editorship of the *Kraj*, a democratic organ that was to be established in Cracow. "Probably I too shall settle down in Cracow because of the stupid Lwów schools. I am sorry for Konrad's capabilities, which are being wasted here, and I am unable even to supervise his lessons."[72]

In the middle of June both Korzeniowskis went to Topolnica in the Stary Sambor district, where Apollo underwent a four-month cure. His letters contain frequent references to his son. "Konradek . . . writes well, without any help from me—and as to loving, he loves those whom I point out to him as worthy." "My little one suffers from a new onset of his old illness typical of children: urinary sand forms in his bladder, causing continuous cramps in the stomach. In such a state of health it is difficult to make him do his lessons, and yet he is already eleven years old and for the last two years has hardly studied at all. Kind as always."[73]

The cure restored some of Apollo's old vitality, but by the middle of October his health again declined. At that time the political groups in Galicia were arguing hotly about the attitude to be adopted toward the government in Vienna and about the range of liberties and autonomous privileges to be demanded from the emperor. The prevailing hope was that conciliatory tendencies toward the central government could be exchanged for greater autonomy for Galicia; in that spirit the regional *sejm* passed a compromise resolution on 24 September.[74] To Apollo, these tactical maneuvers motivated by personal interest seemed repulsive, and his letters of 13 and 14 October to Buszczyński and Kaszewski testify to his extreme irritation.

A life of tiresome struggle—you remember how we embarked on it fourteen years ago—the imprisonment in a rotten Muscovite dungeon, the foul Muscovite exile, and all the personal anguish—you know their measure—all of it has not achieved what a six-month stay in Galicia has done: I am broken, fit for nothing, too tired even to spit upon things.

I am nearing my end; it ought to come with the least expense and trouble: it is not I who have to bear the burden of expense and trouble. . . . Two days of cold and several pieces of good news, a look round at the conditions in which I shall be bringing up Konradek, have destroyed in one blow the results of medicaments and of the several months long treatment. . . . It was my intention to send Konradek to school this year: I have put it off till next year. I am well aware of the advantages of public education for a boy; but judge yourself, my best friend: I arrive at the Gymnasium to enroll my child. The children are just dispersing to their homes for lunch; I find myself surrounded by Polish children; formidable chatter, as of old. I listen and doubt my hearing; strange sounds reach me—Polish among others—but believe me, believe me that I could understand less than half of that childish prattle.[75]

Nevertheless he persevered. He made plans for political and literary works, for a long novel about Polish society from 1854 to 1861, for a collected edition of his poems, and for a complete Polish edition of Victor Hugo's dramas. But his projects were always supplemented with an ironic comment: "Most of the time I am ready to drop, but continue making plans: methinks I am not unlike them."[76] His mood kept changing—doubtless as the result of his illness—but he was getting ready to take up the job of editing for the *Kraj* the sections on Russian and English affairs.

On 1 December he finished the last piece of his work known to us: the fore-word to the drama *Akt pierwszy* [The first act], in which he briefly expounded his views on the social and national functions of literature. "We behold an en-tire generation of writers and poets who hold the quill like a sword. . . . It is difficult to lay the blame for such everlasting weapons upon men who have nothing and ought to regain everything. . . . We, like many others, claim no right to be called writers but have been using our pens for a long time. Let us repeat the words of an Italian patriot and poet [Giosuè Carducci]: 'I am writing now only because I cannot act.'"[77]

It appears Konrad, at eleven, also produced literary pieces charged with patri-otic ideals. A friend of his from those days recalled later that Konrad used to write "plays," usually on the subject of the insurgents fighting against the Mus-covites (the author's favorite headgear was a red and white "Confederate cap"*), to be enacted by his contemporaries. "His most spectacular drama was called *The Eyes of King Jan Sobieski*." Everyone was impressed by his excellent mem-ory and extensive reading; he knew long fragments from Mickiewicz's *Pan Ta-deusz* and *The Ballads* by heart.[78]

In a letter written on Christmas Eve in 1868 his father wrote, "My Konradek is in good health. And this pleases me more than anything else, for his nerves were shaky. He is receiving formal education in accordance with the local school syllabus, although this year he will not attend classes. He is quite ca-pable but has as yet no taste for learning and lacks stability. Admittedly he is only eleven. But before I close my eyes I would like to foresee the course he will follow. He likes to criticize everything from an emotional standpoint. He is also tender and good beyond words." He had private lessons from a pupil from the gymnasium, since Apollo "has by now become incapable of pedagogical work."[79] In spite of his constantly deteriorating health, Apollo took a lively in-terest in the Cracow newspaper, which was scheduled to make its debut toward the end of February. At last, on 20 February, both Korzeniowskis moved to 6 Poselska Street in Cracow.[80] But Apollo's work on the newspaper was only per-functory. His life was coming to an end; he died on 23 May 1869.[81]

The words of his essay on "The Dramatic Element in Shakespeare's Works," which he wrote in 1867—words echoing Friedrich Schiller's formula of fate which exalts man when it pulverizes him—could serve as his epitaph: "By the innate power of his spirit and will man often masters, if only momentarily, events—and then he notices how they become even more sluggish and stub-born on the road he has compelled them to move. And in this struggle, finally, when his life is smashed to pieces, man perishes—but with that quality, with which God has endowed him in the act of creation, intact."[82]

In his introduction to *A Personal Record*, written fifty years later, Con-rad tells of the impression made on him by the "burning of his manuscripts a

---

* As worn by members of the Bar Confederacy, founded in 1768 to fight Russian interference in Poland.

fortnight or so before his death. It was done under his own superintendence. I happened to go into his room a little earlier than usual that evening, and remaining unnoticed stayed to watch the nursing-sister feeding the blaze in the fireplace. My father sat in a deep armchair propped up with pillows. This is the last time I saw him out of bed. His aspect was to me not so much that of a man desperately ill as mortally weary—a vanquished man. That act of destruction affected me profoundly by its air of surrender. Not before death however. To a man of such strong faith death could not have been an enemy."[83]

This expressive fragment often quoted by biographers is, however, like many others in Conrad's reminiscences, at variance with the truth. Twenty years before writing *A Personal Record*, Conrad himself stated in a letter to his friend Edward Garnett that "piles of MS, dramas, verse, prose were burnt after his death according to his last will."[84] Moreover, two pieces of evidence testify that if Apollo had burned or given instructions to burn some papers, they were not his own works. Buszczyński's letter of 19 January 1870 to Kaszewski states that Apollo had put him in charge of all his literary manuscripts.[85] Furthermore, two volumes of Apollo's manuscripts were arranged by Buszczyński and preserved in the Jagiellonian Library in Cracow. Did Apollo really die "a vanquished man" as Conrad remembered (or wished to remember)? It is neither certain nor even very probable. There is no proof of Apollo having renounced his ideals or acknowledging his defeat—only of having become embittered with people and his own infirmity. Thus Conrad's reminiscences ought to be read also as a document of his struggle for his own soul, a struggle that lasted for many years after his father's death.[86]

Apollo Korzeniowski's funeral on 26 May turned into a patriotic demonstration. "Huge crowds surged along the Grodzka and Poselska streets to pay their last respects to the prematurely departed poet and Poland's noble son. The clergy, trade guilds with their banners, students and gymnasium pupils, and representatives of educational societies and of the voluntary fire brigade surrounded the coffin; several thousand people followed in silence." All "had come only to render homage to the ardent fidelity of the man whose life had been a fearless confession in word and deed of a creed which the simplest heart in that crowd could feel and understand."[87]

And so in the middle of his twelfth year Konrad's childhood ended. His father's death, although imminent for some years, must have been a painful shock for the sensitive boy. Contrary to what he wrote later in "Poland Revisited," we know that he wept bitterly at the time.[88] Thirty years later Conrad described his father as "a man of great sensibilities; of exalted and dreamy temperament; with a terrible gift of irony and of gloomy disposition; with strong religious feeling which after the loss of his wife turned into mysticism touched with despair. His aspect was distinguished; his conversation very fascinating; his face in repose sombre, lighted all over when he smiled."[89] His dead father had left him a formidable psychological legacy: an exceptionally intense emotional life; a rigorous and desperate love of his country, and a spontaneous, instinctive belief in democracy; a hatred of the invaders, particularly Russians; inflexible principles that clashed with his volatile moods; a peculiar approach to life's practical problems that was not based on cool perception but consisted rather of absorbing them as if with sudden spasms of his heart, and viewing them always in the light of ultimate aims; a great love of romantic literature; a solitariness imposed by intractable circumstance; and the bitterness of shattered hopes.

Sooner or later Apollo's legacy was bound to collide with the influence of Tadeusz Bobrowski, the boy's guardian. Bobrowski, a wise and honest man, was at the same time reserved and conceited. In his own view he evoked respect rather than affection: "Unable to secure both, I would rather be esteemed than loved." He was, he wrote, "a convinced doctrinaire, deeply confident of the inflexible and unchanging rights and duties of the mind, of critical judgement and free will which make man a master of his own fate and history; I reject all side influences issuing from emotions, passions and other people; through clear thinking I have arrived at a ready formula to meet every problem in life." He shrouded himself, with haughtiness and naiveté, in the mantle of an eighteenth-century rationalist.[90]

What literature and politics were to Apollo, laws, regulations, and accounts were to Tadeusz. His "Document for the information of my beloved nephew Konrad Korzeniowski," written over a number of years, consists largely of long rows of figures interspersed with remarks that, through Apollo's fault and later his son's, financial losses had been incurred or the budget exceeded. Accounts appear in almost all his early letters to Konrad, along with lamentations about the Korzeniowski extravagance. Konrad must have sensed his Uncle Tadeusz's veiled dislike of his father. Bobrowski did not spare hints that his nephew's shortcomings were characteristic of his father and the Nałęcz family in general. By the same token he glorified his own family, praising its common sense, although from his own *Memoirs* we learn that Józef Bobrowski's obstinacy resulted in the loss of thirty thousand rubles over the purchase of an estate and that he died heavily in debt; that he himself frittered away two years at the university; and that his brother, Stanisław, a frivolous philanderer, once arrived home on leave from the army, without horses, with a pawn ticket for his uniform, and three thousand rubles in debt. There is hardly a mention of his uncles, Adolf and Seweryn Pilchowski, scamps in their youth. Contrasting the hotheaded Nałęcz clan with the sensible Bobrowskis, he forgot that all his brothers were hotheads, and that Kazimierz and Stefan held political views similar to Apollo's.[91] Referring to his guardianship, he usually recalled the memory of Konrad's mother, but consistently effaced her patriotic ardor. Characteristically, in the "Document," he stated, ". . . so that you should know that we all loved your Mother and through her you," and only later added "—and your Father."

Tadeusz's unsympathetic attitude toward his brother-in-law was linked with his hostility toward Korzeniowski's political views. Tadeusz opposed the tradition of resistance; he was convinced that if not for the 1863 insurrection ("begot of falsehood and ended in falsehood"), the number of liberal laws introduced by Tsar Alexander II would have increased.[92] Thus his political "realism" was one-sided: he could be a penetrating critic of mistakes made by the conspirators but failed to recognize that appeasement founded on the good will of the occupying nation was equally futile. Although he regarded himself as a patriot and delighted in stressing the cultural superiority of Poles over Russians, his patriotism consisted mainly of adherence to tradition and to the Polish language; it did not lead him to any practical conclusions. True, in 1857 he was very active in a several-hundred-member committee, formed by Polish landowners in the Ukraine, that drafted proposals for laws emancipating the peasantry; he later described in his memoirs the work of this committee. Bobrowski's attitude was grounded in rationalist economic and humanitarian considerations, but he was far from envisaging legal equality, not to mention political rights, for peasants.

Conrad avowed later that Tadeusz had had an enormous influence on him and, not without justification, he regarded that influence as beneficial. But we may see quite clearly that his uncle's authority and example competed quite consciously with his father's. What countless exacerbations and complexes must have arisen in Konrad's mind before his father's shadow receded behind the exigences of life and his guardian's voice.

Konrad's life at first ran in accordance with his late father's wishes. He was looked after by Stefan Buszczyński, his father's closest friend and ideological ally, an eminent publicist whose book *La Décadence de l'Europe* (1867), in which he expressed his liberal beliefs and his admiration for American democracy, won praise from Victor Hugo and Jules Michelet. Konrad was placed in a pension for boys run by one Ludwik Georgeon, in the Fajll's house, on Floriańska Street, a choice that was certainly not accidental since Georgeon was a veteran of the 1863 insurrection.[93] A few weeks after the funeral, Konrad's grandmother, Teofila Bobrowska, moved to Cracow. Later she informed Kaszewski that "the boy's ignorance of the German and Latin languages precluded him from attending other than the second class of the [gymnasium]; we hope he will go into the fourth class next year since his headmaster and the teachers praise his industry, comprehension and application—providing God gives him health—to which end he devotes his spare time. His guardian maintains that he has never known any other child so easy to bring up and with a heart as noble as his; he had surrounded his poor father with most tender attention."[94] Conrad recalled later that at that time he had attended a preparatory school on Floriańska Street; probably the lessons were organized within the Georgeon pension. In the summer his grandmother took him to Bavaria for a water cure in Wartenberg.[95]

The five years that followed constitute the period in Conrad's life about which the least is known. From Bobrowski's notes we learn of the expenses connected with the boy's upkeep; we also know something about his travels during the school holidays, but it is difficult to form a complete picture, all the more so since we lack information about his principal occupation at the time, namely his studies. In 1914 Conrad said that he had left Poland "straight from the fifth class from Saint Anne's Gymnasium in Cracow." He may indeed have left "straight from the fifth class," but it was neither from Cracow nor from St. Anne's Gymnasium. If he attended any Cracow school, which is doubtful considering his illness and the lack of any records, it may have been St. Jacek's Gymnasium, on Sienna Street, where Georgeon had been teaching French.[96] Most likely, however, he took only private lessons from his regular tutor, a student of medicine named Adam Marek Pulman.* It was Pulman who accompanied him to Krynica, a mountain resort, from June to September, in 1870, 1871, and 1872. From 1871 on Konrad received additional educational assistance from an eminent anthropologist, Izydor Kopernicki, who had been a close friend of Konrad's father and a "Red" conspirator from the Ukraine as well as a veteran of the 1863 insurrection.[97] According to all existing evidence, we may assume that Konrad was a mediocre scholar at best. He maintained later that geography had been his favorite subject.

Grandmother Teofila remained in Cracow until January 1870, looking after her ailing grandson.[98] She returned to Cracow in November 1870 and stayed there nearly three years. On 2 August 1870, the Cracow municipal court appointed Teofila Bobrowska the custodian of her "grandson, Konrad Nałęcz-Korzeniowski, a minor," stating that she would be assisted in her guardianship by Count Władysław Mniszek, husband of the late Maria (née Czarnecka), a friend of Ewa Korzeniowska.[99] In this way Stefan Buszczyński was released from his duties, a release which coincided with his departure to Dresden.

Tadeusz Bobrowski, who provided money for Konrad's upkeep, must have had the deciding voice. His attitude toward the boy was at first dry and official. His first letter to Konrad after Apollo's death, written as late as 20 September 1869, sounds like a sermon—a rather striking document considering that the boy was less than twelve years old at the time.

It has pleased God to strike you with the greatest misfortune that can assail a child—the loss of its Parents. But in His goodness God has so graciously allowed your very good Grandmother and myself to look after you, your

---

* Adam Marek Pulman, son of Herakliusz, born at Jurewicze, province of Mozyrz, age twenty-two, entered the Faculty of Medicine at Cracow University in 1868/9 (no. 31); graduated in 1875. Jagiellonian University Archives.

health, your studies and your future destiny. . . . Without a thorough education you will be worth nothing in this world, you will never be self-sufficient.
. . . Therefore, not that which is easy and attractive must be the object of
your studies but that which is useful, although sometimes difficult, for a man
who knows nothing fundamentally, who has no strength of character and no
endurance, who does not know how to work on his own and guide himself,
ceases to be a man and becomes a useless puppet. Try therefore, my child, not
to be or to become such a puppet, but to be useful, hard-working, capable
and therefore a worthy human being—and thereby reward us for the cares
and worries devoted to your upbringing.

Your education has been thought out by us, your needs supplied, it remains for you to learn and to be healthy and even in that matter (although it
chiefly depends on God) if you take heed of the advice of your elders you may
become completely well—not giving way to feelings and thoughts which are
not really proper to your age! [100]

Although in later years Konrad deserved more than once to be thus admon-
ished, it seems highly unlikely that his instability or lack of diligence could already have incurred his uncle's displeasure. Bobrowski's reference to his nephew's oversensitivity is quite significant.

Konrad's friends at that time were "Kocio" (Konstanty), Stefan Buszczyński's
son, a year his senior, and the large Taube family, who lived on the same premises
to which Georgeon's pension had been moved. A biographical legend has it that
Konrad was in love with Janina, one of the Taube sisters (he corresponded with
her later), but a glance at her birth certificate dispels this myth; at the time of
Konrad's departure from Cracow Janina was only eight years old. [101] Conrad's
allusions many years later to the subject of his first loves do not enable us to
identify any of them. We know that among his friends there were also the
slightly older Karolina Taube and Ofelia Buszczyńska, as well as a Miss Ceza-
ryna, the fiancée of a professor; apparently all the pupils at Georgeon's pension
sighed for the beautiful Miss Wyżykowska who lived with the Taubes—but,
after all, if Konrad were in love it did not have to be with somebody whose
existence is known to us. And as to the unhappy love affair bitterly described in
the discarded rough draft of the beginning of *The Arrow of Gold*, it apparently
took place not in Cracow but during his holidays at Krynica. [102]

The tone of the notes and early letters of Tadeusz Bobrowski shows that his
charge was a continual worry to him. The anxiety was probably caused in the
first place by Konrad's health: direct information about his nervous attacks refers precisely to the years spent in Cracow. There were also other problems. The
frail boy betrayed a "talent for cigars," and he defied the authority of adults. [103]
His disposition, which had fitted his lonely existence with his father so well,
must have been ill adapted to everyday life with other people.

The possibility of Konrad going back to his native Ukraine was never considered. As a son of political exiles he would be open to harassment and to many
years of military service. Attempts were made to secure Austrian nationality for
him, but to no avail.* Meanwhile, in the autumn of 1872, the youngster announced his intention of becoming a sailor. Where did he get this idea? The
issue has been magnified by many writers on Conrad, particularly in Poland;
the idea has been treated as exceptional and extraordinary. But what was truly
extraordinary was his later career as a writer. Dreams of faraway voyages and
adventures are rather typical for teenage boys and, even more in those days
than now, distant lands held great fascination.

In the second half of the nineteenth century progress in natural science fostered the belief that it was possible to know and understand everything, and
technological development rendered all parts of the globe gradually accessible.
But the romantic appeal of discovery still persisted, and exploratory voyages
still constituted a challenge to man's courage, inventiveness, and endurance.
The buoyant optimism about science and civilization encouraged explorers, but
the earth did not give up her secrets easily. Each new discovery increased the
fascination with exciting conquests but evoked, at the same time, a feeling of
slight uneasiness. How much more was left to be explored, how many more
opportunities for adventure? People all over the world were captivated by such
expeditions as Leopold McClintock's in the *Fox* (1857–1859), in search for
the lost ships *Erebus* and *Terror*; Conrad recalled later that as a child he had
read McClintock's book.[104]

There were many Poles among the contemporary explorers. Even from Kopernicki, Konrad could have heard about Paweł Edmund Strzelecki, who mapped
the Australian interior, and about Sygurd Wiśniowski, from Podolia, who had
sailed twice around the world. He certainly read in *Wędrowiec* about a veteran
of the 1863 insurrection, Jan Kubary, who since 1869 had been exploring the
Pacific islands collecting exhibits for the Godeffroy Museum in Hamburg.**
Wędrowiec of 28 November 1872 stated that Kubary, setting out for a distant
expedition, wrote from the Atlantic to his mother, "What today happens on
land can evoke nothing but contempt, and seclusion at sea is a hundredfold
more pleasant than life among men." The young traveler professed to prefer

---

* In 1872 Teofila Bobrowska put in an application to the city council to obtain the freedom of the city of
Cracow for Konrad. Permission was granted in a letter of 28 December 1872 on condition of his receiving
Austrian citizenship. Efforts to achieve this end continued for a long time (Bobrowski, "Document") without
success, probably because Konrad had no permission from the Russian authorities to remain abroad permanently and had not been released from Russian citizenship.
** *Wędrowiec*, according to its editors, was "a periodical publishing reports of voyages and expeditions, descriptions of customs and morals of foreign peoples, lives of famous foreigners, stories, translations from
foreign literature, news from the field of natural science, industry and technology, etc."; it was a lively, well-
edited magazine. It published many illustrated descriptions of travels and adventures, mostly in translation
from languages other than Polish.

death in "the deep Ocean" rather than on land because—and here follows a fragment cut out by the censors although the thought is completed by the words "you lie in a free grave." [105] The meaning of this sentiment, with its mood reminiscent of some of Apollo Korzeniowski's poetry, concurs strikingly with Conrad's frequent contrasting of the defiled earth with the purity and freedom of the sea. [106] In any case he did not lack inspiration to set out to sea.

It is difficult to reconstruct Konrad's daily life in Cracow. What books did he read apart from Cooper and Marryat? Did he go to the theatre? In those days Cracow's theatres flourished and he could have seen most of Shakespeare's plays. But he was probably too young to have seen in June 1870 Victor Hugo's *Marion Delorme* in his father's translation, with Helena Modrzejewska (Modjeska) acting the main part. [107] It is also difficult to ascertain the extent to which he was influenced by the then current anti-Romantic, anti-insurrectional, loyalist campaign of Cracow conservatives, whose ideology corresponded with that of Uncle Tadeusz. Konrad must have heard about that campaign; the subject was discussed at the Buszczyńskis, but we shall never know whether it hurt his feelings, aroused contempt, or sowed in him the seeds of bitter resignation. And we cannot know the reaction of the thirteen-year-old boy to France's capitulation to Bismarck's Germany after the Battle of Sedan, a capitulation which in the minds of Konrad's contemporaries destroyed all hope of international developments advantageous to Poland, and deepened the existing mood of resignation. "Until that time Polish hopes were based on an alliance of western countries, France and England, which could draw to their side one of the partitioning powers. . . . It was by no means the January Insurrection which pushed the Polish problem off the European diplomatic scene—but Sedan." [108]

In November or December 1870, Konrad was taken away from Georgeon's pension and moved to his grandmother's flat at 9 Szpitalna Street, where he lived until May 1873. Konstanty Buszczyński recalled that his playmate had a habit of spinning fantastic yarns, whose action always took place at sea and was presented so realistically that the listeners thought it was happening before their eyes. But he was not good at his lessons, and in spite of coaching, excelled only in his beloved geography. [109] On that last point, Conrad's recollections agree with the accounts of his friends.

During those years Uncle Tadeusz was unable to spare much time for his nephew because of long periods he spent abroad for the unsuccessful medical treatment of his daughter Józefa, who died in 1871. Konrad was also in need of medical treatment. Following a doctor's advice, he was sent to Switzerland in May 1873, accompanied by Pulman; a proposed six-week stay lasted twice as long because of a cholera outbreak in Cracow. Konrad and Pulman visited Vienna, Munich, and northern Italy; Conrad claimed to have seen the sea for the first time from the Lido in Venice; he also recalled Milan Cathedral in moonlight. [110] In August, Bobrowski returned to Cracow and took matters in hand.

Having apparently decided that the grandmother's care was no longer adequate and a further stay in Cracow inadvisable, he sent Konrad to Lwów to be looked after by his cousin, Antoni Syroczyński, who ran a boardinghouse for boys orphaned by the 1863 insurrection. The boardinghouse was quite small; group conversation was in French. Bobrowski told Konrad he expected that "the worthy guardianship to which I have entrusted you will help to harden you, which is something that every man needs in this life, and also will provide you with more regular education." [111] It follows, therefore, that in Cracow Konrad's education had not been systematic, but we still cannot establish whether in Lwów he attended a regular school or received private tuition. [112]

Tekla, Antoni Syroczyński's daughter, preserved the following memory: "He stayed with us ten months while in the seventh class at the Gymnasium. Intellectually he was extremely advanced but disliked school routine, which he found tiring and dull; he used to say that he was very talented and planned to become a great writer. Such declarations coupled with a sarcastic expression on his face and with frequent critical remarks, shocked his teachers and provoked laughter among his classmates. He disliked all restrictions. At home, at school, or in the living room he would sprawl unceremoniously. He used to suffer from severe headaches and nervous attacks; the doctors thought that a stay at the seaside might cure him." [113] The picture is completed by the following anecdote preserved by the Syroczyński family. Once, when traveling in a carriage in the company of a couple of venerable old gentlemen, friends of his father's, Konrad cut into their conversation with an unexpected question, "And what do you think of me?" To which they replied, "You are a silly boy who interrupts when adults are talking." [114] Another acquaintance from that period, Jadwiga Tokarska, a year Konrad's senior, recalled that he was very advanced and serious for his age and he used to attend open university lectures on literature and natural sciences, dreamt about distant voyages, and liked to read the *Wędrowiec*. [115] After Cracow, which was then a sleepy city, engrossed in its past and rather provincial, Lwów, the capital of Galicia, presented a marked contrast as a lively center of commerce, culture, and learning.

Konrad's health was still a problem. In March 1874 he was obliged to interrupt his studies. His worst complaints were headaches. Pulman was to take him on an Easter hiking holiday to the Carpathian Mountains. "So you will have to comply with my disposition, abandon illness and sadness in Lwów, and, apart from a small supply of books, you must bring a considerable amount of willingness to jump, run around, go for strenuous walks, show good appetite, etc., etc." His stay in Lwów was expected to last another year or eighteen months, which tallies with Tekla Syroczyńska's statement about Konrad following the course of the next to last class of the gymnasium; later, it was presumed that after that the young man would "start on [his] chosen profession." [116]

But things turned out differently. Perhaps as the result of flirting with Tekla (as maintained by the Syroczyński family tradition) or because of some other conflict with Uncle Antoni, who was both an exacting man and critical of Konrad, or simply on account of ill-health, Uncle Tadeusz removed his nephew from school in September 1874. On 19 September they returned to Cracow, and on 13 October, when all the preparations were completed, the seventeen-year-old Konrad, equipped with clothes and books, set off for Marseilles, for the sea he had long been dreaming about.[117]

Konrad Korzeniowski's departure from Poland was the turning point in his life, and it provokes the most heated arguments. What were the reasons for it? To begin with, it must be stressed that the final decision had to come from Tadeusz Bobrowski, and all his charge could do was to plead and press. Why did he plead? And why was he allowed to leave before finishing his school? Biographers have advanced several suppositions, but not all of them make sense. An unhappy love affair (and we lack any indication of one) would not have been regarded by Bobrowski as a decisive factor. Still less convincing is the conjecture that Konrad may have wanted to escape from Cracow's atmosphere of historical celebrations, from life weighed down with the memories of a glorious past. Nor is it any more likely that he was "consciously cutting himself off from his father's troublesome patrimony, from the world of national struggles and tragedies, or even from the entire world of European culture."[118] The atmosphere in Lwów was quite different, and for Konrad, whose childhood had passed in a climate of persecution, Galicia must have appeared a country of freedom. There is no shred of evidence that he or anyone from his immediate circle regarded the departure to France as a severing of national ties; his uncle would have considered such an argument as absurd, and in fact Conrad never dreamt of escaping from European culture. We have to remember that at the time Poland did not exist on the political map and going abroad for study, work, or general experience was natural for thousands of young Poles of a szlachta or middle-class background. The entire anachronistic hypothesis springs from a tendency to look ahead to Conrad's decision, made more than ten years later, to become an English writer.

Conrad maintained later that his life's aim at that time had been to become a sailor, and only a British one, but one biographer rightly remarks that this statement is at variance with the facts as we know them.[119] What ought to be taken seriously, however, is another statement Conrad made almost in the same breath: his mind was set on the sea—not on becoming a sailor. In other words, he wanted to taste a life of adventure and voyage without the hardships and rigors demanded by the calling. Also, a story from A Personal Record, frequently quoted and often taken literally, about an Englishman on the Furca Pass whose appearance had a direct effect upon the boy's future, is only a delightful literary image, not a reliable historical document.[120] Conrad shapes the scene in his characteristic manner, trying to suggest after the fact that his life was subordinated to preconceived designs.

The young Konrad, egocentric and neurasthenic, a sickly and ambitious dreamer who could not forgive the world for not fulfilling his expectations, and who thirsted for adventure and probably above all for independence and freedom of movement, was impatient to take a leap into the wide and colorful world. Perhaps a youthful depression—aggravated by his unhappy childhood experiences—led to rebellion against the pressures of environment, to a passive resistance, and to a "quiet" aggression.[121] But his uncle, cool and cautious, would not give in to his moods nor let Konrad be guided by whims; he considered everything carefully and must have made his decision soberly, albeit with a trace of impatience. The boy's health was poor, his schoolwork unsatisfactory, his upbringing caused constant problems, and the end to financial outlays was nowhere in sight. Until his departure from Poland, Konrad cost his guardian four and a half thousand rubles—a sum large enough to support an adult reasonably well for several years.[122] Managing his own modest estate, and exhausted by the unsuccessful attempts to save his daughter's life, Bobrowski must have felt weary. And it was difficult to know what to do with the boy, since Syroczyński refused to keep him and his grandmother, nearing the end of her life, could no longer bear the responsibility. To leave the boy to his own devices without any specific duties would increase the risks of his going astray. He could not return to the Ukraine. His application for Austrian citizenship had been refused. And, as we shall see, one of the principal goals Bobrowski set for his nephew was to obtain another citizenship.

It is often suggested that Konrad's poor health prompted the decision to send him to sea. Mrs. Kałuska mentions the danger of tuberculosis; Buszczyński and Mrs. Wojakowska write about migraine headaches and nervous attacks; Bobrowski in his letters asks about Konrad's health repeatedly. The idea that sailor's work should act as medical treatment seems naive. But it was not a question of ordinary work nor of ordinary treatment. Konrad was not sent to toil as a common sailor. His uncle gave him an allowance almost equivalent to the cost of maintenance and schooling in Lwów. And since Konrad's illness was clearly of nervous origin, the doctors supposed that fresh air and physical work would harden him. Also, Tadeusz hoped that the clearly defined duties and rigors of work would teach the boy discipline.

Since he did not want to study, or could not, yet had to support himself, it was essential that he should learn a trade. Konrad's own head was probably full of various projects, but the sober-minded Bobrowski saw him as a sailor-cum-businessman who would combine his maritime skills with commercial activities—better still as a middleman in the huge agricultural products trade.

Such were the most likely considerations and decisive arguments.

What were Konrad Korzeniowski's intellectual achievements on leaving home? He was fluent in French; and as he had followed the gymnasium program, his knowledge of Latin and German must have been tolerably good; he also knew a certain amount of Greek, which was taught beginning with form three; by form five the *Iliad* was being read. It is hard to tell about other subjects, since we do not know how many forms he finished. He probably knew a good deal of history, particularly ancient; and some geography, taught together with history. Possibly it was then that he acquired an interest in physics, although the gymnasium's curriculum stressed languages (for example, in form four seventeen hours a week) and other classical subjects. He was certainly well read, particularly in Polish Romantic literature. The list of set books for school was fairly long, and his father had doubtless enlarged it with some patriotic works.[123]

We shall later get to know the young man's intellectual tendencies and habits. It is worth mentioning here that he belonged to only the second generation in his family that was obliged to earn its living outside the family estates. This can be looked at another way: Conrad was a member of the second generation of the intelligentsia, that peculiar social group that was beginning to play an important part in central and eastern Europe. And so in 1874 he left for Marseilles, the homeless son of political exiles, and an adolescent member of the Polish intelligentsia.

And what was his psychological baggage? Living away from one's natural environment—family, friends, social group, language—even if it results from a conscious decision, usually gives rise to acute internal tensions, because it tends to make people less sure of themselves, more vulnerable, less certain of their own position and of the value of their personalities and achievements. Leaving his home country was for Konrad Korzeniowski not tantamount to shedding all habitual attitudes. Polish szlachta and Polish intelligentsia were social strata in which reputation, one's evaluation by one's own milieu, was felt to be very important, even essential for one's feeling of self-worth. Men strove strenuously to find confirmation of their own self-regard and image in "the eyes of the others" rather than basing them on their own consciousness. Such a psychological heritage forms both a spur to ambition and a source of constant stress, especially if the idea of man's public duties has been inculcated in his mind.

II
· · · · · · · · · · · · ·
IN MARSEILLES
1874–1878

THE JOURNEY must have been enjoyable: a seventeen-year-old boy heading through Vienna, Zurich, and Lyon for Marseilles, free at last from adult supervision, and with his pockets reasonably full. On his way he stopped at Pfäffikon, Switzerland, to visit an old friend of his father, Tadeusz Oksza-Orzechowski, the former plenipotentiary of the Polish National Government in Istanbul. Conrad recalled later how everyone there laughed at his enthusiasm for the sea. "'You want to become a sailor but have you got a knife in your pocket?'" I had not. I knew nothing about it."[1]

Much has been written about Konrad Korzeniowski's stay in Marseilles— tales of fascinating episodes of youthful follies, great romance, and a duel. But this attractive tableau is not supported by documentary evidence; it is the result of a peculiar collaboration of excessive good will on the part of biographers— and Conrad's flights of retrospective imagination. To the French period of his life Conrad devoted two chapters of *The Mirror of the Sea*, a couple of fragments in *A Personal Record*, and *The Arrow of Gold*. The discrepancies between the descriptions of the same persons and facts in *The Mirror of the Sea* and *The Arrow of Gold* ought to warn us against treating those books as valid evidence, particularly if we bear in mind that Conrad vouched for the authenticity of both. And then the contrast that exists between the plot of the novel about the charming Doña Rita and the unfinished novel *The Sisters* where the same two sisters appear as in *The Arrow*, as well as their uncle the Basque priest, the Ortegas, and the painter—at first glance they seem the same and yet they are quite different.[2] What are we to believe?

It is best to believe only the documents. Conrad altered facts, confused dates, and changed effects into causes, even in his private correspondence. Although scholars have shown beyond doubt that his literary works are mostly based on material drawn from real life or from reading, with his imagination playing a lesser part, we should not conclude that whatever we find in those works is a faithful rendering of fact. Conrad's tendency to color and turn into a myth his own past is most apparent in his "autobiographical" works. Thus, these writings are least qualified to be taken literally.

In Marseilles, Korzeniowski was to have been looked after by Wiktor Chodźko, a Pole who sailed on French ships and lived in Toulon. It seems he was temporarily out of town and recommended the young man to a Baptistin Solary, who in turn recommended him to his cousin, the owner of a shipping firm, C. Delestang et Fils.[3] Jean-Baptiste Delestang was a Royalist and in the salon, run by his wife, gathered the local supporters of the Bourbon restoration. This distinguished and snobbish society may have made an impression on Konrad. However, at the beginning of his stay in Marseilles he apparently spent most of his time in the steep, narrow back streets of the old town, and in the port. Ship pilots, whom he always remembered with gratitude, were his first instructors in the art of sailing. He accompanied them to meet the approaching vessels and in time acquired sufficient experience to pilot boats unaided. He grew to love the Mediterranean, "the cradle of sailing," a love that lasted throughout his life.

After two months' stay in Marseilles he set off on his first sea voyage as a passenger on the *Mont Blanc*, a barque belonging to the Delestang firm. The boat was old and, in spite of her grand name, quite small, under four hundred tons. On 15 December 1874 she sailed for Martinique and reached Saint Pierre on 16 February 1875. Korzeniowski stayed there six weeks; on 30 March the *Mont Blanc* started her homeward passage and was back at Marseilles on 23 May.[4]

There were probably two objectives to this voyage: to promote the young passenger's health and to give him a closer look at sailors' work. Chodźko continued to keep an eye on him and received "for his troubles" sixty rubles from Bobrowski.[5] G. J. Resink has advanced a tempting hypothesis that the future author met at that time in Marseilles Arthur Rimbaud, in whose writings he later became deeply interested. It is not impossible, since they both moved in the same circles, but they would have barely a week in which to meet because Rimbaud, who had suffered a sunstroke in Leghorn, arrived at Marseilles— perhaps going straight to the hospital—on 18 June, and on 25 June Korzeniow- ski left again on the *Mont Blanc*, this time as an apprentice.[6]

The barque, commanded by Captain Duteil, arrived at Saint Pierre on the last day of July. She remained in harbor for two months and nothing is known of how the young man spent his time. On 27 September the *Mont Blanc* sailed for Cap-Haïtien, where she arrived on 2 October; she left there for Le Havre on 1 November with a load of logwood. The return passage was difficult; the ship ran into very rough weather and reached port on 23 December damaged, her sails torn.[7] This baptism of sea water must have been unpleasant for Konrad; he left the ship in Le Havre and, losing his trunk with his personal belongings on the way, rushed off for a few days to Paris and then back again to Marseilles.[8] Perhaps he sought the company of nonsailors to recover from his disturbing experiences. The contrast between the environment in which he had grown up and that of professional sailors was enormous. Doubtless he was fascinated by their dissimilarity but vexed by their lack of polish and limited intellectual horizons.

In 1875 Konrad spent five months at sea. This does not appear to have stirred his enthusiasm for his chosen profession. He gave himself over six months' rest from sailing—perhaps he had had enough salt water for the time being or perhaps the temptations on land proved irresistible. Nothing of any importance awaited him in Marseilles; he was a young man able to enjoy his freedom without having to count every penny, and he could also impress landlubbers with his experiences at sea. He visited the theater and the opera and saw the plays of Sardou and Scribe.[9] Theatrical life in Marseilles was flourishing at that time, particularly the opera, housed in the splendid building of the Grand Théâtre; from this period—later he had neither the opportunity nor money—date Conrad's memories of listening to Meyerbeer's works and to his favorite opera, *Carmen*. During Korzeniowski's stay in Marseilles the principal tenor of the opera, Władysław Mierzwiński, sang the part of Don José several times.[10]

"Many hours slipped by in the company of young people of all classes and in the discussion of every conceivable subject in the cafés, which were more numerous then than they are to-day on either side of the Cannebière; or, in a café of the rue Saint-Ferréol, the name of which Conrad, even towards the end of his life, still pronounced with some emotion: the Café Bodoul, the place of which Stendhal said in the *Mémoires d'un touriste*: 'There you could meet all the local haute bourgeoisie.' The café was small but very fashionable about 1875, and refined meals were served on the first floor. An apprentice took his revenge for sea biscuits and the rough time he had had. Polish money encouraged French cooking."[11] The young arrival from Poland was doubtless shown the Café Bodoul's "table de Cracovie," so called for the sake of a pun, *craque*, meaning "humbug."[12] The attractive picture created by Jean-Aubry does not tell the whole truth, since it is highly improbable that Korzeniowski, discussing lofty subjects even in the most exclusive of cafés or relishing lobsters and snails, would squander so quickly all the money scrupulously accumulated by his uncle from the lease of the fertile fields of Kazimierówka. Many years later Conrad gave his wife an account of a marvelous drunken drive in a carriage.[13] Marseilles, a large, rich, lively city, a center of trade and smuggling, and a meeting place between Western Europe and the Levant, swarmed with opportunities and temptations.

Tadeusz Bobrowski sent his nephew an allowance of 2,000 francs a year, but by January 1875 he was obliged to send an additional 250 francs to make up for money that was apparently stolen, and in November of the same year he complied with the request and sent another 300 francs to Le Havre. With time his outlays grew. In the first half of 1876 Korzeniowski spent 1,265 francs above the 1,200 francs taken from his allowance. The sums were not negligible, considering that a lieutenant in the French Navy was paid about 2,000 francs a year, an industrial worker earned 800 to 900 francs, and a craftsman 1,800 on the average. Pan Tadeusz kept sending the required sums to pay the debts and make up the shortage of ready cash but, understandably, he gave vent to his anger. He produced a detailed account showing that in the course of two years Konrad spent the entire third year's allowance.

Here you have the bare facts, based on figures which I do not think you will deny—as each expenditure was made either for you or caused by you. And now, my dear Panie Bracie [literally "Sir Brother," a mode of address used by the *szlachta*. All noblemen were addressed as "Pan," that is, "sir," and together they formed a "brotherhood" of equals.], let us jointly consider if such expenditure on your behalf is and was possible, fair and worthy? . . . Perhaps it seems to you that I can bear such extraordinary expenditure out of love for my 'dearly beloved Nephew'? But this is not the case! My income is around 5,000 roubles—I pay 500 roubles in taxes—by giving you 2,000 francs I am giving you approximately 700 roubles and to your Uncle 1,000 roubles yearly; so I give the two of you about one-third of my income. If therefore I were to give you 300 roubles more per year (as two years have used up the third one), I would have to cut down by half my expenditure on underwear, shoes, clothes, and my personal needs—since my budget for all these things is limited to 600 roubles a year for the very good reason that I cannot have more—there is no more to go round, if I am to fulfill my obligations towards my Brother and Nephew. Is it fair that I should repair your thoughtlessness at the expense of my personal comforts or, I should rather say, my essential needs? Would it be proper for me to reduce the help which I give to my Brother and his children whose right to my heart and help, if not greater (they are six), is certainly not less than yours? I am only too sure that the threefold reply to my threefold question could be only: impossible! and unfair! and unworthy! That will be the answer of your heart, but I wish for an answer of your will—not words, which I have had more than once—but deeds, i.e. the strictest adjustment of your expenditure to the allowance that I have allotted you, and if, in your opinion, this does not suffice, earn some money—and you will have it. If, however, you cannot earn it, then content yourself with what you get from the labour of others—until you are able to supplant it with your own earnings and gratify yourself.[14]

Money was not the only thing the young spendthrift wasted.

You always, my dear boy, made me impatient—and still make me impatient by your disorder and the easy way you take things—in which you remind me of the Korzeniowski family—spoiling and wasting everything—and not my dear Sister, your Mother, who was careful about everything. Last year you lost a trunk full of things—and tell me—what else had you to remember and look after if not yourself and your things? Do you need a nanny—and am I cast in that role? Now again, you have lost a family photograph and some

Polish books—and you ask me to replace them! Why? So that you should take the first opportunity of losing them again!? He who appreciates something looks after it. . . . So, if you do not look after intimate keepsakes (and that after all is a matter of your choice) why do you try to get replacements—and thereby cause somebody trouble? . . . Well, there's your reprimand for your carelessness about looking after your property. You deserve another one, for the carelessness with which you write your letters—I have told you that several times. Could you not possibly keep a supply of paper and write in an orderly fashion—as an orderly person I heartily wish my nephew to be and that is why I give him a dressing-down, which does not prevent me from loving you and blessing you, which I do with all my heart.[15]

What irritated Bobrowski most was Konrad's lack of any sense of responsibility. "Apart from the fact of the expenditure itself, I must say frankly that I did not like the tone in which you refer to what has happened. . . . Certainly, there is no reason for one to take one's life or to go into a Carthusian monastery because of some folly one has committed—even if that folly causes acute pain to someone very close to you!—but a little more contrition would not be amiss and particularly a more thoughtful mode of behavior, which would prove that after a temporary imprudence, reflection and common sense have prevailed! But these latter—my dear—in spite of my great wish to, I have not found—unfortunately!" But the young man, who was apt to send telegrams asking for money and then avoid giving explanations, was not unduly perturbed by that sermonizing, as we can see by his scribbled "Je Vs aime!!!" on the margin of his uncle's letter beside Bobrowski's rhetorical question, "Is it fair?"

Bobrowski forgave, but not without some more stern entreaties.

What is the conclusion to be drawn from this whole recapitulation of our actions? It is this: that you have committed absurdities—that in view of your youth and because it is the first time, all has to be forgiven you—and I, the victim of these absurdities, forgive you with all my heart, on condition, *that it is for the first and last time*!! And I myself, am I wholly innocent? Certainly, I am guilty, because I met your demands too promptly! I also beat my breast and swear to myself that this will be *the first and last* case of such giving way on my part! And I pledge myself to keep my word! And I ask you to remember this—both for yourself and for me. I would have refused my own son outright after so many warnings but to you, the child of my Sister, grandson of my mother, for once, but *only for once*, I forgive you—I save you so that it should not be said that I was too hard on you![16]

Both letters, the second extremely long, reached Konrad on his return from the West Indies, where he had finally sailed on 8 July 1876 as a steward on the barque *Saint Antoine*. The 432-ton sailing ship chartered by Delestang under Captain Escarras made Saint Pierre on 18 August. For the first time in his life Korzeniowski received a salary: 35 francs a month (amounting to one-fifth of his allowance).[17] The first mate was a Corsican of forty-two, Dominic Cervoni, whom Conrad mentioned several times in his works and letters; he was also a prototype for Nostromo. "In his eyes lurked a look of perfectly remorseless irony, as though he had been provided with an extremely experienced soul; and the slightest distension of his nostrils would give to his bronzed face a look of extraordinary boldness. This was the only play of feature of which he seemed capable, being a Southerner of a concentrated, deliberate type."[18] One of the three apprentices in the *Saint Antoine* was eighteen-year-old César Cervoni; he is also described, most unflatteringly, in *The Mirror of the Sea*. It seems, however, that he was not related to Dominic.[19]

From Martinique, the *Saint Antoine* sailed to the South American ports of Cartagena in Colombia and Puerto Cabello and La Guaira in Venezuela. Several days on land provided Conrad with the visual material for *Nostromo*. We do not know what the ship carried; from some of Conrad's later hints it may have been engaged in smuggling—possibly in gunrunning for the conservative rebels in Colombia.[20] Returning to Saint Pierre on 16 September, the *Saint Antoine* left there for Saint Thomas in the Virgin Islands, arriving on 27 September. She left on 12 October with a cargo of coal for Port-au-Prince. The passage lasted two weeks, the ship ran into bad weather, then stayed in port for one month. On 25 November the *Saint Antoine* started on her homeward passage carrying logwood and sugar; she arrived at Marseilles on 15 February 1877.[21]

In one of his uncle's letters awaiting him on return, Konrad read the following admonition: "Please answer all my questions—but not from memory but from my letter—as you are, my young man, very absent-minded and you frequently forget what I have asked you." His questions concerned health, future plans, and, primarily, studies. Bobrowski wished to know what his nephew had learned from Captain Escarras, what studies he was pursuing himself, and whether he was learning English or some other language. He was also interested in the wholesale prices of *les Liqueurs des Iles* and of Havana cigars. "Maybe we could do some small business in these two articles if it should appear that *tout frais compris* [all expenses included] they would still be much cheaper than here locally."[22]

Since all Konrad's letters to Bobrowski went up in flames in 1917 with Kazimierówka manor, we shall never know his answer. Obviously he had intended to set out shortly on another voyage in the *Saint Antoine*, under Captain Escarras: his name was even down on the list of the crew; but when the ship left on 31 March for the Antilles, Korzeniowski had to stay behind because of illness. Captain Escarras wrote to Bobrowski expressing his regret.[23] When Konrad recovered, he began some unknown work which was apparently to bring him sixty francs a month. Judging by the small pay, he must have taken odd jobs; or else he did not disclose to his uncle his full earnings, just as he had made no mention of having received modest pay on the *Saint Antoine*. He questioned his uncle about the Russo-Turkish war, which began on 24 April 1877, but the squire of Kazimierówka rejoined, "I myself cannot tell you anything new as we know absolutely nothing but what our newspapers—which are even less well informed and less informative than yours—tell us. . . . Far away from the scene of the war, away from all question of participation in it, not expecting anything for ourselves either from victory or from defeat, we could only *par amour du roi de Prusse* take an interest in politics and war!"[24]

In July Korzeniowski had a disagreement with Delestang. Bobrowski commented on the incident in his letter of 9 August:

> My dearest boy!
> You have evidently forgotten the national proverb that "the humble calf sucks two mothers." That must have been the cause of your losing your temper—which resulted in a breach with Mr Déléstang. I do not deny that, if things happened the way you describe them, the honourable *épicier* treated you too loftily, unmindful of having before him a descendant of the excellent family of Nałęcz—that's agreed. I see from your account of the talk with him that you have *la repartie facile et suffisamment acérée* in which I recognize your Nałęcz blood—in this tendency to fly into a passion I even detect a drop of Biberstejn blood; unfortunately I do not perceive in this whole affair any trace of that prudent common sense of which on the distaff side you have the right to be proud, deriving it from the House of Jastrzembczyk to which I have the honour to belong. . . . Let us consider this matter coolly. You write that you are looking for employment that would bring you some profit. Mr Déléstang in his majesty condescends to offer you such employment. Common sense should have made you accept this opportunity as he obviously trusted you in spite of your youth and of your being a foreigner; he showed a preference for you over his countrymen and trusted you; you could, when replying to him, have made him feel the unsuitable tone he used; but accepted it, while laying down your conditions both as to present remuneration and as to his making your voyage to India free of charge. . . . you would have profited in three ways: you would not have broken with a man who in one way or another might be useful to you; you would have raised yourself higher in his opinion; you would have earned something;—considerations not without importance!!

Perhaps it was pure coincidence but at the time of the estrangement with Delestang—caused by some awkwardly expressed offer of employment—Konrad gave up the idea of leaving before the middle of August on a voyage to the Antilles.[25] Although his relations with Delestang returned to normal, Korzeniowski wrote to his uncle on 16 August about the lasting quarrel, hinting also at some shady businesses of his ex-patron; Bobrowski urged his nephew to be discreet.[26] Meanwhile, Konrad was basing his hopes for the future on Captain Escarras, for whom he felt great and obviously reciprocated friendship. He counted on sailing with him on his next voyage, but not before the next December. It did not please his guardian, who suggested looking for another job. "Possibly Mr d'Escarras will not be able to take you—in any case to spend a whole year on land cannot be good either for your health or for practising your profession??"

In the same letter of 8 August, Bobrowski for the first time broached two important subjects: Korzeniowski's naturalization abroad, tantamount to obtaining release from Russian citizenship, and the young man's plan to join the British merchant marine. "I do not know to what extent your idea of transferring to the English merchant fleet may be practical. My first question is, do you speak English? As to that I am completely ignorant, since you never answered my question whether you are learning this language. I never wished you to become naturalized in France, mainly because of the compulsory military service which you would have to undergo, God knows for what and for whom. I thought, however, of your getting naturalized in Switzerland and I still think of it. Try then to find out what are the conditions and expense that Swiss naturalization would entail." The project of applying for Swiss citizenship quickly fell through, judging by Bobrowski's next letter, in which Pan Tadeusz supported Konrad's idea of trying for United States citizenship or for "one of the more important Southern Republics."[27]

For a time nothing more was heard of Konrad's plan to join the British merchant service. But as a young man nearing his majority, the problem of settling his legal position was becoming urgent.

The uncle was worried and kept urging him on: "Write to me also how you are. What are you studying? and what will you do with yourself till December? Will you find employment and sail or remain on shore—whatever you do, go on studying and work on your character, my dear boy, for your whole future depends on work."[28] He complained about not getting answers to his repeated questions and scoffed at Konrad's "diplomatic" friends: "Who is the Baron Drużkowicz? The Austrian Consul? And this Japanese consul, who likes you, 'you do not know what for and why'—who may this individual be? Perhaps he could help you to find something in Japan after you get your Master's certificate? Perhaps you will become an Admiral in Japan? Indeed, once you have embarked on a cosmopolitan career such as yours is in the merchant navy, it is unimportant where one is. And I do not see that you are specially attached to the French, which I must say does not displease me—it would sadden me to know that you regarded France as your fatherland."[29]

Korzeniowski's doings in those days are rather obscure. The second half of 1877 and the beginning of the following year represent the truly legendary period of his life. Some facts are undisputed, however. He lived not far from the Opera, in a small *pension* at 18 Rue Sainte; the house, which does not exist today, belonged to Joseph Fagot. Two houses away, in a better-class *pension*, lived Korzeniowski's English friend, Henry Grand, the teacher of English mentioned in Bobrowski's correspondence.[30] In the last autumn of 1877 Konrad collected, in addition to his half-yearly allowance drawn in advance, two thousand francs as a gift from his relative Katarzyna Korzeniowska. Thus he had at his disposal the considerable sum of three thousand francs.[31] In December it transpired that as a foreigner and a Russian subject he had no right to serve on French vessels without permission from the Russian consul. Since he was liable for military service in Russia, there could be no question of the consul's consent; moreover, the affair became generally known. Bobrowski, unaware of the complications, was under the impression that Konrad had set off with Captain Escarras on a voyage around the world. However, at the beginning of March, while he was attending the Kiev trade fair, a request reached him from Marseilles to meet a bill of exchange for one thousand francs; this was followed by a telegram with news of Konrad's being wounded, money needed, and Bobrowski's arrival called for.[32] The telegram had been sent by Korzeniowski's friend Richard Fecht, from Württemberg. Bobrowski was unable to leave immediately, and an exchange of telegrams followed. He learned about his nephew's improved condition and left Kiev on 8 March. He arrived in Marseilles on 11 March and found that Konrad had attempted to take his life but was already almost totally recovered. He paid Konrad's debts, amounting to three thousand francs, and stayed a fortnight in Marseilles, "studying the individual" and investigating the whole affair.[33]

The events that followed are slightly better known. It is necessary now to shift into the past in order to fill in the gaps with the data available from the accounts given by Conrad and Bobrowski. Conrad described twice, in *The Mirror of the Sea* and in *The Arrow of Gold*, how during his stay in Marseilles he was engaged in the smuggling of arms to Spain for the supporters of Don Carlos de Borbón y de Austria-Este, Pretender to the Spanish throne. This, however, seems highly questionable if not impossible. The fights between the supporters of the victorious Alfonso XII and those who favored Don Carlos ended on 27 February 1876; one year later the young king announced a general amnesty for all political opponents.[34] The police archives in Marseilles abound in data on the subject of the Carlists and the tradesmen and ships involved in gunrunning to Spain, but they all concern an earlier period. Franciszek Ziejka examined the police files and press reports and failed to find for 1877 and 1878 a single mention suggesting any kind of Carlist activity in that area.[35] Bobrowski also raises the subject of Korzeniowski's participation in the illicit trading with Spain, which was at first very profitable. But the trade need not have been gunrunning.

Embarking on the supposedly autobiographical tales after thirty years—and in *The Arrow of Gold* after forty years—he embellished his memories, borrowing probably from past adventures of his Marseilles friends. A public admission that his illicit activities, even those as picturesque as smuggling, had been carried out for profit, would be incompatible with the position Conrad wished to occupy in literature. Capt. John Young Mason Key Blunt, a regular cavalry officer who from 1876 served as soldier of fortune in Don Carlos's army, and his mother were real-life people Conrad depicted in *The Arrow of Gold*. One could probably find prototypes of several other characters in that novel.[36] The fact that some characters in the book are derived from authentic people should not lead us to the conclusion that their fates in the novel, particularly their relations with the narrator, M. George-Korzeniowski, are a faithful reflection of real events. It was quite usual for Conrad to use some external characteristics, often also the names, of actual people, but to furnish them with different life histories; such is the case of Almayer, Lingard, Jim, and Kurtz. That in *The Arrow of Gold* ascribed to his fictional enemy, Blunt, the maxim "Américain, catholique et gentilhomme"—an obvious echo of the dedication "Pole, Catholic, *szlachcic*" written by young Konrad on his own photograph offered to grandmother Teofila—is in itself a signal of the complexity of the origin of his fictional characters.[37]

A careful reading of "The 'Tremolino'" and *The Arrow of Gold* reveals that the whole Carlist plot is a sideline, a decoration that does not affect the course of action; its only function seems to be to glamorize and idealize smuggling. Two elements overlap in those books: the author's own recollections, modified in many respects, of the years 1877 and 1878, and his knowledge of Carlist activities and supporters in 1874 through 1876; they may prove more authentic taken separately than taken together.

For the reader it is of no consequence, particularly since *The Arrow of Gold* is Conrad's weakest novel, but biographers have been led up a blind alley.[38] Perhaps one day we will find out more about Captain Duteil, Korzeniowski's accomplice in the smuggling venture, which would throw some light on that mysterious period.[39]

According to the fictional version, the arms were smuggled under the deck of the sailing boat *Tremolino*, owned partly by Korzeniowski himself. He described her alternately as a balancelle, tartan, or felucca but furnished her with two masts; boats of this type are single-masted.[40] Her captain was Dominic Cervoni, the same Corsican who served as first mate on the *Saint Antoine*; one of the crew was his alleged nephew, César. There were a number of successful expeditions from Marseilles to the Costa Brava, but as the result of César's betrayal the Spanish coast guard set a trap for them. To escape capture Korzeniowski purposely wrecked the boat by commanding Cervoni to steer her on the rocks of Cape Creus. This, at any rate, is the story in *The Mirror of the Sea*;

in *The Arrow of Gold* the wrecking of the sailing boat is dismissed with a couple of vague sentences.[41] Conrad apparently told Ford Madox Ford that the disaster had been caused by a drunken innkeeper who forgot to put out a warning signal.[42]

The history of the *Tremolino*, although less improbable than Konrad's participation in the Carlist movement, also evokes certain doubts and needs correcting. Hans van Marle, after detailed research in the archives of the Bouches du Rhône department, ascertained that in the period in question not one out of thirty-five hundred ships that docked at Marseilles bore the name *Tremolino* or was commanded by Dominic Cervoni.[43] And Norman Sherry discovered César Cervoni's son, who confirmed Dominic's proficiency in smuggling but revealed that his father had not been related to Dominic, had not perished in 1878, and had remained on friendly terms with Korzeniowski.[44]

If the *Tremolino* really existed and *if* she was really used for gunrunning, she would probably have gone into one of the many creeks along the jagged French coast rather than into a large patrolled port like Marseilles or Toulon. Van Marle points out that Conrad's great familiarity with the area near Hyères and Golfe de Giens, displayed in *The Rover*, may help us form our conjectures.

Another Marseilles legend concerns Korzeniowski's great love affair. The story is described in *The Arrow of Gold* only; there is no hint of it in any other of his books. In view of the obviously fictional character of this pseudo-autobiographical novel where chronology cannot be reconciled with the documented dates in the author's life, the legend would not be worth considering, but the temptation is irresistible to fill out with romance all the gaps in Conrad's life. Even the usually sober-minded Jocelyn Baines says that "to dismiss the whole Rita story as fabrication would amount to charging Conrad with mythomania."[45] Why speak about "charging"? A novel based on material drawn from one's memories is not a formal declaration and the author is fully entitled to practice "mythomania."

And so we read in *The Arrow of Gold* how after a year of indecision and resistance the beautiful Doña Rita, former mistress of the late painter Henry Allègre and subsequently of Don Carlos himself, submits in body and soul to the narrator of the book, a young enthusiast whose help she secured for the Carlist cause. Their idyll, in a secluded mountain hut, lasts six months and ends when the hero is seriously wounded by a bullet in a duel with a jealous rival, Blunt. There follows a severe illness of many months' duration. Doña Rita departs before the hero regains consciousness but when his life is not in danger.

It would be strange if young Korzeniowski, sensitive, lively, and not impecunious, had no love affairs in a country that seems specially created for the purpose. And we may assume that he experienced in that sphere successes as well as failures: youth and sensitivity ensure both. It may be noteworthy that the idyllic episode in *The Arrow of Gold* is not fully described but only mentioned in a few sentences, giving the impression of an artificially contrived and weakly motivated addition; it has to be accepted at face value. Its credibility is further diminished by the fact that the fictional Rita is not a convincing character; the way she is presented belies the author's assurances about her youthful innocence and spontaneity.

Both in *The Sisters* and *The Arrow of Gold*, Rita is presented as a Basque; her assumed name—"de Lastaola," according to Jean-Aubry, is derived from the name of a mountain pass near Fuenterrabia; her place of birth was supposedly Tolosa, in Vascongadas, a province in northern Spain.[46] Even assuming that the love plot in *The Arrow of Gold* reflects reality to some extent (and the contradictions with "The 'Tremolino'" induce scepticism), once again the Carlist affair element is easy to set apart, since it does not play a vital part in the progress of events. Baines's supposition that arms were smuggled for the Basques makes no geographical sense: why should arms destined for the other end of the Pyrenees be delivered to Catalonia?[47]

We may dismiss without hesitation Jerry Allen's unfounded theory that the object of Korzeniowski's passion and courtship was the Hungarian official mistress of Don Carlos, Paulina Horvath, known as Paula de Somogyi. Baines, and later van Marle, have demonstrated the chronological impossibility of that liaison. Don Carlos met Paula only at the end of 1877; according to the Count de Melgar, the Pretender's secretary who described the romance in his memoirs, Paula at the time spoke only Hungarian and a few words of German.[48]

Much more plausible seems Franciszek Ziejka's hypothesis that the character of Rita's deceased friend Henry Allègre was drawn from the prominent portraitist Louis-Gustave Ricard (1823–1873). Ricard was born in Marseilles, where he had been held in great esteem, but ended his life in obscurity in Paris. It is possible that the fictional Rita de Lastaola owes some of her characteristics to Ricard's mistress, Madame Didier.[49]

It is necessary to discuss these legends and hypotheses in order to remove the veil of fantasy that has obscured Korzeniowski's suicide attempt. Although the theory of the duel still has some followers, it fails to stand up to sober criticism. On his arrival in Marseilles, Bobrowski learned about the suicide attempt from Konrad and Fecht. The followers of the duel theory maintain that Korzeniowski told an untruth and concealed the duel, which he mentioned several times in later life and described in *The Arrow of Gold*.[50] But anyone with a knowledge of the then prevailing moral attitudes will not believe that a young *szlachcic*— and Korzeniowski flaunted his family origin, perhaps not so much out of pride but from a youthful lack of self-confidence, particularly on foreign ground— would camouflage a duel by a suicide. The very fact that Bobrowski had been spreading the news that the injury was sustained in a duel is sufficiently telling. And would Pan Tadeusz, who was clear-headed and sharp-eyed, not get down to the truth of the matter after conferring with his nephew's friends in Marseilles? A duel is not a private, one-man act: at least four persons are involved in it.

One can easily understand Conrad's unwillingness to recall the attempted suicide and his tendency to obliterate that tragic episode. The version of a conflict in which honor was at stake suggested itself automatically: it explained the injury and gave a romantic air to an otherwise embarrassing fact.[51] In any case, there seems no reason why he should have lied to his uncle in March 1878.

Let us hear now what Bobrowski had to say, weighing carefully every word in his letter to Stefan Buszczyński, his own ideological opponent and a friend of the late Apollo:

Suddenly, amidst all the business at the Kiev Fair in 1878, I received a telegram: "Conrad blessé envoyez argent—arrivez." Naturally I could not fly to him straight away like a bird; but having settled my business and having received a reply that Konrad was already better I set off at once from Kiev on the 24 February [old style], and arrived at Marseilles on the 27th. I found Konrad already out of bed and after having had a previous talk with his friend Mr Richard Fecht, a most prudent and worthy young man, I saw the victim in person. And this is what I discovered. Although Konrad had been absolutely certain of accompanying Captain Escarras on his next voyage, the Bureau de l'Inscription forbade him to go on the grounds of his being a 21-year old alien who was under the obligation of doing his military service in his own country. Then it was discovered that he had never had a permit from his Consul—the ex-Inspector of the Port of Marseilles was summoned who in the register had acknowledged the existence of such a permit—he was severely reprimanded and nearly lost his job—which was undoubtedly very unpleasant for Konrad. The whole affair became far too widely known and all endeavors by the Captain and the shipowner proved fruitless (the shipowner, Mr Déléstang, himself told me all this), and Konrad was forced to stay behind with no hope of serving on French vessels. However, before all this happened another catastrophe—this time financial—befell him. While still in possession of the 3,000 fr. sent to him for the voyage, he met his former captain, Mr Duteil, who persuaded him to participate in some enterprise on the coasts of Spain—some kind of contraband! He invested 1,000 fr. in it and made over 400 which pleased them greatly, so that on the second occasion he put in all he had—and lost the lot. This Mr Duteil consoled him with a kiss and then went off to Buenos Aires. He, Konrad, was left behind, unable to sign on for a ship—poor as a church mouse and, moreover, heavily in debt—for while speculating he had lived on credit, had ordered the things necessary for his voyage, and so forth. Faced with this situation, he borrows 800 fr. from his friend Fecht and sets off for Villa Franca [Villefranche], where an American squadron was anchored, with the intention of joining the American service. He achieves nothing there and, wishing to improve his finances tries his luck in Monte Carlo and loses the 800 fr. he had borrowed. Having managed his affairs so excellently he returns to Marseilles and one fine evening invites his friend the creditor to tea, and before his arrival attempts to take his life with a revolver. (Let this detail remain between us, as I have been telling everyone that he was wounded in a duel. From you I neither wish to nor should keep it a secret.) The bullet goes durch und durch [through and through] near his heart without damaging any vital organ. Luckily, all his addresses were left on top of his things so that this worthy Mr Fecht could instantly let me know, and even my brother, who in his turn bombarded me. Well, that is the whole story!

I spent a fortnight in Marseilles, at first investigating the whole affair and then the individual himself. Apart from the 3,000 fr. which he had lost, I had to pay as much again to settle his debts.* Had he been my own son I wouldn't have done it but—I must avow—in the case of my beloved sister's son, I had the weakness to act against the principles I had hitherto held. Nevertheless, I swore that even if I knew that he would shoot himself a second time—there would be no repetition of the same weakness on my part. To some extent also I was influenced by considerations of our national honour, so that it should not be said that one of us had exploited the affection, which Konrad undoubtedly enjoyed, of all those with whom he came into contact. He is lucky with people.

My study of the Individual has convinced me that he is not a bad boy, only one who is extremely sensitive, conceited, reserved, and in addition excitable. In short I found in him all the defects of the Nałęcz family. He is able and eloquent—he has forgotten nothing of his Polish although since he left Cracow I was the first person he conversed with in his native tongue. He appears to know his profession, does not want to and will not change it. In spite of watching him carefully I didn't detect any of the bad habits common among sailors—he drinks hardly anything except red wine—does not gamble (he said that himself and Mr Fecht confirmed never having seen him gambling—the unfortunate incident in Monte Carlo sprang from the thought "first time lucky"). His manners are very good, as if he had never left drawing-rooms—he was very popular with his captains and also with the sailors—more than once have I witnessed scenes of cordial greetings with sailors who call him M Georges. During my stay in Marseilles he was twice called for to bring vessels into the port, for which service he was paid 100 fr. a time. I must therefore regard him as a man who knows his profession. My studies of the individual have not deprived me of the hope that a real man might still be

* In the "Document," Bobrowski lists the repaid debts: banker de Toussaint (for Fecht), 1,706 francs; Mme Bonnard, 1,000; Mme Fagot, the housekeeper, 233; doctor, 70; in all, 3,009 francs, equal to 1,228 rubles. He raised his nephew's allowance to 2,400 francs a year and advanced 1,200 francs for the period from 15 April to 15 October 1878.

made of him—as used to be said—certainly the temperament of the Nałęcz family is predominant in him—and I may be mistaken but I think that unfortunately he has taken after his paternal Uncle rather than after his father. In his face he rather resembles his Mother and is quite a handsome boy; in his build he is more like his Father and is quite robust. In his ideas and discussions he is ardent and original. We Poles, particularly when young, have an innate liking for the French and for the Republic—he, however, does not like them at all and is an imperialist. De gustibus non est disputandum—but several times I couldn't control myself and rebuked him.

Finally, it was decided that he should join the English Merchant Marine where there are no such formalities as in France.[52]

Apparently financial setbacks, sudden and insurmountable difficulties in his professional life, and perhaps an unhappy love fell upon a young man susceptible to youthful depression, thereby producing an acute crisis in self-confidence and plunging him into utter despair. Four years earlier, when Konrad's bad health caused an interruption in his studies, Pulman had to entreat his pupil: "Only do not lose heart, and God forbid you should abandon yourself to despair or apathy."[53] Similar breakdowns and prostration of spirit occurred frequently in Conrad's later life, although never in such a dramatic form. In Marseilles, he must have been crushed by a sense of complete helplessness all the more painful for laying bare the basic frailty of his high-spirited years of freedom. It is well known that attempts to take one's life are often primarily a form of crying for help. It has also been established that suicide or attempted suicide is often the first sign of depression.[54]

The fact that when Bobrowski came to Marseilles, not more than ten days after the accident, he found his nephew out of bed excludes the possibility of Korzeniowski having shot right through his chest, since this would have entailed many weeks of lying down. The expression "*durch und durch* near his heart" should not be taken therefore to mean that the bullet went right through his chest but rather "right through the chest muscle" or between the ribs; it may have gone near the surface, not vertically but diagonally, missing the ventricle and emerging under the shoulder. Either Korzeniowski placed the revolver badly and the bullet went almost parallel to his body, or the suicide was simulated and he never intended to take his own life. The careful preparation preceding the act—the invitation of Fecht and leaving out the list of addresses—points toward the latter possibility, but suicides during depression are usually carefully planned. The difference between serious attempts and ostentatious simulations may be impossible to define. A suicide may want his death but subconsciously not believe in it and half-consciously turn away from its instrument. Even Konrad Korzeniowski himself may have not known the whole truth of his action.

III

THE RED ENSIGN
1878–1886

" THE RED ENSIGN! In the pellucid, colourless atmosphere bathing the drab and gray masses of that southern land, the livid islets, the sea of pale glassy blue under the pale glassy sky of that cold sunrise, it was as far as the eye could reach the only spot of ardent colour—flame-like, intense, and presently as minute as the tiny red spark the concentrated reflection of a great fire kindles in the clear heart of a globe of crystal. The Red Ensign—the symbolic, protecting warm bit of bunting flung wide upon the seas, and destined for so many years to be the only roof over my head." This is how, more than thirty years later, Conrad described his first encounter with the British Merchant Marine ensign.[1] Contrary to the legend he wished to create, his joining an English ship was not the result of a previously formed decision, "if a seaman, then an English seaman."[2] At the same time it was not entirely accidental: in those days over half of all the ships afloat in the world belonged to the British fleet; since sailors were in considerable demand, no special permits were required for the enlistment of foreigners who, as a rule, were less demanding, more tractable, and ready to accept lower wages.[3]

The voyage of the small steamer *Mavis* (763 tons) which Konrad Korzeniowski boarded on 24 April 1878 in Marseilles was somewhat mysterious, unrecorded in the ship's papers. Korzeniowski's name does not figure on the muster roll and he does not mention the *Mavis* on any official lists of the ships on which he served. Before leaving Marseilles he was supposed to give the captain a considerable deposit—500 francs[4]—so he probably joined the ship not as a member of the crew but as an unofficial apprentice.

It is possible to establish, on the basis of *The Shipping and Mercantile Gazette*, that the *Mavis* reached Malta on 27 April and left the next day for Constantinople, arriving there on 2 May, on her way to Kerch in the Crimea; she passed through the straits of Kerch on 6 May heading for Yeysk, on the Sea of Azov; the next information is the date of her return to Lowestoft.[5] It is not, however, the ship's route that is most puzzling, although in the *Mavis*'s papers only the forty-seven-day-long voyage from Marseilles to Lowestoft is recorded.[6] At that time Anglo-Russian relations were tense and the danger of war was still real; the correspondence between Bobrowski and his nephew had to go through Marseilles because letters to England were being officially withheld. Under such circumstances, would a British ship take the risk of entering a Russian port with a subject of the tsar, illegally abroad, among the crew? Many years later Conrad recalled the sight of the Russian army tents near San Stefano, on the sea of Marmara, but he never made the slightest mention of his visit to Russia.[7] Perhaps he went ashore in Constantinople and waited there for the return of the *Mavis*.

The steamer entered the port of Lowestoft on 10 June, and it was there and then that Konrad Korzeniowski set foot on English soil for the first time.[8] The occasion excited no particular emotions since he planned to return to France and enlist in the French navy. To be sure, the voyage on the British steamer must have been rather unpleasant for him. First of all, he did not know the language; that, however, was perhaps not the worst. On the sailing ships of the Delestangs he was in the position of a young apprentice from a good home, a friend of the owner's family; at the end of each voyage he returned to the society of affable and cultured friends. On the *Mavis*, however, blackened with smoke and covered with coal dust, he was just a lonely foreigner. By comparison with the riffraff serving in the British fleet, the simple sailors from southern France must have seemed refined. Probably it was thought on the *Mavis* that "de Korzeniowski" gave himself airs. This might have been the reason for his conflict with Captain William Pine—in which according to Bobrowski the young szlachcic "might have been right."[9] Embittered, Konrad left the ship, apparently forfeiting part of his deposit; either out of curiosity or in search of something to do, or else with the intention of returning to Marseilles, he departed for London; there, with lightning speed, he went through half his ready cash.

Once again it became necessary to appeal to his uncle. But this time he overstepped the limits, and an angry outburst from Pan Tadeusz followed. The very heading on his letter of 8 July looked ominous: "My good Konrad!" Reproaches followed concerning the Marseilles expenses that precluded his uncle from taking his health cure at Marienbad that year.

I would not even mention it—if I knew that all my efforts and privations for you are in a good cause and that you appreciate them. But unfortunately this by no means seems to be the case! Reflect, I pray, if you are still capable of doing it, on what mischief you have done this year, and answer for yourself if even from your own father you could expect such patience and indulgence as you get from me—and whether this should not have reached its limit?

You were idling for nearly a whole year—you fell into debt, you deliberately shot yourself—and as a result of it all, at the worst time of the year, tired out and in spite of the most terrible rate of exchange—I hasten to you, pay, spend about 2,000 roubles, I increase your allowance to meet your needs! All this is apparently not enough for you. And when I make a fresh sacrifice to save you from idleness and to ensure that you could stay on the

CONRAD'S SEA VOYAGES

Voyages as passenger
Voyages as seaman

B. — BANDJARMASIN
F. — FALMOUTH
H. — HULL
L. — LONDON
LO. — LOWESTOFT
M. — MESSINA
P. — PATRAS
PA. — PALERMO
PO. — PORT-AU-PRINCE
S. — SOUTHAMPTON

English ship that you fancied, you leave the ship . . . you travel to London, God knows why, being fully aware that you could not manage by yourself, having nothing and knowing nobody—you then lose half the money you have left and you write to me as if to some school-chum "send me 500 fr. which you can deduct from the allowance";—from which allowance, pray?? —from the one you give yourself? and "advise me what to do in these diffi-cult circumstances." In other words, you treat me like your banker: asking for advice so as to get money—assuming that if I give you advice—which you will or will not follow—I shall also give money for putting my advice into practice! Really, you have exceeded the limits of stupidity permitted to your age! And you pass beyond the limits of my patience! What possible ad-vice can I—so far away—give, not knowing the conditions of your profes-sion in general and the local conditions in particular? When you decided on this unfortunate profession, I told you: I don't want and am not going to chase after you to the ends of the world—for I do not intend nor do I wish to spoil all my life because of the fantasies of a hobbledehoy.

I shall help you, but I warn you that you must persevere in your decision, work, as upon this your whole future depends, I will not allow you to be idle at my expense—you will find help in me, but not for a lazybones and a spendthrift. I told you this when you set out to be a sailor. I repeated it in my letters and I repeated it again in Marseilles—you must think for yourself and fend for yourself, for you have chosen a career which keeps you far from your natural advisers. You wanted it—you did it—you voluntarily chose it. Sub-mit to the results of your decision. You ask for advice in the "present difficult situation"—this I shall not give, for I cannot—I did not send you where you are. I agreed that you should sail on an English ship but not to your staying in England, not to your traveling to London and wasting my money there! I can only give you one piece of advice—not a new one, for I have given it to you a hundred times already, and that is "arrange your affairs within the limits of what I give you, for I will not give you more" . . .

I repeat, it is all the same to me in which navy you work—the choice is your affair. If you decide to join the French Navy I have nothing against it, but until you are 21 do something; don't idle, learn, and don't pretend to be a rich young gentleman. . . .

. . . If you have not secured yourself a position by the age of 24, do not count on the allowance, for I will stop it—I have no money for drones and I have no intention of working so that someone else may enjoy himself at my expense—I wonder if you ever considered how much you have cost me? To facilitate this problem for you I inform you that everything has been carefully noted by me here and that since your parents' death I have spent on you (apart from the 1,100 guldens squandered by you which you had from the

late Mr K and 500 rubles from Mme Korzeniowska) 9,119 rubles. It is a tidy
sum, about 30,000 fr., and up till now what has it produced—nothing!!!
   Write what you are going to do.[10]

Bobrowski did send the money. In the meantime, Korzeniowski, scenting
trouble in advance of the letter, or perhaps unable to see any alternative, returned to Lowestoft, where he stopped at the house of a local acquaintance, a
Frenchman.[11] On 11 July he signed on a 215-ton coastal coal schooner, the
Skimmer of the Sea, giving his name on the contract as "Conrad de Korzeniowski" and "Poland" as the place of birth.[12] The schooner's crew of seven came
from Lowestoft and nearby Pakefield; most men were interrelated and a family
atmosphere prevailed on board. "I can never forget," said Conrad toward the
end of his life, "the friendliness of the Lowestoft people to a strange youngster.
They may have been amused at me but they taught many of a seaman's duties
and the very terms of our sea-speech."[13] He won popularity by bearing the cost
of entertainments and various treats that were obviously not paid out of his
shilling-a-month earnings (the lowest permissible) but out of his uncle's allowance, 160 times higher: even the *Skimmer*'s captain did not earn more. "In
that craft I began to learn English from East Coast chaps each built as though to
last for ever, and coloured like a Christmas card. Tan and pink—gold hair and
blue eyes with that Northern straight-away-there look!"[14]

He served on the *Skimmer* as an A.B. (able-bodied seaman);[15] in theory, this
rank in the merchant service hierarchy was given after four years on the deck,
but the regulations were not strictly observed.[16] Korzeniowski must have presented his seafaring experience in a rather complimentary light. Anyway, he remained on the *Skimmer* only seventy-three days; having made three voyages to
Newcastle and back, he left the schooner on 23 August.

Perhaps the work turned out to be too hard or perhaps he became tired of the
linguistic problems and wanted a breath of fresh air after the salty coal dust. He
then embarked on an energetic correspondence with his uncle, conveniently
"forgetting" that he had already used up in advance half of the allowance assigned to him. This occasioned his guardian to write a sarcastic letter:

I observe that the growing proximity of the payment of your allowance puts
you into a feverish state—which I would call a "fever of receiving." I confess
frankly that I do not experience a similar "fever of giving" and I calmly await
the time of swallowing this pill, which in the present state of my pocket may
cause a certain diarrhea; which, however, will happen soon, so that the
money may be sent to you in time. From your last letter but one, I see that
you expect to get the whole 1,200 fr., as you explicitly show me with a great
knowledge of arithmetic—sorry, I mean the art of addition—how you will
use your 1,200 fr., forgetting that on account of this sum you have already
had 600 fr. . . . If my eyes do not deceive me, I read in your letter of the 15th

July, in which you acknowledge the receipt of 600 fr. (forgetting the 200 fr. due to Richard) the following words: "As for me, I shall have left on the 15th October 400 fr. which I ask you kindly to send me, not more than that, however, as my conscience would not permit me to take a greater sum, after what happened at the beginning of this year." Apparently your conscience is now at rest as you reckon for certain on getting the whole 1,200 fr. If that is so, then it means that what you said in your letter of the 15th July was nothing but an empty phrase—what is the point of it?—whereas the matter in question was a serious one. . . . However, in spite of my past statements to the contrary, once more I shall help you to get back on to the right road—but believe me that this is for the *third and last time*. . . . So manage on it as well you can—firstly pay Richard—for I swear in God's name that I shall give you no more under any pretense—either as an advance or in answer to a request—as I simply cannot. . . . However, as you practise "addition" condescend to add the following figures: Your debts and my journey 1,355, Allowance 15th March: 480, advance in July 240, Allowance 15th October 480—you will arrive at the sum of 2,675 rubles, that is 6,687 francs which is the equivalent of my personal maintenance for 4 years, for I have for myself only 600 rubles annually, which has to suffice me. . . .

Though you may be feverish now, before the wretched money reaches you, I shall also suffer from anxiety till I learn what use you have made of it. Therefore, Panie Bracie, write to me about your intentions and decisions and later on do not forget about your humble servant but fortify him with letters while he labours for your maintenance, for as I have told you in my last letter, I desire the reformation of the sinner and not the getting him out of my mind, thoughts, heart, and pocket; that would have been the easiest way and my concern is to be able to cherish him, love and, what is most important of all, respect him—which is all now up to you.[17]

It seems that at last Korzeniowski determined to look for a more permanent occupation. Following an advertisement in the London *Times* he called on the office of a sailing agent, James Sutherland, in Fenchurch Street. Apparently he had already written to him from Lowestoft. In his essay "Poland Revisited" he gives a colorful description of his first visit to the office where he was to call a number of times in later years:

It was one o'clock in the afternoon, but the day was gloomy. By the light of a single gas-jet depending from the smoked ceiling I saw an elderly man, in a long coat of black broadcloth. He had a grey beard, a big nose, thick lips, and heavy shoulders. His curly white hair and the general character of his head recalled vaguely a burly apostle in the *barocco* style of Italian art. Standing up at a tall, shabby, slanting desk, his silver-rimmed spectacles pushed up high on his forehead, he was eating a mutton-chop, which had been just brought to him from some Dickensian eating-house round the corner.

Without ceasing to eat he turned to me his florid *barocco* apostle face with an expression of inquiry.

I produced elaborately a series of vocal sounds which must have borne sufficient resemblance to the phonetics of English speech, for his face broke into a smile of comprehension almost at once.[18]

Sutherland's business consisted of placing apprentices on ships. Konrad informed his uncle that he had to pay Sutherland a £20 deposit in order to sign a contract for three years: the first for a fee, the second free of charge, the third for a small remuneration; then he was to take the examination for second mate and receive British nationality.[19] Nevertheless on the list of the crew of the beautiful clipper *Duke of Sutherland* which he joined, signing his name again as "Conrad de Korzeniowski," he is mentioned as an ordinary seaman with the ridiculous pay of one shilling a month.[20] Who fooled whom? Sutherland Korzeniowski, Konrad his uncle, or both? We do not know.

The *Duke of Sutherland* had a crew of twenty-three. Although many were experienced sailors, half received the same low wages as Korzeniowski. Indirectly, these low wages resulted from a crisis on the labor market due to a world economic depression.[21] Directly, however, it was brought about because most sailors, the moment they stepped ashore, indulged in wild spending sprees and lived on credit granted them by the "crimps" or boardinghouse owners, often acting in conjunction with publicans and pimps. In due course the crimps would "sell" the indebted and frequently drunk sailors to the captains, collecting from them the money to be deducted later from the men's pay. The English custom of not paying off the crew immediately after completing the voyage but three or five days later favored the process; the sailors, long deprived of the joys of shore life, would get into debt at once by signing IOUs.[22] That state of affairs contributed to the then generally acknowledged deterioration in the standards of sailors' qualifications, particularly those serving on long-distance sailing ships.[23] Often they were recruited from city riffraff, castaways, vagabonds, and waifs; drinking, particularly among the English, was endemic, and foreigners were therefore more willingly accepted. The difference between qualified (A.B.) and ordinary (O.S.) sailors was becoming blurred as the result of the shipowners' reluctance to pay higher wages; the earnings on shore and the pay on the steamers were, as a rule, higher. Very few people chose the sailing profession for the sake of adventure or love for the sea—such spirits would, rather, be attracted by the Royal Navy; the majority of men aboard merchant sailing vessels served out of necessity, for a miserable remuneration.[24]

The *Duke of Sutherland* was a 1047-ton clipper engaged in the transport of wool; when Korzeniowski came on board on 12 October its captain for the first time was a forty-two year old Scotsman, John McKay. Three days later the clip-per departed on Konrad's longest voyage up to then, round the Cape of Good Hope to Australia. The journey lasted 109 days, with unfavorable winds and a gale on the Atlantic. On 26 December the ship passed the Cape; on 31 January 1879 it entered Sydney.[25]

It was Korzeniowski's first genuine service at sea.[26] At that time a sailor's working day lasted twelve hours and was divided into seven watches: the first from 2000 to 2400 hours, the middle watch from 0000 to 0400 hours, the morning watch from 0400 to 0800 hours, then from 0800 to 1200 (noon) and 1200 to 1600; thereafter two "dogwatches": from 1600 to 1800 and 1800 to 2000. The uneven number of watches resulted in a day-to-day rotation of work-ing hours between two teams of the first and second mate respectively. In their free time sailors could sleep, eat, mend their clothes, or rest, but in bad weather they were frequently called upon to help with the watch.

Even in the best of weather the sailors on deck had their hands full. Apart from steering, which was their most difficult and exhausting duty, they had to set, shorten, and take in the sails, check the state of the canvases and rigging, mend tears, scrub decks, and clean the masts. The higher ranks used ordinary seamen for various jobs, particularly for cleaning the crew's quarters. Sailors on watch were not allowed to speak to each other.[27]

It is not surprising that Korzeniowski landed in Sydney in low spirits, which became even lower as the result of a delay of about ten days in the arrival of the five pounds sent at his request by his uncle. He had not realized that on the British ships, contrary to the French vessels, the crew were expected to buy their traveling and working kit out of their own money.[28] He was unprepared for the "uncomfortable conditions on English ships where no one is in the least concerned with the crew's comfort. This fate is shared by all the junior officers who, however, being well aware of the situation knew how to deal with it, while Konrad, having counted on finding the same comfort as he had had on French vessels, did not think about his convenience and consequently had to put up with all the discomfort for 109 days."[29]

The food was worse than on the *Mont Blanc* and *Saint Antoine*; information concerning food supplies in the British merchant marine varies considerably, but there is no doubt that the French paid more attention to their palates.[30] British daily food rations supposedly consisted of a pound of bread, one and a quarter to one and a half pounds of meat (no doubt salted), half a pound of potatoes or vegetables, a little flour and peas, half an ounce each of coffee and tea, two ounces of sugar, and three quarts of water for all purposes. In reality, those moderate guidelines were seldom followed, as the captain could arbitrar-ily introduce food substitutes; moreover the quality of food differed consider-ably from one ship to another.[31]

Clearly life aboard ship was hard. The crew's quarters were not heated and at best possessed primitive lighting; all the sailors slept together, tightly packed on narrow bunks; there was one latrine and sailors washed themselves on deck. The men lived in cramped conditions without any privacy.[32]

Thus thrown together, sailors lived for weeks and months on end, carrying out their monotonous and tiring work, completely cut off from everything beyond the ship. The primitive conditions and boredom had a depressing effect. The spiritual void of their lives was only filled by a constant struggle against the feebleness of their bodies.

When the clipper entered the port of Sydney almost the entire crew was discharged, not because they could not work any longer but because thrifty shipowners, unwilling to pay wages while the ship lay in harbor and knowing that a new crew could easily be found, released as many hands as possible at the end of the journey.[33]

Korzeniowski remained on board probably as the result of an earlier contract. If one is to believe his reminiscences in *The Mirror of the Sea*, he acted as a night watchman throughout the stay in Sydney.[34] The *Duke of Sutherland* was moored at the Circular Quay for four months as the captain could not find a cargo for the return voyage.

Although nothing is known of Korzeniowski's excursions on the Australian mainland, his knowledge of local conditions and even of the slang was revealed later, for instance in his short story "Tomorrow." Moreover, he had time to read and it was then that he became acquainted with Flaubert, through *Salammbô*, which, strangely enough, did not discourage him.[35] He could also plow laboriously through a one-volume edition of Shakespeare. At the same time, he was busy with practical matters. The Antipodes seemed to offer excellent professional and financial possibilities; from hearsay he was tempted by the Malay Archipelago. His uncle reported to Buszczyński:

> Konrad's letters are satisfactory—a liking for his profession and hope of a better future shines through them. He expects to be back in England by September and, not wasting much time, to set off in October again on a voyage to Australia—but this time in order to stay there several years—or at least two. He has it in mind to devote himself to the investigation of trading arrangements on the Archipelago of the Sunda Isles, the beauty and wealth of which he describes with the greatest enthusiasm. In Sydney he became acquainted with some captain famous for his knowledge of the trade with that Archipelago and for his contacts there and well known both in geographical and trading circles. In fact that captain, who is at the same time a shipowner, took a fancy to Konrad and offered him a job—to start with at £5 a month, that is £60 a year—and an officer's keep on the ship—and as I am giving Konrad 2,400 fr., which comes to approximately £100, he would be receiving £150 per annum plus upkeep, which would not be at all bad. His pros-

pects would be: naturalization in England and experience of a trade which he considers profitable—and who knows, maybe in time he would try his luck in this branch of activity? . . . Here I should add—not so much a credit to him as to his gift of languages—that the Polish in Konrad's letters is as good as if he had never left Poland, when in fact, since his departure from Cracow (1874) he has spoken Polish only once—with me in Marseilles.[36]

It is possible that the unnamed captain may have become the archetype of Tom Lingard in *Almayer's Folly*, *An Outcast of the Islands*, and *The Rescue*, whose namesake Korzeniowski never met.

The *Duke of Sutherland* left Sydney on 6 July 1879, apparently sailing around Cape Horn on the homeward voyage.[37]

Korzeniowski arrived in London on 19 October, but in spite of previous statements and plans he disembarked, having evidently lost all desire for long-distance voyages. He brought up once again the idea of returning to the Mediterranean. Bobrowski, complimenting his nephew on thriftiness, since the young man had contented himself with just over half of his allowance, wrote of the Mediterranean projects: "Do as you think! As you wish! I have no knowledge of it. I have read more than once that it is only 'a great lake,' so a sailor enamored as you are of your profession I suppose might like the ocean better. Besides, as I have mentioned before, I would like to see in you a sailor combined with a salesman, and as the roads around here are better trodden and known, I should have thought that the more distant and less known ones would be more appropriate for you. . . . You plan to come to Odessa next year and to see me there. It is difficult to predict what will happen in a year's time—there might be a war— my old self might die. However, neither the one nor the other is in our power to prevent but it is our duty to foresee and avoid unnecessary trouble, and therefore I do not wish you to visit Russia until you are naturalized as an English subject; but what you have not written to me about is whether after passing your examination for second mate you will obtain naturalization. So write to me and clear this up."[38] As a son of exiles and having reached conscription age Konrad was under obligation to do many years of military service in Russia and to go there would have entailed the risk of being treated as a deserter.

In order to sit for the Second Mate examination Konrad needed documents attesting to at least four years' service at sea. That required number of years was still a long way off, but he appealed to his uncle to put in a word on his behalf to M. Delestang about an appropriate certificate.[39] After a two-month stay in England he enlisted on 11 December as an able-bodied seaman on the iron steamer *Europa*. Although fewer qualifications were required on the steamers, the pay was better. He received £3.5.0 a month. On 12 December the steamer departed for Genoa, Naples, Patras, and Palermo from where it returned to London on 29 January 1880.[40] Next day, Konrad left the ship. He felt he had been exploited and he had had a conflict with the captain, A. Munro, about which he complained to his uncle. The incident was reflected in his certificate of discharge; his professional skill was assessed not as "very good" but only "good" (the form offered three possibilities: "very good," "good," and "decline to answer"; professional skill and behavior were judged separately). Among Korzeniowski's testimonials this is the only one to record such a remark.

He also complained of "coughing and occasional fever." That worried Bobrowski to such an extent that in spite of reproaching his nephew for heedless extravagance he offered additional money to cover medical expenses.[41] This time Konrad prolonged his stay in London: first, supposedly in Tollington Park Street near Finsbury Park, where he rented a flat from William Ward;[42] later at 6 Dynevor Road, the address he gave for the next seven years.[43] Dynevor Road is a gray, plain-looking street far from the city's center, in a cheap, unattractive northern district of Stoke Newington. Number 6 still exists. It is a one-story Victorian house like thousands of others along endless miles of streets.

Soon after he left the *Europa*, Korzeniowski met George Fountaine Weare Hope, an ex-merchant service officer, at that time director of a commercial firm in London. This—apparently Konrad's first close contact in England—developed into a long lasting friendship. The two men met in James Sutherland's office, which was frequented by many active and retired merchant navy officers. "I saw him several times before he found a berth and the more I saw him the more I liked him," recalled Hope years later.[44] Little is known about Hope. He seems to have been a simple man with no intellectual or artistic interests, and a lover of sailing;[45] toward Korzeniowski he felt sincere and spontaneous friendship.

Konrad's correspondence with Kazimierówka encountered inexplicable difficulties: several letters sent by Bobrowski in the spring never reached London. Meanwhile Konrad flooded his uncle with letters; in the first half of May he wrote four. Bobrowski commented on the young voyager's new plans:

> You would not be a Nałęcz, dear boy, if you were steady in your enterprises and if you didn't chase after ever new projects. This refers to what you wrote about Mr. Lascalle's proposal that you become his secretary and later make money on the railways! But I would not be myself and your uncle if I did not discourage you from changing professions and did not warn you that such changes make people become "déclassé," who never having warmed a place for themselves nor having built anything for themselves (don't even mention the good of society although it is only fair to think of it), bear a grudge against the whole world for not having succeeded. You must not, Panie Bracie, believe in either good or bad luck. Work and perseverance are the only values that never fail. In the life of every man a momentary success may occur, but a sensible and moderate man will not misuse it but use it, while a thoughtless and stupid man will either miss it or misuse it. But to expect that

success should appear while one is on the threshold of life, and at any time it's needed, without any work or merit, is childish dreaming and a product of our epoch whose only slogan is "enjoyment." You must see it for yourself—does it agree with personal dignity and reason to tie oneself to the fate of another man—however great he might seem—and in this particular case to some American businessman or politician? It is much more dignified and sensible to devote your life and tie your future to a certain profession, putting into it your work and determination. You chose for yourself the profession of seaman,—you can expand on it further by trading—well and good—pursue this as far as you can and you will get somewhere. By changing from one career fortuitously to another you may encounter on your way nothing but buffets and disappointments![46]

Was the writer fully aware of the hardships of the profession chosen by his eccentric nephew? We do not know. One thing is certain, however—his advice and suggestions were to the point and sounded like a prospective plan of morality that Korzeniowski was to realize piecemeal and, eventually, to regard as his own.

Bobrowski raised the subject of naturalization, of taking some citizenship other than Russian; the idea did not seem to appeal to the young man, since his uncle had to use his power of persuasion: "Sooner or later you will have to think about it—but it is always advisable to think and act about such matters at ease rather than under the pressure of circumstances and necessity."

The long-awaited certificate arrived from Delestang, somewhat imprecisely worded but stating clearly that "Conrad de Korzeniowski, native of Poland, entered our service in the month of February 1874 as midshipman on board our vessel the *Mont-Blanc*, then served as lieutenant on board our ship the *St-Antoine* and left this last named vessel after 3 years constant service in the West India and South America trade on the 14th February 1877 and that during that time he gave perfect satisfaction to his superior officers by his sobriety, general conduct and strict application in the discharge of his duties."[47] All this was far removed from the truth. Korzeniowski did not arrive in Marseilles until the second half of October 1874; he made his first half-year sea voyage as a passenger; later he sailed as an apprentice and a steward, not as a "lieutenant"; and the entire duration of his service amounted to thirteen months and five days, not three years. Nevertheless he submitted the document translated and certified by the French consulate in London, together with his application for the examination for second mate in the British Merchant Service.[48] He listed the respective terms of his past employment: the *Mont Blanc*, 1 February 1874 to 1 February 1875; the *Saint Antoine*, 1 February 1875 to 14 February 1877. Together with the certificates from the *Duke of Sutherland* and *Europa*, whose joint terms of service amounted to one year two months, and twenty-two days, the total exceeded the required four years. In reality, however, Korzeniowski had worked as a sailor only two years, five months, and fourteen days, even taking into account his term on the *Skimmer*, which he omitted in the declaration; this included over five months spent on land. Since his work as a steward on the *Saint Antoine* did not in fact fulfill the conditions of the British regulations and since his stay in Sydney ought not to have been counted, his total period of employment amounted to only seventeen months.[49] Nonetheless, he signed a declaration of his statements and of the enclosed documents, risking legal indictment in the event of the fraud being discovered.[50]

Similar cases were obviously not uncommon; the Board of Trade's regulations warned against "tampering" with certificates. The generally low standards of the candidates as well as of the requirements—the minimum age for certification as second mate was seventeen—might have constituted for Korzeniowski some justification. In any case, he took his first step on the ladder by means of deceit and the memory of it, however stifled, must have been irritating.

Konrad attended a special training course conducted by a leading specialist in the field, John Newton, head of the Navigation School in Dock Street, East London, and author of popular examination handbooks, chiefly *Newton's Seamanship Examiner*.[51] The course consisted mainly of questions and answers, from which some were selected later at the examination. Most questions were practical; theoretical knowledge of mathematics and astronomy did not exceed the requirements of the lower forms of secondary schools; it was necessary to remember a certain number of simple mathematical formulae.[52] From Korzeniowski's point of view the most difficult condition to meet must have been that "foreigners must prove to the satisfaction of the Examiners that they can speak and write the English language sufficiently well to perform the duties required of them on board a British vessel."[53]

He passed his examination before Captain James Rankin on 28 May 1880 and three days later received the eagerly awaited certificate.[54] His uncle was delighted:

My dear boy and Officer! Two days ago I got the news (two letters together) about the fortunate outcome of your examination. It has been a profound pleasure and my first reward to learn that you have received that piece of "ass's hide" upon which so many terrible threats were written by the gentlemen of the Board Office in the event of your failing in the duties of your chosen profession, in the hierarchy of which you have now achieved the first step!! I fully share your satisfaction, which you can say arises from a twofold source. Firstly, Dear Sir, you have proved to our country and your own people that you have not eaten your bread in the world for four years in vain; secondly, that you have succeeded in overcoming the difficulties that arise from the language itself, and from your difficult position as a foreigner without any patronage to support you—and all this thanks to Capt. Wyndham, whom may God grant long life for putting the fear of God into you! And yet, that good old fellow of a captain let himself be disarmed, while that kind-hearted professor Newton who encouraged you while not mentioning Wynd-ham's prejudices, and those sailors who rejoiced at your success—they all seem very likeable to me at this moment,—for taking the stranger to their bosom. There are good people everywhere, one must only know how to find them and to attach them to oneself! You cannot complain of any lack of them on your path, from the beginning of your life among strangers.[55]

At that time Korzeniowski still contemplated going to the United States. His uncle did not raise basic objections. "I am not opposed to any of your proj-ects—even if it is to become a Yankee." But he once again exhorted Konrad to remember "what is due to the dignity of the nation and families to which you belong." Quite soon the American plans faded, to the obvious joy of Bobrow-ski, who encouraged his nephew to follow one line of profession and erupted at once into "genealogical" praise: "I see with pleasure that the Nałęcz in you has been modified under the influence of the Bobroszczuki, as your incomparable Mother used to call her own family after she flew away to the Nałęcz nest. This time I rejoice over the influence of my family, although I don't in the least deny that the Nałęczes have a spirit of initiative and enterprise greater than that which is in my blood. From the blending of these two excellent families in your worthy person there should spring a race which by its endurance and wise en-terprise will astound the whole world! Pray God that may happen. Amen!" It appeared, however, that finding a suitable seafaring job was none too easy. Once again Korzeniowski found himself in financial difficulties and his benefac-tor from Kazimierówka was unable to come to his assistance at once.[56]

Not until 21 August did he finally enlist as third mate on an iron clipper, the *Loch Etive*, used mainly in the wool trade. His first pay as an officer was £3.10.0 per month.[57]

The status of a third mate was vague. In the British Merchant Service the distinction between junior officers and seamen was rather blurred, and, when the need arose an officer would often pocket his diploma and work as an or-dinary seaman. The third mate's duties and responsibilities were not clearly stated; his status fell between that of an ordinary sailor and an officer; he was attached permanently to the first mate's watch as his aide and deputy. The crew would taunt him a bit out of contempt and a bit out of envy.[58]

The *Loch Etive* had four officers and twenty-four crew members, eight of them foreigners. On the return journey their number increased to nine, includ-ing one Russian. The captain, forty-eight-year-old William Stuart, was an ex-cellent sailor who from 1863 to 1874 commanded the *Tweed*, a wooden clipper famous for her speed. Now, on the heavier *Loch Etive*, he was trying unsuccessfully to equal his past feats. The era of fast sailing ships was drawing to a close; they could not compete with the speed of steamers, so they were built larger in order to offset the time loss by cheapness of transport. In "Cobwebs and Gossamer" (*The Mirror of the Sea*), Conrad later described, apparently with unusual accuracy, his experiences on board the *Loch Etive*, under the command of a wonder-inspiring but cantankerous captain and a first mate who, on account of impaired hearing, would carry on sail on a ship like "the very devil of a fellow," as the terrifying whistling and creaking of the canvases, ropes and spars strained beyond endurance would fail to reach him.

The *Loch Etive* left London on 21 August. The voyage to Sydney took ninety-four days; the *Loch Etive* entered port on 24 November. The local *Morning Herald* wrote next day: "The beautiful iron clipper ship *Loch Etive* arrived yesterday. . . . The vessel is a high-classed one. . . . She has the appearance of being a thoroughly stanch vessel, and has come into port in capital order. The winds experienced were not of a kind to make a remarkable passage, the best day's performance, however, was 293 miles. The ship left London on August 22, and the Lizards on August 24, with light E. and N.E. winds to latitude 7 degrees North, and then S.W. winds to the Equator which was crossed on September 28. The S.E. trades commenced on the Equator proved moderate, and were parted with in sight of Trinadad [sic] on October 4. Encountered a violent gale from W.S.W. on the 7th, splitting the main topgallantsail, mainsail, foresail, and mizzentopsail. The *Loch Etive* will speedily put out her cargo, and load for London." [59]

The clipper lay in port seven weeks. We know nothing about Korzeniowski's activities at that time. He left Sydney on 11 January 1881; the return voyage lasted 103 days, but the *Loch Etive* outsailed several other wool clippers. [60]

Accounts of daily life on large sailing ships differ sharply. Some authors present it as a tough but wonderful school of life attracting personalities strong and eager for adventure, brave and resourceful souls; others describe the monotonous drudgery that transformed men into moronic bipeds, primitive and dull-witted. [61] Living in constant danger of disablement during routine work, and of death during a storm, a sailor could develop courage as well as absolute indifference to human life. The two aspects are depicted in Conrad's works; it is significant that in his recollections the positive elements, usually flavored with nostalgia, are stronger, while in the fiction the negative aspects prevail.

The attractive features of sea life on the *Loch Etive* under Stuart's command could easily predominate. Good seamanship carried out with precision affords not only professional but aesthetic satisfaction. Basil Lubbock, an expert on the history of clippers, wrote that service on those ships called for "men of courage and grit, men of authority and resource, men of nerve strength and muscle fitness." [62] All those qualities may easily assume the form of brutality, but to Korzeniowski the work on the *Loch Etive* revealed its romantic aspects.

In "Cobwebs and Gossamer" Conrad recalls how on the homeward-bound passage Captain Stuart promoted him to officer of the watch. This information is not certain, however, since it was not recorded, as it should have been according to the regulations, in Korzeniowski's papers. Over forty years later Conrad mentioned that on the passage they encountered in latitude 51° a drifting American whaler, the *Alaska*, to whose crew they threw into the sea a belated Christmas gift parcel.[63] It has been impossible, however, to establish whether and to what extent there was a real basis for another story referring to that same voyage—the last-minute rescue of the crew of a Danish sailing ship, a wreck barely afloat.[64]

The *Loch Etive* entered the port of London on 24 April 1881, and the following day Korzeniowski left the ship.[65] Among the news that awaited him ashore the most sensational concerned the assassination of Tsar Alexander II by a Pole, Ignacy Hryniewiecki. Konrad's allowance was also waiting for him; it was still paid in full—about £46 for six months, more than twice his earnings on the *Loch Etive*.[66]

Bobrowski was extremely pleased with his nephew's return "to the misty shores of hospitable Albion, for which country, by the way, in the depths of my heart, I do not feel a great sympathy" and expounded the following plans: "I expect that during these three years you will sit for at least one examination if not two—and this allowance will enable you to stay several months in London for that purpose . . . should that happen, your Uncle might possibly help you further." Bobrowski also expressed hope of meeting the "dear boy" in the early autumn, which he intended to spend in Wiesbaden taking a cure. "And I have chosen to take it there solely to make it nearer for you to drop in on me, should the opportunity arise." But all this was to depend on Konrad getting a new job, "for I know that staying on shore does not agree with you, and above all that it seems a waste of money to spend an unproductive 3 months on land while waiting for a fortnight's meeting, which although greatly desired by us both, has to be governed by a sensible assessment and judgment of the possibilities; such judgement in no way would diminish or weaken our attachment."[67]

"It pleases me greatly to see your 'professional fervour,' which is proved by the efforts you are making to find a berth," Bobrowski wrote in the same letter. Indeed, for the first time in three years Korzeniowski did not suggest any subsidiary projects. Sailing on the *Loch Etive* must have fired his enthusiasm for seafaring life. The promotion to second mate was essential in order to prepare for the next examination, but otherwise the position on the *Loch Etive* did not get him any closer toward it since one year's charge of the watch was required.[68] The year 1881 brought an immense postdepression boom in sea trade, but there were many jobless sailors looking for work.[69]

Perhaps Sutherland promised the young Pole employment, for on 20 May Konrad wrote to his uncle about the impossibility of arranging a meeting with him in the summer. "I was very pleased that you look with adult determination and common sense at all the difficulties which prevent our meeting, instead of becoming submerged by grief and lamentation, which can lead nowhere except to a loss of energy." He complained about his own failing health and related the repercussions of the pogroms "on the railway line between Kiev and Odessa," which "from the German theoretical 'Judenhetze' took here the practical form of 'thieving.'"[70]

Although he would have preferred to sail into new and unknown parts, Korzeniowski expected to embark on another voyage to Australia toward the end of the summer; on that, the longest, route it was relatively easy to find employment. Meantime he engaged in speculation with Sutherland, a pastime that was soon to get him into trouble. He was in high spirits; his letter to his uncle written on 10 June "was filled with the spirit of energy and enterprise."[71] The postponement of the meeting with the nephew toward whom the ageing recluse felt a growing affection obviously saddened Bobrowski but he did not remonstrate, thinking, in the first place of his charge's future career, as was his wont. He presented him with another project, however:

> As thank God you do not forget your Polish (may God bless you for it, as I bless you) and your writing is not bad, I repeat what I have already written and said before—you would do well to write contributions for the *Wędrowiec* in Warsaw. We have few travelers, and even fewer genuine correspondents: the words of an eyewitness would be of great interest and in time would bring you in money. It would be an exercise in your native tongue—that thread which binds you to your country and countrymen, and finally a tribute to the memory of your father who always wanted to and did serve his country by his pen. Think about this, young man, collect some reminiscences from the voyage to Australia and send them as a sample—the address of *Wędrowiec* is known in Warsaw. Six reports sent from different parts of the world during the year would not take much of your time: they would bring you some benefit and provide you with a pleasant recreation while giving pleasure to others.

Why this appeal evoked no response we do not know, but it was probably not out of indifference to national problems since in Bobrowski's letter written three months later we read: "What you write about our hopes for the future has really delighted me, for I see in it a sign of your interest in our national affairs and of your preoccupation with them in spite of your remoteness."[72]

It is impossible to guess the nature of the young globe-trotter's "speculations on credit" with Sutherland, but they cost him at least his entire half-yearly allowance. That probably gave rise to the fantastic story about an unfortunate accident, loss of luggage, and the several days spent in a hospital that he regaled his uncle with in a letter of 10 August.[73] Allegedly the accident happened on board the clipper *Annie Frost* and Korzeniowski's yarn subsequently became the subject of controversy between biographers. Bobrowski himself believed the story, at least at first.[74]

Whatever Korzeniowski did or planned at the time, employment on the *Annie Frost* was certainly not included. His name is not recorded on the list of the crew, and in his own papers there is no trace of any link with that ship. The *Annie Frost* left London on 31 July on her way to Indochina; there is no record of any accident until the vessel sank in the Atlantic on her return voyage over one year later. Jerry Allen, wishing at all costs to preserve Korzeniowski's good name, advanced a hypothesis that the accident took place on 11 June when the *Annie Frost* suffered damage to her side as the result of the collision with the lock in Le Havre. However, the report of the incident, following which the ship left immediately for London, does not mention any bodily injuries; it would be absurd to suppose that Korzeniowski kept his personal things near the ship's side. Anyway, a glance at the dates makes one reject finally that good-natured but farfetched supposition: on 10 June Konrad wrote from London to his uncle; obviously he had not signed a contract yet but still expected a voyage to Australia.[75]

Evidently Konrad lost all his ready money on speculation, or perhaps simply spent it. Yet he did not wish to harm his reputation, restored with some difficulty, and at the same time was eager to cover up his overlong period of idleness in London, when he had been unable to decide on a visit to his uncle. And so, hastily, he invented the accident, with the questionable supplement that the shipowners had not arranged compensation for the loss of property and that Sutherland offered emergency financial assistance. Bobrowski treated him to another lecture: "I am by no means against speculation, providing it is done with one's own money which one has earned and saved, but I am when it is based on borrowed capital. 'Hope is the Mother of fools and calculation the Father of the sober-minded';—so goes the proverb. Since you are a Nałęcz, beware of risky speculations based only on hope; for your grandfather squandered all his property speculating, and your Uncle, speculating always with other people's money and on credit, got into debt, caused many people disappointments, and died heavily in debt." (The accusation at least as far as it concerned Konrad's grandfather was exaggerated, since he had lost money not through speculations but as the result of insurrections.)

During Bobrowski's health cures at Marienbad (nowadays Mariánské Lázně) and Montreux his correspondence with his nephew became much more frequent. Bobrowski passed on to Konrad the request of an old acquaintance: "Mr. Kopernicki was most solicitous in inquiring about you. I read out your letters to him, having found one waiting for me. He is engaged on a great work which has already brought him European fame: 'Comparative studies of human races based on types of skulls.' This particular branch of science is called

Craniology. He earnestly requests you to collect during your voyages skulls of natives, writing on each one whose skull it is and the place of origin. When you have collected a dozen or so of such skulls write to me and I will obtain from him information as to the best way of despatching them to Cracow, where there is a special Museum devoted to Craniology." [76]

Bobrowski also appealed to Konrad to write to Adam Pulman, living at the time at Sambor, who borrowed money from various people in Cracow and then "turned a deaf ear to all calls for repayment"—Uncle Kazimierz was among those "tricked." "Write to him at Sambor; perhaps that will move him, for to your uncle 600 roubles means a lot. Don't admonish him, just say that you have heard from me of his whereabouts and so you write." [77]

Both correspondents exploited the opportunity offered by Bobrowski's stay abroad to discuss politics freely.

What you write of our hopes based on Panslavism is in theory both splendid and feasible, but it meets great difficulties in practice. You don't take into account the significance which actual numbers have in the affairs of this world. Each of the more influential nations starts by relying apparently on the Panslavic ideal and by forgetting about its own interests—but secretly and almost unconsciously relies on some aspect of its existence which will ensure its leadership. You yourself have fallen into the same error, attributing to our country certain positive qualities, which are partly but not wholly true. And so Russia does not interpret Panslavism otherwise than as a means of russifying all other nations or even converting them to the Orthodox church, justifying themselves by the argument that they have a population of 80 million (which is false). And to our claim that we have a higher culture and a longer history they reply: this was only the life and culture of one class which claimed to be a nation (this contains a grain of truth) and that only she, Russia, will develop the real elements of the people. The Czechs are told: your nation is too small. Both they and we are accused of representing a bastard mixture of East and West while Russia's culture is real, being purely Eastern (and such a one doesn't exist anyway). Other nations are told that they are small and all of Eastern origin as well and should therefore bow to a more numerous nation (Russian, of course!) in order not to perish entirely. They, however, maintain that as they are still in the cradle they are the true representatives of the pure Slavonic idea. And thus the argument goes on without end, with everyone believing himself to be in the right. I am certain that eventually out of this chaos some form of federation will emerge, but by that time I shall be long dead and possibly you will be too. In the meantime, since like pariahs we are deprived of our own political and national rights, we, more than the others, have to preserve our individuality and our own standpoint, till the time comes when Nemesis, as a result of our own efforts, spins out some situation which will give us the right to have a real national existence—and possibly something more.[78]

Bobrowski's musings enable us to trace some basic outlines of the political ideas of his twenty-four-year-old correspondent. Korzeniowski apparently hoped for an improvement of Poland's situation not through a liberation movement but by establishing an alliance with neighboring Slavic nations. This was accompanied by a faith in the pan-Slavistic ideology—surprising in a man who was later to emphasize his hostility toward Russia, a conviction that the superiority of Poland's civilization and her historical traditions would enable her to play a leading role within the pan-Slavistic community, as well as doubts about Poland's chances of becoming a fully sovereign state.

His ideas were not too remote from those held by Bobrowski, although the latter, as usual more shrewd and consistent in criticizing than in positive thinking, rightly perceived in pan-Slavism a tactical tool of the tsarist policy of domination. His own program was reduced to a passive preservation of national identity and a vague definition of "our own efforts"—probably in the economic field. His trust in a future federation of Slavs, incompatible with his avowed scepticism regarding Russia's intentions, took for granted coming to terms with that most oppressive invader and was, in spite of everything, a sign of Russian orientation.

Bobrowski's deliberations could lead only to depressing conclusions: they did not open up any new perspectives, they did not imply any hope; by discrediting Slavistic illusions they fostered inertia and discouragement. All the more so since both correspondents seemed to ignore the social aspects of the problem as if regarding political reality as immobile.

Korzeniowski had trouble finding a second mate position.[79] Eventually he found employment on a small and rather old barque, the *Palestine*. On 19 September he signed on for a voyage to Bangkok at pay of £4 a month.[80] From 15 October his uncle was to send him only half of the previous allowance, rounded up to £50 a year, that is, slightly over his new and hitherto highest salary.[81]

The *Palestine* was manned by three officers and ten hands under the command of the fifty-seven-year-old Captain Elijah Beard. Korzeniowski was not too pleased about his new appointment, judging by his uncle's comments: "It seems to me that you are not very satisfied with your post: is it because being on a 'barque' touches on your honour? Then, of course, £4 a month is disrespectful to your pocket, and, finally, the captain seems to you to be merely a 'creature,' which gives me a sad picture of his intellect. However, perhaps the last point will enable you to distinguish yourself as a 'man conscious of his craft, and useful.' Anyway it's done—proceed in health and return safely. 'Deus te ducat, perducat, et reducat,' as our ancestors used to say when setting out, sabre in hand,—and I say the same, bidding you farewell on your journey on an element unknown to them, embracing and blessing you with all my heart."[82] As it happened, this blessing was well timed; the ship was not only small but rickety. It left London on 21 September; after a stop at Gravesend the barque sailed north on 28 September; because of gales the passage to Newcastle-upon-Tyne took 22 days.

Conrad described his adventures on the *Palestine*, renamed *Judea*, in his short story "Youth," which he was later to call "a feat of memory" and "a record of experience."[83] Although he preserved the names of the captain and first officer, and the general course of events and many details correspond with the facts, as usual a number of things are creations of the author's imagination. There is no documentary evidence of the collision with a steamship in Newcastle; the hero of "Youth" is four years younger than Korzeniowski; there was only one attempt, not several, to leave the port of Falmouth, as the ship was continuously under repair; other and more striking discrepancies will be discussed later.[84]

The ship's grotesque ill-luck, contrasted with the perseverance of her crew, is rendered faithfully. The *Palestine*, with a cargo of 557 tons of coal, left Newcastle for Bangkok on 29 November 1881. Crossing the Channel she met strong gales, lost a mast, and started to leak. The crew refused to continue work and on 24 December it became necessary to return to Falmouth.[85] Bobrowski, who must have received from his nephew a vivid description of the ordeal, was horrified:

Your misfortunes of the past year fill me with despair! I purposely refer to the 'past year,' for I hope and trust that this 'malchance' will leave you alone this year. Certainly your success depends to some extent on chance or luck, but your judgment plays an important part as well. This time at least, after the wreck, cool judgment seems to have deserted you when you accepted such a wretched ship as the *Palestine*. I quite understand, my dear boy, that you decided to do so in order to avoid being a burden to me by a long stay in London, and also by serving as a second officer to qualify for your examination for a first officer. But, my dear boy, you didn't take into account that if as a result of all the mishaps and accidents that are bound to happen in a situation such as yours you should become sick or injured, I would not abandon you! While if you get drowned it will be all the same to you whether you arrive in the 'Valley of Jehoshaphat' with the rank of 2nd officer or that of candidate for 1st officer. I have never considered that I had the right to order you about, especially now that you are 24 years old, but all the same I sincerely advise you not to go to sea in such a lamentable ship as yours. Danger is certainly part of a sailor's life, but the profession itself should not prevent you from having a sensible attachment to life nor from taking sensible steps to preserve it. Both your Captain Beard and you appear to me like desperate men who look for knocks and wounds, while your shipowner is a rascal who risks the lives of 10 good men for the sake of a blackguardly profit.

Consider well, dear boy, what you ought to do. I shall not hold it against you if you decide to return to London and I shall even try to help you, for as you can imagine, I do not want for the sake of saving 300–500 roubles to see you at the bottom of the sea, or ill or, worst of all, injured or crippled with rheumatism for the rest of your life!![86]

Nevertheless, Korzeniowski decided to keep his job on the *Palestine*. His main motive was to obtain the certificate of service in the hard-won position of second officer.[87] The stay on the beautiful Cornish coast could not have been unpleasant, in any case. Konrad made at least one trip to London, where he bought, among other things a volume of Byron's poems; we do not know whether it happened before James Sutherland's death in the spring of 1882.[88] Doubtless he read a good deal; he also frequently exchanged letters with his uncle, who was surprised by the firmness of Konrad's decision. "You are obstinate, my dear lad, or is it the professional code of honour or the customs of the country you are living in that account for your sailing on such a miserable ship and risking your neck? Not being acquainted with either I shall refrain from comment. . . . I should be very pleased if you could return early enough next year for us to meet during the summer. I would very much like to get over to Cracow or Krynica for our meeting so that you could breathe a little of the air of your fatherland. If you get back early enough we could meet in Cracow and then go to Krynica for 4 weeks. If we meet as late as the autumn—then it would be in Lwów where we could also spend 4 weeks together."[89]

Korzeniowski also wrote twice to Kazimierz Bobrowski: first alarmed by Tadeusz's silence and the delay in the half-yearly allowance, then thanking him for a speedy and reassuring reply; his kindhearted uncle Kazimierz was quite touched.[90] Tadeusz, the benefactor of his brother's large family, poked fun at his "successful work in the field of marriage"; in that same letter, and very much à propos, he expounded his philosophy on money matters. "You have now lived for some years in England and have been taking part in the life there and you will have learned to respect money, and it therefore probably surprises you to hear me calling it 'filthy.' This expression is a survival from the 'romantic period' in which I was born and grew up, and to some extent it reflects our national character, a trait which was supposed to show lack of interest in money matters. I presume the latter to be an apparent rather than a real quality, for it arises rather from a carelessness than from a real contempt for money. This is because we did not work to get it but worked rather to squander it! Now our esteem for it has increased, mine possibly more than others, for we have come to realize that it is the 'nervus rerum' and the basis of both the external and inner independence of both an individual and a whole society."[91]

The *Palestine* lay in Falmouth for eight months; the length of stay and the slowness of the overhaul were caused by the stinginess and shiftiness of her owner, John Wilson of London.[92] The sailing dates were changed several times. Korzeniowski planned to sit for his examination for first officer after the voyage and to meet his uncle later. "So it is fixed: after your return and your examination, we shall meet on our native soil! I shall send your autumn allowance to Mr. Ward and if you are still away by next April I shall do the same with the spring one, so that you will be able to take the examination.[93]

Finally on 17 September 1882, one year after leaving London, the barque sailed from Falmouth for Bangkok with the same cargo and a new crew. Korzeniowski was for the first time fully in charge of a four-man watch. However, "in barques of 3–4 hundred ton the second mate is scarcely removed from the foremast hands (although he is a Mr. and has a certain amount of authority)."[94] He was also never at the helm. His responsibility consisted of loading the cargo, and assisting the captain in navigation: "He lives aft, usually having a cabin to himself, and has his meals in the cabin, although generally, and necessarily, after the captain and the chief mate, as he must take charge of the watch on deck while the first mate is below. He is, however, one step up the ladder towards being one day a skipper, although sailors have a saying 'that being second mate doesn't get your hand out of the tar-pot.'"[95] The ambiguous status of the novice second mate required him to be tough and strong-minded, particularly in front of the sailors. "Sailors are always keen to take advantage of a second mate whom they regard as 'everybody's dog.'"[96]

The passage was slow, uneventful, and monotonous.

Nothing unusual occurred until noon of the 11th March, when a strong smell resembling paraffin oil was perceived; at this time the vessel's position was lat. 2 36 S and long. 105 45 E. Banca strait. Next day smoke was discovered issuing from the coals on the port side of main hatch. Water was thrown over them until the smoke abated, the boats were lowered, water placed in them. On the 13th some coals were thrown overboard, about 4 tons, and more water poured down the hold. On the 14th, the hatches being on but not battened down the decks blew up fore and aft as far as the poop. The boats were then provisioned and the vessel headed for the Sumatra shore. About 3 p.m. the S.S. 'Somerset' came alongside in answer to signals and about 6 p.m. she took the vessel in tow. Shortly afterwards the fire rapidly increased and the master of the 'Palestine' requested the master of the 'Somerset' to tow the barque on shore. This being refused, the two-rope was slipped and about 11 p.m. the vessel was a mass of fire, and all hands got into the boats, 3 in number. The mate and 4 seamen in one boat, the 2nd mate with three hands in another and the master in the long boat with 3 men. The boats remained by the vessel until 8.30 a.m. on the 15th. She was still above water, but inside appeared a mass of fire. The boats arrived at Mintok at 10 p.m. on the 15th, and the master reported the casualty to the harbour master.[97]

In "Youth," Conrad dramatized the accident, stretching it out in time and space and giving a different reason for parting with the towing steamer. In the tale the parting appears extremely risky; in reality, however, the disaster took place near shore. The boats did not steer for Java but toward the port of Muntok on Bangka island. When in 1922 Richard Curle triumphantly announced his discovery of the real name of the port where, according to the story, the hero experienced his first fascinating encounter with the exotic East, Conrad protested at once. "It isn't a matter of literary criticism at all if I venture to point out to you that the dogmatic, ex-cathedra tone that you have adopted in your article positively frightens me. As you tell me that you have a copy of the article by you I'll venture to make a few alterations, more to let you see what is in my mind than with any hope of convincing you. . . . The paragraph you quote of the East meeting the narrator is all right in itself; whereas directly it's connected with Mintok it becomes nothing at all. Mintok is a damned hole without any beach and without any glamour and in relation to the parag. is not in tone. Therefore the par. when pinned to a particular spot, must appear diminished—a fake." [98] He was undoubtedly right in remonstrating against a literal and autobiographical approach to his writing, but he himself provoked it by his "author's note." The vehemence of the protest might have been heightened by the fact that the identification of Muntok revealed the greatest exaggeration in the short story: in a dozen or so hours the boats could reach the shore and there was no need to "knock about in an open boat" for "nights and days" nor to remain for "sixteen hours on end with a mouth dry as a cinder" at the steering-oar. It is not surprising, therefore, that after all those years he should forget that he had with him three, instead of two, sailors.

The most interesting discrepancy, however, between the story and reality occurs elsewhere, in a place apparently hitherto unsuspected. The crew Conrad extolled in "Youth" was recruited from "Liverpool hard cases" which not only could work with impressive self-discipline in critical moments, but also display surprising understanding for the beauty inherent in good sailsmanship: "It was something in them, something inborn and subtle and everlasting. I don't say positively that the crew of a French or German merchantman wouldn't have done it, but I doubt whether it would have been done in the same way. There was a completeness in it, something solid like a principle, and masterful like an instinct—a discourse of something secret—of that hidden something, that gift of good or evil that makes racial difference, that shapes the fate of nations." But in fact there was not a single Liverpudlian on the *Palestine*. Five men came from Cornwall, one from Ireland, and the remainder were foreigners—an Australian, a Negro from the Antilles, a Dutchman, and a Norwegian.

In one respect Conrad did not exaggerate: he did acquit himself well. The written certificate drawn up by Captain Beard in Singapore testifies to the fact—"I may recommend him as a sober, honest-man." [99] The recollections of the Irish first officer, H. Mahon, passed on to Hope, were even more favorable— "excellent fellow, good officer, the best second mate I ever sailed with." [100]

The crew of the *Palestine* stayed at Muntok six days. On 21 March they sailed on the S.S. *Sissie* for Singapore where a court of enquiry cleared all the officers and crew of any responsibility for the spontaneous combustion on board. As a matter of fact coal was considered as the most dangerous cargo other than grain. The shipowners, always in a hurry, wanted to take on as much cargo as possible; carelessly loaded, the cargo could easily shift and thereby lessen the ship's stability. 1883 was a record year for accidents at sea: 2,019 seamen's lives were lost—or about 1 percent of those in active service. [101]

Korzeniowski officially signed off the *Palestine* on 3 April, having collected his pay of 171.12 Straits dollars. [102] Throughout the following month he looked in vain for a job that would enable him to sail back to Europe. At that time he became acquainted with Singapore's harbor district, which was to form the scene of several of his books. [103] Eventually, he decided to return as a passenger on a steamer in the middle of April; on 13 May he arrived at Port Said and by the end of the month reached London. [104]

His return was awaited eagerly by Tadeusz at Kazimierówka. Informed by Konrad's letter of 4 April about all the adventures and advised of the date of return by another letter posted in Port Said, he was now getting ready for the meeting, several times postponed, with his globe-trotting nephew. He hoped to go to Cracow for the reunion; nevertheless he stressed the need for Konrad to resolve his passport affairs: "I shall repeat again what I already said in my previous letter: namely, that as you will be staying in London for your examination it would seem most suitable that you should apply then for naturalization and be at last finished with it. . . . I must admit that I should prefer to see your face a little later, and as that of a free citizen of a free country, rather than earlier and still as that of citizen of the world! . . . It is really a matter of your looking after your own best interests." [105]

Quite soon, however, the plans had to be changed because of Bobrowski's stomach troubles and rheumatism. He communicated his latest decision: "We shall meet *in Marienbad*, where I am sure to arrive not later than the 10th/22nd *July*. You should arrive on the 12th/24th of the *same month*, so that I shall have had time to settle in and get our lodgings ready." [106]

Meanwhile Korzeniowski worked for his chief officer's examination, which he intended to take on 4 July. [107] He probably had some tuition from Newton, but nothing came of it since his term of work as second mate was shorter than the required twelve months. Although he had officially served in the *Palestine* nearly eighteen months, the time at sea and in charge of watch—an essential condition—amounted to barely nine and a half months. They added on an extra month but even so Korzeniowski was short by six weeks.[108]

Nothing is known of the meeting after five years between Tadeusz and Konrad. Judging by Bobrowski's letters it was pleasant. A few days after the parting, he wrote, "You were right in supposing that on returning to Toeplitz I was sad and melancholy, sitting down alone to my evening cup of tea, opposite the empty chair of my Admiral!!!"[109] He addressed Konrad as his "Dearest Boy" and thanked him for "an act seemingly of no importance," revealed in the letter posted by the young man from Dresden, on his return journey. "You are mistaken again if you think that your deed would pass me unnoticed! On the contrary, I noticed immediately that you had gone out of your way to give me pleasure." Bobrowski's correspondence became more affectionate and friendly, showing less tendency toward admonition; the prevailing mood is one of intimate understanding. The growing loneliness of the elderly gentleman contributed to this change, as did the passage of time, which somewhat leveled the difference of age. The 1883 meeting certainly marked the beginning of a new phase in their relationship.

There were, apart from the emotional, also other aspects to it. Bobrowski could now, talking to his grown-up nephew, impress him more fully with his own interpretation of national and family history. I suppose that Conrad's idea of his father being a broken man toward the end of his life owed much to Uncle Tadeusz's tirades. Most probably, they were also the source of Conrad's one-sided view of the 1863 uprising as a pointless and unmitigated catastrophe. It is remarkable that it was men of Conrad's generation, and younger, who toward the end of the nineteenth century shaped the powerful legend of heroism and sacrifice which has made the 1863 insurrection both the greatest Polish national calamity and the most stirring patriotic myth.

On 12 August uncle and nephew left Marienbad for Teplice, in Bohemia, where Korzeniowski stayed for two more weeks.[110] In both places they could have met many Poles. On 14 August Konrad sent Stefan Buszczyński the earliest of his surviving letters; it was written on elegant notepaper with the embossed initials CK. He expressed his regret at not having met Buszczyński, who had just left Teplice to go to Venice, apologized for several years of silence, and sent warm greetings for Konstanty Buszczyński, a schoolmate. He ended thus:

I am leaving here for London in a few days; from there I do not know where fate will take me. During the last few years—that is since my first examination, I have not been too happy in my journeyings. I was nearly drowned, nearly got burned, but generally my health is good, I am not short of courage or of the will to work or of love for my profession; and I always remember what you said when I was leaving Cracow: "Remember"—you said—"wherever you may sail you are sailing towards Poland!"

That I have never forgotten, and never will forget!

In the hope that my sins will be forgiven me, and commending myself to your kind memory, I remain, with affection, gratitude, and the highest regards,

Your humble servant,
Konrad N. Korzeniowski[111]

This letter, together with excerpts from Bobrowski's correspondence, allows one to dispense with an occasionally advanced hypothesis that when Korzeniowski left the country he wanted to break once and for all with his Polish past.

At the parting the uncle gave Konrad a present: he paid for his expenses connected with the journey, gave him £25 to cover the cost of naturalization in Great Britain, and added £5. Even more important, he undertook to assign £350 the next spring to pay for Korzeniowski's share in the shipping firm of Barr, Moering and Company in London; Adolf Krieger was the firm's agent. Konrad must have thoroughly acquainted his uncle with the earning prospects of merchant service officers: they were poor and becoming poorer. Land jobs requiring equivalent qualifications brought better pay. On that point all the authors discussing the contemporary social and economic situation of sailors are in full agreement. Frank Bullen in his book *Men of the Merchant Service* has this to say about the first officer: "His pay is so small that he must forego the delights of wife and children if he has only that pay to live on." His words are echoed by Thomas Brassey: "It is not creditable to the shipowners that their officers should be in such abject poverty, that their children are found crowding into asylums originally intended to afford relief to the working seamen."[112]

The position of the officers was made worse by a steady decline in the number of ships. By 1883 the total tonnage of the steamship fleet exceeded that of sailing ships.[113] Steamers were larger, and fewer were needed to transport the same amount of goods; consequently the demand for officers was falling.

The relatively high standard of living in England and possibilities of better earnings on land drew an increasing proportion of more able prospects. The number of foreigners among seamen grew. On 10 September Korzeniowski signed on as second mate (at five guineas a month) on the *Riversdale*, a 1,490-ton clipper. The crew was predominantly Scandinavian.

Unfortunately Bobrowski's letters of the following twenty-one months have been lost, thus limiting our knowledge of Korzeniowski's activities. The voyage in the *Riversdale*, although uneventful by comparison with the one in the *Palestine*, had a personally dramatic ending for him. The ship sailed from London on 13 September, heading for India. She reached South Africa's Port Elizabeth on 7 December and remained there two months, moored at Algoa Bay; she sailed on 9 February 1884. On 8 April she arrived at the port of Madras.[114]

The *Riversdale*'s captain, a forty-two-year-old Scot, Lawrence Brown McDonald, took his wife and sons on the voyage. The captain was despotic and conceited; the officers were kept at a distance, not allowed to express their own views and treated "as machines, to be worked by himself when and as he pleased."[115] It must have created an atmosphere of stress and animosity increased by several months of isolated life on board. McDonald had eye trouble and occasionally suffered from attacks of it. One occurred at night after they had reached Madras. Korzeniowski was sent ashore to fetch a doctor; he was accompanied by a friend of McDonald's, the master of a steamer. Asked by the doctor about the captain's condition, Korzeniowski replied that he thought him drunk. "The impression conveyed to me from the statements of the second officer and a letter from Captain McDonald's wife was that I was going to see a man suffering from delirium tremens," said Daniel Thompson, the physician. But to his surprise McDonald appeared "quiet and rational. . . . Statements made by the second officer were not borne out."

When this master of a steamer repeated to McDonald what Korzeniowski said, the captain became angry and decided to dismiss him. To no avail was even the letter of apology of 12 April in which Korzeniowski withdrew his accusation, expressed his regrets, and assured Captain McDonald that "there was never any intention to cast even the shadow of a suspicion on Captain McDonald's personal or professional character." To the first officer, who evidently privately took his side, Korzeniowski said that his letter was false and that he regretted having written it. The affair dragged on for several days and on 15 April Konrad was relieved of his position. He agreed to have sixty rupees deducted from his pay for the cost of finding a replacement, thereby taking the blame on himself. On the certificate of discharge issued on 17 April, McDonald assessed Korzeniowski's professional ability as "very good" but next to "conduct" wrote "no comment."[116] Later, during a court of enquiry following the stranding of the *Riversdale*, for which McDonald was judged responsible, the captain accused the absent Korzeniowski of failing in his duties, namely for having slept during watch on three occasions, a hardly plausible attempt at self-justification.[117] Anyway, McDonald did not conceal the fact that he had "discharged the second officer for making certain statements to Dr Thompson."

This was not the end of that incident. In a letter from Kazimierz Bobrowski, dated 8 December (probably old style, so in fact 20 December) 1884, we find congratulations on "winning the case against the ex-captain." It refers to Korzeniowski finally being allowed to take his examination for the first mate. Initially, the Marine Board refused to accept his application, put off by McDonald's certificate.[118]

Having left the *Riversdale*, Korzeniowski went at once to Bombay. After only a few days he managed to find a ship: the *Narcissus*, a 1,336-ton clipper, immortalized thirteen years later by the title of his first sea novel. It appeared that the *Narcissus* had sailed from Wales without a second mate; Korzeniowski signed on for the job on 28 April at pay of £5 a month. The ship lay in Bombay over a month and sailed on her homebound passage on 3 June 1884.

Forty years later, Conrad told his first biographer, "The voyage of the *Narcissus* was performed from Bombay to London in the manner I have described." Although the book owes more than its title to this passage, the relation between reality and fiction is presented better elsewhere, in the course of the same conversation. "I do not write history, but fiction, and I am therefore entitled to choose as I please what is most suitable in regard to characters and particulars to help me in the general impression I wish to produce." He said he did not recall the real name of the Negro who had served on the *Narcissus*. "Most of the personages I have portrayed actually belonged to the crew of the real *Narcissus*, including the admirable Singleton (whose real name was Sullivan), Archie, Belfast, and Donkin. I got the two Scandinavians from associations with another ship."[119]

In the real *Narcissus* there were seven Scandinavians; in the book Conrad gives the impression that four foreigners were on board. In fact there were ten—half the entire crew. In Korzeniowski's seafaring days about 15 percent of all merchant service crews were foreign, but on the ships he sailed the proportion was usually higher, between 30 and 60 percent. Work on long-distance sailing ships was by far the hardest, and the English were least willing to enlist on them. Conrad maintained later that in his day foreigners constituted less than one-third of the British Merchant Service but on the ships on which he sailed they formed a "small fraction" only, the crews being "almost exclusively British."[120] In retrospect, he obviously wanted to present his service at sea as unequivocally English in character. He was also consistently silent on the problem of relations between the nationalities.

The assumed Negro in the *Narcissus* was Joseph Barron; on the crew list he put a cross against his name; he died at the age of thirty-five, three weeks before the ship reached Dunkirk. Among the crew there was no sailor called Sullivan or any similar name; Conrad must have had in mind Daniel Sullivan, aged fifty-four, illiterate, with whom he later served in the *Tilkhurst*, on her passage from Singapore to Calcutta. The prototype for Belfast was evidently James Craig, twenty-one, born in Belfast, and for Archie, a twenty-three-year-old Scot, Archibald McLean.[121] Baines supposes that Conrad may have based his Donkin upon Charles Dutton, also illiterate, whose age does not appear on the muster roll (suggesting his illegitimate origin). Dutton sailed on the *Narcissus* from Penarth to Capetown, where he left the ship and landed in prison.[122] Korzeniowski could have heard of his exploits in Bombay or on the return passage.

Considering that the commander of the *Narcissus* had trouble with his crew during their southbound passage—the return voyage was uneventful—it seems that Conrad incorporated into his novel the story heard from Captain Archibald Duncan, a forty-year-old Scot.

According to Baines, the description of life on large sailing ships, as presented in *The Nigger of the "Narcissus,"* is "the distilled essence of Conrad's experience at sea." He adds, "The process of distillation has virtually eliminated all the squalid ingredients . . . the stench below deck, the damp and the cold or the heat, the frequent periods of bad food and of apparently interminable boredom." [123] Nevertheless, *The Nigger*, with its concentration of dramatic events and its theatrical *finale*, gives a more realistic and complete picture of the life at sea than does *The Mirror of the Sea* or any other of Conrad's "autobiographical" works. Writing what purported to be his recollections, Conrad tended to present himself in a way that imparted a mythlike logic to a given chain of events or actions. In *The Nigger* his aim was different, but here too the monotony and squalor of everyday life remained outside his creative perspective.

The *Narcissus* entered the port of Dunkirk on 16 October, and on the following day Korzeniowski signed off. [124] He had with him from India a small monkey, which lost no time in tearing up important papers in the office of Conrad's friend, Adolf Krieger, a partner with Barr and Moering. Not knowing what to do with the pet, he sold it to a merchant. [125] In Krieger's office, £350 awaited Konrad, sent in February by Bobrowski. As the result of paying out this lump sum, expected to lead to permanent, steady income, Tadeusz was to lower Konrad's allowance to £30 a year. [126]

Having at last completed the required length of service, Korzeniowski prepared for his first officer's examination. We do not know his method of study, but he was unsuccessful in his attempt on 17 November, failing in "Day's Work," chiefly in navigation. [127] ("Day's Work" is a twenty-four-hour reckoning based on all the entries in the logbook: the ship's position, speed, and so forth.)

In *A Personal Record* Conrad tells of his three consecutive examinations for officer's degrees but gives no hint of his failures: on the contrary, he writes quite explicitly about his "three ordeals" passed successfully. In 1917 he announced in his letter to A. T. Saunders, "My little vol. of autobiography of course is absolutely genuine": inscribing to somebody else a copy of *A Personal Record* he stated emphatically, "All my examinations were passed in London as related in this book." [128] Here, as in some other respects, the truth was otherwise. What seems puzzling is that he wrote exclusively about the questions pertaining to Seamanship and never mentioned the second part of the examination, written and oral, on the subject of navigation. Van Marle draws attention to the essay "Outside Literature," which gives a perhaps slightly more accurate account. The examiner's assistant hands back to Conrad the page covered with navigational calculations with a discreet hint to recheck the results. True enough, instead of E (East) he had written W (West).[129] But perhaps the error was not detected until the examiner looked at the results. As the examination Konrad failed was a written one, language difficulties could not have played a significant role. J. H. Retinger notes that Conrad "enjoyed talking about his examination . . . although the fact that his English then was not too good rather jarred on his nerves even in remembrance."[130]

The subjects of examination were few and the questions rather easy. When obligatory examinations were introduced in 1850, "the qualification of masters and mates was reduced to one dead level to meet the state of education rather than to create efficiency."[131]

Korzeniowski, possibly coached by a crammer, applied again on 28 November for the examination, which he passed before Captain P. Thompson on 3 December 1884—over four years after his examination for second mate. He immediately boasted about it to uncle Tadeusz and began the search for his next job, which proved a very difficult task.[132]

The years 1885–1888 marked a slump in the shipbuilding industry caused by a fall in demand for new vessels. The number of ships was declining: between 1865 and 1894 the total in England went down by 39 percent, although the tonnage grew threefold. The number of sailors in active service fluctuated slightly, but the demand for officers decreased steadily.[133] Frank Bullen, who served many years as a first officer, maintains at the beginning of his book, *The Men of the Merchant Service*: "I know of no more depressing occupation than that of a capable seaman looking for a ship as officer." In the same book, he describes a significant recollection:

> Before my last voyage I had been prowling about the docks, looking for a ship, until I was in very low water indeed, and glad of almost anything. Yet, as I was married and had one child, there was a minimum wage below which I could not go without the prospect of my dear ones starving. Receiving information that there was a brig in the St. Katherine dock wanting a mate, I hastened down to her, finding the master a pleasant, genial man, and English. I told him my errand, showed my credentials, and was asked what wages I wanted. I suggested £6-10-0 per month, feeling as I did so that I might as well ask for the moon while I was about it. We finally agreed upon £5 15s a month, which made my wife's income while I was at sea about 14s a week. But I went home light-hearted enough in the feeling that I was no longer a sock-slouching mendicant, and that *something* was sure for at least twelve months.
>
> The next morning, when I came on board to work, the skipper told me that he had received an offer from a German, fully certificated, to come as mate for £3 a month, and one from an Englishman, who said that, as he had money of his own, and only wanted to get his time in for master, he would

come for *nothing*. "I didn't take the German," said Captain W——, "entirely because I had given you my word, but because I hold that it is a national crime to permit foreign officers to have charge of our ships, apart altogether from the chance of having them cut the already too scanty wages. And I didn't take the other fellow, because I wanted a man to earn his wages, and I knew that he was likely to earn what he offered to go for—nothing." So I kept the berth, but, as the skipper truly remarked, had the owner known that he was paying much more for my services than there was any necessity for him to do, he would have been very angry.[134]

We do not know whether the foreigner Korzeniowski encountered similar reactions; on the other hand if he never met with obstacles he must have been extremely lucky: a dislike of the "invasion" of foreigners permeates all contemporary sea writing. The fact that Conrad always presented his relationship with his English superiors and employers as free of any national conflict is no proof, since he often smoothed out and retouched his past to render it more consistently positive in meaning.

His search for a job lasted nearly five months. Finally on 24 April 1885, in Hull, he joined as second officer the *Tilkhurst* (a 1,527-ton clipper, the largest sailing ship on which he served), at £5 a month.

Three days later the ship sailed to Cardiff for a cargo of coal; it arrived on 14 May.[135] The same day, Konrad sent a letter to his uncle, who was very worried about his nephew's decision to start on a long voyage to India. "Your whole explanation of the safety of your intended voyage to India, and of your abstinence from wine and rum, which are well known to me and have been well tested, appease me only to the extent to which any irrevocable or already accomplished fact can do."[136] In the following letter he reminded his nephew that his previous expedition to India had had bad effects upon his liver.[137]

It is rather unlikely that Korzeniowski's five-day stay ashore in Cardiff (31 May to 5 June) was caused by doubts about continuing his service on the *Tilkhurst*; he probably simply wanted to spend a short time on land. According to Jean-Aubry, who probably heard it from Conrad himself, a Polish sailor, Komorowski, he had recently met asked Korzeniowski to deliver on his behalf a small sum of money owed by him to a countryman, a watchmaker in Cardiff.[138] The latter turned out to be Spiridion Kliszczewski, an emigré after the 1830 insurrection. He welcomed Korzeniowski enthusiastically. The casual encounter with the watchmaker's family ripened into a long-lasting friendship with the insurgent's son, Joseph Spiridion Kliszczewski, contemporary of Korzeniowski. Spiridion's young grandson, Hubert, was struck by their guest's unusual attire—a frock coat with a flat felt hat, the traditional headgear of Anglican clergy—his strong foreign accent, and refined manners (the last an unusual feature in a sailor).[139]

All Bobrowski's letters since the middle of 1885 have survived. In two of them, written in June and August, the squire of Kazimierówka describes at length his ailments; there is also an interesting literary fragment referring to some metaphor where the young traveler mentioned Barataria—the island whose governor was Sancho Panza. "Let's begin with the 'Barataria' and your explanation of the metaphor, which you did so wittily and in such perfect Polish that reading this part of your letter gave me real pleasure. But I must correct your unjustified assumption: the work of the famous Cervantes is well known to me; in fact, last year in Teplice I read it again."[140]

The *Tilkhurst*, with her cargo of coal, sailed from Penarth on 10 June and reached Singapore on 22 September. The crew once again was largely Scandinavian; the captain was forty-seven-year-old Edwin John Blake.[141] Of Blake Conrad had the best recollections of all his commanders; he depicted Blake as considerably older in *The Mirror of the Sea*: "Well over fifty years of age when I knew him, short, stout, dignified, perhaps a little pompous, he was a man of a singularly well-informed mind, the least sailor-like in outward aspect, but certainly one of the best seamen whom it has been my good luck to serve under."[142] Judging by Conrad's memories, Blake was exceptionally cultured for the captain of a cargo-carrying sailing ship at the time; as a son of a physician he came from an educated background. The atmosphere on the ship must have been exceptional, since only one member of the crew left her in Singapore; it was unusual at the time for sailors to serve a whole voyage on the same ship.[143] Hope mentioned that Korzeniowski was very pleased with his work on the *Tilkhurst* and that the captain reciprocated his feeling. One crew member remembered him as a "queer feller" who always read books.[144]

The unloading in Singapore lasted until 19 October. The sailors as usual passed their time ashore drinking; the last spree before sailing ended in a scuffle, in the course of which one man received a severe blow on the head. Nine days later he committed suicide by jumping overboard.[145] The *Tilkhurst* was then sailing to Calcutta, where she arrived on 21 November. Another stay in port followed, this time to load jute; the homebound passage began on 8 January 1886.

During his stay in India, Korzeniowski sent five letters to Joseph Spiridion. He wrote in English; these letters are his first preserved texts in that language. His English is generally correct but stiff to the extent of being artificial; many fragments, particularly of a more general nature, suggest that the writer's thoughts ran along the lines of Polish syntax and phraseology.[146] The context of those letters is more important, however, since they contain the author's first authentic political and social pronouncements. They indicate a marked change in his attitude from that implied in the correspondence from 1881 to 1883; and they foreshadow the direction of his future evolution. On 13 October he wrote from Singapore:

I saw with pleasure the evidence of improved relations with Germany, the only power with whom an Anti-Russian alliance would be useful, and even possible, for Great Britain. No wonder that in this unsettled state of affairs politics, at least foreign politics, are slightly dull. Events are casting shadows, more or less distorted, shadows deep enough to suggest the lurid light of battlefields somewhere in the near future, but all those portents of great and decisive doings leave me in a state of despairing indifference: for, whatever may be the changes in the fortunes of living nations, for the dead there is no hope and no salvation. We have passed through the gates where "*lasciate ogni speranza*" is written in letters of blood and fire, and nothing remains for us but the darkness of oblivion.

In the presence of such national misfortune, personal happiness is impossible in its absolute form of general contentment and peace of heart. Yet, I agree with you that in a free and hospitable land even the most persecuted of our race may find relative peace and a certain amount of happiness, materially at least; consequently I understood and readily accepted your reference to "Home"—When speaking, writing or thinking in English, the word "home" always means for me the hospitable shores of Great Britain.[147]

Conrad had departed a long way from the "hope for the future" and the "sailing towards Poland" and even from his pan-Slavic ideas. He was left with a painful sense of the hopelessness of the Polish problem and an acceptance of England as a possible place of refuge. Possibly his statements were meant to harmonize to some degree with the opinions or attitudes of the addressee; he did this quite often in his letters. Nevertheless, the theme of hopelessness in the possibility of Poland regaining her independence crops up sufficiently often in Conrad's correspondence and works before 1914 for us to accept this particular pronouncement as an expression of genuine feeling and conviction.

The second political letter, written on 19 December from Calcutta, seems to be more "programmed" by the addressee; this time it deals mainly with British internal affairs, but it is no less catastrophic in tone.

By this time, you, I and the rest of the "right thinking" have been grievously disappointed by the result of the General Election. The newly enfranchised idiots have satisfied the yearnings of Mr Chamberlain's herd by cooking the national goose according to his recipe. The next culinary operation will be a pretty kettle of fish of an international character. Joy reigns in St. Petersburg, no doubt, and profound disgust in Berlin: the International Socialist Associations are triumphant, and every disreputable ragamuffin in Europe feels that the day of universal brotherhood, despoliation and disorder is coming apace, and nurses day-dreams of well-plenished pockets amongst the ruin of all that is respectable, venerable and holy. The great British Empire went over the edge, and yet on to the inclined plane of social progress and radical reform.

The downward movement is hardly perceptible yet, and the clever men who started it may flatter themselves with the progress; but they will soon find that the fate of the nation is out of their hands now! The Alpine avalanche rolls quicker and quicker as it nears the abyss—its ultimate destination! Where's the man to stop the crashing avalanche?

Where's the man to stop the rush of social-democratic ideas? The opportunity and the day have come and are gone! Believe me: gone for ever! For the sun is set and the last barrier removed. England was the only barrier to the pressure of infernal doctrines born in continental back-slums. Now, there is nothing! The destiny of this nation and of all nations is to be accomplished in darkness amidst much weeping and gnashing of teeth, to pass through robbery, equality, anarchy and misery under the iron rule of a militarism despotism! Such is the lesson of common sense logic.

Socialism must inevitably end in Caesarism.

Forgive me this long disquisition, but your letter—so earnest on the subject—is my excuse. I understand you perfectly. You wish to apply remedies to quell the dangerous symptoms: you evidently hope yet.

I do so no longer. . . .

I live mostly in the past and the future. The present has, you easily understand, but few charms for me. I look with the serenity of despair and indifference of contempt upon the passing events. Disestablishment, Land Reform, Universal Brotherhood are but like milestones on the road to ruin. The end will be awful, no doubt! Neither you nor I shall live to see the final crash: although we both may turn in our graves when it comes, for we both feel deeply and sincerely.[148]

Meanwhile, Apollo Korzeniowski must have turned in his grave if he knew what his son was writing. We shall never know how much of it was posturing designed to impress with its gloomy extremism. Some sentences, pompous and trite, seem like self-parody; the whole text appears exaggerated and affected. It is tempting, of course, to supplement and elucidate this diatribe with later, more restrained and mature statements. Too little is known, however, about his outlook in the eighties and about the circumstances relating to the correspondence for us to have the right to give in to that temptation. His attitude is sternly pessimistic, fatalistic, blatantly conservative; his ignorance of certain contemporary political events is striking: he identifies Joseph Chamberlain with social democrats, does not know that the First International has been inactive for nine years—what is more he even does not remember its name. The fear of anarchistic destructive rabble turns up frequently in his letters and writings; its origin could be probably traced not only to the historical and sociological books he had read (Taine, Gustave Le Bon) or to conservative political propaganda, but also to his own experiences with the urban and port mobs he later described with contempt in *The Nigger of the "Narcissus."* Conflicts with the rabble and a decline in the discipline of work among sailors were, it seems, the main reason for the then generally unfavorable attitude of merchant officers toward the incipient trade unions and socialist agitation.

Politics was not the only subject of correspondence with Spiridion. Konrad's mood having changed completely, he forgot about his avowed dislike of the modern age and expounded his project of switching over to whaling.

> And now here I must pray you take also for granted that I am brimful with the most exhaustive information upon the subject. I have read, studied, pumped professional men and imbibed knowledge upon whale fishing and sealing for the last four years. I am acquainted with the practical part of the undertaking in a thorough manner. Moreover, I have the assurance of active help from a man brought up in the trade, and although doing well where he is now, ready to return to his former pursuit [of whales]. Finally I have a vessel in view, on very advantageous terms. And now for ways and means!
>
> Upon that question I want your advice, or rather your opinion upon my plan to raise the necessary capital . . . £1,500 . . . for, you see, although I cannot ask my uncle for the capital, I receive from him and from the London business (which I am advised is daily improving) yearly a sum sufficient for the payment of a premium on a life policy for £2,000, and the interest on the loan. *I suppose* I could raise on the security of the said policy (supposing the interest to be at the rate of 10 per cent) even should the venture for which the loan is destined turn out a dead failure: and I have special reasons to believe that such would not be the case. But let pass! Now, I want your advice on these points:
>
> 1. Is such a transaction for a man in my position at all possible?
> 2. If it is, what is the proper way to go about it? (for I am a very infant in business matters).
> 3. Supposing the plan feasible, do you think, as a cool business man not interested in the matter, that it would be sound to embark upon the undertaking (highly paying, *if successful*, as you know whaling is) on a capital borrowed at 12 percent—for it will come to that with the premium and interest.[149]

Konrad's claim that Bobrowski's allowance together with the profits from the London investment would cover the cost of an insurance policy and interest on the loan (total £180 a year) contradicts other information. The capital placed in Barr, Moering and Company brought only 6 percent interest a year;[150] together with his uncle's allowance he would have barely £51. Whether and how he really imagined himself able to finance this project—typically Nałęcz in style, as his uncle would have said—are impossible to tell. I suspect that he intended to negotiate a loan from the Kliszczewskis, as otherwise he would have written to his partner, Krieger. It is not surprising therefore that his decision on the unlikely project was made subject to the addressee's opinion. Spiridion later told Jean-Aubry that he managed to dissuade his young friend from the enterprise.[151]

Korzeniowski confessed in the same letter that he was "sick and tired of sailing about for little money and less consideration." The idea of whaling was one of the signals that the attraction of a future in the merchant service was waning. His health might have been partly responsible (he complained to his uncle of "dyspepsia" and of being a "weakling"[152]), but the basic considerations were certainly financial and general; the profession did not lead anywhere, ensured no decent living, precluded setting up a family, gave no social status, and forced one into the background of cultural life. Although service on the *Tilkhurst* was one of the most pleasant in his career, he advanced a plan, completely non-seafaring, to remain in London and go into trade.

The *Tilkhurst* arrived in Dundee on 17 June 1886 after an uneventful passage; Korzeniowski signed off that same day.[153] Two letters from his uncle awaited him in London. Bobrowski reported the serious illness of his brother Kazimierz (who died on 2 May), and the resulting heavy financial burdens that prevented him from going abroad and meeting his nephew. "As I deduce from your and Krieger's letters, you intend to devote yourself to trade and stay in London. I would think it only right for you to stay put till you have got quite familiar with the routine of your new occupation and that you should not tear yourself away from it till you have mastered all its difficulties." He suggested an investigation of the London market for wheat flour and granulated sugar. "In both these articles you could with my introduction do big business, providing you were quick and thorough. It would be essential at first to get well acquainted with the market conditions and with the qualities and imperfections of the goods as well."[154] He enquired anxiously about the young man's health and "partnership—will you find it advantageous if you leave the Mercantile Marine?"[155] Both letters carried reminders about "your examination for a captaincy, and also your naturalization;—the final steps in your career, which I still insist on; first get your captain's license and your naturalization, then you can do, Sir, as you please. Your old Uncle will have no choice but to rejoice in your projects and happiness, providing God grants that the former bring about the latter."[156]

In fact Korzeniowski dealt with both matters energetically, although with only partial success. On 28 July, in his first attempt to get his master's diploma, he failed in arithmetic and—once again—in "Day's Work."[157] In his letters to Bobrowski he mentioned the approximate date of examination but later concealed his failure, did not write for almost two months and avoided the subject, prompting his uncle's impatience.[158] He left no hint of any kind in either *A Per-*

sonal Record or anywhere else, presenting the matter quite simply as having passed his master mariner's examination successfully.

The fact that arithmetic was not one of his strong points may be seen by the errors in adding up his terms of service on the examination application forms.[159] His lack of mathematical aptitude and of systematic schooling as well as his natural nervousness may offer sufficient explanation. What is more difficult to comprehend is his failure with the "Day's Work." The requirements were generally considered easy after a short period of coaching; complaints about declining standards were widespread. Six years' service and twenty-one years of age were enough to take the master's examination, which was much easier in England than on the Continent. In Belgium, France, the Netherlands, and Germany, beyond the knowledge required in the British Merchant Service about winds, currents, navigation, nautical astronomy, instruments, and measurements, the candidates were expected to know algebra, geometry, trigonometry, mechanics, physics, steam engines, and one foreign language.[160] In view of the fact that Korzeniowski was certainly not unintelligent, one cannot help suspecting that the roots of the problem were his inadequate knowledge of English and his foreign origin.

The latter obstacle, if that is what it was, was soon overcome. On 2 July he filed the application and on 18 August was granted British nationality. John H. Brady confirmed the details of the applicant's residence at 6 Dynevor Road, and four sureties recommended him: G. F. W. Hope (had "known and been intimately acquainted" with him for "five years past and upwards"), E. A. Poole (one year), John Newton (five years), and John Weston (two years). Another John Weston, sergeant in the metropolitan police, reported, following the enquiries he had made, "Applicant who is about 30 years old, stated that he left Russia when he was 12 years old. He has been 10 years in the British Merchant Service, and now holds an appointment as chief mate." Next to "Remarks" he added: "Applicant is a very respectable person and [worth]y of holding a certificate."[161] The trusting policeman apparently did not check anything and Conrad misrepresented as many as three facts: he was ten years old when he came to Lwów, served only eight years in the British Merchant Service and, until then, had held no position of chief mate.

The naturalization papers changed his position from a tsar's subject staying illegally abroad to a citizen of the world's greatest power, one of the most enlightened countries of Europe. In the eyes of contemporaries, England was the "Mistress of the Seas," the center of the British Empire, the richest country on earth, an industrial power, a giant in the world of finance and trade, the focus of revolutionary discoveries and scientific theories; for many it was a model of inner stability, lawfulness, political moderation, mother of parliaments, a sanctuary for thousands of political refugees. Conrad's cult of his adopted country—whose loyal, albeit not uncritical, citizen he remained until the end—

was based mainly on traditionalism, fair play, and tolerance, as well as on the spirit of adventure displayed in its past. He seemed to prefer the historic England to the contemporary; he appeared somewhat indifferent to the England of industry, trade, and finance.

Even before sitting for the examination, about 10 July, Konrad confided in his uncle his wish to make at least one passage as a captain; nonetheless, as far as one can gather from Bobrowski's words, he was thinking of remaining in London and "working in the Agency." [162] Bobrowski carefully collected all the data and was busy preparing a memorandum on the possibilities of contracting to supply flour and sugar to England from the Ukraine. He sent his report on 9 September, thinking it not too encouraging, "but it is always more pleasant to be surprised by things turning out better than by their being worse than expected." [163]

Nothing is known about the business transactions that kept Korzeniowski occupied throughout the summer and autumn of 1886 (besides working for his second attempt at the examination), but it is clear that they were not very promising, since he decided to approach his uncle with a proposal of making a more substantial investment in London. Bobrowski resented it, although he replied in a jocular tone:

Apparently, my dear fellow, amidst all your business activities in London, you have confused people and facts. I have always told you what I said at the beginning of my memorandum, and I will now repeat it again: I was never either a speculator or a tradesman, for I do not feel that I have the right flair. Having thus for 57 years preserved the innocence of my soul, I have no intention now of selling myself to Mercury or possibly even to the devil himself with the object of exploiting other people's poverty, need, or stupidity! . . . I feel sure, my dear Panie Bracie and nephew, that you would say about me "dementus est," if in spite of the above situation I transferred my funds to England and put them into the hands of a stranger who would pay me a smaller rate of interest,—and above all earn the name of usurer; "Noli me tentare." I would like you to realize that it was not in order to speculate that I parted with some of my "precious metal" and sent it to London—not for speculation but to help my nephew who chose to live there. The Scriptures say: "Where my treasure is, there also is my heart"; and shall I dare to improve on it thus: "Where my nephew is, there is my gold! [164]

He was also anxious to know if the £350 invested two years earlier had been lost.

On 29 October, Konrad informed his uncle of his intention to leave on a voyage of a couple of months. [165] But instead of imparting more details on the subject, he soon announced the long-awaited news of having qualified as master.

Dear boy! Long live the Ordin. Master in the British Merchant Service!! May he live long! May he be healthy and may every success attend him in every enterprise both on sea and on land! You have really delighted me with the news of the 'Red Seal' on your certificate. Not being an Admiral I have no right to give orders to a newly created Master and I leave to his own discretion the solution to the question—whether he is to change his O.M. [Ordinary Master] into E.M. [Extraordinary Master, the highest rank in the British Merchant Marine]??—which depends on your prospects and plans for your future career. As the humble provider of the means for this enterprise I can only rejoice that my groats have not been wasted but have led you to the peak of your chosen profession, in which Mr Syroczyński, the heir to the virtues of the Romans and Greeks, drew twelve years ago such an unfavorable horoscope for the young aspirant to Neptune's service. You are, my dear Sir, now 29 years old and have mastered a profession; it is for you to know and understand what you must do further.[166]

Probably it was this remark or others similarly skeptical that Conrad alluded to in *A Personal Record*, immediately after the account of his last examination; according to his recollection the test went off smoothly, in an atmosphere of a friendly chat.[167] The reality might have been quite different. In order to sit for the second time he applied as a British subject, on 29 October, and the examination took place on 10 November 1886. The application form contains a "personal description of the applicant." Korzeniowski's complexion is defined as dark with dark brown hair and hazel eyes. All that corresponds with other sources. One cannot help, however, being surprised by the entry for his height—5 feet 9½ inches.[168] It would make Korzeniowski a man of considerable height, taller than average among his contemporaries. Almost all written accounts of friends, and his son John's recollections, describe Conrad as of short stature.[169] Thus the story of Korzeniowski's examinations contains yet another mystery, and a symbolic one.

IV
· · · · · · · · · · · · ·
MASTER IN THE BRITISH MERCHANT MARINE
1886–1890

"SOME INSIGNIFICANT BOY, from the borderlands, from an out-of-the way province, from some place called Poland, became a captain in the British Merchant Marine without any backing." Thus Conrad supposedly described himself in 1914 in an interview for *Tygodnik Ilustrowany*.[1] What difference "backing" could have made is difficult to imagine. Anyway, the title did not bring any money by itself. Bobrowski was worried about his nephew's financial situation: "From what you tell me, I see you are a protector of widows and invest their capital well. This is very noble, but for God's sake think of yours also."[2] Unfortunately we do not know who the widow(s) in question was.

The new subject of Queen Victoria did not cease to be a subject of Tsar Alexander III; to obtain release from this honor one had to ask, politely and persistently. So Korzeniowski paid a visit to the Russian embassy—the first of many visits, for the matter was to drag on for a long time; the embassy building, not on nonexistent Chesham Square but in the easily identified Chesham House on Belgrave Square, was introduced later in *The Secret Agent*.[3]

It took Korzeniowski six weeks from his last employment to find another job, one that lasted only five days but provided an opportunity to visit the Kliszczewskis. On 28 December he signed as second mate on an iron frigate, the *Falconhurst*, in which he sailed for £5 from London to Penarth, where he signed off on 2 January 1887.[4] He may have planned a longer voyage on that ship,[5] but at last an opening presented itself for the position of first mate on an iron barque of 1,040 tons, the *Highland Forest*, lying in the port of Amsterdam.

He signed the articles at £7 a month on 16 February, but, according to the *Mirror of the Sea*, he had begun work earlier watching over the loading of cargo delayed by a severe frost, a most unusual occurrence in Holland.[6] "I was . . . biting my fists with impatience for that cargo frozen up-country; with rage at that canal set fast, at the wintry and deserted aspect of all those ships that seemed to decay in grim depression for want of the open water. . . . I was . . . very much alone. . . . Notwithstanding the little iron stove, the ink froze on the swing-table in the cabin, and I found it more convenient to go ashore stumbling

94

over the Arctic waste land and shivering in glazed tramcars in order to write my evening letter to my owners in a gorgeous café in the centre of the town. It was an immense place, lofty and gilt, upholstered in red plush, full of electric lights, and so thoroughly warmed that even the marble tables felt tepid to the touch."[7] This magnificent café, established by a Polish emigré, still exists on Warmoes-straat in the Grand Hotel Krasnopolsky. The cargo was apparently very long in coming, but as to the heavy frost in Amsterdam itself, Conrad exaggerated—the temperature had fallen below the freezing point only between 14 and 18 January and then, after 9 February, only at night.[8]

Continuing his recollections, Conrad tells how, in the absence of the master, he had to supervise the loading of the ship. Unaware of her "stiffness" (and without having made the necessary inquiries), he distributed the weight in the traditional way, which made the ship too stable. This increased the frequency of her side rolls. "Neither before nor since have I felt a ship roll so abruptly, so violently, so heavily. Once she began, you felt that she would never stop, and this hopeless sensation, characterizing the motion of ships whose centre of gravity is brought down too low in loading, made everyone on board weary of keeping on his feet."[9] Possibly the master, former chief mate of the *Highland Forest*, was not blameless; he had not made sure that information about the ship's idiosyncrasies had been passed on.[10] Conrad's suggestion that he super-vised the loading on behalf of the absent captain is misleading, however; stow-age was one of the first mate's regular duties.

The position of the first mate was subordinate to that of the master in terms of authority and legal responsibility, but his duties on board, both in port (when the captain was usually busy on land) and at sea, were more arduous than the master's, and his influence on the ship's fate almost as great. He represented the captain in everything, whether carrying out orders or acting on his own initia-tive. As a rule, he was the one to engage the crew, to supervise the loading and unloading, and to check the freight against the shipping notes. He was respon-sible for the equipment and rigging, sanitary facilities, anchors, and mooring lines. He made entries in the logbook and calculated the position of the ship daily. He was also the only person to have meals at the captain's table—hence, the only person who could establish social contacts with him.[11] The first mate was also in charge of the apprentices; there were four on the *Highland Forest*. One recalled later, "He was always exceedingly kind to us boys, a thing that is not easily forgotten . . . we, like most boys at the age when I was under Mr. Conrad, did not realize what kindness really meant."[12]

The *Highland Forest* had a crew of eighteen, including as many as fourteen foreigners. Her captain was a thirty-four-year-old Irishman, John McWhir (the same name, with an additional *r*, was given by Conrad to the much older mas-ter of the *Nan-Shan* in *Typhoon*). The boat left Amsterdam on 18 February and ran into strong gales. The excessive rolling tired the crew and caused the loss of some spars; as Conrad later wrote, "It was only poetic justice that the chief mate who had made a mistake—perhaps a half-excusable one—about the distribution of his ship's cargo should pay the penalty. A piece of one of the minor spars that did carry away flew against the chief mate's back, and sent him sliding on his face for quite a considerable distance along the main deck. Thereupon followed various and unpleasant consequences of a physical order—'queer symptoms,' as the captain, who treated them, used to say; inexplicable periods of powerlessness, sudden accesses of mysterious pain." [13]

The ship reached Semarang on 20 June. Korzeniowski was sent by a local doctor to a hospital in Singapore, but since he signed off after only ten days, on 1 July, his illness could not have been very serious; the injury and the trying experiences during the voyage caused nagging neuralgic pains. [14] He sent Bobrowski what must have been a very general yet dramatic description of his afflictions; his uncle replied: "My dear boy. I received your letter of 2/14 July yesterday—on the day of the solar eclipse, which was very appropriate because your letter completely eclipsed the good and tranquil thoughts I had had about you. I had expected you by now to stand on your own feet; that I had guided you to the right destination; and after 14 years of work and endeavour you were on the right road. And now 'pas de chance', as you say! And indeed it looks like that if our mariner, who risks death, is later to be faced with the prospect of rheumatism! This is too early for you, and once you have had trouble in your leg I very much doubt if you will ever quite get rid of it. You did not write to me exactly what the trouble is; is it ordinary rheumatism? or sciatica? —or perhaps paralysis? It could be any of these. I am racking my brains to think what it can be!?" [15]

The letter gives no explanation of what actually happened. In the ship's papers (AAC) it has been recorded that Korzeniowski left "by mutual consent" on account of his "bad leg"—but it is not clear whether the illness was a direct or indirect (as the letter seems to suggest) result of an injury or whether he had actually been hit by a flying spar. Obviously, however, his morale must have been low, since he wrote to the Ukraine in such a pessimistic tone.

His uncle rushed to his financial assistance, sending £30 to Krieger's address. The news of Korzeniowski's illness reached Bobrowski at a trying time: apart from an unfavorable economic situation and the fall of the ruble, there was "the tender and increasing attention bestowed on us by Bismarck and Katkov [which gives you] a foretaste of our moral and social situation. He is blessed who can settle down in Patagonia and enjoy the fruits of freedom and civilization—to say nothing of Java or Samoa." [16] ". . . In spite of a good harvest the grain and sugar business is entirely at a standstill. . . . The tax on land has gone up by 30%, and that is without counting the surtax paid by us Poles just because we are Polish, and which amounts to 100% of the basic taxes." [17]

Meanwhile, Korzeniowski left Semarang on 2 July on board the steamship

Celestial; on 6 July he disembarked in Singapore and probably went straight into a hospital for treatment.[18] The European Hospital where he stayed was described later in *Lord Jim*. The hero of the book, injured by a falling spar, also spent some time in the hospital, which "stood on a hill, and a gentle breeze entering through the windows, always flung wide open, brought into the bare room the softness of the sky, the languor of the earth, the bewitching breath of the Eastern waters. There were perfumes in it, suggestions of infinite repose, the gift of endless dreams."[19] It is not known how long he remained in Singapore; by 22 August he had left.

The first mate on the S.S. *Celestial* was a Frederick Havelock Brooksbank, son-in-law of the then well-known merchant and sailor William Lingard, the prototype for Tom Lingard in *Almayer's Folly*, *An Outcast of the Islands*, and *The Rescue*. Korzeniowski never met him personally but heard much about him, mainly from his nephews, James and Joshua.[20] With Brooksbank Korzeniowski became quite friendly, and it was probably through him that he met James Craig, three years his senior, master of a small steamer, the *Vidar*, which made regular voyages between Singapore and the small ports on Borneo and Celebes.[21] James (Jim) Lingard had been living for some years as a trading agent on Borneo, at Berau, on the river Berau Singai.[22]

The *Vidar* (204 tons), commanded by an Englishman, sailed under the British flag and belonged to a well-known and respected old merchant from Singapore, an Arab named Syed Mohsin Bin Salleh Al Joffree.[23] The crew included four whites: Craig, the first mate, and two mechanics, (James Allen and John C. Niven); a Chinese stoker and twelve Malay sailors completed the crew. The ship arrived in Singapore on 19 August from Donggala with a cargo of resin. Shipping documents of the loading and delivery of the cargo have survived among Conrad's papers; we may therefore assume that he had taken up the duties of the first mate while still in port.[24] The *Vidar* left Singapore on 22 August. The steamer made regular voyages, calling at Banjarmasin on Borneo collecting a cargo of coal at Kota Baru on the small insland of Pulau Laut, cutting across the Straits of Macassar on her way to Donggala on Celebes, and returning to Borneo with stops en route at Samarinda, Berau, and Bulungan, the farthest place north. As far as it is known, the *Vidar* called at each port, with the exception of the coaling station in Kota Baru, only once during each voyage. One voyage lasted between seventeen and thirty-five days, and Korzeniowski, according to Norman Sherry's findings, made four of them: 22 August–26 September; 30 September–31 October; 4 November–1 December, and the last one, which ended on 2 January 1888.[25]

The voyages were not unlike the monotonous, thirty-day passages on the steamer *Sofala* described by Conrad in "The End of the Tether," where *Sofala*'s Captain Whalley is gradually losing his eyesight. Apparently Korzeniowski did have trouble with his eyes while serving on the *Vidar*. James Craig, then seventy years old, told this to Jean-Aubry a few months after Conrad's death; but since a great deal of information given by the *Vidar*'s former commander turned out to be inaccurate, this detail has to be noted with certain caution.[26] Nor do we know to what extent the portraits of the two mechanics on the steamer, sketched by Conrad in *The Shadow Line*, are true to life.[27] Korzeniowski's voyages on the *Vidar* were uneventful and calm, unlike the steamer *Nan-Shan*, which he encountered a couple of times in Singapore and which was used for carrying hundreds of Chinese and later immortalized in "Typhoon."[28]

The work on the *Vidar*—particularly when compared with the work on big sailing ships—was easy, not very tiring and well suited for a convalescent. The route presented no problems for the steamer, which had been plying it for several years. Korzeniowski spent 135 days on board the *Vidar*, including approximately 15 in Singapore. A passage took 12 to 13 days each way, not counting the stops en route, so between 20 and 24 days were left for the six ports of call.[29] Since the two trading posts located at Bulungan (the port is Tanjung Selor, as Bulungan is the name of the river and district) and at Berau (Tanjung Redeb, because Berau is the name of a sultanate)[30] belonged to the *Vidar*'s owner, and since both ports also marked the end of the route, one may assume that the steamer made longer stops there, for a day or two each time. If so, this would leave only half a day or less for each remaining port of call, including the coaling station.

What is the use of such detailed calculations? In his letter to W. G. St. Clair, former editor of the daily *Singapore Free Press*, Conrad said, "As you may guess we had no social shore connections. You know it isn't very practicable for a seaman." He developed the same thought in a letter to his publisher, J. M. Dent, written a few days earlier: "But indeed I knew very little of and about shore-people. I was chief mate of the S.S. *Vidar* and very busy whenever in harbour. And anyway I would not have cared to form social connections, even if I had had time and opportunity."[31] Nevertheless, in his memoirs Conrad attributed such importance to his time in the *Vidar* and in his works he gave such prominence to that period that these few months, and particularly the few days spent at Berau have attracted a great deal of attention from biographers and scholars.[32] To no other period of his life has so much time and inventiveness, and so many hundreds of pages of scholarly analysis and speculation, been devoted.

Discounting the six days spent in 1883 in Muntok, it was Korzeniowski's first opportunity to see the East at close range, unconcealed by the façade of port buildings, hotels for whites, European offices, and colonial institutions. On the *Vidar* he penetrated deep inland, steaming up the rivers. Out of the six ports of call, four lay in the interior of the country, the last two as much as thirty miles from the sea: Banjarmasin on the River Barito, Samarinda on the River Kutai, Tanjung Redeb on the River Berau (in those days called the Pantai), and Tanjung Selor on the Bulungan.[33] The rivers Berau and Bulungan form wide and meandering deltas. They spread into numerous branches and canals interspersed with small, flat islands, muddy, full of shallows and bogs, their banks overgrown with thick, tall forests. The landscape is monotonous, and only in clear weather—rare in the hot humid climate where fog occurs daily— is one able to see the hills, a dozen miles away.[34]

Against the primeval natural background of lush, insatiable, and putrefying vegetation, the trading posts must have appeared either as foolish challenges to the invincible forces of the tropics, or as pathetic proof of the vanity of human endeavors. And particularly grotesque must have been the impression made by white men who, cut off from their own civilization, often became deranged drunkards or hopeless cranks. As many as four such men lived at Tanjung Redeb: an old drunken Russian former captain; a young Dutchman, Carel de Veer, another alcoholic; an Englishman, James Lingard, William's nephew; and a Eurasian Dutchman, Charles William Olmeijer, who had lived there for seventeen years.[35]

Olmeijer, under the name of Almayer (a phonetic English transcription), became the protagonist of Conrad's first novel and one of the heroes of the second; he also appears in the autobiographical volume, A Personal Record, where Conrad says, "If I had not got to know Almayer pretty well it is almost certain there would never have been a line of mine in print."[36] But Baines observes (rightly): "This was paying Almayer too big a compliment because when someone is ready to write there will always be an Almayer to hand."[37] In fact, Conrad did not get to know Olmeijer at all well, for neither the pathetic and laughable Almayer from A Personal Record nor the tragic Almayer from Almayer's Folly have much in common with the real Olmeijer. Married to another Eurasian, he had eleven children (not just one daughter) and died in 1900 at the age of fifty-two; as a trader he was both successful and influential.[38]

The fictional Sambir may be located, although with certain adjustments, in the real Berau and Bulungan. However, the detailed research, particularly by Norman Sherry, of tracing presumed prototypes of characters and sources of plots, the persistent search for analogies between the lives of actual people and those of the characters in Conrad's works, all reveal that the connections and similarities are vague. To the readers of Almayer's Folly it is immaterial whether Nina Almayer owes her name to her aunt Ninette Olmeijer, and it is highly unlikely that Korzeniowski ever heard about Ninette or about many other people tracked down by Sherry.[39] A number of similarities simply spring from the similar fates and problems of all Europeans living and working on the Malay Archipelago. The climate, primeval nature, the state of being cut off from their home countries and Western civilization, the potential authority (enforced by contacts with the colonial administration) over the natives, the love affairs with native women, alcohol, nostalgia for Europe, a wish to get rich and return home, or else a shamefaced severing of all connections with their countrymen —most of those elements may be found in the lives of most European settlers at that time. The analogies between the Jim of *Lord Jim* and Jim Lingard are based on such inevitable similarities, just as is the attitude of the fictional half-Dutch Almayer toward his Eurasian daughter.[40]

Conrad used the names of people met at that time, and occasionally their external appearance, in his writings only as fulcra for raising his new fictional world from the vast magma of reminiscences, the books he had read, and his own imagination. Sherry asserts that Conrad's "contact with the Berau trading post was crucial. From it came *Almayer's Folly*, *An Outcast of the Islands*, the second part of *Lord Jim*, and *The Rescue*."[41] This claim seems exaggerated even in the light of his own findings. Books by travelers and diarists played a more significant role as a source of raw material for fiction. Most names of people and places, as well as details depicting local customs and elements of the plot, come from books; they are used in similar ways. Accused of ignorance by Hugh Clifford, an authority on Malaya, Conrad defended himself by referring to printed sources and not to personal observation: "all the details . . . I have taken out (to be safe) from undoubted sources—dull, wise books."[42] In any case, he was not writing reports on his travels or on the books he had read: he cared for the authenticity of material but treated it as raw material to be subordinated to artistic transformations.

It is not for the biographer to trace the origins of characters or plots, but some questions ought not to remain unanswered: Why did Conrad draw so much material for his works precisely from the coast of Borneo? Why does the Malay Archipelago play such an important part as background to his plots? Hitherto the answer has been that the period of work on the *Vidar* provided him with particularly intense and rich experiences, but this theory cannot withstand critical analysis. It rests tacitly on a naive assumption that the more an author writes about something the more extensive must have been his experience in that particular sphere. Moreover, this answer seems to overlook the fact that sea passages of several months' duration and much longer stays in other countries must have left stronger impressions and more memories.

As is usual in such matters, the reasons were various and complex. Several arguments, both psychological and thematic, spoke clearly in favor of choosing the Malayan setting in Conrad's first literary attempts. Malayan reality plays a vital part only in his early works; not counting *The Rescue*, the writing of which was laid aside several times, the last of them was *Lord Jim* (1900). At that time, Conrad, the exile and wanderer, must have been painfully aware of the difficulty that he confessed more than once—the lack of a common cultural background with his readers. Hence the problem: How was Conrad to find a body of experience and a setting that would provide a safe ground, a concrete basis, to enable him to write with a certain amount of authority yet without the risk of discussing matters with which his English readers were too familiar? They had the advantage over him of being intimately acquainted with everyday life in the British Isles as well as in the colonies. Whatever he wanted to write about, wherever he wanted to seek his inspiration, he needed a base in something concrete and familiar: such was the peculiarity of his literary talent. Writing about England, Australia or Singapore would amount to groping half-blind within regions known to him only superficially but well traversed by his readers. The choice of a non-English background suggested itself all the more strongly since it freed him from an embarrassing division of loyalty; in *Almayer's Folly* (and later in "An Outpost of Progress" and "Heart of Darkness") we find many bitter words about colonialism. Above all else, however, such a choice placed Conrad in a position no worse than that of an author born and brought up in England.

As a background for a novel the Malay Archipelago had considerable advantages: the surroundings and customs were exotic; they were made interesting by complicated national, political, and religious interrelations, and the conflicts of different civilizations and competing colonial powers. The Malay states, to a large extent independent, came theoretically under the suzerainty of the Dutch government.[43] Conrad's descriptions are unusually accurate for those days; he was apparently intrigued by the theme of struggles aimed at preserving national independence. The prolific and destructive richness of tropical nature and the dreariness of human life within it accorded well with the pessimistic mood of his early works.

As a fictional subject the Archipelago had been almost unused, and it is worth noting that the reviewers of Conrad's first novels stressed their pioneering quality, noting that the works penetrated regions hitherto unexplored by literature: "No novelist has yet annexed the island of Borneo"; "Borneo, a tract hitherto untouched by the novelist."[44] In short, it was a region where an author in Conrad's position could allow his knowledge and imagination relative freedom.

These considerations influenced the choice of background for Conrad's first novel, *Almayer's Folly*. Later, the Malay motifs acquired in his imagination a place in their own right. Once a fictional world (based on memories and reading) had been created it began to grow spontaneously—a phenomenon common to the works of many writers.

These reflections have led us to anticipate the future—but not too distantly; Korzeniowski started to write *Almayer's Folly* only two years after taking up his berth on the *Vidar*. Captain Craig even mentioned that whenever he entered his chief's cabin for a chat he would find him engaged in writing—most likely, however, he was as yet simply writing letters.[45]

"She was an Eastern ship. . . . She traded among dark islands on a blue reef-scarred sea, with the Red Ensign over the taffrail and at her masthead a house-flag, also red, but with a green border and with a white crescent in it. . . . As to the kind of trade she was engaged in and the character of my shipmates, I could not have been happier if I had had the life and the men made to my order by a benevolent Enchanter.

"And suddenly I left all this."

He calls his decision to give up the job "inconsequential": "It was as though all unknowing I had heard a whisper or seen something."[46] In reality, however, he also had quite rational reasons for resigning. The job offered no prospects for the future, the climate was most disagreeable and there was probably no chance of additional earnings. Moreover the job almost completely cut him off from European civilization. Remaining on the *Vidar* would make sense only if he intended to settle in Singapore or on the Archipelago, but he never entertained such plans. Perhaps he thought already about writing; he probably still wanted to try his luck in business, in London. It is easy to understand why in *The Shadow Line* Conrad left out all rational considerations, making his decision appear quite arbitrary: he wanted to achieve a more marked contrast between impulsive youth and responsible maturity. That "green sickness of late youth" to which he attributed his decision was nothing more than the expression of his unwillingness to spend the rest of his life in ships.

The result of the medical examination to which he submitted on 1 December was satisfactory, and he informed Bobrowski that he had decided for the time being to postpone his return to Europe.[47] Perhaps in January, feeling worse, he remembered his uncle's advice: "Bear your health in mind and at the first sign of a liver attack don't hesitate to return at once—or sooner—for there is nothing like health!" On board the *Vidar* Korzeniowski celebrated his thirtieth birthday. At about that time Bobrowski recorded in his carefully kept "Document": "In view of the fact that in November you will reach the age of thirty, by which time everyone ought to be self-supporting, and moreover because the education of the late Kazimierz's children is costing more, I told you that I must discontinue a regular allowance. This I intend to do and must do. Thus the making of a man out of Mr. Konrad has cost—apart from the 3,600 given you as capital—17,454." The need for a soberly planned future acquired additional urgency. On 4 January 1888, "J. Korzeniowski"—according to the certificate of discharge—signed off the *Vidar* in Singapore.[48]

For two weeks, while waiting for a boat to Europe, he stayed at the Sailors' Home (for officers only). There he had a quarrel with the steward, a certain Phillips, an evangelist and temperance worker and an inspector of brothels—in short a professional do-gooder.[49] Conrad described his stay in *The Shadow Line*, a book he defined as "not a story really but exact autobiography,"[50] a remark that should not be taken as entirely reliable.

"Command is a strong magic," he wrote.[51] Thus, at the first opportunity, he gave up his plan of returning to Europe. He was offered the command of a 346-

ton iron barque, the *Otago*, whose captain had died at sea. The ship, the property of Australian shipowners and registered in Port Adelaide, was in Bangkok and, as her chief mate had no master's certificate,[52] the local British Consul asked the Singapore Harbour Office to send a new commander.

As Norman Sherry has indicated, three of Conrad's works—"Falk," "The End of the Tether," and *The Shadow Line*—contain the same basic situation: a ship lying in Bangkok and a search for a captain to take her over.[53] The main difference in the presentation of other events is this: in "The End of the Tether" the command is offered to one Hamilton, a loafer staying at the Sailors' Home, who turns it down;[54] in *The Shadow Line*, the manager of the Sailors' Home, wanting to get rid of the heavily indebted Hamilton, hatches an intrigue in order to secure for him the command meant for the narrator, that is, Conrad. Sherry advances the hypothesis that the earlier version is close to the truth and that indeed the command was first offered to somebody other than Korzeniowski, whose foreign accent was very strong. The reversal of this order in *The Shadow Line* is in keeping with the atmosphere of the entire story and with the deviations from authenticity introduced to render the principal character-narrator more heroic and to increase the dramatic tension.

On 19 December 1887, Henry Ellis, the Singapore harbor master, handed over to Korzeniowski the following letter to the British Consul in Bangkok:

> Sir,
> I have the honour to acknowledge the receipt of your telegram 'can you engage Master to take 'Otago' from Bangkok to Melbourne salary £14 a month to come here by first steamer and sail at once' to which I replied 'Master engaged proceed "Hecate"'.
> The person I have engaged is Mr Conrad Korzeniowski, who holds a certificate of Competency as Master from the Board of Trade. He bears a good character from the several vessels, he has sailed out of this Port. I have agreed with him that his wages at £14 per month to count from date of arrival at Bangkok, ship to provide him with food and all necessary articles for the navigation of the vessel. His passage from Singapore to Bangkok to be paid by the ship, also on his arrival at Melbourne if his services be dispensed with, the owner to provide him with a cabin passage back to Singapore.
> I consider the above terms are cheap, reasonable, and trust will meet with your approval.[55]

On that same day the newly appointed captain of the *Otago* left for Bangkok on the steamer *Melita*; on 24 January he took his first command.[56] As a rule a captain is busier in harbor than at sea, for while the ship is moored it is his duty to represent the interests of her owners. His basic task is simple: to secure the most profitable freight and to spend as little money as possible. Hence the general principle of cutting short all stops away from home port. This requires speed and energetic activity. Years later Conrad wrote to St. Clair how intensely busy he had been in Bangkok.[57] He tried his best to take the *Otago* out to sea, but over two weeks passed before he managed to do so. And once again we have two literary versions of the delay: in "Falk" it is caused by an unreasonably jealous commander of a tugboat (although the delay of cargo and illness of crew members are also mentioned), and in *The Shadow Line* by difficulties with the firm chartering the ship.

We know nothing of the real nature of those difficulties. The *Otago* had been chartered by Jucker, Sigg and Co., a firm trading in teakwood, which was the *Otago*'s cargo. According to Sherry (who devoted to this subject, "The Delay in Bangkok," one of the most valuable chapters of his *Conrad's Eastern World*), it is unlikely that the non-owner master of a tugboat could refuse his services to anybody.[58] The problems with the firm could arise, among other reasons, from the death at sea of the previous master, John Snadden, unjustly defamed in *The Shadow Line*. Snadden, a co-owner of the *Otago*, had not been on good terms with his partners.[59]

In *The Shadow Line*, the sickness that affected the crew was somewhat overplayed by Conrad. It is true that the ship's steward died, but his death occurred before Korzeniowski's arrival in Bangkok. On the basis of the manuscript of "Falk," Sherry supposes that the steward begged to be allowed to die on board rather than be taken to a hospital; Conrad applied that hearsay story to the first mate on the *Otago*.[60] It is true, however, that there was sickness among the sailors; William Willis, the British Legation doctor in Siam, wrote in his letter to Korzeniowski: "I think it is not out of place on my part that I should state, though not asked by you to do so, to prevent any misapprehension hereafter, that the crew of the sailing ship Otago has suffered severely whilst in Bangkok from tropical diseases, including fever, dysentery and cholera; and I can speak of my own knowledge that you have done all in your power in the trying and responsible position of Master of the Ship to hasten the departure of your vessel from this unhealthy place and at the same time to save the lives of the men under your command."[61]

In spite of Dr. Willis's protestations, the letter sounds as if it were written at the request of the addressee. No doubt the doctor, mentioned by Conrad in *The Shadow Line* as "the only human being in the world who seemed to take the slightest interest in me," knew about the difficult position of the new captain vis-à-vis the shipowners.

Finally on 9 February 1888, the *Otago* left Bangkok, and Korzeniowski experienced for the first time the weight of being responsible "next to God": ". . . the captain of a ship at sea is a remote, inaccessible creature, something like a prince of a fairy-tale, alone of his kind, depending on nobody, not to be called to account except by powers practically invisible and so distant, that they might well be looked upon as supernatural for all that the rest of the crew knows of them, as a rule."[62] He is responsible before the law and to the ship-owners for everything that happens to the ship and on the ship. The crew has to follow with unfailing obedience all orders that comply with the general regulations.[63] Whatever is outside those regulations depends entirely on his will and decision. "His word is law, which nobody must dispute, and which permits of no argument. . . . He stands no watch, comes and goes when he pleases, and is accountable to no one except to his owners. He has entire control of the discipline of the ship; so much so that none of the officers under him have any authority to punish a seaman, or to use any force without the master's order, except only in cases of urgent necessity that admit of no delay. He has to be informed of everything of importance that takes place on board."[64] The responsibility and exclusive power, coupled with relative "inactivity" (in the sense of a lack of regular duties apart from taking bearings when the ship is at sea), lead to loneliness. Even if the captain is on the friendliest terms with his officers, "it is the intimacy of men who are not equals."[65]

Loneliness charged with responsibility was to weigh on Korzeniowski even at the beginning of his command. Owing to calms in the Gulf of Siam, the *Otago* took three weeks to cover the eight hundred sea miles to Singapore. Moreover, the crew suffered from malaria. The *Singapore Free Press* reported on 2 March: "The British bark *Otago*, bound from Bangkok to Sydney with a cargo of rice, put into port here last evening for medical advice as several of the crew are suffering from fever and the Captain wished to get a further supply of medicine before he proceeded on his journey. Dr Mugliston went on board and ordered three of the crew to be sent to Hospital. The vessel is outside the Harbour limits."[66]

Obviously the captain faced considerable difficulties, although not as great or as dramatic as those in *The Shadow Line*. If it had been true that not a single member of the crew was fit for work, as we read in the book, the newspaper would not have failed to print such sensational news.[67] The story about the former captain disposing of the entire stock of quinine is not very probable either: most likely all medicine had been used up, or perhaps the original stock had been insufficient, which would explain the remorse of the narrator in *The Shadow Line*.

A glance at the crew list of the *Otago* reveals other facts that one could not even guess on the basis of *The Shadow Line*. The crew of nine (the captain, two officers, and six sailors) included three Englishmen, one Scot, two Germans, two Norwegians, and a Pole; in short, fewer than half were British. Conrad's first mate, Charles Born, was a German. In the novel Conrad aged Born considerably (in actual fact he was barely three years older than the captain), while making himself younger.[68]

The *Otago* stopped in Singapore for three days. As this would not allow time for both unloading and loading, one has to assume that the information about the ship having come with a cargo of rice is incorrect, in view of the fact that she arrived in Australia loaded with timber. The captain completed the crew which had been decimated by illness: two Englishmen, a Swede, a Dane, and an elderly Negro from the Antilles replaced the two Englishmen and two Germans who had signed off.[69] The British remained in the minority.

On 3 March the ship left the port and headed for Sydney. Korzeniowski's first command was of a barque smaller than the *Mont Blanc* and the *Saint Antoine*; in fact, except for the coaster *Vidar*, it was the smallest he had sailed in. In *The Mirror of the Sea* he praises the experience: "But of the delight of seeing a small craft run bravely amongst the great seas there can be no question to him whose soul does not dwell ashore. . . . The solemn thundering combers caught her up from astern, passed her with a fierce boiling up of foam level with the bulwarks, swept on ahead with a swish and a roar: and the little vessel, dipping her jib-boom into the tumbling froth, would go on running in a smooth, glassy hollow, a deep valley between two ridges of the sea, hiding the horizon ahead and astern."[70]

The *Otago* arrived in Sydney on 7 May 1888. The following day the local *Morning Herald* announced the "Otago, bq., 345 t., Captain Konkorzentowski, from Bangkok February 9" bringing 200 thousand cubic feet of teak. The daily also published a short report of the passage:

> The iron barque *Otago* arrived in port yesterday from Bangkok, with a full cargo of teak. Her captain reports that light winds were had down the Gulf of Siam, with light winds and airs through the China and Java Seas. Passed though the Straits of Sunda on March 15. The S.E. trades were very light and were carried to 26 S. Passed Cape Lewin on April 15, when a very heavy gale from the west was encountered. The gale continued with unabated fury for two days ere it moderated. The barque behaved herself exceedingly well, and beyond plenty of water finding its way on board no damage was sustained. Cape Otway was abeam at 3 a.m. on the 28th ultimo. Wilson's promontory was passed on the 2nd instant. Experienced N.N.E. winds through the Bass's Straits. On Friday and Saturday last a very heavy gale from the westward, the wind going round to the S.S.W., was encountered; the vessel laboured heavily and kept her decks full. The Hornby light was sighted at 8 p.m. on Sunday and the Heads were entered at 9 a.m. yesterday in tow of the *Irresistible*. The *Otago* anchored off Elizabeth Bay.[71]

On his arrival in Sydney, Korzeniowski had a letter, dated 5 May, ready to post to his uncle. The shipowners decided to keep him as master, and on the ninth he officially signed the crew list. The *Otago* remained in port until 22 May, when she left for Melbourne. Arriving there after a difficult and stormy passage, she stayed at anchor in the Melbourne roadstead until 8 June. The following day the local paper *Argus* noted the arrival of a barque *Otago* from

Bangkok via Sydney; it gave the name of the captain as "T. Conrad."[72] After loading 2,750 bags of wheat, the ship left for Sydney on 7 July. She entered the port on 12 July and stayed there until 7 August. The next sea voyage, with a mixed cargo of fertilizer, soap, and tallow, was to Mauritius.[73]

Korzeniowski, nervous and often unsure of himself, decided to test his ability and courage as a master. He who had twice failed his navigation examinations suggested to the shipowners that instead of taking the usual southwestern route he would sail by way of Torres Strait, which separates the Australian continent from New Guinea and was regarded as a more dangerous journey. The route was longer in distance but potentially quicker, and the shipowners gave their consent.[74] The passage, albeit successful, proved not very fast: 6,900 sea miles in fifty-four days. Nowadays the route through Torres Strait is recommended as safer for sailing ships from March to September than the traditional route along the southern coast of Australia.[75]

In "The Secret Sharer" Conrad describes a risky maneuver of the ship, ordered by her newly fledged captain, to whom it gives a sense of control over his craft; for Korzeniowski the passage through Torres Strait was a similar test of his own capacity, except that it lasted longer and could not therefore be as dramatically explicit.

The *Otago* entered the harbor of Port Louis, Mauritius, on 30 September. During the almost two-month-long stay caused by difficulties with the loading, Korzeniowski developed a romantic interest. One of his adventures is described in the story "A Smile of Fortune," a piece that contains obviously autobiographical elements (for example, one of the characters is the same Chief Mate Burns encountered in *The Shadow Line*). The narrator, a young captain, starts to flirt rather ambiguously and surreptitiously with Alice Jacobus, daughter of a local merchant living in a house surrounded by a magnificent flower garden. The narrator behaves as if he had no intention of ever returning to the scene of his conquest. One could dismiss the entire story as purely fictional, but local research has confirmed that in Port Louis at that time, there was a seventeen-year-old Alice Shaw, whose father, a shipping agent, owned the only rose garden in town.[76]

We are better informed about Korzeniowski's other, and more open flirtation. An old friend he had met in Port Louis, Captain Gabriel Renouf of the French Merchant Marine, introduced him to the family of his brother-in-law. Renouf's eldest sister was the wife of Louis Edward Schmidt, a senior official in the colony; with them lived two other sisters and two brothers. Although the island belonged to England, a large number of its inhabitants as well as of the cultural élite consisted of the descendants of the old French colonists. The unusual wanderer's excellent command of the French language and perfect manners opened all doors of local salons to him.

Korzeniowski became a frequent guest at the Schmidts' house, where he often met the Misses Renouf. The young ladies were fascinated by him. Although his behavior was always impeccable and his colorful stories about distant lands and voyages never failed to arouse interest, he would often grow suddenly silent and seemingly absorbed in his own thoughts and, indifferent to the current subject of conversation, he would get up and leave. Or else he would invite the whole family for tea on board the *Otago*, or for a carriage drive to an elegant café in the Jardin des Pamplemousses about six miles away.[77]

One popular drawing room entertainment consisted of filling in questionnaires; the activity, apart from being quite amusing, facilitated courtship. Such an "album of confidences" with Korzeniowski's replies has been preserved by the Renouf family. Although the questions were printed in French, and only French was used in conversation, the captain—probably as a somewhat snobbish joke—wrote his replies in English.

1. Quel est le principal trait de votre caractère?
   Laziness.
2. Par quels moyens cherchez-vous à plaire?
   By making myself scarce.
3. Quel nom fait battre votre coeur?
   Ready to beat for any name.
4. Quel serait votre rêve de bonheur?
   Never dream of it; want reality.
5. Où habite la personne qui occupe votre pensée?
   A castle in Spain.
6. Quelle est la qualité que vous préférez chez la femme?
   Beauty.
7. Que désirerez-vous être?
   Should like not to be.
8. Quelle est votre fleur de prédilection?
   Violet.
9. Dans quel pays voudriez-vous vivre?
   Do not know. Perhaps Lapland.
10. Quelle est la couleur des yeux que vous préférez?
    Grey.
11. Quel est le don de la nature dont vous voudriez être doué?
    Self-confidence.
12. Que préférez-vous dans un bal?
    Not dancing cannot tell.
13. Quelle est votre promenade favorite?
    Hate all "promenades."
14. Que préférez vous, les brunes ou les blondes?
    Both.

15. Quelle est votre plus grande distraction?
    Chasing wild geese.
16. Dites l'état present de votre esprit?
    Calm.
17. Que détestez-vous le plus?
    False pretences.
18. Vous-croyez vous aimé?
    Decline to state.
19. Votre devise?—
20. Votre nom? J. C. K.[78]

The refusal to answer might have concealed some earnest hopes and intentions, and his strange periods of silence could have been caused by shyness or by the entanglement of love. A couple of days before leaving Port Louis, Korzeniowski asked one of the Renouf brothers for the hand of his twenty-six-year-old sister Eugénie. Oddly enough he was unaware of the fact that Eugénie was already engaged to marry her cousin, a pharmacist by the name of Loumeau. After the inevitable rebuff he did not pay a farewell visit but instead sent a polite letter to Gabriel Renouf announcing that he would never return to Mauritius and adding that on the day of the wedding his thoughts would be near them. The marriage ceremony took place as early as January 1889.[79]

The director of the firm chartering the *Otago* in Port Louis was Paul Langlois, young at the time, who recalled forty-two years later his impressions of Korzeniowski, whom he used to meet almost every day during those seven weeks:

In height slightly below average, forceful and very mobile features, passing very rapidly from gentleness to an agitation bordering on anger; big black eyes usually melancholy and dreamy, and gentle as well, except for fairly frequent moments of irritation; a decisive chin, a finely shaped graceful mouth, a thick, well-trimmed dark brown mustache. That was his face—good-looking certainly but, above all, strange in its expression and difficult to forget if you had seen it once or twice.

Apart from his distinguished manners, the most striking thing about the captain of the *Otago* was the contrast between him and other skippers. As a big sugar exporter, I saw ten or so of them every day in the office of "old Krumpholtz," who for over thirty years was the only freight agent in the area. Between ten in the morning and one o'clock in the afternoon, his office, situated on the ground floor of the Mauritius Fire Insurance Co., was the meeting place of all the captains in search of a cargo. And if you remember that in those days, before the sea had been invaded by steamers, there were always fifteen ships or so in port during the sugar season, you can get an idea of the numerous assembly that packed the outer office of "old Krumpholtz" everyday.

Now, those shipmasters generally dressed in ducks, with caps or straw hats on their heads, their faces and hands tanned by sun and saltwater, their nails black with the tell-tale tar of their profession, their language forceful and often coarse, were not models of taste and refinement. Unlike his colleagues, Captain Korzeniowski was always dressed like a dandy. I can still see him (and just because of the contrast with the other sailors my memory is precise) arriving in my office almost every day dressed in a black or dark coat, a vest that was usually light in color, and fancy trousers; everything well cut and very stylish; on his head a black or gray bowler tilted slightly to one side. He invariably wore gloves and carried a cane with a gold knob.

From this description you can judge for yourself the contrast he made to the other captains, with whom, by the way, he was on strictly formal terms, generally not going beyond a greeting. He was not, of course, very popular with his colleagues, who ironically called him "the Russian Count." So much for his physical appearance.

As to his character: a perfect education; very varied and interesting conversation—on the days when he felt communicative, which wasn't every day. The man who was to become famous under the name Joseph Conrad was quite often taciturn and very excitable. On those days he had a nervous tick in the shoulder and the eyes, and anything the least bit unexpected—an object dropping to the floor, a door banging—would make him jump. Today we would call him a neurasthenic, in those days one said a neurotic.

Before his ship was chartered, he would appear at Krumpholtz's only for a few minutes each day, and afterwards not at all. He was always on board his ship, was never to be seen at the Hotel Oriental, where most of the captains took their lunch and spent the afternoon. . . . During this whole stay in Port Louis I don't believe the taciturn Conrad ever took a walk in the country, or—still less—ever made any contact with fashionable society, to which his culture, his perfect education, his impeccably correct manners and the elegance of his appearance would open for him many doors.

Joseph Conrad's English and French were both equally pure and fluent, but he preferred the latter language, which he handled with elegance. Our conversations were always in French.[80]

Langlois's recollection is not entirely accurate in details: he forgot Korzeniowski's beard and he knew nothing about the captain's friendship with the Renouf household; nevertheless the overall description of the physical and psychological aspects of his personality are presented convincingly, faithfully, and in accordance with other testimonies.

In "A Smile of Fortune," when mentioning the "S family," Conrad presents the society at Port Louis in a rather unfavorable light: "the old French families, descendants of the old colonists; all noble, all impoverished, and living a narrow domestic life in dull, dignified decay. The men, as a rule, occupy inferior posts in Government offices or in business houses. The girls are almost always pretty, ignorant of the world, kind and agreeable and generally bilingual; they prattle innocently both in French and English. The emptiness of their existence passes belief."[81] This, as well as other biting comments strewn over the text, sounds like emotional revenge. And yet it is worth noting that of all Korzeniowski's stopping places, including London, the only authentic recollections of his social contacts on land came from Port Louis. And it seems that in no other port did he establish such lively contacts with his own class of people (as one used to say). No doubt he felt more at ease within the French cultural sphere, with which he was to remain closely linked for the rest of his life.

His stay on the island, which ended in emotional discomfiture, brought him some professional success. Although the ship was held up in port longer than planned because of a lack of suitable jute mats to line the hold and protect his cargo of sugar (a fire had just destroyed the port's stock of these special sacks), and although Korzeniowski was forced to accept the freight at the lowest rates, he succeeded in introducing into the agreement a clause whereby the charterers were obliged to cover the possible costs of the pilot and tug up the River Melbourne. Such a clause later became a matter of routine.[82] Apparently he also managed to make a profit on an additional cargo of potatoes, which were at that time fetching a good price in Australia.[83]

The *Otago* left Port Louis for Melbourne on 22 November with a cargo of five hundred tons of sugar[84] and arrived there on 5 January 1889.[85] At Melbourne Korzeniowski found a letter from his uncle saying that his health "is neither good nor bad, swaying from indisposition to robustness—as is usual in an old man of 60." Once again he returned to the subject of his nephew's visit home: "You didn't tell me in your letters how long you think you will stay in Australian waters, but this nevertheless is of great interest to me. I do not wish to influence you either to prolong or to shorten your stay, if you are satisfied with it, but for an old man who has not long to live, time is a matter of some interest as it is also to know that he may possibly see again those who are dear to him—in this particular case: you! Could you not ask Mr Krieger to make inquiries for you at the Russian Embassy in London whether they have news concerning your application for your discharge from subjection?"[86]

For the time being the *Otago* stayed close to the Australian coast. After a month in the port of Melbourne she was towed on 4 February to an anchorage in Port Phillip Bay. It was ten days before she sailed, and the local newspapers cited Guam as the port of destination. It seems that the owners were undecided (or kept changing their minds) about the date and purpose of the journey. On 22 February the *Otago* arrived at Port Minlacowie (today Minlaton) in Spencer

Bay and collected a cargo of wheat. Korzeniowski gave a tea party on board the ship for the wives of local farmers.[87] After another month at anchor, the barque sailed on 21 March around the Yorke Peninsula to Port Adelaide, arriving there on 26 March. That was Captain Korzeniowski's last voyage on the *Otago*; he gave up his job soon after arrival.[88]

Several explanations for that decision have been advanced. Jean-Aubry took seriously Conrad's own statement in "A Smile of Fortune": the owners did not want to let him take the ship to South China and he refused to sail again to Port Louis. Jerry Allen also accepts this.[89] But it had been known long before that the *Otago* would not be sailing to China, and there was no question of her sailing to Mauritius either.[90] Baines suggests that Korzeniowski may have been prompted by a desire to see his uncle, whose letter had awaited him at Port Adelaide; it contained, among others, the particulars concerning Bobrowski's bequest in favor of his nephew.[91] This is possible, although Bobrowski did not insist on his nephew's earlier return. He simply inquired: "How long do you intend to remain with Messrs. Simpson & Sons?"—obviously aware of the fact that Korzeniowski did not intend to stay forever on the *Otago*. Also, Korzeniowski could not have planned to leave immediately for the Ukraine, as it was only on 31 March 1889 that the Russian Ministry of Home Affairs released "the son of a Polish man of letters, captain of the British merchant marine" from the status of Russian subject; the official announcement was published over three months later in *Senatskye Vyedomosti* of St. Petersburg.[92]

Norman Sherry points out the changes of plans on the part of the shipowners, who apparently intended to send the *Otago* from Port Minlacowie to Port Elizabeth, but later redirected her to Port Adelaide. He advances a hypothesis that Korzeniowski had set his mind on sailing to Africa.[93] This theory is founded on Conrad's own anecdote, according to which as a child he had once put his finger on a white spot on the map of Africa and announced, "When I grow up I shall go *there*."[94] But the voyage to a port on the South African coast—the best-known part of the continent—was not quite an expedition to Africa. Moreover, it is hard to tell what difference could have been made by the changed destination of the *Otago*, which eventually left for Brisbane.

All the biographers tend somehow to overlook the fact that Korzeniowski was not a typical seaman; that he did not regard his work at sea as permanent; and, above all, that he had exceptionally wide-ranging interests and cultural needs. Once the first charm of commanding a ship faded, the future writer must have felt the dreariness of sailing in the antipodes, the insufficiency of human contacts restricted as they were to other seamen, so vividly depicted by Langlois, or to the hardly more sophisticated merchants on land. He must have been oppressed by a sense of being cut off from Europe, deprived of newspapers, books, and current news. Even the chances of improving his English were slight: one of his officers on the *Otago* was a German and the other a Finn.[95]

The ship's owners sent Korzeniowski a flattering letter of farewell, dated 2 April 1889, Port Adelaide:

Dear Sir,

Referring to your resignation of the command (which we have in another letter formally accepted) of our bark *Otago*, we now have much pleasure in stating that this early severance from our employ is entirely at your own desire, with a view to visiting Europe, and that we entertain a high opinion of your ability in the capacity you now vacate, of your attainments generally, and should be glad to learn of your future success.

> Wishing you a pleasant passage home,
> We are, dear Sir,
> Yours faithfully,
> Henry Simpson & Sons
> Owners of the Black Diamond Line.[96]

Conrad later recorded his esteem for Australia in a letter to his literary agent, James B. Pinker: "Like all the sailors of the old wool fleet I have the warmest regard for Australians generally, for New South Wales in particular and for charming Sydney especially. Moreover I am a fellow citizen. Haven't I commanded an Australian ship for over two years?"[97] Writing in 1912, Conrad characteristically extended the period of his fourteen-month-long command. In retrospect it sounded impressive, but in actual fact the command of a small barque with a crew of nine could satisfy neither his ambitions nor his needs. Perhaps his carelessness in filling the *Otago*'s Agreement and Account of Crew forms—he skipped dates and other entries—may be taken as indicative of Korzeniowski's growing frustration.

Having left Port Adelaide on 3 April as a passenger on the German steamer *Nürnberg*, Korzeniowski disembarked in Southampton on 14 May.[98] Upon his return to London he rented rooms at Bessborough Gardens, Pimlico, a pleasanter and more central district than the northern outskirts of town from which he moved, not far from the Thames, which at this point still swells and falls in the measured rhythm of the tides.[99]

For him personally the summer of 1889 was a time of low tide. As was usual in his life, a period of intense activity and bold projects was followed by months of indecision and inertia. Unfortunately we know nothing about his moods, because once again there is a gap in Bobrowski's preserved correspondence (from 3 January 1889 to 24 June 1890). Korzeniowski looked for another command but to no avail. There were many others like him without work. Baines points out that "although it was a fine achievement for a Polish gentleman to have become a successful captain in the British Merchant Navy, it was a personal . . . achievement with little significance for anyone but himself."[100] Anyway, his success was rather modest: he had not served as a captain or first mate on any larger vessel, nor had he worked for any firm of importance; sailors who were really successful in their sea career were at his age commanding fairly big craft.[101] His foreign origin and looks were no help to him. Nor had he reached the highest rank in seamanship, that of extra master, which required an additional examination.[102]

For the time being he lived on his savings and a modest income from his share in Barr, Moering and Co., which Bobrowski increased at his request by 400 rubles, bringing the total to almost £400.[103] It is also possible that he was employed in the firm's office, at least on a temporary basis; he was using the firm's address and letterhead.

By the autumn of 1889 Captain Konrad Korzeniowski found an occupation that could compensate for his failures in life and help him cope actively with his inner perplexities. He began to write *Almayer's Folly*. Was it his first literary work? Here too we find Conrad's statements contradictory. Although in *A Personal Record* he maintained unequivocally, "Till I began to write that novel I had written nothing but letters,"[104] he later mentioned privately having written in 1886, for a competition announced by the weekly *Tit-Bits*, a short story that after twenty years was transformed into "The Black Mate." We shall discuss the matter in greater detail in Chapter 11. If he really had written before 1889 anything even similar to "The Black Mate," it would be an additional testimony to his discontent with the seaman's profession, to his frustration, and to his need for cultural contacts that would help him to overcome his loneliness.

In 1903 he wrote to Kazimierz Waliszewski: "I began writing *Almayer's Folly*, just like that, not thinking much what I was doing, in order to occupy my mornings during a rather long stay in London after a three years' cruise in the South Seas."[105] He sailed for a considerably shorter time; perhaps the whole statement is only two-thirds true. He gives a similar account in *A Personal Record*. In his letters and autobiographical confessions he created, for the benefit of his readers as well as himself, a self-portrait: first of a romantic but highly determined youth, then of a brave, enthusiastic, and competent sailor who, out of boredom with enforced inactivity, began to write and went on practicing that difficult profession with the same devotion and concentration he had applied earlier to setting sails and maneuvering ships. On this picture the years spent at sea were meant to shine with the full glow of dreams realized and of genuine achievement; he did not want his decision to become a writer to cast a shadow upon those years. Thus, the son of a writer, praised by his uncle for the beautiful style of his letters, the man who from the very first page showed a professional and serious approach to his work, presented his start on *Almayer's Folly* as a casual and nonbinding incident.

"The conception of a planned book was entirely outside my mental range when I sat down to write; the ambition of being an author had never turned up amongst these gracious imaginary existences one creates fondly for oneself at times in the stillness and immobility of a day-dream: yet it stands clear as the sun at noonday that from the moment I had done blackening over the first manuscript page of *Almayer's Folly* . . . from the moment I had, in the simplicity of my heart and the amazing ignorance of my mind, written that page the die was cast." [106]

And yet he must have felt a pronounced need to write. Every page right from that first one testifies that writing was not something he took up for amusement or to pass time. Just the contrary: it was a serious undertaking, supported by careful, diligent reading of the masters and aimed at shaping his own attitude to art and to reality. Perhaps in retrospect Conrad half-consciously shifted the emphasis: after all, he could not have known that he would become a professional writer, he could not have been sure of his talent. Our explanations and hypotheses concern now only the part writing played in his life; we do not know the sources of his artistic impulses and creative gifts.

Now perforce comes the question that has been asked frequently and sometimes aggressively: why did he write in English? Conrad's own answer is so lofty that it arouses suspicion:

> The truth of the matter is that my faculty to write in English is as natural as any other aptitude with which I might have been born. I have a strange and overpowering feeling that it had always been an inherent part of myself. English was for me neither a matter of choice nor adoption. The merest idea of choice had never entered my head. And as to adoption—well, yes, there was adoption; but it was I who was adopted by the genius of the language, which directly I came out of the stammering stage made me its own. . . . A matter of discovery and not of inheritance, that very inferiority of the title makes the faculty still more precious, lays the possessor under a lifelong obligation to remain worthy of his great fortune. . . . All I can claim after all those years of devoted practice, with the accumulated anguish of its doubts, imperfections and falterings in my heart, is the right to be believed when I say that if I had not written in English I would not have written at all. [107]

Yes, we may and perhaps ought to believe it—but not for the reasons stated by the author. He protests too much. We shall see that "the faculty" (Conrad chooses his words carefully—he is not saying "ability") of writing in English was the cause of many perplexities, difficulties, even despair. The French language, which in many circumstances he would have preferred to use, also tempted him as a literary medium: more than once he advanced the possibility of writing in French. It is true that his English was not a matter of "adoption" but simply a result of partly accidental turns his life had taken. Nevertheless, Conrad wished to infuse his life, and particularly the public aspect of it that he regarded as most precious—his works of fiction—with the sense of an overriding purposefulness; he did not want the tricky problem of language ("tricky" for the English because of the occasionally questioned correctness of Conrad's language, and for Poles because of "patriotic" concerns) to appear to have been determined by external circumstances.

And yet this is exactly what happened: making a start on *Almayer's Folly* Korzeniowski did not "choose" the language. For eleven years he had been in daily contact with English-speaking people, he spoke English, read English books, he even gradually accepted the English point of view on political matters. This does not rule out the possibility that this language of everyday life and work was at the same time his great adventure, revelation, and object of love, all the more powerful because it began in his mature age.

Reading Conrad's later letters to his literary friends, we are struck by the amount of attention he devoted to the analysis of style, to individual words and expressions, to the emotional tone of phrases, the atmosphere created by language. In his letter to Hugh Clifford he explained his theory: ". . . words, groups of words, words standing alone, are symbols of life, have the power in their sound or their aspect to present the very thing you wish to hold up before the mental vision of your readers. The things 'as they are' exist in words; therefore words should be handled with care lest the picture, the image of truth abiding in facts, should become distorted—or blurred." [108]

However different their artistic temperaments may have been, Conrad was following here in the footsteps of Flaubert, who for days on end searched passionately for the right word to render the "essence of the matter." This is the reason, I think, why writing in English may have seemed to Conrad most appropriate: to work in a medium infinitely rich and refined by masterpieces of poetry, resistant like every object that is strange and newly discovered, and at the same time softly pliable because not hardened in schematic patterns of words and ideas inculcated since childhood. At the same time it was a less binding activity, a little like a game: writing in a foreign language admits a greater temerity in tackling personally sensitive problems, for it leaves uncommitted the most spontaneous, deeper reaches of the psyche, and allows a greater distance in treating matters we would hardly dare approach in the language of our childhood. As a rule it is easier both to swear and to analyze dispassionately in an acquired language.

The difference of associations between Polish and English was sharpened by the contrast between the structures of the languages, which follow diverse rhythms and syntactical patterns. For a Pole, English seems a language of immensely rich vocabulary, and one demanding an almost stark concreteness of expression. With its ubiquitous inflections, Polish has a more closely knit syntax, and thus naturally admits of longer sentences; it is rich in adjectives, more sedate in pace, less ambiguous, and tends to the rhetorical. Thanks to its morphological flexibility it can be more easily made to follow closely the flow of one's ideas. To move from one language to the other thus required a remolding of the forms of Conrad's thought and imagination; no doubt he felt this most strongly at the beginning of his writing endeavors, although an analysis of his style reveals the imprint of Polish in all his works.[109]

But even if Conrad had wanted to write in Polish and if his proficiency in his mother tongue had been maintained to a sufficient degree to make creative writing feasible, he would have had to overcome, in addition to all other obstacles, yet another one, practically insurmountable: the Polish novel was at that time in its infancy; its artistic development did not begin until the years when Korzeniowski was sailing the oceans. In his Polish literary heritage the novel was practically nonexistent.

Most probably Conrad wrote the first three chapters of *Almayer's Folly* during the autumn of 1889.[110] At the same time he continued to look for a job. The chances of finding one in England must have been slender, because he began making inquiries on the Continent. He entered into negotiations with an Antwerp-based firm of shipowners, Walford et Cie, on the subject of getting command of a ship on their line trading with the West Indies and New Orleans, but he did not expect to be successful.[111] Barr, Moering & Co. recommended him to a ship broker in Ghent, G. C. de Baerdemaecker, who on 24 September approached Albert Thys, director of the Société Belge pour le Commerce du Haut-Congo, asking about the possibility of finding Korzeniowski a job in Africa. "This gentleman is very warmly recommended to me by friends in London. Besides being a past master of his profession and holding the highest certificates, his general education is superior to that of most seamen and he is a perfect gentleman."[112] The introduction helped, and in the first half of November Korzeniowski traveled to Brussels to meet Thys.[113] The meeting went well to the extent that Thys made a note in the margin of Korzeniowski's letter: "A good captain when we shall need one for the Upper Congo. Get references from Walfords."[114] As the result of an ambiguity in this letter Thys was under the impression that the applicant had been employed by that firm. Korzeniowski later clarified the misunderstanding and gave other references.[115]

Everything indicates that he found his way to Thys accidentally and that the idea of working in Africa presented itself for want of something else. Once this possibility arose, it probably rekindled his old interest, which had been recently revived by a wave of sensational news about the African interior, connected with Henry Morton Stanley's expedition in search of Emin Pasha. Moreover, the work there was well paid, surely better than a command at sea.

For the time being, however, the matter came to a standstill. Thys kept silent for weeks. On 27 December the impatient captain notified the company of his intended trip "to the south of Russia," where the post was unreliable in winter; in view of this he asked for the date when his return would be advisable—but this request also remained unanswered.

In the meantime Korzeniowski could at last pay the long-planned visit to his uncle and his homeland. In spite of his official release from Russian subjection, formalities connected with obtaining his visa took a long time. The applicant was required to produce a copy of the Ministry of Internal Affairs decree. This involved applying to Chernikhov, the last place of his father's exile; the copy arrived with an annotation that it had been made on 18 December 1889 in answer to the request received on 24 October.[116]

Bobrowski, meanwhile, sent his nephew the address of their distant relative Aleksander Poradowski, an emigré of 1863, now settled in Brussels. Korzeniowski then wrote: "I am terribly sorry that I did not know this earlier, as I was in Brussels in October last year. It is possible, however, that before long I shall have to visit Brussels again. . . . I would very much like to be certain that you are in Brussels and that I shall be able to find you there in the course of the next month. . . . I am now more or less under contract to the 'Société Belge pour le Commerce du Haut Congo' to be master of one of its river steamers. I have not signed any agreement, but Mr A. Thys, the director of that Company, has promised me the post. Whether he will keep his promise and when he will send me to Africa, I do not yet know; it will probably be in May."[117]

The expedition to the Ukraine was still in doubt, as he was waiting for the decision of his uncle, who feared bad winter travel conditions. Bobrowski's letter arrived on 20 January, and Korzeniowski wrote to Poradowski, who was gravely ill and waiting for an operation: "I hasten to inform you that in view of the state of your health, I have decided to go home via Brussels. . . . This morning I received, simultaneously with your letter, one from Uncle Tadeusz that says 'come.' However, those villains in the Russian Consulate do not want to grant me a visa—which means further delay, inconvenience, and visits to the Embassy, perhaps to no avail. I shall let you know how I am getting on as soon as I settle matters with these pirates."[118]

By 31 January 1890 he managed to settle the necessary formalities and arrived in Brussels on 5 February,[119] just in time to see Poradowski, who died two days later. The meeting with Poradowski's widow, Marguerite (née Gachet), turned out to be one of the more important events in Korzeniowski's life. The forty-two-year-old "aunt," as he addressed her, was a daughter of a French historian who had settled in Belgium. She was a woman of beauty and charm, highly cultured, well-read, and with good connections; moreover, she was a writer. Her translations from the Polish, as well as her own stories, mostly based on Polish and Ukrainian motifs (the Poradowskis had spent some time in Lwów), had been published since 1880 in the renowned *Revue des Deux Mondes*. It was probably the first time since his childhood that Korzeniowski came in direct contact with someone actively engaged in literature. He took for his journey to Poland her long story *Yaga*, based on the life of Ukrainian peasants and published in Paris in 1888.

He stayed in Brussels for a few days. The Company informed him that in order to take up the promised job he ought to report at the end of April.[120] On 9 or 10 February he arrived in Warsaw. Poradowski, a correspondent of the Warsaw daily *Słowo*, had managed to give him an introduction to the editor-in-chief, Mścisław Godlewski, but Korzeniowski did not find him in his office.[121] This is an intriguing detail: perhaps the budding writer had after all decided to comply with Bobrowski's suggestion to send some articles to the Polish press. He stayed in Warsaw until 12 February, and doubtless met his first cousin Stanisław Bobrowski, a radical university student.[122] Then he paid a two-day visit to Lublin to see his relatives Aniela and Karol Zagórski. On 16 February, driven in a sleigh from Kalinówka railway station, he arrived at Kazimierówka.[123]

Almost immediately they left for Nowochwastów to attend the name-day party of Madame Konstancja de Montrésor. Having arrived there on 18 February they were cut off by snow and had to prolong their stay for several days. "Those were unforgettable days—gathered round a blazing fire we spent long hours listening to Conrad who was talking about his voyages and impressions; he talked in Polish but occasionally lacking a word he would replace it with an English or French expression."[124] In the frequently cited "Document," Bobrowski wrote: "You visited me at Kazimierówka and I am availing myself of this opportunity to hand over to you this statement together with my cordial blessing for your future."

The only preserved trace of the impressions left on Korzeniowski by revisiting his homeland after sixteen years are several pages in *A Personal Record*. Apart from mentioning his two days in Warsaw, he recounts almost exclusively his journey by sleigh from Kalinówka to Kazimierówka and his stay in the snow-covered Ukrainian village. He describes the surprise of the servants on discovering that the visitor from far away had not forgotten his mother tongue; his own sensation of returning to childhood experiences; his uncle's warm-hearted hospitality. And that is all.[125] His two-month stay at Kazimierówka— for he remained there until 18 April—has left no visible signs in his works and correspondence. Even his letters written at that time to Poradowska contain no mention of his surroundings, relations with people, impressions.

Bobrowski's later letters provide some information. We learn that the master mariner had met several distant relatives and many of Uncle Tadeusz's neighbors and friends, who subsequently enquired after the exotic visitor. Konrad also discussed his future plans with his uncle, who was far from enthusiastic about the projected job in Africa. They must also have talked about politics. We may assume that Bobrowski, an appeaser without illusions, did nothing to change his nephew's pessimistic outlook on the future, or rather the lack of future, of Poland—an outlook known to us from Korzeniowski's 1885 letters to Kliszczewski.

Luckily, we have additional testimony concerning the visit: the reminiscences of a diplomat, Jan Perłowski, Korzeniowski's fellow countryman and fifteen years his junior. Perłowski had been one of Tadeusz Bobrowski's legal wards, and he left an interesting portrait of his guardian, whom he characterized as an outstanding personality with a wide range of interests but at the same time a cold and egocentric rationalist. Equally critical, although not devoid of respect, is Perłowski's view of Conrad.

Perłowski took part in one of the social gatherings Bobrowski arranged at Kazimierówka soon after his nephew's homecoming. He reminisces that the traveler was accorded a very warm welcome but succeeded in putting people off by his reticence and indifference: "All the gentlemen were obviously ready to make friends with Conrad but his manner cast a chill. He answered all questions with a strained politeness, he spoke with concentration and listened carefully but one could not fail to notice his extreme boredom. . . . He spoke with a hint of a foreign accent and occasional bursts of our characteristic borderland intonation. . . . He spoke only once to ask about a new railway line which was to link Humań, hitherto cut off from the world, with the port of Odessa. . . . At last there was a subject of common interest." Young Perłowski listened to the conversation with growing irritation and finally asked Korzeniowski how long ago he had left the country. "His eyes glinted. He understood in an instant and answered as if reading my thoughts: 'Ah, well half a life ago!' . . . Then I started telling him about a lady who bore the same name as he did and who years ago had been known all over the Ukraine. I reminded him of Miss Regina Korzeniowska, an outstanding personality combining patriotic feelings, scholarly mind and eccentricity. None less than Julian Bartoszewicz has praised her merits, and humorous anecdotes about her life have entertained even the following generation. . . . I imagined that those reminiscences would interest Conrad and help him cast aside his reserve. The result was quite the opposite. He looked perplexed, made a wry face and began speaking quickly avoiding my subject." Later the two men happened to find themselves alone on a porch where the following scene took place: "Now he approached me, both hands deep in his pockets in the English way, exclaiming with that characteristic merry tone of voice used by the English under similar circumstances: 'A breezy day! Very fine! Isn't it?' I was much younger than Conrad but did not feel impressed by him in any way. . . . Laughing, I replied not too politely: 'Why not say it in Polish?' He lifted his head and turned away with a frown. Several people came out on to the porch and a young puppy with muddy paws rushed towards us jumping. Conrad leaned forward, turned the puppy on its back and petting it for a long while with obvious pleasure, kept on repeating over and over again, partly for the benefit of the dog, partly for me: 'Doggy, doggy, doggy . . . you dirty dog.'" [126]

Perłowski did not know that Regina Korzeniowska was not only Konrad's cousin but also his benefactress: while still a boy he had received from her a present of 500 rubles and, after her death, three times that amount from her sister; the allusion was therefore doubly painful. We may assume that although

Perłowski published his memoirs forty-six years after the event, the general atmosphere of the meeting was rendered faithfully. It is also confirmed by a family anecdote recalled by Tadeusz Garczyński. He had heard from his older relatives that during his visit in the Ukraine Korzeniowski behaved very conde-scendingly toward the local szlachta, who were irritated by his lack of interest in local affairs. Thus, according to a legend, at one party he was treated like an intruder. The two scenes of "patriotic admonitions," one after the other, de-scribed by Perłowski, represented the beginning of a series that continued al-most until the writer's death.

Let us try to imagine it from the point of view of the "culprit." An inhabitant of London, the capital of the richest and most powerful country in the world, comes to a village in the backwoods of the Ukraine. He is a traveler who has seen a great deal and is at present under contract with a huge company, which is supposed not only to profit from trade but also to civilize black Africa. The traveler is a Pole, but without hope that his partitioned motherland will ever become free and unified; he is conscious of the fact that in the modern pros-perous and open world no one is interested in Polish affairs and very few know where that legendary country is, and he is aware that to be continually harping on wrongs, suffering, and oppression evokes, at best, pity mixed with repug-nance. This is not only painful but humiliating for him. In self-defense, he sup-presses all thought about his country, all tender but disturbing memories; he feels inwardly ashamed of his Polish ballast, of that absurd, hopeless anach-ronistic deadweight.

Korzeniowski comes to his home country and the split reaction, typical of the émigré, is only intensified. His emotions, evoked by familiar objects and sounds long unheard, by half-forgotten childhood memories, his shame at having aban-doned it all, clash with his contempt for parochialism and narrow-mindedness, provincial boredom and sentimental intrusiveness. Most of all, however, he is irritated by the open or implied suggestion that he should join the ranks of those men, those relics of the past who heave patriotic sighs and spin out futile dreams about the rebirth of Poland. The stronger the clash, the greater his anger at himself and at others (the mechanism of psychological self-defense quickly redirects grievances outward), the stiffer his manner, the greater his af-fectation and tendency to provoke. Probably the nineteen-year-old interlocutor took Captain Korzeniowski's posturing too much to heart. His chilly manner, indifference, and even contempt concealed shame and anxiety, which although kept under the surface of his consciousness were unextinguished and painfully persistent.

This may explain why the subject of revisiting his motherland was never mentioned in his letters to "Aunt" Marguerite, who, all at once, became the confidante of his most intimate thoughts and feelings. Instead, we find tones of elevated gloom expressed in sentences as if borrowed from Conrad's early works: "Life rolls on in bitter floods, like a dark and brutal ocean under a sky covered with dark clouds, and there are days when the poor souls who have embarked on the disheartening voyage imagine that never has a ray of sun been able to break through that dreary veil; that never will the sun shine again; that it has never even existed! Eyes that the sharp wind of grief has filled with tears must be pardoned if they refuse to see the blue; lips that have tasted the bitterness of life must be pardoned if they refuse to utter words of hope." [127]

The correspondence with Poradowska goes beyond such stirring philosophical allegories, however. Time and again we come across affectionate, direct, well-nigh intimate phrases ("I kiss your hands and embrace you heartily"), rather remarkable considering that the writer and addressee saw each other for only a few days. He takes a keen interest in the future plans of his "dear little Aunt" which "interest him deeply," and he "impatiently" awaits the moment when he will be able to kiss her hands and thank her in person for interceding on his behalf with the Company, which was slow in procuring the promised employment.

Korzeniowski left Kazimierówka on 18 April. On the way back he stopped for two days in Lublin to see the Zagórskis; then he spent some time in Radom with Kazimierz Bobrowski's widow and her children; he arrived back in Brussels on or by 29 April.[128] There he found that the Company's dilatoriness had changed suddenly into a feverish hurry. Its reason was gruesome: the news had just reached Brussels of the murder by local tribesmen on 29 January of Johannes Freiesleben, the Danish master of the steamship *Florida*.[129] Korzeniowski was appointed to take his place.

Shortly afterward he wrote to Karol Zagórski: "If you only knew the devilish haste I had to make! From London to Brussels, and back again to London! And then again I dashed full tilt to Brussels! If you had only seen all the tin boxes and revolvers, the high boots and the tender farewells; just another handshake and just another pair of trousers!—and if you knew all the bottles of medicine and all the affectionate wishes I took away with me, you would understand in what a typhoon, cyclone, hurricane, earthquake—no!—in what a universal cataclysm, in what a fantastic atmosphere of mixed shopping, business, and affecting scenes, I passed two whole weeks." [130]

On 6 May he finally left London for Brussels. Then, following those tender "farewells" and "affecting scenes," probably with Marguerite, he left for Bordeaux by train. On 10 May he stepped aboard the S.S. *Ville de Maceio*[131] and began the most traumatic journey of his life.

V
. . . .
TO THE END OF THE NIGHT
1890

A FEW DAYS before Korzeniowski returned to Brussels from Poland, Henry Morton Stanley, the famed nineteenth-century traveler, delivered a speech in the building of the Brussels Exchange. He had just arrived in great triumph after a successful expedition for the relief of Emin Pasha, who had been cut off by the Mahdist revolt. "What does the greatness of a monarch consist in?" he asked. "If it is the extent of his territory, then the Emperor of Russia is the greatest of all. If it is the splendour and power of military organization then William II takes first place. But if royal greatness consists in the wisdom and goodness of a sovereign leading his people with the solicitude of a shepherd watching over his flock, then the greatest sovereign is your own." [1]

The Congo Free State, extending over a huge area of nearly 900,000 square miles, was under the direct rule of Leopold II, the king of Belgium. It officially became a European dependency in 1885, relatively late, following the decision of the Berlin Congress at which Leopold, the shrewd monarch of a small country, managed to play skillfully against each other the rivalry and jealousy of powerful states. He also knew how to make clever use of slogans about progress, the civilizing mission, and the enlightenment and ennoblement of savages. "To bring civilization to the only part of this globe where it has not yet penetrated, to pierce the darkness which envelops entire populations—is, I dare say, a crusade worthy of this age of progress." [2] Stanley, in King Leopold II's service from 1879 to 1884 as an explorer and administrator on behalf of the Association Internationale pour l'Exploration et la Civilisation en Afrique, last lent his personal authority and propagandistic gift by publishing, among others, a two-volume laudatory report, *The Congo and the Founding of its Free State: A Story of Work and Exploration.* [3]

The Société Anonyme Belge pour le Commerce du Haut-Congo was established on 10 December 1888. The Society had two objectives: to spread the financial burdens of colonization among a body of shareholders and to stimulate the development of the country; and to monopolize trading by the state and to build up an administrative network. Although the Congo had huge potential resources, for the time being the Belgian king was sinking enormous capital, almost his entire wealth, into the building of railway stations and roads. Individuals grew rich, but the state itself did not become self-supporting until 1899.[4] Thus, there was a great demand for energetic organizers; Albert Thys (1849–1915) was among the leading ones.

Did Korzeniowski believe in the official phraseology, and, if so, to what extent? The personal passion he displayed later in his private and public attacks on King Leopold II—he treated no other politician with such venom—suggests the existence of some deep-seated grudge. The irony of "An Outpost of Progress," "Heart of Darkness," and *The Inheritors* is directed mainly at the false pretenses of "civilizing" activity. And in one of Bobrowski's letters written to the Congo, we find a fragment that immediately brings to mind the problems set out in "Heart of Darkness," and seems to show that during his conversations at Kazimierówka Korzeniowski himself took in good faith the "missionary" slogans of the colonizers. Bobrowski wrote, "You are probably looking around at people and things as well as at the 'civilizing' (confound it) affair in the machinery of which you are a cog—before you feel able to acquire and express your own opinion. Don't wait however until it all crystallizes into clear sentences, but tell me something of your health and your first impressions."[5] It is therefore quite probable that Korzeniowski sailed south convinced that he would be participating in an enterprise whose justification was not merely financial.

From Tenerife, the first port of call of the *Ville de Maceio*, he wrote to Poradowska on 15 May. "My dear little Aunt," he began in the mixture of sentimental banter and melancholia that he probably thought becoming, for "the time being I am reasonably happy, which is all one can expect in this rotten world. It was raining on the day we left Bordeaux. A sad day; not a happy departure; haunting memories; vague regrets; still vaguer hopes. I doubt the future. For indeed—I ask myself—why should one trust it? And also why be sad? A little illusion, many dreams, a rare flash of happiness then disillusionment, a little anger and much pain, and then the end—peace! That is the programme and we shall be seeing this tragicomedy to the finish. One must be resigned."[6] Baines calls those phrases "typically Conradian reflections."[7] Indeed, similar thoughts are often found in Conrad's writings, and by and large they expressed his general attitude toward life; in this particular instance, however, they are most likely written for effect, *pour épater sa chère petite tante.*

The tone of another letter, posted from Freetown in Sierra Leone to Karol Zagórski, is entirely different: it has none of the pompous resignation displayed in the correspondence with Poradowska. Writing to his Polish cousin, Korzeniowski postured as a boisterous szlachcic, although the news he was conveying was far from cheerful. Obviously he had not been well briefed by the Society about working conditions in the Congo. "As far as I can make out from my 'lettre d'instruction' I am destined to the command of a steamboat, belonging to M. Delcommune's exploring party, which is being got ready. I like this prospect very much, but I know nothing for certain as everything is supposed to be

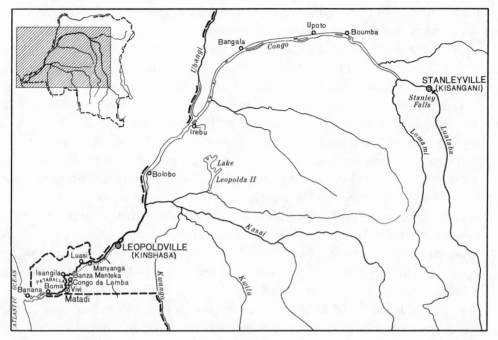

THE CONGO
. . . . caravan trail

kept secret." [8] The fact that he himself had not tried to secure the necessary information may indicate either credulity or the lack of responsibility for which his uncle had reproached him in the past.

One of his fellow passengers on the *Ville de Maceio*, Prosper Harou, was well acquainted with the Central African situation and painted a rather discouraging picture: 60 percent of the employees of the Company resigned their posts before six months were up; others, who could not stand the tropical climate, were quickly sent back to Europe; still others died from various diseases and exhaustion; and only 7 percent completed their three-year contract, such as the one signed by Korzeniowski. Sending this information to Zagórski, Korzeniowski confessed his feelings of apprehension, but commented with bravado, "Yes! But a Polish *szlachcic* cased in British tar! What a concoction! Nous verrons! In any case I shall console myself by remembering—faithful to our national traditions—that I sought this trouble myself." The motif "you sought this trouble yourself" comes to the forefront of Bobrowski's reply to another letter from Korzeniowski, which had been written on the voyage on 28 May: "Firstly, we must fortify ourselves with patience, secondly with a certain amount of optimism;—which will come more easily to me sitting here in Kazimierówka than they will to you. I cannot even rely too much on your 'youth,' when everything seems rosy, for at Christ's age no room is left for illusions. The only consolation you can find in perfecting your perseverance and your optimism amidst your present struggles with life is in the exclamation of Molière with which you are familiar: 'tu l'as voulu, tu l'as voulu, Georges Dandin.'"[9]

The *Ville de Maceio* called at various ports: Tenerife in the Canary Islands, Dakar, Conakry in French Guinea, Freetown, Grand Bassam on the Ivory Coast, Grand Popo in Dahomey, and Libreville in Gabon. Korzeniowski must have had a lot of time for meditation and correspondence. If we are to accept as autobiographical Marlow's confessions in "Heart of Darkness," the voyage was a very lonely one, but not because he was not used to the role of a passenger: he had been one on several occasions and for longer periods of time, for example, a year before on his homeward passage.[10] No, he must have felt lonely because he had just spent three months with his family and friends—an unusual experience for him—and possibly also because he met on board the type of people described in later African novels: nouveaux riches, shady speculators, and businessmen without scruples. Near Grand Popo he saw a French man-of-war, *Le Seignelay*, shelling a Negro camp hidden in the jungle;[11] the incident acquired a symbolic significance in "Heart of Darkness."

On 12 June the *Ville de Maceio* reached Boma, fifty miles up-river from the Congo estuary. The next day Korzeniowski started off in a small steamer for Matadi, thirty miles farther up, the most distant navigable place on the lower reaches of the Congo.[12]

From Boma, on the threshold of the unknown, he sent a long letter to Poradowska, full of sentimental avowals.

> As to events—nothing new. As to feelings—nothing new either. And herein lies the misfortune; for if one could get rid of one's heart and memory (and also brain) and then acquire a new set of those things, life would become perfectly amusing. As it is impossible, life is not so; it is desperately sad! For example: one of the things I wanted to forget, unsuccessfully, was the memory of my charming aunt. Of course this is not possible and consequently I remember and am sad. Where are you? How are you? Have you forgotten me? Are you left alone? Are you working? Especially that! Have you found the forgetfulness and peace of creative, absorbing work? So there. I ask myself all that. You have given my life a new interest and a new affection; I am most grateful to you for this. Grateful for all the sweetness, for all the bitterness, of this priceless gift. I am looking now down two avenues cut in a thick and confused mass of dangerous foliage. Where do they lead? You follow one, I the other. They branch out. Will you find a ray of sunlight, however pale, at the end of yours? I hope you do! I wish it for you! For a long time I have not been interested in the end to which my road takes me. I have walked with my head lowered, cursing the stones. Now I am interested in another traveler. This makes me forget the small annoyances on my own road.[13]

"The annoyances" in the literal sense were to begin soon. We know about them from a diary that Korzeniowski kept for the first sixty-seven days of his

stay in the Congo. It is the only document of its kind among all Conrad materials. The author confined himself almost exclusively to short, factual notes that
enable us to reconstruct with a fair degree of accuracy the various stages of his
journey and the changes of his moods. What adds importance to the diary is the
fact that it is one of Korzeniowski's earliest known English texts. Here and there
are signs of French influence on the vocabulary, and Polish on the syntax, showing that the future writer had not yet completely mastered the English language.

At Matadi, Korzeniowski and Harou were held up for fifteen days by Joseph-
Louis-Hubert Gosse, the manager of the Company's local trading post. Korzeniowski made the following entries in his diary:

"Made the acquaintance of Mr. Roger Casement, which I should consider as
a great pleasure under any circumstances and now it becomes a positive piece of
luck. Thinks, speaks well, most intelligent and very sympathetic.

"Feel considerably in doubt about the future. Think just now that my life
amongst the people (white) around here cannot be very comfortable. Intend
avoid acquaintances as much as possible. . . .

". . . Have been myself busy packing ivory in casks. Idiotic employment.
Health good up to now. . . . Prominent characteristic of the social life here:
people speaking ill of each other." [14]

Many years later he wrote about his having shared a room with Casement
"for some three weeks," but the recollection must be inaccurate; Casement left
Matadi on 24 June and probably did not return until just before Korzeniowski's departure. [15] Roger Casement was at that time employed by the Compagnie
du Chemin de Fer du Congo as a supervisor of the projected building of a railway line from Matadi to Kinshasa. On several occasions Casement and Korzeniowski made joint expeditions into the nearby villages in search of Negro
porters, whose services were acquired by negotiating with the local chiefs. [16]
Casement was very well acquainted with the area, having already spent several
years in the Congo, once at Matadi as the manager of an American camp for
exploratory expeditions directed by General Henry Sanford.

In "Heart of Darkness," which contains a fairly large, albeit unevenly supplied, measure of autobiographical facts, Conrad presented the construction of
the railway line from Matadi as both chaotic and inefficient; he described a line
of chained black prisoner-porters and the grove of death where the sick and
utterly exhausted black workers were left to die slowly. Confusion, stupidity,
and cruelty sum up the fictional picture of that center of civilization. Although
Norman Sherry doubts whether Matadi was in fact so horrifying at that time,
he quotes an account, published in 1907 but relating to the year 1892, of a high
mortality rate among the railroad workers and the fact that blacks were forced
to work against their will; he does not explain why the situation in 1890 should
have been any different. [17]

But to recreate what Korzeniowski did see and experience during his stay in
the Congo, this kind of comparison is not the most important. Even if we estab-

lish what he could have seen and what he did actually see, we have to ask more basic questions: In what categories did he perceive it? How did he understand it? Louis Goffin, the Belgian engineer quoted by Sherry, claims that the enforced labor of the sick and terrified Negroes who were dying at the rate of five a day, was necessary in order to "construct this line of railway, to suppress for ever the far more awful tax of human porterage along this route of the caravans between the Upper and Lower Congo," but he overlooks the fact that the beaten Negroes were interested neither in having a railway line nor in the caravan route for transporting ivory to Europe. Another account cited by Sherry tells of the difficulties involved in finding porters for the construction of that line. An English missionary complained about their lack of subordination and their unwillingness to be moved from their homes.[18] And so once again we are presented with a white man's point of view, which ignores the fact that those porters were hired out by their village chiefs; that they were separated for weeks from their families; that they worked for no or little pay; that they were exposed to disease, mutilation, or death during the long marches with heavy loads; and, finally, that they saw no point in it all. The same situation may be looked at from two entirely opposite points of view: "stupid savages do not want to contribute to progress," or "poor wretches are forced to work till they drop dead."

Korzeniowski never subscribed to the first extreme, but his personal notes reflect an attitude different from that presented in "Heart of Darkness." Jotting down his immediate impressions in his diary and letters, he seemed to have been doing it from the position of a European traveler exposed to discomfort. One may assume that Casement, who was later to become famous for his crusade for humanitarian treatment of the natives in the colonies, told Korzeniowski about the practices of European administrators and traders. But we do not know what Casement's attitude was then and in what categories he saw the problems. After all, he had for many years been one of the cogs in the "civilizing" machinery and, at the time, he was in charge of the construction work on a railway line.

It is evident that Korzeniowski was struck at first by the greed and duplicity of the white bearers of "civilization" eager for quick profits, and by the chaos and stupidity of many of their enterprises. It was only later that he became aware of the outrages perpetrated against the native population and their country.

Matadi was, at that time, an important center of trade, inhabited by well over one hundred Europeans, but, above all, it was a center of communication and transport: the sea routes from the ocean and from Europe crossed the caravan route that lead into the rich interior of the Congo. Although Korzeniowski expected to leave Matadi by 19 June, he did not start on his 230-mile long journey until June 28.[19] Each day he sketched in his diary the road he had covered, marking the bearings and the profile of the terrain, in the belief that the data might be useful in the future. He was rather liberal in assessing the distance covered, sometimes counting as many as three or even more than four miles per hour, which was of course impossible.

Saturday, 28th June.
Left Matadi with Mr. Harou and a caravan of 31 men. Parted with Casement in a very friendly manner. Mr. Gosse saw us off as far as the State station. . . .

Sund[ay], 29th.
Ascent of Pataballa sufficiently fatiguing. Camped at 11h a.m. at Nsoke River. Misquitos [sic].

Monday, 30th.
To Congo da Lemba after passing black rocks. Long ascent. Harou giving up. Bother. Camp bad. Water far. Dirty. At night Harou better. . . .

Wednesday, 2nd July.
Started at 5:30 after a sleepless night. Country more open. Gently andulating [sic] hill. Road good in perfect order. (District of Lukungu.) Great market at 9:30. Bought eggs and chickens.
Feel not well today. Heavy cold in the head. Arrived at 11 at Banza Manteka. Camped on the market place. Not well enough to call on the missionary. Water scarce and bad. Camp[in]g place dirty. . . .

Thursday, 3rd July.
. . . Met an off[ic]er of the State inspecting; a few minutes afterwards saw at a camp[in]g place the dead body of a Backongo. Shot? Horrid smell. . . . Another range parallel to the first mentioned, with a chain of low foothills running close to it. . . . General tone of landscape gray-yellowish (dry grass), with reddish patches (soil) and clumps of dark-green vegetation scattered sparsely about, mostly in steep gorges between the high mountains or in ravines cutting the plain. Noticed Palma Christi—Oil Palm. Very straight, tall and thick trees in some places. Name not known to me. Villages quite invisible. . . .

Friday, 4th July.
Left camp at 6h a.m. after a very unpleasant night. Marching across a chain of hills and then in a maze of hills. At 8:15 opened out into an andulating [sic] plain. . . . Sharp ascents up very steep hills not very high. The higher mountains recede sharply and show a low hilly country. At 9:30 market place. . . .
Saw another dead body lying by the path in an attitude of meditative repose.

In the evening three women of whom one albino passed our camp. Horrid chalky white with pink blotches. Red eyes. Red hair. Features very Negroid and ugly. Mosquitos. At night when the moon rose heard shouts and drumming in distant villages. Passed a bad night.

Saturday, 5th July.
. . . Today fell into a muddy puddle. Beastly. The fault of the man that carried me. After camp[in]g went to a small stream, bathed and washed clothes. Getting jolly well sick of this fun. . . .

Sunday, 6th July.
Started at 5:40. The route at first hilly, then after a sharp descent traversing a broad plain. At the end of it a large market place. At 10h sun came out.

After leaving the market, passed another plain, then walking on the crest of a chain of hills passed 2 villages and at 11h arrived at Nsona. Village invisible. . . .

. . . good camp[in]g place. Shady. Water far and not very good. This night no mosquitos owing to large fires lit all round our tent. . . .

Monday, 7th July.
. . . Walking along an andulating [sic] plain towards the Inkandu market on a hill. Hot, thirsty and tired. At 11h arrived in the M[ar]ket place. About 200 people. Business brisk. No water. No camp[in]g place. After remaining for one hour, left in search of a resting place.

Row with carriers. No water. At last, about 1½ p.m., camped on an exposed hillside near a muddy creek. No shade. Tent on a slope. Sun heavy. Wretched. . . .
Night miserably cold. No sleep. Mosquitos.

Tuesday, 8th July.
The country presents a confused wilderness of hills land slips on their sides showing red. Fine effect of red hill covered in places by dark-green vegetation.[20]

For people unaccustomed to such physical exertions and to the climate, the journey must have been extremely tiring, although the travelers moved at the rate of a dozen or so miles a day, unburdened, and carried by the porters across bogs and rivers in hammocks. On the morning of 8 July they reached Manyanga, where an Englishman, Reginald Heyn, was manager of a transport base.[21] There the travelers stayed seventeen days. "Both have been sick," wrote Korzeniowski in his diary, "most kindly care taken of us." Sherry suggests, erroneously, that the time taken by the march—almost double the normal time—from Matadi to Kinshasa was not entirely justified and that it was the cause of Korzeniowski's conflict with his superiors.[22] However, Korzeniowski's march was by no means a slow one. If we compare the distances he covered with an official itinerary published a few years later for the benefit of caravans traveling from Matadi to Léopoldville, we see that he on the whole walked faster than the instructions suggested.[23] Besides, he was not making the protracted journey alone. The unscheduled halt in Manyanga had taken place with the knowledge of the Society's official and in the company of another of its employees, Prosper Harou, ill at the time, who, although a Congo veteran, fared worse than Korzeniowski. Also, the porters had to be changed in Manyanga and there may have been difficulties with finding new ones.

On the afternoon of 25 July the party started off on their way "with plenty of hammock carriers. H. lame and not in very good form. Myself ditto but not lame."

Sunday, 27th.

Left at 8h am. Sent luggage carriers straight on to Luasi and went ourselves round by the Mission of Sutili.

Hospitable reception by Mrs. Comber. All the missio[naries] absent.

The looks of the whole establishment eminently civilized and very refreshing to see after the lots of tumble-down hovels in which the State and Company agents are content to live. . . .

Tuesday, 29th.

Left camp at 7h after a good night's rest. Continuous ascent; rather easy at first. Crossed wooded ravines and the river Lunzadi by a very decent bridge.

At 9h met Mr Louette escorting a sick agent of the Comp[an]y back to Matadi. . . . Bad news from up the river. All the steamers disabled. One wrecked.

. . . Met ripe pineapple for the first time. On the road today passed a skeleton tied up to a post. Also white man's grave—no name. Heap of stones in the form of a cross.

Health good now.

Wednesday, 30th.

. . . Two hours' sharp walk brought me to Nsona na Nsefe. Market. ½ hour after, Harou arrived very ill with billious [sic] attack and fever. Laid him down in Gov[ernmen]t shimbek. Dose of Ipeca [sic]. Vomiting in enormous quantities. At 11h gave him 1 gramme of quinine and lots of hot tea. Hot fit ending in heavy perspiration. . . . Row with carriers all the way. Harou suffering much through the jerks of the hammock. . . .

Expect lots of bother with carriers tomorrow. Had them all called and made a speech which they did not understand. They promise good behaviour.

Thursday, 31st.

Left at 6h. Sent Harou ahead and followed in ½ hour. Road presents several sharp ascents and a few others easier but rather long. . . . Great difficulty

in carrying Harou. Too heavy. Bother. Made two long halts to rest the
carriers. . . .

Friday, 1st of August 1890.
Left at 6:30 am after a very indifferently passed night. Cold, heavy
mists. . . .
Put up at Gov[ernmen]t shanty.
Row between the carriers and a man stating himself in Gov[ernmen]t employ, about a mat. Blows with sticks raining hard. Stopped it. Chief came
with a youth about 13 suffering from gunshot wound in the head. Bullet entered about an inch above the right eyebrow and came out a little inside. The
roots of the hair, fairly in the middle of the brow in a line with the bridge of
the nose. Bone not damaged apparently. Gave him a little glycerine to put on
the wound made by the bullet on coming out. Harou not very well. Mosquitos. Frogs. Beastly. Glad to see the end of this stupid tramp. Feel rather
seedy. Sun rose red. . . .[24]

It was the dawn of August 2. On that day the caravan arrived at the port of
Kinshasa, the Company's next trade and transport base. The news about the
accidents involving steamers turned out to be only partly true. The *Florida*,
which Korzeniowski was to command, had been seriously damaged on 18 July
but on the twenty-third she was towed to Kinshasa for repair. The boat was
unfit for sailing but in any case Korzeniowski could not have assumed command immediately on an unknown river and in unfamiliar conditions. He was
therefore taken the next day on board the 15-ton river steamer *Roi des Belges*,
commanded by a twenty-five-year-old Dane, Ludvig Rasmus Koch.[25] The *Roi
des Belges* was hurrying off to help another steamer, the *Ville de Bruxelles*,
which on 16 July had got stuck on a root near Upoto.[26]
Before his departure from Kinshasa Korzeniowski posted his sixth letter
from the journey to Uncle Tadeusz, who replied:

I see from your last letter that you feel a deep resentment towards the Belgians for exploiting you so mercilessly. In general there is no love in your
heart for the Latin races, but this time, you must admit, nothing forced you
to put yourself into Belgian hands. You can say to yourself: "Tu l'as voulu,
Georges Dandin"; and if you had paid any attention to my opinion on the
subject when discussing it with me, you would have certainly detected a lack
of enthusiasm in me for this project.
As a traditional Polish szlachcic I value more the certain and less glamorous than a more glamorous uncertainty! In the first place, whatever happened, I ask you most sincerely to calm down and not to get worked up lest it
should affect your liver, "Ne vs gâter pas le sang et le foie." Secondly, let me
observe that by breaking your agreement you would expose yourself to con-

siderable financial loss, and you certainly lay yourself open to an accusation of irresponsibility which may be harmful to your further career. Unless your health becomes affected you should stick it out; at least that is my opinion.[27]

This is the first sign of Korzeniowski's becoming sufficiently displeased with working conditions in the Congo to consider breaking the contract after less than two months. We may guess that the reason directly responsible for it was not the fact that he had been forced, in spite of poor health, to start immediately on another journey, but his personal conflict with the Company's manager, Camille Delcommune, two years younger than himself. Delcommune, who wanted to leave as soon as possible to go up-river, awaited the new captain with impatience. Norman Sherry rightly points to the probability that the real conversation with Delcommune is reflected in the text and manuscript of "Heart of Darkness." "My first interview with the manager was curious. He did not ask me to sit down after my twenty-mile walk that morning. . . . He began to speak as soon as he saw me. I had been very long on the road. . . . He paid no attention to my explanations."[28] Knowing Korzeniowski's touchiness we can imagine how sharply he must have reacted at the reproof; or just at being addressed in a discourteous way; or, simply, at the manager's lack of interest in the reasons for the delay or in Korzeniowski's health. A photograph of Delcommune gives the impression of a bully; his "shipkeeper's" approach could antagonize "the Polish szlachcic cased in British tar," poisoning their relationship right from the start; moreover Korzeniowski's past experiences and impressions could not dispose him well toward the representative of the Company's highest authority in Africa. Alas, they were destined to spend a considerable time together.

The river steamer bearing the majestic name of *Roi des Belges*, in reality a small, clumsy, and noisy contraption resembling a tin box, packed tightly with passengers and the crew, left Kinshasa on 3 August on her way up the Congo.[29] Korzeniowski, watching Koch, got into the habit of recording in detail all navigation instructions, bearings, landmarks, dangerous spots, and so forth in his diary, whose second part consists almost entirely of notes on and sketches of the river bed. When they reached Bangala (later renamed Nouvelle Anvers) on 19 August, his entries stopped, either because he fell ill or because he heard—or decided himself—that he was not going to command a ship on the Congo.[30]

The notes reveal his total preoccupation, both as a potential commander and as a diarist, with the difficulties of navigation, which required constant concentration. "When about the middle of the open snatch steer right across to clear Ganchu's Point. Pass the point cautiously. Stones. . . . Sandbank always covered in the bight. . . . The landing must be approached cautiously on account of stones and snags. Round P[oin]t U cautiously. When entering the reach keep rather on the outer edge of the current following the right shore. Sandbank on left shore not visible. . . . Leave the island to starb[oard] and follow its inner shore to take the narrow p[assa]ge. Sound[in]gs 9 to 5 feet.

This passage is between the m[ai]n land on Port side and 2 islands on star-b[oar]d. Where the 1st is[lan]d finishes there is a sandbank. Steering close in to the islands in a s[ou]nd[ing]s 10 to 5 feet—Steer over to M[ai]n shore and back again." [31] And so it goes, page after page. Constant alertness was all the more needed since the boat advanced with exceptional speed. [32] It covered more than a thousand miles in twenty-eight days.

A reader of Korzeniowski's hastily jotted notes, accompanied by drawings relating mainly to the depth of the current, shallows, promontories, snags, is-lands, and reefs—notes that, apart from the river, concentrate almost exclu-sively on landmarks such as hilltops or trees discernible from afar, and places supplying timber—may easily recapture the sense of complete isolation from the rest of the world, the oppressive solitude, amidst water and jungle, that must have been experienced by the man in command.

Sherry's assertion that, in spite of "Heart of Darkness," Korzeniowski's im-pressions of the journey could not have been "a sense of oppressiveness and isolation" and that the passage up the Congo was "a routine, highly organised venture along a fairly frequented riverway linking quite numerous settlements of trading posts and factories," contrasts strongly with the picture suggested by the established evidence. [33] About two hundred miles above Kinshasa the Congo becomes a huge, elongated lake, interspersed with islands and shoals, with the other bank often invisible. True, the *Roi des Belges* apparently passed six other boats, but what were six small steamers in four weeks' navigation on a river whose banks were mostly hidden by tropical vegetation? In parts, the Congo measures a few miles in width; in others it spreads over ten, twisting and turning before it branches out into yet new creeks, meanders, and bays. It is not even certain whether they actually saw all those ships—at the rate of one every four-and-a-half days. They passed several missions hundreds of miles apart. And as to the villages, Korzeniowski spotted no more than six over a distance of more than five hundred miles. "Heart of Darkness" does not claim to be a dependable traveler's guide, but it does depict the threatening atmosphere of isolation quite convincingly.

In order to support his thesis about the density of population along the upper part of the Congo, Sherry cites statements by Alexandre Delcommune and a Belgian missionary, dating from 1888 and the beginning of 1890. [34] Those state-ments, however, lack substance; moreover, they refer mainly to a relatively short stretch—just over one hundred miles—of the river. Both reports ap-peared in the Brussels *Mouvement Géographique*, which, of course, published only encouragingly optimistic material. Six months after Korzeniowski, a group of traders covered the same route on board the same steamer, and one of them wrote in a letter to Europe: "The country is ruined. Passengers in the steamer *Roi des Belges* have been able to see for themselves that from Bontya, half a day's journey below our factory at Upoto, to Boumba [that is, about two hundred miles along the river] inclusive, there is not an inhabited village left— that is to say four days' steaming through a country formerly so rich, today entirely ruined."[35] This impartial document is valuable not only as geographic information but also as testimony to the effects of Belgian colonization.

On board the river steamer, apart from Koch and Korzeniowski, there was a Belgian mechanic named Gossens, and about twenty-five black crew members (recruited usually from among the Bangalis, not averse to cannibalism). The steamer was a wood-burning vessel, and many hands were needed to keep her running. In addition to two canoes the *Roi des Belges* towed two scows for carrying the wood supply that had to be periodically replenished. Woodcutters worked at night felling and chopping trees in places previously selected. There were also four passengers on board—Camille Delcommune and three agents of the Company (Alphonse Keyaerts, E. F. L. Rollin, and Vander Heyden).[36]

Neither the captain nor—most probably—his assistant had much time for contact with other Europeans on board. J. R. Troup, who on that same *Roi des Belges* took part in one of Stanley's expeditions, left the following description of the working routine of then-Captain Schagerström: "He would be at his post on the bridge, shouting his orders, and we would soon be again on our way . . . Schagerström used to take up his quarters [on the upper deck] from the time we started till we pulled up for the night, some ten hours, and would have his breakfast and lunch sent up to him while he was engaged in piloting us through the intricate channels of the mighty Congo! There was no one to share this task with him, to relieve him of his anxieties."[37]

On 1 September 1890 the party reached Stanley Falls (now Kisangani), which was then an important government station and a district administrative center. It was there that the representative of the government of the Congo Free State lived, and a military detachment was stationed under the command of a white second lieutenant; there were many administration buildings and trade agencies, warehouses with ivory, and so forth. Stanley Falls represented a strategic point not only as the last town in the upper part of the river that could be reached by steamers, but chiefly because of its significant role in the long-lasting conflict between the Arabs and the Belgians.[38] The main object of the Arab penetration of West Africa was the slave trade, which the European countries strongly opposed, thereby helping the natives. This help was, however, only temporary, since European exploitation turned out to be more drastic and even more destructive for the blacks than the old form.

In his essay "Geography and Some Explorers" (1923), Conrad recalls, "The subdued thundering mutter of the Stanley Falls hung in the heavy night air of the last navigable reach of the Upper Congo, while no more than ten miles away, in Reshid's camp just above the Falls, the yet unbroken power of the

Congo Arabs slumbered uneasily. Their day was over. . . . I said to myself with awe, 'This is the very spot of my boyish boast.'"[39]

In place of romance and adventure he found ruthless competition for trade and power, and an organization bent on making quick, huge profits. In place of primordial vegetation, he found a landscape where the jungle, exploding with succulent foliage, contrasted grotesquely with the angular elements of imported architecture. All those European buildings that were a source of pride to the local whites must have given him the impression of façades incongruously superimposed upon the omnipresent density of tropical nature. Even the small misshapen steamer, oozing smoke and shaking and croaking, could be taken for a symbol of the repellent, albeit profitable, European penetration.

After several days in Stanley Falls, Korzeniowski received the following letter of appointment from Delcommune, dated 6 September:

> Mr. Conrad Korzeniowski,
> Captain.
> I have the honor to ask you to take over the command of the SS *Roi des Belges* as of today, until the recovery of Captain Koch.
> Yours etc.
> Camille Delcommune[40]

As a matter of fact, this nomination constitutes the only basis for Conrad's later claim of having commanded a "steamer." The date of departure has not been established, but it may be inferred from the fact that on 15 September the *Roi des Belges* was halfway down the river, and that she reached Kinshasa on the twenty-fourth; thus she probably left Stanley Falls on the seventh or eighth.[41]

The steamer took aboard George Antoine Klein, a twenty-seven-year-old Frenchman suffering from dysentery, who had recently been appointed the Company's commercial agent at Stanley Falls.[42] Klein died during the journey, on 21 September, and was buried at Tchumbiri.[43] His name, later changed to Kurtz, may be found in the manuscript of "Heart of Darkness."[44] Apart from Klein's presence on board, and his death, there seems to be no reason to suppose that he had much in common with the demonic character in the novel.[45]

It is not known whether or for how long Korzeniowski was in command of the ship on the way to Kinshasa. When the *Roi des Belges* arrived in Bangala on 15 September, Captain Koch was already back in charge.[46] Going downstream with the current, the steamer now moved almost twice as fast. There is nothing to indicate that Korzeniowski was still preparing himself for command in the upper part of the Congo. We know that he had no choice but to remain in the company of a man toward whom he felt a strong—and reciprocated—antipathy.

On his arrival at Kinshasa on 24 September, Korzeniowski found a letter

from his Uncle Kazimierz's daughter, Maria Bobrowska, who had just married
Teodor Tyszka, as well as three letters from Madame Poradowska. Without delay he sent back an affectionate letter to his "Dear Maryleczka," "Indeed, I do
not deserve to have a place in your heart—for I am practically a stranger to
you—nevertheless the affectionate words you have written are most precious to
me. I shall carefully preserve them in my heart." Of his plans he wrote, "I am
very busy with all the preparations for a new expedition to the River Kasai. In
a few days I shall probably be leaving Kinchassa again for a few months, possibly even for a year or longer." [47]

Unfortunately, until now no one has established what expedition Korzeniowski had in mind—it has been assumed to be the expedition up the River Lomami,
undertaken several weeks later by Camille Delcommune's elder brother, Alexandre. [48] The expedition up the River Kasai would have followed a different
route, shorter and more explored. Korzeniowski might have thought that he
would sail in one of the Company's steamers, of which there were three. [49] Two
days later, as we learn from his extensive letter to Poradowska, his employers
changed their plans.

No point in deceiving oneself! I definitely regret having come here. I regret
bitterly. With a man's typical selfishness I shall talk about myself. I cannot
·stop myself. To whom should I unburden my heart if not to you? . . .

I find everything repugnant here. Men and things, but especially men. And
I am repugnant to them, too. From the director in Africa, who has taken the
trouble of telling a good many people of his intense dislike of me, down to
the lowest mechanic, all have a gift of getting on my nerves; as a result I am
not as pleasant to them as I might be. The director is a common ivory-dealer
with sordid instincts who imagines himself a merchant while in fact he is
only a kind of African shopkeeper. His name is Delcommune. He hates the
English, and I am of course regarded as one. While he is here I can hope for
neither promotion nor a raise in salary. Anyhow, he told me that promises
made in Europe are not binding here unless they are in the contract. . . .
Anyhow, I cannot expect anything since I have no vessel to command. The
new boat will be finished in June of next year, perhaps. Meanwhile my position here is vague, and I am having troubles because of that. . . .

To crown the pleasures, my health is far from good. *Keep it to yourself*, but
the truth is that going up the river I had the fever four times in two months,
and then at the Falls (its native country) I had an attack of dysentery which
lasted five days. I feel rather weak physically, and a little bit discouraged, and
upon my word I think I am homesick for the sea and want to look again on
the expanse of that salt water which has so often cradled me, which has so
many times smiled at me in the sparkling sunshine of a beautiful day, which
many times too has thrown in my face the threat of death, with a whirl of
white foam whipped by the wind under a dark December sky. I miss all that.

But most of all I regret having tied myself down for three years. True, it is hardly likely that I shall last them out. Either they will pick some groundless quarrel with me to send me home (and on my soul I sometimes wish they would), or another attack of dysentery will send me back to Europe, if not into the other world, which would at last solve finally all my troubles![50]

Looking for a way of leaving Africa without breaking his contract, Korzeniowski turned back to the idea, based on false information, that he could command one of the Company's ocean-going ships.

What was the reason for the conflict with Delcommune and the other employees of the Société Anonyme? Strangely, neither Jean-Aubry nor Baines poses this question, and Sherry confines himself to the already mentioned possibility that the director was antagonized by Korzeniowski's slow journey from Matadi to Kinshasa. This, however, would not justify the profound and reciprocal antipathy affecting the entire staff of the Company. Besides, Korzeniowski was not the only British employee. It is difficult to ward off the suspicion that the explanation lay precisely in those "base instincts" that motivated not only Delcommune but also the Company itself and practically everything else that Korzeniowski had unexpectedly encountered in Africa. "Unreliable" persons, and Korzeniowski must have appeared as such to the speculators, are not admitted to business. In those days the profits of the trading companies exploiting the Congo amounted to several hundred percent of the invested capital per year. To get some idea of their methods of work, it is worth noting that agents were paid high premiums for bringing down the costs of procuring rubber and ivory; thus, massive deliveries of those commodities were made compulsory, and punitive expeditions, made up of members of hostile tribes and cannibals, were launched against noncomplying natives. For the Negroes, however, those enforced deliveries often meant starvation, since they were left with no time to cultivate and harvest their land. Bribery, as well as the disposal of unreliable witnesses, served to conceal those practices.[51]

Ending his letter of 26 September to Madame Poradowska, Korzeniowski wrote, "I am leaving in an hour by canoe for Bamou, to select wood and have it cut for the construction of the local station. I shall remain in the forest camp for 2 or 3 weeks, unless ill. It suits me, rather." Bamou is a village on the French side of the Congo, about thirty miles down the river from Kinshasa. We do not know how long he stayed there, but it is certain that he fell ill. On 19 October he wrote from Kinshasa to Bobrowski that he was unwell and intended to return to Europe. His uncle commented, "I found your handwriting so greatly changed—which I ascribe to the weakening and exhausting effect of fever and dysentery—that I have since then given myself over to far from happy thoughts! I made no secret from you that I was absolutely against your African plans."[52]

On 24 October 1890, four days after Korzeniowski dispatched his letter to Kazimierówka, Captain Duhst, a Dane in the service of the Congo Free State, himself ill at the time and carried in a hammock, made the following entry in his diary: "Camped in a negro town, which is called Fumemba [a day and a half's walk from Kinshasa]. I am in company with an English Captain Conrad from the Kinshassa Company: he is continually sick with dysentery and fever." And again on 27 October: "Marched from 6 morning until 9, when we ate breakfast. We are just on the spot where Lieutenant Puttervelle died and I was ill with fever. Here the ways part, and I took leave of Captain Conrad, who is going to Manyanga and Isangila, and from there to Vivi." By 10 November Duhst was already at Boma, and there he mentioned Korzeniowski for the last time: "Have not seen Captain Conrad since I left him in Manyanga."[53] Sherry writes, "It is possible that Conrad stayed at Manyanga to recuperate, as he did on the upward journey. There can be no doubt at all that Conrad's illness was at its most severe during this last journey over the caravan trail."[54] And he follows with a recollection of Conrad's wife: "I had heard from several of his friends how nearly he had died from dysentery while being carried to the coast when he left the Congo."[55]

And so the expedition came to an end. We know quite well how it began: the initial negotiations and preparations, the bravura and despondency on the passage to Africa, the exhausting march upstream along the great river. Gradually, as Korzeniowski penetrates deeper and deeper into the interior, getting closer to the core of affairs, scented with rubber and gleaming with ivory, he vanishes from sight. The image becomes confused, blurred, obscure. There is something symbolic when a wanderer recedes into the dark regions of our ignorance about his movements and thoughts, simultaneously nearing the end of his dismal experiences and of his own strength.

We hardly know anything about his life during the last months of the year 1890. He was at Kinshasa at the time that the great exploratory expedition of Alexandre Delcommune was starting on its way aboard the *Ville de Bruxelles* and the already repaired *Florida*.[56] He had seen, before his own expedition to Bamou, the members of the Delcommune expedition, whom he was later to describe so caustically in "Heart of Darkness."[57] November is shrouded in obscurity. Of December all we know is that on the fourth he was at Matadi.[58] We do not know when and on what boat he returned to Europe. Toward the end of January he appeared in Brussels; on 1 February he was in London.[59] His letters contain no mention of his recent experiences. Apparently he just wanted to forget.

This period of obscurity, mystery, and struggle against death was also, according to all evidence, the time when the final change took place in Korzeniowski's way of looking at the African reality and the categories of apprehending it. It was only when he supervised the wood cutting at Bamou that he became directly acquainted with the colonizers' methods of work in the country's interior. Later, during his serious and long illness and during convalescence, he could gather up information about what had been going on around him, information that could not be expressed in the simple terms of chaos and individual greed. It was then that he arrived at the verdict, which he was to recall several months before his death, when writing about the Stanley Falls: ". . . the unholy recollection of a prosaic newspaper 'stunt' and the distasteful knowledge of the vilest scramble for loot that ever disfigured the history of human conscience and geographical exploration."[60]

He was depressed and embittered and tried to forget, possibly also because as suggested in "Heart of Darkness" (itself more important as a psychological than a historical and descriptive document), he was aware of having been only a step from himself becoming one of the gang of plunderers. His frequently expressed mistrust of human nature had, I suspect, not only an intellectual but also a personal basis.

Thirteen years later, having made two fictional returns to his African experiences—in "An Outpost of Progress" and "Heart of Darkness"—Conrad wrote to R. B. Cunninghame Graham of wanting to learn Spanish in order to read the lives of conquistadores "If only to forget all about our modern Conquistadores. Their achievement is monstrous enough in all conscience—but not as a great human force let loose, but rather like that of a gigantic and obscene beast. Leopold is their Pizarro, Thys their Cortez and their 'lances' are recruited amongst the souteneurs, sous-offs, maquereaux, fruits-secs [pimps, non-coms, bullies, and failures] of all sorts on the pavement of Brussels and Antwerp." And he ends the letter by suggesting that Graham ought to meet Roger Casement: "He could tell you things! Things I've tried to forget; things I never did know."[61]

In his writer's memory the Congo became fixed forever as a nightmare—all the more difficult to shake off since it was also a reality. I think Jean-Aubry may have been mistaken when he wrote that in setting out for Africa Korzeniowski "cared little about fostering so-called progress."[62] True, he did not care about it later when he began to feel a well-justified disgust with the whole action carried out in the name of progress. He must have been familiar with the manifesto of the Association established in 1884 by "His Majesty the King of the Belgians for the purpose of promoting the civilization and commerce of Africa and for other humane and benevolent purposes."[63] He saw for himself what those "humane and benevolent purposes" meant in practice; how under the guise of "maintaining order" bloody pacifications and hunting for laborers took place; how crops were being destroyed and villages burnt in order to force the natives to work; how minor offences were punished by flogging men or cutting off their hands; and how in every case the main motive of action was the desire for a quick gain. Hence, the origin of Conrad's obvious aversion to colonialism, visible in his works but by no means common in contemporary literature, particularly in England. Until then he had only very superficial knowledge of colonialism, acquired on his sea voyages and travels between the islands of the Malay Archipelago.

The significance of Conrad's African experience is not, however, limited to the fact that it made him one of the fiercest critics of the "white man's mission." From the psychological point of view it is important because this expedition represented his most daring, and in fact his last, attempt to become a *homo socialis*, a cog in the mechanism of society. By accepting the job in the Trading Company, he joined, for once in his life, an organized, large-scale group activity on land.

Contrasting life at sea with life on land is one of Conrad's characteristic motifs. And although in his works the sea has many aspects—from providing a background of sublime beauty for human dramas and reflections to the cruelly indifferent element that cannot be trusted for a single moment—the comparison always comes out in favor of the sea. "Land affairs" are a suspect and dubious medley of events, contradictory desires, low motives, false ideas, and illusory beliefs. The sea represents a realm ruled by simple duties, a clearly defined hierarchy of values, comradeship, and honest good work.

This contrast, and the consequent condemnation of "land affairs," may be traced, both chronologically and causally, to the African episode. By taking up work in the Congo, Korzeniowski realized one of the long series of ideas that had been constantly in his mind from his Marseilles days: to join a profit-making enterprise and, at the same time, to lead a life contained within the framework of a social order. He found the sea both alluring and exciting, but in almost all of his long-term plans that are known to us, we see that he inclined rather toward a life that was at least partly settled and connected with the mainland; he did not want to remain a lonely wanderer.

His only serious attempt to realize those aspirations was the voyage to the Congo, with its tempting visions of making quick profit embellished by the label "in the service of civilization." We must remember that his endeavour was not limited to the long marches in the tropical country nor in steaming up river; it also involved negotiations with the Company's directors, visits to the Brussels head office, discussions and arguments with officials. At the roots of the disappointment that he encountered, at the source of the complete defeat that ended his venture, we find both his illness (one cannot exclude the possibility that it was aggravated by an attack of depression) and his moral protest against the colonizers' practices as he saw them at close range; we observe, too, his inability to coexist with people he despised and whose principles he could neither approve nor tolerate. The result of those experiences was twofold: a condemnation of colonialism and a rejection of the "land-dwelling" community. It is not accidental that the Congo expedition remained an isolated event in Conrad's life. Until his death he remained a recluse in the social sense and never became involved with any institution or clearly defined group of people. To a certain extent it was due to his health, which, never very strong, deteriorated after 1890 to the point of becoming seriously undependable.

VI

· · · · · · · · · · · ·

THE SAIL AND THE PEN
1891–1894

KORZENIOWSKI had expected that "the first sea breeze would restore
him to health," and it seemed at first that his hopes would be fulfilled.
At the end of January 1891, after a few weeks of sea travel, he arrived
in Europe. In spite of swollen legs he felt reasonably well, and a visit to his doctor reassured him that "although a bit anaemic he was otherwise quite healthy."
It was probably then that for the first time he rented the two furnished rooms at
17 Gillingham Street, a small street behind Victoria Station, that were his London base for the next six years.[1]

Once he was settled, Korzeniowski renewed his search for employment. Poradowska, whom he had visited in Brussels after his return from the Congo and
with whom he continued to carry on a lively and affectionate correspondence,
was once again expected to help. "I think I shall be able to go back to work
in six weeks. Provided I find any!? If you think something might be gained by
approaching Pécher, I wish you to know that I am thirty-two years old; have
English Master's Certificate of service in sailing- and steamships; have commanded both, but mainly sailing ships; can produce good references from shipowners and also from London merchants."[2] Korzeniowski was obviously aware
that finding a post was not going to be easy, for he made himself a year younger
and embellished his career: he had commanded a sailing ship only once and
never a steamer, except for the few days going down the Congo when he replaced Captain Koch.

Despite these "improvements" to his record and his genuinely energetic
efforts, Korzeniowski could not find employment. Difficulty walking—"I go
out little, in order not to tire my legs"—created an additional obstacle. He went
to Scotland between 10 and 15 February, but the journey was unsuccessful.
On his return he immediately wrote to Uncle Bobrowski, who answered from
Kazimierówka: "Dear beloved boy! I received your last letter, of the 4/16th
February, on my return from Kiev, and I share with you the regret you feel at
the deformity of your legs (one of which is still swollen while the other is its
normal size) and I also deplore the thinness of your hair, presaging as it does
future baldness. But, in the store of my life's experience, I find no remedy for
this; and we must therefore pass from this touchy matter to the next item on
the agenda, and patiently await whatever the gods of hair-growth decide!"[3]

The gods of hair-growth were to prove quite benevolent; meanwhile, Bobrow-ski, worried about his nephew's health, sent him 300 rubles. The money arrived in London just in time: toward the end of February Korzeniowski had entered the German Hospital at Dalston in northeastern London. He was placed there by one of his earliest London friends, "good old" Adolf Krieger, an American of German origin, seven years his senior.[4] Korzeniowski spent about a month in bed, suffering from gout, neuralgic pains in his right arm, and recurrent attacks of malaria.

Korzeniowski's ailments were less acute than his psychological crisis. It is im-possible to tell now whether his physical afflictions were the cause or the effect; it is certain, however, that all the symptoms mentioned in his letters show that he suffered from pathological depression, and depression, on reaching its crisis, quite often finds an outlet in the form of somatic illness. Bobrowski expressed anxiety at his nephew's being "dispirited and weak," and quite rightly urged him to help the doctors "by not yielding to lassitude or depression—for as you say: 'le moral réagit sur la phisique' [sic]."[5] After his stay in the Congo, Kor-zeniowski's letters to Poradowska, though containing much the same familiar mixture of jokes, lyrical effusions, and skeptical exclamations, acquire a stronger tone of gloomy affectation: in April 1891, for instance, he wrote, "I see everything with such discouragement—everything in black. My nerves have completely gone to pieces."[6]

Even for specialists in direct contact with the patient it is sometimes difficult to diagnose a mental ailment. In the case of a man known only through his works and letters, and the recollections of other people, extreme caution is re-quired. Nevertheless, the evidence indicating that Korzeniowski-Conrad suf-fered from depression in the strict psychiatric sense of the term is so strong that it is nearly impossible to doubt it. Surprisingly, however, no biographer until now has advanced this diagnosis; no definitive proof exists, and, as is usual in psychiatry, the picture as a whole is of greater significance than any element taken separately. The following chapters will record much of the relevant evi-dence, but it will not be specifically produced to support the hypothesis of de-pression. In general I try, as far as it is plausible, to explain Conrad's behavior and moods without reference to his mental malady. After all, he had many real reasons for feeling dejected, for doubting his own strength, for anxiety and in-decision. Nonetheless, the frequency and intensity of his attacks of melan-cholia, the circumstances of their occurrence and the accompanying physical symptoms, call for a general medical explanation. The story of Korzeniowski's early years points the same way: it has been established that early loss of one parent, not to say both of them, frequently foreshadows later depression; and also that most of those who suffer from depression in adult life come from lov-ing families and emotionally warm environments, shattered by a devastating blow.[7]

What are the characteristic symptoms of depression? Sadness; a feeling of incapacity; fatigue; heaviness of limbs; anxiety coupled with listlessness; aversion to any mental or physical activity; continuous self-reproach; thoughts of guilt and punishment; inability to concentrate, sometimes to the extent of stupor; a slowing down of the capacity for work, especially when it is beyond the ordinary routine; frequent and exaggerated symptoms of physical ailments, particularly of the digestive tract; sense of loneliness; fear of madness and of the disintegration of personality (manifesting itself in the vagueness of one's vision of oneself); suicidal tendencies; seeing the bad side of everything; delusions of calamities and disaster; shrinkage of psychological space; loss of vivid imagination; seeing his world in gray and dark colors, and feeling it is unreal and chaotic. Throughout, however, the consciousness remains lucid, and the memory and intelligence are unimpaired.[8]

Those symptoms do not, of course, have to occur simultaneously and with equal intensity. In Korzeniowski's case, however, we observe all the symptoms in the course of the thirty (and more) years for which we have enough biographical material; usually a few symptoms appear simultaneously, indicating an attack of depression. I believe that the first such attack occurred at the beginning of 1891. Since the symptoms for different kinds of depression are very similar it is difficult to establish the character of the one from which Conrad suffered. Moreover, psychiatrists differ in their use of terminology, and there would be no point here in retracing their debates. Korzeniowski-Conrad displayed symptoms of both psychotic and neurotic depression, and had in his background elements typical for both, but neurotic symptoms were decidedly more numerous.[9] Therefore, I believe that in his maturity he was subject to neurotic depression, although at times its bouts look like phases of a manic-depressive cycle with the manic phase attenuated, characteristic of endogenous depression.[10] There are instances of such a cyclical pattern in Conrad's life; for example, in the spring of 1891 a period of stark despondency was followed by a period of exceptional liveliness; but the evidence is hardly decisive, and one can only be sure that from early youth Conrad was prone to melancholia and that in his later years the tendency sometimes took morbid forms.

Toward the end of March Korzeniowski left the hospital. He must have put up a brave front for the sake of his uncle, for Bobrowski wrote on 11 April:

My dear boy! Yesterday I received your last letter, written on the 30 March (your style). Thank the Lord that you have left your bed, but from your description, which you try to make comic, I see that you are still very enfeebled and very exhausted—and the slightest thing may lay you prostrate again. For God's sake, take care of yourself, for I have reason to suppose (you hinted at this indirectly) that you have overtaxed your strength during your stay in Africa, and Mme Marguerite said the same in her letter, and that instead of taking a rest either in Brussels or in London you dashed off to Scotland. Thus I have bad reports about my dear and honoured Sir, in respect of his senseless behaviour towards himself. I appeal for and demand more sense and the utmost prudence in the treatment of my beloved young Master, and I await the fulfillment of my wish!

You have just informed me of the recommendation made by Dr. Ludwig: that you should go to Switzerland. The fact that previously he had in mind the seaside, makes me think that you are very exhausted and he hopes that the bracing air of the Swiss mountains will help you to recover your strength and put on some flesh. Some place like Interlaken or Righi-Culm. If that is the case then we must give up the thought of Kazimierówka. . . . Discuss it all, my dear boy, with the doctor. But do not insinuate anything yourself and do not give any erroneous information about the peculiarities of our climate. Weigh together all the considerations from the point of view of your own advantage and welfare—even if it means something less pleasurable—and decide what you are to do. Switzerland is not very expensive. . . . Write to me, my dear lad, how you stand financially at present; have you still got anything in your pocket? What do they charge for a month's stay in a Maison de Santé? Panie Bracie, let your answer be as sincere as my question is. You know me not to be over-generous, but if there is need for it I shall draw what's necessary to save your health. Parsimony must give way![11]

Konrad's finances must have been poor, because at the beginning of June Bobrowski again sent him 200 rubles. In March he had still felt unequal to negotiating for the command of a small steamship belonging to the Prince Steam Shipping Co. Ltd.[12] He could walk, but his health was not improving and his gloom persisted and deepened. In his letter to Maria Tyszka he complained about his swollen hands, which made writing difficult.[13] "My nerves are disordered, causing heart palpitations and difficulty in breathing," he confided to Poradowska on 1 May. At that time he also sent his uncle a letter "full of sadness and despondency," greatly upsetting the old gentleman. Unable to find employment (or rather unable to undertake any), Korzeniowski remained jobless. He lived on his uncle's money; his future looked dim. The depression persisted. "I am still plunged in deepest night and my dreams are only nightmares," he lamented to Poradowska.[14] Finally he decided to follow his uncle's advice and go to Switzerland for a water cure.

Korzeniowski left London on 20 May for the chosen spa, Champel-les-Bains on the outskirts of Geneva.[15] After an overnight stay in Paris he arrived on 21 May in Champel, where he took a room in La Roseraie, a large, four-storied pension on the River Arve, about half an hour's walk from the center of town. On the twenty-sixth he began water therapy, which soon brought good results. He assured Poradowska that he was feeling "much better, if not quite cured."[16]

As his energy returned, he embarked on the seventh chapter of *Almayer's Folly*.[17] "Thank the Lord you are better and that the cure at Champel is beneficial to you!" was Bobrowski's overjoyed reaction to his nephew's letter of 28 May.[18]

From impatience, or perhaps for the sake of economy, Korzeniowski cut short his treatment on 14 June. Once again he stopped in Paris for one day to visit his "aunt." He also called on her uncle, Dr. Paul Gachet, a physician and art collector who had looked after van Gogh in the last months of the painter's life. The paintings of the Post-impressionists, mainly Cézanne and van Gogh, turned out not to be to Korzeniowski's taste.[19] By 16 June he was back in London. Bobrowski did not approve of how his nephew had hurried his convalescence, and criticized him for foolhardiness: "I hope that Dr Platz did not let you go off too soon or that you didn't run away too soon from him. This is the important question, for indeed I fear a relapse." He did not spare both admonition and advice on professional and financial matters:

> Now we must be careful not to allow your health to deteriorate and to find an acceptable position for you. If, as you say, you have had enough of Africa—although I suppose the Niger is not the same as the Congo—then you are right to have refused. I perceive that you are inclined to settle in London for good, and I see that in this matter you rely on Mr Hope's help: his friendliness and eloquence are to persuade Capt. Noble to resign in favour of Capt. Nałęcz. However, I doubt if things will work out this way . . . I only keep asking myself the question why, having decided to remain in London, you don't take a job with Barr, Möring & Cie? This is how I explain it: you have no capital and not wishing to become a subordinate where you might have been a partner, you have decided to look straight away for other employment. Anyhow, this is the impression I got from a paragraph of a letter you wrote before departing for the Congo. You then informed me of your wish to leave to Mr Krieger whatever sum is left on your account. As it is a weakness shown by all the dreamers known to me to leave a legacy behind them . . . so I deduce that you are, firstly, penniless, and, secondly, a dreamer. Is that so, Panie Bracie?—no offence meant.[20]

Bobrowski's mention of Korzeniowski having been offered employment in Nigeria is the only information on the subject we possess; possibly a small river steamer belonging to the Prince company was to cruise up the Niger.

From 18 to 22 June and 3 to 6 July, Korzeniowski went sailing twice in the Channel and the North Sea on a yacht belonging to his friend, G. F. W. Hope, with whom his relations had been close for several years; Hope's third son, born in 1890, was baptized "Conrad."[21] Korzeniowski's spirits improved considerably, as we see from his uncle's letter: "My heart is overjoyed at reading your last letters from which I can see that you have recovered your old health and humour, which go in harness with you—as indeed with anybody—but particularly in the case of highly strung people." [22]

Unfortunately, this relaxed mood was short-lived; Bobrowski's misgivings turned out to have been true: on 18 July Konrad wrote to his uncle, "I am feeling quite well, although mentally only so so, but this will improve." [23] And by the thirtieth he found himself back in bed, with fever, in a bad physical and mental state. His illness, however, did not last long, and on 4 August he could at last begin to work; in spite of everything, it was in a warehouse and for the firm Barr, Moering and Company. Konrad concealed both his illness and the delay in starting to work from his uncle; meanwhile Bobrowski, at his request, drew up a portrait of his nephew's character and of the traditions of the whole Korzeniowski family:

> Today, you yourself ask me to indicate those shortcomings of your character that I have observed during the thirty-four years of your life, with the help of my "cold reason"; shortcoming that make your life difficult, as you yourself admit. You state in advance that you cannot perceive them yourself, and you therefore request me to conduct this operation upon your person. If this is an oblique way of evoking my assurances, and even of my swearing that I have not perceived even the slightest shortcomings in you and that I consider you perfection without flaw, then forgive me, Panie Bracie, but I shall not say that, because I regard you as an ordinary mortal with ordinary shortcomings, since who is free from them? . . . Well then, I consider that you have always lacked endurance and perseverance in decisions, which is the result of your instability in your aims and desires. You lack endurance, Panie Bracie, in the face of facts—and, I suppose, in the face of people too? This is a trait of character inherited from your Grandfather—your paternal Uncle—and even your Father:—in short the Nałęczs. . . . Your Father was an idealistic dreamer; he certainly loved people and he certainly wished happiness for them—although he usually applied two measures to them:—he was a lenient judge of the poor and the weak of this world—and he was very sharp and pitiless towards the rich and powerful; hence we have a cleavage. They all had a high opinion of themselves and suffered much after their failures—suffered more intensely than appeared or could be expected. Thus, Panie Bracie, you also are subject to these inherited shortcomings and you too bear their punishment. In your projects you let your imagination run away with you—you become an optimist; but when you encounter disappointments you fall easily into pessimism—and as you have a lot of pride, you suffer more as the result of disappointments than somebody would who had a more moderate imagination but was endowed with greater endurance in activity and relationships. This is what I think in this matter, and let me repeat again what I said

in my last letter: these are shortcomings, but even with them one can be loved, while life itself will in time teach you a better perspective when judging people and facts.[24]

Although the squire and jurist from Kazimierówka boasted of his rationalistic impartiality, he was again painting a satirically exaggerated picture. The evaluation of the radical democrat Apollo Korzeniowski by the moderate liberal Bobrowski must of course have been partial and politically conditioned. Given such divergent views, Apollo's ambition was bound to look like egotism to his brother-in-law. As to Konrad himself, Bobrowski, although kind and sagacious, was neither aware of the nature of his nephew's nervous disorder nor able to appreciate the weight of psychological pressure the lonely and sensitive wanderer had to bear. Nevertheless, Konrad was quite ready to agree to a large extent with his guardian; soon after receiving the quoted letter he wrote to Poradowska, "One admires what one lacks. That is why I admire perseverance and fidelity and constancy."[25]

We do not know whether Bobrowski's disquisition was only a general reply to a question or whether it implicitly referred to some recent event. We may guess, however, that Korzeniowski, as was his wont, spent over six months of his half-enforced inactivity making projects too diverse to allow for any directed concentration of energy.

Among those projects and attempts may probably be included translating from the Polish, about which occupation we read in a somewhat mysterious letter, hitherto unnoticed by biographers, written by Andrew De Ternant.[26] Apparently Korzeniowski worked for about two months for an Oxford Street agency, where he translated business letters from "Slavonic languages" into English. The work turned out to be unprofitable. What is more interesting, however, is that Korzeniowski supposedly translated into English some Polish short stories, which he showed to Edgar Lee, the assistant editor of *St. Stephen's Review* (he was probably inspired by the example of Poradowska, who had rendered several tales into French). Mr. Lee, however, rejected the texts because, as De Ternant noted, "all of them were much too revolutionary for a Conservative weekly journal like the *St. Stephen's Review*." It is not possible to guess what Polish short stories Korzeniowski could have translated. If one is to take seriously De Ternant's remark about their "revolutionary" character—presumably only so when judged by the rather mild standards of the time—the most probable works are Stefan Żeromski's early stories, which were published in Warsaw by *Głos*. Anyway, we know too little about the episode to venture more detailed hypotheses. Whatever Korzeniowski did translate, it is obvious that he was attracted to literature.

Apart from his general admonitions, Bobrowski gave Konrad one other specific warning: it concerned his relations with Marguerite Poradowska: "Well, it seems to me that you both fail to see that you are only flirting with each other since the death of poor Oleś—as an old sparrow friendly to you both I advise you to give up this game, which will end in nothing sensible. A worn-out female, and if she is to remarry, it will be with Buls who would give her a position and love—of which he has given proof. It would be a stone round your neck for you—and for her as well. If you are wise you will leave this amusement alone and part simply as friends: if not, however, you have been warned!—and you will not be able to say later on that you were not warned!"[27]

Bobrowski continued his warnings in the next letter: "My Dear Boy, If the Prince of Benevento [i.e., Talleyrand] of 'accursed memory' was right when he said that 'speech (in this case the written word) was given to us to conceal our thoughts,' then, Panie Bracie, you have coped most efficiently with the task, telling me on five whole pages about all the young and old, ugly or beautiful, English women you know, who importune you to flirt with them successfully or unsuccessfully,—God only knows which!—and all this to omit The Only One whom I suspect of such practices with you:—and she not a flat-footed English woman but a certain Margaret well known to me!! There is no need for you to carry into effect the aphorism of that lame Prince and to lie both to me and to yourself, for I am an old bird, and I have got eyes to see with (this time for reading with)."[28]

Had Uncle Tadeusz read Konrad's letters to his "aunt," his anxious suspicion that his nephew was following the slippery path of romance would have been strengthened; affectionate teasing, intimate confidences, and expressions of warm feelings occurred on almost every page. But if the sagacious widower from Kazimierówka could also have seen for himself his nephew's behavior, he would certainly have felt more at ease. Korzeniowski was bold in writing but hesitant in his actions. He visited Madame Marguerite quite often, but only when he was on his way somewhere else, and usually only for a few hours. He had seen her only a few—at most seven—times.[29]

Korzeniowski's friendship with Poradowska was certainly not devoid of erotic feeling, but he, either unwilling or unable to take the decisive step, made up for his practical inactivity in his letters. Possibly his correspondence with Poradowska had a compensatory character; that would explain the recherché tone of his rhetoric. However, it is perhaps best to seek the key to the "Poradowska puzzle" in literature.

Marguerite, a rich, sophisticated, and beautiful society woman nine years his senior, was the only person among Korzeniowski's acquaintances outside Poland who belonged to his own cultural milieu—the milieu to which he was linked by interests, manners, and aspirations. He had had no contact with people of this milieu for at least twelve years—not since he had left Marseilles. (Hope, by all accounts, was a good friend but a man of simple mind.) When

Korzeniowski met Poradowska in February 1890, she already had to her credit two volumes of prose and two stories translated from the Polish.[30] And although some time passed before he told her about his own writings, literary subjects appeared as soon as his fourth letter, written a fortnight after their first meeting. With time they occupied more and more space in his correspondence. He constantly extolled his "aunt's" works and inquired after her literary plans.

The work of a warehouse manager was boring and exhausting. It is difficult to say whether the lack of plans for the future—in the middle of August Korzeniowski still did not know "whether he would stay on shore or go to sea" —was the cause or the effect of his gloom; but one worsened the other. In Konrad's letter of 26 September to his uncle, there was even the sentence, "It is better to die young as in any case one is bound to die sometime."[31]

Bobrowski responded: "To philosophize about death in such a way . . . one must feel 'profondement découragé' or ill—or both. At your age, 'soit dit' at the age of thirty-four—such a philosophy does not even enter the head of anybody young and healthy, and this worries me greatly, my dear lad!"[32]

Korzeniowski struck a similar attitude in his letters to Poradowska: "To tell you the truth I couldn't care less about happiness. I hardly know what it is." He expounded austere and bitter moral and philosophical opinions: "You think me capable of accepting or even admitting the doctrine (or theory) of expiation through suffering. That doctrine, a product of superior but savage minds, is quite simply an infamous abomination when advocated by civilized people. It is a doctrine which, on the one hand, leads straight to the Inquisition and, on the other, offers a chance of bargaining with the Eternal. . . . Anyway, there is no expiation. Each act in life is final and inevitably produces its consequences in spite of all the tears and gnashing of teeth and the sorrow of weak souls who suffer terror when confronted with the results of their own actions. As to myself, I shall never need to be consoled for any act of my life because I am strong enough to judge my conscience instead of being its slave as the orthodox would like us to be."[33] "Once upon a time I was a Christian!" he added a month later.[34] (He later expressed a similar view on the Christian concept of "expiation through suffering," characteristic of Dostoyevsky, in his novels.)

Never before had Korzeniowski lived so long in London—or in any other place since he had left Poland. Those ten months must have been profoundly depressing. They began with an illness, interrupted by the short water cure in Switzerland; they were passed in tense semi-inactivity and in smoky, crowded London—the "cruel devourer of the world's light" as he later called it; in addition, he was on the verge of indigence, without prospects, and almost without close friends. In spite of his occasional jocular protestations and philosophizing, every one of his letters written at that time exudes melancholy. Uncle Bobrowski decided to make short work of it:

My Dear Boy! I begin as usual,—though I should perhaps begin with "My Dear Pessimist" because that at least suggests the aroma which your letters have for some time been bringing me and that and no other is the proper way to address you. I can't say that I am pleased with your state of mind, and having now recognized it for what it is, it is difficult for me to contemplate your future with equanimity; however, I thank you for your openness, and I ask you not to hide from me your real state of mind while this mood persists. . . . After deliberating on the possible causes of your pessimism, I find I can't call it either symptomatic of "youth" or of "old age," for the thirty-four years of your life with all its vicissitudes doubly bear witness against that interpretation; I am therefore obliged to call it "a sickness," and I feel justified in doing so because of your recent experiences in Africa and your ensuing illness during which you had plenty of time for sombre meditations, and because of—as it seems to me—my observation of the structure of your character and mentality. Both in you as an individual and in what you have inherited from your parents I detect the dreamer—in spite of your very practical profession—or perhaps because of it? Perhaps my supposition is wrong, but I think that you had the same pessimistic disposition in Marseilles years ago—only that was against the background of your youth.

As the letter continues we see that Korzeniowski's pessimism and gloomy meditations did not spring from individual or personal matters but from general issues, and that his skepticism was directed at social and philosophical problems. Bobrowski's answer enables us to reconstruct the addressee's point of view which was to remain almost unchanged throughout his life. The letter also represents one of the more significant documents bearing on the sources of certain characteristic Conradian ideas: that Nature is indifferent to man's moral effort; that the contemporary social structure is based on injustice; that "material interests" dominate ethical ideals; that the existence both of an individual governed by a thirst for profit and of a state with imperialist aims is vacuous.

My dear lad, whatever you were to say about a good or bad balance of the forces of nature, about good or bad social relationships, about right or wrong social systems, about the boundless stupidity of crowds fighting for a crust of bread—and ending up in nothingness—none of this will be new!! . . . So that if both Individuals and Nations were to make "duty" their aim, instead of the ideal of greatness, the world would certainly be a better place than it is! And those crowds "aiming instinctively at securing only bread," so detestable to all visionaries, have their raison d'être: to fulfil the material needs of life; and they no longer seem detestable when . . . they embellish their existence, their work, and often even their shortcomings, by some higher moral idea of a duty accomplished, of a love for their family or country to whom they leave the fruit of their endeavours and labours in the form of sacrifices or bequests.

Bobrowski's recommendation was to "obey the order of nature" (although this world leaves much to be desired) with "an understanding of the shortcomings of the order of society." He concluded, "Perhaps you will tell me that what I have said is but the words of a man who has always been comfortable in the world . . . but this is not so—you know this well. I have gone through a lot, I have suffered over my own fate and the fate of my family and my Nation, and perhaps just because of these sufferings and disappointments I have developed in myself this calm outlook on the problem of life, whose motto, I venture to say, was, is, and will be 'usque ad finem.' The devotion to duty interpreted more widely or narrowly, according to circumstances and time—this constitutes my practical creed which—supported as it is by the experience of my sixty years— may be of some use to you?—I shall probably learn the results from your next letters!"[35]

This voluminous letter must have reached Korzeniowski shortly before he decided, on 14 November, to accept the berth of first mate on the passenger clipper *Torrens* (1,334 tons), at the salary of £8 a month. Two days later he left London for Australia.[36] Bobrowski commented on the news, "If I am not mistaken I imagine that you didn't want to take a position below that of a captain and as none came your way you waited in London . . . until at last, bored and tired, you finally decided to accept a less brilliant position, but one which would prevent you from sinking deeper into pessimism. Or perhaps your financial position made you do it?—and 'le fond de votre bourse' was more eloquent than any arguments of your own and your Uncle's logic! In any case, you couldn't have acted more wisely—that is, under the circumstances."[37]

Bobrowski's guesses were certainly right, and they tally with Conrad's reminiscences written thirty years later: "I was then recovering slowly from a bad breakdown, after a most unpleasant and persistent tropical disease which I had caught in Africa while commanding a steamer on the River Congo. . . . I confessed to him [the commander of the *Torrens*] my doubts of my fitness for the post, from the point of view of health. But he said that moping ashore never did any one any good, and was very encouraging."[38]

The *Torrens* was one of the most famous sailing ships of the day. Built in 1875 in Sunderland, she became known during her first fifteen years at sea for remarkably quick crossings from England to Australia; she was the favorite passenger boat on the London–Adelaide line. Thus, Korzeniowski, although taking up employment below the rank of master, found himself, thanks to his friendship with the *Torrens* new commander, W. H. Cope, on a ship of exceptional repute. It was also the first time he had served on a passenger boat. Natu-

rally it was more comfortable than a freighter, the crew was more carefully selected, and, above all, there was the possibility of some social contacts. During
his four long voyages on the *Torrens* Korzeniowski enjoyed a much more cultivated atmosphere than on any ship he had previously served aboard.

After a calm passage of one hundred days, the *Torrens* arrived at Adelaide on
28 February 1892. Letters from Europe brought by faster steamships awaited
Korzeniowski on arrival. In a touching letter which showed that this self-
professed cool rationalist had his moments of undisguised emotion, Bobrowski
wrote: "My Dear Boy! I can't think of a better and more pleasant way of spending the lonely moments of Christmas than by thinking of and talking to you.
For although it will be some time before you read this letter—you will see for
yourself then how in these moments that remind me agreeably of the past, of
my childhood and my parents' home, of youth, of my own home and of those
who were its consolation—my thoughts, orphaned and battered by the trials of
life, are directed towards you and your destiny, seeking in them a vital centre
for my own life which is gradually drawing towards its end. Hence, my dear
lad, according to the custom of our ancestors, I embrace you, bless you, and
wish you all happiness at Christmas and the New Year, which you will already
have celebrated and the arrival of which we are awaiting." [39]

A few days after reaching Australia Conrad wrote to Poradowska, reproaching her for her devotion to some unworthy aunt and invoking repeatedly our
"Creator," the "Almighty," and the "Lord of our souls." [40] Did he in fact reach a
religious turning point during his journey? Later we encounter more than once
his contradictory pronouncements on religious matters.

Korzeniowski spent over one month in Australia. His health was not too
good, and before setting off on his return passage he confided to Poradowska,
"I have been terribly busy during our stay here; this, and a sort of mental torpor which weighs me down, have prevented my writing to you more often." [41]
To his uncle he wrote twice, also in a minor key, renewing Bobrowski's anxiety:
"Firstly, I can't be overjoyed at the news of your indisposition and weariness at
the age of thirty-five—which is not yet old by any means—and I hope that you
will get over it. As to your intention to stay on the *Torrens* another year—you
are the judge and the master in this matter—common sense certainly should
not let you give up a tolerable occupation which you have for an unknown and
uncertain one which you have to seek and possibly in vain." [42]

The same letter contained bad news about Stanisław Bobrowski, the son of
Kazimierz, another of Konrad's uncles. "I can't recollect," Bobrowski wrote, "if
I had already mentioned to you that the poor lad got arrested on the 15 January
this year, accused of some political or rather social propaganda. He is still under lock and key in the Warsaw citadel. It seems to me to be nothing more than
simply a case of unauthorized teaching of artisans—but as there is about it a
tint of nationalism, it becomes complicated. The exceptional ad hoc procedure

is carried out in secrecy and an exceptional penalty may be imposed on the poor devil, ruining his present life—for he was just about to finish the University—and possibly even his whole future." Another generation, the generation of Konrad's contemporaries (Stanisław was born in 1865) was taking up the struggle for independence. We do not know the exact thoughts and feelings on the part of the subject of the most powerful empire in the world, an officer of the British merchant marine, when he read that his first cousin was imprisoned in the same dungeon for the same reason as his own father had been thirty years earlier. It must, however, have made a strong impression on him, since he repeatedly inquired about his cousin.

The *Torrens* left Adelaide on 8 April, and after 147 days, with stops at Capetown (24–25 June) and Saint Helena (14–18 July), arrived in London on 2 September.[43] Korzeniowski stayed there almost two months, undecided about his future. His uncle, noting that his letter exuded "a grey cloud of misgiving and dissatisfaction," commented, "I believe and share your longings for a command, but one cannot expect everything to happen at once. Possibly had you decided to stay for some time in Australia you might have got a command but this would have kept you for a long time or even for ever away from Europe, from me, from your friends—and being endowed with such gifts from heaven 'à la porté de votre main,' speaking in metaphors—you have to wait a bit longer for the realization of your professional hopes."[44]

Korzeniowski's letter to Poradowska echoed his uncle's old admonitions: "When one well understands that in oneself one is nothing and that a man is worth neither more nor less than the work he accomplishes with honesty of purpose and means, and within the strict limits of his duty towards society, only then is one the master of his conscience, with the right to call himself a man."[45] In the same letter he repeated his decision to remain on the *Torrens* "on account of my daily bread," adding that because of numerous duties he would be unable to come to Paris where Poradowska had gone.

We do not know what kept him so busy. To Poradowska he remarked rather vaguely, "My work is not very varied, but none the less it is quite demanding. It could not interest you in the slightest."[46] The four letters he wrote to her at that time sometimes give the impression of literary exercises composed on assigned subjects. This was certainly influenced in part by the addressee's personality; as a rule, Conrad adapted his subject, atmosphere, and even style to the expectations of the person to whom he was writing. And Poradowska was a lady both romantic and learned, as may be seen from the preserved fragments of her letters to Korzeniowski and confirmed by the frank Bobrowski: "I have been besieged as well by Mme Marguerita's voluminous letters which to top it all have been so illegible that I had to read them through a magnifying glass—but I answered every one of them. . . . The little darling is a 'bas bleu' . . . as romantic as a girl of sixteen."[47]

Before leaving England Korzeniowski received two more letters from the Ukraine. "My Dear Boy! The day before yesterday, I received your letter of the 11/23 instant which gave me much pleasure by its gaiety and the news of your good health." The subsequent letter contained news of Stanisław Bobrowski, still imprisoned at Warsaw citadel: "The procedure in his case is exceptional . . . the case is devoid of the elementary principles of defence—the presence of the public and verbal defence. . . . Most probably . . . he will be sent to Siberia for a period. Whichever way it goes he is a lost man—especially as he has studied law—he could never become either a government official, a solicitor, or a notary—not even in Kamchatka!! His whole life has gone off the rails."[48] To "Maryleczka" Tyszka, the prisoner's sister, Korzeniowski wrote, "I can well imagine your anxiety and sorrow. Generally the news from home is far from cheerful."[49]

The *Torrens* left London on 25 October 1892.[50] This time the passage to Adelaide took ninety-eight days. During the voyage one of the passengers aboard, William Henry Jacques, a consumptive Cambridge student traveling for his health, was, according to Conrad's account in *A Personal Record*, the first reader of the still-unfinished manuscript of *Almayer's Folly*.[51]

On 30 January 1893 the *Torrens* arrived at Port Adelaide. Korzeniowski had been ill for a fortnight on the way and had to take a short sick leave. He informed Poradowska:

I have neither plans nor projects. It is quite likely that on my return I shall go to see my uncle; in that case we shall meet again, my dear and good Aunt. If anything prevents me I shall be very sad, for I have grown attached to the idea. I have nursed it for almost three years; it is the only bright spot in the uniform grey of my existence. And this very existence begins to oppress me a bit. It is not the present illness (I am feeling much better now) but the uncertainty of the future—or rather the certainty of the "uniform grey" awaiting me—that causes this discouragement. I know very well that what I have just said, and what I feel, lacks dignity; but at least the feeling is genuine—it is not morbid as I look at the situation without any bitterness. Probably it would be more dignified to face it without breathing a word but one cannot be always perched on the stilts of one's principles.[52]

We have become familiar with similar moods in Korzeniowski's earlier letters. The monotony of a sailor's life distressed him more and more. The expression "uniform grey" may arouse suspicion that his melancholia and bitterness sprang not only from his own experiences and inclinations but also a little from the fin-de-siècle fashion of disillusionment and world-weariness; however, grayness and darkness are also typical colors of depression. In his correspondence with Poradowska there appears yet another notable motif: Korzeniowski's nostalgia for cultivated life, for the broad intellectual interests of his correspon-

dent's milieu. He also wrote to his uncle as many as five times on that journey—
another sign of loneliness.

The *Torrens* left Adelaide on 23 March. Among her passengers were two
young Englishmen returning from Australia and New Zealand: John Galsworthy and Edward Lancelot Sanderson. The twenty-five-year-old Galsworthy, son
of a well-to-do middle-class family, was a newly qualified lawyer. Sanderson
was going to help his father run a preparatory school for boys at Elstree. They
were probably the first Englishmen and nonsailors with whom Korzeniowski
struck up a friendship.

In a letter written to his parents one month after leaving Australia, Galsworthy mentioned his new friend: "The first mate is a Pole called Conrad and is a
capital chap, though queer to look at; he is a man of travel and experience in
many parts of the world, and has a fund of yarns on which I draw freely. He has
been right up the Congo and all around Malacca and Borneo and other out of
the way parts, to say nothing of a little smuggling in the days of his youth." [53] In
his reminiscences, published thirty years later, he described Conrad's looks and
characterized him as a mate: ". . . tanned, with a peaked brown beard, almost
black hair, and dark brown eyes, over which the lids were deeply folded. He
was thin, not tall, his arms very long, his shoulders broad, his head set rather
forward. He spoke to me with a strong foreign accent. He seemed to me strange
on an English ship. . . . He was a good seaman, watchful of the weather, quick
in handling the ship; considerate with the apprentices—we had a long, unhappy Belgian youth among them, who took unhandily to the sea and dreaded
going aloft; Conrad compassionately spared him all he could. With the crew he
was popular; they were individuals to him, not a mere gang; and long after he
would talk of this or that among them, especially of old Andy the sailmaker: 'I
liked that old fellow, you know.' . . . Many evening watches in fine weather we
spent on the poop." [54]

The portrait is complemented and amplified by one of Galsworthy's first literary attempts, *The Doldrums*, written in 1895–1896. [55] There he describes a
ship's physician's death caused by the use of opium and a weakening of the
heart brought about by the heat. The physician on the *Torrens*, thirty-year-old
C. Granville Jackson, did indeed die during the passage, although Galsworthy
had by that time left the ship and the story must have reached him through
Sanderson. Anyway, the hero is the first mate, by the name of Armand, obviously modeled on Korzeniowski. Armand speaks English with a strong foreign accent and occasionally confuses words close in meaning. He has "brown,
almond-shaped Slav eyes," the eyes of "a man who has been to the edge of the
world many times, and looking over—come back again"; "his mouth, between
the close-trimmed, pointed beard and drooping moustaches" has a "cynical
and mournful curve." There is a "melancholy fatalism" in his face ". . . an outcome of his Slav blood." He sits "in his favourite attitude with his hands clasp-

ing his knees, his chin sunk on his chest." He can laugh with that "spontaneous laugh that must have come from his lips even in death, if an idea had commended itself to his sardonic humour." Armand is presented as a man of great experience and philosophical wisdom. He comforts the young passenger, who imagined seeing the doctor die, and explains that he saw "what very few people have seen"—"the twilight of the body, you know, and the dawning of the soul." The fascination with Korzeniowski's unusual personality and the description of the individual features of his mind and body are the most noteworthy elements in this rather insignificant story.

In 1893 Galsworthy was not a writer and was not even thinking of becoming one, but he had a genuine interest in literature. One of the purposes (although unaccomplished) of his journey was to visit Robert Louis Stevenson on Samoa. On the melancholy sailor, Korzeniowski-Conrad, uncertain about his future, the curiosity and sympathy he evoked in Galsworthy and Sanderson must have had a stimulating effect. He may also have become more fully aware of what he was missing by being cut off from congenial society and the wealth of potential human contacts. This mood is evident in his letter to Poradowska, mailed on 17 May from Capetown: "Your life is broadening, Your horizon is extending by all the possibilities of a great agglomeration of human natures whose monotonous variety is measured by infinity; my vision is circumscribed by the dark circle where the blue of the sea and the blue of the sky touch without merging." [56]

In Capetown, where the *Torrens* remained from 17 to 19 May, Galsworthy left the ship to look at the local mines. Sanderson continued his voyage and, judging by their later correspondence, he was the first to develop closer ties with Korzeniowski.

On 26 July 1893, following a smooth but not too fast passage of 126 days, the *Torrens* docked in the port of London, and "J. Conrad Korzemowin," as his name was entered in the certificate of discharge without his knowing it, had completed his last long-distance voyage as a seaman. [57]

In London, letters from his Uncle Tadeusz awaited him, as usual. The old gentleman had for some time been beset by various illnesses and so, in a letter of 22 May, he asked his nephew not to delay his visit to the Ukraine, postponed for the last three years. Bobrowski was to cover all travel expenses. "Probably, as on the previous occasion, you will travel through abominable Berlin, and then take a fast train via Białystok, by-passing Warsaw which is already empty and will be even more so during the summer, and then Brześć to Koziatyń where after waiting a few hours you will have to change on to a modest, partly goods, partly passenger train, which will bring you at 11.30 a.m. to the station of 'Oratów,' which is seven versts [4.6 miles] from Kazimierówka. From Brześć telegraph for horses, but in Russian, for Oratów doesn't receive or accept messages in an 'alien' language." [58]

But in his next letter of 13 July, Bobrowski placed his nephew's welfare over his own pleasure in seeing him. "Consider, my dear lad, at what cost, and I am thinking solely of the cost to you, this visit would take place?—your giving up your present post on the *Torrens*, which you like, and possibly even the chance of obtaining the command of this ship in the event of Capt. Cope succeeding in his endeavours to get the command of a steamship in the future. . . . Judge for yourself, Panie Bracie, the whole question from the point of view of your future career and I shall accept your decision as an indispensable conclusion which concerns both of us and as a professional necessity which is good and well justified—however unpleasant from our personal point of view."[59] Uncle Tadeusz also informed him about the end of the "trial" of Stanisław Bobrowski, who had been sentenced to eighteen months imprisonment, not counting over a year spent under arrest, and sent off to a prison in St. Petersburg.

As we know, Korzeniowski resigned his berth on the *Torrens*, most probably because he had lost all hope of succeeding Captain Cope and possibly because he was weary of the sailor's profession. The exact date of his departure for the Ukraine is not known, but most likely he left England in the first half of August and remained in Kazimierówka for over a month.[60]

In 1899, he noted, in a letter to R. B. Cunninghame Graham: "When I was in Poland 5 years ago and managed to get in contact with the youth of the university in Warsaw I preached at them and abused them for their social democratic tendencies."[61] There is no indication, however, that Korzeniowski stopped in Warsaw on his way to the Ukraine; at all events the students were on vacation at that time, and although one cannot rule out that he met a group of Stanisław Bobrowski's friends (perhaps in Radom), the whole story looks invented or at least magnified.

Only one document has survived from the time Korzeniowski spent at his uncle's estate near Oratów: his letter of 14 September to Poradowska, whom he did not visit either on his way there or back, in spite of grandiloquent promises. We read that he spent five days in bed. "It is nice to be ill here (if one must be ill). My uncle has nursed me as if I were a little child." It appears also that Poradowska, prompted by jealousy, made something in the nature of a scene in one of her letters, to which he replied, "It is quite true that Marysieńka [Ołdakowska, a young distant relative living in the Ukraine] is getting married, but what on earth should I be doing in this marriage affair? I can't believe you were serious in your letter, for it must have seemed strange to you that some one would hurry suddenly from the depths of Australia—without telling a soul—to the depths of the Ukraine to throw himself into the arms of—The whole idea is funny."[62]

His next letter to "Aunt" Marguerite is dated nearly two months later. Korzeniowski was again back in London and was again looking for employment, unsuccessfully: "Since my return from Poland, I spend my days in miserable idleness. You who describe things and men, and so have lifted a corner of the veil, you must know there are times when the mind is asleep, when months slip by, and when even Hope seems dead. I am going through one of those times."[63] A laudatory certificate issued by the commander of the *Torrens* read, "This is to certify that Mr. J. Conrad has sailed with me as Chief Officer for two round voyages between London and Adelaide in the years 91/2/3, I have found him sober honest and trustworthy—as I left him in full charge of the ship while I was away at Melbourne—and shall be glad to hear of his future success in life."[64] But it was of no help.

If we were to graph Korzeniowski's sailing career, or his preliterary life in general, it would be a broken line, but one that climbs between 1874 and 1889. In those fifteen years the succession of certificates and diplomas, a master's licence, and the first command are the salient points. The expedition to Africa stops this upward climb and marks the beginning of a steady and rapid decline. After three years the captain is back to being only second mate, and it is on a ship going nowhere.

Such was Korzeniowski's fate with the 2,097-ton steamer *Adowa*, which was supposed to carry emigrants from France to Canada. He signed on in London on 29 November 1893.[65] On 4 December the *Adowa* put into port at Rouen. She was expected to leave on 9 December for La Rochelle and thence to Canada,[66] but the plan of transporting emigrants fell through and the steamer remained idle in France. Korzeniowski suddenly began to shower his "aunt" with letters; he apparently sensed the precariousness of the situation as early as 18 December and asked Poradowska to make inquiries about the possibility of his getting employment as a pilot on the Suez Canal. Such a job would have provided him with conditions more suited for writing, and this consideration may have been one motive for his appeal. Two days later, mentioning that someone was trying to get him work fishing for pearls on the Australian coast, he returned to the Suez possibility: "The work is light. One is not too far away, and I suppose one can earn a living at it. I ask no more."[67]

Literature is a subject touched upon in all Korzeniowski's letters at this time. Prominence is given to his "aunt's" new novel, *Le Mariage du fils Grandsire*, but on 7 January 1894, acknowledging the receipt of this book, he finished: "If you are a good little girl I shall let you read my story of Almayer when I have finished it."[68] This is the earliest mention of *Almayer's Folly*, but to judge by the way it is phrased, Poradowska must have heard about the book earlier. Korzeniowski may have spoken about his hobby during one of his visits, and now, nearing the end of the novel and therefore viewing it more seriously, he reminded her that he too belonged to the community of writers.

Describing the boredom of his stay at Rouen, Conrad notes in *A Personal Record* that his work on the tenth chapter (of twelve) of *Almayer's Folly* began there.[69] Although in his letters he also complained repeatedly about his inactivity and boredom, the time spent in the old port, situated far inland, was one of active idleness, since apart from writing he must have read a lot—and not only Poradowska. In one of his letters to her he told jokingly how he was taken at the post office for a bomb-carrying anarchist. The joke is significant, considering that Rouen, with the rest of France, was at that time the scene of numerous acts of violence; public opinion was particularly stirred by the affair of Auguste Vaillant, who on 9 December 1893 threw a fairly harmless bomb into the hall of the National Assembly and was sentenced to death on 10 January.

On 10 January, the *Adowa* left Rouen for London.[70] On 17 January, J. Conrad, having for the first time signed his name thus, stepped ashore and unknowingly ended his last service at sea.[71]

Conrad's subsequent professional activity as a seaman consisted of giving evidence six months later before the Board of Trade's Departmental Committee on the Manning of Merchant Ships.[72] One hundred and seventy-six witnesses were interviewed; he was questioned on the tenth day of the hearings. His replies seem competent, though sometimes evasive; one gets the impression that in certain matters the parties did not fully understand each other. Conrad stated quite clearly that the *Adowa* was not sufficiently manned; he considered the manning of the *Skimmer*, *Otago*, and *Torrens* quite satisfactory. The questioning was rigorous, sometimes captious, but in spite of that Conrad allowed himself to depart from the truth in reporting the length of his service and posts held. He maintained that he had spent eighteen months on the Congo River "in command of a steamer," when in fact he had spent only six weeks on the Congo; he also added three months to the period during which he had commanded the *Otago* and claimed that he had made two voyages to Mauritius and two passages through Torres Strait; he lengthened his service on the *Torrens* by three months; and he alleged that he had made a transatlantic voyage in the *Adowa*. In fact it was only to the question of how long he had been at sea that he gave a true answer: about nineteen years.

These distortions of fact in the official statements of a master mariner speaking as a witness and specialist are rather surprising. More understandable perhaps, if not less striking, is Conrad's consistent silence about his service on French ships and about all his continental connections in general. On future occasions Conrad similarly tended to depart from the truth. Let us briefly recapitulate the facts.

From the time he left Cracow in October 1874 to the day he was discharged from the *Adowa* in January 1894, Korzeniowski worked on ships, including long periods in ports, for ten years and almost eight months. He spent just over eight years at sea—nine months of this as a passenger. He served over two and a half years, of which twenty-one months were spent at sea, as a member of the crew (steward, apprentice, sailor). He served eight months as third mate. His longest period of service was as second mate: almost four years, of which only two and a half were at sea. As first mate he had two years and three months service, of which two years were at sea. As captain he served one year and two months, half of that at sea. Of his nearly eleven years at sea, nine months were on steamers.*

So much for statistics. One must also ask to what extent the image of sailors' work as presented in Conrad's autobiographical statements is realistic in a broader sense—that is, irrespective of his own time in service and posts held.

Robert D. Foulke, in his "Life in the Dying World of Sail," attacks the Conradian myth of the beauty and sublimity of life on sailing ships as contrasted with the ugliness and mechanical commerciality of steamships. Foulke points out that Conrad's theory about the sudden and rapid replacement of sail by steam power was exaggerated and that the competition actually lasted several decades, with technical development in both spheres being almost simultaneous. He also notes that Conrad's statement, "It was a swift doom, but it is consoling to know that there was no decadence," was also an exaggeration, since sailing ships were larger, heavier, slower, and harder to handle at the end of the nineteenth century.[73]

Conrad also idealized the quality of life on sailing ships. In his memoirs he never so much as hinted at the dirt, rats, stupefying toil, drunkenness, and fear, or at the heat, cold, and damp that menaced the health of seafarers. Silent, dignified ships without engines cannot fail to appeal to our imagination, but work in them could be lethal to both body and mind. Steamships were less romantic, but few men deliberately chose the sail: in Korzeniowski's time it was simply easier to find work on sailing ships. He, too, tried unsuccessfully more than once to get a berth on a steamship. He was interested in steam engines and knew a lot about their construction, as his younger son John remembers. Only later, in his reminiscences, did Conrad transform dire, though perhaps beautiful, necessity into an inspired choice and present himself as a sailor by vocation.

In "Legends," his last essay, which was unfinished at his death, the author of the soberly realistic *Nigger of the "Narcissus"* asks rhetorically, "What is a 'timid member'" of a crew?[74] The farther Conrad's sea years receded into the past, the more he idealized not only ships but seamen. Historical sources contradict this romantic picture. The last quarter of the nineteenth century was a transitional period marked by an acute crisis in the professional and moral qualifications of the officers and crews of the British Merchant Marine. A great

---

* Here, for greater precision and for the enjoyment of pedants, is a more detailed computation. For simplicity I count 1 month as 30 days. Including his first voyage on the *Mont Blanc* as a passenger and the voyage on the *Mavis* (no data available), he spent 11 years, 2 months, and 3 days on ships. Apart from that, as a passenger he sailed for about 5 months. He spent 8 years, 3 months, and 18 days at sea. His prolonged stays in ports on board ships lasted 3 years, 1 month, and 2 days. Below the rank of officer he served for 2 years, 7 months and 1 day (at sea 1 year, 9 months, and 19 days); as third officer 8 months and 5 days (at sea 6 months and 17 days); as second officer 3 years, 10 months, and 23 days (at sea 2 years, 6 months and 14 days); as first mate 2 years, 3 months, and 14 days (at sea 2 years and 8 days); as master one year, 2 months, and 8 days (at sea 7 months and 21 days); on steamships 9 months and 8 days, not including about 45 days on the *Roi des Belges*.

many accidents were caused by errors committed by the officers, often as a result of incompetence, and this state of affairs was hardly improved by what now seems the surprising lenience of the sea law and marine courts of the period. Captain J. L. Clark of the *Jeddah*—the prototype of the *Patna* in *Lord Jim*— had his certificate of competency as master suspended for three years for abandoning the ship with one thousand passengers on board; the *Riversdale*'s master, L. B. McDonald, who wrecked the ship when he was sixty miles off course during good weather, had his certificate suspended for one year; his first mate's certificate was suspended for only three months.[75] Such lenient verdicts were quite common, and they contrast with Conrad's picture of the strict requirements and the high standards for officers of the merchant navy. Contemporary English authors, writing about the merchant service, judged the situation far more critically.[76]

Unfortunately, there is no evidence to suggest that the sense of professional solidarity and comradeship in dangerous work was indeed part of Korzeniowski's personal experience. It seems more probable that he felt lonely and alienated throughout his service. The vision of life at sea as subordinated, both at times of mortal fear and during ordinary everyday activities, to a clear-cut and unshakable code of professional ethics, the vision of a community bound together by common duties and a common ideal—these are visions of a moral order, not reflections of reality.

"In no other kind of life is the illusion more wide of reality—in no other is the beginning *all* illusion—the disenchantment more swift—the subjugation more complete."[77] In no autobiographical text did the writer of those words bring himself to make such a bitterly frank admission. An open confession, even to himself, of disappointment would have made the ground, none too firm as it was, sway under Conrad's feet. Contrary to the majority of contemporary sailors, he chose his profession of his own free will, on the strength of a youthful dream. And although he pursued his career at sea entirely of his own will, often vacillating and more than once thinking about a change, he devoted almost twenty years of his life—his entire youth and the beginning of maturity— to his first profession. To admit that it had lacked any deep significance would have placed Conrad, a man who was prone to depression in any case, in a desperate situation. A myth of the beauty, dignity, and noble solidarity of his life at sea, not unfounded but exaggerated as all myths are, was the only way to counterbalance the disappointments.

Thus Conrad tried to extract from those twenty years everything precious they could yield—everything and more. But what those years in fact gave him we cannot tell. In such matters we have to agree with Kierkegaard: the subjective personal truth is the essential truth. One thing is certain: Conrad gained an immense range of experience, from stark, helpless fear, disgust, and boredom to ecstatic enjoyment of beauty, a sense of the triumphant efficacy of his own body and spirit, to exhaustion relieved by the consciousness of victory in the struggle against an incomparably stronger elemental opponent.

The biographer must not be misled by idealizations; nor should he take myths for factual accounts. But he ought to try to understand the psychological mechanism that inclined Conrad toward autobiographical flights of fancy: he was raising his own past to the level of a carefully created vision.

In January 1894, Korzeniowski was not aware of having parted with the sea forever. On the contrary, he expected to find a new job quite soon. "I am afraid that I shall have to leave shortly for a long voyage," he wrote to Poradowska.[78] He fell ill, however, and during his convalescence a telegram came from the Ukraine with the news of his uncle's death on 10 February. He wrote, "It seems as if everything has died in me, as if he has carried away my soul with him."[79]

"Dear Captain," wrote Tadeusz Florkowski, one of Bobrowski's wards and an executor of his will, on 21 February, "we have sent you a telegram to London with the sad and painful news about the death of your dear uncle and our much regretted guardian, Tadeusz Bobrowski. It was an unexpected and terrible blow to us all. On Friday 9 February he went to bed in good health and on Saturday 10 February he woke up and, feeling short of breath, called Jaś to rub him with alcohol; then suddenly at 7 o'clock in the morning, with the last word 'attack,' his life ended."[80]

Bobrowski left his estate to the widow and children of his brother Kazimierz. In addition to the table silver and other precious objects and family relics, Konrad inherited a legacy of fifteen thousand rubles in cash to be paid one year after Bobrowski's death. The money had been lent at 8 percent per annum to Konstancja Zaleska; the interest was paid in advance, so Korzeniowski was due to receive twelve hundred rubles at once. The executors of the will cordially invited him to come to the Ukraine, but he remained in London.[81]

Ten years later Conrad declared, "I cannot write about Tadeusz Bobrowski, my Uncle, guardian and benefactor without emotion. Even now . . . I still feel his loss. He was a man of great character and unusual qualities of mind. Although he did not understand my desire to join the mercantile marine, on principle, he never objected to it. I saw him four times during the thirty [sic] years of my wanderings (from 1874–1893) but even so I attribute to his devotion, care, and influence, whatever good qualities I may possess."[82] Was Bobrowski's role in the formation of Conrad's ideas and personality in fact so great and unambiguous?[83]

Certainly it was not an influence based on a similarity of natural propensities and temperaments. Bobrowski gave his own characteristics in his *Memoirs*: "a doctrinaire of the first water, deeply convinced of the unchanging nature of prescribed rights and duties of reason; of critical faculty and free will which make man a master of his own fate and of history; rejecting all side influences like emotions, passions, and environment; possessing ready formulae arrived at through abstract thinking, for coping with all problems of life."[84] The accuracy of this self-portrait, painted with obvious relish, is confirmed in the reminiscences of his contemporaries.

Bobrowski's virtues of sagacity, constancy, will power, and sense of duty cannot be questioned. An efficient administrator, recognized even in his youth as a competent jurist, conscientious and honest, he always believed in the values of planning and of moderation. It is unlikely that Korzeniowski when abroad met people of a cultural and intellectual caliber equal to his uncle's. At the same time, however, Bobrowski was a rather cold man with little tolerance for emotional people; he was also extremely ambitious, and the sense of living among people and affairs below his own intellectual possibilities embittered him. Bobrowski's *Memoirs* reveal a concealed malice; their author obviously enjoyed collecting ridiculous anecdotes, exposing human weaknesses, and relating embarrassing adventures of friends and cousins as a quiet revenge for his own wasted years and unfulfilled aspirations.

He considered himself a patriot but he was an avowed appeaser, opposed to rebellion, conspiratorial activity, and radical reforms. He despised tsarist Russia but lived in peace with the authorities, enjoying their trust; in his *Memoirs* he proudly recalls how during the 1863 insurrection there had not once been a search in his manor, although the activities of his brother Stefan and the political leanings of Ewa and Kazimierz were well known to the police. Tadeusz Bobrowski's participation in the committee debating the abolition of serfdom (1859−1861) won him, from some biographers, the reputation of a progressive, a liberal, even a democrat. In fact, he was progressive only in the context of the conservative gentry from the southeastern territories of the old Polish Commonwealth. A true democrat, such as Apollo Korzeniowski, seemed to Bobrowski an ultraradical visionary. Nevertheless, he tolerated his brother-in-law; he could not fail to recognize Apollo's intelligence and may have even envied him his renown. But he did not like him. Apollo was the very opposite of Tadeusz: emotional and impulsive, he made close friends easily, whereas Tadeusz had none; deeply religious but at the same time a radical "Red"; a rebel and conspirator while Bobrowski was a rationalist, skeptic, and political conformist. Bobrowski regarded Apollo's political and social views as products of his irresponsible fancies and presented him in his letters and memoirs as a wayward daydreamer, without mentioning Korzeniowski's important political activities.[85]

Bobrowski prided himself on being consistently frank in his statements, yet he was not above "correcting" unpalatable facts. Trying to emphasize the contrast (repeatedly stressed in his letters to Konrad) between the reasonable and responsible Bobrowskis and the Korzeniowskis who, according to him, were dreamers and wastrels, Bobrowski whitewashed his own family, which did not lack its own madcaps and rogues.[86] He also markedly toned down his brother

Stefan's radical views. He maintained that Apollo returned from exile a completely broken and resigned man, not mentioning that in spite of everything Apollo remained active in literature and politics. It was also Bobrowski who created the legend about Apollo destroying all his manuscripts before his death; Conrad believed in the story and even recorded it as his own reminiscence.

Intentionally or not, Bobrowski did a great deal to impede Konrad's understanding of his father. His Uncle Tadeusz's stories and opinions must have left Konrad with the impression that Apollo had been an irresponsible fanatic who had ruined the life of his loving wife. The fact that Ewa voluntarily shared her husband's beliefs and activities was glossed over. The couple's joint sacrifice and suffering were presented to Konrad as his father's defeat and his mother's loyal submission. An eleven-year-old boy could not fully understand either his father's actions or his point of view; all Konrad could see were illness, death, frustration, and despair—and all of them pointless, according to his uncle-guardian. So he recalled his parents with bitter sadness.

Konrad's thoughts about Poland must have been similar. For all his sarcasm, Bobrowski was not a pessimist. His position was that of rationalistic fatalism: he believed in the value of "organic" work and of progress, in reconciliation with existing reality and in its gradual transformation. His hopes for the restoration of a Polish state were based on a vague trust in the justice of historical "Nemesis"; he rejected all thought of an armed fight for freedom or even of clandestine political action. But Apollo's son was averse to this kind of passive acquiescence; he abhorred all forms of tyranny and oppression—and did not believe in historical justice. Since his uncle taught him to regard all acts of political resistance as folly, Konrad looked at the future without hope.

Therefore, generally speaking, Bobrowski's formative influence consisted of the clash of his views and propensities with the views, propensities, and personal experience of his nephew. They clashed on several planes. Bobrowski, a fanatic for duty, awoke in the heedless Korzeniowski a sense of responsibility for himself and for others; Bobrowski's sober judgment conflicted with Conrad's daydreaming; rationalistic optimism battled romantic gloom. An appeaser opposed a rebel; a skeptic opposed a naive enthusiast. Almost all Conrad's inner tensions—the painful, uncomfortable, wearisome wealth of his mind—can be associated with this basic contrast between his and his uncle's personalities.

If we are aware of all this inheritance we can more fully appreciate the significance of the fact that Conrad dedicated his first book, *Almayer's Folly* "To the memory of T. B." It was more than a tribute to his guardian and benefactor. The novel about an irresponsible dreamer is, after all, an attempt to come to grips with his own inclinations, for which Bobrowski had frequently reproached him. Also, the book appears to offer the clue to its author's creative attitude: besides a need for compensation, at the root of almost all Conrad's important works we find a struggle against the views toward which he himself was drawn. Thus, writing for Conrad was a moral act on the purely personal plane.

Such seem to have been the lasting results of Bobrowski's influence. The immediate consequence of his death was the break of Conrad's most affectionate and closest personal tie with his family and home country. He found himself alone, without any financial or social support anywhere.

Albert Guerard advanced the hypothesis that Bobrowski's death might have removed "an inhibiting substitute father" who had been an obstacle in the way of Conrad's creative development, thereby speeding up the completion of *Almayer's Folly*.[87] Bernard Meyer also links the end of Conrad's four-year work on the book with the death of his uncle-guardian but associates it with the author's search for consolation in literature.[88] We have seen, however, that in January Korzeniowski was less than three chapters from the end, and that while his literary and intellectual interests grew steadily, his enthusiasm for work at sea was waning. Thus, his concentration on the book was at least partly the continuation of a natural process. Bobrowski's death did play a role in speeding it up, but in a way quite different from those suggested until now. In his letters to Poradowska written in December and January, Conrad had been complaining about a lack of money; this lack was probably why he did not go to his uncle's funeral. But on about 1 May Korzeniowski received the first part of his inheritance, approximately £120. It was the equivalent of fifteen months' salary on the *Torrens*, and so, although he continued his search for work, he could afford a longer period of unemployment and therefore devote much more of his time to writing.

We can follow the progress of his work closely because Conrad's correspondence with Poradowska became much livelier in 1894. In March he paid her a visit in Brussels. By the end of the month he reported, "I am in the midst of struggling with Chap. XI; a struggle to the death, you know! If I give up, I am lost!"[89] In mid-April he went for ten days to Elstree, to the Sandersons, where he began the twelfth chapter of *Almayer's Folly*. On 24 April he informed Poradowska from London,

> It is with a great sorrow that I have to inform you of the death of Mr Kaspar Almayer, which occurred this morning at three o'clock.
>
> It's over! . . . suddenly all those people who have spoken into my ear, moved before my eyes, lived with me for so many years, become a crowd of phantoms, who are growing distant, dim and indistinct, fading away with the sunlight of this brilliant and sombre day.
>
> Since I woke up this morning it seems to me that I have buried a part of myself in the pages lying here before my eyes.[90]

Conrad probably began revising the text and making additions before he finished it. "I find the work of revising my first three chapters not only unpleasant but absolutely painful. And difficult besides! And yet it must be done!"[91] Ted Sanderson and his mother helped him correct the manuscript.[92] Both the original longhand draft of *Almayer's Folly* and the typescript used by the printers have survived. They differ considerably in style and plot—at the beginning of the original version there is no mention of Nina Almayer or her lover Dain; therefore we may assume that there was an intermediate version in which the alterations were made.

Conrad probably finished his revisions by the middle of May. At that time he had a short-lived hope of getting the command of a ship, but nothing came of it.[93] In one of his letters to Poradowska we find a possibly wrong and until now unexplained intimation that the manuscript had already been given to Edmund Gosse, a leading critic. This news may have originated in Conrad's tendency to wishful thinking. In any event, it is certain that on 4 July he did send the typescript to T. Fisher Unwin, a large publishing house in London.[94]

At that time Korzeniowski was again passing through a period of anxiety and depression. His letters to Poradowska teem with complaints and cries of despair. "I am tortured by my nervous disorder which makes me miserable, paralyzes action, thought, everything! I wonder why I exist? . . . I have no courage left to do anything. Just barely enough to write to you."[95] Waiting for the publisher's decision did not improve his mood. He feared that the manuscript might be rejected. For the time being he had no intention of continuing to write. "To tell you the truth I am not interested in the fate of *Almayer's Folly*. It is finished. In any case it could not have been more than an episode of no consequence in my life."[96] But those disavowals were an expression of a momentary opinion: in fact, he was constantly torn between his inability to find employment at sea and his uncertainty about following his literary aspirations.

From that difficult time date Conrad's beautiful words about the thinking man's burden imposed by his personality—words begotten by a momentary mood but expressing a belief he held throughout his life: "We must drag the chain and ball of our personality to the end. This is the price one pays for the infernal and divine privilege of thought; so in this life it is only the chosen who are convicts—a glorious band which understands and groans but which treads the earth amidst a multitude of phantoms with maniacal gestures and idiotic grimaces. Which would you rather be: idiot or convict?"[97]

At the beginning of August, worn out by illness, Korzeniowski suddenly decided to go to Champel for treatment. The water cure proved beneficial. He worried, however, about his funds running low and again appealed to Poradowska for help: "With you I have no false pride or shame, no other feelings but those of affection, of gratitude and trust. If one must put up money for a command, I can deposit 12,000 francs by the first of March 1895, but not before. I am ready to take an examination in Belgium if it is necessary."[98] Although nothing came of those endeavors he somehow managed to carry on without suffering any serious privations until the arrival of the main bulk of his legacy.

Conrad's second cause of worry was *Almayer's Folly*. Weeks passed with no word from the publisher. Conrad, tossed by conflicting emotions, suggested to Poradowska first that the novel should be translated, and then that it should be published as their joint work: "The name 'Kamoudi' in small print somewhere will do. Let your name appear on the title-page—an explanatory note saying that K. collaborated will be enough. Will you agree?" [99]

The same letter from Champel—in which he mentioned his "reading Maupassant with delight"—brought some unexpected and noteworthy news:

> I have begun to write, but only the day before yesterday. I want to make it quite short. Say twenty to twenty-five pages like those of the *Revue*. I am calling it "Two Vagabonds," and I want to sketch in broad outlines, without shades or details, two human wrecks such as one encounters in the forsaken corners of the world. A white man and a Malay. You see that I can't get away from Malays. I am devoted to Borneo. My worst trouble is that my characters are so real. I know them so well that they hamper my imagination. The white man is a friend of Almayer; the Malay is our old friend Babalatchi before he attained the dignity of prime minister and confidential adviser to the Rajah. There it is. But I have no dramatic climax. My head is empty and even the beginning appears difficult! I am not telling you more! I am already tempted to give it up. Do you think one can make a thing interesting without a woman?!

It was the beginning of Conrad's second and much longer novel, *An Outcast of the Islands*. The letter to Poradowska refutes the story (which Conrad later upheld) that it had been Edward Garnett—whom he did not meet until October that year—who had persuaded him to start another novel. As Baines rightly says, Conrad in his reminiscences consistently played down the strength of his desire to write.[100] He always tried to create the impression that he had entered the world of literature by pure coincidence.

Conrad returned to London on 6 September, bringing with him the beginning of *Two Vagabonds*. And once again came an unsuccessful search for work, accompanied by anxious waiting for news from Unwin, to whom he now wrote letters urging a decision. At last came the triumph: on 4 October Conrad received the news that the book had been accepted for publication, with a modest advance of £20.[101] The gates of English literature had opened before Captain Korzeniowski from Berdyczów.

VII
. . . .
WORK AND ROMANCE
1894–1896

ACCORDING TO LEGEND, the discoverer of Conrad's talent was Edward Garnett (1868–1937), who in spite of his youth enjoyed considerable authority as a literary critic and publisher's reader for the house of Unwin. Conrad himself contributed to this legend, which was later perpetuated by Jean-Aubry. In fact, however, the first "official" reader of the manuscript of *Almayer's Folly* was another of Unwin's readers, Wilfrid Hugh Chesson (1870–1952). His opinion was favorable, and the text was passed on to Garnett. "Perhaps I may add," Chesson said twenty-five years later, "that the purely stylistic and academic merits of Mr Conrad's work were even in 1894 too obvious to make the 'discovery' of him by a literary critic much more than an evidence of reasonable attention to his business." [1]

On 8 October 1894 Conrad paid a visit to Unwin's office and met not only the owner of the firm but also both readers. Garnett recalled later:

> My memory is of seeing a dark-haired man, short but extremely graceful in his nervous gestures, with brilliant eyes, now narrowed and penetrating, now soft and warm, with a manner alert yet caressing, whose speech was ingratiating, guarded, and brusque turn by turn. I had never seen before a man so masculinely keen yet so femininely sensitive. The conversation between our host and Conrad for some time was halting and jerky. . . . Conrad, extremely polite, grew nervously brusque in his responses, and kept shifting his feet one over the other, so that I became fascinated in watching the flash of his pointed patent leather shoes. The climax came unexpectedly when in answer to Mr Unwin's casual but significant reference to "your next book," Conrad threw himself back on the broad leather lounge and in a tone that put a clear cold space between himself and his hearers, said: "I don't expect to write again. It is likely that I shall soon be going to sea." A silence fell. [2]

Garnett at once began to persuade Conrad not to give up literature. In his 1919 foreword to *An Outcast of the Islands*, Conrad maintains that it was Garnett who was responsible for the birth of his second novel, but we know that he had begun working on it two months before meeting Garnett. In a letter to Poradowska written two days after his visit to Unwin's, Conrad also presented the matter differently:

At first the two "readers" of the house received me and complimented me effusively (were they by any chance making fun of me?). Then I was led to the head's presence to discuss business. He told me frankly that if I wanted to accept part of the risk of publication I could have a share of the profits. If not, they were giving me £20 and the French rights. I chose the second alternative. "We are paying you very little," he said, "but consider that you are an unknown author and that your book appeals to a very limited public. Then there is the question of taste. Will the public like it? We are also taking a risk. . . . Write something shorter, of the same kind, for our Pseudonym Library, and if it suits us we shall be very happy to give you a much better cheque."

There you are. I am advancing very cautiously with a vagabond under each arm in the hope of selling them to Fisher Unwin. Slave traffic, upon my honor![3]

Thus, although he later maintained that he had been talked into his second novel and that further writing seemed to him at the time rather unlikely, it is obvious that right from the beginning he had been working on *The Two Vagabonds* (*An Outcast*) with publication in mind.

Conrad always insisted that he became a writer by chance, that literature was not a matter of conscious choice nor even a result of some strong inner need. Conrad's efforts to obscure his motives reinforce the hypothesis that for him writing was basically an act of compensation, of correcting, perfecting, or at least complementing his own pre- and extraliterary life. But this compensation for—or, as some say, escape from—the worries and gray humdrum of daily existence into a world created by himself would bring him different but not lesser sufferings, difficulties, and perplexities.

Almost as soon as he began *The Two Vagabonds* he started lamenting in his letters to Poradowska: "I am terribly discouraged. The ideas don't come. I don't *see* either the characters or happenings." ". . . I am completely stuck. I have not written a single word for a fortnight. It's all over, I think. I feel like burning what there is. It is very bad! Worse than bad! This is my deep conviction and not a cry of stupid modesty." "I have burnt nothing. One talks like that and then courage fails. . . . I work a little. I agonize, pen in hand. Six lines in six days."[4]

But the manuscript grew faster than one would expect from these complaints: in two months he wrote five chapters—quite fast for Conrad. By the middle of October, with three chapters finished, he gave the following outline of the book as a whole: "In the first place the subject is the boundless, savage vanity of an ignorant man who is successful but has neither principles nor any motive other than the satisfaction of his own vanity. He is not even faithful to himself. Hence his fall, his sudden degradation into physical enslavement by a completely savage woman. I've seen that! The catastrophe will be brought

CONRAD-KORZENIOWSKI'S EUROPEAN SCENE

about through the intrigues of a small Malay state where the last word is poisoning. The dénouement is suicide, still through vanity. All this will be merely sketched, as I am writing for the Pseudonym Library and my limit is thirty-six thousand words to a volume."[5] The outline came fairly close to the book as we know it, although in its present form there is no suicide, and the number of words is three times greater than Conrad originally expected.

Conrad's literary work consisted not only of writing but also of a careful and studious reading of the masters. "I am afraid I am too much influenced by Maupassant. I have studied *Pierre et Jean*—thought, method and everything— in deepest despair. It seems to be nothing but the mechanics are so intricate that I feel like tearing out my hair. One wants to cry with rage reading it. So there!"[6]

The title had to be changed because another writer, Margaret Woods, had just published a novel called *The Vagabonds*. At the end of December Conrad announced, "The decision is made. I have changed the title. It will be *An Outcast of the Islands*. And the thing itself is changed. Everything is changed except my doubts. Everything—except the fear of those ghosts one evokes and which so often refuse to obey the brain that created them. Well, here is Chap. VIII finished. Four more to come! Four centuries of agony, four minutes of delight, and then the end—an empty head, discouragement, and eternal doubt."[7] Not four but eighteen chapters were to be added.

His torments, which he probably put down to his lack of experience, did not prevent Conrad from looking for employment at sea. In almost every letter he mentioned his hopes and endeavors. He was also afraid that a prolonged stay on land might completely destroy his health. Even the arrival of the proofs of *Almayer's Folly* did not cheer him up: "I am filled with horror. With absolute horror of the printed thing which looks so stupid; worse—senseless." This tendency to feel an aversion, if only temporary, to his every completed work, was to last throughout Conrad's life. But he worked on his first proofreading most conscientiously, introducing many stylistic changes, particularly in the choice of words—at least his third round of corrections for *Almayer's Folly*. Even before the text was set in type he had made about eight hundred changes in the typescript; nearly all involved only one word each.[8] Many of them show that he had still to excise the results of an unconscious pressure of Polish on his English phraseology.

In January 1895, Conrad, then constantly complaining of depression, formed a friendship with Edward Garnett; it developed into a lasting and close relationship. Conrad invited Garnett to his place in Gillingham Street: "The country is quiet just now hereabouts and the inhabitants have given up the practice of cannibalism I believe some time ago. Name day and hour." And Garnett recalled later:

I was introduced to Conrad's snug bachelor quarters where, having placed me in an easy chair, Conrad retired behind a mysterious screen and left me to study the cosiness of the small firelit room, a row of French novels, the framed photograph of an aristocratic lady and an engraving of a benevolent, imposing man on the mantleshelf. On a little table by the screen lay a pile of neat manuscript sheets. I remained conscious of these manuscript sheets when Conrad reappeared and plunged into talk which ranged over things as far removed as the aspects of Malay rivers and the ways of publishers. Conrad's talk that night was a romance; free and swift, it implied, in ironical flashes, that though we hailed from different planets the same tastes animated us. . . . There was a blend of caressing, almost feminine intimacy with masculine incisiveness in his talk . . . Conrad's courtesy was part of his being, bred in the bone, and serving him as a foil in a master's hand, ready for attack or defence.

Conrad showed Garnett the manuscript of *An Outcast of the Islands*: "But when he read aloud to me some new written MS pages . . . he mispronounced so many words that I followed him with difficulty. I found then that he had never once heard these English words spoken, but had learned them all from books!" In one respect the two men seemed to differ: when Garnett advised Conrad to "follow his own path and disregard the public's taste," he was told emphatically, "But I *won't* live in an attic!"[9] Time showed that Conrad wanted neither to live in an attic nor to strive for popularity.

The friendship with Garnett marked a breakthrough in Conrad's social connections in England. Garnett is today forgotten as an author of poetic prose and dramas, but he is remembered as a critic who early recognized and enthusiastically promoted such writers as Conrad, Galsworthy, and D. H. Lawrence. Garnett was eleven years younger than Conrad and already well established in the London intellectual milieu. Son of Richard Garnett, a historian of literature, and married to Constance Garnett, an outstanding translator of Russian novels, Edward was interested in English as well as continental literature. Endowed with a subtle and discerning taste, he had an ability to express his thoughts in a style that was both elegant and caustic. His social and political views were leftist, even socialist; among his friends were revolutionary and anarchist Russian emigrés. For Conrad, a beginner in writing, Garnett's help and kindness were a priceless moral support. Garnett also offered practical advice concerning style, subject matter, and dealings with publishers. Above all, however, Conrad at last had someone to talk to about literature, and thus gradually began to emerge from his state of complete intellectual isolation.

Through Garnett, Conrad also met a literary critic, Edward Verrall Lucas, who recounted later:

[Conrad] was slight and foreign-looking, with manners so punctilious that they made one's own seem almost to be rudeness. . . . In demeanour Conrad was very much the modest author, full of a charming self-depreciation (which he never lost, but which latterly was not always to be taken at its face-value and, indeed, could be almost a weapon), and responding with an embarrassing gratitude to wishes for his success. . . . He spoke with a very strong foreign accent and in sentences not too well constructed. . . . I was never sure of him. Behind that eyeglass what was going on? Was he indeed there at all or away in his study tearing his heart out over his new book? . . . What language he thought in, I cannot say. . . . He had great charm but he never quite convinced his companions he would not be happier alone.[10]

Conrad opened the year by writing his first critical statement: the foreword to *Almayer's Folly*. He challenged the objection to exotic literature as "decivilized," maintaining that the censure arises from a tacitly accepted "contemptuous dislike" for "strange people and the far-off countries." He was eloquent in his defense of a common bond uniting all humanity "no matter where they live; in houses or in huts, in the streets under a fog, or in the forests behind the dark line of dismal mangroves. . . . Their hearts—like ours—must endure the load of the gifts from Heaven: the curse of facts and the blessing of illusions, the bitterness of our wisdom and the deceptive conciliation of our folly."[11] The publisher, however, turned the foreword down, and it did not appear in print until 1920.[12]

Conrad toiled at his writing, and by about 1 February had finished ten chapters of *An Outcast*.[13] But he constantly complained about his health—malaise, lack of appetite, insomnia, and bouts of depression. In the middle of the month he wrote to Poradowska, "I was in bed, in rather bad shape . . . I should have left for Newfoundland on business, but don't feel up to it . . . . Oh God, how black, black, black everything is. This is one of my bad days."[14]

The mysterious business in Newfoundland was probably connected with his plans for investing his inheritance from Uncle Tadeusz, which he had just received. But judging by his letters, he concentrated on writing, passing the finished chapters on the novel to Garnett for his comments; he was always thrilled by words of encouragement or praise. In March his health and mood temporarily improved; between the eighth and fifteenth he spent a few days in Brussels visiting his "aunt." He tried to get *Almayer's Folly* presented to the French public—if not in the form of a translation (which he wanted to do jointly with Poradowska) then at least through an article discussing the novel.[15]

Toward the end of the month he felt worse again. Poradowska's somber mood and her mother's illness added to his anxiety. "Think of me who loves you, suffers and rejoices with you," he wrote on 2 April. He tried to comfort her, taking to heart her literary problems and praising the charming descriptions of the Ukrainian fields in her novel *Marylka*. "I think of your novel as often as of mine."[16] Meanwhile, his work on *An Outcast* was going slowly, amidst doubts and scruples. The number of chapters grew continually. In

December 1894 Conrad thought there would be twelve chapters; on 12 April 1895 the number had risen to "twenty of them . . . if not twenty-one. This time I am giving correct measure"; [17] the final tally was twenty-six.

Tired by recurring bouts of illness and the continual struggle over his book, Conrad decided to go to Champel again.

On 30 April he wrote Poradowska, "I am not at all well. I am getting out of bed and leaving for Champel to take the waters and restore my health. This explains my long silence. You know that when I am not well I have attacks of melancholy which paralyze my mind and will." [18] On the following day, three hours before leaving, he informed Garnett, "I am going to look for Willems in Switzerland. . . . Seriously, I find I can't work. Simply can't! I am going to try what mountain air combined with active fire-hose (twice a day) will do for divine inspiration, I shall try it for about 3 weeks and maybe the lenient gods will allow me to finish that infernal Manuscript." [19]

It is difficult to ascertain whether his worry over the book was the primary reason for his ill health: his ailments were usually psychosomatic. Immediately on arrival at Champel on 2 May, Conrad boasted to Poradowska, "I feel better already." No doubt the fact that on 29 April *Almayer's Folly* had at last been published made a major contribution toward his recovery. After five years of hard work the thirty-eight-year-old writer had made his literary debut.

The book was quite well received: words of praise outweighed unfavorable comments; Conrad was heralded as a talented, original, and promising writer. The word *power* recurred in almost every review. The novel's exotic background attracted the most attention. Conrad was credited with having introduced Borneo into literature; some critics wrote about it tauntingly. The *Spectator* advanced the supposition that he may become "the Kipling of the Malay Archipelago." [20] He was praised for his faithful rendering of realities, although, coming from critics unfamiliar with Indonesia, this was an empty compliment. Widely acclaimed was his ability to evoke mood and atmosphere: the *Daily Chronicle* wrote, "Mr. Conrad has also the art of creating an atmosphere, poetic, romantic. . . . but we have been struck with the book, and know nothing quite like it of recent years." [21] Conrad's form of narration was generally castigated, while the action was described as tangled and too slow; his style was also widely criticized. A respectable weekly, *Athenaeum*, complained that "at times one feels all but stifled by its convolutions," and J. A. Noble, in the even more respectable *Academy*, made the sweeping statement that the book was "much more of a promise than of a performance." [22] H. G. Wells, in his unsigned article in the *Saturday Review*, was one of those who accurately foresaw Conrad's "high place among contemporary story-tellers." [23]

Thus Konrad Korzeniowski, introduced to the reading world as Joseph Conrad, could feel flattered. But the reading world, except for the critics, remained indifferent, and the book did not sell.

On the day of Conrad's arrival at Champel, a twenty-year-old guest, Emilie

Briquel, noted in her diary that "an English sailor who arrived from Neufchatel [Neuchâtel], called Conrad" had been placed at her table.[24] Mlle Briquel came from a well-off and cultured French family; she had arrived with her mother at the pension two weeks earlier.

The sojourn at Champel agreed with the "sailor." His writing progressed faster, as he informed his "Dear and kind Marguerite," announcing that on his way back to England he would stop at Passy, in Paris—where Poradowska had moved—"just for the novel—not for any other reason." He apologized for his short letter, but "I love you none the less for it, you know."[25]

We learn from Emilie's diary why he might have had less time for correspondence: "This evening we played croquet in the garden." And the following day: "Mr Conrad has invited mother and myself to spend a day on the lake with him tomorrow if the weather is good."

The weather held up, and on the evening of 8 May Emilie described her impressions:

I went down before seven o'clock, anxious about the overcast sky. Mr Conrad had gone to town to talk with his boatman and to telephone whether or not we should get ready to go. At about nine the sky cleared up and Mr Conrad arrived in a landau to collect us: Maman, Mlle Simon and me; and the four of us made off for the lake, taking provisions and Maman's folding chair. When we reached the lake, we saw a pretty steamboat with two people on board, a mechanic and a chauffer. They had gone out to fish in the middle of the lake—to think that people had been telling us that fishing was forbidden! We dropped anchor among the reeds near La Belotte and there we lunched very comfortably off our provisions. Afterwards Maman stretched out on her chair, Mlle Simon remained with her in the bow, and Mr Conrad took me back to the back and showed me how to steer. I was delighted to be at the helm. From La Belotte we sailed to Versoix, then to Agnière [Anières], then toward Coppet, crossing the lake in all directions. Mr Conrad supposed we did something like forty kilometres, chasing the small sailboats we came across. Mlle Simon and I took turns at the tiller, but it was to me that Mr Conrad entrusted the difficult task of bringing the boat into harbor and docking. "How wonderful it would be," he said, "to have a little lake-side cottage and a boat of one's own and to be able to spend days on end sailing at random." To my mind it would be real happiness to cut yourself off from the world with the one you love and to be rocked by the waves for hour and hours. I don't think I would ever get bored. At four o'clock we went back and returned by carriage to the hotel after a wonderful drive, no wind, no sun, no rain.

Their friendship grew more intimate. The day after the excursion on the Lake of Geneva, Emilie wrote: "Almost every morning I have breakfast at the same time as Mr Conrad. He is getting nicer and nicer and he listens every day to my playing the piano after breakfast. He at least understands what I play. He is particularly fond of Massenet's *Les phéniciennes*, Saint-Saëns' *Chanson Napolitaine*, Schubert's *Serenade*, and the music of Chopin." The two had long conversations about literature. "Like me he likes Pierre Loti, the poetry of Victor Hugo, and he advised me to read Daudet's *Fromont jeune et Risler aîné* and *Nabob*."[26] They also played croquet and dominoes, and Conrad taught Emilie to play billiards.

The literary side of Conrad's life is presented in his letter to Garnett of 12 May: "I am working every day:—tolerably bad work. Like poor Risler the Elder's cashier 'I haf' no confidence.' . . . I dread the moment when you shall see my *Outcast* as a whole. It seems frightful bosh. I never felt like that even in the first days of my *Folly*. Meantime I live lazily and digest satisfactorily. At my age that last is important. Do not laugh. Your time will come—slowly I hope."[27]

The following day, delighted with a "charming, friendly and understanding" letter from the mayor of Brussels, Charles Buls, Poradowska's longtime admirer to whom Conrad had sent *Almayer's Folly*, he kissed his "dear little aunt" on both cheeks "and would do it for less."[28]

His relationship with Emilie Briquel looked increasingly like a flirtation. Conrad organized excursions, and Emilie sang and played the piano "for him." Her entry of 17 May reads, "I met Mr Conrad in the tram on La Clune, then again in the library and we returned together. That's hardly in accordance with etiquette and convention! In the evening we had a game of billiards and afterwards I played the violin." And next day: "I went into town with Mr Conrad and we came back together on the electric tram."*

To his publisher, Fisher Unwin, Conrad complained, "I am living here in a state of continual exasperation with myself and my work."[29] Nothing in Emilie's diary confirms this mood, however. On the contrary: generally favorable reviews of *Almayer's Folly* and the company of a pleasant young woman seem to have infused Conrad with unusual vigor. And Emilie was obviously charmed by the bearded sailor-writer. Monday, 20 May, was a "great day" for Emilie: she received from Conrad a copy of his novel, with a dedication in English: "To Miss Emily Briquel—whose charming musical gift and everbright presence has cheered for him the dull life of Champel, this book is presented by her most humble, grateful and obedient servant—the Author." On the same day Mlle Briquel resumed her English lessons. And again more walks and conversations . . .

But Conrad's thoughts were already on leaving and seeing his "aunt." On the same Monday he sent Poradowska his congratulations on the Jules Favre literary prize she had been awarded by the Academie Française for her novel, *Les Filles du Pope*, based on Ukrainian and Polish themes. He announced his visit in Passy within a few days. On 25 May he put it off until the beginning of June, complaining of some "passing" indisposition.

---

* Champel is about half an hour's walk from Geneva.

What was the real reason? Possibly uncertainty, doubts, indecision. Although his departure at the end of the month had been planned a long time, now for some reason he tried to dodge the issue. On 26 May Emilie put down in her diary, "We talked a lot all week, but today Mr Conrad received some bad news from a friend of his in London, who had lost part of his fortune; he himself has lost 5,000 francs and has to leave on Thursday, an awful pity, because he is the only one who makes 'La Roseraie' cheerful. My brother Paul has sent him a list of epigraphs for his new novel."

Before parting, Conrad presented Emilie with the music for *Carmen*; he turned the pages while she played. To Paul, his "collaborator," Conrad wrote a letter of thanks:

Your sister received your letter two hours before I left. I am taking the liberty to write to you a few lines to tell you how grateful I am for the trouble you have taken to find an epigraph for my next book. I am impressed by your memory and by the variety of books you have read; after all to produce such a choice like the one you have sent me, you must have read a lot, and carefully.

I hope to have the pleasure of meeting you one day.

Fate has favoured me greatly by allowing me to become acquainted with your mother and sister. I shall cherish the memory of their kindness as a lasting and precious souvenir among those collected during my life of a vagabond.*
Allow me to say: yours ever

J. Conrad.*

The chosen epigraph was to have been the stanza from Victor Hugo:

> Le monde avec ses feux, ses chants, ses harmonies
> N'est qu'une éclosion immense d'agonies
> Sous le bleu firmament
> Un pêle-mêle obscur de souffles et de râles
> De choses de la nuit vaguement sépulcrales
> Qui flottent un moment.**

Conrad promised to visit the Briquel family in Lunéville in the autumn. As he was leaving "La Roseraie," Emilie was "very sad. As if I was losing a true friend, the likes of whom I shall never find again." The following day she mentioned

---

* Conrad must have given Emilie a precise description of the atmosphere of *An Outcast*. Paul Briquel (1877–1922), incidentally, grew up to become quite well known locally as a poet and prose writer, with over a dozen published volumes to his credit.

** "The world with its fires, songs, and harmonies is only an immense hatching of agonies under the blue firmament, an obscure mixture of breaths and rattles, of nightly objects vaguely sepulchral, which fly for a moment" (*La Légende des siècles*, XIII, L'Epopée du ver, lines 577–582). The rhetorical pessimism of these lines fits the mood of *An Outcast* even better than does the tough motto from Calderón's *La vida es sueño* ("Man's worst crime is that he has been born"), but for Conrad the stanza must have evoked particularly painful associations: he had witnessed his father, in exile in Russia, translating fragments of the same *Legend of the Ages*.

her plan to translate *Almayer's Folly* into French, and tried to assess her feelings for Conrad: "For me there are three kinds of love: 1) for the family—I love Maman, I love Paul; 2) the kind I shall have for my husband; 3) friendship, which is how I love Mr Conrad." Although Conrad was placed in the separate category of "friendship," it is revealing merely to find him even included among Emilie's reflections on the varieties of love.

It is perhaps not entirely coincidental that Conrad himself, writing to Garnett barely a week later, brought up the subject of love—quite an unusual thing for him. Following some jokes about his own success (an invitation to dine with his publisher) and the rhetorical question, "What else may I expect?," he added, "True—there is love. That is always new—or rather startling being generally unexpected and violent—and fleeting. Still one must have some object to hang his affections upon—and I haven't." [30]

Apparently he wanted to find such an object but hesitated about the choice. This supposition seems to find some confirmation in a story told by Captain Arthur Burroughs, who, as a fifteen-year-old apprentice, had met Conrad on the *Tilkhurst* (in 1885 or 1886) and remained in contact with him until 1895. Their contact could not have been very close, however, since Burroughs later maintained that Conrad had never commanded a ship. Anyway, Burroughs recounts that in the nineties Conrad used to visit Burroughs's widowed mother, and in her house met one Ida Knight, seventeen-year-old daughter of the Commissioner of Port Darwin in the Falkland Islands. The girl took his fancy, but Mrs. Burroughs's youngest sister, Annette, fell in love with him and made jealous scenes. Conrad, discovering the rivalry, withdrew from the field of battle. This incident apparently took place in the middle of 1895. [31]

Conrad returned to London on 3 June; he must have received Emilie's letter either on the fifth or sixth, but he rushed off the telegram only on the eighth: "Letter only today, thanks. Writing tomorrow to Champel, please leave address with Mürsch [owner of La Roseraie], best wishes for the journey—Conrad." The letter was posted the next day.

> A thousand thanks, dear Mademoiselle Emilie, for your kind and charming letter. It was on my return from Elstree where I had spent three unpleasant days (on the business you know about) that I found an envelope postmarked "Champel," at Barr Moring's. I pounced on it with an enthusiasm easier to understand than to describe and then, with another energetic leap I landed in the telegraph office to let you know—more or less confusedly—why I was so late in replying.
>
> You gave me great pleasure with that phrase in which you wrote that it seemed to you as though "we have lost a true friend." "Lost"—I hope not; but "true friend" are words which make me very proud. Friendship is the most precious thing which one can find in the pilgrimage of life and the traveller who finds it can believe himself to be a favourite of the gods. Our

friendships are the goal and reward of life; they keep us on a straight path—and the memory of them, joyous and sweet, accompanies the fortunate pilgrim; it walks by his side, a tireless and faithful companion, among the cold rocks of the vast solitudes which make up our existence.

Two days later he wrote to Poradowska.

> My dear Aunt,
> Forgive my scandalous silence, but I have had so many annoyances! And also I didn't want to pass on to you the gloom of my troubles. I've carried away such a sweet and charming memory of you—of you happy and peaceful in your nest among the birds. . . . I embrace you most warmly. Yours ever—J. Conrad.[32]

The preceeding letter, affectionate but brief, without confidences and coy endearments like many of the earlier ones—is the last surviving letter from this period; after that there is an almost five-year gap in the extant correspondence with Poradowska. For a biographer the gap is quite catastrophic, since it spans both Conrad's marriage and his final decision to settle in England (in 1896 he was still expressing his intention to live on the Continent); it falls during the difficult period of his apprenticeship as a novelist and of some mysterious contacts with Polish writers; many other things happened during that time about which we are forced to speculate. Why Poradowska destroyed Conrad's letters from that period, which definitely existed, as we know from Conrad's other correspondence, is impossible to tell with certainty.

The months from June 1895 to March 1896 are among the most important and, at the same time, the least-known in Conrad's life.

Let us now try to estimate generally the position of the sailor-writer at a turning point of his life. It should help our understanding of his romantic ventures.

Since leaving his last ship on 18 January 1894, Conrad had had no regular employment, except occasional work with Barr, Moering and Co., the shipping firm where he was a minor shareholder. The inheritance from Uncle Tadeusz—fifteen thousand rubles plus 1,200 in interest—was enough to give him a comfortable living for two to three years. In addition, he probably had some modest savings. The £20 he received for *Almayer's Folly* and £50 for *An Outcast of the Islands* could not be regarded as offering any prospect of economic security in the future. Therefore, although he was now free from immediate financial worries and able to afford a gentlemanlike style of life, he was forced to look for a permanent source of more substantial income. He continued his search for a position as shipmaster, but apart from other obstacles—like a lack of experience with steamships, and his foreign origin—he had constant problems with his health. His other project, one of buying a ship that he would then command himself, also never materialized.

Conrad had to cope alone with those difficulties. To begin with, he was, and remained, a foreigner—both in England and in France. He did not belong to any particular milieu. A motif that frequently recurs in the reminiscences of his old friends is the striking contrast between Conrad and the community of professional officers in the British Merchant Service—in terms of manners, appearance, education and interests. His circle of friends—if one may use this binding term—was very small and rather accidentally chosen. In correspondence and reports we find the same few names mentioned over and over again: the two business partners, G. F. W. Hope (ex-officer of the merchant marine), and an American of German origin, Adolf Krieger; Joseph Spiridion Kliszczewski, son of a veteran from the 1863 insurrection and an emigré, whom Conrad met once in Cardiff; Edward Sanderson, much younger than Conrad, son of a school headmaster; and, finally, the newly met Edward Garnett, the first writer in his group of friends.

By virtue of his origins and upbringing, Conrad belonged to the intelligentsia; he was linked to the same class by his interests, manners, and literary ambitions. But outside Poland he had practically no contacts with people belonging to that class. Poradowska was the sole exception; she had already published four novels (one of them also in German) when Conrad was making his début. Conrad, nine years her junior, was her protégé. Several times, she tried to help him find work, although without success.

Uncle Tadeusz had suspected his former ward of coquetting with Aunt Marguerite as early as in the summer of 1891. Konrad kept denying this but the note of romance rang in his letters often and clearly. All the same it is not easy to assess his attitude toward Poradowska. After he stopped traveling, he wrote her several letters a month; judging by the confidential nature of many of his remarks, he must have regarded her as a person both close to him and understanding; he would also express his concern for her personal and literary affairs. He paid her several visits in Brussels and Paris, although mostly of only one or two days. One may guess that apart from the difference in age he was somewhat disconcerted by Poradowska's position. He was her younger and poorer relation, a beginner in literature, a man without any connection—a very uncomfortable situation for a suitor, as it implied the prospect of a social and financial misalliance for the lady of his choice. Those obstacles could have been surmounted by a strong reciprocal feeling, but probably it was not there. Moreover, Conrad seems to have been on the whole rather shy with women.

Nevertheless, something must have happened about the middle of 1895— and almost certainly it concerned his emotional life. Did Conrad after all propose and meet refusal? Did either of them commit some kind of blunder? Did Poradowska learn about the flirtation with Emilie? Their relations were neither broken nor interrupted, but their correspondence must have become too intimate. One interesting detail which is symptomatic of the many links between Conrad and Poradowska is the fact that the action of *The Sisters*—a novel begun in the autumn of 1895, abandoned in March 1896, and never finished—was to have taken place in Passy, the Paris district where Poradowska rented an apartment. Ukrainian motifs, frequent in Poradowska's writings, also appear in *The Sisters*.*

As for Mlle Emilie Briquel, eighteen years his junior, one thing is clear: Conrad turned her head. The rest remains uncertain. We may, however, use other facts and substantiated guesses to supplement the information found in the girl's diary and in their correspondence.

The Briquel family came from the prosperous *haute bourgeoisie* of Lorraine. One can still sense the richness of their cultural tradition, since their family house in Lunéville, built at the beginning of the nineteenth century, has been preserved. A beautiful garden is guarded by two magnificent sixteenth-century lions, transferred from the Lunéville Castle during its reconstruction. In that castle died the father-in-law of Louis XV, Stanisław Leszczyński, king of Poland and later duke of Lorraine, known affectionately as Le Roi Stanislas. The Lotharingians were traditionally friendly to Poles.

But Konrad Korzeniowski (as he still was on his passport) never even breathed a word about his Polish origin: in Champel he passed for an Englishman. "I shall learn your beautiful language," Paul Briquel wrote to him. Why did Korzeniowski act that way? Perhaps because in England no one would take him for an Englishman: his accent would immediately give him away. And as we know from several independent sources (Garnett, Jessie Conrad, the Kliszczewskis), before 1900 Conrad tried to avoid all conversations on Polish subjects. Or perhaps he thought being English was more consistent with the image of sea dog, writer, and globe-trotter he presented at La Roseraie. Whatever the reasons, the masquerade greatly impeded closer contacts: a visit to Lunéville, for instance, would soon have revealed the truth. All we can do is assume that at first he treated his friendship with the Briquel ladies quite casually. Apart from hiding his original nationality, he probably gave rein to his inclination to invent colorful stories, such as one about the "affair" of the nonexistent Francis described in his letters. Emilie was fascinated, but Conrad put himself in an embarrassing position, whatever his feelings toward the girl were. He himself could not have been quite indifferent—for Emilie occupied too much of his time and attention. The numerous evasions and falsehoods in his letters show that he was unable to find a fitting way out of the tangle without damaging the relationship.

The Briquels were sure that Conrad was about to ask for Emilie's hand—but he was definitely not their idea of a suitor. Perhaps the misunderstanding was caused by Emilie herself suggesting a courtship while at the same time affecting indifference. This possibility cannot be ruled out; but then we would have to

* It may be only a coincidence, but one cannot help noticing that Conrad began writing *The Sisters* in autumn 1895, during the "discreet" stage of his relationship with Poradowska and before he proposed to Jessie—and then stopped writing it shortly before his marriage.

admit that Conrad behaved in a rather lightheaded way. After all, he did pay Emilie marked attentions—he was no callow youth but a seasoned man of the world on the verge of middle age. What seems more likely on the evidence of this irregular but affectionate correspondence is that he was intent on keeping his options open, perhaps waiting for inspiration while simultaneously trying to secure a financial position that would enable him, without embarrassment, to propose matrimony to whatever woman he chose, no matter what her birth had entitled and accustomed her to. Once again, as with Poradowska, all he could offer Emilie was a misalliance, and he was certainly too proud for that.

To return to the chronological order of events: on 3 July Paul Briquel received an answer to the letter he had written a couple of weeks earlier, in which he had also expressed his hope of getting better acquainted with Conrad during the latter's proposed visit to Lunéville, in the autumn. Conrad's reply contained no less than a brief exposition on his view of life. As we shall see from his next letter to Emilie, Conrad himself had doubts about what he had written, and it would not do to accept literally this credo addressed to a poet of barely eighteen, a self-avowed believer in the "old, pessimistic philosophy of the Hindu Nirvana." However, in the stilted phrases we may detect echoes of the fashionable Schopenhauer, as well as some typical elements of Conrad's own intellectual attitude.

> I am using my first free moment to answer your letter. I have been very busy. One must toss in one's cage until the day the doors open up on to the surrounding void.
>
> You have over me the advantage of youth and of superior knowledge of many things I know nothing about. You've read a great deal. And all I've read has been one big, enormous page, a page filled by life completely external, in disregard of one's own personality, faced with various mysterious forces which resist our will. So there you are. I've decided that there lies the only chance of happiness. In a duty fulfilled, in an obstacle overcome—no matter what duty, no matter what obstacle, there lies the refuge of man strayed on this earth, because the reason is weak and short-lived, and the will is eternal and strong. We must serve the master who is stronger, the master never capricious, never erring. But you must not think that I prescribe egoism. One must fulfil tasks that are boring, painful and repulsive; the world must be allowed to proceed; we have to disregard the eternal Error because it contains many Truths in whose triumph we must assist. This is an idea born out of my ignorance. I am sharing it with you. You may perhaps find it useful in your life. Anyhow it cannot do any harm.

At the same time he wrote to Garnett, "I suffer now from an acute attack of faithlessness . . . in anything";[33] his other letters expressed similarly bitter thoughts. He divided his time between Elstree and London, plodding at the growing manuscript of *An Outcast*. Emilie meanwhile was forging ahead with her translation of *Almayer's Folly*. On 10 July she sent off an enthusiastic letter to Conrad with a diffident inquiry about the copyright. He replied immediately:

> Yours is certainly the most delightful letter an author could ever receive. I cannot tell you how very grateful I am and how much I appreciate it. Your judgement, I can assure you, carries great weight with me, because in the end we write for our friends, for the minds and hearts of those who know us, and not for the unknown high priests who publish reviews (usually mistaken) in the papers.
>
> Your praise flatters me and fills me with joy, but also with sadness and regret. Sadness, because I know that I hardly deserve your indulgent assessment, regret at not having done better. On the other hand, your ability to master a foreign language leaves me speechless with admiration. Can it be? So soon? Barely two months have passed since you obtained the book! I really do not know what to admire more: the liveliness of your mind or the strength of your will? your talent or your perseverance!
>
> Believe me, I am deeply touched by this proof of your interest in my book, an interest which is far greater than it merits, by this positive and conclusive proof of your affection. . . . I shall simply say that you have caused me one of the most exhilarating pleasures of my life . . . I am now fighting, grappling, with Chapter 13 of my new book. Then will come the 14th—and after that the deluge. A deluge of doubts, reproaches, regrets and fear on which I shall bob until about some charitable critic throws me a rope of flattery. Otherwise I shall sink like a stone and no more will ever be heard of me. I hope that your brother did not take my idiotic letter amiss. It expressed some reflections in the form of a theory of life whose only value is that it is sincere and supported by the experience of my futile existence. It is also, I feel, fairly honourable. I hope he does not suspect me of preaching to him! Far from it. His letter simply opened the dyke of my thoughts. That is all.[34]

Emilie replied on 20 July with a letter full of compliments about the book, wishes for a pleasant voyage, and assurances that the whole family thought of him constantly. The same day she noted in her diary, "This year in Champel, I met Mr Conrad, I speak about him often and at length, I write to him and I think that I am very fond of him! Perhaps, but I am fond of him as a friend, as an agreeable acquaintance, which cannot be compared to love! I dream of a quiet little nest, of a secluded happiness for two, of the supreme happiness of married love." (Lest this outburst give the wrong impression of Emilie's character, it is as well to make it clear that she was a woman of great vigor and energy; at the age of eighty she could still be seen riding around Lunéville on her bicycle. She died in 1961 at the age of eighty-six.)

Conrad spent the two weeks between 24 July and 7 August sailing on the

Channel and the North Sea in Hope's cutter, the *Illdegonde*.[35] Then he found himself in a whirl of financial affairs. Within a dozen or so days he apparently visited Paris three times, buying and selling claims on South African gold mines, mainly on behalf of Hope's brother-in-law. The description of those triumphant exertions, which is given in a letter to Sanderson, sounds a little too sensational and boastful to be taken as a faithful rendering of facts.[36] Moreover two pieces of information evoke additional scepticism. Conrad claimed that for his services he received 200 shares from the Rorke Roodepoort Gold Mine, and that in addition he bought and sold at a good profit fifty claims on the Black Reef section of the gold-bearing fields at Witwatersrand.[37] "You know that I wanted funds for the base purpose of carrying on a wretched and useless existence. The thing was as honest as such things can be. In fact exceptionally so. It is a first-class property and offered cheap. I could with all due care for my honour (which is my only hereditary property) take it up." The property turned out to be not "first-class," as Rorke Roodepoort Ltd. ceased to exist the following year (the shareholders received back the money they had invested), and the report of the Witwatersrand Chamber of Mines contains no mention of the company's mining activities.[38] A year later it transpired that Conrad had invested almost all his money in some other, probably similar, South African enterprise.

The second bit of news contained in this letter to Sanderson is a typical hoax—not journalistic but epistolary. Naming the people whom he recruited on 8 August in Paris to help him carry out complicated financial machinations, he mentioned "Pascalis of the *Figaro*, Guesde (a deputy), and the bankers Jullien and Epstein. All acquaintances of my young days." I know nothing of Pascalis and Epstein, but the only influential Jullien at the time was, I believe, not a banker but a leftist Republican deputy from the district of Romorantin, Philippe-Emile Jullien (1845–1912). It is rather unlikely that they had met in Conrad's Marseilles days, and it is almost out of the question that Conrad knew Jules Guesde (1845–1922), who had returned from exile a couple of months before Korzeniowski's attempted suicide and had not gone to southern France. It is difficult to imagine that the famous Guesde, a collaborator of Marx, a leader of the Second International, opposed to participation in bourgeois governments, repeatedly imprisoned and banished from the country, and at that time the Socialist deputy for Roubaix, would have anything to do with international financial transactions.

The same letter to Sanderson contains another piece of information, in this case verifiable, about Conrad's signing a contract with Unwin for *An Outcast*. The author was to receive £50 plus 12.5 percent of the proceeds. This business prospect did not look promising, but the publisher, not Conrad, was the loser.

Two days later Conrad wrote to Emilie. He was evasive on the subject of the delay and justified himself by maintaining that he had returned only three days before. Here, too, he gave rein to his imagination, improvising about his expedition to the Atlantic, as far as the Shetland Islands and the Orkneys (in fact he had sailed no farther than the shores of Holland). "As you rightly suppose, I have very much neglected my affairs and am now inundated by work. The book is drawing to an end. But I have other worries. I mean to go back to sea this year. I want to buy a boat, take command and set out on a voyage of two to three years."[39]

This letter marks the onset of a cooling of the relations between Conrad and the Briquels. He left the letter from Emilie's brother unanswered and did not write to Emilie again until 1 October, in affectionate and bantering, but nevertheless once again evasive, terms. He went on about his health and all sorts of financial ventures, while he was really occupied with finishing *An Outcast* and correcting the parts of the manuscript Garnett had criticized.

Repeating the formula he had already used in his letter to Poradowska with regard to *Almayer's Folly*, he informed Garnett:

It is my painful duty to inform you of the sad death of Mr Peter Willems late of Rotterdam and Macassar who has been murdered on the 16th inst at 4 p.m. while the sun shone joyously and the barrel organ sang on the pavement the abominable Intermezzo of the ghastly Cavalleria. As soon as I recovered from the shock I busied myself in arranging the affairs of the two inconsolable widows of our late lamented friend and I am glad to say that—with the help of Captain Lingard who took upon himself all the funereal arrangements—everything was decently settled before midnight. You know what strong affection I had for the poor departed so you won't be surprised to hear that to me—since yesterday life seems a blank—a dumb solitude from which everything—even the shadows—have completely vanished.[40]

Garnett read the last chapters immediately and criticized precisely the scene of Willems's death as being too drawn out and static. Conrad rhetorically admitted a complete failure and promised to prune the text, but, explaining his point of view and intentions, he professed to be unable "to improve what has got itself written."[41]

For the second time the end of a novel left him with a sense of disappointment and unfulfilled intentions. To Edward Noble, who like himself was a sailor turning writer, he wrote about *Almayer's Folly*: "And after all I consider it honestly a miserable failure. Every critic (but two or three) overrated the book. It took me a year to tear the *Outcast* out of myself and upon my word of honour,—I look on it (now it's finished) with bitter disappointment."[42]

Perhaps that was the reason his third novel, *The Sisters*, begun toward the end of 1895, was to be entirely different. Its beginning, amounting to thirty-five printed pages, introduces two plots that remain as yet unconnected. Stephen, a Ukrainian painter settled in Paris, is the hero of the first plot, central and more developed; the second plot evolves around a young Basque girl named Rita, sent from her home village to Paris to be brought up by her family there. In his choice of subject and background Conrad was doubtless influenced by the example of Poradowska: she had written regional stories from the lives of Poles and the Ukrainians, and she was living at Passy, the district where the later action of *The Sisters* was to have taken place. Conrad wanted to reach out for other, nonexotic and nontropical, layers of his experience, but he made an injudicious choice. Stephen came from the same part of Europe as Conrad did, but his national and cultural backgrounds were different, and it turned out that Conrad's knowledge of the subject was practically nil. Apart from making Stephen disappointed with the external aspects of life in the West, he had not much to say about his hero's inner life. For various reasons he refrained from choosing a Polish character; such a choice would have forced him to open old wounds and to expose himself in front of the reader. The Ruthenian hero turned out a fake. He was artificially contrived, and Conrad wrote about him in an artificial, bombastic manner.[43] Garnett saw a fragment of the novel and advised him to discontinue it.[44] Conrad recalled later, "I abandoned The Sisters in despair of being able to keep up the high pitch. . . . I got scared off it thinking it out ahead."[45]

Conrad's occupations toward the end of 1895 and at the beginning of 1896 remain unknown, apart from correcting *An Outcast* and writing *The Sisters*. There is also a gap from 24 September to 22 February in his correspondence with Garnett.

The 1 October letter to Emilie ends with a spirited declaration: "I enjoy every kind of struggle with elements and with people. Struggle means life, and for me the pleasure lies precisely in the struggle itself—never in the victory or in the fruits of victory. That is something I never think about." It echoes in Emilie's diary as an entry under 3 November: "Monsieur Conrad wrote to me once: 'Struggle means life.' Ah, well. I do not agree. For me life is happiness, but happiness that is silent, tranquil, gentle."

Far from trying to cut loose, Conrad went out of his way to preserve a show of affection and was at pains to explain his failure to use the epigraph suggested by Paul in *An Outcast*. His letter of 14 November reads:

> Your kind letter brought me great pleasure and I gather that you are enjoying yourself and that everything at home is all right.
>
> It is good to know that one's friends are having a good time and are happy when one is going through a rough patch. As far as I am concerned I am fed up with the idiotic globe which goes on and on spinning for no good reason. . . .
>
> My poor book met with a sad fate. During my illness I was flooded by proof-sheets which I tried to correct without delay. The title-page with the dedication and the first chapter reached me last. I proof-read the chapter (lying in bed) and asked one of my friends, who was with me at the time, to

check the title-page. He looks, says it is in order and, at my request, marks the whole lot "to go to press," and sends it off. I forget all about it. Two days ago I hear the publisher wants me to come and see the first copy. I go, look and find it well and nicely turned out. I glance at the title. Hell and damnation! There is un (or une) épigraphe in Spanish—a quotation from Calderón, two lines. I raise a storm! They show me the manuscript. True enough! You may remember the difficulties I had with the choice of an epigraph. There were several on that page written for comparison in pencil or pen; one of them was that unfortunate Calderón. I forgot to pass my pen over it. The quotation from Victor Hugo chosen by your brother was not there since I had intended to write it out on the proof-sheet before sending it to the printers. . . .

Well, I've said it all. My most respectful regards for your mother. A friendly handshake for your brother. Please believe me, dear Mademoiselle Emilie, your devoted and obedient servant.[46]

The letter shows that Conrad was anxious to remain on good terms with the Briquel family. At the turn of the year he sent off a bombastic letter of New Year greetings: "If the Master of our souls, the Merciful and Compassionate Master, is pleased to hear the voice of a lonely and blind sinner, he will vouchsafe you long years of calm and comfort, a peaceful and worthy existence, the shelter of dependable feelings, the support of brave and upright hearts. In a word I wish you happiness—but this is a word which I hardly dare express, the thing being so immense, so distant, so elusive, that to wish it seems too presumptuous and futile!"[47]

An acknowledgment of this letter forms the final reference to Conrad in Mlle Briquel's diary, but a mysterious document has survived among her papers: a farewell verse addressed to her by Conrad. According to Briquel family tradition, this is a translation of an English poem sent to Emilie early in 1896. Conrad had apparently been made to understand that, because of the age gap between them and his nomadic life style, he could not hope to win the girl's hand. Here is the poem, which does not lose much in literal translation:

> Why love if departure is near?
> And why part when one is happy?
> Young girl, our paths close for an instant
> Briefly crossed and separate for ever.
> > Your life will pass sheltered from danger,
> > Protected by your mother, later by your husband;
> > You will live simple, sweet and happy,
> > Never leaving your country, serving your God.
> While I have no roots on this earth,
> And in my mind, like in a mystery play,

I see again all I have understood, thought,
And suffered—all I have loved.
    God cast upon me a ray of Genius;
    It is He who holds my pen and makes me write,
    It is He who lets me see the entire harmony
    Of power and beauty, of suffering and love.
Always parting . . . shall I see you one day?
Your happiness and mine follow different routes:
Yours is a simple life beside a hearth
Which you adorn for him who will know how to love you.
    For me—it is to be on the immense sea,
    To devote to it intensely
    All the gifts I have: intelligence and energy;
    For me—it is to sail towards the retreating horizon.
The world is so small—I find it so great.
I am afraid for you; so afraid of the unknown.
The unknown is but a word for me who has seen everything
    But you could die on a long voyage.
    Oh! I am still young and feel at my age
    That the future is mine—the future is God's.

It is most unlikely, not to say impossible, that this poem was actually written by Conrad, who had never tried his hand at verse. The loss of the original would in any case be inexplicable. If any other arguments are needed against Conrad's authorship, there is the work's theistic optimism and mawkish turgidity, not to mention the fact that there is no way of dating it. Being an adieu, it should have followed the last of the extant letters; but there is nothing in the latter to foreshadow such an emotionally charged approach. For all these reasons I personally am sure that the poem was in fact written by Emilie, who ascribed to her "friend" thoughts, views, and attitudes derived from motifs found in his letters and conversation. There emerges here an image of Conrad quite different from the one that appears in his correspondence with Poradowska, Garnett, or Sanderson. But then with Emilie Conrad presumably shed his jaundiced pessimism and posed as a man of action searching out challenges and fiercely contending with the obstacles of life; he exhibited his heroic self-portrait.

For Emilie this rhyming conclusion must have seemed a fitting end to her romantic friendship. For by now she was preparing for marriage: on 10 February she became officially engaged to a local acquaintance, Dr. Edmond Lalitte. News of this event was communicated to Conrad by her mother; apparently he was still regarded as at least a prospective suitor (although a formal rejection is without a doubt no more than a family legend). The situation was at last clear. Conrad, however, took some time before replying.

7th March 1896

Dear Madame Briquel,

I have only just returned from Scotland and read your letter which is so charming and so kind, and above all contains such good news.

Miss Emilie's admirable qualities, your goodness, the affection and sympathy which you were pleased to show me in Champel will always remain among the most precious memories of my life.

Before your daughter there now lies open a sweet and tranquil land of delightful promises. I wish her sun-bathed landscapes, refreshing shade, the warm breezes of an eternal spring along the path of her life. If happiness in this world were apportioned according to deserts, I would have no doubts about Miss Emilie's future. I hope the Merciful Heavens will grant her a long and prosperous life in which she can be a joy to her dear ones and lavish happiness around her through the precious gifts of heart and mind with which she has been endowed.

Please believe me, Chère Madame, when I say that I understand and warmly appreciate the kindness that has dictated the words, so full of friendship, of your letter. I regret my inability to answer it at greater length as I have various pressing engagements, but I wanted to waste no time in sending you and Mademoiselle Emilie my best wishes.

I also am getting married. But that is a long story which I will relate in my next letter, in a few days.

I remain your ever grateful and devoted servant.

Jsph Conrad *

This letter, so stiltedly effusive that it sounds forced, contains the sensational news that Conrad himself was on the point of getting married. What is even more curious is the fact that this is the earliest known reference to any such plans. The possibility of a coincidence cannot be ruled out, but the impression of some connection between both events is difficult to dispel.

Conrad's third romance within the span of a year, the one crowned with complete success and wedlock, was both the quickest and the most mysterious of all.

The only comprehensive and coherent (although unreliable) account of how Conrad came to know and marry Jessie Emmeline George is to be found in Ford Madox Ford's satirical novel, *The Simple Life Limited*.[48] Conrad is represented there as Simeon Brandetski, "possibly Polish, possibly Lithuanian, possibly Little Russian Jew," who settles in England after an eventful life of travel and work in Africa, which has ruined his health; on the advice of a Mr. Parmont (who stands for Garnett) he changes his name to Simon Brandson and becomes a writer. A hopeless sluggard who does not even bother to sit up straight, he hires a secretary to type for him. Since he is a late riser, their work drags on well into

---

* He sent neither the promised letter nor a copy of *An Outcast*; something must have troubled him.

the night. The secretary becomes his mistress—and Brandetski-Brandson is forced to marry her.

Ford's story, published two years after his friendship and association with Conrad were severed, smells of malicious gossip; included in a roman à clef in which most characters combine various traits of living personalities, it cannot be regarded as a valid document. But it should not be ignored, either; it is one of the many proofs that Conrad's strange marriage was "talked about."

Jessie's own account, less sensational and free of any scandalous undertones, is contradictory and fails to clarify some basic facts. The main one is what a sensitive and cultured Pole of aristocratic manners and "gentle birth" saw in a typist of humble origin, one of the many children of a warehouseman and shop-keeper, a girl almost sixteen years younger (she was born 22 February 1873), not well educated or particularly intelligent, or—by Conrad's own account—especially attractive. None of the references to Jessie in Conrad's letters nor even in her own memoirs suggest a strong feeling—and yet matters progressed quickly.

In her first book of reminiscences on Conrad, *Joseph Conrad as I Knew Him*, published two years after the writer's death, Jessie wrote that she had met her future husband in November 1894 through a mutual acquaintance. At their fourth meeting he presented her with a copy of *Almayer's Folly*. The inscription is dated 2 April 1895, which means that Jessie was given one of the advance copies of the novel, published only on 29 April (Poradowska received another one);[49] this suggests a fairly close relationship.

Several months passed before their fifth meeting, during which time Jessie completely lost sight of him. Their friendship grew closer while he finished his work on *An Outcast*. According to Jessie, Conrad frequently asked her to read the manuscript aloud, and these sessions, interrupted by his impatient outbursts, apparently went on for some time.

This chronology does not seem quite convincing: between November 1894 and the presentation of *Almayer's Folly*, five months elapsed during which Jessie says there were four encounters. *An Outcast* was finished on 16 September 1895, which leaves five months into which to fit both a long period of separation and many "reading sessions." Even more confusing is Jessie's claim that Conrad went to take the waters in Champel in December 1895; after an absence of one month Conrad proposed marriage.

In Jessie's second book on Conrad, *Joseph Conrad and His Circle*, published nine years later, the account of events is even more muddled and inconsistent with the real chronology. The most startling detail concerns Mr. and Mrs. Hope. According to Jessie's earlier account, they had introduced Conrad to her; here they are presented as Conrad's friends whom she first met only during her engagement.[50] Jessie's story, like the whole of her book, abounds in dramatic and grotesque incidents; and since she contradicts herself it is all the more difficult to accept her recollections as trustworthy. Nevertheless, certain significant elements occur in both of her accounts: the proposal of marriage takes place after a long interval in their meetings; immediately afterward both of them become unexpectedly ill; Conrad disappears for several days; Jessie is not sure whether to take his proposal seriously—she does not mention it even to her mother; her family is utterly bewildered; Conrad's behavior is perplexing to Jessie, family, and friends (he does not want children, predicts his imminent death, and so on); the engagement is a short one, Conrad suggests the wedding within a week or two, finally they settle on six weeks; there is something strange, even uncanny, in the atmosphere of their relationship.[51]

Following Conrad's letter to Mme Briquel, the next mention of his marital plans comes in his letter of 10 March, to Karol Zagórski in Lublin:

> No one can be more surprised at it than myself. However, I am not frightened at all, for as you know, I am accustomed to an adventurous life and to facing terrible dangers. Moreover, I have to avow that my betrothed does not give the impression of being at all dangerous. Jessie is her name; George her surname. She is a small, not at all striking-looking person (to tell the truth alas —rather plain!) who nevertheless is very dear to me. When I met her a year and a half ago she was earning her living in the City as "Typewriter" in an American business office of the "Caligraph" company. Her father died three years ago. There are nine children in the family. The mother is a very decent woman (and I do not doubt very virtuous as well). However, I must confess that it is all the same to me, as vous comprenez?—I am not marrying the whole family. The wedding will take place on the 24th of this month and we shall leave London immediately so as to conceal from people's eyes our happiness (or our stupidity) amidst the wilderness and beauty of the coast of Brittany where I intend to rent a small house in some fishing village . . . I hope that on the day of my wedding all of you—who are my whole family— will join me in your thoughts.[52]

On 16 March he introduced Jessie to the Garnetts.[53] Garnett expressed his anxiety and warned Conrad against acting rashly: "Conrad's ultra-nervous organization appeared to make matrimony extremely hazardous."[54] Although his arguments, published forty years later, concern Conrad himself, it is significant that Garnett tried to dissuade him from marriage only after he had met Jessie. Conrad replied with a philosophical argument that may be understood as an expression of unwillingness or inability to give a reasonable justification for his decision. "When once the truth is grasped that one's own personality is only a ridiculous and aimless masquerade of something hopelessly unknown the attainment of serenity is not very far off. Then there remains nothing but the surrender to one's impulses, the fidelity to passing emotions which is perhaps a nearer approach to truth than any other philosophy of life."[55]

As I have already said, Jessie's reminiscences neither give a coherent and convincing picture of events nor explain Conrad's motives. Apparently he told her to destroy letters he wrote during their engagement, and so we have been deprived of another source of information. It seems most probable that he met Jessie in an office with which he had business dealings and where she worked as a typist, and also that the intimacy between them (we cannot now know if it went to the point of seduction) developed in the course of her typing some of his manuscripts. Jocelyn Baines suspects that after two years on land, in an alien city, Conrad felt his loneliness more and more acutely, and his choice of a girl without education or cultural background simply reflected his lack of connections with the English intelligentsia.[56] And another thing: in the case of Jessie there could be no question of the bride's financial misalliance—the advantage was all on her side. Although his repeated attempts to find a job had produced no effect, Conrad still had the legacy from his uncle. He was even considering buying a small ship or going into partnership with a shipowner who would give him a command; but that too failed.[57] The sailor's profession was practically closed to him, and that made his plans for marriage more feasible.

Nonetheless, the suddenness of Conrad's decision remains as puzzling to us as it was to Jessie. His haste may have been in some way connected with Poradowska, as Baines suggests, or perhaps with Emilie Briquel: if it is true that he proposed to Jessie six weeks before the wedding, it happened exactly at the time of Emilie's engagement. He need not necessarily have been in love with Emilie, nor even courted her, for the news to have given him an additional and decisive spur.

Jessie recalls the trip by steamer to Grangemouth, Scotland, made by the engaged couple together with Jessie's younger sister Ethel and G. F. W. Hope. Apparently they went to inspect a wooden barque, the 483-ton *Windermere*, which Conrad intended to buy. The main elements of this reminiscence may be verified, but they do little to elucidate the chronology of more important events. For one thing, Jessie places the expedition at the end of their engagement and the return three days before the wedding, while according to the documentary evidence the trip can be fitted only between 18 and 24 February.[58]

The wedding—only a civil ceremony although both came from Catholic families—took place in London on 24 March 1896 at St. George Register Office in Hanover Square. Jessie's mother, Jane George, was one of the witnesses; the others were Hope and Krieger.[59] It appears that Conrad arrived late for the wedding and that his behavior was stiff and strange. He did not conceal his aversion to his wife's numerous siblings while saying his farewells. The young couple spent their evening writing "formal and ceremonial" notifications of their marriage, and then, at two in the morning, the bridegroom insisted on posting those letters. Jessie related that all these proceedings threw her completely off balance. When on the following day the two traveled by train through a tunnel, the sudden flash of a signal light paralyzed her with fear, for she thought that her husband, virtually a stranger, had thrown a bomb.[60]

For Conrad, too, the marriage was a plunge into a strange social, cultural, and psychological world. The burden of loneliness did not disappear, it only changed its shape.

Immediately after the wedding the couple went to Brittany for an unspecified time. The first work completed by Conrad during his honeymoon was a short story, "The Idiots," a naturalistic tale about a wife who kills her husband with a pair of scissors while defending herself from his sexual advances. The work was to provide great fun for all Conrad's future psychoanalytical critics.

VIII

. . . .
STRIVINGS, EXPERIMENTS, DOUBTS

1896–1898

OLORFUL and somewhat implausibly dramatic best characterize Jessie Conrad's description of her honeymoon. One day after their marriage, the Conrads left by train for Southampton, and then by boat for St. Malo, in Brittany.[1] The night crossing of the English Channel was rough, and Jessie found to her consternation that not only she but also her husband, an experienced sea-traveler, suffered from seasickness. When they went ashore in France Conrad kept astonishing Jessie with his strange behavior, and when he ordered rum instead of milk with their pot of tea, she found it "a trifle shocking to my English mind."

After a night at St. Malo, the couple took a bus to Lannion, a small village in northern Brittany, where they registered on 27 March at the Hôtel de France. It was to serve as their base while they looked for a small house to rent. They were after something secluded—"out of the way of absurd French tourists that stream through better known places during July and August"—preferably on an island.[2] A few days after their arrival, Jessie became indisposed, which put Conrad in a state of near panic. He confided to Ted Sanderson's mother, "The dear girl is herself again—nearly—and so am I. For I must tell you, that,—unaccustomed as I am to matrimonial possibilities,—I was alarmed,—not to say horribly scared! However she had convincing proofs of my nursing qualifications: and no doubt in a year or two I will be disposed to take things with much more composure—not to say coolness. But I must tell you under seal of confidence that I would not go through such three days again for a diamond mine!"[3]

The Conrads did not succeed in finding a house on the Ile de Bréhat, famed for its picturesque scenery, but repeated expeditions by chaise along the ragged Corniche de Bretagne resulted in their renting a small house on Ile-Grande which, in spite of its name, is connected with the mainland by a narrow peninsula. The landscape here is rather somber: large patches of flat rocks are interspersed with stumpy weatherbeaten trees; shallows exposed twice a day during low tide reveal an expanse of greenish-brown seaweeds; the sea has a gray tint even in good weather, and under an overcast sky becomes like dark lead. Ile-Grande, where they moved on 7 April, is a country village consisting of stone cottages scattered over rocky hills. The Conrads rented their cottage from Mme Le Bail, whose husband was a stonecutter and seller of granite.* Conrad wrote to Sanderson:

At last, from my new (and very first) home, I write you to say that I am quite oppressed by my sense of importance in having a house—actually a whole house!!—to live in. It's the first time—since I came to years of discretion—that such an event happened in my life.

Jess is immensely amused by the kitchen (the fireplace alone is big enough for her to live in) and spends most of her time trying to talk with the girl (who is a perfect treasure). The kitchen is the most splendid and the best furnished apartment of the palace,—and the only way in or out, anyhow. So we see it pretty often. Our sticks and caps have their domicile there altogether.

The coast is rocky, sandy, wild and full of mournful expressiveness. But the land, at the back of the wide stretches of the sea enclosed by the barren archipelago, is green and smiling and sunny—often even when the sea and the islets are under the shadow of the passing clouds. From beyond the rounded slopes of the hill the sharp spires of many village-churches point persistently to the sky. And the people that inhabits these shores is a people of women— black-clad and white-capped—for the men fish in Iceland or on the banks of Newfoundland. Only here and there a rare old fellow with long hair, forgotten by the successive roll-calls of the sea, creeps along the rock between beaches and looks sad and useless and lone in the stony landscape.[4]

In the upstairs small room, which faced the bay fringed by rocks, Conrad set out to write. But his third novel (not counting the quickly abandoned *Sisters*), whose title he communicated to Garnett one day before the marriage, was to give him the most trouble. Originally it was to be called *The Rescuer, A Tale of Narrow Waters*, with the action set once again in Malaya. Conrad was following Garnett's advice: to stick to maritime and exotic subjects. He planned to finish the book in twelve months, but in fact he grappled with it for as many as twenty-four years.

At first his work progressed with reasonable speed. By 6 April he had finished eleven pages, and one week later he posted twenty-four pages to Garnett—but the accompanying letter was full of doubts: "Is the thing tolerable? Is the thing readable? Is the damned thing altogether insupportable? Am I mindful enough of your teaching—of your expoundings of the ways of the readers? Am I blessed? Or am I condemned? Or am I totally and utterly a hopeless driveller unworthy even of a curse? Do tell the truth. . . . I am ready to cut, slash, erase, destroy, spit, trample, jump, wipe my feet on that MS. at a word from you."[5] Garnett's reaction was enthusiastic, although delayed by illness: "Excellent, oh

---

* In giving his address, Conrad gave their landlady's maiden name, Coadon.

Conrad. Excellent. I have read every word of *The Rescuer* and think you have struck a new note."[6]

It remains unclear whether the difficulties with writing or other distressing factors were the cause (which seems likely) or the effect; at all events, Conrad fell ill suddenly—and now it was Jessie's turn to become alarmed. "By degrees he became more and more incoherent and rambling in his speech, and the shivering fits increased. I became seriously alarmed and sought the aid of my friendly landlady. I could not have been away from him more than a quarter of an hour, but when I returned with the good woman in tow, my husband had gone to bed, fully dressed even to his overcoat—the thick haverlock [sic]. Now he raved in grim earnest, speaking only in his native tongue and betraying no knowledge of who I might be. For hours I remained by his side watching the feverish glitter of his eyes that seemed fixed on some object outside my vision, and listening to the meaningless phrases and lengthy speeches, not a word of which I could understand. . . . All that night Joseph Conrad continued to rave in Polish, a habit he kept up every time any illness had him in its grip."[7]

A few days later his health improved. Their stay in Ile-Grande was diversified by short excursions in a sailing boat, *La Pervenche*, hired from a Captain Le Bras.[8] Conrad was interested in the lives of farmers, as evidenced by the contents of "The Idiots," a story he finished in May ("Peasant Life. Not for babies").[9] The plot might have been invented, but the incidental characters and the whole background are faithfully based on the inhabitants and the landscape of Ile-Grande; even the names have been only slightly changed. It is possible that in writing that story, which stands apart from the rest of his literary output, Conrad was inspired not only by Maupassant but also by his meeting with Charles Le Goffic, a native of Lannion, author of novels on Breton peasant life, and a friend of Anatole France, whose work Conrad admired.[10]

Meanwhile Conrad's work on the novel became his daily torture. "Every day the Rescuer crawls a page forward—sometimes with cold despair—at times with hot hope. I have long fits of depression, that in a lunatic asylum would be called madness. I do not know what it is."[11] It was undoubtedly a bout of depression. The completed first part of the book was dispatched to Garnett on 10 June accompanied by a despairing letter: "I dream for hours, hours! over a sentence and even then can't put it together so as to satisfy the cravings of my soul. I suspect that I am getting through a severe mental illness."[12]

During that trying spring Conrad read carefully the reviews of *An Outcast*; the book, dedicated to E. L. Sanderson, came out on 4 March in an edition of three thousand copies.[13] It was received quite well, although less enthusiastically than *Almayer's Folly*. Critics praised the rendering of exotic atmosphere, the psychology of characters, and the suggestive imagery; they criticized the book's inflated style, convoluted plot, pervading gloom. Struck by an unsigned article in *Saturday Review* ("Perhaps the finest piece of fiction that has been published this year" but "Mr Conrad is wordy . . . he writes despicably. He writes so as to mask and dishonour the greatness that is in him"), Conrad sent a letter to the reviewer; he was pleasantly surprised to learn that the piece came from the pen of H. G. Wells, well known by then for his *Time Machine* (1895). Wells replied politely, taking the opportunity to point at the source of possible future problems: "You don't make the slightest concessions to the reading young woman who makes or mars the fortunes of authors." Thus began Conrad's first acquaintance with a professional English writer; their relationship, however, never developed into a close friendship.[14] Although in his letters to Garnett and Unwin Conrad denied the truth of Wells's accusations, he must have taken them to heart, judging by the relatively economic style of *The Nigger of the "Narcissus,"* probably begun in June.

Conrad was undoubtedly pleased by the response of the critics, but his psychological tension grew along with the increased awareness of the responsibility he bore for his works: once released into the world they lived a life of their own, independent of their author's intentions. Some of the critics' reactions seemed to Conrad rather puzzling, since they revealed ways of interpretation he had never anticipated. Conrad was experiencing both pleasant and unpleasant consequences of being a professional writer—not a novice any more but an author whose output had its own history and evoked definite associations and expectations. "Gone are, alas! those fine days of *Alm:Folly* when I wrote with the serene audacity of an unsophisticated fool. I am getting more sophisticated from day to day. And more uncertain!"[15]

Conrad's awareness of his new status did not make writing any easier. Nine days after completing Part 1 of *The Rescuer*, he confided to Garnett, "Now I've got all my people together I don't know what to do with them. The progressive episodes of the story *will* not emerge from the chaos of my sensations. I feel nothing clearly. And I am frightened when I remember that I have to drag it all out of myself. Other writers have some starting point. Something to catch hold of. . . . They lean on dialect—or on tradition—or on history—or on the prejudice or fad of the hour; they trade upon some tie or some conviction of their time—or upon the absence of these things—which they can abuse or praise. But at any rate they know something to begin with—while I don't. I have had some impressions, some sensations—in my time:—impressions and sensations of common things. And it's all faded."[16] The beginning of Part 2 of *The Rescuer*, "The Shore of Refuge," must indeed have been drawn from imagination, although Conrad probably had just as many recollections to stimulate it as any of those "other writers" whom he envied. Most probably Conrad's complaint was of a more general nature and caused by a growing consciousness of how his earlier wanderings and his present expatriation made him "unable to draw on a body of experience common to his prospective readers."[17]

Six weeks of work brought only twelve more pages of Part 2 of *The Rescuer*.

Meanwhile, however, Conrad was writing a short story more solidly based on his own observations and experiences, and with a less imaginary plot: "An Outpost of Progress," initially titled "A Victim of Progress."[18] Problems arising from his lack of confidence in the solidity of civilization's ethical foundations became for the first time pivotal in the contents of a story. Although "An Outpost of Progress" is exceptional in Conrad's early writings, it heralds his later novels and stories concerned with moral and political issues. At that time Conrad may have also begun to draft his first masterpiece, *The Nigger of the "Narcissus,"* most closely linked with his seafaring experiences, and also artistically innovative. Although by mid-August he temporarily gave up his desperate struggle with the Malay novel, he succeeded in producing within a brief space the time a Malay short story, "The Lagoon."[19]

The period of Conrad's intense and exclusive application to the craft of writing coincided with his initiation into married life. A late marriage, just before the age of forty, was not unusual in those days for a man. But in Conrad's case, all the "normal" difficulties and tensions resulting from a union of two persons of different ages, nationalities, backgrounds, and intelligence were aggravated by his mercurial disposition—tempered by his refined manners and strict sense of decorum—and by the simple fact that he had been leading a solitary existence for over twenty years, without family ties or regular social contacts.

What the first months of their marriage were like, we can only guess. Bernard Meyer thinks Conrad suffered from nervousness springing from his inability to adjust to the sexual aspects of marriage.[20] But this straightforward and unverifiable psychoanalytic hypothesis is by no means necessary to explain the facts. Conrad's bad moods might have been caused by his doubts as to the wisdom of the irrevocable step he had taken, or by the tribulations of writing. At all events, there is nothing in Conrad's letters from that period to suggest enjoyment of life; if they differ in tone from his earlier correspondence it is not because they radiate relaxed serenity but, on the contrary, because they indicate even stronger anxiety and tension. Less than two months after his wedding, Conrad wrote to Garnett about moments when "loneliness becomes insupportable."[21] Mentioning his plan to return to England and settle down in the country, he commented, "A perfectly idyllic but also no doubt a hateful kind of existence."[22] A sardonic acceptance of his own position, coupled with a bitter grimace of distaste, sums up the impression created by Conrad's pronouncements on his personal life.

Jessie's reminiscences do nothing to make us revise this picture. She gives colorful accounts of sailing expeditions along the coast of Brittany; she offers glimpses of family life, and tells how as a young wife she was training to become Conrad's secretary-cum-typist. All that chat, however, is overshadowed by her reflections about the difficulty in understanding her husband's idiosyn-

crasies, strange moods, and unusual behavior. Obviously, Jessie was more surprised, disconcerted, and even bewildered than happy. Life with Conrad must
have been rendered particularly difficult because of his tendency to sullen discontent. "We return in October. . . . Perhaps I will be able to do something
then. But I doubt it. I doubt everything. The only certitude left to me is that I
cannot work for the present. I hope you never felt as I feel now and I trust that
you will never know what I experience at this very moment. The darkness and
the bitterness of it is beyond expression. Poor Jess feels it all, I must be a perfect
fiend to live with—but I really don't care who suffers. I have enough of my own
trouble."[23]

Thus the Conrads' honeymoon summer was not an idyll. In addition to other
difficulties there was a financial disaster: in circumstances that still remain obscure, Conrad lost all, or almost all, his savings. He mentioned it in his letter to
Garnett of 22 July: "I have had a lot of worries. A man I love much had been
very unfortunate in affairs and I also lose pretty well all that remained."[24] According to Baines, the friend was G. W. F. Hope, and the ill-fated venture a
South African gold mine.[25] There is nothing on the subject in Conrad's letters
and documents. Jessie gives a few details, but she cannot be considered a reliable source. According to her, the disaster had taken place two weeks before
their marriage—but this is improbable in light of Conrad's letters from that
period and his confident bearing. Jessie writes that the director of the gold mine
was on his way back to England when his ship sank off the coast of Brittany on
17 June 1896. His death erased the last hope of salvaging at least part of the
capital. That also does not sound very plausible, since the success or bankruptcy of a gold mine does not depend on the life of a traveling director. In any
case, there is another reason why Jessie's statements cannot be accepted in good
faith: almost all her accounts turn out to be misleading when we try to verify
them. She maintains, for example, that the decision to cut short their stay on
the Continent—they had apparently planned to continue it in the Basque country—was made two weeks before their return to England. Yet Conrad had
given the approximate date of their return in a letter written at the end of May.
Jessie describes the feverish search for a house in England while Conrad mentions the renting as a *fait accompli* as early as on 22 August.[26] Similar instances
of misrepresentation may be multiplied, which makes us wary of giving credence to even the simplest, otherwise unverifiable, detail provided by Jessie.[27]

Most probably the Conrads returned to London on 27 September, and while
Conrad remained in his old rooms at Gillingham Street, Jessie stayed for a
couple of weeks or so with the Hopes at Stanford-le-Hope, not far from the
Thames estuary. She was hastily preparing for habitation a semidetached villa
they had rented within walking distance from the Hopes' bungalow.[28] Conrad
wanted to be near the sea and, above all, near his closest and oldest English

friends. But the house was poorly built, damp, and uncomfortable; the Conrads did not like it. Moreover, Jessie furnished it in a way that met with her husband's strong disapproval.

"I preceded him into the room. Alas! there followed some really painful criticisms, sweeping condemnations, indeed, of all or nearly all I had done. I was young, and although we had been married the best part of a year I was too shy and diffident to stand up for myself—as I should have done later. I bowed my head to the storm of invective and thanked God my mother had already departed."[29] Irrespective of the authenticity of Jessie's colorful and frequently grotesque anecdotes about her bewildering husband, the overall impression produced by her reminiscences of those days suggests a definite conflict between Conrad's gentlemanly "continental" manners, habits, and attitudes (often beyond his financial means) and Jessie's insular, petits-bourgeois tastes.

` In spite of the uncomfortable house, work on *The Nigger of the "Narcissus"* progressed quite well. Conrad knew that he was writing an ambitious and innovative book. He wanted to portray the sailors with the same sober understanding that the celebrated French realistic painter Jean François Millet displayed in his presentation of peasants.[30] He did not aim at popularity: "Let [the book's fate] be unpopularity, it *must* be."[31] And although the length of the manuscript exceeded the original expectations by several times, and although the successive deadlines for its completion kept passing, Conrad persevered in his work on the story, which grew into a novel. Nonetheless, in comparison with his past and future tortures, the birth of *The Nigger* was almost painless. Moreover, and most important, Conrad was rarely plagued by doubts during its period of composition, and seemed convinced of its value.

This confident mood braced him for the task of waging war—at Garnett's instigation—against T. F. Unwin, his publisher. Conrad's position was not easy, as he had been on friendly terms with the Unwins.* But the need was pressing: he had already been compelled to borrow money from Galsworthy against future earnings.[32] Thus, when Unwin suggested a £50 advance and a fairly low royalty from the sales, Conrad demanded an advance twice as large, and higher royalties: "I can't afford to work for less than ten pence per hour and must work in a way that will give me this magnificent income."[33] Unwin refused, and Conrad, with considerable help from Garnett, (who, as Unwin's permanent consultant, had to act cautiously and discreetly), began negotiations with other publishers. The discussions concerned not so much his current short stories as his projected novels, to which Conrad attached greater importance. The negotiations with the house of Smith Elder came to nothing, but a more ambitious

* There is little evidence to support F. R. Karl's claim that Conrad despised Unwin as a Jew (*Joseph Conrad: The Three Lives* [New York, 1979], pp. 337, 379), and none that I can find that would indicate that Unwin was indeed Jewish. Conrad's gibes at the "Patron Jew" do not go beyond traditional stereotypes, associating sharp financial practices with Jewishness.

plan succeeded: parts of *The Nigger* were shown to Sidney S. Pawling, a partner in William Heinemann's publishing house, and William Ernest Henley, highly influential in the literary world and editor of the well-known monthly *New Review*; both men became interested. The news of this success provoked an outburst of joyful excitement rare for Conrad: "Now I have conquered Henley I ain't 'fraid of the divvle himself. I will drink to the success of the *Rescuer*. I will even get drunk to make it all safe—no morality! I feel like, in old days, when I got a ship and started off in a hurry to cram a lot of shore-going emotions into one short evening before going off into a year's slavery upon the sea."[34]

Conrad was also pleased by the news that his books had attracted attention in Warsaw;[35] the weekly magazine *Tygodnik Mód i Powieści* published in the following year *An Outcast*—the first translation of Conrad into another language. Unfortunately, very little is known of Conrad's contacts with Poland at that time, but we do know that he used to send his books to various relatives and friends.[36] Only a few of his letters to Aniela and Karol Zagórski have survived. He wrote them on 20 December 1896:

I planned to come to Poland for the holidays—by Poland I mean you. It was a vague and timid plan although the desire behind it was warm enough. I did not write about it—scarcely allowed myself the thought that perhaps it might be possible. Nevertheless the disappointment is acute. . . . In the meantime I must work, for praise does not feed a man (not to speak of a man's wife!). Therefore I have been writing, writing endlessly—and now the sight of an inkwell and of a pen fill me with anger and horror;—but I go on writing! Do not be angry at the long periods of silence. The above is a sample of my state of mind,—and why should I fill your ears with the sound of my complaints? You can be sure if there was any reason for self-congratulations I should at once come running to wag my tail! . . . From the depth of my soul, your brother and servant

Konrad Korzeniowski[37]

The first sentence of this letter could have been written to gratify the recipients, but Conrad, who could not possibly have afforded a trip to Poland, did indeed make an effort to spend Christmas with a Polish family, the Kliszczewskis, in Cardiff. He and Jessie went there on 21 December for a ten-day visit.[38] Many years later Jessie recalled that visit with warm gratitude. She was impressed by the "typically Polish" hospitality and punctilious politeness of their hosts. Yet it was Poland that became the cause of the cooling of Conrad's relations with the Kliszczewskis (although even later Conrad occasionally asked them for loans).[39] Witold Chwalewik recorded in 1932 the version of the incident as preserved in the Kliszczewski's family tradition and corroborated by Jessie's memoirs. "Everybody gathered at table on Christmas Eve and the con-

versation turned to Polish matters. The host addressed the guest, in English for
he was not fluent in Polish, expressing his dearest wish, to see Conrad use his
talent to glorify Poland's name and to depict in his novels the unhappiness of
his native land. Conrad seemed quite annoyed. Throwing up his arms he exploded, at first in French: 'Ah, mon ami, que voulez vous? I would lose my public . . .' He could not make a living by his writing if he were to use it as a tool of
propaganda. It would be impossible for him to write about Poland." On the
whole Conrad left the impression of being touchy, peremptory, and less open
than at their previous encounters. He was allegedly indignant when his host
spoke about Conrad's Polish origin and childhood spent in exile to a journalist
from *The Western Mail*, who was the first man to interview Conrad. The substance of the interview, however, contradicts the Kliszczewskis' assertion that
the information about Conrad's origin had been given without his knowledge;
anyway, the report is so utterly silly that Conrad's irritation seems justified on
more points than one.[40]

Some time later, when a young Polish philosopher, Wincenty Lutosławski,
visited Conrad, a related problem cropped up: why did Conrad not write in
Polish? Coming from Lutosławski, who had himself published in English a voluminous study of the development of Plato's logic, the question implied no
criticism. Conrad apparently answered that he lacked the necessary talent to
contribute to "our beautiful Polish literature"; but his gifts sufficed to enable
him to write in English to secure his daily bread.[41]

Unless Conrad spoke ironically, his affected humility was obviously a defensive gesture. The need to work for money was of course undisputable: stripped
of his savings, unable to find employment in his profession, with a wife to support, his first concern must have been his daily bread. From this angle his argument is irrefutable. Writing on Polish affairs offered no chance of success on the
English publishing market. The motives of his decision to write in a foreign
language we have already considered; by this time the issue was closed. Out of
touch with the life and spoken language of his native country, Conrad—even if
he were able to return and settle in Poland—would encounter insurmountable
difficulties not only in writing but also in adjusting to unfamiliar conditions.
And it is worth bearing in mind that his only relatives lived in the Russian-
occupied part of the country, where literature was hampered by censorship, and
daily life by police supervision.

But there must have been something else behind the reply Conrad gave to the
good-natured and patriotic Kliszczewskis. The son of Apollo Korzeniowski was
sure to recall, at least occasionally, the message contained in his father's "Bap-
tismal Song." The demands placed on him by his heritage clashed with his opinion about the hopelessness of Poland's situation. He wrote to R. B. Cunninghame Graham in 1899, "You who devote your enthusiasm and your talents to
the cause of humanity, you will undoubtedly understand why I must—I need
to—guard my thought intact as the last homage of loyalty paid to a lost

cause." [42] When openly professed, loyalty without hope sounds like an appeal for pity, and Conrad's national pride would not have allowed it. A feeling of shame and of unfulfilled duty fought in him with pessimism and a sense of personal dignity. The well-nigh inevitable consequence of this internal struggle was his aversion to concentrating on his own and his country's miseries.

The Conrads returned from Cardiff on New Year's Day, 1897, and Conrad settled down to intensive work on finishing *The Nigger*. He announced to Garnett on 10 January: "Nigger died on the 7th at 6 p.m.; but the ship is not home yet. Expected to arrive tonight and be paid off tomorrow. And the End! I can't eat—I dream—nightmares—and scare my wife." [43] The novel was finished a week later, [44] but he hesitated about its title. In the manuscript he originally called it *The Nigger of the "Narcissus,"* but in sending it to the publisher he suggested *The Forecastle. A Tale of Ship and Men.* A few days later he changed *Forecastle* to *Nigger*. [45] The book first appeared in print in the *New Review* as *The Nigger of the "Narcissus"—A Tale of the Forecastle*; only in its second book edition (1898) did it bear the final subtitle *A Tale of the Sea*.

Conrad was later to express his satisfaction with the book—a sentiment unusual for him. "Candidly, I think it has certain qualities of art that make it a thing apart. I tried to get through the veil of details at the essence of life." "I am conceited about that thing and very much in love with it." [46] And in the foreword written in 1914 "To my readers in America," he said that *The Nigger* "is the book by which, not as a novelist perhaps, but as an artist striving for the utmost sincerity of expression, I am willing to stand or fall." [47] All the more surprising, therefore, are the literal similarities between some fragments in the last part of *The Nigger* and passages in Maupassant's *Bel-Ami*, particularly in the scene of James Wait's death, where the Maupassantian elements form the artistic and emotional ground of description. [48] But did Conrad consciously, as Paul Kirschner asserts, plagiarize the French writer's impressions, phrases, and images? Perhaps. Less than three years later he vehemently attacked a far less clear case of unacknowledged borrowing by someone else of fictional motifs ("I write strongly—because I feel strongly. . . . One has the right to demand some sort of sincerity and to expect common honesty"). [49] To scold others for the sins we are inclined to commit is not commendable, but it is quite common. Yet it is also possible that "saturated with Maupassant" as he was, he did not fully realize the extent of his imitation. [50] The fact that it was a case of transposing the original text into another language does not predetermine the issue. Conrad could have intentionally translated fragments from Maupassant to inlay his own work with them, or, in moments of great concentration, he could have used images and phrases unconsciously stored in his memory. After all, he had a trilingual mind. In any case, he could not have been aware of his borrowings from Maupassant in June 1898, when he sent Garnett *The Nigger* and *Bel-Ami* simultaneously ("It is simply enchanting to see how it's done"). [51]

Conrad showed Garnett the manuscript of *The Nigger* and continued to work on the text for several weeks after the novel had been finished. As its serial publication was to begin in August, his financial situation did not improve at all. Conrad during that time had practically no income and was compelled to go into debt. Toward the end of 1896 or beginning of 1897, he borrowed £150 from Adolf Krieger—a fact that was to mar their long-lasting friendship.[52] In March he tried unsuccessfully to find £25 to pay off a promissory note; Garnett, moved by Conrad's mournful letter, sent him the necessary sum. The state of being in debt and paying off the most urgent obligations with borrowed money were to last throughout fifteen years. Initially at least, Jessie was not aware of it.

Conrad, high-strung and illness-prone, came to realize that his wife, who could have been his daughter, did not enjoy good health either. He wrote to Garnett that Jessie was ill in bed, "and consequently I am unable to think; for her neuralgia distracts me more than it does herself." He mentioned Jessie's poor health again in April, then in June.[53] The complaint could not have been insignificant; most probably it was psychosomatic in nature, since soon after Jessie had become pregnant, Conrad wrote to Sanderson that, according to the doctor, "it may mend Jess's health permanently—if it does not end her."[54] Jessie presented herself as a person of exceptionally equable disposition, and other sources confirm this opinion; but a juxtaposition of her recollections with those of other persons (such as David Garnett) and with Conrad's letters suggests a certain lack of understanding and a kind of emotional immaturity behind her outer composure. Jessie's tendency to give rein to imagination not only in her memoirs, written years later, but also in immediate accounts—and to assign herself a significant role in various fanciful and dramatic events—indicates a lack of inner balance and a sense of insecurity. Her escape seems to have been into mythomania and a rapidly increasing obesity, which cushioned her against the world's sharp corners. In the early stage of her marriage, which she described as the most difficult, she was not yet capable of adopting such an actively defensive posture. And one can easily imagine that for a simple girl like Jessie life with Conrad was indeed trying and startling; surprise seems to have been her most frequently experienced sensation.

Living in the country, yet less than one hour from the center of London, had great advantages for Conrad. The Hopes were close; sailing was easily accessible; the rent was reasonable. Conrad hated living in town. But even Jessie came to realize—after some time, as she herself admitted—that her husband "must be feeling the isolation from men of his own standard of intellect. . . . I was thankful when one of those most intimate friends, John Galsworthy, Edward Garnett or E. L. Sanderson could be induced to pay us a visit, for a long week-end. The effect of their sympathetic and sustaining presence would lubricate the mental machinery."[55]

The friendship with Galsworthy and Sanderson, begun in 1893, matured into intimacy. Particularly with Ted Sanderson and his fiancée (later wife),

Helen Watson, Conrad exchanged many cordial letters. He would confide his
plans and his writing problems to them, and enjoy their lively reactions to the
works in progress that he sent them. It came as a surprise to Conrad that Galsworthy had literary aspirations, and that Sanderson turned out to be a poet.
Their correspondence thereupon acquired a more professional character: Conrad gave his friends advice and later counseled Galsworthy in his negotiations
with publishers.[56] The Hopes, however, with whom the Conrads made regular
sailing expeditions in the English Channel, remained their closest friends.

In February 1897 Conrad made a new acquaintance who was very important
to him: Henry James sent him his last novel, *The Spoils of Poynton*, with a
warm inscription, and later asked him to lunch in London. "So there is something to live for—at last! He is quite playful about it. Says we shall be alone—
no one to separate us if we quarrel. It's the most delicate flattery I've ever been
victim to."[57]

In the second half of February Conrad made a start on the short story "Karain"—"A Malay thing. It will be easy and may bring a few pence." And indeed, short stories were paying incomparably better than novels; for "Karain"
Conrad was to obtain £40—that is about three times as much per thousand
words than for *An Outcast*.[58] However, the easiness of the task turned out as
usual, to have been illusory. "That infernal story. I can't shake myself free of it,
though I don't like it—never shall! But I can get rid of it only by finishing it
coûte-que-coûte."[59] And although when he sent Garnett the beginning of the
story Conrad declared emphatically, "If you say 'Burn!' I will burn—and won't
hate you. But if you say: 'Correct—Alter!' I won't do it—but shall hate you
henceforth and for ever!"[60]—he altered the text according to the critic's directions. As soon as "Karain" was finished, on 14 April, he sent it off to Unwin. At
the same time he asked Garnett to read it carefully before showing it to magazine editors.[61] Conrad had to wait three months for the story to be placed, but it
was eventually accepted by the respectable *Blackwoods Magazine* in Edinburgh, an event of utmost importance for Conrad's literary career.[62]

"Karain's" principal moral problem, akin to that found in "Lagoon," is a betrayal of friendship. As all readers of Conrad know, the most frequent motif in
his works is a treacherous failure in the performance of one's duties. "I will not
now try to explain what chaotic impulses guided me in writing," he confided to
Garnett.[63]

The writing of "Karain" was interrupted for a certain time by the change of
house for larger, more comfortable, and—at £28 per year—doubtless more expensive quarters in the same locality. The Conrads rented half of "Ivy Walls," a
curious fifteenth-century lath-and-plaster building, shielded from the road by a
row of elm and lime trees. From upper-story windows there was a view of the
Thames and a fairly large orchard adjoined the house. They moved there on 13
March.[64]

The next story, begun in May, was "The Return," Conrad's second attempt (after *The Sisters*) at tackling a contemporary European subject; it was his first and only endeavor to write an "ordinary" tale from the life of contemporary English people.[65] According to Conrad the theme had been suggested by Garnett.[66] He had a very hard time with this story, out of proportion to its length. He complained to Garnett on 18 July, "I go on groping through "The Return." I feel helpless. That thing has bewitched me." And a day later to Sanderson: "I've been ten weeks trying to write a story of about 20 pages of print. I haven't finished yet! and what I've written seems to me too contemptible for words. Not in conception perhaps,—but in execution. This state of affairs spells Ruin, —and I can't help it,—I can't."[67] It was a great relief to him when he finally finished "The Return" on 24 September.[68] But only a few days later he wrote, "I have a physical horror of that story, I simply won't look at it any more. It has embittered five months of my life. I hate it."[69] And when Garnett criticized the artificiality of dialogue, Conrad vowed, "Never more. It is evident that my fate is to be descriptive and descriptive only. There are things I *must* leave alone."[70] "The Return," a story about the disintegration of a middle-class marriage, was to remain Conrad's least favorite piece of writing.

The difficulties with "The Return," coupled with pressing financial needs, prompted Conrad to resume his work on *The Rescuer*, apparently beginning with a change of title into *The Rescue*.[71] Suggesting to William Blackwood on 28 August that he would send him Part 1 of the novel, Conrad anticipated that the book would be finished before 1 February 1898. Ten days later he sent the Scottish publisher the promised text, accompanied by an extensive summary of the entire book. It agrees with the final version, except that at the time Conrad envisioned its length at 90,000 to 100,000 words instead of 150,000. As he openly admitted to Garnett, the novel was supposed to be a "glorified book for boys," but the intentionally unambitious flight did not make the task easier.[72] "I can't get on with the *Rescue*. In all these days I haven't written a line, but there hadn't been a day when I did not wish myself dead. It is too ghastly. I positively don't know what to do."[73]

Edward Garnett, the receiver of these complaints, was an invaluable confidant, comforter, and trusted adviser. "I know you've made me and therefore wouldn't be human if you did not take interest in me. But I like to hear you say so—you can't say it too often. It is balm and nectar and sunshine."[74]

Garnett's counsel concerned the subject matter, composition, and style of Conrad's prose, as well as his negotiations and contracts with publishers. Garnett also suggested books worth reading, including poetry, although Conrad affected complete ignorance of this last.[75] Of greatest value were Garnett's linguistic comments. "The more I write the less sure I am of my English," Conrad confessed to Chesson in January 1898.[76] It is remarkable that although most of his other letters were written in a rather formal style, when addressing Garnett he would make puns, insert colloquial and slang expressions, and sometimes even imitate regional dialects.[77] In those days Garnett read all Conrad's manu-scripts, writing remarks in their margins and correcting errors (he did not spot all of them).[78] That was why Conrad could let himself go before Garnett, dis-playing his ability to use expressions outside standard English.

Among the most valuable results of Conrad's association with Garnett were his contacts with William Blackwood, owner of an old and reputable Edin-burgh publishing house, and with David S. Meldrum, Blackwood's London ad-visor. The idea of offering "Karain" to Blackwood occurred to Garnett in April 1897; he thought it "destined by Providence for *Blackwood's Magazine*."[79] Fol-lowing lengthy negotiations—Conrad asked £40 for the story and Blackwood accepted his terms only in August—"Karain" appeared in the November issue of the magazine, marking the start of five years of fruitful collaboration. *Black-wood's Magazine*, a carefully edited monthly, fairly conservative in its literary tastes, earned its reputation by publishing several great Victorian novelists; at that time it was favored particularly by professional men both in Britain and her dominions. Conrad wrote to Garnett, "All the good moments—the real good ones in my new life I owe to you—and I say it without a pang; which is also something of which you may boast, O Wiser than the serpents. You sent me to Pawling—you sent me to Blackwoods—when are you going to send me to heaven? I am anxious to depart soon so as not to be too late for the next batch of immortals—but I don't care to go without an introduction from you."[80]

In August 1897 Conrad formed one of the most important and peculiar friendships of his life. Greatly impressed by "An Outpost of Progress"—a scath-ing criticism of the colonial system—published in *Cosmopolis* in June and July, Robert Bontine Cunninghame Graham wrote Conrad a letter. Graham was at the time a well-known traveler, writer, publicist, and radical politician.[81] An exchange of letters, rich in intellectual, political, and social argument, soon de-veloped into a lifelong friendship. Cedric T. Watts, the editor of Conrad's letters to Cunninghame Graham, described this friendship as an "expanding para-dox," but it was only an apparent paradox; in analyzing it, several persistent misunderstandings concerning Conrad's outlook and character are clarified.

Cunninghame Graham came from an old aristocratic Scottish family. After studying in Brussels, he went in 1869 to South America where, with some inter-vals, he spent nearly fifteen years traveling and trying unsuccessfully to trade in horses and cattle. In 1878 he eloped with Gabrielle de la Balmondière, daughter of a French father and Spanish mother (Graham himself was part Spanish). In 1882 and 1885 he stood for Parliament, both times without success. In 1886 he won a seat as a Liberal, and throughout the following six years was the most radical member of the House of Commons, a champion of laws protecting fac-tory and farm workers, an advocate of nationalized industry and of free univer-sal education, and a fierce critic of colonialism. He was imprisoned for six weeks for taking part in a huge illegal leftist demonstration in Trafalgar Square on 13 November 1887 ("Bloody Sunday"). After 1892 he became active as a publicist, first for the Trade Unionist publication *People's Press* and later for the leftist *Saturday Review*. Slightly built, wiry, and strikingly handsome, impetuous yet extremely well-mannered, he was famed for his bravado, altruism, and the pride he took in his own appearance.

It is customary to attribute to Conrad views unequivocally conservative and antisocialist, partly on the grounds of his letters to Kliszczewski from the years 1885 and 1886. It may therefore seem surprising that he formed such a close friendship with Graham, an advocate of general strike and revolution and a participant in the Congress of the Second International in Paris (1889). From January 1898 on, after a few letters headed "Dear Sir" and "My dear Sir," Conrad addressed Graham as "Cher ami" or "Très cher ami"; in a letter to Graham's mother he spoke of him as "my friend, *the* friend." Many years later Richard Curle recalled, "In each other's company they appeared to grow younger; they treated one another with that kind of playfulness which can only arise from a complete, unquestioning, and ancient friendship. I doubt whether the presence of any man made Conrad happier than the presence of Don Roberto."[82]

Graham was undoubtedly closer to Conrad than Garnett or Galsworthy, who held far more moderate views. Conrad and Graham had a great deal in common; Baines rightly points to their skepticism of human nature, their hatred of tyranny and exploitation, their exasperation at the stupidity of individuals and institutions.[83] But over and above all that, both men had a negative attitude to the social and economic order of the day—and both objected to it on the same grounds: that it was based on the dominance of money and "material interest." Both noblemen stood for the chivalric ethics of honor and loyalty, and both abhorred bourgeois morality; and although Conrad did not attack it "from the left," considering his cult of work and duty, he was not after all an advocate of a feudal reaction. The attitudes inherited from Scottish earls or the Polish *szlachta* were alike in inculcating a sense of responsibility for their society. Graham acted out this sense in his political activity, while Conrad struggled to give it expression in his writings. Although the two men differed in their conduct, their fundamental beliefs were closer to each other than to those, for instance, of Garnett, a leftist liberal who hobnobbed with international anarchists but who was, above all, a disgruntled and embittered bourgeois littérateur.[84]

Conrad, a Briton by choice and naturalization, an immigrant not uncritical and yet loyal, must have felt more at ease in the company of someone who had un-English manners, a liking for the Romance nations (he himself frequently admitted to a weakness for them)—one who, in short, was as "international" in all respects as Graham.[85] It appears also that Cunninghame Graham was Conrad's only close British friend who sympathized with oppressed nations and who did not regard the "national idea" as anachronistic but rather as an essential element of culture. Conrad's main objection to the contemporary social democrats was their disregard for the rights of once-conquered nations to independence.

Lastly, Graham was Conrad's first intellectual friend of about his own age: the five years' difference between them (Graham was older) was insignificant compared with the ten to sixteen years that separated Conrad from his younger friends Garnett, Galsworthy, Sanderson, Ford, and Crane. Also, as Cedric Watts has put it, "When Graham first approached Conrad it was the latter who was relatively obscure and the former who . . . was the celebrated and influential public figure; 'a friend at court,' as Conrad told Garnett." "An Outpost of Progress" was preceded in *Cosmopolis* by Kipling's "Slaves of the Lamp" from the volume *Stalky & Co*, which glorified English imperialist morality. Writing to Conrad, Graham juxtaposed the two stories and attacked Kipling. The tone of Conrad's reply was modestly ironic: "Mr Kipling has the wisdom of the passing generations—and holds it in perfect sincerity. Some of his work is of impeccable form and because of that little thing he shall sojourn in Hell only a very short while. He squints with the rest of his excellent sort. It is a beautiful squint; it is an useful squint. And—after all—perhaps he sees round the corner? And suppose Truth is just round the corner like the elusive and useless loafer it is? I can't tell. No one can tell. It is impossible to know. It is impossible to know anything tho' it is possible to believe a thing or two." [86] Here Conrad's discreet irony is also aimed at Graham's own assertiveness. Not until later, following their first encounter on 26 November 1897, did their correspondence acquire a directness unusual for Conrad and become a means of exchanging serious thought. [87]

Conrad expressed his views on the duties of art and on human solidarity—shared by Graham—for the first time in the preface to *The Nigger*. He probably wrote it in August, interrupting his struggle with *The Rescue*. "I want you not to be impatient with it and if you think it at all possible to give it a chance to get printed," he appealed to Garnett. [88] The preface appeared at the end of *The Nigger* when it was serialized in the *New Review*; it was not included in the first book editions of the novel. [89] Later, however, it became his best-known theoretical piece, and the sentence about the rendering of "the highest kind of justice to the visible universe" is almost proverbial today. Much attention has been given to the problem of the influence of other writers on this preface; echoes of Maupassant, Walter Pater, and even Schopenhauer have been detected—but most important in the essay is a precise description of Conrad's own views. [90]

This artistic manifesto is by no means coherent and clear; like all proclamations of its kind it becomes more concrete when set side by side with the practice to which it may be referred. The trouble is that the Preface cannot be regarded as a complete and reliable summing up of the artistic experiences and principles that guided Conrad in the writing of *The Nigger*. Certain elements of the Preface do not easily connect with this novel, and that is probably why

Conrad did not insist on having it printed in the book edition. Also, in view of the fact that his other works, dissimilar to *The Nigger*, were completed much later, after months of futile struggle with *The Rescue*, his programme must be interpreted in fairly general terms: as an exposition of principles which may be realised in various ways.[91]

The Preface, partly polemic in tone, was directed against the carefree attitude, then common in England, toward the technique of novel writing. Conrad, Flaubert's disciple, postulated artistic cohesion and responsibility for every word: "A work that aspires, however humbly, to the condition of art should carry its justification in every line" says the first sentence of the Preface. And further, "It is only through an unremitting never-discouraged care for the shape and ring of sentences that an approach can be made to plasticity, to colour, and that the light of magic suggestiveness may be brought to play for an evanescent instant over the commonplace surface of words: of the old, old words, worn thin, defaced by ages of careless usage."

Conrad's artistic programme is usually called literary impressionism. This is somewhat misleading, since the term *impressionism* applied to literature is ambiguous. In Conrad's case it can refer neither to concentrating attention on momentary sensual stimuli or moods, nor to the creation of a simple illusion of reality. "To snatch in a moment of courage, from the remorseless rush of time, a passing phase of life, is only the beginning of the task." The aim of the artist is to arrive at a different truth than a faithful recording of sensations and feelings: the artist ought to penetrate to deeper, hidden meanings. The basis of Conrad's "impressionism" is his striving after suggestiveness; to evoke in the reader specific moods or visions—not by means of mirrorlike descriptions or reports communicated to the intellect, but by direct appeal to feelings and imagination. Conrad is therefore, in fact, closer to symbolism than to impressionism in painting. "Such an appeal to be effective must be an impression conveyed through the senses; and, in fact, it cannot be made in any other way, because temperament, whether individual or collective, is not amenable to persuasion."

The aim of art is not "in the clear logic of a triumphant conclusion; it is not in the unveiling of one of those heartless secrets which are called the Laws of Nature." Conrad repeats here the romantic contrasting of "dead truths" with "the heart" to which the artist addresses himself; he also rejects the "scientific" aspirations of naturalism. According to Conrad, art appeals, above everything, to emotions. To judge by his later correspondence with Graham, Conrad was convinced that rational knowledge and intellectual study of nature are ethically barren and lead to extreme skepticism in life; he believed that the only firm basis for human bonds can be found in emotions. The artist "speaks to our capacity for delight and wonder, to the sense of mystery surrounding our lives; to our sense of pity, and beauty, and pain; to the latent feeling of fellowship with all creation—and to the subtle but invincible conviction of solidarity that knits together the loneliness of innumerable hearts, to the solidarity in dreams, in joy, in sorrow, in aspirations, in illusions, in hope, in fear, which binds men to each other, which binds together all humanity—the dead to the living and the living to the unborn." For Conrad the moral aim of art consisted in the stirring up of this profound sense of solidarity based on immemorial tradition: "One may perchance attain to such clearness of sincerity that at last the presented vision of regret or pity, of terror or mirth, shall awaken in the hearts of the beholders that feeling of unavoidable solidarity; of the solidarity in mysterious origin, in toil, in joy, in hope, in uncertain fate, which binds men to each other."

Assigning to literature such responsible and worthy tasks does not lead to lifting it onto an idealized pedestal: Conrad compared the work of a writer to that of a farmer and a craftsman. An important supplement to that conception of the artist-craftsman may be found in a fragment of the Preface omitted on Garnett's advice: "For in art alone of all the enterprises of men there is meaning in endeavour disassociated from success . . . and ideals are practically un-reachable except by the very great who can command the sanction of recognized success. To others the consciousness of a worthy aim is everything; in it is conscience, dignity, truth, honour—the reward and the peace."[92] Conrad's characteristic tendency to link the cult of work with an antipathy for the prag-matic morality of success is reflected in his idea that the meaning of the writer's work consists not in acquired renown but in the sincere and diligent pursuit of his aims; this idea is essential for understanding Conrad's attitude toward his own writing. He defended his point to Garnett: ". . . but I think that the eight lines at the end (of the paragraph struck out) conveying the opinion that in 'art alone there is a meaning in endeavour as apart from success' should be worked in somehow. And whether your wisdom lets me keep them in or not I tell you plainly . . . that there is the saving truth—the truth that saves most of us from eternal damnation."[93] But Garnett, who had his own complexes, did not regard this fragment as a courageous *credo* proclaiming the worth of one's own crea-tion, but as a timid defence; finally Conrad gave up and the fragment was omitted.

In the same August Conrad began a correspondence with a childhood friend, Janina de Brunnow née Taube, whom he had seen for the last time over twenty years earlier in Cracow. Now she lived on her husband's estate, Rudawa, near Brzostowice, in Grodno Province, in the Russian part of Poland. In his second letter Conrad sent her a general report on himself. The description of his busy life, of the publishers competing for his favors, and of floods of correspondence was somewhat exaggerated. "I have acquired a certain reputation—a literary one—but the future is still uncertain because I am not a popular author and I shall probably never become one. . . . I do not dream of making a fortune and anyway it is not something to be found in an ink-well. However, I must confess that I dream of peace, of a little recognition and of devoting to Art the rest of a life that would be free from financial worries."

". . . I have little or no contacts at all in society, I correspond . . . with a lot of people." [94]

True enough, Conrad's social contacts consisted mainly of an exchange of letters. In the summer of 1897 he began a lively correspondence with William Blackwood, the fifth in line of a family owning a distinguished firm of Scottish publishers, known for their policy of cultivating the most outstanding story-tellers of the time. The principal topic of those letters was Conrad's literary plans. Encouraged by the publisher's warm reception of "Karain," Conrad sent him the finished part of *The Rescue*. As the rights of the book edition belonged to Heinemann, Blackwood was unable to accept the novel. But for the next several years he was the chief recipient of Conrad's work, and a patient, under-standing, tactful, and generous confidant of all Conrad's literary and financial troubles. Their friendship, unlike Conrad's relationship with the Unwins, never reached the stage of social contacts between the two families, but some of Blackwood's letters exude genuine warmth. Blackwood was not only the owner of the firm but also the editor of the "Maga," as *Blackwood's Magazine* was nicknamed. Occasionally Conrad would give him unfailingly flattering opin-ions about a particular issue of the periodical. His first commentary (4 Septem-ber 1897) sounds rather artificial, as if its author felt obliged to pass judgment on every text. As a result he covered the whole issue in a manner both forced and banal. One of his statements concerned a Mrs. Oliphant, a well-known but mediocre novelist who also happened to be the author of the official history of the Blackwood publishing house. Conrad declared that "she was a better artist than George Elliot," incidentally making a significant spelling mistake in the pseudonym of an author with whose works he was probably only vaguely acquainted. [95]

Conrad also corresponded with Blackwood's London adviser, David Mel-drum. Sidney Pawling, Heinemann's adviser, Meldrum, and, of course, Garnett, Unwin's adviser, were practically the only guests whom the Conrads invited to their house; thus, rather unusually, Conrad entered the intellectual and literary milieu through the world of publishing. Apart from them he knew only a few people in London, where he used to go mainly on business.

A sudden change, not unlike a burst of some elemental force, was brought about by Conrad's meeting—through Pawling—with Stephen Crane. The young American was very different from Conrad's staid English friends. The son of a learned Methodist minister and of an activist in the temperance movement, Crane rebelled against his family tradition. At first he worked as a journalist and war correspondent, interrupting his work for various love affairs and merry-making. He was a man of impetuous decision but given to melancholy; amorous and extravagant; sensitive and unpredictable; although rather small and slight, he loved sports and physical contests. Passionately devoted to literature, he left the United States angered by lack of recognition; in England he ridiculed the parochialism of the natives. He arrived in England from Greece with Cora Stewart, the ex-proprietress of a shady night spot in Jacksonville, Florida. Deeply attached to Stephen, intelligent and unselfish, Cora could not become his legal wife because the second of her two previous husbands had refused to divorce her, but she used Crane's name.[96]

Although fourteen years Conrad's junior, Crane made his debut as a novelist two years before Conrad did; *The Red Badge of Courage* had earned him a notable reputation upon its publication in 1895. Having read *The Nigger* in instalments, Crane wanted to meet its author. Conrad for his part had also been reading Crane's work, of which he thought very highly ("I *do* admire him. I shan't have to pretend").[97] Their acquaintance, begun in London with an interminable peripatetic conversation that Conrad described in his preface to Crane's biography twenty-five years later, soon blossomed into a warm friendship. The talk concerned literature: from the start it was clear that the bond between these two contrasting men was their enthusiastic and deeply serious approach to writing. Each of them, aware of his own artistic originality, valued the other's opinion all the more. Conrad sent Crane the galley proofs of *The Nigger* and took great pleasure in his appreciation: "The book is simply great. The simple treatment of the death of Waite [sic] is too good, too terrible. I wanted to forget it at once."[98] Although the fragment selected by Crane for particular praise owes most to Maupassant, Conrad confessed in his reply, "If I've hit *you* with the death of Jimmy I don't care if I don't hit another man. . . . When I feel depressed about it I say to myself 'Crane likes the damned thing'—and am greatly consoled. . . . I am not more vile than my neighbours but this disbelief in oneself is like a taint that spreads on everything one comes in contact with; on men on things—on the very air one breathes."[99]

Conrad in his turn was enthusiastic about Crane's stories: "'A Man and Some Others' is immense. I can't spin a long yarn about it but I admire it without reserve. It is an amazing bit of biography. I am envious of you—horribly."[100] But his admiration was not without reservations: in a letter to Garnett he argued five days later, "He is *the only* impressionist and *only* an impressionist. Why is he not immensely popular? With his strength, with his rapidity of action, with that amazing faculty of vision—why is he not? He has outline, he has colour, he has movement, with that he ought to go very far. But—will he? I sometimes think he won't. . . . He is the master of his reader to the very last line—then—apparently for no reason at all—he seems to let go his hold. It is as if he had gripped you with greased fingers. His grip is strong but while you feel the pressure on your flesh you slip out from his hand—much to your own surprise."[101]

There is all the more reason, therefore, to draw a distinction between Conrad's allegedly "impressionistic" literary programme contained in the Preface to *The Nigger* and Crane's variety of impressionism. Let us recapitulate: for Conrad the impressionistic method of writing was one of several literary means; he accused Crane of treating that means as an end in itself. The similarity between the two authors may be seen rather in their preoccupation with the problem of moral stance and in their bent for irony—in Crane's writings more straightforward and mainly suggested by the style of his descriptions.

After finishing "The Return," Conrad wrote almost nothing for several months; it was the longest unproductive period since he had begun *An Outcast*. He tried to continue *The Rescue* but with results no better than before. His lack of success with "The Return" irritated him: it was his first short story that no magazine wanted to publish. Although personally displeased with the work, in his letters to Unwin he attributed its failure to the narrow-minded rigidity of the editors.[102] Finally he included it in a volume of short stories that on 24 November he decided to call *Tales of Unrest*.[103] Conrad's relations with his first publisher were steadily deteriorating, but he could still count on Blackwood and Pawling.[104]

The Nigger of the "Narcissus," dedicated to Garnett—to whom Conrad had also paid a compliment by giving a leading character, Singleton, Garnett's mother's surname—officially came out on 2 December, but two days earlier Conrad had sent a copy to Henry James with an accompanying letter in French: "Chèr Maître, You've allowed me to send you my book. Here it is. It has the virtue of being short. I lived through it."[105] The critics were more consistent in their favorable reception of *The Nigger* than of Conrad's earlier novels.* *Books and News Gazette* expressed the opinion that the author "has given us the most artistic and natural picture of sea-life that has yet appeared in literature." Critics praised the descriptions and emphasized the novelty of approach to the subject; some protested against the excessive brutality of vocabulary and action. "The tale has no plot and no petticoats," summed up the *Academy*, but the lack of conventional elements of fiction was regarded as one more mark of

---

* William L. Courtney's review in the *Daily Telegraph* (8 December 1897), in which he claimed that *The Nigger* showed the influence of Crane's *Red Badge of Courage*, elicited from Conrad a rebuttal, full of elaborate politeness. In his letter of 9 December Conrad disclaimed any allegiance to realism or naturalism and expressed artistic intentions close to symbolism. Donald W. Rude pointed at the contrast between this letter and Conrad's Christmas postcard to the Cranes, where Courtney's review is dismissed as asinine. But there is an undercurrent of irony below the surface of profuse compliments, addressed to Courtney—who had maintained, for instance, that the "living personages" of *The Nigger* speak as they "would have talked, without any squeamishness on the part of the author in deference to our sensitive and refined ears." This is a ridiculous assertion. (See Donald W. Rude, "Joseph Conrad, Stephen Crane and W. L. Courtney's review of *The Nigger of the 'Narcissus,'*" *English Literature in Transition*, 21 (1978): 188–197. Conrad's letter to Courtney was published by David R. Smith, "'One Word More' about *The Nigger of the 'Narcissus,'*" *Nineteenth-Century Fiction* 23 (1968): 208–209; postcard to the Cranes in R. W. Stallman and Lillian Gilkes, eds., *Stephen Crane: Letters* [New York, 1960], 157–158.)

the book's originality. The *Spectator*, however, spoke for many others when asserting that "Mr Conrad is a writer of genius; but his choice of themes, and the uncompromising nature of his methods, debar him from attaining a wide popularity." [106]

The prediction of the lack of popularity was to be fulfilled with painful accuracy, and meanwhile Conrad's financial situation was steadily deteriorating. Although he frequently professed his indifference to reviewers' opinions, words of praise gave him obvious pleasure and even improved his mood enough to make him report to Garnett on 23 December, "I am writing the *R*! I am writing! I am harrassed with anxieties but the thing comes out." [107] In the same letter he mentioned the enthusiastic response of Arthur T. Quiller-Couch, the well-known novelist and critic. Quiller-Couch, although he did not know Conrad personally, wrote to him directly, announcing his forthcoming favorable review. Conrad replied immediately. "Writing in a solitude almost as great as that of the ship at sea the great living crowd outside is somehow forgotten. . . . Only a small group of human beings—a few friends, relations—remains to the seaman always distinct, indubitable, the only ones who matter. And so to the solitary writer. As he writes he thinks only of a small knot of men—three or four perhaps—the only ones who matter." [108]

The significant passage about loneliness and the small group of those for whom an author writes expresses Conrad's frequently recurring and Stendhal-like view of the author's attitude toward his readers. Conrad repeated his statement almost word for word three days later in a letter to Ted Sanderson. But surely the conflict between material needs and fidelity to his own artistic vision was not the one that tormented Conrad most. Rather, it was again a sense of being lost and an uncertainty of his final purpose. "Life passes and it would pass like a dream were it not that the nerves are stretched like fiddle strings. Something always turns up to give a turn to the screw. Domestic life would be tolerable if,—but that soon will be over. The larger life (including many large hopes) rolls on like a cart without springs,—that is, jolting me fearfully. It's true also I never knew how to drive. . . . you know where you're driving to. A great thing,—in fact everything! But I don't." [109]

Conrad wrote several other effusive letters at that time. He was not a recluse by choice. The loneliness of an artist and an emigré weighed heavily upon him —hence his readiness to discuss the moral and technical aspects of fiction; hence his need of friendship and of confidences, borne out by facts from his life and by recurrent motifs in his work. "For where can we lay down the heaviness of our trouble but in a friend's heart?" says Arsat, the hero of "The Lagoon." For Conrad friends had to replace family and milieu; only they could give him a sense of belonging, allay his anxieties, and help combat his indecision. But when Conrad, without a shred of enthusiasm, awaited the arrival of his child, he was encountering two ultimate difficulties in his new literary life: creative impotence and a lack of money. And while his new friendships were not yet firmly established, the old ones were proving insufficient.

Conrad had two old intimate friends, Hope and Krieger, but his relationship with the latter was beginning to deteriorate. On 5 December he wrote to Garnett, "My soul is like a stone within me. I am going through the awful experience of losing a friend. Hope comes every evening to console me but he has a hopeless task. Death is nothing—and I am used to its rapacity. But when life robs one of a man to whom one has pinned one's faith for twenty years the wrong seems too monstrous to be lived down." [110] The losing of a friend presented here in such dramatic terms was in fact a long process, since in the next year Conrad dedicated to Krieger his *Tales of Unrest*; he corresponded with Krieger for a few more years and in 1904 presented him with a copy of *Nostromo* inscribed "from his affectionate friend." [111] It appears that money was at the root of the conflict: Conrad had borrowed a considerable sum from Krieger and was unable to pay it back.

Besides his debts, Conrad was short of money for his current expenses. On 7 January 1898 he announced to Garnett, "That I must borrow money somewhere is very evident," asking whether it would be proper for him to turn to Pawling for an advance, for the unfinished *Rescue*, that would bring him "bread and *peace*." [112] For although in his Christmas letter to the Zagórskis (his first to them that year) Conrad maintained, "Things are going better at present. That I shall some day attain material success there is no reason to doubt," this was purely verbal consolation. And, he added, "The worst is that my health is not good. *Les nerfs, les nerfs!* Uncertainty torments me. . . . I fear that 'before the sun rises, the dew will have destroyed the eyes.'" [113]

For Conrad these months, scanty in written pages, were a period of intensive reading and reflection. Several letters penned at that time to Cunninghame Graham are among the most interesting Conrad ever wrote; they represent his first attempt to express his mature views on human nature and on man's place in the universe. Later, he modified his opinions, changing the emphasis here and there, but the basic ideas remained the same. Conrad's pronouncements are not a methodical exposition of his theories; they are a combination of personal confessions and polemic arguments; many statements have their origin in momentary moods. He uses images, parables, metaphors, irony, rhetorical questions, exaggeration, and understatement—hence the frequent contradictions in attempted reconstructions of his thoughts by critics and biographers. Let us try to arrange them, concentrating on the most characteristic components.

The scientific picture of the world, whose reliability Conrad never questioned, does not provide grounds for ascribing some meaning to reality, nor does it give any basis for regarding some values or ideals as better or more sensible than others. Science tells us, "Understand that thou art nothing, less than a shadow, more insignificant than a drop of water in the ocean, more fleeting than the illusion of a dream." The universe is like a huge machine:

It evolved itself (I am severely scientific) out of a chaos of scraps of iron and behold!—it knits. I am horrified at the horrible work and stand appalled. I feel it ought to embroider—but it goes on knitting. You come and say: "this is all right; it's only a question of the right kind of oil. Let us use this—for instance—celestial oil and the machine shall embroider a most beautiful design in purple and gold." Will it? Alas no. You cannot by any special lubrication make embroidery with a knitting machine. And the most withering thought is that the infamous thing has made itself; made itself without thought, without conscience, without foresight, without eyes, without heart. It is a tragic accident—and it has happened. You can't interfere with it. The last drop of bitterness is in the suspicion that you can't even smash it. In virtue of that truth one and immortal which lurks in the force that made it spring into existence it is what it is—and it is indestructible!

It knits us in and it knits us out. It has knitted time space, pain, death, corruption, despair and all the illusions—and nothing matters.

There is a chasm between nature and man—Nature is perfectly indifferent to Humanity, and vice versa:

The mysteries of a universe made of drops of fire and clods of mud do not concern us in the least. The fate of a humanity condemned ultimately to perish from cold is not worth troubling about. If you take it to heart it becomes an unendurable tragedy. If you believe in improvement you must weep, for the attained perfection must end in cold, darkness and silence. In a dispassionate view the ardour for reform, improvement for virtue, for knowledge, and even for beauty is only a vain sticking up for appearances as though one were anxious about the cut of one's clothes in a community of blind men. Life knows us not and we do not know life—we don't know even our own thoughts.

And men are hopelessly weak:

Into the noblest cause men manage to put something of their baseness; and sometimes when I think of You here, quietly, You seem to me tragic with your courage, with your beliefs and your hopes.[114]

Our consciousness, which sets us apart from other living creatures, is also the source of the tragedy of our fate:

We can't return to nature, since we can't change our place in it. Our refuge is in stupidity, in drunkenness of all kinds, in lies, in beliefs, in murder, thieving,

reforming—in negation, in contempt—each man according to the prompt-
ings of his particular devil. There is no morality, no knowledge and no hope;
there is only the consciousness of ourselves which drives us about a world
that whether seen in a convex or a concave mirror is always but a vain and
fleeting appearance.[115]

The last sentence sounds like a distant echo of a subjective idealist; but in fact
Conrad did not question the existence of material reality; all he maintains is
that while consciousness makes man aware that he is not entirely part of the
natural order of things, it does not give him any rationally dependable instructions on how to behave.

Discussing Graham's projects of radical social reform, Conrad wrote:

What you want to reform are not institutions—it is human nature. Your faith
will never move that mountain. Not that I think mankind intrinsically bad. It
is only silly and cowardly. Now *You* know that in cowardice is every evil—
especially that cruelty so characteristic of our civilization. But without it
mankind would vanish. No great matter truly.[116]

How are we to understand those statements? In the spirit of Schopenhauer as
some suggest? The different echoes of opinions of that eloquent whiner are a
result of Conrad's moodiness and his knack of adopting catchy notions and expressions, rather than of a genuine similarity of beliefs. When Conrad was
gloomy and downhearted, he was particularly prone to use Schopenhauer's
phraseology, widely popular at the time. It is possible, of course, that he had
read *The World as Will and Idea*, but the analogies with Schopenhauer seem
mostly verbal. Conrad's conception of human nature was different: more historical and social, and not deterministic; he did not think that man's personality was given to him irreversibly, nor that it was unchangeable. He recognized
the immense role played by irrational factors, but his understanding of the will
was quite different from that of Schopenhauer: more traditionally, he regarded
the will as a factor that shaped and changed man's character. Conrad perceived
malevolence and egoism no less acutely than the German philosopher, but he
did not consider them universal. His ethics were based on the principles of responsibility, duty, and solidarity—not on compassion, against which he lashed
out in *The Nigger*. This novel may be interpreted as anti-Schopenhauerian in its
apotheosis of work, authority, group responsibility and fidelity to tough social
principles. Conrad was much closer to the sophisticated skepticism of Anatole
France; in his letters to Graham are several thoughts reminiscent of France's
Father Jerome Coignard.[117] The contention about the basic unchangeability of
man's flawed nature belongs to the tenets of Catholicism. But for the right interpretation of the quoted sentences and views it is most important to place
them among Conrad's other pronouncements and his literary work as a whole.

Only then shall we understand the grounds of his protests, the consequences of his skepticism, and the foundations of his irony.

"Of course reason is hateful—but why? Because it demonstrates (to those who have the courage) that we, living, are out of life—utterly out of it."[118] As we can see, the cause of reason's "hatefulness" is that it leads to a desperate and proud recognition of the insignificance of human fate. Reason enables the chosen—that handful of the convicts Conrad mentioned once in a letter to Poradowska—to reject all illusions about the privileged position of mankind in the order or disorder of the universe. But reason is not man's only faculty. Although Conrad did not name will and emotions, they played an important part in his vision of the world: the values of loyalty and honor, which he mentioned several times, are obviously not intellectual values.

Therefore, to say that some ideals are unpopular and difficult, or even unattainable, does not imply their rejection. To regard an ideal as unpracticable or tragically inaccessible was not, for Conrad, tantamount to its condemnation. Reading his works we have to bear this constantly in mind so as not to lose, in our age ruled by considerations of efficiency and utility, the sight of what is essential for Conrad's ethical position. "You with your ideals of sincerity, courage and truth are strangely out of place in this epoch of material preoccupations. What does it bring? What's the profit? What do we get by it? These questions are at the root of every moral, intellectual or political movement." But he soon added, "I am more in sympathy with you than words can express." And again, "There are no converts to the ideas of honour, justice, compassion, freedom."[119]

The impossibility of achieving "conversion" is a reproach directed at men, not at ideas. Men, not values, are the subject of Conrad's skepticism.

Conrad, high-strung and inclined to depressions, was apt to express himself in tones of extreme despondency. This has to be remembered; not everything he said ought to be taken literally. At any rate, he was not a nihilist and never questioned the validity of all moral ideals. He accused Graham of naiveté: "You want from men faith, honour, fidelity to truth in themselves and others. You want them to have all this, to show it every day, to make out of these words their rule of life. The respectable classes which suspect you of such pernicious longings lock you up and would just as soon have you shot. . . . What makes you dangerous is your unwarrantable belief that your desire may be realized. This is the only point of difference between us. I do not believe. And if I desire the very same things no one cares."[120] Thus it is clear that doubts did not concern "faith, honour, and fidelity to truth" but the chances of persuading men to be guided by these values. As for himself, he obviously wanted to remain faithful to them. The psychological consequences of such a moral attitude were indeed hard to bear: to preserve unpractical fidelity, even if only as an ideal, demanded a constant effort of will. It is certainly easier to cultivate total skepticism, which usually changes smoothly into cynicism or mere indifference; thus Schopenhauer could live comfortably while proclaiming the meaninglessness of everything. But Conrad placed himself in the position of a soldier defending a doomed outpost.

What Conrad says in his letters ought always to be interpreted in relation to their psychological background. The author's protean moods have to be constantly borne in mind. Conrad's letters to Graham are not a formal declaration of a programme but an impassioned discussion with a friend. What Conrad attacks is primarily the historical optimism of the aristocrat-socialist. His own knowledge, and personal as well as national experience, filled him with skepticism. Again and again he would repeat that he looked at history from a point of view entirely different from that of the British, who were accustomed to success. Take the following quotation: "Yes. We Poles are poor specimens. The strain of national worry has weakened the moral fibre—and no wonder when you think of it. It is not a fault; it is a misfortune."[121] These words are an important complement to and explanation of the views expressed in his letters to Graham in late 1897 and early 1898.

Letters from that period as well as those written to Graham later point to yet another subject worth consideration. Conrad wrote to Sanderson about his meeting with Cunninghame Graham: "We talked in two languages." From January 1898 on, writing to Graham, he used French headings; many of his letters were bilingual—written in English and French.

English was Konrad Korzeniowski's third language (not counting Latin and German). Ford Madox Ford (Hueffer) mentioned that this was often evident during their many years of close relationship. Conrad would occasionally say, "There's a word *so and so* in Polish to express what I want." Usually, however, they would talk in French, especially when discussing theoretical issues and technical problems of literary craft.[122] His friends generally agree that throughout his life Conrad spoke with a marked foreign accent; equally unanimous is the opinion that his spoken French was very good. He was well aware of his linguistic shortcomings: "But you know I am shy of my bad English," he wrote to Graham in January 1898.[123] This lack of confidence extended to the written language. He made grammatical errors, for example, using *will* instead of *shall*, or *like* instead of *as*; he sometimes stretched English syntax to the breaking point, shaping his sentences after the Polish or French fashion; now and then he made spelling mistakes. He appealed to Hope to check yachting terminology in the manuscript of *The Rescue*.

As Conrad was not a French man of letters, to write and speak French was less of a commitment for him, quite apart from the fact that he often felt more competent in that language. Therefore he liked to write whole letters in French or throw in French expressions, sentences, and longer fragments. He tended to do the same in his Polish correspondence: he would switch over to French when writing to the Zagórskis, and all his letters to Janina de Brunnow and Zygmunt Szembek are in French.[124] It is significant that he used French for the inscriptions of his books presented to Henry James. Conrad regarded James as the greatest living writer in English, and addressing him in an "international" language was, perhaps, an expression of a certain humility and result of the fear of making a mistake; he also conversed with James in French.[125]

René Rapin, who made a detailed study of those of Conrad's French texts that were available to him, summed it up: "As I had to demonstrate with all possible supporting evidence to refute G. Jean-Aubry's exaggerated assertions in this respect, Conrad makes frequent and at times quite serious mistakes in French. Conrad himself was worried that his French was that of a foreigner. But apart from the fact that a great number of his faults . . . are such as many French people would indeed commit and do commit when writing offhand, suffering from bad health, living outside France, when worried, nervous or tired—these faults . . . strike the reader far less . . . than the natural ease, often even extraordinary aptitude, for expressing himself in a language which was neither his mother tongue nor the language in which he thought, wrote, and lived during his forty-six years as seaman and later as English writer."[126] Thus, Jean-Aubry's claim that Conrad could have been a French writer is obviously exaggerated: English was the only language in which Conrad showed his verbal versatility and inventiveness; nevertheless, his mastery of a third tongue confirms Conrad's uncommon gift for languages no less than his ability to retain fluency in his second.

The range of Conrad's French usage helps us understand the role this language played in his mature life. The vast majority of French fragments woven into English texts consists of either colloquial and vivid expressions pithily rendering the writer's thought or sentences concerning general or abstract problems, particularly political and moral. Almost all philosophical remarks in Conrad's letters are formulated in French. Thus, French for him was a language of social immediacy, and also a language of theoretical discourse. We may assume that he read philosophical books mostly in French—whether they were ancient classics, or Pascal and Rousseau, or Moleschott and Schopenhauer. Besides, it is worth remembering that the French syntax is much closer to the Polish than to the English; and the intellectual traditions of the two countries are also closer to each other.

Ending his bitterly skeptical letter to Graham—the same in which he wrote, "Life knows us not and we do not know life"—Conrad added a postscript: "This letter missed this morning's post because an infant of male persuasion arrived and made such a row that I could not hear the Postman's whistle. It's a fine commentary upon this letter! Still I feel remorse." As we recall, his lack of enthusiasm about his prospective heir had been evident earlier. "Jessie is very happy with this expected event," he wrote to the Zagórskis; he himself never expressed similar feelings. The situation did not change after the birth of Borys: Conrad assured Mrs. Brooke that Jessie was "in the seventh heaven" but refrained from disclosing his own sentiments.[127] Not for long though. Although Jessie's memoirs in this respect also are not quite credible—according to her story, Conrad, supposed to fetch the doctor, assured him that there was no need to hurry, accepted his invitation to lunch, and returned only after two messengers had been sent to bring him and the doctor to the house—she seems to render faithfully the general atmosphere of confusion and irritability.[128] It is enough to read some of Conrad's comments about the birth of his son, made in letters to his friends. On 16 January to Galsworthy: "I feel relieved greatly and hope to do some work now." The same day to Chesson: "The house was in a state of disorganization. . . . However the fuss is over thank God." And to Crane: "A male infant arrived yesterday and made a devil of a row. He yelled like an Apache and ever since this morning has been on the war path again. It's a ghastly nuisance." A few days later to Garnett: "Jess sends her love to Mrs Garnett and desires me to state that the baby is a very fine baby. I disclaim all responsibility for that statement. *Do* you really think the volume [*Tales of Unrest*] *will do*?" Again a week later: "My wife shall want to show the blessed baby to your wife. I hate babies."[129] The following year he confided to Helen Sanderson: "I don't mind owning I wished for a daughter. I can't help thinking she would have resembled me more and would have been perhaps easier to understand. . . . at the age of thirteen months he [Borys] is an accomplished and fascinating barbarian full of charming wiles and of pitiless selfishness. It is not his innocence but his unconsciousness that makes him pathetic—besides making him just bearable."[130]

Conrad was certainly not called upon to help with the baby. Jessie's mother arrived for the confinement, and Jessie's younger sister Dorothy (Dolly) stayed with the Conrads for six months to help. Conrad's relations with his mother-in-law were not good; one may gather this even from Jessie's guarded remarks about her mother's inability to understand Conrad's eccentricities.

Errors in dating his son's birthday further testify to Conrad's subconscious disapproval of the event. In a letter to Zagórska he explained the origin of the name he decided to give his son: "The baby was born on the 17th of this month . . . he has dark hair, enormous eyes—and looks like a monkey. What upsets me is that my wife maintains that he is also very much like me. . . . He will be christened in the Chapel of the Cloister of the Carmelites in Southwark (London). The principle on which his name was chosen is the following: that the rights of the two nations must be respected. Thus, my wife representing the Anglo-Saxons chose the Saxon name Alfred. I found myself in an embarrassing situation. I wanted to have a purely Slavonic name, but one which could not be distorted either in speech or in writing—and at the same time one which was not too difficult for foreigners (non-Slavonic). I had, therefore, to reject names such as Władysław, Bogusław, Wieńczysław etc., I do not like Bohdan: so I decided on Borys, remembering that my friend Stanisław Zaleski gave this name to his eldest son, so that apparently a Pole may use it."[131] Borys was indeed baptized, but not until a year later. And there was never a Carmelite cloister in the Southwark parish. It remains unknown whether Conrad ever realized that the name he chose for his son was typically Russian; the Zagórskis' reply to his letter is unknown.

At the beginning of 1898, Conrad's relations with Crane became closer. The writers were fascinated by each other's personalities. Crane could have been charmed by Conrad's courtly manners, coupled with a deeply cultured and versatile mind, by his fundamentally serious approach to the problems of life and literature coexisting with an inclination to grotesque humor. Crane, in turn, displayed a captivating spontaneity, freshness, and incisiveness of perception, the courage of an adventurer coupled with the subtlety of an artist. Their second meeting had to be delayed because Jessie was in the final weeks of her pregnancy, but Crane wrote to suggest that they collaborate on a play (at that time theatrical success was highly profitable). Conrad demurred but was obviously flattered. "I have no dramatic gift. *You* have the terseness, the clear eye, the easy imagination. You have all—and I have only the accursed faculty of dreaming. . . . But if by any chance . . . you should really, honestly, artistically think I could be of some use—then my dear Crane I would be only too glad to work by your side and with your lead."[132]

Nothing came of the project, but Conrad's notes, dated 12 February 1898, on the subject of the Franco-Prussian War, discovered a few years ago, were probably prepared for Crane, who was then working on a series of articles called "Great Battles of the World."[133]

On 19 February, the Conrads, together with Borys and Dolly, arrived for a fortnight's stay at Ravensbrook, Crane's house in Oxted, Surrey. The visit, a great success, furthered friendly relations between the two families. Garnett recalled later:

Conrad's moods of gay tenderness could be quite seductive. On the few occasions I saw him with Stephen Crane he was delightfully sunny, and bantered "poor Steve" in the gentlest, most affectionate style, while the latter sat silent, Indian-like, turning enquiring eyes under his chiselled brow, now and then jumping up suddenly and confiding some new project with intensely electric feeling. At one of these sittings Crane passionately appealed to me to support his idea that Conrad should collaborate with him in a play on the theme of a ship wrecked on an island. I knew it was hopelessly unworkable, this plan, but Crane's brilliant visualization of the scenes was so strong and infectious that I had not the heart to declare my own opinion. And Conrad's sceptical answers were couched in the tenderest, most reluctant tone. I can still hear the shades of Crane's poignant friendliness in his cry "Joseph!" And Conrad's delight in Crane's personality glowed in the shining warmth of his brown eyes.[134]

They were also thinking out plans for jointly renting a house in Brittany for the summer, and together pondered over their financial troubles.[135] Himself penniless, Conrad arranged an advance from Blackwood for Crane, who was always spending much more than he earned. This enabled the young American to hurry off to the States. Crane, determined to know the smell of gunpowder and rub shoulders with death, did not want to miss the opportunity offered by the war with Spain over Cuba and the Philippines.[136] He was ready to join in any capacity—as a volunteer or a reporter. Conrad's support for Crane's ambitions shows him as a truly loyal friend, since he himself was outraged by the war and sided with Spain.

Visiting the Cranes and the Garnetts (3–4 March) provided Conrad with a welcome diversion from his daily worries. "I feel that if there is no break I will go crazy or go out altogether." "I've been rather seedy lately—all worry I think. But I am going to put my worries aside and have a real good time with you," he told Crane in a letter. Above all, he felt besieged by troubles, mainly financial: "Everybody here is in rude health at which I am sorry because of the enormous appetites which is so expensive—and the stores running low at that." [137] Forced to appeal for a loan, he turned to Spiridion, while at the same time looking desperately around for a source of income. He wrote an article about Alphonse Daudet, who had recently died. As Ian Watt shows, it is a brilliant piece of criticism, combining praise of Daudet's achievement, couched in terms of ironical dismissal of the elitist view of literature, with a trenchant assessment of Daudet's limitations. About that time Conrad also wrote a piece on Kipling; it was never published, and is thus the only nonepistolary text of Conrad's which certainly existed, but which has remained unknown—regrettably, since it would be interesting to see what Conrad thought about that talented glorifier of imperialism.[138]

Conrad continued to plod on with *The Rescue*, but progress was slow. He stuck to it only because the text represented a considerable outlay of work and could be shown to publishers. "That damned and muddy romance. I am getting on—and it is very very bad. Bad enough I sometimes think to make my fortune." [139] However, when Pawling managed to sell the book rights to McClure of New York for £250 (£100 to be paid in advance), Conrad's joy was mixed with horror at the thought of the approaching deadline when the finished work had to be submitted to the publishers. He assured Pawling, "I shall go right ahead with the story and hope to finish it in five months—at the outside, probably in four." But barely a week later he complained to Graham, "The worst is the book is not finished yet and must be delivered end July at the latest." [140] The novel was soon to become the real curse of his life—all the worse for having already been paid for.

One of the difficulties might have been the very subject of *The Rescue*. Its hero, the famous Captain Tom Lingard, is honor-bound to help Hassan and Immada regain their native country. But, charmed by an English woman, Mrs. Travers, Lingard is deflected from his purpose by the temptation of a different kind of life. He is torn by conflicting loyalties, and his Malay friends end up as losers. Consciously or subconsciously Conrad may have associated this situation with his own duties toward his own country—duties that he brushed aside, attracted by a different kind of life.

The first nine months of 1898 must have been the most difficult period for Conrad since he had left the sea. At the beginning of February he received from Lublin the sad news about the death of Karol Zagórski, a relative with whom he had preserved a closer and apparently warmer relationship than with his first cousins of the Bobrowski family. In reply to the widow's telegram, he sent a long and compassionate letter in which we find a characteristic fragment about "confessing": "And in difficult moments the thought that a day will come when I shall be able to confess to him my whole life and be understood: this thought was my greatest consolation. And now this hope—the most precious of all—is extinguished for ever." [141]

The lack of somebody close to lean on and confide in was particularly oppressive for Conrad. The whole course of his life and the kind of profession he finally chose had deprived him of the possibility of everyday contact with the communal life of a stable human environment. Solitude fosters depressive tendencies and sharpens their effects. It seems that in those months he was indeed on the verge of a complete breakdown. "I did not write because I was beastly seedy—nerve trouble—a taste of hell. . . . An extreme weariness oppresses me. It seems as though I had seen and felt everything since the beginning of the world. I *suspect* my brain to be yeast and my backbone to be cotton. And I *know* that the quality of my work is of the kind to confirm my suspicions. I would yell for help to anybody—man or devil if I could persuade myself that anybody would care—and, caring, could help. Well. No more." [142] Although visiting friends had a good effect on his condition and the good news from Pawling about the sale of the American rights of *The Rescue* brought temporary relief, on 22 March he had to cancel his meeting with Crane, which had been set for the twenty-fifth in London; again, "nervous trouble" was the cause, and his doctor advised him to avoid all excitement. [143]

The direct cause, aggravated by the situation at home, was the ill-starred *Rescue*. "To tell you the truth I hate the thing with such great hatred that I don't want to look at it again," he wrote to Garnett on 21 March, thanking him for the corrections and remarks concerning a fragment of the manuscript.

I shall certainly go on—that is if I can. The best about the work is that it is *sold*. They've got to take it. But the thought that such rubbish is produced at the cost of positive agony fills me with despair.

Eight days later he complained again about his nerves:

> Since then I've been better but have been unable to write. I sit down reli-
> giously every morning, I sit down for eight hours every day—and the sitting
> down is all. In the course of that working day of 8 hours I write 3 sentences
> which I erase before leaving the table in despair. There's not a single word to
> send you. Not one! And time passes—and McClure waits—not to speak of
> Eternity for which I don't care a damn. Of McClure however I am afraid. . . .
> I seem to have lost all *sense* of style and yet I am haunted, mercilessly haunted
> by the *necessity* of style. And that story I can't write weaves itself into all I see,
> into all I speak, into all I think, into the lines of every book I try to read. . . . I
> tried to correct Part II, according to your remarks. I did what I could—that is
> I knocked out a good many paragraphs. It's so much gained. As to alteration,
> rewriting and so on I haven't attempted it—except here and there a trifle—
> for the reason I could not think out anything different to what is written.
> Perhaps when I come to my senses I shall be able to do something before the
> book comes out. As to the serial it must go anyhow. . . . That's how things
> stand today; and to-morrow would be more mysterious if it were not so
> black! I write you a nice cheery letter for a good-bye: don't I, dear old fellow.
> That's how we use our friends. If I hadn't written I would have burst.[144]

The fear of McClure did not help much, and although Conrad assured Garnett in June, "I intend to write nothing else," it was more a case of creating
appearances than making a real effort. He kept confessing his absolute inability
to "imagine" anything in the novel, and while swearing to persevere he worked
on something else.[145]

On 26 March 1898, the *Tales of Unrest* were published, marking the end of
Conrad's connection with T. Fisher Unwin. The volume was reasonably well
received by the critics, although almost all reviewers complained about the
"unbearably gloomy" tone and the too stark realism of the stories. The *Spectator* disliked the presentation of Malays as morally superior to Europeans. And
the critic for *Literature* described the dwellings of Conrad's muse:

> On the walls prints depicting the failures and the tragedies of the world, hag-
> gard debauchees and their drunken wives, murders, suicides, and the living
> horrors of grinding, loveless poverty. Bookshelves filled with vast tomes of
> psychology leading nowhere and teaching nothing. Hard chairs and a large,
> plain deal table littered with medicine bottles and anatomical specimens. In
> every corner a close, stuffy, unhealthy smell. . . . Here we are told art has
> made its home, and on those hard chairs are seated its true votaries. The art-
> ist must devote himself to the truth and to nothing but the truth—but not to
> the whole truth. He must shut his eyes . . . to the tempting voices of love and
> happiness . . . until at last by due abstinence from the pleasures of the world,
> by a rapt contemplation of misery and sin, he may attain to the true aesthetic
> life.

Conrad was, then, subjected to much the same accusations as had been raised against his naturalist masters. Such opinions must have discouraged readers, in spite of all the praise of Conrad's artistic attainments.[146]

The respectable *Academy* printed a particularly favorable review, and soon after, its editor asked Conrad to write an article on the *Studies in Brown Humanity* by Hugh Clifford, the British Resident in Pahang, Malaya. By mid-April Conrad sent in the quickly written review, which expressed his high opinion of England's role in Malaya and in other colonies, although, as a matter of fact, he had seen very little of the British colonies. This led to his long-lasting friendship and correspondence with Clifford, a well-educated and talented man and ranking civil servant in various British colonies. In the meantime, Conrad wrote another short article deserving special attention. On 4 June, the newly established weekly *Outlook*, which had published his short essay on Daudet, with its thoughts on the poignant futility of human affairs, printed his notes on the *Sea Stories* by Frederick Marryat and James Fenimore Cooper. Reading Marryat, wrote Conrad, awakened one's regret for the bygone romanticism and zest for adventure of youth; it evoked admiration for the loyalty and sense of duty in his heroes. He confessed that Marryat and Cooper had been the favorite authors of his boyhood. Marryat enchanted him with his "youthful glamour, the headlong vitality"; Cooper fascinated him with his profound understanding of human nature and with artistic insight; he never regretted having been under their spell.[147]

One day before this article-tribute-confession appeared in print, Conrad finished "Youth," one of his best short pieces.[148] Anyone who remembers the mood of the story and the recurrent verbal motifs will notice the analogy with ideas and expressions of the essay on Marryat and Cooper. As we do not know exactly when Conrad wrote the article and when he started to work on "Youth," we cannot establish a definite relationship. But I suspect that Conrad, working on *The Rescue*, which was intended as a "glorified book for boys," looked for inspiration to the authors whose books had charmed his childhood; and his musing about their novels adumbrated both the idea and the general mood of his own story.[149]

Conrad almost certainly started his work on *Lord Jim* even earlier. Be that as it may, the appearance of these manuscripts on his table indicate that Conrad's creative impasse was finally being overcome. In "Youth," we are first introduced to Marlow, the narrator. This character, peculiar to Conrad and important for the shaping of his artistic personality, continues to evoke great interest among his critics as well as biographers. Indeed, Marlow's origin has both literary and psychological aspects.

It is not easy to separate one from the other. Those elements of Conrad's literary programme which brought him close to French realists and naturalists clashed with the Romantic tradition and the idea of moral and political commitment that he had brought from Poland, as well as with his own stormy and emotional temperament. Marlow's artistic and literary origins and the general problem of "a story within a story" have attracted much attention. Polish critics have pointed, quite justly, to the affinity between this particular convention and the *gawęda* ("yarn"), a very popular genre in Poland; thus the Polish tradition was perhaps singularly conducive to Conrad's development of this particular form of narrative. For a biographer, however, the psychological aspect is more important: in what way did the advent of Marlow help Conrad to overcome his crisis? He did not use Marlow again for some time, and then a decade later he reintroduced him in *Chance*—but in the reader's mind this narrator remains a most characteristic element of Conrad's art.

Tale-tellers had appeared earlier in Conrad's works—in "The Lagoon" and "Karain." But stories put in the mouths of Malays, whom Conrad did not know too well, could have but a limited subject range and had, perforce, to have been exotic. The paramount difficulty that Conrad experienced in his work at that time was to find some clearly defined attitude or point of view. He complained about a decline in his sense of style and form, about the vagueness of his imagination, his inability to think clearly and articulate what he wanted to say, about a lack of faith in his own work.[150] The intensity and perseverance of those symptoms showed them to reflect more than just a temporary ebb of creative powers; it was not simply a case of having problems with literary workmanship. The cause seems to have been more deeply rooted: it was an identity crisis.

Sensitivity and excitability shown since childhood (and later his unrestrained changes of mood) accounted for Conrad's difficulties with creating a coherent identity. For an orphan, exile, and wanderer, the task was particularly, almost hopelessly, hard. A person who matures within his own stable family and social environment unconsciously absorbs definite traditions and beliefs, adopts concepts, ways of feeling and of expressing himself. Associating with his environment, which undergoes gradual but continuous natural changes, he can compare his emotions, views, ideals, and dreams with the reactions they evoke among his relatives and friends. His peers' approval would be an acknowledgment to him of his own maturing personality; disagreements with friends and environment would make him assert the distinct character of his individuality. Early in life, Conrad, thrown from place to place since childhood, lost his home, and on leaving Poland found himself in an international socio-cultural vacuum. As a young man and adult he associated with people completely different from the gentry and intelligentsia with whom he had grown up. Following his difficult and lonely years at sea he suddenly plunged into a middle-class and at the same time marginal existence in England. The British merchant marine was a school of life for him, but it was a one-sided and insufficient education for a writer and intellectual. Now, after so many years, the lonely man and wanderer settled down and established a family; the sailor dropped anchor in a quiet village; the marine officer changed, with difficulty, into a man of letters; and the exile tried to take root in an alien country. This last was perhaps most important. These factors were more than sufficient to cause a great difficulty in defining for himself who he really was and wanted to be; and, consequently, it was also difficult to establish a consistent point of view that would enable him to impose some order upon the multitude of real and imagined facts.

Conrad wanted to belong to English literature and to England. This choice was unambiguous and explicit. But he did not want to, or did not know how to—it comes to the same thing—be fully immersed in the English environment. Even had he wanted to, it would have been made impossible by the English tendency to keep foreigners at arm's length—there are many allusions to this fact in Conrad's own books. He had his reservations about even a purely psychological immersion. Family memories rankled in his mind; he had a lively sense of Polish and continental cultural continuity. In short, he was aware of his own dissimilarity and strangeness—yet he strove for the comforting sense of belonging. How many stories and reminiscences there are about Conrad's efforts to become a real English gentleman! They are always a bit comic or ironic: Conrad was never fully successful in his attempts; something would always give away his foreignness.

Marlow, a model English gentleman, ex-officer of the merchant marine, was the embodiment of all that Conrad would wish to be if he were to become completely anglicized. And since that was not the case, and since he did not quite share his hero's point of view, there was no need to identify himself with Marlow, either emotionally or intellectually. Thanks to Marlow's duality, Conrad could feel solidarity with, and a sense of belonging to, England by proxy, at the same time maintaining a distance such as one has toward a creation of one's imagination. Thus, Conrad, although he did not permanently resolve his search for a consistent consciousness of self-identity, found an integrating point of view that enabled him, at last, to break out of the worst crisis of his writing career. It did not happen all at once; it was a long and difficult process, not free from hesitation and worry. Obviously, Conrad did not realize immediately the possibilities Marlow was opening for him. Only five months after he had finished "Youth" he again used his new hero. Yet at the beginning of *Lord Jim* Marlow does not appear and nothing seems to foreshadow his coming.

An immediate escape from the impasse would have been something like a miracle. Conrad felt hopelessly involved in *The Rescue*, and also beset by financial worries; a change in his method of writing required time. The £40 he had received from Blackwood on 11 June (£35 for "Youth" and £5 as an advance for *Lord Jim*) gave only temporary relief to his budget. Although the exact figures are not known, the Conrads spent quite a lot and lived above their means. Judging by Conrad's letters, their tastes and habits, although not extravagant, were nevertheless quite refined and costly. Throughout his life—at least when not at sea—Conrad was a gourmet, and the quality of food had a direct impact on his moods. Consolation provided by good cooking and delicacies had to be paid for. The Conrads also helped Jessie's family, and her siblings spent long periods of time at the Conrad home.[151]

In July the last part of the advance from McClure was due, but the end of the novel was nowhere in sight. Conrad, unable to find other work or means of income, made far-reaching plans, warmed by his success with "Youth": "I've sold (I think) the sea things to B. for £35 (13,000 words). Meldrum thinks there's no doubt—but still B. must see it himself. . . . I think *Jim* (20,000) "Youth" (13,000) "A Seaman" (5,000) "Dynamite" (5,000) and another story of say 15,000 would make a volume for B. here and for McC. there."[152] But it was the proverbial counting of chickens before they were hatched. (*Lord Jim* was then to be a long short story; "A Seaman" was probably the later "The End of the Tether"; "Dynamite" eventually became *Chance*—and all of them ended up as works of novel length.) At any rate, he had to give priority to *The Rescue*.

"I am in a state of deadly, indecent funk. I've obtained a ton of cash from a Yank under, what strikes me, are false pretences. The Child of the Screaming Eagle is as innocent as a dove. He *thinks* the book he bought will be finished in July while I know that it is a physical and intellectual impossibility to even approach the end by that date. He sends on regular checks which is—according to his lights—right: but I pocket them serenely, which—according to my lights— looks uncommonly like a swindle on my part," wrote Conrad to Sanderson on 15 June.[153] McClure paid him a visit a few days later (18 and 19 June) and apparently postponed the deadline for the delivery of the text. Soon afterward McClure offered *The Rescue* to Clement Shorter, the editor of *Illustrated London News*, who was ready to serialize the novel. This opened up before Conrad the possibility of a considerable additional income and, above all, of popular success. At the same time, however, it meant that the book had to be finished promptly, since its publication was to begin on 1 October.[154]

Conrad took care to cultivate good relations with his publishers—he also invited Meldrum on 24 June—but was unable to find a way out of his predicament. He was perennially short of money. In spite of that, and in spite of the fact that Dolly was still with them, the Conrads looked unsuccessfully for a servant, because Conrad was worried that Jessie was overworked. "The poor girl is doing all the housework, nursing and cooking, herself. She is very cheerful about it but it makes me miserable to see her toiling like this from morning to night. Oh! for a success, a beastly popular success! I long for it on that account," he lamented to Cora Crane.[155] Quite possibly Meyer is right when he says that Conrad felt jealous of the time devoted by Jessie to their son, who was teething at the time and howled all day.[156] I suppose, however, that his "lordly" habits, plus a normal wish to isolate himself from the "precious and insufferable" child, played a greater part than did jealousy.

He was torn between contradictory desires: to continue the novel that had been already paid for or to abandon it for the sake of other works.[157] Now and again he would be beset by doubts whether he had done the right thing in deciding to become a writer. "Why the devil did I ever begin?"[158] From the middle of July he looked, with Cunninghame Graham's support, for employment at sea. He assured Graham that "Jess . . . is as anxious for the sea as I am." On 19 July he spoke with Sir Francis Evans, the director of the Union Line. On 3 August he waxed apologetic about "my silly desire to get out to sea added to your occupations." On 27 and 28 September he made a special trip to Glasgow and returned slightly more hopeful. But all those attempts, fruitless in the end, were undertaken in a desperate mood. "So I must write or burst. It is too awful. Half the book is not written and I have only to 1st Nover to finish it! I could not take a command till December because I am in honour bound to furnish the story to time. Yet to get to sea would be salvation. I am really in a deplorable state, mentally. I feel utterly wretched. I haven't the courage to tackle my work," he grieved to Graham on 26 August.[159]

Again it is impossible to tell to what extent his depression was the cause or the result of living in "his own hell," which consisted of an inability to write, a lack of money, and family worries. Conrad was obviously in a state of prostration. "I feel suicidal. . . . All is darkness," he unburdened his heart to Garnett.[160] A fortnight later, grateful for Garnett's comforting words and his praise of a new fragment of *The Rescue*, Conrad tried to convince himself that the worst was over. But his forced cheerfulness only lasted for a few sentences. "I must be getting well since, looking back, I see how ill, mentally, I have been these last four months. The fear of this horror coming back to me makes me shiver. As it is it has destroyed already the little belief in myself I used to have. I am appalled at the absurdity of my situation—at the folly of my hopes, at the blindness that had kept me up in my gropings. Most appalled to feel that all the doors behind me are shut and that I must remain where I have come blundering in the dark," he wrote to Garnett on 18 August.[161]

Letters from that period, particularly those written in August, show Conrad's continual fight to preserve a clear mind and resist mental disintegration. He wrote to Graham, "I would pray . . . for a little forgetfulness. Say half an hour. Oh bliss." "If this miserable planet had perception a soul, a heart, it would burst with indignation or fly to pieces from sheer pity. . . . I am writing coglionerie [nonsense] while I don't know how the Teufel [devil] I am going to live next month. The very sea breeze has an execrable taste. . . . I wish you would come to shoot me."[162] And to Helen Sanderson: "Dates are knocked over like ninepins: proofs torn to rags. . . . The last shred of honour is gone—also the last penny. The baby, however, is well. He is singing a song now. I don't feel like singing—I assure you. My head feels as if full of sawdust. Of course many people's heads are full of sawdust—the tragic part of the business is in my being aware of it. . . . I am like a tight-rope dancer who, in the midst of his performance, should suddenly discover that he knows nothing about tight-rope dancing. He may appear ridiculous to the spectators, but a broken neck is the result of such untimely wisdom." [163]

Conrad's psychological torment abated only toward the end of September. His spirits were revived by the expedition to Glasgow. While there, he was fascinated by an X-ray apparatus and his encounter with John McIntyre, a pioneer of radiology, with whom he talked about the vibrations of waves as the only real basis of human consciousness. Ending a lively letter to Garnett in which he described his Glasgow experiences, Conrad announced, "I feel less hopeless about things and particularly about the damned thing called *The Rescue*." [164] And two weeks later he reported, "I've destroyed all I did write last month but my brain feels alive and my heart is not afraid now. Permanent state?—who knows. Always hope." [165] This state of mind was anything but permanent, but there was an evident change for the better. It was a sign of conquering the depression with some help from external factors. "Ultimate" deadlines came and went, but the sky did not fall. Conrad's relations with his publishers remained good. McClure showed supreme patience and even gave Garnett a job as a result of Conrad's mediation; the *Illustrated London News* decided to postpone publication of *The Rescue* until April, and Conrad began to feel he had plenty of time ahead of him. In September he probably borrowed more money from Krieger—and it was only at the end of October that he was again compelled to appeal to Galsworthy for help. [166] Moreover, and perhaps above all, he decided to move. He rented a cottage from a young writer he had recently met, Ford Madox Hueffer. Pent Farm was in Kent, near Hythe, one of the ancient Cinque Ports, some sixty miles from London. It was an ordinary one-storied red brick house with a steep roof, and it stood next to farm buildings. Although old, it looked gray and uninteresting compared with the attractive Elizabethan cottage, Ivy Walls, which the Conrads occupied in Stanford-le-Hope. Pent Farm had its advantages, however: it was smaller, cheaper (at £25 a year), and drier than Ivy Walls; besides, although the farm itself was isolated, the Cranes, Wellses, and Henry James lived in the vicinity.

"We are only five kilometres from the sea. The railway station is 3 kilometres away. . . . Behind the house are the hills (Kentish Downs) which slope in zigzag fashion down to the sea, like the battlements of a big fortress. . . . On the other side of the little garden stretches out quiet and waste land intersected by hedges and here and there stands an oak or a group of young ash trees. Three little villages are hidden among the hillocks and only the steeples of their churches can be seen. The colouring of the country presents brown and pale yellow tints—and in between, in the distance one can see the meadows, as green as emeralds." [167]

Most importantly, the change of domicile was linked in Conrad's mind, as though symbolically, with a change in mood. His situation did not improve, and his old troubles remained—but it was as if he broke out from a magic circle. He was not certain if this escape would be successful. Ten days before moving, he wrote to Graham's mother, "Early next year, when that torment is over [writing *Rescue*]—and I am hardly able to realize that such a time will ever come—I will without scruple use and abuse everybody's goodwill, influence, friendship to get back on the water. I am by no means happy on shore. . . . I am haunted by the idea I cannot write." [168]

On the whole, however, he was optimistic. The move took place on 26 October. [169] Shortly after, Conrad's most productive period began.

IX

FORD, THE PENT, AND JIM
1898–1900

CONRAD met Ford Madox Hueffer at the beginning of September 1898* at the Garnett's new house in the country, The Cearne, near Limpsfield, Surrey.[1] Hueffer, who at the time occupied himself with gardening, lived next door.

> Conrad came round the corner of the house. I was doing something at the open fireplace in the house-end. He was in advance of Mr Garnett who had gone inside, I suppose, to find me. Conrad stood looking at the view. His hands were in the pockets of his reefer-coat, the thumbs sticking out. His black, torpedo beard pointed at the horizon. He placed a monocle in his eye. Then he caught sight of me.
>
> I was very untidy, in my working clothes. He started back a little. I said: "I'm Hueffer." He had taken me for the gardener.
>
> His whole being melted together in enormous politeness. His spine inclined forward; he extended both hands to take mine. He said:
>
> "My dear faller...Delighted...Ench...anté!"[2]

The direct result of their meeting was the plan for the Conrads to sublet the Pent from the Hueffers. Immediately on his return from Glasgow, Conrad wrote to his new friend to confirm the decision: "This opportunity is a perfect

---

* F. R. Karl elaborates a hypothesis, originally proffered by Eloise Knapp Hay, that Conrad met Hueffer as early as in May 1898 (*Joseph Conrad: The Three Lives* [New York, 1979], pp. 426–427). It rests mainly on the existence of three Conrad letters, assumed to have been written in the summer of 1898 on paper with the Pent Farm letterhead. In fact, one of the three, to David S. Meldrum, was certainly written not on 10 August 1898, but a year later (see note 41, chapter 9). One of "17 May 1898" to Clifford I know only from Jean-Aubry's not quite reliable edition (G. Jean-Aubry, *Joseph Conrad: Life and Letters* [London, 1927], 1:237). The third is a letter to Galsworthy which, as Karl says, "we can date as June 28," and which he describes as "a key document in dating the meeting of Conrad and Ford as having occurred before September" (Karl, *Joseph Conrad*, pp. 427 and 940). Since we are not told on what the dating is based, the reasoning smacks of a petitio principii.

The negative evidence, speaking against both an earlier meeting between the two writers and an earlier association of Conrad with Pent Farm, is quite strong. There exist many letters unquestionably written in the summer of 1898 and dated, in Conrad's hand, from Stanford-le-Hope (for example, one to Cora Crane of 27 June, R. W. Stallman and Lillian Gilkes, eds., *Stephen Crane: Letters* [New York, 1960], pp. 182–183). Moreover, Conrad's earliest letters to Hueffer (29 September, 2 and 6 October 1898, all at Yale) sound like letters to a new acquaintance, and the letter of 2 October indicates a lack of familiarity with Pent Farm (Conrad is planning "a preliminary look around" and inquires if there is any coal or other burning material on the premises).

godsend to me."[3] The arrangement was quickly concluded; meanwhile the two men devised a more daring and incomparably more momentous scheme: they decided to embark on a literary collaboration.

Ford Hermann Hueffer was born on 17 December 1873 at Merton, Surrey. His father, Franz Hüffer, had emigrated from Germany to England four years before and changed his name to Francis Hueffer; he was a distinguished musicologist and music critic for *The Times*. Ford's mother, Catherine, was the daughter of the well-known Pre-Raphaelite painter Ford Madox Brown. The boy was brought up in the atmosphere of a cult of the arts and of tolerance for eccentricity—providing it was justified by talent. Ford had a flair for writing (he made his debut at eighteen with a fairy tale, *The Brown Owl*), read a lot, and from an early age felt quite at home in the English literary milieu; he had, however, a very shaky sense of his own identity. Wells described him later: "What he is really or if he is really, nobody knows now and he least of all; he has become a great system of assumed personas and dramatised selves."[4] The most glaring symptom of this inner lack of stability was his mythomania, which increased with age, manifesting itself first in petty bragging and later in highly involved stories about his own exploits and achievements. He gradually altered even his surname: when Conrad first met him he was already signing himself Ford Madox Hueffer, and after World War I he changed to Ford Madox Ford; for the sake of simplicity I shall call him Ford Madox Ford throughout.

A gawky, heavily built, fair-haired youth, at the age of twenty he eloped with seventeen-year-old Elsie Martindale, daughter of a well-known pharmacologist. Interested in intellectual and artistic novelties, Ford established social contacts with members of the Fabian Society. In March 1898 the Fords moved from Pent Farm to Gracie Cottage, in the immediate neighborhood of The Cearne, to be closer to the circle of Russian emigrés, mostly anarchists, who flocked around the Garnetts; among the initiated, the district became known as "Dostoyevsky's corner." There Ford devoted his time to his latest passion: the cultivation of vegetables and the breeding of ducks; he also worked on a historical novel, *Seraphina*. It was Richard Garnett who had suggested to him the plot, based on the adventures of one Aaron Smith, who had been a prisoner of Cuban pirates at the beginning of the nineteenth century.[5] Ford wrote fast and easily; by then he had already published *The Shifting of the Fire* (1892), three collections of fairy tales, a book of poetry (1893), and a biography of his maternal grandfather: none of these, however, were the kind of works that would establish his position in the publishing market.

Baines calls the arrangement with Ford "the most important event in Conrad's literary career."[6] This is, I believe, an exaggeration: Conrad's friendship with Garnett had a greater impact on what and how he wrote—but Baines in turn underestimates the psychological importance of the "non-literary" aspect of Conrad's association with Ford.

The origin of their decision to collaborate has often been discussed by Con-

rad's and Ford's biographers. Both writers also made their own comments—
although misleading—on the subject. Ford, as was his wont, exaggerated:

> Conrad confessed to the writer that previous to suggesting a collaboration he
> had consulted a number of men of letters as to its advisability. He said that he
> had put before them his difficulties with the language, the slowness with
> which he wrote and the increased fluency that he might acquire in the process
> of going minutely into words with an acknowledged master of English. . . .
> He stated succinctly and carefully that he had said to Henley . . . "Look here.
> I write with such difficulty: my intimate, automatic less expressed thoughts
> are in Polish; when I express myself with care I do it in French. When I write I
> think in French and then translate the words of my thoughts into English.
> This is an impossible process for one desiring to make a living by writing in
> the English language. . . ." And Henley, according to Conrad on that eve-
> ning, had said: "Why don't you ask H. to collaborate with you? He is the
> finest stylist in the English language of today. . . ." The writer, it should be
> remembered, though by ten or fifteen years the junior of Conrad was by some
> years his senior at any rate as a published author, and was rather the more
> successful of the two as far as sales went. Henley obviously had said nothing
> of the sort.[7]

Neither—let us add—did Conrad. And although it is true that Ford made his
debut three years ahead of Conrad, who was sixteen years his senior, his position in the publishing market and his critical reputation could not have been
compared with Conrad's.

As to Conrad, five years later he wrote to Kazimierz Waliszewski, "I collaborated on it [*Romance*] at a time when it was impossible for me to do anything
else."[8] This is not true either, because during the time he was collaborating with
Ford on *Romance*, he wrote "Typhoon," "Amy Foster," and "To-morrow"—in
fact an entire volume of his own stories, and good ones at that.

There is no doubt that the idea of collaboration came from Conrad, although
it may have been suggested by Garnett.[9] Conrad wrote explicitly in an apologetic letter to William E. Henley:

> When talking with Hueffer my first thought was that the man there who
> couldn't find a publisher had some good stuff to use and that if we worked it
> up together my name, probably, would get a publisher for it. On the other
> hand I thought that working with him would keep under the particular devil
> that spoils my work for me as quick as I turn it out (that's why I work so slow
> and break my word to publishers), and that the material being of the kind
> that appeals to my imagination and the man being an honest workman we
> could turn out something tolerable—perhaps; and if not he would be no
> worse off than before. It struck me the expression he cared for was in verse;
> he has the faculty; I have not; I reasoned that partnership in prose would not

affect any chances he may have to attain distinction—of the real kind—in verse. It seemed to me that a man capable of the higher form could not care very much for the lower. These considerations encouraged me in my idea. It never entered my head I could be dangerous to Hueffer in the way you point out. The affair had a material rather than an artistic aspect for me. . . . As for myself I meant to keep the right to descend into my own private little hell— whenever the spirit moved me to do that foolish thing—and produce alone from time to time—verbiage no doubt—my own—therefore very dear. This is the truth—the whole truth.[10]

Henley, who, as we may easily guess from Conrad's peroration, wrote poetry and not prose, was not the only writer to be dubious about Conrad's partner-ship with Ford; Wells also sounded a warning.[11] Later, after *The Inheritors* was finished, Henry James allegedly described the Conrad-Ford collaboration as "inconceivable," "like a bad dream which one relates at breakfast."[12] Wells thought that association with Conrad might spoil Ford's career. Henley also can be assumed to have been concerned for the effect on Ford's career; it was natural to fear that Ford, the younger of the two and still not fully formed as an artist, would be dominated by his more mature colleague. James, on the other hand, who regarded Ford as light-minded, might have been anxious lest he lead Conrad astray with his rash projects.

For the sake of clarity three aspects of the problem ought to be distinguished: Why did Conrad suggest collaboration? Why did Ford accept his suggestion? And how and why did their partnership survive several years? There is little connection between the last aspect and the first two, because from the time the decision was made until the time it was brought into effect, a whole year was to pass. Baines rightly remarks that literary partnerships were not unusual at the time. For Conrad, who four years earlier had suggested collaboration to Pora-dowska, it was an arrangement that promised to solve several psychological dif-ficulties and one professional one. In his first preserved letter to Ford, Conrad described himself as a "self-made philosopher and a pilgrim on the stony path of Art."[13] He felt lonely on his pilgrimage; he was firmly established neither in the English literary milieu nor in literature as a profession; his sense of malad-justment in the role of writer was frequently revealed in his letters. With a neighbor who could be his regular partner in work and discussion and who shared his passionate interest in the art of the novel, Conrad could fend off loneliness and, at the same time, gain a firm foothold in the world of literature. And since Conrad's greatest problem was that he worked slowly and sometimes was unable to write at all, a connection with Ford, who wrote with speed and ease, was particularly attractive.

The most important argument in favor of the arrangement must have been the opportunity to perfect his English by acquiring a keener sense of the shades of meaning and emotional associations linked with words, expressions, or rhythms. Until then the two principal sources of Conrad's knowledge of English were the colloquial language of the sailors and the books he read; that left substantial areas where he was insecure.

The financial aspect brought to the fore in Conrad's letter to Henley was certainly important, but not decisive. Conrad did not want to write simply "for money"; he looked for help to overcome the difficulties that hampered his productivity. At any rate, whatever the advantages of partnership, financial profit was not to be one of them.

Ford's financial position was much better than Conrad's, but for him too the arrangement was to prove advantageous. In spite—perhaps also because—of his numerous and varied prospects, Ford had difficulty finding publishers, and on several occasions it was Conrad's name that paved the way for him.[14] It is significant that their collaboration applied exclusively to works that had been begun or to a large extent already written by Ford himself. Conrad's contribution never amounted to more than one-third of the whole piece. Viewed from this angle, Conrad simply helped to correct and put finishing touches on Ford's own novels, also lending his name to promote their sale. Ford, on the other hand, took no part in reshaping or carrying out Conrad's projects. His motives were certainly not pecuniary. He was convinced, quite rightly, that he could help Conrad, and helping others was one of his life's passions. With all the faults and failings of his character, he was a kindly man, always ready to oblige a friend. Affording protection to others boosted his rather precarious sense of his own importance. Moreover, the projected partnership looked sufficiently exciting to appeal to his imagination.

Conrad had known Ford only fleetingly when he suggested collaboration; the decision was almost a leap in the dark. The partnership lasted several years, however—although not without moments of tension; and close friendship survived for more than a decade. Several factors apart from those just mentioned played a part. Ford wrote in one of his semifabulous volumes of memoirs: "Conrad had very strongly the idea of the Career. A Career was for him something a little sacred: any career." As we continue reading we realize that Ford, as usual showing facts in a singularly fluctuating light, has distorted as much as he has elucidated. Conrad was intent not on the idea of a Career but on the idea of Good Professional Work: to use Ford's own words, Conrad regarded it as a "crime" not to squeeze "the last drop of blood out of your subject when you are writing a book: the real crime against the Holy Ghost."[15] This striving for perfection, which was eventually to add to the conflict between the two writers, fascinated Ford for several years and provided the main grounds for their endless literary debates.

Ford, who in later years posed as a typical English gentleman, at this time emphasized his continental heritage and connections. Although his "Germanism" was largely theoretical, as he was brought up and educated entirely in England, his snobbery, coupled with his cult of French literature, made him into a kind of honorary foreigner. Conrad, on the other hand, was a genuine foreigner. Their joint sense of being outsiders is best illustrated by Ford's frequently quoted anecdote: "Once we were sitting in the front row of the stalls at the Empire. . . . On that night at the Empire there was at least one clergyman with a number of women: ladies is meant. . . . And, during applause by the audience of some *too* middle-class joke one of us leaned over towards the other and said: 'Doesn't one feel lonely in this beastly country!' . . . Which of us it was that spoke neither remembered after: the other had been at that moment thinking so exactly the same thing."[16] *Si non è vero, è ben trovato*. One may add that in England at the time everything foreign was generally regarded with contempt, and France was synonymous with debauchery and moral decay.[17]

Bernard Meyer listed the supposed similarities between Conrad and Ford: their lack of emotional balance, nervousness, hypochondria, digestive disturbances, tendency toward chronic depression, obsessive preoccupation with suicide.[18] The list is not entirely convincing: their gastric troubles were not more frequent than average, and anyway are typical symptoms of hypochondria; if their sullen moods were a form of depression then it is misleading to talk of hypochrondria. "Physical suffering," says Antoni Kępiński, "can be understood more easily than psychological, both by the patient and by other persons"— therefore depression characteristically manifests itself in somatic pains.[19] Suicidal thoughts are also typical of depressives.

A tendency to depression and emotional instability usually hinders the development of a close friendship; since it did not have an adverse effect on this particular relationship, an explanation is called for. Both Conrad and Ford were aware that loneliness increases depression. Observing the same states in one another, they probably felt less embarrassed. Outwardly, Ford was in a better position—his place in society, his finances, and his command of English were superior. He was also less agitated and better reconciled to the world and to himself. Conrad, in turn, bolstered himself internally by the consciousness that psychologically he was the stronger of the two. Although himself of mercurial and unstable disposition, he did not celebrate his changeability the way Ford did. Although he too had fits of mythomania, his myths were not, like Ford's, an expansion of his own various incarnations, of the many visions of his own possibilities; they were efforts to integrate, retrospectively, his life into a cohesive whole; to smooth out and unify the discrepancies within his inclinations and actions.

Ford was fascinated by Conrad to the point of worship. We can perceive this attitude through all the clouds of exaggeration and distortion of facts in almost everything he wrote about Conrad. Conrad, on the other hand, seems never to have regarded Ford on a par with such close friends as Graham, Garnett, or even Crane. It is difficult to rid oneself of the suspicion that he considered Ford

a likable, extremely gifted but superficial featherbrain who notoriously confused the form with the essence of the matter. This opinion seems to be confirmed by Ford's own memoirs; although colorful and amusing to read they
contain an overwhelming amount of twaddle. His reminiscences have practically no documentary value—even if only on account of numerous contradictions and different versions of the same events. Some of the purely descriptive
parts seem fairly close to the truth, however superficially presented. This is how
Ford depicted Conrad:

> He was small rather than large in height; very broad in the shoulder and
> long in the arm; dark in complexion with black hair and a clipped black
> beard. He had the gestures of a Frenchman who shrugs his shoulders fre-
> quently. When you had really secured his attention he would insert a monocle
> into his right eye and scrutinise your face from very near as a watchmaker
> looks into the works of a watch. . . . He spoke English with great fluency and
> distinction, with correctitude in his syntax, his words absolutely exact as to
> meaning but his accentuation so faulty that he was at times difficult to under-
> stand and his use of adverbs as often as not eccentric [Note: adverbial forms
> are much more common in Polish than in English]. . . . He gesticulated with
> his hands and shoulders when he wished to be emphatic, but when he forgot
> himself in the excitement of talking he gesticulated with his whole body,
> throwing himself about in his chair, moving his chair nearer to yours. Finally
> he would spring up, go to a distance, and walk backwards and forwards
> across the end of the room. . . . His reading had been amazingly wide and his
> memory was amazingly retentive. . . . Yet Conrad never presented any ap-
> pearance of being a bookish, or even a reading man. He might have been
> anything else: you could have taken fifty guesses at his occupation, from pre-
> cisely ship's captain to say financier, but poet or even student would never
> have been among them.[20]

The move to Pent Farm opened a period of new and much livelier social contacts for Conrad. His interesting neighbors contributed toward it in some measure, but in spite of his financial difficulties there was also a steady trickle of
guests from London. Clearly, Conrad looked for company, as if trying to erase
the summer breakdown from his memory.

Among Conrad's neighbors, the most important was H. G. Wells. After a two-
year gap in correspondence, Conrad wrote to him from The Cearne on 6 September. It was a humble and warm reply to Wells's letter criticizing "Youth." Five
days later Conrad hastened to announce, "I am writing in a state of jubilation
at the thought we are going to be nearer neighbours than I dared to hope a
fortnight ago." Wells was living at the time with his second wife, Jane, on the
Kentish coast at Sandgate, less than half an hour by horse-trap from the Pent.[21]
The first visits came to nothing; the Wellses were not at home. Conrad called on

the seventeenth; then he unsuccessfully tried to invite Wells for 26 November; and on 23 December he went to Sandgate with Ford, missing Wells on the way:

So we went despondently. And by the by, there was an Invisible Man (apparently of a jocose disposition) on your doorstep, because when I rang (modestly), an invisible finger kept the button down (or in, rather) and the bell jingling continuously to my extreme confusion (and the evident surprise of your girl). I wish you would keep your creations in some kind of order, confined in books or locked up in the cells of your brain, to be let out at stated times (frequently, frequently, of course!) instead of letting them wander about the premises, startling visitors who mean you no harm—anyhow my nerves can't stand that kind of thing—and now I shan't come near you till next year. There!

Coming back we found your card. We haven't cards. We ain't civilized enough—not yet. But the wishes for the health, happiness and peace of you both I am writing down here in mine and my wife's name are formulated with primitive sincerity, and the only conventional thing about them is the time of their voicing prescribed by the superstitions of men. Thus are we the slaves of a gang of fools unable to read your work aright and unwilling to buy a single entire edition of any of mine.[22]

This was only the beginning of their acquaintance. The next extant letter to Wells is dated 6 January 1900; not until later years did relations between the two writers become closer.

Conrad had at the time a high opinion of Wells. He called him a "Realist of the Fantastic": "He is a very original writer, romancier du fantastique, with a very individualistic judgement in all things and an astonishing imagination."[23] Conrad felt a genuine admiration for Wells's intellectual energy and was impressed by his ability to combine serious and original themes with a straightforward—today we would say journalistic—realism. Although Conrad's own way of writing was quite different, their interests at that time converged at many points: Conrad, although in a less "professional" way, was also deeply interested in the foundations of human knowledge, future of science, theory of evolution, and cosmogony. Wells's mind was clearer and better versed in abstract thinking; but it was also simpler and more conventional. He did not reciprocate Conrad's admiration. Even allowing for the fact that his opinions grew more pungent with time, his remarks about Conrad in the *Experiment in Autobiography* show that he never really understood or tried to understand him. Wells described Conrad visiting Sandgate with his family, "cracking a whip along the road, driving a little black pony carriage as though it was a droshky and encouraging a puzzled little Kentish pony with loud cries and endearments in Polish, to the dismay of all beholders. We never really 'got on' together. . . . I found therefore something as ridiculous in Conrad's *persona* of a romantic adventurous un-mercenary intensely artistic European gentleman carrying an exquisite code of unblemished honour through a universe of baseness . . . he had set himself to be a great writer, an artist in words, and to achieve all the recognition and distinction that he imagined should go with that ambition, he had gone literary with a singleness and intensity of purpose that made the kindred concentration of Henry James seem lax and large and pale."[24]

Wells's memory fixed an image of Conrad far more grotesque than that of Ford's recollections.

> At first he impressed me, as he impressed Henry James, as the strangest of creatures. He was rather short and round-shouldered with his head as it were sunken into his body. He had a dark retreating face with a very carefully trimmed and pointed beard, a trouble-wrinkled forehead and very troubled dark eyes, and the gestures of his hands and arms were from the shoulders and very Oriental indeed. He reminded people of Du Maurier's Svengali and, in the nautical trimness of his costume, of Cutliffe Hyne's Captain Kettle. He spoke English strangely. Not badly altogether; he would supplement his vocabulary—especially if he were discussing cultural or political matters—with French words; but with certain oddities. He had learnt to read English long before he spoke it and he had formed wrong sound impressions of many familiar words; he had for example acquired an incurable tendency to pronounce the last *e* in these and those. He would say, "*Wat* shall we do with *thesa* things?" And he was always incalculable about the use of "shall" and "will." When he talked of seafaring his terminology was excellent but when he turned to less familiar topics he was often at a loss for phrases.[25]

At least three other reminiscences referring to the first years of Conrad's stay at the Pent complement this portrait. C. Lewis Hind, the editor of *The Pall Mall Budget*, recalled, "With Wells I always associate Conrad, due, I suppose, to the afternoon we spent years ago, on the sands at Sandgate, Kent. . . . It was a marvel to me then, and always has been, how so un-English a man in temperament, looks, and utterance as Conrad should be able to write such perfect English. . . . That afternoon he dug his fists into the sand, I remember, and said 'Ah, if only I could write zee English, good, well! But you see, you will see.' We have seen."[26]

Edwin Pugh, who later visited Conrad a few times at the Pent, met him for the first time at a literary dinner in London.

> He came at me with a sort of sinuous grace, with a sort of writhing servility; and he looked—it is the only word to use, if I am to translate my first impressions of Conrad accurately—simian. His head was a little askew and seemed somehow to be unduly sunken between his unusually high shoulders. His forehead, which was of a cold, shining whiteness, receded sharply from his

heavy brows. The rest of his face was dully flushed, his cheeks thickly inter-
laced with tiny purplish veinings. And one had a feeling of forced geniality in
the flash of his large white teeth through the bristling amplitude of his moustache and beard.

   Then, as if by a flashlight of inspiration, I had another impression—an impression of huge strength in reserve, of something smoulderingly fiery in his
dark brown eyes, of pain and weariness and the sort of high courage and yet
latent exasperation which all that kind of thing induces in the very bone,
blood and flesh of all men who have seen and suffered and lived with a kind
of savage pungency.

Pugh also mentioned Conrad's strong foreign accent and the wrong usage of *as*,
like, *who*, *whom*, *that*, and *which*.[27]

The most suggestive recollection is the one written by Henry-D. Davray,
Conrad's future translator into French, and his correspondent for many years.
One day while on an excursion with Wells, Davray found himself at a small
country railway station.

   Suddenly, from nowhere, appears a strange personage, accosts my companion, greets him with a shower of words barely interrupted during the ceremony of introduction carried out by my English friend. With passionate and
energetic gesticulation, the new arrival vents his indignation at the absence of
an employee who would hand over to him a long-awaited parcel of books.

   This was not how I imagined Joseph Conrad. He is not a seafaring traveller, a Viking of impressive stature, of prudent and forceful gestures. He is
slightly less than average in height; his head is sunken between large bulging
shoulders which seem to shorten his torso lengthening his legs. But the head
is unforgettable and one looks at nothing besides. His high open forehead,
large aquiline nose, on both sides deep lines disappearing in a pointed beard
which elongate even more the perfect oval of his face. His brown eyes beneath two black lines of his thick brows draw our attention. When he happens to open his eyes wide they shine with a strange expression but more
often they remain half covered by the lids as if to filter part of the light, or of
the sunglare on the waves. When he looks at his interlocutor, his gaze becomes sharp, penetrating and deep; then suddenly it loses its intensity as if he
saw what he had been seeking.

   Having discharged his wrath, Conrad turned to me and almost without a
transition, dropping his English—which although spoken quickly and fluently
had a strongly marked accent—he apologized for his outburst, in French, with
great ease and no trace of an accent.[28]

Conrad "loved his house and took pride in it as if he had built it."[29] The
farmhouse, shaded by an enormous chestnut tree, had an air of having been

lived and worked in from time immemorial. The surrounding scenery was somewhat monotonous but the location had the double advantages of easy accessibility and rural seclusion; moreover, friends lived not far away. Conrad developed, perhaps under Ford's influence, an interest in the history of that particular part of Kent; he was aware of the three traditions that coexisted there: agriculture, contraband, and sailing.

He wrote to Zagórska, "We live like a family of anchorites. From time to time a pious pilgrim belonging to la grande fraternité des lettres comes to pay a visit to the celebrated Joseph Conrad—and to obtain his blessing. Sometimes he gets it and sometimes he does not, for the hermit is severe and dyspeptic et n'entend pas la plaisanterie en matière d'Art! At all events, the pilgrim receives an acceptable dinner, a Spartan bed—and he vanishes."[30] In fact, however, Conrad's life at the time was far from that of a hermit. It suffices to count casual remarks in Conrad's letters to see that he entertained almost every weekend: Ford, Galsworthy, Garnett, Graham, Hope, Meldrum, Pugh, and others. For Jessie it meant a heavy load of extra work, but by now she had help in the house: a permanent maid and usually one of her sisters or her mother as well.[31]

Edgar Jepson got the impression that "his family [was] an oppression that kept him irritable."[32] Perhaps Jepson exaggerated, but neither the rare remarks scattered in Conrad's letters nor the recollections of other witnesses, for example David Garnett, nor Jessie's memoirs, contain any indication of Conrad deriving pleasure from having a wife and child, or of his active participation in family life. One of the causes might have been the fact that his relations with Jessie's mother and sisters were, at best, correct.[33] Little is known of the Georges' visits to the Pent: the subject was never mentioned in Conrad's letters and barely hinted at in Jessie's books. The Georges belonged to a different world, and Jessie, instead of bridging the gap, was a bone of contention: for them she was somebody who had betrayed the family by submitting to the domination of an incomprehensible foreign eccentric; in Conrad's view she not only dragged behind her a tail of petty bourgeois connections but herself had difficulties in getting attuned to a life subordinated to Art.

Conrad's trips to London were now less frequent, which certainly helped to cut down his expenses. Life in the country was very cheap, and so was domestic help. Nevertheless, the Conrads must have been spending more than he earned: in the last nine months of 1898 he published only "Youth." Unless he was then using up some savings we know nothing about, he must have been forced to borrow money, and probably not only from Galsworthy.

A few days after moving to the Pent, Conrad, himself penniless, attempted to obtain a loan from Blackwood or some other publisher for the Cranes. Stephen Crane sailed to New York in April, and thence to Cuba. By the middle of August Cora lost touch with him; it was rumored that he was missing. Cora, who looked after the widow and three children of the American novelist Harold

Frederick, found herself without means of support; then news reached her that Stephen, too, was in financial straits and could not pay for his return passage. Conrad tried to obtain an advance from Blackwood, offering as guarantee, among other things, his own future works. But the publisher, to whom both writers had been in debt, refused; Macqueen's reply was negative as well.[34] Conrad felt helpless; his letters to Cora bear out his true concern for both the Cranes.

"We are here—over a week now and the place is a success. . . . I feel hopeful about my own work. Completely changed," he wrote to Garnett from the Pent on 7 November.[35] We do not know, however, what he was working on at that time, if he was working at all; the only mention of the subject is rather vague: "I get on dreamily with the *Rescue*, dreamily dreaming how fine it could be if the thought did not escape, if the expression did not hide underground, if the idea had a substance and words a magic power, if the invisible could be snared into a shape."[36] The collaboration with Ford did not get beyond the stage of preliminary discussions and plans either. Conrad wrote to him on 12 November, "The acceptance of our joint work is assured as far as Pawling is concerned. McClure I guess is all right. We must serialise next year on both sides of the pond." Contrary to Baines's supposition, this remark referred to *Romance* (still called *Seraphina*), and not to *The Inheritors*. Conrad was in no great hurry to read it: "I would be very pleased to *hear Seraphina read*. I would *afterwards* read it myself." Almost two years passed before they set down to reshaping Ford's half-baked stuff.[37]

Theoretically Conrad ought to have been working on *The Rescue* and on *Lord Jim*, promised to Blackwood. The story of the growth of what is today Conrad's most popular work is far from simple. We may only guess, although with a fair amount of probability, when the piece was begun.

The first draft of the story, initially called *Jim: a Sketch*, was penned, peculiarly enough, in a thick, leather-bound album which had belonged to Conrad's grandmother, Teofila Bobrowska.[38] The title, carefully written out in round-hand, announces: "Miscellaneous Poems." There are twelve of them, all from the first quarter of the nineteenth century, almost all mediocre, and most by authors today forgotten. Bobrowska covered twenty-five pages with these verses. One of them is a rhyme by Józef Korzeniowski (1797–1863), entitled "When You Are Happy!" Freely translated, the last stanza reads: "But if my visionary forebodings which so often lead me astray would give me back my country, I would be the happiest of men."

Having turned over six leaves we come to the draft of *Jim*. Probably soon after he had begun the story, Conrad added "Tuan"—the Malay word for *Lord*—to the title. *Tuan Jim: a Sketch* fills twenty-eight pages, with numerous corrections and deletions. The text corresponds approximately to a part of Chapter 1, and to Chapter 2, of the book as we know it today, but it clearly foreshadows the future course of events and the hero's role in Patusan. In the margins the writer kept a careful count of words; obviously he had magazine publication in mind, since in book editions the length is of lesser importance. After "1300," however, there is a jump to "3300"—thus almost two thousand words must have been written elsewhere.[39] The characterization of Jim as an inexperienced and imaginative young merchant marine officer, and later ship chandler's clerk, corresponds to his portrayal in the final version. There is, however, no trace of Marlow. Among Conrad's works, the style of the fragment and the form of narration most resembles "An Outpost of Progress."

The first mention of *Jim* appears in Conrad's undated letter to Meldrum (which I have ascertained was written on 3 June 1898), where he announced sending a completed part of the story. He mailed it—eighteen pages of typescript—the next day. Conrad planned the work to be twenty to twenty-five thousand words long (about seventy typed pages). The part he sent off probably comprised what had been written in Bobrowska's album, plus those additional two thousand words. As "Youth" was completed on 3 June, we may assume with near certainty that the beginning of *Jim* was written before that tale. How long before is impossible to say, but since Conrad was usually quick to inform others of his projects, and almost never discarded once-begun manuscripts, we may safely assume that *Tuan Jim* did not remain in his drawer for long. April 1898 may be therefore regarded as the most likely starting date.[40]

The first signal is followed by a six-month pause. Not before December did Conrad mention working on the story, and his two references are vague; in February 1899 he assured Blackwood that he would do everything possible to finish *Jim* (as a short story of twenty to thirty thousand words) in April.[41] This long interval, which was not the last, later became the basis of the apocryphal and largely untrue story of *Lord Jim*'s birth which Conrad presented in his 1917 author's note to the novel.[42]

Considering that for six months from the time he finished "Youth" Conrad wrote nothing or almost nothing, it is surprising how little he complained in the autumn of 1898. The buoyant mood connected with his move to the Pent and his fairly good health lasted in spite of a lull in his creativity. Not until December did he again begin to complain. At the beginning of the month he suffered an attack of rheumatism; it was not accidental that it happened at the time when he was "eating [his] heart out over the rottenest book that ever was—or will be"—meaning *The Rescue*, which he was soon to lay aside for twenty years.[43]

The state of reasonable balance that Conrad managed to achieve was rather precarious, as indicated by a sudden attack of despondency, almost black despair, in his 9 December letter to Graham: "It seems to me I am disintegrating slowly. Cold shadows stand around."[44] In his Christmas letter to Zagórska he wrote, "Since the month of January! I have been in such a state that I have been unable to write anything. It was not until November that I started to work." This long letter was in reply to her appeal for his help in writing articles on contemporary English literature, and for securing Wells's permission to translate *The Invisible Man*. Besides invectives against popular authors who make easy money by writing to suit the public taste, the letter mentions only two English authors of distinction: there is an acid comment on George Moore, and a very complimentary remark about Wells.[45] Later Conrad sent Zagórska a batch of cuttings from literary magazines, some of which, confiscated by Russian censors, never arrived.[46]

Although Conrad had already begun his long novel, and received an advance for it, as well as for what he thought was going to be a short story, sometime around 15 December he started on a third piece—"Heart of Darkness."[47] He presented his latest work to the publisher: "It is a narrative after the manner of *youth* told by the same man dealing with his experience on a river in Central Africa. The *idea* in it is not as obvious as in *youth*—or at least not so obviously presented. . . . The title I am thinking of is "The Heart of Darkness" but the narrative is not gloomy. The criminality of inefficiency and pure selfishness when tackling the civilizing work in Africa is a justifiable idea. The subject is of our time distinctly—though not topically treated. It is a story as much as my *Outpost of Progress* was but, so to speak 'takes in' more—is a little wider—is less concentrated upon individuals."[48]

Obviously Conrad did not want to put Blackwood off, but his soothing assurances sound quite grotesque when juxtaposed with the cheerless gravity and complex problems of his politically trenchant story. The resemblance to "Youth" is also rather superficial: Marlow in "Heart of Darkness" is a far richer personality; and not only the atmosphere but also the symbolism in the new story reveal its basic dissimilarity to "Youth" in nearly every sentence.

Conrad took up the subject of the Congo at a time when the name of that country, after having been much in the public eye, had disappeared almost completely from the press; a fresh influx of sensational news did not begin again until January 1899.* At the roots of the story we can discern not only undercurrents of doubt about Europe's "civilizing action" in Africa but also an anxiety about man's place in nature—particularly about the relationship between morality on one hand and nature and evolution on the other. Ian Watt pointed out the concurrence between Conrad's ideas and Thomas H. Huxley's celebrated lecture, "Evolution and Ethics" (1893), on the persistent presence of the animal in man and the unavoidable conflict between the demands of nature and of human endeavors, between Man's order and the order of nature. "Let us understand, once and for all, that the ethical progress of society depends, not on imitating the cosmic process, still less in running away from it, but in combat-

---

* For example, there were only three mentions of the Congo Free State in *The Times* in the last quarter of 1898; there were five extensive reports in January 1899.

ing it."[49] What in Huxley constituted a break with the traditions of optimistic hedonism characteristic of the natural sciences of the day gives the impression in Conrad of being a consistent element of his tragic and skeptical world view, expressed in his letters to Graham. Those as well as other letters show his interest in cosmogony, which led him to similarly somber conclusions. The ideas of the recently deceased Huxley might have attracted Conrad's attention all the more easily from the fact that Huxley had been a professional colleague, having served as a young man for five years (1846–1850) as a doctor on board a sailing warship.

The work on "Heart of Darkness" went relatively smoothly, although Conrad could not refrain from complaining of his inability to write. He declared to Crane, "It *is* rotten—and I can't help it." Twice he informed Garnett that he was writing for money—a fine example of posturing. He was indeed in financial difficulties: again he had to ask Blackwood for an advance on the still undelivered manuscript.[50] On 31 December he assured the publisher that he had spent the last ten days working on a story for *Maga* which would have been finished but for Borys's illness and would be ready in a few days. Conrad expected it to be twenty thousand words long. On 2 January he said the same to Meldrum, with one small difference: "I began the story for *Maga* 10 days ago."[51] "Heart of Darkness" was to have been included in one volume with "Youth" and *Jim*. As usual, Conrad finished it later than predicted (on 6 February 1899), and it turned out longer: thirty-eight thousand words.[52] In the last weeks of writing he confided to Ford, "The story I told you of holds me. It grows like the genii out of the bottle in the Tale."[53]

The year 1899 began well: on 13 January Conrad was informed of a prize for the *Tales of Unrest* awarded to him by the literary weekly *Academy*, to which Garnett and Lucas were regular contributors. "Have you seen *it! It! The Academy*. When I opened the letter I thought it was a mistake. But it was too true, alas. I've lost the last ounce of respect for my art. I am lost—gone—done for—for the consideration of 50 gs. . . . Ah if I could only write! If I could write, write, write! But I cannot. No 50 gs. will help me to that," exclaimed Conrad in a letter to Garnett.[54]

The second piece of good news was Stephen Crane's return to England; before long Crane moved closer to the Conrads, to a medieval mansion, Brede Place, in Sussex. On 29 January Borys's postponed christening took place; the ceremony, a purely family affair that left no trace in the correspondence, was carried out in the Roman Catholic Church of the Virgin Mary of Good Counsel at Hythe, and the boy received the name Alfred Borys Leo.[55]

Soon afterward Conrad found himself under great financial pressure: Krieger demanded the return of his loan of £150 (or £180). Conrad appealed for help to Meldrum, to whom he even forwarded his creditor's letter. Only three days later, Blackwood, informed of the situation by his adviser, dispatched £100—in addition to the £60 advance for "Heart of Darkness." [56] "You have removed an immense load from my mind by your kind and sympathetic action," Conrad wrote gratefully, but he did not repay the entire debt. In the same letter he discussed in detail the volume that would include three stories: "Youth" (thirteen thousand words), "Heart of Darkness," and *Jim* (twenty to thirty thousand). He also mentioned his plans for two further stories: "First Command" (subsequently *The Shadow Line*) and "A Seaman" (probably "The End of the Tether"). [57]

The first of three instalments of "Heart of Darkness" appeared in *Blackwood's Magazine* in February, evoking understandable enthusiasm in Cunninghame Graham. Perhaps it was the passage where the French man-of-war wantonly shells the African jungle—as well as the political interests Conrad and Graham shared—which prompted Graham to invite Conrad to the speaker's platform at an 8 March mass meeting of pacifists, organized by the Social Democratic Federation. Conrad refused to come to the rostrum, but he attended the meeting and, "revolted a little," listened to speeches by Graham, Jaurès, Wilhelm Liebknecht, Émile Vandervelde, and others. [58] The meeting was part of an international socialist action opposed to the convening, at the initiative of Tsar Nicholas II, of a peace conference in The Hague. Liebknecht described the initiative as a "fraud." Socialists regarded the tsar's proposals as a smoke screen for his autocratic and predatory policies, and the conference itself as a gigantic bluff to divert attention from the true aims and practices of bourgeois governments. [59]

Conrad's letter to Graham declining the invitation, written one month before the meeting, contained his most extensive political declaration to date. It is not an orderly, coherent exposition, but an emotional outburst: "This letter is as incoherent as my life." It was not for the first time that his friend's naive, as he thought, optimism provoked him to impulsive and sweeping statements. Conrad's feelings are expressed unambiguously while his ideas, sometimes contradictory, have to be plucked from his heated rhetoric.

"Man is a malicious animal. His malice has to be organized. Crime is an essential condition of organized life. Society is basically criminal—otherwise it would not exist. Egoism saves everything—absolutely everything—all that we abhor and all that we love. And everything holds together. That is precisely why I respect extreme anarchists. 'I wish for general extermination'—Excellent. It is fair as well as obvious." [60] Eloise Knapp Hay has—needlessly—made an inventive effort to find logical justification for Conrad's opinion on human wickedness. [61] First of all we ought to detect in it an echo of Anatole France's Père Coignard's words: "Man is by nature a very malicious animal and societies are abominable because he puts his genius into creating them." [62] The irony of Conrad's pronouncement is fully evident in his phrases about the anarchists; it ought to be taken as a caustic satire and not as a serious philosophical evaluation.

Obviously, Conrad's condemnation referred to contemporary society, whose materialistic attitude he had criticized a year earlier in his letters to Graham: to the society that shapes such men as the characters of "An Outpost of Progress," Carlier and Kayerts, and whose product was Kurtz in "Heart of Darkness." The egoism of which Conrad wrote is neither Stirnerian nor Schopenhauerian, although the term itself might have occurred to Conrad as a result of reading one of these philosophers.[63] Both the evil and the good, Conrad believed, are basically created by individuals. Society institutionalizes the evil, in the form of profit seeking, and the good can be saved only in defiance of depersonalizing pressure of the masses. But only a few sentences later Conrad used the term *egoism* in a different sense.

At any rate, antisocial sarcasm and glorification of "egoism" were discarded the moment Conrad announced the need for "a definite principle," which he identified with the "national idea." This is precisely where we see how the univocal character of his emotions tended to impose order upon his fragmentary thoughts. "Even if the national idea brings suffering and serving it results in death, this is still better than serving the shadows of an eloquence that is dead precisely because it has no body. Believe me when I tell you that for me these problems are extremely serious—much more so than for Messrs Jaurès, Liebknecht & Co. . . . I look at the future from the depth of a very black past and I find that nothing is left for me except fidelity to a cause lost, to an idea without future." He continued by asserting that matters that interested Graham did not leave him indifferent: "Only [my] concern lies elsewhere, [my] thought follows another route, [my] heart desires something else."

It was Conrad's hopeless fidelity to the memory of Poland that prevented him from believing in the idea of "international fraternity," which he considered, under the circumstances, to be just a verbal exercise. Russian emigrés and representatives of German socialists were to speak from the platform. Against the first Conrad harbored the grievance that they talked about freedom and preached world brotherhood while keeping silent on the subject of his own oppressed nation. A significant remark, unintentionally justifying Conrad's attitude, may be found in Garnett's reminiscences: "I was told . . . that he was a Pole, and this increased my interest since my Nihilist friends, Stepniak and Volkhovsky, had always subtly decried the Poles when one sympathized with their position as 'under dog.'"[64] Conrad accused social democrats (in the case of Jaurès, unjustly) of actions directed toward a weakening of "the national sentiment the preservation of which [was his] concern"; of attempting to dissolve national identities in an impersonal melting pot. He even boasted of having warned a group of Warsaw students against them.

Conrad's distrust of democracy, that "very beautiful phantom," sprang from a different source. He did not know, he said, "what evils it is destined to remedy"; this means he doubted whether the propagation of democracy as an aim in itself could solve any problems. He thought that in view of the weakness of human nature and of the "criminal" character of contemporary society, democracy offered boundless opportunities for demagogues and charlatans. Antidemocratic gibes have won him the reputation of a conservative among the majority of Conrad scholars. I consider this an oversimplification: his opposition to democracy was not political, but sprang from theoretical, philosophical, and psychological misgivings. It was not an opposition in the name of autocracy, aristocracy, monarchy, oligarchy, or other forms of government. In deriding contemporary democracy Conrad was not setting something better against it—in this respect he was not unlike the early Anatole France. And in his distrust of all political doctrines and general theories he very much resembled his own father.

Toward the end of January Conrad went to London for two days and, "in the strictest confidence," presented to Meldrum the project of "a great novel about the Ana Baptists."[65] This was the sole mention of a plan that never materialized; meanwhile *Romance* lay untouched. In the middle of February the pressure to finish work on *The Rescue* was removed: the *Illustrated London News* dropped its plan of publication. McClure, who had paid a considerable advance, remained friendly and patient.[66] Conrad received two new offers. In May, Algernon Methuen approached Conrad to suggest publishing a book; Conrad, however, indebted to Blackwood and McClure, who were waiting for *The Rescue* and *Lord Jim*, replied that under the circumstances "to talk about any future work of mine would be futile and not very sincere. Nevertheless I am very grateful to you for your generous suggestions."[67] In August, James B. Pinker, Stephen Crane's literary agent, offered to take over Conrad's affairs. Conrad at first answered in the negative. His reply is the earliest of over one thousand letters he was to write to Pinker: "My method of writing is so unbusinesslike that I don't think you could have any use for such an unsatisfactory person. I generally sell a work before it is begun, get paid when it is half done and don't do the other half till the spirit moves me. I must add that I have no control whatever over the spirit—neither has the man who has paid the money."[68]

From the same period dates one of the strangest letters Conrad wrote: an "ecclesiastic" letter to Helen Sanderson. It is worth quoting a few sentences; we do not know how closely they reflect Conrad's views, but, at any rate, they show to what length Conrad would go to suit his correspondents' expectations. He, who never revealed any interest in religion, declares himself a champion of the Church as of the watch tower of unshakable, uncompromising faith: "The unrest of human thought is like the unrest of the sea, disturbing and futile. . . . But a church should be like a rock in the midst of an ocean—unmoved. The mad individualism of Nietsche [sic] the exaggerated altruism of the next man tainted with selfishness and pride come with their noise and froth, pass away and are forgotten. Faith remains; . . . Truth is immovable—it is eternal, it is one; and a church as the repository of the highest truth cannot listen, cannot absorb what is unstable, complex and doomed to die." [69]

Conrad promised Blackwood in February that he would do his best "to finish *Jim* in April." [70] It would seem that, freed from the immediate pressures of money troubles and time limits, he should have set energetically to work on the book—all the more eagerly since Blackwood wanted to print it in the June issue. But five months passed with only one mention of Conrad writing anything at all. On 31 March he informed Garnett, "I write! I write! I write! Certainly. Write quick. Not quick enough to make up for the frightful leeway." The same letter, explaining his prolonged inactivity, carries a vivid picture of his depression: "Gout. Brought on by—by—by agitation, exasperation, botheration. . . . The fright is growing on me. My fortitude is shaken by the view of the monster. It does not move; its eyes are baleful; it is as still as death itself—and it will devour me. . . . I am alone with it in a chasm with perpendicular sides of black basalt. Never were sides so perpendicular and smooth, and high." [71] Only on 6 July did Conrad send to Meldrum the first two chapters and part of the third of *Lord Jim*, in what must have been the new version. [72] It was not enough even for one instalment; nevertheless Conrad still intended to finish the story in July, expecting it to run to forty thousand words, twice as long as he had anticipated in February, and approximately the same length as "Heart of Darkness."

During that rather mysterious five-month lull in creative work—but not before May—there reached Conrad rumors about, or even perhaps texts of, a discussion in which, unknowingly, he was the focal point. The discussion took place in the Polish weekly *Kraj*, published in St. Petersburg; it was initiated by Wincenty Lutosławski, a well-known philosopher and the author of a huge book in English on the development of Plato's logic. Lutosławski, who lectured and published mostly outside Poland, visited Conrad in the summer of 1897, having received his address from Henry James. Lutosławski recounted later, "His welcome was exceedingly warm, and he introduced me to his English wife, at that time very young, whom he called 'my girl.' He invited me to stay overnight and after his wife had retired for the night, we changed from English into Polish and I soon realized that after all those years of wandering in the world, Conrad Korzeniowski retained a good command of his native tongue." They apparently talked late into the night. [73]

In his article "The Emigration of Talent," Lutosławski praised those who emigrated to earn their living or to take advantage of the opportunities, particularly academic, unavailable in their native country. He maintained that it was unfair to accuse outstandingly gifted people who had left their country of "disloyalty," because staying at home would have wasted their chances of serving humanity and promoting the glory of their homeland. To illustrate his point he adduced only one example:

Recently a position of distinction in English literature was gained by a compatriot of ours, Mr. Konrad Korzeniowski, known under the pen-name of
Joseph Conrad, an emigré from 1863. His novels are marked by a Polish-
style nobleman's panache intensified by many years of sailing round the islands of the Pacific. During my visit to his country place near London, I put
to him a simple question: "Why don't you write in Polish?"—"I value our
beautiful Polish literature too much to bring into it my clumsy efforts. But for
the English my gifts are sufficient and secure my daily bread."

Lutosławski continued by arguing that since Polish books are published in relatively small editions,

those who remain at home out of duty and have to write for their living must
lower the level of their work and instead of cultivating their talents allow
them to wither away. The same authors should follow Konrad Korzeniowski's example and master the English language which is universally known,
and write for their living in English instead of Polish. Thus, they would have
enough time left to communicate to their compatriots their best thoughts,
expressed in the most perfect form in their mother tongue.[74]

The article, whose simplicity bordered on crudeness, contained obvious falsehoods and distortions, the more strange and reprehensible because Lutosławski
had received a letter from Conrad, outlining the latter's family background.[75]
Conrad was not an emigré from 1863 and did not leave Poland as an adult. If in
the course of conversation with his pushy visitor Conrad did, in fact, say anything like the quoted sentence, it must have been on his part an attempt to cut
short Lutosławski's inquisitive questions. Whatever doubts Conrad might have
had about the merits of his work, his approach to it was always deeply serious
and responsible. And writing never gave him financial security. The suggestion
that Polish writers ought to "master" the English language and write in both
Polish and English is ridiculously naive. And the phrase about the "withering of
talent" sounds offensive with regard to writers in Poland, and quite absurd
when set against Sienkiewicz's world-wide success.

Significantly, the editors of the politically appeasing *Kraj* deemed it necessary
to publish a statement dissociating the paper from Lutosławski's views. In the
same issue there appeared a reply by Tadeusz Żuk-Skarszewski, a regular contributor. The main counterattack, however, was launched by Eliza Orzeszkowa,
an eminent novelist and one of the country's moral authorities. Not a "na-
tionalist," as sometimes described, but a leading liberal, an advocate of the
emancipation of Jews, a friend of Ukrainian writers who were trying to assert
their cultural identity, this well-educated woman, one of the more enlightened
minds in the Europe of her day, forced by the Russian government to live in the
provincial town of Grodno, was also a champion of patriotic obligations. In a

long and highly emotional article under the same title, "The Emigration of Talent," she expressed her objection to the emigration of gifted people, arguing that participation in the life of one's home country is one's principal duty, even if it entails suffering and self-denial.

> Let us stand by our principles! The most able, and the least able; in joy, and in suffering; in pleasant and unpleasant circumstances; we must always stand by our principles for otherwise all of us, every single one of us, on account of singular gifts or unusual suffering will obtain a passport from his conscience and off he will go!

Alluding to Lutosławski's article, she sharply attacked Conrad:

> Speaking of books I must say that this gentleman who writes popular and very lucrative novels in English has almost caused me a nervous breakdown. My gorge rises when I read about him. Why . . . creative talent forms the very head of the tree, the pinnacle of the tower, the life-blood of the nation. And to take away that flower, to remove that pinnacle, to drain away that life-blood from the nation in order to pass it on to the Anglo-Saxons who anyway lie on a bed of roses just because they pay better! It is even hard to think about it without shame! And to make matters worse, that gentleman bears the name and possibly is a very close descendant of Józef Korzeniowski whose books when I was a teenager brought tears to my eyes, the first tears of compassion, and fired me with my first noble enthusiasm and good resolutions. But over Mr. Konrad Korzeniowski's novels no Polish teenager will ever shed a single altruistic tear or make a noble resolution.[76]

It is almost certain that the news of the discussion in *Kraj* reached Conrad promptly. Lutosławski himself probably sent him his own articles, and possibly others as well. This seems to be borne out by a letter Conrad wrote to Józef Korzeniowski (no relation to himself), custodian of the Jagiellonian Library in Cracow, on 14 February 1901: "And please let me add, dear Sir (for you may still be hearing this and that said of me), that I have in no way disavowed either my nationality or the name we share for the sake of success. It is widely known that I am a Pole. . . ."[77] Quite improbable, however, sounds Conrad's statement to Aniela Zagórska, made fifteen years later, that Orzeszkowa had written to him on the subject. ("I don't want anything of hers," he reportedly snarled in reply to Zagórska's suggestion that he should read one of Orzeszkowa's books.)[78] Conrad's memory in matters concerning his own life was notoriously treacherous and, assuming that Zagórska remembered his words accurately, he probably confused the ill-fated article with a letter. Or perhaps he did not even see the actual article but read about it in someone else's letter from Poland. Orzeszkowa was definitely not the kind of person who would write aggressive letters to strangers.

It has been suggested that Orzeszkowa's accusation of national desertion had influenced the content of *Lord Jim*. This hypothesis, first advanced by Józef Ujejski, has been upheld by other critics.[79] Is it really supportable? The themes of betrayal, escape, neglect of important duty, appeared in Conrad's earlier writings. He was obviously haunted by them from the very beginning of his literary life: we find this motif in *An Outcast*; it forms the center of the plots of "The Lagoon," "Karain," and *The Rescue*. It is clearly outlined in even those first twenty-eight pages of *Tuan Jim* that were written by the spring of 1898. Conrad did not need a new stimulus to be driven into that kind of an obsession. Nor is it clear in what way Orzeszkowa's attack could cause the original story of Jim to have been extended. Parts of the text written after May 1899 contain no new elements that would necessarily result from the discussion in *Kraj* rather than from the intrinsic needs of the artistic structure and moral contents of the novel—needs shaped already in its original outline. At most we may assume that the discussion in *Kraj* intensified Conrad's desire to demonstrate how immensely difficult it is to acquire knowledge about another man and a full understanding of his motives.

One can scarcely doubt, however, that Conrad was deeply hurt by Orzeszkowa's article. To be sure, the person most responsible for the outbreak of the whole storm was Lutosławski, who gave a grotesquely false image of Conrad's situation and his reasons for writing in English, thus making Orzeszkowa's accusations partly beside the point. But an unjustified accusation may still smart, especially when it touches a raw nerve. Conrad had confessed to Lutosławski, "I have written so much about the dead! But I suppose that by writing about those deceased I can let you, Dear Sir, know best the living man. . . . I have lived among strangers, but not with strangers, and wandering around the world I have never left the 'Country of Memories.'"[80] These words help us to understand why Conrad was throughout his life disturbed by the thought that he had not abided by his parents' heritage. Ten years later he wrote in *A Personal Record*, "It would take too long to explain the intimate alliance of contradictions in human nature which makes love itself wear at times the desperate shape of betrayal. . . . And perhaps there is no possible explanation."[81] This was probably his most sincere reply to the *Kraj* article, and it is hardly a defense.

That summer Conrad, with Crane, bought a small sailing boat, *La Reine*, from Hope. The boat was moored at Rye and used for excursions in the Channel.[82] The Cranes and the Conrads exchanged frequent visits. Borys learned to walk on the slopes of Brede, and Crane, having decided that the boy needed a dog, presented him with one of his many puppies, "named Pizanner because he was black and utterly mongrel in shape." In honor of the toreador from *Carmen*—an opera Conrad was fond of whistling arias from—the puppy was renamed Escamillo and became a favorite of the entire family.[83]

Meanwhile the work on *Lord Jim* followed its usual Conradian course, with changing timetables and moods, and with incessant turmoil of anxiety. July had passed, but Conrad was barely at the beginning of Chapter 5, where Marlow's narrative begins. And it was then that Conrad mentioned for the first time the possibility that *Jim* would be longer than "Heart of Darkness"; he also asked for another £50 in advance.[84] The later story of his work on *Lord Jim* looks like a pursuit of the receding horizon: the number of pages keeps growing, the end is forecast in one month, two weeks, one week, but the dates are constantly put off, the text swells several times above the expectations—and the end still does not come.

Conrad experienced his usual doubts. Although in his letters to his publisher he several times expressed satisfaction with the results of his work, in other letters, and much more frequently, he gave vent to quite contrary thoughts and feelings. "I am like a man who has lost his gods. My efforts seem unrelated to anything in heaven and everything under heaven is impalpable to the touch like shapes of mist. Do you see how easy writing must be under such conditions? . . . Every image floats vaguely in a sea of doubt—and the doubt itself is lost in an unexplored universe of incertitudes." "I *feel* it bad; and, unless I am hopelessly morbid, I can not be altogether wrong. . . . I am weary of the difficulty of it. The game is not worth the candle; of course there is no question of throwing up the hand. It must be played out to the end."[85]

On 22 August, with twenty thousand words written and believing himself to be halfway through (he had arrived at Chapter 6), Conrad assured Blackwood, "I devote myself exclusively to *Jim*. I find I can't live with more than one story at a time. It's a kind of literary monogamism."[86] The first instalment of the story, called *Lord Jim: a Sketch*, appeared in the October issue of *Blackwood's Magazine*. It comprised the first four chapters. Conrad, aware of their introductory character, was worried.[87] He thought that the whole story would fit into four numbers, but although he wrote to Meldrum on 18 October that *Jim* was reaching its climax (he was certainly referring to the description of the hero's escape in Chapters 9 and 10), the "climax" passed and the text continued to grow. Serialization put Conrad under pressure to keep to the appointed dates. Meanwhile, however, the "sketch" grew far beyond the planned length. Luckily, Meldrum was a Conrad enthusiast, and Blackwood showed not only tolerance but kindness and understanding. At any rate, the story's exceptional qualities soon became evident. Conrad was exhausted by the race against time but he resolutely plodded on toward the goal, although it kept changing its shape and the road leading to it grew longer. "It would be to my interest to cut [*Jim*] short as possible, but I would just as soon think of cutting off my head." On 24 October he announced that he would close *Lord Jim* within five instalments, approximately twelve chapters. But on 8 November he contemplated an additional instalment, declaring that "no amount of sacrifice seems too much for him." On 25 November, when he was finishing Chapter 13, he assured Meldrum that the whole book would "of course" be ready by the end of the year.[88]

Meanwhile, in spite of his professions of literary monogamy, Conrad occasionally deserted *Jim*—against his own will—to collaborate with Ford. Until then their partnership had existed only in theory: they would meet, talk, discuss plans, bait the hook to publishers. There were some tensions, and also grievances on the part of Ford. Conrad showed little enthusiasm. "Why didn't you come?" he wrote to Garnett. "I expected you and fate has sent Hueffer. Let this be written on my tombstone."[89]

Ford began *The Inheritors* in the summer of 1899. On 6 October he brought the first chapters of the novel to the Pent. Elsie Ford wrote that Conrad was "upset with the novel" and evidently set Ford to rewriting it.[90] "There is not a chapter I haven't made him write twice—most of them three times over," he boasted later to Garnett.[91] To Ford's reproaches that he was doing little, Conrad replied on 12 November:

> I am sorry your wife seems to think I've induced you to waste your time. I had no idea you had any profitable work to do—For otherwise effort after expression is not wasted even if it is not paid for. What you have written now is infinitely nearer to actuality, to life, to reality than anything (in prose) you have written before. . . . Beautiful lines do not make a drawing nor splashes of beautiful colour a picture. . . . If I had influence enough with the publishers I would make them publish the book in your name alone—because the *work* is all yours—I have shared only a little of your worry. . . . Whether I am worth anything to you or not, it is for you to determine. The proposal certainly came from me under a false impression of my power of work. I am much weaker than I thought I was but this does not affect you fundamentally. Heinemann (and McClure too I fancy) are waiting for our joint book and I am not going to draw back if you will only consent to sweat long enough.[92]

Jessie complained that the Fords spent over two weeks with their daughter at Pent Farm, causing general inconvenience. ("No doubt our guests suffered quite as much as I did," wrote Jessie, and Mizener comments pithily, "clearly with disbelief."[93]) Conrad's correspondence, however, indicates that the visit must have been much shorter.

Conrad's participation in *The Inheritors* consisted almost entirely of advising Ford, or rather inciting him to revise the manuscript, and of negotiating with publishers.[94] Ford was responsible for both the idea and almost the entire text.[95] Conrad's name helped sell the book. Work on the novel lasted until 16 March 1900. Heinemann in England and McClure in the United States accepted it: "It [the story] seems to have produced a very good impression on . . . [the] readers. There's something in it no doubt. *What*, exactly, I can't say myself," wrote Conrad to Meldrum.[96] In his letter to Garnett he was even more brutally frank:

> I consider the accept: of the *Inh*[ors] a distinct bit of luck. Jove! What a lark! I set myself to look upon the thing as a sort of skit upon the sort of political

(?!) novel, fools of the Morley Roberts sort do write. This in my heart of hearts. And poor H. was dead in earnest! . . . This is collaboration if you like! Joking apart the expenditure of nervous fluid was immense. There were moments when I cursed the day I was born and dared not look up at the light of day I had to live through with this thing on my mind. H. has been as patient as no angel had ever been. I've been fiendish. I've been rude to him; if I've not called him names I've *implied* in my remarks and the course of our discussions the most opprobrious epithets. He wouldn't recognise them. 'Pon my word it was touching. And there's no doubt that in the course of that agony I have been ready to weep more than once. Yet not for him. Not for him.[97]

The encouraging telegram sent on the same day to Ford is steeped in hypocrisy: "Splendid reports of novel original popular great hopes society hit McClure takes serializing in both countries . . . my heartiest congratulations."[98]

A better mutual understanding and a more productive collaboration did not develop before 1901. It is rather unlikely that the discussions about *The Inheritors*, "long and heated . . . lasting well into many nights," concerned the art of the novel—the book is both too feeble and too contrived for that.[99] The authors' attention must have centered on the style itself, pale and hopelessly insubstantial. Possibly those conversations left in Ford's easily fermenting memory the impression that Conrad had a "dislike for the English language, contempt for English as a prose language" and that "he used to declare that English was a language in which it was impossible to write a direct statement."[100]

Undoubtedly they discussed politics, which next to literature was Conrad's greatest intellectual passion and at the same time constituted the most interesting—in fact the only lively—element of *The Inheritors*, a satirical fantasy à clef. The theoretical (because not developed) theme of the book—the inevitable defeat of political idealism when confronted with pragmatism—and the declared (but not achieved) atmosphere of historical inevitability and the fall of tradition were subjects close to Conrad's thought and heart. Moreover, both villains of the novel, the hypocritical Leopold II, king of the Belgians, represented as the speculating duc de Mersch, and the aggressive imperialist Joseph Chamberlain, portrayed as the ruthless and cunning Gurnard, had for years been objects of his antipathy. It is not clear, however, whether Conrad really valued the traditional English conservatives more highly. The fictional Churchill, a noble idealist, is supposed to portray Balfour, but seems to have just as many characteristics of Balfour's uncle, the marquis of Salisbury (at that time prime minister), with whom he collaborated closely and whom he later succeeded. And Conrad sneered at Salisbury.[101] At any rate, according to Ford, "The British Empire was for him the perfection of human perfections, but *all* its politicians, all its public officials, police, military officers . . . port admirals and policies were of an imbecility that put them in intelligence below the first lieu-tenant of the French navy that you could come across." As usual Ford overshot, just as he exaggerated out of all proportion Conrad's very real francophilia, maintaining that his friend considered the French the "only European nation who knew how to colonise." [102]

The first serious test of Conrad's psychological loyalty to Great Britain was the Boer War, which broke out on 11 October 1899. Among his close friends, the Garnetts and Graham were openly, even violently, opposed to Chamber-lain's aggressive policy, which was supported by Salisbury's cabinet. Conrad's letters reveal three different attitudes: that of concerned citizen, that of loyal defender of the crown, and that of sarcastic critic of a dirty war.

To Sanderson, who was soon commissioned and sailed off to Africa in Janu-ary, Conrad complained about the pointlessness of the war, which he believed was not directed against the real source of danger threatening England; he had Russia in mind. The war was therefore unworthy of sacrifices, and since of ne-cessity "ruthless repression" would follow in its wake, "the situation will be-come repugnant to the nation." He pondered several times the strong and weak points of particular English commanders; he worried about defeats and con-gratulated Helen Sanderson on the victories that brought her husband's return closer. All his remarks carried a note of genuine sorrow and anxiety, whereas any signs of jingoism or warlike spirit met with his scorn and contempt. [103]

To Zagórska Conrad defended government policy: "That they [the Boers] are struggling in good faith for their independence cannot be doubted; but it is also a fact that they have no idea of liberty, which can only be found under the En-glish flag all over the world. *C'est un peuple essentiellement despotique*, like by the way all the Dutch. This war is not so much a war against the Transvaal as a struggle against the doings of German influence. It is the Germans who have forced the issue. . . . You are mistaken in saying that it is the Government who sends soldiers. The English Government has no right to make a single English-man move, if he does not consent to it. Le pour et le contre of this issue have been weighed not only in the conscience of the people but of the whole race." [104]

It is obvious that this was a desperate attempt at self-defense; the son of Apollo Korzeniowski found it hard to admit that by his own choice he had become a citizen of a country engaged in a war aimed primarily at enlarging the empire. Hence the doggedness of his arguing: the conflict was not "forced" by Ger-many. True, the Boers did not want to give equal rights to British settlers, but the phrase about Dutch "despotism" sounds grotesque and shameful when set beside Conrad's own words in a letter to Graham of 14 October: "If I am to believe Kipling this is a war undertaken for the cause of democracy. *C'est à crever de rire* [Makes one die laughing]." To both Graham and Garnett he called the war "idiotic," and he later complained that it made him feel depressed, disgusted, and "done for." Undoubtedly Conrad was at his most sincere when he confessed to Zagórska that his feelings on the matter were "very complex"—and his most accurate rendering of these feelings was to Graham: "Now the fun has commenced, I trust British successes will be crushing from the first—on the same principle that if there's murder being done in the next room and you can't stop it you wish the head of the victim to be bashed in forthwith and the whole thing over for the sake of your own feelings."[105] Unfortunately the British army betrayed his hopes.

The vexation caused by the war lowered Conrad's spirits. His doubts about *Lord Jim* and his general discontent with himself recur in almost all his letters from that period.

> I am unutterably weary of thinking, of writing, of seeing, of feeling, of living.
>
> Doubts assail me from every side. The doubt of form,—the doubt of tendency,—a mistrust of my own conceptions,—and scruples of the moral order.
>
> I am at work, but my mental state is very bad,—and is made worse by a constant gnawing anxiety.
>
> The leaden hours pass in pain but the days go in a flash; weeks disappear into the bottomless pit before I can stretch out my hand and with all this there is an abiding sense of heavy endless drag upon the time. I am one of those who are condemned to run in a circle. . . . I have lost all sense of reality; I look at the fields or sit before the blank sheet of paper as if I were in a dream. Want of mental vigour I suppose.[106]

Such confessions are typical of a man suffering from depression; the sense of guilt, a constant factor, is particularly characteristic.[107] This sense is most openly revealed in Conrad's long letter to Sanderson of 12 October:

> I am always looking forward to some date, to some event, when I finish this: before I begin that other thing,—and there never seems to be any breathing time, not because I do much but because the toil is great. I try at times to persuade myself that it is my honesty that makes the burden so heavy, but, alas! the suspicion will force itself upon one that, may be, it is only lack of strength, of power, of an uplifting belief in oneself. . . . My dear Ted, you have much to forgive me: but try to imagine yourself trying your hardest to save the School (God forefend) from downfall, annihilation, and disaster: and the thing going on and on endlessly. That's exactly how I am situated: and the worst is that the menace (in my case) does not seem to come from outside but from within: that the menace and danger or weakness are in me —in myself alone. . . . I fear! I fear! . . . I am now trying to finish a story which began in the Oct. No. of *Blackwood*. I am at it day after day, and I want all day, every minute of a day, to produce a beggarly tale of words or perhaps to produce nothing at all. And when that is finished . . . I must go

on, even go on at once and drag out of myself another 20,000 words, if the boy is to have his milk and I my beer (this is a figure of speech—I don't drink beer, I drink weak tea, and yearn after dry champagne) and if the world is not absolutely to come to an end.[108]

Conrad's melancholia made writing more difficult; the slow pace of work produced a sense of guilt; the sense of guilt deepened his gloom. Conrad tortured himself in a vicious circle of depression, sinking in "lugubrious meditations," reproaching himself for "weak will" and "ultra-Slav nature" (this last obviously in a letter to a compatriot—to foreigners he vehemently protested at being classified a Slav).[109] The sufferings of soul changed, in the natural course, into body ailments, and in January he fell severely ill: "Malaria, bronchitis and gout. In reality a breakdown."[110]

All that time Conrad was beset by his usual financial worries, always earning less than he was spending, but he seldom mentioned these troubles.[111] The death on 28 November of Hope's son, a boy of seventeen, victim of a sex-motivated murder, was a painful shock. The Conrads left immediately to look after their friends and later took them into their home for a time.[112]

The Conrads paid fairly frequent visits to Brede Place where Crane, up to his ears in debt and work, besieged by unwanted guests, led a half-bohemian, half-courtly existence. The big house, only partly inhabited and furnished, had the reputation of being haunted. Crane decided to celebrate the end of 1899 with a big party open to the local population. The crowning attraction of the evening was to have been the staging of a burlesque, *The Ghost*, allegedly written by ten authors, including Conrad, James, Gissing, Wells, and the host himself. Conrad's real contribution to the entertainment, which lasted three days, is unknown.[113] We may only guess that he was shocked by a race on broomsticks organized by Wells, and all the fun and games (for which Crane paid with a hemorrhage that marked the beginning of the last stage of his illness) did nothing to dispel the "gloom" of Conrad's existence.[114] A few days later he wrote to Graham, "I am pretty miserable—nothing new that! But difficulties are as it were closing round me; an irresistible march of blackbeetles I figure it to myself. What a fate to be ingloriously devoured."[115]

Meanwhile *Lord Jim* progressed along its winding spiral. As late as 17 December Conrad believed that he would finish it by the end of the year. On 26 December he supposed that although the story considerably exceeded forty thousand words, it would not be long enough for separate publication. On 3 January 1900 *Lord Jim* already had seventeen chapters, and the author expected to send off the last part of the text in the second half of the month. Four days later he dispatched Chapter 18. At the end of January he fell ill and, blaming his sickness for the delay, promised that Chapter 20 would be the last. He thought that ten quiet days were all he needed to bring the story to a close.[116]

There followed, however, an interruption lasting several weeks. In order to re-lax Conrad even visited Wells for a couple of days, but he announced on his return that his "distaste to every form of literary exertion persists."[117] The in-terval, apparently caused by depression, probably occurred after Chapter 18, that is, before Marlow's visit to Stein. On 27 February he sent off two new chapters, most likely the nineteenth and twentieth, introducing Stein. Fourteen more pages followed on 3 March, before another month-long interval during which he decided to develop the report of Jim's success in Patusan.[118] The seesaw of Conrad's mood is illustrated in the same letter to Garnett in which he had made fun of Ford's strenuous exertions over *The Inheritors*: "I am old and sick and in debt—but lately I've found I can still write—*it* comes! *it* comes!—and I am young and healthy and rich.

"The question is *will* I ever *write* anything?

"I've been cutting and slashing whole parts out of Jim. How bad oh! HOW BAD! Why is it that a weary heaven has not pulverised me with a wee little teeny weeny thunderbolt?"[119]

Five days later he wrote to Ford, "My aunt is coming on Monday to stay a week, I would be awfully glad if your wife and yourself could come on Wednes-day to lunch. . . . I am of course anxious very anxious to introduce my 'collab-orateur' to the good woman who represents to me so much of my family—she had known so many of them on whom no eye of man'll rest again."[120]

Poradowska's visit—Conrad's first meeting with his "aunt" after five years—was a great success. Jessie was enthusiastic: "She was, I think, the most beauti-ful woman I had ever seen." She must have been impressed by Poradowska's worldliness and captivated by her warm and open personality. Conrad appar-ently suggested to Poradowska, who traveled alone, that if necessary his wife could help her dress. According to Jessie, Poradowska, immensely amused, turned down the offer and delivered a little speech on the subject of the many duties that a hard-working housewife must fulfil.[121] One may easily guess that in fact the only bewildered person must have been Jessie, who had never met with the life-style of wealthy women. Poradowska helped the Conrads to solve a long-standing family problem: thanks to her intercession Jessie's younger sis-ters, Dorothy and Ethelinde, were placed at low fees at a convent school in Slough, near Windsor. Conrad probably contributed to their maintenance.[122]

Poradowska brought with her a hint of France and the Continent; of elegant connections, and the wide world. Conrad was easily persuaded to spend a vaca-tion in Belgium "to take a month's rest because wasting the paper makes me quite silly," as he wrote to Davray. And he added, "I think often of you working in your anthill over there; while I am here, lonely as a mole, burrowing, bur-rowing without break or rest, never emerging into the open."[123]

Conrad interrupted his work for one day to see a dying friend. Stephen Crane, in a hopeless state, was being transferred from Brede to Badenweiler in the Black Forest. The journey had to be broken for one week at Dover to let the patient gather strength for the crossing. On 16 May Conrad saw him for twenty minutes; Crane was very weak and was in isolation.[124] Perhaps Conrad never learned about Crane's last letter, which was an appeal on his behalf: "My condition is probably known to you. . . . I have Conrad on my mind very much just now. Garnett does not think it likely that his writing will ever be popular outside the ring of men who write. He is poor and a gentleman and proud. His wife is not strong and they have a kid. If Garnett should ask you to help pull wires for a place on the Civil List for Conrad please do me the last favor. . . . I am sure you will."[125] "Though the word is discredited now and may sound pretentious, I will say that there was in Crane a strain of chivalry which made him safe to trust with one's life," wrote Conrad over twenty-five years later.[126]

Work on *Lord Jim* filled the second quarter of 1900. On 3 April Conrad declared that he was beginning the last chapter, which would be finished on the twelfth. On that date he moved the goal one week forward and suggested some cuts to the publisher if the work was too long; luckily, Blackwood declined the offer. Conrad kept complaining about his "dog's life," but his writing seemed to gather momentum: about 10 May he sent off the beginning of Chapter 31. The Patusan part of the plot continued to develop, but without any hint of the ending. On 15 May Blackwood drew the obvious conclusion from the evolution of the "sketch" and suggested publishing *Lord Jim* as a book. Conrad agreed, estimating that the novel would come to about 100,000 words (it has 130,000). He also changed the title to *Lord Jim: A Tale.*

The signing of the contract must have given Conrad a great sense of liberation, since during the last couple of months of work he wrote as much as fifteen chapters, 28 percent of the entire book. An analysis of the text, however, shows that the last quarter of the novel is consistently linked with the preceding chapters. Toward the end of Chapter 21, Marlow announces, "My last words about Jim shall be few." Although he does not keep his promise, what follows is structurally cohesive. Most probably no one unaware of the history of the novel's rise would guess that its author had so many different visions of its length.

Conrad's last error of judgment occurred on 9 July, when he again announced the end—this time to come on the twelfth of that month. On the fourteenth, he informed Blackwood: "The last word of Lord Jim is written."[127] He related the final stage of the struggle to Galsworthy:

The end of *L.J.* has been pulled off with a steady drag of 21 hours. I sent wife and child out of the house (to London) and sat down at 9 a.m. with a desperate resolve to be done with it. Now and then I took a walk round the house, out at one door in at the other. Ten-minute meals. A great hush. Cigarette ends growing into a mound similar to a cairn over a dead hero. Moon rose over the barn, looked in at the window and climbed out of sight. Dawn broke, brightened. I put the lamp out and went on, with the morning breeze blowing the sheets of MS. all over the room. Sun rose. I wrote the last word and went into the dining-room. Six o'clock I shared a piece of cold chicken with Escamillo (who was very miserable and in want of sympathy, having missed the child dreadfully all day). Felt very well, only sleepy; had a bath at seven and at 1.30 was on my way to London.[128]

Ewa Korzeniowska in 1862.

Apollo Korzeniowski in 1862.

Parish church in Oratów where Apollo Korzeniowski and Ewa Bobrowska were married, 8 May 1856. Photograph taken about 1975.

Carmelitan monastery in Berdyczów. Etching by Napoleon Orda.

Nowy Świat Street in Warsaw about 1860. The Korzeniowskis lived in the tenth house from the right.

A log house in Vologda similar to the one where the Korzeniowskis lived during their exile there. Photograph taken in 1977.

A neo-Gothic pavilion in the Lubowidzkis' park at Nowochwastów (allegedly the house where Joseph Conrad was born). Drawing by Napoleon Orda.

Konrad Korzeniowski in 1863.

Dedication in verso of photograph 8: "To my dear Granny who helped me send pastries to my poor Daddy in prison—grandson, Pole-Catholic, and szlachcic, Konrad."

Robert Korzeniowski (?) in typical attire of an 1863 insurgent.

Stefan Bobrowski and Antoni Syroczyński.

First and last page of Regina
Korzeniowska's letter to Konrad
Korzeniowski, 26 November 1865.

Tadeusz Bobrowski about 1870.

APOLLO KORZENIOWSKI

Ofiara moskiewskiego
męczeństwa
ur. 21 Lutego 1820
um. 23 Maja 1869

Apollo Korzeniowski's
tombstone: "A victim of Muscovite martyrdom."

Teofila Bobrowska.

Konrad Korzeniowski in 1874.

Circular Quay, Sydney.

Dynevor Road, London. Conrad lodged here, 1880–1886. Photograph taken in 1957.

Konrad Korzeniowski in 1883 at Marienbad.

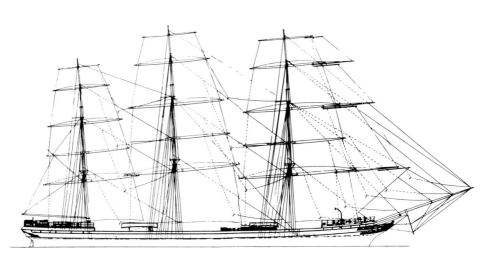

Design of the construction of the *Narcissus*.

Tanjung Redeb; on the left, the house of William Charles Olmeijer, Conrad's Kaspar Almayer.
Photograph taken in 1903.

Sambaliung on the River Kelai, Borneo.

Aniela Zagórska with daughters Aniela and Karola.

Marguerite Poradowska.

Two pages from the second part of Conrad's *Congo Diary*.

The *Torrens*.

Conrad with five apprentices on the deck of the *Torrens*.

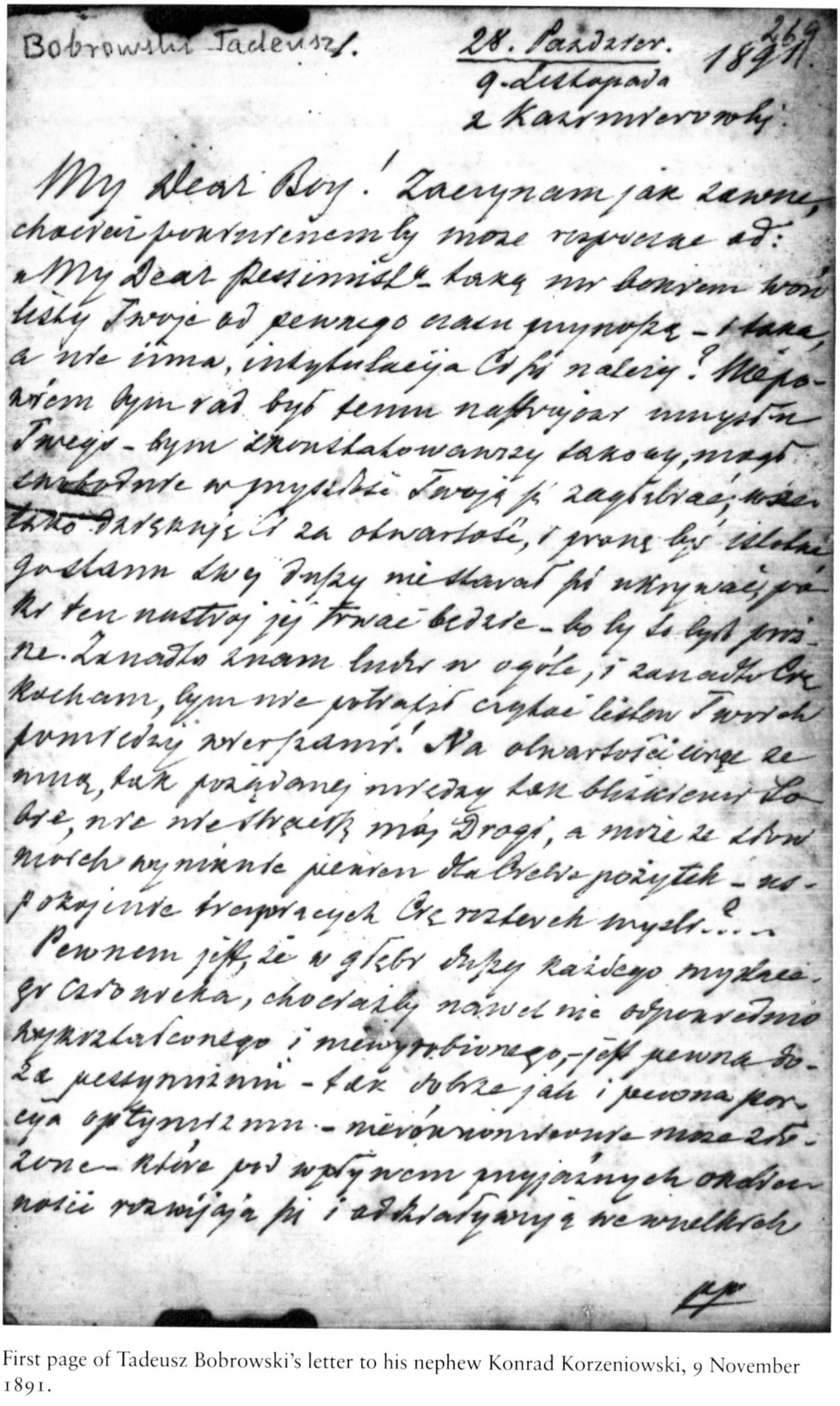
Bobrowski Tadeusz. 28. Październ. 1891. 269
9 Listopada
z Kazimierówki:

My Dear Boy! Zaczynam jak zawsze, chociaż powinienem by może rozpoczać od: "My Dear pessimist" - taką mi bowiem woń listy Twoje od pewnego czasu przynoszą - i taka, a nie inna, intytulacyja Ci się należy! Nie po-wiem bym rad był temu nastrojowi umysłu Twego - bym skonstatowawszy takowy, mógł chłodnie w przyczyny Twoje się zagłębiać; wszelkako dziękuję Ci za otwartość, i proszę byś szlachetnego stanu swej Duszy nie starał się ukrywać, póki ten nastrój jej trwać będzie - bo by to było próżne. Zanadto znam ludzi w ogóle, i zanadto Cię kocham, bym nie potrafił czytać listów Twoich pomiędzy wierszami! Na otwartości więc ze mną, tak pożądanej między tak bliskiemi sobie, nic nie straciesz mój Drogi, a może ze słów moich wyniknie pewien dla Ciebie pożytek - uspokojenie trapiących Cię czarnych myśli....

Pewnem jest, że w głębi duszy każdego myślącego człowieka, chociażby nawet nie odpowiednio wykształconego i niewyrobionego, - jest pewna doza pessymizmu - tak dobrze jak i pewna porcya optymizmu - nierównomiernie może złożone - które pod wpływem przyjaznych okoliczności rozwijają się i atrofiują we wszelkich

First page of Tadeusz Bobrowski's letter to his nephew Konrad Korzeniowski, 9 November 1891.

Conrad's certificate of discharge from the *Adowa*, his last ship.

Emilie Briquel.

1 oct. 1895.
17. Gillingham St
London. S.W.

Chère Mademoiselle Briquel.

Je couvre ma tête avec
des cendres, je déchire mon
paletot, j'enlève mes souliers
— pour un rien je me
mettrai une corde au cou —
pour approcher le tribunal
de Votre miséricorde. L'Indigne
(c'est moi) ose à peine prendre
la plume pour répondre à Votre
si bonne lettre de 8 sept^bre !
Quand je regarde la date en
tête de cette page j'ai la sensation d'avaler un morceau de
fer rouge. Puis je m'attendre
au pardon ?

Si Vous saviez comme j'ai
été occupé ! D'abord j'étais
occupé à être malade. Ce n'est
pas une occupation bien active (puisqu

Conrad's letter to Emilie Briquel.

Jessie George in 1896, before her marriage to Joseph Conrad.

The house of Mme Le Bail in Ile-Grande, where the Conrads stayed during their honeymoon. Photograph taken in 1975.

The gardens of Le Peyrou in Montpellier.

Arthur Marwood.

Capel House, where the Conrads lived, 1910–1919. Photograph taken in 1957.

Joseph Conrad in 1912.

Jessie, John, and Joseph Conrad in 1912.

Joseph Conrad with his son John.

Józef Hieronim Retinger in 1912.

Otolia Retinger, née Zubrzycka.

Ellen Glasgow and Joseph Conrad in June 1914.

John Conrad (right) and Robin Douglas in 1914.

Apollo Korzeniowski's grave.

Conrad with Aniela Zagórska (daughter) in Zakopane in 1914.

Borys Conrad in military uniform.

Jane Anderson.

From the right: Joseph Conrad, Jessie, Jane Anderson, and John Conrad.

Drawing room at Oswalds.

Conrad with Karola Zagórska at Oswalds in summer 1920.

Conrad in 1923.

Joseph Conrad's grave. Photograph taken in 1957.

X

. . . .

DIFFICULT MATURITY

1900—1904

ON 20 JULY Conrad hurried off, forgetting even to send letters ready for posting to Blackwood and Meldrum, with Jessie and Borys for a month's holiday in Belgium, where they were awaited by the Fords and their daughter. Ford met them in Ostend; from there all six of them proceeded first to Bruges and then to Knocke-sur-Mer, to the Grand Hôtel de la Plage.[1] Conrad felt "exhausted mentally and very depressed,"[2] but he could not even think of resting, as he still had to prepare a clean copy of *Lord Jim*'s ending and to proofread the successive instalments of the novel. Moreover, he hoped to work with Ford on *Seraphina*.

Nothing came of their plans, however; about 1 August Borys fell seriously ill with dysentery. Ford helped Jessie look after the sick child, and years later she still recalled with gratitude the devotion shown by the man whom she otherwise detested. "He was always at hand to shift my small invalid, fetch the doctor or help with the nursing." Conrad, plunged into distress, had an attack of gout. It could have been a symptom of depression—or its cause, since rheumatic ailments often lower the spirits. Exhausted by their holiday, the Conrads returned to the Pent about 20 August.[3]

Ford joined them there, and the two writers set to work for a few weeks on *Seraphina*—to the obvious displeasure of Conrad, whose mind was elsewhere. "Bosh! Horrors!" Ford reports him as saying.[4] About the middle of September Conrad began writing "Typhoon," although originally he thought about starting *First Command*.[5] The story about the captain of the *Nan-Shan* and the coolies fighting under the deck was meant to be short and written in a short time: on 8 October Conrad promised to send off the finished text in a week. As usual, it took him longer. On 27 November he was complaining, "The typhoon is still blowing. I find it extremely difficult to express the simplest idea clearly. It is a sort of temporary fog on the brain."[6] In the end, "Typhoon" was not finished until January.

In September Conrad got in touch with James B. Pinker (1863–1922), the literary agent, whose offer he had gently turned down a year earlier. In taking this step he was obviously tempted by the prospect of securing, through advance payments, a more regular flow of cash, and also of being free from the necessity of finding publishers and negotiating his contracts. In addition, his

268 · · DIFFICULT MATURITY

second collaborative work with Ford needed particularly adroit, businesslike handling. Although as early as 19 September Conrad assured Pinker that *Seraphina* was "nearing completion," its progress was slow; and while both authors were pinning their hopes on the book, they were in fact—and Conrad particularly—concentrating on their own work.[7]

The association with Pinker's firm lasted throughout Conrad's life, and although his relationship with the agent was at times stormy, Conrad relied on his continuous financial help. Pinker was "a short sturdy man, clean-shaven, with a plump ruddy face, deceptive spectacles, and close-cropped whitening hair. . . . His calm . . . his ability to sit with an interested expression and say nothing but 'Oh' and 'Yes' while another person blethered his heart out, were all invaluable assets to an intermediary of genius."[8] Not an intellectual, Pinker had neither particular artistic interests nor sophisticated literary taste, but he was known for his flair for spotting new talents and for his ability to deal ruthlessly and successfully with editors and publishers.

Conrad's first letters to Pinker—and he was to write almost thirteen hundred—had already established a pattern that was to last throughout their correspondence. The writer reported on the work in progress; almost always prophesied an early finish (almost always far off the mark); complained of various physical and mental ailments; unfolded his ideas for short stories and novels planned for the near future. Some of those stories took ten years to produce; others never materialized. If Conrad had been able to work even for only five years in accordance with his own predictions, he would have completed almost his entire output for the years 1900–1924. This permanent discrepancy between self-imposed standards and real possibilities produced a state of constant stress; it also gave rise to fits of self-recrimination, characteristic of neurotic depression. Entangled in a vicious circle of mental suffering, Conrad yearned above all else for a moment's respite. Unexpectedly, and quite unwarranted by its context, we find this yearning in a passage of "Typhoon" about a "heart, which is incorrigible, and of all the gifts of the earth—even before life itself—aspires to peace."[9]

He must have felt all the more exhausted as the rhythm of his life from the autumn of 1898 to the summer of 1914 was determined almost entirely by the single factor of his work on successive books. Conrad's rare trips to the Continent in the course of the first nine of those years did little to change that rhythm, which was accompanied by a succession of good—and more often bad—moods, and of improved—but mostly worsening—health. If his life in those years is dull and, over long periods of time, sadly monotonous for the biographer (and the reader), how extremely depressing it must have been for Conrad when he contrasted his writing life with his earlier years of freedom and constant change.

Literature—his own works and those of his correspondents—became the most frequent and well-nigh sole subject of his letters. This applies particularly to his letters to Galsworthy: by about 1900 Conrad became Galsworthy's closest confidant and adviser, a meticulous and kindly reader of his novels and stories—always praising them to excess. His critical remarks were carefully veiled by such elaborate phrases and metaphors that it is sometimes difficult to ascertain what he in fact disapproved of and what improvements he suggested.[10] Anyway, it seems certain that it was Conrad who advised Galsworthy to read Maupassant and Turgenev.[11]

The description of friendship between those two very different writers must be rather lopsided, since very few letters from Galsworthy to Conrad have survived. Nothing is known of how Galsworthy reacted to praise and what advice he sought. His own opinion of Conrad's works we know solely from his later reminiscences and retrospective assessment. It seems obvious that Galsworthy could only very inadequately fathom the intellectual content and virtuosity of his friend's works; he did not share Conrad's philosophical interests, artistic ambitions, or his interest in the pursuit of new forms of fiction. Galsworthy's superficial approach to Conrad's prose is shown by the fact that he regarded Conrad chiefly as a "painter's writer . . . a pure artist (there is practically nothing of the moralist in him)," and believed that in his books "nature is first, man second."[12] Conrad, on the other hand, must have been aware of the distance separating him from the creator of the Forsythes, but whenever he commented on Galsworthy's works, it was always in praise.

It would, however, be an unjust simplification to regard their familiarity as founded, on Conrad's part, in the pleasure he felt in patronizing the literary career of an English gentleman—one from whom, moreover, he often borrowed money. The tenor of Conrad's letters written over the period of almost thirty years, and the recollections of their mutual friends, show that he felt a genuine friendship for Galsworthy. It was a friendship toward a man very different from himself, self-controlled, practical, solid, not too profound, but of great integrity. Galsworthy, for his part, was particularly fascinated by the compressed energy of the high-strung Conrad, so much in contrast with his own calm and restraint.

I think I never saw Conrad quite in repose. His hands, his feet, his knees, his lips—sensitive, expressive, and ironical—something was always in motion, the dynamo never quite at rest with him. His mind was extraordinarily active and his memory for impressions and people most retentive, so that he stored with wonderful accuracy all the observations of his dark-brown eyes, that were so piercing and yet could be so soft. . . . His sense of humour, indeed, was far greater than one might think from his work. He had an almost ferocious enjoyment of the absurd. Writing seemed to dry or sardonise his humour. But in conversation his sense of fun was much more vivid; it would leap up in the midst of gloom or worry, and take charge with a shout. . . . He was an extremely quick judge of a man. I remember a dinner convoked by me, that he might meet a feminine compatriot. The instant dislike he took to that individual was so full of electricity that we did not dine in comfort. The dislike was entirely merited. This quick instinct for character and types inimical to him was balanced by equally sure predilections, so that his friendships were always, or nearly always, lasting—I can think of only one exception. He illustrated vividly the profound truth that friendship is very much an affair of nerves, grounded in instinct rather than in reason or in circumstance, the outcome of a sort of deep affinity which prevents jarring.[13]

The last instalment of *Lord Jim* appeared in *Blackwood's Magazine* on 15 October 1900, and the book edition came out on the same day. Conrad, extremely agitated, awaited the reaction: "If you've written to me about L.J.," he appealed to Garnett, "keep back your letter for a week. I am in a state bordering on distraction. Most unhappy about it and yet idiotically exalted."[14] To his friend's criticism he answered with self-flagellation, "Yes! you've put your finger on the plague spot. The division of the book into two parts which is the basis of your criticism demonstrates to me once more your amazing insight; and your analysis of the effect of the book puts into words precisely and suggestively the dumb thoughts of every reader—and my own. . . . For what is fundamentally wrong with the book—the cause and the effect—is want of power. . . . I mean the want of illuminating imagination. I wanted to obtain a sort of lurid light out of the very events. . . . I've been satanically ambitious, but there's nothing of a devil in me, worse luck. The *Outcast* is a heap of sand, the *Nigger* a splash of water. *Jim* a lump of clay. A stone, I suppose will be my next gift to the impatient mankind."[15]

Conrad's self-criticism was made easier and less painful by the fact that the first reviews were enthusiastic. Soon he described himself as a "spoiled child of the critics."[16] *Lord Jim* was acclaimed as the author's "greatest" work, "entirely original" and bringing Conrad "into the front rank of living novelists." The *Speaker*'s reviewer maintained that the "apparent artlessness about the arrangement of the book" was designed to distract the reader from the "mere external events of the tale" and make possible the introduction of multiple points of view.

Most critics, however, were confused by the novel's structure and complained of the involved and obscure method of narration. The author of a review in the *Academy* objected to Marlow's storytelling, claiming that the monologue would have lasted eleven hours. The *Pall Mall Gazette* complained of the novel's "formlessness"—the breaking up of the narrative into two parts (the episode with the *Patna* and the remaining "dispensable" rest) and declared that *Lord Jim* was "more than a little difficult to read." And so the praise was based on intuitive reaction rather than on understanding—and again the "difficulty" of the book was stressed. *Literature* even declared that Conrad "cannot write what is commonly understood as a novel." [17] Thus, in spite of the critics' praise, the popularity of *Lord Jim* was quite modest. True, the first impression, of 2,100 copies, was sold out in two months, but the next one, of only 1,050 copies, lasted four years. [18]

A letter from Henry James, received at the beginning of November, pleased Conrad more than all the reviews put together. He described it as "absolutely enthusiastic" and, sending it on to Garnett, he waxed rapturous in an accompanying letter: "A draught from the Fountain of Eternal Youth. Wouldn't you think a boy had written it? Such enthusiasm! Wonderful old man, with his record of wonderful work!" [19] To appreciate his reaction we must remember that in Conrad's personal pantheon James occupied the unique position of the only living author to whom he referred as the "Master."

Lord Jim brought applause but no additional income. At first the sales did not even cover Blackwood's advance. "Typhoon" was not finished, a lot more work had to be put into *Seraphina*, and a story supplementing the volume *Youth* (for which he had also received an advance) was not even begun. Meanwhile, Conrad's creditor, presumably Krieger, again demanded the repayment of an old debt. Conrad resorted for the first but not the last time to a complicated and costly method that would enable him to borrow a bigger sum. He drew two life insurance policies of £500 each; the annual premium for both of them came to just over £35. (In compliance with the insurance company regulations, Conrad had to pass a medical examination; his health was pronounced satisfactory, except for gout. [20]) Using the policies as a security, he wished to obtain a five-year loan at 5 percent from the Standard Life Insurance Company. He needed two sureties as a guarantee of regular payments of the premiums and interests. One of them came from Galsworthy ("He has plenty of money and a great affection for me," Conrad assured Meldrum; the former claim was greatly exaggerated). For the second surety Conrad decided to appeal to Blackwood ("I find it easier to put myself under obligation to you than to any other man—a fact not particularly fortunate for you perhaps—but illustrative of my feelings."). At first the loan was to be £150, but as the negotiations progressed, so did Conrad's appetite; after four weeks the sum grew to £250. And so Conrad's payments for the policy and loan came to almost £48 annually—twice as much as the rent for his house. Blackwood agreed and, under pressure from Conrad, lent him an additional £50. Conrad promised to repay this as soon as the formalities with the insurance company were over, but he did not keep his word. [21] These complicated manoeuvres cost a great deal of time and trouble, but they succeeded in bringing Conrad some temporary financial relief.

Conrad had, therefore, many reasons to feel grateful to Blackwood. He wrote to him on 30 December: "You have made the last year of the Old Century very memorable to me, by your kindness. I am alluding to the production of Lord Jim . . . . As it went on I appreciated more and more your helpful words your helpful silence and your helpful acts; and this feeling shall never grow old, or cold or faint."[22] But it was precisely from that time on that his relations with the old Edinburgh publisher began to cool.

Conrad made a fair start in the new year. On 11 January 1901 he finished "Typhoon," and four days later Pinker sent him £100 as an advance for its magazine publication, which did not begin until January of the following year.[23] Next Conrad began "Falk," which the agent had been told about on 8 October 1900. About this time he also had a small accident when driving his horse-cart—Conrad was an absent-minded and erratic driver—but its main victim was the old mare.[24]

In January 1900, at Garnett's request, Conrad had written a letter about his parents and ancestors and the atmosphere of the struggle for independence in which he had been brought up. "Tempi passati, brother! Let them go," he concluded.[25] Now, exactly a year later, a voice from the past reached him again. Józef Korzeniowski, an official in the Jagiellonian Library in Cracow, sent him, at Marguerite Poradowska's request, a copy of Tadeusz Bobrowski's *Memoirs*, published in Lwów a year earlier. We do not know why Conrad did not receive the book directly from the publisher; perhaps his contact with the executors of his uncle's will had been broken off. In later years Conrad read the *Memoirs* carefully, drawing from them material for his own writing.

The librarian Korzeniowski had been informed by Poradowska about the literary achievements of his namesake and sent with the book ceremonious expressions of regard. Conrad reacted with elaborate modesty, and—doubtless referring to the earlier controversy about the emigration of talent—made the unsolicited declaration: "It is widely known that I am a Pole and that Józef Konrad are my two Christian names, the latter being used by me as a surname so that foreign mouths should not distort my real surname—a distortion which I cannot stand. It does not seem to me that I have been unfaithful to my country by having proved to the English that a gentleman from the Ukraine can be as good a sailor as they, and has something to tell them in their own language. I consider such recognition as I have won from this particular point of view, and offer it in silent homage where it is due."[26] Such a declaration presented the problem in the best possible way, but that Conrad himself was not altogether convinced is suggested by the fact that he later returned to the subject more than once.

In February and March of 1901, Conrad's spirits and productivity flagged again. He complained of either "getting stale or becoming an idiot"; he lamented over a violent chill that attacked his liver, face, and back, but principally his "intellect which became withered"; he had to have a tooth extracted, which seemed to him "like the beginning of the end." The presence of his ailing mother-in-law might have aided to his own indisposition.[27] At any rate, Ford and *Seraphina* prevented Conrad from devoting his time exclusively to his own work. Short periods of collaboration in December in the Pent and in March at Aldington where the Fords lived—or rather were cooped up—allowed very little progress on their work. In April Ford reappeared at the Pent, and about 10 May the Conrad family went for a fortnight's working visit to the Fords' new house at Winchelsea. After Conrad had finished "Falk" there, both writers concentrated on their struggle with *Seraphina*.[28]

But not for long: Conrad's imagination was aroused by an anecdote related by Ford in *The Cinque Ports*, published in the autumn of 1900. Ford mentioned there a shipwrecked sailor from a German merchant ship who, washed ashore in Kent, unable to communicate in English and driven away by the local country people, finally found shelter in a pigsty.[29] Conrad reshaped the anecdote into a moving story about a young peasant from the Tatra Mountains, Yanko Gooral, a survivor from a ship carrying emigrants to America. Yanko's unsurmountable foreignness among the English villagers forms the psychological pivot of the action: they fear the unfamiliar and the unknown, and the sensitive stranger is crushed by the consciousness of absolute loneliness and isolation. An auto-biograhical component is evident here. Bertrand Russell regarded this story as the key to Conrad's psychology. One of the titles that Conrad considered, "The Husband," emphasizes another aspect of the story's personal meaning. Yet another title contemplated by Conrad was "A Castaway," but he eventually decided to bring to the fore the character of Yanko's dull-witted wife, Amy Foster, and thus stress what he regarded as the keynote of the story, the "incompatibility of races." The story, begun in May at Winchelsea, was finished on 18 June.[30]

In May and June Conrad and Ford were constantly visiting each other to collaborate on *Seraphina*. The text grew by fits and starts. Their method of work, exciting as well as risky, showed that the attitudes of both partners were basically incompatible and the concurrence of their aims was quite illusory. Whatever psychological nourishment Conrad derived from his association with Ford —and it was considerable—artistically the collaboration turned out more important for the junior partner. As Raymond T. Brebach says, the typescript version of *Seraphina* written by Ford before Conrad's demands forced him to rework it shows that Ford "did not have a clear conception of how to construct an internally consistent and coherent plot, how to introduce characters, or how to describe action vividly and directly." Conrad's letters to Pinker of 7 June and 7 November carried the same news: that *Seraphina* had been finished.[31] The two letters referred to different drafts. In the spring of that year the novel was still almost entirely Ford's own product, but, although ostensibly complete, it was clearly unfit for publication. Conrad's threefold contribution was to consist of giving advice, correcting the existing text, and adding fragments jointly or individually conceived. Ford, apart from joint consultations, was expected to read and correct fragments written by his collaborator.

Jessie viewed all this without enthusiasm. The presence of two authors under one roof and at one dining table was very trying. She recalled later:

> For hours after I had gone to bed the voices would reach me through the floor. Sometimes the tones would appear to mingle in pleasant accord, their ideas flowing easily, amused laughs and chuckles. At others sounds of wordy strife and disagreement penetrated to my ears, and raised voices came distinctly into my room. . . .
>
> The small house seemed at times full to overflowing and there were days when the two artists with their vagaries, temperaments and heated discussions made it seem rather a warm place. Still, to give F.M.H. his due, he was the least peppery of the two, being a native of a less excitable nation and his drawling voice made a sharp contrast with the quick, un-English utterances of the fellow collaborator.[32]

All the indications are that when the two writers were together their collaboration consisted only of discussions. Those must have been both pleasant and stimulating, but to judge by their stylistic and artistic differences, when it came to actual writing each man worked alone. *Seraphina* was intended as an adventure story, but it was written with care for aesthetic effect. As Conrad confided later to Waliszewski, "The idea we had was purely aesthetic: to depict in an appropriate way certain scenes and certain situations. Also it did not displease us to be able to show that we could do something which was very much en vogue with the public at the moment."[33] But the satisfaction of this last ambition was denied them; how could the writer concentrate on artistic description of pure adventure when such reflections floated in his mind: "How often the activity of our life is the least real part of it!"[34] For an author of adventure novels that kind of admission smacks of literary suicide.

It was not surprising, therefore, that Blackwood did not accept *Seraphina* for serialization—sweetening the refusal with his readiness to print an article on any literary or artistic subject of Conrad's choice. David Meldrum, Blackwood's literary adviser, who was very kindly disposed toward Conrad and was inclined to accept the text, thus summed up his impressions of the book: "The fault of the thing, stated in a word, is that it is Hueffer's story and Conrad's telling; and that the dramatic intensity, while there, appears a little forced." Neither Blackwood nor Meldrum had, in fact, read Part 3, which had been mainly written by Conrad.[35] The novel at the time consisted of four parts, the last of which was today's Part 5; the present Part 4 did not yet exist.

Meanwhile, the first product of the Ford-Conrad collaboration, *The Inheritors*, came out on 26 June 1901. The critics' reception was cool and the public's was indifferent. Conrad tried to instill Ford with optimism, quoting Pawling's enthusiastic reaction and reporting Galsworthy's and Poradowska's praise.[36] It soon became apparent, however, that the book was a failure.

The most favorable notice appeared in *The New York Times Saturday Book Review*, but the critic, obviously impressed by Conrad's name on the title page, took it to be yet another work, quite unlike the previous ones, by that outstanding author. Ford's authorship was disregarded, and the novel was interpreted as a satire on "some of the most cherished traditions and achievements of Englishmen."[37] Conrad found himself in a doubly uncomfortable position: he was praised for a novel that came almost entirely from Ford's pen and that he did not value; and further he was viewed as an author who wanted to criticize traditions dear to his adopted countrymen. This led Conrad, in what was to remain the sole occasion in his life, to reply to a review in a letter to the editor, making a gallant stand on behalf of his partner: "The elder of the authors is well aware how much of these generously estimated qualities the book owes to the younger collaborator." He also cleared up the misunderstanding about his alleged attack on English traditions. And, probably in order to add some weight to the letter, he gave a short exposition of his own views on science, art, the mystery of existence, ethics, and the role of the novelist.

Conrad's basic ideas are contained in a few concise sentences:

> Science . . . is not concerned with truth at all, but with the exact order of such phenomena as fall under the perception of the senses. Its conclusions are quite true enough if they can be made useful to the furtherance of our little schemes to make our earth a little more habitable. The laws it discovers remain certain and immovable for the time of several generations. But in the sphere of an art dealing with a subject matter whose origin and end are alike unknown there is no possible conclusion. The only indisputable truth of life is our ignorance. Besides this there is nothing evident, nothing absolute, nothing uncontradicted; there is no principle, no instinct, no impulse that can stand alone at the beginning of things and look confidently to the end. Egoism, which is the moving force of the world, and altruism, which is its morality, these two contradictory instincts, of which one is so plain and the other so mysterious, cannot serve us unless in the incomprehensible alliance of their irreconcilable antagonism. . . .
>
> Fiction, at the point of development at which it has arrived, demands from the writer a spirit of scrupulous abnegation. The only legitimate basis of creative work lies in the courageous recogniton of all the irreconcilable antagonisms that make our life so enigmatic, so burdensome, so fascinating, so dangerous—so full of hope. They exist! And this is the only fundamental truth of fiction. . . . The mood does not matter. It is only the writer's self-forgetful fidelity to his sensations that matters. But, whatever light he flashes on it, the

fundamental truth remains, and it is only in its name that the barren struggle of contradictions assumes the dignity of moral strife going on ceaselessly to a mysterious end—with our consciousness powerless but concerned sitting enthroned like a melancholy parody of eternal wisdom above the dust of the contest.[38]

Conrad's views on the aims of fiction and the duties of the novelist are basically the same as those expressed in the preface to *The Nigger*. Here, however, the stern postulate of complete "self-denial" tends to assign to the writer the role of a faithful but almost passive transmitter of his sensations. Also, because of the relative brevity of the statement, the assumption that fidelity toward one's own sensations is tantamount to fidelity toward objective, nonpsychological reality is emphasized all the more strongly. In practice, however, Conrad does not seem to have been guided by such a solipsistic assumption. It might have expressed, in an exaggerated form, his philosophical wariness, but it was not an element of his creative attitude.

The statements about science, seemingly casual, deserve some attention. We detect in them a note of modern skepticism toward the claims of nineteenth-century science—as if Conrad had read, as indeed he might have done, the works of an outstanding critical philosopher of science, Émile Boutroux. Conrad's skepticism extends to metaphysics as well: he was a declared agnostic. The phrases on egoism and altruism appear to express his personal conception; if they contain distant echoes of his philosophical readings (Hobbes, Guyau?), those have been changed out of all recognition.

The failure of *The Inheritors* precipitated another financial crisis. It was the only book Conrad published in 1901, and the money borrowed in December had already evaporated. On 7 June, and still before "Amy Foster" was finished, he made a dramatic appeal to Pinker: "You will have to advance something on that too if you don't want me to roll over on my side and give up writing altogether. It's awful. Awful."[39] Then Conrad decided to repeat the manoeuvre of six months ago by obtaining a loan on the strength of his life insurance policy. This time the creditor was Ford—in spite of the objections of Robert Garnett, who was looking after his financial affairs. Conrad obtained £100 from his friend: "Many thanks to you for staving off the impending annihilation."[40]

In November Conrad calculated that in 1901 he had received £240 from Pinker.[41] Adding up his income (£300 and £100 in loans, £240 from Pinker, and a small sum for the second edition of *Lord Jim*), we see that Conrad had that year at his disposal a little over £650, a large part of which was taken up by debts and interest. Was he spending very much by contemporary standards? Yes and no. At that time in England and Wales taken together, only 400,000 people declared an income above £400 per year; fewer than a million earned over £160. The average income per capita was about £40 per year; average earnings were barely over £90; only 2.5 percent of the gainfully employed earned over £2 per week. Mrs. C. S. Peel, author of the popular book *How to Keep House*, calculated that £1 a week was sufficient for a "very good living" of one person. Servants were cheap: the maid at the Pent was not paid more than £20 per year.[42]

According to the statistics Conrad's small family was among a small group of relatively affluent people. But in those days the differences in living standards between the classes were so enormous that they are now difficult even to imagine. Maintaining a family on the level of what was then regarded as middle-class propriety cost incomparably more than mere accommodation, food, and even servants. Furniture and furnishings, good-quality clothes, entertaining, books and magazines, trips to London, and various small luxuries would consume dozens of pounds. One could therefore spend less, or even several times less, than the Conrads, but only at a risk of dropping out of the "better class" of people; and this might have meant a public admission of poverty, which might attract attention in cultured circles. Conrad, uncertain of his position in English society, dreaded the possibility of such a stigma. His regard for appearances was strengthened by the traditional Polish tendency to indulge in hospitality well above one's means, as well as by the carefree attitude toward money characteristic of sailors and artists; and these considerations kept pushing him to the verge of bankruptcy.

The last months of 1901 were spent on alterations and additions to *Seraphina*. Conrad brought Part 3 to completion;[43] in continuing the story of Kemp's adventures, he added the most colorful and dramatic part of the novel, Part 4. Ford reshaped the end;[44] he wrote to Elsie, "We're getting ahead. . . . Conrad has actually killed Don Rodrigo and I am just surrendering Kemp to the Admiral. C. was so obviously depressed at the idea of my departing or rather so elated at that of my remaining that I thought that since I hadn't to go up to London that I'd stay."[45]

Conrad also made a start on a short story, "To-morrow," the idea of which he got from Ford.[46] His mood fluctuated. On 15 November, Olive Garnett, Edward's sister, visited the Pent with Elsie Hueffer. "Conrad spoke very despondingly about his work, said he often had a mind to return to the sea . . . but he had gout in the foot, and it wd. not be honourable to engage. Afterwards he became more cheerful. We dined together . . . Conrad was most hospitable, most simple in a good mood, Elsie said. He told us we had wound him up."[47] Already, then, Conrad was presenting what was actually the result of his inability to find a suitable berth as though it were the consequence of his own decision to give up the sea.

Young Ernest Dawson, who had met him at Wells's, was under the impression that Conrad "in those days . . . resembled *de jure* sovereign, sure of his rights, but with his claim to the succession not yet before the world, and he was proud to the verge of arrogance." The lapse of twenty-five years (Dawson wrote his reminiscences in 1928) simplified his interpretation, concealing the essence of the matter behind appearances. Conrad's proud bearing probably reflected as much his sense of his own worth as his self-defense against constant inner turbulences and his awareness of the precariousness of his social and financial position. We shall see more than once how his outbursts of near-arrogance always had a defensive undercurrent. He felt his triple weakness: as an unsuccessful artist, as a man suffering from depression, as an alien.

Dawson recalls their first meeting:

On the Sunday, after luncheon, Conrad arrived in a dog-cart. The day was rough, and he wore a peaked cap of maritime cut, which, with his jacket and trousers of stout blue cloth, gave him somewhat of the aspect of a pilot. Apart from details of costume, you knew him quickly for a sailor: as quickly for a *sahib*. He stood an inch or two below middle height but never looked small, his square, high breadth of shoulders and short neck gave an impression of a compact power. His face was sallowish, the skin weathered and puckered round the full dark eyes by habitual staring into the night or over the brightness of the sunlit sea. The hair and clipped, pointed beard were wiry and almost black. He wore an eyeglass, which he seldom used; when he did screw it into his eye the effect was slightly incongruous. . . . He smoked almost incessantly and always cigarettes; at that time he rolled them for himself. . . . Conrad's manners were courtly. The word is used here without any implication of stiffness or formality. . . . he always seemed to bring a breath of the Great World. . . . Those of his readers who heard him speak were continually surprised because he could not utter two words in English without betraying that it was not his mother tongue. And there were certain words which he, so to speak, declined to learn.[48]

The Conrads, with Borys, spent Christmas, the last week of 1901, and the first of 1902 with the Fords at Winchelsea. Unfortunately, on 17 December, during his birthday party, Ford had had an unpleasant accident: a chicken bone got stuck in his throat.[49] Conrad, again perplexed by his own problems, lamented to Meldrum:

Seraphina seems to hang about me like a curse. There is always something wrong turning up about that story. . . . It is now a satisfactory piece of work but not quite rearranged and adjusted all through to the changes in action and in the reading of characters which I have introduced. Hueffer was to do all that—instead of which he goes and tries to swallow a chicken bone, gets nearly choked, awfully shaken up, unable to work and so on. I could have wept. . . . The past has been a disastrous year for me. I have wasted—not idled—it away, tinkering here, tinkering there—a little on *Rescue*, more on that fatal *Seraphina* with only three stories (50000 w) finished and *two* others begun lying in a drawer with no profit or pleasure to anybody. . . . I am, as soon as ever I can, going to work for *Maga* at last. My idea is to do some autobiographical matter about Ships, skippers, and an adventure or two. . . . *Youth* style upon the whole. . . . And in this connection do you think Mr B'wood would advance me £50 after I send in say 5000 words.[50]

The preceding constitutes the first known reference to *The Mirror of the Sea*. But what had been planned as a short story evolved along quite different lines. The second of "the two others begun" was never written; Conrad described its subject to Pinker: "The *other* is the story of a barge collision on the Thames and trial in court arising therefrom. A rather funny affair which happened lately."

The same January letter contains a dramatic appeal for help in the form of £40 as one more advance on *Seraphina*. Again, and not for the last time, Conrad used a desperate threat as the final argument: "Really all these anxieties do drive me to the verge of madness—but death would be the best thing. It would pay off all my debts and there would be no question of MS. Really if one hadn't wife and child I don't know—There are also some pressing bills. Damn. And with all this my bodily health is excellent. It is the brain only that is fagged."[51] Pinker, however, refused to budge and instead of money sent a reprimand in which he mentioned Conrad's "failure." Incensed, Conrad reacted with a long letter in which he, in turn, was angry, apologetic, and offended. "Were you as rich as Croesus and as omnipotent as all the editors rolled into one I would not let such a tone pass without resenting it in the most outspoken manner. And don't write me of failure, confound it, because you and I have very different notions of failure." Only Wells's intervention by wire, after he had visited Conrad and seen the manuscripts of *Seraphina* and "To-morrow," induced Pinker to relent.[52] But the crisis was only temporarily suspended. Toward the end of February Conrad suggested that his life insurance policy be bought out by Pinker; Conrad would then pay it off with his stories. Pinker agreed, sending the required sum; the exact amount is not known but it must have been two or three hundred pounds.[53] At any rate that lasted no longer than Blackwood's loan. Conrad must have been paying some of his outstanding debts; by the summer he was again penniless.

On 16 February 1902 he finished "To-morrow" and at once sent it off to Pinker. Conrad presented this short story as "Conrad adapted to the needs of a magazine." Earlier, on 28 January, he had assured Blackwood of his readiness to proceed with the completion of the *Youth* volume, but meanwhile the work on *Seraphina*, whose title was changed in February to *Romance*, continued.[54] The authors visited each other by turns: Ford would come to the Pent or Conrad would go to Winchelsea. They finished writing—or so at least they thought

—on 10 March at Ford's place. "*Seraphina* is finished and gone out of the house she has haunted for this year past. I do really hope it will hit the taste of the street—unless the devil's in it."[55]

The devil, it turned out, did not neglect his duties. Pinker's endeavors to place *Seraphina* for serial publication produced no effect. Conrad meanwhile, in spite of his fits of depression ("I am not fit to live in the world"), possibly aggravated by Blackwood's rejection of "Falk" ("What's wrong with that damn thing? They seem to treat it as though it had the pest"),[56] set out to grapple energetically with his own writings. The first of them was "The End of the Tether," destined for Blackwood and at first bearing a dreary title, suggested by Ford, "The End of the Song." The earliest reference to this story dates from 17 March.[57] On the very same day Conrad announced to Pinker that his next work would be . . . *The Rescue*.[58] Few people could equal Conrad in the art of wishful thinking.

It was not a sign of presumptuousness but, on the contrary, of a constant lack of self-confidence. Conrad was only half joking when he wrote to Ford:

> I have from personal experience a rooted mistrust towards our work—yours and mine—which is under the patronage of a Devil. For indeed unless beguiled by a malicious fiend what man would undertake it? What creature would be mad enough to take upon itself the task of a creator? It is a thing unlawful. *Une chose néfaste*, carrying within its own punishment of toil, unceasing doubt and deception.

The collaboration with Ford, which he occasionally shirked and complained about, helped him overcome the loneliness of the task and of the punishment.

> Those interrupted relations must be taken up again. The cause of my illness is as usual the worry about stuff that won't get itself written. . . . I miss collaboration in a most ridiculous manner. I hope you don't intend dropping me altogether. . . . I don't know how it is but with the end of Seraphina everything in the world seemed to come to an end.[59]

The importance of the moral support Conrad derived from his collaboration with Ford is further shown by his doleful letter to Garnett of 10 June. "I have now lost utterly all faith in myself, all sense of style, all belief in my power of telling the simplest fact in a simple way. . . . I am trying to write now [a thing] called the *End of the Tether*—an inept title to heartbreaking bosh. Pawling's vol. shall follow at a decent interval: four stories of which *Typhoon* is the first and best. I am ashamed of them all; I don't believe either in their popularity or in their merit. Strangely enough it is yet my share of *Romance* . . . that fills me with the least dismay."[60]

Such an attitude might have been expected to make it very difficult for Conrad to defend his work when the need arose; but when William Blackwood pointed out in the course of a conversation that hitherto he had been a loss to the firm, Conrad set forth an elaborate apology.

I admit that after leaving you I remained for some time under the impression of my "worthlessness"; but I beg to assure you that I've never fostered any illusions as to my value. . . . That—labouring against an anxious tomorrow, under the stress of an uncertain future, I have been at times consoled, re-assured and uplifted by a finished page—I'll not deny. . . . For the rest I am conscious of having pursued with pain and labour a calm conception of a definite ideal in a perfect soberness of spirit. . . .

I've rejected the idea of worthlessness and I'll tell you, dear Mr Blackwood, on what ground mainly. It is this—that, given my talent (which appeals to such widely different personalities as W. H. Henley and Bernard Shaw—H. G. Wells and professor Yrgö Hirn of the Finland University—to Maurice Greiffenhagen a painter and to the skipper of a Persian Gulf steamer who wrote to the papers of my "Typhoon"—to the Ed of PMM to a charming old lady in Winchester—given my talent, the fundamental and permanent failure could be only the outcome of an inherent worthlessness of character. Now my character is formed: it has been tried by experience. . . .

[The] incidental remark . . . that the story ["The End of the Tether"] is not fairly begun yet is in a measure correct but, on a large view, beside the point. For, the writing is as good as I can make it (first duty), and in the light of the final incident, the whole story in all its descriptive detail shall fall into its place—acquire its value and its significance. This is my method based on de-liberate conviction. I've never departed from it. I call your own kind self to witness and I beg to instance Karain—Lord Jim (where the method is fully developed)—the last pages of Heart of Darkness where the interview of the man and the girl locks in—as it were—the whole 30000 words of narrative description into one suggestive view of a whole phase of life, and makes of that story something quite on another plane than an anecdote of a man who went mad in the Centre of Africa. . . .

Out of the material of a boys' story I've made *Youth* by the force of the idea expressed in accordance with a strict conception of my method. And however unfavourably it may affect the business in hand I must confess that I shall not depart from my method. . . .

I am *modern*, and I would rather recall Wagner the musician and Rodin the Sculptor who both had to starve a little in their day—and Whistler the painter who made Ruskin the critic foam at the mouth with scorn and indig-nation. They too have arrived. They had to suffer for being "new." And I too hope to find my place in the rear of my betters. But still—my place. My work

shall not be an utter failure because it has the solid basis of a definite intention—first: and next because it is not an endless analysis of affected sentiments but in its essence it is action (strange as this affirmation may sound at
the present time) nothing but action—action observed, felt and interpreted
with an absolute truth to my sensations (which are the basis of art in literature)—action of human beings that will bleed to a prick, and are moving in a
visible world.

This is my creed.[61]

Conrad regarded himself as modern, but his "modernity" was not contempo-
raneous with his times: contrary to the prevailing fashion he was against descriptions of unique states of consciousness; he wanted to be a writer of action,
not of psychological dissections. The remark about absolute fidelity to one's
sensations clearly harks back to his earlier statements; but, true to his own
practice, Conrad brought to the forefront another postulate: to shape every
work consciously in such a way that its overall structure not be determined by
the plot but that, conversely, the plot be subordinated to the overall artistic
purpose.

The unpleasant exchange with Blackwood had concerned Conrad's new financial proposal, or rather request. In desperation, Conrad had decided to
make yet another attempt to put his affairs in order. For the last few months his
situation had been steadily worsening. In March, and again in June, he was
compelled to refuse to leave the Pent, which had been sublet from Ford: "I am
afraid we can't afford to move from here. Simply can not."[62] Ford, responsible
for paying the rent, usually had to do it from his own none too deep pocket. It
is possible, however, that Conrad covered the cost of the repairs that were carried out in the spring of 1902. "The Pent has been done thoroughly outside;
floors mended inside also the defects of inner walls."[63] By the end of May 1902
Conrad was for a while insolvent, but he somehow managed, probably thanks
to a short-term loan, to pay an insurance company his debt of £250, incurred in
January 1901.[64] He was then able to relieve Blackwood of his suretyship. Four
days later he offered to sell the publisher for £350 the copyright of *Lord Jim*
and the *Youth* volume—the latter still incomplete. Blackwood declined, and it
was probably in this context that he spoke of Conrad's being a loss to the firm.
Conrad in turn suggested selling the said copyright for £50 in cash and a loan
of £300—again secured by his life insurance policy. Blackwood turned down
this request as well, commenting rightly that to sign away his copyrights would
have been, in the long run, disadvantageous to Conrad himself.[65]

Conrad, evidently very hard-pressed, immediately approached Heinemann
with the same proposal and simultaneously appealed for help to Galsworthy.[66]
The latter did not disappoint him, but his means were insufficient to do more
than tide Conrad over.[67] Meanwhile, another misfortune occurred.

In April and May Conrad had worked on "The End of the Tether." On 20 May about twenty thousand words were written and, expecting the story to be thirty thousand words long, he promised to finish it by 20 June. On 5 June he made the same prediction as to its length.[68] But on the twenty-third disaster struck. "Last night," he wrote to Ford, "the lamp exploded here and before I could run back into the room the whole round table was in a blaze—Books, cigarettes, MS. alas! The whole second part of 'End of the Tether' ready to go to Edinburgh. The whole! The fire ran in streams and Jess and I threw blankets and danced on them."[69] The fire upset all Conrad's plans for future work, plans that had included the continuation of *The Rescue* and making a start on the "Mediterranean novel."[70]

Did the burned manuscript in fact represent the whole (or "all but" as he wrote to Galsworthy) of "The End of the Tether"? This is doubtful, and for three reasons. First, Conrad usually sent off completed copy piecemeal, particularly to Blackwood, who paid separately for each successive instalment. It is therefore very unlikely that Conrad would have withheld as many as twenty thousand words for any length of time. Second, the alleged re-creation of the text in fact took more time than the writing of the original version: the first version had supposedly been completed in some three months, between the middle of March and 23 June, while the reconstruction of the destroyed manuscript took nearly twice as long, from 24 June until 15 October. Third, "The End of the Tether" is fifty thousand words and thirteen chapters long—not ten chapters as Conrad told Blackwood in his letter about the accident.[71] It is of course possible that the story grew in the process of re-creation, but it is more likely that the destroyed manuscript did not contain the entire story and that Conrad, in arrears as usual, wanted to draw at least one benefit from the disaster: to cover up the traces of his erroneous estimates in respect of both the time taken up by writing and the length of the piece.

All that did nothing to alleviate Conrad's immediate problems but, as in a Western, relief came when things were at their worst: at the beginning of July the Royal Literary Fund awarded Conrad a grant of £300.[72] It was probably only a coincidence that the grant was made soon after the accident with the lamp, but the news about it might have speeded up the committee's decision.[73] Several documents recommending Conrad for the grant are extant: Sidney S. Pawling's memorandum; an outline of Conrad's life written by Edmund Gosse, the secretary of the Fund; and Henry James's two letters, one private and one official, addressed to Gosse. Gosse's sketch of Conrad's life fairly bristles with inaccuracies: "Born in Warsaw. Parents sent to Siberia. Escaped to England. . . . Commanding large trading vessels to all parts of the world," and so forth. Both Pawling and Gosse attribute Conrad's resignation from a career at sea to the weakening of his eyesight. This last information could have been supplied only by Conrad himself; the only supporting evidence consists of the motif of failing vision in "The End of the Tether," and also of the fact that Conrad was greatly interested and knowledgeable in optics.[74] Both recommendations mention that Conrad was paying the fees for his sisters-in-law at a school near Windsor.

The terms of James's support are of great interest. In his private letter he wrote, "I lose not an hour in responding to your request about Conrad—whom I had not in the least known to be in the state you mention. It horrifies me more than I can say, and I applaud to the echo your attempt to do something for him." James's official letter in support of granting Conrad financial assistance brimmed over with eloquent praise of Conrad's work: "one of the most interesting and striking of the novelists of the new generation," "real literature, of a distinguished sort," "*The Nigger of the Narcissus* is in my opinion the very finest and strongest picture of the sea and sea-life that our language possesses— the masterpiece in a whole class; and *Lord Jim* runs it very close." However, as Ian Watt observes, "James's praise is curiously qualified by the distance of his tone."[75] The remark that Conrad's sea stories "approximate more than anything we have to the truth and beauty of the French Pierre Loti" would have certainly pained Conrad, while the modern reader may wonder at the superficiality of James's judgment. Both James's letters reveal his sense of the social distance separating him from Conrad, whom he regarded primarily as an exotic foreigner and former sailor. In writing "the case seems to me unique and peculiarly worthy of recognition," James surely implies that the value of Conrad's work lay mainly in its singularity; and a remark made later, "poor queer man," seems to betray the true nature of his attitude toward the author of *The Nigger*.[76]

Temporarily liberated from the pressure of debts and immediate expenses, Conrad spent the following few months writing or rewriting "The End of the Tether." The instalments were supposed to be ready by definite dates, as the first part had already appeared in the July issue of *Blackwood's Magazine*. Conrad raced against time, sending the copy to Edinburgh—usually at the last minute, occasionally so late that he had to forgo the proofs or even the typing out of his manuscript. Again he had to apologize for delays and for the overgrowth of the story, which certainly suffered from the conditions of its birth. The tale of Captain Whalley, who trusts in God and in man's natural goodness and who decides to conceal the deterioration of his sight to continue the support of his daughter, is both dramatic and moving—but it is also decidedly long-drawn-out and verbose, overburdened with authorial comments, and flattened by a liberal dose of melodrama.

I suspect that these faults may be ascribed to Ford. In his memoirs Ford tells how he helped Conrad in the reconstruction of the destroyed manuscript, picking up his pen whenever the author's own strength flagged. Conrad apparently even rented a house near Ford's to facilitate their cooperation. "At two in the morning the mare . . . was saddled. . . . The stable-boy was to ride to the junction with the manuscript and catch the six in the morning mail train. The soup kept hot; the writers wrote. By three the writer had done all that he could in his room. He went across the road to where Conrad was still at it. Conrad said: 'For God's sake. Another half hour: just finishing." And so forth in the same sensational style.[77] Since the original manuscript of "The End of the Tether" has not been preserved, it is impossible to establish the real extent of Ford's participation, although the fact itself is indisputable.

Oddly enough, Jessie Conrad, herself fond of dramatic effects, makes no mention of the disaster caused by the fire. According to her, Ford's role was only passive and the greater part of the story "was written against time in a little cottage in Winchelsea, near the house of the Hueffers. Conrad would remain writing far into the night . . . refreshed at intervals by Ford Madox Hueffer, who would appear from time to time armed with a bottle and a few sandwiches or biscuits and cheese. Almost at daybreak he would retire, worn out, and I would take up the work with the typewriter."[78] In actual fact, however, Conrad worked mostly at the Pent. All in all the Conrads made only two or three visits to Winchelsea for a total of three or four weeks, and the ill-starred story was at last finished there on about 15 October.[79] Actually, it was only almost finished, because Conrad made some additions to the last pages, in proofreading before he wrote, "Now the story is properly finished as originally contemplated."[80]

Apart from Ford and Elsie, Conrad saw hardly anyone at that time. Even his contacts with Garnett became looser; Galsworthy he corresponded with but met only infrequently. "Four or five months ago G.B.S. towed by Wells came to see me reluctantly and I nearly bit him." Shaw shocked Conrad on this occasion with stories about his drunkard father.[81] The unsuccessful visit is also mentioned by Jessie. Wells in his autobiography describes another scene characteristic of all three participants and of his own attitude toward Conrad:

> When Conrad first met Shaw in my house, Shaw talked with his customary freedoms. "You know, my dear fellow, your books won't *do*"—for some Shavian reason I have forgotten—and so forth.
>
> I went out of the room and suddenly found Conrad on my heels, swift and white-faced. "Does that man want to *insult* me?" he demanded.
>
> The provocation to say "yes" and assist at the subsequent duel was very great, but I overcame it. "It's humour," I said, and took Conrad out into the garden to cool. One could always baffle Conrad by saying "humour." It was one of our damned English tricks he had never learnt to tackle.

Perhaps indeed he never learned it, but such occasions must have made him aware of his ineluctable foreignness. In turn Wells himself was taken in by the story that Conrad had tried to persuade Ford to call Wells to a duel; a typical Fordian fabrication.[82]

Not only Blackwood but also Ford had waited impatiently for the completion of "The End of the Tether," since *Romance* had to be shortened to give it a chance of serialization. Pinker had been insisting on cutting it since May,[83] but Ford procrastinated in order to give Conrad time to finish "The End of the Tether." Only on 26 November was Conrad able to inform Pinker that after "four days and one whole night" they shortened *Romance* almost by half, adding, "All that's likely to be most popular is preserved."[84] To no avail: no periodical wanted to publish the novel.

At the end of October and beginning of November Conrad and Jessie had a few days' break in London. Conrad described it as a week of "dissipation," but apart from meeting Galsworthy, he probably spent most of his time in libraries.[85] In spite of several declarations that from now on he would continue the work on the novel begun six years earlier which he "must" finish before March, it seems he did nothing with *The Rescue*.[86] Eventually, he sent it to Ford pleading for . . . rescue. In vain.[87]

Conrad's imagination, which in June 1902 prompted him to make plans for "a novel of intrigue with the Mediterranean, coast and sea, for the scene," now moved him, as if casually, to South America. Towards the end of November he began mentioning a new story. *Nostromo* was originally planned as a rather short piece, about the length of "Karain."[88] In several letters Conrad mentioned that the length of thirty to forty thousand words (that of "Heart of Darkness" for instance) suited him best.[89] On 26 November he informed Pinker of having started on a "short story." At the beginning of January he reported that he had been working on it since Christmas.[90]

Meanwhile, *Youth—A Narrative and Two Other Stories*, dedicated to Jessie and comprising in addition to the title piece "Heart of Darkness" and "The End of the Tether," at last appeared (on 13 November). The reception was mixed: from enthusiastic *Spectator* (Hugh Clifford) to hostile *Speaker* (John Masefield). On the whole the first two pieces were rated better, although "Heart of Darkness" caused the critics some problems. The *Manchester Guardian* deemed it necessary to stress that "it must not be supposed that Mr Conrad makes attack upon colonisation, expansion, even upon Imperialism." Some judgments were strikingly contradictory: the *Times Literary Supplement* praised Conrad's zest, the picturesqueness of the narrative and the vividness of descriptions—precisely the qualities that Masefield found lacking.[91] No one predicted popularity, but *Youth* sold slightly better than *Lord Jim*: the first two editions (November 1902 and February 1903) amounted to 4,200 copies.[92]

For Conrad the most important reactions to the *Youth* volume were three in number: the long, intelligent, and well-balanced article by Garnett in *Academy and Literature* (which considerably influenced later criticism); the equally extensive and friendly review in the *Athenaeum* by A. J. Dawson; and Gissing's letter to Edward Clodd, who showed it to Conrad. The only perceptive analysis of "Heart of Darkness" was done by Garnett, who recognized the fundamental theme of the story as the "deterioration of the white man's morale, when he is let loose from European restraint, and planted down in the tropics as an 'emissary of light' armed to the teeth, to make trade profits out of the 'subject races.'" Garnett was also the first critic to compare Conrad with Dostoyevsky. Dawson's unsigned article, although more general, stressed Conrad's ability to link intellectual and moral incisiveness with creating and sustaining an atmosphere. As for the novelist George Gissing, dying of tuberculosis at Saint-Jean-de-Luz, he wrote to his friend, "No man at present writing fiction has such grip of reality, such imaginative vigour, and such wonderful command of language, as Joseph Conrad. I think him a *great* writer—there's no other word. And, when one considers his personal history, the English of his books is something like a miracle." [93]

Praise made Conrad happy but did not dispel his wary self-criticism. In his warm letter of thanks to Gissing, whom he had met once at Wells's several months before, he confessed, "After forty it is easier to spurn away blame than to embrace the fair form of praise. There is a talking spectre, a ghostly voice whispering incessantly in one's ear of the narrow circle circumscribing all effort, of the shortness of one's vision and of the poverty of one's thought." [94] And replying to Ernest Dawson (the critic's brother), who had also mentioned "greatness," he wrote, "I doubt if greatness can be attained now in imaginative prose work. When it comes, it will be in a new form; in a form for which we are not ripe as yet. Till the hour strikes and the man appears, we must plod in the beaten track." [95] Conrad's modest disclaimer need not to be taken too literally; he surely did explore unbeaten tracks, and was not unaware of the novelty of his endeavors.

The approaching holidays provoked Conrad to one of his rare and unpredictable utterances about religion. This time he was jokingly blasphemous: "J. [George] B'wood sent me word that the thing sells decently and that if the Christmas does not kill it or if. . . .

"It's strange how I always, from the age of fourteen, disliked the Christian religion, its doctrines, ceremonies and festivals. Presentiment that some day it will work my undoing, I suppose. Now it's quite on the cards that the Bethlehem legend will kill the epic [*Youth*], and the bogie tale ["Heart of Darkness"], and the touching, tender, noble captain Newcome—Colonel Whalley thing. Hard. Isn't it? And the most galling feature is that nobody—not a single Bishop of them—believes in it. The business in the stable isn't convincing; whereas my atmosphere (vide reviews) can be positively breathed." [96] One sees at a glance that Conrad had read a great deal of Anatole France.

In December 1902 Conrad felt so unwell, dispirited, and dissatisfied with himself that he was unable to work. On 23 December he left with Jessie and Borys for Winchelsea, where they planned to stay a week or longer. But Conrad was still sick, and they returned home after only a few days. [97] The next occasion for celebration occurred in mid-January: a joint birthday party for Christina Hueffer and Borys. The plans for the festivities survive in two amusing letters by

Conrad. They show that in spite of Jessie's constantly smoldering irritation with the Hueffers and Conrad's continuous financial worries and difficulties with writing, the two families shared moments of complete relaxation amidst children's games and elaborate make-believe.[98]

Little is known about everyday life at Pent Farm. Jessie's recollections, crammed with figments and inaccuracies, are so rich in dramatized emotions and so poor in factual data that they cannot provide a basis for reconstructing the ordinary run of things. We learn more from Borys's short and not always reliable memoirs, but his recollections refer to later years, except for a few bits of information about relations with Jessie's family—a subject she herself hardly ever broached. According to Borys, of all Jessie's siblings (four sisters and four brothers), his father liked only Ethel, seventh in order of age, who "acted from time to time as voluntary, unpaid governess to her youngest brother my Uncle Frank, her young sister Nellie, and myself." Conrad was also fond of Jessie's old aunt, Miss Alice Sex: "She was highly intelligent and a brilliant conversationalist; and I believe she was the only person entirely unconnected with the literary world who was ever invited to join in those long and animated discussions behind the closed door of his room, which often lasted till the small hours of the morning." Neither father nor son felt any affection toward Jessie's mother, "a grim-featured old lady who habitually wore an expression of disgust and disapproval which seemed to me to be entirely in keeping with her character." She, in turn, was not "upon the best of terms" with her son-in-law—"In fact they detested one another."

On one occasion Mrs. George met with an unpleasant accident at the Pent which "must have put the final seal upon the antipathy which already existed between them." One day at dawn Grandmother George suffered from indigestion:

> The toilet facilities at the Pent were housed in a separate building of considerable size; having been designed by the architect, if any, upon what one might describe as social and family lines inasmuch as it provided adult accommodation for two and, at an appropriately lower level, juvenile accommodation for one. It also possessed a heavy oak door fitted with two iron hasps through which the occupant, or occupants, were supposed to pass a piece of wood, thus forming a crude bolt. It was towards this building that Grandmama directed her steps, but her movements attracted my Father's attention as he sat writing at his desk. He immediately seized his rifle and rushed out of the front door at about the same moment as Grandmama emerged from the back entrance. Seeing no sign of an intruder, he proceeded to make a reconnaissance. Grandmama must, in her turn, have heard the noise of his approach and fled, with the result that they would appear to have made one or more circuits of the house before Grandmama recovered her wits sufficiently to run

for shelter in the toilet building. Unfortunately, she omitted to make use of the wooden bolt and my Father, having as he thought, run the intruder to earth, burst into the building shouting: "Come out you—Damn you."[99]

In spite of primitive sanitation, considerable distance from the town and shops, and difficulties with putting people up for the night, Jessie later came to regard the years spent at the Pent as the happiest of her married life.[100] Conrad did not share her view. In his mind the Pent must have been associated primarily with incessant grind and mounting debts. But it was at Pent Farm that Conrad wrote the books that establish his greatness and determine his position—his indispens-ability—in the history of twentieth-century European literature. These books were born in anguish and toil comparable only to Flaubert's creative agony. But Flaubert did not have to borrow money to keep body and soul together.

Luckily for himself, Conrad was as yet unaware that the book he was begin-ning would be his longest and hardest to write. The background (and partly the action) of his previous novels and short stories had been mostly based on his own experiences and memory. The characters had been relatively few and the area in which the action occurred, though large geographically, had been fairly narrow socially. Now, in *Nostromo*, with his imagination sustained by barely a few days' personal observations and by extensive reading, Conrad was creating a huge country, its history, all social classes, political parties, and over twenty protagonists. For a writer who regarded fidelity to the real world as his princi-pal duty, the effort required was indeed exorbitant.

At first Conrad joked that the book would be "silly and saleable."[101] He had hoped to sign simultaneous contracts for serial and book rights, but the pub-lishers (Harper) agreed only to a book edition.[102] At any rate, Conrad was ap-prehensive about having to meet set deadlines and had ensured in advance that Ford would be ready to "stand by and save an instalment or two should I be suddenly laid out on my back by gout—say."[103] In January 1903 *Nostromo* was planned as a long short story (thirty-five thousand words); but by March it was to be a short novel of sixty to seventy thousand words—to be finished by the end of June: "If I can finish N in 3 months I am saved for a time. And if then I can finish Rescue by Dec. next I am saved altogether. The question is—can I make the effort. Is it in me"—Conrad confided in Ford, asking in the same letter for a copy of Alexandre Dumas' biography of Garibaldi, echoes of which can be heard even in the earliest chapters of *Nostromo*.[104] His misgivings proved closer to the mark than his projects, this time for dental reasons. Conrad's fear of dentists—recalled by both sons—and the resulting neglect of his teeth used to bring about sporadic attacks of pain, inflammation, and swelling; these in-fections had a disastrous effect on his entire organism; nervous tension sought release in episodes of gout; and one such episode prostrated Conrad in mid-March.

Romance was at last accepted by the publishers Smith Elder. And even then Conrad had to defend the text against cuts, traveling to London to support Ford in the negotiations. In April Ford came to the Pent and together they drudged at the proofs.[105]

It was probably at about that time that Hugh Clifford succeeded in "luring him [Conrad] forth to a luncheon at the Wellington Club, . . . to meet Thomas Hardy, Edmund Gosse, Edward Clodd, Frank Swettenham, Sir John Rodger, Sidney Brookes, Arthur Legge and Sir Maurice Cameron, all of whom were ardent admirers of his work."[106] Of these, Conrad already knew Clodd and Gosse, at least from correspondence; among the others he probably maintained later contacts only with Swettenham, the great expert on Malaya.

In another London club, the Savile, Conrad met Henry Newbolt, a respected historian and poet, and an admirer of *Lord Jim*. Newbolt remembered the encounter:

> The man himself did not disappoint me. One thing struck me at once—the extraordinary difference between his expression in profile and when looked at full face. In both aspects it was an oriental face: but while the profile was aquiline and commanding, in the front view the broad brow, wide-apart eyes and full lips produced the effect of an intellectual calm and even at times of a dreaming philosophy. Then came a sharp surprise. As we sat in our little half-circle round the fire, and talked on anything and everything, I saw a third Conrad emerge—an artistic self, sensitive and restless to the last degree. The more he talked the more quickly he consumed his cigarettes, rolling them so fast one after another that the fingers of both hands were stained a deep yellow almost as far as the palms. And presently, when I asked him why he was leaving London after a stay of only two days, he replied that he could never be more than a day or two in London, because the crowd in the streets so terrified him. "Terrified? By that dull stream of obliterated faces?" He leaned forward with both hands raised and clenched. "Yes, terrified: I see their personalities all leaping out at me like *tigers*!" He acted the tiger well enough almost to terrify his hearers: but the moment after he was talking again wisely and soberly as if he were an average Englishman with not an irritable nerve in his body.[107]

Conrad's lively contacts with publishers and their advisers were now being replaced by his dealings with Pinker. Even to Blackwood Conrad sent an official letter informing him—without any reference to the debt and to their years of friendly association—that from now on all financial matters would be dealt with by the agent. Not surprisingly, the patient creditor felt hurt.[108]

The volume *Typhoon, and Other Stories*, dedicated to R. B. Cunninghame Graham, was published on 22 April 1903. Two days later Olive Garnett noted in her diary, "Arranged to meet Ford at Gatti's; found Conrad with him, come up to town for the day. Conrad genial; drank the health of Typhoon in coffee." [109] The book was received well, at times even enthusiastically. It caused fewer misunderstandings than Conrad's previous works, although some critics had rather astonishing associations (for example, with Tolstoy and Gorki!); and a few reviewers were confused by the diversity of contents and atmosphere of the stories. M. H. Vorse of the *Critic* pointed out that Conrad harmed his popularity by holding himself aloof from the literary and journalistic milieu, avoiding interviewers and all forms of advertising.[110] Conrad valued his good reputation among his fellow writers and fostered it; Gissing, for instance, wrote to Wells, "Conrad sent me his *Typhoon* volume, and I was delighted with it. He is a strong man." [111] But apart from this, Conrad, very conscious of the uniqueness of his biography and afraid of becoming a public curiosity, did his utmost to preserve his privacy. This was no doubt partly responsible for the fact that, despite being hailed by the critics as an important writer of established reputation and authority, Conrad remained largely unknown to the wider public.

In the tight circle of his close literary friends, Conrad held the position of a master. He advised Elsie Hueffer how to translate Maupassant: "There are three requisites for a good translation of M. Imprimis she must be idiomatic, secundo she must be idiomatic, and lastly she must be idiomatic. For in the idiom is the *clearness* of a language and the language's force and its picturesqueness—by which last I mean the picture-producing power of arranged words." [112] He corrected Ford's introduction to the volume of Elsie's translations, criticizing his showy and careless wording.[113] In the case of Galsworthy he played a more substantial role by reading and commenting on his friend's manuscripts and giving advice on style and construction. He helped choose the title *The Island Pharisees*; consoled Galsworthy when the novel was turned down by Blackwood; and ultimately recommended it successfully to Heinemann.[114] Frederick Karl says rightly that Conrad may have been aware of the contrast between his own desperate battling with creative difficulties and the "somewhat dilettantish struggle with literature" of Galsworthy—a writer of clearly defined and consciously planned themes, aims, and artistic means. But Karl is surely mistaken when he claims that Conrad lacked genuine interest in his friend's work.[115] Even the sense of his own literary superiority did not rule out the watchful and loyal attention he unsparingly devoted to Galsworthy's career as a writer.

It was quite natural, however, that the problems of others should pale in comparison with his own agonies over *Nostromo*. Conrad was crushed by the size of the novel, and the strain on his imagination consumed his entire mental and physical energy. At the time of writing *Nostromo* Conrad gave the impression of someone being wasted by a constant loss of blood, and from among his statements about his ongoing work one could collect a poignant anthology on authorial suffering.

13 May: "I am here fixed to slave and groan for months. Harpers got the book of which *not a quarter* yet is written. I am indeed appalled at myself when I think what rotten contemptible bosh it must and shall be."

8 July: "I've sent off up to 25000 words yesterday in a storm of toothache. My very neck is stiff with it but I am going on without stoppage."

22 August: "To work in the conditions which are, I suppose, the outcome of my character mainly, is belittling, it is demoralizing. I fight against demoralization, of which fight I bear the brunt and my friends bear the cost. . . . I feel myself strangely growing into a sort of outcast. A mental and moral outcast. I hear nothing—I think of nothing—I reflect upon nothing—I cut myself off." "I have never worked so hard before—with so much anxiety."[116]

One day when he had sent off a "half" (in fact only one-fourth) of the text and taken a brief respite from his labors, Conrad felt particularly aware of his loneliness and needed to confide in someone: "So there, half is ready—and I am half dead and quite stupid," he wrote to Davray. "Loneliness is overtaking me: it absorbs me. I see nothing, I read nothing. It is like a kind of tomb which is also hell where one must write, write, write. One wonders if it is worthwhile—because in the end one is never satisfied and never finished."[117]

A visit from William Rothenstein provided a welcome diversion. Though only thirty-two, he was already a well-known portrait painter and asked Conrad to sit for him; in the summer of 1903 he produced the earliest known portrait of Conrad. Conrad liked the painting, now in the National Portrait Gallery in London, very much.[118] The visit marked the beginning of a lasting friendship. Rothenstein had wide interests, money, and many connections; on several occasions he helped Conrad in his financial troubles. Initially, however, it was Conrad who gave businesslike advice, suggesting Pinker as the painter's agent. "I hold that an artist should obtain the uttermost farthing that can be got for his work—not on the ground of material satisfaction but simply for the sake of leisure which, it seems to me, is a necessary condition of good work."[119] There was an undercurrent of bitterness beneath these lofty words: Conrad was convinced, and no doubt rightly, that if he had some time to spare his own writing would have improved.

Rothenstein later recounted his first impressions:

With his piercing eyes and keen, deeply-lined bearded face, in some ways he looked like the sea captain, but his nervous manner, his rapid, excited speech, his restlessness, his high shoulders, did not suggest the sailor. I accepted him at once as an artist; never, I thought, had I met anyone with a quicker apprehension, with such warmth of intellectual sympathy, sympathy which came half-way to meet everything one said. . . .

There was always an element of strain in Conrad—an excitability, which may have been individual, or may have been Polish—I cannot say. . . . While

Conrad was extremely courteous and understanding by nature, his nerves sometimes made him aggressive, almost violent; and like most sensitive men, he was strongly affected, either favourably or disagreeably, by others. . . . His gallantry to Jessie was a true sailor's chivalry. What others had, she should have too. . . . when he liked people he would admit no faults; indeed, he was inclined to flatter—perhaps this was a Polish trait—both in speaking and writing.[120]

The work on *Nostromo* was now and then interrupted by the proofreading of *Romance*, finished by Conrad and Ford in September. Ford added a rhymed epigraph to the novel, dedicated to Elsie and Jessie.[121] At the last moment Conrad hotly disputed Ford's suggestion to put the dates of writing the book as 1896–1903: "It opens a wide door to disparagement to anybody minded for that game. . . . The apparent want of proportion will be jumped upon. Sneers at collaboration—sneers at those two men who took six years to write 'this very ordinary tale'—whereas R. L. S[tevenson] singlehanded produced his masterpieces etc., etc. . . . Moreover we did not collaborate six years at that. We began in Dec. 1900 and finished in July 1902 really. The rest is delay; horrid delay—because we could not get ourselves printed sooner. Why intrude our private affairs for the grin of innumerable swine? . . . Even Flaubert was not six years writing Mme Bovary which *was* an epoch making volume."[122]

Romance came out on 16 October. The reception was kind but on the whole rather cool: the critics were unanimous in blaming the faults on Ford; the public remained impassive.[123] Before the dreams of the two partners about wealth and popularity were finally dispelled, Conrad had already tried to distance himself from *Romance* as if to guard himself against the possibility of failure:

I consider *Romance* as something of no importance; I collaborated on it at a time when it was impossible for me to do anything else. . . . There were moments when both Hueffer and I were very gay while working on this construction. Nevertheless we took pains with the technical side of the work. You will admit that it is well written.

. . . H. and I wanted to try our hand in view of a serious novel which we plan to write some day. As a pivot for the action we conceived a picture by an old and famous painter, and the base, wicked intrigues surrounding a great man who had been successful but just because he was a supreme artist remained misunderstood. A great deal can be made out of a subject such as this, expressing the thoughts on art which hover over us and on the materialism which creeps into life. . . . H. has a well-founded knowledge of these problems thanks to a family tradition, and also to his own research, and also de visu for he had been a very close friend of Ford Madox Brown during the last six years of his life. I am telling you this, my dear Sir, under the seal of secrecy.[124]

The preceding is the only reference we know to this unrealized project of a "serious novel" about a painter. The reason Conrad mentioned it at all—perhaps indeed the source of the whole idea—is probably that he was desperately tired by his wrestling with *Nostromo*. Again he unburdened himself to Galsworthy: "The book ought to have been finished by now. Had it been so I could have existed; now it seems as if the thing had gone too far to be retrieved. . . . I exhort myself dishonestly to write anything, anything, any rubbish—and even *that* I cannot do just as if I were cursed with a delicate conscience. But no! It's powerlessness and nothing else alas!"[125] He spread before Pinker and himself alluring projects for another, "easy" book—the later *Mirror of the Sea*, reeling off a series of titles for planned sketches: "Gales of Wind," "Up Anchor," "Yards and Masks," "The Cut of the Sails," "The Web of Ropes," "Old Timbers," "Round the Compass," "The Chance of Landfalls," and so on.[126]

Those were, however, only titles and dreams. The everyday reality was dominated by the struggle for each successive thousand words that were paid for by successive attacks of gout. Every few weeks Conrad's health would fail, and by the end of November 1903 he was again in a state of dejection. "Your good letter found me in bed," he wrote to J. M. Barrie, "and though I've crawled out of it today I remain still recumbent and am writing this on a pad with a horrid fountain pen. Another week lost out of the few left to me for the silly book I am writing now—if the thing can be called a book at all. I am afraid it shall be more in the nature of printed matter. A certain amount of cheap sincerity there is in it, some shadow of intention too (which no one will see), and even an artistic! purpose—but all this makes for failure, since I've never felt that I had my subject in the palm of my hand: I've been always catching at it all along; and I shall be just catching at it to the end. That state of feeling leads one to sheer twaddle."

To Galsworthy Conrad gave a less florid but more precise description of his condition: "No work done. No spring left to grapple with it. Everything looks black, but I suppose that will wear off, and, anyhow, I am trying to keep despair under. Nevertheless I feel myself losing my footing in deep waters. They are lapping about my hips.

"My dear fellow, it is not so much the frequency of these gout attacks, but I feel so beastly ill between, ill in body and mind. It has never been so before. Impossible to write—while the brain riots in incoherent images. It is sometimes quite alarming."[127]

He continued to work: there was no alternative. A month later he confessed to Harriet Capes, a Roman Catholic writer who specialized in children's books, "My mind struggles with a strange sort of torpor, struggles desperately while the sands are running out. That is the most terrifying thought of all. They are running out—and there is nothing done; nothing of what one desires to do."[128]

Not surprisingly, on 31 December he summed up the completed year in one word—"disastrous."[129]

Twice during that gloomy autumn the echoes of his Polish and African past reached Conrad. Kazimierz Waliszewski, a Polish historian living in Paris, asked him for biographical data and copies of books in connection with a major article he was going to write about his fellow countryman turned English writer. Conrad answered readily, and two months of correspondence ensued. He declared, "I consider it a great happiness and honour to return to my home country under your guidance (if I may express myself thus). And if you are prepared to take my word for it and say that during the course of all my travels round the world I never, in mind or heart, separated myself from my country, then I may surely be accepted there as a compatriot, in spite of my writing in English."[130] It is worth adding that he indeed wanted to be known in Poland; for example, he asked Blackwood to send a copy of *Youth* to *Chimera*, the leading Polish literary magazine at that time.[131]

In another letter to Waliszewski, Conrad confessed, "Both at sea and on land my point of view is English, from which the conclusion should not be drawn that I have become an Englishman. That is not the case. Homo duplex has in my case more than one meaning. . . .

"The circle of my readers is very small. Life has now become much harder. I write with difficulty, slowly, crossing out constantly. What a foul profession!"[132]

In October Conrad had a visit from Roger Casement, who was then preparing a report on the situation in the Congo, sharply critical of Leopold II's administration; it was published on 15 February 1904 by the Foreign Office. The authorities of the Congo Free State, wishing to refute in advance Casement's charges, maintained among other things that the cutting off of hands for minor offenses was not a colonial practice but a result of native customs. Conrad confirmed Casement's accusations: "It is an extraordinary thing that the conscience of Europe which seventy years ago has put down the slave trade on humanitarian grounds tolerates the Congo State today. It is as if the moral clock had been put back many hours. . . . now I suppose we are busy with other things; too much involved in great affairs to take up cudgels for humanity, decency and justice."[133] Although Conrad refrained from joining the anti-Leopold campaign ("I am only a wretched novelist inventing wretched stories and not even up to that miserable game"), he gave Casement encouragement and an eloquent recommendation to Graham: "He is a limpid personality . . . I have always thought that some particle of Las Casas' soul had found refuge in his indefatigable body. . . . He could tell you things! Things I've tried to forget; things I never did know."[134] On 3 January Casement visited Conrad at the Pent and passed a "delightful day."[135]

The new year, 1904, brought a distinct improvement of health and a sudden spurt of activity. Conrad continued his work on *Nostromo*—its first instalment was supposed to appear on 29 January in the popular *T. P.'s Weekly* (Conrad agreed to have the text shortened and renounced reading proofs). At the same time he began writing the "sea sketches" that were to become *The Mirror of the Sea*.[136] On 17 January he left with his family for London. They took a flat in Kensington, at 17 Gordon Place. Undoubtedly this was a costly venture and far beyond their means, particularly since Conrad's bank, Watson & Co., failed and Conrad was faced with the need to pay off his considerable overdraft of nearly £200.[137] What lured him to London? There were probably two reasons, reinforcing each other. Conrad wanted to be close to Ford, on whose moral support and literary help he counted, particularly with *The Mirror of the Sea*. Also, as he was emerging from depression, he certainly longed for a change in his surroundings and daily routine.

In Ford's case the move to London was also a financially risky step; for him too the principal motive was a desire for change, for broader social contacts and the stimulation of the metropolis.[138] Ford's enthusiasm could easily have influenced Conrad; the flat he rented was near the house taken by the Hueffers. There were even plans for the families to do their cooking jointly, in spite of Conrad's obvious and—as it turned out—well-justified misgivings, which were certainly shared by Jessie, who always felt ill at ease in the artistic and intellectual atmosphere cultivated by Ford and Elsie.[139] Jessie's antipathy toward that couple, which is quite evident in both her books of memoirs, could have arisen merely from a legitimate sense of her own inferiority of interests, education, talent, and social polish; from time to time the Hueffers no doubt aggravated matters by letting her feel it.

A few days after their arrival in London, Jessie had an accident that had disastrous long-lasting consequences: she fell on the pavement, damaging both her knees.[140] Undoubtedly, her considerable weight as well as earlier problems with her legs made the case serious. She had hurt one of her knees at the age of sixteen, and apparently as early as 1896 she suffered from it again; she had also had a painful fall in March 1903.[141] Medical help and intensive treatment, at first only external, were now necessary. It was the beginning of Jessie's permanent disability.

But the accident and the resulting troubles did not weigh Conrad down; nor did the consequent expenses. It seems that following his period of depression, he was in a state of euphoria. He led an active—for him—social life, both with the Hueffers and independently. He frequently met his recent acquaintance Sidney Colvin, the director of the British Museum library and an influential critic of art and literature. At Colvin's instigation and with Ford's considerable assistance, Conrad transformed his short story "To-morrow" into a one-act play, *One Day More*.[142] Conrad also sat for a portrait painted by George Sauter,

Galsworthy's brother-in-law. With Galsworthy himself, whose study was near-by, there was an almost daily exchange of visits.[143]

Conrad also wrote a short piece, "A Glance at Two Books," which for some reason was never corrected and published in his lifetime.[144] The article was in praise of Galsworthy's *Island Pharisees* and W. H. Hudson's *Green Mansions*, rather paradoxically joined to an ironical criticism of the English tradition of novel writing: "The national English novelist seldom regards his work—the exercise of his Art—as an achievement of active life by which he will produce certain definite effects upon the emotions of his readers, but simply as an instinctive, often unreasoned, outpouring of his own emotions. He does not go about building up his book with a precise intention and a steady mind. It never occurs to him that a book is a deed, that the writing of it is an enterprise as much as the conquest of a colony. He has no such clear conception of his craft. Writing from a full heart, he liberates his soul for the satisfaction of his own sentiment; and when he has finished the scene he is at liberty to strike his forehead and exclaim: 'This is genius!'"[145] This is not quite fair; Conrad, for instance, overlooks Jane Austen. He takes up the position of an impartial authority entitled to pass judgment. The idea that a "book is a deed" refers, consciously or not, to Polish Romantic writers. There is no trace in his article of his usual uncertainty and lack of self-confidence. On the contrary: coming from a foreigner whose own writing constituted a negation of the English tradition described above, Conrad's statements sound almost impudent. Perhaps it was this that made him refrain from publishing the piece.

Two weeks earlier Olive Garnett, who attended one of Ford's literary parties, recorded Conrad's words: "I am at the top of the tree."[146] The words reflect the same consciousness of his artistic eminence as "A Glance at Two Books." Conrad's few letters written during his stay in London (to Colvin, Waliszewski, Wells) also express a mood different from the one he was in toward the close of the previous year. Even his lamentations are on a lighter note. He told Wells of his work:

> I've been working at *Nostromo*, besides writing a play in one act (based on my To-morrow story) on the suggestion of S. Colvin, who has been very friendly. Another acquaintance which I owe to you, my dear fellow, in the long list of your good offices.
>
> I've started a series of sea sketches and have sent out P[inker] on the hunt to place them. This must save me. I've discovered that I can dictate that sort of bosh without effort at the rate of 3,000 words in four hours. Fact! The only thing now is to sell it to a paper and then make a book of the rubbish. Hang!
>
> So in the day Nostromo and, from 11 p.m. to 1 a.m., dictation.[147]

Ford presented the situation in a different light: "Indeed a great part of his *Mirror of the Sea* was just his talk which the writer took down in a shorthand of his own extemporising, recalling to Conrad, who was then in a state of great depression, various passages of his own relating."

In his later recollections Ford put the matter more floridly and dramatically:

> *The Mirror and the Sea* and *A Personal Record* were mostly written by my hand from Conrad's dictation. Whilst he was dictating them, I would recall incidents to him—I mean incidents of his past life which he had told me but which did not come freely back to his mind because at the time he was mentally ill, in desperate need of money, and, above all, sceptical as to the merits of the reminiscential form which I had suggested to him. The fact is I could make Conrad write at periods when his despair and fatigue were such that in no other way would it have been possible to him. He would be lying on the sofa or pacing the room, railing at life and literature as practised in England, and I would get a writing pad and pencil and, whilst he was still raving, would interject: "Now then, what was it you were saying about coming up the Channel and nearly running over a fishing boat that suddenly appeared under your bows?" and gradually there would come "Landfalls and Departures."[148]

Neither in this essay (which Conrad began and perhaps completed himself at the Pent) nor in any other do we find the scene on the Channel, but this is a detail of minor importance beside the exaggeration in the whole picture. However, although Ford as usual magnified his part—nine out of fifteen essays in *The Mirror of the Sea*, including the two best, were written in his absence—his contribution to the six earliest essays ("Landfalls and Departures," "Emblems of Hope," "The Fine Art," "Cobwebs and Gossamer," "The Weight of the Burden," and "Overdue and Missing") cannot be doubted. I suppose that the idea for the whole series came from Ford; in terms of literary technique the book is more Fordian than Conradian. In addition to supplying the idea Ford probably helped Conrad spin out the parts by asking questions or suggesting the development of a theme. At any rate, Conrad felt under an obligation to share with Ford the fees received for the publication of the first essays in periodicals.[149]

But even apart from Ford's influence, *The Mirror of the Sea* is a novelty among Conrad's books: for the first time he conceived a volume devoid of artistic ambitions, neither designed to develop his craft as a writer nor to continue the confrontation of moral and political ideas with observed reality that characterizes his earlier work. It is true that Conrad's ideas for short stories did occasionally have a more popular and anecdotal character than his finished pieces; and it seems that in his search for subjects he was at times motivated by prospects of salability and popularity; but as soon as Conrad set about the task, other factors usually played the decisive role: artistic responsibility and "rendering justice" to the theme. Both the conception, however, and the execution of *The Mirror of the Sea* were deliberately those of a book quick to produce and easy to read. To be sure, Conrad evoked the name of Turgenev, whom he venerated, when announcing that the volume would be "something in the spirit of Turgeniev's *Sportsman's Sketches*, but concerned with ships and the sea with a distinct autobiographical and anecdotal note running through what is mainly meant for a record of remembered feelings"—but this was a decoy to lure publishers.[150] In fact, only the final essays, written in 1905, testify to the author's greater artistic ambitions.

It may seem puzzling that Ford—contrary to the existing evidence—maintained that Conrad had suffered from depression when dictating the essays. I suspect that he projected over the months spent in London the recollection of Conrad's previous period of depression, or the one that followed later. More importantly, he extended on Conrad the memory of his own state of mind; he went as far as saying that the first quarter of 1904 was "the most terrible period in both their lives." Ford's nerves were getting out of hand; by April his condition was quite bad and a complete nervous breakdown followed in July.[151]

Conrad's own high spirit did not last long either. While Jessie returned to the Pent with Borys on 4 March, he stayed behind in town, "bound fast by the necessities of dictation."[152] It appears from his letters to Pinker, however, that not a single essay was written between 4 and 29 March.[153] There survived, though, a sixteen-page manuscript with a fragment of the fifth chapter of Part 2 of *Nostromo* penned that time by Ford:* starting from the words "The *Porvenir* must have a long and confident article" to "She did not answer. She seemed tired and they . . ."[154] As Arthur Mizener rightly remarks, the fragment does not give the impression of having been dictated; it was apparently composed by Ford according to Conrad's instructions. Ford's explanation of the origin of the piece is as follows: "Whilst I was living in London with Conrad almost next door and coming in practically every day for meals, he was taken with so violent an attack of gout and nervous depression that he was quite unable to continue his instalments of *Nostromo* that was then running as a serial in T.P.'s weekly. I therefore simply wrote enough from time to time to keep the presses going—a job that presented no great difficulties to me."[155] Mizener notices that many minor factual errors in Ford's text, corrected in the book edition, could not have been made by Conrad, and comments, "What Ford did was to write a brief passage in which he made sure nothing significant happened, a set of variations on matter already invented by Conrad in a plausible imitation of Conrad's style. That certainly called for considerable intimacy with the story and

---

* As Hans van Marle points out in a forthcoming paper, such dating of this fragment presents a difficulty: it implies growth of the text fairly slow before and fairly rapid afterward. Still, I believe that ascribing the piece to any other time poses even more problems: Conrad neither needed nor had much opportunity for Ford's close collaboration on *Nostromo* prior to their coming to London.

considerable ingenuity, but it did not require Ford to create anything in the style of Conrad's imagination. That Ford could do the job he set himself with comparatively little difficulty is evident from the modest amount of revision in the manuscript. It is a pity he did not resist the temptation to point out that this task 'presented no great difficulties to me,' but it is true." [156]

Conrad returned to Pent Farm toward the end of March. [157] Soon after, Ford also left London, tired and on the verge of nervous collapse. Jessie, an invalid, awaited Conrad's return home. Deeply distressed, he wrote to Meldrum, "My poor wife who has been complaining of not feeling very well ever since last Oct. was found to have a valvular defect of the heart. . . . The doctors in consultation have sent her to bed for six weeks both for her heart and her knee. She certainly can't walk and it looks bad; it looks as if she were to be a helpless cripple. The words as I write give a shudder. . . . She has been now laid up for 3 weeks. Her heart seems better; but now, after all her anxieties and shocks she had, her nerves are giving way and as I write to you in her bedroom she is lying lightheaded and groaning with neuralgia in all the limbs. . . . Half the time I feel on the verge of insanity. The difficulties are accumulating around me in a frightful manner." [158] Again money was short, even for current expenses. [159] Since the sea sketches promised quicker money, Conrad speedily produced three more. [160] As Jessie was unable to take dictation and do the typing, Pinker found Conrad a secretary, Miss Lillian Hallowes, who worked for him for the next twenty years. Borys thus describes her: "She was a tall willowy female, then I think about thirty, with a supercilious manner and a somewhat vacant expression. She also had very thick long brown hair which she wore in an insecurely anchored bun on the nape of her long neck, which used to wobble about as she moved, in a most intriguing manner and finally disintegrate, leaving her hair free to cascade over her shoulders—usually at the most inappropriate and embarrassing moments." [161] She turned out to have been a "great help," Conrad assured Pinker. [162]

Now all Conrad's energy was concentrated on *Nostromo*. He completed Part 2 on 24 April; [163] thus 40 percent of the whole remained to be written. Work advanced painfully but, for Conrad, at a fairly good pace, although he laid the novel aside three times during the summer to do some minor pieces. In May he wrote a short introduction to Maupassant's *Yvette and Other Stories*, translated by Ada Galsworthy—at the time his friend's lover and one year later his wife; Conrad must have been privy to the secret about the long-lasting romance, hidden from the world during the lifetime of John's father to spare him the shock of a divorce in the family (Ada, born Cooper, was the wife of Arthur Galsworthy, John's first cousin). Conrad's introduction praises Maupassant's masterly realism, his "justice and courage." [164]

In July, at Garnett's request, Conrad wrote an article about Anatole France's *Crainquebille*, a eulogy of another (and very different) French favorite of his. [165]

A few days later Conrad informed Pinker that he had ready two-thirds of an essay on the Thames, later called "The Faithful River."[166] Here, as in his other sketches in *The Mirror of the Sea*, Conrad wove some general reflections into his reminiscences and descriptive yarns. Occasionally, those reflections function as statements summing up the writer's fundamental ideas—hence their value as hints for the interpretation of Conrad's works. In "The Fine Art," such a personal declaration of belief is the sentence on the nonutilitarian sense of the "honour of the craft," which, while it imposes exigent demands, also upgrades professional work to the level of an art. And in "The Faithful River," amidst the somewhat pompous and ornate musings about the "souls of ships" "impatient of confinement," we find this magnificent Conradian statement: "And faithfulness is a great restraint, the strongest bond laid upon the self-will of men and ships on this globe of land and sea."[167]

Conrad kept assuring Pinker that six weeks was all he needed to finish *The Mirror of the Sea*—but he could not lay *Nostromo* aside for that long. Meanwhile, his income fell very short of his expenses, and he had already received money from Pinker for works as yet unwritten. "Speaking of money," Conrad wrote to Pinker on 3 May 1904:

> There shall be but little or nothing from Nostromo for me when I've finished. I shudder to think how deep I am in your debt. But Nostromo ought to put me right even if I must call upon you again before the end which is near. As to the immediate "afterwards" the book of sketches must be made to provide for that. Is Harvey going to take it? Should he do so and (the contract being signed) should I take out another policy on my life (for six months say) I suppose you could raise some money for me on it at once. . . . I can't exist very long in this penury. I've some small liabilities to meet which must be attended to. . . . And besides my wife will have to get a change directly she can be moved by rail without risk of undoing all the good the six weeks in bed have undubitably done to the limb. To prevent her becoming a cripple is worth any sacrifice even from the point of view of my peace of mind.[168]

Pinker could not or did not want to arrange a loan for Conrad, and the negotiations with George Harvey, the director of Harper's, dragged on for a long time. Conrad turned for help to Rothenstein. He asked for a short-term loan of £100 to £150, guaranteed once again by his life insurance policy. Rothenstein decided to try to find a more permanent solution to Conrad's difficulties and appealed for assistance to various friends, among them Henry Newbolt ("Conrad has *no one* to fall back on"). Newbolt, in turn, approached Gosse, the secretary of the Royal Literary Fund, who informed the Prime Minister, Arthur Balfour, about Conrad's difficult situation. This was the beginning of the endeavors that bore fruit a year later in the form of a government grant for Conrad.[169] Meanwhile, Rothenstein succeeded in collecting £200. Conrad, "overwhelmed by [his] good fortune," suggested, "I think you ought to take charge of my debt in the sense that the policy shall be made over to you and the repayments also shall be made to you." [170]

The whole manoeuvre was hardly completed when a rumor spread through London literary circles, rendered plausible by Rothenstein's activities—that Pinker was keeping Conrad in tight check. The forebearing agent felt hurt and in self-defense wrote to Wells about

> an incident that occurred last week. Conrad came up and finding me out . . . asked Heinemann to give him a sovereign "to enable him to get home." Heinemann offered him about £7 royalties standing to his credit. Conrad said he must send that to me, but if H. would let him have a pound and tell me that he had done so, C. could get home and would put it right with me another day. Conrad told me all this when he called two days after, and one can quite see how the incident might be utilized to produce the impression that poor Conrad was in penury and that I was treating him with less than humanity. As a matter of fact Conrad always borrows a sovereign whenever he comes in. . . . In truth I have never refused Conrad any sum that he has asked for, and if it were not a breach of confidence to give the figures, I would be only too delighted for anyone to see the details of my dealings with him. [171]

The rumor, however, must have persisted, for a month later Conrad himself, probably at Pinker's request, addressed a denial to Edmund Gosse.

> It has come to my isolated ears that it is given out at large, that it is said—in what exact words I don't know, but said in effect, that "Pinker deals harshly with Conrad." Such a statement injurious to Pinker, becomes by implication an aspersion upon Conrad in a way which I need not point out to your insight. . . . Without troubling to trace what is said to its source, I am extremely anxious that you should not believe it. . . . I have no taint in my character either of vice, indolence or subserviency which could ever make me the victim of such a situation as is implied in that piece of baseless gossip. . . . [Pinker] has known me for six years. He has stepped gallantly into the breach left open by the collapse of my bank: and not only gallantly, but successfully as well. He has treated not only my moods but even my fancies with the greatest consideration. . . . He cannot take away the weariness of mind which at the end of ten years of strain has come upon me; but he has done his utmost to help me to overcome it by relieving the immediate material pressure—and the even more disabling pressure of human stupidity. [172]

Conrad must have felt the burden of his debt to Ford particularly heavily, because Ford was then suffering from a deepening nervous crisis that was to end in a serious and long-lasting depression. Toward the end of July, when he still hoped that Ford would be able to work, Conrad sent him an offer for a story he had received from Northern Newspapers Syndicate: "By same post with your letter comes the enclosed. I was going to fling it into the paper basket. Still—if you have something written that you do *not* care for *in the least* send it on." [173] Conrad was thus prepared, when necessary, to put his own signature to his friend's work. But in a week Ford had to be sent off to Germany for treatment. [174] A few weeks later Conrad wrote him a solicitous and reassuring letter, suggesting among other things that if Ford were to write literary correspondence from Germany, he would take care of the typing and then place the articles in journals. [175]

"*Je tombe de fatigue*"—he wrote at the end of June. "I have been half dead. I am now in the night and day writing stage. I am simply in despair," he announced a month later. And again after another four weeks: "The last month I worked practically night and day, going to bed at three and sitting down again at nine. All the time at it, with the tenacity of despair." He seems to have sustained his imagination with supplementary reading of tangential interest: this would explain borrowings from Anatole France in his characterization of Decoud on the verge of suicide, based on France's words about Prosper Mérimée. [176]

Nostromo was finished on 30 August at the Hopes' home at Stanford-le-Hope. All the Conrads had gone there on the twenty-eighth, following Conrad's dramatic adventures with a tooth extraction. Conrad related that he "worked all day. In the evening dear Mrs Hope (who is not used to that sort of thing) gave me four candles and I went on. I finished at 3." [177]

Three days later he confessed to Rothenstein, "What the book is like, I don't know. I don't suppose it'll damage me: but I know that it is open to much intelligent criticism. For the other sort I don't care. Personally I am not satisfied. It is something—but not *the* thing I tried for. There is no exultation, none of that temporary sense of achievement which is so soothing. Even the mere feeling of relief at having done with it is wanting. The strain has been too great, has lasted too long. But I am ready for more. I don't feel empty, exhausted. I am simply joyless—like most men of little faith." [178]

For the next three weeks he revised and polished the text for the book edition—adding substantial fragments at the end. [179] Then came the proofs. [180] So Conrad worked on, consoled by thoughts of his imminent sojourn in London, necessary for Jessie's health (she was still suffering from heart trouble), and of his cherished plan to seek the southern sun in Morocco or Capri. [181]

XI

. . . .

UPHILL

1904–1909

T HE STATE of Jessie's knees was not improving; her left knee required hospital treatment. On about 10 October the Conrads went to London and stayed for almost three months. At first they lived at 10 Prince's Square, in Bayswater—the future whereabouts of Old Nelson (or Nielsen), the father of the unfortunate Freya of the Seven Isles; on 20 October they moved closer to Galsworthy, to 99B Addison Road, a charming street with trees, adjacent to Holland Park.[1] Medical examination of Jessie's joints lasted several weeks and produced conflicting opinions. Jessie was finally placed in a nursing home where she was operated on by Bruce Clarke on 24 November.[2] Initially it seemed that the operation was successful;[3] later, however, it appeared that the state of the damaged limb had become even worse.

Meanwhile the book edition of *Nostromo*, dedicated to Galsworthy, came out on 14 October. Galsworthy recalled later that Conrad regarded this novel as his most important work, and he apparently told Cecil Roberts that the book was the one "dearest to his heart."[4] Conrad also often declared his dismay at the way *Nostromo* had been received by the critics and the public.[5] Having put so much work and energy into the most "imagined" of his novels—a novel less based on memories and reading than any of his others—he was very disappointed, although as Norman Sherry rightly observes, some of the reviews were favorable: "Conrad was misunderstood, even attacked, but he was also praised." Conrad's bitterness was not due to his excessive touchiness; perhaps he cherished two hopes—that the book would attain popularity and thus relieve him from his constant financial worries and/or that *Nostromo*'s intellectual content and artistic innovation would not go unnoticed by the critics and would thus at least afford its author some professional satisfaction. However, the public showed only a feeble interest and the reviews evinced a lack of understanding of the book's structure and ideas. Among the few exceptions was Garnett's penetrating article in the *Speaker*: Garnett turned out to be the only critic who perceived the book's real theme. The *Times Literary Supplement*, on the other hand, in a review published a week after the book came out, called it an "artistic mistake" and criticized its wordiness and shapelessness. There were many similar accusations. Praise was usually vague and superficial—the *British Weekly*, for instance, recommended *Nostromo* as an adventure story.[6] The lack of understanding was perhaps even more unpleasant than the lack of applause: Conrad used to find in the opinions of others an acceptance or rejection of both his image of his own work and his personality itself.

Having finished *Nostromo*, Conrad wanted to continue with the South American theme. In Captain Basil Hall's *Extracts from a Journal, written on the Coasts of Chili, Peru, and Mexico in the years 1820, 1821, 1822,* Conrad found a story about a pirate named Vincente Benavides. He initially intended to use it as a basis for a cycle of short tales entitled "Benavides." The first, twenty-five hundred words long and intended for the monthly *Strand*, was probably completed on 8 November.[7] For an unknown reason—probably *Strand*'s rejection—the story was later reshaped into "Gaspar Ruiz."[8] "Benavides" was undoubtedly written for money; even the final version is primitive and garish, but Conrad spent an inordinately long time on it: the first twenty-five hundred words took at least three weeks to write. Earlier still, and possibly faster, he had written a solemn, eulogistic essay on Henry James, calling him a "historian of fine consciences," a chronicler of intense moral battles fought in the souls of his protagonists.[9] He compared the novelist's art to "rescue work" aimed at snatching from obscurity "vanishing phases of turbulence" in order to endow them "with the only possible form of permanence in this world of relative values— the permanence of memory." And, significantly, in this article about a creative artist Conrad took the opportunity to express his admiration for mankind's "pride, its assurance, and its indomitable tenacity."[10]

He also continued his work on the sea sketches. In the autumn of 1904 he finished "The Faithful River" (originally "London River, the Great Artery of England")[11] and wrote "Cobwebs and Gossamer" (initially called "Tallness of the Spars").[12] But all that was minor work. For almost six months after finishing *Nostromo*, Conrad was unable to concentrate on any more serious undertaking. His health was poor, and he complained of fits of breathlessness and gout.[13]

Although it arose from necessity, the stay in London had its good side: it gave Conrad an opportunity to meet his old friends more often and to make new acquaintances. Jessie reproachfully recalled, with obvious exaggeration, that the night before she entered the nursing home thirty people came to dinner. Among the guests were the painters Augustus John and Henry Tonks, both of whom William Rothenstein had introduced to Conrad.[14] At the beginning of December Ford, on his way back from Germany, stopped in London.[15] On 14 December Conrad took him to see Albert Tebb, a physician in whom he had great confidence and who had been looking after Jessie and Borys.[16] We know nothing about the treatment—Ford's story is as usual both colorful and fantastic—but it proved quite successful. From the outset Conrad must have been optimistic about his friend's prospects, since on 21 December he assured Pinker that if *The Rescue* were to appear in instalments in *Pall Mall Magazine*, Ford would be ready to help.[17]

Conrad needed consolation; his financial situation was again becoming desperate, chiefly owing to the costs of Jessie's treatment. He borrowed money from Rothenstein and had to apologize to Elsie Hueffer for a delay in repaying an overdue debt to her, explaining that his credit with Pinker had been exhausted.[18] His plans for future books were vague. Now and again in his letters there are references to a novel due to be written before next June, but no traces of his work on it exist.[19] It is impossible even to establish which novel he had in mind. He also planned to supplement the volume of sea sketches with articles on literary subjects and to have them published together as *The Mirror of the Sea: Action and Vision.*[20]

In order to speed Jessie's recovery and at the same time break away from the state of creative prostration that worsened his money troubles, Conrad decided to visit Capri for a few months. The idea was obviously of the "like cures like" type: in order to make up for time wasted, he had to devote weeks to preparing for the journey itself and to settling down in Italy; then, of course, he had to raise new loans for the expedition. Capri was probably suggested by Galsworthy, who was staying with his future wife Ada at nearby Amalfi. Given Jessie's condition, the choice of Capri was not a wise one, since walking on the hilly island is difficult even for people with strong legs; Conrad presumably thought climate was the paramount consideration. In those days Capri was neither as commercialized and crowded nor as expensive as it is today—the Conrads paid £28 a month for three people; but staying far from the nearest town meant engaging a nurse to care for Jessie.

The Conrads returned from London to the Pent on 7 January and left for Italy six days later.[21] On the evening of the thirteenth they arrived in Paris (stopping, ironically enough, at the Hôtel St. Petersbourg) and set out the next day on a very tiring journey. Jessie, unable to walk, had to be transported in an armchair, and this produced many exciting moments. At Dover the porters had had great difficulty in lifting her onto the boat; at the railway station in Rome the chair was removed from under her before she was properly set on her feet inside the carriage, and she had to clutch a handhold and hang on above the steps while Conrad's "hair stood on end and the nurse nearly fainted."[22] On Sunday, 15 January, the travelers reached Naples, where they had to wait five days for the weather to improve. Conrad later wrote to Galsworthy that it was "impossible to land Jessie at Capri if the sea was at all rough as the steamer does not come alongside the jetty; and the transfer from the steamer to small boat and from boat to shore required smooth water for safety. Perhaps the difficulty was not so great as all these people—the hotel keeper, the steamboat officials and the headman at Cook's—tried to make me believe."[23]

The delay produced a large hotel bill, which immediately forced Conrad to borrow money in Naples. The journey alone cost £12 a person;[24] one day after arrival, Conrad asked Galsworthy for an instant loan, acknowledging that "the whole expedition is a mad thing really, for it rests upon what I am not certain of—my power to produce some sixty thousand words in 4 months. I feel sick with apprehension at times." [25] The Conrads reached Capri on the evening of 20 January, and a friend of Davray's, Canon Pietro Ferraro, was there to welcome them and offer his assistance. [26] The Conrads made their home in the center of the village, at the Villa di Maria. In addition to Ada and John Galsworthy, who came by boat to pay a visit, Conrad found company in Norman Douglas, an ex-diplomat and future writer who at that time primarily occupied himself with botany and was a prodigy of erudition in everything Mediterranean. Years later Conrad presided over the beginnings of Douglas's literary career. Conrad also made the acquaintance of a fellow countryman, Count Zygmunt Szembek, with whom he later corresponded, and of Dr. Giorgio Cerio, a local physician who took care of Jessie's leg with good results. In the library of Dr. Ignazio Cerio, Giorgio's brother, Conrad found many interesting historical publications and manuscripts, and his readings there led him to conceive the idea of writing a novel about the fighting around Capri between the French and the English in 1808. [27] Conrad had been attracted to the Napoleonic era for many years before he finally took up the subject in two late novels—*The Rover* and *Suspense*, the latter of which remained unfinished.

The Conrads' stay on Capri began badly. The nurse, a Miss Jackson, whom Conrad could not stand and Jessie did not particularly like, fell ill on her arrival and needed attention. [28] In the end she had to be sent back to England. These unexpected complications upset Conrad completely and made it impossible for him to focus on his work. Then he apparently came down with influenza, followed by spells of insomnia; [29] at the end of March he was laid up with a toothache. [30] But the chief cause of Conrad's inability to write, which he constantly bemoaned, was not so much physical as mental, and he attributed his lack of concentration to life on Capri. In letters to Pinker—which offered excuses for not sending the text and at the same time asked for money —Conrad blamed his difficulties on poor health and hot weather; other letters were devoted to finding fault with the scenery, the climate, and the local population. To Davray he confessed, "The beauty of Capri makes me languid and I think I have done nothing. Absolutely nothing. It is delightful but is becoming dangerous." [31] After more than three months on the island the balance was not much better: "I've done nothing. And if it were not that Jessie profited so remarkably I would call the whole expedition a disaster. This climate, what between tramontana and sirocco has half killed me in a not unpleasant languorous melting way. I am sunk in a vaguely uneasy dream of visions, of innumerable tales that float in an atmosphere of voluptuously aching bones." [32]

The real reason for Conrad's inability to write was probably rooted in himself: he was unable to overcome his irresolution and find a subject that would arrest his attention or a literary form that would hold his fleeting ideas. He kept

assuring Pinker that his thoughts revolved around a "novel." This novel may
have been the future *Chance*, originally called "Dynamite Ship" or "Explosives."[33] But at the time Conrad thought of it as a short story.[34] Conrad also
vaguely pondered a book about the "bay of Naples, Capri, Sorrento, etc.—
places visited every year by the English and Am^can tourists." Such a book, in his
opinion, would have a "better chance of popularity. That is what I must aim at
in the measure of my forces."[35] In the end, however, all he wrote was the political essay "Autocracy and War."[36]

Conrad first mentioned the essay, the most extensive and ambitious political
statement he ever made, as early as 12 January 1905, when he asked Davray for
"a book on Russia—recent—serious."[37] He maintained then that he would
write "Autocracy and War" "to keep the pot boiling," but this could hardly
have been true, since political articles paid less than fiction and Pinker, moreover, was by no means sure of being able to place the essay. Behind a mask of
facetious nonchalance, Conrad was trying to conceal his deep involvement with
the questions raised and the fact that he was expressing his own political credo.

Initially the essay's title was to be "'The Concord of Europe' . . . a sort of
historical survey of international politics from 1815 (The Vienna Congress)—
with remarks and conclusions tending to demonstrate the present precarious
state of that concord and bringing the guilt of that precariousness to the door of
Germany—or rather of Prussia."[38] In the course of writing, Conrad's emphasis
shifted: the title changed, and the focal point of the essay became Russia, to
which Conrad devoted over half his text.

We know that Conrad was passionately concerned with politics: this is mentioned several times by Ford; Conrad's correspondence with Graham testifies to
it; and it is confirmed by several of his works, starting with *Almayer's Folly*.
Baines is mistaken in assuming that "it may well be that *Nostromo* had stimulated Conrad to think particularly about political subjects."[39] On the contrary,
Nostromo only revealed his concern with these matters more fully; it was, of
course, a concern quite natural for someone from a country where politics was
a matter not only of everyday existence but also of life and death. Moreover,
Conrad himself came from a social class that claimed exclusive responsibility
for state affairs, and from a very politically active family. It was by no means his
mysterious "Slavic temperament," as Frederick Karl calls it, which made Conrad see political problems in terms of a continuous struggle between law and
violence, anarchy and order, freedom and autocracy, material interests and the
noble idealism of individuals;[40] it was Conrad's historical awareness. This
awareness endowed Conrad with a clear perception, exceptional in the Western
European literature of his time, of how winding and constantly changing were
the front lines in these struggles.

The starting point for Conrad's reflections was the Russo-Japanese War; he
finished the article one month before the battle of Tsushima. The war destroyed

the old myth of Russian might, and it precipitated the fall of tsardom. Germany, with its aggressively imperialist ambitions, was ready to fill the newly created vacuum. "Autocracy and War" begins with a statement about Russia's incurable weakness and ends with warnings against Prussia, the dangerous aggressor in the future European war. Within that framework Conrad inserted a characterization of Russia's political and governmental traditions, and some meditations on Europe's recent past and its contemporary condition.

Conrad presented the Russian state as a monster that crushed its own subjects and was devoid of both any historical justification and any prospect for evolutionary development. His words echo those of P. Ya. Chaadayev (1793–1856), an early Russian "dissident." Conrad had probably learned about Chaadayev's views from Astolphe de Custine's famous book *Russia in 1839*, but he may have absorbed them from Apollo Korzeniowski and Stefan Buszczyński; both de Custine and Apollo had been influenced by the same Polish Romantic poets.[41] Conrad wrote that the "rigid monstrosity of tsardom" made revolution in Russia inevitable, but the lack of any democratic tradition and the backwardness of Russia's masses made it impossible to expect the revolution to have any salutary effect. Conrad regarded the formation of a representative government as impossible and foresaw a transition from autocracy to dictatorship. Although he explicitly stated that Russians were not to be blamed for their cruel fate, Conrad argued that their tragically anomalous political heritage deprived them of any right to speak up "on a single question touching the future of humanity, because from the very inception of her being the brutal destruction of dignity, of truth, of rectitude, of all that is faithful in human nature has been made the imperative condition of her existence." The sentence follows directly after a critical allusion to Dostoyevsky ("Some of the best intellects of Russia, after struggling in vain against the spell, ended by throwing themselves at the feet of that hopeless despotism as a giddy man leaps into an abyss."). It was clearly leveled at the enthusiasm shown by the Garnetts and their entourage for everything Russian.

Conrad aimed at an impersonal tone for his reflections; when first printed in the *Fortnightly Review* the article carried the motto "*sine ira et studio*" [without anger and ardor]. The passage about the partition of Poland was even accompanied by the reservation "without indulging in excessive feelings of indignation at that country's partition,"[42] and although Russia and Prussia, Poland's principal oppressors, were targets of Conrad's passionate attacks, the accusations brought against them were only of a general character. Conrad accused tsardom of tyranny toward its own people and the conquered nations; he described Prussia as a predatory imperialist state consumed by conceit and endangering world peace. But the Western countries, the traditional center of Europe, were not held up as the good contrasted with the Russian evil. Instead, Conrad saw Europe as torn by antagonistic trends engendered by economic rivalry and commercial selfishness. It would be in vain for a Russian revolution to seek advice or help from a materialistic and egoistic Europe that armed itself in preparation for wars far more brutal than those of the past.

A few months after the essay was published, Conrad's awareness of the danger of a total war brought about by national envy and economic rivalry inspired him to include an emphatic antiwar sally in his essay "The Nursery of the Craft."[43] Here, as in his other political pronouncements, Conrad displayed his characteristic distrust of all contemporary governments. This mistrust sprang from two sources. First, Conrad considered all political institutions intrinsically defective, even if they were born of noble motives and lofty ideals; institutions inevitably ossify and degenerate as a result of the inherent weakness of human nature. Second, Conrad thought that the newest system of government—democracy—had decided "to pin its faith to the supremacy of material interests" and had thereby repudiated historical and moral traditions for the sake of mercantile advantage. "Autocracy and War" shows that Conrad's political values were national independence, continuity of traditions, unconstrained development of institutional forms, and the subordination of economic affairs to moral ideals; at the same time it is quite clear from this that Conrad saw no possibility of all his postulates being realized in the foreseeable future. Conrad's attitude was quite atypical at this time, since the prevailing mood in European politics was optimistic. True, the optimism of the Germans and the British was based on different premises, and the complacency of the middle class was opposed by the hopes of the radical left—but neither those who endorsed the status quo nor those who anticipated a revolution associated their visions with catastrophe.

After finishing "Autocracy and War"—ten thousand words, "the work of one month in nearly four"—little time was left for Conrad in Capri.[44] But an exciting piece of news reached him about 20 March and touched off a few months of commotion in his life and in his correspondence. Thanks to Rothenstein's endeavors, which Conrad had known about as early as the summer of 1904, he received a grant of £500 from the Royal Bounty fund.[45]

What ensued is so characteristic of Conrad's life and attitudes that it deserves a detailed description. The royal grant, intended to relieve the financial problems that distracted Conrad from his work, in fact gave rise to endless worries, annoyances, and loss of time.

Conrad's first reaction was a loftily humble letter of thanks to Gosse: "I have often," he wrote, "suffered in connection with my work from a sense of unreality, from intellectual doubt of the ground I stood upon. This has occurred especially in the periods of difficult production. I had just emerged from such a period of utter mistrust when Rothenstein's letter came to hand revealing to me the whole extent of *your* belief . . . I need not tell you that this moral support of belief is the greatest help a writer can receive in those difficult moments which

Baudelaire has defined happily as 'les stérilités des écrivains nerveux'." [46] How-ever, even Gosse's acclaim and the prospect of a shower of gold did not cure Conrad's "sterility." We may guess that the news excited him and gave rise to plans that had little to do with writing. Not for many years had Conrad had a sum as large as £500—perhaps one year's expenses—at his disposal; and when, on 11 April, he received Gosse's official notification of the size of the grant, he answered in an ingratiating tone: "For the rest, I may say that the way of return having been so unexpectedly made smooth, I am more anxious than ever to get back to Pent Farm, under whose lowly (and imperfectly watertight) roof five volumes have had the audacity to get themselves written. I've done very badly here. It's all very well for Englishmen born to their inheritance to fling verse and prose from Italy back at their native shores. I, in my state of honourable adop-tion, find that I need the moral support, the sustaining influence of English at-mosphere even from day to day." [47]

Conrad evidently expected to receive the money while he was still in Italy, but Gosse, as soon as he learned from the prime minister how large the sum involved was, approached Henry Newbolt, for his advice: "To whom should the money be paid, and when? Is it advisable to send it in a lump to Conrad? Should it be placed in the hands of a friend, as trustee? For instance, yourself?

"I should like to prevent his doing something sudden and silly with it, at the same time I don't want to 'froisser' his sensitive temperament." [48]

Newbolt's reply has not been preserved, but he must have shared Gosse's ap-prehension about Conrad's extravagance; in the end he and Rothenstein—both safely and comfortably well-off—were appointed trustees to supervise the dis-bursement of the grant.

For a time Conrad was unaware of all this and waited impatiently for the money to arrive. On 1 May he wrote to Rothenstein's wife urging her to get £150 sent off immediately. He justified his request by the absolute necessity of returning home: "The Stage Society offers to perform my little play *To-morrow* in June this year. I think it is really a chance for me, it may lead to the end of all my financial troubles for if the play produces a good impression I may place the 3 acts I've been carrying in my head for the last seven years. Now it is necessary for me to be back in *England* as soon as possible to carry out the alterations insisted upon." [49]

Conrad's reasoning was farfetched: he had not been summoned by the Stage Society, and the success or failure of a one-act play could hardly determine the fate of a three-act play as yet unwritten (of which this is the only mention); in any case other letters show that the date of the Conrads' return had always been fixed for the middle of May. [50] But Conrad, up to his ears in debt, probably found himself with no money either to stay in Capri or to go back to England, and he could not turn to Pinker for help, because he had failed to send him the promised manuscript.

At any rate, £100 of the requested sum finally arrived, and on 12 May the Conrads started their return journey. They went by boat from Naples to Marseilles, where they met Poradowska and Robert d'Humières, a French aristocrat, man of letters, and translator of *The Nigger of the 'Narcissus.'* After a two-day stay, from the fifteenth to the seventeenth, and a night in Paris, the Conrads arrived at the Pent on 18 May.[51]

Conrad must have heard about the appointment of Newbolt and Rothenstein as trustees just before leaving Italy, for he exploded with bitterness and indignation in a letter sent to Gosse from Marseilles: "The whole affair has assumed an appearance much graver and more distressing than any stress of my material necessities: the appearance of 'Conrad having to be saved from himself'—the sort of thing that casts a doubt on a man's sense of responsibility, on his right feelings, on his sense of correct conduct."[52] He demanded a hearing. (Conrad had earlier posted a similarly "hysterical" letter to Rothenstein.[53])

Gosse sent a calm yet reproachful reply straight to Pent Farm. He explained that the appointment of trustees was a normal procedure and turned down the request for an interview. Conrad's anger changed into apologetic embarrassment. "Your chiding—severe as it is—I take as meekly as if it were wholly deserved. Nothing could please me more than to discover that I've made a silly ass of myself."[54] To Newbolt, by no means a close acquaintance, he addressed an elaborately polite appeal for a hearing. His later correspondence on the subject presents a sometimes embarrassing mixture of humiliation, wounded pride, cunning, affected humility, and a desire to obtain the largest possible sum of money in the shortest possible time.

The requested meeting with Newbolt took place on 25 May, and Conrad wrote him a long letter afterward. He argued, "In my view of the grant made to me I start from the principle that the first and main intention has been to procure for me the ease of mind necessary for tranquil and steady writing." This is why he appealed for £250 immediately needed to pay off his most urgent debts; from a short list it seems that, apart from his obligations to Ford, Galsworthy, Pinker, and Rothenstein, his debts amounted to over £450, including nearly £200 from his overdraft at Watson's bankrupt bank. Pleas and arguments alternate with self-justification: Conrad cited Jessie's illness as the principal cause of his debts; his poor health and the precariousness of his own life, on which his invalid spouse and young child depended, also figured in his plea; he concluded with diffident thanks to Newbolt for his words of encouragement during their conversation.[55]

To Conrad's surprise and annoyance—for he had meanwhile acquired some new furniture[56]—Newbolt, instead of writing an appropriate check, suggested that a solicitor should be appointed to negotiate a reduction of the payments due.[57] Conrad, hardly able to conceal his indignation, rejected the proposal outright: he did not want to admit his bankruptcy; he did not want the public to take him for an irresponsible bohemian; he did not want to cause losses to his creditors; and of course he did not want to lose his credit. The desire to preserve his good name was bolstered by purely practical considerations: "It would be *bad business*, making my position much worse for the future." He was thankful for Newbolt's solicitude and apologized for having caused trouble, but his argumentative repetitiveness indicates that he found it difficult to control his temper.[58] Without giving Newbolt time to reply, Conrad sent another, even more dramatic letter four days later. This time he appealed for tolerance, faith, and an understanding of his situation. Once again he argued that it would be "impracticable" to refer the matter to a solicitor. After expressing doubts about his own literary merits he claimed that it was only the thought of his wife and child that had made him accept the grant; it was not, he wrote, "because they were in any immediate want, but because I wished to give myself a chance of remaining with them as long as possible." In addition to this emphatic hint at the possibility of his premature death, Conrad pleaded that he should not be discredited as an irresponsible spendthrift; he recalled his foreign origin and the resultant loneliness: "Pray remember that from the nature of things I cannot count upon the moral support one's family, connections, the opinion of numerous early associates, gives one against the hasty judgement of the world. Except for the woman who trusted me and the child not yet old enough—thank God—to understand all the uncertainty of his future, I am so alone that you two stand in virtue of your charge in the position that only the nearest of blood could occupy with perfect safety to myself."[59]

Newbolt and Rothenstein gave in not to Conrad's arguments but to his stubbornness, to the extent of allowing him to pay off his debts at full rate and without a solicitor's mediation.[60] The haggling was embarrassing to all concerned and revealed a complete lack of mutual comprehension. The trustees, prompted by common sense and the best intentions, treated Conrad as an impractical bohemian. As Rothenstein told Newbolt, "He seems to me, like so many artists, to have muddled his life quite unnecessarily."[61] Neither of them realized that Conrad was not a bohemian at all but an uprooted *szlachcic* obsessed with the need to preserve the appearance of wealth and largesse, unable to understand how two men of integrity could regard debts incurred on the strength of a gentleman's word as a matter to be bargained through solicitors. The incident exposed a cultural barrier: for Conrad debts could be left unpaid if one had no money, but it was wrong to deny them or wrangle over the amount due.

Conrad's expostulations about his foreign origin and lack of family and social setting also help us understand why he lived well above his means or needs. Quite simply, he always felt socially insecure; Rothenstein even saw his insecurity as a hysterical sense of persecution. The pressure of conventional class expectations would have been powerful even for an Englishman; the social historian Peter Laslett writes about the English middle class of the period, "A third of the population was trying to live in a way that only a seventeenth of the population could live."[62] But in Conrad's case three factors, national, personal, and social, converge: the traditional Polish impulse to cut a dash even if it meant going into debt; the personal inability to economize; and the silent pressure to imitate the life style of the wealthy middle class to avoid being branded as a denizen of the abyss of poverty, an abyss then regarded as "unthinkable and only to be approached by the statistician or the poet," as E. M. Forster put it a few years later.[63]

On 9 June Conrad sent Newbolt a list of his creditors—at least those he wanted to pay off at once out of the Royal grant. The total came to £260 (Conrad made mistakes in his addition and wrote "270" twice). The largest items were the partial repayment of his overdraft at the bank (£50), the outstanding rent for his house (£45), doctors' fees (£60), and various debts with local shopkeepers and tradesmen (£85).[64] The money was to be paid in a somewhat complicated manner: Conrad would send Newbolt addressed envelopes into which the latter put signed checks for the appropriate sums; Conrad, in turn, would endorse the checks and pass them on to his creditors. I think that the humility, bordering on obsequiousness, of Conrad's later letters to Newbolt concealed his stifled fury at having to go through so many requests, explanations, justifications, and avowals. Even Rothenstein found this affected humility irritating.[65] But one may ponder what would have happened if Conrad had not received the grant, especially as on 16 June he had already admitted that his financial situation was not "perfectly sound."[66] Conrad received the rest of the grant in £15 to £20 instalments until 10 April 1906.[67]

From 25 to 27 June three evening performances and two matinées of *One Day More* were given at the Royal Theatre; it was billed along with Miss Laurence Alma Tadema's *New Felicity*. Conrad's one-act play had a similar reception to that of most of his novels. Max Beerbohm hoped it would not be "the only alms that Mr Conrad will bestow on our needy drama"—pointing out, however, that "the play is a tragedy, set in modern times; and that fact alone is, of course, enough to damn it in the eyes of most critics."[68] Thus once again Conrad had produced a fine work with little chance of financial success.

Conrad's own attitude toward the piece was oddly ambiguous. He displayed great concern but maintained that the adaptation had been done purely for money; he was excited about his chances of success on the stage while at the same time announcing, "I don't think that I am a dramatist"; he complained that the play was taking up a lot of his time and energy but considered it of marginal importance in relation to his basic work; George Bernard Shaw's approval pleased him but in a detached way; and in spite of promises (to Galsworthy, for example) he refrained for a time from further dramatic experiments.[69]

Conrad's ambivalence may be easily explained by the fact that *One Day*

More had been written in collaboration with Ford.[70] The draft, forty-three pages long, written in Ford's hand (probably at the beginning of 1904), survives at Cornell University. In his letters to Pinker, Ford, although treating the play as a joint enterprise with Conrad, was prepared to waive his authorship: "Certainly you can say the play is by self & Conrad—C., that is, will do more to it if there is a reasonable certainty of its being accepted—&, for all I sh^d care, he c^d call it quite his own."[71] This in fact was what Conrad did. Asked by Colvin about the authorship, Conrad first sounded Ford out about his position and, having made certain that Ford would not give a conflicting version, assured Colvin that Ford's participation had been limited to "taking out the dialogue of the story in a typewritten extract for my use and reference. The play, as can be shown by the MS., has been written entirely in my own hand. . . . I've always looked upon the play as mine . . . You may take it from me that no one collaborated in that play so much as yourself."[72] Eleven days later Conrad lamely explained to Ford, "I hadn't the pluck to write to you, not even after the telegram about the play—not after your good letter which saddened me a little and augmented my desire to see you very much. . . . If I inquired what you wished done re play, it was mostly from the feeling that you did not like the thing anyhow. And as I feel also it's going to fail in the end, I could not without your distinct authorization associate you with what I believe will be a sort of '*four*.'"[73] Ford evidently did not consider the matter important and decided to let bygones by bygones.

During the summer Conrad wrote two more essays for *The Mirror of the Sea*: "In Captivity," finished soon after his return from Capri,[74] and the best essay in the book, "Initiation," probably finished in July.[75]

Conrad also published a short essay, "Books," about novel writing. Eight years after the preface to *The Nigger*, he was tackling a similar theme; but although he had meanwhile published a few excellent books, including two great novels, he sounded less confident now. "Books" is a somewhat chatty essay; a few passages are banal and others are excessively convoluted. Apart from some praise for Stendhal and a plea for compassion and tolerance for human weaknesses and failings—a plea that is a little startling from the future author of "The Informer" and *The Secret Agent*—what deserves attention is Conrad's repudiation of the nihilism and pessimism of which he is sometimes suspected: "It must not be supposed that I claim for the artist in fiction the freedom of moral Nihilism. I would require from him many acts of faith of which the first would be the cherishing of an undying hope. . . . What one feels so hopelessly barren in declared pessimism is just its arrogance. It seems as if the discovery made by many men at various times that there is much evil in the world were a source of proud and unholy joy unto some of the modern writers. That frame of mind is not the proper one in which to approach seriously the art of fiction. . . .

To be hopeful in an artistic sense it is not necessary to think that the world is good. It is enough to believe that there is no impossibility of its being made so." [76]

It appears that paying off most of his debts put Conrad in a happier frame of mind. That at least was Garnett's impression; he wrote to Galsworthy, "In fact, I think Conrad is especially well just now." [77] Judging by complaints about his health that Conrad made soon after, however, his buoyant mood did not last long. [78] It is doubtful whether he was then writing anything apart from the essays; perhaps bits of *Chance*, nothing more. Conrad mentioned to Newbolt his intention of writing articles on international politics for the *Monthly Review*, and he also asked him for advice on a projected essay about Lord Nelson. [79] The political articles never got written, and Conrad did not finish "The Heroic Age," an essay for the centenary of the battle of Trafalgar, until 20 September. It was then that Conrad informed Pinker that "*Chance* simmers slowly on to be ready by the end of the year." [80]

Conrad was still unable to concentrate on one piece at a time and worked in snatches, experimenting and exploring in various directions. The essay on Trafalgar does not match the rest of *The Mirror of the Sea*; and "The 'Tremolino,'" the last sketch written for the volume, is, in fact, a separate tale. This sketch, somewhat surprisingly, originally formed the second part of a longer piece called "The Inland Sea," whose first part consisted of the largely reflective "Nursery of the Craft." This first part contains statements characteristic of Conrad's philosophy, for example, "It is we alone who, swayed by the audacity of our minds and the tremors of our hearts, are the sole artisans of all the wonder and romance of the world." [81] Conrad finished "'Tremolino'" on 6 October, assuring Pinker that from now on he would devote his time solely to *Chance*. [82] Two weeks later, however, he reported that he was at work on "Benavides," that is, "Gaspar Ruiz."

The final version of this tale was probably finished around mid-October. The text contains the well-known Polish proverb "Man discharges the piece, but God carries the bullet," presented as one that "evolved out of the naive heart of the great Russian people." Gustav Morf ascribes this misattribution to Conrad's striving for popularity: "He was firmly convinced that any association with Poland could only dim his prospects. Russian literature, on the other hand, had become very popular in England. . . . Anything Russian seemed fashionable." [83] I do not think one can attribute such crass motives to Conrad— and not only because a few months earlier he had spoken out in "Autocracy and War" against the current fashion for things Russian. It is even more significant that the context in which the proverb appears is clearly sarcastic: "Some proverbs are simply imbecile, others are immoral. The proverb . . . 'Man discharges the piece, but God carries the bullet' is piously atrocious, and at bitter variance with the accepted conception of a compassionate God. It would

indeed be an inconsistent occupation for the Guardian of the poor, the innocent, and the helpless, to carry the bullet, for instance, into the heart of a
father."[84] The literal interpretation of the proverb departs from the traditional:
it is a question not of God choosing the victims of his projectiles but of the
frequent disjunction between the aims and the results of human endeavors. If
Conrad had attributed the proverb to the Poles, the entire fragment would have
turned into a wanton insult leveled at his native country; the change avoided
this and enabled him to vent his spleen at the Russians.

In the autumn Conrad again bewailed his unsatisfactory health and the even
more unsatisfactory results of his work. "It is all very monstrous—my news is,"
Conrad wrote to Wells on 20 October 1905. He continued:

> I stick here fighting with disease and creeping imbecility—like a cornered rat,
> facing fate with a big stick that is sure to descend and crack my skull before
> many days are over. If I haven't been to see you (which I admit is beastly and
> ungrateful) I haven't been to see anyone else—except Ford, and of course, the
> indispensable Pinker . . . As to Ford he is a sort of life-long habit of which I
> am not ashamed, because he is a much better fellow than the world gives him
> credit for. . . . As to working regularly in a decent and orderly and indus-
> trious manner, I've given that up from sheer impossibility. The damned stuff
> comes out only by a kind of mental convulsion lasting two, three or more
> days—up to a fortnight—which leaves me perfectly limp and not very happy,
> exhausted emotionally to all appearance, but secretly irritable to the point of
> savagery.[85]

Ford was staying in London at the time, mostly at Dr. Tebb's house. He felt
better, and the success of his book, *The Soul of London*, published in the summer of 1905, greatly bolstered his spirits. When Conrad showed him the beginning of *Chance*, about fifteen thousand words (less than one-tenth of the
novel), Ford pronounced it "something magnificent," adding that "it's really
like to do . . . the trick of popularity—this time."[86] Later he was very proud of
his prophecy, although he had to wait eight years for its fulfillment.

Conrad's relationship with Wells had a peculiar character. They did not see
each other often. Conrad's letters expressed admiration and amity and his
praise of Wells's books, particularly the newly published *Kipps*, was effusive—
but his admiration and amity give the impression of being directed at a representative of a different biological species, at an athlete competing in an entirely
different game. No one, according to Conrad, had until then attempted to define just what that different kind of game was; in spite of all his compliments,
he, too, refrained from doing so.[87] An anecdote related many years later by St.-
John Perse to Igor Stravinsky provides an apt, even if not wholly accurate, illustration of Conrad's attitude toward a different, more "practical" brand of
writer: "Conrad once told me about a dinner he had had sometime in the coun-

try with Shaw, Wells, Bennett. When these *savants cyniques* of the literary industry talked about writing as 'action,' poor Conrad, horrified, left the table, pretending he had to catch an earlier train. He told me later . . . , 'Writing, for me, is an act of faith. They all made me feel so dowdy.'"[88]

Conrad's letters to Galsworthy were always warm and more open than those to Wells. The vagueness of his praise of *The Man of Property* published in February 1906—and he praised the novel both privately and publicly—seems to spring not from a sense of the distance that separated him from Galsworthy but rather from a fear that the book could only be praised if one refrained from probing too deeply under its surface.[89] Conrad's exchange of letters with Garnett became less frequent after 1902; only one survives from the two-year period between the autumns of 1904 and 1906. They certainly met, even if only at the Tuesday lunches organized by Garnett at the Mont-Blanc Restaurant in Gerrard Street, but much less often. They knew each other too well and respected each other too much to be content with mere social courtesies, and their differences in outlook and ways of thinking, particularly in political matters, made a really close friendship difficult. One may imagine how aroused Garnett must have been by "Autocracy and War."

Late autumn of 1905 turned out to be a season of illness for the Conrad trio. First Jessie, who was pregnant and suffering from occasional heart palpitations, had a nervous breakdown.[90] When at the end of November the Conrads went to London to seek Dr. Tebb's advice, Borys contracted scarlet fever and had to be hospitalized. The Conrads moved to 32 St. Agnes Road, near Kennington Park in South London. Jessie must have been feeling better by that time, because she was able to look after the boy, who remained in the hospital until 3 January. Conrad's turn came in December, when a bad attack of gout laid him up for a fortnight that included Christmas Day.[91] Then Borys suddenly developed heart trouble on the day of their return to the country and later was burned by disinfectant.[92]

In addition to the nervous strain, all this cost Conrad a lot of money, and he was forced first to ask that the payments out of the almost exhausted government grant be speeded up and then, when that was not enough, to appeal to Galsworthy for a loan.[93]

In spite of these calamities Conrad succeeded in producing three short stories at the end of 1905: "An Anarchist," "The Informer," and "The Brute"; he was aware that his haste had an adverse effect on the quality of these works, which were, he said, "produced hastily, carelessly in a temper of desperation."[94] "An Anarchist" had been completed in December, probably before the gout attack; "The Informer" was written in five days between 27 December 1905 and 1 January 1906.[95] Both stories show Conrad's growing fascination with the phenomenon of militant anarchism. "The Informer" was to have been called "Gestures," a title explained by a statement that sounds quite topical today: "An idle and selfish class loves to see mischief being made, even if it is made at its own expense. Its own life being all a matter of pose and gesture, it is unable to realize the power and the danger of a real movement and of words that have no sham meaning."[96] "The Brute" is one of Conrad's weakest works; it was certainly finished by 21 February 1906, and since Conrad had not mentioned it before producing "An Anarchist" and "The Informer," we may surmise that he wrote "The Brute" in January 1906.[97]

Conrad began the year with the following balance sheet: the essays for *The Mirror of the Sea* had been written but required reshaping and correcting; four very different tales of uneven quality were ready for a new volume of collected short stories; the projected novel was at a standstill and what was written was only of short-story length; finally, the results of several new experiments in writing were discouraging. In short, there was nothing in Conrad's workshop to presage the birth of a new book in the near future. His creative lassitude had persisted for almost eighteen months, and the financial situation was once again nearing disaster.

To change the atmosphere and mend the family's health, the Conrads again decided to travel south. Their sojourn in Italy, although not very successful, may have reawakened Conrad's taste for a milder climate and for the Continent; Jessie's pregnancy settled the question.[98] They chose to go to Montpellier, a charming old Languedoc health resort, elegant but less expensive than Biarritz or Cannes, the regular haunts of the wealthy English.

On 9 February, the Conrads left England for a three-month stay abroad.[99] They lived at the Hôtel Riche et Continental, whose windows look out over Montpellier's square, the Place de la Comedie, popularly called The Egg. Conrad was in excellent spirits and immediately started on what he envisaged as a third short story about anarchists. Its title was to have been "Verloc," and Conrad worked at it in surroundings that made a grotesque contrast with the content of his tale: he sat in a plane tree–lined avenue, against the sunny wall of the beautiful Le Peyrou Gardens, where elegant visitors to the spa took their daily walks.[100]

The work on "Verloc" was interrupted until 5 March by the task of arranging and editing the essays for *The Mirror of the Sea*.[101] Conrad dedicated the book to Mrs. Katherine Sanderson, Edward's mother. The collection lacks unity; neither its title nor its subtitle (*Memories and Impressions*) covers the whole content. It is a case of two conventions coexisting, not always to mutual advantage: memoirs of the past tinged with sentiment keep uneasy company with essays on particular "sea subjects." Conrad felt more at ease and his writing was more interesting in the former—but he had greater ambitions and was probably aware that, given the unexceptional nature of his own sea experiences, his personal reminiscences alone would not make an outstanding book, so he tried to interweave his personal memories with general reflections. He found himself in a dilemma when the publisher, Methuen, asked for a characterization of the book. In Conrad's vaguely phrased reply one can detect a hesitation between the need for a catchy formula to promote the sales and an awareness of the book's weakness; he even forbade the publisher to quote his remarks.[102]

Having arranged the texts for *The Mirror of the Sea*, Conrad resumed work on "Verloc." The progress was slow. On 5 March he conceived it as a "longish story" of about eighteen thousand words (the length of "Karain"). A month later he mentioned the same length and, in self-defense, tried to justify his slow pace to Pinker: "The conduct of such a story requires no small amount of meditation—not upon questions of style and so on—but simply upon what is fit or is unfit to be said. It is easy with a subject like this to produce a totally false impression. Moreover the thing has got to be *kept up as a story* with an ironic intention but a dramatic development." At the same time Conrad worked, or rather intended to work, on a shorter tale, also "anarchistic," about a "bomb in a hotel"; in spite of his repeated announcements, it was never written.[103]

In the end, the results of Conrad's work at Montpellier were rather unsatisfactory, and he described his consequent misery to Galsworthy: "I am trying to put off this horrid dread of the future which oppresses me. I am dispirited by that feeling of mental exhaustion of which I cannot get rid at all now. I have learned to write *against* it—that's all. But you you [sic] may imagine this effort of will—the sense of failure." "And yet perhaps those days without a line, nay without a word, the hard, atrocious, agonizing days are simply part of my *method* of work." He made no attempt to justify his slow progress—on the contrary, he indulged in self-flagellation: "14,000 words was all I could achieve. It's simply disaster and there's nothing in them, it seems to me, the merest hack novelist could not have written in two evenings and a half. I doubt not only my talent (I was never so sure of that) but my character. Is it indolence—which in my case would be nothing short of baseness—or what? No man has a right to go on as I am doing without producing manifest masterpieces. It seems I've no excuse under heaven or on earth. Enough!"[104]

This outpouring of self-critical anxiety was connected with Conrad's awareness that his financial situation was once again becoming desperate. He repeatedly had to appeal to Pinker for advances ("notwithstanding that I do not send you any fresh copy") and for money to settle newly incurred debts.[105] The royal money came to an end. Rothenstein's remark in his letter to Newbolt about Conrad being in exactly the same straits as the year before greatly irritated the addressee and confirmed his original fears about Conrad's methods of using the grant.[106]

From the financial point of view, the journey to southern France was no doubt an extravagance, but money problems and the slow pace of work did not spoil Conrad's mood. "Joseph Conrad," recalls Jessie, ". . . was another creature when the sun shone on him."[107] Conrad's worship of the Mediterranean sun is also mentioned by Ida Sée, Borys's French teacher in Montpellier.[108] And Montpellier offered more than a salubrious climate and the pleasures natural to a picturesque town with a rich history near the sea; it also offered a social life in which Conrad did not stand out because of his foreign accent and his somewhat peculiar foreign looks. It was a return of a European to Europe, of a man with a "better-class" background to his own milieu. It meant staying in a good hotel, frequenting cafés, then nonexistent in England, and living in the center of an attractive, cultivated town whose size was not overpowering even for a provincial visitor. In all likelihood, if not for a lack of funds, the Conrads would have prolonged their stay. Borys took lessons not only in French but also in riding: "From the very first day he had an excellent seat and a most amusing assurance on horseback. I daresay he inherits the instinct from his Polish ancestors."[109]

The Conrads returned to England on 14 April. Jessie's pregnancy ran its normal course and significantly, Conrad's attitude toward the birth of their second child differed from his reactions eight years earlier. His letters to friends were free from complaints and forebodings. To Rothenstein he wrote facetiously, "I feel very shy and blushing at being let in for that thing at my venerable age."[110] Jessie also remembers that her husband "was more pleased this time than he had been when the first one was coming."[111] In May, however, her own patience and self-control were severely tried.

Ford suggested that the Conrads move to the Hueffers' temporarily unoccupied house, the Bungalow, at Winchelsea. Jessie suspected that behind this offer was Ford's hidden design to get the Conrads permanently settled in his neighborhood, to provide a distraction for his "domestic affairs, which were not exactly to his liking."[112] (Jessie was referring to the gradual disintegration of Ford's marriage.) In July 1905 Elsie discovered that Ford had been having a love affair with her sister, Mary Martindale, and after that time she and Ford lived mostly apart.[113] Perhaps Jessie was right about Ford's intentions; his attempts three years later to get the Conrads involved in his next major love affair seem to confirm her suspicions. But one can also see more immediate and obvious reasons why the two writers wanted to be near each other. Ford needed Conrad's collaboration on "The Nature of a Crime," a piece of kitsch produced for money; Conrad, for his part, needed Ford as a source of information, suggestions, and, above all, encouragement for his work on *The Secret Agent*.[114]

And so the Conrads left for Winchelsea on 11 May and stayed there twelve days.[115] Ford would come down from London for weekends. On 17 May he mentioned in a letter to Elsie that he and Conrad were doing "a rather larky collaboration." *The Nature of a Crime* was something of a phantasy on Ford's real life, at that time torn between his wife and his mistress. As Thomas Moser says, Ford tried to make Conrad help him to "write a love letter to a married woman whose situation resembled Elsie's." In the end, however, Ford had to write practically the whole of *The Nature of a Crime* himself.[116] According to Jessie, "Every conceivable thing happened that fortnight to make me regret coming to Winchelsea. The two long week-ends that F.M.H. had stipulated he should come down were the longest I have ever known, and a fit punishment for any sins I might have ever committed, or even contemplated." The examples of Ford's misbehavior cited by Jessie sound rather pathetic. These trivial conflicts betray, on the one hand, the happy-go-lucky attitude of a bohemian intellectual, and, on the other hand, the pettiness of a simple-minded woman, no doubt particularly touchy because of her advanced pregnancy. We behold Ford blocking with his body the entrance to a railway carriage, or trying to dry his not-too-clean Panama hat in the oven above a roast, or closing the door to the stuffy and hot kitchen where Jessie is preparing tea, and—the epitome of all horrors—covering himself in bed for the night with Conrad's evening suit.[117] Ford was also feeling the strain: "Conrad and Jessie go on Wed.,—and I've not pressed them to stay: they're rather exhausting."[118]

It was probably during this ill-fated visit that Conrad met Arthur Pierson Marwood. The contact was to prove of great value and importance to him.[119] Marwood, who had been living at Winchelsea for about a year, came from a Yorkshire county family. Although he lacked both profession and university education—because of poor health he had to leave Cambridge in the second year of his studies—Marwood was a man of a most impressive intellect and personality.[120] Archibald Marshall wrote of him, "He read voluminously, and seemed to have forgotten nothing of what he ever had read. He was the most remarkable instance of the encyclopedic mind that I have ever come across. There seemed to be no subject upon which he did not possess a store of detailed information. He wrote with difficulty and wrote very little, but he had a clear and convinced appreciation of literary values."[121] Ford had met Marwood and later used him as a model for Christopher Tietjens, the ideal English gentleman and hero of four of his novels; he remembered him as "the heavy Yorkshire squire with his dark hair startlingly silver in places, his keen blue eyes, his florid complexion, his immense, expressive hands and his great shapelessness. He used to say of himself beside Conrad's small vibrating figure: 'We're the two ends of human creation: he's like a quivering ant and I'm an elephant built out of meal sacks.'"[122] Conrad and Marwood became close friends but unfortunately only a few letters survive, and we know rather little about him.

The Conrads decided to go to London sometime before Jessie's confinement and to stay in the house lent them by the invaluable Galsworthy. They proposed, first to Dr. Tebb and then to Rothenstein, to take over the Pent. Nothing came of it in the end, but Conrad's letter to Rothenstein helps us imagine the conditions of the Conrad's daily existence:

Five bedrooms above, two and the big kitchen below—with everything need-ful in it except *the bed sheets* which we take up to London. Stove's in good order—water first rate and no possible smells to affect the chicks; with the wooden house (where you worked on my head) for them to play in when they are tired of the fields.

A good-natured ass called Andrews stays in *our* service to clean knives, boots, light kitchen stove in the morning, fetch water from well, give infor-mation, and drive the trap which holds four with a kiddy or two thrown in. . . . Andrews has a sort of cubicle for himself. . . . The sanitary arrang^ts are primitive as you know, and there is no bathroom—but the good-natured ass above mentioned is trained to carry hot and cold water upstairs and in due course to empty the sponge baths. There is also a tin bath suitable for baby.[123]

The Conrads came to London on 10 July to stay for almost two months.[124] It was a big move, with heavy luggage, numerous chests, boxes, and stocks of food.[125] Their second son was born on 2 August, and in honor of Galsworthy he was named John and nicknamed Jack. "My dear Ada," wrote Conrad to his friend's wife, "I have lately made the acquaintance of a quiet, unassuming, ex-tremely ugly but upon the whole a rather sympathetic young man. A lady I like very much introduced him to me and I am very anxious to secure your and Jack's friendly reception for him when you return. His name is John Alexander Conrad and he arrived here at 9.30 a.m. to-day in a modest and unassuming manner which struck me very favourably. His manner is quiet—somnolent, his eyes contemplative, his forehead noble, his stature short, his nose pug, his con-tenance ruddy and weather-beaten. Altogether I think already that he will be quite a valuable acquisition for our little circle. I feel already (9 p.m.) a good deal of affection for him."[126] Other close friends received equally cheerful let-ters, but barely two weeks later Conrad again struck a doleful note: "I am the only painful person of the crowd. But that is my usual state which is a natural one for a man trying to squeeze some trickle of silly fiction out of a dry, saw-dusty brain. It is, I assure you, a very horrid operation which should be forbid-den by law on humanitarian grounds."[127]

Conrad was working on *The Secret Agent*—one of the novels that took him the least time to write and evoked relatively few complaints, although he had originally conceived of it as a story. Pinker arranged its serialization, which be-gan on 6 October in—such are the ironies of the literary market—*Ridgway's: A Militant Weekly for God and Country*, an American popular magazine. The first version of the novel was completed by the beginning of November.[128]

Twenty years later, in his Author's Note, Conrad gave an exceptionally can-did and detailed account of his sources for the story. In his comments made at the time of writing *The Secret Agent*—he showed the manuscript to Galsworthy before publication—Conrad kept silent about his sources and obstinately repudiated not only any political, social, or philosophical motives but even any desire to present the anarchists in a satirical light: "I had no idea to consider Anarchism politically; or to treat it seriously in its philosophical aspect, as a manifestation of human nature in its discontent and imbecility. The general reflections whether right or wrong are not meant as bolts. . . . As to attacking Anarchism as a form of humanitarian enthusiasm or intellectual despair or social atheism, that—if it were worth doing—would be the work for a more vigorous hand and for a mind more robust, and perhaps more honest than mine."[129] And to his publisher Algernon Methuen he wrote with greater self-confidence: "I confess that in my eyes the story is a fairly successful (and sincere) piece of ironic treatment applied to a special subject—a sensational subject if one likes to call it so. And it is based on the inside knowledge of a certain event in the history of active social or philosophical intention. It is, I humbly hope, not devoid of artistic value. It may even have some moral significance."[130]

And yet the political substance of the book appears quite obvious. So why did Conrad protest? One may only speculate that he did not want *The Secret Agent* to be taken as a roman à thèse or as a topical report on contemporary anarchists. Such an approach would obscure the more general significance of the book, the contrast between order and anarchy. "All these people are not revolutionaries—they are Shams," Conrad later wrote to Graham, delighted with that radical's praise. "By Jove! If I had the necessary talent I would like to go for the true anarchist—which is the millionaire. Then you would see the venom flow. But it's too big a job."[131] Claiming that his novel was not a satire on the anarchists, Conrad may have wanted to hint at something he dared not say publicly: that the Russian embassy, the English police, and the Home Office were objects of no less ridicule: "There are about half a dozen anarchists, two women and one idiot. Besides, all the others are imbeciles, including the head of the chancellory, Minister of State and the Police Inspector."[132]

Meanwhile *The Mirror of the Sea* came out on 4 October to good, sometimes even enthusiastic reviews by critics and fellow writers. It was praised by Wells, Lucas, and, unexpectedly, Kipling. Galsworthy pronounced it "one of the finest books of our time; and in it an episode called 'Initiation' the *very* finest thing written on the sea in our day."[133] Henry James, having received the volume with a modest and deferential dedication in French, reacted with a recherché effusiveness (also partly in French): "J'en suis tout confus, my dear Conrad, and can only thank you and thank you again. But the book itself is a wonder to me really—for it's so bringing home the prodigy of your past experiences: bringing it home to me more personally and directly, I mean, the immense treasure and the inexhaustible adventures. No one has *known*—for intellectual use—the things you know, and you have, as the artist of the whole matter, an authority that no one has approached. . . . Nothing you have done has more in it. . . .

You stir me, in fine, to amazement and you touch me to tears, and I thank the powers who so mysteriously let you loose with such sensibilities, into such an undiscovered country—*for* sensibility." [134]

This kind of acclaim—being praised for his deviation from the ordinary experience of a writer—had its dangers. The image being shaped of Conrad as a writer of sea stories and the exotic was to give him a wide but short-lived, shallow, and misleading kind of popularity. Conrad, sensing that danger, wrote to his French translator, "The critics have been vigorously swinging the censer to me. I believe that most of them had intended to wipe my nose. Some took the opportunity to give a kick to that poor *Nostromo* who had been buried alive two years ago. Do you remember? Behind the concert of flattery, I can hear something like a whisper: 'Keep to the open sea! Don't land!' They want to banish me to the middle of the ocean." But with all the praise, *The Mirror* sold less than fifteen hundred copies in England. [135]

With *The Secret Agent* finished, Conrad, as always after a period of intensive creative work, complained of depression—evidently the "depression of un-shouldering." [136] All the same he managed to devote a great deal of attention to a patient analysis of Garnett's play *The Breaking Point*. Conrad's long letter of 17 November shows his capacity for serious and detailed critical discussion—sweetened by compliments—when the work in question was still in draft form and it was not too late to make changes in it. In the case of Garnett's artificial and pretentious piece, the task must have been particularly thankless. [137] Presently he resumed his own work and, probably on 4 December, finished "Il Conde," a short story presumably based on an experience of Count Zygmunt Szembek. [138] On 16 December the Conrads left again for Montpellier, this time for a longer stay. Two more people accompanied them on the journey: Jessie's cousin, Miss Wright, as nurse and helper, and a maid. [139] On the way they stopped for a day and a half in Paris to meet Mme Poradowska, her brother Charles Gachet, and Davray. [140]

The first weeks of their stay passed very pleasantly. The weather was beautiful, "cold, calm dry brilliant." [141] Conrad's letter to Ford struck a lyrical note: "I am better in this sunshine. The landscape around is magic all subtle, all of colour alone. The villages perched on conical hills stand out against the great and sweeping lines of violet ranges as if in an enchanted country. The beauty of this land is inexpressible and the delicacy of colours at sunset and sunrise beyond the power of men to imagine. . . . And every day as I go about entranced, I miss you more and more. You ought to see this. . . . I am drunk with colour and would like dearly to have you to lean upon. I am certain that with no other man could I share my rapture.

"Work at a standstill. Plans simply swarming in my head but my English has all departed from me." [142]

This was not surprising: Conrad was busy revising the French translations (by Poradowska and Davray) of his stories from *Tales of Unrest*, an occupation he obviously enjoyed.[143] The family made excursions to Palavas-sur-Mer and visited the beautiful twelfth-century cathedral at Maguelone, right on the seashore. In one characteristic expedition they found the road blocked by an upturned cart loaded with vine shoots. Conrad first made his driver climb down and help the cursing farmer get his mule to move, then stunned the man with joy by giving him a louis-d'or to "make up for the trouble and the waste of time."[144] Borys resumed his riding and French lessons and also started fencing. Conrad, for his part, was learning Spanish; he also made at least one interesting acquaintance. As the story goes, Conrad, "a little quiet bearded man who smelled of an old mariner," introduced himself to one Louis-Charles Eymar, a traveler and local painter, whom he met in the still-existing Café Riche. He gave his "difficult name," and it was only years later that Eymar learned from Valery Larbaud that he had met a famous writer.[145] Apparently there was also a female orchestra playing at the Café Riche, and one of the musicians attracted Conrad's attention; she later served as the model for Lena in *Victory*.[146]

In the municipal library Conrad rummaged about for books about Napoleon on Elba. He was already fascinated by the subject that he would take up in his last novel. Meanwhile his interest in the Napoleonic era found expression in "The Duel," a short story begun in January and finished on 11 April.[147] It was Conrad's first historical piece, one in which he tried to "capture the spirit of the Era." With all the lightness of its sensational plot, he placed the action firmly within contemporary political reality, as the impressive conversation with Fouché bears out.[148] He was also helping Jessie put the finishing touches to her "work of art"—a cook book for "a small house"; he furnished a foreword, comical in a rather strained way.[149]

Chance remained dormant. As late as 14 May 1912 the manuscript numbered only 164 pages (the finished work numbered 1,252).[150] As always, Conrad complained about the slow tempo of his work, writing to his Franco-Polish "aunt," "I am lazy like all Poles. I prefer to dream about a novel than write it. The dream is always much more beautiful than the printed reality. Moreover English is for me still a foreign language and its use requires a formidable effort on my part."[151] Meanwhile Pinker, who now and again supplied Conrad with money, was making repeated demands for the finished parts of the manuscript. Conrad, with nothing to send, kept giving evasive answers, complaints mingled with reports about purportedly well-developed projects: "I will make it interesting enough, you may well trust me for that. But please don't place it *too soon*. . . . I want time. . . . I wish to reach a certain point from which I will be able to dictate for a little while. All that part is maturing very fairly, and a month of dictating will give a famous shove to the thing. I intend to give up the month of May to that; which month, by the bye, I wish to spend in London. But of that I will tell you later. Then June, Aug. Sept. Oct. in the Pent driving hard, and exclusively at it will bring into view of the conclusion, which last I tell you frankly *I haven't* got as yet. But by that time it will be there." [152] He was more than four years off the mark.

Toward the end of January 1907 a new series of illnesses began. It appeared that Borys had to be operated on for adenoids but instead he came down with a severe case of measles followed by a mysterious lung ailment. Pneumonia, bronchitis, and tuberculosis were suspected in turn and in the beginning of March Conrad expressed his despair to Galsworthy: "This is the tenth night I haven't slept. I don't mean to say I have had no sleep in all that time, but I hang about his room all night listening and watching. I simply can't go to bed. Then in the afternoon I throw myself down on the sofa and sleep from sheer weariness. For four days I haven't written anything. Jessie is wholly admirable, sharing herself between the two boys with the utmost serenity." [153] Baines observes that Conrad's state of acute anxiety must have been increased by the memory of the cause of his parents' deaths. [154]

Fortunately the tests for tuberculosis proved negative. But Conrad, frightened by Borys's proneness to lung infections, decided to increase the boy's resistance to disease by postponing the family's return to England and spending the spring in Switzerland. [155] In a long letter to Pinker, who would have to finance the venture, Conrad set forth his arguments. A stay in Switzerland complemented by a water cure would benefit both the boy and himself: he had not suffered from gout for fourteen months and it would be worthwhile to make this improvement permanent. The best place to go would be Champel, where he had worked before. And as for Borys: "If it is to be Switzerland I much prefer Geneva now than Davos-Platz later on, where the modern Dance of Death goes on in expensive hotels." Thus they could go to Champel in the middle of April and return to England in September. On 21 March he would accompany Miss Wright and the maid back to Paris; there he would pick up the Conrads' old housemaid, Nellie Lyons; this would mean one person less to support. He was convinced that there would not be even a "single day" of delay with *Chance*, which had been progressing quite well lately. But of course he would need money now, and he could not send the completed chapters yet because they might be needed for further work on the novel. [156]

Pinker accepted the plan. The Conrads remained in Montpellier until mid-May, however, extending their stay in France for another month, probably for financial reasons. During that time Conrad finished "The Duel" and continued to say he would reach the end of *Chance* in a few months. This would have been the only way to stop his debts from climbing; Conrad was trying to reassure Pinker-the-creditor, but he himself was tormented by doubts, and there are no signs that the novel was in fact progressing.

There were other reasons for the plan. Conrad did not feel like returning to Pent Farm—the house was not large enough for so many people; also, in spite of the modest rent, the distance from the nearest town increased the cost of keeping up a decent standard of living. Not surprisingly, after a few reasonably uneventful weeks, on about 1 May Conrad suffered another attack of gout, and began to sink into despair again. "The state of worry in which I am living—and writing—is simply indescribable," he wrote to Galsworthy. "It's a constant breaking strain. And you know that materials subjected to breaking strain lose all elasticity in the end . . . It seems to me I have a lump of mud, of slack mud, in my head. . . . Have been in bed, feeling very beastly for five days. The nervous collapse is considerable. Can't react somehow. I drag about with an arm in the sling, hopeless, spiritless, without a single thought in my head. Borys is coughing a lot and I avow that the sound robs me of the last vestiges of composure." [157]

Borys's cough heralded a new disaster. He had whooping cough, which he soon passed on to his younger brother. The illness had developed just before the family left Montpellier on 15 May; a few days later Conrad informed Pinker that he needed to pay the hotel bill of 1,100 francs (about £55), adding, "And please don't scold me, because I have just now as much as I can bear. Here I am stranded again with baby at its last gasp with whooping cough. . . . The poor little devil has melted down to half his size. Since yesterday morning he has had a coughing fit every quarter of an hour or so and will not eat anything. We'll have to resort to artificial feeding very soon. Of course *La Roseraie Hôtel* won't take us now. . . . Really I haven't got my share of the commonest sort of luck. . . . My dear Pinker I feel that all this is almost too much for me." [158]

If we are to trust Jessie's version, Conrad frequently lost his head during these family crises; she recalled, "At each development this time it really seemed that I could endure no more, yet as soon as I saw that poor Joseph Conrad showed signs of a collapse, I became once again efficient and calm." Conrad even added to the confusion by setting his mattress on fire after falling asleep with a cigarette, or losing his wallet; anyway, at night, he usually slept soundly, unaware of what was going on. [159] But Jessie, who often boasted about her extremely accurate memory, is consistently guilty of so many misrepresentations and fabrications designed to present herself in the role of an indomitable heroine that one is wary of fully accepting her portrayal of Conrad as a hysterical bungler. Conrad, for his part, spared no praise of his wife's attitude under difficulties: "Jessie has been simply heroic in the awful Montpellier adventure, never giving a sign of anxiety not only before the boy, but even out of his sight; always calm, serene, equable, going from one to the other and apparently never tired though cruelly crippled by her leg, which is not in a good condition, by any means. But how long she will last at it I don't know." [160]

Jessie somehow survived, and only years later let out her torrent of complaints. Conrad, on the other hand, reached the limits of his psychological endurance by the end of May. His letters to Galsworthy and Rothenstein reveal that the series of illnesses sometimes completely upset his mental and emotional stability. On 28 May Conrad wrote to Rothenstein, "Poor baby is simply melting away in our hands. It's heartbreaking business to look at him. But this is not all. Four days ago Borys, who had really never been himself since that attack of measles, got laid hold of by an attack of rheumatism in both ankles. . . . And all this time with a whooping cough which jerks him all over as he lies in bed. I break into cold perspiration whenever I hear him cough, for I know how horrible is the pain of a jarred rheumatic limb." [161] In early June Conrad informed Galsworthy:

I read to him all day and attend to him the best I can with one arm, because my left, since my last gout, isn't much use: and what I can do with it is done at the cost of a good deal of pain. Now and then I steal an hour or two to work at preparing the *Secret Agent* for book form. And all this is ghastly. I seem to move, talk, write in a sort of quiet nightmare that goes on and on. I wouldn't wish my worst enemy this experience. . . .

From the sound next door (we have three rooms) I know that the pain has roused Borys from his feverish doze. I won't go to him. It's no use. Presently I shall give him his salicylate, take his temperature and shall then go to elaborate a little more the conversation of Mr Verloc with his wife. It is very important that the conversation of Mr Verloc with his wife should be elaborated—made more effective, don't you know—more *true* to the situation and the character of these people.

By Jove! I've got to hold myself with both hands not to burst into a laugh which would scare wife, baby and the other invalid—let alone the lady whose room is on the other side of the corridor! [162]

On 17 June Conrad again wrote to Galsworthy:

Borys does not get on at all. Symptoms of bronchitis at the top of left lung have declared themselves since the 15th, and there is the pleurisy too. With this a hectic fever well characterized and rapid emaciation with a cough. It is his 22nd day in bed. Things could not look much more ugly. Another doctor is coming this afternoon.

I am keeping up, but I feel as if a mosquito bite were enough to knock me over. Good God! If I were to get it now, what would happen! As it is I don't know very well what will happen. It will be nothing good anyway—even at best. [163]

A similar letter so alarmed the Fords that they were ready to come to Champel to help. Conrad, declining their offer, assured Elsie that "one has complete faith in you and Ford." [164]

It was not until 24 June that Borys's temperature finally went down and his recuperation began. [165] Thus serious illnesses had dragged on for full five months, and Conrad had sufficient cause to bemoan his run of bad luck and utter exhaustion. Unable to adopt a stoic attitude, he wrote many letters that border on hysteria; they presumably exaggerate the family misfortunes and his own nursing activities. On the other hand, Jessie's biased portrait of her husband as a man whose excitability and egocentrism only made matters worse shows that she was insensitive to the psychological stresses to which Conrad was subjected—the exasperations of creative writing and his awareness of the family's hopeless financial situation, which Jessie never even mentions. Conrad, for his part, was again caught in a vicious circle: Borys's illness hindered his work; his own slowness at writing increased his debts; they in turn aggravated the strain and worsened his depression; and his dejection in the face of his son's suffering was the final paralyzing burden.

Quite apart from all these considerations *Chance* had to be laid aside because Conrad was busy revising *The Secret Agent*—"a distinctly new departure in my work. And I am anxious to put as much 'quality' as I can in that book which will be criticised with some severity no doubt—or *scrutinised* rather I should say. Preconceived notions of Conrad as sea writer will stand in the way of its acceptance." [166] In the middle of May the proofs for the book edition arrived, and Conrad immediately complained to Pinker, "I have almost cried at the sight. I thought it was arranged beyond doubt that I was to have *galley slips* for my corrections. Instead of that I get the proofs of set pages! Apart from the cost of corrections, which will be greatly augmented through that, there is the material difficulty of correcting clearly and easily on small margins." [167] Despite the practical difficulties with the sheets and the consequent addition to his psychological strain, Conrad added over one-fourth of the text of the novel, making it artistically more homogeneous, chiefly by consistently observing the principle "to render, not to report." He added all of Chapter 10 (the Assistant Commissioner's conversations with Sir Ethelred and Mr Vladimir) and considerably expanded Chapters 11 and 12. [168] The book was dedicated to Wells. "Considering that the time passes and that I am not likely to improve much by keeping on this earth I think the moment for this small proof of very great affection to be given has come. Hereby I ask for permission!" [169]

In the final weeks at Champel, Conrad took a water cure, which he claimed was most beneficial. "But I am worried incessantly with thoughts of the future." [170] The "future" consisted of the far from finished *Chance*, of plans for another novel, and of the growing debts to Pinker. He meant to have *Chance* ready for the printer at the beginning of December, and the next novel by August 1908. "I cling to it desperately. It must be done." [171] In order to set his finances in some semblance of order, and probably also to safeguard himself in the event of not submitting promised texts on time, as had repeatedly happened, Conrad suggested to Pinker a bilateral agreement based on a preagreed budget, which he solemnly promised not to exceed. The proposed sum of £800 a year included £50 for the rent, £614 for household expenses and Borys's school, and £126 for doctors' bills.[172] Pinker was supposed to cover current expenses with weekly checks and quarterly payments, "all to fall strictly within the limit, as it has been estimated, and not a penny more."[173]

While accepting the principle of a prearranged budget, Pinker reduced it to £600. Conrad was to write "80,000 *at least* being the words of a *novel* not short stories" in the course of twelve months.[174] The "financial year" was to begin on 10 August but Conrad at once asked the agent for an exception to the rule in the form of an additional £60 to cover his debts in Hythe and the neighborhood. "We must end this damnable outing now as soon as possible. . . . We could start from here on the 10th. . . . I would go on the 8th, providing always you pay the people in Kent before I return, in accordance with the enclosed list. . . . No more trips abroad. I am sick of them."[175]

On the return voyage Conrad, according to Jessie, again caused trouble and spread confusion: he forgot the time of departure, perused a bookstall instead of buying sandwiches for the journey, and then once more lost his wallet.[176] The family was back in the Pent on 12 August, and Conrad immediately began to look for a new house. He considered moving to Hampshire, near Winchester, where their friend Harriet M. Capes lived. The Conrads had had their eye on a house on Colden Common, but physicians and friends apparently dissuaded them from taking it because the damp climate of southern England was considered injurious to Conrad's health.[177] On 10 September the Conrads left for Bedford, "40 minutes from St Pancras and many times a day. It is 2½ miles from Luton: a farmhouse of a rather cosy sort without distinction of any kind, but quite 500 ft above the sea—which is what we both want. Its name is Someries."[178] "We have abandoned the Pent to its green solitude—*to its rats*. There's a chapter closed." Conrad was leaving the Pent under the cloud of his extant debt to Ford, from whom he had sublet the house. Ford, financially not less strapped than Conrad, apparently considered exerting legal pressure on Pinker, to force him to pay his client's debt. It is difficult to say whether the threat was serious, or just one of Ford's fleeting phantasies. Conrad protested to Galsworthy, "My conduct to Ford is not so base as it looks"; he himself was entirely powerless.[179]

Someries, with its six bedrooms, was much larger than the Pent but also noisier, and the farm laborers living nearby filched vegetables from the garden. The biggest advantage of the new house was probably its proximity to London—but that, in turn, attracted guests, sometimes unwanted; no doubt that was one of the reasons Jessie disliked Someries from the start. Her description of the move from the Pent is another tirade about Conrad's impracticality, his lack of organization, and his habit of demanding good food and peace for his work, regardless of unfavorable circumstances.[180] Very soon Conrad also began to criticize the new house as depressing.[181] The difficulty of getting reaccustomed to the doubtful pleasures of the English winter—in the summer he praised the "bracing" climate of Bedfordshire—was certainly a contributing factor.[182]

The Secret Agent was published on 12 September. The subject, the place of action, the modest size and clear structure of the book ought to have made the critics' task easier and their attitude more agreeable, but in fact the reception of *The Secret Agent* was worse than that of *Nostromo*. Some good or even enthusiastic reviews appeared—the one in the *Times Literary Supplement* deserves particular attention, as does the unsigned article by Garnett in *The Nation*. But the praise was outweighed by expressions of disappointment and, at times, by ludicrously unfair accusations, often contradictory and sometimes strikingly typical of the reviewers' social prejudices. Many critics referred to Conrad's foreign origins; the book's difficulty and inaccessibility to the "ordinary reader" was again stressed, with or without reproach. The novel sold poorly: in England less than three thousand copies in five years; in the United States twenty-five hundred in seven.[183]

Conrad, while declaring that he was not expecting great popularity, had counted on at least a reasonable financial success. He confessed, "I have some hopes of my new book"; he even expected it "to produce some sensation."[184] But he had to sum up the fate of *The Secret Agent* very differently: "The S.A. may be pronounced by now an honourable failure. It brought me neither love nor promise of literary success. I own that I am cast down. I suppose I am a fool to have expected anything else. I suppose there is something in me that is unsympathetic to the general public . . . Foreigness [sic] I suppose."[185] The reception of *The Secret Agent* crystallized what Conrad had long feared—that he would be classified as a curio, a writer interesting by virtue of his unique experiences and background. To be sure, Conrad contrasted himself with Kipling, the exemplar of a *"national* writer" who "speaks of *his compatriots"*—while he, Conrad, wrote *"for them,"* that is, for the English; but he made the comparison in a letter to a Frenchman.[186] When his foreignness was pointed out by the English, he found it galling, particularly when he was referred to as a Slav. Garnett did it as many as four times in his review and topped it off by drawing an absurd comparison with Chopin.

When at the beginning of October Garnett, whose play *The Breaking Point* had been taken off the theater bill by the censor's office, asked for an article attacking that institution, Conrad agreed at once but added, "I've been so cried up of late as a sort of freak, an amazing bloody foreigner writing in English (every blessed review of S.A. had it so—and even yours) that anything I say will be discounted on that ground by the public—that is if the public, that mysterious beast, takes any notice whatever—which I doubt."[187] And when Garnett counseled moderation in attack, warning that the action—many writers were coming out against censorship—might prove ineffective, Conrad sent a cutting reply: "You remember always that I am a Slav (it's your idée fixe) but you seem to forget that I am a Pole. You forget that we have been used to go to battle without illusions. It's you Britishers that 'go in to win' only. We have been 'going in' these last hundred years repeatedly, to be knocked on the head only—as was visible to any calm intellect. But you have been learning your history from Russians no doubt."[188] Garnett later censored "The Censor of Plays" by deleting such sentences as "He can go out in the morning, this grotesque magistrate of a free commonwealth, catch a donkey on Hampstead Heath, lead him into his study and sit him down in his curule chair. Has not Caligula made his horse a consul? He can do that and there is no one to say him nay. Perhaps indeed no one could detect the difference."[189] The whole article is written in a tone of sarcastic hyperbole. It is not a defense of the freedom of belles-lettres or theater plays but a passionate plea, presented in political and cultural terms, for freedom of expression in general. Conrad was displeased with Garnett's deletions, although he had authorized him to make cuts: "I did not discuss the point for fear that Edward (who declares himself Irish) should tell me that (as a Slav) I know nothing of the English temper in controversy."[190]

At the time, Conrad's chief work in progress was *Chance*; as late as the beginning of November 1907 he was still hoping to finish it before the New Year.[191] His next book was to have been a volume of short stories, but Conrad thought that the tales that were later collected in *A Set of Six* did not make a coherent whole. In its place he visualized a volume including only five of the stories: "Gaspar Ruiz," "Anarchist," "The Informer," "The Brute," and "Il Conde"; "The Duel," Conrad wrote, was to be left as a seed for another volume: "I have material for another military story about the same length and we could publish the two together when the time comes. It would be something distinctive. Military stories of a hundred years ago.. See?"[192] He also contemplated writing a "big novel with London for background and . . . another which is nothing less than European in scale."[193]

In early December, with the progress of *Chance* still very slow, Conrad began a new short story which was to be ready soon after Christmas. His terms for it, in a letter to Pinker, are interesting: "It's the one about the revolutionist who is blown up with his own bomb."[194] The work was then called "Razumov," and it quickly began to expand. "It is a more difficult job than I thought," Conrad wrote to Pinker on 30 December. Perhaps the concept of a novel on a European scale became linked in the course of writing with that of the story about a Russian revolutionary, intended originally as the nucleus for yet another volume of short stories. It was to have been an essentially serious piece: "a contribution to and a reading of the Russian character. . . . Here is given the very essence of things Russian. Not the mere outward manners and customs but the Russian feeling and thought. . . . And I think the story *is* effective. It is also characteristic of the present time. Nothing of the sort had been done in English. The subject has long haunted me. . . . The fact is my dear Pinker I haven't yet given my measure. I am not thinking of the writing—the style. It is something else that I am thinking of—what may be called 'my powers.' You know well that in fact nobody who was 'aware' of my literary existence expected anything like the *Secret Agent*. Well there is more—and different things too—in me yet."[195]

This proud and promising statement exposed Conrad's practical dilemma. He planned to write a short piece begun almost by chance; at the same time he was embarking on a huge and ambitious project. The host of problems associated with Russia and the contrasts between autocracy and democracy, which had been pent up in his mind for a long time, could not be disposed of without a major writing effort. The subject of *Chance* had to pale in comparison: the consciousness of new artistic and intellectual possibilities was surely exhilarating. Therefore, in spite of assuring Pinker that *Chance* would be "done faster now," Conrad abandoned it for a longer period of time. After spending one month on "Razumov," he realized that it was going to be a fairly long work. He summarized it to Galsworthy: "The Student Razumov (a natural son of a Prince K.) gives up secretly to the police his fellow student, Haldin, who seeks refuge in his rooms after committing a political crime (supposed to be the murder of de Plehve). First movement in St Petersburg. (Haldin is hanged of course.)

"2nd in Genèva [sic]. The Student Razumov meeting abroad the mother and sister of Haldin falls in love with that last, marries her and, after a time, confesses to her the part he played in the arrest and death of her brother.

"The psychological developments leading to Razumov's betrayal of Haldin, to his confession of the fact to his wife and to the death of these people (brought about mainly by the resemblance of their child to the late Haldin), form the real subject of the story."[196]

Conrad grumbled about his health; at the end of November he even maintained that sickness had made him unable to work since August.[197] But he made use of the proximity of London, both for visiting friends there and, apparently more frequently, for receiving friends at his home. One of the guests, who was becoming a good friend, was Sidney Colvin.[198] Another visitor was J. C. Tarver, author of a book on Flaubert.[199] Norman Douglas also came; Conrad encouraged him and offered him advice in the first stages of his literary career. It seems that his contacts with Ford were mainly by correspondence: Elsie was seriously ill at the time and Ford commuted between his London flat and Winchelsea.[200] Conrad's trips to London were not regular, but he occasionally attended the Tuesday luncheons at the Mont-Blanc Restaurant.[201] During those gatherings, in which Belloc, Chesterton, Galsworthy, Marwood, and Edward Thomas (among others) participated, Conrad met a journalist and editor, Archibald Marshall. "Conrad . . . made the deepest impression upon me," Marshall later wrote. His magnificent head, surely one of the handsomest that was ever set on a pair of shoulders, if you are to take into account what a face reflects of the spirit that enlightens it, his dignity, austerity, kindness of heart, even his irritabilities, made him an unforgettable figure. I had no personal experience of those irritabilities, but used to hear enough about them, and they all seemed part of him, for nobody ever took his work as a writer more to heart than he did, and it was because he almost agonized over it that little outside impingements upon his brain annoyed him, like midge bites."[202] A reporter from *T.P.'s Weekly* who interviewed Conrad at the time was struck mainly by his excitability: "He is abnormally highly-strung. He is sensitive, intensely susceptible to any slight jarring from outside. His nerves seem to be all on end. . . . He dislikes certain broad types of people virulently, and says so in a downright fashion. At such times he sloughs his elaborately courteous demeanour he reveals himself as a man of devastating force of character. He grows fierce, passionate, violent . . . triumphant and obliterating and sweeping away his calculated suavity of speech."[203]

Around this time Conrad, through Garnett, struck up a friendship with a budding writer, Stephen Reynolds, whom Conrad invited for Christmas. Their common interest, in addition to literature, was the sea. Reynolds, who for health reasons had been living on the Devon coast for a few years, acquired first-hand knowledge about the work of local fishermen and devoted the rest of his life mainly to improving their lot.[204]

Summing up his past achievements and assessing the current state of his affairs at the close of 1907, Conrad wrote several times that he was "beginning" his fiftieth year;[205] in fact he had ended it on 3 December. The situation looked rather dismal: his health was poor and his work, in spite of continued effort, progressed slowly; Conrad's books still failed to win any broad acclaim, so his financial position remained desperate. Back in September Conrad had found himself in the disagreeable situation of being unable to repay his debt to Ford, who needed money urgently.[206] Conrad rendered a financial balance sheet of his writing career to Galsworthy:

> Eleven novels. If each had averaged £1000 I would have now 5000 in hand. For casting up all I owe you, other debts, the balance against me with P. (£1572 to date) and the grant I had together with all I have earned it works out at £650 per year in round numbers. Even if I have made a mistake of a 100 a year too little, which is improbable (for however carelessly I counted I am not likely to have underestimated all I had by 1200 pounds st), this is not outrageously extravagant. And in this, there's Jessie's illness, all of my own— (the year wasted when writing *Nostromo*, when I had six fits of gout in eleven months)—and this last fatal year with Borys abroad.
>
> That last was very bad—for pressed by necessity (when a child is ill one does not stop to count) I have had to use all the money remitted by Pinker— it was none too much—and have left a lot of bills unpaid in Kent.[207]

These calculations and confidences were the preface to yet another request for a loan—£60 to be paid in instalments by Pinker. They provide a good example of how Conrad's confused thinking in money matters was usually hidden under the appearance of sober calculations. Conrad had not, in fact, produced eleven novels, but eleven volumes, including the collections of short stories and *Romance* (mainly written by Ford). If each volume had in fact brought him £1,000 and if in fact Conrad had been spending only £650 a year, after thirteen years—counting from the time of publishing *Almayer's Folly*—he would actually have earned a reserve of not £5,000 but only half that sum.[208] There can be no doubt that he had really been spending a good deal more; it is also known that at the start of his writing career he still had considerable capital. The unpaid bills in Kent had little to do with Borys's illness; the debts had been incurred before the journey to France, and Borys's sickness began two months later. Conrad's whole attitude toward money and its management was bound to land him in trouble.

The arrangement with Pinker, in the abstract very convenient, in practice proved a pitfall, because Conrad, working more slowly and needing more money than he expected, plunged deeper and deeper into debt. The terms of the agreement compelled Conrad to appeal to Pinker for help; but each such appeal was a new irritation and further poisoned their relationship. The conflict came to a head early in 1908. Soon after the New Year Conrad asked Pinker for additional payments amounting to £37.[209] On 13 or 14 January Pinker announced in conversation that he was unable to make additional outlays and wanted to revise the existing agreement. Conrad reacted with a lengthy letter on what the new agreement—more complicated and less inflexible—was to be. Conrad would seek a loan (Galsworthy, although not named, was the intended lender) of £260 for six months, with Pinker providing the security. In exchange Conrad would undertake never to demand any advance payments exceeding one-third of the commercial value (for serialization and book edition) of *Chance*, which he promised to finish for July. Moreover, Pinker was to pay him £100 immediately and commit himself to cover bills amounting to £130 over a six-month period. The bills included Borys's school fees of £16 a quarter, the rent for the house, instalments on the furniture, and so forth. Conrad embellished the new budget with self-defensive—and mythologizing—reflections:

> However I think that you have a fixed impression that Conrad to "inability to work" too much gives way! It is not so. You have said: *you all* (literary men I suppose) *talk like that. Other people have to work whether they can or not.* I beg to point out that I am not a literary man. In 1890 coming out the hospital after 6 months illness I managed for 4 months the Straw Plait Warehouse of Barr Moering and Co, introduced a new system altogether both as to book keeping and stowage. I have now a letter from Simpson and Sons in Adelaide telling me that for years before I took command the *Otago* barely earned her insurance. The two years I had her that ship paid 16% on her actual value. So I know what all sorts of work mean. It is extraordinary that people who

understand that a carpenter can't make a box if somebody keeps on jogging his elbow will say that no jog of any sort should matter to a mind.[210]

Two days later, probably annoyed at not having received a reply, Conrad again wrote to Pinker:

I feel every time I write as if I were begging. I don't like it. It grows impossible. Here out of this months nominal money I have paid 4 months coal practically. This sort of thing won't do. . . . Nobody can say I have a vice— gambling or drink to lead me astray. It may be that I don't *count* my money very well.

After this sensational discovery, Conrad went on to suggest that Pinker should pay him the agreed sums not by cheques but in cash, at the rate of £40 a month.

As it is I take money from my wife for this and that and then of course I must come to you for cheques. I hate it. And perhaps I do take too much. Perhaps I don't *count* strictly enough. When one does not *see* what one spends one is apt to spend too much. Though this is not an admission of extravagance.[211]

By then the debt to Pinker was enormous; according to Conrad's own estimate it equaled almost two and a half years' expenses. Thus it is not surprising that Pinker put off making new payments while demanding the manuscript. On 13 February Conrad became desperate:

13 vols since 1895 when my first book was published are no sign of indolence—considering too that there are such vols as Lord Jim—the *Youth* collection, the Outcast—the Secret Agent and considering too that at least ⅓ of the time should be deducted for illness, depressing in itself and treated too usually by most depressing remedies.

I've been drenched with Colchicum since last October and I have enough of it. I have begun what I am told may be a radical cure with some new drugs. This last attack, the 5th since Oct. has been brought on by the medicine and I've felt very ill for 3 days. Now it is passing away apparently and I am going to persevere for another 40 days so as to eradicate all poison out of the system—if it can be done. I am telling you all this not because I think it interesting but because it has some bearing upon my future production.

I want to know whether you will pay Borys' school fees for the current term. They amount to £16.18.9. If I don't hear on Sat. I shall take it that it is impossible. . . .

I referred to you some time ago a proposal from a firm of Literary Agents for the rights of trans: into French. I want to be sure that you have not disposed of any rights because the Mercure de France is inclined to negotiate in that respect for the whole of my work. I have also proposals for working in French and I don't feel too old to make a fresh start. In the general uncertainty of what is to happen to me the idea doesn't seem so very bizarre. Rather interesting in fact. . . .

The furniture people are reminding me that the Jan. inst. 2.0.5 has not been paid. If they come here to take the things away, I will have to finish Razumov in French—I am afraid—wherein I shall not have to fear the competition of A. Bennett, that true Parisian.[212]

It is unlikely that Conrad's grotesque and melodramatic threat of changing over to writing in French was intended as blackmail. After all, Pinker had nothing to fear. The threat was more probably an outlet for Conrad's dreams of escape, of breaking out of the vicious circle; and Conrad cannot really have believed what he said. He may have enjoyed correcting the French translations of his works; but, as he himself wrote in November 1909 to the translator of *The Nigger*, Robert d'Humières, "I always had but one literary language as if I were born English."[213]

The budget was temporarily patched up by the loan and the checks from Pinker, but in March Conrad had to appeal to the Royal Literary Fund for a grant. He asked Wells to support his application, and on 16 April Conrad was able to inform him that he had received £200.[214]

Under those circumstances it was not surprising that the beginning of 1908 passed in a doleful mood. Throughout January Conrad was racked with gout; in February he thought, incorrectly, that he had phlebitis.[215]

An additional and ever present worry was Jessie's condition; she walked with increasing difficulty. Conrad's attitude toward family life took a subtle but perceptible turn for the better in the eighteen months that followed the birth of their second child. His letters mention his children more often and with greater affection, and he devoted more time and attention to them. As Borys grew older communication and companionship developed, and then there was the shared experience of the boys' illnesses at Montpellier and Geneva. Another reason for Conrad's changing attitude may have been that the family was no longer a triangle in which father and son competed against each other for Jessie's attention; the pattern of mutual connections and responsibilities became more complex, particularly after Jessie's illness. At the beginning of the school year Borys was placed in a private preparatory school in Luton. Although it was only three miles from Someries, he went as a boarder, probably to relieve Jessie from some of her duties; he came home only for weekends. In February Conrad wrote of Borys to Poradowska, "He is a very brave boy, very loyal, a little pessimistic, a little moody, but deeply affectionate towards his family. He adores John Alexander—who reciprocates in his own fashion." And to Galsworthy he noted, "[Borys] has a good report from school."[216]

As an immediate measure to mend his budget Conrad wrote "The Black Mate" in January and February.[217] The story was published in the April number of *London Magazine*. It is a trivial piece and was not included in any collection that Conrad published. It was, however, to become the subject of a marital controversy now impossible to untangle. In 1922 Conrad wrote to Pinker, "I don't remember whether I told you that I wrote that thing in '86 for a prize competition, started, I think, by *Tit Bits*. It is an extraneous phenomenon. My literary life began privately in 1890 and publicly in 1895 with *Almayer's Folly*, which is regarded generally as my very first piece of writing. However, the history of 'The Black Mate,' its origin etc., etc., need not be proclaimed on housetops, and *Almayer's Folly* may keep its place as my first serious work."[218] Not long after, when signing a copy of a collector's edition for Richard Curle, Conrad made a more guarded statement: "My memories of this tale are confused. I have a notion that it was first written some time in the late eighties and retouched later."[219] He might have withdrawn the unambiguous version presented to Pinker because of Jessie, who categorically denied it, claiming that she had been the one who suggested the plot of the story.[220] The weekly *Tit-Bits* indeed used to run competitions but not for short stories, only for reminiscences. The manuscript of "The Black Mate" (at the British Library) shows no signs of being a reshaped version of an earlier draft. Perhaps Conrad had in fact written something for *Tit-Bits* and later connected it with the artistically primitive tale suggested by his wife.

At any rate the story was indeed an "extraneous phenomenon." Conrad's serious attention was absorbed by *Razumov*, which kept on growing beyond original plans. In March Conrad announced that "Raz. will be 43000 words. You may take this estimate as pretty correct."[221] A few days later he believed he was writing the last chapter.[222] A week later he was pondering the title: "Mrs Atherton wrote a novel entitled *Rezanov* some time ago—very much the same sound. Only my title has a significance whereas hers probably has not. My story deserves a better title than a man's name."[223] As the weeks went by the most frequently mentioned subject in Conrad's letters to Pinker was his need of money; although on 10 April he informed *Harper's Magazine*, "I am now struggling with the end of a long novel of Russian life," in May he announced to Pinker, "I can't let you have Razumov yet. That story must be worked out as it is worth it."[224] Since at the end of September Conrad estimated *Razumov's* length to be sixty-two thousand words—slightly more than *The Nigger* and less than half the final version of *Under Western Eyes*—only some fifty odd pages can have been written from March to September. "I have it all in my head and yet when it comes to writing I simply can't find the words," Conrad wrote to Garnett.[225]

The slowness of "production," as Conrad called it, was bound to result in yet another conflict with Pinker. This one broke out in July. Conrad wrote to Pinker—on the office paper, and presumably, therefore, after an interview—"You must not treat me as a journeyman joiner. Am I to understand that if the book is not finished by say 10 or 15 then you will drop me on the 19th of August. I don't inquire whether it is you *can't* or *won't*. From the practical point of view it amounts to the same thing. . . . If your idea is that my stuff is unsalable then all I can say is that *I* haven't made it so. . . . Consider whether it would be good policy (from a practical point of view) to drive me away. . . . I can't believe that my reputation has gone to pieces suddenly."[226]

Meanwhile Pinker was in a position to sell to Methuen a volume of six stories. Writing to the publisher, Conrad allowed that "it's difficult to find a general definition of the stories. . . . All the stories are stories of incident—action —not of analysis. All are dramatic in a measure but by no means of a gloomy sort. All, but two, draw their significance from the love interest—though of course they are not love stories in the conventional meaning. They are not studies—they touch no problem. They are just stories in which I've tried my best to be *simply entertaining*."[227] Conrad was obviously on the defensive, determined to safeguard himself against the usual attacks of the critics. This determination was so strong that it made him not only degrade such unquestionably analytical stories as "Il Conde" and "An Anarchist" but also introduce a contradiction into the letter itself by describing "The Duel" as "an attempt to realize the spirit of the Napoleonic Era."

Conrad was right, however, to believe that this time he was giving the public and the critics a more readily acceptable book. He even made it easier by supplying each story with a "signal" subtitle designed to set the public's reaction on the right course.[228] The volume—dedicated to Miss Capes and published on 6 August—was received well; the critics did not find it difficult or incomprehensible and they made no gloomy forecasts about its lack of popularity. There was a growing awareness that Conrad held a significant position in English literature, but this was coupled by a sense of his elusive "oddity," and so the epithet "Slav" persisted. Conrad retorted to Garnett, "But let me ask is my earnestness of no account? Is that a Slavonic trait? And I am earnest, terribly earnest. Carlyle bending over the history of Frederick called the Great was mere trifle, a volatile butterfly, in comparison. For that good man had only to translate himself out of bad German into the English we know whereas I had to work like a coal-miner in his pit quarrying all my English sentences out of a black night."[229]

Conrad found Robert Lynd's review in the *Daily News* particularly galling because it touched on his two tender spots: that he had abandoned his native country and that he wrote in an adopted language.

Mr Conrad, as everybody knows, is a Pole, who writes in English by choice, as it were, rather than by nature. According to most people this choice is a good thing, especially for English literature. To some of us, on the other hand, it seems a very regrettable thing, even from the point of view of English literature. A writer who ceases to see the world coloured by his own language —for language gives colour to thoughts and things in a way that few people understand—is apt to lose the concentration and intensity of vision without which the greatest literature cannot be made. It was a sort of nationalism of language and outlook that kept wanderers like Turgenieff and Browning from ever becoming cosmopolitan and second rate. . . .

Mr Conrad, without either country or language, may be thought to have found a new patriotism for himself in the sea. His vision of men, however, is the vision of a cosmopolitan, of a homeless person. Had he but written in Polish his stories would assuredly have been translated into English and into the other languages of Europe; and the works of Joseph Conrad translated from the Polish would, I am certain, have been a more precious possession on English shelves than the works of Joseph Conrad in the original English, desirable as these are.[230]

Conrad's response to this devastating review was a dejected letter to Garnett: "It is like abusing a tongue-tied man, for what can one say. The statement is simple and brutal; and any answer would involve too many feelings of one's inner life, stir too much secret bitterness and complex loyalty to be even attempted with any hope of being understood."[231] Soon, however, Conrad did attempt an answer: I am convinced that there is a link between Lynd's painful attack and the genesis of A Personal Record. The supposition sometimes advanced—that Conrad wanted to justify himself in the eyes of Poles or to rid himself of a sense of guilt toward his homeland—might be valid if his retrospective confessions were not so clearly addressed to English readers. It was only one month after Lynd's review that Conrad began A Personal Record, a work in which he presents to the English public his anomalous origins and experiences while refuting the accusation of being a renegade.

The idea for the book occurred to him during conversations with Ford. Conrad's assurances that the idea came from Ford himself should not be taken too seriously: I think he simply wanted to safeguard himself against suspicions of self-defense and egotism.[232] For some time he had been considering a move farther away from London and back to Kent;[233] he took his whole family to Aldington, close to Ford and Marwood, for three weeks (29 August to about 20 September).[234] It was from there that he wrote to Pinker, "If you will help to clear me out of that damned Luton place I promise to contribute toward it by a series of papers for the English Review, without the slightest check to my other work. Hueffer suggested them to me and offered to take me down from dictation. I've done the first of which you will receive a proof in a few days for securing copyright in Am. . . . There are to be intimate personal autobiographical things under the general title (for book form perhaps) of The Life and the Art."[235]

Less than three weeks later Conrad produced a far more detailed description of the contents of his reminiscences in another letter to Pinker: "To make Polish life enter English literature is no small ambition—to begin with. . . . To reveal a very particular state of society, bring forward individuals with very special traditions and touch in a personal way upon such events for instance as the liberation of the serfs (which in the number of people affected and in the general humanitarian significance is a greater fact of universal interest than the abolition of Negro Slavery) is a big enterprise. And yet it presents itself easily just because of the intimate nature of the task, and of the 2 vols. of my uncle's *Memoirs* which I have by me, to refresh my recollections and settle my ideas. . . .

"A mere casual suggestion has grown into a very absorbing plan."

And he added significantly: "It may be, so to speak, *the* chance of a lifetime . . . for my acceptance as an English writer is an accomplished fact."[236]

The seemingly debonair tone of the reminiscences made it possible for Conrad to touch upon painful and embarrassing subjects, as if from behind a screen of discreet self-irony. Although he once claimed in a letter to Harriet Capes that he was "unreservedly frank," Conrad was conscious that he used a protective shield of ironic distance. His frankness, as he declared in the same letter, would be transparent only to "friends": "I lay my temperament quite bare before the world in the assurance that the world at large will never perceive the whole extent of my sincerity."[237]

Conrad's auto-mythological posturings should not be taken at face value either artistically or psychologically. Artistically they form just one element of a broader structure; psychologically they are symptoms of insecurity and uncertainty. Perhaps the best illustration of that double entendre occurs in *The Mirror of the Sea*. Conrad begins the essay "The Nursery of the Craft" with the words "Happy he who, like Ulysses, has made an adventurous voyage"—a translation of the opening line of Joachim Du Bellay's famous sonnet, part of the cycle *Les Regrets*. If we do not realize this, or do not remember the rest of the poem, we interpret Conrad's whole fragment as a hymn to adventurous voyaging; but for Du Bellay Ulysses's full happiness includes returning home after all travels, "to live among his relatives till the end of his age"; ten lines of the sonnet are devoted to regrets of being far from one's homeland, and it ends with an expression of preference for "the old country's delights" over "sea air."[238] The Mediterranean had been wonderful, to remember it was thrilling, but Conrad could not forget that, for him, there was no home to return to.

When Sidney Colvin criticized the conversational reserve of *A Personal Record*, Conrad replied: ". . . this defect saves the pangs of my shyness."[239] More than that, the reserve also facilitated personal mythmaking; it allowed Conrad to shape and project into his own past his vision both of himself and of Poland and his attitude toward it. The Conrad we see emerging from the pages of *A Personal Record* is a man who, although brought up in a completely different, old, rich, and precious tradition, was preordained, as it were, to become a sailor and later an English writer. The transition from life at sea to life at a writing desk is presented as accidental and yet logical because it was in keeping with Conrad's temperament and interests. Poland is depicted in a nimbus of romantic heroism but also in a tragically hopeless situation. "It has been the fate of that credulous nation to starve for upwards of a hundred years on a diet of false hopes." The fate of Poles was like that of his great-uncle Nicholas, heroic but pitiable: "My grand-uncle Nicholas, of the Polish landed gentry, *Chevalier de la Légion d'Honneur*, etc. etc. . . . in his young days, had eaten the Lithuanian dog. . . . let us charitably remember that he had eaten him on active service, while bearing up bravely against the greatest military disaster of modern history, and, in a manner, for the sake of his country."[240] This was how Conrad described his native tradition. He could be proud of it but at the same time portray his departure from it as an act founded on the tragic awareness of the hopelessness of remaining faithful to his Polishness alone.

Ford maintained later that he had written *A Personal Record* from Conrad's dictation. This can only apply to a few fragments. Neither the style nor the fact that several sections were translated from Bobrowski's *Memoirs* support Ford's claim; besides, collaboration would have been difficult, since during most of the time when the text was being written the two authors lived in different places.[241]

It was not only when he was writing his reminiscences that Conrad was concerned with how his readers saw him; there was, for example, the characteristic way in which he reacted to a critical essay that Arthur Symons tried to publish. Symons praised Conrad as a consummate artist but presented him as a writer who delighted in scenes of cruelty and brutality. Conrad objected strongly: "I may say that there are certain passages which have surprised me. I did not know that I had 'a heart of darkness' and an 'unlawful' soul . . . I did not know that I delighted in cruelty and that the shedding of blood was my obsession."[242] One can surmise here the natural anxiety of a man who had touched the fringes of mental illness and now read about his morbid inclinations in an article by a critic who himself suffered occasional lapses into insanity; but Conrad's denial may have been mainly motivated by his desire to disassociate himself completely from the kind of exhibitionism and lack of psychological balance that he attributed to Dostoyevsky. Conrad was pleased when Symons's article was rejected—although, hypocritically enough, he professed to sympathize with its author.[243]

The origins of *A Personal Record*, initially published as *Some Reminiscences*, are closely linked with that of the *English Review*, the excellent monthly founded by Ford with borrowed money. The periodical attracted new talent and played a role in modernizing English literature. From the outset Conrad participated in all its organizational and editorial activities; for instance, at the beginning of August he approached Norman Douglas on behalf of the periodical, asking him for the manuscript of *The Isle of Typhoeus*.[244] Apart from Conrad, Ford's closest collaborators included Wells and Marwood; the latter supplied considerable capital, which was soon squandered through Ford's wild mismanagement.[245] Conrad's friendship with the Marwoods was by then intimate. Conrad maintained his regard for Wells, as we can see from a letter he wrote on 25 September: "No one *can* be more honest intellectually—and the very young—the workers of our more distant hopes—perceive this at once. And as your grip on every side of the question is very firm—a thing too they require—they repay your high qualities by a sort of mental devotion. It is an enviable fate. On the other hand there is your mastery of the art—that side of your writer's genius which contains infinite possibility."[246] Although they were separated by essential differences in social and philosophical views and in their approach to literature, Conrad loyally tried to enter into the spirit of Wells's work and to understand its intentions and merits.

The first number of the *English Review* was due in December. At the beginning of November Conrad, out of friendship to Ford and undoubtedly excited by the momentous event, invited the entire editorial group to Someries. For Jessie it meant confusion in the house and extra expenses—an uncalled-for upheaval.[247] Years later Conrad wistfully recalled to Ford:

> The early *E.R* is the only one literary business that, in Bacon's phraseology, "came home to my bosom." The mere fact that it was the occasion of you putting on me that gentle but persistent pressure which extracted from the depths of my then despondency the stuff of the *Personal Record* would be enough to make its memory dear. Do you care to be reminded that the editing of the first number was finished in that farmhouse we occupied near Luton? You arrived one evening with your amiable myrmidons and parcels of copy. I shall never forget the cold of that night, the black grates, the guttering candles, the dimmed lamps—and the desperate stillness of that house, where women and children were innocently sleeping, when you sought me out at 2 a.m. in my dismal study to make me concentrate suddenly on a two-page notice of the *Ile des Pingouins*. A marvellously successful instance of the editorial tyranny![248]

That short and enthusiastic article about Anatole France was, apart from a chapter from the *Reminiscences*, Conrad's second contribution to the December issue. It is also one more proof of his steady antisentimentalist and antimodernist tastes. Although in many respects Conrad wrote within the Romantic tradition, he favored clear and analytical literature and valued skepticism and rationalism. It was from this perspective that he derided Tolstoy in a letter to Galsworthy: "The gratuitous atrocity, of, say, *Ivan Illyith* [sic] or the monstrous stupidity of such a thing as the *Kreutzer Sonata*, for instance; where an obvious degenerate not worth looking at twice, totally unfitted not only for married life but for any sort of life, is presented as a sympathetic victim of some sort of sacred truth that is supposed to live within him."[249] In another letter Conrad ridiculed the modernists: "D'Annunzio, that dreary, dreary *saltimbanque* [humbug] of passion (out of his original Italian of which I know *nothing*), and Maeterlinck the farceur who has been hiding an appalling poverty of ideas and hollowness of sentiment in wistful baby-talk."[250] Such criticisms are less surprising when we remember that, according to Jean-Aubry, Conrad was a lover of Voltaire.[251]

That autumn Conrad was also wrestling with the spirit of Voltaire's ideological adversary, Rousseau, whose statue and intellectual legacy play such a notable part in *Under Western Eyes*. The growth of the novel continued to be slow. On 14 October Conrad sent Chapters 4 through 6 to Pinker (that is, Chapters 1 through 3 of Part 2); by November all of Part 2—half the book—had been finished.[252] In December Conrad informed Pinker that the whole novel was complete and only the last part needed typing. This, however, was evidently an attempt to extricate some money from Pinker, since on the twenty-eighth of that month Conrad wrote disconsolately to Colvin, "I am finishing a confounded difficult novel. But how long that bone will be sticking in my gizzard I can't tell."[253] It was to stick there for another year.

During this time *Chance* was rarely mentioned; it had to wait its turn. The theater again tempted Conrad with visions of high royalties such as those earned by Barrie and Galsworthy; Conrad apparently intended to write another play. He boasted to Pinker: "The theatrical people have been after me ever since last December."[254] It is in fact very doubtful if Conrad was really approached in this way, and the attractions of the stage were really alien to Conrad; as he avowed to Ada Galsworthy, "I don't understand much of the theatre; my own imagination is so tyrannical that the stage can never attain for me the necessary force of illusion."[255]

Pinker was growing restless; it was no use trying to get extra money from him. In an attempt to escape his supervision, Conrad addressed to Ford a lengthy and complicated justification of his request that the money for *A Personal Record* be sent directly to him and not through his literary agent. "In my state of absolute dependence on Pinker," Conrad explained, "I must be very cautious for, should he refuse making even the present absolutely insufficient advances where would I be? It's a perfect agony. I don't think that this is anything he can object to, for after all the whole thing is a voluntary service—a generosity on your part even to the point of you taking me down from dictation."[256] Ford paid Conrad £85 in checks and probably at least £40 in cash.[257]

In spite of its author's claims, *A Personal Record* was not produced easily and quickly; nor is it true that it did not slow down Conrad's other work. At the end of November 1908 Conrad was busy with Chapter 4. Two weeks later, in an apparent attempt to pacify Pinker, Conrad assured him, "This is the end of *Remins*[es]. The Review, counting one paper with another has, say 32000 words; I hold some 8000 which got written in the course of composition but which I keep back from serialisation altogether but which count for book form."[258] Those eight thousand words were doubtless the future "Prince Roman" finished two years later. In due course three more chapters were added to *A Personal Record*—despite Pinker's lack of enthusiasm, due chiefly to his difficulties in selling the copy. Pinker's agent in New York communicated an opinion that was probably typical of contemporary editors and publishers: "An editor to whom I showed them to-day, who was very much interested in the idea, said that he was very much disappointed, but found there was too much about life in Poland and about Mr Conrad's uncle, and very little about himself and about how he came to write, which is really what people would be interested in."[259]

Throughout 1908 Conrad often complained of gout. Jessie's knee also continued to cause her suffering and anxiety; by the autumn her condition had deteriorated so much that another operation was considered.[260] The boys were a source of increasing joy and pride to their father, however. Conrad wrote to Galsworthy on 30 November, "Borys looks better and Jack is very well. This morning I said to him: 'Show me your fists,'—when all of a sudden with the word 'punch' he hauled off and hit me in the jaw straight from the shoulder. I was never so surprised in my life. Borys, on the point of going off to school, was inexpressibly delighted. 'Won't he know how to fight by and by!' Such, my dear boy, are the delights of paternity."[261] But Conrad's family life, like his writing, was constantly threatened by financial worries. As he wrote to Ada Galsworthy, "I have just received the accounts of all my publishers, from which I perceive that all my immortal works (13 in all) have brought me last year something under five pounds in royalties."[262] Worse still, at this time Conrad feared—even awaited—a sudden death. "I expect neither fame nor fortune," he wrote in reply to Davray's New Year 1909 greetings. "I have no time to wait. I even doubt whether Mr d'Humières will complete his translation of *Nigger* before my death."[263] He was most open about his fears and anxieties in a letter to Poradowska: "I ask myself what will happen to those poor people when I am gone. Without family, without money, even without friends. I have mismanaged my life. I did not know any better—because I certainly wanted to. And perhaps it has not been possible to make it different."[264]

The last months at Someries were as gray and monotonous as the English winter. In the first days of March 1909 the family moved to Aldington, where Ford had rented them four rooms above a local butcher's shop.[265] Borys later recalled that "the slaughter house and the shed where the bacon was cured were situated at the back of the house directly under the bedroom windows. The squealing of the pigs on the weekly 'killing' days together with the smell from the old-fashioned curing shed must have been very trying for my Father."[266] It was the most uncomfortable and least spacious lodging ever occupied by the Conrads; Conrad's own study consisted of a windowless cubicle.

The beginning of the Conrads' stay at Aldington was marred by illness. Right after they moved in Conrad came down with influenza and missed the first night of Galsworthy's *Strife*; he eventually saw the play at the end of March.[267] In April, Dr. Clifford Hackney, the family's new physician, promised to cure Conrad of gout. "It was time that something were done gout affecting my head too frequently of late. The improved health would mean easier, quicker work—and that's all I care for, for neither of pain nor death I am afraid," declared Conrad to Pinker.[268] His working pace was still slow. Conrad claimed in January that *Razumov* was nearly finished, but that was more wishful thinking than reality. In the first week of March he added another instalment to the *Reminiscences*.[269]

Meanwhile, the *English Review* flourished artistically while it dried up financially. Ford shone as the editor of a distinguished magazine, exciting admiration in some people but antagonizing others by his conceit and mythomania. Conrad's attitude toward his friend was also changing. In the autumn of 1908 and in January 1909 he confided to Ford that he was "longing" to see him, and generally spoke of him in the most affectionate terms ("my *intimé*," "I am anxious for Ford to make a success," "He is a brave fellow and a man of talent").[270] But in March some new, skeptical undertones appeared. On the sixth he advised Douglas confidentially how best to tackle the editors of the *English Review* about the publication of *The Syren Land*. Later in the month, continuing the same subject, he commented, "The fact is that H.[ueffer] loves to manage people."[271] We can only guess at the probable cause of this evolution. Conrad was not the only close friend of Ford who, at the same time, reexamined his attitude toward him. At the end of January a clash occurred between Ford and Wells; its reasons were financial, but Ford's haughty manner and absurd naiveté in business matters aggravated the conflict. Soon Ford quarreled with Garnett and Stephen Reynolds, other mutual friends of him and Conrad.[272]

Conrad was prepared to tolerate snobbery, posturing, and other eccentricities as long as they appeared to him as harmless, half-prankish excesses of an artistic temperament. But when Ford behaved that way in his public capacity as the chief editor of the *English Review*, Conrad regarded it as a sign of a lack of consideration for others' feelings and personalities. Moreover, his past links with Ford were bilateral: they were friends and collaborators. Now Ford, as editor, was a man of the world, perambulating in a horse cab all over London and patronizing young writers; he became a self-appointed hub of a large circle of people, and Conrad felt himself being drawn into a web of multiple interrelationships. Their respective attitudes had to undergo a change, unavoidably creating a certain distance between them, but the vivid memory of their former closeness resulted in a mutual oversensitivity about potential snubs.

When on Easter Sunday 1909 Ford nonchalantly invited himself, his wife, and Conrad's physician, Rober D. Mackintosh, to dinner at the Conrads, he met with Jessie's strong opposition, supported by her husband, who explained to Dr. Mackintosh, "I beg you not to put an unfavourable interpretation on this perfectly open confidence; and to believe that as far as you are concerned any day, any hour in which you come to see us will ever be considered fortunate. But I had really to make a stand against that mania for managing the universe, worse even in form than in substance."[273]

These, however, were minor incidents. The first serious conflict was precipitated by the Hueffers' marital discord. At the end of March Elsie, increasingly worried about Ford's avoidance of her (he was having an affair with Violet Hunt at the time), complained to him that Marwood had been making advances to her for some time. It is impossible to tell to what extent the charge was justified. Elsie, who had previously complained to Marwood about her unhappy marriage, now, for tactical and psychological reasons, confided in Ford, wishing to lure him back to Aldington, where she was living with their two daughters.[274] Both the Hueffers tried to involve the Conrads in their complicated intrigues.

Conrad refused to believe the charges about Marwood. "My view of M is that he is a galant-homme in the fullest sense—absolutely incapable of any black treachery."[275] Conrad was also highly indignant at the suggestion that the gossip about the Hueffers' love affairs affected his attitude. In late April or early May he protested to Ford, "Against that [suggestion] I oppose an unqualified denial; and as this denial expresses the exact truth I warn you that I demand to be believed without any reservations or doubts whatever. I had heard nothing about you and Elsie except what passes current in ordinary conversation." He flatly refused to comply with Elsie's plan that Ford should move for a week to the Conrads' house: "I said at once: no. That can not be. If you are reconciled so completely Ford's place when he is in Aldington is in the cottage. What is the end of such a proposal; what object, what purpose can be served by re-creating an equivocal situation? By such juggling with the realities of life an atmosphere of plots and accusations and suspicions is created. I can't breathe in situations that are not clear. I abhor them. They are neither in my nature nor in my tradition, nor in my experience. I am not fine enough for them. We are a pair of silly innocents."

In the same letter Conrad congratulated Ford on the May number of the *English Review* and expressed his past misgivings about Ford's behavior as editor—which was "indeed mere talk but talk which upset and discomposed me utterly." He concluded with a stern yet friendly admonition referring to the Marwood affair: "It strikes me my dear Ford that of late you have been visiting what might have been faults of tact, or even grave failures of discretion in men who *were* your admiring friends with an Olympian severity. A man who not often takes liberties ventures to ask you now whether it is worth while. Unless words are wind, facts are mist, the confidence you've given me a mere caprice of fancy, and unless an absolute loyalty of thought and act on my part contra mundum gives no privilege I have the right to warn you that you will find yourself at forty with only the wrecks of friendships at your feet."[276]

Two days later Conrad poured out his troubles to Galsworthy: "We have fallen here into a most abominable upset: the execution of Marwood by Ford and Elsie. . . . For weeks poor Marwood looked as if after a severe operation. . . . We couldn't keep the horrid affair off us anywhow—what with E coming with horrid details and revelations (I told her plainly I could not believe what she said—and she only smiled) which it was impossible to silence and the poor M's whom we *had* to listen to out of common humanity."[277] On top of it all Conrad was not feeling well at that time—he blamed it on "the English spring."[278]

Conrad obviously felt irritable and hurt, but his annoyance would probably have been assuaged fairly soon, particularly since much of the blame rested on Elsie. However, after scarcely three weeks, Ford, who was also easily aroused, fanned the flame with an insolent letter in which he rebuked Conrad for not having received Willa Cather, then on the staff of *McClure's Magazine*, on whose financial support Ford counted. Again, Elsie's gaucherie was partly responsible, but Conrad was incensed by the undeserved reprimand. "What the devil do you mean? Come my dear chap. You know very well that I knew *nothing whatever* of your relations, of your friendship, of your regard for Miss C—I didn't even remember the lady's name. . . . Stop this nonsense with me Ford. It's ugly. I won't have it."[279]

Ford's behavior in that trifling affair was unfortunately typical of him, and by that time Conrad must have been aware that his friend paid little attention to the time and feelings of others. The incident strengthened Conrad's critical attitude toward Ford and his doubts about any future collaboration with the *English Review*. "I have been fed up in this connection of late till my gorge rises at the thought of it," Conrad wrote Galsworthy on 5 June.[280] He clearly tried to keep his distance from the periodical.[281] According to Mizener, Conrad had decided to discontinue writing his reminiscences for the *English Review* but all he did at first was to have Ford informed that owing to bad health he would be unable to send further instalments.[282] We have no proof, however, of the decision being so conscious and clear-cut. Conrad probably hesitated about what to do next; he did not even know whether writing for the *English Review* would bring him any money.[283] On 13 May he informed Harriet Capes that "the fate of the E. Review hangs in the balance . . . only a sale to some plutocrat ambitious of that sort of prestige can save the Review from extinction."[284] Under those circumstances a genuine illness at the end of May might have settled the matter almost automatically. Conrad lamented in mid-June, "This fit of gout has literally ruined me by stopping my work at a critical moment."[285] And to

Galsworthy he explained, "I was prevented from giving an instalment of my *R'ces* to the June No. of the *English Review,* on which I counted to pay for Borys's schooling. . . . I made desperate efforts to do something but could not finish two pages—not two pages!—in time." [286] Conrad described the events to Garnett in similar terms, although we may easily imagine that he in fact felt relieved and had no intention of resuming his contributions. [287]

Ford further inflamed the situation by publishing a note in the July number of the *English Review:* "We regret that owing to the serious illness of Mr Joseph Conrad we are compelled to postpone the publication of the next instalment of his *Reminiscences.*" The dramatic tone of the announcement and the implied obligation annoyed Conrad. His opinion of Ford had by then become decidedly negative—partly because of Elsie's complaints, which, however irksome, were clearly justified. [288] Ford was carrying on two affairs simultaneously: with Violet Hunt and with his "secretary," Gertrud Schlablowsky—trying by every possible means to force his wife to divorce him. [289] Conrad wrote to Perceval Gibbon, "Totally unconnected with her I have had various reports of Ford's doings. His furies, his agonies, his visits to various people of distinguished quality and his general carryings on like a spoilt kid—together with a report of the male and female devotions attending upon his mental and moral convulsions." [290] Conrad must have made some response to the announcement in the *English Review,* but his letter on the subject has not survived. Neither has Ford's reply, although we may guess at its tone of haughty rebuke from Conrad's retort. It begins, "Dear Hueffer"—although for eleven years they had been on a first-name basis. Then Conrad continued:

> If you think I have discredited you and the *Review*—why then it must be even so. . . . But as writing to a man with a fine sense of form and a complete understanding, for years, of the way in which my literary intentions work themselves out, I wish to protest against the words—*Ragged condition.*
>
> It is so little *ragged* to my feeling, and in point of literary fact, that in the book (if the book ever appears) the *whole* of the contribution to the *E.R.* as it stands now without the addition of a single word shall form the Part First.
>
> It expresses perfectly my purpose of treating the literary life and the sea life on parallel lines with a running reference to my early years. . . . It begins practically with the first words of appreciation of my writing I ever heard and ends with the first words ever addressed to me personally in the English tongue. . . .
>
> The *E.R.* I hear is no longer your property and there is, I believe, another circumstance which for a purely personal reason (exceptionally personal I mean) makes me unwilling to contribute anything more to the *E.R.* [291]

The "purely personal reason," to which Conrad returned several times, must have been a reference to David Soskice's participation in the sale of the *English*

Review. Soskice, Ford's brother-in-law, was a Russian political emigré of anarchistic persuasion, and a shrewd businessman.[292] Conrad disliked him intensely, but this part of his explanation sounds particularly unconvincing.

Conrad's letter to Ford was tantamount to an open break of their close friendship. A few days later Conrad unburdened himself to Pinker: "He's a megalomaniac who imagines that he is managing the Universe and that everybody treats him with the blackest ingratitude. A fierce and exasperating vanity is hidden under his calm manner which misleads people. . . . I do not hesitate to say that there are cases, not quite as bad, under medical treatment."[293]

For a time Conrad could not decide what to do with his *Reminiscences*. They were too short to be published under a separate cover and no editor was interested in their serialization. He sounded Lucas: "Since you have mentioned my *Reminiscences* I am emboldened to ask your advice as to continuing them. . . . I am thinking of a volume (or even two short vols of say 65000 words each) for later on, with an interval of a couple of years. I know that the form is unconventional, but it is not so unusual as it seems. . . . My case (as before the public) being not only exceptional but even unique, I felt I could not proceed in cold blood on the usual lines of an autobiography."[294] Lucas, Methuen's adviser, apparently offered no encouragement. Equally unsuccessful was Conrad's attempt to arouse the interest of Harper and Brothers of New York. Their delay in replying prompted Conrad to write an angry letter; it was one of those outbursts of wounded pride that reveals the other side of Conrad's personality, a side no less genuine than the self-torment and doubt that we are so familiar with: "Be good enough to understand distinctly that I no longer care in what sense your answer is worded, nor yet whether you ever publish or not another line of my writing; but from a regard for the dignity of English Letters in which I occupy a recognized position, I will not let pass what looks like a deliberate slight without calling upon You for such an expression of regret as the least spark of good feeling may prompt you to offer."[295] Yet at the close of the year he was still asking Davray for advice: "I have an idea to write 30000 words more to make a volume. Do you think it is worthwhile."[296] But it was not until three years later that Conrad began work on his memoirs again.

The spring of 1909 brought at least one pleasant surprise: an enthusiastic voice from across the Atlantic. James Gibbon Huneker, an outstanding critic, was the first American man of letters—not counting the expatriate Crane—to establish a correspondence with Conrad. A polonophile and author of a well-known book on Chopin, Huneker began by sending Conrad a volume of biographical studies of great men of culture, suggesting that he regarded Conrad as one of them. When Conrad's polite letter of thanks revealed that they both were great admirers of Flaubert, Huneker repeated, "You are the English (and the Polish) Flaubert."[297] The comparison must have made sweet music in Conrad's ears. He had written solemnly, "Yet [if] there is one point in which I resemble that great man, it is in the desperate heart-breaking toil and effort of the writing, the days of wrestling as with a dumb devil for every line of my creation. And poor Flaubert had no wife and children, he had neither himself nor others to feed on the vain words which survive him for your delight and mine."[298]

Conrad's estrangement from Ford and his somewhat loosened contacts with Garnett and Graham were largely compensated for by some new acquaintances of a later generation. In addition to Stephen Reynolds (born 1881) and Edward Thomas (born 1878), a poet and literary critic who earned his living by journalism, there was Perceval Gibbon (born 1879), a gifted writer, energetic reporter, and motorcycle fan. Gibbon soon became almost a member of the Conrad household. Jessie even described him as "perhaps the closest and for both Joseph Conrad and for me, the most intimate [friend]." "Uncle Reggie" (Gibbon's unused first name was Reginald) was also adored by both Conrad boys. Gibbon was youthful, bursting with energy, and known for his sharp wit; his attitude toward Conrad was one of respect and filial protection.[299] In August the Conrads spent about a fortnight as the guests of Gibbon and his wife at Trosley, near West Malling, in Kent.

"I want change, for this hole is growing more odious to me every day," confessed Conrad to Galsworthy in July.[300] The summer of 1909 was passing in an atmosphere of gloom, amidst attacks of gout and worsening financial troubles. In May Conrad had had to apologize to Douglas for being unable to repay a short-term loan.[301] In mid-June he had claimed that he had not written a word for a month.[302] In a doleful letter to Galsworthy, he gave vent to self-pity: "Well it [an attack of gout] was pretty bad: the horrible depression worst of all. It is rather awful to lie helpless and think of the passing days, of the lost time. But the most cruel time is afterwards, when I crawl out of bed to sit before the table, take up the pen—and have to fling it away in sheer despair of ever writing a line. And I've had thirteen years of it, if not more. Anyway, all my writing life. I think that in this light the fourteen vols (up-to-date) are something of an achievement. But it's a poor consolation."[303]

To get out of his financial quagmire—his debts now totaled £2,250—he devised, at Gibbon's instigation, a new plan of speculation with his life insurance policies; it turned out to be impracticable, however.[304] His attempt to obtain another government grant, on which he had counted, also proved unsuccessful.[305] Not until September was Conrad able to earn anything—12 guineas "on the side" from the *Daily Mail* for a short article called "The Silence of the Sea," on the subject of lost ships.[306] In October he had a larger payment: 832 francs for the French edition of *The Nigger*.[307]

It is hard to tell how fast the text of *Razumov* was growing. Conrad kept complaining, even at Trosley, about his inability to write, but it seems that by October three-quarters of the book was ready, and Conrad promised to finish it in three weeks.[308] Meanwhile, as Conrad was struggling with his vision of

Russia, he received a letter—an echo of his past. It was from a Captain Carlos M. Marris, who for twenty-one years had lived in the East, married a Malay princess in Penang, and was now undergoing medical treatment in England. Marris, disgusted with the English climate and customs, sent a chatty epistle interlarded with Malay expressions and full of names of places and ships known to Conrad. Marris praised *The Mirror of the Sea* which, according to him, was very popular among the British officers of the Merchant Marine in Malayan waters; he waxed nostalgic about the disappearance of European sailing ships from the Eastern seas; and he related his adventures about smuggling arms to Malays who were fighting the Dutch. Marris hoped that Conrad would "give . . . some more tales of the East" and diffidently inquired about the possibility of visiting Conrad.[309] He came to Aldington at the end of September, and Conrad recounted his visit to Pinker: "It was like the raising of a lot of dead—dead to me, because most of them live out there and even read my books and wonder who [the] devil has been around taking notes. My visitor told me that Joshua Lingard made the guess: 'It must have been the fellow who was mate in the *Vidar* with Craig.' That's me right enough. And the best of it is that all these men of 22 years ago feel kindly to the Chronicler of their lives and adventures. They shall have some more of the stories they like."[310]

And they did. The direct outcome of the visit was "The Secret Sharer," a short story that took its author back to the Far East. Some critics produce a psychoanalytical thread to tie the inception of the story to Conrad's estrangement from Ford. As it is impossible to either confirm or refute this kind of hypothesis, the existence of some sort of link—as in the form of an analogy between Conrad's and the protagonist's achievement of self-sufficiency—cannot be ruled out. The more obvious connections, however, seem to be with Marris's visit and with the fact that both Conrad and Pinker urgently needed money; there was, moreover, a well-paid market for short stories, particularly in the United States. Conrad himself maintained that he had written the story "for the very purpose of easing the strain."[311] And *Razumov* still required a good deal of work.

The material for "The Secret Sharer" had been preserved in Conrad's memory for many years.[312] The story was written at the end of November and the beginning of December.[313] Several titles were considered: "The Secret Self," "The Other Self," or "The Secret Sharer"—"but that," Conrad wrote of the last, "may be too enigmatic." It appears that Pinker made the final choice.[314] The story was written immediately after a period of acute depression, which Conrad described to Rothenstein in a letter of 15 November: "The last year and a half has been like hell, from which I have just emerged thanks to a good volunteer doctor who took me in hand, I believe, only just in time. But twenty months have gone already over a novel and now I *must* finish it—or I am totally undone. I daren't budge from the desk. . . . The fourteenth year of my writing life draws to an end, and when I look at the result I am appalled. I speak from a worldly point of view, but then we live in the world and its weights and measures impose themselves upon our judgment—yes, even upon our feelings."[315]

Writing to Galsworthy he waxed turgid: "Sufficient moral tenacity is all I pray for, not to save me from taking to drink, because I couldn't even if I wanted to, but from the temptation to throw away the oar. And I have known some good men do that too, saying: 'It's no use.' Then was my turn to keep the boat head to sea for fourteen solid hours. Yes. *Moi qui vous parle* have done that thing just thirty years ago—all but. I wish sometimes I had remained at sea, which, had I honestly stuck to it, would no doubt be rolling now over my head."[316]

Shortage of money and the difficulties with *Razumov* seem to have been the chief causes of Conrad's despondency. But he wrote "The Secret Sharer" with unusual speed and announced delightedly to Reynolds, "We are fairly well. I am working at last! After something like a year of futile agony." There was a similar buoyancy in a letter to Galsworthy: "I have been working rather well of late. I took off last week to write a short story . . . And no gout so far! I am aware of a marked mental improvement. Only 2 years of no worse health would put me nearly right with the world."[317]

Very soon, however, Conrad was again bogged down in *Razumov*. At that stage of the novel he must have experienced an intensified conflict between his antipathy to the revolutionaries and his awareness that only they could dislodge the fossilized autocratic system and its power—obtuse in its ways of governing and sophisticated in its methods of suppressing the opposition. The question of Russia's future—the same question which he had wrestled with in "Autocracy and War"—demanded with growing urgency that Conrad take a more clearly defined stand; what he saw ahead was blood and darkness.

He tried to concentrate entirely on his work, did not budge from Aldington, and refused an offer to visit Rothenstein. To his friends, and probably to himself, he even exaggerated this state of lasting isolation.[318]

We may only guess what made Pinker's attitude toward Conrad harden again: the end of year was drawing near and with it the closing of the balance sheets; he probably thought that since Conrad could produce a short story quickly there was no reason for him to delay the novel; and he may simply have grown impatient. At any rate, on 18 December, Pinker replied to a letter requesting additional money by demanding that Conrad send batches of copy regularly; he also refused to make an advance payment on "The Secret Sharer" and threatened that unless he received the end of the novel within a fortnight, the weekly £6 checks would stop.

"If he does that I shall fling the MS of Raz[umov] in the fire—and see how he

likes that," Conrad exploded in a letter to Gibbon.[319] He repeated this melodramatic threat, which he turned into a jest a few days later,[320] in a letter to
Galsworthy:

> I have been nearly out of my mind ever since. If he says *yes*—that was what
> he meant I wonder if I can restrain myself from throwing the MS in the fire. It
> is outrageous. Does he think I am the sort of man who wouldn't finish the
> story in a week if he could? . . . this gratuitous ignoring of my sincerity in
> spirit and also in fact is almost more than I can bear. I who can hardly bear to
> look at the kids, who without you could not have held the boy at school even
> —I wouldn't finish the book in a week if I could—unless a bribe of six
> pounds is dangled before me!—I sit twelve hours at the table, sleep six, and
> worry the rest of the time, feeling the age creeping on and looking at those I
> love. For two years I haven't seen a picture, heard a note of music, hadn't a
> moment of ease in human intercourse—not really. And he talks of *regular
> supplies of manuscript* to a man who in these conditions (taking all the time
> together, ill and well) sends him MS at the rate of 7,600 words a month . . . I
> don't complain, dear Jack. I only state it as an argument—for when people
> appraise me later on with severity I wish you to be able to say:—I knew him
> —he was not so bad. . . . I assure you I feel sometimes as if I could drop
> everything and beat at the door—you understand. The thing is that, so far, I
> don't. But I feel now that if he stops the miserable pound a day I *must* throw
> the MS in the fire. And indeed why not. It's nothing—it's a mere swindle—
> it's no good to me. . . . I am at the present moment unable to write a line.
> One must secure a certain detachment which is beyond me. I can hardly sit
> still. If it wasn't for dear Jess—well I don't know.[321]

These must indeed have been difficult times for Jessie, although her story about
the stealing and saving of the manuscript of *Under Western Eyes* is, I think,
only a product of her imagination kindled by the memory of her husband's
rhetorical threats.[322]

In Conrad's reply to Pinker, fury sometimes prevailed over despair.

> Had you answered simply I can't or I won't do what you ask for there would
> have been nothing to be said. But in a manner which is nothing short of con-
> temptuous you seem to be holding out a bribe—next week forsooth!—as
> though it were a bone to a dog to make him get up on his hind legs. . . . In
> the course of those 23½ months, as two *honourable* professional men can
> testify, from July last year to August of this, I've had five severe attacks of
> gout—which means that actually I was either utterly disabled or sickening
> for it or recovering from it. That's twelve months, but as I often worked when
> far from fit—yet with temp above 100°—when most men would be utterly

unable to do anything—yes and creative work too—let us deduct only 8 months, which would leave 16 months of effective health and works out at the average of 11630 w. per month. Out of the total there were 40000 words which you told me: 'I can do nothing with that' with an air as if it were dirt which it isn't, you know. But never mind that. And all that time there wasn't a day when I got up without thinking of you and went to bed without thinking of my work in relation to you.

Raz. wants 15–20 thous. words more and shall get it as fast as I can write them. You have the story. Sell it. . . . Raz. when handled may cover two fifths or perhaps more of my indebtedness and that for next year a scheme of work may be arranged which would bring quick returns for the immediate needs and would allow at the same time a long novel to be kept going. I've now all *Chance* in my head as a Malay sea tale. That's what health is good for. I am not a confounded hypocondriac [sic] in search of sympathy.[323]

Pinker's reaction was certainly conciliatory; at any rate Conrad's mood soon improved. Perhaps the out-and-out polemic with his agent, the literary self-examination, and the fortifying letters from his friends had a tonic effect. At all events Conrad convinced himself that he was not to be blamed for the whole situation and wrote in high spirits to Gibbon, "I am going to slave like anything. . . . And then I shall come to see you whooping and singing savage war-songs with an eagle's feather in my hair and Pinker's scalp at my waist. Amen!"[324] On the last day of 1909, although laid up with influenza, Conrad assured Meldrum that his health "has wonderfully improved in the last six months." In the same letter there is an unusually calm reference to Ford: "I am not likely to see anything of him in the future. He's aggrieved—not I. But that is not worth talking about. Still after eleven years of intimacy one feels the breach."[325] The phrasing sounds strangely ambiguous because "feeling the breach" may apply to Ford as well as to Conrad. But Conrad's remarks to Norman Douglas were explicit and resentful: "The very echoes of the great upheaval have died out. Hueffer goes about lying exuberantly about everything and everybody. . . . 'everything is over but the stink' as they say after fireworks."[326]

In January 1910 Conrad energetically set about finishing *Razumov*. Unfortunately only three letters to Pinker, all undated, survive from that month.[327] The new title, *Under Western Eyes*, probably occurred to Conrad about the middle of the month. The typescript bears the date 22 January 1910, and this may be taken as the date Conrad finished the novel. It was neither his biggest nor the one that took him the longest to write, but it was perhaps the one that caused him more anguish than anything else he ever wrote.

XII

. . . .

CRISIS AND SUCCESS
1910–1914

CONRAD delivered the finished and typed (but uncorrected) text of *Under Western Eyes* to Pinker at once, undoubtedly expecting an advance.[1] Jessie mentions that he was in a state of unusual excitement and irritation when he left home. We can easily imagine the fatal conversation: Conrad asked for money, explaining at the same time that the novel was not yet ready to be shown to editors and publishers. When Pinker offered resistance, possibly reproaching him for failing to abide by the conditions of their agreement (that is, for constant delay in submitting the finished copy), Conrad's mounting irritation increased his usually strong accent or even made him use an incorrect expression. The agent, also aroused by the altercation, told him to speak English. The remark offended Conrad deeply.[2]

After spending the night at Galsworthy's home, Conrad returned to Aldington in a very bad mood. He began sorting out the manuscript but it was obvious to Jessie that he did not feel well.

It is not clear from her memoirs when he actually fell ill; it must have happened toward the end of January.[3] The symptoms were alarming: an attack of gout in his whole body, high fever, loss of consciousness—again he frightened his wife by raving in Polish—and, worst of all, a complete nervous breakdown. In response to Pinker, who apparently demanded the text, Jessie explained, "Only two hours before Conrad was taken ill he absolutely forbade me to touch the MS which he has arranged after a great deal of trouble." Together with her letter she even enclosed Dr. Hackney's certificate dated 3 February: "I am of opinion that Mr Conrad is much too ill to attend to any sort of work or to undergo the slightest mental exertion. He will not be anything like well for another ten days."[4] To her friends Jessie wrote openly, "Conrad has had a complete nervous breakdown and gout. Gout everywhere, throat, tongue, head. There are two swellings on the back of his head as big as my fist. Poor boy, he lives the novel, rambles all the time and insists the Dr and I are trying to put him into an asylum."[5] "Poor Conrad is very ill and Dr Hackney says it will be a long time before he is fit for anything requiring mental exertion . . . he lives mixed up in the scenes and holds converse with the characters [from *Under Western Eyes*]. I have been up with him night and day since Sunday week and he, who is usually so depressed by illness, maintains he is not ill, and accuses the Dr and I of trying to put him into an asylum." [6] Conrad's delirious fears must have been caused by his illness, diagnosed as "complete nervous breakdown . . . that has been coming on for months." [7] The patient's state seemed so alarming that Jessie summoned Borys from school; he was appalled at his father's appearance. [8]

Bernard Meyer advances a hypothesis that Conrad suffered from a psychosis caused by an acute infectious toxic process, or an "Infection-Exhaustion Psychosis." [9] It is not quite convincing, because it explains neither the first symptoms of gout nor the subsequent period of three months' intellectual incapacity. It seems more likely that Conrad's illness was psychiatric from the beginning and that the physical symptoms were of a derivative nature. He had long been subject to depression, and in this case several causes coincided to bring it about: the sudden relaxation which usually followed the completion of a major work; financial difficulties; the shock caused by his row with Pinker; and—to my mind the most important—his emotional involvement in the contents of *Under Western Eyes*. As early as December 1909 he wrote to William Rothenstein about his "terrible moral stress" during the two years of working on the novel. [10] I suppose the "nervous breakdown" was, in fact, severe depression associated at the beginning with typical states of anxiety and delusions of persecution.

Meyer is also of the opinion that the contents of *Under Western Eyes* contributed to Conrad's nervous breakdown, but he attributes Conrad's deep emotional involvement to a "hidden sense of identification [with the Russians] expressing a fundamental Slavic unity"; in short, to Conrad's sense of "Slavonism" and to his ambivalent feelings toward Dostoyevsky. There is, however, not a shred of evidence to prove that Conrad took seriously the existence of an imaginary cultural or political bond between the Slavs; it is also difficult to believe that an emotional ambivalence toward another writer could have upset him to such an extent. What Karl lists as elements of a "Slavonic tradition" which Conrad "shared" with Dostoevski—"secrets, conspiracies, meetings with police and police agents . . . murderous crimes committed against officials or society"—are, in fact, elements common as well in Italian, Irish, Hungarian, and many other cultures, whenever there was political oppression, social inequality, and a struggle for national independence. [11]

When, after the publication of *Under Western Eyes*, Conrad argued about the book with Garnett, he appealed to him to "look beyond the literary horizon where all things sacred and profane are turned into copy." In order to understand his attitude to the novel we must remember that it does not treat of literary fictions or of the author's personal problems, or even of his hostility toward the Russian colossus. *Under Western Eyes* is a book about the real problems of the political life and death of a huge empire, on whose fate also depended the fate of Poland—a fact well known and remembered by Conrad. In "Autocracy and War" he could permit himself to write that for Holy Russia the only possible way of reform was suicide; but here he knew that was rhetoric. And since he saw no hope for Russia, he saw none for Poland. Moreover, *Under Western Eyes* sets forth a dramatic confrontation:

> History not Theory.
> Patriotism not Internationalism.
> Evolution not Revolution.
> Direction not Destruction.
> Unity not Disruption.[12]

Conrad had every sympathy with the first group of watchwords, but at the same time he saw clearly that within the realm of tsarist Russia these principles were thoroughly pernicious. Thus he had to struggle—to no avail—with his own deeply rooted opinions. There was probably no other book whose content was as difficult for him to accept or, at least, to come to terms with. *Nostromo* depicts a grim social reality dominated by powerful "material interests," but its action takes place in an imaginary world. *The Secret Agent* is no less gloomy, but Conrad was able to preserve an ironic distance from its contents. Conrad, who in all his other novels and major stories managed to reason with himself and with some elements of his philosophy, in *Under Western Eyes* found himself face to face with a black wall of hopelessness raised by the real world. Even the book's narrator, the English teacher of languages, had not set up a protective barrier between the author and his work. That feeling of helplessness associated with guilt might be expected to lead to a severe depression in a person of Conrad's constitution.

Meyer sees another (and according to him more important) cause of Conrad's illness in the disintegration of the friendship with Ford; the immediate reaction was supposedly delayed by Conrad's concentration on *Under Western Eyes*.[13] To my mind the psychoanalyst exaggerates Conrad's obsession with Ford. The break had taken place several months earlier and Conrad showed no signs of suffering. His view of Ford's character at that time was such that he could not have wished for a renewal of their old intimacy. Nonetheless, the fact that during the period of acute nervous strain that eventually reached its climax in illness he could not rely—as he had in the past—on the understanding and moral support of a forbearing and clear-sighted friend must have worsened his state. Jessie was a devoted nurse but not a partner with whom he could share his thoughts and worries. Under the circumstances, the Russophile Garnett could not be of much use (although he did visit Conrad toward the end of his illness[14]). Graham was abroad at the time. Galsworthy, although, as it seems, Conrad's closest friend then, was not very well suited for the role of confidant, as he probably failed to understand the causes of Conrad's deep-seated confusion and perplexity. He did help financially, however.[15]

When at the very beginning of May Conrad emerged from his illness, he was more than ever in need of friendship, warmth, affection, and contact with people. One of the outward signs of this need was the cheerful and almost enthusiastic letter inviting for an initial visit a journalist and novelist from South Carolina, Francis Warrington Dawson, who had an introduction from Ted Sanderson.[16] It was the beginning of a lifelong friendship with the highly educated American (then thirty-two), who lived most of his life in France.

Conrad was eager to return to social life, although the size of his home did not allow for guests staying overnight and the train trip to London took two hours. He himself was still unfit to undertake the journey. He confided by way of letters:

> And I need greatly to have my morale boosted. I fell ill at the end of January. . . . three months in bed! . . . I drag myself from one room to another with the help of a stick, which is rather sad! but here I am back at work for eight days and I manage passably.[17]

> I am but a wretched convalescent as yet, after all. Two painful ankles and one painful wrist (the left luckily) keep me in a state of uneasy irritation. I just can hobble along for a few yards. My voice too has not come back properly. . . . I am thus coming back to the world. Yet that isn't exactly it. It's very much like coming out of one little hell into another. Don't think I am ungrateful to Gods and men (and of all men to you) by saying this. One can't help that feeling. I am glad enough to have changed one hell for another—for I do not feel either helpless or hopeless. On the contrary there is a sort of confidence—but indeed it may be only the sign of an incipient softening of the brain! However, I am glad enough to feel it on any terms. Anything better than black depression, which may be the sign of religious mania.

> About this same brain: it is not equal to prolonged effort. I am writing this in 10 minute snatches. That's the limit at present. Nevertheless I am going to begin to-morrow a short story—if the devil's in it. It's to be comical in a nautical setting and its subject is (or *are*) potatoes. Title: A Smile of Fortune. May it be a good omen! Only, I don't quite believe in omens.[18]

> I am too lame (in both feet) to come and see you in London. I am also somewhat shaky all over. It seems I have been very ill. At the time I did not believe it, but now I begin to think that I must have been. And what's more, I begin to see that the horrible nervous tension of the last two years (of which even my wife knows nothing) had to end in something of this sort.
> Perhaps it was the only way of relief?[19]

> Can't concentrate for more than 1/2 hour at a time. How to write long or short stories under this disability I don't know. But they must be written and

shall be. It'll be, no doubt, very delightful. . . . I am keeping a tight hand on myself for fear my nerves go to pieces.[20]

Against Pinker Conrad bore a grudge. "As it can't have escaped your recollection that the last time we met you told me that I 'did not speak English' to you I have asked Robert Garnett to be my mouthpiece—at any rate till my speech improves sufficiently to be acceptable."[21] Meanwhile Galsworthy continued to help financially and Robert Garnett, Edward's brother, read the manuscript and also arranged with Pinker that Conrad was to get £3 for every thousand words delivered, plus £1 for every thousand words on completion of each book.

On 11 May Conrad finished correcting *Under Western Eyes*. The changes in the manuscript confirm the hypothesis about Conrad's exceptional psychological commitment to the contents of this work.[22] Three kinds of changes are the most significant: elimination of critical remarks made by the Russians about England and the West generally, about the parliamentary "tyranny of numbers" and the quiet but soulless life of societies governed democratically (as if the author had tried to adopt a more approving attitude toward the West); omission of all evidence that would betray his personal involvement with presented events; obscuration of the similarities between Razumov's dilemmas and the author's own perplexities.

Borys helped sort out the manuscript, which moved Conrad greatly. A week later he began his next work, "A Smile of Fortune." It differs profoundly from the Russian novel in its subject, background, mood, reliance on inspiration derived from Maupassant, and also by the overt presence of an autobiographical element.[23] Conrad continued here his return to the Far Eastern seas, which he began in "The Secret Sharer." He also continued in the sense that the narrator, who is easily identified with the author, since no distance between them is indicated, has control over the situation, emerging victorious from all the difficulties and temptations, just as the captain-narrator in "The Secret Sharer" comes off triumphant (albeit only at the last moment) from all moral and professional problems. This is a noteworthy aspect, since in Conrad's earlier works similar situations did not arise and even when the hero managed to overcome all obstacles (as MacWhirr in "Typhoon"), the happy end was usually accompanied by an ironic question mark. Thomas Moser suggests that in writing "The Secret Sharer" Conrad seemed to be announcing to Ford, "I can manage without you, my former partner."[24] This is quite possible, although Leggatt's strong personality bears little resemblance to the volatile, bragging Ford. Perhaps Conrad was simply trying to persuade himself of his own strength and ability to guide his affairs unaided. Anyway the psychological role of "A Smile of Fortune" seems obvious: after months of helplessness, of being confined to his room in the depth of depression, the writer opens a window onto the world of old freedom; looking back he presents himself as a master of the situation and avenges the rebuff he met with twenty-two years earlier on Mauritius, as well as more recent humiliations.

Here we should interrupt the chronological account to give some attention to a question from the borderland of biography and literary criticism: did the crisis of 1910 mark a turning point in Conrad's life and work? If so, to what extent?

There is a widespread opinion nowadays that after 1912 Conrad's works were not on the same high level as before. Although it would be difficult to defend the thesis that all his later works are of a lower standard, it cannot be denied that his literary output between 1896 and 1910 surpasses in quantity as well as quality that of the next fourteen years. The judgment that the "later" Conrad is worse than the "earlier" was made first by Virginia Woolf and soon after by Galsworthy. Following a low ebb in Conrad's popularity, the theory revived again in the years of renewed critical and scholarly interest in the writer. It has been formulated in different ways by Albert Guerard, Douglas Hewitt, and Thomas Moser.[25] Their books make apparent the risk of linking aesthetic evaluations with biographical hypotheses: once we accept that the lowering of standards was caused by an event in the author's life, we automatically tend to argue that all his works written after that event are inferior.[26] The thesis of "decline" has been fully documented and forcibly set forth, as the very title implies, by Moser in *Joseph Conrad: Achievement and Decline*. It coexists there with an expanded argument purporting to demonstrate that love was Conrad's "uncongenial subject" because of various complexes that are revealed by psychoanalysis. According to Moser, when Conrad wrote about love he became artificial, awkward, and, quite often, garishly banal. One can easily perceive that both theses support one another: in Conrad's later writing women occupy far more space than in his works from the years 1897 to 1909.

Moser and other scholars bypass the specific character of Conrad's poetics, however. Whether because of the traditions from which he could draw inspiration (love played a rather insignificant part in Polish literature[27]) or because of his conscious decision (he disliked contemporary novels dealing with sex[28]), the problems of love occupied a place of secondary importance in his books. This did not necessarily spring from a warped personality, or inhibitions or complexes. We would have stronger grounds for thinking so if his presentation of love and women had been tied up with some basic discords in his vision of the world, his moral views, or his concept of human relations. But this was not the case. I believe that Conrad opposed the emphasis on erotic themes in literature because he was convinced that it would overshadow more vital and serious problems. Among the subjects that concerned him most—responsibility, sense of duty, guilt, justice, freedom, honor, solidarity, anarchy, order—masculine-feminine affairs were not in the forefront. Love and amorous episodes usually occurred, as in Scott or Sienkiewicz, in the form of impulses competing with moral motivations (although not always: see, for example, *Under Western Eyes* and *Victory*). Moreover, and perhaps primarily, Conrad did not know much about women, for reasons that may be easily explained by his biography from the age of eight. His marriage increased his experiences but kept them lamentably one-sided.

If, therefore, the subjects of love and women indeed coincide with a lowering of Conrad's artistic standard, which is not always the case, the reason is probably more involved than some hidden psychological complex. There may be at least three other causes: Conrad's ignorance of women; his regard of those themes as of secondary importance; and the pressure of stereotypes—more difficult to reject precisely because the subject was treated as a side issue. The last may even account for the fact that in his later writing he dealt with women and love more frequently, since the subjects held a promise of broader popularity without requiring greater artistic and intellectual concentration from him; after all, it is easier to be less original and to accept fixed patterns than to create against readers' expectations and contemporary literary fashions. Thus, love in Conrad's later writings may be taken rather as a *symptom* of his weariness than as the *cause* of his decline.

Bernard Meyer's valuable contribution consists of producing the first detailed description of Conrad's illness in the winter of 1910, indicating not only the moment of actual crisis but also the concrete biological and psychological reasons that could account for the future decline of his literary powers. Meyer seems, however, so preoccupied with pursuing various psychoanalytical hypotheses that he neglects one typical postdepressive reaction that may explain the later changes in Conrad's creative temper: namely, when emerging from depression, the patient sets in motion self-defensive mechanisms. The most obvious one is to reject all thoughts and things that brought about the illness or are associated with it. It is not a sudden switch to a different personality but a psychological process that may consolidate, pendulate, or transform itself. As we know, Conrad had been subject to depressions before. The winter of 1910, by bringing the worst crisis of all, provoked the strongest reaction. It was not a turning point though, but the beginning or perhaps rather solidifying of certain tendencies in his psychological makeup. Explaining the change in Conrad's mind and work by the phenomenon of "projection," a "psychological device which consists in the attribution to influences or agencies beyond the self of those attitudes, feelings, impulses, and thoughts which reside within the subject's own mind" sounds ingenious but prompts two objections.[29] First, it is begging the question. Were the main causes of Conrad's torment really internal? Did his psychological tensions originate in his own mind, or were they forced upon him by his experience, by his perception of the tragedies of human existence, individual and communal? I think that Conrad was not an egocentric, and what he worried about was more often than not external reality—hard, unalterable facts. Second, it is not easy to distinguish between "projection" as a literary device (as exemplified by the diabolical trio of Mr. Jones, Ricardo, and Pedro in *Victory*) and as a psychological stratagem. The example of *Victory* is telling: although the Evil is made so blatantly "external," nobody can doubt that the essential philosophical and moral conflict takes place in Axel Heyst's mind.

Meyer presents both Conrad the artist and Conrad the man, after 1910, as a rather disagreeable and uninteresting person. He does so, it seems, on the basis of certain latent assumptions that are worth revealing, since they crop up quite frequently: when they are brought to light their falseness becomes obvious; left to act from concealment they cause considerable harm. It is implied that simplifications shown in literary works are a proof of the author's simple-mindedness; that the writer is as it were morally guilty of producing worse books; that artistic defects are a sign of intellectual primitivism. Such conclusions about the author cannot obviously be based on his works. Even if Conrad the man had suffered a decline—and, after all, Bertrand Russell, André Gide, Paul Valéry, and Valery Larbaud met him later than 1910 and were impressed by his mind—the supporting evidence would have to be found elsewhere.

A somewhat different accusation is voiced against Conrad quite openly: that in his later years he turned from sober skepticism, gnawing doubts, and moral analysis to preaching slogans about virtue and duty.[30] It is virtually an accusation that he betrayed his own beliefs. This is unjust. The values endorsed and advocated in Conrad's later works are without exception present in the books written in the heyday of his creativity. The difference consists not in substituting one set of values for another but in shifting the emphasis, a shift that was neither sudden nor arbitrary. From depicting such definite ideals as fidelity, honor, solidarity, and a sense of duty together with the entire ballast of doubts that they may entail and all the fatal consequences they sometimes bring upon the heroes and people close to them, he moved to the approval of an ideal more steadfast and less wrought with dilemmas. It was not a case of changed values and convictions. Suffice it to look at Conrad's letters or at his essay "Books," written in 1905, to find that he was always ready to "affirm" "a few very simple ideas." One can surmise that having gone through hell in writing *Under Western Eyes* he felt that his worst battles had been left behind, that he had fought enough both intellectually and emotionally. Or else he may simply have grown tired, and come to lack the energy to continue his old struggles.

Exhaustion was the dominating motif in Conrad's postdepression correspondence. He made great efforts to change his mood. The most important step was to move into another house. His frequent changes of home were usually symptoms of a search for a psychological regeneration; to each move he attached hopes of improvement, in regard to his own work as well as general living conditions. Staying in the country he resigned himself to seclusion, restricted stimuli, monotony. He might have known intuitively that he was reducing his own psychological space, a factor contributing to depression.[31] By moving from Aldington to Capel House in Orlestone near Ashford, only eight miles from the Pent, he entered a different world. "It may be folly to take it—but it's either that or a break-down; for my nerves are just on the balance. I require perfect silence for my work—and I can get that there."[32]

Capel House, a one-storied seventeenth-century residence surrounded by a garden, was the prettiest house inhabited by Conrad. According to Borys Conrad, it was also "undoubtedly the happiest of the Conrad homes"; his father described it as "sympathetic."[33] The country around it is flat but richly wooded, with an atmosphere of rustic elegance. The only drawback is the dampness caused by ponds and ditches encircling the house, remnants of the old moat. The great asset of the house, however, was its size: it gave freedom to work and to put up guests for the night. Conrad could feel like a country squire, master of his small manor house in that "most peaceful nook in Kent."[34] The rent was £45 a year.[35] The move took place on 21 June in Conrad's absence; he was still not strong enough and went to stay with Gibbon in Trosley. "He rushed me about on his side-car motor-bike, storming up hills and flying down vales as if the devil were after him. I don't know whether that is particularly good for the nerves, but on return from these excursions I felt ventilated, as though I were a bag of muslin, frightfully hungry and almost too sleepy to eat."[36]

Conrad was welcomed home by a surprise offer from the *Daily Mail* to become a regular contributor for its literary section. He accepted it readily because he badly needed money.[37] Three of four quickly written articles appeared at weekly intervals during July.* The reason he stopped writing is not known. Most probably the collaboration was terminated by the editor, since the essays, bordering on literary criticism of recently published books, are dull, superficial, and wordy to the extent of making us suspect that their author suffered from distraction. It may be said in fairness that Conrad was aware of it. He felt such a lack of self-confidence that through Gibbon's intervention he secured, in case of need, the ghostwriting help of Edward Thomas, whom he barely knew. Thomas lived nearby and supplemented his meager income by journalism. Conrad confided to Thomas, "I have done already two papers and each time I felt as I sat down to it that the feat was utterly impossible. They are, I may say, the products of despair and, as was to be expected from that condition, unspeakably fatuous. . . . I am trying for cold raillery and can achieve nothing but the vulgar tongue in the cheek. . . . Later, say after 3 months, some other trick'll have to be found."[38]

It could not have been anything else but the temptation of easy earnings that

* "The Life Beyond" (16 July), "A Happy Wanderer" (23 July), and "The Ascending Effort" (30 July). Jessie's account (*JCC*, pp. 152–153) is inaccurate: it was the first and not the fifth article that did not appear.

prompted Conrad to correspond on the subject of collaboration over some musical; mercifully, nothing came of it.[39] His financial worries were somewhat relieved by the award on 9 August of a permanent government grant of £100 a year (the so-called Civil List Pension) "in consideration of his merits as a writer of fiction." The wording was restrained; a year later William Butler Yeats was granted £150 annually "in recognition of his distinguished literary attainments, and his eminence as a poet."[40]

Apart from exhaustion Conrad's mood in the summer of 1910 was dominated by doubts about his own strength and the fear of a relapse. He tried to work but was not too successful at first. "I did not really start till July. June's work was mere fooling—not on purpose of course. I was still too limp to grasp the subject and most of the pages written then have been cancelled in typescript. It was strangely nerveless bosh."[41] His feeling of indecision is shown by his reactions to the proposal of having *Chance* published in instalments by the *New York Herald*. In Ceylon, Gordon Bennett, the owner of the newspaper, had met Hugh Clifford, who encouraged him to read three volumes of Conrad, toward whom Clifford was very well-disposed.[42] In August the editor of the *Herald* approached Conrad about the possibility of printing the novel. At first Conrad wanted to agree, but later he became beset by doubts—probably he did not feel able to deliver his copy on time. He turned down the offer, although he needed money badly and was anxious to pay off Pinker in order to "part" with him.[43] The agreement with the *New York Herald* was not signed until a year later.

In the meantime, he concentrated on short stories. In August he sent Pinker a note about a planned volume to be called *Tales of Experience*. The opening story was to be "The Secret Sharer"; he intended also to include "A Smile of Fortune" and two projected stories, "The Reef" (later renamed "The Planter of Malata" but in a different form) and "Character."[44] "A Smile of Fortune" was completed on or just before 2 September.[45] It was followed in the same month by "Prince Roman," which must have existed, at least in draft form, since December 1908.[46]

Partly based on Bobrowski's memoirs, "Prince Roman" contains Conrad's significant declaration about Poland, "That country which demands to be loved as no other country has ever been loved, with the mournful affection one bears to the unforgotten dead and with the unextinguishable fire of a hopeless passion which only a living, breathing, warm ideal can kindle in our breasts for our pride, for our weariness, for our exultation, for our undoing."[47] Beautiful and moving words, which express a tragic love devoid of hope, and one that, although faithful, leads straight to a painful state of numbness. "There is something monstrous in the thought of such an exaction," stated Conrad, and once again we see to what desperate conclusions his recollections and meditations had led him. However hard Conrad-Korzeniowski tried to suppress thoughts about Poland, his sense of hopelessness on the subject, upheld by the diagnosis made in *Under Western Eyes*, could not but darken his spiritual horizon.

Moreover, it became evident, not for the first time, that the subject of Poland, on which he was so sensitive, was of small interest to the public. Pinker, who by then had no problems placing Conrad's stories, had trouble placing "Prince Roman."[48]

In October Conrad started writing "The Partner," a short story that caused him serious doubts from the beginning; he finished it in the first week of December but was still making additions and alterations in March 1911.[49] In December 1910 he began "Freya of the Seven Isles," inspired by a story told by Captain Marris. He worked on it until the end of February, trying simultaneously to get on with *Chance*.[50]

Edward Thomas spent a few days with the Conrads in August 1910. On his return home, in a state of exhaustion—he had made the journey by bicycle—he wrote to his friend Gordon Bottomley, "Conrad . . . looks something like Sir Richard Burton in the head, black hair, and moustache and beard and a jutting out face, and pale thin lips extraordinarily mobile among the black hair, flashing eyes and astonishing eyebrows, and a way of throwing his head right back to laugh."[51]

At that time Conrad probably did not laugh often. Also, he did not grumble as he had before, but a mood of weariness and fatigue tinted his letters. "Life is very difficult." He worried about Jessie's health and blamed the deterioration of her knee on the exertion and nervous tension during his own long illness.[52] Galsworthy was his most faithful intimate. Conrad, however, seemed to have been painfully aware of the inability to establish a deep mutual understanding with him; he put it down, tactfully, to the "general weakening of my grasp over things" or to the lack of regular personal contacts.[53] His encounters with Garnett were also rare; it seems that in the second half of 1910 he never visited London, but he kept Garnett affectionately in mind and was grateful for all his signs of friendship.[54] Gibbon and Marwood, however, were frequent guests. We know relatively little about Gibbon; only a few letters to him have survived; according to Borys Conrad, Gibbon moved later to Guernsey, away from literary circles, and all his papers were burned by the Germans in 1940.[55] More is known about Marwood, although also little in view of the role he played in the lives of Conrad and Ford. Richard Curle recollected, "He had, I think, the deepest and clearest analytic brain I have come in contact with. . . . Every week he used to spend an afternoon with Conrad, and to hear those two discussing literature and history was something of which I can never hope to hear the like again. Marwood was a burly Yorkshireman, whose appearance belied the subtlety of his intelligence, but once he started to talk one listened in an enthralled silence. He was very wise and very profound and C. found his conversation immensely stimulating."[56] Ford later expressed his opinion in almost identical terms.[57] Marwood ailed through most of his life, so Conrad and he might have had a good deal of understanding for each other's afflictions.

In Conrad's complaints, always characteristic of his letters, appeared a new note: his sensation of having changed. Writing to Garnett, he reminded him of being his "literary child," born in 1894: "And so you've kept my letters! Have you! Ah my dear you'll never meet the man who wrote them again. I feel as if I had somehow smashed myself."[58] To Symons he confided, "My days of fine things are done I fear; still one must go on."[59] And also: "Life—an awful grind. The feeling that the game is no longer worth the candle. . . . and yet [I] must go on spinning out of myself like a disillusioned spider his web in a gale."[60] His constant problems with writing seem to have changed their character. The work, although as laborious as ever, becomes more monotonous and grinding. The dramatic intervals in his creativity, caused by an inability to cope with a given book, gradually disappear. It less often gets stuck in a particularly difficult place or on a complicated problem. He does not put aside unfinished books, and his writing acquires greater continuity. He must also concentrate more fully than before. This is why he apologized to Galsworthy and Garnett for not being able to read their new works until his own were finished.[61]

Not until he completed "Freya" in March 1911 did he express his opinion—favorable but with some critical remarks—about Galsworthy's *The Patrician*, Garnett's play *Jeanne d'Arc*, and *The Siren Land* by Douglas, whom he tried to patronize. His reaction to a letter from Ford was also very friendly;[62] perhaps he did not know yet that Ford had just published under the name of Daniel Chaucer a roman à clef with rather malicious caricatures of Conrad, Jessie, and Garnett (see p. 191 of this book). Conrad never spoke on the subject, although it is hard to imagine that he never read *The Simple Life Limited*. Writing his letter he might simply have been prompted by compassion for the unfortunate fellow entangled in marital and divorce problems (Ford was even imprisoned for his apparent failure to pay alimony). It is also possible that Conrad arrived at a tolerant view of his ex-friend's novel under the influence of Marwood, who had been Ford's accomplice for a brief time in guarding the secret of the pseudonym.[63] Be that as it may, Conrad soon took vengeance by attributing what were clearly Ford's traits of character to one of the protagonists of *Chance*, the great financier-crook de Barral.[64]

Early spring brought another crisis: ". . . full 3 weeks—no two consecutive ideas, no six consecutive words to be found anywhere in the world. I would prefer a red hot gridiron to that cold blankness . . . The most horrible nightmare of an existence . . . with not a page, not half a page in all that time!"[65] There may have been two external reasons for the crisis: a shortage of money and the renewed threat of an operation on Jessie's leg.[66] Once again financial help came from Galsworthy.[67] There is no detailed record of Conrad's income and his expenses at that time, but considering that from 1 July 1910 to March

1911 he forwarded to Pinker seventy-two thousand words which brought him £288, and that in addition he was receiving money for the serialization of *Under Western Eyes* and "A Smile of Fortune," as well as £100 a year from the government, his total income was not smaller than in the previous years, and amounted to over £600 on an annual scale. Such a sum was considerably higher than the average earnings of a contemporary counsel for the defense, doctor, or dentist (£478; £395; £368) but much lower than of the best-paid 10 percent of the representatives of those professions (£1,820; £1,200; £1,140).[68] Such a wide range of incomes indicates the possibility of being able to live on a modest budget and of being dangerously close to the temptation to overstep one's means: a few ill-considered purchases, the choice of a more expensive doctor or a better private school, could bring financial ruin.

In early May 1911 Conrad made a fresh start on *Chance*. The copy grew quickly; none of his bigger works progressed at such a speed. In the course of the first fortnight he wrote twelve thousand words ("a record"—he wrote to Douglas, prompted by "a sort of dull desperation"), and on 19 June he thought himself almost halfway through the novel. In fact, it was barely over one-fourth—forty-seven thousand words.[69]

During the summer, in connection with a planned book edition of *A Personal Record*, Conrad wrote a long introduction to the volume, "A Familiar Preface."[70] It presents the vision of his own personality that he wished to convey to his readers; a secondary theme is the psychology of expressing his own feelings and convictions. His self-portrait consists of two dualities: the Anglo-Polish and the nautical-literary. The first is silently implicit and present only as an object of allusions; although Conrad states that the years of his youth were for him "the days when [his] habits and character [were] formed," he does not analyze their lasting influence. The second duality is explicit and even emphasized by dating the beginning of his literary activity as late as 1893. Declaring the existence of both dualities, Conrad suggests that in spite of everything they reveal a basic consistency, even cohesion. As one of the fundamental characteristics of the author's personality, "A Familiar Preface" presents his restraint in expressing deep affections and strong emotions. A paradoxical statement, since the "Preface" is opened by a declaration of irrationalism, by an expression of distrust in the force of a reasoned argument: "Nothing humanely great—great, I mean, as affecting a whole mass of lives—has come from reflection." However, neither here nor elsewhere is Conrad's irrationalism a triumphant belief, as it is in Bergson. Rather, it is a defensive attitude, like that of contemporary French sociologists. Conrad does not say intuition and feelings are the keys to truth, but that it is easier to influence men by the appropriate sound of a word than by reasoning. Therefore, the issue of restraint in expression is not a problem of revealing or hiding a truth, but a problem of communicating with the reader.

This restraint has two sources, one psychological, the other moral. It does not stem from coldness, but from pride: "There can be nothing more humiliating than to see the shaft of one's emotion miss the mark of either laughter or tears." In *A Personal Record* this refers, most likely, mainly to feelings connected with Poland; we know that even that little he told there about his homeland met with indifference from both publishers and readers. Moreover, unrestrained exposure of emotions in literature carried, according to Conrad, the risk of losing full control of oneself and of falling into artistic falsehood; Conrad protests here against the noisy emotionalism of modernist literature, and perhaps also against Dostoyevsky's psychological exhibitionism.

This restraint, however, is not caused by indifference, and need not lead to resignation from expressing one's beliefs. At this point of the confession comes the statement: "Those who read me know my conviction that the world, the temporal world, rests on a few very simple ideas; so simple that they must be as old as the hills. It rests notably, among others, on the idea of Fidelity."[71]

This fragment has been quoted so often that it belongs to Conrad's best-known pronouncements, but its meaning is sometimes distorted. Not infrequently the sentences that follow are overlooked: "At a time when nothing which is not revolutionary in some way or other can expect to attract much attention I have not been revolutionary in my writings. The revolutionary spirit is mighty convenient in this, that it frees one from all scruples as regards ideas. Its hard, absolute optimism is repulsive to my mind by the menace of fanaticism and intolerance it contains." Thus "fidelity" acquires a more concrete meaning by being contrasted with the cult of revolution and the optimistic dogma of change: it means remaining faithful to tradition, history, human experience. Conrad's formula expresses neither a formal dictate of fidelity nor any arbitrary ideology, but rather humility in the face of man's age-old moral heritage. It is not a new, sudden revelation of truth but a discreet suggestion. Just look— Conrad is saying—in spite of my great caution in displaying feelings and beliefs (and it is obvious that only beliefs supported by feelings deserve to be trusted), one can—and you should—notice in all my works a deeply rooted opinion that human reality is arranged according to "a few very simple ideas." You should perceive that I see and express human affairs in terms of certain values which have served many generations to judge their actions and guide their conduct.

Meanwhile, the *English Review* and the *North American Review* were publishing *Under Western Eyes* in instalments. Conrad's relations with the *English Review* were not particularly good at that time; in June he even had an argument with its editor, Austin Harrison.[72] Then Pinker's *faux pas* soon put a certain awkwardness into Conrad's relations with Garnett. As it happened, a New York monthly, *The Century*, had rejected "Freya of the Seven Isles" in March, because of its "overpowering gloom." In July, Pinker, who had hitherto been

unsuccessful in placing the story in other American magazines, sent it to Garnett, disregarding the latter's recent appointment as reader for *The Century*.
Apparently Garnett told Pinker that he had seen the story "years ago," where-
upon Conrad announced with indignation that this was a "thundering lie."[73] It
is possible, however, that he suspected Pinker of having twisted Garnett's reply,
perhaps unintentionally, in order to cover up his own tactlessness. And so he
apologized to Garnett for the whole affair: "I have expressed to Pinker my view
of his sending to you a story rejected already by the Century. It was not fair
either to you or me. As to faking a 'sunny' ending to my story I would see all
the American Magazines and all the American Editors damned in heaps before
lifting my pen for that task."[74]

In the summer Jessie's knee improved markedly. The new surgeon decided
against an operation, and the several-month-long treatment originally planned
to begin in September turned out to be unnecessary.[75] But problems with Borys
began. In May 1910 he failed a special examination that would have made him
eligible for university education, and on 6 June 1911 he failed the entrance examination to a private secondary school at Tonbridge.[76] Thus the way to general education was practically closed to him. Conrad then thought of making
his son follow his own example, at least partly, by sending him to sea.* However, because of Borys's shortsightedness he was only accepted by the Royal
Navy training ship, the *Worcester*, after special intervention, and without any
chances of becoming a sailor—just for a period of mathematical and technical
training. On 22 September Conrad took Borys to the ship, which was moored
at Greenhithe. "Poor Mons. B. looked to me a very small and lonely figure on
that enormous deck, in that big crowd, where he didn't know a single soul. It is
an immense change for him. Yes. He did look a small boy. Couldn't make up
my mind to leave him and at last I made rather a bolt of it. I can't get him out of
my eyes. . . . in Maidstone I wrote a letter to Borys, which I am certain must
have comforted him to receive this morning."[77] Half-jokingly he considered the
future of the five-year-old John, for whom Sanderson promised a place at
Elstree. "I would have to cut Jessie into small pieces before I could take the kid
away from her now. But in another 3–4 years' time she will be ready to stand
the pang of separation like a sensible woman. By that time too the monkey'll be
thoroughly spoiled. Elstree shall be his salvation."[78]

Conrad complained to Galsworthy about life having become a "dead pull"
and said he was "beginning to get used to it";[79] yet he did not lack contacts with
people. There was Agnes Tobin, a rich young Californian poetess and patron
of writers (particularly of Arthur Symons, who lived near Orlestone). She had
already paid Conrad a visit at the beginning of February, leaving behind a

---

* As Borys never showed any deeper intellectual interests or aptitude, Karl's speculations (*Joseph Conrad*,
p. 696) that Conrad may have been "selling Borys short," or possibly was even envious of an "educated older
son," seem to me entirely gratuitous.

"delightful scent of intelligence and charm";[80] in July she brought André Gide and Valery Larbaud to Capel House.[81] Both were already quite well acquainted with Conrad's works. Their visit, which marked the beginning of Conrad's life-long friendship and correspondence with Gide, was one of the signs of recognition accorded Conrad by young French writers converging round the *Nouvelle Revue Française*: Copeau, Ghéon, Gide, Larbaud, Rivière, Schlumberger. They were all united by a dislike of literary modernism. This cult of Conrad fans had no equivalent in England. In September Tobin again stayed a week with the Conrads;[82] the extremely favorable impression she made on Conrad is testified to by the dedication of *Under Western Eyes*—to the person "who brought to our door her genius of friendship from the uttermost shore of the west." *

Norman Douglas's visit to Capel House was much less pleasant; he arrived suddenly on 12 August suffering from a severe attack of jaundice. He had just returned from Italy where he had been living, and he found himself homeless in England. Conrad vented his indignation in a rather hysterical letter to Galsworthy: "My head swims—and in truth I am as near distraction as is consistent with sanity. Should he die I shall have to bury him I suppose. . . . I have seen and tended white men dying in the Congo but I have never felt so abominably helpless as in this case."[83] Nonetheless the Conrads did look after Douglas for about a week before placing him in a hospital at Ashford. Obviously they did not let him feel the trouble he was causing; he returned again on the twenty fourth for four days of convalescence, and their relations remained friendly.[84] Conrad must have known by then of Douglas's pederastic tendencies, but until Douglas's affairs grew into a scandal, Conrad was entirely loyal to him;[85] during school holidays in later years he and Jessie took care of Robin Douglas (four years older than John Conrad), left by his father to fend for himself.

Under Western Eyes was published on 5 October 1911. It was received with respect but little understanding and enthusiasm. Sales in both England and the United States were fairly low, lower than those of *The Secret Agent*.[86] Even the best-disposed critics regarded the problems set out in the novel as purely Russian, distant and foreign, and the basic political conflict escaped their notice. The reviewer in the *Pall Mall Gazette*, having acknowledged that *Under Western Eyes* ranked with Conrad's best works, announced in the next sentence that "Haldin's crime merited the swift and degrading execution that was its punishment."[87] To contemporary English readers, the novel's gloomy mood seemed to flow from the author's soul and not from the presented reality. D. H. Law-

---

* Conrad did not, however, "renew" his correspondence with Wincenty Lutosławski (as Karl claims in *Joseph Conrad*, p. 705); he only answered (on 2 July 1911 [*Conradiana*, no. 13 (1981): 21–22]), in a highly ironical tone; his single letter contained a request to keep secret Lutosławski's visit to Pent Farm fifteen years before. Nor did Lutosławski himself "return to the controversy" with Orzeszkowa in 1911 (Karl, *Joseph Conrad*, p. 705). Anyway, Conrad was, by then, known in Poland from several translations and studies, some of them remarkably perceptive.

rence's reaction was typical: "Conrad . . . makes me furious—and the stories are *so* good. But why this giving in before you start, that pervades all Conrad and such folks—the Writers among the Ruins. I can't forgive Conrad for being so sad and for giving in." [88]

The author's foreign origin was again brought up. The reviewer in the *Pall Mall Gazette* gently drew attention to some grammatical errors; Ford, in his lengthy and laudatory essay, wrote that "this preoccupation with the idea of the point of honour is very foreign—so foreign that it has obviously come to this author with his foreign blood." [89] A novel suggestion that the author was Jewish appeared in the *Morning Post* review. Conrad was annoyed: "It is an absurd position to be in, for I trust I have no contemptible prejudices against any kind of human beings and yet it isn't pleasant to be taken out of one's own skin, as it were, by an irresponsible chatterer." [90]

He was even more vexed, however, by the easily predictable reaction of Garnett, who wrote a very loyal review for *The Nation* but accused Conrad of "hate" in a private letter. Conrad's sarcastic reply betrayed suppressed anger: "There's just about as much or as little hatred in this book as in the *Outcast of the Islands* for instance. . . . You are so russianised, my dear, that you don't know the truth when you see it—unless it smells of cabbage-soup when it at once secures your profoundest respect. I suppose one must make allowances for your position of Russian Ambassador to the Republic of Letters. . . . But it is hard after lavishing a "wealth of tenderness" on Tekla and Sophia, to be charged with the rather low trick of putting one's hate into a novel. . . . Is it possible that you haven't seen that in this book I am concerned with nothing but ideas, to the exclusion of everything else?" [91] At the same time he confided to Edward's sister, "The fact is that I know extremely little of Russians. Practically nothing . . . I crossed the Russian frontier at the age of ten. Not having been to school then I never knew Russian." [92] A few months later he returned to the Russian subject in a calmer tone, thanking Garnett for his wife's translation of *The Brothers Karamazov*. "Of course I was extremely interested. But it's an impossible lump of valuable matter. It's terrifically bad and impressive and exasperating. Moreover, I don't know what D. stands for or reveals, but I do know that he is too Russian for me. It sounds to me like some fierce mouthings from prehistoric ages. I understand the Russians have just "discovered" him. I wish them joy. Of course your wife's translation is wonderful. . . . But indeed the man's art does not deserve this good fortune. Turgeniev (and perhaps Tolstoi) are the only two really worthy of her." [93]

A Personal Record was due to come out a few weeks after *Under Western Eyes*. At first Conrad intended to entitle it *The Double Call: An Intimate Note*.[94] Polish exoticism must have acted as a deterrent, however, for in November no publisher could be found for the volume.[95] It was eventually published at the end of January 1912 by Nash in barely one thousand copies under the title

Some Reminiscences, later changed to *A Personal Record*. It is the only book of Conrad's not dedicated to anyone. The American edition appeared slightly earlier (19 January) and was considerably bigger: twenty-five hundred copies.[96] American reviews were more favorable and, on the whole, more perceptive than the English.

This was characteristic: success came to Conrad from across the ocean. In August, *Harper's Magazine* made persistent requests for short stories; in November *Metropolitan Magazine* offered as much as two thousand dollars for "Freya."[97] Conrad's luck was turning at last. At the same time, through the good offices of Agnes Tobin, John Quinn, a New York lawyer and collector, managed to establish contact with Conrad, whose works he greatly admired. Quinn offered to purchase manuscripts. He began in August by buying *An Outcast of the Islands* (for £30) and "Freya"; other transactions soon followed.[98] Business relations with the ambitious lawyer quickly developed into a close friendship, and for Conrad the sale of the manuscripts was for several years a source of additional income that did not require any new work. But Conrad, in spite of growing profits that were largely consumed by his huge debt to Pinker, was still forced to borrow money.[99]

Although in November and at the beginning of December his health was rather poor, his work on *Chance* showed steady progress.[100] He was already looking ahead to his future books: the "Mediterranean" novel, or two, possibly three, short stories.[101] On 12 December he wrote to Pinker, with whom his estrangement was gradually healing: "I *see* my end right enough but the putting it down with some effect is the very devil. And of course I have ominous twinges of toothache. Ever since *Lord Jim* (inclusive) the end of every long novel has cost me a tooth. I wouldn't mind losing two teeth to get this end done quickly." On 29 January 1912 *Chance* started appearing in instalments in the *New York Herald*. Conrad finished it two months later: "On the 25th March, the last words were written at 3.10 a.m., just as my working lamp began to burn dimly and the fire in the grate to turn black. . . . I went out and walked in the drive for half an hour. It was raining and the night was still very black."[102] The manuscript of the novel, which is in the Berg Collection at the New York Public Library, is dated 3 June 1911–12 March 1912. The first date is obviously fictitious; the second may refer to the rewritten "nicer" version of the ending, mentioned in an undated letter to Pinker.

Conrad's statement about *Chance*, made one year later, is often quoted as a proof of his loss of self-criticism. "I have been very anxious—but I am so no longer. . . . As to what *it is* I am very confident. As to what will happen to it when launched—I am much less confident. . . . And it's a pity. One doesn't do a trick like that twice."[103] We must remember, however, that the letter was written to his literary agent, in whom, on principle, he never confided his doubts. Writing several months later to Lady Morrell, he openly expressed his uncertainty about the value of *Chance*.[104] Both in the first and the final stage of writing he confessed to "making a start with stuff in which I don't believe" and then of "no longer [having] the consciousness of doing good work";[105] he also asked Henri Ghéon to tell Gide, "Conrad has written a long (and stupid) novel since his visit. It's *disgusting* to even say it—try and imagine what it was like writing it! I have become disgusted with myself, with paper, with ink—with everything!"[106]

In the December number of the *English Review*, Ford published a comprehensive essay on "Joseph Conrad." Like all Ford's critical writing it was impressionistic, chatty, and uneven, but it contained a few penetrating observations and some statements that must have given Conrad great pleasure: about the "desperate sort of remorselessness" in posing moral problems in his works, about the weight attached to the idea of honor, and about the splendor of Polish traditions, which brought Conrad closer to the Elizabethan traditions in English literature.[107] Pleasantly surprised, Conrad reacted with a warm, almost affectionate letter: "I am infinitely touched by what you say and by the accent you have found to express what may be critically just and true but to a certainty is the speech of a friend. What touches me most is to see that you do not discard our common past. These old days may not have been such very 'good old days' as they should have been—but to me my dear Ford they are a very precious possession. In fact I have nothing else that I can call my own."[108] He even went so far as to acknowledge the nonlegalized union between Ford and Violet Hunt, to whom he courteously referred as "your wife." In February he wrote her a nice, politely humorous letter expressing pleasure at an invitation and promising an early visit—which he never made.[109] He addressed Miss Hunt as "Mrs Hueffer," possibly assuming that the divorce between Elsie and Ford had already taken place. (Two months later the legitimate holder of the title brought an action against Violet Hunt for using Hueffer's name.) Conrad's feelings toward both Ford and Hunt were ambiguous, however. It seems that his polite phrases in correspondence were designed to maintain a safe distance; and in his letter to Galsworthy he wrote about the visit that "the great F.M.H. with the somewhat less great V.H." paid him shortly after New Year.[110]

Conrad's writing, as if freed from its old inhibitions, progressed at greater speed, thereby bringing an improvement in his financial situation. He estimated that *Chance* and the volume of short stories that was to appear in 1912 would reduce his debt to Pinker by £900; moreover, the publishers were paying a higher than ever percentage from the sale of his stories (25 percent).[111] Not surprisingly, his relationship with Pinker was rapidly returning to its old familiarity. "You must not be angry! Nobody is ever angry with me now. It is well known that you can't get Conrad to answer any letter in decent time. It is the only blot on his character—but a large one."[112] On the day *Chance* was completed they met for lunch in London, and later Conrad summed up: "I've carried

from our meeting the impression that there is now no misunderstanding between us." [113]

After a few days the feeling of elation passed, and a fortnight of prostration
followed.[114] For several weeks Conrad was unable to start a new work or even
decide what he was going to write. He had signed a contract with Harper and
Brothers for a long novel, estimating that it would take him between twelve and
eighteen months to write; it seems he had in mind a book on Napoleon in Elba.
"I am still in doubt about the form. Whether a narrative in the first person or a
tale in the third." [115] Again he began considering a follow-up to his reminiscences; in spite of his own protestations, he may have doubted whether the slim
volume presented a distinct unit. He suggested submitting to the *English Review* over the course of eighteen months a series of six or seven sketches as a
continuation of *A Personal Record*, "under the general title of Some Portraits
family & others—my uncle the conspirator, two marriages, episodes of the liberation of our peasants and of the '63 rising and so on." [116]

The monthly's serialization of *Chance* was Conrad's condition, and the project fell through when Harrison failed to take up the offer. Instead, the *English
Review* published two long articles, written in April and June, about the sinking of the *Titanic*; Conrad attacked the shrill publicity about the steamer being
"unsinkable," as well as the neglect of safety rules by the money-grubbing
shipowners.[117] The old sailor felt indignant at the cheap ecstasies about the heroic behavior of the *Titanic's* crew. "I attach no exaggerated value to human
life. But I know it has a value for which the most generous contributions to the
Mansion House and "Heroes" funds cannot pay. . . . Death has its sting. . . . I,
who am not a sentimentalist think it would have been finer if the band of the
Titanic had been quietly saved, instead of being drowned while playing—
whatever tune they were playing, the poor devils." [118]

At the beginning of May Conrad at last settled down to work on a short story
whose development was to be exceptionally complicated. For a long time it was
called "Dollars," and Mr. G. Berg was its leading character.[119] It eventually resulted in two works: a short story, "Because of the Dollars," and the novel *Victory*. They are similar in two respects: in both the good old Captain Davidson
plays the part of a general observer of events, and in both a "woman of ill repute" gives her life to save the hero. Because of those similarities it is difficult to
establish at what stage the two plots parted ways in their author's imagination.

Conrad's need for making friendly confidences found a new and unexpected
outlet in 1912 in his correspondence with Quinn. One may wonder what induced Conrad to such effusiveness—with a touch of posturing—toward a lawyer thirteen years his junior whom he had never met, who grew up in entirely
different circumstances, and who knew little about literature. Perhaps it was
precisely this difference of background, in addition to the fact that Quinn was a
complete alien in the English literary circles where Conrad felt always ill at ease.

Contacts with Quinn were like being in a confessional, where the face of the confessor cannot be seen. No doubt Conrad respected Quinn's outstanding professional competence and sober intellect. Perhaps subconsciously he wanted to recompense Quinn for his willingness to buy the manuscripts. "The hundred pounds will pay last year's doctor's bill and cover my overdraft at my bank. They save me from the necessity of putting aside the work I am busy with now to write a couple of silly stories for the magazines."[120] It is possible, however, that the intimate tone, apparent for the first time in Conrad's letter of 27 March announcing the finish of *Chance*, was prompted by the mood of the moment. As to Quinn, who was a bit of a cultural snob, the familiarity with Conrad was flattering; in the course of time he began advising the writer—even on literary matters.

One must admit that Conrad sounded encouraging. He confessed, "It has never entered into my head to put forward either the pains or the importance of my labours as something exceptional. I am the less likely to exaggerate to myself my difficulties because I have followed different occupations; and I am far from ascribing to literary work any sort of special merit—or special difficulty. I am only getting a little tired of it. After sixteen years it is excusable; for, in that lapse of time, illusions get tarnished a bit and one's imaginative machinery begins to show signs of wear. It works, but it creaks—which is annoying—and also a little alarming for a man who has to depend entirely on it for everything. I can't go on living on my reputation."[121] In another letter he wrote bitterly about partners and with reserve about marriage: "Truly, partnerships are the very devil—with a few exceptions. I verily believe that marriage is a less risky transaction. But you must not take this opinion as encouragement to change your state. I've been lucky but it's a fact that there are advantages in playing a lone hand which one should not forego lightly."[122]

Since the transactions with the manuscripts provided an opportunity to ponder the fate of books written years earlier, Conrad's letters to Quinn contain information about his past as well as current works. As early as 1911 Quinn bought the manuscript of *Under Western Eyes*, among others; in March 1912 Conrad sent him *The Secret Agent* and "The Brute." "Karain" sank with the *Titanic*; in its place Conrad dispatched the manuscript of "The Informer." *Chance* followed in May, and in December fragments of *Nostromo*, *Lord Jim*, and "Heart of Darkness," with a simultaneous offer of other manuscripts. Conrad's business letters radiate commercial charm:

> The principal object of this letter my dear Quinn is to bring to your notice the MSS we discovered during our search amongst a welter of all sorts of papers and which are enclosed here for your inspection. One is the MS of my only play founded on the story *To-morrow* . . . If you examine it you will see that it is somewhat of a literary curiosity—and at any rate it is the only

attempt of Conrad's at dramatic form . . . no other text (it was never printed)
of it is in existence . . .

Frankly I had just as soon stick to it as long as I live; it will be always worth
something; but as you have the story (together with the others of that volume) I am willing to let you have the play if you care to pay £40 for the 60 pp
. . . On my side I engage myself that if I ever write another play big or little
you shall have the MS of it for nothing.

But this is not all. Examining various boxes which have not been opened
for years . . . we found the complete MS of the Nigger—the story by which,
as creative artist, I stand or fall, and which, at any rate, no one else could
have written. A landmark in literature, I can safely say, for nothing like it has
been ever done before. I want £80 for this MS and if it hadn't been for this
bad year (I have done nothing for nearly six months) no money would have
bought it. I would have kept it by me for the sake of old associations and
then left it to the MSS Dept. of the British Museum. They preserve many less
significant MS there. And that is what I will do should you not feel disposed
to acquire it for your collection.

He went on, declaring later:

> With the fragments and this special lot you shall really hold everything I have
> written (barring *Mirror of the Sea* which was mainly dictated) and there can
> be no further discoveries because there is nothing more to discover. As to
> what I may write in the future I can only repeat that no MS of mine shall be
> either sold or given away to any one during my lifetime and as long as you
> don't part with your collection.[123]

As it happened various items kept turning up later, like *The Sisters*, fragments
of *Romance*, and others.

Conrad's improved financial position was soon reflected by his purchase of a
car, a second-hand two-seater Cadillac, "a worthy and painstaking one-cylinder
puffer which amuses us very much."[124] There were three potential drivers:
Jessie, Conrad, and Borys, who, unable to reach the pedals, had to drive standing. It was he, in fact, who soon became the expert chauffeur. Jessie was calm
behind the wheel and, according to Borys, much more competent than his father, who was a reckless and nervous driver and had frequent, although luckily
minor, accidents. In connection with Conrad's motoring adventures Borys observed a certain psychological regularity applicable to Conrad's whole life, including his seafaring years: "His complete calm and apparent air of detachment
in face of any sudden and unexpected happening, in contrast to his excessive
agitation over trivialities, always fascinated me."[125] Conrad's ability to mobilize
all his psychological and physical resources in moments of real danger, combined with an almost hysterical excitability and touchiness in matters of every-

day trifles, is amply documented. In his literary period, particularly in later years, he had very few opportunities to demonstrate the first characteristic, while the second became more and more trying, especially for Jessie who, judging by her memoirs, regarded it as the dominating feature of her husband's personality.

In time the new acquisition had the effect of enlivening the Conrads' social contacts, but in the summer of 1912 they still refrained from excursions beyond their immediate neighborhood. One of their rare guests was young Alexis Saint-Léger Léger, the eminent French poet (writing under the name of St.-John Perse); he came to Conrad with an introduction from Agnes Tobin and stayed for a few days. Nine years later he wrote from Peking:

> I too have lost nothing of what I have carried away with me from your home—such as the fragments of our first intimate conversations in the evening, in your small study downstairs where you suffered the terrible attack of gout . . .
>
> Again I am leaning with you over the old family album which displays your entire Polish childhood. I am again listening as you recite the first lines of Edward Lear's nonsense rhymes where, as you assured me, I was more likely to find "the spirit of great adventure" than among the best sea writers like Melville. I can still hear you becoming irritable at my passion for Dostoyevski and my lack of taste for Turgenev. And once again I am surprised by your confession that the French authors you feel closest to are Molière and Zola. Finally you flare up when you hear me repeat that I regard you as the only poet of the sea, when your intention has been to extol nothing but the ship itself, man's creation against the sea—like a bow drawn against destiny or a violin set against the night.[126]

Even in 1947 St.-John Perse preserved a clear recollection of his visit, which he described in very similar terms to Jean-Aubry:

> Conrad denied that he was a poet of the sea, and protested that he loved not the sea, but the ship, the triumph of skill, or more simply of man, over the sea! . . . He would also surprise me by his imaginative taste for the life of society, for a very eighteenth-century-like curiosity about the role of women behind the course of events.[127]

Throughout August and September Conrad complained about his poor health and low spirits. "I have not been very well and more crippled mentally than physically even. I must go through these depressing periods; there is no cure for them apparently."[128] He lamented to Gide, "I well know I have written myself out."[129] Nevertheless, he continued to work, slowly, sending Pinker successive batches of "Dollars" fairly regularly. On 29 July he estimated its length at twenty-five thousand words; on 12 September he declared that it would amount to forty thousand "but not more"; by 1 October he predicted seventy thousand and hoped to finish it before December. A few days later he announced that he was writing not a short story but a short novel, and he sent Pinker the summary of *Victory*.[130] He assured him that he had not forgotten "the long novel" on Elba. On 3 September he even announced that he had "formally" begun it, but this was only a declaration of good intentions.[131]

In spite of complaining about being downcast, he made trips to London and received guests at home.[132] He continued to see Warrington Dawson, and on 12 October he had a visit from another American, James Gibbons Huneker, who recalled being received by "a man of the world, neither sailor nor novelist, just a simple-mannered gentleman, whose welcome was sincere, whose glance was veiled, at times far-away, whose ways were French, Polish, anything but 'literary,' bluff, or English."[133]

On 14 October '*Twixt Land and Sea* was published; the book was dedicated to Captain C. M. Marris. The English edition of thirty-six hundred copies exceeded not only that of *Under Western Eyes* but all of Conrad's previous books—a sign of his growing popularity.[134] Originally the volume was to comprise four stories.[135] Fortunately "The Partner" was eliminated; the three remaining tales were "A Smile of Fortune," "The Secret Sharer," and "Freya of the Seven Isles." The critics were unanimous in their approval, and the reception of this volume may be regarded as a landmark in Conrad's quest for popularity; for the first time there were no complaints about the work being difficult and no warnings about its gloom. The return to the exotic and to sea adventures was generally welcomed; Conrad was praised for abandoning complicated artistic experiments and for "shaking himself free" from the "lamentable" influence of Henry James; his masterful simplicity evoked admiration. Each of the three stories had its devotees, who claimed it as the best. (The author himself valued "The Secret Sharer" most highly: "I daresay Freya is pretty rotten. On the other hand The Secret Sharer, between you and me, is *it*. Eh? No damned tricks with girls there. Eh? Every word fits and there's not a single uncertain note. Luck my boy. Pure luck."[136]) The *Standard*'s literary critic voiced the general opinion when he declared, "No volume that Mr Conrad has ever published could offer more unmistakable proof of his genius."[137]

Throughout the autumn Conrad complained of gout. To each of his correspondents he gave a different account of the duration of his new attack; it began between 20 September and 15 October and lasted at least until the end of November.[138] Despite everything those autumn months turned out rather well for Conrad. His most recent volume was his greatest publishing success. Arnold Bennett sent him such an enthusiastic letter about *Under Western Eyes* that Conrad felt quite overwhelmed. "It is indeed a rare happiness for a craftsman to evoke such a response in a creative temperament so richly gifted and of a sincerity so absolutely above suspicion as all your work proclaims you to be. . . . It is difficult to answer a letter like yours my dear Bennett. . . . I shall show your letter to my oldest boy when he comes home for his holidays and then I shall deposit it for preservation in the copy of Nostromo . . . The joy your praise of that novel has given me is immense." [139]

In November he made the acquaintance of two men, both a generation younger than himself, who considerably influenced the remainder of his life. The first was Richard Curle (born in 1883), journalist, literary critic, and writer. Their friendship had a literary origin. The second was Józef Hieronim Retinger (born in 1888).

Curle wrote an article on Conrad's works for the newly established monthly publication *Rhythm*; Edward Garnett showed it to Conrad before printing. Conrad was extremely pleased by the essay and expressed a wish to meet the author. Read today, Curle's piece evokes more embarrassment than admiration. It is naive in its enthusiasm and generalities, and the criticism, whether favorable or adverse, seems equally superficial. According to Curle both "Heart of Darkness" and *Nostromo* are very poorly constructed and in both Conrad seems to have forgotten about the existence of readers. What made Conrad like this essay? Probably three things: a lack of a general formula that would "place" him; a stress on his unique and unrepeatable qualities ("it's not much use trying to compare Conrad to anyone"); and the praise of the *impression* that his works created. [140] When, a few months earlier, Stephen Reynolds published a comprehensive study on Conrad and the sea literature, he argued against interpreting the special character of Conrad's writings in terms of his foreign origin (as had been done by Ford, among others) and emphasized instead the significance of the positive ideals of conduct adopted from the British maritime tradition. This diagnosis, which substituted seamanship for foreignness as the key to his work, could not please Conrad too much, and his compliments about Reynold's article were rather tepid. [141] His attitude was always negative whenever anyone tried to interpret his works by a single formula. Curle's stressing of his "astonishing power of visualization" and of his gift by which "everything he touches starts throbbing" were forms of praise that accorded well with Conrad's aesthetic intentions as set out in his preface to *The Nigger of the "Narcissus."*

Conrad's first meeting with Curle took place at the Mont-Blanc Restaurant. [142] Soon after, he asked him to stay overnight at Capel House. [143] Conrad's relations with Curle, whom even a year later he described as a "queer creature," were based at first on an understanding of mutual advantages: [144] Conrad wanted to have a critical summing up of his literary output; and the enthusiastic budding writer cleared the way for himself by helping Conrad. [145] Intimate friendship developed with time. A few years later Curle began to visualize himself in the part of Boswell to Conrad's Dr. Johnson. Judging by Curle's memoirs he was a Boswell with an untidy memory; his shrewdest psychological observation was that he had never penetrated the mystery of Conrad's personality.[146] Curle's book about the last twelve years of Conrad's life shows common sense and is admiring, affectionate, messy, verbose, and superficial.

Retinger, too, later published his memoirs—lively, scintillating, witty, and seldom reliable.[147] Introduced to Conrad by Arnold Bennett, he came with his wife to Capel House for a few days and frequent meetings followed.[148] Retinger, the son of a successful Cracow lawyer, had been educated in Paris. He had personal charm and social ease. In Cracow he occupied himself mainly with literary criticism as the editor of a respectable and attractively presented, albeit short-lived, monthly magazine on art and literature, but he also had political ambitions. He came to London in the autumn of 1912 in order to awaken sympathy for the cause of Poland's independence.[149] He may at first have tried to enlist Conrad's support, but to no avail (Conrad soberly judged the chances for success of such an action as hopeless). Soon Retinger published a skillfully written brochure with information about Poland and Prussia; in it, without directly assailing either Austria or Russia, he affirmed Poland's right to national self-determination.[150] A few years later Conrad recalled, "He was very often here for week-ends and talked to me openly of his hopes. Both himself and his wife gained very soon our regard and affection."[151] Young Otolia Retinger contributed most effectively to Conrad's reestablishment of closer relations with his fellow countrymen.

Teodor Kosch, who met Conrad in 1914, recalls, "At first even Mr Retinger spoke with Conrad only in English. Conrad told us (me and my wife) how the change occurred: having met Retinger Conrad invited him to lunch. During the conversation at table it transpired that Mr Retinger was in London with his wife; Conrad felt disconcerted at not having invited her . . . he accompanied Retinger to his London flat to apologize. This is how Conrad put it: 'I was received by the lovely Madame Tola who stretched out her hand addressing me in Polish' and he added that ever since that moment he and Retinger spoke Polish. My wife remembers well all those details because she had known Mme Tola from Cracow."[152]

Conrad enjoyed his meetings and long conversations with the Retingers.[153] If we judge by two extensive letters about the future of Constantinople written at that time, one might think that he was attracted by the young man's passion for politics, which he shared. Surprisingly, however, Retinger maintains that Conrad took little interest in politics.[154] A possible explanation may be that what Retinger regarded as politics—the behind-the-scenes activities of politicians—evoked the greatest doubts in Conrad.

Early in 1913 the Retingers were invited to spend a weekend at Conrad's home. Otolia Retinger's ingenuous reminiscences seem to render well the atmosphere of Capel House and the impression Conrad made on new acquaintances:

The rooms in Capel House were not large. Comfortable, old-fashioned furniture made them look very cosy. On the ground floor were the dining-room, living-room, the boys' room, what was called the den, full of tools, stones, in short: treasures. The first floor consisted of bedrooms and a guest-room—a large room with a low ceiling and wide windows facing the garden. . . .

Nelly, the maid, knocked at seven o'clock bringing a cup of fragrant tea and toast. After that one could still sleep before breakfast was served downstairs at about nine.

Jessie in her blue dressing-gown presided over the important ritual: making toast, pouring out coffee, offering various kinds of marmalade.

Conrad may have been still a bit out of sorts. No one knew how he slept or how he felt because his hospitality and politeness were always unfailing. . . .

We spent long evenings sitting near the fire. Conrad would liven up. Sometimes he talked about distant seas and ports but most likely about his early youth and family.

He was also fond of talking about literature; his favourite authors were the French masters of the word whom he admired. On those occasions he liked to speak French. In English he always had a marked foreign accent. He spoke Polish clearly with a charming Ukrainian accent. Sometimes, unable to find a word, he would switch into French.

We tended to forget about the time as the evening hours slipped by unnoticed. In the glowing circle of the fire Conrad would evoke a new, strange world. He never told fantastic stories about unusual adventures; he hated showiness, easy effects and all posing.

And yet he knew how to create a unique atmosphere, full of subtle charm. His dark eyes with drooping lids radiated a powerful spirit and individuality. Images of peculiar suggestiveness and colour emerged through his nervous manner and broken sentences. . . .

He was subtle in the extreme, a sensitive observer, an aesthete, thinker and above all a poet. Sometimes he was tragic, difficult and complex in his moodiness; sometimes he was simple, warm-hearted, intimate. But he always looked at the world through his own heroic eyes; he always approached life from its romantic side."[155]

At the end of 1912 Conrad wrote "The Inn of Two Witches," probably the most trivial of his short stories.[156] Untypical in its subject matter (gruesome adventures on land of an English sailor during the 1813 war in Spain), it apparently echoed a contemporary history Conrad had read.[157] There is an amusing autobiographical detail in an allusion to a treatise on the sugar industry written years before by Tadeusz Bobrowski.[158] Work on what was to be *Victory* but was still called *Dollars* continued uninterrupted. Conrad considered giving it yet another title, *The Man in the Moon*—"only the public would misunder-stand."[159] Still believing the novel to be short, he kept giving close dates of its completion: Christmas 1912; the end of January 1913; the end of February 1913: "the end is near"; and the same again on 14 April.[160] He felt anxious: "My manner [of writing] is evolving into something new to which I am not used. The work in such conditions comes with difficulty and the doubt as to his [its] value is worrying."[161] By February 1913 the plot of "Because of the Dol-lars" became sufficiently clear in Conrad's mind to make him mention the pos-sibility of writing a very short story, "the real *Dollars* tale."[162]

Conrad did not want to delay writing the novel in spite of the fact that short stories were more profitable in the short run, and his financial situation, al-though improved, was still precarious and his debt to Pinker quite substantial. The cost of running Capel House with three servants must have been consider-able. When in March 1913 Ford asked for the £100 he had lent ten years earlier (plus £40 interest for eight years), Conrad promised to pay back the £40 within six to twelve months, and the basic debt within three years.[163] According to Conrad's letter to Ford, his debt to Pinker was diminishing and, apart from that, his remaining debts amounted to barely £200. To Quinn, who invited Conrad to New York and kept urging him to take a rest, Conrad answered with haughty exaggeration that when he had got up in March (!) 1910 after a four-month illness, he was £2,700 in debt, while now he owed less than £600. "If I had indulged in holidays this result could not have been attained"—and his health would not have been better. "I want peace and intense concentration, conditions I can only find at home."[164] The fees for Borys's school were still paid for by the sale of manuscripts to Quinn; luckily, in spite of several assur-ances to the contrary, new ones kept turning up.[165]

Quinn suggested to Conrad the publication of his collected works. Conrad's reaction was enthusiastic and he at once began to spin out dreams of a twenty thousand–copy edition and a £10,000 payment.[166] Visions of high royalties must also have induced him, neither for the first nor last time, to try to write a play in collaboration with Perceval Gibbon. The subject of the play is un-known, and the project seems to have come to an end after one fragment of the first act.[167]

Toward the end of the winter all four Conrads contracted influenza and bronchitis. Borys spent a month in the school infirmary.[168] Work on *Victory* slowed down particularly, since Conrad had simultaneously to prepare *Chance* for a book edition. He finished correcting on 30 May[169] but later rewrote the first chapter once again and added the epigraph suggested by Marwood.[170] At the same time Conrad had a violent quarrel with the publisher, Algernon Me-thuen, who maintained that the agreement had been signed for a book half its length. Conrad was annoyed at being reproached; Methuen fanned the flames by reminding Conrad that his books were none too profitable, and Conrad almost broke the contract. During an acrimonious exchange of letters Methuen pointed out that, when signing a long-term agreement, he hoped for sea tales, which had brought Conrad some popularity, and not for novels of *The Secret Agent* or *Under Western Eyes* type.[171] Although in the end both were to make good profits, Conrad's attitude toward Methuen remained cool. Conrad established contact with an American publishing firm, Doubleday, Page and Company, an association that turned out to be of great importance in the future. Frank Nelson Doubleday, director of the house, visited Conrad in the early spring; later dealings were taken over by a young and energetic editor, Alfred A. Knopf, who was most favorably disposed toward Conrad. Conrad's long letter of July 1913 to Knopf, in which he discussed his future relations with Doubleday, testifies to the weight he attached to winning greater popularity. He went so far as to use almost comical arguments; repudiating artistic virtuosity, he declared, "My style, which may be clumsy here and there, but is perfectly straightforward and tending towards the colloquial, cannot possibly stand in the way of a large public." In order to promote the sales of *Chance* he suggested a publication of Curle's short study of his work, and a simultaneous reissue, in a cheap edition, of *A Personal Record*.[172] Behind Conrad's lofty words about his position in literature there might have lurked the feeling of not being able to count much on further achievements but rather on the profits derived from his accumulated literary capital.

In mid-April Conrad again expressed confidence that the new novel was "drawing to an end." This comforting illusion remained with him for many months, although at the same time he complained that his work was "confoundedly difficult." On 12 June he assured Pinker that the book would be finished within six weeks. In July he moved the deadline to August, consoling himself, contrary to the truth, "But it has always been so. A quick book followed by a slow book. But the prospect for the Mediterr[anean] novel is good on that principle."[173] He kept sending Pinker the copy in batches ("the usual miserable 3000 words"), fairly regularly even when he was complaining to friends of not being able to write.[174] In the second half of July his work was interrupted by proofreading *Chance*, which he finished on the twenty fourth; on the next day he suffered a severe attack of gout.[175] Possibly it was caused by rereading the book. He was extremely apprehensive about its prospects, and remarks like "*of its kind*, it isn't a thing that one does twice in a lifetime!" smack of self-consolation.[176] "I've just passed two sets of proofs of Chance. My brain's muddled, my spirits depressed. I had to read that stuff so many times over that I have lost all belief in it."[177] Conrad was certainly much better aware than his readers of the duality of the story: the plot of de Barral-Flora-the Fynes and the plot of Flora-Anthony-Powell are intertwined rather mechanically; the author was conscious that the novel comprised elements of two different books, written at different times. Simplifying, he reminded Pinker, "It was written in 1907 and the rest of the novel in 1911–12. And it did not belong to that novel—but to some other novel which will never be written now I guess."[178] Moreover, *Chance* was the first of Conrad's books not to have a clearly defined thematic center. True, the contrasts between semblance and reality recur throughout the story, but they assume such diverse shapes (de Barral's fraud and the well-nigh Calderónian domination of formal commands and obligations over the emotions and experiences of Flora and her husband) that instead of having a cohesive effect they produce at best the general impression of a comedy of errors.

Thus there were reasons for Conrad's anxiety, particularly since he was aware at the same time of his declining strength and of the hitherto unencountered opportunity of winning wider acclaim. All this might account for his sudden physical and spiritual breakdown, following the completion of the proofs. Jessie wrote to Warrington Dawson, "The house presented a curious aspect the other night: Conrad his hands dug deep in his hair—cursing I'm afraid—printers—proof readers etc, casting collar and tie into the waste paper basket, and slowly relaxing into utter despair. It was a task but with my help he finished it in a fortnight. He sends you his love and is of course very much depressed now that it is over and very worried as to his work in hand. It is awfully difficult to cheer him up but I am trying very hard."[179] And Conrad confided to the long-unseen William Rothenstein, "Everything seems to grow so difficult! . . . I am tired my dear Will—and I daren't own it to myself as I would stop—which I musn't do. It is as if the game weren't worth the candle, already more than half-burned down, while necessity drives one to save every gleam of flickering light . . . There are 30,000 words at least to write and I can't come to grips with the thing. No combination of words seems worth putting down on paper."[180] A month later he was again in a similar mood, complaining of still being "absolutely rotten."[181]

In spite of all this, the summer of 1913 was not a bad time for Conrad. Throughout May, June, and July he felt reasonably well, hardly complaining of his health in his letters. His social life was lively and diversified as never before. Apart from old friends and acquaintances, new ones turned up. Although exhausted by difficulties in his work, he gave his time generously to younger recruits to the world of literature. Unfortunately, apart from Norman Douglas, they were writers of questionable talent, like E. L. Grant Watson, whose first novel Conrad read carefully in manuscript before giving advice and comments;[182] another was Warrington Dawson whose bloodless writings Conrad corrected and altered, also acting as an intermediary with the publishers.

Dawson, a faithful admirer of Conrad who was always welcomed by Jessie, introduced them to his friend, John Powell, a talented pianist. Conrad, a music lover and devotée of *Carmen* and of Meyerbeer, had not been to an opera or concert for years but went twice to London to the recitals given by the young

American, whom he later often invited to his home.[183] At Capel House Powell apparently played Chopin for hours.[184] Dawson and Powell tried to get Conrad to join the Fresh Air Art Society, started by a group of musicians whose aim was to fight aesthetic effeminacy and to combine physical and spiritual health in art. After reading the group's manifesto—a document oozing with pompous naiveté—Conrad declined, explaining his refusal in a letter containing a short outline of his philosophical and artistic creed. He repeated his belief that it was impossible to understand the essence of either reality or life: both science and art penetrate no further than the outer shapes; the superiority of art based on the artist's fidelity to his own feelings consists of compelling us to look and feel, while science formulates theories. He added two new pronouncements: "What I believe in most is responsibilities of *conduct*"; "Suffering is an attribute, almost a condition of greatness, of devotion, of an altogether self-forgetful sacrifice to that remorseless fidelity to the truth of his own sensations at whatever cost of pain or contumely."[185] Both sound like confessions; it is hard to tell if they carry more pride or bitterness.

Having a car made it easier both to welcome guests, who could now be fetched from the station, and pay visits. Henry James sent one of his usual elaborate letters with an invitation to Rye, thirteen miles away: "I hear with fond awe of your possession of a (I won't say life-saving, but literally life-making) miraculous car, the most dazzling element for me in the whole of your rosy legend. Perhaps you will indeed again, some July afternoon, turn its head to Lamb House, and to your, my dear Conrad, and your Wife's, all far more faithfully than you can lately have believed even by whatever stretch of ingenuity, Henry James."[186] But when the Conrads arrived James was apparently not in the mood to see them and gave orders to say he was out.[187]

The sting of this unpleasant incident was assuaged by a visit from two aristocrats, Lady Ottoline Morrell and Bertrand Russell, who were lovers at the time. Although it was Russell, already a well-known philosopher and mathematician, who drew Lady Ottoline's attention to Conrad's books, she had already met the writer. It appears that James was the unwilling intermediary. Lady Ottoline Morrell, née Cavendish-Bentinck, then aged forty, was a society woman of vital temperament, intellectual ambitions, sharp intelligence, biting wit, and vigorous love life.

In her diary she described her first visit to Conrad and its comical preliminaries, which illustrate to what extent James's social snobbery could obscure his perceptions. When she confided to him her wish to meet Conrad,

Henry James held up his hands in horror . . . I remember best some of his exclamations and expostulations: "But, dear lady . . . but dear lady . . . He has lived his life at sea—dear lady, he has never met 'civilized' women. Yes, he is interesting, but he would not understand you. His wife, she is a good cook. She is a Catholic as he is, but . . . No, dear lady, he has lived a rough life, and is not used to talk to," an upward movement of the arms had to describe who—and it was, of course, myself . . . I found Conrad himself standing at the door of the house ready to receive me. How different from the picture Henry James had evoked, for Conrad's appearance was really that of a Polish nobleman. His manner was perfect, almost too elaborate; so nervous and sympathetic that every fibre of him seemed electric . . . He talked English with a strong accent, as if he tasted his words in his mouth before pronouncing them; but he talked extremely well, though he had always the talk and manner of a foreigner . . . He was dressed very carefully in a blue double-breasted jacket. He talked on apparently with great freedom about his life— more ease and freedom indeed than an Englishman would have allowed himself. He spoke of the horrors of the Congo, from the moral and physical shock of which he said he had never recovered . . . she [Jessie] seemed a nice and good-looking fat creature, an excellent cook, as Henry James said, and was indeed a good and reposeful mattress for this hypersensitive, nerve-wrecked man, who did not ask from his wife high intelligence, only an assuagement of life's vibrations. . . . He made me feel so natural and very much myself, that I was almost afraid of losing the thrill and wonder of being there, although I was vibrating with intense excitement inside; and even now, as I write this, I feel almost the same excitement, the same thrill of having been in the presence of one of the most remarkable men I have known. His eyes under their pent-house lids revealed the suffering and the intensity of his experiences; when he spoke of his work, there came over them a sort of misty, sensuous, dreamy look, but they seemed to hold deep down the ghosts of old adventures and experiences—once or twice there was something in them one almost suspected of being wicked. I was amused some years later when I was talking to a dear old Canterbury canon's wife . . . who had known Conrad and who was obviously fascinated by him, to hear her say, "But I am afraid he might drag me down to Hell and I don't want to go there." To which I laughingly replied, "I would willingly go with Conrad." But then I believe whatever strange wickedness would tempt this super-subtle Pole, he would be held in restraint by an equally delicate sense of honour. . . . In his talk he led me along many paths of his life, but I felt that he did not wish to explore the jungle of emotions that lay dense on either side, and that his apparent frankness had a great reserve. This may perhaps be characteristic of Poles as it is of the Irish.[188]

Lady Ottoline's candid description of Jessie and her role seems quite justified. It is borne out by Garnett.[189] On the whole Conrad's friends and acquaintances did not hold a high opinion of his wife. She was indifferent to literary and intellectual pursuits and at her husband's side seemed almost a simpleton; her narrow-minded domesticity shocked not only such artistic Bohemians as Ford. Retinger was the only one to praise Jessie unreservedly in his memoirs: "[She] was without exception the best and most perfect woman I have ever had the good fortune to know." Retinger, however, who otherwise had a preference for male company, judged Jessie not as an equal partner and life companion of Conrad but as an ideal housewife. "She would not have been different had he been a junior clerk or a shopkeeper. She treated him just as a beloved human being, rather queer, who had to be taken care of." [190] In that she was indeed irreplaceable, and it is doubtful whether a person with more refined qualities could have endured her husband's wayward disposition and temperamental outbursts. The two of them lived on different planes, but Conrad's deep loyalty and Jessie's simple patience diminished the friction.

One month after her first visit, Lady Ottoline brought Russell to Capel House. Russell later described his first encounter with the Conrads. "My first impression was one of surprise. He spoke English with a very strong foreign accent, and nothing in his demeanour in any way suggested the sea. He was an aristocratic Polish gentleman to his fingertips. . . . At our very first meeting, we talked with continually increasing intimacy. We seemed to sink through layer after layer of what was superficial, till gradually both reached the central fire. It was an experience unlike any other that I have known. We looked into each other's eyes, half appalled and half intoxicated to find ourselves together in such a region. The emotion was as intense as passionate love, and at the same time all-embracing. I came away bewildered, and hardly able to find my way among ordinary affairs." [191]

The liking was reciprocal. The friendship and correspondence that followed lasted, in spite of intervals, almost until the end of Conrad's life, and Russell's philosophical writings met with his enthusiasm: "You have reduced to order the inchoate thoughts of a life-time and given a direction to those obscure mouvements d'âme which, unguided, bring only trouble to one's weary days on this earth. For the marvellous pages on the worship of a free man the only return one can make is that of a deep admiring affection, which, if you were never to see me again and forget my existence tomorrow will be unalterably yours usque ad finem." [192] Russell looked with incomparably greater optimism than Conrad on the possibilities of scientific and philosophic knowledge, so it may be a little rash to regard Conrad's compliments as an expression of his complete approval of Russell's philosophy. Nevertheless, the admirer of Anatole France may have been attracted by the philosopher's sober rationalism, his anti-speculative and antimetaphysical attitudes, his striving for clarity, and passionate defense of the dignity of the free human mind.

In spite of all the distractions and complaints about his slowness, Conrad was making good progress with his work. By 11 July he had 370 pages of manuscript ready, and on 15 September 651. [193] But although he kept promising an early finish, he was only halfway through the book. In October he decided to change the hero's name and add the subtitle *An Island Story*.[194] He still occasionally mentioned his intention of starting the "Mediterranean" novel before the end of the year; the publication of *Chance*, planned for September, was put off, probably for commercial reasons, and twenty copies were released in order to secure the copyright.[195] Conrad continued to work on the new novel until November, when "the spirit moved me to begin suddenly a short story—title The Assistant."[196] The title was soon changed to "The Planter of Malata," and the story was finished on 14 December.[197] Conrad began another story immediately—that "real Dollars tale"; he considered calling it "The Dollars" or "The Spoiled Smile" but finally decided on "Because of the Dollars." It was finished by 8 January 1914.[198] The intended title for the new collection of stories was *Tales of Hearsay*.[199] As if to celebrate his working ability, Conrad bought a bigger car, a four-seater Humber, in mid-December.[200]

Or was it perhaps his good intuition? The popularity of *Chance*, the "girl-novel" as he called it, published on 15 January 1914, by far exceeded that of any other of his books.[201] The reviewers treated it with respect and often enthusiasm, although not without reservations and adverse criticism. The *Athenaeum* and the *Times Literary Supplement* pointed out a strong element of melodrama; Robert Lynd complained that it bored him; others, as in the past, criticized the complicated structure of the narrative, which even Garnett considered slightly artificial. The *Glasgow News* quipped that "*Chance* suggests a formidable scaffolding that people watch being constructed intricately for days, only to find that at the end it was designed for nothing more than the placing of a weathercock on a steeple."[202]

However, the decisive factor in the popularity of the book was neither critical opinion nor publicity. Garnett supposed later that "the figure of the lady on the jacket of *Chance* did more to bring the novel into popular favour than the long review by Sir Sidney Colvin in The Observer."[203] I daresay there were deeper reasons as well: that same Garnett described *Chance* as "the most insular of Conrad's works," and this book undoubtedly has more in common with the English literary tradition than any of his other novels.[204] But the closest to the truth was probably the author himself when he mentioned as factors contributing to the novel's popularity the heroine and "a steady run of references to women in general all along."[205] After all, women constituted a majority of the reading public, and Conrad's previous works could not count on their enthusiastic reception. In fact, the success even of *Chance* was not all that enormous: all in all thirteen thousand copies were sold in England in two years.[206] It represented a considerable sale for "good literature" but could not stand comparison with really mass editions.

Conrad scored a success with the public that was buying expensive books (*Chance* sold in England for 6 shillings and in the United States for $1.35), a public about which he had written not long before to Norman Douglas, "Don't forget that the S[aturday] R[eview] is meant for the most contemptible part of the populace, that which fills the more respectable streets."[207] *Lord Jim* boasted a larger edition and a wider range of readers: it also came out in January, with fifteen thousand copies priced at 1 shilling, in spite of Conrad's resistance: "I would much prefer a new edition at 6/—leaving the Democracy of the book-stalls to cut its teeth on something softer."[208]

But he was not greedy for money. All memoirs confirm that he was inclined to great, sometimes unreasonable generosity and a lack of ostentation and acquisitive instinct. Curle described with disapproval Conrad's lack of regard for his own comfort and worldly possessions. But at the same time Conrad hated poverty, which restricted his freedom of action, and he was utterly exhausted by the debts that had been trailing him for years. His bad health, both physical and mental, made him anxious about the future and, at times, overconcerned about deriving profits from books he had written long before.[209] His behavior remained, however, that of a man for whom money was only a means; the more he had, the more quickly he went through it. On 12 February 1914 he admitted to Pinker that he was overdrawn by as much as £234.[210]

"I celebrated the publication of *Chance* after the time-honoured custom, by a beastly bout of gout which laid me up for a week," wrote Conrad to Graham;[211] it was apparently a nervous reaction. At the success of the book he looked with a hint of melancholy: "How I would have felt about it ten or eight years ago I can't say. Now I can't even pretend I am elated. If I had *Nostromo*, *The Nigger*, *Lord Jim* in my desk or only in my head I would feel differently no doubt."[212]

And yet it was *Chance* which gave rise to the only criticism that "affected [him] painfully," as he later confided to Quinn.[213] It appeared in a long article by Henry James, "The Younger Generation," published in March and April 1914 in the *Times Literary Supplement*.[214] Although James described Conrad as a "genius" and placed him high in the middle generation of English writers, he criticized his new novel for its artificial construction and excessive subordination of content to form. According to James, the method of indirect narration in *Chance* is almost an aim in itself, and a driving force of presented events. Coming from James this was an accusation of clumsy apprenticeship, and, not surprisingly, these words hurt Conrad, who regarded James as the only living master in English. But he took no offense, and during the summer partook at last of that lunch at Lamb House which had given James the occasion for a display of rhetorical flourish in his letters.[215]

The sting was blunted by the fact that James placed Conrad on the opposite pole to Leo Tolstoi, in whose writings he perceived and sharply condemned the dominance of content over form, a complete subordination of the means of presentation to the subject. By coincidence, at that time Conrad, too, spoke disapprovingly about the great Russian—although for a different reason. To the suggestion of his "disliking" Tolstoi, he responded by an attack against Christianity: "*Dislike* as definition of my attitude to Tols. is but a rough and approximate term. . . . his anti-sensualism is suspect to me. . . . Moreover the base from which he starts—Christianity—is distasteful to me. Great, improving, softening, compassionate it may be but it has lent itself with amazing facility to cruel distortion and is the only religion which, with its impossible standards, has brought an infinity of anguish to innumerable souls—on this earth."[216] Is this an echo of Russell's free-thinking essays?

Soon after the publication of *Chance*, there appeared the first critical book on Conrad's fiction: *Joseph Conrad, A Study*, by Richard Curle. Conrad was pleased with it, although he kept his more effusive compliments for a letter of consolation written to the author, who had received rough treatment from his critics. Curle's study now seems very superficial and naive. His interpretation of Conrad's works was at times pathetically simpleminded; Douglas Hewitt is right when he says that Curle obscures "the finest aspects of Conrad's work."[217] Do Conrad's compliments, however, indicate his basic agreement with the views expressed by Curle, who declaimed about the romantic aura of adventure, about emotions, "the soft atmosphere of triumphant love" (in "The End of the Tether"!), about Marlow "the bore," "naive belief in goodness," and the basic "simplicity" of Conrad the writer?[218] Hewitt's conclusion that this is so seems rash. I think that Conrad's reaction to his young admirer's study was shaped mainly by two factors: his notorious loyalty to friends and his belief that the simplifications in this obviously popularly oriented little book would act as bait. Of course, one should not rule out the possibility that to soothe his tortured soul he acquiesced to the mollifying statements that emphasized the "positive" aspects of his work; and yet that same Conrad had talked recently with Russell. Besides, Curle wrote also about the tragedy hidden in Conrad's irony and about the underground world of "darkness and unrest" in his books. He stressed the importance of heroism and of defending honor—of all that enables us to overcome the chaotic madness of this world. And probably the fact that Curle detected in *Lord Jim* a "passionate and melancholy Pole" made Conrad forgive him even the epithet "Slavonic."

At the beginning of February Conrad signed a lucrative contract with *Munsey's Magazine* for the serialization of "an island tale";[219] he planned to finish it by mid-April.[220] He already had seventy-five thousand words; in December he had estimated the length at one hundred thousand, more than fifteen thousand fewer than he finally wrote.[221] He complained to Pinker, "That tale is the very devil to manage. It has too many possibilities." And he immediately consoled him, as well as himself, "It won't be so with the next novel which I have been thinking out for five years at odd times."[222] The book he had in mind was, of course, the "Mediterranean novel." In the second half of March he estimated having twenty thousand words more to write; it was clear that he could not finish on time, and on 5 May he expected to work on it for another month.[223]

He allowed himself only one literary—or rather journalistic—deviation: another catastrophe took place at sea and Conrad again produced an extensive article, followed by a polemical letter to the editor. Its content was predominantly professional, but he did not let the occasion go by without making several sarcastic remarks on the subject of politicians and the exaggerated reliance on technical improvements, which could never fully replace the efficiency and inventiveness of seamen.[224] During his short visit to London to deliver his article to the *Illustrated London News*, Conrad met Pinker, and a characteristic clash took place between them. Conrad, who was at that time discussing his income with the tax collector, asked Pinker to specify the sum deducted by him to cover interest on the long-term debt. Pinker answered sharply and then apologized. For Conrad, the apology itself demanded an explanation. "I have too much sense to resent a sharp word from a man with whom I am in close confidential and friendly relations. A fellow who can't stand a moment of brusqueness in a friend is not a dignified person. He is simply effeminate. It's women that are perpetually on the look-out for slights and pin-pricks. The apology for something I obviously did not resent was not necessary. . . . But if the apology was offered from mere pity with the thought—'poor Conrad can't very well resent anything I like to do' then I assure you that if ever I thought you were attempting to wound and slight me intentionnally [sic], I wouldn't go home and brood over it but I would openly express my feelings there and then."[225]

In June a new distraction was provided by a visit from the American novelist Ellen Glasgow, who found her way to Conrad through Warrington Dawson. Her visit was immortalized in several of Dawson's photographs: Jessie, impressively stout, makes a face as if she were inflating herself as a joke; Conrad, in spite of the sunny summer weather, is wearing either long drawers or bandages on his knees, under the trousers, of course—the stick is another reminder of his gout.[226] Dawson also took a picture of twelve-year-old Robin Douglas, a member of the Conrad household at the time. From 1914 to 1916 he spent many months at Capel House, theoretically as a playmate for John, but in reality as a ward during the more adventurous periods of his father's life. The lot of a cuckoo's nestling is not always a pleasant one, but Robin remembered with gratitude the atmosphere at Capel House: "I was brought up by them as a member of the family and as such was chidden equally with the two sons and, on occasions, felt the weight of Joseph Conrad's nautical hand across the seat of my pants." He praised Jessie: "She was the real genius of that household . . . it was she who kept the wheels turning smoothly; she who could soothe away the savage frown on Conrad's brow and cause a twinkle to gleam through his monocle—through her flair for cooking; it was she who preserved the peace at all times among all members of her household." Conrad lived in Robin's memory as irritable and temperamental; he worked in his dressing gown and slippers and when called to lunch became annoyed, cursed, threw bread pellets into the fireplace and calmed down gradually only as the meal progressed.[227] Surprisingly, Jessie, affectionately remembered by Robin, for whom she replaced his almost unknown natural mother, gave the boy a bad character and maintained that his articles about the Conrad household were "desperately untrue."[228]

The Conrads' younger son, accustomed from an early age to live a life of his own, interested in plants, animals, and, later, mechanical and architectural constructions, was not causing his parents much trouble. "John," wrote Conrad to Galsworthy, "lives up trees mostly or in the ponds. Wet and scratched." It was different with Borys, to whom his father had in those days to devote much time and attention. The boy had completed his training on the *Worcester* and starting on 10 May was reading for the University of Sheffield entrance examination.[229] It was to take place on 1 July, and Conrad accompanied his son to raise his spirits. He himself, in turn, was deriving moral support from Curle, who went with them both. They remained in Sheffield until 10 July, but Borys failed.[230]

This happened after *Victory* was finished. The title of what had been for so long a nameless novel was finally assigned three days after the last words of the text were written.[231] Then Conrad spent three weeks correcting the first three parts of the book.[232] As Andrzej Busza has demonstrated, the end of *Victory* bears a striking resemblance to the last sentences of Żeromski's *History of a Sin* [*Dzieje grzechu*, 1908]; the similarity is so close that a connection between the two seems indisputable—particularly as there are also a number of similarities in the plot and the presentation of characters, and we also know from a later letter of Conrad's that he had read the book.[233] Was he aware of borrowing?— we do not know. The fact that nine years later he chose the end fragment for public reading brings to mind his boasting about the description of Wait's death in *The Nigger*, which was in fact taken over from Maupassant. Perhaps Conrad, who normally wrote with great difficulty, derived satisfaction from the ease with which he "created" those scenes, never admitting, even to himself, that they were only "re-created."

Anyway, this is not the end of the story. Żeromski's novel shows some analogies with Anatole France's *Le Lys rouge* (1834), phrases of which Conrad apparently knew by heart and from which he also borrowed elements of Lena's character, the vision of female Christian martyrdom, and a fragment of the final chapter of *Victory*. Owen Knowles writes, "Conrad, under pressure and overtired at this late stage of the novel, decided to take the shortest and quickest route to his final destination." However, according to Frederick R. Karl, the manuscript of *Victory* demonstrates Conrad's considerable artistic versatility: it is more realistic and ironical than the final version. Karl argues that Conrad not only preserved his literary skills and maintained a firm grip on his aims, but boldly tackled what is often considered his weakest subject, the male-female relationship.[234]

Conrad's contracts for *Victory* were remunerative: all in all £1,850 for the serialization and advances for the book edition. Together with the profit from *Chance* and the high income from short stories, Conrad was at last able to pay off his debt to Pinker and promise, "There shall be three or four hundred in hand, with a vol. of short stories ready to publish—as a stand-by. Tho' I feel frightfully shaken, my head is now above water in a measure."[235] This time he erred to his own disadvantage.

It was now possible to think of holidays; there were prospects of a trip to the United States, but, after seven years in England, the first destination was to be Poland.[236]

XIII

VOYAGE TO POLAND
1914

IN HIS ESSAY "Poland Revisited," Conrad tries to explain why in the last weeks before the outbreak of World War I he remained unmindful of what was happening in international affairs. He accounts for his unawareness by saying that he was fully absorbed at the time by his personal problems—finishing and correcting *Victory* and Borys's exams—and also by the desire that "possessed" him to go to Poland: "My eyes were turned to the past, not to the future."[1]

The invitation to Poland came from the Retingers, formally from Mrs. Emilia Zubrzycka, mother of Otolia Retinger. She owned a small country estate, Goszcza, near Cracow but on the Russian side of the boundary between the partitioned Polish territories.[2] The psychological ground for the visit had been prepared by Conrad's increasingly lively contacts with Poles. In the spring of 1914 he quite often met Józef Retinger, who managed a Polish Bureau on Arundel Street in London.[3] Retinger also arranged for the only interview Conrad gave in Polish and for a Polish periodical. The interviewer, Marian Dąbrowski, was evidently a little awed by the great writer, and in places his report does not sound quite reliable, although the text was apparently authorized by Conrad.

According to Dąbrowski, Conrad spoke good Polish, without a trace of an accent. Asked about his views on Poland's "immortality," he answered:

> The immortality of Poland? No one doubts it. English critics—and after all I am an English writer—whenever they speak of me add that there is in me something incomprehensible, inconceivable, elusive. Only you can grasp this elusiveness, and comprehend what is incomprehensible. This is Polishness, Polishness which I took from Mickiewicz and Słowacki. My father read *Pan Tadeusz* aloud to me and made me read it aloud. Not just once or twice. I used to prefer *Konrad Wallenrod*, *Grażyna*. Later I preferred Słowacki. You know why Słowacki? *Il est l'âme de toute la Pologne, lui.*

And he added at the close of the interview:

> But there burns in me *your immortal fire*: small, insignificant, just a *lueur*, but it is there. When I ponder the present political situation, *c'est affreux*! I can't think of Poland often. It feels bad, bitter, painful. *It would make life*

unbearable. The English say "Good luck" when they part. I cannot say this to you. But in spite of everything, in spite of imminent annihilation, *we live*. Two personal things fill me with pride: *that I, a Pole, am a master of the British merchant marine, and that I can write, not too badly, in English.*

Conrad also confessed that "something pulls him to Poland" and that he would willingly go there if it were not for his gout.[4] Earlier, lack of money had been a much more serious obstacle, ever since his journey to Poland in 1893, when he had gone to see his uncle for the last time. According to Otolia Retinger, her husband's persuasion played a decisive role in Conrad's return to Poland. The invitation came in the spring, and in June Conrad decided to accept it.[5] Shortly before that he had had another visitor from Poland. Sometime in May young Artur Rubinstein paid a visit to Capel House, introduced by Norman Douglas.[6] Rubinstein turned out to have been a friend of Aniela Zagórska, Conrad's cousin, who at that time kept a pension at Zakopane, a mountain resort in southern Poland. The pension was frequented by several celebrities, among them Józef Piłsudski, the future Polish head of state. Rubinstein had stayed there in the summer of 1913, and Conrad questioned him eagerly about Zagórska, whom he had not seen for twenty years, and about her two daughters, now young women.[7] Undoubtedly, the news about the Zagórskie strengthened Conrad's wish to go to Poland; he probably planned to visit Zakopane as well.

The invitation to his motherland aroused changing, ambivalent, and sometimes stormy emotions in Conrad. "I feared. But [. . .] I was pleased with the idea of showing my companions what Polish country life was like; to visit the town where I was at school before the boys by my side should grow too old, and gaining an individual past of their own, should lose their unsophisticated interest in mine." He confessed to Galsworthy that the prospect of the voyage "caused such an excitement in the household that if I had not accepted instantly I would have been torn to pieces by my own wife and children." On the other hand Conrad was wary of committing himself unequivocally: "As to this Polish journey, I depart on it with mixed feelings. In 1874 I got into a train in Cracow (Vienna Express) on my way to the sea, as a man might get into a dream. And here is the dream going on still. Only now it is peopled mostly by ghosts and the moment of awakening draws near."[8]

It is easy to see through this fluctuation of moods. Conrad's last visit to Poland, over twenty years before, had been part of his earlier life: he had not been a writer, nor settled, nor even quite English. Cracow lay even further back; he had not been there for forty years. So the voyage promised to be one of confrontation: not only of memories with reality, but also of his old with his new self, and of his past with his present allegiance.

Conrad planned to spend six weeks in Poland.[9] Retinger took responsibility for all travel arrangements. The Conrad foursome and both Retingers departed on 25 July, the day Austria-Hungary rejected Serbia's conciliatory reply to its ultimatum. They left London by train for Harwich and from there went by boat to Hamburg; traveling by train, and particularly changing trains, was very tiring for Jessie. The steamer's master made Conrad angry, both by his enthusiasm for everything German and by his incredulity with regard to Conrad's specialist's maritime knowledge.[10] Disembarking in Hamburg on the morning of 27 July, they went sightseeing around the port and then visited Hagenbeck's famous zoo. Continuing by train, they spent the night in Berlin, where an atmosphere of militaristic excitement was rife. On 28 July the war between Austria-Hungary and Serbia began.

The travelers arrived in Cracow that evening and stopped at the Grand Hotel on Sławkowska Street.[11] After supper Conrad and the Retingers went out for a walk. "We stepped out of the portal of the hotel into an empty street, very silent, and bright with moonlight. . . . I felt so much like a ghost that the discovery that I could remember such material things as the right turn to take and the general direction of the street gave me a moment of wistful surprise." Along side streets they went to Floriańska Street and, following the old itinerary of little Konradek, walked up to St. Mary's Square, the center of the old city. "The Square, immense in its solitude, was full to the brim of moonlight." They stopped to wait for the traditional hourly bugle call from the church's tower; "The unequal massive towers of St. Mary's Church soared aloft into the ethereal radiance of the air, very black on their shaded sides, glowing with a soft phosphorescent sheen on the others."

They had to wait for a long while, and Mrs. Retinger began to worry that perhaps the trumpeter would not play. But he did. Conrad stiffened with emotion. The Retingers, on both his sides, took his hands. He squeezed them in his own, and then thanked his friends for having persuaded him to come. They felt, for the first time since the beginning of their journey, that he was relaxed and genuinely glad.

"There was not a soul in sight, and not even the echo of a footstep for our ears." The wandering along the pavements of the ancient city was changing into a pilgrimage to scenes of nearly half a century ago. Conrad remembered his father's last weeks. "It seemed to me that if I remained longer there in that narrow street I should become the helpless prey of the Shadows I had called up. They were crowding upon me, enigmatic and insistent, in their clinging air of the grave that tasted of dust and of the bitter vanity of old hopes."[12]

Conrad's recollections of his stay in Cracow, written in 1915 and 1918, have to be treated cautiously as biographical documents, not only because their author confuses the dates and chronology of current events, but primarily because —for reasons I shall later try to explain—his account there of his own and other people's moods is contradicted by his own letters written in the summer of 1914.[13]

Although the war on the Serbian front had begun—however sluggishly—until the first days of August it could have seemed that the conflict would not spread. Austria in particular did not wish it to. The Austro-Russian frontier remained open.[14] Waiting for the whole international situation to clear up, Conrad spent his first two days in Cracow sightseeing and taking his older son around the city. Together they paid a visit to the Jagiellonian Library and were shown by its keeper portfolios with manuscripts and letters of Apollo Korzeniowski.[15] They also went to Rakowice Cemetery and there, for the only time in his life, Borys saw his father kneel down and pray—at Apollo's grave.[16]

Much has been written, often rashly, about Conrad's subconscious antagonism toward his father, but it has been forgotten that such an antipathy is frequently born of a feeling of guilt. If the thought that he had strayed far from his father's spiritual legacy was sometimes painful for Conrad then a natural, self-defensive reaction to that pain would have been anger, anger at that oppressive model of heroic selfless martyrdom. But that anger would have been a reactive, and not a primal, sentiment; and a few months later Conrad recounted his father's funeral with proud and somber affection.

The first acquaintance of old times Conrad met was Konstanty Buszczyński, the son of his first guardian. They recognized each other, to their mutual joy, in the hotel's dining room on the second night of Conrad's stay in Cracow. Buszczyński invited the whole Conrad family to Górka Narodowa, near Cracow, where he owned a seed-producing farm. On the day of their visit there, 31 July, general mobilization was declared; roads and streets filled with recruits and requisitioned horses.[17]

In the prevailing atmosphere of general excitement Conrad doubtless spent much of his time discussing politics. The people with whom he was in touch represented a variety of opinions, from cautious conservatives to the leftist followers of Piłsudski. Piłsudski commanded a Polish Legion, formed on Austrian territory with the aim of fighting for an independent Poland; the legion was mobilized during the night of 1 to 2 August. The mood in Cracow was almost universally buoyant: for Poland, a major conflict between the powers which had partitioned it presented its only chance of regaining national unity, even if it were a unity under an Austrian protectorate. And as long as the fires of war did not spread out to the West and England was not involved on the side opposite Austria-Hungary, Conrad could share that boisterous feeling without major reservations.

There was, however, an immediate danger of getting stranded in a battle zone: Cracow was just a few miles from the Russian border and all civilian transport was about to be suspended. A journey across Europe, awash with mobilized millions, with the invalid Jessie and ill John, was obviously too risky to contemplate. Conrad decided, therefore, to take "all the unlucky tribe to Zakopane . . . out of the way of all possible military operations. I had rather be stranded here, where I have friends, than try to get away and be caught perhaps in some small German town in the midst of the armies." [18]

They left on 2 August, the day of Russian general mobilization and of the proclamation of the state of emergency in Germany. [19] In Zakopane they stopped first at a big pension, Stamary, and after a few days moved to Zagórska's Konstantynówka. [20] During the next few weeks Conrad's main worry was again lack of money—for paying bills and, eventually, for buying return tickets. He asked Galsworthy and Pinker for cash in letters sent via a roundabout route. He was, however, still optimistic. "My health is good. I am getting a mental stimulus out of this affair—I can tell you! And if it were not for the unavoidable anxiety I would derive much benefit from the experience," he wrote to Pinker on 8 August. [21] At that moment the war between Germany and Great Britain had been going on for four days, that between Russia and Austria-Hungary for three, and war between Great Britain and Austria had not yet been declared.

Conrad did not complain about his health, enjoyed meeting people, and regularly frequented local cafés. [22] He also sat for a portrait painted by Dr. Kazimierz Górski, a physician he had met at Stamary. [23] Although he was still not widely known in Poland at that time, he aroused a lot of interest both as a famous writer and as an exotic compatriot from far away. He easily charmed new acquaintances, especially women; some, however, frowned at him. Bronisława Dłuska, sister of the physicist Maria Curie-Skłodowska, openly scolded him for having used his great talent for purposes other than the better future of his motherland. [24] But thirty-three-year-old Aniela Zagórska, the elder of two sisters, idolized Conrad, kept him company, and provided him with books. Apparently he read a lot in Polish at the time, particularly the novels and stories of Bolesław Prus, a leading late-nineteenth-century writer. He refused, however, to read anything by Orzeszkowa—"Don't bring my anything by that hag," he growled; evidently the memory of her attack on him in 1899 still rankled. [25] But generally he was in a relaxed mood. He was always ready to tell stories and was a spellbinding raconteur. Although Conrad claimed to be telling about his own adventures at sea and in exotic lands, he would weave in large fragments of his own stories and novels. [26] Zagórska introduced to him several Polish writers, intellectuals, and artists who had also taken refuge in Zakopane. Unfortunately, the extant reminiscences of these encounters contain little more than banalities and assurances that Conrad was fluent in Polish.

Conrad's political conversations are a little better known; of course, political subjects were the most hotly debated at that time. The Zagórskie were enthusiasts of Józef Piłsudski. His Legion was now fighting on the Russian front alongside the Austrian forces, but Piłsudski considered it the nucleus of an army of a future sovereign state of Poland. Conrad must have felt uncomfortable when talking to the adherents of this political line: he was certainly for the restoration of a Polish state, but Austria was at war with Great Britain.

Dr. Teodor Kosch, a young Cracow lawyer who met Conrad very often at that time, remembered later that it had been difficult for Conrad to reconcile his conviction that England would be ultimately victorious with the view that Polish hopes for independence would be best served by a military and political alliance with Austria-Hungary.[27] Conrad's mental dilemma was undoubtedly made more distressing by the fact that Russia was an ally of England.

Kazimierz Górski remembered that Conrad was skeptical about any independently active role played by Poles in the war. Górski was taken aback by the calm detachment with which Conrad expressed his opinion that neither France nor England realized the importance of the Polish problem for European stability. Conrad also maintained that "the Polish question could be positively solved only if Russia were beaten by Germany and Germany by England and France."[28]

That was exactly what happened in the end, and also what Piłsudski apparently counted on. This paradoxical convergence of outlooks elucidates the basic ideas of a political document that Conrad composed during his stay in Poland. In spite of his doubts and misgivings, he wanted to do something for his country of origin after his return to England. To marshal his own thoughts and to facilitate future discussions, he expounded the principles of his political plan for the future in a four-page memorandum in Polish.[29] His main goal was to persuade British public opinion that the Polish right to national unity should be recognized by both the victorious and the defeated powers. Conrad saw the best prospects for Poland's future in a merger of the lands occupied by Russia and Prussia with those ruled by Austria-Hungary; within this last monarchy Poles would possess autonomy and counterbalance the German element. One of Conrad's premises was that the long-range interests of Great Britain and Austria-Hungary did not in fact clash with each other.

Conrad's friends in Zakopane and his whole environment there kept directing his attention toward Polish problems and issues. But distant England was also there, represented by his wife and sons. Of these three only Borys, who spoke fluent French and thus could communicate with most of these new friends, felt happy amidst the entire flurry of events, excited by visions of adventure and by youthful love affairs. His younger brother was rather lonely and required constant attention. Jessie kept losing her head to the turmoil of unfamiliar words, faces, and objects. What confused her in the first place was that she did not understand Polish, and French was not her forte either. She was thus reduced to relying on guesses as to the meaning of the scenes she watched. Her reminiscences indicate that she was often mistaken in her understanding of the events she witnessed and the intentions of people she met. Besides, for the first time since her honeymoon in Brittany, she was in a country that was poor and backward in comparison with England or France. A few minutes after they had arrived in Cracow, she remembered, "I rather turned my nose up when we left the station; the road paving seemed extremely primitive, and the odour of stables and bad draining was somewhat sickening. Conrad noticed my expression. He turned to me rather sharply, remarking, 'This is not England, my dear; don't expect too much.'"[30] (Evidently, they both forgot about London's East End.) Moreover, she had no idea what war could be like and took everything that differed from established peaceful order as an outcome of wild chaos and a sign of utter cataclysm.

She wrote in her memoirs, "I understood my husband so much better after those months in Poland. So many characteristics that had been strange and unfathomable to me before, took, as it were, their right proportions. I understood that his temperament was that of his countrymen."[31] This sounds promising, but in the end boils down to explaining one incomprehensibility by another: in Jessie's eyes, Poles are hospitable and on the whole quite nice, but most of them behaved like lighthearted, irresponsible hysterics. Nevertheless, she remembered her stay in Zakopane without resentment.

News from the fronts and capitals seeped to the mountain retreat after great delays, frequently distorted by gossip, censorship, and propaganda. Moreover, the Polish-language press was loathe to write about German successes on the Western front: national sympathies were with the French. Anyway, the Eastern front was a more immediate concern, especially as the Russian offensive at the beginning of September was initially successful. The Russians captured Lwów and came close to Cracow, bypassing it on the north. Conrad's Polish friends watched these developments with grave anxiety.

As a British subject, Conrad had been liable to be interned by Austrian authorities after the declaration of war between Austria-Hungary and Great Britain; he had thus far been sheltered by his Polish name and connections, but the threat remained. More pressing was lack of money, for which he again appealed to Pinker, using Frederick C. Penfield, the American ambassador to Vienna, as an intermediary. Of course, Conrad's position would have been made much more vulnerable if the front had drawn nearer to Zakopane. To make things worse, with the passing of summer and the onset of the rains and mists of autumn, Conrad began to suffer from gout and was compelled to spend whole days in bed, almost entirely incapacitated; for about a year, rheumatism, if it was in fact rheumatism, had affected his right hand as well.[32]

These were sufficient reasons for trying hard to obtain permission and the means to leave for a neutral country. Efforts to this end succeeded at the beginning of October. On 1 October Conrad received five hundred guldens from Penfield.[33] Five days later he obtained official permission to go "by train or automobile" from Nowy Targ (the district town near Zakopane) to Vienna.[34]

The Conrad family, looked after by Stanisław Zajączkowski, their friend from Cracow, left Zakopane in the night of 7–8 October. First they drove in a highlander's cart; both the carriage and its driver horrified Jessie, but the ride to Nowy Targ passed without a hitch. The train from Nowy Targ to Cracow, a distance of sixty-five miles, took eighteen hours; they arrived early on the morning of 9 October.[35] Conrad was well aware of the risks of travel across war-ridden countries ("You ought to think yourselves lucky to have the Channel between you and what is going on in Europe now," he wrote to Pinker[36]); as a result he apparently wondered whether they should not return to Zakopane.[37] Nevertheless, after a stop of twelve hours or so, they continued their trek and on the evening of the tenth, in a train full of wounded soldiers, the Conrads arrived in Vienna.[38]

On arrival Conrad was immediately laid up by an attack of gout, which lasted four days, undoubtedly caused by the nervous tension during the passage. Still, in spite of his illness, on the thirteenth he held a long conference with Marian Biliński, whose brother Leon was the Austro-Hungarian minister of finance. They discussed "the Polish question in general—in detail and exhaustively, for some hours, and how it might be put before a European Congress, and the hopes, fears, and possibilities connected with it." Five days later Conrad paid Biliński a visit: "We talked again for an hour or more mainly about how the Polish question should be presented in England. It will be difficult in view of the course of events . . . It will be necessary to look around, sound the hearts and minds of influential people and only then start to act, if any action is possible in this question which is so close to our hearts."[39]

In the meantime Jessie, with Borys's assistance and the help of an interpreter, recovered from the goods depot of Vienna's railway station two trunks that had been lost on the way from Berlin to Cracow.[40] Thus a citizen of a hostile country was given back her luggage, lost several weeks before and a good few hundred miles away.

Conrad also discussed the current political situation with Penfield, who did not spare his help and advice. After receiving an assurance from the police commissioner that there were no official objections to their crossing the Austrian border, the whole family left Vienna on 18 October for Milan, via Cormons.* On the twentieth they were in Italy, which was still neutral.[41]

From Milan Conrad wired Pinker for more money. At last supplied with cash, the Conrads went to Genoa to look for a suitable boat; at that time the

---

* Borys Conrad's claim that his father proved on this occasion that he could speak German "with great fluency" (My Father, p. 97) sounds exaggerated. Conrad certainly remembered some German from his school days, but it is unlikely that he ever knew that language well or that he retained good command of it. And completely incredible is Borys's story that the Conrads were stopped at the Austro-Italian frontier by German guards. Austria-Hungary, although a German ally, was a sovereign country and such incursion was simply impossible.

sea blockade of the British Isles was still ineffectual. Conrad spent his short stay in Genoa sightseeing in the city and port, which he later made the scene of *Suspense*. On the twenty-fifth they left on the Dutch steamer *Vondel*.[42]

Amidst all travel arrangements Conrad was not forgetting his political mission. He wrote to Kosch, "As far as I can judge, the islanders [the British] understand our situation quite well. There is of course no grievance against Aus[tria]."[43] And on 2 November, a few hours before arriving in London, he promised Biliński, "Tomorrow I shall straight away endeavour to meet some influential people in the world of journalism. . . . I do not want you to think that I am treating the matter in any way casually. We shall probably be staying in London a whole week so as to meet people, discuss things, and weigh up the situation."[44]

Two days later Arnold Bennett noted in his diary that Pinker "had seen Conrad that morning, just returned from Austrian Poland. C. had no opinion of Russian army, and had come to England to influence public opinion to get good terms for Austria! As if he could."[45]

XIV

. . . .

THE WAR AND THE
MEMORIES
1914–1919

"ON REACHING HOME I just rolled into bed and remained there till yesterday, in a good deal of pain but mostly suffering from a sort of sick-apathy which I am trying now to shake off," wrote Conrad to the Galsworthys on 15 November 1919.[1] After coming back from Poland Conrad was ailing almost until the end of January.[2] His complaints were both physical—the usual gout—and psychological: dejection and discouragement induced by "the thoughts of this war [that] sit on one's chest like a nightmare. I am painfully aware of being crippled, of being idle, of being useless."[3] In the five months after his return to England he wrote only one short essay, "Poland Revisited."[4]

Despite its title, almost half of the piece deals with Conrad's journey itself, from London across the North Sea and Germany, not with his stay in Cracow and Zakopane. In the essay Conrad harked back to his first arrival in England, spinning distant associations as if trying to stifle the present and its more pressing thoughts. When writing about Cracow, he plunged into memories from forty years ago; they are moving but inaccurate—for instance, Conrad spent only the last four months of his father's life in Cracow with him, not the last eighteen. Moreover, the atmosphere of Conrad's recent journey underwent a significant change in the telling. In "Poland Revisited" Conrad's Polish friends and interlocutors are presented as depressed, even despairing and resigned: there is talk of "final catastrophe," lack of "all hope and even of its last illusions," a feeling of "Ruin—and Extinction." Similarly, Conrad wrote to Quinn a little later, "I've had to stand for two months the strain of living amongst the Poles who see with dismay the ruin of their hopes. For this indeed is the end no matter what manifestoes [sic] are issued or what promises are being held out. The situation doesn't stand being thought about."[5]

Here Conrad's picture not only distorts reality but turns it upside down; Conrad projects his present depressed mood onto past events and feelings, which had actually been quite different. Conrad must have encountered some pessimists in Poland, but they had been in the minority; and all the contemporary sources agree that during his visit to his motherland Conrad had been moderately optimistic. What was the cause of this emotional *volte-face*? On his return to England Conrad must have been painfully struck by the utter indifference to the question of Polish independence both in British official circles and in the public in general. It was now becoming impossible for Conrad to ignore the fact that Britain's foreign policy toward Poland had traditionally been unsympathetic. As late as September 1914 His Majesty's Government officially announced that it regarded Poland's future and her possible self-government as Russia's internal affair.[6] The guiding principle of British policy was: "In no way to offend the Eastern ally, by no means to arouse Russia's suspicions—the existence or non-existence of a Polish state was of no consequence for either British trade or British politics."[7] And Conrad was deeply convinced that England would emerge from the war victorious. Under the circumstances, the plans Conrad had made in Zakopane and Vienna to arouse sympathy in England for Poland's struggle for independence appeared unrealistic and would inevitably lead to humiliation and a sense of divided loyalty. And so, partly because of his tendency to adopt tragic attitudes and partly out of self-justification, Conrad attributed his own sense of hopelessness to the Poles he had met during his visit. In a letter to Quinn of 15 April 1915 he hinted rather definitely that it was precisely the gloomy thoughts about Poland's situation which had brought on his long state of prostration; the explanation sounds convincing.

Still, Conrad was unable to forget Polish affairs, for they continued to demand his personal decisions. Ignacy Paderewski, a member of the Relief Committee for War Victims in Poland, which had been formed on 9 January 1915 at Vevey, Switzerland, called upon Conrad to join the committee. Conrad replied by telegram, "With all deference to your illustrious personality must decline membership Committee where I understand Russian names are to appear."[8] His refusal was received badly. The committee tried to maintain its purely charitable and nonpolitical character, although it did not always succeed, and Conrad's disinclination to cooperate was taken as a sign of his indifference to national matters. This interpretation was both unjustified and injurious, for it was Conrad's serious approach to the Polish question and to his own public role that made him reject the invitation. The committee received ostentatious support from the Russian ambassadors—Izvolsky in Paris and Benckendorf in London—who wanted to make its activities seem a purely "internal" Russian affair; consequently the committee unwittingly found itself forced to operate according to the principle adopted by the allied powers by which the Polish question was placed in Russian jurisdiction. Conrad's view, as we know, was entirely different. It was probably Retinger who drew Conrad's attention to the significance of the Russian ambassadors' patronage. Retinger arrived in England just before 1 September and immediately plunged into energetic, although none too sensible, political activities.[9] He went next to the United States but was back again in Europe by December, commuting between

London and Paris. Retinger did not belong to any political organization or group, but he consistently upheld the idea of Polish sovereignty vis-à-vis all three partitioning powers.

To Mrs. Iris Wedgwood, the wife of a new friend, Ralph Wedgwood, a wealthy industrialist, Conrad confided, "It seems almost criminal levity to talk at this time of books, stories, publication."[10] But for Conrad writing was an escape from gloomy thoughts, in addition to a means of earning money: on 1 January 1915 his debt to Pinker amounted to £230.[11] Despite his considerably improved financial situation, Conrad could not expect to live only on the royalties from his old books. In the first place he was planning to complete *The Rescue*, which he had begun and laid aside a long time ago.[12] Before that, however, Conrad had embarked on another project which he had mentioned as far back as 1899: "I've carried it in my head for years under the name of First Command. . . . An early personal experience thing."[13] In the same letter of 3 February 1915 he spoke to Pinker of his intention to write a "military tale" set in Spain and based on an episode from his youth; this was obviously a reference to what was to become *The Arrow of Gold*. *First Command*, the future *Shadow Line*, had perhaps already been begun in February, but its progress was slow— all the slower for Conrad's simultaneous work on *The Rescue*.[14] There were also disheartening periods of creative sterility; to his friends Conrad confessed to what sound like the classic symptoms of morbid depression: "I am wretched and coughing dismally. Gouty bronchitis I suppose. Still I am trying to write—I don't know what and I don't know what for—really. The very sunlight seems sinister."[15]

From the point of view of publishing, the year 1915 was exceptional: two volumes of his writings appeared—to Conrad's discontent, however, because he was afraid that the critics would make unfavorable comparisons between them.[16] *Within the Tides*, dedicated to the Wedgwoods, came out on 24 February; the following month *Victory* was published in the United States. The new volume of stories had as good press as the previous one, showing that the critics judged Conrad more on the strength of his acquired reputation than on perceptive reading of his current work. Even "The Inn of the Two Witches" was praised, and "The Partner" most of all. W. L. Courtney's criticism in the *Daily Telegraph*, about which Conrad complained, was an exception. Conrad himself seems to have been somewhat embittered by his current popularity: "'The Planter of Malata' alone earned eight times as much as 'Youth,'" he wrote to Galsworthy, "six times as much as 'Heart of Darkness.' It makes one sick."[17]

Although Capel House lay only a hundred miles as the crow flies from the front in Flanders, the war at first had little effect on the life of the Conrads in the sheltered English countryside. Now and again guns could be heard practicing near Dover; occasionally recruits marched by. Jessie recalled that after her return from Poland, being at home gave her the impression of a "fantastic dream." [18] Conrad must have frequently thought about his isolation from the terrible realities of the front. Contrary to many contemporary writers, he neither idealized nor glorified the war; his letters and writings show no trace of having been influenced by official propaganda or such writing matter as A. J. Dawson's mawkish "sketches from the front." [19] But the war as such was not a shock for Conrad. He was neither surprised nor embittered by the news of hundreds of thousands being killed and maimed, or of large parts of various countries being devastated; he had predicted the cataclysm or, at least, he had foreseen in *The Mirror of the Sea* and in "Autocracy and War" the origins, aims, and means of a future European war.

And so life followed its usual course. From time to time the Conrads went for short visits to London; in May they bought a new car. [20] In Conrad's letters to Pinker there appeared, as usual, suggestions for nonliterary and profitable projects: the latest being a film adaptation of "Gaspar Ruiz"—as if to expose more fully the utter trashiness of the story. [21] *The Shadow Line* advanced at a slow pace. Although on 24 June Conrad expected to complete it in a few days, he did not yet anticipate its ultimate length. At the same time he promised to finish *The Rescue* before the end of the year. [22]

Conrad's involvement with current events was still confined to Polish affairs. He lent money to Retinger for his political work—keeping it a secret from Jessie. ("As I haven't contributed anything to *that* cause I should like to be useful in the way of a loan.") [23] Conrad also recommended August Zaleski to Austin Harrison, editor of the *English Review*, as a possible contributor of an article on the economic situation in Eastern Europe. [24] Zaleski represented Piłsudski in England, and the anti-Russian circles of Polish irredentists in general.

In response to a letter from the secretary of the Polish Association in London, Conrad thanked him for the "brotherly acknowledgement of Polishness with which, in the depth of my soul, I have never parted," [25] but when the association asked Conrad to take part in a public meeting, he firmly refused, giving his weak voice as an excuse. [26] Was this merely a subterfuge? To some extent yes, since no one had ever noticed Conrad's voice having failed him before; but he resorted to it not because of the Polishness of the organizers but because of the Englishness of the audience. A few months later, and even more emphatically, Conrad used the same excuse to turn down Quinn's suggestion that he should read fragments of his books in public. In 1922 Conrad confessed the real reason for his refusal in a letter to another American, Elbridge L. Adams: "I am not very anxious to display my accent before a large gathering of people. It might affect them disagreeably . . . if it were not for that . . . I would love nothing better than to give readings from my works." [27]

Borys's presence at Capel House was an everyday reminder of the reality of the war. After some months of reluctant studies for yet another entrance examination for Sheffield University, he tried his luck again at the end of June; Conrad accompanied him as before. This time Borys passed, but he already had made up his mind to volunteer for the army.[28] Thanks to Cunninghame Graham's intercession and to his certificate from the *Worcester*, Borys was granted a commission in spite of being only seventeen and a half. He was gazetted second lieutenant on 20 September.[29] Conrad hoped that the period of training in the Mechanical Transport Corps would last for about one year; he ordered a pair of field glasses for Borys and even lent him his car for the period he was to spend in the training center at Grove Park.[30]

The parting with his son prompted Conrad to write, "I am driven nearly distracted by my uselessness." He deplored his own inability to "work in this war atmosphere. Reality, as usual, beats fiction out of sight."[31] Throughout the autumn Conrad often grumbled about Jessie's and his own health, complaining that he was spending most of the time in bed.[32] This was an exaggeration, although not as great as Conrad's declaration in a letter to Gide that he had written "nothing—absolutely nothing" that year.[33] To be sure he had not much to show, but Conrad's feeling that he had "all the starch taken out" made him minimize even what little he had. According to calculations Conrad made on 26 October, he had written only twenty thousand words in 1915.[34] If that was indeed the case, then nothing apart from half of *The Shadow Line* was done before that date. But Conrad was not feeling well at the time. Jessie unburdened herself to Pinker: "He is better today, only weak and very unreasonable. I feel sure you will not misunderstand me when I say that he is like a spoiled child." She appealed to the agent to suggest to Conrad that he should dictate in order to speed up his writing, which was impeded by a painful arm.[35]

It seems that *Victory*'s good reception brought at least a temporary improvement in Conrad's health and mood. Dedicated to Perceval and Maisie Gibbon, the novel came out in England on 24 September and was a great popular success.[36] Galsworthy, who did not particularly like it ("*Victory* is something of a triumph for his hypnotic faculty, for it's not really good"), visited Conrad soon after its publication and "thought him looking better than for a long time."[37] Apparently to celebrate the success, Conrad and Jessie went on a three-day jaunt to London; they even went to see *Romeo and Juliet*.[38] The reviews of *Victory* were on the whole very favorable. It is noteworthy, however, that the critics who had had such difficulty identifying the essential merits of Conrad's art in his earlier works astutely pointed out the weaknesses of *Victory*: a heady dose of melodrama, facile allegory, cautious subtlety in the characterization of some protagonists, and crudity in the development of others.[39] Conrad did not comment on those charges in his letters, but among his works *Victory* remains artistically apart. At all events Conrad maintained that he did not care for the book "very specially."[40]

The Shadow Line was at last completed on 17 December. The next day Conrad wrote to Curle: "Looked at as a whole it isn't bad. I laboured hard at the last; and I feel unexpectedly well (for me) now it is all over." [41] I suspect, although the evidence is only circumstantial, that the story became "stuck" during the summer when its end seemed within sight. Later Conrad was spurred on to write by the knowledge that Borys, to whom the story was dedicated, might be sent off to the front at any moment. Borys's training in England had lasted only a short time, and from the middle of November a transfer of his unit to France was expected on short notice. [42]

The Shadow Line carries the subtitle *A Confession*. In spite of Conrad's claim in a letter to Sidney Colvin, the story is not an "exact autobiography," although it is indeed based to a large extent on his reminiscences. [43] These reminiscences dated from the time when he had been at the height of his physical powers, readiness to venture, and professional skill. Its autobiographical content and simplicity of structure, its intellectual concentration and expressiveness, as well as its synthesis of the typically Conradian moral and psychological problems—these elements combine to form a paradoxical contrast, certainly invigorating for Conrad, with the moods of distraction, depression, and sterility that had weighed on him throughout 1915.

The new year, 1916, at first brought no change. Conrad complained that his "mentality [seemed] to have gone to pieces" and that he was a "strangely useless personality." [44] But he went to London quite often, though apparently not on business, which may explain his constant lack of money. [45] He tried to take care of his health. For a time he even gave up cigarettes and took up the pipe, which he "detested," in order to cut down on smoking. "All in the interest of more (and better) work," he explained to Pinker virtuously. [46] Conrad actually did little work, however, and was dissatisfied with its results. In February and March he wrote a short story, "The Warrior's Soul" (formerly "The Humane Tomassov"), but he did not wish to have it published at once: "I feel so dissatisfied that I keep it back for a little while longer." [47] A year later he decided that the story was not really "*done*" and called it a "pot-boiler." [48] It is actually a rather unexpected piece for Conrad: until then he had never spoken sympathetically about the Russians or the Russian army, and here a young Russian officer is presented as a noble and idealistic hero—as if Conrad were trying to show his lack of prejudice as a writer.

At any rate, the story failed to raise his spirits: "I find work, properly speaking, impossible," he confided to Garnett, whom he had not seen for a long time. [49] But he derived great pleasure from reading a little book about his literary output by an American, Wilson Follett: "I am simply delighted by it. It's the first intelligent attempt to understand the fundamental ideas of my work—a successful attempt, too." [50] Conrad praised it more than Curle's study, and without reservation. Follett's booklet has by now fallen entirely into obscurity, mainly, it seems, because of its exasperatingly "poetic," convoluted and pompous style. The book contains a number of shrewd and revealing observations, however: Follett underscored the fundamental intellectual coherence of Conrad's works, exposed the ever-present conflict beween man and his will on the one hand and the indifferent world of nature on the other; he also pointed out the crucial importance for Conrad of the principle of human solidarity and took note of Conrad's artistic contribution to English prose.[51]

Simultaneously with Follett's booklet another newcomer from overseas appeared in Conrad's household: a beautiful young woman with flaming orange hair, brimming over with temperament and daring ideas.[52] She was Jane Anderson, a journalist from Arizona, married in a nonbinding way to the composer Deems Taylor. At the time she was working as a war correspondent in England and France. An admirer of Conrad and a budding novelist herself, she had tried earlier to secure an invitation to Capel House through Wells and Lord Northcliffe, owner of the large newspaper syndicate, but Conrad was ill at the time. Finally Jane Anderson succeeded when her colleague, Gordon Bruce, a correspondent for the *New York Herald*, charmed Jessie at the unveiling of Jo Davidson's bust of Conrad. (Conrad had not felt well enough to go to London.)[53] On the same day as her visit to Capel House, when her impressions were still fresh, Jane sent back a long and enthusiastic report to Deems Taylor in New York:

> We turned into a grey road with deep ruts in it and saw, on a little rise, a very old brick cottage with old-fashioned flowers in a small garden. There was also a monstrous tropical tree with stiff branches. And there was a moat, rather a deep moat in places, which broadened into a pool by the wall. We crossed over a little bridge and drew up before a faded green door with a knocker. A maid admitted us, a very smart maid with a billowing white collar and a timid smile. . . . Then in the next room I heard a conversation and a hurried bustling. Then the door burst open and I saw a man's head and shoulders rising above the furniture of a little dining-room. It was Conrad, only it was an older, more agitated Conrad than I had thought about. He seized both my hands, and looked at me; he considered Gordon, who was standing behind me.
>
> "Ah!" he said. "You haf come for the day." He was glad!
>
> It was afterwards that I understood all of this, all of this precipitancy, this agitation, this unmistakeable nervous excitement. It seems that he has a fear of trespassers, a real fear of new faces and gestures. He had been afraid of this luncheon.
>
> While he took us across the dining-room to the livingroom beyond he was talking—talking very fast and making tremendous motions with his hands and his shoulders. His voice is very clear and fine in tone, but there is an accent which I have never heard before. It is an accent which affects every word,

and gives the most extraordinary rhythm to phrases. And his verbs are never right. If they are in the place they should be—which is seldom—they are without tense; a new facet for the miracle.

The room to which he took us was a low room, rather crowded with furniture. A big fire blazed in a narrow fireplace. By a little couch there was the woman they had all told me about, a big woman with very fine grey eyes and a quick, generous smile. She came slowly to meet us, walking with a cane. The black dress was unmistakeably foreign in cut and in texture, and she wore six bold bracelets on each wrist. Her arms were very white. I don't know what she said, but I looked at her and she looked at me, and I loved her. And I'm not given, all in a minute, to loving folks exactly.

Then I said how glad I was that I could come down.

"It's Conrad," she said. "He's afraid of new faces." At which Joseph Conrad set himself to being hospitable—it was, all that he did, all that he said, inexplicably alien to England. It was not that he was foreign; it was simply that he was not English. He asked us if we would sit down, and he made one of these great gestures which included the small room. "This," he said, and pointed to the window where his desk stood, "is my study, my chair where I wrote *Victory*. And this"—he looked at the little black piano—"is the moosic room. As for where you stand, it is Mrs. Conrad's drawing-room. Our house is not a great house."

. . . His head is extraordinarily fine in the modelling, although the forehead is not high. There are certain planes above the eyes, however. It is the pose of his head, which is a little sunken into his shoulders, which gives the impression of strength. His mouth, although not clearly defined under the grey moustach [sic], is full but sensitive. But it is his eyes which are the eyes of genius. They are dark, and the lids droop except in moments of intense excitement. They are dark brown, in which the pupil does not show. And there is in them a curious hypnotic quality.

. . . "We will talk," he said suddenly, "but not of ze war." Then he told the history of this war, and of other wars; told it with his gestures, and his shoulders, and those extraordinary flashes in his eyes. He said that his faith in the French, and all of his hope for them, had been fulfilled; that the signs of decay were not decay. They were but the imperfections that marked fine fruit; that in England there was the goodness which is the foundation of strength. "But for Russia," he said, "there can be no hope. I came to Russia many times. It is great but in numbers. It has grown, it has flowered. But it is rotten before it is ripe."

. . . Then there was the long afternoon, and I went for a walk with the youngster and a remarkable friend of some fourteen years who is on holiday from school [Robin Douglas]. . . . Then there was tea afterward, and while

Conrad was away from a little bit, Jessie Conrad showed me some old photographs of a little boy who sat in a great carved chair and wore a Russian tunic with flowers embroidered in the hem of it. He was staring straight out ahead of him and looking at the world with rather large and astonished eyes. This was Conrad, aged five.

Then, at the end of it all, Mrs Conrad showed me certain things she made, clothes and such, with fine stitches in them and white embroidery such as fine ladies wore some fifty years ago. And I loved her for her great ignorance in such matters. And she told me how she had met Conrad, and of a long honeymoon in a tramp cutter off the coast of Brittany, and of the first book which was sent off to a publisher because a friend who was without literary discernment said to send it there. And how, when it was forgotten, and Conrad was making plans to be off to sea again, a postcard came to say that it was accepted . . . a bit of a postcard for *Almayer's Folly*.[54]

The main interest of the letter is not its confirmation of how Jessie would invent fantastic stories about Conrad but that while confirming Rebecca West's verdict that Jane was a "good natured, silly, melodramatic ass," it exhibits Jane Anderson's journalistic shrewdness. The visit marked the beginning of Jane's ambiguous friendship with Jessie, Conrad, and Borys, and also with Joseph Retinger. At first, however, it provided only a momentary distraction.

Conrad had at the time an additional reason for grief: the fatal illness of Marwood, who died in mid-May.[55] A few days later Conrad wrote to Gide, "My health, my dear friend, has been rather poor. At the moment I am knocked down flat by gout. . . . It's disgusting. My thoughts revolve ineffectually without getting anywhere. What survives in me, however, is an unshaken trust in the future, a deep conviction that the shadow of Germanism will be wiped out from the face of this earth on which I wandered so much."[56] And Borys was indeed engaged in "wiping out" the Germans, although not very effectively; he was stationed near Armentières, close to the front line.

Conrad soon emerged from his long-lasting torpor; toward the end of May his health became considerably better. "I am speaking of my body. The mind perhaps will follow," he wrote to Pinker.[57] The summer of 1916 did in fact prove active and eventful.

Negotiations concerning a complete edition of Conrad's works by Doubleday in the United States and by Heinemann in England began as early as February. Quinn also took part in the negotiations and even had a conflict with Pinker; Conrad took his agent's side against Doubleday and Quinn: his attitude toward the American publisher was at that time distinctly cool. Both Conrad and Pinker wanted money, but, for reasons of "both sentimental and of a practical order," they preferred to postpone the edition until the end of the war; and indeed this was what finally happened.[58] Conrad also insisted that "all reference to the sea" ought to be avoided in the edition; he did not wish to be presented as a "writer of the sea—or even of the tropics."[59]

Talks and correspondence on the subject of a stage adaptation of *Victory* by Macdonald Hastings were also under way in early 1916. It is difficult to reconstruct the progress of these negotiations because the crucial letters are undated. Hastings approached Conrad at the beginning of 1916. Conrad was initially interested in a collaboration but then backed out. Probably in April Hastings produced a draft of the adaptation, but Conrad did not like it much. In July, Henry B. Irving, at that time the manager of the Savoy in London, approached Conrad with a similar proposal to adapt *Victory*, but Conrad gave him an evasive answer, saying that he must wait for the text of the first adaptation.[60] When Hastings showed him the first act, Conrad decided that although he did not like "the whole thing," from the box-office point of view its success was a "cert." To Pinker Conrad made no secret that he regarded the theater primarily as a source of income; but at the same time he was excited by the possibility of getting acquainted with a new medium. Hastings, he wrote, "asks for assistance. Very well. One can talk to him anyhow and I may learn a few things on this occasion. . . . I intend to make my profit in the way of knowledge this time and get into close touch with the stage. Who knows? . . .

"You will admit I have some faculty of dialogue. . . . the bulk [of my work] *is* dramatic. And if I can only learn to adapt my faculty for dialogue and drama to the conditions of the stage, then . . . I am not ossified yet. I am still impressionable and can adapt my mind to various forms of thought—and, perhaps, of art."[61]

But Conrad's attention was at that time only infrequently focused on art. Politics kept invading his life from two directions, one of which was quite unexpected. On 21 April Roger Casement was arrested near Dublin, a few hours after he had stepped ashore from a German submarine. Although he had returned with the intention of calling off the Irish insurrection against England, he was accused of treason. Conrad, as we shall see, had little sympathy for the Irish cause and regarded the Dublin Easter Rebellion as a stab in the back of an England fighting for her very life. On 24 May Conrad wrote to Quinn, an Irish sympathizer, "One only wonders in one's grief, what it was all for? With Britain smashed and the German fleet riding the seas, the very shadow of Irish Independence would have passed away. The Island Republic (if that is what they wanted) would have become merely a strongly held German outpost—a despised stepping-stone towards the final aim of the Welt-Politik."[62] Conrad had hoped that Casement would not be given the death sentence, but when Casement was condemned to be hanged, Conrad refused to join in the appeal for clemency signed by many English writers, including Galsworthy.[63] Conrad was frequently criticized for this refusal and was accused both of the chauvinism characteristic of the nonnative and of hostility toward "perverts" (the authorities had been secretly circulating fragments of Casement's diaries that revealed his homosexuality). However, on other occasions Conrad also showed that he did not feel he had the right to speak out publicly as an Englishman. The view that he was prejudiced against homosexuals is also unfounded; among his better friends were several: Douglas, Gide, Stephen Reynolds, and Walpole. In any case, I think it most unlikely that the Home Office sent the excerpts from Casement's diary to Conrad. Four years later, in a conversation recounted by Karola Zagórska, Conrad justified his position: "Casement did not hesitate to accept honours, decorations and distinctions from the English Government while surreptitiously arranging various affairs that he was embroiled in. In short: he was plotting against those who trusted him."[64]

Karola Zagórska, Aniela's younger sister, a thirty-two-year-old singer, was paying a brief visit to Capel House at this time. She noted a resemblance between John—Conrad asked her to call him Janek, a Polish diminutive—and the photograph of his grandmother, Ewa Bobrowska. Zagórska recalls how on one of their walks Conrad "asked slowly in a voice charged with emotion:

"'Will you forgive me that my sons don't speak Polish?'

"Instinctively, as quickly as possible, not to leave those words hanging in suspense, I began saying that after all it had happened in a most natural way as their mother was English . . . 'I'm grateful to you for not holding it against me,' he added." They also talked about the future of Poland. Zagórska believed that after the war Poles would be free; Conrad was dubious whether they would become "entirely free."[65]

The skepticism that Bobrowski had inculcated was a permanent feature of Conrad's temper. In this case, however, his doubts about the cause of Polish freedom may have been partly based on the current political situation, and, to an even greater extent, on his awareness of the British government's position. In the summer of 1916 the outlook for Poland was bad. The British government still considered the Polish question Russia's internal affair. The Russian government was not inclined to make any concessions; in July, indeed, Sergei Sazonov, the minister of foreign affairs, was forced to resign mainly because of his "softness" toward Polish claims. On the other side of the front lines, Piłsudski openly demanded recognition of the Polish legions as cadres of a future independent army, and neither Austria nor Germany would consent to that. However, Conrad's young friend Retinger was not to be deterred from his efforts to "internationalize" the Polish question by inducing French and British politicians to take the initiative in the matter. In a letter to Curle on 20 August 1916, Conrad was full of admiration: "Retinger's activities go on at white heat—personal success immense, political what it can be and indeed better than one would have thought it possible in the hopeless state of the Polish question. He created for himself certain titles to a hearing by accomplishing a brilliant piece of work last month as an unofficial intermediary between the Br. and Fr. Governments."[66]

Retinger persuaded Conrad to assist him, and under his influence Conrad wrote and presented to the British Foreign Office a memorandum concerning the restoration of the Polish state as a hereditary monarchy under the joint protectorate of England and France. Conrad said in the memorandum that Polonism cannot be reconciled either with the detested Germanism or with the entirely alien "Russian Slavonism." In spite of her captivity Poland has survived as an outpost of Western civilization and the restoration of her statehood is the West's moral duty. Conrad argued that Poland ought to regain her independence from the hands of her Western friends "with the fullest concurrence of Russia." Over the reestablished Polish Commonwealth of Nations, England and France ought to hold a joint protectorate for twenty years, maintaining a naval station on the Polish coast. Russia ought to participate formally in the guarantees "on such a footing as will allay to the fullest extent her possible apprehensions and satisfy her national sentiment." Poland would occupy a permanent place in the "Anglo-Franco-Russian alliance."[67] Conrad's moral and theoretical arguments could have been effective only if they had had the support of some political organization and military force, but Conrad and Retinger had only moral reasons and good intentions; they could not and did not command any political backing. Commenting on a conversation Conrad and Retinger had had at the Foreign Office with George Russell Clerk, a middle-ranking official, Conrad wrote to Retinger:

I recall that from the very beginning he gave you clearly to understand that it would be difficult for England to discuss Polish affairs anywhere else but in Petrograd, although the British would willingly listen to Polish requests.

To your concrete question whether the British Government (in agreement with France) would consent in general to the idea of a protectorate (tripartite) he replied: let the Poles first make a clearly defined request. This does not need to be over-enthusiastic—a properly argued request will suffice, supported by important personalities representative as far as possible of all political and social trends in Poland. *Only then* could the question of Poland's future be raised in the sense of the memorandum which you left him. . . . The problem that lies ahead of you is that of obtaining the agreement to this project of all Polish parties.[68]

Such an agreement, of course, was impossible. The memorandum did not reflect the programme of any of the political groups active in Poland at the time; it was more in the nature of a compilation and as a result was not very realistic. It was absurd to suppose that Russia would consent to the reestablishment of the Polish Commonwealth of Nations. Conrad's historical moralism is understandable and typical, but as a man active in politics Retinger ought to have known that the most noble thoughts have no practical meaning if they are suspended in a theoretical vacuum. This kind of objection was raised against the memorandum left at the Foreign Office, whose officials called it "unrealistic," "impractical," and a "hopeless solution"; Lord Grey, the foreign secretary, commented curtly, "Quite impossible. Russia would never share her interests in Poland with Western Powers."[69] Nevertheless, it seems that the document did not pass entirely unnoticed; we can find its echoes in an anonymous memorandum prepared at the Foreign Office in the autumn of 1916, at the request of Herbert Henry Asquith, the prime minister.[70]

Conrad had probably hoped that his note would have some influence on the attitude of the British government. He explained to Christopher Sandeman, a wealthy and influential journalist, that if the idea of rebuilding Poland under the Anglo-French protectorate were accepted, "I could be sure—when closing my eyes on this sublunary scene—that the Poles could never be drawn into antagonism to England."[71] This was the first occasion that Conrad had come into direct contact with British governmental authorities, and his decision, some two weeks later, to participate as an observer in the British war effort was no doubt directly connected with his activities on behalf of the Polish cause. Participation in the British war effort might do something to strengthen his political influence in Polish matters, but Conrad must have also been affected by the fact that his son had gone to the front. As an officer in a mechanical transport unit attached to the heavy artillery, Borys took part in the battle of the Somme and dreamed of being promoted to the rank of lieutenant.[72] Ford, too, had been in France since the middle of July, and also behind the front lines, with his battalion transport. During the battle of the Somme Ford suffered a severe nervous breakdown as a result of shell shock; he later wrote three long letters to Conrad with vivid descriptions of his war experiences.[73]

Conrad's immediate contact was with the war at sea and lasted two months. On 14 September he left for the naval station at Lowestoft on the east coast; he visited the port, watched firing practice, and was received with great hospitality: "I was made to feel at home," he wrote, "as much as if I belonged to all those services [the Navy, the Reserve, the Naval Flying Corps]." Conrad was extremely excited and at the same time very tired by all this unaccustomed activity.[74] On the morning of 16 September he left on a two-day trip aboard the minesweeper *Brigadier*. Then on the morning of 18 September he went to the Royal Naval Air Station at Yarmouth where he spent eighty minutes in a Short patrol biplane; he was later to describe his experience in a separate article entitled "Flight."[75] Even climbing into the cabin of the hydroplane was something of a problem for the aging Conrad; as to the flight itself, it was in those days— only thirteen years after the Wright brothers—sufficiently unusual and dangerous for Conrad to conceal it from Jessie.

After a ten-day rest Conrad set off again on a short trip to the Royal Navy shipyards in Scotland.[76] His meetings and conversations with the officers there stimulated him to write his only story based on the war. This story, "The Tale," was finished on 30 October.[77] It combines a characteristically Conradian set of moral problems with a rather non-Conradian method of writing and in this is not unlike Conrad's early piece, "The Return." "The Tale" is certainly a marked contrast to the military stories then common, and resembles rather the later literature of the *Good-bye to All That* kind; it kindles in the reader not a fighting spirit but profound uncertainty.

Three days after finishing "The Tale," Conrad again went north, this time to Edinburgh and the nearby port of Granton. The following day was stormy, but Conrad went to sea in a boat engaged in mending the nets that were set as protection against enemy submarines. The rain and gale forced the boat to return to port after a few hours. "I was never so pleased in all my sea-life to get into shelter," Conrad wrote to Jessie. On the following day he accompanied Admiral James Startin to the Firth of Forth on an inspection tour of the fortifications and to watch firing practice. "While we were at it 3 divisions of our newest destroyers came in from sea. It was an exceedingly fine sight."[78]

On 6 November Conrad started off on a longer, twelve-day expedition in the H.M.S. *Ready*, an armed brigantine disguised as a merchant ship to lure German submarines into a trap (she was one of the so called Q-boats). The brigantine sailed under the Norwegian flag; on Conrad's suggestion she was officially rebaptized the *Freya*.[79] On the third day of the voyage Conrad sent Pinker, by patrol boat, a letter written in telegraphic style:

"All well.
Been practice-firing in sight of coast.
Weather improved.
Health good.
Hopes of bagging Fritz high."[80]

The ship's commander, Captain J. G. Sutherland, later wrote an entire book about the voyage; it clearly disconcerted Conrad by its pomposity and its profusion of irrelevant padding; the expedition itself had been uneventful, with no enemy ships sighted. Conrad gave Lieutenant Osborne some help with navigation and in the evenings read Hartley Withers's *War and Lombard Street*—a tribute to the part played by the main English banks in the war effort. The brigantine put Conrad ashore at Bridlington on 17 November.[81] Jessie tells, with many dramatic embellishments, how her husband was immediately arrested, probably as a suspected foreigner. It is hard to believe her story, because Conrad had been put ashore by a minesweeper whose officers he later entertained to breakfast; Sutherland mentions only that a policeman came to the hotel to check on the unknown arrival.[82]

At all events, Jessie's memoirs from that period are exceptionally confused and full of contradictions. She also may have cut out some fragments when the text was already being set, and thus made her account less comprehensible.[83] Some of the confusion was connected with Miss Jane Anderson. The friendship, begun in April, had blossomed quickly. Conrad was undoubtedly attracted by the beautiful American; Jessie, too, enjoyed her company, at least in the first months. Conrad wrote to Curle that Jane had "an European mind" and that she was "yum-yum"; he also described Jane as their "adopted . . . big daughter."[84] It seems that Jane spent about a month convalescing at Capel House; the exact dates are difficult to establish because the chronology of Jessie's reminiscences contradicts what we know about the sequence of events.[85] During Conrad's trip to Lowestoft in September, Jane accompanied Jessie and John to Folkestone. In his letters to Jessie, Conrad wrote at great length about Jane as the "woman you have affection for." He appealed to Jessie to give her moral support to Jane, "personally as a woman," should the latter encounter professional setbacks. A postscript to one of these letters reads, "Give my love to Jane and if the signs are propitious you may even go as far as a hug, or something of the kind. I wish I was there to see it. I never cared to see you kissing other women as you know. But this one is different."[86] Two weeks later, reporting that Lord Northcliffe, Jane's patron, had "obviously cooled down a lot," Conrad indulged in curious equine metaphors: "The dear Chestnut filly is obviously put out. Am trusting the dearest dark-brown mare to steady that youngster in her traces."[87]

According to Jessie, the young American "was very fond of the boy [John], and he of her, and as I have said, I was sufficiently interested in her to be glad of her company, and anything was better than having no one to talk to." But apparently from the very beginning Jessie had been aware that Jane attached great importance to the impression she made on men.[88] This is confirmed by Borys, who met Jane in Paris in 1917 and immediately became infatuated, despite his father's warnings "not to make a damned fool" of himself.[89] Miss Anderson (or Mrs. Taylor, as Borys says, "depending apparently on the situation in which she found herself at any given time") was then carrying on an affair with Retinger, whom she had met at Capel House; she was perhaps responsible for the breakup of his marriage.[90]

There can be no doubt that Conrad was also not immune to Jane's charms. Jessie tells about finding her husband's love letter; and in a confused way she also seems to imply that Jane herself had boasted about Conrad's overtures.[91] It is hard to understand why Jane should have said anything about this to her, considering she did not wish to break off her relations with either of the Conrads. I believe that the stories of Jane's confession and of Conrad's letter to her, left in a book at Capel House, are figments of Jessie's imagination. It is much more probable that Jessie had found her husband's letter among Jane's papers and that the discovery prompted her to force the scene she describes. She apparently confronted Conrad with the incriminating letter and he, angrily but without a word, threw it into the fire—and then immediately promised to fulfill one of Jessie's old desires for some sort of gift.

It is not easy to guess to what lengths the flirtation, or love affair, between the young Jane and the aging Conrad went. Conrad's letters to Curle and Pinker appear to indicate that he doted on her; the tone of his letters to Jessie, in which affectionate references to Jane appear side by side with a husbandly concern for his wife, make one doubt whether his conscience was entirely clear. Retinger, who knew quite a lot about the whole affair, denied that there was a romance between Conrad and Jane. But he denied it in a way that prompts us to ask what Conrad's sex life was like. Retinger said that Conrad had not previously known women like Jane but that he had had various "affaires louches" [suspect, shady affairs]; he refused to comment further, taking refuge behind the statement that "gentlemen are discreet."[92] And Conrad himself on the subject of sex was indeed so exceptionally discreet in an old-world way that his reticence has occasionally provoked suspicion: was the erotic side of life closed to him entirely? Did he suffer from some abnormality or deeply rooted inhibition? Borys, when asked, burst out laughing. "What a nonsense," he said, and made a promising start: "My father and I—we were always quite frank to each other about our relations with women." But he did not want to say anything more.

I think that we ought to respect Conrad's reticence—all the more since we have to rely on guesswork. Perhaps Conrad was simply and consistently a faithful husband, which in view of Jessie's health would have condemned him to long years of celibacy or semicelibacy. However, not only Retinger's and Borys's veiled hints and Ford's romanticized gossip counsel skepticism. Conrad's reaction at being shown his love letter to Jane, as described by Jessie, also makes one wonder: "he had flung it on the fire, and turning to me suggested a way of procuring something I had expressed a wish for. A usual form of any penitence, that followed no accusation and no apology."[93] Along with the fact that Conrad felt very much at ease in cabarets and nightclubs—all this is in keeping with the stereotype of the husband who now and again amuses himself on the side; but we lack clear evidence.[94] At any rate it seems that Eros did not play an important part in Conrad's spiritual life. It is impossible to tell why; we know too little of that aspect of his life even to attempt to answer the question whether this resulted from some traits of Conrad's personality or was due to some enforced separation of his emotional and sexual life, or was simply a consequence of depression, which usually lowers sexual potency and desire.

We do now know exactly how long Jane Anderson's close friendship with the Conrads lasted. In December 1916 Conrad recommended her most emphatically to Pinker:

> I am sending you a selection of the short stories she published in Munsey's and Harper's Mags from 1909 to 1912. It's very young stuff of course. . . .

She tells me that there is also a lot of unpublished stuff (MS) and some verse —which I haven't been allowed to see. The best point about her is that though very earnest about her production she has not got the slightest conceit about her. . . . The novel she has planned being essentially autobiographical may make a success by a sort of wild sincerity that will be the distinctive mark of it I guess; for that is her great characteristic. She has gifts but her personality is inwardly in such a tangle that one can't tell what all these gifts will amount to in the end. Personally she lacks judgment and determination in the conduct of her life. But she is as frank and open as a woman can be, I believe, and all her instincts are rather generous than otherwise. With all her airs of independence and her consciousness of her own intellect you will find her a most amenable creature and by no means naturally ungrateful.[95]

Conrad's letters to his son paved the way for the meeting between Jane and Borys in Paris in July 1917.[96] Conrad commented later on the young man's infatuation: "If he must meet a 'Jane' it's better he should meet her at nineteen than at twenty-four."[97] And as late as November 1917 Conrad wrote to Pinker that he hoped Jane would be able to come from Paris to cheer up Jessie, who was awaiting an operation: "It will [be] good for Jessie to whom she is very devoted. It will be a fine opportunity to show the devotion."[98]

About that time Norman Douglas got himself into trouble with the law: this sexually versatile Epicurean had been more and more openly breaking away from accepted norms of behavior. In December 1915, Conrad, who had been paying for his friend's younger son's education, had worried about Douglas's situation and appealed to mutual friends for tolerance.[99] Now, having learned about Douglas's arrest on 25 November 1916 on the charge of molesting a sixteen-year-old boy, Conrad exploded in a letter to Pinker: "I wish to goodness the fellow had blown his brains out. He has been going downhill for the last 2 years and I did once or twice ask him most seriously to consider his position. But it was impossible to do anything for him. Lately he has been avoiding us all . . . I don't know if the *Worcester* will keep the boy. It's simply awful to think of that poor boy. Of course we'll have him for Xmas. We must. But what to say to him!" Conrad adds that the "bail has been peremptorily refused," and this renders questionable Compton Mackenzie's allegation that Conrad himself refused to put up bail for his friend.[100] Anyway Douglas was soon released and, jumping bail, left England for good before the trial began.[101]

On 24 December 1916 Conrad confessed to Major Gardiner, "On landing (on the 17th) I had to disentangle a good many affairs of my own and then I passed through a period of depression—which is hardly over yet."[102] He grieved about the war—the end of the year had brought the Allies either setbacks or stagnation on the front, and the changes in the British cabinet failed to raise Conrad's spirits.[103] Paul Fussell writes of this period, "A terrible gloom overcame everyone at the end of 1916. It was the bottom, even worse than the end of 1915."[104]

The war was also claiming more and more of Conrad's friends and acquaintances. Ford wrote pathetic letters from a hospital in Rouen—he said that he had been gassed; in fact he was afraid of his commander, but his suffering was nevertheless very real;[105] Edward Thomas had volunteered for front-line service and on 10 December came to say good-bye to Conrad; four months later he was killed near Arras.[106]

Perhaps Conrad felt tired after his tour of the ports and of voyages in small vessels; it is even more likely that he had grown weary of the futility of these activities. Apart from the short article "Flight," his travels produced only a slightly longer essay entitled "The Unlighted Coast." It was written for the Admiralty, probably in December 1916, but was not published during Conrad's lifetime—possibly because it contained no trace of propaganda and not even much optimism. This failure must have discouraged Conrad from further efforts, and, despite his own occasional mention of projects, he did not write any more articles about the war.[107] Before Christmas Conrad discussed the stage adaptation of *Victory* with Hastings. Then he made plans, never realized, to write a short story before the middle of January; he also declared his intention to resume work on *The Rescue* "and stick to it till the end which I can see now pretty clearly."[108]

This turned out to be another optical illusion. Only the adaptation of *Victory* got done. In January Conrad wrote to Hastings, "You can have no conception of my ignorance in theatrical art. I can't even imagine a scenic effect but reading your adaptation, I, even I, felt something what I imagine to be the scenic emotion, come through to me—got home."[109] Conrad nevertheless made a number of detailed suggestions and showed great interest in the casting. He corresponded on the subject with Pinker, Irving, Colvin, Sandeman, and most of all with Catherine Willard, whose mother, Grace Willard, had been supplying Conrad with period furniture, old silver, and glass. His letters to the young actress, whom he called "dear child," abound in not wholly paternal playfulness and endearments. But apparently Jessie had her eye on the girl as a candidate for daughter-in-law.[110] Conrad confessed to Miss Willard his "desperate resolve to turn dramatist."[111] He suggested that Hastings should translate the dramatized version of *Victory* into French; and he contemplated making stage adaptations of parts of *Nostromo* or *Under Western Eyes*.[112] Conrad also planned to collaborate with Hastings on an original play, set in Italy, about a forged painting by an old master.[113] This theatrical interest was, as before, motivated by financial considerations; Conrad's bank account was once again overdrawn and in spite of a "fair" state of health he complained to Doubleday: "Mentally I am without much grip on my work."[114] And once again he felt restless and in need of a change of surroundings: he was already considering leaving Capel House.[115]

In January 1917 Borys arrived on his first ten-day leave. Conrad was clearly proud of his son's "good-tempered, imperturbable serenity in his manner, speech and thoughts—as if nothing in the world could startle or annoy him anymore." And continuing along the same line to Quinn: "He looks wonderfully robust and has developed a respectable moustache. . . . We got on extremely well together. We talked not only of war but of the other two W. Where the fellow got his taste for wine I cannot imagine. As to Women, Cunninghame Graham . . . wrote to me with great glee that he found the boy 'très dégourdi' and that he thought he 'will be un homme à femmes like you and I for he has a way with them.'" [116]

The Shadow Line, dedicated to "Borys and all others who like himself have crossed in early youth the shadow-line of their generation—With Love," came out on 19 March 1917.[117] Clement Shorter, who had followed Conrad's literary career from its beginning, declared in *The Sphere*: "A new book by Mr. Joseph Conrad is a literary event to many of us, and so it has been for nearly a quarter of a century. Since Mr. George Meredith died and Mr. Thomas Hardy ceased to write novels no novelist other than Mr. Conrad has appeared who has been able to give me that particular thrill—the thrill which came to an earlier generation as each of the novels of Dickens and Thackeray came from their publishers. And it was gratifying to find that with his eighteenth book, *Victory*, Mr. Conrad became not only one of the favourite novelists of the elect but one of the favourite novelists of the many."[118] Most other critics wrote in the same tone. Some misunderstandings, as usual, occurred. To Conrad's annoyance a few reviewers detected in the story the presence of supernatural forces. And the praise was not unanimous: the *Times Literary Supplement*, for instance, complained that the "moral overbalances the story." All in all, however, *The Shadow Line* strengthened Conrad's position as a classic author, "one of the great ones, not of the present, but of the world."[119]

Sidney Colvin published a particularly enthusiastic article in the *Observer*.[120] Conrad attached great importance to Colvin's opinion and had tried to influence it in several letters, mainly concerning the story's autobiographical content. Conrad declared that "there can be no possible objection to your recognizing the autobiographical character of that piece of writing . . . If you will notice I call it *A Confession* on the title page."[121] On the other hand Conrad did not want "that little piece to be recognized *formally* as autobiographical. It's *tone* is not. But as to the underlying *feeling* I think there can be no mistake."[122]

On 18 March Conrad suggested to Colvin the following self-interpretation, which has been frequently quoted: "Perhaps you won't find it presumptuous if after 22 years of work, I may say that I have not been very well understood. I have been called a writer of the sea, of the tropics, a descriptive writer, a romantic writer—and also a realist. But as a matter of fact all my concern has been with the "ideal" value of things, events and people. That and nothing else. The humorous, the pathetic, the passionate, the sentimental *aspects* came in of themselves—*mais en vérité c'est les valeurs idéales des faits et gestes humains qui se sont imposés à mon activité artistique* [but in truth it is the ideal values of human acts and deeds which have impressed themselves on my artistic activity]." Those words are not unambiguous, and it seems impossible to determine the exact meaning Conrad attached to them. I believe, however, that it is a mistake to maintain that Conrad was intent on extolling ideals and glorifying man's inherent nobility. The content of his books as well as of his other pronouncements suggests that his intention was to seek out the fundamental principles that guide people in their actions; by "values" he meant these "deeper" underlying principles, and by "ideals" human values that were not "material" needs, impulses, and aims.

In Conrad's statements on the war and on international political events there is no trace of a belief that lofty moral ideals play a decisive role in the behavior of individuals and nations. On the contrary, Conrad never joined in the chorus of enthusiastic supporters of "the war in the defense of justice and civilization," and he carefully avoided jingoistic phraseology. Apart from the single exception of his essay "Poland Revisited," Conrad never allowed himself to be carried away by the fervor of anti-German propaganda; he ridiculed the "bawlings of our statesmen at Mme Germania" and treated the shrill, simplistic exhortations of the press with contempt.[123] After the United States entered the war in April 1917,[*] Conrad wrote caustically to Quinn, "Here we don't fight for democracy or any other '-cracy' or for humanitarian or pacifistic ideals. We are fighting for life first, for freedom of thought and development in whatever form next."[124] And in a letter to Hugh Walpole he firmly stated: "I am not an idealist . . . My hopes are of a strictly limited kind."[125]

Conrad's "hopes" here were for the end of the war. For the Allies the first months of 1917 were unfavorable, and the general mood in England was one of weariness and discontent. German submarines kept inflicting enormous losses on Allied and neutral fleets; the French front was bleeding but virtually immobile; in Romania the German and Austrian armies were advancing; and Russia was on the verge of collapse. The fossilized despotic system had been toppled by the "February" (8–16 March) revolution, and Russia's further contribution to the war against the Central Powers became uncertain. Conrad worried about the weakening of the Allies, and his reaction to the pro-revolutionary enthusiasm of the liberal press was cool.[126] "The immediate result is to eliminate it as an active factor from the war. . . . There is no government of any sort there now," he wrote to Quinn in May.[127] His attitude did not arise from sympathy with the old régime or from a predilection for political stability as such. Despite

---

[*] Although Conrad initially opposed the U.S. entering the war (letter to Eugene Saxton, 18 March 1916, quoted by Karl, *Joseph Conrad*, pp. 781–782), he welcomed the "young Alliance," called it "a great piece of luck for Gt Britain," and expressed his admiration for American troops (letters to W. T. H. Howe of 15 June and 16 August 1917, NYPL).

his frequent sallies against democracy, Conrad acknowledged in a historical discussion with Colvin the greatness of Léon Gambetta, a prominent French democrat, and stated that "the greatest figure of the times through which we have lived was The People itself, *la Nation*. For 150 years the French people has been always greater (and better) than its leaders, masters and teachers. And the same can be said of the English—indeed it's manifest in what we see today. The two great figures of the West!"[128]

In Russia Conrad feared a terrible blood bath. Writing to Walpole on 18 May, Conrad's thoughts turned to his native country: "I feel startled when I remember that my foster-brother is an Ukranian peasant. He is probably alive yet. What does he think? I am afraid that what he thinks bodes no good to the boys and girls with whom I used to play and to their children. Are those gracious Shades of my memory to turn into blood-stained Spectres? *C'est possible, vous savez*. And those houses where, under a soul-crushing oppression, so much noble idealism, chivalrous traditions, the sanity and the amenities of Western civilization were so valiantly preserved,—are they to vanish into smoke? *Cela aussi est très possible*."[129]

The fall of Imperial Russia at last opened up the possibility of the Allies placing the Polish question in an international context. The governments of Great Britain, France, and Italy greeted with approval the declaration of the Russian Provisional Government on 30 March 1917, which clearly acknowledged Poland's right to independence. Conrad viewed those developments with his usual skepticism. To Sandeman he wrote, "The Russian proclamation is very fine but—2/3rds of the Polish territory (on the basis of the 1772 frontier) are in German hands. And peace will have to come soon."[130]

In May Conrad confided to Garnett, "Impossible to start myself going, impossible to concentrate to any good purpose. It is the war—perhaps? Or the end of Conrad simply? I suppose one must end someday, somehow." And to Curle he had moaned earlier, "I simply *can't* write."[131] Conrad was suffering from his usual attacks of gout but, to judge by his letters, his health was on the whole not too bad. It is worth noting, however, that when Conrad worked on a book his health tended to become more important to him, and so his medical comments and complaints inevitably increased. It was his mental state that created problems at the time. "But, you know, to speak openly I feel at times that I am not quite myself," he confessed to Pinker.[132] Nevertheless Conrad renounced the annual government subsidy from the so-called Civil List Pension.[133]

All Conrad wrote in the first seven months of 1917 were three prefaces. Two were to his own works: to the new edition of *Lord Jim* and to the volume *Youth*; the third, in the form of a letter, was to Garnett's study of Turgenev. In this last Conrad paid tribute to his favorite "profoundly, whole-souledly national" writer, not missing the opportunity to contrast Turgenev with the abominable Dostoyevsky.[134] The preface to *Lord Jim* is defensive: Conrad rejected the charges that the book was too drawn-out and that Jim's "acute consciousness of lost honour" was a symptom of morbidity. In his note to the *Youth* volume, Conrad stressed the authenticity of the stories as based on his personal experiences and observations; this was later to become the dominant motif of his author's notes.[135]

Not until the end of July did Conrad settle down to a bigger piece of work.[136] This was yet another short story which grew into a novel: *The Arrow of Gold*. Its title was changed several times. The draft of the beginning is called "The Laugh"; the piece was conceived in the form of "selected passages from letters."[137] Conrad wrote the first ninety-four pages in longhand; the rest he dictated.[138] This apparently speeded up the work, but, according to the critics, had a disastrous effect upon Conrad's style. The material for the new book harked back to his days in Marseilles forty years ago, and in the first pages of the draft, which were later omitted, he went even farther back into the past, to his adolescent loves in Poland. Ewa Korzeniewska advances an interesting hypothesis that a letter of May 1914 from Tekla Turska, Conrad's friend in Lwów in the years 1868–1874, may have provided the novel's initial stimulus. A fragment of the First Note to *The Arrow of Gold*, which is about "the writer's childhood's friend," seems to support this theory.[139]

At first Conrad worked at a good pace; as early as mid-August he informed Pinker that the story would not be shorter than *The Shadow Line*.[140] (Unfortunately, most of Conrad's letters from 1917 are dated only with the day of the week, which makes reconstruction of an exact chronology extremely difficult.) On the last day of December, bemoaning his frequent attacks of gout and bronchitis, Conrad wrote self-critically to Sanderson, "And all through it, with groans and imprecations, I have been working every morning. You can imagine what sort of stuff that is. No colour, no relief, no tonality; the thinnest possible squeaky bubble. And when I've finished with it, I shall go out and sell it in a market place for 20 times the money I had for the *Nigger*."[141] But confessions of this kind were for friends only; what Pinker heard were assurances that the "story without a name is progressing well."[142]

As the war dragged on, compulsory blackouts and restrictions on travel rendered Capel House more and more isolated, and Conrad lamented the lack of visitors. To his great joy Garnett came for a few days in May, and later that month Conrad wrote to him, "Seriously my dear fellow it was comforting and warming to have you here, all to myself, and laugh, and ironise, and squabble with you as in the days when the wine was still red and women more than a mere memory of smouldering furies (of all sorts) and diabolic eccentricities. It's true that we always treated those subjects literarily. The loftiness of your sentiments and the austerity of your demeanour intimidated me. Even now during your visit I wanted once to be impertinent to you and simply couldn't do it. The Prestige! Your undying prestige! . . . If you think there are many men for whose words I care enough to get furious with them you are mistaken. There is in fact only one—yourself." [143]

In September Borys arrived on ten days' leave. His brother John had been at a boarding school at Ripley Court in Surrey since September 1916, and came home only for holidays. [144] Jessie's health was a source of constant anxiety for the whole family. She suffered pain in her knee and her obesity was making matters worse; she could hardly walk even on crutches. Conrad was very worried by her condition. At the beginning of November 1917 it was decided that Jessie would be put through a detailed medical examination; the possibility loomed that her leg would have to be amputated. Medical treatment made it necessary to move to London for a few months.

In October, shortly before the move, Conrad wrote a lengthy and "very intimate" Author's Note to the new edition of Nostromo. [145] In a half-jocular tone, intertwining real events with elements of fiction, he linked the action of Nostromo with his own personal experiences. The fragment devoted to Antonia Avellanos, "modelled" on his first love, indicates Conrad's readiness to revert to memories of his years in Cracow; at the same time, however, the passage also casts doubt on the credibility of his "confessions"; the portrayal of his first love here differs sharply from her description in the first pages of the draft of The Arrow of Gold.

In London, the Conrads rented a flat in a boardinghouse in Marylebone Road (4c Hyde Park Mansions), not far from Jessie's nursing home (3 York Place, near Baker Street). They moved there about 20 November. [146] After a few days the doctors were able to dispel the fear of amputation; Jessie was instead to undergo a long course of physiotherapy. After a few weeks in the nursing home she had her entire leg immobilized with a heavy metal splint. [147] Conrad grumbled at first about his cold and general seediness but clearly was pleased with their escape from rural isolation, enjoying a life that, for him, was socially very active—although at times, when gout made it impossible for him to go out, he felt cut off from the world. Conrad often met Galsworthy, Garnett, the Colvins, and Hastings; old friends like Ted Sanderson; and new ones like Hugh Walpole. [148] Walpole, the thirty-four-year-old novelist and journalist who had recently returned from Russia, noted on 21 January, "Conrad even better than I had expected—looking older, very nervous, rather fantastic and dramatic somehow—his eyes I think—an intellectual Corsair. He talked eagerly, telling me all kinds of things about his early life." [149] Young Cecil Roberts, a wealthy and well-connected amateur writer whom Conrad had met in Grace Willard's salon, formed a somewhat different impression of Conrad, probably influenced by his own predilection for aristocratic company: "His profile was a triangle, coming to a point where grew the trim beard. His eyes were sunk, and slant lidded. They brightened like the eyes of a bird when he looked at you. He was handsome, not in the virile manner of the seaman, but with the air of a diplomat, of a familiar of the Faubourg St. Germain. He was, in short, the Polish aristocrat, cosmopolitan, who belonged equally to a dinner-table at an English Embassy, the Bois de Boulogne, the Tiergarten or the Prater. Dressed in a double-breasted blue serge suit, with monocle swinging on its thin cord, he had the air of a member of the Corps Diplomatique, and yet something much more." [150]

Conrad was working at the time on the future *Arrow of Gold*. He applied himself assiduously to his task, "at the rate of four of my pages per day—but without pleasure and only feeling now and then in touch with my subject." [151] Apparently he confided to Garnett his doubts about going on with the novel, but Garnett was definitely encouraging and gave his "critical reasons"—we do not know what they were. [152] By 3 January 1918 Conrad had written twenty-six thousand words of the story, which he considered to be "about half at most"; [153] it was actually less than one-fourth. Although at first he was content that dictation was speeding up his work, while dictating he became excited to the point of shouting, which made concentration and remembering the whole given fragment very difficult. [154] In the middle of February Conrad visualized the novel as consisting of four parts, three to four chapters each; the final result is five parts of three, four, four, five, and eight chapters respectively. The novel was still without a title. Conrad wrote to S. A. Everitt, Doubleday's publicity agent:

> Lots of titles pass though my head (in my idle moments—which are few) but not one of them gives me the exact feeling of rightness. If it had been a book in French I believe I would have called it *L'Amie du Roi*, but as in English (The Friend of the King) the gender is not indicated by the termination, I can't very well do that. People would think perhaps of a friend with a great beard and that would be a great mistake. The title of *The Goatherd*, which would have been possible too, is open to the same objection. They would be both a little misleading, because the connection of the story both with goats and kings is very slender. *Two Sisters* would be a title much more closely related to the facts, but I don't like it. It's too precise and also too commonplace. On the other hand, *Mme de Lastaola* is foreign in appearance, besides looking pretentious. *The Heiress*, which is closest to the facts, would be the most misleading of all; and it is also very unimaginative and stupid. We must wait for the title to come by itself.
>
> As you see, the above are all connected with a woman. And indeed the novel may be best described as the Study of a Woman who might have been a very brilliant phenomenon but has remained obscure, playing her little part in the Carlist war of '75–6 and then going as completely out of the very special world which knew her as though she had returned in despair to the goats of her childhood in some lonely valley on the south slope of the Pyrenees. The book, however, is but slightly concerned with her public (so to speak)

activity, which was really of a secret nature. What it deals with is her private life: her sense of her own position, her sentiments and her fears. It is really an episode, related dramatically and in the detailed manner of a study, in that particular life. That it is also an episode in the general experience of the young narrator (the book is written in the first person) serves only to round it off and give it completeness as a novel.[155]

At that stage, then, Conrad did not suggest, as he would later, that the book's content was autobiographical. The date "'75–6" corresponds with the history of the Carlist war, but it makes young Korzeniowski's participation in it impossible: his mysterious and dramatic adventures took place two years later. The time of the action as well as the characterization of the heroine also argue against the possibility that she was modeled on Paula de Somogyi, whom Don Carlos had not met until 1877. The return to the subject of the "two sisters"—no doubt the same ones he had written about in 1896—suggests that they were real-life characters, firmly fixed in Conrad's memory. It seems that as the novel progressed the author injected into it with growing ardor his own experiences and feelings, by and large, I think, only imaginary. This would explain why Conrad concentrated his attention on the hero and narrator, and why he later described the book as a confession. It is noteworthy that Jessie later maintained that The Arrow of Gold "seems to belong more to me than any of the others, inasmuch that had it not been for me, it would certainly never have been written."[156] A cynic may be inclined to give a sigh of relief that Jessie did not influence her husband's writing more often—she also took the credit for "The Black Mate"; but joking apart, Jessie's claim must serve as a caution against treating The Arrow of Gold too seriously.

Conrad worked rather fast on the novel, and almost without interruption. It seems that the only other piece written at this time was "Tradition," which was posted to the Daily Mail on 4 March. Its short text, extolling the bravery and sense of duty of the merchant marine, brought Conrad as much as 250 guineas from Lord Northcliffe, the press magnate.[157] A week later, on Conrad's election to London's exclusive Athenaeum Club, the same wealthy admirer paid out the £40 membership fees.[158]

On 15 February, just before their return to Capel House, Galsworthy paid the Conrads a visit in London, noting later in his diary, "All Conrads very well."[159] As usual, this state of affairs was not a lasting one. "I can't think consecutively," Conrad complained to Garnett a few weeks later, "and the few distressed thoughts that are knocking about in my head I am totally unable to put into words. It's a most distressing and depressing state to be in. One marches staggering along the very edge of despair hour after hour, day after day, feeling that one will never get anywhere."[160]

No doubt the international situation, and particularly the events on the front, were causing Conrad much anxiety. He broached these subjects only rarely, usually limiting himself to generalities or short remarks about new appointments among the commanding generals and admirals. The only exception was the Polish question, which Conrad discussed at greater length. In February 1918, three months after the October Revolution and one month after President Wilson's famous declaration listing an independent Poland among the military aims of the United States, Conrad wrote to Quinn:

> Whatever happens Russia is out of the war now. The great thing is to keep the Russian infection, its decomposing power, from the social organism of the rest of the world. In this Poland will have to play its part on whatever lines her future may have to be laid. And at the same time she will have to resist the immense power of Germanism which would be death too, but in another shape. Whether that nation over-run, ruined and shaken to the very foundations of its soul will rise to this awful task I really don't know. What assistance she will be able to get from the Western world nobody can tell. Never was there such a darkness over a people's future, and that, don't forget, coming after more than a century of soul-grinding oppression in which apart from a few choice spirits the Western world took no interest. Fine words have been given to it before. And the finer the words the greater was always the deception. One evening in August in 1914 in a dimly lit, big room I spoke to a small group of Poles belonging to the University and the political life of the town of Cracow. . . . I had the courage to tell them: "Have no illusions. If anybody has got to be sacrificed in this war it will be you. If there is any salvation to be found it is only in your own breasts, it is only by the force of your inner life that you will be able to resist the rottenness of Russia and the soullessness of Germany. And this will be your fate for ever and ever. For nothing in the world can alter the force of facts."
>
> And if I had to speak to them tomorrow I would repeat those very words. I don't remember now what Mr Wilson said in his latest utterance. There is an awful air of unreality in all the words that are being flung about in the face of such appalling realities.[161]

Three elements in these reflections deserve to be stressed: Conrad's skepticism, bordering on pessimism, about Poland's future; his vision of Poland as Europe's bulwark separated from the West by "Germanism"; and his clear-sighted awareness of the fact that Poland could not expect consistent support from the Allies because their attitude will always be determined by their own interests. Conrad's bitter mistrust might have been influenced by the new Soviet government's publication of secret agreements between the Tsarist government and the Western Allies; these agreements really amounted to new partition of the Polish territory.[162]

On 21 March a powerful German offensive against the British lines began, and contact with Borys was lost for ten days. According to Conrad it was the "most anxious time of [his] life." He feared that Borys and his unit had been mopped up by the enemy forces.[163] Both Conrad parents were relieved to learn that after the front had resettled Borys's battery had been withdrawn for a rest behind the lines. The young lieutenant was satisfied with his own performance and that of his subordinates, and Conrad felt proud of his son: "It was awful, he says and goes on to add 'and yet I enjoyed it in a way.' What could a Napoleon's officer say more—or less? There is a military vein imbedded somewhere in that child's temperament."[164]

Conrad must have written several scores of letters to Borys, but only a few have come to light. One of these letters, referred to in note 163, dates from this period. It is cordial but somewhat stiff, as if the author were consciously adopting a pose, uncertain of his position vis-à-vis the recipient. This, of course, is only a hypothesis, but it seems to fit in both with later patterns of the father-son relationship, as well as with Borys's memoirs, which testify to their affection and concern for one another but do not suggest any deeper mutual understanding or strong spiritual bond. It seems that Conrad's attitude toward his younger son was more direct and spontaneous, both when he half-jokingly complained about his "little sprite" or John's "little monkey" tricks and when he wrote affectionately after a visit to the Ripley Court boarding school: "It was sad to behold the dear little pagan in the Eton jacket and horrible round collar. Those people are really full of kindness and tact . . . but they have not the slightest conception of what he is. They will understand him presently when he has become like one of themselves. But I shall always remember the original— the only genuine John—as long as I live."[165]

Although Borys was out of danger for the time being, Conrad was inevitably depressed by the generally unfavorable state of the war. "My heart is like lead. I don't think I had many illusions from the first; but this is so different even from a mere half of what one was led to expect," he confided to his old friend Helen Sanderson.[166] *The Arrow of Gold* grew fast, providing Conrad with a welcome escape in work. (The novel was given this title in May, although in August Conrad could still not decide between *The Arrow of Gold* and *The Lost Arrow*.) On 16 April he informed Pinker: "The end is near. It will in the long run reach 75.000 words . . . It will be something either good or bad but at any rate won't be mediocre."[167] To Helen Sanderson, Conrad wrote, "It's probably rubbish";[168] whether this was affectation or clairvoyance we cannot tell. By 9 May he had finished the first chapter of the fifth and last part; Conrad thought that two more chapters would bring it to a close and hoped to finish them within one week.[169] He added seven more, however, developing the most melodramatic part of the book—that in which the hero and narrator, M. George, woos the heroine by means of defending her from his rival, J. K. M. Blunt. On 27 May Conrad believed that only ten to fifteen more pages were needed; he worked in a great hurry, and the main text was finished on the fourth, the First Note on the eleventh, and the Second Note, concluding the book, on the fourteenth of June.[170] Judging by the fact that Conrad expected to have written the Second Note in one day, this fragment of the novel—and thus the tale of the lovers' romantic idyll and of the duel—flowed from his pen at the last moment.

Conrad's fast pace of writing must have kept him in a good mood. Galsworthy, who visited Capel House with his wife, noted in his diary on 26 May: "Conrad very well, and cheery."[171] A few days later Walpole, too, found Conrad in high spirits: "Conrad simply superb. A child, nervous, excitable, affectionate, confidential, doesn't give you the idea anywhere of a strong man, but *real* genius that is absolutely *sui generis*. . . . Said end of 'Secret Agent' an inspiration. . . . Doesn't think end of 'Victory' anything but inevitable. Wanted to put *everything* into 'Lord Jim.'"[172] Conrad's sociability during the last stages of work was for him exceptional—usually when completing a long novel he would withdraw into himself; moreover, he did not get ill after finishing the book; these are surely indications that Conrad's emotional involvement in *The Arrow of Gold* was not very deep.

After another weekend, Walpole, whom Conrad described later as "the most intimate of my younger friends,"[173] noted, "A very happy day, although Conrad is in many ways like a child about his various diseases, groaning and even crying aloud. He said some interesting things: about Gissing turning over the manuscript of 'Amy Foster' and saying in a melancholy voice: 'Ah! I envy you that!' . . . That he can't read Wells, Bennett or Galsworthy—in fact, reads no one now. That it is his ambition after the war to get a yacht and sail down the Thames."[174]

Walpole had written one of the first books on Conrad, published in 1916. Conrad did not read it until June 1918—or, at any rate, it was only then that he wrote about it to the author. The slim book is adulatory, banal, and stupendously naive; Conrad acknowledged it with a few polite platitudes, but he went out of his way to repudiate two of Walpole's assertions that he considered patently false: that he had hesitated whether to write in English or in French, and that he had modeled his work on Flaubert. Conrad's denial of the first point seems the more convincing, although his overemphatic protests evoke suspicion: "It is absurd. When I wrote the first words of A[lmayer's] F[olly] I had been already for years and years *thinking* in English. I began to think in English long before I mastered, I won't say the style (I haven't done that yet), but the mere uttered speech. . . . You may take it from me that if I had not known English I wouldn't have written a line for print in my life. C[lifford] and I were discussing the nature of the two languages and what I said was: that if I had been offered the alternative I would have been afraid to grapple with French, which is crystallized in the form of its sentences and therefore more exacting and less appealing . . . But there was never any alternative offered or even dreamed of." Actually the possibility of writing in French had been mentioned several times in Conrad's earlier letters and projects; now he tried to cover up his tracks. As to the second point, Conrad's denial of the influence of Flaubert is unconvincing. His assertions that he read *Madame Bovary* "only after finishing A.F. as I did all the other works of Flaubert and, anyhow, my Flaubert is the Flaubert of *St. Antoine* and *Ed[ucation] Sent[imentale]*: and that only from the point of view of the rendering of concrete things and visual impressions" are obviously untrue; they may have been prompted by a wish to erase from his literary biography any elements which might detract from his reputation as a classic of the English literary tradition.[175]

It was probably for the same reason that Conrad maintained to Ernest Rhys that he had read Maupassant too late to have been influenced by him.[176]

Meanwhile Jessie's suffering grew worse, although she tried to conceal her pain from her husband to spare him the worry.[177] The truth was soon out, however, and after *The Arrow of Gold* had been finished the Conrads left for London, putting up again at Hyde Park Mansions. On 26 June Jessie was placed in a nursing home in Devonshire Terrace.[178] To her great joy Borys had obtained a fortnight's special leave and came to London two days before her admission to the clinic. On 27 June, Jessie's knee was operated on by Sir Robert Jones, a well-known surgeon from Liverpool.[179] The operation was declared successful, but Jessie had to remain in the nursing home for six weeks. During that time both Conrad and Borys came down with influenza; Borys even had to postpone his return to France.[180] Conrad complained to Jessie, "Everything is infinitely horrible to go through without you to boss the show and cheer one's heart with your dear eyes. I worry a bit about you being in so much pain. Still to think of you making such splendid recovery does cheer one."[181]

Jessie for her part grumbled to Pinker about Conrad's crotchets: "Don't think I am unsympathetic but I do feel irritated with him. Dr Mackintosh says there are several stumps to come out that cause all this gouty trouble, that isn't gout really. The thing is to persuade him to see a first-rate dentist and have a proper anaesthetic and have them removed. What chance do you think we have of getting him to have it done?"[182] In his family Conrad's fear of dentists was notorious.

While Jessie treated Conrad like a capricious child in her letters, he in turn complained to his confidant, who was no doubt amused by the role of comic duplicity assigned to him: "Jessie had not her cheque today and has struck me for a loan. I will never see it back—of course."[183] (Jessie received her money directly from Pinker and had her own bank account.)

At the beginning of July 1918 Conrad once more set about writing the novel that he had begun twenty years earlier. "With any sort of luck the Rescue will be finished this year. I am reading it over now for the 20th time at least. I must try to catch on to the old style as much as possible. But if I can't it will have to be done anyhow," he assured Pinker.[184] Gone now were Conrad's high standard of self-criticism and his principle of fidelity to the truth of one's own feelings; their place was taken by a determination to use up all his remaining resources.

First, however, he wrote two essays: a short one, "First News," in which he recounted the beginning of his stay in Poland in 1914 and the arrival of the news about the outbreak of war; and a longer one, "Well Done," praising the courage of the men of the Merchant Service.[185] Pinker, probably dubious about the prospects of *The Rescue*, recommended a continuation of the subject taken up in "First News." But Conrad had reservations: "Your suggestion for developing the Polish episode is helpful and I would accept it at once if it weren't for the thought that I could hardly avoid in that case touching on the political side of the present situation which I am very shy of doing, both in regard to its effect in this country and also in Poland, where everything I write does make its way. It may be absurd shrinking but there it is."[186] Conrad was reluctant because he viewed Poland's situation with a pessimism that, judiciously enough, he was unwilling to make public; in any case, he no longer had any close adviser on Polish affairs, because Retinger had left England for the continent, and there had been no news of him for a long time. Retinger's silence was probably caused by the breakup of his marriage—he kept that from Jessie—and his romance with Jane Anderson. In the late summer of 1918 Retinger, who evidently had stepped on too many toes when running his self-appointed errands for the Polish cause, found himself banished from the territory of the Allied Powers. He went to the Basque country, and in his penniless condition appealed from there for Conrad's help.* Conrad immediately dispatched £100 and asked Hugh Walpole to use his influence to obtain permission for Retinger to return to England: "The question for me is to save this, in many respects, lovable human being broken in health and in fortune from perishing miserably as if abandoned by God and man. For that is how the situation looks to me. If we could get him over here we would look after him."[187] Walpole and Bennett intervened on his behalf, but it is unclear whether Retinger ever returned to England before 1923.[188]

Conrad's generosity toward Retinger, his financial help to Dr. Tebb, and the costs of the funeral for the "faithful Nellie," which Conrad also paid, did not come out of a fat purse.[189] We can see from his correspondence with Pinker that Conrad's earnings could barely keep pace with his expenses. Evidently, driven to extremes by a sudden necessity, and contrary to his promise made years ago to Quinn, Conrad sold the manuscript of *The Arrow of Gold* and the typescript of the dictated parts of *Rescue* (the latter still uncompleted). The deal leaked out a year later and caused a sudden cooling in Conrad's relations with Quinn.[190]

---

* The cause of Retinger's banishment remains unclear; it seems to have been due to intrigues within various Polish political groups in France; Retinger was not closely associated with any and thus was an easy target of attack. He left France sometime between April and August.

After the Conrad's return to Capel House in the middle of August it transpired that the improvement in Jessie's condition had been short-lived; she was still unable to walk.[191] The first half of October was again devoted to medical examinations in London.[192] From there Conrad sent a family report to Curle, then working in Africa: "The present disposition of the family forces is as follows: Mr and Mrs J. Conrad are going to retreat to Capel House next week, according to plan. Lt. B. Conrad is advancing in Flanders with the 2nd Army and is much bucked up. Master John Conrad is interned in a preparatory school in Surrey for his third term and is now reconciled to his horrible situation. I can't tell you very much about further operations, beyond the fact that they include a frontal attack upon *The Rescue*, which was indeed begun some time ago but, I am sorry to say, has been pushed feebly and has died out for a time. However, in the present more favourable circumstances it shall be taken up with a vigour and is expected to achieve a success by January next at the latest."[193]

A week later Borys suffered shell shock, and, after being gassed slightly during an artillery bombardment, had to be hospitalized.[194] The war now seemed nearly over, and Conrad wrote to Pinker on 25 September, "It looks indeed as if out there we were out of the wood at last. It is at home that I can't help feeling that we are still in the dark about the truth of the situation. Those strikes are really inexcusable and seem to me either the result of moral blindness or of a very sinister recklessness of purpose, strangely un-English—at least, as I have understood the character of Englishmen in the past. It may be simply a lack of imagination, a kind of stupidity, but it's hard to believe that it is nothing else but that."[195] Large-scale, well-organized strikes were becoming more frequent in the summer of 1918; the working class, impervious to patriotic slogans about national solidarity, protested against social inequality; and this made the tasks Conrad saw standing before England at the end of the war impossible to fulfill. He wrote to Walpole, "Great and very blind forces are set free catastrophically all over the world. This only I know, that if we are called upon to restore order in Europe (as it may well be) then we shall be safe, at home too. To me the call is already manifest—but it may be declined on idealistic or political grounds. It is a question of courage in the leaders, who are never as good as the people."[196]

These interventionist illusions, somewhat inconsistent with Conrad's bitter political skepticism, must have soon disappeared. Conrad greeted the end of the war with a joyless distrust, very different from the general mood of national euphoria. As he wrote gravely to Garnett, "A cloud of unreality hangs about men, events, discourses, purposes. The very relief from long-drawn anguish is touched with mistrust as it were if not a delusion then at least a snare."[197]

Conrad did not spell out the reasons for his gloom. True, his attitude to President Wilson's idealistic principles was openly and somewhat acidly dubious,[198] but surely those principles did not present a threat. I think the cause of Conrad's pessimism may be found in his essay "The Crime of Partition" and in his letter to Hugh Clifford of 25 January 1919, which forms a kind of supplement to it. These two texts constitute Conrad's most extensive postwar political pronouncements.

In spite of divisions and suspicions bred by 123 years of partition, Poles quickly rallied around the government, headed by Józef Piłsudski, who was on 8 November 1918 released from a German jail. Thanks to his contacts with Władysław Sobański, the London representative of the Polish National Committee, Conrad was well informed about the British government's attitude toward the reborn Polish state.[199] He certainly knew about the delay in the formal recognition of the Polish state by the Allied Powers—it eventually took place on 24 February 1919; he also knew that Prime Minister Lloyd George, and Foreign Secretary Balfour, were unsympathetic to Polish territorial aspirations. When he wrote "The Crime of Partition" in December 1918, Conrad must have been aware that his views clashed with official British policy.[200] He outlined the history and consequences of the partitions of Poland in the eighteenth century, claiming that the political "crime," by absorbing the attention and the military power of the enemies, had saved revolutionary France from subjugation. He praised the government and parliamentary traditions of the old Poland, which, in his view, had always been an outpost of the West. He angrily rejected the accusations that the new Polish state was guilty of territorial expansion. And as to Poland's independence, Conrad stated categorically that Poles did not owe it to anyone but to themselves.[201]

Conrad's statements to Clifford, a high official of His Majesty's government, were even more caustic; he wrote with suppressed fury:

As to Poland, I have never had any illusions and I must render the Poles the justice to say that they too had very few. The Polish question has been buried so long that its very political importance is not seen yet. In this war it had not been of episodic importance. If the Alliances had been differently combined the Western Powers would have delivered Poland to the German learned pig with as little compunction as they were ready to give it up to the Russian mangy dog. It is a great relief to my feelings to think that no single life has been lost to any of the fronts for the sake of Poland. The load of obligation would have been too great; . . . The only justification for the reestablishment of Poland is political necessity, but that has never been very clearly seen except by a superior mind here and there, both in France and England. Nothing serious or effective will be done. Poland will have to pay the price of some pretty ugly compromise . . . The mangy Russian dog having gone mad is now being invited to sit at the Conference table, on British initiative! The thing is inconceivable, but there it is. One asks oneself whether this is idealism, stupidity or hypocrisy? I do not know who are the individuals immediately responsible, but I hope they will get bitten. The whole paltry transaction of conciliating mere crime for fear of obscure political consequences makes one sick. In a class contest there is no room for conciliation.

Conrad had opened this tirade with a paragraph containing his declaration of loyalty:

Of course my concern is for England, which engages all my affections and all my thoughts. I look at all the problems and incertitudes of the day from that point of view and no other.[202]

Set against the rest of the letter, this declaration acquires a sarcastic meaning—Poland was in fact not only the center of Conrad's attention and the principal cause of his vexation but also the factor determining his entire outlook.

The line taken by Lloyd George's government was in keeping with traditional British foreign policy in Eastern Europe: England's sole object was to play Germany and Russia off against one another. An independent Poland would have created complications by introducing a new and unknown factor; Balfour was for a long time against the establishment of a sovereign Polish state. Conrad's attack on the invitation to Soviet Russia to participate in the peace conference can be understood only as a manifestation of his fear that the fate of Poland—still officially unrecognized at the time Conrad wrote to Clifford—would be decided in negotiations with former partitioning powers. Conrad's bitterness was sharpened by his awareness that three years earlier he himself had not believed that Poland could be reborn without the help of England and France.

Conrad, who spoke out so forcefully, with strong conviction supported by historical knowledge, in defense of Polish rights to national independence, would not accord the same rights to the Irish—presumably because their tradition of statehood was so much more remote.[203]

Conrad did not busy himself only with politics. In the autumn of 1918, making the most of a spell of better health, he worked hard on *The Rescue*.[204] Although maintaining that "this writing is an odious business,"[205] he finished Part IV by the end of November.[206] He even thought that *The Rescue* could be published before *The Arrow of Gold*.[207] Hoping to have *The Rescue* ready by January,[208] Conrad looked ahead to his cherished project of a Napoleonic novel: "[It] may take 18 months in writing. I would like too to have a look at Elba and Corsica before I get too deep into the tale—say next winter."[209]

In an ingratiating business letter to Doubleday, Conrad made a statement which, with all its exaggerations, contains an element of truth: "I am sufficient of a democrat to detest the idea of being a writer of any 'coterie' of some small self-appointed aristocracy in the vast domain of art or letters. As a matter of feeling—not as a matter of business—I want to be read by many eyes and by all kinds of them, at last. I pride myself that there is no sentence of my writing, either thought or image, that is not accessible . . . to the simplest intelligence that is aware at all of the world in which we live." [210] Indeed, although his "accessibility" had been at least debatable, Conrad had never been, and never wanted to be, a fashionable or an elitist writer.

Nevertheless, the collected edition that he discussed with Doubleday was intended, for economic reasons, to come out first in a limited, luxury edition: Conrad undertook to write separate "Author's Notes" for whatever volumes had not, until then, had prefaces. On 29 January he wrote the Note to *An Outcast*. [211] Like those which followed, it is written in a chatty confessional tone and deals largely with the origin of the work; these Author's Notes, though pleasant to read, must not be taken too seriously, because Conrad was primarily concerned not with recording the facts faithfully but with recounting colorful anecdotes and autobiographical legends that would endow his seafaring and writing life with a coherent pattern. The story about the origin of *An Outcast*, a book Conrad allegedly began only because Garnett had asked him "why not write another," constitutes a myth designed to establish that Conrad's impulse to write had been far from overpowering; the note suggests that the choice between sailing and writing had depended on his conscious decision, and that beginning his second novel and consequently becoming a professional writer had been determined by compliance with Garnett's suggestion.

In the first days of January 1919 Conrad suffered a bad attack of gout that left him bedridden for nearly three weeks. [212] Jessie's account and comments are most characteristic. She quotes Conrad's affectionate letter to her written in his bedroom on the first floor, and scoffs, "This letter would give anyone the impression that he was ill miles away, whereas he was only lying in a room upstairs in the same house." [213] Jessie was herself at the time unable to walk and suffering from bronchitis. In her reminiscences she treats her husband's illness as a simple case of malingering brought on by his annoyance at the death of a maid; she adds, "Some quite ordinary change in the domestic staff disturbed Joseph Conrad greatly." This "quite ordinary change" was the death of "the faithful Nellie" who had worked with the family from 1900; (actually she died while Conrad had already been in bed a fortnight and a few days after the above-mentioned letter). [214] Conrad was indeed most upset by their maid's illness. [215] Jessie's sickness and her imminent surgery constituted "a crushing worry"; he confided to Pinker that the anxiety was giving him "most horrid sleepless nights of late." [216] Jessie was different. She was harsh and often malicious in her dealings with servants. Plucky in her own illness, she was intolerant of the sufferings of others. A drink now and again undoubtedly helped her to bear the pain. In later years Jessie's drinking became more frequent and sometimes caused embarrassing scenes.

Borys had been convalescing at his parents' house since early December. [217]

Gas poisoning and contusions had caused psychological shock and nervous disorder; he had fits of melancholy and sudden terrors at night. Finally he was given a disability pension of £150 a year. Jessie believed that Borys ought to be sent off on a long trip "to rouse him from the state of moody indolence." In her memoirs she accuses Conrad of being unable or unwilling to understand the need for such an action.[218] The accusation is unfounded for at least three reasons. First, Jessie herself says that Borys relaxed by falling asleep in her armchair, that is, in close proximity to his mother; second, she also relates that his younger brother's company had a soothing effect on Borys's nerves; and last, Borys could not in any case travel at the time because his leave from the army was only temporary, and he was not demobilized until April 1919.[219] Conrad had been trying for some time to find work for his son. But given Borys's lack of eagerness, his poor qualifications, and growing unemployment in England, the task proved very difficult. Borys was passive and at best contemplated further studies. At first Pinker tried to find a job for Borys, and later Curle did his best to help, for many months and in various ways.[220]

On 7 February the Conrads left for London for a new series of medical examinations. They traveled in a rented car because their new Studebaker was an open car and Jessie was still troubled by bronchitis.[221] Conrad had anticipated a longer stay in town, but after the surgeons had decided that Jessie's knee ought to get better without an operation, they were back in Capel House within a week.[222]

Conrad now energetically resumed work on The Rescue, which had been interrupted by an attack of gout. The novel had been appearing since 30 January in the weekly Land and Water. "I hope one of those two books will make a hit [The Rescue and The Arrow of Gold]—I mean a money hit," Conrad confessed to Pinker. "I fancy it is The Rescue, which is picturesque and at the same time more conventional, that will prove the best spec. of the two." Conrad was anxious to shake himself free from financial worries. "Perhaps at least we shall win to comparatively placid years, where there will be no other problems but quiet writing for me and leisurely, astute and successful negotiating for you. Shall I ever get into real smooth water and you have no longer to stand by ready with ropes and lifebuoys watching my flounderings anxiously?"[223]

It is in the light of such thoughts and moods that we must read Conrad's opinions on the merits of the "romantic presentation" of the plot.[224] These reflections reveal just as clearly as Moser's critical analysis that Conrad had little idea of what the central action of The Rescue was supposed to be. "Romanticism" became his authorial incantation: "I have thrown into that tale, as into a desperate fight, all that I am, all that I have, in the way of romantic vision, expression, and feeling. That is the artistic aim of the story," he confessed to young Roberts.[225] And to Doubleday he announced, "I mean to make the critics sit up with it—whether to bark or to bless I don't know—but sit up, anyway."[226] To Wise, Conrad confessed, "I myself, without being elated, think fairly well of the story. The romantic feeling is certainly there: but whether I can manage to keep the interest of the tale going—that's another question."[227] Thus he was not without doubts, which, as usual, he expressed most openly to Garnett.[228] Nevertheless, Conrad must have had quite a good opinion of *The Rescue*, because he even discussed with Pinker the possibility of an earlier book edition that would be in time to be considered by the Nobel Prize committee; on 15 February Conrad wrote to him, "I think sincerely that 'Rescue' has a particular quality. Novels of adventure will, I suppose, be always written; but it may well be that 'Rescue' in its concentrated colouring and tone will remain the swan song of Romance as a form of literary art."[229]

The same letter to Pinker contains a statement symptomatic of how Conrad saw his own special position in English society. Conrad had heard that members of the Athenaeum Club intended to suggest—confidentially of course— that Conrad be given the Order of Merit, the highest and most rarely awarded distinction open to him. Kipling was another candidate, and Conrad wrote, "I feel strongly that K. is the right person, and that the O.M. would not perhaps be an appropriate honour for me who, whatever my deepest feelings may be, can't claim English literature as my inheritance."

The work on *The Rescue* progressed at a speed that Conrad himself described as "a record"—in one day he wrote as many as nineteen hundred words. As usual the novel kept swelling beyond expectations: on 22 February Conrad thought he would have to write fifty more pages, but on 12 March he was only on the second chapter of Part VI—as many as ninety pages from the end.[230] He planned to finish the book in April. The speed of work was not, however, a result of concentrated attention; Conrad kept mentioning his cherished project of a Napoleonic novel "very much in my mind all the time." He also announced his intention to write a short story directly after completion of *The Rescue*.[231]

Leaving Capel House caused some interruption of Conrad's work. "The house is upside down. An earthquake is nothing to it. It does not last so long."[232] The owner of Capel House had died and his son wished to live there. With Borys as the driver, Conrad had been touring the countryside for some months, looking for another place.[233] As nothing suitable could be found, the Conrads had to rent a furnished house, Spring Grove, near Wye. It was a small seventeenth-century manor, with beautiful Adam fireplaces; too large for the family's needs, it was very suitable for receiving numerous guests—mostly Borys's friends—and for housing servants under the same roof. For some reason—perhaps because of its size and the constant coming and going of visitors—Conrad considered Spring Grove "odious."[234] The family moved in on 25 March 1919.[235]

On the following day, the first performance—delayed by Irving's illness—of

Victory took place at the Globe Theatre in London; the play was a moderate success.[236] Conrad did not feel like going to the show but took this opportunity to tell Pinker that he intended to write an original play, "that play with which I propose to surprise you before we both get too old to care a hang what happens on or off the stage."[237]

On 11 April Conrad told Pinker, "Begun also penultimate chapt. of *Rescue.* The last will be very short. I am by no means sick of the R. but oh! what a relief it will be!"[238] As it happened Conrad still had to write three chapters, not one.[239] A few days later he produced another eulogistic essay about the merchant marine, "Confidence." This time the piece was purely journalistic, without any personal reminiscences.[240] Next, Conrad fell ill again and was unable to work for three weeks: "I am afraid it will be some time before I can see anybody, at any rate a stranger, here. . . . My health is very precarious and I want to talk to you about the future" he told Pinker. Later he thanked him: "My mind has been set at rest by our long talk."[241]

On 25 May *The Rescue*, begun twenty-three years earlier, was at last finished.[242] It seems that Garnett was less than enthusiastic about the text, which had been appearing in *Land and Water.* Conrad explained to his old friend, "It was the instinct (not the sense—the instinct) of what you have discerned with your unerring eye that kept me off the R. for 20 years or more. That—and nothing else. My instinct was right. But all the same I cannot say I regret the impulse which made me take it up again. I am settling my affairs in this world and I should not have liked to leave behind me this evidence of having bitten off more than I could chew. A very vulgar vanity. Could anything be more legitimate?"[243]

In the summer of 1919 Conrad corrected *The Rescue* for the book edition and wrote Author's Notes to the next four volumes of the collected edition: *Tales of Unrest, Typhoon and Other Stories, The Mirror of the Sea,* and *A Personal Record.*[244] In the first two Notes Conrad tells about the origins of the stories included in these collections; he dissociates himself unobtrusively but quite clearly from "The Idiots" and "The Return." In the third Note Conrad exalts the texts written a dozen or so years earlier and downplayed by him at that time to his friends and to Pinker. Now he claims they are deeply personal and "most sincere disclosures," while expressing pleasure at the fact that they were so well received and understood. The longest Note is that to *A Personal Record*; it discusses in some detail how Conrad had come to write in English. Just as he had a year earlier in his letter to Walpole, Conrad claims that he had never faced a choice between English and French:

Well, yes, there was adoption; but it was I who was adopted by the genius of the language, which directly [as] I came out of the stammering stage made me its own so completely that its very idioms I truly believe had a direct action on my temperament and fashioned my still plastic character.

By creating one more autobiographical myth Conrad was at the same time trying to explode the fallacy of describing him as a "Slav"; this theme provoked an
impassioned tirade in praise of Polishness:

> Nothing is more foreign than what in the literary world is called Sclavonism,
> to the Polish temperament with its tradition of self-government, its chival-
> rous view of moral restraints and an exaggerated respect for individual
> rights: not to mention the important fact that the whole Polish mentality,
> Western in complexion, had received its training from Italy and France and,
> historically, had always remained, even in religious matters, in sympathy
> with the most liberal currents of European thought. An impartial view of hu-
> manity in all its degrees of splendour and misery together with a special re-
> gard for the rights of the unprivileged of this earth, not on any mystic ground
> but on the ground of simple fellowship and honourable reciprocity of ser-
> vices, was the dominant characteristic of the mental and moral atmosphere
> of the houses which sheltered my hazardous childhood:—matters of calm
> and deep conviction both lasting and consistent, and removed as far as possi-
> ble from that humanitarianism that seems to be merely a matter of crazy
> nerves or a morbid conscience.[245]

Conrad's dream of being liberated from the stress of immediate financial
need was finally realized in June 1919—at least for a time. He sold the film
rights to his works for the very considerable sum of £3,080.[246] At the same time
The Arrow of Gold, dedicated to Curle, which had been published in the
United States on 12 April, was selling extremely well; and there was still *The
Rescue* in reserve. As Conrad had no urgent writing commitments, the social
life at Spring Grove flourished; groups of friends and acquaintances flocked in
for weekends. Conrad himself made frequent trips to London.[247] From 11 to
14 July the entire Conrad family visited the Hopes in Fingringhoe near Col-
chester.[248] In the summer of 1919 Conrad enjoyed a few months of exceptionally good health, and his letters were almost free from complaints; in June
he said he felt "considerably better," and in August Walpole found him in
"great form."[249]

Conrad felt that his old friendship with Garnett, which had languished from
1902 to 1916, was still alive, and he liked to recall its beginnings and its lasting
quality.* He praised Garnett's "trusted and uncompromising soul," his "wonderful insight" and "unimpaired wisdom." Replying to Garnett's letter recol-
lecting the commencement of *The Rescue*, Conrad wrote on 12 March 1919 of
"a strange impression of having always lived under [Garnett's] eyes," and later
assured him of his "absolute confidence."[250] Among his younger friends he saw
Curle most often; Conrad wrote about him, "He is a little eccentric and a little

---

* In a reversal of roles, in May 1918 Garnett sounded Conrad about helping him avoid possible conscription
(Carolyn G. Heilbrun, *The Garnett Family* [London, 1961], pp. 114–115). Conrad explained that he lacked
appropriate connections (letter to Garnett, 16 May 1918, E. Garnett, *Letters*, p. 281).

trying, but his friendship is above suspicion." [251] Relations with Jean-Aubry, whom Conrad had probably met through Retinger, were steadily growing closer; Jean-Aubry, Conrad's translator into French, was later to become his first biographer. [252] In his reminiscences Conrad shows no signs of old age or illness:

> Although he was of medium height, the size of his chest, the sturdiness of his body, the way his triangular head was tilted back and set deeply between his broad shoulders, the bold and fine structure of his face, the firm design of his jaw, the occasional lifting of his lip baring his teeth, and the penetrating gaze fixed either on a distant point or on the eyes of the interlocutor—everything about him conspired to give an impression of strength, an aroused strength ready to expand, similar to the strength of the most noble beasts of prey. Under his drooping eyelids which at times made him look drowsy or day-dreaming, his eyes retained such a piercing expression that one could not doubt their constant alertness.
>
> At the very first encounter one was struck by the power emanating from him as well as by the exceptional charm of his manners. His way of bowing, his wordly and reverent attitude towards women, the gracious cordiality with which he clasped one or both your hands between his, obviously contrasted not only with the habitual British stiffness but even more with the uncouth behavior of many of our contemporary writers.

Jean-Aubry did not doubt that Conrad's courteous manners betrayed his Polish origin. [253]

Frequent meetings with friends and busy social life could not, however, re-press Conrad's awareness that the best years of his life had passed beyond recall and that both the present and the future lacked any purpose that would arouse his energies. Thus Conrad requested Gide, "Think of me sometimes with friend-ship, my dear Gide. There now, I am getting sentimental . . . I've seen the an-nouncements of *Almayer's Folly*—and thought I was dreaming. The man who wrote it is not dead yet but he is thoroughly buried. And he still shudders from time to time, the poor devil." [254] Conrad expressed his anxiety most frankly in a surprisingly open letter to Warrington Dawson: "I have la sensation du vide. Not perhaps le Vide Eternel, though after sixty one may well begin to grow aware of it a little, but of a certain inward emptiness. For 25 years I've been giving out all that was in me. But apart from that I have the feeling of approach-ing isolation. I don't say loneliness; I shall, I imagine be always looked at now—but from a distance, as if set apart by my predestined temperament like some strange animal confined within a fence for public view. Through my fault—or is it simply Fate?—I have missed all along the chances of closer contacts." [255] The sincerity of this confession is confirmed by the fact that Conrad let himself be so outspoken to a man who did not belong to the circle of his closest friends.

The letter to Dawson helps us to understand the significant evolution that took place in Conrad's attitude toward *The Arrow of Gold*. As we remember, in the first stages of writing Conrad put no stress on the autobiographical character of the novel, and while writing *The Arrow* he never spoke about it with any special emphasis. The change in Conrad's attitude occurred only after the book's publication in England on 6 August 1919. The novel lacked the authenticity of emotions that could, perhaps, have created a great love story out of several loosely woven plots; Conrad tried to confer that authenticity *ex post facto* by giving *The Arrow of Gold* an allegedly autobiographical character. Conrad knew that the story as told was remote from his experiences in Marseilles, and he could not fail to realize that it lacked a focal point. Perhaps he also sensed the disappointment of his friends. Galsworthy confided to Garnett, "I can find no real *feeling* in *The A of G*. . . . *Youth* has glamour, this hasn't a speck of it . . . there it is, a sumptuous assembling of things meant to fuse and live, and the spark left out."[256]

Conrad feared the reactions of the critics; he listened to their voices perhaps more intently than ever before, adopting at once a defensive attitude.[257] Indeed, the reception was not enthusiastic; and although *New Statesman* called Conrad the leading English novelist after Hardy, even that reviewer voiced reservations; three weeks after the book had been published, W. L. Courtney summarized in *The Daily Telegraph* almost all the objections that were to be brought against it later: a lack of cohesion, poor characterization of both protagonists, diffusiveness, and so on.[258] Conrad shielded himself in advance by trying to impose upon his readers the vision of the book as a personal confession—particularly by exerting his influence upon Colvin, who was expected to review it for the *Observer*. To Galsworthy Conrad wrote, "Never before was the act of publication so distasteful to me as on this occasion."[259] And to Colvin he insisted repeatedly:

> The first notices . . . are very poor, puzzle-headed, hesitating pronouncements . . . A very unsatisfactory send-off.
>
> Your question raises a delicate problem. A man of your *savoir-faire*, your sense of literary *convenances* and your *homme-du-monde* tact, is best fit to judge how the autob'al note, if struck, may affect the world—and the man.
>
> With all deference then I venture to suggest that the view of its being a study of a woman, *prise sur le vif* (obviously, you may say) and also the story of young, very young love told with a depth of emotion pointing to experience is what you perceive, what impresses you—which makes the "quality" of the book. This said with your authority will amount to a confession—a sufficient confession to a not particularly delicate world.

And apologizing for errors in the syntax, he added:

> I have never been able to read *these* proofs in cold blood. Ridiculous! My dear (as D. Rita would have said) there are some of these 42-year-old episodes

of which I cannot think now without a slight tightness of the chest —*un petit serrement de coeur*. What a confession!²⁶⁰

In such terms Conrad tried to conceal behind a haze of alleged autobiographical and emotional revelations the fact that the book was both sterile and impersonal. The Author's Note, written later, takes the same line; and such artificially created emotional myths must surely have strengthened Conrad's inward sense of futility.

Conrad was again dreaming about the Mediterranean novel, the great ambition of his last years. He was afraid that he might not finish it. He joked in a letter to Gide, "There will always be fools who will say: he aimed so high that he was bound to crack up. A beautiful epitaph. Forgive all my sins (including *The Arrow of Gold*)."²⁶¹

Originally *The Arrow of Gold* was to have been dedicated to Quinn; then Conrad decided to offer to him his future Napoleonic novel.²⁶² But shortly after Conrad had made this promise, his relations with Quinn cooled as a result of the disclosure that Conrad had been selling his manuscripts to Wise, and also— to a lesser degree—Quinn's none too successful attempts to mediate between Conrad and Doubleday in the negotiations concerning a collected edition. Conrad henceforward treated his collector and admirer rather stiffly and condescendingly, and after 1919 their correspondence became more and more formal before petering out in October 1922, just a few months before they might have met during Conrad's visit to America.²⁶³

On 28 August 1919 the Conrads again went to London to see a surgeon about Jessie's knee. The examinations were very painful and another operation was pronounced necessary.²⁶⁴ One week earlier Conrad had signed a contract for the rental of a new house, Oswalds, in Bishopsbourne near Canterbury; he described it to Pinker as a "house, 2 cottages, 3 gardens—all complete—£250 a year."²⁶⁵

XV

. . . .

HOPE AND RESIGNATION

1919–1924

THE MOVE to Oswalds in Bishopsbourne took place early in October 1919, during a railway strike.[1] Thanks to Borys's inventiveness—he managed to hire a lorry and get some porters to help in return for free beer—the move did not take too long, although even after two weeks Conrad was still complaining that the new house was unfit for normal use.[2] Conrad spoke about the strike with contempt, insisting that the railwaymen were quite passive and interested only in resuming work as soon as possible; he does not seem to have taken note of the fact that the strike ended with their victory.[3]

Oswalds was a large house—the largest of all the houses ever occupied by Conrad; it was nearly a century old, shaded by elm trees, with a garden surrounding it on three sides and walls overgrown with ivy. The only drawback—quite serious in Conrad's opinion—was that the house was in a hollow enclosed by woods, and the only more distant view was of a cemetery ajoining the village Romanesque stone church.

On the ground floor apart from some smaller rooms there were two drawing rooms, one large and one small, a dining room, Conrad's study, and some smaller rooms; the bedrooms were on the first floor. Because the Conrads did not have enough furniture to fill such a large house, Grace Willard got another opportunity to display her talents. She supplied two fireplaces (apparently by Adam), three second-hand Aubusson carpets, some old Italian upholstered furniture, and several other items. Conrad wrote to Pinker, "It seems to me I am dreaming a strange and aesthetic dream in the atmosphere of a curio shop. It's very funny."[4]

Soon after the move, in the middle of October, Conrad ended a four-month hiatus by beginning intensive work on a stage adaptation of *The Secret Agent*; Act 2 was concluded on 10 November, and Act 3 on 22 November.[5] But Conrad soon began to have doubts about the whole enterprise, and wrote to Pinker, "As I go on in my adaptation, stripping off the garment of artistic expression and consistent irony which clothes the story in the book, I perceive more clearly how it is bound to appear to the collective mind of the audience a merely horrible and sordid tale, giving a most unfavourable impression of both the writer himself and of his attitude to the moral aspect of the subject. . . . I will confess that I myself had no idea of what the story was till I came to grips with it in this process of dramatization. Of course I can't stop now. . . . I have resolved that since the story is horrible I shall make it as horrible as I possibly can. If there is any salvation for it, it may possibly be found just in *that*. But I have not many illusions on that score."[6] Conrad's unreasonable obstinacy, which ought to have been checked by his artistic conscience, may be explained only by his desire to squeeze everything possible out of what he had in stock—a desire obviously reinforced by his failing imaginative power.

A sharp, almost arrogant, letter to Gide about the French translation of *The Arrow of Gold* constitutes another example of Conrad's wayward unreasonableness at this time. Gide, who had been responsible for getting Conrad translated into French, had consigned the translation of *The Arrow of Gold* to his friend, Mme Maus, but Conrad, meanwhile, had promised it to Jean-Aubry. In his letter Conrad carped at Gide's attempts at placatory humor and even reviled the whole idea of entrusting his work to a female translator: "If my writings have a distinct character it lies in their virility—in their spirit and method of expression. No one has denied me that. And you throw me to women!" He fumed, "One would think that you're taking me for a fool,"[7] forgetting that he had never objected to the earlier "feminine" translations. Conrad must have been looking forward to his future collaboration with Jean-Aubry on revising the French translations (whether done by Jean-Aubry or by others) of his works.[8] His irritation must have been caused not only by the promise he had given to Jean-Aubry, but also by a desire to have a close friend for translator. It was only thanks to Gide's patience that the conflict was eventually resolved peacefully.

On 27 November all four Conrads traveled via London to Liverpool, where Jessie was at last to undergo an operation. Sir Robert Jones performed it on 2 December, and, after a few days, it was pronounced successful.[9] Conrad reported, "We may hope that poor Jessie's troubles are nearing their end." "Everything is going on so well . . . Of course I feel happy. . . . All this seems too good to be true and I have a dread of some beastly development. But every one assures me that it isn't likely."[10]

During their stay in Liverpool, from 30 November to 24 December, Conrad complained that he was unable to do any kind of work.[11] He interrupted his adaptation of *The Secret Agent* and felt incapable even of reading proofs of *The Rescue*.[12] The University Club, however, managed to persuade him to attend a banquet in honor of the merchant marine; there Conrad met Captain David Bone, whom he had corresponded with. The two men boosted each other's morale and eventually Bone induced Conrad (who kept objecting because of his "not impeccable diction") to make a speech in praise of British sailors. This was Conrad's first public speaking appearance.[13]

After returning to Bishopsbourne Conrad fell seriously ill. On 20 January 1920 he wrote to Colvin, "I assure you that for a month very nearly I haven't had the energy to command my thoughts and resolution enough to lift a pen and try. . . . I can't imagine what has brought on me that long fit of the very blackest depression unless it be a very beastly little ailment (of an inflammatory nature) the first touch of which I felt in London on our passage home. It is passing off now; but by this time my old friend the gout has come along to keep me company. . . . I don't want to do anything. If you were to peep magically into my study you would see me sitting absolutely motionless like a crabbed, unasiatic-looking Buddha—and not even twirling my thumbs—all day long."[14] This sounds like a passage from a psychiatry textbook: the immobility for which Jessie so often reproached her husband is a classic symptom of depression.[15]

Conrad was ill for a month, but he finally set about doing the proofs of *The Rescue*; he worked on them from the middle of January until 24 February. Again he expressed hope of writing a short story soon.[16] All that he produced, however, was the Note to *The Secret Agent*, in which he alluded to the stage adaptation of the novel. The Note also hints of at least some of his sources for the plot. To be sure, Conrad, as usual, stressed how he drew on his imagination and his own experiences for new material, while trying to cover up the extent of his readings and borrowings. But even so, this part of the Note is more credible than Conrad's mythologizing "confessions" both about *The Mirror of the Sea* and his moods before beginning *The Secret Agent*.[17] Soon after writing the Note, on 15 March, Conrad finished the first version of his stage adaptation of the novel.[18] He continued to work on the text. "I've managed to ram everything in there except the actual cab-drive. It was very interesting to do—and perfectly useless," he told Galsworthy.[19] Deep down, however, Conrad could hardly have been wholly convinced about this "uselessness"; he not only carried on negotiations with theater managers but also corresponded with Aubry about translating the play into the French.[20]

In the first days of April Conrad wrote the Author's Note to *A Set of Six*.[21] It deals almost exclusively with the sources for the stories, and he tells us how "Il Conde" was inspired by a tale told by "a very charming old gentleman" he met in Italy; Conrad was consciously reticent about the origins of "The Informer" and "An Anarchist"; and he is particularly interesting about that often underestimated story "The Duel," saying that he had tried there to capture the spirit of the Napoleonic epoch.

Meanwhile "poor Jessie," who in February had been troubled by shingles, and at the beginning of May by bronchitis, was again suffering acute pains in her knee. On 31 March Sir Robert Jones performed another operation, this time in Canterbury.[22] It was supposed to be "the last time"; Jessie's condition showed an almost immediate improvement after the surgery and Conrad assured Eric Pinker (James's son) that "the trick was done this time." However, on 27 April, barely one week after she had left the hospital, Jessie's condition deteriorated, raising the possibility of another operation. Conrad was obviously worn out by these repeated hopes and disappointments, while even Jessie's apparently inexhaustible patience was wearing down.[23] The new trouble was diagnosed as pereostitis. On 5 May, this time at Oswalds, Jones cut and cleaned the wound, warning that yet another operation might be needed.[24]

Amidst all the disturbance a welcome diversion was provided by a visit from Karola Zagórska, Aniela's younger sister.[25] Conrad enjoyed talking with his attractive thirty-seven-year-old cousin, although their conversations sometimes produced violent emotional discords. Apparently on one occasion, when Conrad had confessed his deep regard for her parents, Karola cried out excitedly, "'But you are even happier than I am, because the lives of your parents were truly great and beautiful. They gave to their country all they could. As long as Poland exists every generation will cherish their memory. Just think of it. . . .'

"Konrad glanced at me abruptly: A magnificent glow lit up his face. But suddenly it was gone and before I realized Konrad had left me."

On another occasion Karola assured Conrad that her childhood had not been overshadowed by a sense of captivity and that she had grown up with a feeling of inner freedom and belief in the future independence of Poland.

"'But a great many did not want to wait. Their belief in freedom was a creative force—so they fought and perished. And about the majority of them no one will ever hear anything.'

"Suddenly I became frightened. Konrad pushed me aside, stood up, moved the chair away noisily, walked to his desk and began looking through a pile of papers. Then he turned round and glared straight at my face, looking positively forbidding. His lips twiched . . . It seemed he was about to flare up but gradually his face became calm and serious. He turned away completely composed.

"'Pardonnez-moi,' he said abruptly."

Zagórska reported an even more poignant episode. She had brought with her a popular history of Poland, published in 1847. It was inscribed "To Karolek Zagórski from Ewelina and Apollon Korzeniowski. May God let him love nothing but what is his own and his native land's." Bearing in mind Conrad's extreme sensitivity on the subject, she decided not to give him this bitter souvenir of their family past.[26] And she behaved prudently, it seems: Conrad did not like feeling forced.

On 17 February 1920, Eustachy Sapieha, the first minister of reborn Poland to the Court of St. James, sent Conrad a letter, urging him to initiate and chair a "club of friends of Poland," a British equivalent of the Anglo-Polish Society, formed in Warsaw in November 1919; its objective was to inform English public opinion about Polish affairs and foster cultural exchange. Conrad declined, politely but firmly: "I am not the right sort of person to take the initiative in that matter. . . . I have led a retired life. I have formed no social relations. I am ill now."[27]

However, this correspondence, and the emotional conversations with Karola Zagórska, found an immediate echo in Conrad's letter to Quinn of 2 March.

Conrad said that it made him happy to think about a reborn state which "has one heart and one soul . . . The magic sense of independence is the cause of that union without reserves and regrets which enables that three times devastated and impoverished country to put forth its physical strength, and on the very morrow of rising from its grave to take up its old historical part of defender of civilization."[28] A few weeks later Conrad answered, in the same vein, an appeal from the Committee for the Polish Government Loan, active in the United States, with an emphatically worded cablegram: "For Poles the sense of duty and the imperishable feeling of nationality preserved in the hearts and defended by the hands of their immediate ancestors in open struggles against the might of three Powers and in indomitable defiance of crushing oppression for more than a hundred years is sufficient inducement to come forward to assist in reconstructing the independence, dignity and usefulness of the reborn Republic."[29]

Karola Zagórska brought the news that her sister Aniela had been working for some time on a translation of *Almayer's Folly*—she was at first helped by Stanisław Ignacy Witkiewicz, later a well-known writer—and that Aniela would also like to take on the responsibility for publishing Conrad's other works in Polish.[30] Although Aniela was a woman and although Conad had not seen anything done by her, he willingly agreed, and even encouraged a certain freedom in translation.

Conrad wrote to her on 10 April 1920.

> I give you my best and completest authority and right to translate all my works into Polish.
>
> You are authorized to give or to refuse permission and to decide all matters concerned therewith, using your own judgement and taking decisions in my name.
>
> I should be happiest if you yourself had the wish and the time to translate at least those books which you like. I know from Karolcia that you worked on *Almayer's Folly*—possibly even too conscientiously! My dear, don't trouble to be too scrupulous about it. I may tell you (in French) that in my opinion "il vaut mieux interpréter que traduire" [it is better to interpret than to translate]. My English is not at all literary. I write idiomatically. Je me sers des phrases courantes qui, après tout, sont celles avec lesquelles on se garde le mieux contre "le cliché." Il s'agit donc de trouver les équivalents. Et là, ma chère, je vous prie laissez vous guider plutôt par votre tempérament que par une conscience sévère. Je vous connais. J'ai foi en vous. Et vraiment Conrad vu à travers Angèle, ça ne sera pas déjà si mauvais. Inspirez vous bien de cette idée . . . [I use current expressions which, after all, are the best defense against "cliché." It is, then, a question of finding the equivalent expressions. And there, my dear Aniela, I beg you to let yourself be guided more by your

temperament than by a strict conscience. I know you. I have faith in you. And indeed Conrad seen through the eyes of Aniela will by no means be so bad. Take heart from this idea.]

Later Conrad formally and unconditionally signed over to the Zagórski sisters his translation rights and copyright for Poland and Russia.[31]

On 11 May he announced to Pinker, "I am tackling in good earnest today the Elba Novel and mean to continue from day to day if the heavens fall."[32] The heavens remained in their place, but four days later Conrad confessed to Curle his inability to get "any kind [of prose] out of myself."[33] In May he wrote only the Author's Notes to *Under Western Eyes* and *The Shadow Line*.[34] The former departs from the usual character of his other Author's Notes. With the exception of a declaration, somewhat contradicting his previous statements regarding his ignorance of things Russian, that the book's content was the result of his "general knowledge fortified by earnest meditation," Conrad gave no information about his sources but expressed his belief in the novel's topicality and asserted that its vision had been confirmed by recent political events. "The ferocity and imbecility of an autocratic rule rejecting all legality and in fact basing itself upon complete moral anarchism provokes the no less imbecile and atrocious answer of a purely Utopian revolutionism encompassing destruction by the first means to hand, in the strange conviction that a fundamental change of hearts must follow the downfall of any given human institutions. These people are unable to see that all they can effect is merely a change of names. The oppressors and the oppressed are all Russians together; and the world is brought once more face to face with the truth of the saying that the tiger cannot change his stripes nor the leopard his spots."[35]

The American edition of *The Rescue* came out on 21 May and the English on 14 June; the novel was dedicated to Frederick R. Penfield, the former American ambassador to Vienna. In one letter to Garnett, Conrad called the novel a "patched book"; in another he confessed that he would quite readily forget *The Rescue*'s existence if it were not for "your interest, the thought and time you've given to it." Even to his publishers Conrad spoke about *The Rescue* with a certain hesitation, stressing its possible success rather than its merits.[36] And when Walpole criticized one of the novel's protagonists, Mrs. Travers, he heard in reply, "Of course, mon cher, it is not very good. I did my best work long ago!"[37] Nevertheless, *The Rescue* had an enthusiastic press; Katherine Mansfield in the *Athenaeum* also joined the admiring chorus; only Virginia Woolf in an unsigned review in the *Times Literary Supplement*, and an anonymous critic in *The Nation* of New York, voiced reservations.[38]

Virginia Woolf confessed in her diary, "I was struggling, at this time, to say honestly that I don't think Conrad's last book a good one. I have said it. It is painful (a little) to find fault there, where almost solely, one respects. I can't help suggesting the truth to be that he never sees anyone who knows good writing from bad, and then being a foreigner, talking broken English, married to a lump of a wife, he withdraws more and more into what he once did well, only piles it on higher and higher, until what can one call it but stiff melodrama."[39] Thomas Moser is right in saying that her remarks are very perceptive; but they also tend to simplify the issues. It is true that Conrad's accent became much more marked in his old age,[40] and that his capacity to absorb and make imaginative use of new material was gone. On the other hand it was precisely in the last years of his life that it became possible for Conrad to escape from his rural seclusion and enjoy a much wider social life—to travel, visit friends, and invite them to Oswalds. It is true that Conrad's contacts in England were almost entirely restricted to lesser writers; but this was not the result of conscious choice, but of the fact that such English writers as Joyce, D. H. Lawrence, E. M. Forster and Aldous Huxley—unlike Claudel, Gide, Larbaud, St.-John Perse, Valéry, Thomas Mann, and Stefan Żeromski—showed little interest even in Conrad's best works. Among the leading English writers of the older generation only Bennett and Galsworthy had been paying friendly attention to his novels and stories, and they were very remote from him spiritually. Meanwhile the aging Conrad, physically enfeebled, tired out by sickness, and withered as an artist, retained an undiminished thirst for approval, sympathy, understanding, and affection; it was perhaps even greater than before.

Conrad's mental fatigue and the decline of his creative powers also brought a change in the nature of his relations with friends and acquaintances. Only rarely did he seek a dialogue or discussion; he would persistently ask for conversation, but the ensuing talk usually consisted of his own monologues. Walpole, at the time an eager listener, wrote uncharitably a few years later, "Conrad never said anything very interesting in his last years; he was too preoccupied with money and gout. He was only thrilling when he lost his temper and chattered and screamed like a monkey."[41] Conrad's favorite company consisted of such patient admirers as Jean-Aubry and Curle, in whom he conveniently found not only moral but also practical support; they in fact took upon themselves many of his everyday affairs. The support of Jean-Aubry and Curle allayed Conrad's sense of decadence and alleviated his inner conflicts, facilitating thereby his reconciliation with all that which, through lack of strength, he was unable to process in his mind or imagination. This was precisely the reason why toward the close of his life Conrad tolerated the company of so many "uncritical worshippers," as Rothenstein calls them.[42] Nevertheless, as his conversations with Bertrand Russell show, Conrad was still able to participate in a serious exchange of ideas when in contact with a first-class mind. The "blame" for the situation described by Virginia Woolf was not wholly Conrad's. He had remained an outsider in England, but over the course of many difficult years the fortitude he needed to bear his own isolation finally began to fail him.

On 8 June Conrad again informed Pinker that he was "getting on" with the Napoleonic novel, provisionally called *The Isle of Rest*. He made a few trips to the British Museum in London to read historical books recommended by Jean-Aubry.[43] By the end of the month Conrad thought that his "grip on the novel grows with every added page." In July he assured Walpole that the work was indeed progressing, but when Walpole saw fragments of the second chapter, he was surprised by the number of "foreign phrases" in the draft.[44] At all events the progress made on the novel in June had soon been checked by a sudden attack of gout; for a week Conrad felt "as flat (and as soft) as a pancake."[45]

Jessie's knee had to be cut open again at the end of June; the operation was repeated on 24 July, and this time, at last, the surgeon successfully removed the source of infection. One month after the last operation Jessie began to walk— and soon she was even able to go up and down the stairs.[46]

Jessie's treatment, supervised by a celebrated and titled surgeon and carried out by a special live-in nurse, was expensive. And not only Jessie's treatment depleted Conrad's finances; the more he earned the more easily he spent. Thus, although the collected limited edition—fifteen hundred sets in England and the United States—brought £2,205 and $12,000 (£5,500 in all), and the royalties from *The Arrow of Gold* and *The Rescue* were high, Conrad continually tried to secure additional income, outside Pinker's control, by selling his manuscripts. How different from his former letters to Quinn is the tone of Conrad's correspondence with T. J. Wise at this time. Offering him four Author's Notes and four essays, Conrad wrote, "Personally I am indifferent whether they remain in England or go to the U.S." When Wise paid £150 for the stage version of *The Secret Agent*, Conrad wrote jubilantly to Curle, "God knows I wanted this cash." Conrad also arranged the publication of a collector's edition of the volume of prefaces to his own works—it was to bring him £380 more. "Every little bit counts. Money runs out like water! I am quite nervous."[47]

With age Conrad became obsessively anxious about money—a trait common among elderly people, and typical among victims of depression. The latter, however, also tend to find a "liberating" release in extravagance. In the course of two years, 1919–1920, Conrad spent well over £8,000, a huge sum even considering the rise in prices immediately after the war.[48]

Conrad's generous hospitality added to the expenses: he often invited guests for a few days' stay and was fond of giving elegant Sunday luncheons. John Powell, whom he had not seen for a few years, came in June to give a private concert, at which he played his own *Rhapsodie Nègre*, and Chopin.[49] According to both Zagórska and Jean-Aubry, Conrad was a great admirer of Chopin's music. Apparently he sometimes whistled motifs from the *Mazurkas* or *Nocturnes* and considered "Polishness" the distinct feature of Chopin's music.[50]

Powell's recital took place in the drawing room, which Karola Zagórska has described:

It was a lovely room. White and blue Chippendale furniture, white and gold Empire style pieces covered with yellow satin. Near the door leading to the garden a piano stood as if waiting to be played. Above the fireplace an old painting of the Dutch school; on each side of the large window oval mirrors in carved, gilt frames reflected the ceiling, furniture and an Aubusson carpet on the floor. There was an old desk, and crystal vases full of narcissus in the spring, then tulips and later roses.

Karola, who spent almost six months at Oswalds, liked Conrad's study best of all the rooms in the house.

You entered it from the hall on the right. It was a large room with light walls and two large windows. . . . The largest wall in the room was covered with bookshelves—from the floor to the ceiling; and in addition here and there stood shallow bookcases full of books. Between the windows, Konrad's secretary sat at the desk and took dictation from him. . . . In the middle of the room, closer to the fireplace, stood a large round table and next to it an armchair with a light-colored cretonne loose cover. It was Konrad's usual place for dictating, correcting manuscripts, sitting with his family or friends. . . . Opposite the armchair stood a small, cozy couch also covered with light-colored cretonne. I used to spend hours sitting on it and talking with Konrad . . . On top of the bookcase behind the armchair stood various photographs. There was Borys in uniform, and several friends of Konrad's; among them Cunninghame Graham, Galsworthy and Edward Garnett. . . . Photographs of Konrad's wife and his uncle-guardian Tadeusz Bobrowski stood on the mantelpiece. And above hung a valuable print of the port of Marseilles in the seventeenth century. On the wall opposite the door a coloured woodcut by Jastrzębowski depicted Marshal Piłsudski on horseback. . . . The fire was always lit even during summer.[51]

The portrait of Piłsudski is significant. During the Polish-Soviet war of 1920 Conrad was well informed about Poland's situation and watched events closely. When the Polish army was suffering defeats in June and July, he "could not" talk about Poland; much dispirited, he would confide to Zagórska that he was "unable to breathe."[52] But even in mid-August, when the Red Army approached Warsaw, aiming to "carry the flame of the Revolution" to Germany and the West, Conrad did not express his anxiety publicly. He must have known about Lloyd George's unsympathetic attitude toward Poland, and the Labour party's threat of a general strike to prevent any attempt to send supplies to the Polish army; but he kept silent.[53] Were his lips sealed by a double loyalty, a loyalty that forbade him to make any open attack on his own government and much of English public opinion? Was it Conrad's grim pride and his intense dislike of asking for help? Or was it his deep-rooted pessimism under the guise of sullen passivity? I think that the decisive factor was his lack of faith. Conrad had been accustomed to think of Poland as lost forever, and any news of defeat pushed him back into a state of hopelessness. But whatever may have been the causes of his silence, the neglect of his country must later have cast a shadow over his conscience.

Karola Zagórska left Oswalds on 15 August, the critical day in the Polish-Soviet war. On the day of her departure, Conrad, for the first time in may days, apparently, was in better spirits. The two of them talked about the situation on the front, and as soon as Karola arrived in London, she sent Conrad a newspaper with the headline "Piłsudski crushes the enemy." Conrad was a great admirer of Piłsudski.[54] They had both grown up in the shadow of the 1863 insurrection; but while its failure left Conrad with the trauma of defeat, for Piłsudski, ten years younger, the uprising was a legend that imposed a duty of patriotic action.

In July, a big Liverpool shipping firm, the Ocean Steam Ship Company, approached Conrad for his opinion on the projected construction of a sailing ship to be used as a training ship for the merchant marine. Conrad felt highly gratified, and wrote to the firm's managing director: "To be still recognized after all these years as a seaman by the head of a House known so long and so highly honoured on the wide seas touches me deeply."[55] Within a few days he composed an extensive "Memorandum on the Scheme for Fitting out a Sailing Ship for the Purpose of Perfecting the Training of Merchant Service Officers Belonging to the Port of Liverpool." Conrad stressed the moral value of service on sailing ships for future officers not only as sailors but as men. More than once he referred to his experiences on the *Torrens*. The *Torrens*, of course, was a passenger ship and therefore particularly clean and comfortable; Conrad's choice of this example might have served to justify his praise of the physical work and the general living conditions on old sailing ships, a praise belied, for instance, by *The Nigger*. In a letter accompanying the "Memorandum" Conrad set out his pedagogical principles. A training ship, he wrote, should inculcate the traditions of the sailor's profession and thus perform the same function that a classical education does on land. Conrad continued:

> The public school man, even if he devotes himself to literature afterwards, has no immediate practical, and as it were, *material* use for the classical lore he has acquired. . . . He will only have gained a more liberal conception of his attitude to life and a strong inner feeling of that continuity of human thought, effort and achievement which is such an inspiring and at the same time such a steadying element in national existence . . . A year, or a year and a half, of training in a sea-going sailing ship I would regard for a boy destined for the sea as a course in classical practice of the sea. . . . He will have acquired the old lore of the sea, which has fashioned so many generations

down to his very fathers and in its essence will remain with the future generations of seamen, even after the day when the last sail and the last oar have
vanished from the waters of our globe.[56]

Meanwhile, the manuscript of what was then significantly entitled *The Isle
of Rest* grew slowly; by August Conrad had only reached the third chapter.
"The Nap[ic] novel is in its 3 chap[t]. All very lame and unsatisfactory—so far," he
complained to Curle. No theater was interested in putting on *The Secret Agent*;
and Conrad's reaction was like that of the fox to the sour grapes: "If one is to
condescend to that sort of thing well then, all considered, I prefer Cinema to
Stage. The Movie is just a silly stunt for silly people— but the theatre is more
compromising since it is capable of falsifying the very soul of one's work both
on the imaginative and on the intellectual side—besides having some sort of
inferior poetics of its own which is bound to play havoc with that imponderable
quality of creative literary expression which depends on one's individuality."[57]

In accordance with these opinions Conrad embarked on a film script based
on "Gaspar Ruiz," entitled *Gaspar the Strong Man*. His collaborator was—of
all people—Pinker, and they began working together at Deal, on holiday, for
the first three weeks of September. The script was finished on 29 October in
Bishopsbourne;[58] it has not survived, and, no doubt luckily, was never filmed.

On their first day at Deal Conrad was delighted by a chance encounter with a
sailor who had served with him on the *Riversdale*. This friend, Baker, owned a
small sailboat, and during the following days they made short trips in the Channel with John as a third. Fourteen-year-old John watched his father with amazement and admiration as, with "all his infirmities forgotten, and his strength returned in an almost miraculous way," he climbed rope ladders and without a
moment's hesitation jumped from the yawl onto the accommodation-ladder of a
ship they visited—although, as Conrad confessed to his son, he had never
learned to swim: "J. C. changed completely when on board, seemed to have
eyes in the back of his head." Conrad also made use of the occasion to subject
John to a drastic treatment aimed at curing his seasickness: the boy was made
to sit in a small boat "anchored where the swell seemed worst" and fish for dabs
with cold bacon fat on a line; when he felt ill, he was taken ashore and made to
walk; when he felt better he had to return to the dinghy. It worked.[59]

During holidays Conrad much enjoyed the company of his younger son,
whom he missed very much when he was away at school. He taught John to
play chess—Conrad himself was apparently an excellent player—discussing
each move in detail according to Capablanca's handbook.[60]

At the beginning of October Conrad wrote his last Author's Note: to the volume *Notes on Life and Letters*, which was being prepared with Curle's help.[61]
In the Note Conrad declared his "constitutional inability" to expose his private
life. And in the fragment where he announced his "receding from the world,"

caused by the relentless passage of time, he stated disarmingly, "This volume (including these embarrassed introductory remarks) is as near as I shall ever come to *déshabillé* in public."[62]

After the operation of 24 July, the state of Jessie's leg improved sufficiently to enable her to walk, "still on crutches but with the confidence that she will soon throw them off. It is a return to life for her, and—to tell the truth—for me as well. From 1917 I have lived in a kind of nightmare, unable to see its end," wrote Conrad to Gide. And he joked in a letter to Harriet Capes, "She's growing more active, restless, mischievous, independent, debonnaire, outspoken, and generally Shakespearian, every day."[63] Meanwhile, Conrad's own health was not too good. At the beginning of November he suffered an attack of gout and then felt unwell throughout the autumn.[64] The Napoleonic novel was at a standstill.[65] But he translated Jean-Aubry's article "Joseph Conrad's Confessions" into English, and adapted another of his stories, "Because of the Dollars," for the stage: he described it as "a play for Grand Guignol (English), 2 acts, 3 scenes. It will play forty minutes. Subject: Laughing Anne (Because of the Dollars)."[66] This short play was not staged at the time but Conrad's labors were not entirely wasted—because Wise bought the manuscript for £100.[67]

Although Conrad complained about his health and was unwilling to accompany Jessie to London, where she spent a week in November, he continued to lead a fairly active social life receiving guests and spending occasional weekends with the Pinkers at Reigate. About 20 December three Polish visitors came to Oswalds: the well-known composer Karol Szymanowski; the Polish chargé d'affaires in London, Konstanty Skirmunt; and a musician, Jan Effenberger-Śliwiński. Conrad and Szymanowski discovered that their families in the Ukraine had known each other very well.[68]

Toward the close of 1920 Conrad's mood turned gloomy. He confided to Garnett, "I have done nothing—can do nothing—don't want to do anything. One lives too long. Yet cutting one's throat would be too scandalous besides being unfair to other parties." Conrad struck a similar note in his letters to Rothenstein and Galsworthy.[69] Indeed, Conrad's 1920 harvest was very scanty: a few prefaces, less than three chapters of the novel, and two or three adaptations of his old pieces. Although gout now troubled him less than a dozen or so years earlier, there could be no doubt that age was taking its toll.

Conrad intended to make an energetic start in 1921. On 2 January Borys was to begin work in a radio-electric firm belonging to a Dr. Mackintosh.[70] Until then the young man had been in no hurry to find permanent employment; not particularly industrious by nature, Borys was still suffering the aftereffects of his war experiences in the form of sudden fits of terror. Jessie was unaware of her son's affliction, but Conrad knew about it and worried greatly about his future. He paid Borys an allowance enough to live on, and, in addition to occasional smaller sums of money, gave him £1,000 as capital.[71] On 21 January

John was placed in a good boarding school at Tonbridge. As for the elder Conrads, they were planning a car trip to Corsica. The main purpose of the journey was to help Jessie's recovery in a dry, warm climate. "She needs it, and it may do me good too,—but I doubt it," wrote Conrad to Rothenstein.[72] Shortly before departure a problem arose with Conrad's passport. He had never formally changed his surname ("I have not and do not intend [to] divest myself of it for sentimental reasons," he stated), but this time he asked that his passport be issued in the name of Conrad in order, as he said, to avoid complications on the way. Pinker had to intervene at the last moment with the officials in the Passport Office.[73]

The Conrads left on 23 January, accompanied by a nurse and a chauffeur. Borys was proud of having found an experienced driver for his parents; Jessie, on the other hand, considered him a "raw yokel." Jessie's account of the journey is another of her fantastic and peevish tales of woe about her grumpy, hysterical, and obtuse husband.[74] On the first leg of their journey they visited the battlefields near Armentières with Borys, and Conrad would interrupt his son's war stories, although he himself had asked Borys to recount his experiences. Jessie's explanation was that the "details were often too vividly described for his father to endure"; but it is more likely that Conrad was too impatient at his son's tendency to exaggerate.

In Rouen Jessie and Conrad parted with Borys, who, after a few days in Paris, returned to work in Mortlake. Borys's seat in the car was taken by Jean-Aubry, in whose company they reached Lyons via Orléans. In the course of the previous year or so the Frenchman had become one of the Conrads' closest and most intimate friends. Jean-Aubry translated Conrad, wrote laudatory articles about him, gave advice about continental publishers, and, above all, was a most willing participant in endless conversations. He wrote to Valéry Larbaud, "I frequently see Joseph Conrad who is kind enough to show an interest in and even an affection for me. . . . We often spend weekends together chatting about hundreds of things. He has an admirable mind and is altogether an adorable man."[75] Conrad was indeed very fond of Jean-Aubry's company, now and again stressing the specifically national aspect of their relationship, as when he thanked him for a walking stick: "Anglo-Saxonism is inappropriate here; please let me embrace you in a Franco-Polish fashion for your present. It is the nicest walking-stick in the world."[76]

Jean-Aubry's presence made this part of the journey more pleasant, and on 23 February Conrad wrote: "We missed you a lot, really a lot, after Lyons." Conrad sent Pinker a description of their subsequent drive to Montélimar: "We found a magnificent sunset over these wild and barren peaks. Then night set in and we had to lower the car as it were foot by foot under an amazingly starry sky, creeping down in perfect solitude into a sort of purple-black abyss which was in fact the Valley of the Rhône. . . . Great fun—to look back upon."[77]

In the afternoon of 30 January the travelers arrived in Marseilles, where Conrad took Jessie to the scenes of his youthful adventures. After a few pleasant days they took a boat for Ajaccio. The weather there was foul: "Cold. Wet. Horrors." They found the Grand Hôtel d'Ajaccio et Continental smart ("an atmosphere of intense good form pervades the place") but uncongenial. Three weeks later Conrad told Jean-Aubry, "This expedition is not quite the success we expected it to be. . . . I am nervous, irritable, bored—and so forth. La familia del Signor P[inker] is here. Miss Hallowes is arriving in a week's time. We have made no excursions. The afternoons are rather cold. The hotel is abominable. The Corsicans are charming . . . but the mountains with all those paths which wind and wind endlessly along the coast get on my nerves. One feels like howling."[78] Conrad complained about "my moral depression which I cannot shake off"; thus the change of surroundings did not help him at all. For Jessie, on the other hand, the stay on Corsica proved beneficial: "Jessie likes Corsica. She walks about with a stick and looks well."[79] In March, when the weather got warmer, the Conrads made many inland excursions—but they did not go to Bastia, from where Conrad could have taken a boat to the nearby island of Elba.

Conrad was rather sarcastic about the other hotel guests—it was the first time he had stayed under the same roof with a large group of wealthy English tourists; but Jessie says that they renewed a friendship with Sir Maurice Cameron, a colonial official, and made a new acquaintance, Alice Kinkead, a young Irish painter, affectionately called Kinkie, who was later a frequent visitor at Oswalds. Their closest contacts were with the Pinkers. Jessie recalls that "Mr Pinker had a knack of soothing my husband in difficult moods, who needed either sympathetic indulgence or tolerant disregard. Mr Pinker's wonderful voice was a joy and a delight to us all." On one occasion, however, it was Pinker who provoked Conrad's sudden anger. There was no electricity that day and dinner took place by candlelight. Conrad, ill-tempered for some reason, had been first to retire, but Jessie and the rest of the company stayed up late. Returning to their rooms they spontaneously formed a procession, each person carrying a candle. "J.B. Pinker walked first, the flickering light from his candle falling on his white head. His wonderful voice rose in a sacred chant and the waiters—all Swiss—fell into line with clasped hands or making the sign of the Cross. . . . Mr Pinker, deadly serious and filling the place with his voice, proceeded right to the door of our private sitting-room. Suddenly my husband flung it open and said icily: 'Yes, and I'm a Catholic, aren't I?'"[80] Jessie took this to be another one of Conrad's unpredictable eccentricities; there are several indications, however, that Conrad's attitude to religion was at that time undergoing a change. Such a change is indicated by the character of the parish priest in *The Rover*; and it is attested to by two other pieces of evidence. John Conrad relates that his father once took him to the church next to Oswalds, and there announced that profanity was the domain of the devil and that he,

Conrad, although nonpracticing, believed in God as "all true seamen do in their hearts."[81] And when Gordon Gardiner suggested that Conrad join a club whose members were in principle supposed to belong to the Anglican church, Conrad replied, "I was born a R.C. and though dogma sits lightly on me I have never renounced that form of Christian religion. The booklet of rules is so, I may say, theological that it would be like renouncing the faith of my fathers."[82]

It so happened that H.-R. Lenormand, a young French playwright and enthusiastic admirer of Dostoyevsky and of psychoanalysis, was staying in Ajaccio at the time. He presented himself to Conrad with an introduction from Robert d'Humières. Three years later he recalled how Conrad had confessed to him his inability to work: "The only really tragic cry that a writer may make 'I cannot work anymore!' was repeated almost every day during our conversations." Conrad could apparently express his most persistent anxieties to a little-known writer, and he confided to Lenormand that he thought continually about his death and had no hope of finishing the novel for which he wanted to gather material on Corsica. "I cannot find words which correspond to my thoughts. I am never sure of what I affirm. I am stupid." Lenormand was shocked by Conrad's refusal to read Freud, whose books he had lent him, or to discuss the subconscious motives influencing the behavior of his characters. Whenever Lenormand broached the subject, Conrad would recoil, "I am only a tale-teller," and then complain, "I am too conscious, I have lost all innocence." Even after admitting that he had always been fascinated by the father-daughter relationship, Conrad did not want to analyze *Almayer's Folly* from this point of view. "I do not want to reach the *depths*. I want to treat reality like a raw and rough object which I touch with my fingers. That is all," he allegedly said.[83] Evidently Lenormand failed to understand that by rejecting the temptation of psychoanalytical speculations, Conrad remained faithful to his artistic principles: he conceived his own role and duty as a writer to lie in depicting reality, not in seeking mysterious clues; in recording facts, not in imposing interpretive schemes upon them.

In spite of everything, Conrad later judged his sojourn on Corsica to have been quite successful. He had read a great deal and "picked up some good stuff for the novel."[84] Moreover, Conrad's creative sterility might have been easier to bear away from home, and away from the moral pressure experienced in the quiet of his own study. The Conrads hastened their departure from Corsica, fearing the possibility of a railway strike in England. They left Ajaccio on 7 April and were back in England on the tenth.[85] Waiting there was a long letter from St.-John Perse and the first reviews of *Notes on Life and Letters*, published on 25 March. St.-John Perse, the French poet and at the time secretary of the French Legation in Peking, wrote to Conrad about his impressions of China; recalling his visit at Capel House, he assured Conrad, "I think of you often, dear friend, and I wish that the old gout leaves you immediately, today, in order to preserve for your work the entire freedom of your spirit."[86]

Among the reviews of the *Notes on Life and Letters*, E. M. Forster's article "The Pride of Mr Conrad" was to gain a perhaps excessive fame because of its author's reputation and because of his opinion that Conrad "is misty in the middle as well as at the edges, that the secret casket of his genius contains a vapour rather than a jewel . . . No creed, in fact. Only opinions, and the right to throw them overboard when facts make them look absurd."[87] Alas, we know nothing about Conrad's reaction to this judgment. Other reviewers stressed Conrad's dislike of intimate revelations, and his tendency to keep readers at arm's length. Conrad must have been gratified by these comments, which were so consistent with his intentions and disposition. The critic of the London *Bookman* named the political essays as being of the greatest value and interest; considering that many of Conrad's views were completely new to the English tradition this was a perceptive judgment that could not but please Conrad.[88]

The Conrads found Borys again unemployed, apparently because of his firm's bankruptcy. At any rate, Borys needed his father's money even when he had a job; Jessie enigmatically mentions that his letters were "rather disquieting generally."[89] Borys's financial dependence and general instability had already lasted for two and a half years and were to continue still longer, further contributing to Conrad's worries.

It is not known how much money Conrad was spending on subsidizing various friends and members of the family. Only fragmentary data have been preserved—Jessie's mother received £12.10.0 a month, Karola Zagórska £120 and later £200 a year—but all in all the sum must have exceeded several hundred pounds a year.[90] The household expenses had by then grown to £2,300; this included Jessie's £728 shopping allowance; £500 for rent and gardening expenses; £400 for electricity, heating, and the car. Although Conrad's earnings that year came to £4,264, the sum left after subtracting all other expenditures could not have been very large.[91]

But there was enough to receive guests. They came to Oswalds almost every weekend and there was often someone staying for shorter or longer visits during the week. Miss Kinkead spent the first days of June at Oswalds and soon after Conrad wrote a eulogistic and evasive foreword, with hardly a word about painting, to a catalogue of her Corsican and Irish landscapes.[92]

The Conrads frequently exchanged visits with the Pinkers. Lord Northcliffe, who charmed Jessie with tales about his mother, also often came to Oswalds. Conrad's fear of strangers had obviously subsided, but his social contacts were mainly superficial; this was more satisfying for Jessie, who could now be a hostess without having to exert herself in the kitchen, than for Conrad, for whom these contacts brought much-needed distraction but seldom developed into more intimate relationships. In his letters to old friends, by now absorbed by their own careers, families, and worries, Conrad rarely omitted the opportunity to hark back to the days of close intimacy: "Dearest Jack, you have written me a letter of the dearest kind. Yes,—talk. But could we talk? Could we recapture the fine (though by no means careless) rapture of the early days? A sense of unreality creeps over all things—I am speaking for myself—which a life of industrious, say, stock-broking would not have left behind . . . perhaps!"[93] Conrad also missed Curle, who had been away from Europe for a year, and was happy to welcome him back in June. Curle was like a third son for Conrad, and the closest to him because of their common interests—Borys and John were indifferent to literature and the arts in general; and his relationship with Curle was free from conflict—even Curle's unsuccessful marriage had the effect of drawing them closer.

John Conrad's *Times Remembered* contains a revealing fragment about his father waking him up occasionally in the middle of the night to play chess: "I would feel his hand on my shoulder and hear him ask me to come down for a game. I would put on my dressing-gown and slippers, brush my hair and descend to the study to find the chessboard set out and a glass of lemon tea waiting for me. Sometimes, after playing a few moves he would get up and walk to his desk, sit down and start writing."[94] Such sudden need for human company is quite common among depressive artists who, left to themselves and their excruciating struggle, feel unable to bear the pain of loneliness.

Conrad tried to take up his work on the "Mediterranean" novel but found it difficult: "I can't get my teeth into the novel. I am altogether in the dark as to what it is about. I am depressed and exasperated at the same time and I only wish I could say to myself that I don't care. But I do care. A horrid state." As usual, Conrad was more optimistic with Pinker, informing him on that same day that he had made "a good start with the novel" and boasting two days later of having just written fifteen hundred words.[95] The discrepancies in Conrad's statements reflect in part his wish to give Pinker the impression that he was being more productive than he was, and in part his constant changes of mood. On the whole, however, he was telling the truth when he reflected that "what with one thing and another, I don't feel very happy";[96] and the chief cause was probably his inability to "get his teeth into the novel."

Perhaps this was why, quite unexpectedly, Conrad began translating from Polish. In May 1921 Bruno Winawer, a columnist and writer of comedies and an excellent popularizer of contemporary physics, sent Conrad his newly published short play *The Book of Job*, asking Conrad for help in finding a translator. Conrad answered evasively, painting an exaggerated picture of his helplessness ("I do not know a single actor or actress, director or capitalist entrepreneur, nor in fact anything that is the theatre's") and promised nothing except to investigate the possibilities when time allowed. However, when he wrote his first letter to Winawer on 12 June, Conrad must not only have decided to translate Winawer's play himself, but even made considerable progress; nine days later he offered Wise the manuscript of the translation.[97] On 27 June Conrad gave the text to Norman McKinnel, with whom he had been negotiating the staging of *The*

Secret Agent; but only two months later did he divulge the whole truth to Winawer and send him the translation.[98]

Such secretiveness was unusual for Conrad. He probably wanted to give Winawer a pleasant surprise; he might also have hoped to be able to announce his success in placing the play in some theater. The decision to translate this particular piece was partly accidental: Winawer's book arrived at the time when Conrad could not bring himself to work on his own novel and, for the sake of distraction, he probably decided to have a go at translating from his mother tongue. Conrad wrote to Winawer that he found *The Book of Job* very amusing; he probably did, as the play is quite funny, although it is also insubstantial and contrived, a little like a series of sketches put together. Some ideas and scenes, however, might have been particularly to Conrad's taste: bitter attacks against contemporary materialism; the satirical presentation of society's contempt for the protagonist, Dr. Herup, an inspired and eccentric scientist; and also Herup's playful mysogyny. Conrad was certainly acting in good faith when he later tried to persuade Allan Wade, a theater producer, that the play was pretty good and should do well on stage. Conrad also thought of arousing the public's interest by putting the translator's name on the bill as Mr. X, though without concealing his identity. "What I would like is that when it gets as far as the bill stage Mr X should remain, while at the same time everybody would know who Mr X is."[99]

Had the text been more obviously difficult Conrad would certainly not have attempted the translation. But the language is easy, colloquial, slightly individualized. Particularly Herup and a snobbish Jew, "Bolo" Bendziner, have their characteristic ways of speaking. Conrad, who had had little contact with everyday spoken Polish, simplified the dialogue, left out Herup's scientific expressions, and missed many amusing nuances.[100] The action in the original is quite clearly set in contemporary Warsaw, somewhere between elegant society and the demimonde; this specific cultural setting is lost in the translation. Conrad left out many accents of topical satire in the presentation of the dramatis personae and ignored not only the ungrammatical speech (which might have escaped him) of some characters but even the Jewishness of two of them, Bolo and Mosan. Now and then Conrad is accused of anti-Semitism; apart from other evidence, the fact that he translated Winawer's comedy also shows this accusation to be unfounded: the author's Polish-Jewish origin must have been well known to Conrad.*

Winawer was pleased with the translation,[101] but in spite of Conrad's efforts

---

* F. R. Karl writes that Conrad's "attitude towards Jews was altered by his association with Pinker" (*Joseph Conrad: The Three Lives* [New York, 1979], p. 867). But he offers no evidence for Pinker being Jewish or Conrad thinking him Jewish. For Karl the main instance of Conrad's "anti-Semitism" was the latter's contemptuous attitude toward Unwin—but Unwin certainly was not Jewish. (See Philip Unwin, *The Publishing Unwins* [London, 1972], p. 11).

The Book of Job was never staged in England, and the English version was published only after the translator's death.

In the summer of 1921 Conrad felt "fairly well,"[102] but wrote little. On 27 July he published a short article on "The Dover Patrol" in *The Times*; it dealt with the contribution of local merchant seamen to the war effort.[103] "I am trying desperately to get on with the novel," Conrad wrote to Curle on 31 August, but in fact a month later he had only arrived at page 210, which means that he had not yet completed Part 2 of *Suspense*.[104]

Social life, however, flourished. The Pinkers spent weeks on end at Oswalds, and Sidney Cockerell, Curle, Hope, Walpole, and many others paid frequent visits. It is impossible to tell to what extent those social activities hindered Conrad's work and to what extent they merely helped him forget his inability to write. "I wish I could exclude all sounds and sights from my life and devote myself for the next 25 days to that novel which has not even a name. The sun, the wind, the little birds, the electric pump, everything seems to get in the way. It's like trying to fight off a cloud of gnats," he moaned.[105] Five days later he laid the "novel without a title" aside and started a new piece, the future *Rover*.[106] But here, too, Conrad made no appreciable headway, and after two months barely fifty-five hundred words had been set down on paper. The story was supposed to be about twelve thousand words long (the same length as "Amy Foster"); Conrad intended to have it finished by February 1922 and to put it in one volume with "Prince Roman"—the February deadline was connected with Pinker's projected voyage to the United States. By the middle of December, with the title already decided upon, Conrad announced his intention to "make that tale as long as possible, within the long short-story limits . . . that by itself it may fill up the volume of short stories up to their proper market capacity."[107] The same anxious concern about earnings, connected with his sense of declining strength, prompted Conrad to sell Wise the manuscript of the still-unfinished novel and to contemplate various special and luxury editions that could bring large royalties.[108]

Apart from all else, money opened the way to escape, even if only temporarily, from everything. In November 1921 Mrs. Kate Meyrick, an energetic provider of nightlife for fashionable London, opened her best-known club, the "43," at 43 Gerrard Street. In spite of frequent conflicts with the police, caused mainly by the violation of licensing hours, Mrs. Meyrick found favor in the eyes of high society: all three of her daughters (and collaborators in business) were eventually married off to lords. Among the patrons of the "43" were the painter Augustus John, the sculptor Jacob Epstein, the writer J. B. Priestley, boxing champion Georges Carpentier, and many other celebrities. Mrs. Meyrick recalled, "Joseph Conrad was another early visitor. With his short rough beard, his clothes of nautical cut and his twinkling eyes, he looked exactly what he was—an ex-sailor. I fell at once under the influence of his charm and simplicity; he was so direct, so completely natural. I used to feel I wanted to leave my work and just talk to him. He seemed attracted to me, too, for he said on leaving that he hoped soon to come again for a longer chat. Sad to say, however, that never came to pass. Whenever he visited the club after that the crowds of other people kept us all too hard at work for a chance of any real conversation."[109]

Whatever Conrad's pastimes, he was painfully aware of his mental decrepitude.[110] He was pleased to receive Russell's fundamental book on the philosophy of knowledge, *The Analysis of Mind*, but although he read it with great enthusiasm he was unable to maintain a continuous discussion about it with its author. Russell gave Conrad another quite unexpected pleasure by naming his son after him. Conrad wrote, "I am profoundly touched—more than I can express—that I should have been present to your mind in that way and at such a time."[111]

Conrad had no doubt as to the main cause of his permanent sadness. He wrote nostalgically to Graham, "Ever since I saw You in London I have been seedy and often in pain; which I would not mind much but for the depression (consequent on the inability to work seriously)—which I can not somehow shake off. Your letter so full of friendship and appreciation was a great moral tonic. . . . You have been one of my moral supports through my writing life . . . Yours with the greatest affection."[112]

Conrad's erstwhile friendship with Ford was, on his side at least, defunct. Conrad replied promptly to Ford's request to settle some old accounts, at once sending £20, claiming that he was unable to send more because, allegedly, for the last two years his writings had brought him no money. He clearly tried to keep Ford at a distance,[113] although he was not as forthright and consistent about it as he was with Elsie Hueffer who, quite unexpectedly and for reasons known only to herself, had tried, a year earlier, to revive the friendship that had been broken off many years before. Conrad answered politely that he considered it pointless.[114]

"I could not work properly the whole of last year—I could not even concentrate my thoughts without a great effort. This makes me worried and fretful. Je ne suis pas très heureux ma chère," Conrad wrote on 27 January 1922 to Aniela Zagórska in a macaronic Polish-French letter.[115] (Inability to concentrate on any kind of work that is not routine and automatic is another characteristic symptom of depression.[116]) The new year also started off badly: "For about a month I have been in bed with influenza complicated by an attack of gout. C'était charmant. Only today I have come down to my study, where everything somehow looks strange and uninviting."[117] Before Conrad had the time to recover from his last illness, he was struck by a new blow: on 8 February 1922 James B. Pinker died suddenly in New York. The news made a deep impression on Conrad. "Twenty years' friendship and for most of that time in the constant interchange of the most intimate thoughts and feelings created a bond as strong as the nearest relationship," read Conrad's cable to the bereaved son. Conrad also confided his feeling of deep loss to Walpole; and when the latter had published a moving obituary, Conrad threw his arms round Walpole's neck and embraced him when they met in London. Conrad was well aware how much he owed to Pinker, who for so many years had shown his trust in him by extending generous financial support.[118]

Eric Pinker inherited his father's business, and with it the running of Conrad's affairs—"But it will never be the same," Conrad wrote to Karola Zagórska.[119] The irreplaceable Curle helped Conrad sort out his finances.[120] "My financial situation is a bit shaky. Pinker was an optimist. For the last two years my expenses were too big and now I shall have to suffer for it," he told his cousin in Poland.[121] Eric Pinker, like his father before him, had to look after Borys's affairs as well. In August 1921 Borys at last found work with a London car-dealing firm, run by colleagues from the army. But by March he was again in trouble and Conrad had to rush to his aid.[122]

On 20 March Conrad told Curle, "I have been working hard ever since you left the house, dictating in the morning, correcting all the rest of the time." At the beginning of April his gout became worse and he had to remain in bed—but this time he continued to work. He dictated lying down and kept assuring Eric Pinker that he was in good spirits. On 10 April he got out of bed and two weeks later sent off chapters 4, 5, and 6 of *The Rover*.[123] At that time Conrad carried on an extensive correspondence about *The Secret Agent* and *The Book of Job* with Allan Wade. As when writing earlier to Galsworthy, he did his best to point out the merits of his play. But in the first place he referred to its "excessively Conradian" quality, and thus to what could be associated with, rather than what was contained by, the text. Conrad also admitted that precisely because he was not a playwright, he was counting on a *succès de curiosité*.[124] J. Harry Benrimo of the Ambassadors Theatre probably cherished similar hopes when he decided some months later to stage *The Secret Agent*.

Meantime the news of Conrad's translation of Winawer's piece must have gotten around, and from several sides Conrad was being approached about translations of Polish writers' work. Garnett sounded him about a novel, *The History of a Sin*, by Stefan Żeromski, at that time a leading Polish novelist. Conrad's reaction was negative: "Honestly I don't think it will do for translation. . . . The whole thing is disagreeable and often incomprehensible in comment and psychology. Often it is gratuitously ferocious. You know I am not squeamish. The other work the great historical machine is called *Ashes* (Popioły). Both of course have a certain greatness—the greatness of a wild landscape—and both take too much for granted in the way of receptivity and tolerance."[125] Nevertheless he wrote Zagórska, "Be so kind, my dear, as to remember me to Mr. Żeromski and give him my deeply sincere regards. C'est un Maître! The impression left by his personality has remained vivid in my memory."[126] More and more books by contemporary Polish writers kept arriving. We do not know which of them Conrad read, but he certainly did read, and with great interest, Zofia Kossak-Szczucka's *The Blaze*, a stirring documentary about the Bolshevik Revolution in the Ukraine.[127]

Desmond MacCarthy, a prominent English critic and essayist, visited Conrad in the spring of 1922. MacCarthy recalls in his *Portraits*:

> The length of his head from chin to crown struck me, and this was accentuated by a pointed greyish beard, which a backward carriage of his head on high shoulders projected forwards. Black eyebrows, hooked nose, hunched shoulders gave him a more hawk-like look than even his photograph had suggested. His eyes were very bright and dark when he opened them wide, but unless lit and expanded by enthusiasm of indignation, they remained half-hidden, and as though filmed in a kind of abstruse slumberous meditation. Very quiet in voice and gesture, somewhat elaborate in courtesies, his manner was easy without being reassuring. He had the kind of manners which improve those of a visitor beyond recognition. He was very much the *foreign* gentleman. He evidently expected others not only to respect his dignity (that went without saying) but their own. I surmised that, like his own people, the Poles, and like the Irish, he might be lavish in compliment, but that anyone would be a fool who did not divine that his delicious generosity of praise might hide reserves of caustic severity. Following the sea had not left a trace of bluffness in his manner. His talk was that of a man who cares for what is delicate, extreme, and honourable in human nature—and for the art of prose. Intellectually, he seemed something of a Quietist; he did not enjoy provoking discussion.[128]

This "quietist" attitude may have been in Conrad simply an aspect of his politeness, a part of his exquisite manners—sometimes baffling to his less-well-bred interlocutors—which John Conrad remembers so well.[129]

However, when in April Curle sent Conrad the manuscript of his article "Joseph Conrad in the East," Conrad did start a discussion himself. In a friendly but forcible way, he attacked two of Curle's ideas: first, the suggestion that there exists a close link between the contents of Conrad's works and their origin—particularly their authentic, local background (Conrad's own Author's Notes had been partly responsible for this idea); second, Curle's descriptions of Conrad as a gloomy and tragic writer. Even earlier, feeling apprehensive about the subject of Curle's article, Conrad had tried to draw attention to his other, and by no means exotic, interests: "You may just as well say, which is a truth, that I do read biography and memoirs. History has a fascination for me. Naval, military, political." Curle, a professional journalist, tended to interpret Conrad as if he were a writing globe-trotter. Conrad protested: "It is a strange fate that everything that I have, of set artistic purpose, laboured to leave indefinite, suggestive, in the penumbra of initial inspiration, should have that light turned on to it and its insignificance (as compared with I might say without megalomania the ampleness of my conceptions) exposed for any fool to comment upon or even for average minds to be disappointed with." For other and clearly commercial reasons, Conrad insisted that Curle cross out the sentences about: "gloom, oppression, and tragedy. . . . That reputation, whether justified or not, has deprived me of innumerable readers . . . I absolutely object to being called a '*tragedian*.' The thing is shocking." Conrad entered his own corrections on the copy which he had received, and also asked Curle to add that his books had "the quality of interest—as the m-in-the-s understands it—the interest of surprise, of story etc." [130] Curle meekly complied with all the recommendations. In this way Conrad himself promoted a shallow understanding of his own works, and in this case all the more pointlessly since Curle was writing not for the popular press but for a high-brow audience.

In May Conrad went to London several times, and later visited the Pinkers. A letter to Garnett, however, gave a doleful report on his state of mind: "As soon as I get away from home I seem to go to pieces mentally and physically." He complained about his current work, which he still expected to be a long short story: "I will make you a signal about joining company . . . directly *The Rover* has ceased to rove—and be damned to him. You have no idea how that fellow and a lot of other crazy creatures that got into my head have also got on my nerves. I have never known anything like this before. I have been infinitely depressed about a piece of work, but never so exasperated with anything I have had to do." Nevertheless he continued to work, and quite fast at that. During May and June he produced ten chapters—two-thirds of the novel. "The whole thing came on me at the last as through a broken dam. . . . Could hardly bear to speak to anybody." [131]

Conrad described *The Rover* later as "a thing of sentiment—of many sentiments." [132] Indeed this was the only book written in the closing years of his life which engaged many of the author's deepest sentiments: his nostalgia for the Mediterranean, his dislike of revolution, and his acquired English patriotism which is in constant contrast to the austere and yet spontaneous attachment to man's native soil shown by the novel's French hero.

Conrad finished writing *The Rover* on 27 June; until 16 July he corrected and supplemented the text, bringing the total number of chapters to sixteen. [133] The novel, he reported to Galsworthy, "has gone out of the house: and it's like waking up out of a nightmare of endless effort to get out of a bog." [134]

Even before he finished revising the text, Conrad had to go to London for a week. Borys again had made a mess of his affairs and had run up heavy debts. "I hope I received the shock with becoming fortitude. One does not want to quarrel with one's son as long as one still keeps some belief in him. It is a crippling affair for me. One could get the money by extra work but in this affair the element of time is important."[135] To Jean-Aubry, Conrad deplored the "bitter disappointment" and the "depressing atmosphere" of the "difficult affair"—although his letter to Borys, written shortly afterward, while brief and matter-of-fact, shows no signs of resentment.[136] We do not know how large the sum involved was, but it was exactly at this time that Conrad had to apply to his bank for a loan of £500.[137] Luckily Borys soon found permanent and well-paid employment: in mid-August he began work in Coventry, for Daimler, the car manufacturers.[138] As it transpired, he immediately drew practical conclusions from this turn in his affairs.

.It was probably the perturbations caused by Borys which prompted Conrad to settle the problems of his inheritance; on 1 August he drew up his will. His beneficiaries were Jessie, with three-fifths of the income from the residuary trust funds, and his two sons, with one-fifth each of the income. The trust itself was to be administered by the will's executors, Ralph L. Wedgwood and Richard Curle.[139] Thus Jessie's income, although liberally apportioned, was to be kept in check: she could not use the capital.

As long before as January 1920 Curle had asked Conrad to write a preface to his *Wanderings*, a volume of travel articles; at the time Conrad talked him out of this idea, arguing that it would look too much like favoritism. Now Curle, who was putting the final touches to his new volume, *Into the East*, repeated his request and Conrad, deeply indebted to him, was unable to refuse. In the last week of July he wrote the preface in the form of an essay about travel books in general.[140] That done, he consoled himself with the thought that he would at last be able to concentrate, without impediments, on his "half-written" Mediterranean novel, which he would complete by the beginning of the next year.[141] Physically he felt "pretty well," and believed the improvement to be lasting.[142] At the same time, however, he sounded a despondent note in a letter to Galsworthy: "My very soul is aching all over. My fault of course."[143] For several months he wrote nothing. "I've lived and that's enough," he told Jean-Aubry laconically.[144] Neither the visit he and John had paid to Robert Jones in Liverpool nor an excursion to northern Wales helped him shake off his depression.[145] He was wrestling with his disability. As he unburdened himself to Curle, "I have been doing nothing but thinking—absorbing myself in constant meditation—over the novel. It's almost there! Almost to be grasped. Almost ready to flow over the paper—but not quite yet. I am fighting off depression. A word from you would help."[146]

At the beginning of October Conrad became very excited by the preparations for the staging of *The Secret Agent*. The very fact that the play had been accepted was enough to stimulate Conrad to consider further stage adaptations. "I don't know, my dear, whether it ever struck you that there is a very possible play in the *Arrow*. . . . there is the drama contained in *Western Eyes* of which, as a matter of fact, I have the first and last act in my head very definitely indeed." Conrad's wish to find a substitute, in the form of reprocessing his old works, for writing new pieces of which he was becoming incapable, is clearly visible, although he found other reasons: "There is a fascination in doing a thing like that over again in another medium; that is, if one were certain of intelligent interpretation. And if later people were suddenly to begin to say 'Here is Conrad been writing those blessed tales and now, after thinking some of them over for fifteen years, he attempts to show us how they ought to be told on the stage'—well, my career as a whole is exceptional enough to have that evolution in it, too, recognized as a manifestation of creative art." Eric Pinker, however, appealed to Conrad to remain faithful to the novel, and managed to dissuade him from this venture.[147]

At first Conrad was quite pleased with the rehearsals. In time, however, he became more and more uneasy: he argued with the director about the cuts, although later he maintained that he had introduced them himself; he was irritated by the acting of some roles, and complained that "these people will never be able to understand the piece—let alone learn it reasonably well before Thursday"; and he confessed that he was "quite downhearted" and "exceedingly annoyed by this damned play."[148] Conrad attended all the rehearsals, including the dress rehearsal. This intimate acquaintance with the stage made an unsettling impression on him: "An air of unreality, weird unreality, envelops the words, the ideas and the arguments we exchange, the familiar words of the play, the figures of the people; clings to the very walls, permeates the darkness of the fantastic cavern which I can by no means imagine will ever contain anything so real as an audience of men and women." A couple of days before the first night he told Garnett, "The thing has been marvellously vulgarised. I don't know whether to laugh or to swear."[149] On the first night, 2 November, Conrad stayed at home, apparently because of a cough, but he sent along Jessie, who was delighted with her outing. Conrad remained in London overnight, impatiently awaiting news from the theater; but he did not go to any of the ten performances.[150]

The play received a bad press and the public remained indifferent. The critics were inclined to pick at the text, while on the whole praising the acting. When comforted by friends, Conrad assured them that the flop did not worry him— but actually it was a case of keeping a stiff upper lip. In trying to explain the failure of the play he changed his tune, and far from blaming the actors admitted that he had not been fair to them. He insisted, however, that "even a play written by an angel could not have stood up against the weight of a unanimous press," and added words of sympathy for the actors.[151] Asked by the *Evening Standard* what he thought about the unfavorable reception of *The Secret Agent*, Conrad answered magnanimously, "I think no playwright has ever been executed with such consideration and friendliness, so that I don't even feel guilty. The only painful part of it is the loss of the hard work of everyone concerned being wasted." [152] His ultimate consolation was the fact that he had anticipated failure. [153]

On the day *The Secret Agent* was removed from the bill, Conrad finished, as if symbolically, his essay "Outside Literature"—a eulogy of the clear and precise prose of the Notices to Mariners, which are written in a style that can be objectively evaluated. [154]

A few weeks earlier, in a long letter, Conrad discussed the programme of political reforms in China which was contained in Bertrand Russell's book, *The Problem of China*. Convinced at the time that it was both legitimate and necessary to introduce socialist reforms, Russell had argued for the establishment in China of a kind of an oligarchy of sages who would then reshape the society in the right spirit. Conrad protested, explaining his own distrust of political panaceas:

> I have never been able to find in any man's book or any man's talk anything convincing enough to stand up for a moment against my deep-seated sense of fatality governing this man-inhabited world. . . . The only remedy for Chinamen and for the rest of us is the change of hearts, but looking at the history of the last 2000 years there is not much reason to expect that thing, even if man has taken to flying—a great "uplift" no doubt but no great change. He doesn't fly like an eagle, he flies like a beetle. And you must have noticed how ugly, ridiculous and fatuous is the flight of a beetle.

A quarter of a century had passed since his polemic with Graham but Conrad still did not believe in the spontaneous goodness of human nature. The same skepticism that made him doubt whether men could rid themselves of their faults and weaknesses by embracing correct opinions made him sharply oppose the system of government advocated by Russell:

> If a constitution proclaimed in the light of day, with at least a chance of being understood by the people, is not to be relied on, then what trust could one put in a self-appointed and probably secret association (which from the nature of things must be above the law) to commend or condemn individuals or institutions? . . . There is not enough honour, virtue and selflessness *in the world* to make any such council other than the greatest danger to every kind of moral, mental and political independence. It would become a centre of delation, intrigue and jealousy of the most debased kind. No freedom of thought, no peace of heart, no genius, no virtue, no individuality trying to raise its head above the subservient mass, would be safe before the domination of such a council, and the unavoidable demoralisation of the instruments of this power. [155]

It seems that in spite of his earlier scoffing at democracy, Conrad considered it to be a better system after all. This conclusion is borne out by Conrad's comments on the success of the Labour party, which had emerged from the elections of 15 November 1922 as the second largest party in the United Kingdom and thus acquired the status of being the official opposition. He wrote to a friend on 20 November, "I don't know that the advent of class-parties into politics is abstractly good in itself. Class for me is by definition a hateful thing. The only class really worth consideration is the class of honest and able men to whatever sphere of human activity they may belong—that is, the class of workers throughout the nation. . . . But if class-parties are to come into being . . . I am glad that this one had a considerable success at the elections."[156]

Conrad complained to Russell about his "unaccountable depression." When writing a month later to Sandeman, he was in the same mood, and quoted an anonymous American: "Life is just one damned thing after another." He declared himself bored with "the stupidity of the whole thing" he was working on—because he "must." He insisted that he "must" finish the novel by April or even March.[157] By mid-December forty-five thousand words were down on paper (Parts 1 and 2; thus in fourteen months he had dictated barely nineteen pages) and he had at last decided on a provisional title—*Suspense*.[158]

Insurmountable difficulties with writing—with what for years had provided the very meaning of his life—produced a visible incongruity in Conrad's behavior, a discrepancy noticed by Walter Tittle, a graphic artist who visited Conrad in November 1922. "He spoke much of fatigue, and his eyes showed evidence of it, and he talked nervously of much to do and little time to do it. Yet his manner was gay and exceedingly animated; his utterances came in a romping torrent with a very considerable expenditure of nervous energy. . . . Alertness, burning energy, humour, transcendent intelligence, and abundant kindliness are there. When he gives of himself there is no stinting."[159] Social contacts had to make up for the loss of artistic creativity.

Conrad's reading at the time was apparently confined to Proust, who had died on 18 November 1922.[160] In December Conrad wrote a fine note, praising the Frenchman's "veiled greatness," consisting of masterly analysis carried to the point where it becomes creative. Jean-Aubry believed that Conrad, next to José Ortega y Gasset, had been the first writer to have truly appreciated Proust; it testifies to Conrad's lasting spiritual agility that he was able to take Proust up so late in his own life. Throughout the twenties Conrad's reading of French literature was particularly extensive. This was partly connected with his work on the "French" historical novels, *The Rover* and *Suspense*; but he also read contemporary writers such as Gide, Larbaud, Valéry, and many others.[161]

It was at this time that Conrad made the acquaintance of two distinguished Frenchmen: Paul Valéry and Maurice Ravel. He met them both in the London salon of Lady Colefax, and they immediately felt a strong mutual attraction. "The two of them were charming to me," Conrad told Gide. "The moment I saw Valéry I felt a real affection for him"—and he promptly invited the poet to Oswalds, where Valéry came in October. Conrad met Ravel again in April

1923, and in October of the same year both the composer and the poet visited Oswalds. They had a lively discussion about the fighting qualities of the British and French navies at the time of Napoleon—a subject close to Conrad's heart because of *The Rover*. Valéry was astonished by Conrad's "horrible" accent in English.[162]

The steadily growing renown and prestige among writers and critics across the Channel which Conrad was enjoying ("Boom in J.C. in France," he boasted to Curle[163]), were not only a source of immediate pleasure but also fostered Conrad's hopes for the Nobel Prize. Significantly, it was apparently the French and Swedes—and not the English—who favored Conrad's candidacy. Conrad, greatly stirred by the possibility of the prize, thought that the publication of *The Rover* would enhance his chances.[164]

Conrad never made any public statements on the subject of what was being written about him at the time, and only rarely, more rarely indeed than in the past, would he comment about it in private. The only problem on which he was outspoken was his alleged "Slavonism." When his enthusiastic admirer Mencken used this term to describe his attitude, Conrad protested vehemently. In a letter to George T. Keating he called Mencken's words "mere parrot talk," and perorated, "I wonder what meaning he attaches to the word. Does he mean by it primitive natures fashioned by [a] byzantino-theological conception of life, with an inclination to perverted mysticism? . . . Racially I belong to a group which has historically a political past, with a Western Roman culture derived at first from Italy and then from France; and a rather Southern temperament; an outpost of Westernism with a Roman tradition, situated between Slavo-Tartar Byzantine barbarism on one side and the German tribes on the other; resisting both influences desperately and still remaining true to itself to this very day."[165] Thus for Conrad "Slavonism" was evidently synonymous with Dostoyevsky-ism.

A year later he again argued this point in a letter to Charles Chassé: "The critics detected in me a new note and as, just when I began to write, they had discovered the existence of Russian authors, they stuck that label on me under the name of Slavonism. What I venture to say is that it would have been more just to charge me at most with 'Polonism.'"[166]

To hint at his Polish heritage, Conrad placed his Nałęcz coat of arms on the cover of the complete edition of his works; with this purpose in mind he had even ordered the appropriate volume of an armorial.[167] Meanwhile, thanks to the efforts of Aniela Zagórska, a selected edition of Conrad's writings—the first collected edition of his works in translation—began appearing in Poland. Aniela Zagórska's translation of *Almayer's Folly* opened the series, and the leading Polish writer, Stefan Żeromski, who exercised a considerable moral authority over his country, wrote the preface. Żeromski brushed aside the question, frequently raised in Poland, of Conrad's "defection" from Polish culture: "No one has the right to interfere in his decisions. It may be taken as a matter of chance that his crib stood here." Moreover, he declared with magnanimous exaggeration that "not a single thread links Joseph Conrad's purely artistic heritage to Polish literature." But he described in lofty and highly emotional terms Conrad's family tradition and the martyrdom of his parents, and advanced the hypothesis ("rather risky perhaps," as he himself admitted) that Conrad created as if in two languages, arriving at English words through Polish thoughts and images, and that it was from the Polish that he took the music of his phrases.[168]

Conrad thanked Żeromski for the preface: "I confess that I cannot find words to describe my profound emotion when I read this appreciation from my country, voiced by you, dear Sir—the greatest master of its literature.

"Please accept, dear Sir, my most sincere thanks for the time, thought, and work you have devoted to me and for the sympathetic assessment which disclosed a compatriot in the author." He signed himself J. K. Korzeniowski.[169]

Conrad took a lively interest in the translations. Trusting Aniela Zagórska, he generally accepted "in advance all changes." The finished translation left him "satisfied and even more than satisfied," and he was right in his assessment: Zagórska's work was indeed outstanding.[170] But Conrad also regarded as "really very good" Leon Piwiński's mediocre translation of "Il Conde," which had been sent to him for perusal. Conrad suggested several changes which demonstrate that although in some instances his sense of shades of meaning and style in Polish was excellent, it was in general uneven and incomplete.[171] The pressure of using and hearing English had brought about a deterioration in his Polish syntax—as his few letters in Polish testify; they also show that whenever he wanted to express a more complex idea, he resorted to French expressions.

Toward the end of 1922 Conrad again found himself in financial straits; he even advanced the idea of moving to southern France where living was cheaper and some English taxes could be evaded.[172] Pressed by necessity he accepted the proposal of his American publisher, Frank Nelson Doubleday—called Effendi from his initials—to give a few talks in the United States. His visit there was supposed to stir up interest in his works and boost sales. Doubleday issued the invitation when they met for lunch in London on 6 December. "I must confess," wrote Conrad to Karola Zagórska, "that I am not really keen on this trip. But it's a must. Everyone says that it will greatly improve my business affairs."[173] This consideration apparently mastered Conrad's fear of public appearances; and at least America was not England, and there his accent would matter less. His talks were to be held in private homes, and for invited audiences only.[174]

From 1 January 1923 Conrad applied himself zealously to the novel. For a few weeks he did not even complain about his health. But although he worked "with desperate determination," he was dissatisfied with the results.[175] "No doubt the anxiety itself prevents me in a way to reach my best. I find life rather a trial just now."[176] And Conrad kept worrying so much because he was conscious of the fact that "my reputation hangs on its [*Suspense*'s] quality." "It is a big piece of work—the biggest since 'Western Eyes.'"[177] At the beginning of March he arrived at the end of Part 3 and decided to have a short break; now he planned to have the novel finished by September or October 1923.[178]

During the break Conrad hastily produced two articles about Stephen Crane: a longer introduction to Crane's biography written by Thomas Beer, and a short preface to a new edition of *The Red Badge of Courage*.[179] The first is an affectionate recollection of his friend; Conrad was not satisfied with the piece: he described it to Pinker as "mostly twaddle," claiming also to have made use there of material for the continuation of his *Personal Record*, which "I have had long in my mind."[180]

As the time of departure for the United States approached, Conrad's interest in the expedition kept diminishing, and he admitted his lack of enthusiasm to his friends: "But the less I think of it the better, or I may die of funk before I put foot on that distant shore."[181] Nevertheless he was preparing notes for talks he intended to give, particularly for one about the affinities between the novel and the film.[182] Also, to test himself and to gain practice, he decided to give a speech at the annual meeting of the Lifeboat Institution.[183]

Conrad left Oswalds on 16 April. First he visited his old friend Hope, who was recovering from a stroke. On the seventeenth he made his public appearance at the Aeolian Hall in London. The guests of honor were lifeboat crews from Lowestoft; Conrad reminisced flatteringly (and inaccurately) about how he had served under the red ensign the first time on a sailing ship from Lowestoft. That evening he met Arnold Bennett and Maurice Ravel for dinner. On 20 April Conrad, accompanied by Curle, left London for Glasgow, and the following day sailed on the *Tuscania*. Her captain, David Bone, was an old friend of Conrad's and the brother of Muirhead Bone, a popular illustrator whom Conrad also knew, and who was also on board as passenger.[184]

Jessie was again suffering acute pain in her unfortunate knee. On the day of Conrad's departure from London she was examined by Robert Jones, who issued an optimistic prognosis. Conrad wrote to the surgeon that without his wife he would feel like a "lost sheep." He reported the course of his voyage to Jessie, saying that "the passage was good and M. Bone has been looking after me like a good fellow," and confessing that he was longing for her and the boys. He also missed Curle's help and his soothing support. In spite of his low spirits Conrad managed to write a short article "My Hotel in Mid-Atlantic"; contrary to the title, it consists mainly of Conrad's recollections of intercontinental voyages he had made on the *Torrens*. Here, Conrad's contempt for the boredom of modern travel in idle comfort found discreet but unambiguous expression.[185]

The *Tuscania* reached New York on 1 May. "I will not attempt to describe to you my landing, because it is indescribable. To be aimed at by forty cameras held by forty men that look as if they came out of the slums is a nerve-shattering experience. Even D'day looked exhausted after we had escaped from that mob— and the other mob of journalists."

Conrad wrote to Jessie a few days later, after he had recovered his composure, "Then a Polish deputation—men and women (some of these quite pretty)—rushed me on the wharf and thrust enormous nosegays into my hands. Eric nobly carried two of them. Mrs D'day took charge of another. I went along like a man in a dream and took refuge in D's car."[186] He had never before been the center of public interest on such a scale. As a rule he had avoided journalists and defended his privacy; now every movement he made and every word he uttered was carefully watched and reported. And although Doubleday shielded Conrad from intrusions and protected him from becoming overtired, he was at the same time anxious to make full use of Conrad's visit for publicity purposes. At that time Conrad was better known to the American than to the English reading public, and so newspapermen were out to feed their readers with as many personal details, singularities, and "intimate" statements of the famous author as possible. Thus Conrad was a popular celebrity in the public eye, which he had never been in England; hence his bewilderment. Journalists tended to stress, as something exotic, the seaman side in Conrad; and he himself also consistently avoided all "literary" questions and kept saying that he was not "a literary man"—but "a seaman, and never anything else."[187]

Luckily, Conrad did not stay in New York but at Doubleday's private residence, Effendi Hill, at Oyster Bay on Long Island. There he rested for a few days after the voyage. Powell came for a visit and on 3 May gave a private recital. One evening F. Scott Fitzgerald, who lived nearby at Great Neck and was already well known as the author of *This Side of Paradise*, together with Ring Lardner decided to tell Conrad of their admiration. But it was not easy to break through Doubleday's protective barriers; and so the two writers hit upon the scheme of performing a dance on the lawn in front of the Doubleday's residence in order to attract attention in a manner that was both subtle and artistic. Unfortunately, they were chased away for drunken and disorderly behavior.[188]

From 5 May on Conrad was constantly on the move. That very day he gave a talk to the staff of the Doubleday Company at Garden City. But he spoke too softly and his audience, unaccustomed to Conrad's Anglo-Polish accent, understood nothing—even the stenographers were at a loss.[189] Then followed a round of daily receptions, meetings, press conferences. On 9 May Conrad was entertained at lunch by Colonel E. M. House, the influential politician and former advisor to President Wilson. There he met Ignacy Paderewski, the famous pianist and Polish statesman, of whom he apparently said later, "What an outstanding man . . . in half an hour I learned from him more about my motherland than I had within the last fifteen years of my life."[190] The sojourn in the New

York area also offered an obvious opportunity to meet Quinn. But Conrad, guilty for having behaved badly toward him, could not bring himself to face his former confidant. This lapse made the breakdown of their friendship final. Ford later gave a kindhearted explanation of Conrad's behavior: "Conrad was afraid to see him . . . He was a sick man himself . . . And he was told Mr Quinn had a violent temper . . . The publishers advised him not to see him." [191]

On 7 May Conrad held his first press conference, with nineteen journalists who had been invited to Effendi Hill by Doubleday. He was troubled by gout: his left arm and right leg were thickly wrapped in wool scarves and he leaned heavily on his stick. The journalists noticed immediately that Conrad was more agitated and flustered than they were. He tried to make his answers to their oral and written questions polite and even jocular, but it was evident that at times he could hardly control his irritation. He refused to speak about the technical problems of writing, about the composition of novels, or about the meaning of his works, maintaining that all he had to say he had written in his books. He made the impression of a diplomat rather than a writer or former sailor. His replies as taken down by the reporters are mostly banal, many sounding like self-quotations. [192]

Three days later, after an informal meeting with students of Columbia University organized by the lecturer in Polish, Dr. Wojciech Zygmunt Morawski-Nawench, and dinner at the house of a wealthy and fashionable hostess, Mrs. Curtiss James, on the corner of Park Avenue and 67th Street, Conrad read fragments of *Victory* before two hundred invited guests.

Under the glare of electric lights hanging from the chandelier . . . a man with a beard stood on the raised dais. He had the hunted look of a hare about to be strangled by a poacher. His breath came in gasps, his voice shook. . . . Little by little the ballroom with the hygienic tapestries and cleaned primitifs slipped away. The mist of sea-blue horizons blotted out even the presiding figure in the straight-backed Spanish leather chair with her alarming slant of concentrated attention. The halting voice took on the power and assurance of its vision . . . An hour passed. And then another thirty minutes . . . A few tired business men had slipped out on the points of their toes to lean in the stone doorways, muttering something about getting a cigarette, but they did not quite leave the ballroom. After all, this was the greatest writer of the English language, or almost (some people put Joyce first, but they were obscene), of his day, they kept reminding themselves. What a pity, though, that his pronunciation was so bad . . . For Conrad spoke English with a guttural Polish twist. Good came out ringingly as "gut," and blood as "blut," which fitted in curiously with the complex beauties of his phrases . . . He had been talking now for nearly two hours and a half. And so on until the end where the heroine Lena dies: capturing the very sting of death Conrad's voice broke . . . he was moved to sudden tears. Conrad and all who had followed him there, drunk on Conrad.

This is how one of the guests, Countess Palffy, described the reading;[193] in spite of her enthusiasm, she remembered the reading as lasting twice as long as it really had.

Conrad was pleased with the evening. He told Jessie, "It was a most brilliant affair, and I would have given anything for you to have been there and seen all that crowd and all that splendour, the very top of the basket of the fashionable and literary circles. . . . I gave a talk and pieces of reading out of *Victory*. After the applause from the audience, which stood up when I appeared, had ceased I had a moment of positive anguish. . . . There was a most attentive silence, some laughs and at the end, when I read the chapter of Lena's death, audible snuffling."[194]

The reading, however, left Conrad very tired. He took a few days' rest and backed out of other public engagements. He complained of having lost the ability to enjoy new environments and meetings with strangers; he was clearly exhausted. On 15 May the Doubledays took him by car to Boston. On their way they stopped in New Haven to meet William Lyon Phelps, a professor of English at Yale. Conrad in a friendly mood granted an interview to two young students.[195] On 16 May the party arrived in Boston; they put up for five days at the Copley Plaza Hotel and toured the neighboring countryside. Afterward Conrad spent a couple of days in Elbridge Adams's country house, and on 24 May returned to Oyster Bay. Conrad was tired out by constant traveling and the "infinite kindness," which he found "overwhelming."[196] Of course, in front of his hosts he preserved his courteous manners and thanked them for their "American large-heartedness and generosity."[197] He lamented his fate only to Jessie, whom he had to assure that she was constantly in his thoughts and that it was only his lack of time and energy which prevented him writing letters more often than every four or five days. He was impatient, he said, to return home to her: "I think of nothing else. The time seems interminable and yet the visit is a success."[198]

Conrad spent the remaining few days at Effendi Hill. The kindly Doubledays decided to accompany him back to England. They sailed on 2 June on the *Majestic*, and arrived in Southampton a week later.[199] Conrad summed up his impressions in a letter to Winawer: "Entre nous, I felt all the time like a man dans un avion, in a mist, in a cloud, in a vapour of idealistic phraseology; I was lost, bewildered, amused—but frightened as well . . . Obviously some power is hidden behind it—great power undoubtedly—and certainly talkative. Its chatter reminds one of a well-trained parrot. It makes me shiver! . . . I may be wrong . . . I have feelings of great friendship towards many people there. . . . Indeed, one month is not enough to comprehend such a complicated machinery. Perhaps a whole life would not be sufficient."[200]

The cloud of idealistic phraseology, however, was raining gold. Doubleday guaranteed Conrad an income of £4,000 a year, or even more, for three years; and this was for book sales only. Yet Conrad was still worrying about his finances. His present budget swelled to £3,500 a year, including the rent of £250, Jessie's expenses and housekeeping money £730, and Conrad's personal fund £2,160, which covered among others the salaries of his secretary and of Jessie's nurse, Miss Audrey Seal, Karola Zagórska's allowance, and so on.[201] Hundreds of pounds went on doctors' bills. Conrad's anxiety was mainly caused by the thought that he was living on his literary capital, and that he was unable to increase it. He did his best, therefore, to put it to the fullest use, taking a keen interest in various publishing enterprises, from limited bibliophile issues to school editions.[202]

The first weeks after Conrad's return home were overshadowed by a more immediate distress. Jessie disclosed that Borys had married without his parents' knowledge. She had learned about it before Conrad's voyage but had kept it secret from him, apparently to spare his nerves. The marriage had taken place on 2 September 1922. Borys, who, thanks to his father, had just managed to extricate himself from his debts, and who had barely started in his new job, did not inform his parents of the event. Knowing how Conrad worried about his future, Borys probably felt that his marriage would be regarded as a sign of his extreme irresponsibility.[203] Besides, he feared that his parents would not approve of his choice of wife, whom he had met when she was working in an officers' mess in France.[204] Keeping the secret called for countless evasions and lies; Borys's financial crisis in July 1922 was probably connected with the affair, and therefore required special efforts to conceal the facts. The truth was apparently revealed in a letter from Borys's mother-in-law to Jessie; the bridegroom was evidently ashamed of the situation he had created and could not bring himself to make an open admission.

The rest of the story is known to us from two partly contradictory accounts left by mother and son. The latter, although sketchy, sounds more credible. Jessie, upon learning about the marriage, forbade Borys to see his father until she broke the news herself. This was why Borys neither saw his father off nor greeted him on his return from the United States; Conrad was greatly saddened by his absence.[205] The strangest element in the whole affair is Jessie's interpretation of the reasons which made Borys keep the marriage secret. "I have heard it often argued that a man should have only himself to please, and nobody should choose his wife for him, and this I heartily endorse. But his father was a desperately unreasonable man. This concealment he could not be expected to understand or accept as a more prosaic Englishman would. . . . I had known ever since the boys began to grow up that their natural inclinations would be diffi-

480··HOPE AND RESIGNATION

cult for my husband to realize, and the knowledge that his son had been married for eight months—in secret—would need a good deal of getting used to,
for Joseph Conrad to accept the fact. I knew that I myself had received a shock,
something in the nature of a blow in the chest, but I could have recovered from
it very soon. Not so my husband."[206] Thus Jessie confuses two issues: Borys's
independent decision to marry, and his concealment of this decision; and she
thereby puts the entire blame on Conrad. However, despite Jessie's claims, the
relationship between father and son suffered much less than that between Borys
and herself, because Borys blamed his mother for unnecessarily prolonging the
whole awkward situation.[207]

It is therefore difficult to take literally Jessie's typically highly dramatized description of Conrad's reaction to the news. Conrad was told about his son's
marriage a day after his return.[208] Undoubtedly, he was deeply shaken by his
son's secretiveness and gave vent to anger at this unprovoked humiliation. But
only the following day he wrote quite calmly to Pinker, "Marrying is not a
crime and one can not cast out one's son for that. I believe that this particular
marriage is foolish and inconsiderate, I shall not conceal my opinion when I
write. My confidence is shaken but I will not *assume* the worst." And although
a few days later he thought that "the more this affair is looked into the less
satisfactory it appears," he at once granted Borys an allowance of £50 a quarter.[209] "I had written to him informing him of the payments . . . in recognition
of his new status . . . I said in my letter 'you may look upon it as a wedding
present.' I made no statement about the future, but I expressed forcibly my
opinions as to his personal history for the last two years, adding that the only
good point were his sincere endeavours to find something to do and his apparent success in his present berth which I hoped he would keep."[210] Conrad
paid for the affair with a few days' in bed at the end of June.[211]

Jessie grumbled to Pinker, "He is ill and terribly unreasonable as usual."[212]
With age Conrad's moods were indeed becoming more capricious and unpredictable. After a weekend at Oswalds Walpole noted in his diary, "[Conrad]
much odder than I've ever known before, bursting into sudden rages about such
nothings as the butter being salt, and then suddenly being very quiet and
sweet." His comment, perhaps unfair, was: "Too many women in this house
and too many secret feelings."[213] To Conrad's constitutional excitability and the
changes of mood which arose out of his depression and were aggravated by
frequent illness and pain was now added the fretfulness of old age. But there was
also, I believe, a deeper motive for Conrad's unexpected and rather pointless fits
of temper which Jessie describes so unsparingly; he was half-consciously aware
of the fact that even in his own home he was surrounded by somewhat alien
people who did not truly understand him. He often gave vent to this feeling in
bouts of capriciousness and gratuitous scenes that constituted a safety valve,
and at the same time they dispersed the central conflict of their mutual mal-

adjustment, the conflict Conrad did not know how (nor perhaps wish) to solve. Jessie, thanks to her uncomprehending simplicity, was enveloping her husband as if in a cocoon which blunted both external and internal stimuli.[214] Still, her letters to friends support the impression she made on at least some of Oswalds' visitors: that she was prone to boss Conrad.[215]

With the onset of affluence Jessie's life became physically easier, but psychologically rather more difficult. Disability made domestic chores, which she liked and had been accustomed to, almost impossible; the presence of servants made them unnecessary. Relieved of her duties she felt deeply bored. Her interests were limited: she did not read; she was not even much interested in sightseeing when on a car trip; and since she was now spending much more time in the drawing room than in the kitchen, the difference between her intellectual level and that of her husband was more evident to their guests. Sir Christopher Cockerell (son of Sydney), who was in his teens when he came to Oswalds with his parents, remembers that "Conrad's wife did not seem to be an equal partner." Conrad he remembers as a rather small man, "extremely well dressed, with a perfectly trimmed beard and an elegant beautiful figure." He had memorable eyes, "which looked out almost fiercely."[216]

On 3 July Conrad sent Pinker a short article, "Christmas Day at Sea," based rather loosely on his memories. A week later he reported, "I have plunged into Suspense. Well there is only that to think of and stick to."[217] But he did not "stick" to it for long, as the manuscript grew only a little. In August Conrad returned again to his seafaring days and wrote a nostalgic essay, "The *Torrens* —A Personal Tribute."[218]

He became unable to tackle any entirely fresh work and paid increasing attention to the presentation and "positioning" of old. Curle was preparing a comprehensive article occasioned by Doubleday's collected edition—and again sent his text to Conrad for perusal. This time Conrad objected to the excessive stressing of his connections with the sea.

> I was in hopes that on a general survey it could also be made an opportunity for me to get freed from that infernal tail of ships, and that obsession of my sea life which has about as much bearing on my literary existence, on my quality as a writer, as the enumeration of drawing-rooms which Thackeray frequented could have had on his gift as a great novelist. After all, I may have been a seaman, but I am a writer of prose. . . . That the connection of my ships with my writings stands, with my concurrence I admit, recorded in your book is, of course, a fact. But that was biographical matter not literary. . . . you know yourself very well that in the body of my work barely one-tenth is what may be called sea stuff.

To this Conrad added in his next letter to Curle: "This damned sea business keeps off as many people as it gathers in." He suggested a simple and felicitous interpretive formula: "My manner of telling, perfectly devoid of familiarity as between author and reader, aimed essentially at the intimacy of a personal communication."[219] This was the first adumbration of the later critical notion that Conrad was an "impressionist" writer.

Conrad explained to Curle: "You understand that the moment is perhaps critical. It may fix my position with the buying public." He carefully selected—again pushing the sea element into the background—the photographs to be used for frontispieces in the consecutive volumes of Doubleday's edition of his works. *Almayer's Folly* was preceded by a photograph of Tadeusz Bobrowski.[220]

The strain in family relations did not last for long. On 15 July Borys and his wife paid their first visit to Oswalds. "As far as this sort of thing can be satisfactory it was satisfactory. I was glad to have it over. We must now hope for the best," wrote Conrad to Pinker.[221] Borys remembers that his father greeted his daughter-in-law "with his usual elaborate courtesy, putting her at ease immediately." Jessie describes the visit in her customary theatrical fashion; the most interesting element of her account is the story of Conrad personally supervising all preparations and even driving to Canterbury to do special shopping for the occasion as if he intended to host "God knows whom." Conrad could not have been so frightfully distraught as she believed, because on that very day he wrote two long letters, including a very amusing one to a little girl.[222] And the whole visit could not have passed badly: the young Conrads came back on 30 July and remained at Oswalds for a few days. Conrad confessed to Jean-Aubry, "One had to smooth out this rather silly situation. The two people primarily concerned give the impression of being perfectly matched. Jessie accepted her fate with grace. So did I—in my own fashion. The incident is closed—and everyone feels greatly relieved." Borys's position was certainly improved by the fact that on 23 July he became the manager of Daimler's warehouse in London.[223]

John had in the meantime finished his secondary school and Conrad decided to improve his son's French. The plan was to send the seventeen-year-old boy to Le Havre, where Jean-Aubry's father lived, to lodge with the large family of a Protestant pastor, the Reverend Bost. In mid-September (11–15) they all went to see the place; Conrad reported to Doubleday: ". . . a house where there are eight young people and no carpets on the stairs, and the atmosphere is intellectually severe and domestic—of the high thinking and plain living sort. If in these surroundings he doesn't pick up French of the best sort then there is no hope for him in this world."[224] Conrad also went to see André Gide at Cuverville, but did not find him home.[225]

Although he was satisfied with the results of the trip, Conrad paid for it with a few days in bed.[226] A week after his return from France he confided gloomily to Galsworthy, "I have done nothing worth speaking of lately—a long lately. And that is terrible."[227] Conrad hoped to have *Suspense* finished by winter—but he found he was unable to do any work on this novel. He was pleased when in November he managed to write "Geography and Some Explorers," an essay that turned out to be his last substantial piece of work.[228] When just a little earlier Ford—who had become editor of the *transatlantic review* newly founded in Paris—asked for a contribution to his monthly, Conrad replied, "I am afraid the source of the *Personal Record* fount is dried up. Thanks for your proposal. I'd like to do something for the sake of old times—but I daresay I am not worth having now." And later added, "I haven't got two ideas in my head. Times are changed and I have changed with them." Conrad wished his former friend every success, and even consented to have his letter, nostalgically recounting the early days of the *English Review*, published by Ford. He showed little eagerness to have *The Nature of a Crime* reprinted: "If you think it advisable to dig up this affair, well, I don't see how I can object."[229]

Among the guests flocking that summer to Oswalds was another Pole who had settled in England and was rapidly acquiring world renown: Bronisław Malinowski, the cultural anthropologist. Apparently he and Conrad had been in friendly contact for several years.[230] One autumn day Lady Ottoline Morrell—this time accompanied by her husband—came for another visit, after a ten-year interval:

> It was a perfectly happy day. We found him in a pleasant country house on the edge of a park, an old-fashioned house with large low rooms, which he had furnished with great distinction and with something of the air, it seemed to me, of a Polish château. . . . As we sat round a large table at tea he talked with even more freedom [than at their first encounter] and I felt easier than before. He sat by me and told me . . . how he came to England, he did not know anything of the language . . . Frequently in his talk this love of England and the English would recur. He specially liked simple young men who went into the Army and the Navy; clear, true and direct; he delighted in their fairness of mind. They were the people, he said, with whom he got on most easily—"not the learned or the intellectuals."

They talked also about Conrad's journey to Poland.

> When we first arrived Conrad brought up a little chair and sat down to talk to me about all this, but his wife at once came and sat on my other side and showed me page by page of a little book of snapshots of this journey—dull, ill-focused, conventional little photographs—and it was only with the greatest difficulty that I made myself polite to her. But I knew he was very exacting that she should be treated with proper respect.[231]

Hugh Walpole spent the weekend of 20–21 October at Oswalds and took part in the Sunday dinner, at which Mrs. Harding, Jean-Aubry, Richard Curle, and Paul Valéry were also present. He noted in his diary: ". . . jolly talk in the evening, mostly damning everyone, but Conrad's eyes lit over Fenimore Cooper and over Proust, who stirred him to deep excitement." Conrad was "in great form."[232] Walpole introduced Cyril Clemens, a cousin of Mark Twain, to Oswalds. Clemens noted a few interesting bits of conversation. Conrad apparently said, "In everything I have written there is always one invariable intention, and that is to capture the reader's attention." He confessed that the book he most liked to read over and over again was *Don Quixote*: "Certain maxims from the work I find myself frequently quoting, such as: 'The brave man carves out his own fortune and every man is the son of his own works.'"[233]

Conrad's "great form" lasted but a short time. At the beginning of November he fell ill again and was ailing, with only brief interruptions, until the first days of January 1924.[234] "Too much pain to think, too much pain to read—and almost to care," he wrote to Bennett.[235] Conrad's old physician, Dr. Fox, diagnosed a weakening of the heart muscle, which manifested itself in fluttering and arrhythmia. "This accounts for that unshakeable despondency of which I complained to you more than once," Conrad tried to console himself in a letter to Curle. He complained most of a persistent cough.[236]

And Conrad was again worried by the state of his finances. His budget, although by no means tight, was constantly exceeded; it is not surprising, since when going to London, for instance, Conrad would stay at the very expensive Curzon Hotel. Thus he again had to look for additional income. For a thousand-dollar fee he inscribed appropriate sentences on copies of the first edition of his works belonging to a young American collector, George T. Keating.[237] When in mid-November Borys, whose wife was expecting a child, asked his father to lend him £75 (apart from his normal allowance), Conrad turned to Walpole for an endorsement of a loan from Borys's bank. He explained that he did not wish to endorse it himself: "If I come forward in the usual way my bank manager is bound to know what is being done and of course E[ric] P[inker] too. I have nothing against them . . . But not a long time ago I was made to hear—or feel rather—that I was a weak person and exploited at that." The fact that he kept this letter secret from Jessie indicated that he was also hiding his action from her. (In his next letter to Walpole Conrad confessed that Jessie had called him—in Polish!—a donkey.)[238]

These new financial problems happened to coincide with the news about the astonishing prices paid for Conrad's manuscripts from John Quinn's collections, which had been auctioned in New York. Manuscripts of novels were sold for several thousand dollars apiece; short stories fetched over one thousand, articles a few hundred—often more than their author's fee had been.[239] Quinn made an excellent profit, probably in the vicinity of 1,000 percent. In a letter to Doubleday Conrad allowed himself to gibe: "Did Quinn . . . enjoy his glory in public and give graciously his hand to kiss to the multitude of inferior collectors who never, never, never dreamt of such a coup?" He certainly did not know that Quinn was mortally ill; but anyway it was unfair of him to criticize the

New York lawyer for not having kept his promise by letting his collection disperse, because Conrad himself had not stuck to his voluntary undertaking not to sell his manuscripts to anybody else. Besides, Conrad realized that the sensational sale constituted an excellent advertisement for his books.[240]

This publicity undoubtedly helped to produce the record success of *The Rover*. The novel, dedicated to G. Jean-Aubry, was published on 1 December in the United States and two days later in England. Sales were excellent: the first British printing ran to forty thousand copies.[241] Conrad himself did not think too highly of his last book ("which certainly is not remarkable," he wrote to Sandeman) and Garnett's praise came as a nice surprise. Aptly criticizing the character of Scevola as "half-grotesque" and "a failure," Conrad confessed that while working on *The Rover* he had been conscious of the possibility of developing a conflict between Peyrol and a worthy adversary but he did not feel up to this ambitious design. He also admitted that if he had not dictated but written "with pen and ink," he would have probably come nearer to expressing his intentions.[242]

The reception given *The Rover* was, all in all, the reverse of how Conrad's books had been received twenty-five or fifteen years earlier: now popular acclaim and sales were high, while the voices of the reviewers were cool and censorious. H. J. Brock in the *New York Times Book Review* called the novel "commercial," artificial and sugary; Raymond Mortimer said in *The New Statesman* that *The Rover* was "downright bad," pale and lifeless; these were typical opinions.[243] Conrad could perhaps have treated these accusations with irony if he had written an easy and popular book on purpose; but such was not the case.

The new year 1924 began joylessly. "*Entre-nous* I feel as if I were fighting my Verdun battle with my old enemy. It isn't that the symptoms are unusually severe, but it goes on and on . . . I begin to wonder whether I have sufficient reserves. But I am not hopeless," wrote Conrad to Arnold Bennett.[244] On 6 January Conrad sat for a portrait painted by Walter Tittle (now at the National Portrait Gallery in London); "Conrad was very gay and happy at the diversion of the studio, and he was constantly jumping up to look over my shoulder to see the progress of the work which fascinated him greatly."[245] The next day the Conrads took the first ride in their new car: a second-hand Daimler, which had previously belonged to the duke of Connaught. It cost £200 and had been procured by Borys, who felt very proud of being of service to his parents and to his firm at the same time.[246] A few days later Borys's son Philip was born, and the arrival of a grandson seems to have "finally restored the old intimacy" between Conrad and Borys. Conrad paid all expenses connected with the child's birth and kept showering the young couple and their baby with gifts. Jessie did not like this at all, and her relations with her son and daughter-in-law remained cool for quite a long time.[247] One week after Philip had been born Conrad and

Jessie went to see him ("The baby is really quite nice. Everything looks quite satisfactory there"). Some time later Borys and his family paid a visit to Oswalds.[248] Conrad's only worry was Borys's poor health and the recurrence of his "neurasthenic symptoms."[249] He also grieved for Jessie, although he tried to keep this from her.[250] Only John, prospering in Le Havre, caused no anxiety.[251]

At the end of January Conrad felt better. The outward sign of improved spirits was that he started to make plans: he wanted to go to southern France in September, and even thought of spending the summer in Biarritz.[252] In the first place, however, he wished to assail *Suspense*.

"What a lot of work there is to do yet! . . . I feel fairly hopeful," he wrote to Curle on 1 February 1924; and two days later Conrad declared to Pinker, "I am concentrating all my thoughts on the Novel, which certainly by the time it is done will be a biggish thing—I mean in matter and size." The critics, he explained, had been disillusioned with *The Rover* because they had been expecting "the great 'Mediterranean novel.'"[253] *Suspense* does in fact concern itself with a very vast array of psychological, historical, political, and cultural problems; in this it is comparable only to *Nostromo*, and possibly to *Under Western Eyes*. These problems include Napoleon as the animator of powerful national and social movements; the contrast between the civilizations of England, France, and Italy; the socio-cultural changes in Europe after the French Revolution; Italy's strivings for national independence; the love between half-siblings. The novel was very ambitious, and this must have made Conrad's inability to write even more excruciating: "It's like a chase in a nightmare," he wrote, "weird and exhausting." After March 1923 Conrad managed to put down on paper only one overdrawn chapter of the novel, amounting to less than fifty pages of print.

Nor was Conrad able to tackle any other work; as he complained to Galsworthy: "I'll have to write two [short stories] presently (to complete a vol.) and I am incapable of finding a subject—even for one. Not a shadow of a subject!"[254] Such were Conrad's feelings even while both he and Jessie considered that he was "in good form."

Conrad remained in comparatively fair health throughout March.[255] Toward the end of the month he sat for Jacob Epstein, whose bust is undoubtedly Conrad's most impressive portrait. An admirer of Conrad's work, Epstein remembers in his autobiography that the nervous and volatile writer was not an easy model, although he did his best to pose patiently: "His glance was keen despite the drooping of one eyelid. . . . He was crippled with rheumatism, crotchety, nervous and ill. He said to me 'I am finished.' There was pathos in his pulling out of a drawer of his last manuscript to show me that he was still at work. There was no triumph in his manner, however, and he said that he did not know whether he would ever finish it. 'I am played out,' he said, 'played out.'" Conrad often repeated the word *responsibility*. He said he knew nothing about the visual arts. When they talked about literature, and Epstein mentioned *Moby*

Dick, Conrad burst out indignantly: "'He knows nothing of the sea. Fantastic, ridiculous!' When I mentioned that the work was symbolical and mystical: 'Mystical, my eye! My old boots are mystical!' 'Meredith? His characters are ten feet high!' D. H. Lawrence had started well, but had gone wrong. 'Filth. Nothing but obscenities.'"[256] Conrad was satisfied with the bust. Epstein "has produced a wonderful piece of work of a somewhat monumental dignity, and yet—everybody agrees—the likeness is striking," he wrote to Doubleday.[257]

The mood Conrad expressed in his conversations with Epstein was not a fleeting one, and he soon fell ill again. Even the preface he composed with great difficulty in April to a volume of his *Shorter Tales* testifies to that. It is wholly devoted to attempts to justify his having consented to this particular selection of his stories being put together and published; the writing emanates weariness and defensiveness; we may doubt if it ever encouraged anyone to read the volume.[258]

Ford dragged Conrad into another undertaking which he did not have heart for: to publish *The Nature of a Crime* in a separate volume, with prefaces by both collaborators. Ford's motives were complex. He was certainly aware that at that moment all Conrad's works possessed a high market value and wished to cash in on that himself. Primarily, though, his reasons were psychological. After years of painful experiences before and during the war, and of chaos in his personal affairs during which his artistic sterility had been aggravated by nervous breakdowns, Ford was just returning to the life of literature and original writing; and being published side by side with Conrad would boost his morale if only because it would remind everybody, himself included, of the flourishing time of the *English Review*, the time when he had collaborated with the now unquestioned master of English prose. In addition, Ford was truly and deeply attached to Conrad, needed his friendship, and sought opportunities to renew their old intimacy. But for that Conrad felt no inclination. Even if he had, it would have meant overcoming Jessie's hostility: she hated Ford and suspected her husband of being gullible and soft.[259]

These conflicting attitudes sometimes led to tragicomic developments. When in February Ford proposed to come to Oswalds "between two trains," Conrad did not refuse the invitation, but when Jessie answered Ford's wire, she gave him the times of the most inconvenient trains. Ford, however, was not to be discouraged, and after the visit, beguiled by Conrad's politeness, he concluded that the old friendship had been restored.[260] Conrad, for his part, reported to Pinker, "We met as if we had seen each other every day for the last ten years. . . . As we talked pleasantly of old times I was asking myself, in my cynical way, when would the kink come." In his next letter he summed the situation up: Ford "wants to be friendly in personal relations with me. In fact, *entre nous*, too friendly."[261] Keeping him at a distance was luckily made easier by the fact that Ford now lived in Paris. They met again only once, on 30 April 1924, when

Ford evaded the Conrad defense by arriving unexpectedly at Oswalds. Jessie fulminated, "That odious Hueffer has just turned up. J.C. wanted to bring him up here for tea but I declined as what is the use of letting him get very friendly again. I dislike him profoundly."[262]

The business of having *The Nature of Crime* republished, complicated as it was because of copyright problems, dragged on and on, although Conrad, much irritated, tried to speed it up and accepted all proposed conditions. Ultimately Conrad and Ford settled not only the matter of the tale but also that of their two co-authored novels: they were both entitled to include them in their collected editions, sharing half each the royalties for the respective volumes— which was very advantageous to Ford, who never had a collected edition of his works issued; in addition, Conrad made over to Ford all the rights to translations of *The Inheritors* and *Romance* into European languages.[263] In May Conrad wrote the short preface to *The Nature of a Crime* Ford had asked for; it turned out to be his last completed piece of work;[264] Conrad only refused his consent to a transparently mercenary project to have the tale included in the volume of *Best Stories of 1924*.[265]

At the beginning of May Jessie thought that Conrad was feeling better, although she complained as usual that he was "unreasonable." She herself was preparing for another operation on her knee, to take place in June. An additional complication was the necessity of looking for a new house, as they were to leave Oswalds in September.[266] Conrad grieved at his inability to work. The whole world looked "flat and stale—but I have not given it up. I've given up nothing, but what the brutal years have robbed me of," he avowed to Doubleday.[267] But even such declarations were becoming increasingly difficult. Conrad confided to Gide, "For almost four years I have not written anything worthwhile. I wonder if it is the end. Perhaps."[268]

Undoubtedly it struck Conrad as paradoxical that it was the first socialist government in British history, the Labour party cabinet of Ramsay MacDonald, which offered him a knighthood. Conrad declined, but with a fine courtesy: "In conveying to you my sincere thanks I venture to add, that, as a man whose early years were closely associated in hard toil and unforgotten friendships with British Working men, I am specially touched on this offer being made to me during Your premiership."[269] Why did Conrad decline? I suppose that a sufficient reason was his consciousness of coming from an old noble family; Conrad may have felt that accepting the new title would look like a renunciation of that ancient heritage. But Conrad seems to have been averse to public honors in general; he had already refused to accept the honorary degrees offered him by Cambridge, Durham, Edinburgh, Liverpool, and Yale universities.[270]

At the beginning of June, while Conrad was anxiously awaiting Jessie's operation, two meetings with Polish compatriots provided a welcome distraction. First Miss Irena Rakowska, daughter of Conrad's distant relative Maria Ołdakowska, came to Oswalds with her friend, another young Polish girl; the two of them spent several weekends at Oswalds. She later remembered that Conrad, an engaging and attentive host, planned and organized sightseeing excursions and other entertainment for them. "He himself would prepare and serve breakfast—bacon and eggs—for everybody. It was his usual job, not only when there were visitors in the house. He would not skip it even while he was suffering fits of depression. Then nobody dared to talk. Conrad himself would nervously jingle the cutlery, 'so as to make something to be happening.'" He told Rakowska that his sons were not interested in literature (and Borys confessed to her that he had "read nothing"). Apparently Conrad wanted John to marry a Polish girl and to learn Polish. Rakowska recalls that Conrad expressed a desire to return to Poland;[271] Jessie also mentions this wish, and R. L. Mégroz, who talked to Conrad in November 1922, writes that "had he lived longer it is almost certain that Conrad would have returned and settled in the dream-burdened land of his fathers." Jean-Aubry, on the other hand, apparently never heard of any such project, and Curle, Conrad's other closest friend in the last years of his life, categorically denied that Conrad ever mentioned such an intention.[272] The truth probably lies in between. Especially when he was emerging from depression, Conrad was wont to devise lots of various stimulating and "liberating"—if only momentarily—plans, without considering them really seriously. There is no evidence that he ever made enquiries as to the practicality of his return to Poland; on the contrary, just before he died he had decided to rent a house in Kent for the next few years.

Conrad's attitude toward Poland remained a tangled one. He was glad to receive an invitation to an official lunch at the Polish legation in London; but when Konstanty Skirmunt, the Polish envoy, asked him to become honorary president of the reestablished Literary Association of the Friends of Poland, Conrad refused, pleading that he was in poor health and lived far from London and from public life altogether. To Roman Dyboski, who was at that time Lecturer in Polish at London University, Conrad added that he thought propagandistic efforts did not become Poland's historical and cultural dignity.[273] There was an element of shirking in Conrad's refusal: an honorary president would presumably not have had much to do besides allowing his name to be used; still, Conrad was probably not quite sure what the association was going to do and did not want to give its action a blanket endorsement. It must be said also that the Poles sometimes behaved a little equivocally toward him as if wanting to stress—with reproach—his foreignness. Although the conversation at the diplomatic lunch was at first in Polish and Conrad seemed quite happy with that, Dyboski, who had earlier written to Conrad in English, switched to English. And when Stefan Pomarański, a young Warsaw archivist, sent Conrad some newly discovered documents, manuscripts, and a pencil portrait of Apollo Korzeniowski, he enclosed a letter in English with gently veiled reproofs. On the basis of his books, wrote Pomarański, Conrad seemed "very foreign" to him. He wanted the collection of documents and manuscripts "to return to Poland some day . . . For us in Poland it will always be a sacred national memory." Surprisingly, Conrad took this very well; he answered with a warm letter in Polish, signing himself Konrad Korzeniowski. He agreed to become an honorary member of the Polish Geographic Society and announced that he wished to become a member of the Mianowski Foundation, which was subsidizing scholarly research and literature in Poland.[274]

Jessie's operation took place in Canterbury on 13 June. It was considered a success, but she was told to remain in the hospital until 24 July.[275] Conrad, himself unwell and not always able to visit Jessie in Canterbury, wrote to her frequently.[276]

He tried to work, but in vain. On 2 July he complained to Curle, "Am trying to fight off a fit of severe depression which has taken me by the throat, as it were." And next day he confessed to Ernest Dawson, "I feel (and probably look) horribly limp and my spirits stand at about zero. Here you have the horrid truth. But I haven't been well for a long time and *strictly entre nous* I begin to feel like a cornered rat. No more at present."[277]

Then Conrad braced himself and, encouraged by Curle, began work on the essay about "Legends"; in three weeks, however, he managed to write only four pages. He was very glad when Jessie came back home, although she was immobilized upstairs, and had an open wound in her knee. On 26 July Irena Rakowska and her friend Krystyna Świeżawska came again for a weekend; they took a few snapshots.[278]

Curle came for the following weekend on Friday, 1 August. Conrad was in a sociable mood, appearing well and in high spirits. "My mind seems clearer than it has been for months," he said, "and I shall soon get hold of my work again." On Saturday Conrad drove with Curle to have a look at a house he wanted to rent. On the way there he was seized by a pain in his chest; it was undoubtedly caused by a heart attack, but Dr. Fox, called from Ashford, ascribed it to acute indigestion. In the evening Borys came with his wife and son; they also brought John along. Conrad asked to have the baby, Philip, brought to him at once; he felt worse again and had increased difficulty breathing. Another physician came, this time from Canterbury, but he did not find reason for alarm either. After the doctor left, Conrad's breathing became even more spasmodic and painful. Later that night, Conrad's suffering became difficult to bear, and he asked to be left alone.

In the morning of 3 August, after a bad night, Conrad seemed easier. He joked and called encouragingly to Jessie. At 8.30 A.M., when he was sitting alone in his room, propped up in a chair, they heard a cry and the fall of a body. He was dead.[279]

The funeral, held according to Roman Catholic rites and preceded by a mass in Saint Thomas Church, took place on 7 August in Canterbury.[280] Not many people were present: the family, a few friends, Edward Raczyński as the representative of the Polish government. It was not a great occasion, although it took place among great crowds. "To those," wrote Edward Garnett, "who attended Conrad's funeral in Canterbury during the Cricket Festival of 1924, and drove through the crowded streets festooned with flags, there was something symbolical in England's hospitality and in the crowd's ignorance of even the existence of this great writer. A few old friends, acquaintances and pressmen stood by his grave."[281] Conrad's body was laid to rest at the edge of the cemetery, under a simple obelisk of gray granite, on which Conrad's names are chiseled in a version which demonstrates how uncertain was Jessie's grasp of her husband's background: Joseph Teador Conrad Korzeniowski.[282] The headstone's rectangular form stands out starkly among neighboring crosses.

English literature paid Conrad his finest tribute in the words of Virginia Woolf: "Suddenly, without giving us time to arrange our thoughts or prepare our phrases, our guest has left us; and his withdrawal without farewell or ceremony is in keeping with his mysterious arrival, long years ago, to take up his lodging in this country. For there was always an air of mystery about him. It was partly his Polish birth, partly his memorable appearance, partly his preference for living in the depths of the country, out of earshot of gossip, beyond reach of hostesses so that for news of him one had to depend upon the evidence of simple visitors with a habit of ringing door-bells who reported of their unknown host that he had the most perfect manners, the brightest eyes, and spoke English with a strong foreign accent."[283]

She saw Conrad, from a distance, as an isolated stranger. Cunninghame Graham remembered his lost friend as a man of striking genius, within whom "an inward fire seemed to be smouldering ready to break out."[284] And Conrad was finally burned out by this inward flame—burned out but not vanquished. The lines from Edmund Spenser, which Conrad had chosen as the epigraph to *The Rover*:

> Sleep after toyle, port after stormie seas,
> Ease after warre, death after life, does greatly please"

and which were inscribed on his tombstone, may seem apt—but only if we take them out of their context in *The Faerie Queene*. Spenser has these words spoken by Despayre, who is soliciting the Red Cross Knight to commit suicide.[285] Conrad knew such allurements only too well, but despair, although it was often his mood, was not his concluding judgment.

Epilogue

. . . .

TEOFILA BOBROWSKA prophesied that her grandson would grow up to be "a man of great heart." And Conrad was one. He scorned sentimentality and effusiveness; his manner of portraying emotion in his works was full of restraint; skepticism and irony are far more characteristic of his writing than tenderness, enthusiasm, or passion. And yet he was a deeply emotional man.

In what I think is the most revealing fragment of his memoirs, Conrad's younger son John tells how his father liked to play with him in the garden—for instance at sailing toy boats on a pool—but as soon as anyone else turned up in the vicinity, Conrad would quickly disappear or pretend to be busy with something else. Ian Watt has rightly observed that Conrad wanted to love and be loved. But the conditions in which he grew up—his dramatic and gloomy childhood, unsettled youth, long years spent among tough seamen, and later his life among the English, well-known for their reserve ("underdeveloped hearts" in E. M. Forster's famous diagnosis)—taught him to be wary of showing his emotions or even his need of them. He opened up rarely and only to his closest friends.

One might think that his strongest and most permanent feelings were directed not toward people but toward ideas. His letters become most passionate when he writes about the tragedy of existence, the weakness of human nature, political violence, fidelity to lost causes, human dignity, the weight of moral responsibility, and the rigid demands of Art. But St.-John Perse's remark that among all the writers he knew Conrad was "the most human" was not unfounded. In private life he could be quite warm-hearted, although he never waxed sentimental; and a genuine compassion and deep involvement in the fate not of mankind as a whole but of particular human beings showed through the layers of irony and grotesque. "Homo duplex has in my case more than one meaning." Obviously, the "one meaning" refers to the Anglo-Polish duality. But perhaps it was not the most important one. Contrasts between loneliness and a need for friendship, understanding, and compassion; and also the contrast between alienation and a cult of traditional and national bonds, were other dualities that weighed on Conrad's fate.

Dozens of letters testify to the emotional needs of the recluse. Letters were to him a substitute for direct contact. Each exchange of correspondence appeared to establish new links, new kinds of mutual relations: hence the diverse character of letters that Conrad would send different people.

An alienated émigré, he was haunted by a sense of the unreality of other people—a feeling natural to someone living outside the established structures of his family, milieu, and country. He therefore described the work of a novelist as an expression of "conviction of our fellow-men's existence," as an act of faith in the reality of human fellowship, of which he wrote in the Preface to *The Nigger of the "Narcissus."*

That the idea of honor was of paramount importance for Conrad's ethical thinking has been observed many times—although not always with sympathy or even understanding—both by his contemporaries and by later critics. It is worth remembering here that this supposedly abstract ideal implies solid empirical grounds. One cannot preserve honor in mind alone; one cannot "sin" against it in thought; one cannot gain it by words. Real men and concrete deeds are needed. Thus believing in the reality of others was for Conrad also morally essential. And morally essential for him also was the belief in the existence of a class of men who could serve as arbiters of honor: men who testify to one's honor or to the lack of it. Understandably, for a man as alienated and uprooted as he was, this class was a semimythical one: the class of "us"—in his works consisting mainly of seamen.

Throughout almost his entire life Conrad was an outsider and felt himself to be one. An outsider in exile; an outsider during his visits to his family in the Ukraine; an outsider—because of his experiences and bereavement—in Cracow and Lwów; an outsider in Marseilles; an outsider, nationally and culturally, in British ships; an outsider as an English writer. Ford described him as a Pole from another epoch; Bennett as "an Easterner"; Ernest Dawson as somebody more at home in French than in English literature; and Conrad called himself (to Graham) a "bloody foreigner." At the same time, this novelist writing in English and regarded as an outsider attached great importance to continuity and tradition, and also to national culture. The two writers whom he praised most eloquently, Maupassant and Turgenev, he called "intensely national." He regarded "national spirit" as the only truly permanent and reliable element of communal life.

Conrad made such frequent use of his own memories as literary material that one is strongly tempted to treat his life and work as one whole, and on the same plane. Thus Conrad's "view of the world" or some elements of this view are usually described by citing in one breath both his private and public statements, fragments from letters and sentences from books. Only methodological purists would object to such an approach if it were not for the fact that in the end we get a picture both incoherent and misleading. Automatically and uncritically linking the two spheres, literature and private life, it throws a distorting light upon their mutual relationship. Conrad used his own experiences as raw material, but the finished product should not be treated in the same way as raw material.

Another reason why this should not be done is that many of Conrad's letters were written under the influence of depression. He tried—to my mind usually with success—to eliminate the effects of that illness from his literary works as far as possible. In his letters he showed less constraint and self-control, and, anyway, he could not control himself there. It is well known that pessimism, lack of self-confidence, a weakened sense of one's identity ("vagueness of self-portrait"), and a darkened picture of the world are characteristic symptoms of depression, just as is an intensified sense of physical pain. All that must be taken into consideration, just as when describing somebody's face we would not omit the fact that a tooth infection has just made it swollen.

One of the symptoms of a depressive disposition is a high degree of reliance on the sympathy and love of others, which are required to maintain a favorable sense of oneself. Some persons look for a substitute in the form of a dominant goal, the attainment of which could give them a feeling of their meaningfulness, of their inherent worth. Conrad's passionate devotion to his art can be interpreted also in these terms; but for a writer the search for such a supreme goal involves the risk of getting ensnared in a vicious circle—because it makes his feeling of self-realization dependent on success, and at the same time isolates him further and further in his solitary toil. The reader of this book will remember many passages that illustrate this quandary and Conrad's awareness of it.

"Man . . . is a product of circumstances and their victim," Conrad wrote in one of his works. He himself was not an exception to this rule, but throughout his life he tried hard to break away from the power of circumstance. He kept changing his decisions and at least five times suddenly altered the course of his life: departing from Poland; leaving France; going to Africa; beginning to write; and getting married. In each case the escape from the pressure of circumstances was both forced upon him and made easy. And in each case the escape turned out to be only illusory because the sense of mastering one's fate may be found only in the consistent pursuit of a once-chosen way. That is exactly why Conrad tried to invest his own autobiographical legend with precisely such consistency.

The legend was an attempt to make his life meaningful. But Conrad's works as a whole—and after all his autobiographical legend forms only a small part of it—represent an attempt to find the meaning of human existence in general. He wrote so many times about "illusions" which must be cherished "lest men should renounce their life early"; he expressed so many times his distrust of man's thinking; he made such sarcastic remarks about the "consolatory influence" of action which "is the enemy of thought and the friend of flattering illusions"—that many critics suspected him of being a nihilist and of denying the very possibility of finding such a meaning. This suspicion, however, springs from the naiveté of the interpreters. Conrad is skeptical about the human mind and scientific cognition because, according to him, no intellectual process per se can give meaning to human reality. A knowledge of Nature, perfectly indifferent to man, does not supply us with directives on how to live; nor does it reveal any moral values. Conrad writes about "illusions" because he believes that all ideals are created by man and only by man, that they are all man's own conception and have no confirmation outside man's life. But it is neither resignation nor lack of hope that dictate those skeptical remarks. On the contrary: Conrad is convinced that human life may have a meaning—but it is for us to confer it. That meaning is not derived from intellectual knowledge, but it is an expression of faith; it will not result from any deliberation but from an effort of will. Conrad does not leave the substance of faith and the direction of effort to the individual's own judgment. Their point of reference is explicitly stated: it is the principle of fidelity. Fidelity to human solidarity and fidelity to mankind's moral heritage.

For Conrad, writing was not tantamount to the setting forth of truths previously laid down, but an act of wrestling with himself in an attempt to reconcile the contradictions that tore him from within; a struggle with problems that preyed on his mind; an effort to come to terms with the magma of his own personality. His work was the result of searching for truth "manifold and one." Conrad's private letters contain reports of the search and struggle, incomplete reports, sometimes quite contradicting the final outcome.

We, Conrad's readers, may look at his life as at a battlefield. And recognizing his greatness as a writer we may also see his greatness as a man who, for our benefit, derived so much beauty and such a wealth of ideas from his suffering.

Abbreviations

References to Conrad's works are to Dent's Collected Edition (London, 1946–1955). Texts not included in that edition, hitherto the most complete, have been collected in Conrad, *CDAUP*.

Berg	Berg Collection, New York Public Library, New York City.
Birmingham	Birmingham University Library, Birmingham, England.
BL	Ashley Collection, British Library (British Museum), London.
Colgate	Colgate University Library, Hamilton, New York.
Conrad, *CDAUP*	Joseph Conrad. *Congo Diary and Other Uncollected Pieces*. Edited and with comments by Zdzisław Najder. Garden City, N.Y., 1978.
Cornell	Cornell University Library, Ithaca, New York.
CPB	Zdzisław Najder, ed. *Conrad's Polish Background: Letters to and from Polish Friends*. Translated by Halina Carroll. London, 1964.
Duke	William R. Perkins Library, Duke University, Durham, North Carolina.
Harvard	Houghton Library, Harvard University, Cambridge, Massachusetts.
Indiana	Lilly Library, Indiana University, Bloomington, Indiana.
JCC	Jessie Conrad. *Joseph Conrad and His Circle*. London, 1935.
JCKH	Jessie Conrad. *Joseph Conrad As I Knew Him*. London, 1926.
LL	G. Jean-Aubry. *Joseph Conrad: Life and Letters*. 2 vols. London, 1927.
Macpherson	Copies of Joseph Conrad's letters to Norman Douglas, received from the late Kenneth Macpherson.
Mursia	Originals in possession of Dr. Ugo Mursia in Milan.

NYPL   Manuscript Division, New York Public Library, New York City.

Princeton   Princeton University Library, Princeton, New Jersey.

Rosenbach   Philip H. and A. S. W. Rosenbach Foundation, Philadelphia.

Texas   The Humanities Research Center, University of Texas at Austin.

Wspomnienia i studia   Barbara Kocówna, ed. *Wspomnienia i studia o Conradzie.* Warsaw, 1963.

Yale   Beinecke Rare Book and Manuscript Library, Yale University, New Haven, Connecticut.

Notes

I. IN THE SHADOW OF ALIEN GHOSTS: 1857–1874

1. Testimony of the Korzeniowski family from Podolia, MS 6577/IV, vol. II, Jagiellonian Library, Cracow. Kasper Niesiecki traces the family back to the Poznań region, from which Piotr, a captain of horse, moved to Livonia about 1600; subsequently his son Mateusz moved to the Bracław district. *Herbarz polski* [The Polish armorial], edited by K. Łodzia-Czarniecki (Gniezno, 1881), 1:773.

2. Aleksander Jełowicki, *Moje wspomnienia* (Warsaw, 1970), pp. 181, 220, 221. Robert's and Hilary's dates of birth are unknown. Robert was the oldest; Hilary must have been grown up in 1849, as he was then looking for a wife, according to Apollo's letter to Tadeusz Bobrowski of 11 May 1849 (old style). MS 2889, National Library, Warsaw. From the same letter comes one of the two remarks about Korzeniowski's sister, hitherto overlooked by biographers.

3. Tadeusz Bobrowski, *Pamiętniki* [Memoirs], 2d ed., edited by Stefan Kieniewicz (Warsaw, 1979), 1:363.

4. Henryk Golejowski, in *Pamiętnik* [Memoirs] (Cracow, 1971), 2:286–301, gives a bad character to Robert Korzeniowski, describing him as shifty, cruel, and immoral. This judgment refers to Robert in his early twenties; it is difficult to guess to what extent this opinion was influenced by the fact that the two men were political opponents, Korzeniowski representing more radical views.

5. Marian Dubiecki, *Na kresach i za kresami* [In borderland and beyond] (Kiev, 1914), pp. 192–193.

6. Stefan Buszczyński, *Mało znany poeta* [Little-known poet] (Cracow, 1870), p. 8.

7. Bobrowski, *Pamiętniki*, 1:426.

8. Bobrowski, *Pamiętniki*, 2:72.

9. Roman Taborski, *Apollo Korzeniowski—ostatni dramatopisarz romantyczny* [. . . the last Romantic dramatist] (Wrocław, 1957), p. 148; also Bobrowski, *Pamiętniki*, 2:54–56.

10. Apollo Korzeniowski [anonymously], "Polska i Moskwa. Pamiętnik," *Ojczyzna* (Leipzig, 1864), no. 51.

11. Taborski, *Apollo Korzeniowski*, p. 154.

12. Apollo Korzeniowski's poems to his betrothed, dated from Terechowa, 6 and 10 July 1855, MS 6794/II, Jagiellonian Library.

13. Date of the wedding in Apollo Korzeniowski's letter to Władysław Górski, 1 July 1856, MS 7811, Jagiellonian Library. The anecdote about an argument with the parish priest has been preserved in the family tradition and passed on by Tadeusz Garczyński, a relative by marriage.

14. Tadeusz Bobrowski, a record kept from 1869 to 1890, *Dla wiadomości Kochanego Siostrzeńca mojego Konrada Korzeniowskiego*, MS 6391, Jagiellonian Library; henceforth referred to as "Document." He locates Derebczynka in the Mohylów district.

15. MS 6794, Jagiellonian Library. Copy made by hand by Teofila Bobrowska, Ewa's mother.

16. MS 6794/II, Jagiellonian Library. Poem dated 16 May 1859, Żytomierz.

17. Bobrowski maintains that one-third of the money for the lease was given by Apollo's mother-

in-law, that the Korzeniowskis lost everything, and Teofila Bobrowska almost everything ("Document" and *Pamiętniki*, 2:91). The latter seems inaccurate, since Apollo had means to support his family at Żytomierz and Warsaw, and was able to pay his share in the publishing partnership. In his letters to Kaszewski (20 January and 9 July 1860, MS 3057, Jagiellonian Library), he relinquished his author's fees, so he could not have been penniless. Later, he financed the launching of a periodical in Warsaw; somebody may have been helping him.

18. Bobrowski, *Pamiętniki*, 1:426, and "Document."

19. Bobrowski, *Pamiętniki*, 2:90–91.

20. Apollo Korzeniowski to Karol Szajnocha, Żytomierz, [n.d.] 1859, MS 6518/II, Ossolineum, Wrocław. One of the things he mentions is his intention to write a play, *Rejtan*. On his family: "I have a wife who shares with me the whole life of her soul. . . . She helps me in everything and is often an inspiration to me. Our child is my hope for the future that I shall leave behind me a heart which will beat at once as mine does after my years of anguish, and that he will become what I have always dreamt to be."

21. 18 May 1861. Ewa's letter to her husband and Teofila Bobrowska's to her son-in-law, were published by S. Pomarański, *Kobieta Współczesna*, 1931, nos. 16–22. The preinsurrection atmosphere at Żytomierz, charged with Polish patriotism, the manifestations to commemorate those killed in Warsaw, and so forth, are described in Vladimir Korolenko's memoirs, *Istoria moego sovremennika* [The history of my contemporary] (Warsaw, 1906), vol. 1.

22. Cf. S. Kieniewicz, *Powstanie Styczniowe* [The January insurrection] (Warsaw, 1972), p. 104.

23. Ewa Korzeniowska to Apollo Korzeniowski, 19 June and 8 July 1861.

24. As reported by J. Perłowski, "O Conradzie i Kiplingu," reprinted in *Wspomnienia i studia*, p. 116.

25. Bobrowski, *Pamiętniki*, 1:427.

26. Bobrowski, *Pamiętniki*, 2:464.

27. Taborski, *Apollo Korzeniowski*, pp. 104, 105.

28. Apollo Korzeniowski to Władysław Zawadzki, MS 3455/II, Ossolineum. The date of the letter: 8 October 1861, established on the basis of Korzeniowski's letter to Szajnocha, posted simultaneously, MS 5877/II, Ossolineum.

29. Kieniewicz, *Powstanie Styczniowe*, pp. 196 and 747.

30. The explanation of the real name of the Committee, ibid., p. 207.

31. *A Personal Record*, p. x. The quoted fragment comes from the Author's Note written in 1919. Conrad objects to his father being called a "Revolutionist," and this probably prompted him to assert, contrary to the facts, that "the secret National Committee intended primarily to organize moral resistance to the augmented pressure of Russianism." In fact, the committee had more far-reaching aims and was preparing for an insurrection.

32. Ewa Korzeniowska to Antoni Pietkiewicz, 19 November 1861, *Ruch społeczno-polityczny na Ukrainie* [Socio-political movement in the Ukraine] (Kiev, 1963), p. 176.

33. E. Korzeniowska to Władysław Górski, 6 January 1862, MS 8711/IV, Jagiellonian Library.

34. Public Records Office in Warsaw, part II, no. 4091. Dr. Franciszka Ramotowska has drawn my attention to this document. The results of the investigation passed to the Court on 4 April 1862. Cf. Kieniewicz, *Powstanie Styczniowe*, pp. 169–171 and 192–199.

35. The summary of the verdict reads as follows: "Prikazano vislat Korzeniowskiego i zhenu iego na zhitelstvo v g. Perm, pod strogij nadzor Politsii." The fact that Ewa Korzeniowska had also been sentenced to exile was disclosed by Rafał Blüth in his article, "O tragicznej decyzji kra-

kowskiej Konrada Korzeniowskiego," *Verbum*, no. 2 (1936), reprinted in *Wspomnienia i studia*. Blüth examined the records of the court case, which, at that time, were still complete. Bobrowski ascribes the leniency of the verdict to the fact that the investigating commission was headed by Colonel E. Rozhnov, an army friend of Stanisław Bobrowski.

36. Bobrowski, *Pamiętniki*, 2:457, gives another version of the incident: "On the journey, one station before Moscow, the Korzeniowski's little son became ill, and when the escorting guards refused them permission to break the journey, the desperate parents announced that nothing short of physical force would make them continue. A sympathetic traveler, on his way to Moscow, promised to send a doctor, and Korzeniowski, recalling that he had a friend in Moscow, a Dr. Młodzianowski, a university professor who, at one time, had been his tutor at Winnica, sent an appeal for help through the traveler. Thus, the kind Aesculapius soon arrived and saved the child from acute meningitis."

37. *Tygodnik Ilustrowany*, no. 4 (1920). The Korzeniowskis lived at Vologda in Deviatkov's house, on Bolshaya Kozlenskaya (or Kozlyonaya, today Uritskego) Street. The wooden house was demolished in the late 1960s. The address is in Korzeniowski's letters to the Zagórskis, 27 June 1862, and to Mr. Budkiewicz's bookshop at Żytomierz, 22 October 1862 (both at the Ossolineum). The location of the house was established by Valentin Panov in "Dom Deviatkowa i sovremenniki Dzh. Konrada" [Deviatkov's house and J. Conrad's contemporaries], *Krasnyi Sever* (Vologda), 14 September 1977.

38. Michał Rolle, *In illo tempore. . .* (Brody-Lwów, 1914), pp. 47–49.

39. Longin Panteleev, *Vospominanya* [Memoirs], 1903.

40. Entries concerning the Korzeniowskis are preserved in the police records in the public records office at Vologda; they were published by Panov, "Po sledakh Dzhozefa Konrada" [In J. Conrad's footsteps], *Krasnyi Sever* (Vologda), 10 March 1976. The first entry for 1862 reads, in the section "Information on the subject of persons under police surveillance, not deprived of the right to live in the town of Vologda": "No. 54. An inhabitant of Volhynia province, Polish writer Apollo Korzeniowski, born in Podolia province, age 40. His wife Evelina Osipovna, born in Kiev province, age 30. Under surveillance from 20 June 1862. Subject to secret surveillance of unlimited duration. Has no occupation in the town of Vologda. Sent from Lublin province. For maintenance draws no money from the treasury. Has with him his wife and son. His conduct is good, so is his wife's."

41. Apollo Korzeniowski to the Zagórskis, 14 October 1862, *Tygodnik Ilustrowany*, no. 20 (1920).

42. Rosenbach.

43. Yale. The date 6/17 L. 1863, one day's mistake, probably February [luty] because he spent July [lipiec] at Nowochwastów.

44. The entry in police records (no. 53 for 1863), published by Panov, "Po sledakh." Bobrowski, *Pamiętniki*, 2:458, incorrectly gives the date of the move as summer 1863.

45. Apollo Korzeniowski to the Zagórskis, 27 March 1863, *Tygodnik Ilustrowany*, no. 20 (1920).

46. Buszczyński, *Mało znany poeta*, p. 5, maintains that Captain Korzeniowski died on his way to Różycki's detachment, about 1 May 1863. Bobrowski, *Pamiętniki*, 1:430, gives the date of death as spring 1864, the time when Korzeniowski solicited help in Dubno for the imprisoned Hilary; but the remark about a Russian regimental orchestra playing at the funeral (as the deceased man was an ex-officer) makes this date rather improbable, since such a gesture could have been possible only before the insurrection in the Ukraine.

47. *A Personal Record*, p. 24.

48. "Polska i Moskwa. Pamiętnik ××× zaczęty 186..." [Poland and Muscovy. Memoirs of ××× begun in 186...], *Ojczyzna* (Leipzig), nos. 27–29, 31, 34–36, 42–52 (1864). The editor presented the anonymous author as dead. Karl Marx expressed similar thoughts a few years later: "There is but one alternative for Europe. Either the horde of Asiatic barbarians, led by Moscow, will fall like an avalanche on Europe—or else Europe must rebuild Poland, and by establishing a twenty-million strong barrier of heroes gain the breathing space necessary to achieve its social rebirth." K. Marx and F. Engels, *Werke* (Berlin, 1975), 16:204.

49. *A Comedy of Errors*, published by *Kłosy*, 1866; *Hard Times*, *Gazeta Polska*, 1866 to 1867. About *Les travailleurs de la mer*, mentioned later by Conrad, only some references have survived.

50. Apollo Korzeniowski to Kazimierz Kaszewski, 28 February 1865, 26 February 1865; Korzeniowski and Ewa Korzeniowska to Kaszewski, 8 March 1865. Letters to Kaszewski are in MS 3057, Jagiellonian Library.

51. Bobrowski, "Document," *CPB*, p. 185; from the middle of March, Teofila and Tadeusz Bobrowski were also at Chernikhov.

52. Bobrowski, *Pamiętniki*, 2:8.

53. Ibid., 2:18. He draws a comparison between Ewa and her younger sister Teofila, who died in 1851. Conrad included this fragment, almost to the letter, in *A Personal Record*. In his letter to Kazimierz Waliszewski (5 December 1903, *CPB*, p. 239) he writes about his mother: "I can hardly remember her, but judging by what I heard about her and by the letters she wrote to her brothers—which I read later—she must have been a woman with uncommon qualities of mind and spirit."

54. Korzeniowski to Kaszewski, 10 June 1865, 18 September 1865.

55. Korzeniowski to Kaszewski, 1 February 1866.

56. Joseph Conrad, "The Books of My Childhood," *CDAUP*, p. 77.

57. M. Dąbrowski, "Rozmowa z J. Conradem" [A chat with J. Conrad], *Tygodnik Ilustrowany*, no. 16 (1914).

58. Regina Korzeniowska to Konrad Korzeniowski, dated "Winnica 1865 on Saint Konrad's Day," Yale; the money was actually a joint gift from Regina and her sister Katarzyna.

59. Korzeniowski to Kaszewski, 18 September 1865.

60. The shortage of money, the need to earn by translating, and the difficulties with getting paid were frequent subjects in Korzeniowski's letters to Kaszewski. In September 1865 he asked Kaszewski to sell the desk he had left in Warsaw to cover the cost of books for Konrad; in December he asked for the sale of other small items. During Ewa's terminal illness, Tadeusz Bobrowski paid to Apollo Ewa's part of the inheritance from her brother Stefan. From April 1865 until Apollo's death Bobrowski paid the Korzeniowskis 400 rubles a year for their maintenance (Bobrowski, "Document").

61. Korzeniowski to Kaszewski, 31 October 1865, 18 February 1865.

62. 6/18 January 1866, *Tygodnik Ilustrowany*, no. 20 (1920). To Kaszewski he wrote on 31 January 1866: "Although I am not a man of letters in the strict sense of the term, God has blessed me—or punished me—by an instinct and I feel how distressing and unbearable the position of writers with an honest vocation must be in this post-cataclysmic era." The motif of a deeply felt sympathy for the sufferings of the nation is always present in his letters.

63. Korzeniowski to Kaszewski, 31 December 1866: "My poor Konradek has been ill for five months; at present he is with his Granny receiving treatment in Kiev."

64. Bobrowski, "Document," *CPB*, p. 185; Korzeniowski to Władysław Wóycicki, 14 December 1866, MS 7832, Jagiellonian Library; Korzeniowski to Kaszewski, 19 February and 29 June 1867.

65. Information contained in Tekla Wojakowska's (née Syroczynska, daughter of Antoni) not-always-reliable recollections, Stefan Czosnowski, "Conradiana," *Epoka*, no. 1363 (1929), reprinted in *Wspomnienia i studia*.

66. Information comes from three sources: (1) In Tadeusz Bobrowski's letter to Conrad, 2 December 1891, we read about the eleven-year-old son of Kazimierz Bobrowski: "The youngest, Michaś, may be suffering from the same illness as you were—anyway he had a similar fit to yours in the autumn. The only difference is that the symptoms appeared much later than in your case and this makes one wonder if he will grow out of it by the age of fourteen, as you did." In the next letter, of 7 January 1892, he doubts whether Michaś will be able to attend school "for he is still ill—possibly threatened by a mental illness" (*CPB*, pp. 158, 160). (2) Mrs. Tekla Wojakowska, a cousin of the Korzeniowskis, who met Konrad in 1868 and saw him frequently for ten months in 1873–1874 (he was at that time in her father's care), recalls: "He used to suffer from severe migraine headaches and nervous attacks." (3) Konstanty Buszczyński, Stefan's son, who was Konrad's friend from 1869 to 1873 in Cracow, said in an interview given in 1920: "He was sickly, too, and very nervous, and given at times to epileptic seizures" (George P. Putnam, "Conrad in Cracow," *Outlook* [New York], 3 March 1920).

According to Bobrowski the attacks stopped in 1871; Mrs. Wojakowska maintains that Konrad suffered from them at sea as well, but she is not always reliable. Buszczyński does not specify the dates but says that as a sailor Korzeniowski was "the very picture of health." Probably the epileptic fits occurred in 1865 or 1866 and lasted slightly longer than Bobrowski remembered. Other indispositions, such as headaches, which hindered Konrad's studies, kept recurring later as well.

Conrad was probably alluding to his illness when he said that the exams at school "for certain reasons, happened to be [for him] a more difficult task than for other boys" (*A Personal Record*, p. 43).

67. Documents are in MS 6391, Jagiellonian Library. I am giving the dates in the new style. Róża Jabłkowska is incorrect in her theory that Korzeniowski's release was the result of the *ukaze* of 17 May 1867 to discontinue the investigations and to set free the prisoners accused of participating in the 1863 insurrection whose cases had not been closed (*Joseph Conrad* [Wrocław, 1964], p. 29): the verdict on Korzeniowski was legally valid and his case closed in May 1862.

68. Bobrowski, "Document," *CPB*, p. 187.

69. Korzeniowski to Kaszewski (from Lwów), 23 March 1868.

70. *Dziennik Literacki*, no. 14 (1868).

71. Korzeniowski to Buszczyński, 17 March 1868, MS 2064, vol. 1, Polish Academy of Sciences Library, Cracow.

72. Korzeniowski to Buszczyński, 16 May 1868, MS 2064, vol. 1, Polish Academy of Sciences Library. Similar opinions in a letter to Kaszewski, 23 March 1868.

73. Korzeniowski to Buszczyński, 10 May, and an undated letter from Topolnica, MS 2064, vol. 1, Polish Academy of Sciences Library, Cracow; to Kaszewski, 20 April, 10 May, and [24 June 1868].

74. S. Kieniewicz, *Historia Polski 1795–1918* (Warsaw, 1968), p. 310.

75. Korzeniowski to Kaszewski, 14 October 1868, announcing his departure for Lwów "on Saturday." In an undated letter to Buszczyński, MS 2064, vol. 1, Polish Academy of Sciences Library, he mentions his departure "in four days' time," which makes it possible to establish the date.

76. Korzeniowski to Buszczyński, 29 October 1868, MS 2064, vol. 1, Polish Academy of Sciences Library.

77. A. Nałęcz Korzeniowski, *Akt pierwszy. Dramat w jednej odsłonie* [The first act. A drama in one scene] (Lwów, 1869), p. vi. The drama itself is poor.

78. The recollections of Mrs. Jadwiga Kałuska (née Tokarska), quoted by R. Dyboski, "From Joseph Conrad's Youth," *Czas*, no. 196 (1927), reprinted in *Wspomnienia i studia*. Kałuska's account sounds plausible on the whole. The address of her father, a doctor, at Ormiańska Wyżna no. 121, had been given by Apollo to Kaszewski on 14 October 1869, with the request to have his letters sent there. The first part of the reminiscences of Mrs. Tekla Wojakowska, daughter of Antoni (Czosnowski, "Conradiana," reprinted in *Wspomnienia i studia*), relate to the same period. They contain among others the following often quoted fragment: "Once when I was visiting them I found Apollo sitting motionless in front of his wife's portrait. He never stirred on seeing us and Konradek who was accompanying me put his finger to his lips and said: 'Let us cross the room quietly. Father spends every anniversary of mother's death sitting all day and looking at her portrait; he does not speak or eat.'" But Apollo did not spend a single anniversary of his wife's death in Lwów. Also, the Korzeniowskis did not live in a gloomy flat in the Żółkiewski suburb, as Mrs. Wojakowska would have them, but in the center of Lwów, at 11 Szeroka Street (later Kopernik Street). This undermines the credibility of her recollections. The information about staging plays, given by Mrs. Kałuska, is confirmed not only by Mrs. Wojakowska but by her uncle, Leon Syroczyński (*LL*, I: 2).

79. Korzeniowski to Kaszewski, 24 December 1868.

80. Korzeniowski to Buszczyński, 7 February 1869, MS 2064, vol. 1, Polish Academy of Sciences Library.

81. Certificate of death in All Saints Church, Cracow, no. 298.

82. Apol[lo] N[ałecz] K[orzeniowski], "Studia nad dramatycznością w utworach Szekspira" [Studies on the dramatic element in Shakespeare's works], *Biblioteka Warszawska*, April 1868, p. 14.

83. *A Personal Record*, p. xi.

84. Conrad to Edward Garnett, 20 January, 1900, Edward Garnett, *Letters from Conrad, 1895 to 1924* (London, 1928), p. 168.

85. "I am in the possession of all unpublished manuscripts of the late Apollo Korzeniowski whom you honored with your friendship." Buszczyński lists, among others, some otherwise unknown translations of Shakespeare's dramas. MS 6490/IV, Jagiellonian Library.

86. Those reminiscences cannot be regarded as documentary evidence: most accounts of events require correction, and there are also surprising omissions. For example, Conrad never mentioned that his last year in Poland had been spent in Lwów; in *A Personal Record* he wrote that in 1873 his tutor "took his degree of the Philosophical Faculty" and later entered medical school. In fact, Pulman studied medicine from the beginning to the end (1868–1875). In "Poland Revisited" Conrad mentioned his wintertime walks to school in Cracow in 1868—but he arrived in Cracow toward the end of the winter in 1868 and did not attend school at that time.

87. "Poland Revisited," *Kraj*, no. 70 (1869): 169.

88. Teofila Bobrowska to Kaszewski, 12 June 1869, MS 3057, Jagiellonian Library.

89. Conrad to Garnett, 20 January 1900.

90. Bobrowski, *Pamiętniki*, 1:116 and 2:27. Frederick Karl's statement (*Joseph Conrad: The Three Lives* [New York, 1979], p. 87) that Bobrowski was an admirer of the French Revolution and a "minor league Dostoevski" is groundless. Bobrowski was an antirevolutionary and would have abhorred Dostoyevski's emotionalism.

91. Bobrowski, *Pamiętniki*, 1:195, 357; 2:8, 23, 24.

92. Ibid., 1:441–443. But he too was, for once, "stirred by deeper feeelings," as recalled by August Iwański, Sr., *Pamiętniki* [Memoirs] (Warsaw, 1968), p. 154, when in 1861 he offered, unsolicited, a financial contribution to an insurgent army.

93. Documents of Georgeon and his wife, MS 344/59, Jagiellonian Library.

94. Bobrowska to Kaszewski, 12 June 1869.

95. Bobrowski, "Document"; Jean-Aubry and later biographers place Wartenberg in Bohemia, but the only health resort of that name lies in Upper Bavaria.

96. Konrad Korzeniowski's name does not appear on any of the documents of St. Anne's Gymnasium, preserved in Cracow District State Archives; these records give a complete list of pupils for the relevant classes and school years. Nor can his name be traced on the list of pupils in the Memorial Book published for the three-hundredth anniversary of the founding of St. Anne's Gymnasium (Cracow, 1888). The list does not include the names of boys who were Konrad's friends at the time (Buszczyński, the brothers Taube). L. Krzyżanowski ("Kiedy Conrad po raz pierwszy widział morze i gdzie chodził do szkoły?," letter to the editor of Wiadomości Literackie, no. 454 [1932]) informs us that T. Żuk-Skarszewski discovered in the minutes of the meetings of St. Anne's teaching staff (no. 29, 17 September) the following note: "Józef Korzeniowski has passed the entrance examination to class IV" (GLN, no. 19/51/, State Archives, Cracow). In all known documents, however, Apollo Korzeniowski's son has always been referred to as "Konrad"; it is therefore doubtful that the entry refers to him. The matter cannot be resolved because the minutes of the teachers' meetings for the years 1865–1873 have not been preserved. "Józef Korzeniowski's" name does not appear on the lists of pupils, so, apparently, having passed the examination he did not become a regular pupil. If the entry does refer to Konrad Korzeniowski, he was two years behind the normal age of pupils in form IV. And since Korzeniowski's name cannot be traced among those pupils who sat for their entrance examination in 1869, one may assume that his grandmother Teofila's letter refers either to a "private" examination for pupils outside the school, or to St. Jacek's Gymnasium—the other Cracow gymnasium. The latter's documents were destroyed by fire during World War II, but in the thirties they had apparently been scrutinized without success (Krzyżanowski, "Kiedy Conrad."). The problem of Conrad's school history has been discussed at length by A. Busza, "Conrad's Polish Literary Background and Some Illustrations of the Influence of Polish Literature on His Work," Antemurale, 1966, pp. 244–247. Busza is inclined to believe that Conrad was a pupil at St. Anne's.

I suppose that Conrad remembered the name of a well-known Cracow gymnasium where he was to have gone or whose curriculum he followed and mentioned it in order to conceal his illness and the fact that he had not gone to school. The sentence quoted is taken from the interview given to Dąbrowski, "Rozmowa z J. Conradem."

97. Krzyżanowski, "Kiedy Conrad"; Busza, "Conrad's Polish Literary Background," pp. 142–144.

98. Kazimierz Bobrowski to Konrad Korzeniowski, 25 December 1869, Yale; S. Buszczyński to J. I. Kraszewski, 19 January 1870, MS 6490/IV, Jagiellonian Library.

99. Bobrowski, "Document," CPB, p. 188; court appointment of legal guardians, MS 6391, Jagiellonian Library.

100. Bobrowski to Korzeniowski, 20 September 1869, MS 2889, National Library, Warsaw; this MS contains all Bobrowski's letters to his nephew (CPB, pp. 35–36).

101. Born at Kalnik, 1865. Information obtained from her daughter, Mrs. de Virion, by Miss Monika Gronkiewicz. Janina's sister Karolina was three years older than Konrad.

102. MS of "R.L.," Yale. It says that the protagonist was in love for the first time "towards the end of summer, during his last school holidays."

103. Bobrowski to Konrad Korzeniowski, 26 October 1876, CPB, p. 44.

104. "Geography and Some Explorers," Last Essays, p. 11. McClintock's book appeared two years later (1859) than Conrad maintained, and he probably read it in French, since no Polish translation had been published.

105. *Wędrowiec*, no. 152 (1872). Kubary's book, *Obrazki z wysp żeglarskich*, came out in Warsaw in 1873. On another Polish traveler to the Pacific islands, Piotr Wereszycki, see J. Dürr, "Józef Conrad na drodze do Polski" [Joseph Conrad on his way to Poland], *Ruch Literacki*, no. 8 (1932). But Konrad was not in a great hurry to embark on such long journeys.

106. In *Nostromo*, for instance, "the sea, which knows nothing of kings and priests and tyrants, is the holiest of all. . . . The spirit of liberty is upon the waters," p. 341.

107. J. Got, *Teatr krakowski pod dyrekcją A. Skorupki i S. Koźmiana* (Wrocław, 1962), p. 147. Modrzejewska played in Cracow theaters until May 1872.

108. S. Kieniewicz, *Adam Sapieha* (Lwów, 1939), p. 224.

109. K. Buszczyński's recollections included in: G. P. Putnam, "Conrad in Cracow," *Outlook*, 3 (March 1920).

110. Bobrowski, "Document," *CPB*, pp. 191–192; *A Personal Record*, pp. 38 and 43; Conrad to E. Garnett, 29 March 1898, E. Garnett, *Letters*, p. 126.

111. Bobrowski, "Document," *CPB*, p. 192. For the information about the boarding school I am indebted to Tadeusz Garczyński.

112. The research carried out at my request by Dr. W. Borys in Lwów archives yielded no result.

113. *Wspomnienia i studia*, pp. 87–88.

114. The anecdote comes from T. Garczyński.

115. *Wspomnienia i studia*, pp. 39–40.

116. Adam Pulman to Konrad Korzeniowski, 14 March [1874], Yale.

117. Bobrowski, "Document," *CPB*, p. 193. The date of departure established thanks to Bobrowski's letter to Konrad, 26 October 1876, *CPB*, p. 39.

118. R. Blüth, "O tragicznej decyzji krakowskiej Konrada Korzeniowskiego" [On Konrad Korzeniowski's tragic decision in Cracow], *Wspomnienia i studia*, p. 399. Blüth's essay contains, however, many penetrating remarks on the subject of Conrad's early life. Similar hypotheses concerning the departure were advanced also by other scholars, for example, S. Zabierowski, *Conrad w Polsce* [Conrad in Poland] (Gdańsk, 1971), pp. 39–52.

119. Baines, *Joseph Conrad*, p. 32.

120. Pulman's letter shows that the decision about the departure was made in March 1874 and Konrad's holiday in Switzerland had taken place one year earlier.

121. Painful childhood experiences are a frequent factor in the aetiology of depression (A. Kępiński, *Melancholia* [Warsaw, 1974], p. 208). It is possible that Korzeniowski's psychological complaints had, at first, a reactive character. On the rebellious form of youthful depression, see Kępiński, *Melancholia*, p. 15.

122. Counting from Apollo's death. Precise data in Bobrowski, "Document," *CPB*, p. 193. A further 525 rubles spent had been given to Konrad by the Korzeniowski sisters.

123. *Sprawozdanie C. K. Dyrekcji Gimnazjalnej przy Św. Annie w Krakowie z roku szkolnego 1869* [Report of the I. R. Direction of the St. Anne's Gymnasium of school year 1869], (Cracow, 1869); same for the year 1870 (Cracow, 1870); same for the year 1871 (Cracow, 1871); *Sprawozdanie Dyrektora c. k. Gimnazjum Nowodworskiego czyli Św. Anny w Krakowie za rok szkolny 1873* [Report of Director of the I. R. Nowodworski alias St. Anne's Gymnasium in Cracow for school year 1873] (Cracow, 1873). Stefan I. Możdżeń, "Podręczniki w galicyjskich szkołach średnich (1860–1885)" [School manuals in Galician secondary schools (1860–1885)], *Acta Universitatis Wratislaviensis*, no. 248; *Prace Pedagogiczne VII* (Wrocław, 1875), pp. 33–

59. Religious instruction occupied two hours a week; pupils read a condensed edition of the Bible prepared by A. Tyc.

II. IN MARSEILLES: 1874—1878

1. M. Dąbrowski, "Rozmowa z J. Conradem" [A chat with J. Conrad], *Tygodnik Ilustrowany*, no. 16 (1914).

2. It may be useful to compile a short list of similarities and contradictions between the respective versions. In *The Sisters* (1896), the characters are Stephen, a Ruthenian painter, and two sisters of Basque origin. One sister has been brought up in the country by an uncle, a sullen, fanatical priest; the other has been looked after by another uncle, Ortega, an orange merchant in Paris. The names of the sisters, Rita and Teresa, are the same as in *The Arrow of Gold*. Rita is charming and popular; all we know about Teresa is that her uncle wants her to become a nun. In *The Mirror of the Sea* ("'Tremolino,'" 1905), Rita is a delightfully volatile creature, an ex-mistress of a Paris painter, and in close relationship with Don Carlos and J. K. M. Blunt. The sailing ship *Tremolino* belongs to a syndicate of four: Conrad and his three friends, one of them an American, J. K. M. Blunt. In *The Arrow of Gold* (1917—1918) Rita is the embodiment of "the women of all time"; she is noble, beautiful, and wistful. Her relations with the deceased painter Henry Allègre who left her a big legacy are shrouded in mystery. She is naive, wise, and unapproachable. Her cousin, Ortega, the son of an orange merchant, has been pestering her from childhood with his love, transformed by time into mad jealousy. Rita's sister is a stupid and cunning bigot. The *Tremolino* belongs to the narrator, whose implacable enemy is Blunt; other friends are not mentioned.

3. H. van Marle, "Young Ulysses Ashore: On the Trail of Konrad Korzeniowski in Marseilles," *L'Epoque Conradienne* (1976), pp. 23—34.

4. Jocelyn Baines, *Joseph Conrad: A Critical Biography* (London, 1960), p. 34; Jerry Allen, *The Sea Years of Joseph Conrad* (New York, 1965), pp. 315—316; *Le Sémaphore de Marseille*, 16 December 1874 (information supplied by H. van Marle).

5. Bobrowski, "Document," *CPB*, p. 194.

6. G. J. Resink, "Axel Conrad en Martin Rimbaud," *Forum der Letteren* (1971), pp. 41—46; van Marle, "Young Ulysses."

7. Baines, *Joseph Conrad*, p. 34; Allen, *The Sea Years*, p. 316.

8. Tadeusz Bobrowski to Konrad Korzeniowski, 26 October 1876, *CPB*, p. 39. Unless otherwise stated, all Bobrowski's letters are dated here in new style. *LL*, 1 : 33.

9. *LL*, 1 : 34; Baines, *Joseph Conrad*, p. 35.

10. F. Ziejka, "Marsylskie dni Conrada" [Conrad's days in Marseilles], *Miesięcznik Literacki*, no. 10 (1975): 72—73.

11. G. Jean-Aubry, *Vie de Conrad* (Paris, 1947), p. 59.

12. Ziejka, "Marsylskie dni Conrada," pp. 71—72.

13. *JCKH*, p. 123.

14. Bobrowski to Korzeniowski, 26 October 1876.

15. Bobrowski to Korzeniowski, 27 September 1876 (9 October 1876), *CPB*, p. 36.

16. Bobrowski to Korzeniowski, 26 October 1876.

17. Allen, *The Sea Years*, p. 316.

18. *The Mirror of the Sea*, p. 163.

19. Norman Sherry, *Conrad's Western World* (Cambridge, 1971), pp. 163–164.

20. Allen, *The Sea Years*, p. 24. It is impossible to uphold Allen's assertion that the *Saint Antoine* sailed as far as Colón, Panama. In order to cover in twenty-nine days the route from Saint Pierre to Puerto Cabello to La Guaira to Cartagena to Saint Pierre, including the stops in ports, the ship had to make about two thousand sea miles, exceeding the normal sailing speed. To reach Colón would mean covering an additional six hundred miles. It is virtually impossible, therefore, to accept as valid Bobrowski's information (letter to Buszczyński, 24 March 1879, *CPB*, p. 175) that Korzeniowski had visited New Orleans. It is probable, although difficult to verify, that the ship was used for gunrunning (*LL*, 1:37). However, Allen's supposition that the arms may have been used in the battle at Los Chancos (31 August) is unfounded because it would not have been possible to deliver them on time as far inland.

21. Allen, *The Sea Years*, pp. 316–317.

22. Bobrowski to Korzeniowski, 26 October 1876.

23. Baines, *Joseph Conrad*, p. 42; Bobrowski to Korzeniowski, 22 June 1877, *CPB*, p. 45; Bobrowski to Buszczyński, 24 March 1879.

24. Bobrowski to Korzeniowski, 22 June 1877.

25. Ibid. and 8 August 1877, *CPB*, p. 47.

26. Bobrowski to Korzeniowski, 14 September 1877, *CPB*, p. 50.

27. Ibid.

28. Bobrowski to Korzeniowski, 8 August 1877.

29. Bobrowski to Korzeniowski, 14 September 1877.

30. Van Marle, "Young Ulysses"; Bobrowski mentions Grand in a letter to Buszczyński, 24 March 1879.

31. Bobrowski, "Document," and letter to Buszczyński, 24 March 1879; Konrad Korzeniowski, receipt for money received from Katarzyna Nałęcz Korzeniowska, dated 12/24 March 1878, Marseilles, *Echo Tygodnia*, no. 31 (1929).

32. In the "Document," Bobrowski records that the news of his nephew's injury reached him in Kiev in February, meaning of course the old style date, since in his letter to Buszczyński, 24 March 1879, he states that he left Kiev on 24 February [8 March, new style], some time after receiving the news and exchanging telegrams in Marseilles. Thus Konrad's attempted suicide probably took place on 1 or 2 March.

33. See Bobrowski to Buszczyński, 12/24 March 1879. Fecht, as Hans van Marle has established, was five years older than Korzeniowski.

34. See, for example, *Diccionario de historia de España* (Madrid, 1968), 1:687. See also Baines, *Joseph Conrad*, pp. 52–53; van Marle, "Young Ulysses."

35. Ziejka, "Marsylskie dni Conrada," pp. 75–76.

36. Henry Grand (Henry C. in *The Mirror of the Sea*) apparently served as a model for Mills (*LL*, 1:40–41); according to Jean-Aubry, Prax represents the sculptor Frétigny (*Vie de Conrad*, p. 60).

37. Compare *The Mirror of the Sea*, p. 157 to *The Arrow of Gold*, p. 18. Conrad was in possession of the photograph of himself that he had dedicated to his grandmother probably after 1890.

38. See chapter XIV, pp. 428–429 and 444–445.

39. Duteil's documents contain no record of employment from 14 April 1877 to 7 November 1878; in Dominic Cervoni's documents there is a blank after 14 October 1877. Baines, *Joseph Conrad*, pp. 52–53.

40. Van Marle, "Young Ulysses"; compare Ugo Mursia, "Włoskie dzieje kilku statków Josepha Conrada," *Nautologia*, no. 4 (1976): 51–52.

41. *The Mirror of the Sea*, pp. 155–183; *The Arrow of Gold*, p. 256.

42. Ford Madox Ford, *Joseph Conrad: A Personal Remembrance* (London 1924), p. 85.

43. Van Marle, "Young Ulysses."

44. Sherry, *Western World*, pp. 163–167. This is how the son of César Cervoni describes in his letter to Sherry the first meeting between his father and Conrad: "One day, when my father was on board the *Saint Antoine* my father saw a slim and very distinguished man arrive in the company of his fellow countryman Dominic Cervoni. . . . Dominic Cervoni said that the gentleman had been put on board by the firm as super-cargo and he recommended him to my father's care. . . . The Captain . . . told him in patois to take care of the man and to spare him too many contacts with the other members of the crew."

45. Baines, *Joseph Conrad*, p. 54.

46. Jean-Aubry, *Vie de Conrad*, p. 69: "un passage en pays basque près de la Bidassoa." The Bidassoa is a small river, thirty miles long, running along a part of the border between France and Spain and emptying into the Bay of Biscay near Fuenterrabia. The name *Lastaola* does not appear in geographical dictionaries.

47. Baines, *Joseph Conrad*, p. 53.

48. Ibid., p. 56, and van Marle, "Young Ulysses."

49. Ziejka, "Marsylskie dni Conrada," p. 74.

50. I published the letter from Bobrowski to Buszczyński as long ago as 1957 (*Życie Literackie*, 6 October, no. 40); in spite of that the theory of the duel is still supported by Allen, *The Sea Years*, pp. 85–93 and W. Chwalewik, "Conrad in the Light of a New Record," *Kwartalnik Neofilologiczny*, no. 1 (1971): 51–55. Allen adduces mainly *The Arrow of Gold*; also a remark by Richard Curle, p. 44, which may have been based on that same novel; and indirectly Aniela Zagórska, "A Few Reminiscences on Conrad," *Wspomnienia i studia*, p. 96, who recalls that Conrad confessed to her (in a way that seems to me rather unconvincing) how he had been wounded in a duel but managed to "fracasser la patte" of his opponent. Van Marle, "Young Ulysses," rightly points out that Blunt could not have served seventeen years in the cavalry with one of his arms "smashed." Edmund Pugh, referred to by Chwalewik, maintains that Conrad described to him a duel with swords, and even bared his chest; but Pugh makes no mention of the scar ("Joseph Conrad As I Knew Him," *T. P.'s and Cassell's Weekly*, 23 August 1924). John Conrad, in his memoirs, *Joseph Conrad: Times Remembered* (Cambridge, 1981), p. 181, tells that he once noticed some scars on his father's chest: "Just below his left shoulder in the pectoral muscle, the white weals looked as though they had been made with a sword or cutlass. There were two about an inch long, tapering together towards the top and another pair about the same length forming a cross slightly below and to the left of the first pair. They appeared to be quite clean, straight cuts but I could not see whether there were any marks of stitches." Conrad gave his son to understand that those were marks left from a duel with sidearms. The description of the scars does not suggest cut wounds; it is hard to imagine that Korzeniowski's adversary slashed him again and again in the same place; the blade must have cut through his clothes as well. One may consider sword thrusts, but then the scars would be found on the same level, and apart. The description suggests surgical cuts and not scars left by bullet wounds. In my interpretation I have made use of the information supplied by the surgeon, Professor Witold Rudowski. Conrad's scar was situated on the left side of his body, while bullet wounds received in duels are usually on the right side.

51. Ziejka suggests that the description of the duel in *The Arrow of Gold* was influenced by a real duel, with swords, that took place on 3 December 1877 in Montredon between Clovis Hugues and Joseph Daime ("Marsylskie dni Conrada," pp. 74–75). Hugues, a communard, leftist poet and journalist, and later a radical socialist deputy, was married—but only before a registrar—to Jeanne Royannez, later a well-known sculptor. Daime, the editor of *L'Aigle*, a Bonapartist paper, wrote that she was Hugues's mistress. The duel ended with Daime's death; Hugues, who at first escaped abroad, returned to France and was found innocent by the court in Marseilles, in February 1878. Jean-Aubry maintains that Conrad knew Hugues personally (*LL*, 1:35); would the biting remarks in *The Arrow of Gold* (for example pp. 71–72) about the "Red" journalist be aimed at him?

52. The origin of Bobrowski to Buszczyński, 24 March 1879, is as follows: Adam Pulman, Conrad's old tutor, alarmed by gossip, wrote to Buszczyński on 10 March 1879. Buszczyński, who had known nothing about the young Korzeniowski, wrote to Bobrowski, who then responded.

53. Pulman to Korzeniowski, 14 March 1874, Yale; see also Bobrowski to Korzeniowski, 9 November 1891, *CPB*, p. 153.

54. See Antoni Kępiński, *Melancholia* (Warsaw, 1974), pp. 144–145.

III. THE RED ENSIGN: 1878–1886

1. At the end of *A Personal Record*, pp. 137–138, Conrad recounts having seen the red ensign on a square-topsailed cargo steamer, the *James Westoll*, but the ship of that name was not built until 1884, and it had only two masts (Jerry Allen, *The Sea Years of Joseph Conrad*, p. 13). Conrad probably had in mind the steamer *James Watson*, which arrived in Marseilles on 10 December 1875, five days before he left on the *Mont Blanc* (H. van Marle bases this information on *Lloyd's List*, 15 December 1874).

2. *A Personal Record*, p. 122.

3. R. L. Cornewall-Jones, *The British Merchant Service* (London, 1898), pp. 270–271.

4. Tadeusz Bobrowski to Konrad Korzeniowski, 28 May 1878, *CPB*, p. 52. Bobrowski also corresponded on the subject with Fecht, to whose address he had been sending money (T. Bobrowski to Konrad Korzeniowski, 8 July 1878, *CPB*, pp. 53–56); the deposit was probably authentic.

5. *Shipping and Mercantile Gazette*, 4, 11, 13, 28 May, and 11 June 1878. Information from Hans van Marle.

6. AAC (Agreement and Account of Crew), *Mavis*, BT 100/35, Public Record Office, London.

7. Joseph Conrad to J. de Smet, 23 January 1911, *LL*, 2:124. He mentioned the *Mavis* only once (*A Personal Record*, p. 39), also recalling the strong Scottish accent of the second engineer; in fact, however, the second engineer came from Cornwall (AAC, *Mavis* and a letter from van Marle to the author, 23 October 1975).

8. *LL*, 2:47. After him Baines, Allen, and others give the date as 18 June, but it does not concur with AAC, *Mavis* and the *Shipping and Mercantile Gazette*, which both give the date as 10 June. Bobrowski in his letter of 8 July (*CPB*, pp. 53–56) refers to Korzeniowski's letter of 9 June, posted after his trip from Lowestoft to London; the only explanation of that date may be the fact that Bobrowski, who for everyday purposes used the old-style calender, "translated" for his own use the date of his nephew's letter (21 June) into the old style and then forgot about it.

9. Bobrowski, "Document," *CPB*, p. 198, and letter to Korzeniowski, 8 July 1878. F. R. Karl, *Joseph Conrad: The Three Lives* (New York, 1979), p. 182, gives the name of the *Mavis*'s master as Munnings but fails to reveal the source of his information, which is not substantiated by AAC, *Mavis*.

10. T. Bobrowski to Korzeniowski, 8 July 1878.

11. Mrs. G. F. W. Hope to J. T. Babb, 7 March 1928, Yale; Hope's reminiscences of Conrad kindly made available by Norman Sherry.

12. AAC, *Skimmer of the Sea*; Certificate of Discharge, Yale.

13. AAC, *Skimmer*, and Conrad's speech at the meeting of the Lifeboat Institution, 17 April 1923, *CDAUP*, pp. 110–112.

14. Conrad to R. B. C. Graham, 4 February 1898, Cedric T. Watts, ed., *Joseph Conrad's Letters to R. B. Cunninghame Graham* (Cambridge, 1969), p. 75; he affirms there that it happened "twenty-two years ago." Compare Conrad to de Smet, 23 January, 1911.

15. Certificate of Discharge, Yale.

16. E. Blackmore, *The British Mercantile Marine: A Short Historical Review* (London, 1897), pp. 146 and 194; Cornewall-Jones, *British Merchant Service*, p. 263.

17. T. Bobrowski to Korzeniowski, 14 September 1878, *CPB*, pp. 56–58, in reply to Korzeniowski to T. Bobrowski, 28 August and 1 September 1878.

18. *Notes on Life and Letters*, pp. 152–153; he maintains here, however, that it was his first visit to London.

19. T. Bobrowski to Buszczyński, 24 March 1879, *CPB*, p. 175.

20. AAC, *Duke of Sutherland*, BT 100/121, Public Record Office.

21. See, for example, R. C. K. Ensor, *England 1870–1914* (Oxford, 1936), p. 111; W. Flamant and J. Singer-Kérel, *Modern Economic Crises* (London, 1968), p. 34.

22. R. D. Foulke, "Life in the Dying World of Sail, 1870–1910," *The Journal of British Studies* 3, no. 1 (1963): 129–130.

23. Ibid., p. 127.

24. Ibid., pp. 126–127; Cornewall-Jones, *British Merchant Service*, pp. 270–271; Blackmore, *British Mercantile Marine*, p. 158.

25. AAC, *Duke of Sutherland*, and Jerry Allen, *The Sea Years of Joseph Conrad* (New York, 1965), pp. 157–158.

26. As Józef Miłobędzki rightly observes in *Conrad w żeglarskiej kurcie* [Conrad in a sailor's jacket], (Gdańsk, 1972), p. 10.

27. F. T. Bullen, *The Men of the Merchant Service* (London, 1900), pp. 287–293; Cornewall-Jones, *British Merchant Service*, pp. 296–298.

28. Gerald Morgan, "Nauclerus," a dissertation on the sea aspects of Conrad's life and works, manuscript made available by the author.

29. T. Bobrowski to Buszczyński, 30 May 1879, *CPB*, p. 179.

30. Cornewall-Jones, *British Merchant Service*, p. 271: "Most British ships are better victualled than foreign ships"; Foulke, *Dying World*, p. 113: "British ships—notorious the world over for poor and scanty food."

31. Cornewall-Jones, *British Merchant Service*, pp. 266–267.

32. Foulke, *Dying World*, pp. 111–112.

33. Ibid., p. 129; compare Allen, *The Sea Years*, pp. 101–102, 112.

34. Conrad, *The Mirror of the Sea*, pp. 121–127; but in 1916 he said that he had been relieved from his duties at his own request; J. G. Sutherland, *At Sea with Conrad* (Boston, 1922), p. 95.

35. Conrad to J. G. Huneker, 16 April 1909, Dartmouth College Library, Hanover, New Hampshire.

36. Bobrowski to Buszczyński, 30 May 1879. According to Hans van Marle, this seaman, merchant, and geographer was most probably William Henry Eldred (1819–1897), a founding member of the Geographical Society of Australasia. Eldred left England in 1839; as early as 1848 he owned and commanded a ship; in 1848–1850 he sailed Indonesian waters; later he was active in the trade between Australia and Chile (van Marle to the author, 13 May 1981).

37. Van Marle's conclusion, based on an analysis of the voyages of the vessel in the years 1873–1877 and on references in Conrad's texts. Letter to the author, 14 July 1976. Compare *The Mirror of the Sea*, pp. 78–79. Apart from Korzeniowski and the officers, only four sailors completed the southbound passage, among them one Swede and two youths (AAC). On the certificate of discharge (Yale) Korzeniowski's name is recorded as C. Kokenonski.

38. T. Bobrowski to Korzeniowski, 7 November 1879, *CPB*, pp. 58–60, in reply to letter of 20 October.

39. Blackmore, *British Mercantile Marine*, p. 146; T. Bobrowski to Korzeniowski, 7 November 1879. The phrase "I sent to M. Déléstang a very lofty letter asking him for a testimonial for you . . . now you must write to him" shows that it was not a matter of a simple confirmation of facts but of a favor.

40. AAC, *Europa*, BT 100/19, Public Record Office. Signing on, he gave his name as "Konrad Korzeniowski," signing off as "Conrad Korzeniowski"; the certificate of discharge (Yale) is issued in the name "K. Koreinowski," age 21.

41. T. Bobrowski to Korzeniowski, 12 February 1880, *CPB*, p. 60, in reply to letter of 2 February.

42. Hope's reminiscences; Ward's name turns up in Bobrowski's letters from 22 August 1881 to 11 August 1882—he sent Korzeniowski's money to Ward's address. *CPB*, pp. 75–87.

43. Van Marle, "Conrad's English Lodgings, 1880–1896," *Conradiana* 8, no. 3 (1976): 257–258.

44. Hope's reminiscences, regarded by Norman Sherry as proof of Conrad's faithful rendering of his personal experiences in "Heart of Darkness." *Conrad's Western World* (Cambridge, 1971), p. 132. Actually the reminiscences, in everything that is not based on facts directly available to Hope, have minimal documentary value, since they are quite obviously based on what Hope read in Conrad's books about his experiences.

45. Richard Curle, *Caravansary and Conversation: Memories of Places and Persons* (London, 1937), p. 153.

46. T. Bobrowski to Korzeniowski, 30 May 1880, *CPB*, p. 62, in reply to letters of 1, 6, 11, and 16 May received simultaneously.

47. Photocopy of the original, *LL*, 1: after p. 38; English translation in Norman Sherry, *Conrad and His World* (London, 1972), p. 20. The French *pilotin* ("apprentice") was translated as "midshipman."

48. This application and those following, as well as Korzeniowski's ups and downs at the examinations, are described by Hans van Marle, "Plucked and Passed on Tower Hill: Conrad's Examination Ordeals," *Conradiana* 8, no. 2 (1976): 99–109. The original documents are in the General Register and Record Office of Shipping and Seamen, Cardiff, Wales. The application form is signed "Konrad de Korzeniowski."

49. See, for example, Blackmore, *British Mercantile Marine*, pp. 148 and 194. Service "before the mast," that is, as ordinary seaman at sea, was required.

50. See *Regulations Relating to the Examinations of Masters and Mates in the Mercantile Marine* (London, 1881), pp. 6–8.

51. John Newton, *Newton's Seamanship Examiner; Being the Seamanship Required of Candidates for Masters and Mates Certificates of Competency*. On p. 117 all possible examination questions and answers are given (56 pages for Second Officer, 30 for First Officer, 20 for Master). Lessons with Newton are mentioned by Bobrowski in his letter of 17 June 1880, *CPB*, pp. 64–66.

52. Newton's other handbook was *Newton's Guide to the Board of Trade Examinations of Masters and Mates of Sailing Ships and Steamships in Navigation and Nautical Astronomy*, 6th ed. (London, 1881). It gives 136 pages of text and replies to twelve possible sets of examination questions on navigation and nautical astronomy. Blackmore wrote in 1897, "The young aspirant [for second mate], on discovering that no education was required beyond a mere knowledge of figures, troubled himself no more about the matter until, having put in his four year time, he went to the nearest 'crammer' to be coached for an examination, all the tricks of which the crammer knew beforehand, and this is a rule which has continued to the present day." *British Mercantile Marine*, p. 184.

53. *Regulations*, p. 5.

54. Conrad tells of this examination in *A Personal Record*, pp. 112–114, and also in *Chance*, pp. 4–6; in both cases he stresses its long duration.

55. T. Bobrowski to Korzeniowski, 17 June 1880, *CPB*, pp. 64–66.

56. T. Bobrowski to Korzeniowski, 28 June (old style = 10 July 1880), *CPB*, pp. 66–67, in reply to letter of 13 June.

57. AAC, *Loch Etive*, BT 100/42, Public Record Office. The first officer who in *The Mirror of the Sea* appears as P. (pp. 39–45) was actually William Purdu from Glasgow.

58. Bullen, *Merchant Service*, pp. 144–145; Cornewall-Jones, *British Merchant Service*, pp. 261, 287.

59. *Sydney Morning Herald*, 25 November 1880.

60. AAC, *Loch Etive*; T. Bobrowski to Korzeniowski, 13 May 1881, *CPB*, p. 67.

61. Foulke, *Dying World*, pp. 108–110.

62. Basil Lubbock, *The Last of the Windjammers* (Glasgow, 1929), 1:1.

63. "Christmas Day at Sea," *Last Essays*, pp. 29–34. The recollection requires several corrections: it cannot refer, as the text implies, to 1879, because that year Korzeniowski was in the Mediterranean; if it refers to 1881 (as indicated, among others, by the presence of the whaler *Alaska* on the Southern Ocean, west from New Zealand, as established by van Marle), it has to be at the end of January. Curle's supposition, in the introduction to Conrad's *Last Essays*, that the recollection refers to the passage on the *Duke of Sutherland* to Australia, and not from Australia as Conrad writes, is incompatible with the bearings given by Conrad; the course around the Cape of Good Hope did not run so far south.

64. "Initiation," *The Mirror of the Sea*, pp. 128–148.

65. Joining the *Loch Etive* he had signed himself "Konrad Korzeniowski," on leaving it, "Conrad Korzeniowski." On the certificate of discharge (Yale), the name is given as "Konrad Corzen," born 1858.

66. Bobrowski, "Document."

67. T. Bobrowski to Korzeniowski, *CPB*, pp. 67–69.

68. Blackmore, *British Mercantile Marine*, p. 194.

69. G. Fitzgerald, "A Hundred Years of Rates," *The Nautical Magazine*, 127 (January 1932): 73–79.

70. T. Bobrowski to Korzeniowski, 30 May 1881, *CPB*, pp. 69–70, in reply to letter of 20 May.

71. T. Bobrowski to Korzeniowski, 28 June 1881, *CPB*, p. 71, in reply to letter of 10 June; 15 August 1881 (from Marienbad), 26 May 1882; *CPB*, pp. 72–75, 84–86; 15 August was in reply to a letter of 10 August received 14 August.

72. T. Bobrowski to Korzeniowski, 28 June 1881 and 23 September 1881, *CPB*, pp. 71–72 and 79.

73. T. Bobrowski to Korzeniowski, 15 August 1881.

74. On 15 August 1881 Bobrowski maintained, "It seems to me that the owners of the *Anna Frost* [sic] in negotiating compensation for the ship should have included compensation for the things lost by her officers." And on 26 May 1882 he reminded his nephew, "You have still left unanswered my repeated question: did you get any compensation from the owner for the loss of your belongings in the *Anna Frost*. Answer, please. And if you didn't—give the reasons."

75. Jocelyn Baines, *Joseph Conrad: A Critical Biography* (London, 1960), p. 69; Allen, *The Sea Years*, pp. 151–153.

76. T. Bobrowski to Korzeniowski, 15 August 1881; Korzeniowski replied at once, suggesting the ways of getting the skulls. T. Bobrowski to Korzeniowski, 22 August 1881, *CPB*, pp. 75–76.

77. T. Bobrowski to Korzeniowski, 30 August/10 September 1881, *CPB*, pp. 77–78; one of the dates is wrong. Since the letter was written in Montreux, where the Gregorian calendar was used, the date 10 September is probably correct.

78. T. Bobrowski to Korzeniowski, 23 September 1881 (from Montreux-Vernet), *CPB*, pp. 79–80.

79. T. Bobrowski to Korzeniowski, 10 September 1881.

80. AAC, *Palestine*, BT 100/4, Public Record Office. Captain Beard is entered as "continuing" his service; Conrad's claim in "Youth" that it was his first command may refer only to the ship and not to that particular passage.

81. Bobrowski, "Document."

82. T. Bobrowski to Korzeniowski, 23 September 1881.

83. *Youth*, pp. vi–vii; the Author's Note dates from 1917.

84. *Shipping and Mercantile Gazette*, 10 February 1882, stated that the *Palestine* left Falmouth on 8 February; on 11 May it reported that the vessel was still in Falmouth.

85. The report of the Court of Enquiry investigation, 2 April 1883, Singapore, attached to AAC, *Palestine*. Fragments first published by Baines, *Joseph Conrad*, pp. 70–72; the full text published by Norman Sherry, *Conrad's Eastern World* (Cambridge, 1966), pp. 297–298. The date of return to Falmouth, *Shipping and Mercantile Gazette*, 26 February 1882.

86. T. Bobrowski to Korzeniowski, 20 January 1882, *CPB*, pp. 81–82.

87. See T. Bobrowski to Korzeniowski, 11 August 1882, *CPB*, p. 87.

88. The volume of Byron's works is mentioned by Hope in his reminiscences, probably on the basis of "Youth"; the recent death of Sutherland is referred to by Bobrowski in his letter of 26 May 1882, *CPB*, pp. 84–86, in reply to letter of 11 May. According to Hope, J. H. Brady took over the running of the firm.

89. T. Bobrowski to Korzeniowski, 26 May 1882.

90. Kazimierz Bobrowski to Korzeniowski, 30 April 1882. The reasons for Tadeusz's silence (absence from home and loss of a letter from Korzeniowski) is explained in letter of 24 April 1882 in reply to letters of 3 February and 12 April. MS 2889, National Library, Warsaw.

91. T. Bobrowski to Korzeniowski, 26 May 1882.

92. Bobrowski here supports the testimony of "Youth": "The tergiversations of your Mr Wilson are not to my liking either." 11 August 1882, *CPB*, p. 87.

93. Ibid.

94. Cornewall-Jones, *British Merchant Service*, p. 285.

95. Blackmore, *British Mercantile Marine*, p. 170; Cornewall-Jones, *British Merchant Service*, p. 286.

96. Bullen, *Merchant Service*, pp. 134–139.

97. The Court of Inquiry report, Singapore, attached to AAC, *Palestine*.

98. Joseph Conrad to Richard Curle, 24 April 1922, Indiana. Curle withdrew from the text all fragments called in question by Conrad.

99. Original in Yale, reproduction, *LL*, 1:74. In AAC, *Palestine*, he twice signed himself Conrad Korzeniowski; on the certificate of discharge (Yale) his name entered as C. Korzeniowski.

100. Hope's reminiscences.

101. Blackmore, *British Mercantile Marine*, pp. 122 and 133.

102. Sherry, *Eastern World*, p. 25.

103. Ibid., pp. 25–29.

104. Passage through Suez: T. Bobrowski to Korzeniowski, 5 June 1883, *CPB*, pp. 88–89; Sherry's supposition that Korzeniowski was on board the steamer *Leon XIII* (*Eastern World*, p. 29) cannot be upheld, as the vessel did not pass through the Suez Canal until 28 May. Van Marle's detailed research shows that three steamers could be considered: the German *Lydia* and the British *Merionetshire* and *Diomed*. The first had only two passengers. The *Merionetshire* left Singapore on 18 April and arrived in London on 29 May; the *Diomed* left on 19 April and arrived on 30 May. Van Marle's to author, 18 December 1975.

105. T. Bobrowski to Korzeniowski, 5 June 1883 (from Kiev, although dated "Kazimierówka"), *CPB*, pp. 88–89, in reply to letters of 4 April from Singapore and 13 May from Port Said.

106. T. Bobrowski to Korzeniowski, 24 June 1883, *CPB*, pp. 90–91, in reply to letters of 5 and 13 June.

107. T. Bobrowski to Korzeniowski, 9 July 1883, *CPB*, pp. 91–92, in reply to letter received 25 June.

108. T. Bobrowski to Korzeniowski, 31 August 1883: "You must make certain, my dear lad, that the B. of Trade will be satisfied with 6 weeks, so that you do not have any more trouble." *CPB*, pp. 93–95.

109. T. Bobrowski to Korzeniowski, 31 August 1883.

110. Bobrowski establishes the date of arrival at Teplice in his letter of 31 August: "I am to stay here the full 4 weeks, that is till the 28th August/9 September."

111. Korzeniowski to Buszczyński, 14 August 1883, *CPB*, pp. 205–206.

112. Bobrowski, "Document" and letter of 31 August 1883. Bullen, *Merchant Service*, pp. 14 and 87; T. Brassey, *British Seamen as Described in Recent Parliamentary and Official Documents* (London, 1877), p. 326.

113. B. R. Mitchell, *Abstracts of British Historical Statistics* (Cambridge, 1962), p. 21.

114. AAC, *Riversdale*, BT 100/16, Public Record Office, and Allen, *The Sea Years*, p. 320.

115. The report of the court proceedings, quoted in a detailed account of the whole affair in G. Ursell's, "Conrad and the *Riversdale*," *Times Literary Supplement*, 11 July 1968.

116. Certificate of Discharge, Yale. On the certificate and the AAC, *Riversdale*, "Conrad Korzeniowski."

117. On the night of 28 April, in good weather, the ship went sixty miles off course; the logbook contains many contradictions. McDonald was suspended from command for twelve months (Ursell, "*Riversdale*").

118. Minutes of the Local Marine Board, London, 1884. Application to be examined granted to Konard Korgeniowski (sic) (information from van Marle).

119. *LL*, 1:77; the conversation took place in June 1924.

120. "Well Done," *Notes on Life and Letters* (written in 1918), pp. 179–181. Statistical data on Merchant Marine, Foulke, *Dying World*, p. 128.

121. AAC, *Narcissus*, BT 100/40, Public Record Office; Allen, *The Sea Years*, p. 321; Ian Watt, *Conrad in the Nineteenth Century* (Berkeley, 1979), p. 90, doubts whether Barron was a native of Georgia, as Allen claims, and argues convincingly that he probably came from the Leeward Islands; it is not certain whether he was black.

122. Baines, *Joseph Conrad*, pp. 76–77.

123. Ibid., p. 77.

124. On the certificate of discharge, "Conrad Korzeniowski"; on AAC, *Narcissus*, both times signed "Conrad Korzeniowski."

125. Hope's reminiscences.

126. Bobrowski, "Document."

127. Van Marle, "Plucked and Passed."

128. Conrad to A. T. Saunders, 14 June 1917, Sherry, *Eastern World*, pp. 295–296; catalogue of auction at Anderson Gallery in New York, 15–16 November 1926, quoted by van Marle, "Plucked and Passed."

129. "Outside Literature," *Last Essays*, pp. 41–42.

130. J. H. Retinger, *Conrad and His Contemporaries* (New York, 1943), p. 48.

131. Blackmore, *British Mercantile Marine*, p. 182.

132. K. Bobrowski to Korzeniowski, 8 December 1884 (old style = 20 December), *CPB*, pp. 95–96. The writer had learned three days earlier from his brother Tadeusz about Konrad having passed the examination.

133. Blackmore, *British Mercantile Marine*, pp. 133–134.

134. Bullen, *Merchant Service*, pp. 11–12 and 225–226.

135. AAC, *Tilkhurst*, BT 100/41, Public Record Office.

136. T. Bobrowski to Korzeniowski, 13 June 1885, *CPB*, pp. 96–98, in reply to letter of 14 May.

137. T. Bobrowski to Korzeniowski, 14 August 1885, *CPB*, pp. 98–99, in reply to letter of 3 June.

138. *LL*, 1:78.

139. Ibid., pp. 78–79; H. S. Kliszczewski, "Conrad w moim domu rodzinnym" [Conrad in my family home], *Wiadomości*, no. 33/34 (1949).

140. T. Bobrowski to Korzeniowski, 13 June 1885, p. 97.

141. AAC, *Tilkhurst*.

142. "Landfalls and Departures," *The Mirror of the Sea*, p. 9.

143. Allen, *The Sea Years*, pp. 171–172.

144. Ibid., p. 173.

145. Ibid., p. 172.

146. See Baines, *Joseph Conrad*, p. 78, which refers to Maria Danilewicz.

147. *LL*, 1:8–81. "Events" which "are casting shadows" in a reference to the worsening of the Anglo-Russian relations as a result of the Russian penetration in Afghanistan.
   Signatures on letters to Spiridion: 27 September, Conrad N. Korzeniowski; 13 October, the same; 25 November, Conrad Korzeniowski; 19 December, Konrad H. Korzeniowski; and 6 January, J. Conrad and C.K. The next to last form, repeated in the address (Mr. J. Conrad, 2nd Mate, ship *Tilkhurst*, Sailor's Home, Dundee), is the first recorded case of Korzeniowski's use of his future pen name. I suppose he followed the example of the addressee: Joseph Spiridion Kliszczewski used his second name, in Anglicized spelling, as surname.

148. Ibid., 1:83–85. Following the reform of 1884, which enfranchised landless workers, among others, the number of voters in Great Britain increased from three to five million. In the November 1885 election, the Liberals, after five months in opposition, again gained a majority in Parliament. The radical wing, led by Joseph Chamberlain, played a decisive role in the campaign. The brochure "The Radical Programme," published at his instigation in July 1885, carries demands, rejected by other Liberals, for land reform designed to increase the number of landholders and for future separation between the Anglican church and the state. Chamberlain was soon to become a leading imperialist and conservative politician. He did not even dream of paving a way for socialist reforms; on the contrary, he regarded himself as a defender of property. "I am putting the rights of property on the only firm and defensible basis. I believe that the danger of property lies in its abuse," he said in his preelection speech at Ipswich, 14 February 1885. One of the first modern electoral manipulators, he knew how to use phraseology with public appeal for purposes that were often contrary to what his observers imagined.

149. Korzeniowski to Spiridion, 25 November 1885 (from Calcutta), *LL*, 1:82.

150. T. Bobrowski to Korzeniowski, 18 December 1887, *CPB*, pp. 119–120.

151. *LL*, 1:79.

152. T. Bobrowski to Korzeniowski, 6 July 1886, *CPB*, pp. 104–105, in reply to letter received on 2 July.

153. AAC, *Tilkhurst*; on two consecutive lists he signed himself: Conrad Korzeniowski, Konrad Korzeniowski, and twice Conrad Korzeniowski.

154. T. Bobrowski to Korzeniowski, 5 April 1886, *CPB*, p. 101, in reply to letter of 8 January. The plan to remain in London is, of course, quite contrary to the whaling project proposed simultaneously to Spiridion, whose negative reaction reached Korzeniowski after his return to England. One should therefore place an extra question mark next to that plan.

155. T. Bobrowski to Korzeniowski, 24 April 1886, *CPB*, p. 103.

156. T. Bobrowski to Korzeniowski, 5 April 1886, *CPB*, p. 100.

157. Van Marle, "Plucked and Passed." Korzeniowski's failure at the examination is apparent in his application for a second examination.

158. T. Bobrowski to Korzeniowski, 20 July 1886, *CPB*, pp. 106–107; 9 November 1886, *CPB*, p. 112.

159. The errors are listed in detail by van Marle, "Plucked and Passed."

160. Blackmore, *British Mercantile Marine*, p. 243.

161. Naturalization papers, H.O. 144/177/A 44314, Public Record Office, London, first located by Hans van Marle, to whom I owe this information. Conrad wrote to his uncle on 25 August. See T. Bobrowski's letter of 9 September 1886 in reply, *CPB*, p. 109.

162. T. Bobrowski to Korzeniowski, 20 July 1886, p. 106.

163. T. Bobrowski to Korzeniowski, 30 September 1886, *CPB*, p. 111.

164. T. Bobrowski to Korzeniowski, 9 November 1886, *CPB*, p. 112, in reply to letters of 21 September and 29 October.

165. Ibid.

166. T. Bobrowski to Korzeniowski, 26 November 1886, *CPB*, pp. 113–114.

167. *A Personal Record*, pp. 117–121.

168. Van Marle, "Plucked and Passed."

169. Borys Conrad maintains in a letter to van Marle, 10 March 1976, that his father was 5 feet 7 inches tall (170cm), but even that seems an overestimate.

IV. MASTER IN THE BRITISH MERCHANT MARINE: 1886–1890

1. See Joseph Conrad, "The Books of My Childhood," *CDAUP*, p. 77. Many sentences in the interview do not sound authentic.

2. Tadeusz Bobrowski to Konrad Korzeniowski, 26 November 1886, *CPB*, p. 114.

3. Ibid.; according to Bobrowski's later remarks, Korzeniowski had already put in an application for his release from citizenship.

4. AAC, *Falconhurst*, BT 100/49, Public Record Office, London. For a considerable time his service on the *Falconhurst* escaped the attention of the biographers; the first to describe it in detail were E. A. Bojarski and H. R. Stevens, "Joseph Conrad and the *Falconhurst*," *Journal of Modern Literature* (1970): 197–208.

5. This is suggested by Hope's memoirs.

6. AAC, *Highland Forest*, BT 100/51, Public Record Office.

7. *The Mirror of the Sea*, p. 49.

8. I owe this information to Hans van Marle, letter to author, 18 December 1975.

9. *The Mirror of the Sea*, p. 53.

10. The matter is discussed in detail by J. Miłobędzki, *Conrad w żeglarskiej kurcie* (Gdańsk, 1972), pp. 16−18.

11. E. Blackmore, *The British Mercantile Marine: A Short Historical Review* (London, 1887), p. 170; R. L. Cornewall-Jones, *The British Merchant Service* (London, 1898), pp. 286−288.

12. *LL*, 2:187−189.

13. *The Mirror of the Sea*, pp. 54−55. The only information concerning the difficulties with loading and the subsequent accident comes from Conrad himself; by and large it seems probable.

14. AAC, *Highland Forest*. On the list of the crew signatures: Conrad Korzeniowski and J. Conrad Korzeniowski; on the certificate of service the name entered is J. C. Korzeniowski.

15. Bobrowski to Korzeniowski, 20 August 1887, reply to letter of 14 July received on 19 August. The letter indicates that Korzeniowski complained about his situation and asked for advice (*CPB*, p. 117).

16. Bobrowski to Korzeniowski, 17 April 1887, *CPB*, p. 116.

17. Bobrowski to Korzeniowski, 18 December 1887, reply to letter of 3 November received on 16 December, *CPB*, p. 120.

18. Norman Sherry, *Conrad's Eastern World* (Cambridge, 1966), p. 27.

19. *Lord Jim*, p. 12.

20. Sherry, *Eastern World*, pp. 28, 89−118.

21. Conrad's letter to W. G. St.Clair of 31 March 1917 (published by Sherry in *Eastern World*, pp. 316−317)—generally polite but compare sardonic remarks about St.Clair in Conrad's letter to Dent, 27 March 1917, *LL*, 2:186−187.

22. Sherry, *Eastern World*, pp. 89−118; and Andrzej Braun, *Śladami Conrada* (Warsaw, 1972), pp. 439−441, 478, 498.

23. Sherry, "Conrad and the *Vidar*," *Review of English Studies* (1963), pp. 157−158. The Arab's name has been differently transcribed; I follow Sherry's version.

24. Yale. The consignee of goods was Babalatchie—hence the origin of the name (but of nothing else) of Conrad's fictional hero.

25. Sherry, *Eastern World*, p. 30.

26. "The End of the Tether," especially pp. 166−167; Craig's reminiscences; *LL*, 1:93−100; errors corrected by: John Dozier Gordan, *Joseph Conrad: The Making of a Novelist* (Cambridge, Mass., 1940), p. 36; Sherry, *Eastern World*, particularly pp. 30−31; and Braun, *Śladami: Conrada*, pp. 40−42.

27. *The Shadow Line*, p. 6; Niven here called Nieven, the first mechanic left without name.

28. Sherry, "Conrad and the *Vidar*," p. 163.

29. The calculation: the passage Donggala-Singapore, 7−8 days; at the same speed (but taking into account slower progress on river) Donggala-Samarinda-Bulungan, 4−5 days; the passage would have been longer if the ship had called also at Banjarmasin. Compare Jerry Allen, *The Sea Years of Joseph Conrad* (New York, 1965), pp. 190−191 and 336. I assume here that the *Vidar* stopped at each port in turn only in one direction.

30. Braun, *Śladami Conrada*, pp. 431 and 474.

31. Conrad to St. Clair, 31 March 1917, Sherry, *Eastern World*, p. 317; and to Dent, 27 March 1917, *LL*, 2:186.

32. Allen (*The Sea Years*, p. 190) thinks that Conrad spent "over 3 weeks" in Berau, which is not possible; even Sherry's supposition that he would spend three days there on each voyage, that is, a total of twelve days, requires the assumption that he never stopped at any other port for a whole day.

33. Sherry, *Eastern World*, p. 121.

34. After Braun, *Śladami Conrada*, pp. 424, 428–431, 451, 453–455, based on his own description and surveyor's data.

35. Allen, *The Sea Years*, pp. 217–230; she relies here on field research by R. Haverschmidt.

36. *A Personal Record*, p. 87.

37. Jocelyn Baines, *Joseph Conrad: A Critical Biography* (London, 1966), p. 89.

38. Allen, *The Sea Years*, pp. 220–222. Although the author maintains that Conrad reproduced in his fictional Almayer the "prominent traits" of Charles Olmeijer and that "in essence the life of Almayer in *Almayer's Folly* and *An Outcast of the Islands* bore strong resemblance to that of the real Olmeyer," this is contradicted by her other statements.

39. Sherry, *Eastern World*, pp. 90–91.

40. Ibid., pp. 135–136.

41. Ibid., p. 30. Braun is much more cautious (*Śladami Conrada*, p. 428).

42. Conrad to William Blackwood, 13 December 1898, William Blackburn, ed., *Joseph Conrad: Letters to William Blackwood and David S. Meldrum* (Durham, N.C., 1958), p. 34.

43. J. S. Holmes and Hans van Marle, "Joseph Conrad in Indonesia," typescript of a lecture delivered at Münster University, 1962.

44. *Daily News*, 25 April 1895 and *Critic*, 11 May 1895. After Sherry, ed., *Conrad: The Critical Heritage* (London, 1973), pp. 47, 50.

45. *LL*, 1:98. Contrary to Jean-Aubry's assertion, incautiously repeated by Baines (*Joseph Conrad*, p. 90), Korzeniowski corresponded at the time not only with his uncle but also with Krieger and probably with other friends in England. Doubtless he wrote more than the average officer of the merchant service.

46. *The Shadow Line*, pp. 4 and 5.

47. Bobrowski to Korzeniowski, 13 January 1888, reply to letter of 1 December 1887, *CPB*, p. 120.

48. Certificate of Discharge, Yale; the list of the *Vidar*'s crew is not known.

49. Sherry, *Eastern World*, p. 183.

50. Conrad to James B. Pinker, Sunday [1917], NYPL. He wrote similar letters to Pinker, 3 February 1915, and to John Quinn, 24 December 1915, ibid.; compare also Conrad to Sidney Colvin, 27 February [1917], *LL*, 2:182, and Sherry, *Eastern World*, p. 211.

51. *The Shadow Line*, p. 29.

52. Contrary to what we learn in *The Shadow Line*, the chief officer of the *Otago* received his master's certificate on 29 June 1888 (Sherry, *Eastern World*, p. 268).

53. Ibid., p. 212.

54. "The End of the Tether," pp. 199–200.

55. The original in Public Record Office, London; first published by Sherry, *Eastern World*, p. 216. Letter dated 19 January 1888, the same date on the memorandum from Ellis to Korzeniowski (presently at Yale): "This is to inform you that you are required to proceed today in the SS

Melita to Bangkok and you will report your arrival to the British Consul which will show that I have engaged you to be Master of the *Otago* in accordance with the Consul's telegram on a voyage from Bangkok to Melbourne." The arrival of the *Hecate* was delayed, hence the change of ship (Sherry, *Eastern World*, p. 215).

56. Sherry, *Eastern World*, p. 217.

57. Conrad to St. Clair, 31 March 1917.

58. The actual tugboat called *Bangkok* was commanded by Captain Saxtrop and belonged to Windsor, Rose and Co. (Sherry, *Eastern World*, p. 238).

59. The chapter "Conrad's Predecessor on the *Otago*," ibid., pp. 218–227.

60. The steward's name was John Carlson (AAC, *Otago*; Sherry, *Eastern World*, pp. 230–232). Sherry mistakenly assumes that Conrad, when writing *The Shadow Line*, had access to the MS of "Falk," the MS had been sold in 1912 to John Quinn (Conrad to Quinn, 1 July 1912, NYPL). Carlson died on 16 January 1888 of cholera, in a hospital (AAC, *Otago*).

61. William Willis to Korzeniowski, Yale; the letter, dated Bangkok, February 1888, has been reproduced several times.

62. *Chance*, p. 288.

63. Blackmore, *British Mercantile Marine*, p. 217.

64. Cornewall-Jones, *British Merchant Service*, p. 289.

65. Ibid., p. 290.

66. Sherry, *Eastern World*, p. 247. Another press item gave the captain's name as Korgemourki.

67. Sherry also quite rightly questions the truth of the story of the arrival on the *Otago* of as many as five doctors from the men-of-war standing in the port. One of them was German (ibid., pp. 246–247), and possibly Korzeniowski had been in direct contact with her captain: in his already quoted interview with M. Dąbrowski he said, "They had to recognize me as a captain!" But the "pride" resulting from this fact is probably just a journalistic embellishment.

68. AAC, *Otago*. Allen is mistaken when she maintains that Korzeniowski was helped by the cook, a Dutchman by the name of Veilvom, apparently the only healthy man on board (*The Sea Years*, p. 249). The cook, one Verborg, signed off the *Otago* in Newcastle on 25 July 1887 (AAC) and so could not have been the prototype of the faithful Ransome. Sherry erroneously perceives Ransome's model in a sailor called Pat Conway (*Eastern World*, p. 248). The sailor's name was Pat Conroy, and his pay was higher than that of the others not because he performed the duties of a steward but because he was an A.B. seaman (AAC). Ransome strikes me not as a character based on recollections but as a fictional partner of the protagonist, whom he complements. Among the crew there was not a single middle-aged sailor who could serve as a prototype for the gray-haired Gambril.

69. AAC, *Otago*. The sailors came from four different ships and not, as suggested in *The Shadow Line*, from one shipwreck.

70. *The Mirror of the Sea*, p. 75. The reminiscence refers to the passage from Mauritius to Australia, between the islands of Saint-Paul and Nouvelle Amsterdam, and Cape Otway.

71. *Sydney Morning Herald*, 8 May 1888. In fact the *Otago* passed through Sunda Strait as early as 11 March, as has been established by van Marle on the basis of the newspaper report in *Java-Bode* of 13 March 1888 (letter to the author, 18 December 1975).

72. L. Paszkowski, "Conrad w portach Australii" [Conrad in Australian ports], part 2, "Kapitan barku *Otago*," *Wiadomości* (London), 10 September 1967. This valuable article, hitherto overlooked by biographers, has been made available by Zygmunt Brocki. Paszkowski records one more instance of the captain using the name of "Conrad"—entered as "Comrad"—in the book

of pilots on the river Yarry, on 2 July. He also lists various versions of the name as it appeared in the press: Konkorzentowski, Korsenowaski, Korzoniowski, and in one case H. Conrad; occasionally the spelling was correct.

73. Ibid. He knew about this journey on 29 June (Bobrowski to Korzeniowski, 14 September, *CPB*, p. 125).

74. In his essay "Geography and Some Explorers" written in 1923, Conrad tells of the proposal, the shipowners' consent, and his own thoughts and feelings. Among his papers (Yale) there is a map of Torres Strait but not the "quoted" letter to the shipowners, which is doubtless apocryphal.

75. Miłobędzki, *Conrad w żeglarskiej kurcie*, pp. 27–28.

76. Article by P. J. Barnwell about Conrad in the *Dictionary of Mauritian Biography*, no. 4, 1942, p. 109.

77. Jean-Aubry, *Vie de Conrad* (Paris, 1947), pp. 135–138, on the basis of local research done by Auguste Esnouf, who wrote under the pen name of Savinien Mérédac.

78. Mérédac, "Joseph Conrad chez nous," *Radical* (Port-Louis), 7 August 1931.

79. Barnwell in *Dictionary of Mauritian Biography*, and Jean-Aubry, *Vie de Conrad*, p. 138.

80. P. Langlois to A. Esnouf, cited in Mérédac, "Joseph Conrad et nous," *Essor*, 15 February 1931. Jean-Aubry, quoting the characterization (*Vie de Conrad*, pp. 133–135) omitted, the sentence about Conrad's shortness.

81. "A Smile of Fortune," pp. 34–35.

82. Mérédac, "Joseph Conrad et nous."

83. This, at least, is his version given in "A Smile of Fortune," pp. 86–88. According to Paszkowski, only the cargo of sugar was reported in the press, so the potatoes may well have been transported on the captain's own account ("Conrad w portach Australii").

84. Barnwell, *Dictionary of Mauritian Biography*.

85. Sherry, *Eastern World*, p. 35.

86. Bobrowski to Korzeniowski, 24 September 1888, reply to letter of 6 August 1888, *CPB*, p. 125.

87. Paszkowski, "Conrad w portach Australii"; Sherry, *Eastern World*, p. 35; about the teaparty, Conrad to A. T. Saunders, 14 June 1917, Sherry, *Eastern World*, p. 295.

88. Jean-Aubry, *Vie de Conrad*, p. 140, gives 26 March as the date of the resignation but supplies no source of this information. Judging by the date 2 April on the letter from the shipowners, it must have happened in the last days of March. Among Korzeniowski's certificate of service the one from the *Otago* is missing. AAC carries no date of the termination of employment. *Lloyd's Register* for 1888 gave the name of the *Otago*'s captain as Korneowski.

89. Jean-Aubry, *Vie de Conrad*, p. 140; Allen, *The Sea Years*, pp. 260–261.

90. Paszkowski, "Conrad w portach Australii," established that the *Otago* under Captain E. Trevett had left on 16 April for Brisbane, then for New Zealand, and in June was again back in Sydney.

91. Bobrowski to Korzeniowski, 3 January 1889, reply to letter of 18 November 1888, *CPB*, pp. 127–128. The inheritance of fifteen thousand rubles was deposited as a loan in order to avoid death duties.

92. Department of Foreign Affairs of the Ministry of Internal Affairs, no. 3880, letter to the Governor of Chernikhov, dated 19 March 1889 (old style), the copy among Konrad Korzeniowski's papers in the Jagiellonian Library, MS 6391. Ibid. the cited number of the *Vyedomosti*, no. 49 of

29 June (new style 11 July) 1889; the date of 20 May given by Jean-Aubry, *LL*, 1:117, and repeated by Baines, *Joseph Conrad*, p. 101, is not correct.

93. Sherry, *Eastern World*, pp. 36–37. The information concerning the projected journey to Port Elizabeth is doubtful because, according to the *South Australian Register* which gave it (Paszkowski, "Conrad w portach Australii"), the *Otago* was to sail first to Guam and only from there to South Africa—thus it would have been a very odd route to take.

94. *A Personal Record*, p. 13. The same in "Heart of Darkness," p. 52, and in "Geography and Some Explorers," pp. 16–17.

95. AAC, *Otago* (second, for the voyage to Mauritius): first mate Charles Born, Germany; second F. Totterman, Finland. In "Falk" (p. 154) the second officer is referred to as "Tottersen or something like that," but in the MS of the story Totterman. Compare Sherry, *Eastern World*, p. 249.

96. *LL*, 1:116. The *Otago* was that firm's only ship.

97. Conrad to Pinker, 9 April 1912, NYPL.

98. Van Marle to author, 18 December 1975. As Sherry has established, the entry on the passenger list reads "Captain Conrad" and not Captain Korzeniowski (*Eastern World*, p. 37).

99. *A Personal Record*, p. 73.

100. Baines, *Joseph Conrad*, p. 101.

101. For example, Captain W. H. Angel (Robert D. Foulke, "Life in the Dying World of Sail: 1870–1910," *Journal of British Studies*, no. 1 [1963]: 132); William Stuart at thirty-one master of the famous *Tweed*; Wallace who at twenty-seven became captain on the still more famous *Cutty Sark*.

102. It is possible that he sat for that examination as well; the documents recording failed examinations have not been preserved.

103. Bobrowski, "Document," *CPB*, p. 201.

104. *A Personal Record*, p. 68.

105. Conrad to Kazimierz Waliszewski, 20 November 1903, *CPB*, p. 238.

106. *A Personal Record*, pp. 68–69.

107. Author's Note to *A Personal Record* (written in 1919), pp. v–vi.

108. Conrad to Hugh Clifford, 9 October 1899, *LL*, 1:280.

109. I have to confess that I do not know what Frederick Karl means when he calls Polish "a highly formal language, much more restricted because of its morphology than English" (*Joseph Conrad: The Three Lives* [New York, 1979], p. 191). If "highly formal" is understood as referring to the relative stringency of grammatical rules, then Polish is not more formal than, for example, French or German; morphology, inflection and the abundance of modes of word formation (prefixes, suffixes, diminutives, augmentatives, verbal aspects, and so forth) testify to something quite opposite to restriction.

110. Aleksander Janta, "The First Draft of *Lord Jim* and Conrad's letters in American Collections," in *Conrad żywy* (London, 1957), pp. 214–216. On the back of the first page of the fourth chapter Korzeniowski wrote a rough draft of his letter to G. Sobotkiewicz, 29 March 1890, *CPB*, p. 208.

111. Jean-Aubry, *Vie de Conrad*, p. 145; Korzeniowski to Thys, 4 November 1889, Jean-Aubry, *Joseph Conrad: Lettres françaises* (Paris, 1929), pp. 25–26; he notified them of having given up his negotiations with Walford.

112. Jean-Aubry, *Vie de Conrad*, p. 146.

113. Barr, Moering and Co. to Thys, 31 October 1889, Jean-Aubry, "Joseph Conrad au Congo," *Mercure de France*, vol. 183 (1925): 297, Korzeniowski to Thys, 28 November 1889, Jean-Aubry, *Lettres françaises*, p. 26.

114. Korzeniowski to Thys, 4 November 1889.

115. Korzeniowski to Thys, 28 November 1889.

116. Jagiellonian Library, MS 6391.

117. Korzeniowski to Aleksander Poradowski, 16 January 1890, *CPB*, pp. 206–207.

118. Korzeniowski to Poradowski, 20 January 1890, *CPB*, p. 207.

119. Korzeniowski to Marguerite Poradowska, 4 February 1890, René Rapin, ed., *Lettres de Joseph Conrad à Marguerite Poradowska* (Geneva, 1966), p. 60.

120. Korzeniowski to Thys, 11 April 1890, Jean-Aubry, *Lettres françaises*, p. 29.

121. Korzeniowski to Poradowska, 11 February 1890, Rapin, *Lettres*, p. 60. The frequently repeated information that the editor-in-chief of *Słowo* was Sienkiewicz is incorrect; after 1887 the magazine was edited by Godlewski.

122. Compare Conrad to R. B. Cunninghame Graham, 8 February 1899, Cedric T. Watts, ed., *Joseph Conrad's Letters to R. B. Cunninghame Graham* (Cambridge, 1969), p. 116.

123. The date of the arrival is given by Bobrowski, "Document." Information concerning the journey in Korzeniowski to Poradowska, dated "Saturday 14 February" (from Lipowiec, about twenty-five miles from Kazimierówka). He became confused in the conversion of dates: 14 February new style was a Friday and not a Saturday (and 2 February, Sunday, old style); the letter was written in the evening of Saturday, 15 February. (He left Lublin on 14 February in the evening and arrived the next day at Kalinówka, between Koziatyn and Winnica.)

124. K. de Montresor to Jean-Aubry, 18 November 1927, Yale.

125. *A Personal Record*, pp. 19–23 and 26–27. Conrad's reference to a "very modernist review, edited by the very young and patronised by the highest society" (pp. 19–20) in Warsaw, may be an echo of what Korzeniowski had heard about *Życie* in 1887 to 1888, when Zenon Przesmycki (Miriam) was its literary editor.

126. J. Perłowski, "O Conradzie i Kiplingu" [On Conrad and Kipling], *Przegląd Współczesny*, no. 4 (1937). Reprinted (incomplete) in *Wspomnienia i studia*, pp. 110–131.

127. Korzeniowski to Poradowska, 23 March 1890, Rapin, *Lettres*, p. 64.

128. The expected date of 29 April is in Korzeniowski to Poradowska, 14 April 1890, Rapin, *Lettres*, p. 65; Jean-Aubry ("Joseph Conrad au Congo," pp. 302–303), without foundation, gives 24 April as the date of arrival in Brussels.

129. Sherry, *Conrad's Western World* (Cambridge, 1971), p. 17.

130. Korzeniowski to Karol Zagórski, 22 May 1890, *CPB*, p. 211.

131. Sherry, *Western World*, p. 23.

V. TO THE END OF THE NIGHT: 1890

1. Speech of 24 April 1890, G. Martelli, *Leopold to Lumumba: A History of the Belgian Congo, 1877–1960* (London, 1962), p. 124.

2. Speech by King Leopold II at the African Geographic Conference in Brussels, September 1876. Cited in Jocelyn Baines, *Joseph Conrad: A Critical Biography* (London, 1960), p. 107.

3. *The Congo and the Founding of its Free State: A Story of Work and Exploration*, vols. 1 and 2 (London, 1885).

4. Ruth M. Slade, *English-Speaking Missions in the Congo Independent State (1878–1908)* (Brussels, 1959), p. 238; *The Times* (London), 16 January 1899.

5. Tadeusz Bobrowski to Konrad Korzeniowski, 24 June 1890, in reply to a letter from Tenerife, 15 May 1890, *CPB*, pp. 128–129.

6. René Rapin, ed., *Lettres de Joseph Conrad à Marguerite Poradowska* (Geneva, 1966), p. 66.

7. Baines, *Joseph Conrad*, p. 111.

8. Korzeniowski to Karol Zagórski, 22 May 1890, *CPB*, p. 211.

9. Bobrowski to Korzeniowski, 22 July 1890, in reply to letter of 28 May, posted from Libreville probably on 9 June, *CPB*, p. 130. The 28 May letter contains the information about Korzeniowski's three-year contract.

10. "Heart of Darkness," p. 61; see Norman Sherry, *Conrad's Western World* (Cambridge, 1971), p. 25.

11. Korzeniowski to Kazimierz Waliszewski, 16 December 1903, *CPB*, p. 242.

12. Conrad, *CDAUP*, p. 7. If the date on the letter to Poradowska (see note 13) is correct, Korzeniowski arrived at Boma in the evening. Libreville is about 550 sea miles away from Boma, and the steamer would need at least three days to cover the distance.

13. Rapin, *Lettres*, p. 67. Korzeniowski says that he began writing the letter in Libreville on 10 June as the ship was leaving the port, in order to have it ready for posting in Boma.

14. Conrad, *CDAUP*, p. 7.

15. Korzeniowski to J. Quinn, 24 May 1916, NYPL.

16. Brian Inglis, *Roger Casement* (London, 1973), p. 31.

17. Sherry, *Western World*, pp. 32–33. I consider anachronistic Sherry's remark about the improbability, from the point of view of hygiene, of the existence of the "grove of death."

18. Ibid., pp. 36–37.

19. Korzeniowski to Marguerite Poradowska, 18 June 1890, Rapin, *Lettres*, pp. 68–69. The only explanation may be the fact that he was held up by Gosse, a Belgian ex-officer who died six months later (G. Jean-Aubry, *Vie de Conrad* [Paris, 1947], p. 158).

20. Conrad, *CDAUP*, pp. 7–11.

21. Jean-Aubry, *Vie de Conrad*, p. 160.

22. Sherry, *Western World*, pp. 45–47.

23. *Carte des routes de portage dans la région des chutes du Congo*, dressée par le lieutenant Louis, chef de bureau à l'Etat du Congo, n.p., n.d. [1894?].

24. Conrad, *CDAUP*, pp. 12–15.

25. Sherry, *Western World*, pp. 56 and 399–401. The *Roi des Belges* was assembled in Leopoldville in 1887 (ibid., p. 57).

26. Ibid., p. 50 (from *Mouvement Géographique*, 2 November 1890).

27. Bobrowski to Korzeniowski, 9 November 1890, reply to letter of 3 August, received on 6 November via London, *CPB*, p. 133. Previous letters reached Bobrowski from Tenerife, Libreville, Banana (at the estuary of the Congo), Matadi, and Manyanga; only the reply to the second of these letters has survived.

28. "Heart of Darkness," pp. 73–75; Sherry, *Western World*, pp. 45–46. In the manuscript the conversation is reported in the form of a dialogue.

29. Contrary to Jean-Aubry's statement (*Vie de Conrad*, p. 161) and Sherry's doubts (*Western World*, p. 40) based on a notice in *Mouvement Géographique*, Conrad's diary proves unquestionably that the ship left on 3 August. This date appears on the first page of Part 2, and the date 4 August refers to the second day of the journey.

30. I have established the place where the diary stops on the basis of a detailed map; about his illness, Korzeniowski wrote to Poradowska on 26 September 1890 (Rapin, *Lettres*, p. 69).

31. Conrad, *CDAUP*, pp. 22–24, 37.

32. Sherry, *Western World*, p. 49.

33. Ibid., pp. 51 and 61. Sherry's suggestion that the impressions Conrad wanted to evoke in the readers of "Heart of Darkness" correspond with his impression of the Congo (p. 61) is unfounded, and paying the Negroes their "wages" in copper wire, as described in the story, is no less grotesque for having been in reality a common practice.

34. Ibid., p. 51.

35. Edmund D. Morel, *King Leopold's Rule in Africa* (London, 1904), p. 39.

36. Sherry, *Western World*, pp. 56 and 59–60. Wood was not cut every day, as the author assumes; inferring from Korzeniowski's diary, it seems to have been cut approximately every two or three days.

37. J. R. Troup, *With Stanley's Rear Column* (London, 1890), p. 125, quoted in Sherry, *Western World*, p. 58.

38. Sherry, *Western World*, pp. 64–69.

39. Conrad, *Last Essays*, p. 17.

40. Jean-Aubry, *Vie de Conrad*, p. 164.

41. Table of shipping reprinted from *Mouvement Géographique* in Sherry, *Western World*, p. 377.

42. LL, 1:136.

43. Sherry, *Western World*, p. 77.

44. John Dozier Gordan, *Joseph Conrad: The Making of a Novelist* (Cambridge, Mass., 1940), p. 37.

45. There has been much speculation about the origin of Kurtz. Jean-Aubry, with his habitual naïveté, linked Kurtz with the real Klein; Jerry Allen found him reminiscent of Major E. M. Barttelot, a British member of Stanley's 1888–1890 expedition; Sherry points at the analogies between Kurtz and a leading agent of the Société du Haut Congo, A. E. C. Hodister. Both these latter sources seem quite possible, but they are not indispensable. The model for Kurtz was supplied on the one hand by literary and philosophical tradition, on the other by the behavior of a great many Europeans in Africa. In the end, as a character with his own specific life history, Kurtz is the author's own creation.

46. Otto Lütken, "Joseph Conrad in the Congo," *The London Mercury* 22, no. 127 (1930): 40–43. The author, a Danish captain who also served in the Congo, relies on a diary kept by another Dane, Captain Duhst, who lay ill at Bangala and was visited by Koch. The latter never mentioned that someone else had taken over command of the *Roi des Belges*. Duhst's entry is dated 17 September 1890; since the *Roi des Belges* reached Bangala on the fifteenth and left on the sixteenth, one may assume that Koch visited his countryman on the sixteenth and Duhst made the entry the following day.

47. Korzeniowski to Maria Bobrowska, 24 September 1890, *CPB*, pp. 212–213.

48. Jean-Aubry, *Vie de Conrad*, pp. 167–168; Baines, *Joseph Conrad*, p. 118; Sherry, *Western World*, pp. 73–76. Distinguishing these two expeditions explodes the theory of a sharp contrast in mood between Korzeniowski's letters of 24 and 26 September.

49. Sherry, *Western World*, p. 376.

50. Korzeniowski to Poradowska, 26 September 1890, Rapin, *Lettres*, pp. 70–72.

51. Morel, *King Leopold's Rule*, passim; Morel, *Red Rubber* (Manchester, 1906), passim; the Casement Report, released in 1904 by the British government as "Correspondence and Report from His Majesty's Consul at Boma Respecting the Administration of the Independent State of the Congo"; also Neal Ascherson, *The King Incorporated, Leopold II in the Age of Trusts* (London, 1963), especially pp. 195–203, 241–260. Morel tends to exaggerate in his generalizations, but his books contain a great deal of documentary material.

52. Bobrowski to Korzeniowski, 27 December 1890, *CPB*, p. 134, reply to letter of 19 October, received on 24 December.

53. Lütken, "Conrad in the Congo," p. 41. Manyanga lies on both banks of the Congo, seventy-five miles as the crow flies from Matadi. In order to get to Isangila and Vivi one had to cross over to the right bank. Isangila lies about twenty miles from Vivi, the first "capital" of the Congo Free State. Vivi lies on the west bank, opposite Matadi. Duhst's last entry is not very clear, for it would appear from it that after parting on 27 October, he and Korzeniowski met once again at Manyanga. Eugène-Jean-Baptiste-Guillaume Puttevils, whose name Duhst misspells, died on 17 June 1889 and was buried at Nsona na Nsefe. See *Biographie Coloniale Belge* (Brussels, 1951), 3:719–720.

54. Sherry, *Western World*, p. 88.

55. *JCC*, p. 13.

56. *Mouvement Géographique*, 3 May 1891.

57. Sherry, *Western World*, p. 85.

58. *LL*, 1:141.

59. Korzeniowski to Poradowska, [1 February 1891], Rapin, *Lettres*, p. 77; and Poradowska to Korzeniowski, 4 February 1891, ibid., p. 210.

60. *Last Essays*, p. 17; see also Conrad to T. F. Unwin, 22 July 1896, Yale: "All my bitterness of those days, all my puzzled wonder as to the meaning of all I saw—all my indignation at masquerading philanthropy . . ."

61. Joseph Conrad to R. B. Cunninghame Graham, 26 December 1903, Dartmouth College Library, Dartmouth College, Hanover, New Hampshire.

62. Jean-Aubry, *Vie de Conrad*, p. 158.

63. Morel, *King Leopold's Rule*, p. 12.

VI. THE SAIL AND THE PEN: 1891–1894

1. Tadeusz Bobrowski to Konrad Korzeniowski, 27 December 1890, *CPB*, p. 134; Korzeniowski to Marguerite Poradowska, 1 February 1891, René Rapin, ed. *Lettres de Joseph Conrad à Marguerite Poradowska* (Geneva, 1966), p. 77. The address is given for the first time in the letter to Poradowska of 15 September 1891; its context indicates that Korzeniowski has already lived there for some time. According to G. F. W. Hope, Conrad lived on Gillingham Street after leaving the German Hospital (Norman Sherry, *Conrad's Western World* [Cambridge, 1971], p. 90).

In his correspondence Korzeniowski used mostly the address of the firm Barr, Moering and Co., 36 Camomile Street, London E.C. (near Liverpool Street Station).

2. Korzeniowski to Poradowska, Sunday [1 February 1891], Rapin, *Lettres*, p. 78. The name of the shipping firm in Antwerp was in fact Ed. Pécher et Cie.

3. Tadeusz Bobrowski to Korzeniowski, 10 March 1891, answering the letter of 26 February, *CPB*, p. 136.

4. Most information on Krieger has been collected by Sherry (*Western World*, pp. 327–334). The German Hospital is on Ritson Road, London E. 8. Korzeniowski's doctor there was Rudolf Ludwig.

5. Bobrowski to Korzeniowski, 24 March 1891, reply to letter of 5 March, *CPB*, p. 137.

6. Korzeniowski to Poradowska, 14 April 1891, Rapin, *Lettres*, p. 83.

7. See, for example, George W. Brown and Tirvil Harris, *Social Origins of Depression* (London, 1978), passim.

8. Eliot Slater and Martin Roth, *Clinical Psychiatry*, 3rd ed. (London, 1969), pp. 194, 207–210; Antoni Kępiński, *Melancholia* (Warsaw, 1974), pp. 130–152.

9. For instance, feelings of guilt and inadequacy, chronic pessimism, and agitated behavior are typical of neurotic depression. Psychotic depression is often related to a past deprivation by death, neurotic to a past loss by separation (Brown and Harris, *Depression*, p. 285).

10. Slater and Roth, *Clinical Psychiatry*, p. 188; Kępiński, *Melancholia*, pp. 1–9, 44–51.

11. Bobrowski to Korzeniowski, *CPB*, pp. 139–140. Evidently Bobrowski made an error when computing the date in New Style.

12. Ed. Pécher et Cie were chartering agents for this firm. Korzeniowski to Poradowska, 30 March 1891, Rapin, *Lettres*, p. 82.

13. Korzeniowski to Maria Tyszka, 15 April 1891, *CPB*, p. 213.

14. Korzeniowski to Poradowska, 1 May 1891 and 10 May 1891, Rapin, *Lettres*, pp. 83–84. Conrad mentions the same period—moving his illness by half a year and making it last for six months—in a letter to E. Dawson, 25 June 1908, *LL*, 2:69–70.

15. Bobrowski to Korzeniowski, 6 and 27 June 1891, *CPB*, pp. 140–141, 143.

16. Korzeniowski to Poradowska, 3 June 1891, Rapin, *Lettres*, p. 86.

17. John Dozier Gordan, *Joseph Conrad: The Making of a Novelist* (Cambridge, Mass., 1940), p. 179.

18. Bobrowski to Korzeniowski, 6 June 1891, reply to letters of 20 and 28 May.

19. He wrote to Poradowska on 2 July 1891, "The atmosphere was too nightmarish with those paintings of the Charenton school" (Rapin, *Lettres*, p. 87). Le Charenton is the name of a well-known insane asylum near Paris.

20. Bobrowski to Korzeniowski, 27 June 1891, reply to letter of 14 June, *CPB*, pp. 143–144. The fact that when leaving for Africa Conrad wanted to leave Krieger his share in the firm as a "legacy" arouses a suspicion that he might have owed his friend money, perhaps the equivalent of that share (4,000 rubles, or about £460). We shall hear further about Conrad's debt to Krieger, but not about his share.

21. Korzeniowski to Poradowska, 22 June and 2 July 1891, Rapin, *Lettres*, pp. 86–87. Letter of Mrs. Muriel Dobree (daughter of G. F. W. Hope) to Mrs. J. C. L. Pugh, 2 March 1949, quoted in J. C. L. Pugh, "Some Sidelights on Joseph Conrad," *The Thurrock Historical Society Journal*, no. 5, Autumn 1960, p. 55.

22. Bobrowski to Korzeniowski, 1 July 1891, in reply to letter of 24 June, *CPB*, p. 145.

23. Quoted in Bobrowski to Korzeniowski, 30 July, ibid., p. 148.

24. Ibid., pp. 147–148.

25. Korzeniowski to Poradowska, 26 August 1891, Rapin, *Lettres*, p. 90.

26. Andrew De Ternant, "An Unknown Episode in Conrad's Life," *New Statesman and Nation*, 28 July 1928, p. 511. De Ternant writes about the "early 'nineties," but, as *St. Stephen's Review* ceased publication in 1892, the information may refer only to the preceding year.

27. Bobrowski to Korzeniowski, 30 July 1891, *CPB*, p. 148. Charles Buls (1837–1914), a long-time suitor of Poradowska both before her marriage and after the death of her husband, was the mayor of Brussels from 1881 to 1899.

28. Bobrowski to Korzeniowski, 26 August 1891, *CPB*, p. 149. The lame Prince of Benevento was the French statesman Charles Maurice de Talleyrand-Périgord, who repeatedly changed his political allegiance; he was unfriendly to Poland.

29. In January 1890 on his way to Poland; in April on his way back; in May 1890 he came to Brussels twice but it is not certain whether he saw Poradowska; in January 1891 on his way from Africa (this time for two days); in May on his way to Champel; in June coming back from his cure. Bernard Meyer's calculation (*Joseph Conrad: A Psychoanalytic Biography* [Princeton, 1967], p. 107) is therefore wrong. In his letter of 30 September 1891 (Rapin, *Lettres*, p. 93), Korzeniowski called seeing Poradowska "a beautiful dream"—but he could have made the trip in a few hours.

30. Bibliography of Poradowska's works in Rapin, *Lettres*, pp. 216–217.

31. Sentence quoted in Bobrowski to Korzeniowski, 8 October 1891, *CPB*, p. 150.

32. Ibid.

33. Korzeniowski to Poradowska, 15 September 1891, Rapin, *Lettres*, p. 92.

34. Korzeniowski to Poradowska, 16 October 1891, ibid., p. 94.

35. Bobrowski to Korzeniowski, 9 November 1891, *CPB*, pp. 152–156.

36. Conrad to Poradowska, 14 November 1891, Rapin, *Lettres*, p. 95; AAC, *Torrens*, BT 100/39, Public Record Office, London.

37. Bobrowski to Korzeniowski, 2 December 1891, reply to letter of 20 November, *CPB*, p. 156.

38. "The *Torrens*: a Personal Tribute," in *Last Essays*, p. 27.

39. Bobrowski to Korzeniowski, 7 January 1892 (26 December 1891 in Old Style), *CPB*, p. 159.

40. Korzeniowski to Poradowska, 5 March 1892, Rapin, *Lettres*, p. 100.

41. Korzeniowski to Poradowska, 6 April 1892, ibid., p. 101.

42. Bobrowski to Korzeniowski, 14 May 1892, reply to letters of 4 and 24 March, *CPB*, pp. 161–162.

43. AAC, *Torrens*.

44. Bobrowski to Korzeniowski, 18 September 1892, reply to a letter from London, n.d., *CPB*, p. 164.

45. Korzeniowski to Poradowska, 4 September 1892, Rapin, *Lettres*, pp. 102–103.

46. Ibid., p. 104.

47. Bobrowski to Korzeniowski, 18 September 1892, *CPB*, p. 165.

48. Bobrowski to Korzeniowski, 17 October 1892, reply to letters of 2 October and 6 October, ibid., pp. 166 and 168.

49. Korzeniowski to Tyszka, 8 September 1892, ibid., p. 214.

50. J. Conrad Korzeniowski signed up the same day (AAC, *Torrens*).

51. *A Personal Record*, pp. 15–18. Apparently he had by that time written nine chapters of *Almayer's Folly*; Jacques encouraged him to continue the novel. Conrad's recollections here are not quite reliable, however. He maintains that Jacques died either in Australia or on his return journey on another ship; in fact he sailed back to England with Conrad on board the *Torrens*. Jacques was born 6 April 1869, studied in Cambridge 1888–1891, died 19 September 1893 (*Alumni Cantabrigienses*, pt. II, vol. 35 [Cambridge, 1947], p. 543).

52. Korzeniowski to Poradowska 3 February 1893, Rapin, *Lettres*, pp. 110–111.

53. H. V. Marrot, *The Life and Letters of John Galsworthy* (London, 1935), p. 88.

54. John Galsworthy, *Castles in Spain* (New York, 1927), pp. 101–103.

55. Galsworthy, *Forsytes, Pendyces and Others* (London, 1935), pp. 187–206. The dying doctor is the son of a Yorkshire parson and is returning home after several years of wandering; possibly another source of Jim in *Lord Jim*. The real C. G. Jackson died 28 June 1893 (AAC, *Torrens*).

56. Korzeniowski to Poradowska, 17 May 1893, Rapin, *Lettres*, p. 112.

57. Certificate of Discharge, Yale. Both AACs of the *Torrens* and the first certificate of discharge have "J. Conrad Korzeniowski" written in; on the AACs "Korzeniowski" is in quotation marks.

58. Bobrowski to Korzeniowski, 22 May 1893, reply to letter of 19 March from Adelaide, *CPB*, p. 170.

59. Bobrowski to Korzeniowski, 13 July 1893, reply to letter of 17 May from Capetown. This is the last preserved letter of Bobrowski. Ibid., pp. 171–172.

60. See Korzeniowski to Poradowska, 17 May and 14 September 1893, Rapin, *Lettres*, pp. 112–113. The journey from London, via Vlissingen, Berlin, Eytkühnen, Białystok, and Brest, lasted over two days.

61. Conrad to Cunninghame Graham, 8 Februry 1899, Cedric T. Watts, ed., *Joseph Conrad's Letters to R. B. Cunninghame Graham* (Cambridge, 1969), p. 116.

62. Korzeniowski to Poradowska, Rapin, *Lettres*, pp. 112–113. Marysieńka is Maria Ołdakowska, a niece of Aleksander Poradowski; Korzeniowski had met her during his earlier visit to the Ukraine.

63. Korzeniowski to Poradowska, 5 November 1893, ibid., pp. 113–114.

64. The certificate is dated London, 17 October 1893 (Yale).

65. Certificate of discharge, *Adowa*, Yale.

66. Korzeniowski to Poradowska, 6 December 1893, Rapin, *Lettres*, p. 115.

67. Korzeniowski to Poradowska, 18 and 20 December 1893, ibid., pp. 115–116.

68. Korzeniowski to Poradowska, 7 January 1894, ibid., p. 123.

69. *A Personal Record*, pp. 3–6.

70. Korzeniowski to Poradowska, 9 January 1894, Rapin, *Lettres*, p. 123.

71. Certificate of discharge, *Adowa*.

72. The report of the investigation was discovered and published by Edmund A. Bojarski, "Conrad at the Crossroads: From Navigator to Novelist with New Biographical Mysteries," *The Texas Quarterly*, Winter 1968, pp. 15–29.

73. "Legends," in *Last Essays*, p. 46; R. D. Foulke, "Life in the Dying World of Sail," *The Journal of British Studies* 3, no. 1 (1963): 107–108 and passim.

74. "Legends," p. 47.

75. Other examples of incompetence and of marine court verdicts are given in Foulke, "Dying World," pp. 132–133.

76. For example, Thomas Brassey, *British Seamen as Described in Recent Parliamentary and Official Documents* (London, 1877), p. 311, considered British masters inferior to Scandinavian masters in point of "education, professional knowledge, manners, and steadiness."

77. *Lord Jim*, p. 129.

78. Korzeniowski to Poradowska, 20 January 1894, Rapin, *Lettres*, p. 124.

79. Korzeniowski to Poradowska, 18 February 1894, ibid., p. 126.

80. Tadeusz Florkowski to Korzeniowski, 21 February 1894, no. 2889, National Library, Warsaw.

81. Jessie Conrad maintains that at the news of his uncle's illness Conrad hurried to the Ukraine (*JCC*, p. 10), but his correspondence with Poradowska and the letters of Florkowski and Zaleski exclude the possibility of such a voyage.

82. Conrad to K. Waliszewski, 5 December 1903, *CPB*, p. 239.

83. There is more about Conrad's relations with his uncle and about the influence of Bobrowski's *Memoirs* on Conrad's work in my essay, "Conrad i Bobrowski," in *Nad Conradem* (Warsaw, 1965), pp. 46–69.

84. Bobrowski, *Pamiętniki* [Memoirs] 2nd ed., (Warsaw, 1979), 1:301.

85. See Stefan Kieniewicz, *Powstanie Styczniowe* [The January insurrection] (Warsaw, 1972), pp. 169–171, 192–199, 206–207.

86. Rafal Blüth, "Dwie rodziny kresowe" [Two borderland families], *Ateneum*, no. 1 (1939); Aleksander Janta, "Skąd fatalne dziedzictwo Conrada?" [Whence Conrad's fatal inheritance?], *Wiadomości* (London, 1959), no. 22.

87. Albert Guerard, *Conrad the Novelist* (Cambridge, Mass., 1959), p. 11.

88. Meyer, *Conrad*, pp. 103–104.

89. Korzeniowski to Poradowska, Thursday, [22 or 29 March 1894], Rapin, *Lettres*, p. 127.

90. Korzeniowski to Poradowska, Ibid., p. 129.

91. Korzeniowski to Poradowska, 2 May 1894, ibid., p. 132.

92. M. E. Reynolds, *Memories of John Galsworthy* (London, 1936), p. 26; Jocelyn Baines, *Joseph Conrad: A Critical Biography* (London, 1960), p. 134.

93. Korzeniowski to Poradowska, Thursday, [17 May 1894], Rapin, *Lettres*, p. 133.

94. In the typescript of *Almayer's Folly* (W. B. Leeds Collection, New York), the author's name is given as "Kamudi." Korzeniowski chose this pen name, meaning "rudder" in Malay, because he had in mind the possibility that the novel would be included in Unwin's Pseudonym Library. Books published in that series were much shorter, however. Descriptions of the manuscript (Rosenbach) and typescript are given in Gordan, *Conrad*, pp. 112–129, 182–183.

95. Conrad to Poradowska, Friday, [20 July? 1894], Rapin, *Lettres*, p. 136.

96. Conrad to Poradowska, 12 July 1894, ibid., p. 135.

97. Conrad to Poradowska, Friday, [20 July? 1894].

98. Conrad to Poradowska, Saturday, [18 August? 1894], Rapin, *Lettres*, p. 139.

99. Ibid.

100. Baines, *Joseph Conrad*, p. 141.

101. Conrad to Poradowska, 4 October 1894, Rapin, *Lettres*, p. 142.

VII. WORK AND ROMANCE: 1894–1896

1. Wilfred Hugh Chesson, letter to the editor, *To-day* 5 (1919): 152. It was with Chesson that Conrad conducted his early correspondence concerning the text, corrections, and proofreading of *Almayer's Folly*. See Ugo Mursia, *The True "Discoverer" of Joseph Conrad's Literary Talent and Other Notes on Conradian Biography* (Varese, 1971).

2. Edward Garnett, ed. *Letters from Conrad, 1895 to 1924* (London, 1928), pp. vii–viii.

3. Joseph Conrad to Marguerite Poradowska, 10 October 1894, René Rapin, ed., *Lettres de Joseph Conrad à Marguerite Poradowska* (Geneva, 1966), pp. 143–144.

4. Conrad to Poradowska, 23 October 1894; 26 November or 3 December 1894; second half of December 1894, ibid., pp. 145, 150, 151.

5. Conrad to Poradowska, Monday morning, ibid., p. 148. The numbering of chapters was later changed; it is therefore uncertain on which part of the novel he was then working.

6. Ibid., pp. 146–147.

7. Conrad to Poradowska, 27 December 1894, ibid., p. 151.

8. Ibid.; John Dozier Gordan, *Joseph Conrad: The Making of a Novelist* (Cambridge, Mass., 1940), pp. 112–129; and Floyd Eugene Eddleman and David Leon Higdon, "The Typescript of Conrad's *Almayer's Folly*," *Texas Studies in Literature and Language* 18, no. 1 (1976): 98–123.

9. Conrad to Edward Garnett, 4 January 1895, E. Garnett, *Letters*, p. 3; ibid., pp. ix–x, xiii, xix.

10. Edward Verral Lucas, *Reading, Writing and Remembering* (London, 1932), pp. 145–146.

11. *Almayer's Folly*, pp. vii–viii.

12. The "lady—distinguished in the world of letters," criticized by Conrad in his foreword, was Alice Meynell (1847–1922); Conrad identified her in his note added to the foreword in the first volume of his *Works*, published by Heinemann (London, 1921), p. x. The story of the foreword's manuscript is told by David Leon Higdon in "The Text and Context of Conrad's First Critical Essay," in *Joseph Conrad: Commemorative Essays*, ed. A. Gillon and L. Krzyżanowski (New York, 1975), pp. 97–105. Higdon believes that Conrad wrote his first Author's Note "in late 1894" and that it "had been written by 4 January 1895." This is far from certain, as the first mention of the note is Conrad's promise, in his letter to Garnett, 4 January 1895, to "send on the preface tomorrow" (E. Garnett, *Letters*, p. 3).

13. Conrad to Poradowska, Wednesday, [30 January or 6 February? 1895], Rapin, *Lettres*, p. 157.

14. Conrad to Poradowska, Saturday, [16 or 23 February 1895], ibid., p. 158.

15. Conrad to T. Fisher Unwin, 12 March 1895, from Brussels, Yale.

16. Conrad to Poradowska, 2 April 1895, Rapin, *Lettres*, p. 159; Good Friday, [12 April 1895], ibid., p. 160.

17. Conrad to Poradowska, 27 December 1894 and [12 April 1895], ibid., pp. 151 and 160.

18. Conrad to Poradowska, 30 April 1894, ibid., p. 160.

19. E. Garnett, *Letters*, p. 8. Willems is the main hero of *An Outcast of the Islands*.

20. *Spectator*, 19 October 1895; a very late review.

21. *Daily Chronicle*, 11 May 1895.

22. *Athenaeum*, 25 May 1895; *Academy* 15 June 1895.

23. *Saturday Review*, 15 June 1895. The reception of *Almayer's Folly* is more extensively discussed by Gordan, *Conrad*, pp. 271–276, and Norman Sherry, *Conrad: The Critical Heritage* (London, 1973), pp. 5–8; Sherry reprints thirteen reviews on pages 49–61.

24. Excerpts from Emilie Briquel's diary and texts of letters to her and her family are all based on the originals in possession of her daughter, Mme Françoise Meykiechel.

25. Conrad to Poradowska, 6 May 1895, Rapin, *Lettres*, p. 162.

26. Almost at the same time, Conrad alluded to Daudet's novel in a letter to Garnett. In February he contemplated sending Daudet a copy of *Almayer's Folly* (Rapin, *Lettres*, p. 158).

27. Conrad to Garnett, 12 May 1894, E. Garnett, *Letters*, p. 9.

28. Conrad to Poradowska, 13 May 1894, Rapin, *Lettres*, p. 161. Conrad sent Buls, a well-known patron of the arts, a copy of *Almayer's Folly* anonymously, wanting the mayor to assume that the book was coming from Poradowska. He was not pleased when she revealed the sender.

29. Conrad to Unwin, 18 May 1895, Yale.

30. Conrad to Garnett, 7 June 1895, E. Garnett, *Letters*, p. 10.

31. D. Homer, "Conrad: Two Biographical Episodes," *Review of English Studies* 18 (1967): 54–56.

32. Conrad to Poradowska, 11 June 1895, Rapin, *Lettres*, pp. 164–165.

33. Conrad to Garnett, [July 1895], E. Garnett, *Letters*, pp. 11–12.

34. Conrad to Emilie Briquel, 14 July 1895.

35. Conrad to Briquel, 14 July 1895; Conrad to Edward Sanderson, 24 August 1895, *LL*, 1:177. Unwin was also invited but declined (Conrad to Unwin, 9 July 1895, Brotherton Collection, University of Leeds Library).

36. Conrad to Sanderson 24 August 1895, *LL*, 1:176–179.

37. This refers to the actually existing Black Reef, exploited by, among others, the firm called "Minerva," which occupied land adjacent to Rorke's plots. Minerva mined gold from November 1895 to September 1896, but with little success. F. R. Hatch and J. A. Chalmers, *The Gold Mines of the Rand* (London, 1895), pp. 54–55; *Witwatersrand Chamber of Mines Annual Report* (Johannesburg, 1896 and 1897).

38. *Register of Defunct and Other Companies, Removed from the Stock Exchange Official Year Book* (London, 1898), p. 421; *Witwatersrand Chamber of Mines* (1896, 1897, 1898); H. van Marle's research in the Public Record Office in London (BT 31/6380/45056) indicates that Conrad's name does not appear on the list of shareholders.

39. Conrad to Briquel, 26 August 1895.

40. Conrad to Garnett, 17 September 1895, E. Garnett, *Letters*, pp. 12–13.

41. Conrad to Garnett, Tuesday, [24 September 1895], ibid., pp. 15–17.

42. Conrad to Edward Noble, 28 October 1895, *LL*, 1:183. It is, however, worth noticing that Conrad was trying to comfort the addressee.

43. The origins and contents of *The Sisters* and the reasons for Conrad's laying this novel aside are discussed more extensively in Zdzisław Najder, "*Siostry* Conrada," *Teksty* 2, no. 2 (1972): 67–81.

44. Conrad to Garnett, Monday, [23 March], and 9 April 1896, E. Garnett, *Letters*, pp. 23, 26.

45. Conrad to John Quinn, 18 July 1913, NYPL.

46. The explanation seems farfetched, but it is not improbable. Conrad corrected the first pages about 20 October; on the twenty-second, before leaving London, he sent Unwin the forgotten dedication (Conrad to Unwin, 22 October 1895, Rosenbach). The short motto from Calderón barely fits on the title page; the quotation from Hugo would have had to be placed elsewhere. Conrad might have simply forgotten about it. He could have inserted it during the second proof-reading in January (Conrad to Unwin, 29 January and 1 February 1896, Rosenbach) but did not.

47. Conrad to Briquel, 29 December 1895.

48. Published under the pseudonym Daniel Chaucer, London 1911. See Arthur Mizener, *The Saddest Story: A Biography of Ford Madox Ford* (New York, 1971), pp. 212–214, 558, and Thomas C. Moser, *The Life in the Fiction of Ford Madox Ford* (Princeton, N.J., 1980), pp. 91–98.

49. Conrad to Poradowska, 2 April 1895, Rapin, *Lettres*, p. 159.

50. Both Mr. and Mrs. Hope claimed to have known Jessie since she was a child. Frances Ellen Hope to J. T. Babb, 7 March 1928, Yale.

51. *JCKH*, pp. 100–106; *JCC*, pp. 9–10.

52. Conrad to Karol Zagórski, *CPB*, pp. 215–216.

53. Conrad to Garnett, Wednesday, [11 March 1896], E. Garnett, *Letters*, p. 22.

54. E. Garnett, *Letters*, p. xxii.

55. Conrad to Garnett, Monday, [23 March 1896], E. Garnett, *Letters*, p. 23.

56. Jocelyn Baines, *Joseph Conrad: A Critical Biography* (London, 1960), p. 171.

57. E. Garnett, *Letters*, pp. xxi–xxii.

58. *JCC*, pp. 18–19. In verifying her account and establishing the probable dates, Hans van Marle's help was essential.

59. Baines, *Joseph Conrad*, p. 170, and information from Borys Conrad. The only wedding present we know about was from the Unwins, received as early as 20 March. Conrad acknowledged it in a grateful letter, signed J. Conrad Korzeniowski (Conrad to Mrs. E. J. C. Unwin, 20 March 1896, County Record Office, Chichester, Essex, Cobden MS 972).

60. *JCC*, pp. 19–21.

VIII. STRIVINGS, EXPERIMENTS, DOUBTS: 1896–1898

1. Jessie Conrad maintains in *JCKH* (p. 25) that they left the evening after their wedding, in *JCC* (p. 19) that they left the next day. Since ferries between Southampton and St. Malo operated on

Mondays, Wednesdays, and Fridays (*Bradshaw's Continental Railway Guide* [March 1896], p. 728) and the Conrads arrived at Lannion on March 27, the latter version is correct.

2. Joseph Conrad to Edward L. Sanderson, 28 March 1896, Yale.

3. Conrad to Mrs. Sanderson, 6 April 1896, *LL*, 1:187. Note that the final disclaimer had a factual ground of sorts, because G. F. W. Hope's brother-in-law, with whom Conrad had some business connections, was a shareholder in a diamond mine.

4. Conrad to Sanderson, 14 April 1896, *LL*, 1:188.

5. Conrad to Edward Garnett, Monday, [13 April 1896], Edward Garnett, *Letters from Conrad, 1895 to 1924* (London, 1928), p. 27.

6. Ibid., p. xxiii.

7. *JCC*, p. 26.

8. *JCKH*, pp. 31–32.

9. Conrad to T. Fisher Unwin, 22 May 1896, Brotherton Library, Leeds.

10. Information from M. Pierre Strnisté, Ile-Grande.

11. Conrad to Garnett, 2 June 1896, E. Garnett, *Letters*, p. 34.

12. Conrad to Garnett, 10 June 1896, ibid., pp. 36–37.

13. Theodore G. Ehrsam, *A Bibliography of Joseph Conrad* (Metuchen, N.J., 1969), p. 293.

14. Wells's review in *Saturday Review*, 16 May 1895, reprinted in Norman Sherry, ed., *Conrad: The Critical Heritage* (London, 1973), pp. 73–76; Conrad to Wells 18 May, Illinois University Library, Urbana, Illinois; Wells's reply, undated, in G. Jean-Aubry, ed., *Twenty Letters to Joseph Conrad* (London, 1926), n.p.

15. Conrad to E. Sanderson, 21 November 1896, *LL*, 1:196.

16. Conrad to Garnett, 19 June 1896, E. Garnett, *Letters*, pp. 37–38.

17. Joycelyn Baines, *Joseph Conrad: A Critical Biography* (London, 1960), p. 174.

18. Conrad to Garnett, 22 July 1896, E. Garnett, *Letters*, p. 41.

19. Conrad to Garnett, 14 August 1896, ibid., p. 47.

20. Bernard C. Meyer, *Joseph Conrad: A Psychoanalytic Biography* (Princeton, N.J., 1967), p. 118.

21. Conrad to Garnett, 22 [= 24] May 1896, E. Garnett, *Letters*, p. 32.

22. Conrad to Unwin, 9 August 1896, Brotherton Collection.

23. Conrad to Garnett, 5 August 1896, E. Garnett, *Letters*, p. 45.

24. Conrad to Garnett, 22 July 1896, ibid., p. 42.

25. Baines, *Joseph Conrad*, p. 471.

26. Conrad to Vernon Weston, 26 May 1896, Yale; to Unwin, 22 August 1896, NYPL; *JCC*, pp. 41–42. Also Conrad's letter to Garnett, written immediately after his return to England (n.d.), E. Garnett, *Letters*, p. 48, indicates that the house had been already rented and the Conrads were to move in in a week.

27. For example, contrary to Jessie's claim (*JCC*, p. 28), Conrad was sending *The Rescuer* to London in manuscript, not in typescript form; also, her description of the allegedly desperate state of Conrad's documents (*JCC*, p. 34) does not agree with their condition today.

28. In his letter to Unwin of 22 August, Conrad gives the planned date of return as 28 September; in others he mentioned the end of September (to Mrs. Brooke, 29 July 1896, Texas) or beginning of October. Jessie remembers that they came back on a Sunday (*JCC*, p. 41), therefore probably on 27 September. James Whitaker, *Joseph Conrad at Stanford-le-Hope* (Stanford-le-Hope, Essex, 1978), pp. 5–7.

29. *JCC*, pp. 43–44.

30. Conrad to Arthur T. Quiller-Couch, 23 December 1897, the Reverend Foy F. Quiller-Couch.

31. Conrad to Garnett, Sunday, [29 November 1896], E. Garnett, *Letters*, p. 61.

32. Conrad to John Galsworthy, 12 October 1896, Birmingham, thanking him for a check for £20.

33. Conrad to Unwin, 19 October 1896, Yale.

34. Conrad to Garnett, Monday morning, 7 December 1896, E. Garnett, *Letters*, p. 62.

35. Conrad to Garnett, 16 November 1896, ibid., p. 59.

36. See Conrad to Aniela Zagórska, 12 June 1896, and to J. de Brunnow, 2 October 1897, *CPB*, pp. 216, 220.

37. Conrad to the Zagórskis, 20 December 1896, ibid., p. 217.

38. Conrad to Garnett, 19 December 1896, E. Garnett, *Letters*, p. 63; to Unwin, 1 January 1897, Brotherton Library.

39. Conrad to Joseph Spiridion, 5 April 1897, Berg (£20) and 23 February 1898, Rosenbach (£5).

40. Witold Chwalewik, "Józef Conrad w Kardyfie" [Joseph Conrad in Cardiff], *Ruch Literacki*, no. 8 (1932), reprinted in *Wspomnienia i studia*. See also *JCC*, p. 49, and Hubert S. Kliszczewski, "Conrad w moim domu rodzinnym" [Conrad in my family home], *Wiadomości* (1949), nos. 33–34. The interview appeared in *The Western Mail*, 1 February 1897.

41. W. Lutosławski, "Emigracja zdolności" [Emigration of Talent], *Kraj*, no. 12 (1899), reprinted in *Wspomnienia i studia*; "Odwiedziny u Conrada" [A vist at Conrad's], *Tygodnik Wileński*, no. 1 (1925).

42. Conrad to R. B. Cunninghame Graham, 8 February 1899, Cedric T. Watts, ed., *Joseph Conrad's Letters to R. B. Cunninghame Graham* (Cambridge, 1969), p. 118 (the original is in French).

43. Conrad to Garnett, 10 January 1897, E. Garnett, *Letters*, p. 67.

44. Probably on 17 January, as on the nineteenth he wrote to Garnett, "I have been in bed two days. A cheap price for finishing that story." Ibid., p. 69.

45. Conrad to Garnett, Thursday, [21 January 1897], ibid., p. 71; to Helen Watson, 27 January 1897, *LL*, 1:200.

46. Conrad to Watson, 27 January 1897; to Graham, 9 August 1897, Watts, *Letters*, p. 48.

47. First published in the 1914 (Garden City, N.Y.: Doubleday, Page) edition of *The Nigger*; later reprinted in all American editions but not included in the Dent Collected Edition.

48. Paul Kirschner, *Conrad: The Psychologist as Artist* (Edinburgh, 1968), pp. 200–205.

49. Conrad to Blackwood, 8 November 1899, William Blackburn, ed., *Joseph Conrad: Letters to William Blackwood and David S. Meldrum* (Durham, N.C., 1958), p. 73. The concurrence, probably accidental, concerns two short stories: John Buchan's "The Far Islands" and Kipling's earlier "The Finest Story in the World."

50. Conrad to H.-D. Davray, 22 August 1903, G. Jean-Aubry, ed., Joseph Conrad: *Lettres françaises* (Paris, 1933), p. 51.

51. Conrad to Garnett, Saturday, [4 June 1898], E. Garnett, *Letters*, p. 130 (erroneously dated May 1898).

52. Date of the loan: Meldrum says in his letter to Blackwood of 9 February 1899 (Blackburn, *Letters*, p. 48) that it was given "two or three years ago." On 12 October 1896 Conrad borrowed £20 from Galsworthy and then for several months did not mention any financial difficulties, although he was not earning any money from his writing.

53. Conrad to Garnett, Thursday, [21 January], and 2 June 1897, E. Garnett, *Letters*, pp. 70 and 83–84; to Spiridion, 5 April 1897, Berg.

54. Conrad to E. Sanderson, 19 July 1897, *LL*, 1:207.

55. *JCC*, pp. 50–51.

56. Conrad's first comments on Sanderson's verse are in his letter of 21 November 1896 where he discusses *An Episode of Southern Seas* (*LL*, 1:195). Extensive comments on another poem are in his letter to E. Sanderson, 14 October 1897, Yale. About Galsworthy he wrote to Unwin, "A friend of mine Jack Galsworthy has been down here to tell me that you are going to publish a vol. of short stories by him. The sly dog never told me he wrote. He is a first rate fellow, clever, has seen the world" (Birmingham). As his letter to Garnett of 19 February 1897 shows, however, it was Conrad who directed his friend to Garnett, Unwin's literary adviser.

57. Conrad to Garnett, Friday, [19 February 1897], E. Garnett, *Letters*, p. 75.

58. Conrad to Garnett, Sunday, [7 February 1897], ibid., p. 73. Although on the very same day he informed Unwin that he had begun the story, twelve days later he wrote to Garnett, "I shall try to begin that short story to-day." To Garnett Friday, [19 February 1897], ibid., p. 76. See Lawrence Graver, *Conrad's Short Fiction* (Berkeley-Los Angeles, 1969), p. 25, on payment comparison.

59. Conrad to Garnett, Wednesday, [24 March 1897], ibid., p. 80.

60. Conrad to Garnett, 28 February 1897, ibid., p. 76.

61. Conrad to Garnett, ibid., p. 81.

62. Conrad to Garnett, 18 July 1897, ibid., p. 85.

63. Conrad to Garnett, [20 April 1897], ibid., p. 82.

64. Conrad to Garnett, 12 March [1897]: "We shift camp at 7 a.m. tomorrow," ibid., p. 79. Mrs. J. C. L. Pugh, "Some Sidelights on Joseph Conrad," *The Thurrock Historical Society Journal*, no. 5 (Autumn 1960), pp. 52–56; Whitaker, *Conrad at Stanford-le-Hope*, pp. 9–12.

65. Conrad to Garnett, 2 June 1897: "I *must* go on now with the *Return*," ibid., p. 84.

66. Conrad to Garnett, 27 September [1897], ibid., p. 92.

67. Conrad to Garnett, 18 July 1897, ibid., p. 86; to E. Sanderson, 19 July 1897, *LL*, 1:206–207.

68. Conrad to Garnett, 24 September [1897], E. Garnett, *Letters*, p. 90.

69. Conrad to Garnett, 27 September [1897], ibid., p. 92; he repeated this verdict four months later (to Garnett, Monday evening [24 January 1898], ibid., p. 120).

70. Conrad to Garnett, Wednesday, [29 September 1897], ibid., p. 94.

71. The title was changed between 11 June and 28 August. See Baines, *Joseph Conrad*, p. 194.

72. Conrad to Garnett, 8 October 1897, E. Garnett, *Letters*, p. 96.

73. Conrad to Garnett, Monday evening, [11 October 1897], ibid., p. 100.

74. Conrad to Garnett, [14 October 1897].

75. Conrad to Garnett, Thursday, [21 January 1897], ibid., p. 70. Ten months later, however, he waxed enthusiastic writing about *Shorter Poems* of Robert Bridges, whom he considered a much better poet than Tennyson (to Garnett, 26 November 1897, ibid., p. 106).

76. Conrad to Chesson, 16 January 1898, Yale.

77. See, for example, Conrad to Garnett, 25 and 27 October, 6 November, and 7 December 1896, E. Garnett, *Letters*, pp. 51–54, 56, 62.

78. Conrad to J. Quinn, 8 December 1912 and 18 July 1913, NYPL. But see, for example, *Almayer's Folly* [capitals added]: "It may be supposed that Dain Maroola was not exceptionally delighted with his prospective mother-in-law, NOR that he actually approved of that worthy woman's appetite for shining dollars" (p. 67); "But Abdulla, after the first shock of surprise, with THE old age's dislike for solving riddles, showed a becoming resignation" (p. 109). See also *Tales of Unrest*: "She, to give her individuality FAIR PLAY, took up all manner of philanthropism" (p. 121); ". . . while his familiar ghosts are not easy to propitiate BY casual wayfarers upon whom they long to wreak the malice of their human master" (p. 189).

79. E. Garnett, *Letters*, p. xxviii.

80. Conrad to Garnett, 28 August 1897, ibid., p. 89.

81. It was Graham's mother, Anna Elizabeth Bontine, who drew his attention to Conrad (Conrad to Bontine, 16 October 1898, *LL*, 1:252).

82. Conrad to Bontine, 22 November 1898, ibid., 1:256; Herbert Faulkner West, *A Modern Conquistador: Robert Bontine Cunninghame Graham: His Life and Works* (London, 1932), p. 114.

83. Baines, *Joseph Conrad*, p. 198.

84. David Garnett's presentation of his father's intellectual attitude (*The Golden Echo* [London, 1953], p. 69) suggests an interesting analogy with the similarly defeatist and escapist stance of the father of Axel Heyst, the main hero of Conrad's *Victory*.

85. An example of these sentiments was Conrad's attitude during the Spanish-American War. "Will the certain issue of that struggle awaken the Latin race to the sense of its dangerous position? [. . .] But, perhaps, the race is doomed? It would be a pity. It would narrow life, it would destroy a whole side of it which had its morality and was always picturesque and at times inspiring. The others may well shout Fiat lux! It will be only the reflected light of a silver dollar [. . .]" (to Graham, 1 May 1898, Watts, *Letters*, p. 84). He apparently disregarded Spanish exploitation of Cuba and the Cubans' aspirations to national independence.

86. Watts, *Conrad and Cunninghame Graham* (Farnham, 1978), p. 5. Conrad to Graham, 5 August 1897, Watts, *Letters*, p. 45.

87. Conrad to Garnett, 26 November [1897], E. Garnett, *Letters*, p. 105.

88. Conrad to Garnett, Tuesday, [24 August 1897], ibid., p. 87.

89. The history of the Preface, which Conrad for a time wanted to publish as a separate article, is described briefly in John Dozier Gordan, *Joseph Conrad: The Making of a Novelist* (Cambridge, Mass., 1940), p. 239.

90. See Baines, *Joseph Conrad*, p. 188; G. J. Worth, "Conrad's Debt to Maupassant in the Preface to *The Nigger of the 'Narcissus*,'" *Journal of English and Germanic Philology* 54 (1955): 700–704; Kirschner, *Conrad*, pp. 272–274; Frederick R. Karl, *A Reader's Guide to Joseph Conrad* (New York, 1969), pp. 24–27.

91. It was indeed in *The Rescue* that Conrad tried to realize his principles. "It will be . . . a deliberate attempt to get in some artistic effects of a graphic order," to Blackwood, 28 August 1897, Blackburn, *Letters*, p. 6.

92. Gordan, *Conrad*, p. 238.

93. Conrad to Garnett, 28 August 1897, E. Garnett, *Letters*, p. 88.

94. Conrad to Janina de Brunnow, 2 October 1897, *CPB*, p. 219.

95. Conrad to Blackwood, 4 September 1897, Blackburn, *Letters*, p. 8.

96. John Berryman, *Stephen Crane* (London, 1950).

97. Conrad to Garnett, [14 October 1897], E. Garnett, *Letters*, p. 102.

98. Stephen Crane to Conrad, 11 November 1897, R. W. Stallman and Lillian Gilkes, eds., *Stephen Crane: Letters* (New York, 1960), pp. 149–150.

99. Conrad to S. Crane, 16 November 1897, ibid., pp. 151–152.

100. Conrad to S. Crane, 1 December 1897, ibid., p. 154.

101. Conrad to Garnett, 5 December 1897, E. Garnett, *Letters*, p. 107.

102. Conrad to Unwin, 5 November, Yale; 24 November, Duke; 26 November, Indiana; and 11 December 1897, Yale.

103. "It's a title that embraces all the stories and most of Life" (Conrad to Unwin, 24 November 1897, Duke).

104. See Conrad's letters to Blackwood of 30 October 1897, Blackburn, *Letters*, p. 15, and to Garnett, [6 November 1897], E. Garnett, *Letters*, p. 104.

105. Neill R. Joy, "A Note on the Naming of Singleton in *The Nigger of the 'Narcissus,'*" *Conradiana* 8 (1976): 77–80. Conrad to Henry James, 30 November 1897, Jean-Aubry, *Lettres françaises*, p. 34.

106. Gordan, *Conrad*, p. 285; Sherry, *Conrad*, pp. 11–14, 82–100.

107. Conrad to Garnett, 23 December 1897, E. Garnett, *Letters*, p. 112. But three days later he wrote to Sanderson: "I declare solemnly to you that for all that I haven't done anything for ages" *LL*, 1:218.

108. Conrad to Quiller-Couch, 23 December 1897.

109. Conrad to E. Sanderson, 26 December 1897.

110. Conrad to Garnett, 5 December 1897, E. Garnett, *Letters*, pp. 107–108.

111. Norman Sherry, *Conrad's Western World* (Cambridge, 1971), p. 330. It is not clear to what extent Conrad exaggerated his indebtedness to Krieger and his creditor's insistence. I would guess that he also used Krieger as a cover for his other debts and obligations.

112. Conrad to Garnett, 7 January 1898, E. Garnett, *Letters*, p. 116.

113. Conrad to Mrs. Aniela Zagórska, 20 December 1897, *CPB*, p. 221.

114. Conrad to Graham, 14 and 20 December 1897, 14 and 23 January 1898, Watts, *Letters*, pp. 54–57, 65, 68.

115. Conrad to Graham, 31 January 1898, ibid., pp. 70–71.

116. Conrad to Graham, 23 January 1898, ibid., p. 68.

117. Kirschner, *Conrad*, pp. 230–232. Kirschner does not list all concurrences, nor does he mention essential differences, for example, in their views on honor. Some opinions of Father Coig-

nard seem to complement Conrad's own ideas: "Les vérités découvertes par l'intelligence demeurent stériles. . . . C'est par le sentiment que les semences du bien sont jetées sur le monde. La raison n'a point tant de vertu. . . . Il faut, pour servir les hommes, rejeter toute raison . . . et s'élever sur les ailes de l'enthousiasme" Anatole France, *Oeuvres complètes* (Paris, 1926), 8: 510–511.

118. Conrad to Graham, 14 January 1898, Watts, *Letters*, pp. 64–65.

119. Conrad to Graham, 23 January and 15 June 1898, ibid., pp. 68, 89.

120. Conrad to Graham, 20 December 1897, ibid., pp. 56–57.

121. Conrad to Graham, 5 March 1898, ibid., p. 79.

122. Ford Madox Ford, *Joseph Conrad: A Personal Remembrance* (London, 1924), p. 158; see also p. 37.

123. Conrad to Graham, 14 January 1898, Watts, *Letters*, p. 64. Two days later he repeated the same sentence in a letter to Chesson, Yale.

124. On 16 October 1896 Conrad dedicated to James, in English, a copy of *An Outcast*, Texas; 30 November 1897, in French, a copy of *The Nigger*, Harvard (he wrote *pénétrer* without accents); then about 1 September 1906, again in French, a copy of *The Mirror*, Jean-Aubry, *Lettres françaises*, p. 77.

125. Leon Edel, *Henry James: The Master, 1901–1916* (Philadelphia, 1972), p. 48.

126. René Rapin, ed., *Lettres de Joseph Conrad à Marguerite Poradowska* (Geneva, 1966), p. 53.

127. Conrad to Graham, 15 January 1898, Watts, *Letters*, p. 65; to Zagórska, 20 December 1897, *CPB*, p. 221; to Brooke [16 January 1898], Texas.

128. *JCC*, p. 57. Conrad's postscript to his letter to Graham, 14/15 January, contradicts this story.

129. Conrad to Galsworthy, Sunday, [16 January 1898], *LL*, 1:223, to Chesson, 16 January 1898, Yale; to S. Crane, 16 January 1898, Stallman and Gilkes, *Crane*, p. 169; to Garnett, [24 January] and [2 February 1898], E. Garnett, *Letters*, pp. 121–122.

130. Conrad to Helen Sanderson, 22 February 1899, *LL*, 1:272.

131. Conrad to Zagórska, 21 January 1898, *CPB*, p. 223. The baptism was to have taken place on 14 February (Conrad to Brooke, 25 January 1898, Texas), but for unknown reasons was postponed.

132. Conrad to S. Crane, Wednesday, [12 January 1898?], Stallman and Gilkes, *Crane*, p. 167. See also Conrad to E. Sanderson, 3 February 1898, *LL*, 1:227.

133. The notes were published, with a valuable commentary, by Norman Sherry in the *Times Literary Supplement*, 25 June 1970. Conrad saw Crane in London on 2 February (see Stallman and Gilkes, *Crane*, p. 170), and the two fixed the date of the Conrads' visit at Oxted (Conrad to Garnett, [2 February 1898], E. Garnett, *Letters*, p. 122). Conrad wrote to S. Crane on 15 February, "I shall bring a lot of paper and you shall find a pen."

134. E. Garnett, *Letters*, pp. xv–xvi.

135. Conrad to S. Crane, letter dated mistakenly 5 February 1898 instead of 5 March, Stallman and Gilkes, *Crane*, p. 171. After his stay at Crane's house Conrad addressed Crane by his first name.

136. Crane left London about 10 April (Blackburn, *Letters*, p. 21; Stallman and Gilkes, *Crane*, pp. 178–179). The war began on 21 April.

137. Conrad to S. Crane, 15 February 1898, Stallman and Gilkes, *Crane*, pp. 175–176; to Garnett, [2 February 1898], E. Garnett, *Letters*, p. 123.

138. Ian Watt, *Conrad in the Nineteenth Century* (Berkeley-Los Angeles, 1979), pp. 48–49. Conrad, "Alphonse Daudet," *Outlook*, 9 April 1898. Conrad described his article about Kipling ("Concerning a Certain Criticism" as "a chatter about Kipling provoked by a silly criticism" (to E. Sanderson, 3 February 1898, *LL*, 1:228). It was certainly a reaction to the review of Gabriele D'Annunzio's *Trionfo della Morte*, in which Arthur Symons accused Kipling's *Captains Courageous* and Conrad's *Nigger* of having "no idea" behind them; see Baines, *Joseph Conrad*, pp. 183, 472.

139. Conrad to Garnett, [2 February 1898], E. Garnett, *Letters*, p. 122. Through Garnett Conrad tried to have *The Rescue* serialized in *Saturday Review*; to Garnett, Monday, [10 January 1898], ibid., p. 118; and to Graham, 14 January 1898, Watts, *Letters*, pp. 63–64.

140. Conrad to Pawling, 27 February 1898, Heinemann (publisher's archives), London; to Graham, 5 March 1898, Watts, *Letters*, p. 79.

141. Conrad to Zagórska, 6 February 1898, *CPB*, p. 224 (original in French).

142. Conrad to Graham, 16 February 1898, Watts, *Letters*, pp. 77–78.

143. Conrad to Cora Crane, Tuesday, [17 March 1898], see also 24 March, Stallman and Gilkes, *Crane*, pp. 176, 178.

144. Conrad to Garnett, Monday, [21 March], and 29 March [1898], E. Garnett, *Letters*, pp. 125–127. Garnett was going to Italy.

145. Conrad to Garnett, Saturday, [4 June], and Tuesday, [7 June 1898], ibid., pp. 130, 135.

146. Gordan, *Conrad*, pp. 291–294; Sherry, *Conrad*, p. 14. Wobbly grammar and erroneous use of *like* instead of *as* were also criticized, Sherry, *Conrad*, p. 103.

147. Conrad, "An Observer in Malaya," *Academy*, 23 April 1898; "Tales of the Sea," *Outlook*, 4 June 1898.

148. Conrad to H. Sanderson, 3 June 1898, *LL*, 1:238.

149. Marlow in "Youth"—simple, nostalgic, presented almost without distance—is quite different from the pensive and complex Marlow in "Heart of Darkness" and *Lord Jim*; this seems to support my hypothesis about the origins of "Youth."

150. Conrad to E. Sanderson, 23 March 1898, Yale; to Garnett, Tuesday, [12 July 1898], E. Garnett, *Letters*, p. 133; to C. Crane, 27 June 1898, Stallman and Gilkes, *Crane*, pp. 182–183, and so forth. Although Jessie's memories of that period abound in the usual fantasies, we may accept as true their general tenor: Conrad was having great difficulty in settling down to the role of a family man, and his behavior at that time was particularly capricious.

151. *JCC*, pp. 61–63, 141. Conrad often invited guests, when in London ate in good restaurants, at least sometimes in reserved rooms; see Conrad to Garnett, Wednesday, [12 October 1898], E. Garnett, *Letters*, p. 140.

152. This important letter to Garnett is dated only "Saturday." E. Garnett places it in May (*Letters*, pp. 130–131), but since "Youth," finished on 3 June, is listed as ready, the earliest possible date is 4 June. See also Blackburn, *Letters*, p. 22.

153. *LL*, 1:240.

154. Conrad to Meldrum, 20 June 1898, Blackburn, *Letters*, p. 25; to Graham, 26 August 1898, Watts, *Letters*, pp. 101–102. These accounts contradict Conrad's later simplified and at the same time more colorful version of the events (to Tils, 25 November 1918, NYPL).

155. Conrad to C. Crane, 27 June 1898, Stallman and Gilkes, *Crane*, p. 183.

156. Bernard C. Meyer, *Joseph Conrad: A Psychoanalytic Biography* (Princeton, 1967), pp. 126–130.

157. For example, Conrad to Quiller-Couch, 13 July 1898 (original in possession of Foy F. Quiller-Couch).

158. Conrad to Graham, 27 August 1898, Watts, *Letters*, p. 103. See also to Meldrum [11 August 1899]: "I ask myself whether I am fitted for that work" (Blackburn, *Letters*, p. 27).

159. Conrad to Graham, Saturday, [probably 8 July], 19 July, 3 August and 26 August 1898, Watts, *Letters*, pp. 91–93, 100–102. See also Baines, *Joseph Conrad*, p. 213.

160. Conrad to Garnett, 3 August 1898, E. Garnett, *Letters*, pp. 133–134.

161. Conrad to Garnett, dated only "Saturday," ibid., pp. 134–135.

162. Conrad to Graham, 26 August and 27 August 1898, Watts, *Letters*, pp. 101, 103.

163. Conrad to H. Sanderson, 31 August 1898, LL, 1:247.

164. "All day with the ship-owners and in the evening dinner, phonograph, X rays, talk about *the* secret of the Universe, and the nonexistence of, so called, matter. The secret of the universe is in the existence of horizontal waves whose varied vibrations are at the bottom of all states of consciousness. If the waves were vertical the universe would be different. . . . Therefore it follows that two universes may exist in the same place and in the same time—and not only two universes but an infinity of different universes—if by universe we mean a set of states of consciousness. . . . *all matter* being only that thing of inconceivable tenuity through which the various vibrations of waves (electricity, hear, sound, light, etc.) are propagated, thus giving birth to our sensations— then emotions—then thought" (Conrad to Garnett, 29 September 1898, E. Garnett, *Letters*, pp. 136–137). Cedric Watts suggests that these ideas contributed to the conception of the "Fourth Dimensionists" in *The Inheritors*, the novel on which Conrad later collaborated with Ford (*Letters*, p. 108). Conrad's visit at McIntyre's is also described by Neil Munro, *The Brave Days: A Chronicle from the North* (Edinburgh, 1931), pp. 113–114. McIntyre had made the first phonographic recording of Paderewski's playing (p. 109), and Conrad's visit was to the accompaniment of a recorded concert by the Polish pianist.

165. Conrad to Garnett, Wednesday, [12 October 1898], E. Garnett, *Letters*, p. 141.

166. Postponing the serialization of *The Rescue*: Conrad to Meldrum, 12 October 1898, Blackburn, *Letters*, p. 30. The September loan from Krieger is only hypothetical (though probable, because for several weeks Conrad did not complain of the lack of money although he was not earning any). Loan from Galsworthy: Conrad to Galsworthy, 28 October 1898, Birmingham.

167. Conrad to Zagórska, 18 December 1898, CPB, pp. 226–227.

168. Conrad to Bontine, 16 October 1898, LL, 1:251–252.

169. Ibid., and Conrad to Ford, Friday, [21 October 1898], Yale.

IX. FORD, THE PENT, AND JIM: 1898–1900

1. Conrad to H. Sanderson, 31 August 1898, LL, 1:248; and to H. G. Wells, 6 September 1898, ibid., 1:248–249.

2. Ford Madox Ford, *Return to Yesterday* (London, 1931), p. 52.

3. Conrad to Ford Madox Ford, 29 September 1898, Yale.

4. H. G. Wells, *Experiment in Autobiography* (London, 1934), p. 617. See also Thomas C. Moser, "From Olive Garnett's Diary: Impressions of Ford Madox Ford and His Friends, 1890–1906," *Texas Studies in Literature and Language* 16 (1974): 516–521.

5. Arthur Mizener, *The Saddest Story: A Biography of Ford Madox Ford* (New York, 1971), pp. 39–40, 530–531.

6. Jocelyn Baines, *Joseph Conrad: A Critical Biography* (London, 1960), pp. 214–215.

7. Ford, *Joseph Conrad: A Personal Remembrance* (London, 1924), pp. 36–37.

8. Conrad to Kazimierz Waliszewski, 8 November 1903, *CPB*, p. 236.

9. Mizener, *Saddest Story*, p. 42.

10. Conrad to William E. Henley, 18 October 1898, Baines, *Joseph Conrad*, pp. 217–218.

11. Ford to Wells, 1 August 1920, Richard M. Ludwig, ed., *Letters of Ford Madox Ford* (Princeton, 1965), p. 119.

12. An undated entry in Olive Garnett's diary, Leon Edel, *Henry James: The Master, 1901–1916* (Philadelphia, 1972), p. 47.

13. Conrad to Ford, 29 September 1898.

14. For example, Conrad to Ford, 12 November 1899, Yale; to James B. Pinker, 19 September 1900, Berg.

15. Ford, *Joseph Conrad*, pp. 124, 128.

16. Ibid., pp. 239–240.

17. Samuel Hynes, *The Edwardian Turn of Mind* (Princeton, 1968), pp. 307–310.

18. Bernard C. Meyer, *Joseph Conrad: A Psychoanalytic Biography* (Princeton, 1967), p. 137. Here Meyer uses a nonspecialist term, *chronic depression*, and thus probably has in mind a tendency to depressed moods rather than a specific disease. From the psychiatric point of view Ford's case looks different: he often displayed symptoms typical of manics.

19. Antoni Kępiński, *Melancholia* (Warsaw, 1974), p. 8.

20. Ford, *Joseph Conrad*, pp. 11, 34–35, 56.

21. Conrad to Wells, 11 September 1898, *LL*, 1:249. Norman Mackenzie and Jeanne Mackenzie, *The Time Traveller: The Life of H. G. Wells* (London, 1973), p. 141.

22. Conrad to Wells, 23 December 1898, *LL*, 1:263.

23. Conrad to Wells, 4 December 1898, ibid., 1:259; and to Aniela Zagórska, 25 December 1898, *CPB*, p. 229.

24. Wells, *Experiment in Autobiography*, pp. 527, 530, 529.

25. Ibid., p. 525. Svengali is a Hungarian musician and sorcerer, the hero of George Du Maurier's *Trilby* (1894); Captain Kettle is the hero of sea adventure stories by Charles Hyne.

26. C. Lewis Hind, *Naphtali* (London, 1926), p. 73.

27. Edwin Pugh, "Joseph Conrad as I Knew Him," *T.P.'s and Cassell's Weekly*, 23 August 1924.

28. Henry-Durand Davray, "Joseph Conrad," *Mercure de France*, no. 175 (1 October 1924), pp. 33–34.

29. Ernest Dawson, "Some Recollections of Joseph Conrad," *The Fortnightly Review*, no. 130 (August 1928), p. 205.

30. Conrad to Zagórska, 18 December 1898, *CPB*, p. 227.

31. On 17 November 1898 Conrad wrote to Wells that they had been compelled to dismiss their maid whose "temperament was too artistic" (*LL*, 1:254). The absence of a maid would cause a break in the Conrads' social life; see Conrad to Clifford, 24 May 1899, ibid., 1:277.

32. Edgar Jepson, *Memories of an Edwardian and Neo-Georgian* (London, 1937), p. 142.

33. Borys Conrad, *My Father: Joseph Conrad* (New York, 1970), p. 13. Also his letter to the author, 5 August 1975.

34. R. W. Stallman and L. Gilkes, eds., *Stephen Crane: Letters* (New York, 1960), pp. 179–197.

35. Conrad to Edward Garnett, 7 November 1898, Edward Garnett, *Letters from Conrad, 1895 to 1924* (London, 1928), pp. 141–142.

36. Conrad to Ford, Saturday, [12] November 1898, Yale.

37. Ibid., and 17 November 1898, Yale.

38. The album, now in the Houghton Library, Harvard, is described by Alexander Janta, "A Conrad Family Heirloom at Harvard," in *Joseph Conrad: Centennial Essays*, ed. Ludwik Krzyżanowski (New York, 1960), pp. 87–109.

39. Ibid., p. 101. It was probably an addition to what we know as Chapter 1, and certainly a retroactive addition, since the jump in numbers is not reflected in the text itself.

40. Eloise K. Hay put forward the hypothesis that *Tuan Jim* had been written as early as 1896, during Conrad's stay in Brittany ("*Lord Jim*: From Sketch to Novel," in Conrad, *Lord Jim*, ed. Thomas C. Moser [New York, Norton, 1968], pp. 426–428). I am not persuaded by her arguments. She ignores the initially rapid growth of the text; her claim that as late as February 1899 Conrad thought only about the *Patna* episode is unfounded; her dating of the basic change in the design of the story as between February and July 1899 seems arbitrary, and so forth. My hypothesis that *Tuan Jim* was written in Spring 1898 can be supported by the fact that a note concerning *The Rescue* on the back of page 28 of the album refers to Chapter 5 of Part 3, the part Conrad was working on at that time. On the back of pp. 29–31 Conrad scribbled a sketch of Part 1 of a drama, with the action in Renaissance Ferrara; his first dramatic projects orginated, as far as we know, under the influence of his talks with Crane in early 1898.

41. Conrad to Blackwood, 13 December 1898, William Blackburn, ed., *Joseph Conrad: Letters to William Blackwood and David S. Meldrum* (Durham, N.C., 1958), pp. 33–34; Blackburn believes that the hint referred to "Heart of Darkness," but Conrad wrote about a story of thirty thousand words. To Blackwood, 14 February 1899, ibid., p. 51.
     Much confusion concerning the chronology of Conrad's work on *Lord Jim* has been caused by Blackburn's uncritical acceptance of the date written by Conrad on his letter to David Meldrum: "Friday 10 Aug 98" (ibid., pp. 26–27). However, 10 August 1898 was a Wednesday; and the letter is dated from Pent Farm, where Conrad moved on 26 October 1898 (see ibid., p. 30!); Conrad mentions in the text the proofs of the second instalment of *Lord Jim*, whose publication began in November 1899. Thus the correct date of this important letter is [11 August 1899]. Conrad's error in the day's date resulted probably from the fact that his writing of the letter spanned two days.

42. *Lord Jim*, p. viii. It is not true that his "first thought was of a short story, concerned only with the pilgrim ship episode." He did not initially write "a few pages," but much more. And his statement that when he "sat down to it [he] knew it would be a long book" is false with regard to all the three times he started his work on *Lord Jim* anew: June 1898, February 1899, July 1899.

43. Conrad to Wells, 4 December 1898, *LL*, 1:260. In the next few years there are occasional mentions of *The Rescue* in Conrad's letters, but never in a context indicative of actual work on the novel.

44. Conrad to R. B. Cunninghame Graham, 9 December, 1898, Cedric T. Watts, ed., *Joseph Conrad's Letters to R. B. Cunninghame Graham* (Cambridge, 1969), p. 111.

45. Conrad to Zagórska, *CPB*, p. 229.

46. Conrad to Zagórska, 12 April 1899, ibid., p. 231.

47. Conrad to Garnett, [18 December 1898], E. Garnett, *Letters*, p. 142.

48. Conrad to Blackwood, 31 December 1898, Blackburn, *Letters*, pp. 36–37. He estimated the length as twenty-thousand words.

49. Thomas H. Huxley, *Collected Essays* (London, 1894), 9:46–116. See Ian Watt, *Conrad in the Nineteenth Century* (Berkeley-Los Angeles, 1979), pp. 162–163. Professor Watt's book contains the most extensive and penetrating discussion of the intellectual sources and ideological perspectives of "Heart of Darkness."

50. Conrad to Crane, 13 January 1899, Stallman and Gilkes, *Crane*, p. 205; to Garnett, [18 December 1898] and 13 January 1899, E. Garnett, *Letters*, pp. 142, 147; to Meldrum, 2 January 1899, Blackburn, *Letters*, p. 38.

51. Conrad to Blackwood, 31 December 1898, to Meldrum, 2 January 1899, Blackburn, *Letters*, pp. 36–37.

52. Ibid., p. 45.

53. Conrad to Ford, Tuesday, 4 January 1899, Yale. The "Tale" is "The Brass Bottle," by T. A. Guthrie ("F. Anstey"), published in *Punch*.

54. Conrad to Garnett, 13 January 1899, E. Garnett, *Letters*, p. 147. Blackburn, *Letters*, pp. xxii and 42, maintains erroneously that Conrad knew about the prize in September. However, the words, "this unexpected piece of real good fortune," in Conrad to Wells, 6 September 1898, *LL*, 1:248, refer not to the prize, about which Garnett would have been the first to know, but to the letter from Wells Conrad received at The Cearne. Blackburn is right in assuming that Conrad would not have kept the secret from his friends; but in his letter to S. Crane, dated 13 January 1899, Conrad says that he heard about the prize "only today." In their note to this letter Stallman and Gilkes explain erroneously that the sentence, "You haven't lost time in looking up the old Academy," refers to the weekly's issue of 17 December 1898; in fact, "old" is here used as a decorative epithet.

55. According to the certificate of baptism in Borys Conrad's possession.

56. Conrad to Meldrum, 10 February and to Blackwood, 12 February, Blackwood to Meldrum, 13 February 1899, Blackburn, *Letters*, pp. 49–52.

57. Conrad to Blackwood, 14 February 1899, ibid., pp. 54–55. In his letter to Meldrum written the same day Conrad also mentioned "'Equitable Division' (a story of a typhoon)," ibid., p. 56; it is the first hint of "Typhoon."

58. Watts, *Letters*, p. 120.

59. Barbara Tuchman, *The Proud Tower* (New York, 1965), pp. 231, 163.

60. Conrad to Graham, 8 February 1899, Watts, *Letters*, pp. 116–118. Characteristically, he wrote the essential parts of the letter in French.

61. Eloise Knapp Hay, *The Political Novels of Joseph Conrad* (Chicago, 1963), pp. 17–27.

62. Conrad: "L'homme est un animal méchant. Sa mechanceté doit être organisée. Le crime est une condition nécéssaire de l'existence organisée. La société est essentielment criminelle ou elle n'existerait pas." France: "Il était persuadé l'homme est naturellement un très méchant animal, et que les sociétés ne sont abominables que parce qu'il met son génie à les former." *Les opinions de*

M. Jérôme Coignard (Paris, 1920), p. 20. The analogy was first noticed by Watts, *Letters*, p. 121. In Conrad's sarcastic remarks about "brotherhood" there are echoes of France's words about cowardice as a condition of peace (*Les opinions*, p. 120).

63. For Max Stirner (1806–1850), a German individualist and anarchist philosopher, the ego had an absolute value and was a law unto itself. Schopenhauer regarded the state as a means used by egoism to curtail its own excesses (see, for example, *The World as Will and Idea*, 2, §47).

64. E. Garnett, *Letters*, p. vi.

65. Conrad to Ford, Monday, [30 January 1899], Yale; Meldrum to Blackwood, 2 February 1899, Blackburn, *Letters*, p. 44.

66. Conrad to Garnett, Tuesday, [21 or 28 February 1899], E. Garnett, *Letters* p. 148.

67. Conrad to A. Methuen, 25 May 1899, *LL*, 1:277.

68. Conrad to Pinker, 23 August 1899, ibid., 1:278.

69. Conrad to H. Sanderson, 22 July 1899, Yale.

70. Conrad to Blackwood, 14 February 1899, Blackburn, *Letters*, p. 55.

71. Conrad to Garnett, 31 March 1899, E. Garnett, *Letters*, p. 150.

72. Conrad to Meldrum, 6 July 1899, Blackburn, *Letters*, pp. 58–59.

73. "Odwiedziny u Conrada," *Tygodnik Wileński*, no. 1 (1925). Lutosławski described his visit four times: in *Kraj* (see note 74), in the article quoted here, in *The Blue Peter*, no. 12 (1930), and in his autobiography, *Jeden łatwy żywot* [One easy life] (Warsaw, 1933), pp. 214–215. Jessie Conrad's report is grotesque even by her own standards (*JCC*, p. 53). Lutosławski was undoubtedly an eccentric, but full of charm, to which his social successes in many European countries testify. He knew Jessie's side of the story when he wrote about her in his autobiography: "She was a woman without breeding and education, and neither her husband nor I paid any attention to her when we started talking in Polish."

74. *Kraj*, no. 12 (1899), reprinted in *Wspomnienia i studia*. In *Tygodnik Wileński* (see note 73), there is a slightly different version of Conrad's reply: "To write in Polish! That is a great thing, to do that one has to be a writer like Mickiewicz or Krasiński. I am an ordinary man and write to earn mine and my wife's living, in the language of a country where I have found my refuge." It is obvious that these words did not express Conrad's actual opinions; but it is hard to say whether he pretended, or was falsely understood—or whether Lutosławski forgot what he had heard.

75. Conrad to Wincenty Lutosławski, 9 June 1897, *Przekrój*, 18 January 1981.

76. *Kraj*, no. 16 (23 April 1899); reprinted in *Wspomnienia i studia*, pp. 16–30.

77. Conrad to Józef Korzeniowski, 14 February 1901, *CPB*, p. 234.

78. Zagórska, "Kilka wspomnień o Conradzie" [A few reminiscences of Conrad], *Wiadomości Literackie*, no. 51 (1929); Conrad's retort is quoted by Józef Ujejski, *O Konradzie Korzeniowskim* (Warsaw, 1936), p. 17.

79. Ujejski, *Konradzie Korzeniowskim*, pp. 18–24. Ujejski did not know of the existence of the *Tuan Jim* fragment. Anybody tempted to look for influences and analogies should remember that between Jim's flight and Konrad Korzeniowski's "desertion" there is at least one fundamental difference: the former was a discrete, single act, done in a state of awareness diminished by fear, the latter a long-lasting and conscious process.

80. Conrad to Lutosławski, 9 June 1897.

81. *A Personal Record*, p. 36.

82. Stallman and Gilkes, *Crane*, pp. 225, 282. Jessie claims, probably unjustly, that Crane never paid his share (*JCC*, p. 74).

83. Edith R. Jones, "Stephen Crane at Brede," *Atlantic Monthly*, July 1954, p. 60. See also B. Conrad, *My Father*, pp. 33–34.

84. Conrad to Meldrum, 31 July 1899, Blackburn, *Letters*, pp. 59–60.

85. Conrad to Garnett, 16 September and 26 October 1899, E. Garnett, *Letters*, pp. 152–153.

86. Conrad to Blackwood, 22 August 1899, Blackburn, *Letters*, p. 64.

87. Conrad to Garnett, 26 October 1899, E. Garnett, *Letters*, p. 155.

88. Conrad to Meldrum, 25 November 1899, Blackburn, *Letters*, pp. 67–75.

89. Conrad to Garnett, Good Friday, [31 March 1899], E. Garnett, *Letters*, p. 151.

90. Mizener, *Saddest Story*, p. 51.

91. Conrad to Garnett, 26 March 1900, E. Garnett, *Letters*, p. 169.

92. Conrad to Ford, Sunday, [12] November [18]99, Yale.

93. *JCKH*, p. 113; Mizener, *Saddest Story*, p. 51.

94. See, for example, Conrad's note on the margin of the letter from McClure, 23 November 1899, Yale.

95. Conrad to Ford, 31 March 1900, Yale: "The literary quality (and most other things) is all *your own* in the book." Similarly in a much later inscription in Wise's copy of the novel, Baines, *Joseph Conrad*, p. 240.

96. Conrad to Meldrum, 3 April 1900, Blackburn, *Letters*, p. 89.

97. Conrad to Garnett, 26 March 1900, E. Garnett, *Letters*, p. 169. In spite of Conrad's advice ("You'll have to burn this letter"), Garnett published it in full in 1928, and Ford felt deeply hurt (Mizener, *Saddest Story*, pp. 54–55).

98. Conrad to Ford, 26 March 1900, Yale. The novel was never serialized.

99. *Notes by Joseph Conrad written in a set of his first editions in the possession of Richard Curle* (London, 1925), p. 21.

100. Ford, *Joseph Conrad*, pp. 211–213.

101. Conrad to S. Kliszczewski, 12 April [1898], *LL*, 1:274 (Jean-Aubry wrongly dates this letter 1899); to Graham, 19 December 1899, Watts, *Letters*, p. 128.

102. Ford, *Joseph Conrad*, pp. 48, 241.

103. Conrad to Edward Sanderson, 26 October and 28 December 1899, *LL*, 1:285–286, 289; to the Sandersons, 19 January 1900, Yale; to H. Sanderson, 17 March 1900, *LL*, 1:294.

104. Conrad to Zagórska, 25 December 1899, *CPB*, p. 232.

105. Conrad to Graham, 14 October and 19 December 1899, 28 July 1900, Watts, *Letters*, pp. 126–127, 135; to Garnett, 15 January 1900, E. Garnett, *Letters*, p. 163.

106. Conrad to Galsworthy, 2 September 1899, *LL*, 1:278; to E. Sanderson, 26 October and 28 December 1899, ibid., 1:287, 289; to Graham, 19 January 1900, Watts, *Letters*, p. 131.

107. Kępiński, *Melancholia*, p. 123.

108. Conrad to Sanderson, 12 October 1899, *LL*, 1:282–283 (original of letter, Yale).

109. Conrad to Galsworthy, 21 December 1899, Maria Danilewiczowa, ed., *Joseph Conrad: Listy do Johna Galsworthy'ega* (London, 1957), p. 6; to Zagórska, 25 December 1899, *CPB*, p. 232.

110. Conrad to Graham, 13 February 1900, Watts, *Letters*, p. 132.

111. For example, Conrad to Meldrum, 22 August 1899, Blackburn, *Letters*, p. 62; to Galsworthy, 12 October 1899, Birmingham (thanking him for a check for £20).

112. Conrad to Meldrum, 3 December 1899, and footnote, Blackburn, *Letters*, p. 76.

113. John Dozier Gordan, "The Ghost at Brede Place," *Bulletin of the New York Public Library*, no. 56 (1952), pp. 591–595. There are no contemporary reports of Conrad's participation in either the spectacle itself or its preparation.

114. Stallman and Gilkes, *Crane*, pp. 244–255.

115. Conrad to Graham, 4 January 1900, Watts, *Letters*, p. 129.

116. Blackburn, *Letters*, pp. 77–86. Conrad's illness lasted until 11 February.

117. Conrad to Ford, 17 February 1900, Yale.

118. Blackburn, *Letters*, pp. 87–88.

119. Conrad to Garnett, 26 March 1900, E. Garnett, *Letters*, pp. 169–170.

120. Conrad to Ford, 31 March [1900], Yale.

121. *JCC*, p. 70.

122. To Poradowska: Conrad, 16 April, Jessie, 10 May 1900, René Rapin, ed., *Lettres de Joseph Conrad à Marguerite Poradowska* (Geneva, 1966), pp. 171–172; S. Pawling to E. Gosse, June 1902, Yale.

123. Conrad to Henry-Durand Davray, 10 June 1900, G. Jean-Aubry, ed., *Joseph Conrad: Lettres françaises* (Paris, 1929), p. 40.

124. Cora Crane to Wells, 15 May 1900, Stallman and Gilkes, *Crane*, p. 284: Conrad to Galsworthy, Thursday, [17] May 1900, *LL*, 1:294 (wrongly dated as 7 May).

125. S. Crane to Sanford Bennett, 14 May 1900, Stallman and Gilkes, *Crane*, pp. 283–284.

126. "Stephen Crane," *Last Essays*, p. 100.

127. Conrad to Blackwood, 14 July 1900, Blackburn, *Letters*, pp. 89–103.

128. Conrad to Galsworthy, Friday, [20 July 1900], *LL*, 1:295. In London, Conrad gave the end of *Lord Jim* to Meldrum, who immediately sent the manuscript to be typed (Meldrum to Blackwood, 14 July 1900, Blackburn, *Letters*, p. 104).

X. DIFFICULT MATURITY: 1900–1904

1. Joseph Conrad to John Galsworthy, [20 July 1900], *LL*, 1:295–296; *JCC*, p. 71; Conrad to William Blackwood, 23 July 1900, William Blackburn, ed., *Joseph Conrad: Letters to William Blackwood and David S. Meldrum* (Durham, N.C., 1958), p. 107.

2. Conrad to R. B. Cunninghame Graham, 28 July 1900, Cedric T. Watts, ed., *Joseph Conrad's Letters to R. B. Cunninghame Graham* (Cambridge, 1969), p. 135.

3. *JCC*, p. 71; Conrad to Galsworthy, 11 August 1900, *LL*, 1:296.

4. Arthur Mizener, *The Saddest Story: A Biography of Ford Madox Ford* (New York, 1971), p. 59.

5. Conrad to Galsworthy, 19 September 1900, Birmingham; to David Meldrum, 1 September 1900, Blackburn, *Letters*, p. 109. *First Command*, which later became *The Shadow Line*, he mentioned several times, from 14 February 1899, Blackburn, *Letters*, p. 56.

6. Conrad to James B. Pinker, 8 October 1900, Berg; to Meldrum, [27 November 1900], Blackburn, *Letters*, pp. 115–116.

7. Date on the MS, Harvard.

8. Frank Swinnerton, *An Autobiography* (London, 1937), pp. 242–243.

9. *Typhoon and Other Stories*, p. 52.

10. See, for example, Conrad to Galsworthy, 16 January 1898 about *Jocelyn*, LL, 1 : 224; and 11 November 1901 about *Man of Devon and Other Stories*, ibid., 1 : 301–302.

11. See H. V. Marrot, *The Life and Letters of John Galsworthy* (London, 1935), pp. 136, 154.

12. Galsworthy to R. H. Mottram, 4 August 1906, in R. H. Mottram, *For Some We Loved* (London, 1956), p. 82; Galsworthy, "Joseph Conrad: A Disquisition," *Fortnightly Review*, April 1908, cited in Norman Sherry, ed., *Conrad: The Critical Heritage* (London, 1973), p. 205.

13. Galsworthy, *Castles in Spain* (New York, 1927), pp. 117, 113, 123–124.

14. Conrad to Edward Garnett, Friday, [2 November? 1900], Edward Garnett, *Letters from Conrad, 1895 to 1924* (London, 1928), p. 171.

15. Conrad to Garnett, 12 November 1900, E. Garnett, *Letters*, pp. 172–173. See Garnett to Galsworthy, 15 November 1900: "I have attacked Conrad critically, *re* last two-fifths and the end of *Lord Jim*. He more than accepts what I have said: he goes too far in acceptance" (E. Garnett, ed., *Letters from John Galsworthy* [London, 1934], p. 24).

16. Conrad to Blackwood, 19 December 1900, Blackburn, *Letters*, p. 122.

17. John Dozier Gordan, *Joseph Conrad: The Making of a Novelist* (Cambridge, Mass., 1940), pp. 294–297; Sherry, *Conrad*, pp. 16–17, 111–128.

18. Blackburn, *Letters*, p. 199. Following editions (525 copies each) came out in 1904 and 1905, and later in 1914, after the success of *Chance*—at that time 15,000 copies were issued.

19. Conrad to Meldrum, Tuesday, [27 November 1900], Blackburn, *Letters*, p. 115; to Garnett, 12 November 1900, E. Garnett, *Letters*, p. 173. James's letter has been lost.

20. Conrad to Meldrum, Tuesday, [27 November 1900].

21. The pertinent correspondence in Blackburn, *Letters*, pp. 117–124. W. Blackwood had agreed to guarantee £200 but received and signed a form for £250.

22. Conrad to W. Blackwood, 30 December 1900, Blackburn, *Letters*, p. 123.

23. Conrad to Pinker, 15 January 1901, Berg.

24. Conrad to Galsworthy, Tuesday, [January? 1901], Maria Danilewiczowa, ed., *Joseph Conrad: Listy do Johna Galsworthy'ego* (London, 1957), p. 9; see also *JCKH*, p. 111.

25. Conrad to Garnett, 20 January 1900, E. Garnett, *Letters*, p. 168.

26. Conrad to Józef Korzeniowski, 14 February 1901, *CPB*, p. 234.

27. Conrad to Galsworthy, 27 February, 6 March, and 24 March 1901, Birmingham.

28. Mizener, *Saddest Story*, pp. 69, 537; Conrad to W. Blackwood, 24 May 1901, Blackburn, *Letters*, p. 126. See also Ford's letter to Galsworthy of March 1901, in Richard M. Ludwig, ed., *Letters of Ford Madox Ford* (Princeton, 1965), p. 15.

29. F. M. Hueffer, *The Cinque Ports* (London and Edinburgh, 1900), p. 163. See Mizener, *Saddest Story*, pp. 69–70 and 537, for Ford's claim that "Amy Foster" had originally been his own story which Conrad rewrote.

30. Conrad to Pinker, 7 June, and Sunday evening, [16 June 1901], Berg; to Galsworthy, 20 June 1901, *LL*, 1:300. Conrad's letter to Davray of 2 April 1902 states that Yanko was conceived of as a Pole (G. Jean-Aubry, ed., *Joseph Conrad: Lettres françaises* [Paris, 1929], p. 44).

31. Raymond T. Brebach, "The Making of *Romance*: A Study in Literary Collaboration," *Dissertation Abstracts International*, 37:2191A. Conrad to Pinker, 7 June and 7 November 1901, Berg; in his letter to Pinker of 19 September 1900 Conrad had claimed that the novel was "nearing completion" (Berg).

32. *JCC*, p. 66.

33. Conrad to Kazimierz Waliszewski, 8 November 1903, *CPB*, p. 236. See also to W. Blackwood, 24 May and 4 July 1901, Blackburn, *Letters*, pp. 126, 129.

34. Conrad and Ford, *Romance*, p. 335.

35. Meldrum to W. Blackwood, 5 August 1901, Blackburn, *Letters*, p. 131; W. Blackwood to Conrad, 15 August 1901, ibid., p. 132.

36. Conrad to Ford, Tuesday, [1 July 1901], *LL*, 1:313, and 19 July 1901, Yale.

37. *The New York Times Saturday Book Review*, 13 July 1901; Hueffer's name is mentioned only in a bibliographic note.

38. Letter of 2 August, published 24 August 1901, Conrad, *CDAUP*, pp. 73–76.

39. Conrad to Pinker, 7 June 1901, Berg.

40. Conrad to Ford, 11 July, 19 July, and Thursday, [25 July 1901], Yale. Mizener, *Saddest Story*, pp. 64–65, tells the story relying, among other sources, on letters from Robert Garnett to Conrad hitherto inaccessible to other scholars. The new policy was apparently a £500 twin of another that Conrad had drawn in December with the same purpose in mind. The money he now borrowed from Ford was to pay the first rate of the loan that he had taken at that time and also for the premium on the new policy; Conrad to Ford, 19 July 1901.

41. Conrad to Pinker, 7 November 1901, Berg. It consisted of £100 for "Typhoon," £60 for "Falk," £40 for "Amy Foster," and £40 for Conrad's share in *Seraphina*.

42. Marghanita Laski, "Domestic Life," in *Edwardian England 1901–1914*, ed. S. Nowell-Smith (London, 1964), pp. 142, 166; A. L. Bowley, *Wages and Income in the U.K. since 1860* (Cambridge, 1937), p. 42; E. H. Phelps Brown and Margaret H. Browne, *A Century of Pay* (London, 1968), appendix 3. Statistical data refer to years 1900 and 1901.

43. Conrad to Pinker, 7 November 1901, Berg.

44. The change in numbering the parts of *Seraphina* caused some trouble to Conrad's and Ford's biographers (see Jocelyn Baines, *Joseph Conrad: A Critical Biography* [London, 1960], p. 270; Mizener, *Saddest Story*, p. 72). As late as the summer of 1901, the novel consisted of four parts but ended, as it does now, with Kemp's trial. While continuing to write Part 3, Conrad expanded it into another, which became Part 4—and the last, written by Ford, Part 5.

45. Mizener, *Saddest Story*, pp. 72–73.

46. Baines, *Joseph Conrad*, p. 269.

47. Thomas C. Moser, "From Olive Garnett's Diary: Impressions of Ford Madox Ford and His Friends, 1890–1906," *Texas Studies in Literature and Language* 16 (1974): 524–525.

48. Ernest Dawson, "Some Recollections of Joseph Conrad," *The Fortnightly Review*, 1 August 1928, pp. 204–208. Date of their meeting: after the publication of *Lord Jim* and after Wells's Spade House in Sandgate had been finished in December 1900.

49. Mizener, *Saddest Story*, p. 73.

50. Conrad to Meldrum, 7 January 1902, Blackburn, *Letters*, pp. 137–139. W. Blackwood refused the advance and politely reminded Conrad of his £50 debt, extant since December 1900 (ibid., p. 142).

51. Conrad to Pinker, 6 January 1902, Berg.

52. Conrad to Pinker, 8 January 1902, Berg; Baines, *Joseph Conrad*, p. 268.

53. Conrad to Pinker, 25 February and 23 [in fact, 22] March 1902, Berg. Conrad's deal with Pinker enabled Conrad to release Galsworthy from his obligation to pay half of Conrad's yearly insurance premium (Conrad to Galsworthy, 10 March 1902, Birmingham).

54. Conrad to Pinker, 16 February 1902, Berg; to W. Blackwood, 28 January 1902, Blackburn, *Letters*, p. 140 (in the same letter Conrad proposed "Falk" for serialization); to Pinker, 25 February 1902, Berg.

55. Conrad to Galsworthy, 10 March 1902, Birmingham. Conrad's letters of the same day to Bennett, (*LL*, 1:302–303) and of 16 March to Pinker (Berg) indicate that he was staying in Winchelsea at the time.

56. Conrad to Pinker, 23 March 1902, Berg; to Ford, Sunday, [9 March 1902], Yale.

57. Conrad to Elsie Hueffer, Monday, [17] March 1902, Yale. By 10 April the title had been changed to the present one; to Davray, Jean-Aubry, *Lettres françaises*, p. 48.

58. Conrad to Pinker, 16 and 17 March 1902, Berg.

59. Conrad to Ford, Wednesday, [24 April 1902], and 15 April 1902, Yale.

60. Conrad to Garnett, 10 June 1902, E. Garnett, *Letters*, pp. 183–184.

61. Conrad to W. Blackwood, written the day of their meeting, 31 May 1902, Blackburn, *Letters*, pp. 152–156.

62. Conrad to Ford, Monday, [24 March] and 10 June 1902, Yale. On 15 April Conrad thanked Ford for not giving notice to the owner of Pent Farm, Richard Hogben. The rent, supplies of farm produce, and keep of the pony cost £50 per annum; Conrad to Newbolt, 1 June 1905, Mursia.

63. Conrad to Ford, 24 June 1902, Yale (second letter of that date).

64. Conrad to Meldrum, [31 May 1902], Blackburn, *Letters*, p. 151; to Galsworthy, 1 June 1902, Birmingham.

65. As above, and W. Blackwood to Conrad, 3 June 1902, Blackburn, *Letters*, pp. 156–157; also p. xxvi.

66. Details in Conrad to Galsworthy, 11 June 1902, Birmingham.

67. Conrad to Galsworthy, 19 June 1902, Birmingham.

68. Conrad to George Blackwood, 20 May, and to W. Blackwood, 5 June 1902, Blackburn, *Letters*, pp. 147, 157.

69. Conrad to Ford, 24 June 1902, Yale (first letter). See also to Galsworthy, 25 June 1902, *LL*, 1:304, and to Garnett, Thursday, [August 1902], E. Garnett, *Letters*, p. 185.

70. Conrad to W. Blackwood, 5 June 1902, Blackburn, *Letters*, pp. 157–158.

71. Conrad to W. Blackwood, 24 June 1902, ibid., pp. 158–159. Conrad's and Blackwood's calculations of the text's length were markedly different: what Conrad described as 14,000 words (to W. Blackwood, 20 May) contained only 10,000 (Blackwood to Conrad, 26 June 1902, Blackburn, *Letters*, pp. 148, 158). Taking this adjustment into account leads to the conclusion that Conrad had to reconstruct and/or write about 40,000 additional words. Chapters 11–13 are very long and constitute over two-fifths of the whole text (about 20,000 words).

72. Blackburn, *Letters*, p. xxvii, and Baines, *Joseph Conrad*, p. 285; Conrad to Royal Literary Fund, 11 July 1902, Public Record Office, Royal Literary Fund, File 2629.

73. Blackburn believes (*Letters*, p. xxvii) that the grant was allotted because of the news about the fire. This, however, would have required almost incredibly swift action by all concerned. Conrad would have to have informed Clifford immediately by an unknown letter of 24 June, Clifford to have contacted Gosse personally, and Gosse to have written to James on 25 June.

74. Pawling's memorandum and Conrad's *vita* by Gosse, Yale; James's private letter, BL; James's official letter, also of 26 June 1902, in Blackburn, *Letters*, pp. 200–201. J. G. Sutherland, *At Sea with Joseph Conrad* (Boston, 1922), p. 63. Also, in verso of copy of T. E. Lawrence's letter to F. N. Doubleday, received 3 May 1920, Conrad listed, among other books wanted: *Physiology of Vision*, F. W. Eldridge Green (Yale).

75. Ian Watt, "Conrad, James and *Chance*," in *Imagined Worlds: Essays on Some English Novels and Novelists in Honour of John Butt*, ed. Maynard Mack and Ian Gregor (London, 1968), p. 307.

76. Leon Edel, *Henry James: The Master, 1901–1916* (Philadelphia, 1972), p. 493.

77. Ford Madox Ford, *Joseph Conrad: A Personal Remembrance* (London, 1924), pp. 243–244; see also his *Return to Yesterday* (London, 1931), p. 227.

78. *JCKH*, p. 115.

79. Visits to Winchelsea: probably in the first half of July (Mizener, *Saddest Story*, pp. 79, 539); at the end of July and beginning of August (Conrad to W. Blackwood, 3 August 1902, Blackburn, *Letters*, pp. 163–164); in mid-October, when they remained until the twenty-second or twenty-third (Conrad to Garnett, 17 October 1902, E. Garnett, *Letters*, pp. 185–186).

80. Conrad to W. Blackwood, 5 November 1902, Blackburn, *Letters*, p. 168.

81. Conrad to Garnett, Thursday, [August? 1902], E. Garnett, *Letters*, p. 185.

82. Wells, *Experiment in Autobiography* (London, 1934), pp. 622, 630.

83. Conrad to Ford, Thursday, May 1902, BL. This contradicts Mizener's claim (*Saddest Story*, p. 80) that Pinker succeeded in convincing Conrad of the necessity of cuts only in September.

84. Conrad to Pinker, 26 November 1902, Berg; Ford to Pinker, 28 November 1902, Ludwig, *Letters of F. M. Ford*, p. 16.

85. Conrad to W. Blackwood, 5 November 1902, Blackburn, *Letters*, p. 168. See also to Elsie Hueffer, 4 November 1902, Yale; and Galsworthy to Garnett, 5 November 1902, *Letters from Galsworthy*, p. 44.

86. Conrad to Pinker, 26 November 1902, Berg; same day to Northern Newspapers Syndicate, Berg; to W. Blackwood, 4 December 1902, Blackburn, *Letters*, p. 171; to Ernest Dawson, 12 December 1902, *LL*, 1:308.

87. Conrad to Ford, 2 January 1903, Baines, *Joseph Conrad*, p. 286.

88. Conrad to W. Blackwood, 5 June 1902; to Galsworthy, Thursday, *LL*, 1:308. Jean-Aubry dates this letter as "early 1903," but it was probably written in November 1902.

89. Conrad to Meldrum, Friday, [autumn 1902], to W. Blackwood, 4 December 1902, Blackburn, *Letters*, pp. 170–171.

90. Conrad to Pinker, 5 January 1903, Berg.

91. Gordan, *Conrad*, pp. 298–302; Sherry, *Conrad*, pp. 129–142; Sherry reprints the reviews by Garnett, Masefield and (unsigned) by A. J. Dawson in *The Athenaeum*, whose authorship reveals Conrad's letter to E. Dawson of 3 February 1903, Yale.

92. Blackburn, *Letters*, p. 199.

93. George Gissing to Edward Clodd, 30 November 1902, in Ernest Clodd, *Memoirs* (New York, 1916), p. 186.

94. 21 December 1902, Pierre Coustillas, "Conrad and Gissing," *Cahiers d'Etudes et de Recherches Victoriennes et Edouardiennes* 2 (1975): 43–44.

95. Conrad to E. Dawson, 12 December 1902, *LL*, 1 : 308.

96. Conrad to Garnett, 22 December 1902, E. Garnett, *Letters*, pp. 188–189. Captain Whalley is the hero of "The End of the Tether," Colonel Newcome a hero of Thackeray's *The Newcomes* (1855).

97. Date of departure: telegram to Elsie Hueffer of 23 December 1902, Yale; Conrad's mood and his intention of staying longer at Winchelsea: to Galsworthy, 22 December 1902, Birmingham; date of return: to Galsworthy, 1 January 1903, Birmingham, and same day to Meldrum, Blackburn, *Letters*, p. 175.

98. Conrad to Elsie Hueffer, Thursday, [8 January 1903], and to Ford, Sunday evening, [11 January 1903], Yale.

99. Borys Conrad, *My Father: Joseph Conrad* (New York, 1970), pp. 13, 25–27; also B. Conrad's letter to the author, 5 August 1975.

100. *JCC*, p. 74.

101. Conrad to Ford, 2 January 1903, Yale.

102. Conrad to Galsworthy, 16 February and 2 April 1903, Birmingham.

103. Conrad to Galsworthy, 16 February 1903. See also to Ford, 23 March 1903, Yale: "I do not doubt of your assistance in my efforts."

104. Conrad to Pinker, 5 January 1903, Berg (here the title *Nostromo* is mentioned for the first time); to Ford, 23 March 1903; to Meldrum, 23 March 1903, Blackburn, *Letters*, p. 177.

105. Conrad to Pinker, 20 April 1903, Berg; Mizener, *Saddest Story*, p. 73.

106. Hugh Clifford, "Joseph Conrad: Some Scattered Memories," *The Bookman's Journal and Print Collector* 11 (October 1924): 5.

107. Sir Henry Newbolt, *My World As in My Time: Memoirs 1862–1932* (London, 1932), p. 300.

108. Conrad to William Blackwood and Sons, 16 February 1903, Blackburn, *Letters*, p. 175.

109. Moser, "From Olive Garnett's Diary," p. 526.

110. Sherry, *Conrad*, pp. 18–19, 143–158; *The Critic*, September 1903, p. 280; comparison with Tolstoy and Gorki in *The Speaker*, 6 June 1903.

111. Gissing to H. G. Wells, 31 August 1903, Royal A. Gettman, ed., *George Gissing and H. G. Wells: Their Friendship and Correspondence* (London, 1961), p. 215. Gissing also wrote a long

and complimentary letter to Conrad, 9 May 1903 (G. Jean-Aubry, ed., *Two Letters from George Gissing to Joseph Conrad* [London, 1926]).

112. Conrad to Ford, Saturday, [June 1902], Yale.

113. Conrad to Elsie Hueffer, n.d. but probably September 1903, Yale. See to same, 1 October 1903, Yale: "If it's one of his little jokes I am sorry that he let himself become folâtre before the high altar."

114. Marrot, *Galsworthy*, pp. 156-160. Conrad also discussed Galsworthy's novel with Ford (Conrad to Galsworthy, 22 April 1903, Danilewiczowa, *Conrad*, p. 11).

115. Frederick R. Karl, "Conrad-Galsworthy: A Record of Their Friendship in Letters," *Midway*, Autumn 1968, pp. 92-93. *The Island Pharisees* appeared in 1904; *The Man of Property*, which Conrad also read and discussed in his letters, appeared two years later. In later years Galsworthy did not show Conrad his works before they were published; he probably felt more sure of himself by then. This is the main reason why there are no comments on those subsequent works in Conrad's letters to Galsworthy. Galsworthy's opinion about Dostoyevsky, whom he placed below Turgenev and Tolstoy, is regarded by Karl as an example of his non-Conradian taste (p. 93), but it actually reflects Conrad's own assessment exactly.

116. Conrad to Garnett, 13 May 1903, E. Garnett, *Letters*, p. 190; to Elsie Hueffer, Wednesday, [8 July 1903], Yale; to Galsworthy, 22 August 1903, *LL*, 1:317; to Pinker, 22 August 1903, *LL*, 1:316.

117. Conrad to Davray, 22 August 1903, Jean-Aubry, *Lettres françaises*, p. 50.

118. Conrad to William Rothenstein, 22 July and 13 October 1903, Harvard. Watts wrongly places Rothenstein's visit about the end of September or early October (*Letters*, p. 147).

119. Conrad to W. Rothenstein, 11 September 1903, Harvard.

120. W. Rothenstein, *Men and Memories: 1900-1922* (London, 1932), pp. 41-43, 157.

121. Conrad to Harriet M. Capes, 26 December 1903, Yale.

122. Conrad to Ford, [September 1903], Yale. In the end, *Romance* was published without dates of its writing.

123. See, for example, *Athenaeum*, 7 November 1903, and *The New York Times Saturday Book Review*, 14 May 1904.

124. Conrad to Waliszewski, 8 November 1903, *CPB*, pp. 236-237.

125. Conrad to Galsworthy, Friday, [29 October? 1903], Birmingham.

126. Conrad to Pinker, Thursday [autumn 1903], Berg.

127. Conrad to J. M. Barrie, 23 November 1903, NYPL; to Galsworthy, 30 November 1903, *LL*, 1:322.

128. Conrad to Capes, 26 December 1903.

129. Conrad to Barrie, 31 December 1903, NYPL; the same expression in Conrad to Meldrum, 26 December 1903, Blackburn, *Letters*, p. 179.

130. Conrad to Waliszewski, 15 November 1903, *CPB*, p. 237.

131. Conrad to W. Blackwood, 22 December 1902, Blackburn, *Letters*, p. 174.

132. Conrad to Waliszewski, 5 December 1903, *CPB*, pp. 240-241.

133. Conrad to Roger Casement, 21 December 1903, B. L. Reid, *The Lives of Roger Casement* (London, 1976), pp. 54-56. See Peter Singleton-Gates and Maurice Girodias, *The Black Diaries:*

An Account of Roger Casement's Life and Times With a Collection of His Diaries and Public Writings (New York, 1959), p. 175; Brian Inglis, *Roger Casement* (London, 1973), p. 79.

134. Conrad to Graham, 26 December 1903, Watts, *Letters*, p. 149.

135. Singleton-Gates and Girodias, *The Black Diaries*, p. 189.

136. Conrad to Pinker, 12 December 1903, Berg. Conrad had started to write the sea sketches before coming to London (to Ford, Monday, [11 January 1904], BL). Baines errs in assuming that three articles for *The Daily Mail* were planned and counted as separate (*Joseph Conrad*, p. 292); in fact, they constituted two essays included in *The Mirror*. A brief chronology of the growth of texts: until 4 March 1904, six essays ("Landfalls and Departures," "Emblems of Hope," "The Fine Art," "Weight of the Burden," "Overdue and Missing," "The Grip of the Land"); until 18 September 1904, three more ("The Character of the Foe," "Rulers of East and West," "In Captivity"); in July and November 1904, "The Faithful River"; in Autumn 1904, "Cobwebs and Gossamer"; in July 1905, "Initiation"; in September and October 1905, the last three ("The Nursery of the Craft," "The 'Tremolino,'" "The Heroic Age").

137. About the bank's collapse: Conrad to Ford, Friday evening, [14 January 1904], Yale, and to Wells, 7 February 1904, *LL*, 1:326–327. Conrad's estimates of his overdraft varied between nearly £200 (to Elsie Hueffer, 2 September 1904, Yale) and £250 (to A. Krieger, 15 March 1904, Norman Sherry, *Conrad's Western World* [Cambridge, 1971], p. 395). Conrad used the necessity to repay his overdraft in the failed bank immediately as an excuse to delay payment of his other debts (to Elsie Hueffer, 2 September 1904), but in fact as late as June 1905 he still owed money to the receivers of Watson and Co. (Conrad to Newbolt, 1 and 9 June 1905, Mursia).

138. See Mizener, *Saddest Story*, p. 85.

139. Conrad to Ford, Monday, [10 January 1904], BL, with an extensive argument against sharing their meals.

140. Conrad to Alice Rothenstein, 23 January 1904, Harvard.

141. *JCKH*, p. 47; Conrad to Ford, 23 March 1903, Yale.

142. Conrad to Sidney Colvin, Tuesday, [February 1904], Rosenbach, and 4 March 1904, Duke; to Wells, 7 February 1904, *LL*, 1:326–327. On Ford's share: Conrad to Colvin, 28 April 1905, *LL*, 2:17.

143. Conrad to Colvin, Tuesday, [February 1904], and 4 March 1904.

144. Published only posthumously, included in Conrad, *Last Essays*. MS is dated 2 March 1904 (Gordon Lindstrand, "A Bibliographical Survey of the Literary Manuscripts of J. Conrad," *Conradiana* 2, no. 2 [1969–1970]: 106–107). The article was probably intended for *Blackwood's Magazine*.

145. Conrad, *Last Essays*, p. 132.

146. Entry, 13 February 1904, Moser, "From Olive Garnett's Diary," p. 527.

147. Conrad to Wells, 7 February 1904, *LL*, 1:326–327.

148. Ford, *Joseph Conrad*, p. 30; Ford, *Return to Yesterday*, pp. 286–287.

149. Conrad to Ford, [29 May 1904], Baines, *Joseph Conrad*, pp. 290–291; to Elsie Hueffer, 19 September 1904, Yale: "Cheque (endorsed) enclosed here is for Ford's proportion of Sketches—nothing to do with the loan. Please do not trouble with a receipt. . . . Mark: on acct. of two sketches disposed of up to now (serial)."

150. See, for example, Conrad to Pinker, 6 January 1902, Berg. Conrad to George Harvey, 15 April 1904, Yale.

151. Ford Madox Ford, *Joseph Conrad: A Personal Remembrance* (London, 1924), p. 212; Thomas C. Moser, *The Life in the Fiction of Ford Madox Ford* (Princeton, 1980), pp. 53–56.

152. Conrad to Colvin, 4 March 1904, Duke.

153. Conrad to Pinker, 4 March and 29 March 1904, Berg. The latter makes one wonder whether the essay "The Grip of the Land," apparently finished the night of 3–4 March, was in fact written down by Ford. Conrad says in the letter that it is ready but not typed; Miss Hallowes would have been unable to decipher Ford's private "shorthand."

154. *Nostromo*, pp. 175–185. Mizener describes the MS and the controversy it aroused (*Saddest Story*, pp. 89–91). He only errs, I believe, in dating the fragment for mid-February. It appeared in *T.P.'s Weekly* of 9 April, and if Ford wrote it to help Conrad meet the deadline, he need not have done it before early March.

155. Mizener, *Saddest Story*, pp. 90–91.

156. Ibid., pp. 91 and 541.

157. Conrad to Pinker, 29 March 1904, Berg.

158. Conrad to Meldrum, 5 April 1904, Blackburn, *Letters*, pp. 179–180.

159. For example, on 5 April he had to ask Galsworthy for five guineas (Conrad to Galsworthy, Birmingham).

160. Conrad to Pinker, 18 April 1904, Berg.

161. B. Conrad, *My Father*, p. 14.

162. Conrad to Pinker, 3 May 1904, Berg; the information about Miss Hallowes's salary (paid by Pinker)—£1.5.0 weekly—from the same source.

163. Conrad to Ford, [25 April 1904], Yale.

164. Date of writing according to Conrad to Pinker, 17 May 1904, Berg; the introduction is included in *Notes on Life and Letters*.

165. Date according to Conrad to Garnett, 6 July 1904, E. Garnett, *Letters*, pp. 192–193. It was published in *The Speaker*, 16 July 1904, and later included as the first part of an essay about Anatole France in *Notes on Life and Letters*.

166. Conrad to Pinker, 11 July 1904, Berg.

167. *The Mirror of the Sea*, pp. 24–25, 111.

168. Conrad to Pinker, 3 May 1904, Berg.

169. W. Rothenstein to Newbolt, 9 and 22 June 1904, Gosse to Newbolt, 26 June and 7 July 1904, Mursia.

170. Conrad to W. Rothenstein, 27 June 1904, *LL*, 1:330 and Harvard.

171. Pinker to Wells, 18 July 1904, Yale.

172. Conrad to Gosse, 19 August 1904, *LL*, 1:331–332.

173. Conrad to Ford, 29 July 1904, Yale.

174. Moser, "From Olive Garnett's Diary," pp. 528–529.

175. Conrad to Ford, 5 September 1904, Yale.

176. Conrad to W. Rothenstein, 27 June 1904, *LL*, 1:330; Conrad to Ford, 29 July 1904, Yale; Conrad to W. Rothenstein, 3 September 1904, *LL*, 1:336. Owen Knowles, "Conrad, Anatole

France, and the Early French Romantic Tradition: Some Influences," *Conradiana* 11, no. 1 (1979): 41–42.

177. Conrad to Galsworthy, 1 September 1904, *LL*, 1:334.

178. Conrad to W. Rothenstein, 3 September 1904.

179. See Karl, "The Significance of the Revisions in the Early Versions of *Nostromo*," *Modern Fiction Studies* 5 (Summer 1959): 129–144.

180. Conrad to W. Rothenstein, 24 September 1904, Harvard.

181. Conrad to Galsworthy, 23 September 1904, Birmingham.

XI. UPHILL: 1904–1909

1. Joseph Conrad to R. B. Cunninghame Graham, 7 October 1904, Cedric T. Watts, ed., *Joseph Conrad's Letters to R. B. Cunninghame Graham* (Cambridge, 1969), p. 156; Conrad to James B. Pinker, 18 and 19 October 1904, Berg.

2. Conrad to Alice Rothenstein, 17 November 1904, Harvard; to Ford Madox Ford, 22 November 1904, Yale; to Marguerite Poradowska, 15 December 1904, René Rapin, ed., *Lettres de Joseph Conard à Marguerite Poradowska* (Geneva, 1966), p. 182.

3. Conrad to E. V. Lucas, 1 December 1904, Indiana.

4. John Galsworthy in George T. Keating, ed., *A Conrad Memorial Library: The Collection of George T. Keating* (Garden City, N.Y., 1929), p. 138; Cecil Roberts, *Half Way* (London, 1931), p. 218.

5. See, for example, *JCKH*, pp. 53–56, 120.

6. Norman Sherry, *Conrad: The Critical Heritage* (London, 1973), pp. 20, 159–180.

7. Conrad to Pinker, 18 October, 8 November, 21 December 1904, and n.d. from the same period (in the last Conrad mentions the "Banavides cycle"), Berg; length of the piece: to Ford, 22 November 1904, Yale.

8. Jocelyn Baines, *Joseph Conrad: A Critical Biography* (London, 1960), p. 321.

9. Essay probably finished on 15 October; see Conrad to Ford of this date, Yale.

10. *Notes on Life and Letters*, pp. 11–19.

11. Conrad to Pinker, 31 October 1904, Berg; and to Ford, 22 November 1904, Yale.

12. Conrad to Pinker, 31 October 1904; and 5 February 1905, *LL*, 2:11.

13. Conrad to William Rothenstein, 24 October 1904, Harvard; to Pinker, 21 December 1904, Berg.

14. *JCC*, p. 89.

15. Thomas C. Moser, "From Olive Garnett's Diary: Impressions of Ford Madox Ford and His Friends, 1890–1906," *Texas Studies in Literature and Language*, no. 3 (1974):530.

16. Arthur Mizener, *The Saddest Story: A Biography of Ford Madox Ford* (New York, 1971), pp. 101–102.

17. Conrad to Pinker, 21 December 1904.

18. Conrad to W. Rothenstein, 3, 25, and 30 November 1904, Harvard; to Elsie Hueffer, Tuesday, [22 or 29 November? 1904], Yale.

19. Conrad to Lucas, 1 December 1904, Indiana; to Pinker, 21 December 1904.

20. Conrad to Pinker, 4 January 1905, Berg.

21. Conrad to Henry-Durand Davray, 28 December 1904 and Tuesday, [12 January 1905], G. Jean-Aubry, ed., *Joseph Conrad: Lettres françaises* (Paris, 1929), p. 68; to Galsworthy, 14 January 1905, from Paris, Birmingham.

22. Conrad to David Meldrum, 22 January 1905, William Blackburn, ed., *Joseph Conrad: Letters to William Blackwood and Davis S. Meldrum* (Durham, N.C., 1958), p. 182.

23. Conrad to Galsworthy, 21 January 1905, *LL*, 2:9.

24. Appendix B, Conrad to Henry Newbolt, 9 June 1905, Mursia.

25. Conrad to Galsworthy, 21 January 1905.

26. Jean-Aubry, *Lettres françaises*, p. 68.

27. Conrad to Pinker, 22 February 1905, *LL*, 2:13; see also to Zygmunt Szembek, 8 December 1906, *CPB*, p. 249.

28. *JCC*, pp. 91–96; Conrad to Meldrum, 22 January 1905; to Pinker, 5 February 1905, *LL*, 2:10.

29. Conrad to Pinker, 23 February 1905, Berg; to Davray, 12 March 1905, *LL*, 2:12–13.

30. Jessie Conrad to Norman Douglas, 25 March 1905, Macpherson.

31. Conrad to Davray, 12 March 1905, Jean-Aubry, *Lettres françaises*, pp. 70–71.

32. Conrad to Ford, 9 May 1905, *LL*, 2:19.

33. Conrad to Pinker, 5 February 1905 (Jean-Aubry interprets this erroneously as referring to *The Secret Agent*), and 12 and 24 April 1905, Berg. The MS of the novel (Berg) has its original title *Explosives—A Ship-Board Tale* erased.

34. Conrad to Galsworthy, 5 May 1905, *LL*, 2:18, and Birmingham. Conrad says here that he "has begun" a short story; Jean-Aubry supposes, mistakenly, that it was "The Brute." In his letter to Pinker of 12 May (Berg) Conrad writes that he has the "Explosives" ready.

35. Conrad to Pinker, 23 February 1905.

36. Mailed to Pinker with Conrad to Pinker, 24 April 1905.

37. Conrad to Davray, 12 January 1905, Jean-Aubry, *Lettres françaises*, p. 69.

38. Conrad to Pinker, 23 February 1905. Thus his criticism of German assertiveness preceded Wilhelm II's well-known belligerent speech in Tangiers (31 March).

39. Baines, *Joseph Conrad*, p. 318.

40. Frederick R. Karl, "Conrad—Galsworthy: A Record of Their Friendship in Letters," *Midway*, Autumn 1968, p. 94.

41. More extensively on this subject: A. Busza, "Rhetoric and Ideology in *Under Western Eyes*"; E. Crankshaw, "Conrad and *Russia*"; Z. Najder, "Conrad and Rousseau: Concepts of Man and Society"; all in Norman Sherry, ed., *Joseph Conrad: A Commemoration* (London, 1976), pp. 85, 90, 100–102, 107–109.

42. *Notes on Life and Letters*, pp. 99, 95.

43. *The Mirror of the Sea*, pp. 149–151.

44. Conrad to Galsworthy, 5 May 1905.

45. Edmund Gosse to Newbolt, 26 June 1904, W. Rothenstein to Newbolt, 4 July 1904, Mursia. The official name of the fund is the Royal Bounty Special Service fund. The award has always been either given in trust or used for buying a life insurance. The money was made available by the minutes of 26 April 1905 and paid out to trustees by the Paymaster General on 3 May 1905 (information from Hans van Marle; Public Record Office, T 1/10268A/8033 and PMG 27/63).

46. Conrad to Gosse, 23 March 1905, LL, 2:14.

47. Conrad to Gosse, 11 April 1905, ibid., p. 15. In accordance with the government's wishes, Conrad promised to be discreet, but he informed Galsworthy about the grant, giving its size as "something like 300" (8 May 1905, ibid., p. 18).

48. Gosse to Newbolt, 6 April 1905, Mursia.

49. Conrad to A. Rothenstein, 1 May 1905, Harvard.

50. Conrad to Davray, [12 January 1905], Jean-Aubry, Lettres françaises, p. 70; to Sidney Colvin, 28 April 1905, LL, 2:17.

51. Conrad to Szembek, 16 May and Monday, [22] May 1905, CPB, pp. 245–247; to Galsworthy, 8 May 1905, LL, 2:19.

52. Conrad to Gosse, 16 May 1905, Yale.

53. W. Rothenstein to Newbolt, Monday, [15 May 1905], Mursia; Conrad's letter to Rothenstein has not been preserved. The whole affair is described by Newbolt, My World As in My Time (London, 1932), pp. 300–312, and by Rothenstein, Men and Memories (London, 1932), 2:61.

54. Conrad to Gosse, 19 May 1905, Yale.

55. Conrad to Newbolt, 23 May from London and 25 May 1905 from Pent Farm, Mursia.

56. Conrad to Pinker, 5 March 1906, Berg.

57. A copy of Newbolt to Conrad, 30 May 1905, was sent to Rothenstein; W. Rothenstein to Newbolt, 31 May 1905, Mursia.

58. Conrad to Newbolt, 1 June 1905, Mursia.

59. Conrad to Newbolt, 5 June 1905, Mursia.

60. W. Rothenstein to Newbolt, 3 and 5 May 1905, Mursia; copy of Newbolt to Conrad, 7 June 1905, Mursia.

61. W. Rothenstein to Newbolt, 24 May 1905, Mursia. Rothenstein, who later must have mercifully destroyed Conrad's letters to him, was swayed in turn by the arguments of Conrad and of Newbolt.

62. The Listener, 28 December 1961.

63. E. M. Forster, Howards End (New York, Vintage, n.d.), p. 45.

64. Conrad to Newbolt, 9 June 1905 and appendices, Mursia; on 16 June he thanked Newbolt for checks received, Mursia.

65. W. Rothenstein to Newbolt, 14 June 1905, Mursia.

66. Conrad to Newbolt, 16 June 1905.

67. Conrad to Newbolt, 10 April 1906, Mursia; to W. Rothenstein, same date, Harvard.

68. Max Beerbohm, "Mr. Conrad's Play," Saturday Review, 8 July 1905. He was sharply critical of Tadema's play.

69. Conrad to Galsworthy, 30 June 1905, LL, 2:20–21.

70. This was first pointed out by David Harvey, in his unpublished bibliography of Ford; see Mizener, *Saddest Story*, pp. 107–109.

71. Ford to Pinker, n.d. (probably early 1905), quoted by Mizener, *ibid.*, p. 108.

72. Conrad to Colvin, 28 April 1905, *LL*, 2:17.

73. Conrad to Ford, 9 May 1905, ibid., p. 20.

74. William Blackwood to Pinker, 6 June 1905, Blackburn, *Letters*, pp. 184–185; Conrad to Galsworthy, 30 June 1905, *LL*, 2:20. "In Captivity" (nos. 33 and 34 of *The Mirror*) clearly consists of two thematically distinct pieces; this is apparently why Conrad wrote to Galsworthy that he had written "Two *Mirror* papers."

75. MS (Rosenbach), with the original title "Their Character" crossed out, is dated 4 July. Pinker sent a copy to Blackwood on 5 September, Blackburn, *Letters*, p. 186.

76. *Notes on Life and Letters*, pp. 8–9. To Edward Garnett Conrad wrote, "I am rather ashamed of the silly thing I had to send to the *Speaker*; tho' I think that to say it contains all my philosophy of life is a severe hit. . . . I wasn't even aware I had it" (20 July 1905, Edward Garnett, *Letters from Conrad, 1895 to 1924*, [London, 1928], p. 199).

77. E. Garnett to Galsworthy, July 1905, E. Garnett, ed., *Letters from John Galsworthy* (London, 1934), p. 94.

78. For example, Conrad to Douglas, 18 October 1905: "I haven't had more than 3 weeks of decent health in the whole time since I left Capri" (*LL*, 2:24).

79. Conrad to Newbolt, 19 July 1905, Mursia.

80. Conrad to Pinker, 20 September 1905, Berg. Cuts in the Nelson essay started Conrad's angry exchange of letters with the editors of *The Standard* (Yale).

81. *The Mirror of the Sea*, p. 151.

82. Conrad to Pinker, 6 October 1905, Berg.

83. Gustav Morf, "Polish Proverbial Sayings in Conrad's Work," in Róża Jabłkowska, ed., *Conrad Colloquy in Poland 5–12 September 1972* (Wrocław, 1975), pp. 89–90. Morf cites another instance of Conrad ascribing a Polish proverb to the Russians: in *Victory*, "when a guest enters the house, God enters the house" (p. 358). Morf does not explain this other mystification; an explanation similar to the one given for the "Gaspar Ruiz" case would obviously have been wrong, as *Victory* was written after *A Personal Record* and "Prince Roman," where Conrad is quite open about his Polishness. Morf does not notice, either, that in *Victory* the proverb is used ironically, referring to a trio of bandits.

84. *A Set of Six*, p. 18.

85. Conrad to H. G. Wells, 20 October 1905, *LL*, 2:25–26. The novel mentioned was not, as Jean-Aubry assumed, *The Secret Agent*, but *Chance*. That Conrad's bad mood was not momentary is attested to by his other letters, for example to Galsworthy, 23 September, Maria Danilewiczowa, ed., *Joseph Conrad: Listy do Johna Galsworthy'ego* (London, 1957), p. 13.

86. Ford quoted by Olive Garnett, Moser, "From Olive Garnett's Diary," p. 531; also Ford to Pinker, n.d., Mizener, *Saddest Story*, p. 110.

87. See Conrad to Wells, 20 October and 28 November 1905, *LL*, 2:26 and 29.

88. Igor Stravinsky and R. Croft, *Dialogues and a Diary* (New York, 1963), p. 196. The same anecdote also contains the only critical remark about Conrad's command of French I have come across; apparently St.-John Perse called Conrad's French *épouvantable* ("dreadful").

89. Conrad to Galsworthy, 31 January 1906, Birmingham; Conrad, "John Galsworthy," *Outlook*, 31 March 1906 (included in *Last Essays*, pp. 125–131).

90. Conrad to Ada Galsworthy, 31 October 1905, Birmingham: "His [doctor's] verdict is nervous breakdown of a sort"; to Colvin, 26 December 1905, Duke.

91. Conrad to Colvin, 26 December 1905; to Galsworthy of the same date, *LL*, 2:29–30.

92. Conrad to Meldrum, 5 January 1906, Blackburn, *Letters*, p. 187; to Galsworthy, Thursday, [4 January 1906], Danilewiczowa, *Conrad*, p. 14, and 11 January 1906, Birmingham.

93. W. Rothenstein to Newbolt, 28 November and 3 December 1905, Mursia; Conrad to Galsworthy, 29 December 1905, Birmingham.

94. Conrad to Galsworthy, 29 December 1905.

95. Conrad to Galsworthy, 26 December and 29 December 1905; to Pinker, 1 January 1906, Berg. The MS of "The Informer" (Rosenbach) is dated 11 January 1906, however, and this date is supported by Conrad's letter to Galsworthy of the same day, Birmingham.

96. Conrad to Pinker, 1 January 1906; *A Set of Six*, p. 78.

97. Conrad to Pinker, 21 February 1906, Berg.

98. Ibid.

99. Conrad to W. Rothenstein, 7 February 1906, Harvard.

100. Conrad to Pinker, 13 February 1906, Berg; F. J. Temple, "Joseph Conrad à Montpellier," in C. Thomas, ed., *Studies in Joseph Conrad* (Montpellier, 1975), pp. 14–15.

101. Conrad to Pinker, 5 March 1906, *LL*, 2:30.

102. Conrad to Algernon Methuen, 30 May 1906, ibid., p. 34.

103. Conrad to Pinker, 5 March 1906; also 4 April 1906, Berg.

104. Conrad to Galsworthy, 22 March 1906, Birmingham, and 9 April 1906, *LL*, 2:33.

105. Conrad to Pinker, 5 March 1906, Berg. Conrad's new creditors were the same merchants in Hythe and its vicinity whom he had listed in his financial report to Newbolt a year before; the debts amounted to £70.

106. W. Rothenstein to Newbolt, 3 and 5 April 1906, Mursia.

107. *JCC*, p. 111.

108. Ida R. Sée, "Joseph Conrad à Montpellier," *Le Petit Méridionel*, 6 September 1924.

109. Conrad to Pinker, 5 March 1906.

110. Conrad to W. Rothenstein, 7 February 1906, Harvard.

111. *JCC*, p. 109.

112. Ibid., p. 112.

113. Mizener, *Saddest Story*, p. 109.

114. Ibid., pp. 113–114. That Ford influenced Conrad in his work on "The Informer" and *The Secret Agent* is beyond doubt (see Norman Sherry, *Conrad's Western World* [Cambridge, 1971], pp. 148, 206–210); however, his claim that he also co-authored fragments of the novel cannot be substantiated. It is also worth remembering that Conrad's interest in anarchists predated by several years his meeting Ford; see Conrad to Poradowska, Sunday, [7 January 1894], Rapin, *Lettres*, pp. 122–123.

115. Date of departure: Conrad to Galsworthy, 11 May 1906, Birmingham; date of return: Ford's letter to his wife, dated by Mizener between 9 and 20 May, Mizener, *Saddest Story*, p. 115.

116. Moser, *Life in Fiction of Ford*, p. 67. Mizener, *Saddest Story*, pp. 118–119, 545. A short fragment, about four hundred words, in Conrad's hand is preserved at Yale. Conrad kept Ford's MS for the whole summer 1906 but did nothing to it.

117. *JCC*, pp. 112–116.

118. Ford to Elsie Hueffer, n.d., Mizener, *Saddest Story*, p. 115.

119. The approximate date of Marwood's arrival at Winchelsea was given to me by Thomas Moser. Jessie Conrad dates his first visit as July 1906 (*JCC*, p. 116).

120. *Alumni Cantabrigienses* (Cambridge, 1951), part 2, vol. 4, p. 348; Archibald Marshall, *Out and About* (London, 1934), pp. 278–279.

121. Marshall, *Out and About*, p. 275.

122. Ford, *It Was the Nightingale* (Philadelphia, 1933), pp. 207–208. Ford's memories of Marwood are very inaccurate; see, for example, Marshall, *Out and About*, pp. 276–279.

123. Conrad to W. Rothenstein, Sunday, [24] June [1906], Harvard.

124. Conrad to Galsworthy, 7 July 1906, Danilewiczowa, *Conrad*, p. 15; on 24 August Conrad wrote that they would leave the house "on the end of Augst or say 2d Sept" (ibid., p. 17).

125. Conrad to Galsworthy, 7 July 1906.

126. Conrad to A. Galsworthy, 2 August 1906, *LL*, 2:35–36.

127. Conrad to Harriet M. Capes, 15 August 1906, Yale.

128. Conrad to Methuen, 7 November 1906, *LL*, 2:38; to Davray, 8 November 1906, Jean-Aubry, *Lettres françaises*, p. 77; to Garnett, same date, E. Garnett, *Letters*, p. 200. The editors of *Ridgway's* cut the text to suit their readers; see Emily K. Dalgarno, "Conrad, Pinker, and the Writing of *The Secret Agent*," *Conradiana* 9, no. 1 (1977):50–51.

129. Conrad to Galsworthy, 12 September 1906, *LL*, 2:37.

130. Conrad to Methuen, 7 November 1906, ibid., 2:38.

131. Conrad to Graham, 7 October 1907, Watts, *Letters*, p. 170.

132. Conrad to Davray, 8 November 1906, Jean-Aubry, *Lettres françaises*, p. 78.

133. Galsworthy, to Garnett, 30 September 1906, E. Garnett, *Galsworthy*, p. 122. See Galsworthy to Conrad, same date, in G. Jean-Aubry, ed., *Twenty Letters to Joseph Conrad* (London, 1926); also letters of praise from Kipling, Lucas, and Wells in the same collection. See also reviews in *Athenaeum*, 27 October; *Outlook*, 13 October; *Spectator*, 1 December; and the *Times Literary Supplement*, 12 October 1906.

134. Conrad's dedication in Jean-Aubry's *Lettres françaises*, p. 77; James's letter of 1 November 1906, in Jean-Aubry, *Letters to Conrad*.

135. Conrad to Davray, 8 November 1906, Jean-Aubry, *Lettres françaises*, p. 78. Lawrence Graver, *Conrad's Short Fiction* (Berkeley and Los Angeles, 1969), p. 148.

136. Conrad to Galsworthy, 15 November 1906, Danilewiczowa, *Conrad*, p. 19: "I am in a state of such depression as I have not known for years." Also to Garnett, 20 November 1906, E. Garnett, *Letters*, p. 210. To Graham, 31 December 1906, Watts, *Letters*, p. 165: "A horrid almost suicidal depression . . ." A curiously bland letter of condolence sent to Graham after his wife's death attests to Conrad's exclusive concentration on *The Secret Agent* in the final weeks of his work on the novel (4 October 1906, Watts, *Letters*, p. 164).

137. Conrad to Garnett, 17 November 1906, E. Garnett, *Letters*, pp. 201–209.

138. Baines, *Joseph Conrad*, pp. 340, 483.

139. Conrad to Pinker, 26 February and 13 March 1907, *LL*, 2:42, 46; Borys Conrad, *My Father: Joseph Conrad* (New York, 1970), p. 50.

140. Conrad to Davray, 5 December 1906, Jean-Aubry, *Lettres françaises*, p. 80; to Poradowska, 7 December 1906, Rapin, *Lettres*, pp. 184–185.

141. Conrad to Graham, 31 December 1906.

142. Conrad to Ford, 8 January 1907, copy at Cornell.

143. Conrad to Davray, 20 and 30 December 1906, 8 January 1907, Jean-Aubry, *Lettres françaises*, pp. 81–84.

144. Sée, "Conrad à Montpellier."

145. Temple, "Conrad à Montpellier," pp. 16–17; Frida Weissman, ed., *Valery Larbaud, G. Jean-Aubry: Correspondance 1920–1935*, (Paris, 1971), pp. 48, 62.

146. Author's Note, *Victory*, pp. xv–xvii; *LL*, 2:4.

147. Conrad to Pinker, 25 January 1907, *LL*, 2:41, and 13 April 1907, Berg.

148. Conrad to Methuen, 26 January 1908, *LL*, 2:66. Hans van Marle has established that the source of the story's main plot, mentioned by Conrad in Author's Note, *A Set of Six*, is to be found in the French periodical *L'Audience*, 1858 (van Marle to the author, 14 July 1976).

149. Conrad to Ernest Dawson, 3 January 1907, Yale; to Ford, 25 January 1907, BL.

150. Conrad to John Quinn, 24 May 1912, NYPL; MS of *Chance*, Berg.

151. Conrad to Poradowska, 5 January 1907, Rapin, *Lettres*, p. 186.

152. Conrad to Pinker, 26 February 1907, *LL*, 2:42.

153. Conrad to Galsworthy, 5 March 1907, ibid., p. 44.

154. Baines, *Joseph Conrad*, p. 342.

155. In Conrad to Pinker, 13 March 1907 (*LL*, 2:45), the Swiss venture is presented as a suggestion of Dr. Grasset, Borys's doctor; but in an earlier letter to Galsworthy (5 March), Conrad mentions the Swiss cure as his own project. I suppose he suggested it to the physician.

156. Conrad to Pinker, 13 March 1907, Berg. In *LL*, 2:45, Jean-Aubry omitted a long fragment concerning financial matters and also the sentence "Miss Wright is such a fool."

157. Conrad to Galsworthy, 6 May 1907, *LL*, 2:47.

158. Conrad to Pinker from the Hôtel de la Poste, Geneva, 18 May 1907, ibid., p. 48.

159. *JCC*, pp. 122–126.

160. Conrad to W. Rothenstein, 28 May 1907, *LL*, 2:50–51.

161. Ibid.

162. Conrad to Galsworthy, 6 June 1907, ibid., pp. 51–52.

163. Conrad to Galsworthy, 17 June 1907, ibid., pp. 52–53.

164. Conrad to Elsie Hueffer, 15 June 1907, Mizener, *Saddest Story*, p. 127.

165. Conrad to Galsworthy, 27 June 1907, Danilewiczowa, *Conrad*, p. 22.

166. Conrad to Pinker, 6 May 1907, Berg.

167. Conrad to Pinker, 18 May 1907. He had indeed asked Methuen for galleyproofs (Conrad to Methuen, 7 November 1906, *LL*, 2:38).

168. Harold E. Davis, "Conrad's Revision of *The Secret Agent*: A Study in Literary Impressionism," *Modern Language Quarterly* 19 (1958):244–254; Dalgarno, "*The Secret Agent*," pp. 51–53.

169. Conrad to Wells, 30 July 1907, University of Illinois, Urbana.

170. Conrad to Pinker, 27 July 1907, Berg.

171. Conrad to Pinker, 3 August 1907, Berg. For this next novel Conrad expected to get £1,600 (to Pinker, 30 July 1907, Berg [partly printed in *LL*, 2:54–55]).

172. Conrad to Pinker, 30 July 1907.

173. Conrad to Pinker, 3 August 1907.

174. Conrad to Pinker, 13 August 1907, Berg.

175. Conrad to Pinker, 30 July 1907. Pinker did not meet this request. In September Conrad begged him again: "Pray stretch a point. This will clear me completely and make life a different thing altogether" (Monday, [30?] September [19]07, Berg).

176. *JCC*, pp. 127–128.

177. Conrad to Capes, 13 and 20 August 1907, Yale.

178. Conrad to Capes, 10 September 1907, Yale.

179. Conrad to Henry James, 20 September 1907, *LL*, 2:55. Conrad to Galsworthy, 15 September 1907, Birmingham.

180. *JCC*, pp. 129–131.

181. Conrad to Elsie Hueffer, 1 January 1908, Yale.

182. Conrad to E. Dawson, 25 June 1908, *LL*, 2:70.

183. Ian Watt, ed., *Conrad: "The Secret Agent", A Casebook* (London, 1973), pp. 26–58. Graver, *Conrad's Short Fiction*, p. 148.

184. Conrad to Pinker, 18 May 1907; to W. Rothenstein, 21 August 1907, Harvard; to Pinker, 30 July 1907.

185. Conrad to Galsworthy, 6 January 1908, *LL*, 2:65.

186. Conrad to Davray, 26 January 1908, Jean-Aubry, *Lettres françaises*, p. 87.

187. Conrad to Garnett, Friday, [4 October 1907], E. Garnett, *Letters*, p. 212.

188. Conrad to Garnett, Tuesday, [8 October 1907], ibid., pp. 216–217.

189. Ibid., p. 216. "The Censor of Plays" was published in *The Daily Mail*, 12 October 1907, and later included in *Notes on Life and Letters*.

190. Conrad to Galsworthy, 24 October 1907, *LL*, 2:62.

191. Conrad to D. Welch, 7 November 1907, Dartmouth College Library, Dartmouth College, Hanover, New Hampshire.

192. Conrad to Pinker, Tuesday, [29 October? 1907], Berg.

193. Conrad to Welch, 7 November 1907.

194. Conrad to Pinker, 4 December 1907, Berg.

195. Conrad to Pinker, 7 January 1908, Berg.

196. Conrad to Galsworthy, 6 January 1908.

197. Conrad to Galsworthy, 27 November 1907, Birmingham.

198. Conrad to Colvin, 11 October 1907, University of Buffalo; *JCC*, p. 131.

199. Conrad to Galsworthy, 17 February 1908, Danilewiczowa, *Conrad*, p. 23. The book was J. C. Tarver, *Gustave Flaubert as Seen in His Works and Correspondence* (London, 1895).

200. Mizener, *Saddest Story*, pp. 130–131 (but the Christmas party mentioned here took place only a year later, see ibid., p. 547, note 13).

201. See Conrad to Garnett, 12 December 1908, E. Garnett, *Letters*, p. 227.

202. Marshall, *Out and About*, p. 143.

203. Quoted in Norman Sherry, *Conrad and His World* (London, 1972), pp. 93–94.

204. Stephen Reynolds to Pinker, 17 December 1907, R. Wright, ed., *Letters to Stephen Reynolds* (Richmond, 1923), p. 101. See also Conrad to Galsworthy, 17 February 1908.

205. For example: to Poradowska, 1 January 1908, Rapin, *Lettres*, p. 187; to Galsworthy, 6 January 1908; to Davray, 3 February 1908, Jean-Aubry, *Lettres françaises*, p. 89.

206. Conrad to Galsworthy, 15 September 1907, Birmingham. Here Conrad mentioned the possibility of a legal action on Ford's part.

207. Conrad to Galsworthy, 6 January 1908.

208. In his letter to Pinker, 7 January 1908 (Berg), Conrad said that for the last twelve years he spent, "including everything," £650 a year. But 12 × 650 = 7,800; thus out of the mythical £11,000, only 3,200 would have been left.

209. Conrad to Pinker, 7 January 1908; and n.d., written between 9 and 12 January, Berg.

210. Conrad to Pinker, 14 January 1908, Berg. See also letter of the same date to Galsworthy, Birmingham, with many details of his dismal financial position. Conrad must have spent most of that day writing these letters.

211. Conrad to Pinker, 16 January 1908, Berg.

212. Conrad to Pinker [13] February 1908 (letter dated "Thursday 12 Feb. 1908," but 12 February was a Wednesday), Berg. Conrad wanted Davray to take care of all French translations of his works (to Davray, 3 February 1908).

213. Conrad to Robert d'Humières, 11 November 1909, Y. Guérin, "Huit lettres inédités de Joseph Conrad à Robert d'Humières," *Revue de Littérature Comparée* (1970), pp. 367–392.

214. Conrad to Wells, 27 March and 18 April 1908, University of Illinois. In the former Conrad stated that within the last year he had earned only £420. See Baines, *Joseph Conrad*, p. 285.

215. Conrad to Galsworthy, 17 February 1908; and 20 February 1908, *LL*, 2:67.

216. Conrad to Poradowska, 5 February 1908, Rapin, *Lettres*, p. 189; to Galsworthy, 6 January 1908. (Jean-Aubry in *LL*, 2:64–66, published only about a half of this long letter).

217. Conrad to Pinker, Thursday (probably 23 January 1908) and Friday (probably 31 January 1908), also 12 February 1908 (by which time the story had been completed), Berg.

218. Conrad to Pinker, 19 January 1922, *LL*, 2:264.

219. Baines, *Joseph Conrad*, p. 84.

220. Keating, *Conrad Memorial Library*, p. 365.

221. Conrad to Pinker, Wednesday, [11?] March 1908, Berg.

222. Conrad to Pinker, 17 March 1908, Berg.

223. Conrad to Pinker, 23 March 1908, Berg.

224. Conrad to the editor of *Harper's Magazine*, 10 April 1908, J. Pierpont Morgan Library, New York; to Pinker, Wednesday, [May 1908], Berg.

225. Conrad to Garnett, 28 August 1908, E. Garnett, *Letters*, p. 226.

226. Conrad to Pinker, n.d. (end of July), Berg.

227. Conrad to Methuen, 26 January 1908, *LL*, 2:66.

228. At least one of the reviewers, Anderson Graham of *Country Life*, a publication unfriendly to Conrad, saw through this game and sharply criticized the volume. His whole article (unsigned) is based on a juxtaposition of the subtitles of the stories with their content. Reprinted in Sherry, *Conrad*, pp. 217–219.

229. Conrad to Garnett, 28 August 1908, E. Garnett, *Letters*, p. 225. Conrad repeated the miner simile in his letter to Arthur Symons, 29 August 1908, *LL*, 2:84.

230. *The Daily News*, 10 August 1908, reprinted in Sherry, *Conrad*, pp. 210–211.

231. Conrad to Garnett, 21 August 1908, E. Garnett, *Letters*, p. 223.

232. See Conrad to Wells, 2 September and 3 November 1908, University of Illinois.

233. See, for example, Conrad to Wells, 27 March 1908, University of Illinois; to Pinker, Tuesday, [18?] August 1908, Berg.

234. Conrad to Symons, 29 August 1908; and to Pinker, 18 September 1908, Berg.

235. Conrad to Pinker, 18 September 1908.

236. Conrad to Pinker, Wednesday, [7?] October 1908, Berg.

237. Conrad to Capes, 13 May 1909, Yale.

238. *The Mirror of the Sea*, p. 51. Joachim Du Bellay, *Les Regrets* (1558), sonnet 31: "Heureux qui, comme Ulysse, a fait un beau voyage . . . Et puis est retourné, plein d'usage et raison, Vivre entre ses parents le reste de son âge! . . . Plus me plait . . . que l'air marin la douceur angevine."

239. Conrad to Colvin, 28 December 1908, *LL*, 2:93.

240. *A Personal Record*, pp. 46, 34–35.

241. Ford to Keating, n.d. [December 1936], Richard M. Ludwig, ed., *Letters of Ford Madox Ford* (Princeton, 1965), pp. 267–268. Mizener's more modest claim that "Conrad dictated much of the second instalment of the *Reminiscences* to Ford" (*Saddest Story*, p. 166) is also only a hypothesis for which Mizener does not give any supporting evidence. Mizener's supposition that Conrad resorted to Bobrowski's *Memoirs* because of his own "bad memory" (*Saddest Story*, p. 554) is unjustified: practically all the quotations and borrowings pertain to matters that he could not have known first-hand.

242. Conrad to Symons, Monday, [24 August 1908], *LL*, 2:73. See also to Garnett, 28 August 1908, E. Garnett, *Letters*, pp. 225–226; Douglas Hewitt, *Conrad: A Reassessment* (Cambridge, 1952), pp. 120–121.

243. Conrad to W. Rothenstein, 4 November 1908, Harvard.

244. Conrad to Douglas, 2 August 1908, Texas.

245. Mizener, *Saddest Story*, pp. 160–163.

246. Conrad to Wells, 25 September 1908, University of Illinois.

247. *JCC*, p. 131.

248. Conrad to Ford, 23 October 1923, *LL*, 2:323.

249. Conrad to Galsworthy, Wednesday, [26? August 1908], ibid., p. 77.

250. Conrad to Galsworthy, 24 October 1907.

251. Jean-Aubry, *Lettres françaises*, p. 144.

252. Conrad to Pinker, 13 October 1908, Berg; to Galsworthy, 30 November 1908, *LL*, 2:90.

253. Conrad to Pinker, Wednesday, [9?] December 1908, Berg; to Colvin, 28 December 1908.

254. Conrad to Pinker, 30 September 1908, Berg.

255. Conrad to A. Galsworthy, n.d. [about 29 March 1909], Birmingham.

256. Conrad to Ford, 17 December 1908, BL.

257. Checks signed by Ford, Berg. Before 17 December there were five checks, totaling £60; however, in Conrad's letter the sum with which Pinker was to debit Conrad is given as £100.

258. Conrad to Pinker, 25 November, and Wednesday, [9?] December 1908, Berg.

259. P. R. Reynolds to Pinker, 12 November 1908, NYPL. See also Conrad to Pinker, 15 April 1909, Berg.

260. Conrad to Lucas, 6 October 1908, *LL*, 2:89; to Capes, same date, Yale; to Poradowska, 3 November 1908, Rapin, *Lettres*, p. 190. To W. Rothenstein, 4 November 1908, Conrad mentioned the possibility of an amputation.

261. Conrad to Galsworthy, 30 November 1908, *LL*, 2:91.

262. Conrad to A. Galsworthy, 17 January 1909, ibid., p. 94. Of course that was Conrad's income apart from Pinker's advances, which were paid off with royalties for each consecutive work separately.

263. Conrad to Davray, 2 January 1909, Jean-Aubry, *Lettres françaises*, p. 96.

264. Conrad to Poradowska, 3 November 1908, Rapin, *Lettres*, p. 191.

265. Conrad to Douglas, 6 March 1909, Texas.

266. B. Conrad, *My Father*, p. 60.

267. Conrad to Galsworthy, 6 March 1909, Danilewiczowa, *Conrad*, p. 24, and 29 March 1909, *LL*, 2:96.

268. Conrad to Pinker, 15 April 1909, Berg.

269. Conrad to A. Galsworthy, 17 January 1909; to Galsworthy, 6 March 1909.

270. Conrad to Ford, 10 October 1908, copy at Cornell; to Douglas, 29 September 1908, *LL*, 2:86; to Garnett, 13 December 1908, E. Garnett, *Letters*, p. 227; to Davray, 2 January 1909.

271. Conrad to Douglas, 6 March 1909, and Sunday evening, [18 or 25 March 1909], Texas.

272. Mizener, *Saddest Story*, pp. 161–165. J. D. Osborne, "Conrad and Stephen Reynolds," *Conradiana* 13 (1981):59–63.

273. *JCC*, pp. 138–139; and Conrad to Mackintosh, Easter Sunday, [11 April] 1909, Colgate.

274. See Mizener, *Saddest Story*, pp. 180–183; however, Mizener erroneously dates Conrad's letter to Ford of Wednesday evening, [28 April or 5 May 1909], Berg, as March 31; he is also wrong in implying that Conrad stopped writing his reminiscences in April (ibid., pp. 553–554, notes 27 and 34).

275. Conrad to Galsworthy, 30 April 1909, Birmingham.

276. Conrad to Ford, Wednesday evening [28 April or 5 May 1909]. Date indicated by references to the May issue of the *English Review* and also by Conrad to Galsworthy, 30 April.

277. Conrad to Galsworthy, 30 April 1909.

278. Conrad to Douglas, Tuesday, [4? May 1909], Texas.

279. Conrad to Ford, 20 May 1909, Berg.

280. Conrad to Galsworthy, 6 June 1909, *LL*, 2:98.

281. Conrad to Lucas, 14 June 1909, ibid., p. 99.

282. Mizener, *Saddest Story*, p. 186.

283. Conrad to Ford, 20 May 1909; "Am I to be paid for this article? I don't urge it. I simply want to know." There were seven instalments of the *Reminiscences* (December 1908–June 1909); the last of six checks, signed by Ford, is dated 29 March 1909 (Berg). See also Conrad to Douglas, 18 May 1909, Texas.

284. Conrad to Capes, 13 May 1909, Yale.

285. Conrad to Galsworthy, 5 June 1909, *LL*, 2:97; to Douglas, 18 June 1909, ibid., p. 100; to Capes, 8 June 1909, Yale. It would be absurd to assume that it was an elaborate cover-up.

286. Conrad to Galsworthy, 13 July 1909, *LL*, 2:101.

287. Conrad to Garnett, 19 July 1909, E. Garnett, *Letters*, p. 232; but see to Lucas, 23 June 1909, *LL*, 2:100, where he writes, with no regret, that the publication of the *Reminiscences* in the *English Review* has "come to an end."

288. See Moser, "Conrad, Ford, and the Sources of *Chance*," *Conradiana* 7 (1975):216.

289. Mizener, *Saddest Story*, pp. 175, 189. Elsie's visits: Conrad to Perceval Gibbon, [11 July 1909], to Maisie Gibbon, [18 July 1909], NYPL.

290. Conrad to P. Gibbon, [11 July 1909].

291. Conrad to Ford, 31 July 1909, *LL*, 2:101–102.

292. "A Russian has got hold of the *ER* and I can not contribute any more" (Conrad to Galsworthy, 7 September 1909, Birmingham). In another letter to Galsworthy (n.d., Birmingham) he called Soskice a "horrid Jew."

293. Conrad to Pinker, Wednesday, [4? August 1909], Berg.

294. Conrad to Lucas, 23 June 1909. N.B. the *English Review* text of the *Reminiscences* has only 45,000 words.

295. Conrad to Harper and Brothers, 17 October 1909, Colgate. See also to Pinker, 10 October 1907, *LL*, 2:61, about Tauchnitz, the German publishers.

296. Conrad to Davray, 23 December 1909, Jean-Aubry, *Lettres françaises*, p. 99.

297. James Gibbon Huneker to Conrad, 22 June 1909, in Jean-Aubry, *Letters to Conrad*. Huneker's volume of essays: *Egoists: A Book of Supermen* (New York, 1909).

298. Conrad to Huneker, 18 May 1909, *Modern Philology* 52 (1955):224–225.

299. See *JCC*, p. 132; B. Conrad, *My Father*, pp. 63–64.

300. Conrad to Galsworthy, 30 July and 7 September 1909, Birmingham.

301. Conrad to Douglas, 18 May 1909.

302. Conrad to Douglas, 18 June 1909.

303. Conrad to Galsworthy, 5 June 1909, *LL*, 2:98.

304. Conrad to P. Gibbon, 19 July and Saturday, [25? September 1909], NYPL.

305. Conrad to Pinker, Monday, [4? October 1909], *LL*, 2:103. See also his characteristic remarks about his "mendicancy" and governmental bureaucracy, to Galsworthy, Monday night, [15 November?] 1909, ibid., p. 105.

306. Conrad to Pinker, Monday, [4? October 1909].

307. Conrad to d'Humières, 29 October 1909, Guérin, "Huit lettres."

308. The promise made in Conrad to Pinker, Tuesday, [12? October 1909], Berg. Text of *Razumov*; in his letter of Monday [4? October 1909], Conrad stated that in the last 20 months he had written nearly 160,000 words; in the letter of 20 December 1909 (Berg), he said that in 23½ months he had written 187,000 words, of which 130,000 were for *Razumov*. The novel had in its original form nearly 145,000 words; at the beginning of October there were probably about 100,000.

309. Carlos M. Marris to Conrad, 18 July 1909, Yale. See Conrad to Hugh Clifford, 19 May 1910, *LL*, 2:109.

310. Conrad to Pinker, Monday [4? October 1909]; see also to P. Gibbon, Saturday, [25? September 1909].

311. See, for example, P. R. Reynolds to Pinker, 22 May 1909 (Berg), with the news that several periodicals wanted to publish Conrad's short stories and promised high fees. Conrad to Pinker, 20 December 1909, Berg.

312. Norman Sherry, *Conrad's Eastern World* (Cambridge, 1966), pp. 253–257.

313. Conrad to Galsworthy, 14 December 1909, Birmingham; and to P. Gibbon, 19 December [1909], NYPL. In both, Conrad states that he wrote the story "in ten days," but this is an exaggeration: it certainly took longer than that.

314. Conrad to Pinker, n.d. (before 14 December 1909), Berg.

315. Conrad to W. Rothenstein, 15 November 1909, *LL*, 2:103.

316. Conrad to Galsworthy, Monday night, [15 November 1909], ibid., p. 106.

317. Conrad to S. Reynolds, 27 November 1909, NYPL; and to Galsworthy, Friday, [3 or 10 December 1909], Birmingham. The swift change of Conrad's mood is already evident in his letter to Galsworthy of 19 November, Birmingham.

318. Conrad to W. Rothenstein, 17 December 1909, *LL*, 2:104; but see also to P. Gibbon, [25 September 1909], and to S. Reynolds, 27 November 1909.

319. Conrad to P. Gibbon, 19 December [1909].

320. Conrad to P. Gibbon, Wednesday, [29 December 1909], Berg.

321. Conrad to Galsworthy, 22 December 1909, Birmingham (quoted in Baines, *Joseph Conrad*, pp. 359–360). Calculation in the letter to P. Gibbon of 19 December:

Therefore in two years I stand thus *to date*

Ms pages of Raz[umov]   130000
Black mate   10
Story as above
　Secret Sharer   12
Re[miniscence]s   35
_____
187000

Conrad forgot here that he had placed the *Reminiscences* without Pinker; also, the agent could not sell *Razumov* before he had received the whole text—Conrad himself was against such premature transaction to Pinker, [4? October 1909].

322. *JCC*, pp. 141–142. Jessie places the incident a little later, after the novel had been completed.

323. Conrad to Pinker, 20 December 1909, Berg. The 40,000 words mentioned here are of the *Reminiscences*.

324. Conrad to P. Gibbon, Wednesday, 29 December [1909].

325. Conrad to Meldrum, 31 December 1909, Blackburn, *Letters*, p. 191.

326. Conrad to Douglas, 23 December 1909, Texas.

327. The letters are as follows:
   1. Thursday, probably 6 January 1910 but possibly 31 December 1909 (Berg). Conrad mentioned here the epidemic of influenza about which he wrote to Meldrum on 31 December. He proposed publishing in the United States a volume of *Alternate Stories*, containing three sea stories: "The Brute," "The Other Self" ["Secret Sharer"], and "The Black Mate"; and three land stories: "Gaspar Ruiz," "An Anarchist," and "Il Conte"[!].
   2. Wednesday, probably 12 January 1910 (Berg). He proposed *Under Western Eyes* as the new title.
   3. Thursday, probably 20 January but possibly a week later (Texas). He promised to bring the last pages on Monday and explained that *Under Western Eyes* was the title of the novel and not of the volume of stories.

XII. CRISIS AND SUCCESS: 1910–1914

1. Joseph Conrad to James B. Pinker, Thursday, probably 20 January but possibly a week later, Texas; Conrad probably went to London on Monday, 24 January 1910.

2. *JCC*, pp. 140–141, and Conrad to Pinker, 23 May 1910, Berg. Jessie's account of the disagreement and of the beginning of Conrad's illness (pp. 141–146) is in many respects exaggerated and can serve only as an additional source. Her own letter to Pinker, 3 February 1910 (Berg), does not agree with the story of Conrad's alleged wish to burn the manuscript of *Under Western Eyes*. Also, there is no telegram in Pinker's archives although she mentions one in *JCC*.

3. Jessie Conrad to David S. Meldrum, 6 February 1910, William Blackburn, ed., *Joseph Conrad's Letters to William Blackwood and David S. Meldrum* (Durham, N.C., 1958), p. 192; she tells of having looked after Conrad from 30 January. Admittedly, in his letter to Galsworthy, 31 March 1910 (Birmingham), Conrad wrote about his ten-week-long illness, which would mean that it began on 20 January, but to Davray, 3 May, he wrote that he fell ill at the end of January.

4. Jessie Conrad to Pinker, 3 February 1910; Dr. Clifford Hackney's certificate, Berg.

5. Jessie Conrad to Alice Rothenstein, 6 February 1910, Harvard.

6. Jessie Conrad to Meldrum, 6 February 1910.

7. Quoted in Jessie Conrad to Pinker, 3 February 1910.

8. Borys Conrad, *My Father: Joseph Conrad* (New York, 1970), pp. 60–61.

9. Bernard C. Meyer, *Joseph Conrad: A Psychoanalytic Biography* (Princeton, 1967), p. 207.

10. Conrad to William Rothenstein, 17 December 1909, *LL*, 2:104.

11. Meyer, *Conrad*, pp. 212–214. The only argument cited by Meyer (after Eloise Hay) in support of the thesis of Conrad's sense of "Slavonism" is that at one time he held pan-Slavonic views.

But that was almost thirty years earlier and even then Uncle Bobrowski dismissed the pan-Slavonic theory as a political slogan convenient for tsardom; Frederick R. Karl, *Joseph Conrad: The Three Lives* (New York, 1979), p. 680.

12. *Under Western Eyes*, p. 66.

13. Meyer, *Conrad*, pp. 207–210.

14. John Galsworthy to Edward Garnett, 24 April 1910, *Letters from John Galsworthy: 1900–1932*, ed. Edward Garnett (London, 1934), p. 177.

15. Conrad to Galsworthy, 31 March 1910. This is the only extant letter from the time of the illness, probably written during a momentary improvement. Conrad wrote that he was still feeling very weak both physically and mentally but would try to prepare the manuscript of *Under Western Eyes* for the publishers. He did not start on it, however, until a month later.

16. Conrad to Francis Warrington Dawson, 21 May 1910, Dale J. B. Randall, *Joseph Conrad and Warrington Dawson: The Record of a Friendship* (Durham, N.C., 1968), pp. 129–130. In the introduction to this book, Randall gives a detailed account of the friendship's origin, (pp. 29–36).

17. Conrad to H.-D. Davray, 3 May 1910, G. Jean-Aubry, ed., *Joseph Conrad: Lettres françaises* (Paris, 1929), p. 100.

18. Conrad to Galsworthy, 17 May 1910, Birmingham.

19. Conrad to Hugh Clifford, 19 May 1910, *LL*, 2:109. Meyer regards the words "the last two years" as an allusion to the deterioration of the relationship with Ford (*Conrad*, p. 207); in fact, however, it proves that Conrad did not regard his estrangement with Ford as the cause of his nervous breakdown. Their relationship began to be strained a year before his illness, and Jessie was well aware of it. In his letter to W. Rothenstein of 17 December 1909, *LL*, 2:104, Conrad wrote of having worked for two years at the novel hindered by illness and a "terrible moral stress."

20. Conrad to W. Rothenstein, 20 May 1910, Rothenstein, *Men and Memories* (London, 1939), 2:159–160.

21. Conrad to Pinker, 23 May 1910, Berg. Conrad's correspondence with Edward Garnett's lawyer-brother Robert has not been made available.

22. MS, Yale. The corrections, particularly the deletions, have been analyzed by R. Davis, "*Under Western Eyes*: 'The Most Deeply Meditated Novel,'" *Conradiana* 9, no. 1 (1977):59–74.

23. Conrad to Galsworthy, 17 May 1910; see also to Norman Douglas, 28 June 1910, *LL*, 2:113; Paul Kirschner, *Conrad: The Psychologist as Artist* (Edinburgh, 1968), pp. 220–223.

24. Letter from Thomas C. Moser to the author, 4 November 1976.

25. Virginia Woolf, *The Common Reader* (London, 1925), first published in the *Times Literary Supplement*, 14 August 1924; Galsworthy, *Castles in Spain* (New York, 1927), first published in *Scribner's Magazine*, January 1925 (Galsworthy privately expressed a similar opinion in 1919 [letter to E. Garnett, 8 September, E. Garnett, *Letters from Galsworthy*, p. 236] but stressed that it was confidential); Albert Guerard, in *Joseph Conrad* (New York, 1947), confines Conrad's best period to the years 1897–1904; also *Conrad the Novelist* (Cambridge, Mass., 1958); Douglas Hewitt, *Conrad: A Reassessment* (Cambridge, 1952); Moser, *Joseph Conrad: Achievement and Decline* (Cambridge, Mass., 1957).

26. More on the subject in Najder, *Nad Conradem* [Reading Conrad] (Warsaw, 1965), pp. 37–40.

27. See Najder, "The Development of the Polish Novel: Functions and Structure," *Slavic Review*, December 1970, pp. 651–662.

28. For example, Conrad to E. Garnett, 2 September 1921, E. Garnett, *Letters*, p. 309; Jacob Epstein, *An Autobiography* (London, 1955), p. 74.

29. Meyer, *Conrad*, p. 221.

30. Ibid., p. 222. Meyer repeats, in a simplified version, the thesis advanced more cautiously by Moser, *Joseph Conrad*, pp. 131–178. Moser, arguing shrewdly with the critics who regard Conrad's late works as his most valuable intellectual achievement, does not claim that Conrad's "thinking deteriorated" after 1912.

31. See Antoni Kepiński, *Melancholia* (Warsaw, 1974), pp. 49–50.

32. Conrad to Galsworthy, 17 May 1910.

33. Borys Conrad, *Coach Tour of Joseph Conrad's Homes in Kent* (not in print, 1974); Conrad to Edward Sanderson, 2 September 1910, *LL*, 2:115.

34. *Notes on Life and Letters*, p. 148.

35. Conrad to Galsworthy, 17 May 1910. Conrad often had trouble paying his rent (Randall, *Conrad and Dawson*, p. 39).

36. Conrad to Galsworthy, 26 June 1910, *LL*, 2:112.

37. Ibid.

38. Conrad to Edward Thomas, 13 July 1910, Berg. The first article was supposed to deal with hypnosis; its text has not been preserved.

39. Conrad to an unknown addressee, 29 July 1910, in private hands, Honolulu. The action of the thirty-minute play was to take place on board a ship.

40. *The Times*, 7 July 1911.

41. Conrad to Galsworthy, 27 August 1910, *LL*, 2:114–115.

42. Clifford, "Joseph Conrad: Some Scattered Memories," *The Bookman's Journal and Print Collector*, October 1924, p. 5.

43. Conrad to Davray, 10 August 1910, Jean-Aubry, *Lettres françaises*, p. 104; to Galsworthy, 8 September 1910, *LL*, 2:119, and 27 August 1910, Birmingham (sentence omitted in Jean-Aubry).

44. Conrad, "Note" for Pinker, August 1910, Berg.

45. Conrad to E. Sanderson, 2 September 1910.

46. On 1 October 1910 he acknowledged the receipt of money from Pinker for the text (Berg); to Pinker, Wednesday, [9 December 1908], Berg.

47. "Prince Roman," p. 51. The first person plural includes the unnamed narrator, a Pole, who may be identified with Conrad. Although he states (p. 30) that Prince Roman married in the same year (1828) that his father was born (when Apollo was in fact eight years old), he weaves into the story the recollection of his own visit to the prince with Bobrowski, who mentions it in his *Pamiętniki*, 2:387, but dates it 1859.

48. Paul R. Reynolds to Pinker, 28 May 1909 and 28 July 1911, Berg.

49. Conrad's doubts were expressed in a letter to Galsworthy, 27 October 1910, *LL*, 2:119–122. The date of completion comes from a letter to Pinker of 10 December 1910, in which he acknowledges the receipt of money; on additions, to Pinker, 2 and 4 March 1911, Berg.

50. Charles M. Marris to Conrad, 18 July 1909, Yale. The question of using Marris's information, as well as later slurring over the traces in the preface to *'Twixt Land and Sea*, has been

looked at more closely by van Marle. Also Conrad to Pinker, 26 December 1910, 8 and 28 February 1911 (the same day he sent off the MS of "Freya"), Berg.

51. Edward Thomas to Gordon Bottomley, 26 August 1910, R. G. Thomas, *Letters from Edward Thomas to Gordon Bottomley* (London, 1968), p. 207.

52. Conrad to Galsworthy, 27 October and 1 November 1910, LL, 2:119–122.

53. Conrad to Galsworthy, Tuesday, [8 November 1910], H. V. Marrot, *The Life and Letters of John Galsworthy* (London, 1935), p. 351.

54. Conrad to E. Garnett, 22 November 1910, E. Garnett, *Letters from Conrad, 1895 to 1924* (London, 1928), pp. 233–234. The half-joking supposition that Garnett was becoming "cantankerous" expressed in a letter to Galsworthy of 27 October (Birmingham; fragment omitted in Jean-Aubry) is not inconsistent with the content and tone of this letter, since it refers to an argument by correspondence between Garnett and Galsworthy on the subject of *The Patrician* (Marrot, *Galsworthy*, pp. 301–302).

55. B. Conrad, *Coach Tour.*

56. Richard Curle, *Caravansary and Conversation: Memories of Places and Persons* (London, 1937), p. 275. See also Conrad to Galsworthy, 5 February 1911, Birmingham.

57. Ford Madox Ford, *Return to Yesterday* (London, 1931), pp. 371–375.

58. Conrad to E. Garnett, 12 January 1911, E. Garnett, *Letters*, pp. 237–238.

59. Conrad to Arthur Symons, 7 February 1911, LL, 2:125.

60. Conrad to Ford, 29 March 1911, Berg.

61. Conrad to Galsworthy, 1 November 1910 (Jean-Aubry deleted this part of the letter); to E. Garnett, 12 January 1911. Conrad made an exception for Wells, to whom he wrote on 20 January 1911 a eulogistic letter which is, however, so unspecific that it is not certain to which work it refers (University of Illinois, Urbana).

62. See Conrad to Ford, 29 March 1911.

63. P. A. Bartlett, "Letters of Ford Madox Ford," *The Saturday Review of Literature*, no. 15 (1941), pp. 3–4.

64. Moser, "Conrad, Marwood, and Ford: Biographical Speculations on the Genesis of *The Good Soldier*," *Mosaic* 8, no. 1 (1974):220; "Conrad, Ford, and the Sources of *Chance*," *Conradiana* 8, no. 3 (1976): 215–216.

65. Conrad to Galsworthy, Sunday, [14? May 1911], LL, 2:129 and Birmingham. Moser ("Conrad, Ford, and *Chance*," p. 214) infers that "re-awakened feelings about Ford" played an important part in this crisis. This seems to disagree with the chronology of events: the crisis lasted from the beginning of March to the end of April; Ford's *Simple Life Limited* was published on 15 February but Conrad's friendly letter to him was written right in the middle of his illness.

66. At the end of March it seemed that the operation would be imperative in May (Conrad to F. W. Dawson, 28 March 1911, Randall, *Conrad and Dawson*, p. 136); later it was put off until September (to Galsworthy, Sunday, [14? May 1911]).

67. Conrad to Galsworthy, 28 March 1911, LL, 2:127–128.

68. Guy Routh, *Occupation and Pay in Great Britain, 1900–1960* (Cambridge, 1965), pp. 62, 64. The income of the upper 25 percent in those professions was approximately £680, £700, and £600 respectively.

69. Conrad to Galsworthy, Sunday, [14? May 1911]; to Douglas, 2 June 1911, Texas; to Pinker, 19 June 1911, Berg.

70. Conrad to T. Fisher Unwin, 17 May 1911, Berg.

71. "A Familiar Preface," *A Personal Record*, pp. xix–xx.

72. Conrad to Pinker, 27 June 1911, Berg.

73. Conrad to Garnett, 18 and [29] July 1911, E. Garnett, *Letters*, pp. 245–247; and to Pinker, 9 August 1911, Berg. Jocelyn Baines assumes that Conrad took Pinker's account seriously, but there are no grounds for this assumption (*Joseph Conrad: A Critical Biography* [London, 1960], pp. 377–378).

74. Conrad to E. Garnett, 4 August 1911, E. Garnett, *Letters*, pp. 247–248.

75. Conrad to E. Sanderson, 7 June 1911, *LL*, 2:130–131.

76. Conrad to Galsworthy, Sunday, [14? May 1911]; and B. Conrad, *My Father*, p. 73.

77. Conrad to Galsworthy, 23 September 1911, *LL*, 2:135. See also B. Conrad, *My Father*, pp. 73–74, and Conrad to Ford, 21 December 1911, NYPL.

78. Conrad to E. Sanderson, 9 June 1911, Yale.

79. Conrad to Galsworthy, 28 July 1911, Birmingham.

80. Conrad to Symons, 7 February 1911.

81. R. Mallet, ed., *Paul Claudel et André Gide: Correspondance 1899–1926* (Paris, 1949), p. 333.

82. Conrad to John Quinn, 25 September 1911, NYPL.

83. Conrad to Galsworthy, 11 a.m. Friday, [18 August 1911], *LL*, 2:133–134; and to Elsie Hueffer, 24 August 1911, Yale.

84. Mark Holloway, *Norman Douglas: A Biography* (London, 1976), p. 186.

85. See Conrad to Dawson, 17 August 1911, Randall, *Conrad and Dawson*, p. 138.

86. The book version was about 30,000 words shorter than the serialized text (Karl, *Joseph Conrad*, p. 703). In London, 3,000 copies were issued; two weeks later in New York, 4,000 (Theodore Ehrsam, *A Bibliography of Joseph Conrad* [Metuchen, N.J., 1969], p. 319). In England, 4,112 copies were sold in the two years after publication (Baines, *Joseph Conrad*, p. 380).

87. 11 October 1911, reprinted in Norman Sherry, *Conrad: The Critical Heritage* (London, 1973), p. 227, as is the review in the *Morning Post* of 12 October (pp. 231–232).

88. D. H. Lawrence to Garnett, 30 October 1912, D. H. Lawrence, *Collected Letters*, ed. H. T. Moore (New York, 1962), 1:152. The next letter shows he had *Under Western Eyes* in mind.

89. Hueffer, "Joseph Conrad," *English Review*, no. 12 (December 1911). Reprinted in Sherry, *Conrad*, p. 243.

90. Conrad to Galsworthy, 15 October 1911, *LL*, 2:136. Conrad did not "significantly misread" the review, as Karl maintains (*Joseph Conrad*, p. 703). He did not claim that the reviewer had said that Conrad was Jewish, but only that the passage was "incomprehensible" unless understood as hinting at Conrad's Jewishness.

91. Conrad to E. Garnett, 20 October 1911, E. Garnett, *Letters*, pp. 248–250. See also to Davray, 10 March 1909, Jean-Aubry, *Lettres françaises*, p. 97: "It is written from the English point of view, of course, but sympathetically, at least I hope so."

92. Conrad to Olive R. Garnett, 20 October 1911, E. Garnett, *Letters*, pp. 250–252.

93. Conrad to Garnett, 27 May 1912, ibid., pp. 260–261.

94. Conrad to Unwin, 17 May 1911. The publication by Nash was announced for October in letters to Galsworthy, 23 September 1911, *LL*, 2:135, and to F. W. Dawson, 30 September 1911, Randall, *Conrad and Dawson*, p. 139.

95. Conrad to W. Dawson, 25 November 1911, Randall, *Conrad and Dawson*, p. 144. Randall assumes (mistakenly) that Conrad referred to *'Twixt Land and Sea*.

96. Ehrsam, *Bibliography*, pp. 295 and 310.

97. Conrad to the editor of *Harper's Magazine*, 23 August 1911, Pierpont Morgan Library, New York; P. R. Reynolds to Pinker, 8 November 1911, Berg.

98. B. L. Reid, *The Man from New York: John Quinn and His Friends* (New York, 1968), p. 113. Conrad to Quinn, 24 August, 25 September, and 3 November, NYPL; to Galsworthy, 11 a.m. Friday, [18 August 1911], Birmingham.

99. Conrad to Douglas, 30 October 1911, Macpherson, and 26 February 1912, Texas.

100. Conrad to Symons, 11 December 1911, *LL*, 2:137.

101. Conrad to Pinker, Thursday and Sunday [November 1911], Berg.

102. Conrad to Quinn, 27 March 1912, NYPL. Date of completion confirmed in letter to Galsworthy, 27 March 1912, Birmingham.

103. Conrad to Pinker, Sunday, [1 June 1913], *LL*, 2:146 (with wrong date of 2 June).

104. Conrad to Ottoline Morrell, 17 February 1914, Texas.

105. Conrad to Ford, 29 March 1911; and 2 February 1912, Harvard.

106. Conrad to Henri Ghéon, 22 November 1911, *Conradiana* 8, no. 3 (1976): 221.

107. Ford, "Joseph Conrad." In answer to the contentions about Conrad's sudden conversion after 1911 from moral doubts to "affirmation," it is worth noting that in 1911 Ford saw him as an unequivocal moralist of honor.

108. Conrad to Ford, 21 December 1911, NYPL.

109. Conrad to Violet Hunt, Sunday evening, [18 February 1912], BL. Arthur Mizener writes that "the Conrads . . . were invited in as frequently as possible" (*The Saddest Story: A Biography of Ford Madox Ford* [New York, 1971], p. 220). No trace of any visit remains, however, and some letters testify against this statement, for example: to Ford, 2 February, Harvard; to Pinker, 9 April, Berg; to Graham, 14 April 1912, Cedric T. Watts, ed., *Conrad's Letters to R. B. Joseph Cunninghame Graham* (Cambridge, 1969), p. 177. Letters of Sunday evening, 18 February 1912 and 27 March 1912 (copy at Cornell), which Karl identifies as written to Elsie Hueffer (*Joseph Conrad*, p. 712), Conrad in fact wrote to Violet Hunt.

110. Conrad to Galsworthy, 27 March 1912, *LL*, 2:138.

111. Ibid., and 28 June 1912, ibid., p. 141.

112. Conrad to Pinker, 9 April 1912, Berg.

113. Conrad to Pinker, Wednesday, [27 March 1912], Berg.

114. Conrad to Gide, 14 April 1912, Jean-Aubry, *Lettres françaises*, p. 117.

115. Conrad to Pinker, Saturday, [11 May 1912], Berg. See also to F. Watson, 24 May 1912, *LL*, 2:139.

116. Conrad to A. Harrison, [May 1912], Rosenbach. See also to E. Garnett, 27 January 1912, E. Garnett, *Letters*, p. 259.

117. Conrad suggested an article on 16 April, immediately after the catastrophe, which took

place on the night of the fourteenth, to the editor of *Nash Magazine*, who offered it unsuccessfully to a New York daily; (Randall, "Conrad Interviews," *Conradiana* 2, no. 1 (1969): 19–22.

118. "Certain Aspects of the Admirable Inquiry into the Loss of the Titanic," *Notes on Life and Letters*, pp. 247–248.

119. Conrad to Pinker, n.d., [May 1912], Berg; to Quinn, 10 May 1912, NYPL; to Pinker, Thursday, [6 June 1912], Berg. In the last he estimated the length of the story at eighteen thousand words.

120. Conrad to Quinn, 9 February 1913, Reid, *Man from New York*, p. 127.

121. Conrad to Quinn, 1 July 1912, NYPL.

122. Conrad to Quinn, 29 July 1912, NYPL.

123. Conrad to Quinn, 8 December 1912. See also 18 July 1913, NYPL.

124. Conrad to Sidney Colvin, 13 August 1912, Duke; see also B. Conrad, *My Father*, pp. 70–71.

125. B. Conrad, *My Father*, pp. 79–80.

126. St.-John Perse to Conrad, 26 February 1921, St.-John Perse, *Oeuvres complètes* (Paris, 1972), pp. 885–886.

127. St.-John Perse to Jean-Aubry, 19 September 1947, Yale, published by J. Vidan, *Conradiana* 2, no. 3 (1969): 17–22; Roger Little, "Saint-John Perse and Joseph Conrad: Some Notes and an Uncollected Letter," *Modern Language Review* 72 (1977): 811–814.

128. Conrad to S. Reynolds, 31 August 1912, Berg; see also to Pinker, Tuesday night, [8 October 1912], Berg.

129. Conrad to Gide, 16 August 1912, Jean-Aubry, *Lettres françaises*, p. 122.

130. Conrad to Davray, 29 July 1912, ibid., p. 121; to Pinker, 9 July, 23 July, 19 August, 3 September, 12 September, and 1 October 1912, Berg.

131. Conrad to Pinker, 3 September and 1 October 1912; to Quinn, 12 November 1912, NYPL.

132. See, for example, to F. W. Dawson, 12 August and 23 August 1912, Randall, *Conrad and Dawson*, p. 149; to Symons, 12 September 1912, Virginia.

133. J. G. Huneker, *Steeplejack* (New York, 1920), 2:128. See also Conrad to Huneker, 7 October, 9 October, and 16 October 1912, Baker Library, Dartmouth College, Hanover, New Hampshire.

134. Ehrsam, *Bibliography*, p. 317.

135. Conrad to Galsworthy, 28 June 1912, *LL*, 2:141, to Pinker, [6 July 1912], Berg.

136. Conrad to E. Garnett, 5 November 1912, E. Garnett, *Letters*, p. 263. See also to Galsworthy, Monday, [November 1912], *LL*, 2:143–144. To Edith Wharton, who suggested a translation of *The Secret Agent* into French, he wrote, "The thing is so particularly English, in moral atmosphere, in feeling and even in detail—n'est-ce pas?" (24 December 1912, Yale). Writing four days later to Davray, however, he favored the idea of the translation (Jean-Aubry, *Lettres françaises*, p. 123).

137. The *Standard*, 25 October 1912; see also Sherry, *Conrad*, pp. 30 and 251–258; *Bookman* (New York), March 1913, p. 85; *Review of Reviews* (New York), 13 June 1913; *Outlook* (New York), 15 March 1913.

138. On 27 October he wrote to Quinn that he had been ill for five weeks; to Garnett on 5 November for three weeks; to Quinn on 6 November one month; to Colvin on 21 November two months; to Curle on 23 November six weeks.

139. Conrad to Arnold Bennett, 25 November 1912, University College Library, London, in response to Bennett to Conrad, 22 November 1912, G. Jean-Aubry, ed., *Twenty Letters to Joseph
Conrad* (London, 1926).

140. Curle, "Joseph Conrad," *Rhythm*, November 1912, pp. 242–255. Curle's contention that
in the article he "expressed, above all, [his] admiration for Nostromo" is misleading and exaggerated (*The Last Twelve Years of Joseph Conrad* [London, 1928], p. 1). See Conrad to Garnett,
16 October 1912, Virginia; also to Curle, 6 November 1912, the original in the possession of the
recipient's son.

141. S. Reynolds, "Joseph Conrad and Sea Fiction," *The Quarterly Review*, July 1912, pp.
159–180; Conrad to S. Reynolds, 31 August 1912, Berg. (Evasively, he attributed to illness his
delayed reaction to Reynolds's article.)

142. Curle, *Last Twelve Years*, p. 2.

143. Conrad to Curle, 23 November 1912, Curle, *Conrad to a Friend: 150 Selected Letters from
Joseph Conrad to Richard Curle* (London, 1928), p. 3; *Last Twelve Years*, pp. 3–4.

144. Conrad to Dawson, Tuesday, [December 1913], Randall, *Conrad and Dawson*, p. 162.

145. See early letters to Curle, and to Alfred Knopf, 20 July and 24 August 1913, *LL*, 2:
146–150.

146. Curle, *Last Twelve Years*, pp. 12–13, 44–45.

147. J. H. Retinger, *Conrad and His Contemporaries* (New York, 1943). Even the date of meeting Conrad is wrongly given as 1909 (p. 65).

148. Conrad to Bennett, 17 November 1912, *LL*, 2:142.

149. About Retinger's intentions Bennett wrote to Conrad, who reacted skeptically to the possibility of such an action (to Bennett, 17 November 1912). Retinger maintained later that he
acted in the name of the Supreme National Committee (John Pomian, ed., *Joseph Retinger:
Memoirs of an Eminence Grise* [London, 1972], p. 14), but the committee was not established
until 16 August 1914.

150. Retinger, *The Poles and Prussia* (London, no date, probably the winter of 1912–1913).

151. Conrad to Walpole, 31 August 1918, Texas.

152. Letter from T. Kosch to the author, 10 October 1958. Mme Otolia Retinger says she first
saw Conrad at the railway station in Ashford when she and her husband visited Capel House
(O. Zubrzycka [O. Retinger], "Syn dwu ojczyzn" [A son of two countries], *Iskry*, no. 8 [1931]).
This is not inconsistent with Kosch's account—Mrs. Retinger was not present at the first meeting
between Conrad and Retinger.

153. Zubrzycka, "Syn dwu ojczyzn."

154. Open letter from Conrad to the editor of *The Times*, 7 November 1912; private letter of
that period to the same, both in Conrad, *Last Essays* pp. 149–154. Conrad's particular interest
in Constantinople was probably due not only to the part played by Russia in the Balkans but also
by the fact that Perceval Gibbon had been sent to the Bulgarian front as a war correspondent; to
Colvin, 21 November 1912, Yale. Retinger, *Conrad and His Contemporaries*, pp. 77–79; see
also p. 167.

155. Zubrzycka, "Syn dwu ojczyzn."

156. Conrad to Pinker, Tuesday evening, [17 December 1912], and [23 December 1912], Berg.
In spite of the date "June 1913" placed by Conrad at the end of the finished story, his letter to
Pinker, 20 February 1913 (Berg), refers to the work as finished, and it was published in March of
that year in *Pall Mall Magazine*.

157. See Baines, *Joseph Conrad*, p. 390.

158. *Within the Tides*, p. 132.

159. Conrad to Pinker, [27 January 1913], Berg.

160. Conrad to Pinker, 2 November 1912, Monday morning, [27 January 1913] (when he thought he had finally reached the end), Saturday, [22 February 1913], [12–14 April 1913], Berg; to Davray, 6 April 1913, Jean-Aubry, *Lettres françaises*, p. 126. Many of Conrad's letters of that time addressed to Pinker were incompletely dated but stamped with the received date at Pinker's London office. I date several of them differently than does Karl.

161. Conrad to Curle, Friday, [31 March 1913], Curle, *Conrad to a Friend*, p. 6.

162. Conrad to Pinker, 20 February 1913.

163. Conrad to Ford, 27 March 1913, BL. Ford was suddenly driven into a corner by Marwood's demand to return the £440 lent in 1908 to cover the costs of Elsie's operation. Conrad explained the Marwood's insistence by his illness during winter and his wish to put his own financial situation in order. Ford's biographers suspect other reasons (Mizener, *Saddest Story*, p. 232; Moser, "Conrad, Marwood, and Ford," pp. 219–220; note that the tenor of Conrad's letter does not indicate a new hostility). Ford suggested to Conrad that in exchange for £40 in cash he would transfer the entire debt to Marwood; Conrad refused: "the very idea is painful to me."

164. Conrad to Quinn, 9 February 1913, NYPL.

165. Conrad to Pinker, 28 April 1913, Berg; to Quinn, 18 July 1913, NYPL.

166. Conrad to Galsworthy, 12 April 1913, *LL*, 2:145.

167. Conrad to Pinker, Sunday night, [27 April 1913], letter received 2 May, Monday, 2 a.m., [5 May 1913], and Whitsun, [11 May 1913], Berg. Probably he had discussed earlier the project of a similar collaboration with Norman Douglas; Conrad to Douglas, Sunday, [16 March 1913], Randall, *Conrad and Dawson*, p. 154.

168. Conrad to Douglas, Sunday, [16 March 1913]; to Poradowska, 12 April 1913, René Rapin, ed., *Lettres de Joseph Conrad à Marguerite Poradowska* (Geneva, 1966), p. 201.
dowska (Geneva, 1966), p. 201.

169. Conrad to Pinker, Friday, [30 May 913], Berg.

170. Conrad to Pinker, [12 April 1913], Berg.

171. Conrad to Pinker, [12 April 1913], Berg; the file with copies of correspondence between Conrad and Methuen on the subject of the publication of *Chance*, Yale.

172. Conrad to Knopf, 20 July 1913, *LL*, 2:146–149.

173. Conrad to Pinker, letters received 14 April 1913, 10 July 1913, Whitsun, [11 May 1913], and Thursday, [12 June 1913], Berg.

174. As, for example, with the letter received by Pinker on 10 July he sent 3,000 words, and the same again with the letter of 12 July; but on 2 August he maintained to Symons (*LL*, 2:149) that he had not done anything for one month, and the same in an undated letter to Dawson (*Conrad and Dawson*, p. 167).

175. Conrad to Pinker, received 25 July 1913, Berg; Jessie Conrad to F. W. Dawson, 28 July 1913. Randall, *Conrad and Dawson*, p. 166; to Symons, Saturday, [2 August 1913].

176. Conrad to Knopf, 20 July 1913, *LL*, 2:143.

177. Conrad to Curle, Friday, [25 July 1913], Curle, *Conrad to a Friend*, p. 9.

178. Conrad to Pinker, Sunday, [1 June 1913], *LL*, 2:145–146.

179. Conrad to F. W. Dawson, 25 July 1913, Randall, *Conrad and Dawson*, pp. 165–166.

180. Conrad to W. Rothenstein, 2 August 1913, Harvard.

181. Conrad to Pinker, Tuesday evening, [9 September 1913], Berg.

182. E. L. Grant Watson, *But to What Purpose* (London, 1946), pp. 148–151.

183. Galsworthy, *Castles in Spain*, p. 110.

184. Randall, *Conrad and Dawson*, pp. 60–61.

185. Conrad to F. W. Dawson, 20 June 1913, ibid., pp. 159–161; the whole affair discussed, ibid., pp. 66–74.

186. Henry James to Conrad, 19 June 1913, Jean-Aubry, *Twenty Letters*.

187. Ian Watt, "Conrad, James and *Chance*," Maynard Mack and Ian Gregor, eds., *Imagined Worlds: Essays on Some English Novels and Novelists in Honour of John Butt* (London, 1968), pp. 311–312, 319.

188. Ottoline Morrell, *Memoirs: A Study in Friendship, 1873–1915*, ed. R. Gathorne-Hardy (New York, 1964), pp. 232–235. The date of the visit (5 or 7 August) is based on Jessie's letter to Lady Ottoline, 30 July 1913 (Texas).

189. E. Garnett, *Letters*, p. xxii: "calming him and taking the daily trials and rubs of life off his shoulders."

190. Retinger, *Conrad and His Contemporaries*, pp. 70, 73–74.

191. Bertrand Russell, *Autobiography, 1872–1914* (New York, 1968), pp. 278–279, 281. The account is supported by Morrell, *Memoirs*, p. 236.

192. Conrad to Russell, 22 December 1913, Russell, *Autobiography*, p. 302.

193. Conrad to Pinker, Friday morning, [11 July 1913], and Monday, [15 September 1913], Berg. The MS (Texas) numbers 1,139 pages.

194. Conrad to Pinker, letter received 11 October 1913, Berg; to Knopf, 22 October 1913, Rosenbach.

195. Doubleday's publicity booklet: *Joseph Conrad—A Sketch* [1924], with annotations by Jessie Conrad, in possession of the author.

196. Conrad to Pinker, Saturday, [November 1913], Berg.

197. Date on the MS (Berg) confirmed by letter to Wicken (editor of the *Metropolitan Magazine*), 11 December 1913, Berg.

198. Conrad to Gide, 8 January 1914, Jean-Aubry, *Lettres françaises*, pp. 130–131. Although the previous day he had told Curle that he would finish it "before Monday," that is, 12 January, he probably wanted to postpone his visit. The story's title was decided very late; Conrad wrote about it to Pinker on 1 July 1914 (Berg).

199. Conrad to Pinker, no date, [13? December 1913], Berg.

200. Conrad to Pinker, Monday, 7 or 14 December 1913, Berg; B. Conrad, *My Father*, p. 85.

201. Conrad to Huneker, [April 1913], Dartmouth.

202. *Glasgow News*, 3 February 1914, reprinted in Sherry, *Conrad*, p. 283, as are the unsigned review by Garnett in *The Nation*, 24 January 1914, and Lynd in the *Daily News*, 15 January 1914; see also *Athenaeum*, 17 January 1914, and the *Times Literary Supplement*, 15 January 1914.

203. E. Garnett, *Letters*, p. xx.

204. Introduction to *Conrad's Prefaces to His Works* (London, 1937), p. 34.

205. Conrad to Pinker, received 8 April 1913, Berg.

206. Sherry, *Conrad*, p. 30.

207. Conrad to Douglas, 16 December 1912, Macpherson.

208. Conrad to G. Blackwood, 6 February 1913, Blackburn, *Letters*, p. 193; data concerning publication, p. 199.

209. See Conrad to F. W. Dawson, 17 February 1914, Randall, *Conrad and Dawson*, p. 176: "The peace of my future years, the fate of the children hangs in the balance—for I can't write forever and there is not much time left to pursue fortune to follow up a first success."

210. Conrad to Pinker, 12 February 1914, Berg. See also Thursday, [1915], Berg.

211. Conrad to Graham, 23 January 1914, Watts, *Letters*, p. 178. Confirmed by letters to E. Garnett, 28 January (E. Garnett, *Letters*, pp. 263–264), and to Bennett, 29 January, *LL*, 2:151.

212. Conrad to Galsworthy, 19 March 1914, *LL*, 2:151–152. He expressed a similar mood in a letter to Morrell, 17 February 1914, Texas.

213. Conrad to Quinn, 16 May 1914, NYPL.

214. 19 March and 2 April, reprinted later in *Notes on Novelists* (New York, 1914); see Watt, "Conrad, James and *Chance*," pp. 314–319.

215. Leon Edel, *Henry James, 1901–1916, The Master* (Philadelphia, 1972), p. 493.

216. Conrad to E. Garnett, 23 February 1914, E. Garnett, *Letters*, pp. 264–265.

217. Douglas Hewitt, *Joseph Conrad: A Reassessment* (Cambridge, 1952), pp. 124–126.

218. Curle, *Joseph Conrad, A Study* (London, 1914), passim.

219. Conrad to Russell, 7 February 1914, McMaster University, Hamilton, Ontario.

220. Conrad to W. Rothenstein, 17 February 1914, Harvard.

221. Conrad to F. W. Dawson, 17 February 1914; to J. W. Gilmer, 10 December 1913, Berg.

222. Conrad to Pinker, 19 February 1914, Berg.

223. Conrad to Galsworthy, 19 March 1914; also 5 May 1914, *LL*, 2:154.

224. *Illustrated London News*, 6 June, and *Daily Express*, 10 June; both texts appeared jointly in *Notes on Life and Letters* under the title "Protection of Ocean Liners," pp. 249–259.

225. Conrad to Pinker, 4 June 1914, Berg.

226. Ellen Glasgow's visit described by Randall, *Conrad and Dawson*, pp. 84–86; ibid., reproductions of photographs.

227. Robin Douglas to Mr. Chamberlain, 17 August 1935, Yale; and "My Boyhood with Conrad," *Cornhill Magazine*, January 1929, pp. 20–28.

228. Jessie Conrad to J. T. Babb, 6 December 1935, Yale.

229. Conrad to Galsworthy, 24 June 1913, Birmingham; to Rothenstein, 17 February 1914; to Galsworthy, 5 May 1914.

230. Conrad to Curle, Monday, [29 June 1914], Curle, *Conrad to a Friend*, p. 26; to Galsworthy, 25 July 1914, *LL*, 2:156–157; Jessie Conrad to F. W. Dawson, 3 July 1914, Randall, *Conrad and Dawson*, p. 182; B. Conrad, *My Father*, p. 88.

231. Conrad to Pinker, 1 July 1914, Berg; date of completion in letter to Galsworthy, 25 July 1914.

232. Conrad to Pinker, 1 July 1914; to Curle, 22 July 1914, Curle, *Conrad to a Friend*, p. 27.

233. Andrzej Busza, "Conrad's Polish Literary Background and Some Illustrations of the Influence of Polish Literature on His Work," *Antemurale* 10 (1966):216–233. The first person to point out in print the similarities between *Victory* and *The History of a Sin* was Julian Krzyżanowski ("O tragedii na Samburanie" [About the tragedy in Samburan], *Pion*, no. 50 1934). Anna and Jarosław Iwaszkiewicz have informed me that the analogies had been "talked about" in Warsaw directly after the publication of the first Polish edition of *Victory* in 1931. Conrad wrote to E. Garnett on 2 September 1921: "I have just read through the Żeromski novel you mean: History of a Sin. Honestly I don't think it will do for translation . . . The whole thing is disagreeable and often incomprehensible in comment and psychology" (E. Garnett, *Letters*, pp. 308–309). I do not suspect that Conrad consciously tried to cover up his tracks by opposing the English translation of Żeromski's *kitsch*, but I do not doubt that he had read it earlier.

234. Jean-Aubry, *Lettres françaises*, p. 12; Owen Knowles, "Conrad, Anatole France, and the Early French Romantic Tradition: Some Influences," *Conradiana* 11, no. 1 (1979):54–58. Karl; *Joseph Conrad*, pp. 756–769.

235. Conrad to Galsworthy, 5 May 1914; see also P. R. Reynolds to Pinker, 3 February and 27 February 1914, Berg.

236. Conrad to Quinn, 22 July 1914, NYPL.

XIII. VOYAGE TO POLAND: 1914

1. *Notes on Life and Letters*, p. 144.

2. Conrad to John Galsworthy, 25 July 1914, *LL*, 2:157.

3. According to Otolia Retinger, the bureau, which occupied only one room, spread information about Poland; its address in Conrad's letter to Pinker, 8 August 1914, ibid., p. 160.

4. Marian Dąbrowski, "Rozmowa z J. Conradem" [A talk with J. Conrad], *Tygodnik Ilustrowany*, 25 April 1914. Adam Mickiewicz (1798–1855) and Juliusz Słowacki (1809–1849) are the two greatest poets of Polish Romanticism and the two most respected national moral authorities of the nineteenth century. *Pan Tadeusz* (1834) is Mickiewicz's most famous work, a national epic. *Konrad Wallenrod* (1827) is a short epic poem about a Lithuanian noble who, to revenge his plundered country, becomes Grand Master of the Teutonic Order and treacherously destroys its might. *Grażyna* (1823) is a heroic poem about a Lithuanian princess who dies leading her knights to battle against German invaders.

5. O. Zubrzycka [O. Retinger], "Syn dwu ojczyzn" [A son of two countries], *Iskry*, nos. 8–10, (1931); also information given to me by Mrs. Retinger.

6. John S. Lewis, "Conrad in 1914," *The Polish Review* 20, nos. 2–3 (1975):217–219.

7. Arthur Rubinstein, *My Young Years* (New York, 1973), pp. 416–417.

8. *Notes on Life and Letters*, pp. 145–146; to Galsworthy, 25 July 1914. Similarly, to Harriet Capes, *LL*, 2:155.

9. Conrad to Galsworthy, 25 July 1914.

10. *Notes on Life and Letters*, pp. 158–159; *JCKH*, p. 65; J. H. Retinger, *Conrad and His Contemporaries* (New York, 1943), pp. 148–149.

11. The date of arrival in Cracow can be established on the basis of Mrs. Retinger's reminiscences (Zubrzycka, "Syn dwu ojczyzn"). See also *JCKH*, pp. 66–67.

12. *Notes on Life and Letters*, pp. 164–170. Conrad says there that he took Borys along and that they went via Sławkowska Street straight to the Square. Borys neither mentions nor remembers that walk. Retinger, *Conrad and His Contemporaries*, pp. 150–151, says that both he and Borys accompanied Conrad and that Conrad insisted on taking a roundabout route, which had been his habitual one as a boy. This last is confirmed by Mrs. Retinger's recollections, imparted to me, which sound most reliable. According to her, Borys was left at the hotel.

13. For example, he gives the date of their arrival in Cracow as 1 August ("First News," *Notes on Life and Letters*, p. 174); the German ultimatum to Belgium (2 August, but published in Cracow on 6 August) as three days later (*ibid.*, p. 170); mobilization in Austria-Hungary (31 July) as a day later (ibid., p. 171); and dates the declaration of war on the same day—it is unclear which declaration, however: between Germany and Russia (1 August) or Austria and Russia (5 August).

14. *Ilustrowany Kurier Codzienny*, 1 August 1914. Mrs. Retinger encountered no difficulties in going by train to Słomniki (station across the border, closest to her mother's estate) and back. She regards the dramatic stories about night escapades across the frontier told by Jessie (*JCKH*, pp. 73–74) and Borys (*My Father: Joseph Conrad* [New York, 1970], pp. 91–93) as greatly exaggerated.

15. *Notes on Life and Letters*, pp. 175–176; *A Personal Record*, p. ix.

16. Borys Conrad to Hans van Marle, 15 March 1976.

17. *JCKH*, pp. 70–71; B. Conrad, *My Father*, pp. 89–90.

18. Conrad to Galsworthy, 1 August 1914, *LL*, 2:158.

19. Ibid., and *Ilustrowany Kurier Codzienny*, 2 August 1914.

20. Professor Karol Górski to the author, 16 January 1957.

21. Conrad to Pinker, 8 August 1914, *LL*, 2:160.

22. B. Conrad, *My Father*, p. 95.

23. Karol Górski's letter to the author, 16 January 1957.

24. Letter of Dr. Teodor Kosch, who witnessed the scene, to the author, 10 October 1958.

25. Aniela Zagórska, "Kilka wspomnień o Conradzie" [A few reminiscences of Conrad], *Wspomnienia i studia*, pp. 93–94. Zagórska's memoirs contain a fair dose of patriotic hagiography.

26. Zagórska, ibid., p. 95, remembers a tale corresponding to chapter 2, part II of *The Rescue*; Henryk Jasieński remembers another, corresponding to chapter 2, part V of *Romance* (Barbara Kocówna, "Żywa tradycja Conradowska" [Conrad's living tradition], *Przegląd Humanistyczny* 5, no. 1 [1961]:173–174).

27. Kosch, "Memoriał Conrada (Korzeniowskiego) w sprawie polskiej w czasie wielkiej wojny" [Conrad's memorandum on the Polish question of the time of the Great War], *Czas*, no. 89 (1934); also conversations with the author.

28. Kazimierz Górski, "Moje spotkanie z Josephem Conradem" [My meeting with Joseph Conrad], *Przegląd Wołyński*, 17 January 1932.

29. *CPB*, pp. 303–304.

30. *JCKH*, p. 68.

31. Ibid.

32. Górski, "Moje spotkanie"; Jessie Conrad to Pinker, 30 September 1913, Berg.

33. *CPB*, p. 255.

34. Kosch, "Powrót Conrada do Anglii—ze wspomnień o Conradzie" [Conrad's return to England—from my reminiscences of Joseph Conrad], *Tygodnik Powszechny*, no. 30 (1960). Travel permit for J. Konrad Korzeniowski, Cracow, Jagiellonian Library, MS 6391.

35. Conrad to Mrs. Aniela Zagórska and Miss Aniela Zagórska, Friday, [9 October 1914], *CPB*, p. 252; to Galsworthy, 15 November 1914, *LL*, 2:163.

36. Conrad to Pinker, 15 September 1914, *LL*, 2:161.

37. *JCKH*, p. 85.

38. Conrad to Kosch, 18 October 1914, *CPB*, p. 253; and to Galsworthy, 15 November 1914.

39. Conrad to Kosch, 18 October 1914.

40. *JCKH*, pp. 88–89; B. Conrad, *My Father*, pp. 97–99.

41. Conrad to Stanisław Zajączkowski, Sunday, 18 October 1914, *CPB*, pp. 254–255; to Kosch, 20 October 1914, ibid., p. 256.

42. Telegram, Conrad to Pinker, 24 October 1914, Berg; letters to Kosch, 22 October, to Biliński, 24 October and 3 November, to Zajączkowski, 24 October 1914, *CPB*, pp. 256–258.

43. Conrad to Kosch, 22 October 1914.

44. Conrad to Biliński, 3 November 1914; *CPB*, pp. 258–259.

45. Arnold Bennett, *Journals*, ed. Newman Flower (London, 1932), 2:108.

XIV. THE WAR AND THE MEMORIES: 1914–1919

1. Joseph Conrad to John Galsworthy, 15 November 1919, *LL*, 2:163.

2. Conrad to Iris Wedgwood, 28 January 1915, ibid., p. 168; Jessie Conrad to James B. Pinker, 20 December 1914, Berg.

3. Conrad to Ralph Wedgwood, 15 November 1914, *LL*, 2:162.

4. Although on the last page of the MS. (Yale), Conrad wrote "11 Dec^{er} 1914," his later correspondence indicates that it was this date he began writing the piece; he completed it probably in March 1915. It appeared in the *Daily News*, March 29 and 31 and April 6 and 9, in four instalments titled: "The Shock of War," "To Poland in War-time," "The North Sea on the Eve of the War," and "My Return to Cracow."

5. *Notes on Life and Letters*, p. 171; to John Quinn, 18 April 1915, NYPL.

6. Kenneth J. Calder, *Britain and the Origins of the New Europe, 1914–1918* (Cambridge, 1976), p. 23.

7. Janusz Pajewski, *Wokół sprawy polskiej. Paryż-Lozanna-Londyn 1914–1918* [Around the Polish question. Paris-Lausanne-London 1914–1918] (Poznań, 1970), p. 171.

8. *Archiwum polityczne Ignacego Paderewskiego* [The political archives of Ignacy Paderewski], ed. W. Stankiewicz and A. Piber (Wrocław, 1973), 1:67.

9. See Arnold Bennett, *Journals*, ed. Norman Flower (London, 1932), 2:96.

10. Conrad to Iris Wedgwood, 28 January 1915, *LL*, 2:168.

11. Conrad to Pinker, 20 March 1915, Berg.

12. Conrad to Pinker, 19 January 1915, Berg.

13. Conrad to Pinker, 3 February 1915, Berg; see also to William Blackwood, 14 February 1899,

William Blackburn, ed., *Joseph Conrad: Letters to William Blackwood and David S. Meldrum* (Durham, N.C., 1958), p. 54.

14. Conrad to Pinker, 24 June 1915, Berg.

15. Conrad to Galsworthy, 10 April 1915, Birmingham; see also to Richard Curle, 20 April 1915, Richard Curle, ed., *Conrad to a Friend: 150 Selected Letters from Joseph Conrad to Richard Curle* (London, 1928), p. 33; and to Galsworthy, 18 May 1915, Birmingham.

16. Conrad to Pinker, 19 February 1915, Berg.

17. See *Athenaeum*, 6 March 1915; *Daily Telegraph*, 3 March 1915; *Spectator*, 6 March 1915; *Nation* (New York), 10 February 1916; *Publisher's Weekly* (New York), 19 February 1916. Also Conrad to Galsworthy, n.d., *LL*, 2:164.

18. *JCC*, p. 191.

19. A. J. Dawson, *Some Battle Stories* (London, 1916). Conrad had known Dawson for about fifteen years.

20. Conrad to Curle, 5 March [1915] and Wednesday [May 1915], Curle, *Conrad to a Friend*, pp. 32, 34.

21. Conrad to Pinker, 29 March 1915, Berg.

22. Conrad to Pinker, 24 June 1915, Berg.

23. Conrad to Pinker, Monday, 11[=12] May 1915, Berg.

24. Conrad to Austin Harrison, 19 August 1915, Rosenbach. The article was not published.

25. 1 June 1915, A. Busza, "Dwa nieznane listy Conrada" [Two unknown letters of Conrad], *Wiadomości* (London), no. 31, (1973).

26. 27 September 1915, ibid. Conrad wrote, "Since a severe illness four years ago I have lost my voice entirely, and even in ordinary conversation I am sometimes compelled to whisper."

27. Conrad to Quinn, 14 March 1916, NYPL: "About 5 years ago after an attack of gout I lost my voice completely. It fails me even in ordinary conversation if it is at all prolonged. A sustained effort such as a lecture or reading is out of question." Also to Elbridge L. Adams, 20 November 1922, *LL*, 2:283.

28. Conrad to Pinker, 24 June 1915; to F. W. Dawson, 11 August 1915, Dale J. B. Randall, *Joseph Conrad and Warrington Dawson: The Record of a Friendship* (Durham, N.C., 1968), p. 185.

29. Borys Conrad, *My Father: Joseph Conrad* (New York, 1970), pp. 106–108; Conrad to R. B. Cunninghame Graham, 15 September 1915, Cedric T. Watts, ed., *Joseph Conrad's Letters to R. B. Cunninghame Graham* (Cambridge, 1969), p. 181.

30. Conrad to Sidney Colvin, Sunday, [19 September 1915], Yale; to F. N. Doubleday, 17 September 1915, Princeton. It was probably Ford's request for Conrad's old field glasses (Conrad to Ford Madox Ford, Monday, [30 August 1915], *LL*, 2:169) that gave Conrad the idea of buying binoculars for his son.

31. Conrad to F. W. Dawson, 11 August 1915; to Doubleday, 17 September 1915.

32. Conrad to William Rothenstein, 26 October and 18 December 1915, Harvard.

33. Conrad to André Gide, 18 November 1915, G. Jean-Aubry, ed., *Joseph Conrad: Lettres françaises* (Paris, 1929), p. 132.

34. Conrad to W. Rothenstein, 26 October 1915.

35. Jessie Conrad to Pinker, 9 November 1915, Berg.

36. Conrad to Harriet M. Capes, 25 September 1915, Yale. Conrad wrote here that on the day of publication the two first impressions of *Victory* were sold out.

37. Galsworthy to Edward Garnett, 15 October 1915, *Letters from Galsworthy: 1900–1932*, edited by E. Garnett, p. 221.

38. Conrad to Curle, 7 October 1915, Curle, *Conrad to a Friend*, p. 38.

39. *New York Times Book Review*, 28 March 1915; G. Gould in the *New Statesman*, 2 October 1915; *Glasgow Evening News*, 7 October 1915; Norman Sherry, *Conrad: The Critical Heritage* (Cambridge, 1973), pp. 31–32 and 285–303.

40. Conrad to Capes, 18 December 1915, Yale.

41. Conrad to Curle, 18 December 1915, Curle, *Conrad to a Friend*, p. 40.

42. Conrad to Gide, 18 November 1915; and to G. Taube, 24 November 1915, Jean-Aubry, *Lettres françaises*, pp. 132–133.

43. Conrad to Colvin, [17 February] 1917, *LL*, 2:182 (wrongly dated as 27 February).

44. Conrad to W. F. Dawson, 12 February 1916, Randall, *Conrad and Dawson*, p. 188.

45. Letters to Pinker, written at that time, and especially those sent from London (and thus during his escapades in town) usually contain requests for additional sums of money. See also Conrad to Curle, 12 April 1916, Indiana (the relevant fragment is omitted in Curle's edition), where Conrad mentions a debt.

46. Conrad to Pinker, Wednesday, [February 1916], Berg.

47. Conrad to Pinker, 30 March 1916, Berg.

48. Conrad to Colvin, 2 April 1917, Yale. Conrad said here that he "got the hint" for the story in Philippe de Ségur, *Histoire de Napoléon et de la Grande Armée en 1812* (1824).

49. Conrad to Garnett, Thursday, [3 April 1916], E. Garnett, *Letters from Conrad, 1895 to 1924* (London, 1928), p. 267.

50. Conrad to Pinker, Tuesday, [April 1916], Berg; also to W. Rothenstein, to whom he sent Follett's booklet, 19 June 1916, Harvard.

51. Wilson Follett, *Joseph Conrad: A Short Study of His Intellectual and Emotional Attitude toward his Work and of the Chief Characteristics of His Novels* (Garden City, N.Y., [1915]).

52. The characterization of Jane Anderson is taken from Rebecca West's letter of 19 May 1959 to Ian Watt. Professor Watt, with John Halverson, had collected material for an article about Jane Anderson; he kindly gave me copies of his most important findings.

53. Conrad to Curle, Tuesday, [14 April 1916], Curle, *Conrad to a Friend*, p. 51; *JCC*, p. 195. See also Conrad to Pinker, Tuesday, [February? 1916], Berg.

54. J. Anderson's letter to Deems Taylor, 19 April 1916, copy from Ian Watt and John Halverson. I quote about one-quarter of the text.

55. Conrad to Curle, Saturday, [20 May 1916], Curle, *Conrad to a Friend*, p. 52 (wrongly dated 21 May). Jessie's account that Conrad did not want to visit his dying friend alone (*JCKH*, p. 135; it is accepted as true by Bernard Meyer, *Joseph Conrad: A Psychoanalytic Biography* [Princeton, 1967], p. 247) is at least partly fabricated. She says that she "had not left [her] room for more than a month," but in fact she has recently been to London to see Davidson's exhibition. It is also not true that they did not have a car at that time. Curle remembers that he and Conrad went to

see Marwood a few days before he died (*The Last Twelve Years of Joseph Conrad* [London, 1928], pp. 172–173).

56. Conrad to Gide, 19 May 1916, Jean-Aubry, *Lettres françaises*, p. 135.

57. Conrad to Pinker, 8 June 1916, *LL*, 2:172. But see also 23 July to Garnett about the difficulty of any mental work, E. Garnett, *Letters*, p. 267.

58. Conrad to Doubleday, 3 July 1916, Princeton; to Quinn, 15 July and 10 August 1916, NYPL. In April, Conrad prepared the text of *Almayer's Folly* for the planned collected edition (John Dozier Gordan, *Joseph Conrad: The Making of a Novelist* [Cambridge, Mass., 1940], pp. 116–129, and David L. Higdon and Floyd E. Eddleman, "Collected Edition Variants in Conrad's *Almayer's Folly*," *Conradiana* 9 (1977):77–103.

59. Conrad to Doubleday, 19 May 1916, copy in NYPL.

60. R. D. Evans, "Dramatization of Conrad's *Victory* and a New Letter," *Notes and Queries*, March 1961, pp. 108–110; Conrad's letter to Irving, 19 July 1916, ibid.

61. Conrad to Pinker, Wednesday, [August? 1916], *LL*, 2:172–173.

62. Conrad to Quinn, 24 May 1916, NYPL.

63. Conrad to Quinn, 15 July 1916, NYPL.

64. Karola Zagórska, "Ze wspomnień o Conradzie" [Recollections of Conrad], *Twórczość*, no. 8, 1969, p. 110; the recorded conversation took place in 1920. Cunninghame Graham expressed a very similar opinion in his letter to H. W. Nevinson of 27 November 1928 (A. F. Tschiffely, *Don Roberto* [London, 1937], pp. 391–393).

65. K. Zagórska, "Pod dachem Konrada Korzeniowskiego (Josepha Conrada)" [Under the roof of Konrad Korzeniowski], *Kultura*, nos. 2 and 3, 10 and 17 January 1932.

66. Conrad to Curle, 20 August 1916, Curle, *Conrad to a Friend*, p. 55; see also to Christopher Sandeman, 31 August 1916, *LL*, 2:174–175. Retinger himself deplored, in retrospect, his inexperience at that time. His biographer, John Pomian, writes astutely that Retinger's "credentials and his mandate could also be doubted and contested both by his own compatriots and by his Western hosts, if only they chose to do so. As is always the case with exiles in similar circumstances, he would be accepted as a representative spokesman only if there was no one better at hand, and in so far as it pleased people to give him credence. Should he come to be regarded as a nuisance he could easily be dubbed a pretentious youngster and brushed aside. In this ambiguous situation he should have acted warily. He did not always do so; which ultimately proved his downfall" (*Joseph Retinger: Memoirs of an Eminence Grise* [London, 1972], p. 29).

67. "A Note on the Polish Problem," in *Notes on Life and Letters*, pp. 134–140. The original memorandum, as presented at the Foreign Office, has been located by Hans van Marle in the Public Record Office in London (FO 371/1747, 1916). It differs in a few points from the published text, which—understandably, since it appeared in 1921—does not specify that the reborn Poland should be a monarchy, does not mention an Anglo-French naval base, and so forth; *Joseph Conrad Today* 4, no. 1 (October 1978): 97, 100–101.

68. Conrad to Joseph Retinger, 21 August 1916, *CPB*, pp. 260–261.

69. I owe this information to Hans van Marle.

70. See Pajewski, *Wokół sprawy polskiej*, pp. 179–180.

71. Conrad to Sandeman, 31 August 1916.

72. Conrad to H. Sanderson, 16 July 1916, Yale; to Garnett, 23 July 1916, E. Garnett, *Letters*, p. 268.

73. Arthur Mizener, *The Saddest Story: A Biography of Ford Madox Ford* (New York, 1971), pp. 284–288.

74. Conrad to Pinker, Saturday, 15[=16] September 1916, Berg; see also to Jessie Conrad, 10 P.M. Friday, [15 September 1916], *LL*, 2:178–179.

75. Conrad to Pinker, Saturday, 15[=16] September 1916; *Notes on Life and Letters*, pp. 209–212.

76. Conrad to Jessie Conrad, 29 September 1916 and Sunday, [1 October 1916], Joseph Conrad, *Letters to His Wife* (London, 1927), pp. 21–22, 25. Jocelyn Baines confuses this trip with another a month later (*Joseph Conrad: A Critical Biography* [London, 1960], p. 408).

77. Date on manuscript; Hodgson and Co., London, *A Catalogue of Books, Manuscripts, and Corrected Typescripts from the Library of the late Joseph Conrad* (London, 1925). Writing to Pinker on Tuesday, [31 October 1916], Conrad described the piece as "very Conradesque indeed" (Berg).

78. Conrad to Jessie Conrad, Sunday, [5 November 1916], from Edinburgh, *LL*, 2:177–178.

79. J. G. Sutherland, *At Sea with Joseph Conrad* (Boston, 1922), p. 39.

80. 8 November 1916, *LL*, 2:179.

81. Conrad to Gordon Gardiner, 24 December 1916, Harvard; Sutherland, *At Sea with Conrad*, p. 145.

82. *JCC*, pp. 202–204; Sutherland, *At Sea with Conrad*, p. 146.

83. The deleted fragment should have followed p. 205 of *JCC*; on the next two pages Jessie refers to it a few times.

84. Conrad to Curle, 20 August 1916, Curle, *Conrad to a Friend*, p. 54.

85. According to Jessie (*JCC*, pp. 204–205), Jane Anderson came to Capel House to recuperate some time after Conrad's return from his voyage on the *Ready*, and thus not before the end of November; but she writes that *afterward* Jane accompanied her and John to Folkestone while Conrad went to Lowestoft and Yarmouth—in mid-September.

86. Conrad to Jessie Conrad, 14 September 1916 and [15 September 1916], Conrad, *Letters to His Wife*, pp. 14, 17, 19.

87. Conrad to Jessie Conrad, 29 September 1916, ibid., p. 21–22.

88. *JCC*, p. 196, 205.

89. B. Conrad, *My Father*, pp. 121–125.

90. Ibid., and Pomian, *Joseph Retinger*, p. 38.

91. *JCC*, pp. 207–208.

92. Information from Ian Watt.

93. *JCC*, pp. 207–208.

94. B. Conrad, *My Father*, p. 88; see also chapter 15 this book.

95. Conrad to Pinker, Sunday evening, [10 or 17 December? 1916], Berg. Conrad's words about Jane's uncertain future proved prophetic. In the 1930s, if not before, she became a German spy, and during World War II took part in German propaganda broadcasts.

96. Conrad to W. T. H. Howe, 16 August 1917, NYPL.

97. Conrad to Pinker, Tuesday, [about 1 August 1917], Berg.

98. Conrad to Pinker, Wednesday, [7? November 1917], Berg.

99. Conrad to Pinker, 7 February 1915, Berg; to Capes, 18 December 1915.

100. Conrad to Pinker, Monday, [4 December 1916], Berg; Compton Mackenzie, *My Life and Times. Octave Five: 1915–1923* (London, 1965), p. 92.

101. Mark Holloway, *Norman Douglas: A Biography* (London, 1976), pp. 229–232.

102. Conrad to Gardiner, 24 December 1916, Harvard.

103. Conrad to Sandeman, [30] November 1916, *LL*, 2:176–177; to J. M. Dent, 4 December 1916, ibid., p. 180; to Graham, 3 January 1917, Watts, *Letters*, p. 185.

104. Paul Fussell, *The Great War and Modern Memory* (London, 1975), p. 14.

105. Ford wrote to Conrad on 19 December 1916 from the Red Cross Hospital in Rouen: "As for me, c'est fini de moi, I believe, at least as fighting is concerned—my lungs are all charred up and gone . . . one lives under the shadow of G[ustave] F[laubert] here. After all you began yr literary career here—and I jolly near ended mine here too—And I assure you I haven't lost a jot of the immense wonder at the immensities you bring down onto paper" (Richard M. Ludwig, *Letters of Ford Madox Ford* [Princeton, N.J., 1965] p. 79). See also Mizener, *Saddest Story*, pp. 291–292.

106. Eleanor Farjeon, *Edward Thomas: The Last Four Years* (London, 1958), pp. 232–233.

107. On the first page the MS has the inscription "1st and only Admiralty Paper"; G. Lindstrand, "A Bibliographical Survey of the Literary Manuscripts of Joseph Conrad," part 3, *Conradiana* 2, no. 3 (1969–1970):161. His letter to Pinker of Monday, [December 1916], shows that Conrad originally planned to write more articles (Berg).

108. Conrad to Pinker, n.d., [about 1 December 1916], Berg. In the same letter Conrad asked Pinker for £80 of assistance money for Jessie's mother and sisters; all Jessie's brothers were at the front.

109. Conrad to Macdonald Hastings, 25 January 1917, Colgate.

110. B. Conrad, *My Father*, pp. 143–144. See also Conrad's letters to Grace Willard: 11 April 1917, NYPL; Easter Monday, [16 April] 1917, *LL*, 2:188–189; 30 April 1917, ibid., pp. 191–192.

111. Conrad to Willard, 19 April 1917, *LL*, 2:189.

112. Conrad to Pinker, written in verso of Hastings's letter of 5 May 1917, 25 May 1917, and n.d., Berg.

113. Conrad to Pinker, Sunday [1917] and 19 February 1918, Berg. Baines supposes it was the same play which Conrad had outlined in his grandmother's album, next to the draft of *Tuan Jim* (*Joseph Conrad*, p. 489); however, in that play all the protagonists are Italian, while in the play planned with Hastings all the protagonists were supposed to have been English.

114. Conrad to Pinker, 1 February 1917, Berg; to Doubleday, 22 January 1917, Princeton.

115. Jessie Conrad to Pinker, 16 February 1917, Berg.

116. Conrad to Quinn, n.d. (received 12 February 1917), NYPL. Borys arrived around 10 January (see Conrad to Graham, 17 January 1917, Watts, *Letters*, p. 186, and to Doubleday, 22 January 1917).

117. Conrad to Pinker, 19 March 1917, Berg. Conrad initially wanted to publish *The Shadow Line* in one volume with "Prince Roman," and even drafted a special preface, which has not been preserved: to Pinker, n.d., [1916], Berg, and Sunday, *LL*, 2:181–182. The dedication of *The*

Shadow Line apparently caused some misunderstandings (*JCC*, p. 194), as some readers saw in it an allusion to death.

118. *The Sphere*, 14 April 1917, signed CKS; quoted in Sherry, *Conrad*, pp. 32–33. See also Conrad's letter to Clement Shorter, 31 December 1916, BL.

119. *Times Literary Supplement*, 22 March 1917. Other opinions: Sherry, *Conrad*, pp. 32–33, 304–312.

120. Colvin, "Mr Joseph Conrad," *Observer*, 25 March 1917.

121. Conrad to Colvin, 18 March 1917, *LL*, 2:184.

122. Conrad to Colvin, Wednesday, [21 March 1917], Yale.

123. Conrad to Sandeman, 15 September 1917, *LL*, 2:197.

124. Conrad to Quinn, 6 May 1917, NYPL.

125. Conrad to Hugh Walpole, 18 May 1917, *LL*, 2:194.

126. Conrad to Hugh R. Dent, 19 March 1917, ibid., p. 188; to Colvin, 23 March 1917, Yale; to Pinker, 31 March 1917, Berg. See also Bennett, *Journals*, 2:108 (4 November 1914), and Conrad to Colvin, 12 November 1917, *LL*, 2:198.

127. Conrad to Quinn, 6 May 1917.

128. Conrad to Colvin, Saturday, [21 April 1917], *LL*, 2:190.

129. Conrad to Walpole, 18 May 1917, ibid., p. 194. His prophecy was fulfilled a few months later when Kazimierówka—at that time owned by Stanisław Bobrowski, a socialist and former political prisoner—was burned down by rabble.

130. Conrad to Sandeman, 3 April 1917, ibid., p. 188.

131. Conrad to Garnett, [2 May 1917], E. Garnett, *Letters*, p. 270; to Curle, 27 March 1917, Curle, *Conrad to a Friend*, p. 57.

132. Conrad to Pinker, Wednesday night, [1917], Berg.

133. Conrad to the Paymaster General, 2 June 1917, Public Record Office, T1/12178/29480/18.

134. *Notes on Life and Letters*, pp. 45–48; see also Conrad to Garnett, [2 May 1917], E. Garnett, *Letters*, pp. 268–270.

135. The new edition of *Lord Jim* was issued in June by Blackwood; the new edition of *Youth* was published by Dent.

136. Conrad to W. Rothenstein, 2 August 1917, Harvard.

137. Conrad to Pinker, n.d., with the proposed title *R. L., Selected Passages from Letters*, Berg; to Pinker, Wednesday [1917] asking the agent what he thought "from a business point of view" about a preface to the novel "in the form of a letter taking a wide sweep around the subject." The text of *The Laugh* was only partly used by Conrad in *The Arrow of Gold*, for example, in the First Note to the novel. Possibly the "tale," the typing of which Conrad mentions in his letter to Pinker of [27 June 1917], was *The Laugh*.

138. MS of *The Laugh* and TS of *Rita Lastaola, a Tale*, Yale; Conrad to Pinker, Wednesday, [August? 1917], Berg.

139. Conrad, *The Arrow of Gold*, p. 3. E. Korzeniewska in her notes to M. Dąbrowska, *Szkice o Conradzie* [Essays on Conrad] (Warsaw, 1974), pp. 255–256; as she explains, it seems impossible that Tekla Turska was the same person as Tekla Wojakowska née Syroczyńska (see chapter 1).

140. Conrad to Pinker, 15 August 1917, Berg.

141. Conrad to the Sandersons, 31 December 1917, *LL*, 2:198. About his poor health see, for example, Conrad to Sandeman, 15 September 1917.

142. Conrad to Pinker, 1 January 1918, Berg.

143. Conrad to Garnett, Friday, [18 May 1917], E. Garnett, *Letters*, pp. 272–273 (one sentence omitted; original, Texas).

144. Conrad to Garnett, 27 October 1917, ibid., *Letters*, p. 274; John Conrad to the author, 8 March 1977.

145. "Très intime," Conrad to Curle, 2 December 1917, Curle, *Conrad to a Friend*, p. 59.

146. Conrad to Colvin, 12 November 1917, *LL*, 2:198; to Hastings, 24 November 1917, Colgate; Jessie Conrad to Pinker, 6 November 1917, Berg.

147. Conrad to Pinker, 1 P.M. Sunday, [25 November 1917], Berg; to Colvin, 30 November 1917, Duke; see also Jessie Conrad to Pinker, 13 November 1917, Berg; and B. Conrad, *My Father*, pp. 127–131.

148. See H. V. Marrot, *The Life and Letters of John Galsworthy* (London, 1935), pp. 433–434, 439–440; Conrad to Garnett, Sunday, [30 December 1917] (dated erroneously 3 December), 6 January, 31 January, and 16 May 1918, E. Garnett, *Letters*, pp. 274, 279–280, 282; to Colvin, 30 December 1917, Duke; to Hastings, 19 December 1917, Colgate; and so forth.

149. Rupert Hart-Davis, *Hugh Walpole* (London, 1952), p. 168.

150. Cecil Roberts, *Half Way* (London, 1931), p. 215. Roberts says that he first met Conrad in 1919, but Conrad's letter to Garnett of 16 May 1918 (E. Garnett, *Letters*, p. 282) shows that they met in early 1918.

151. Conrad to Garnett, 6 January 1918, E. Garnett, *Letters*, p. 279. That would make about eight hundred words per day; compare *A Personal Record*, p. 69.

152. Garnett, *Letters*, p. 280.

153. Conrad to Pinker, 3 January 1918, Berg.

154. Conrad expressed satisfaction with dictating in his letter to Pinker to Wed[nesday, Autumn 1917], Berg; Jessie told Mégroz about Conrad's shouting (Rodolphe Louis Mégroz, *Joseph Conrad's Mind and Method* [London, 1931], p. 90); Moser points out the bad consequences of dictating (*Joseph Conrad: Achievement and Decline* [Cambridge, Mass., 1957], pp. 207–208). Conrad's letter to Garnett of 6 January 1918 (Garnett, *Letters*, p. 279) indicates that, apart from *The Laugh*, he wrote at least a part of the novel in longhand.

155. Conrad to S. A. Everitt, 18 February 1918, *LL*, 2:201.

156. *JCKH*, p. 147.

157. Conrad to Pinker, 4 March 1918, Berg. Lord Northcliffe wired to Conrad on 6 March: "There is obviously some mistake dear master in the suggestion that you should be paid only 50 guineas for anything you may care to write" (Berg).

158. Conrad to Pinker, 14 March 1918, Berg.

159. Marrot, *Galsworthy*, p. 440.

160. Conrad to Garnett, 27 March 1918, E. Garnett, *Letters*, p. 281.

161. Conrad to Quinn, 6 February 1918, NYPL.

162. Pajewski, *Wokół sprawy polskiej*, pp. 77–79.

163. Conrad to Borys Conrad, 27 April 1918, Boston Public Library. See also Conrad to Colvin, 27 March 1918, Colgate.

164. Conrad to Colvin, 28 April 1918, Duke.

165. Conrad to Galsworthy, Monday, [25 February 1918], *LL*, 2:220. John Conrad helped me to establish the date of this letter, which Jean-Aubry had placed in 1919.

166. Conrad to H. Sanderson, 20 April 1918, ibid., p. 203.

167. Conrad to Pinker, 16 April 1918, Berg. On 22 August 1918 Conrad rejected as "unlucky" the title *Doña Rita*; in another letter to Pinker, of Saturday, [31 August], he proposed *The Lost Arrow*; later, on Tuesday, [3? September], he asked Pinker to choose between *The Lost Arrow* and *Arrow of Gold* (all letters Berg).

168. Conrad to H. Sanderson, 20 April 1918.

169. Conrad to Pinker, 9 May 1918, Berg.

170. Conrad to Pinker, 27 May, 4 June, and 11 June 1918, Berg; to Curle, 9 October 1918, Curle, *Conrad to a Friend*, p. 61.

171. Marrot, *Galsworthy*, p. 442.

172. Hart-Davis, *Hugh Walpole*, p. 171.

173. Conrad to Quinn, 18 September 1919, Texas.

174. Hart-Davis, *Hugh Walpole*, p. 176.

175. Conrad to Walpole, 7 June 1918, *LL*, 2:206. On Conrad's early reading of Flaubert see, for example, his letter to Poradowska of 6 April 1892, René Rapin, ed., *Lettres de Joseph Conrad à Marguerite Poradowska* (Geneva, 1966), p. 101.

176. Ernest Rhys, "An Interview with Joseph Conrad," *The Bookman* (New York), 56 (December 1922):407.

177. Jessie Conrad to Pinker, 5 June 1918, Berg: "I have managed to hide the fact that I am nearly crazy with pain, I knew it would take all the backbone out of him." See also B. Conrad, *My Father*, p. 131.

178. Conrad to Colvin, 25 June 1918, in possession of Fred B. Johnson.

179. Conrad to Colvin, 27 June 1918, Indiana; B. Conrad, *My Father*, p. 133.

180. Conrad to Gide, 6 July 1918, Jean-Aubry, *Lettres françaises*, p. 141.

181. Conrad to Jessie Conrad, 5:30 P.M. [6? July 1918], Conrad, *Letters to His Wife*, p. 43.

182. Jessie Conrad to Pinker, 25 July 1918, Berg.

183. Conrad to Pinker, Sat[urday], from Capel House, Berg.

184. Conrad to Pinker, 5 July [1918], Berg.

185. The former was certainly written in July; the latter is mentioned in Jessie's letter to Pinker of 31 August 1918 (Berg), in which she says that she is trying to persuade Conrad to finish it. Both were published in August.

186. Conrad to Pinker, 25 September 1918, *LL*, 2:208.

187. Conrad to Walpole, 31 August 1918, Texas; to Pinker, Saturday morning, [31 August 1918], Berg.

188. Conrad to Walpole, 17 September 1918, Texas; Jessie Conrad to Retinger, 23 August 1923, PAN Library, Cracow.

189. On Nellie Lyons's funeral, see Conrad to Pinker, 21 January 1919, Berg; in verso of a letter from Emilio Cecchi dated 26 March 1919, Conrad asked Pinker to give or lend £50 to Dr. Tebb, Jessie's former physician.

190. Conrad to Thomas J. Wise, 2 October 1918, *LL*, 2:209, and 2 December 1918, BL; to Quinn, 29 September 1919 and 2 March 1920, NYPL.

191. Conrad to Walpole, 16 August 1918, Texas; to Gardiner, 9 September 1918, Harvard; to Quinn, 6 October 1918, NYPL.

192. Conrad to Pinker, 25 September 1918; to Wise, 2 October 1918; to Morley Roberts, 17 October 1918, courtesy of Mr. Cecil Roberts. Conrad and Miss Hallowes stayed at the Norfolk Hotel.

193. Conrad to Curle, 9 October 1918, Curle, *Conrad to a Friend*, p. 62.

194. Conrad to B. Conrad, 21 October 1918, Boston Public Library; to Colvin, 21 October 1918, Barrett Library, University of Virginia.

195. Conrad to Pinker, 25 September 1918.

196. Conrad to Walpole, 11 November 1918, *LL*, 2:211.

197. Conrad to Garnett, 22 December 1918, E. Garnett, *Letters*, p. 285. In a similar vein to the Galsworthys, 24 December 1918, *LL*, 2:215–216.

198. Conrad to Sandeman, 17 October 1918, ibid., p. 210.

199. Conrad to Pinker, 12 and 15 November 1918, Berg.

200. On British policy toward Poland see Maria Nowak-Kiełbikowa, *Polska—Wielka Brytania w latach 1918–1923* (Warsaw, 1975), pp. 56–62.
Conrad wrote to Pinker that he "wasn't particularly for *that* one ["The Crime of Partition"] to appear in Engd" (11 April 1919, Berg). He addressed the piece to the American public. "I like the Americans for one thing: they are friendly towards Poland," Conrad told Karola Zagórska (n.d. [March 1923], *Twórczość*, no. 8 (1969) p. 106).
In January 1919 Conrad had a long conversation on Polish subjects with Antoni Czarnecki, editor of *The Daily News* in Chicago. The account of this talk, published five years later in *Ameryka-Echo* (Toledo, Ohio, 31 August 1924, p. 11), contains many factual errors and is generally unreliable.

201. The typescript, very heavily corrected by hand, is dated 12–27 December 1918 (Yale). In *Conrad and His Contemporaries* (New York, 1943) Retinger maintained that "The Crime of Partition" was "based" on his "books," *La Pologne et l'Équilibre européen* and *Considérations générales sur l'avénir économique de la Pologne* (pp. 173–174). This is probably why Baines says that Conrad wrote his article "urged" by Retinger and on the basis of Retinger's pamphlet (*Joseph Conrad*, p. 414). However, only about a page and a half of Conrad's text shows analogies with Retinger's booklets (see *Notes on Life and Letters*, pp. 119–121 and J. H. Retinger, *La Pologne* [Paris, 1916], pp. 22–27).
In "The Crime of Partition," Conrad twice alluded to Retinger—as "a young Pole coming to me from Paris" and "my young friend"—*Notes on Life and Letters*, p. 126.

202. Conrad to Clifford, 25 January 1919, *LL*, 2:216–217.

203. Conrad to Quinn, 16 October 1918, NYPL. Conrad scornfully accused the Irish of rejecting all possibilities of conciliation and wrote about his own credentials: "I, who also spring from an oppressed race where oppression was not a matter of history but a crushing fact in the daily life of all individuals, made still more bitter by declared hatred and contempt."

204. Conrad to the Galsworthys, 24 December 1918: "I haven't had any gout for a long time." But Conrad's letter to Clifford of 25 January 1919 was written after an attack of gout.

205. Conrad to W. Rothenstein, 24 October 1918, Harvard.

206. Conrad to Pinker, 21 November 1918, Berg.

207. Conrad to Pinker, 4 December 1918, Berg.

208. Conrad to Doubleday, 21 December 1918, *LL*, 2:215.

209. Conrad to Pinker, 6 December 1918, Berg.

210. Conrad to Doubleday, 21 December 1918. Conrad met Doubleday for the first time on 2 January 1919; Conrad to Doubleday, 31 December 1918, Princeton.

211. Conrad to Pinker, 30 January 1919, *LL*, 2:218.

212. Conrad to Pinker, 7 January 1919, Berg, and 30 January 1919.

213. *JCC*, p. 213. Conrad's letter, ibid., and in Conrad, *Letters to His Wife*, p. 45 (wrongly dated February 1919).

214. Conrad to Pinker, 21 January 1919, Berg; see also Conrad to Pinker, 13 March 1907, *LL*, 2:46.

215. Conrad to Galsworthy, 16 December 1918, Birmingham.

216. Conrad to Pinker, 18 January 1919, Berg.

217. Conrad to Symons, 9 December 1918, Barrett Library, University of Virginia; B. Conrad, *My Father*, p. 138.

218. *JCC*, p. 212.

219. Conrad to Doubleday, 17 April 1919, *LL*, 2:221; B. Conrad, *My Father*, p. 153. In February Borys had been ordered to Denmark Hill Hospital to be treated for neurasthenia (Conrad to Pinker, 1 March 1919, Berg).

220. Conrad to Pinker, 1 March 1919; to Pinker, 19 March 1919, Berg—Conrad wrote here that he hoped to send Borys to Cambridge Engineering School "where everybody *must be* an earnest worker"; to Pinker, 22 December 1918, Berg. To Curle, Thursday, [19 June 1919]; Friday, [27 June 1919] (wrongly dated 28 June); 7 July 1919; Tuesday, [8 July 1919]; 24 August 1919, Curle, *Conrad to a Friend*, pp. 65–69, 73–74. All jobs involved were in mechanical engineering firms.

221. Conrad bought the car in early January for £180 (to Pinker, 7 January 1919); about their trip to London Conrad wrote to Pinker, 30 January 1919.

222. Conrad to Garnett, 8 February 1919, E. Garnett, *Letters*, p. 285.

223. Conrad to Pinker, 30 January 1919.

224. Conrad to Pinker, 31 December 1918, Berg.

225. 15 February 1919, Mr. Cecil Roberts.

226. Conrad to Doubleday, 24 February 1919, Princeton.

227. Conrad to Wise, 16 February 1919, BL.

228. Conrad to Garnett, 12 March 1919, E. Garnett, *Letters*, pp. 286–287.

229. Conrad to Pinker, 15 February 1919, Berg.

230. Conrad to Pinker, 19 February 1919, Berg; to Doubleday, 22 February 1919, Princeton; to Pinker, Monday, 11[=12] March 1919, Berg.

231. Conrad to Pinker, 19 February 1919; to Pinker, 21 March 1919, Berg.

232. Conrad to Pinker, 21 March 1919; see also *JCC*, pp. 215–216.

233. Conrad to Borys, 21 October 1918, Boston Public Library; to Pinker, 8 November 1918, Berg; B. Conrad, *My Father*, pp. 138–139.

234. Conrad to Garnett, 7 July 1919, E. Garnett, *Letters*, p. 288.

235. Conrad to Pinker, 26 March 1919, Berg.

236. Robert O. Evans, "Dramatization of Conrad's *Victory*: A New Letter," *Notes and Queries*, n.s. 8 (March 1961): 108–110. Ibid. an amusing quotation from a letter of Miss Marie Löhr, the play's producer: Conrad was "an enchanting man. Spoke very little English."

237. Conrad to Pinker, 26 March 1919.

238. Conrad to Pinker, 11 April 1919, Berg.

239. See Conrad to J. C. Squire, 9 May 1919, Berg. Conrad said here that he had 24,800 words of Part VI written and that he needed another 10,000 words or less; thus he had ready six chapters of Part VI.

240. The MS (BL) is dated 17 April 1919. Conrad began the piece on 11 April (letter to Pinker of this date, Berg).

241. Conrad to Pinker, 30 April and 9 May 1919, Berg.

242. Conrad to Pinker, 25 May 1919, Berg.

243. Conrad to Garnett, 7 July 1919, E. Garnett, *Letters*, pp. 287–288. See also to Garnett, 24 September 1919, ibid., p. 289.

244. Conrad to Doubleday, 17 April 1919, and 30 July 1919, Princeton. Author's Note to *A Personal Record* is dated 25 September 1919, MS Princeton.

245. *A Personal Record*, pp. v–vii.

246. Conrad to Pinker, 17 June 1919, Berg, and to Curle, Thursday, [19 June 1919].

247. See, for example, Conrad to Colvin, 20 June 1919, Duke; to Curle, Friday, [27 June 1919], and 7 July 1919, Curle, *Conrad to a Friend*, p. 68; to Walpole, Monday, [14 July 1919], Texas.

248. Conrad to Colvin, 11 July 1919, Yale.

249. Conrad to Curle, Thursday, [19 June 1919]; Hart-Davis, *Hugh Walpole*, p. 187 (Walpole's note dated 10 August).

250. Conrad to Garnett, 22 December 1918, 12 March, and 7 July 1919, E. Garnett, *Letters*, pp. 284, 286–288; see also p. xxxiii.

251. Conrad to Quinn, 26 May 1919, NYPL.

252. The cover of Retinger's pamphlet *La Pologne et l'Équilibre européen* carries the announcement of a book—apparently never written—*La Réalité polonaise*, co-authored by Retinger and G. Jean-Aubry. Jean Aubry changed his name to G. (for nothing) Jean-Aubry. See Conrad to Jean-Aubry, 3 November 1917, 30 May 1919, and 13 November 1919, Jean-Aubry, *Lettres françaises*, pp. 138, 145, 149–150.

253. G. Jean-Aubry, "Souvenirs," *Nouvelle Revue Française*, no. 12 (1 December 1924), pp. 673–674.

254. Conrad to Gide, 20 August 1919, Jean-Aubry, *Lettres françaises*, p. 147.

255. Conrad to F. W. Dawson, 22 September 1919, Randall, *Conrad and Dawson*, p. 198.

256. Galsworthy to Garnett, 5 and 8 September 1919, E. Garnett, *Letters from Galsworthy*, pp. 235–236.

257. Conrad to Curle, Thursday, [19 June 1919]; to Pinker, 7 and 14 August 1919, *LL*, 2:225 and 227.

258. *New Statesman*, 16 August 1919; *Daily Telegraph*, 29 August 1919; both reviews reprinted in Sherry, *Conrad*, pp. 321–325. See also Conrad to J. C. Squire, 21 August 1919, *LL*, 2:228.

259. Conrad to Galsworthy, 8 August 1919, *LL*, 2:226.

260. Conrad to Colvin, 7 August 1919 and Wednesday, [6 August? 1919], ibid., pp. 224, 229.

261. Conrad to Gide, 20 August 1919.

262. Conrad to Quinn, 10 April, 30 April (wire), and 26 May 1919—where Conrad said that he mentally calls *The Arrow* "Quinn's book"—NYPL.

263. Conrad to Quinn, 31 July and 29 September 1919, 2 March 1920, 27 October 1922, NYPL. In 1921 Conrad did not write a single letter to Quinn.

264. Conrad to Curle, 24 and 30 August 1919, Curle, *Conrad to a Friend*, pp. 73–75.

265. Conrad to Pinker, 21 August 1919, Berg.

XV. HOPE AND RESIGNATION: 1919–1924

1. The strike lasted from 1 to 6 October; it was not a "general strike", as reported in *JCC*, p. 216. Conrad's first letter from Oswalds was to James B. Pinker, 8 October 1919, Berg.

2. *JCC*, p. 216; Borys Conrad, *My Father: Joseph Conrad* (New York, 1970), p. 151.

3. Conrad to Sidney Colvin, 15 October 1919, Duke; compare A. J. P. Taylor, *English History 1914–1945* (Oxford, 1965), p. 141.

4. Conrad to J. Pinker, 29 January [1920], Berg. Compare B. Conrad, *My Father*, p. 152.

5. Conrad to John Galsworthy, 3 September 1919, Birmingham; to Colvin, 15 October 1919; to J. Pinker, 11 November 1919, *LL*, 2:233; to Richard Curle, Saturday, [22 November 1922], Richard Curle, *Conrad to a Friend: 150 Selected Letters from Joseph Conrad to Richard Curle* (London, 1928), p. 82.

6. Conrad to J. Pinker, 11 November 1919, pp. 233–234.

7. Conrad to André Gide, 4 November 1919, Bibliothèque Doucet, Paris. Conrad's letters to Gide not included in G. Jean-Aubry, ed., *Joseph Conrad: Lettres françaises* (Paris, 1929) were edited by Gabrijela and Ivo Vidan, "Further Correspondence between Joseph Conrad and André Gide," *Studia Romanica et Anglica Zagrabiensia* 29–32 (1970–71):523–536.

8. See Jean-Aubry, "Souvenirs," *Nouvelle Revue Française*, 23 December 1924, p. 678.

9. Conrad to William Rothenstein, 24 September 1919, Harvard.

10. Conrad to Edward Garnett, 8 November 1919, Edward Garnett, *Letters from Conrad, 1895 to 1924* (London, 1928), p. 291; to Curle, 12 December 1919, Curle, *Letters to a Friend*, pp. 84–85.

11. Conrad to Curle, Wednesday, [24 December 1919], Curle, *Conrad to a Friend*, p. 86 (dated erroneously 26 December).

12. Conrad to Curle, 12 December 1919.

13. David Bone, "Memories of Conrad," *Saturday Review of Literature*, 7 November 1925, p. 286.

596 · · NOTES TO PAGES 448–451

14. Conrad to Colvin, 20 January 1920, Barrett Library, University of Virginia, Charlottesville, Virginia.

15. See E. Slater and M. Roth, *Clinical Psychiatry* (London, 1969), pp. 207–208.

16. Conrad to Curle, 19 January and 24 February 1920, Curle, *Conrad to a Friend*, pp. 90 and 92; to J. Pinker, 24 February 1920, Berg.

17. The MS of the Note is dated 25 February–3 March 1920, Yale. On the sources of *The Secret Agent* see Norman Sherry, *Conrad's Western World* (Cambridge, 1971), pp. 205–324.

18. The MS is dated 15 March 1920 (BL).

19. Conrad to Galsworthy, 28 March 1920, *LL*, 2:238; compare to Curle, 18 March 1920, Curle, *Conrad to a Friend*, p. 96.

20. Conrad to Jean-Aubry, 14 June 1920, *LL*, 2:240; to J. Pinker, 17 July 1920, Berg. See also to Galsworthy, 28 March 1920; to J. Pinker, 18 November 1920, *LL*, 2:250.

21. The MS is dated 9 April 1920 (Yale).

22. Conrad to J. Pinker, 15 February 1920, Berg; to Ernest Dawson, 8 March 1920, Yale; to J. Pinker, 27 March 1920, Berg; to Galsworthy, 28 March 1920, also 4 April 1920, Birmingham.

23. Conrad to Garnett, 4 and 27 April 1920, E. Garnett, *Letters*, pp. 293–294; to Galsworthy, 20 April 1920, *LL*, 2:239; to Eric Pinker, 17 April [1920], Berg.

24. Conrad to Gordon Gardiner, 5 May 1920, Harvard.

25. Conrad to Curle, 26 February 1920, *Conrad to a Friend*, p. 92. Conrad had been helping Karola financially since September 1919, when he sent her £100, using Poradowska as the intermediary; to J. Pinker, 5 February 1920, Berg.

26. Karola Zagórska, "Pod dachem Konrada Korzeniowskiego (Josepha Conrada)" [Under the roof of Konrad Korzeniowski], *Kultura*, nos. 2 and 3, (1932).

27. Conrad to Eustachy Sapieha, 20 February 1920, Tadeusz Bobrowski, *Listy do Conrada*, ed. Róża Jabłkowska (Warszawa, 1981), pp. 255–256.

28. Conrad to John Quinn, 2 March 1920, NYPL; fragment in *LL*, 2:237, wrongly dated 24 March.

29. Cablegram dated 26 April 1920; Conrad, *CDAUP*, p. 94.

30. I owe this information to Professor Daniel Gerould.

31. Conrad to Aniela Zagórska, 10 April 1920, *CPB*, pp. 261–262. The relevant document in Berg; Conrad sent it to J. Pinker on 31 August 1920; officially endorsed by the Polish Legation in London, it was mailed to Zagórska on 19 January 1921 (see *CPB*, p. 265).

32. Conrad to J. Pinker, 11 May 1920, Berg.

33. Conrad to Curle, 15 May 1920, Curle, *Conrad to a Friend*, p. 104.

34. Corrected TS of the former is dated May 1920 (Yale); about finishing the latter Conrad wrote to Wise on 24 May 1920 (Yale). Author's Notes to *'Twixt Land and Sea*, *Victory*, and *Within the Tides* were ready by that time, as the same letter indicates. They had been written in 1920.

35. Conrad, *Under Western Eyes*, p. x.

36. Conrad to Garnett, [27 April 1920] and 11 July 1920, E. Garnett, *Letters*, pp. 294–295; to H. R. Dent, 24 June 1920, *LL*, 2:242.

37. Rupert Hart-Davis, *Hugh Walpole*, (London, 1952), p. 195 (note of 18 July 1920).

38. *Athenaeum*, 2 July 1920 (Katherine Mansfield later included this review in her *Novels and Novelists* [London, 1930]); *The Nation*, 12 June 1920. See Norman Sherry, *Conrad: The Critical Heritage* (London, 1973), pp. 34–35, 329–345; on pp. 332–335, V. Woolf's review in the *Times Literary Supplement*, 1 July 1920.

39. Note of 23 June [1920], quoted by Thomas C. Moser, *Joseph Conrad: Achievement and Decline* (Cambridge, Mass., 1957), p. 209.

40. R. B. Cunninghame Graham in his Preface to *Tales of Hearsay*, p. ix.

41. Hart-Davis, *Hugh Walpole*, p. 286.

42. W. Rothenstein, *Men and Memories: 1922–1938* (London, 1939), p. 28.

43. Conrad to J. Pinker, 8 June 1920, Berg; to Curle, 14 June 1920, Curle, *Conrad to a Friend*, p. 108; to Jean-Aubry, same date, *LL*, 2:240.

44. Conrad to J. Pinker, 28 June 1920, Berg; Hart-Davis, *Hugh Walpole*, pp. 194–195.

45. Conrad to J. Pinker, 14 June 1920, Berg.

46. Conrad to Garnett, 11 July 1920; to Lady Colvin, 24 July 1920, Duke; to Jean-Aubry, 26 August 1920, Jean-Aubry, *Lettres françaises*, p. 157; to Harriet Capes, 31 August 1920, Yale.

47. Conrad to Thomas J. Wise, 30 September 1919, BL; to Curle, 8 April 1920, Indiana, and 22 November 1920, Curle, *Conrad to a Friend*, p. 120; see also to Curle, 9 October 1920, ibid., p. 118, and to J. Pinker, 27 February 1920, Berg.

48. Conrad to J. Pinker, [22 January 1921], Berg: "I didn't know I threw £8.000 in a little more than two years." The sum mentioned consisted only of money paid out by Pinker; the total of Conrad's actual income must be raised by about £1,000; for example, in the summer of 1920 Conrad received £450 from Quinn (Conrad to Curle, 18–23 August 1920, Indiana).

49. The date, June 19–20, can be established on the basis of Conrad's letters to Curle of 14 and 22 June, Curle, *Conrad to a Friend*, pp. 109–110, and to Francis Warrington Dawson of 9 July 1920, Dale J. B. Randall, *Joseph Conrad and Warrington Dawson: The Record of a Friendship* (Durham, N.C., 1968), p. 201.

50. K. Zagórska's notes on Conrad's attitude toward music, National Library, Warsaw, MS 9219 Ac.; G. Jean-Aubry, "Joseph Conrad and Music," *The Chesterian*, no. 42 (November 1924):37–42.

51. K. Zagórska, "Ze wspomnień o Conradzie" [Recollections of Conrad], *Twórczość*, no. 8 (1969), pp. 108–110.

52. K. Zagórska, "Pod dachem Konrada."

53. If he wished, Conrad could have published in the most influential newspapers such as *The Times* and the *Daily Mail*, if only because of his friendship with Lord Northcliffe. Nor was there any lack of occasion for private activities in the Polish cause; for example, in the first days of August he visited Lady Northcote at her residence, Eastwood Park, and talked there to Lady Gwendolen Cecil, wife of Lord Cecil of Chelwood, the Under Secretary of State in the Foreign Office, a man rather unfriendly to Poland. Conrad wrote to Curle after this visit: "The Duchess of Albany was there and also Lady Gwendolen Cecil—and *she* was very interesting and friendly. . . . Altogether a very pleasant experience" (18 August 1920), Curle, *Conrad to a Friend*, p. 112.

54. K. Zagórska, "Pod dachem Konrada." On Zagórska's departure Conrad gave his cousin some money and undertook to pay her a yearly allowance of £120; to Pinker, 11 August 1920, Berg.

55. Conrad to Lawrence Holt, 20 July 1920, *LL*, 2:244. Conrad may have known that John Holt, head of the firm at that time, was the only member of the Liverpool Chamber of Commerce

who assisted Edmund D. Morel's campaign against the Congo atrocities in the early 1900s; see Neal Ascherson, *The King Incorporated* (London, 1963), p. 247.

56. Conrad to Holt, 25 July 1920, *LL*, 2:246.

57. Conrad to Curle, 18–23 August 1920, Curle, *Conrad to a Friend*, p. 112; ibid., p. 114.

58. The MS is dated 14 September–8 October 1920 (Yale), but Conrad's letters to Curle of 9 October (Curle, *Conrad to a Friend*, p. 116) and to Wise of 1 November (Jean-Aubry, *LL*, 2:249) testify that the work lasted longer. Lillian Hallowes recorded in her notebook (now at the Bodleian Library, Oxford): "*Gaspar Ruiz* begun Sept. 14th 1920 at Deal (with J. B. P.). Finished typed copy Oct. 29th 1920 (at Bishopsbourne)." Conrad asked Wise to remain discreet: "It may not after all be accepted—though it was written at the request of Laski Film Players Co—and I don't like to have a failure (should it turn out to be that) publicly known" ([24] October 1920, BL). About the stay in Deal (at the Great Eastern Hotel), Conrad to Capes, 31 August 1920, and to Curle, 9 October 1920.

59. John Conrad, "Some Reminiscences of My Father," in *Conrad żywy* [The living Conrad], ed. Wit Tarnawski (London, 1957), pp. 25–29.

60. John Conrad, *Joseph Conrad: Times Remembered* (Cambridge, 1981), p. 164.

61. Conrad to Curle, 9 October 1920.

62. *Notes on Life and Letters*, p. vi.

63. Conrad to Gide, 1 November [19]20, Jean-Aubry, *Lettres françaises*, pp. 151–152 (erroneously dated 1 February); to Capes, 17 November 1920, Yale.

64. Conrad to Jean-Aubry, 8 November 1920, Jean-Aubry, *Lettres françaises*, p. 160; to Garnett, 16 December 1920, E. Garnett, *Letters*, p. 299.

65. Conrad to Curle, 22 November 1920.

66. Conrad to Jean-Aubry, 10 December 1920, Jean-Aubry, *Lettres françaises*, p. 162. The article was published in *Fortnightly Review*, May 1921.

67. Conrad to Wise, 3 and 6 January 1921, BL. In the first letter Conrad informed Wise that he had finished the adaptation, "calculated to play in about 50 minutes," on 16 December "with a view to the *Little Theatre*." The discrepancy between this letter and Conrad's letter to Jean-Aubry of 10 December results from the fact that from his manuscript first draft Conrad dictated a revised and expanded text for typing.

68. Karol Szymanowski, *Z listów* [From the letters], ed. T. Bronowicz-Chylińska (Cracow, 1958), pp. 198–199.

69. Conrad to Garnett, 16 December 1920; to Rothenstein, 17 December 1920, *LL*, 2:251; to Galsworthy, 17 January 1921, Birmingham.

70. Conrad to Walpole, 26 December 1920, Texas (fragment deleted in *LL*, 2:252); to Curle, 22 January 1921, Curle, *Conrad to a Friend*, p. 122.

71. B. Conrad, *My Father*, pp. 154–156; Conrad to J. Pinker, 20 January 1921, Berg. That Conrad was aware of his son's illness is shown in his letter to Doubleday, 7 February 1924, *LL*, 2:339.

72. Conrad to Rothenstein, 17 December 1920, *LL*, 2:251.

73. Conrad to J. Pinker, letter dated "23.1.21 Sat. morg.," [22 January 1921].

74. B. Conrad, *My Father*, pp. 157–158; *JCC*, pp. 221–236. There are also several errors in Jessie's chronology of events.

75. Jean-Aubry to Valery Larbaud, 8 September 1920. *Valery Larbaud, G. Jean-Aubry: Correspondance 1920–1935*, ed. Frida Weissman (Paris, 1971), p. 12. See also *JCC*, p. 214.

76. Conrad to Jean-Aubry, 21 March 1920, Jean-Aubry, *Lettres françaises*, p. 153.

77. Conrad to Jean-Aubry, 23 February 1921, ibid. p. 164; to J. Pinker, 30 January 1921, *LL*, 2:254.

78. Conrad to Eric Pinker, 5 February 1921, *LL*, 2:254–255; to Jean-Aubry, 23 February 1921.

79. Conrad to K. Zagórska, 6 March 1921, *CPB*, p. 266; compare to Garnett, 18 March 1921, E. Garnett, *Letters*, pp. 306–307.

80. *JCC*, pp. 227–228.

81. John Conrad, *Joseph Conrad: Times Remembered*, p. 152.

82. Conrad to Gardiner, 8 October 1923, Harvard.

83. H.-R. Lenormand, "Note sur un séjour de Conrad en Corse," *Nouvelle Revue Française*, 12 (1924):666–671.

84. Conrad to J. Pinker, Monday, [4 April 1921], Berg; see also to Gide, 5 August 1921, Jean-Aubry, *Lettres françaises*, p. 166.

85. Conrad to J. Pinker, [4 April 1921]; to Garnett, Monday, [11 April 1921], E. Garnett, *Letters*, p. 307. Contrary to Jessie's claim (*JCC*, pp. 235–236), the strike did not occur.

86. St.-John Perse to Conrad, 26 February 1921, St.-John Perse, *Oeuvres complètes* (Paris, 1972), p. 889.

87. Published anonymously in *Nation and Athenaeum*, 19 (March 1921):881–882; reprinted as "Joseph Conrad: A Note" in *Abinger Harvest*, 1936.

88. G. S., "Conrad the Statesman," *Bookman* (London), 60 (April 1921):33–34.

89. B. Conrad, *My Father*, p. 158; Conrad to E. Pinker, 5 February 1921, Berg; *JCC*, p. 230.

90. Jessie to E. Pinker, 25 March 1924, Berg; Conrad to T. Marynowski, 8 September 1921, *CPB*, pp. 271–272.

91. Conrad to J. Pinker, 18 April 1921, Berg.

92. Conrad to J. Pinker, 24 May 1921; Foreword to "Corsican and Irish Landscapes [of Alice S. Kinkead]," in the catalogue published by The United Arts Gallery, London, in November 1921, reprinted in Conrad, *CDAUP*, pp. 96–97.

93. Conrad to the Galsworthys, 10 May 1921, *LL*, 2:256.

94. John Conrad, *Joseph Conrad: Times Remembered*, p. 165.

95. Conrad to the Galsworthys, 10 May 1921, ibid., p. 257; to J. Pinker, 10 and 12 May 1921, Berg.

96. Conrad to Galsworthy, 8 June 1921, *LL*, 2:259.

97. Conrad to Bruno Winawer, 12 June 1921, *CPB*, p. 267; to Wise, 21 June 1921, BL. On 1 July Conrad sent Wise both the MS and the typescript of the translation, for which he received £100; to Wise, 1 July 1921, BL. The MS is dated 25 June 1921 (BL).

98. Conrad to J. Pinker 27 [June] 1921, *LL*, 2:260; to Winawer, 10 August 1921, *CPB*, pp. 268–270.

99. Conrad to Allan Wade, 9 April 1922, *LL*, 2:270–271.

100. See Róża Jabłkowska, *Joseph Conrad* (Wrocław, 1961), pp. 350–351.

101. Conrad to J. Pinker, 6 September 1921, Berg; to Winawer, 20 September 1921, *CPB*, p. 272.

102. Conrad to A. Zagórska, 21 August 1921, *CPB*, p. 271.

103. The MS is also dated 27 July (BL); the article was later included in *Last Essays*.

104. Conrad to Curle, 31 August 1921, Curle, *Conrad to a Friend*, p. 127; to J. Pinker, 30 September 1921, Berg; MS of *Suspense*, BL.

105. Conrad to J. Pinker, 4 October 1921, Berg. By the end of October Conrad wanted to have three hundred pages of the manuscript of *Suspense* written (to J. Pinker, 30 September 1921).

106. Date on the MS of *The Rover*, Yale.

107. Conrad to J. Pinker, 9 and 19 December 1921, Berg. Conrad had difficulty finding a title for this strangely composed volume (to J. Pinker, 6 February 1921, Berg).

108. Wise paid £100 for the MS of *The Rover* (Conrad to Wise, 18 November 1921, BL). See also to Rothenstein, 17 December 1921, Harvard, about the project of a luxury edition of *The Mirror of the Sea*, illustrated with photographs.

109. Mrs. [Kate] Meyrick, *Secrets of the 43* (London, 1933), pp. 41–42.

110. Conrad to Curle, 10 November 1921, Curle, *Conrad to a Friend*, p. 133.

111. Conrad to Bertrand Russell, 18 November 1921, Bertrand Russell Archives, McMaster University, Hamilton, Ontario.

112. Conrad to Cunninghame Graham, 6 December 1921, Cedric T. Watts, ed., *Joseph Conrad's Letters to R. B. Cunninghame Grahame* (Cambridge, 1969), p. 191.

113. Conrad to Ford Madox Ford, 6 and 15 December 1921, Yale.

114. Conrad to Elsie Hueffer, 29 November 1920, Yale.

115. Conrad to A. Zagórska, 27 January 1922, *CPB*, p. 277.

116. See Slater and Roth, *Clinical Psychiatry*, p. 207.

117. Conrad to A. Zagórska, 27 January 1922.

118. Conrad to E. Pinker, 10 February 1922, *LL*, 2:265; Hart-Davis, *Hugh Walpole*, p. 219.

119. Conrad to K. Zagórska, 22 February 1922, *CPB*, p. 279.

120. Conrad to Curle, 22 March 1922, Curle, *Conrad to a Friend*, p. 139.

121. Conrad to A. Zagórska, 19 April 1922, *CPB*, p. 280.

122. Conrad to E. Pinker, 23 March 1922, Berg; see also to Curle, 22 March 1922.

123. Conrad to Curle, Monday 6 p.m., [20 March 1922], Curle, *Conrad to a Friend*, p. 138; to E. Pinker, 8, 10, and 24 April 1922, Berg.

124. Conrad to Galsworthy, 8 June 1921, *LL*, 2:257–258; to Wade, 4 and 9 April 1922, ibid., pp. 267–270.

125. Conrad to Garnett, 2 September 1921, E. Garnett, *Letters*, p. 309.

126. Conrad to A. Zagórska, 14 December 1921, *CPB*, p. 277. He used similar words in a letter to Winawer, 12 April 1922, *CPB*, p. 280.

127. Conrad to A. Zagórska, 24 November 1922, *CPB*, p. 284. Sale catalogues of Conrad's library (Heffer's No. 251 of 1925 and No. 267 of 1926, Hodgson's of 13 March 1925) list several

books in Polish and about Poland. Some of them Conrad received from their authors, others he evidently bought, as, for example, George Brandes's *Poland* (London, 1903).

128. Desmond MacCarthy, *Portraits* (London, 1931), pp. 68–69.

129. John Conrad, *Joseph Conrad: Times Remembered*, pp. 151, 185–186.

130. Conrad to Curle, [5] and 24 April and 2 May 1922, Curle, *Conrad to a Friend*, pp. 140–145, 148. Curle deleted the fragment about "tragedian"; original letter in Indiana. Compare Conrad to Graham, 31 January 1898, Watts, *Letters*, pp. 70–71.

131. Conrad to Garnett, 24 May 1922, E. Garnett, *Letters*, p. 313; to Curle, 29 June 1922, Curle, *Conrad to a Friend*, p. 151. Conrad apologizes here for his silence, but his avowals of inability to speak and write are exaggerated: he had played host to Jean-Aubry within the last few days (17–20 June) and had written other letters. However, when trying to evoke sympathy, Conrad—not surprisingly—tended to exaggerate, as we see in other letters; see, for example, to Jean-Aubry, 27 May 1922, Jean-Aubry, *Lettres françaises*, p. 170.

132. Conrad to Garnett, 21 November 1923, E. Garnett, *Letters*, p. 328.

133. Conrad to E. Pinker, 27 June and 20 July 1922, Berg. The MS is dated 16 July 1922 (Yale). Writing to Wise on 20 July he offered the draft of *The Rover* for £150 (BL).

134. Conrad to Galsworthy, 7 August 1922, *LL*, 2:274.

135. Conrad to Graham, 7 July 1922, Watts, *Letters*, pp. 193–194.

136. Conrad to Jean-Aubry, 9 August 1922, Jean-Aubry, *Lettres françaises*, pp. 171–172; Conrad to Borys, 16 August 1922, Yale.

137. Conrad to E. Pinker, 10 August 1922, Berg. Compare Jessie Conrad to F. W. Dawson, 18 May 1926, Duke.

138. Conrad to Curle, 24 July 1922 and 2 January 1923, Curle, *Conrad to a Friend*, pp. 154, 171; B. Conrad, *My Father*, p. 162.

139. The original of Conrad's will is preserved in Somerset House, London; Hans van Marle kindly gave me a copy.

140. Conrad to Curle, Tuesday, [6 or 13 January 1920], and 24 July 1922, Curle, *Conrad to a Friend*, pp. 87–89 and 153.

141. Conrad to Doubleday, 3 August 1922, Princeton; to E. Pinker, 12 August 1922, Berg.

142. Conrad to Doubleday, 3 August 1922; to Curle, 23 August 1922, Curle, *Conrad to a Friend*, p. 154.

143. Conrad to Galsworthy, 7 August 1922.

144. Conrad to Jean-Aubry, 22 September 1922, Jean-Aubry, *Lettres françaises*, p. 173.

145. *JCC*, p. 239; Conrad to Curle, 18 September 1922, Curle, *Conrad to a Friend*, p. 155.

146. Conrad to Curle, 1 October 1922, Curle, *Conrad to a Friend*, p. 157.

147. Conrad to E. Pinker, 8 October 1922, *LL*, 2:276–277, and 12 October 1922, Berg.

148. Conrad to Curle, [October 1922], Curle, *Letters to a Friend*, p. 160; to J. Harry Benrimo, 21 October 1922, Yale, and 27 October 1922, *LL*, 2:277–278, but compare to Garnett, Tuesday, [31 October 1922], E. Garnett, *Letters*, p. 317; to Jean-Aubry, 27 October 1922, Jean-Aubry, *Lettres françaises*, pp. 178–179.

149. Conrad to Wade, 30 October 1922, Brotherton Library, Leeds; to Garnett, Tuesday, [31 October 1922].

150. Rodolphe Louis Mégroz, *A Talk with Joseph Conrad* (London, 1926), p. 31; Conrad to E. Pinker, 11 November 1922, Berg; to Galsworthy, Tuesday, [14] November 1922, *LL*, 2:282.

151. Conrad to H. A. Jones, 7 November 1922, *LL*, 2:279. Similar statements appear in all Conrad's letters of that period.

152. *The Evening Standard*, 8 November 1922, p. 9.

153. Conrad to Gardiner, n.d., Harvard; to Winawer, 23 November 1922, *CPB*, p. 283. Indeed, on 17 January 1921 Conrad had written to Christopher Sandeman, "I foresee for it a 'frost' modified—or tempered—by a certain amount of curiosity on the part of a small section of the public; with the conclusion on the part of the critics that 'Conrad can't write a play'" (*LL*, 2:253).

154. Conrad to Pinker, 11 November 1922.

155. Conrad to Russell, 23 October 1922, Bertrand Russell Archives.

156. Conrad to E. L. Adams, 20 November 1922, *LL*, 2:285.

157. Conrad to Sandeman, 21 November 1922, *LL*, 2:285–287; to Doubleday, 15 December 1922, Princeton.

158. Conrad to E. Pinker, 14 December 1922, Berg (*The Suspense*); to Doubleday, 15 December 1922.

159. Walter Tittle, "Portraits in Pencil and Pen. III. Joseph Conrad," *The Strand Magazine*, June 1924, p. 546. The visit took place on 12 November; see Conrad to E. Pinker, 11 November 1922.

160. Conrad to Sandeman, 21 November 1922.

161. Conrad to C. K. Scott Moncrieff, 17 December 1922, *LL*, 2:291–292. "Proust as Creator" was published in *Marcel Proust: An English Tribute*, ed. C. K. Scott Moncrieff (London, 1923), pp. 126–128; reprinted in Conrad, *CDAUP*, pp. 105–106. See also Conrad to J. C. Squire, 30 November 1922, Indiana. Jean-Aubry, "Souvenirs," *Nouvelle Revue Française*, 12 (1924):679. See, for example, Conrad to Gide, 5 August 1921, Jean-Aubry, *Lettres françaises*, p. 165; to Jean-Aubry, 20 December 1922, ibid., p. 180; Jean-Aubry, "Des heures anglaises," *Cahiers du Sud*, 1946, p. 135.

162. Jean-Aubry, "Des heures anglaises"; Conrad to Gide, 28 December 1922, Bibliothèque Doucet, Paris; to E. Pinker, 9 April 1923, Berg. P. Valéry, "Sujet d'une conversation avec Conrad," *Nouvelle Revue Française*, 12 (1924):663–665.

163. Conrad to Curle, 2 January 1923, Curle, *Conrad to a Friend*, p. 171.

164. See Conrad to E. Pinker, 30 December 1922, Berg. Jean-Aubry writes about the efforts of Conrad's French and Swedish friends to secure the Nobel prize for him in *Lettres françaises*, p. 193.

165. Conrad to George T. Keating, 14 December 1922, *LL*, 2:289; original in Mr. Keating's possession.

166. Conrad to Charles Chassé, 31 January 1924, ibid., p. 336.

167. Conrad to A. Zagórska, 7 March and 11 April 1923, *CPB*, pp. 288–289 and 291.

168. S. Żeromski, preface to the selected edition of Conrad's works in Polish, in: J. Conrad Korzeniowski, *Fantazja Almayera* (Warsaw, [1922]), pp. vii–xix. Suggesting that the musical rhythms of Conrad's prose are non-English in origin, Żeromski refers to Curle's *Joseph Conrad: A Study* (London, 1914).

169. Conrad to Żeromski, 25 March 1923, *CPB*, p. 289.

170. Conrad to A. Zagórska, 10 April 1920, 21 August 1921, 30 December 1922, *CPB*, pp. 261–262, 271, 285.

171. See Wacław Borowy, *Studia i rozprawy* (Wrocław, 1952), 2:61–72.

172. Conrad to Curle, 8 December 1922, Curle, *Conrad to a Friend*, pp. 167–169. On 6 January 1923 Conrad wrote to Curle: "The hard times are beginning with a vengeance" (p. 172).

173. Conrad to K. Zagórska, [March 1923], *Twórczość*, no. 8 (1969), p. 106. The date of Conrad's meeting with Doubleday from Conrad's letter to Curle of Tuesday, [5 December 1922], Curle, *Conrad to a Friend*, p. 166.

174. Conrad to Doubleday, 8 December 1922, Princeton.

175. Conrad to Curle, 6 January 1923; to Adams, 22 January 1923, *LL*, 2:294; to A. Zagórska, 12 February 1923, *CPB*, p. 288.

176. Conrad to Curle, Friday, [2 February 1923], Curle, *Conrad to a Friend*, p. 173.

177. Conrad to Pinker, [2]3 March 1923, Berg.

178. Conrad to Doubleday, 13 March 1923, *LL*, 2:297.

179. The preface to Beer's book was written between 12 and 23 March 1923; Conrad to Curle, 12 March and 23 March 1923, Curle, *Conrad to a Friend*, pp. 174–176 (the second letter is wrongly dated by Curle as 22 March, original at Indiana). Conrad's preface to *The Red Badge of Courage*, titled "His War Book," is dated by Wise, who bought the MS from Conrad, 29 March 1923 (Gordon Lindstrand, "Literary Manuscripts of Joseph Conrad," *Conradiana* 2, no. 2 (1969–1970), p.107).

180. Conrad to E. Pinker, 22 and 23 March 1923, Berg.

181. Conrad to Garnett, 10 March 1923, E. Garnett, *Letters*, p. 322.

182. Conrad to E. Pinker, 9 April 1923, *LL*, 2:302; see A. T. Schwab, "Conrad's American Speeches and His Reading from *Victory*," *Modern Philology* 62 (1965):342–347.

183. Conrad to Doubleday, 9 April 1923, Princeton; the text of the speech is published in Conrad, *CDAUP*, pp. 110–112.

184. Conrad to E. Pinker, 9 April 1923; see also to Doubleday, 13 March 1923, Curle, *The Last Twelve Years of Joseph Conrad* (London, 1928), pp. 179–180.

185. To R. Jones, 19 April 1923, *LL*, 2:305; to Jessie 20–30 April 1923, ibid., pp. 305–306; to Curle, 29 April 1923, Curle, *Conrad to a Friend*, p. 180. "My Hotel in Mid-Atlantic," renamed "Ocean Travel," is included in *Last Essays*, pp. 35–38. Conrad did not miss this chance of embellishing his seafaring past, either. He says that during his sea years "it never occurred" to him that he "might be a passenger some day"; but he had been one even then, and more than once.

186. Conrad to Jessie Conrad, 4 May 1923, *LL*, 2:307–308.

187. William V. Constanzo, "Conrad's American Visit," *Conradiana* 13, no. 1 (1981): 13–14.

188. Arthur Mizener, *The Far Side of Paradise: A Biography of F. Scott Fitzgerald* (New York, 1959), pp. 173–174.

189. Schwab, "American Speeches," p. 342. Conrad's notes are confused and lack a central focus (Indiana).

190. Jean-Aubry, "Stosunek Conrada do muzyki" [Conrad's attitude to music], *Muzyka*, no. 5 (1926), p. 207. The date of the lunch is recorded in Conrad's diary of his stay in the U.S., kept by a secretary of Doubleday's, in possession of Philip Conrad.

191. Ford Madox Ford, *It Was the Nightingale* (Philadelphia, 1933), p. 309.

192. See Randall, "Conrad Interviews," *Conradiana*, 2, nos. 2 and 3 (1969–1970): 86–89, 122.

193. Eleanor Palffy, "Drunk on Conrad," *Fortnightly Review*, October 1929, pp. 534–538.

194. Conrad to Jessie Conrad, 11 May 1923, *LL*, 2:309–310.

195. Conrad to Borys Conrad, 6 May 1923, Jocelyn Baines, *Joseph Conrad: A Critical Biography* (London, 1960), p. 430; see also to Curle, 11 May 1923, Curle, *Conrad to a Friend*, p. 182, and to Jessie Conrad, 14 May 1923, *LL*, 2:311. W. L. Phelps, *Autobiography* (New York, 1939), pp. 753–754; Randall, "Conrad Interviews," no. 1, pp. 75–80.

196. Conrad to Jessie Conrad, 18 and 24 May 1923, *LL*, 2:312–314.

197. Conrad to Adams, 31 May 1923, ibid., 315.

198. Conrad to Jessie Conrad, 24 May 1923; see also Conrad's cable to Jessie, 25 May 1923, Princeton.

199. Conrad to Curle, 18 May 1923, Curle, *Conrad to a Friend*, p. 184.

200. Conrad to Winawer, 9 September 1923, *CPB*, pp. 292–293.

201. Conrad to E. Pinker, 11 June 1923, Berg.

202. For example, to Doubleday, 10 July 1923, Princeton.

203. The date of the marriage was established by Hans van Marle; B. Conrad, *My Father*, p. 162.

204. Jessie's attitude toward her daughter-in-law was decidedly hostile; see her letter to F. W. Dawson, 18 May 1926, Duke.

205. *JCC*, pp. 242 and 253–254; B. Conrad, *My Father*, p. 163. Jessie maintains that she only forbade Borys to disclose his marriage before Conrad's return from America (*JCC*, p. 245); this, however, does not explain Borys's absence, because he had been a frequent visitor at Oswalds (last time on 8 April, Conrad to Curle, 10 April 1923, Curle, *Conrad to a Friend*, p. 177).

206. *JCC*, pp. 242–243. When we remember what Conrad wrote to Pinker about Jane Anderson and Borys it is impossible to question his understanding of his son's "natural inclinations"; for her part, Jessie wrote with such scorn about the courtship between her nurse and their chauffeur (*JCC*, p. 249) that we may doubt her own reliability on such matters.

207. B. Conrad, *My Father*, p. 163; compare *JCC*, p. 245.

208. *JCC*, pp. 255–258.

209. Conrad to E. Pinker, 11 and 14 June 1923, Berg. This contradicts Jessie's account, compare *JCC*, p. 260.

210. Conrad to E. Pinker, 21 June 1923, Berg.

211. Conrad to Pinker, 27 June 1923, Berg; to Colvin, n.d. [4 July? 1923], Keating, *A Conrad Memorial Library: The Collection of G. T. Keating* (Garden City, N.Y., 1929), pp. 360–361.

212. Jessie Conrad to E. Pinker, 24 June 1923, Berg.

213. Hart-Davis, *Hugh Walpole*, p. 215.

214. Conrad was undoubtedly aware of his wife's intellectual limitations, but he was extremely discreet on this subject. The only signals, gently veiled, I find in his letters to Garnett—who, it is important to remember, had warned him against his marriage. In February 1897 Conrad joked patronizingly about Jessie's futile attempts to understand James's *Spoils of Poynton*; twenty-four

years later he wrote that Jessie possessed "an admiring understanding of [Garnett's] personality reached by God knows what mysterious intuitive process" (13 February [1897], [11 April 1921], E. Garnett, *Letters*, pp. 74–75, 308).

215. Reminiscences of Mr. Charles Harding, as reported by Hans van Marle.

216. From Sir Christopher Cockerell's letter to Hans van Marle.

217. Conrad to E. Pinker, 2 July 1923, Berg; to Pinker, 9 July 1923, Berg.

218. MS is dated 29 August 1923 (Yale); the date is confirmed by Conrad to Curle, 1 September 1923, Curle, *Conrad to a Friend*, p. 203.

219. Conrad to Curle, 14 and 17 July 1923, ibid., pp. 188–189, 191, 196. Curle's article appeared anonymously in the *Times Literary Supplement*, 30 August 1923, as "The History of Mr Conrad's Books."

220. See two lists of frontispieces drawn up by Conrad for Doubleday, dated 20 and 27 August 1923, Princeton.

221. Conrad to E. Pinker, 18 July 1923, Berg.

222. B. Conrad, *My Father*, pp. 163–164; *JCC*, pp. 260–261; Conrad to Miss Lorna Watson and to Doubleday, 15 July 1923, *LL*, 2:318–320.

223. Conrad to Jean-Aubry, 5 August 1923, Jean-Aubry, *Lettres françaises*, p. 186; to Curle, 30 July 1923, Curle, *Conrad to a Friend*, p. 199; to Doubleday, 13 August 1923, Princeton.

224. Conrad to Doubleday, 4 October 1923, Princeton. The trip to Le Havre took place 10–16 September (Conrad to Curle, 1 September 1923 and 20 September 1923, Curle, *Conrad to a Friend*, p. 206).

225. Conrad to Gide, 16 October 1923, Jean-Aubry, *Lettres françaises*, p. 191; John Conrad, *Joseph Conrad: Times Remembered*, p. 208.

226. Conrad to E. Pinker, 20 September 1923, Berg.

227. Conrad to Galsworthy, 23 September 1923, Birmingham.

228. Conrad to Gide, 16 October 1923; to Curle, 12 November 1923, Curle, *Conrad to a Friend*, pp. 218–219. Conrad began writing the essay about 1 November and completed it on 12 November; to Curle, 2 November 1923, ibid., p. 213, and 12 November 1923.

229. Conrad to Ford, 23 October 1923, *LL*, 2:323, and 10 November 1923, Yale. See also Baines, *Joseph Conrad*, p. 432 and Mizener, *The Saddest Story: A Biography of Ford Madox Ford* (New York, 1971), pp. 329, 332.

230. I owe this information to Wiktoria Karnicka, Malinowski's friend. In 1913 Malinowski offered Conrad a copy of his *The Family among the Australian Aborigines* with a dedication in Polish (Heffer, Catalogue No. 251, Cambridge, 1925).

231. Ottoline Morrell, *Memoirs: A Study in Friendship*, ed. R. Gathorne-Hardy (New York, 1964), pp. 236–238.

232. Hart-Davis, *Hugh Walpole*, p. 236. Compare Conrad to Grace Willard, 25 October 1923, NYPL.

233. Cyril Clemens, "A Chat with Joseph Conrad," *Conradiana* 2, no. 2 (1969–1970): 98.

234. Conrad to Curle, 5 November 1923, Curle, *Conrad to a Friend*, p. 215; to E. Pinker, 26 November 1923, Berg; to Doubleday, 7 January 1924, *LL*, 2:331.

235. Conrad to Arnold Bennett, 20 December 1923, ibid., p. 330.

236. Conrad to E. Pinker, 8 November 1923, Berg ("pronounced flabbiness of heart"); to Curle, 12 November 1923 ("flabby heart, fluttering and missing about every fourth beat").

237. Conrad to E. Pinker, 27 January 1924, Berg; to Keating, 18 January 1924, Yale. Conrad's inscriptions are reproduced in Keating, *Conrad Memorial Library*.

238. Conrad to Walpole, 18 and 19 November 1923, Texas.

239. "Conrad Manuscripts: Notes on Sales," *Times Literary Supplement*, 22 September 1923. See also Baines, *Joseph Conrad*, p. 433.

240. Conrad to Doubleday, 20 November 1923, *LL*, 2:324; to Garnett, 21 November 1923, E. Garnett, *Letters*, p. 328.

241. Philip Unwin, *The Publishing Unwins* (London, 1972), p. 47.

242. Conrad to Sandeman, 21 November 1922; to Garnett, 4 December 1923, E. Garnett, *Letters*, pp. 330–333.

243. *New York Times Book Review*, 2 December 1923; *New Statesman*, 15 December 1923. See Sherry, *Conrad*, pp. 36, 349–362. There were exceptions: T. E. Lawrence wrote to Sydney Cockerell on 13 January 1923 that *The Rover* is "a very good book" (T. E. Lawrence, *Letters*, ed. David Garnett [London, 1938], p. 450).

244. Conrad to Bennett, 2 January 1924, *LL*, 2:331.

245. Quoted from Tittle's unpublished diary, Richard P. Valer, "Walter Tittle and Joseph Conrad," *Conradiana* 12, no. 2 (1980): 98.

246. Conrad to the Doubledays, 7 January 1924, *LL*, 2:332; to Doubleday, 28 January 1924, Princeton; B. Conrad, *My Father*, pp. 164–165.

247. Ibid., p. 163; *JCC*, pp. 264–265.

248. Conrad to Curle, 16 January 1924, Curle, *Conrad to a Friend*, p. 229; to Jean-Aubry, 3 February 1924, Jean-Aubry, *Lettres françaises*, p. 195.

249. Conrad to Doubleday, 7 February 1924, *LL*, 2:339.

250. Conrad to Curle, 27 December 1923, Curle, *Conrad to a Friend*, pp. 224–225.

251. Conrad to Galsworthy, 22 February 1924, *LL*, 2:340.

252. Conrad to Keating, 28 January 1924, Yale; to Adams, 26 March 1924, *LL*, 2:341; to E. Pinker, 8 April 1924, Berg.

253. Conrad to Curle, 1 February 1924, Curle, *Conrad to a Friend*, p. 230; to E. Pinker, 3 February 1924, Berg.

254. Conrad to Galsworthy, 22 February 1924.

255. Jessie Conrad to E. Pinker, 24 February 1924, Berg; Conrad to Doubleday, 27 March 1924, Princeton.

256. Jacob Epstein, *An Autobiography* (London, 1955), p. 74.

257. Conrad to Doubleday, 27 March 1924.

258. Conrad sent the preface on 30 April (to Doubleday 8 May 1924, Princeton). About the composition of the volume see Conrad to Doubleday, 7 February 1924, and to E. Pinker 12 February 1924, Princeton. See also Donald W. Rude, "Conrad as Editor: The Preparation of *The Shorter Tales*," in *Joseph Conrad: Theory and World Fiction* (Lubbock, Texas, 1974), pp. 189–196.

259. Jessie Conrad wrote to E. Pinker on 24 February 1924, "I am looking forward to your eloquence when you voice your opinion of F. M. H. I don't think J. C. knows the depths of his base mind yet. And as Karola [Zagórska] would say he has a base *exterior*."

260. Conrad to E. Pinker, 3 February 1924, Berg (fragment deleted from *LL*, 2:337); Pinker's telegram to Conrad announcing Ford's visit, 4 February 1924, Yale; Mizener, *Saddest Story*, p. 336.

261. Conrad to E. Pinker, 4 and 7 February 1924, Berg; see Baines, *Joseph Conrad*, p. 432, and Mizener, *Saddest Story*, p. 336.

262. Jessie Conrad to E. Pinker, 30 April 1924, Berg; Conrad to E. Pinker, 1 May 1924, Berg.

263. Conrad to Ford, 2 May 1924, Yale.

264. Conrad finished the preface on 14 May (date on MS, Yale) and sent it to Ford with the letter of 17 May 1924, Yale.

265. Conrad to E. Pinker, 20 July 1924, *LL*, 2:347.

266. Conrad to A. Zagórska, 28 April 1924, *CPB*, p. 298; Jessie Conrad to E. Pinker, 4 May 1924, Berg.

267. Conrad to Doubleday, 8 May 1924, Princeton.

268. Conrad to Gide, 30 May 1924, Jean-Aubry, *Lettres françaises*, p. 200.

269. Conrad to R. J. MacDonald, 27 May 1924, Berg.

270. Conrad letter to the Vice-Chancellor of Cambridge University, 15 March 1923, Fitzwilliam Museum, Cambridge; Conrad to Doubleday, 13 March 1923; to E. Pinker, 22 March 1923, Berg.

271. Barbara Kocówna, "Żywa tradycja Conradowska" [Conrad's living tradition], *Przegląd Humanistyczny* 5, no. 1 (1961): 177–178; Irena Rakowska-Łuniewska, "U Konrada Korzeniowskiego" [At the home of Konrad Korzeniowski], *Pion*, no. 50 (1934).

272. *JCC*, p. 271; Mégroz, *A Talk with Joseph Conrad*, pp. 63–64; Curle, *Last Twelve Years*, p. 184.

273. The lunch took place on 11 June, Conrad to Curle, [10 June 1924], Curle, *Conrad to a Friend*, p. 238. Alma Tadema, Jean-Aubry, and Edward Raczyński, among others, were present. Conrad consented only to have his name listed as one of the initiators of the restitution of the Association (which was never realized). Roman Dyboski, "Spotkanie z Conradem" [My encounter with Conrad], *Czas*, no. 71 (1932); Edward Raczyński, "Spotkanie w poselstwie w Londynie" [A meeting at the Polish legation], *Wiadomości* (London), nos. 33–34 (1949).

274. Stefan Pomarański to Conrad, 22 June 1924, Yale; Conrad to Pomarański, 28 June 1924, *CPB*, p. 299.

275. Conrad to E. Pinker, 6 and 15 June 1924, Berg; to R. Jones, 10 July 1924, *LL*, 2:346; to Jean-Aubry 22 July 1924, Jean-Aubry, *Lettres françaises*, p. 203.

276. Most of these letters have been included in Conrad's *Letters to His Wife*; a few, undated and unpublished, are in the Sterling Library, Senate House, London University.

277. Conrad to Curle, 2 July 1924, Curle, *Conrad to a Friend*, p. 239; to E. Dawson, Thursday 4[=3] July 1924, Yale.

278. Conrad to Curle, 8 and 22 July 1924, Curle, *Conrad to a Friend*, pp. 240–241; *JCC*, p. 274; Conrad to Jean-Aubry, 22 July 1924.

279. Curle, *Last Twelve Years*, pp. 219–239; JCC, pp. 274–276. The cause of death was apparently a heart attack. Conrad's health had undoubtedly been undermined by his neglected teeth (see JCC, p. 275).

280. Baines, *Joseph Conrad*, p. 436. At the time of his death the value of Conrad's estate was £20,045, *The Times*, 17 November 1924.

281. E. Garnett, ed., *Letters from J. Galsworthy*, Introduction, pp. 14–15. Herbert F. West, who described the funeral in "Joseph Conrad's Funeral," in the *Saturday Review of Literature* (6 September 1924), wrote that the procession filing out after the mass, was "singularly small" and that only half a dozen cars and three or four persons walking accompanied the hearse to the cemetery. The photographs taken at the cemetery (Duke) show not more than fifty people present.

282. In JCC, p. 7, Jessie gives Conrad's names as "Joséf Teador Konrad Korzeniowski." Teador is, of course, a misspelling of Teodor (Theodore in English).

283. Virginia Woolf, *Collected Essays* (London, 1968), 1:302. Written in August 1924.

284. R. B. Cunninghame Graham, "Inveni Portam: Joseph Conrad," *Saturday Review* (London), 16 August 1924, pp. 162–163. This essay has been reprinted as, alternately, "Inveni Portam" and "Inveni Portum"—the latter seems to be the correct version, because the text indicates that Graham had in mind *portus* ("port," "haven") and not *porta* ("gate"). Whether he intended to allude to the medieval adage "*Inveni portum: spes et fortuna valete*" is doubtful.

285. Edmund Spenser, *The Faerie Queene*, bk. 1, canto 9, stanza 40.

Bibliography

Allen, Jerry. *The Sea Years of Joseph Conrad*. New York, 1965.

Askenazy, Szymon. *Uwagi* [Remarks]. Geneva, 1916.

———. *Uwagi* [Remarks]. Warsaw, 1924.

Baines, Jocelyn. *Joseph Conrad: A Critical Biography*. London, 1960.

Bartlett, P. A. "Letters of Ford Madox Ford." *The Saturday Review of Literature*, no. 15 (1941).

Bennett, Arnold. *Journals*. Edited by Newman Flower. Vols. 1 and 2. London, 1932.

Berryman, John. *Stephen Crane*. New York, 1950.

Blackburn, William, ed. *Joseph Conrad: Letters to William Blackwood and David S. Meldrum*. Durham, N.C., 1958.

Blackmore, E. *The British Mercantile Marine: A Short Historical Review*. London, 1887.

Blüth, Rafał. "O tragicznej decyzji krakowskiej Konrada Korzeniowskiego" [On Konrad Korzeniowski's tragic decision in Cracow]. *Verbum*, no. 2 (1936).

———. "Dwie rodziny kresowe" [Two borderland families]. *Ateneum*, no. 1 (1939).

Bobrowski, Tadeusz. *Pamiętniki* [Memoirs]. Vols. 1 and 2. 2nd ed. Warsaw, 1979.

Bojarski, Edmund A. "Conrad at the Crossroads: From Navigator to Novelist with New Biographical Mysteries." *The Texas Quarterly*, Winter 1968.

Bojarski, E. E., and Stevens, H. R. "Joseph Conrad and the *Falconhurst*." *Journal of Modern Literature*, October 1970.

Bone, David. "Memories of Conrad." *The Saturday Review of Literature*, 7 November 1925.

Borowy, Wacław. "Conrad krytykiem polskiego przekładu swojej noweli 'Il Conde'" [Conrad as critic of a translation of his tale "Il Conde"]. *Studia i rozprawy*. Vol. 2. Wrocław, 1952.

Bowley, A. L. *Wages and Income in the United Kingdom since 1860*. Cambridge, 1937.

Brassey, Thomas. *British Seamen as Described in Recent Parliamentary and Official Documents*. London, 1877.

Braun, Andrzej. *Śladami Conrada* [In Conrad's footsteps]. Warsaw, 1972.

Brown, E. H. Phelps, and Browne, Margaret H. *A Century of Pay*. London, 1968.

Bullen, Frank T. *The Men of the Merchant Service*. London, 1900.

Busza, Andrzej. "Conrad's Polish Literary Background and Some Illustrations of the Influence of Polish Literature on His Work." *Antemurale* 10 (1966).

———. "Dwa nieznane listy Conrada" [Two unknown letters of Conrad]. *Wiadomości*, no. 31 (1973).

Buszczyński, Stefan. *Mało znany poeta* [Little-known poet]. Cracow, 1870.

Calder, K. J. *Britain and the Origins of the New Europe, 1914–1918*. Cambridge, 1976.

Chwalewik, Witold. "Józef Conrad w Kardyfie" [Joseph Conrad in Cardiff]. *Ruch Lite-racki,* no. 8 (1932).

———. "Conrad in the Light of a New Record." *Kwartalnik Neofilologiczny,* no. 1 (1971).

Clemens, Cyril. "A Chat with Joseph Conrad." *Conradiana* 2, no. 2 (1969–1970).

Clifford, Hugh. "Joseph Conrad: Some Scattered Memories." *The Bookman's Journal and Print Collector,* no. 10 (1924).

Conrad, Borys. *My Father: Joseph Conrad.* New York, 1970.

———. *Coach Tour of Joseph Conrad's Homes in Kent.* Joseph Conrad Society pamphlet, 1974.

Conrad, Jessie. *Joseph Conrad As I Knew Him.* London, 1926.

———. *Joseph Conrad and His Circle.* London, 1935.

Conrad, John. "Garść wspomnień o moim ojcu" [Some reminiscences of my father]. In *Conrad żywy,* edited by Wit Tarnawski. London, 1957.

———. *Joseph Conrad: Times Remembered.* Cambridge, 1981.

Conrad, Joseph. *Letters to His Wife.* Preface by Jessie Conrad Korzeniowska. London, 1927.

Cornewall-Jones, R. L. *The British Merchant Service.* London, 1898.

Coustillas, Pierre. "Conrad and Gissing." In *Studies in Joseph Conrad,* edited by Claude Thomas. Montpellier, 1975.

Curle, Richard. "Joseph Conrad." *Rhythm,* November 1912.

———. *Joseph Conrad: A Study.* London, 1914.

———. "The History of Mr. Conrad's Books." *Times Literary Supplement,* 30 August 1923.

———. *The Last Twelve Years of Joseph Conrad.* London, 1928.

———. *Caravansary and Conversation: Memories of Places and Persons.* London, 1937.

———, ed. *Notes by Joseph Conrad written in a set of his first editions in the possession of Richard Curle.* London, 1925.

———, ed. *Conrad to a Friend: 150 Selected Letters from Joseph Conrad to Richard Curle.* London, 1928.

Dąbrowski, Marian. "Rozmowa z J. Conradem" [A talk with J. Conrad]. *Tygodnik Ilustrowany,* no. 14 (1914). Reprinted in Maria Dąbrowska. *Szkice o Conradzie* [Essays on Conrad]. Warsaw, 1974.

Dalgarno, Emily K. "Conrad, Pinker and the Writing of *The Secret Agent.*" *Conradiana* 9, no. 1 (1977).

Danilewiczowa, Maria, ed. *Joseph Conrad: Listy do Johna Galsworthy'ego* [Letters to John Galsworthy]. London, 1957.

Davis, Harold E. "Conrad's Revision of *The Secret Agent:* A Study in Literary Impressionism." *Modern Language Quarterly,* September 1958.

Davray, Henry-Durand. "Joseph Conrad." *Mercure de France,* 1 October 1924.

Dawson, Ernest. "Some Recollections of Joseph Conrad." *The Fortnightly Review,* 1 August 1928.

De Ternant, Andrew. "An Unknown Episode of Conrad's Life." *New Statesman and Nation,* 28 July 1928.

Douglas, Norman. *Looking Back.* London, 1931.

Douglas, Robin. "My Boyhood with Conrad." *Cornhill Magazine*, no. 1 (1929).

Dubiecki, Marian. *Na Kresach i za kresami* [In borderland and beyond]. Kiev, 1914.

Dürr, Jan. "Józef Conrad na drodze do Polski" [Joseph Conrad on his way to Poland]. *Ruch Literacki*, no. 8 (1932).

Dyboski, Roman. "Spotkanie z Conradem" [My encounter with Conrad]. *Czas*, no. 71 (1932).

Edel, Leon. *Henry James: The Master, 1901–1916*. Philadelphia, 1972.

Ehrsam, Theodore G. *A Bibliography of Joseph Conrad*. Metuchen, N.J., 1969.

Epstein, Jacob. *An Autobiography*. London, 1955.

Evans, R. D. "Dramatization of Conrad's *Victory* and a New Letter." *Notes and Queries*, March 1961.

Farjeon, Eleanor. *Edward Thomas: The Last Four Years*. London, 1958.

Fitzgerald, G. "A Hundred Years of Rates." *The Nautical Magazine*, January 1932.

Flamant, M., and Singer-Kérel, J. *Modern Economic Crises*. London, 1968.

Fleishman, Avrom. *Conrad's Politics*. Baltimore, 1967.

Follett, Wilson. *Joseph Conrad: A Short Study of His Intellectual and Emotional Attitude Toward His Work and of the Chief Characteristics of His Novels*. Garden City, N.Y., 1915.

Ford, Ford Madox. "Joseph Conrad." *The English Review*, December 1911.

———. *The Simple Life Limited*. London, 1911.

———. *Thus to Revisit*. London, 1921.

———. *Joseph Conrad: A Personal Remembrance*. London, 1924.

———. *Return to Yesterday*. London, 1931.

———. *It Was the Nightingale*. Philadelphia, 1933.

Forster, Edward Morgan. *Abinger Harvest*. London, 1936.

Foulke, Robert D. "Life in the Dying World of Sail: 1870–1910." *The Journal of British Studies* 3, no. 1 (1963).

Galsworthy, John. "Joseph Conrad: A Disquisition." *Fortnightly Review*, 1 April 1908.

———. *Castles in Spain*. New York, 1927.

———. *Forsytes, Pendyces and Others*. London, 1935.

Garnett, David. *The Golden Echo*. London, 1953.

———. *The Flowers of the Forest*. London, 1955.

Garnett, Edward, ed. *Letters from Conrad: 1895 to 1924*. London, 1928.

———, ed. *Letters from John Galsworthy*. Saint Clair Shores, Minn., 1971.

Gee, John A., and Sturm, Paul J., eds. *Letters of Joseph Conrad to Marguerite Poradowska*. New Haven, Conn., 1940.

Gettman, Royal A., ed. *George Gissing and H. G. Wells: Their Friendship and Correspondence*. London, 1961.

Golejowski, Henryk. *Pamiętnik* [Memoirs]. Vols. 1 and 2. Cracow, 1971.

Gordan, John D. *Joseph Conrad: The Making of a Novelist*. Cambridge, Mass., 1940.

———. "The Ghost at Brede Place." *Bulletin of the New York Public Library*, no. 12 (1952).

Górski, Kazimierz. "Moje spotkanie z Josephem Conradem" [My meeting with Joseph Conrad]. *Przegląd Wołyński*, no. 3 (1932).

Got, Jerzy. *Teatr krakowski pod dyrekcją A. Skorupki i S. Koźmiana* [Cracow theater under the directorship of A. Skorupka and S. Koźmian]. Wrocław, 1962.

Guerard, Albert. *Conrad the Novelist*. Cambridge, Mass., 1959.

Guérin, Yves. "Huit lettres inédites de Joseph Conrad à Robert d'Humières." *Revue de Littérature Comparée*, no. 3 (1970).

Hart-Davis, Rupert. *Hugh Walpole*. London, 1952.

Hay, Eloise K. *The Political Novels of Joseph Conrad*. Chicago, 1963.

———. "*Lord Jim*: From Sketch to Novel." In J. Conrad, *Lord Jim*, edited by Thomas C. Moser. New York, 1968.

Hewitt, Douglas. *Conrad: A Reassessment*. Cambridge, 1952.

Higdon, D. L. "The Text and Context of Conrad's First Critical Essay." In *Joseph Conrad: Commemorative Essays*, edited by A. Gillon and L. Krzyżanowski. New York, 1975.

Higdon, D. L., and Eddleman, F. E. "Collected Edition Variants in Conrad's *Almayer's Folly*." *Conradiana* 9, no. 1 (1977).

Hind, C. Lewis. *Naphtali*. London, 1926.

Holloway, Mark. *Norman Douglas: A Biography*. London, 1976.

Homer, D. "Conrad: Two Biographical Episodes." *The Review of English Studies*, February 1967.

Hueffer, Ford Madox. *The Cinque Ports*. Edinburgh and London, 1900.

Huneker, James Gibbons. *Steeplejack*. New York, 1920.

Hynes, Samuel. *The Edwardian Turn of Mind*. Princeton, 1968.

Inglis, Brian. *Roger Casement*. London, 1973.

Iwański, August. *Pamiętniki* [Memoirs]. Warsaw, 1968.

Jabłkowska, Róża. *Joseph Conrad*. Wrocław, 1961.

Janta, Aleksander. "Pierwszy szkic *Lorda Jima* i listy Conrada w zbiorach amerykańskich" [The first draft of *Lord Jim* and Conrad's letters in American collections]. In *Conrad żywy*, edited by Wit Tarnawski. London, 1957.

———. "Skąd fatalne dziedzictwo Conrada?" [Whence Conrad's fated heritage?]. *Wiadomości*, no. 22 (1959).

———. "Conrad's 'Famous Cablegram' in Support of A Polish Loan." *The Polish Review*, no. 2 (1972).

Jean-Aubry, G. "Souvenirs." *Nouvelle Revue Française*, no. 12 (1924).

———. *Joseph Conrad au Congo*. Paris, 1925.

———. "Stosunek Conrada do muzyki" [Conrad's attitude to music]. *Muzyka*, no. 5 (1926).

———. *Joseph Conrad: Life and Letters*. Vols. 1 and 2. London, 1927.

———. "Des heures anglaises." *Cahiers du Sud* (1946).

———. *Vie de Conrad*. Paris, 1947.

———, ed. *Twenty Letters to Joseph Conrad*. London, 1926.

———, ed. *Two Letters from George Gissing to Joseph Conrad*. London, 1926.

———, ed. *Joseph Conrad: Lettres françaises*. Paris, 1929.

Jełowicki, Aleksander. *Moje Wspomnienia* [Reminiscences]. Warsaw, 1970.

Jepson, Edgar. *Memories of an Edwardian and Neo-Georgian*. London, 1937.

Jeż, Teodor Tomasz [Zygmunt Miłkowski]. *Od kolebki przez życie* [From cradle through life]. Vols. 1 and 2. Cracow, 1936.

Jones, Edith R. "Stephen Crane at Brede." *The Atlantic Monthly*, July 1954.

Karl, Frederick R. "The Significance of the Revisions in the Early Versions of *Nostromo*." *Modern Fiction Studies*, Summer 1959.

———. "Conrad—Galsworthy: A Record of Their Friendship in Letters." *Midway*, Autumn 1968.

———. *A Reader's Guide to Joseph Conrad*. New York, 1969.

———. "Conrad, Wells, and the Two Voices." *Proceedings of the Modern Language Association*, October 1973.

———. "Conrad and Pinker." In *Joseph Conrad: A Commemoration*, edited by Norman Sherry. London, 1976.

Keating, George T., ed. *A Conrad Memorial Library: The Collection of George T. Keating*. Garden City, N.Y., 1929.

Kępiński, Antoni. *Melancholia*. Warsaw, 1974.

Kieniewicz, Stefan. *Adam Sapieha*. Lwów, 1939.

———. *Powstanie Styczniowe* [The January insurrection]. Warsaw, 1972.

Kieniewicz, Stefan, Janczewski, Z., Majewski, K., Awejde, O., Daniłowski, W., eds. *Zeznania śledcze o powstaniu styczniowym* [Evidence given in inquiries concerning the January insurrection]. Wrocław, 1956.

Kirschner, Paul. *Conrad: The Psychologist as Artist*. Edinburgh, 1968.

Kliszczewski, Hubert S. "Conrad w moim domu rodzinnym" [Conrad in my family home]. *Wiadomości*, nos. 33 and 34 (1949).

Koc, Barbara [Barbara Kocówna]. *Conrad—opowieść biograficzna* [Conrad—a biographical tale]. Warsaw, 1977.

Kocówna, Barbara. "Dwa listy M. Poradowskiej do J. Korzeniowskiego" [Two letters of M. Poradowska to J. Korzeniowski]. *Kwartalnik Neofilologiczny*, no. 4 (1959).

———. "Żywa tradycja Conradowska" [Conrad's living tradition]. *Przegląd Humanistyczny*, no. 1 (1961).

———, ed. *Wspomnienia i studia o Conradzie* [Reminiscences and studies on Conrad]. Warsaw, 1963.

Korolenko, Vladimir. *Istoria moego sovremennika* [History of my contemporary]. Vol. 1. Warsaw, 1909.

Kosch, Teodor. "Memoriał Conrada (Korzeniowskiego) w sprawie polskiej w czasie wielkiej wojny" [Conrad's (Korzeniowski's) memorandum on the Polish question of the time of the Great War]. *Czas*, no. 89 (1934).

———. "Powrót Conrada do Anglii—ze wspomnień o Conradzie" [Conrad's return to England—from my reminiscences of Conrad]. *Tygodnik Powszechny*, no. 30 (1960).

Krzyżanowski, Julian. "O tragedii na Samburanie" [About the tragedy in Samburan]. *Pion*, no. 50 (1934).

Krzyżanowski, Ludwik. "Kiedy Conrad po raz pierwszy ujrzał morze i gdzie chodził do szkoły" [When Conrad saw the sea for the first time and which school he attended]. *Wiadomości Literackie*, no. 32 (1932).

———, ed. *Joseph Conrad: Centennial Essays*. New York, 1960.

Laski, Marghanita. "Domestic Life." In *Edwardian England 1901–1914*, edited by S. Nowell-Smith. London, 1964.

Lawrence, D. H. *Collected Letters*. Edited by H. T. Moore. Vol. 1. New York, 1962.

Lawrence, T. E. *Letters*. Edited by David Garnett. London, 1938.

Lenormand, Henri-René. "Note sur un séjour de Conrad en Corse." *Nouvelle Revue Française*, no. 12 (1924).

Leśnodorski, Bogusław. "List Conrada w sprawie Polski z roku 1916" [Conrad's letter of 1916 about Poland]. *Twórczość*, no. 12 (1957).

Lewis, John S. "Conrad in 1914." *The Polish Review*, nos. 2 and 3 (1957).

Lindstrand, Gordon. "A Bibliographical Survey of the Literary Manuscripts of Joseph Conrad." *Conradiana* 2, nos. 1, 2, and 3 (1969–1970).

Lloyd, George David. *The Truth about the Peace Treaties*. Vol. 1. London, 1938.

Lubbock, Basil. *The Last of the Windjammers*. Vol. 1. Glasgow, 1929.

Lucas, Edward V. *Reading, Writing and Remembering*. New York, 1932.

Ludwig, Richard M., ed. *Letters of Ford Madox Ford*. Princeton, 1965.

Lütken, Otto. "Joseph Conrad in the Congo." *The London Mercury*, no. 5 (1930).

Lutosławski, Wincenty. "Emigracja zdolności" [Emigration of talent]. *Kraj*, no. 12 (1899).

———. "Odwiedziny u Conrada" [A visit at Conrad's]. *Tygodnik Wileński*, no. 1 (1925).

———. *Jeden łatwy żywot* [One easy life]. Warsaw, 1933.

MacCarthy, Desmond. *Portraits*. London, 1931.

Mackenzie, Compton. *My Life and Times. Octave Five: 1915–1923*. London, 1966.

Mackenzie, Norman, and Mackenzie, Jeanne. *The Time Traveller: The Life of H. G. Wells*. London, 1973.

Mallet, R., ed. *Paul Claudel et André Gide: Correspondance 1899–1926*. Paris, 1949.

Marle, Hans van. "Conrad's English Lodgings, 1880–1896." *Conradiana* 9, no. 3 (1976).

———. "Plucked and Passed on Tower Hill: Conrad's Examination Ordeal." *Conradiana* 8, no. 2 (1976).

———. "Young Ulysses Ashore: On the Trail of Konrad Korzeniowski in Marseilles." *L'Epoque Conradienne* (1976).

Marrot, H. V. *The Life and Letters of John Galsworthy*. London, 1935.

Marshall, Archibald. *Out and About*. London, 1934.

Martelli, G. *Leopold to Lumumba: A History of the Belgian Congo, 1877–1960*. London, 1962.

Mégroz, Rodolphe Louis. *Joseph Conrad's Mind and Method*. London, 1931.

Mérédac, Savinien. "Joseph Conrad chez nous." *Radical*, 7 August 1931.

———. "Joseph Conrad et nous." *L'Essor*, 15 February 1931.

Meyer, Bernard C. *Joseph Conrad: A Psychoanalytic Biography*. Princeton, 1967.

Miłobędzki, Józef. *Conrad w żeglarskiej kurcie* [Conrad in a sailor's jacket]. Gdańsk, 1972.

Mitchell, B. R. *Abstracts of British Historical Statistics*. Cambridge, 1962.

Mizener, Arthur. *The Far Side of Paradise: A Biography of F. Scott Fitzgerald*. New York, 1959.

———. *The Saddest Story: A Biography of Ford Madox Ford*. New York and Cleveland, 1971.

Morel, Edmund D. *King Leopold's Rule in Africa*. London, 1904.

———. *Red Rubber*. Manchester, 1906.

Morf, Gustav. *The Polish Heritage of Joseph Conrad*. London, 1930.

———. "Polish Proverbial Sayings in Conrad's Work." In *Joseph Conrad Colloquy in Poland*, edited by Róża Jabłkowska. Wrocław, 1975.

————. *The Polish Shades and Ghosts of Joseph Conrad*. New York, 1976.

Morrell, Ottoline. *Memoirs: A Study in Friendship*. Edited by R. Gathorne-Hardy. New York, 1964.

Moser, Thomas C. *Joseph Conrad: Achievement and Decline*. Cambridge, Mass., 1957.

————. "Conrad, Marwood, and Ford: Biographical Speculations on the Genesis of *The Good Soldier*." *Mosaic*, no. 1 (1974).

————. "From Olive Garnett's Diary: Impressions of Ford Madox Ford and His Friends, 1890–1906." *Texas Studies in Literature and Language*, no. 3 (1974).

————. "Conrad, Ford, and the Sources of *Chance*." *Conradiana*, no. 3 (1975).

Mottram, R. H. *For Some We Loved*. London, 1956.

Możdżeń, Stefan I. "Podręczniki w galicyjskich szkołach średnich (1860–1885)" [School manuals in Galician secondary schools]. *Acta Universitatis Wratislaviensis*, no. 248 (1975).

Munro, Neil. *The Brave Days: A Chronicle from the North*. Edinburgh, 1931.

Mursia, Ugo. *The True "Discoverer" of Joseph Conrad's Literary Talent and Other Notes on Conradian Biography*. Varese, Italy, 1971.

————. "Włoskie dzieje kilku statków Josepha Conrada" [The Italian history of some of Joseph Conrad's ships]. *Nautologia*, no. 4 (1976).

Najder, Zdzisław. *Nad Conradem* [Reading Conrad]. Warsaw, 1965.

————, ed. "Joseph Conrad's letters to Roger D. Casement," *Polish Perspectives*, no. 12 (1974).

————, ed. *Conrad's Polish Background: Letters to and from Polish Friends*. Oxford, 1964.

Nettels, Elsa. *James and Conrad*. Athens, Ga., 1977.

Newbolt, Henry. *My World As in My Time: Memoirs 1862–1932*. London, 1932.

Newton, John. *Newton's Guide to the Board of Trade Examinations of Masters and Mates of Sailing Ships and Steamships in Navigation and Nautical Astronomy*. 6th ed. London, 1881.

————. *Newton's Seamanship Examiner*. 16th ed. London, 1882.

Nowak-Kiełbikowa, Maria. *Polska—Wielka Brytania w latach 1918–1923. Kształtowanie się stosunków politycznych* [Poland—Great Britain in the years 1918–1923. Formation of political relations]. Warsaw, 1975.

Orzeszkowa, Eliza. "Emigracja zdolności" [Emigration of talent]. *Kraj*, no. 16 (1899). Reprinted in *Pisma krytycznoliterackie*, edited by Edmund Jankowski. Wroclaw, 1959.

Pajewski, Janusz. *Wokół sprawy polskiej. Paryż-Lozanna-Londyn 1914–1918* [Around the Polish question. Paris-Lausanne-London 1914–1918]. Poznań, 1970.

Palffy, Eleanor. "Drunk on Conrad." *The Fortnightly Review*, October 1929.

Panov, V. "Po sledakh Josefa Konrada" [On Joseph Conrad's footsteps]. *Krasni Sever*, 10 March 1976.

————. "Dom Devyatkova i sovremenniki J. Konrada" [Devyatkov's house and J. Conrad's contemporaries]. *Krasni Sever*, 14 September 1977.

Paszkowski, Lech. "Conrad w portach Australii" [Conrad in Australian ports]. *Wiadomości*, 10 September 1967.

Perłowski, Jan. "O Conradzie i Kiplingu" [On Conrad and Kipling]. *Przegląd Współ-czesny*, no. 4 (1937).

Phelps, W. L. *Autobiography*. New York, 1939.

Piszczkowski, Tadeusz. *Anglia a Polska 1914–1939* [England and Poland 1914–1939]. London, 1975.

Pobóg-Malinowski, Władysław. *Najnowsza historia polityczna Polski* [Recent political history of Poland]. Vol. 2. London, 1967.

Pomian, J., ed. *Joseph Retinger: Memoirs of an Eminence Grise*. London, 1972.

Pugh, Edmund. "Joseph Conrad as I Knew Him." *T. P.'s and Cassell's Weekly*, 23 August 1924.

Putnam, George P. "Conrad in Cracow." *Outlook*, 3 March 1920.

Raczyński, Edward. "Spotkanie w poselstwie w Londynie" [A meeting at the Polish legation in London]. *Wiadomości*, nos. 33 and 34 (1949).

Rakowska-Łuniewska, Irena. "U Konrada Korzeniowskiego" [At the home of Konrad Korzeniowski]. *Pion*, no. 50 (1934).

Randall, Dale B. J., ed. *Joseph Conrad and Warrington Dawson: The Record of a Friendship*. Durham, N.C., 1968.

———. "Conrad Interviews." *Conradiana* 2, nos. 1, 2, and 3 (1969–1970); *Conradiana* 3, no. 2 (1971–1972); *Conradiana* 4, no. 1 (1972).

Rapin, René, ed. *Lettres de Joseph Conrad à Marguerite Poradowska*. Geneva, 1966.

Rawita-Gawroński, Franciszek. *Rok 1863 na Rusi: Ukraina, Wołyń, Podole* [The year 1863 in Ruthenia: The Ukraine, Volhynia, Podolia]. Lwów, 1903.

Regulations Relating to the Examinations of Masters and Mates of the Mercantile Marines. London, 1881.

Reid, B. L. *The Man from New York: John Quinn and His Friends*. New York, 1968.

Resink, G. J. "Axel Conrad en Martin Rimbaud." *Forum der Letteren* (1971).

Retinger, J. H. *La Pologne et l'Equilibre européen*. Paris, 1916.

———. "Moje wspomnienia o Conradzie: podróż do Polski" [My reminiscences of Conrad: The journey to Poland]. *Wiadomości Literackie*, no. 49 (1934).

———. *Conrad and His Contemporaries*. New York, 1943.

Reynolds, M. E. *Memories of John Galsworthy*. London, 1936.

Reynolds, Stephen. "Joseph Conrad and Sea Fiction." *The Quarterly Review*, July 1912.

Rhys, Ernest. "An Interview with Joseph Conrad." *The Bookman*, December 1922.

Roberts, Cecil. *Half Way*. London, 1931.

Rothenstein, William. *Men and Memories*. Vols. 1, 2, and 3. London, 1932 and 1939.

Routh, Guy. *Occupation and Pay in Great Britain, 1900–1960*. Cambridge, 1965.

Rubinstein, Arthur. *My Young Years*. New York, 1973.

Rude, Donald W. "Conrad as Editor: The Preparation of *The Shorter Tales*." In *Joseph Conrad: Theory and World Fiction*. Proceedings of the Comparative Literature Symposium, 7. Lubbock, Texas, 1974.

Russell, Bertrand. *Autobiography, 1872–1914*. New York, 1968.

Said, Edward W. *Joseph Conrad and the Fiction of Autobiography*. Cambridge, Mass., 1966.

St.-John Perse. *Oeuvres complètes*. Paris, 1972.

Schwab, A. T. "Conrad's American Speeches and His Reading from *Victory*." *Modern Philology*, May 1965.

Sée, Ida R. "Joseph Conrad à Montpellier." *Le Petit Méridional*, 6 September 1924.

Sherry, Norman. "Conrad and the *Vidar*." *Review of English Studies*, May 1963.

——. *Conrad's Eastern World*. Cambridge, 1966.

——. "A Conrad Manuscript." *Times Literary Supplement*, 26 June 1970.

——. *Conrad's Western World*. Cambridge, 1971.

——, ed. *Conrad: The Critical Heritage*. London, 1973.

——, ed. *Joseph Conrad: A Commemoration*. London, 1976.

Singleton-Gates, P., and Girodias, M., eds. *The Black Diaries*. New York, 1959.

Skarbek, Hanna. "Dwie godziny u J. Conrada" [Two hours with J. Conrad]. *Wiadomości Literackie*, no. 38 (1924).

Slade, Ruth M. *English-Speaking Missions in the Congo Independent State (1878–1908)*. Brussels, 1959.

Slater, E., and Roth, M. *Clinical Psychiatry*. London, 1969.

Sprawozdanie C. K. Dyrekcji Gimnazjalnej przy św. Annie w Krakowie z roku szkolnego 1869 [Report of the I. R. Directorate of the St. Anne's gymnasium in Cracow for the school year 1869]. Cracow, 1870, 1871, and 1872.

Sprawozdanie Dyrektora C. K. Gimnazjum im. Nowodworskiego czyli św. Anny w Krakowie za rok szkolny 1873 [Report of the Director of the I. R. Nowodworski alias St. Anne's gymnasium in Cracow for the school year 1873]. Cracow, 1873.

Stallman, R. W., and Gilkes, Lillian, eds. *Stephen Crane: Letters*. New York, 1960.

Stanley, Henry M. *The Congo and the Founding of its Free State: A Story of Work and Exploration*. Vols. 1 and 2. London, 1885.

Stravinsky, Igor, and Croft, R. *Dialogues and a Diary*. New York, 1963.

Sutherland, J. G. *At Sea with Joseph Conrad*. Boston, 1922.

Swinnerton, Frank. *An Autobiography*. London, 1937.

Szymanowski, Karol. *Z listów* [From the letters]. Edited by T. Bronowicz-Chylińska. Cracow, 1958.

Taborski, Roman. *Apollo Korzeniowski—ostatni dramatopisarz romantyczny* [Apollo Korzeniowski—the last romantic dramatist]. Wrocław, 1957.

Tarnawski, Wit. *Conrad, człowiek—pisarz—Polak* [Conrad: man, writer, Pole]. London, 1972.

——, ed. *Conrad żywy* [The living Conrad]. London, 1957.

Taylor, A. J. P. *English History 1914–1945*. Oxford, 1965.

Teets, Bruce, and Gerber, Helmut. *Joseph Conrad: An Annotated Bibliography of Writings about Him*. De Kalb, Ill., 1971.

Temple, F. J. "Joseph Conrad à Montpellier." In *Studies in Joseph Conrad*, edited by Claude Thomas. Montpellier, 1975.

Thomas, Claude, ed. "Cahiers d'Etudes et de Recherches Victoriennes et Edouardiennes." In *Studies in Joseph Conrad*, edited by Claude Thomas. Montpellier, 1975.

Thomas, R. G. *Letters from Edward Thomas to Gordon Bottomley*. London, 1968.

Tittle, Walter. "Portraits in Pencil and Pen. III. Joseph Conrad." *The Strand Magazine*, June 1924.

Tschiffely, A. F. *Don Roberto*. London, 1937.

Tuchman, Barbara. *The Proud Tower*. New York, 1965.

Ujejski, Józef. *O Konradzie Korzeniowskim* [On Konrad Korzeniowski]. Warsaw, 1936.

Unwin, Peter. *The Publishing Unwins*. London, 1972.

Urnov, Dmitri. "Vakhta Josefa Konrada" [Joseph Conrad's watch]. *Vokrug Sveta*, no. 2 (1972).

Ursell, Geoffrey. "Conrad and the *Riversdale*." *Times Literary Supplement*, 11 July 1968.

Valéry, Paul. "Sujet d'une conversation avec Conrad." *Nouvelle Revue Française*, no. 12 (1924).

Vidan, Gabrijela, and Vidan, Ivo. "Further Correspondence between Joseph Conrad and André Gide." *Studia Romanica et Anglica Zagrabiensia*, nos. 29–32 (1970–1971).

Vidan, Ivo. "Thirteen Letters of André Gide to Joseph Conrad." *Studia Romanica et Anglica Zagrabiensia*, no. 24 (1967).

Watson, E. L. Grant. *But to What Purpose*. London, 1946.

Watt, Ian. "Conrad, James and *Chance*." In *Imagined Worlds: Essays on Some English Novels and Novelists in Honour of John Butt*, edited by Maynard Mack and Ian Gregor. London, 1968.

——, ed. *Conrad: "The Secret Agent," A Casebook*. London, 1973.

Watts, Cedric T., ed. *Joseph Conrad's Letters to R. B. Cunninghame Graham*. Cambridge, 1969.

Weissman, Frida, ed. *Valéry Larbaud, G. Jean-Aubry: Correspondance 1920–1935*. Paris, 1971.

Wells, H. G. *Experiment in Autobiography*. London, 1934.

West, Herbert Faulkner. "Joseph Conrad's Funeral." *Saturday Review of Literature*, 6 September 1924.

——. *A Modern Conquistador: Robert Bontine Cunninghame Graham*. London, 1932.

Woolf, Virginia. *The Common Reader*. London, 1925.

Worth, G. J. "Conrad's Debt to Maupassant in the Preface to *The Nigger of the 'Narcissus.'*" *The Journal of English and Germanic Philology*, no. 4 (1955).

Wright, R., ed. *Letters of Stephen Reynolds*. Richmond, Va., 1923.

Zabierowski, Stefan. *Conrad w Polsce* [Conrad in Poland]. Gdańsk, 1971.

Zagórska, Aniela. "Kilka wspomnień o Conradzie" [A few reminiscences of Conrad]. *Wiadomości Literackie*, no. 51 (1929).

Zagórska, Karola. "Pod dachem Konrada Korzeniowskiego (Josepha Conrada)" [Under the roof of Konrad Korzeniowski]. *Kultura*, nos. 2 and 3 (1932).

——. "Ze wspomnień o Conradzie" [Recollections of Conrad]. *Twórczość*, no. 8 (1969).

Zawodziński, Karol Wiktor. "Nieuwzględnione motywy decyzji życiowej Conrada" [Overlooked motives of Conrad's vital decision]. *Wiadomości Literackie*, no. 39 (1927).

Zdrada, Jerzy. *Jarosław Dąbrowski*. Cracow, 1973.

Żeromski, Stefan. "Joseph Conrad," preface to *J. Conrad-Korzeniowski, Pisma wybrane*, vol. 1, *Fantazja Almayera*, Warsaw, 1923. Reprinted in Żeromski's *Dzieła*, edited by Stanisław Pigoń, *Pisma literackie i krytyczne*, Warsaw, 1963.

———. "Joseph Conrad." *Wiadomości Literackie*, no. 33 (1924). Reprinted in Żeromski's *Dzieła*, edited by Stanisław Pigoń, *Pisma literackie i krytyczne*, Warsaw, 1963.

———. "Autor-Rodak" [Author-compatriot]. Naokoło Świata, no. 2 (1925). Reprinted in Żeromski's *Dzieła*, edited by Stanisław Pigoń, *Pisma literackie i krytyczne*, Warsaw, 1963.

Ziejka, Franciszek. "Marsylskie dni Conrada" [Conrad's days in Marseilles]. *Miesięcznik Literacki*, no. 10 (1975).

Zubrzycka, O. (Otolia Retingerowa). "Syn dwu Ojczyzn" [A son of two countries]. *Iskry*, nos. 8–10 (1931).

Bibliographical Note

Early versions of several chapters in this book were originally published separately in various periodicals.

Chapter 1   "Polskie lata Conrada," *Twórczość* 1956, no. 11.
              "Konrad Korzeniowski we Lwowie i Krakowie," in *Studia Conradowskie*, Katowice, 1976.

Chapter 2   "Conrad w Marsylii," *Życie Literackie* 1957, no. 4.

Chapter 3   "Czerwona bandera Conrada-Korzeniowskiego," *Wiedza i Życie* 1958, no. 12.
              "Czerwona bandera," *Twórczość* 1976, no. 12.

Chapter 4   "Kapitan brytyjskiej marynarki," *Życie Literackie* 1962, no. 37.
              "Kapitan Korzeniowski z 'Otago'," *Odra* 1976, no. 7/8.

Chapter 5   "Do kresu nocy," *Nowa Kultura* 1960, no. 30.
              "Conrad in the Congo," *Polish Perspectives* 1961, no. 1.

Chapter 6   "Żagiel i pióro," *Twórczość* 1973, no. 8.

Chapter 7   "Conrad romansowy," *Twórczość* 1972, no. 7.
              "Conrad in Love," *Polish Perspectives* 1972, no. 11.

Chapter 8   "Próby, poszukiwania, rozterki," *Literatura na Świecie* 1974, no. 7.
              "Conrad in 1898," *Cahiers d'Etudes et de Recherches Victoriennes et Edouardiennes*, 2, Montpellier, 1975.

Chapter 12   "Kryzys i sukces," *Twórczość* 1977, no. 8.

Chapter 13   "Podróż do Polski," *Twórczość* 1979, no. 5.

Name Index

Academy (London weekly), 176, 216, 229, 250, 270

Academy and Literature, 286

Adams, Elbridge L., 408, 478, 584, 602–604, 606

Adelaide, 153–157, 160, 336

Adowa (steamship), 160–161, 530

Africa, 112, 119, 121, 135, 139–141, 152, 153, 160, 181, 186, 191, 195, 249, 261, 435, 494

Aftanazy, Roman, 10n

Ajaccio, 459, 460

Alaska (whaler), 69, 513

Aldington, 273, 346, 347, 353, 354, 357, 365

Alexander II (tsar), 13, 30, 69

Alexander III (tsar), 94, 122

Alfonso XII, 47

Algoa Bay, 81

Allen, James, 97

Allen, Jerry, 50, 71, 112, 507–511, 514, 516, 517, 519–521, 526

Ambassadors Theatre (London), 466, 470

America, 205, 209, 273

Amsterdam, 94, 95

Anderson, Jane (Jane Taylor), 411–413, 419–421, 585, 587, 604

Andrews (the Conrads' servant at Pent Farm), 323

Andy (sailmaker in the Torrens), 157

Angel, W. H., 523

Annie Frost (clipper), 71, 514

Antilles, 44, 45

Antwerp, 140

Argus (Melbourne daily), 106

Armentières, 413, 458

Ascherson, Neal, 527, 598

Ashford (Kent), 372, 577

Asquith, Herbert Henry, 417

Athenaeum (London club), 429, 440

Athenaeum (London weekly), 176, 286, 390, 451, 554, 562, 579, 584, 597

Atherton, Gertrude, 339

Austen, Jane, 297

Australia, 62, 70, 101, 106, 107, 111, 113, 153–155, 157, 159, 160, 521, 522

Austria-Hungary, 25, 382, 398–403, 403n, 404, 415

Babalatchie, 519

Babb, James T., 511, 534, 580

Bacon, Francis, 344

Badenweiler, 264, 265

Baerdemaecker, G. de, 117

Baines, Jocelyn, 10n, 49, 50, 82, 83, 99, 112, 113,

138, 169, 194, 201, 210, 237, 239, 247, 308, 327, 506–510, 514, 516, 517, 520, 523–525, 527, 531, 532, 534, 535, 537, 538, 541–543, 547, 550, 552, 555, 557, 558, 563, 565, 569, 574, 578, 587, 588, 592, 604–608

Baker (sailor in the Riversdale), 456

Balfour, Arthur James, 260, 301, 436, 437

Bamou, 138, 139

Banana, 525

Bangala, 133, 136, 526

Bangka strait, 76, 77

Bangkok, 73, 74, 76, 103–105, 521

Bangkok (tugboat), 521

Banjarmasin, 97, 98, 519

Barnwell, P. J., 522

Barr, Moering and Company, 80, 83, 89, 114, 117, 147, 148, 180, 181, 336, 524, 528

Barrie, James Matthew, 294, 345, 554

Barron, Joseph, 82, 516

Bartlett, P. A., 573

Barttelot, Edmund Musgrave, 526

Baudelaire, Charles, 311

Beard, Elijah, 73, 74, 76, 78, 514

Bedfordshire, 331, 332

Beer, Thomas, 475, 603

Beerbohm, Max, 314, 559

Belgium, 168, 264, 267

Belloc, Hilaire, 334

Benavides, Vincente, 305

Benckendorf, Alexandr, 406

Bennett, Enoch Arnold, 318, 338, 380–382, 404, 432, 434, 452, 475, 484, 485, 493, 551, 577, 580, 583, 589, 605, 606

Bennett, Gordon, 366

Bennett, Sanford, 548

Benrimo, J. Harry, 466, 601

Berau, 97–99, 520

Berdichev. See Berdyczów

Berdyczów, 7, 10, 10n, 169

Berg, Fyodor, 20

Bergson, Henri, 369

Berlin, 87, 158, 398, 403, 530

Bezak, Alexandr, 19

Białystok, 158

Biarritz, 486

Biliński, Leon, 403

Biliński, Marian, 403, 404, 583

Bishopsbourne, 456, 598

Bismarck, Otto von, 34, 96

Bizet, Georges:
  Carmen, 41, 179, 386

Blackburn, William, 541, 544, 545, 549, 552, 553

Hackney, Clifford, 347, 357, 570
Hague, The, 251
Hall, Basil, 305
Hallowes, Lillian, 300, 459, 556, 592, 598
Halverson, John, 585
Hamburg, 398
Harding, Charles, 605
Harding, Mrs., 483
Hardy, Thomas, 290, 423, 444
Harou, Prosper, 125, 127, 129, 131, 132
Harper and Brothers, 301, 351, 376, 568
Harper's Magazine, 339, 374, 420, 566, 575
Harris, Tirvil, 528
Harrison, Austin, 370, 376, 408, 575, 584
Hart-Davis, Rupert, 590, 591, 594, 596, 597, 600, 604, 605
Harvey, David, 560
Harvey, George, 301, 555
Harwich, 398
Hastings, Macdonald, 414, 422, 427, 588, 590
Hatch, F. R., 533
Haverschmidt, R., 520
Le Havre, 40, 41, 71, 482, 486, 605
Hay, Eloise Knapp, 236n, 251, 544, 545, 570
Hecate (steamship), 103, 521
Heilbrun, Carolyn G., 442n
Heinemann, William (publishing house), 203, 214, 259, 282, 291, 302, 413
Henley, William Ernest, 203, 238, 239, 281, 543
Hewitt, Douglas, 362, 392, 566, 571, 580
Heyden, Vander, 135
Heyn, Reginald, 130
Higdon, David Leon, 532, 586
Highland Forest (barque), 94, 95, 518, 519
Hind, C. Lewis, 244, 543
Hirn, Yrgö, 281
Hobbes, Thomas, 276
Hodgson and Co. (London), 587
Hodister, A.E.C., 526
Hogben, Richard, 551
Holland, 187, 261
Holloway, Mark, 574, 588
Holmes, James S., 520
Holt, Lawrence, 597, 598
Homer, 38
Homer, Douglas, 533
Honoratka, 4
Hope, Conrad, 147
Hope, Frances Ellen, 192, 303, 442, 511, 534
Hope, George Fountaine Weare, 64, 78, 91, 147, 182, 186, 192, 194, 201, 206, 218, 222, 246, 257, 303, 442, 464, 475, 511, 512, 515, 516, 518, 527, 534, 535
Horvath, Paulina. *See* de Somogyi, Paula
Hôtel Riche et Continental (Montpellier), 319
House, Edward Mandell, 476
Howe, W.T.H., 424, 587
Hryniewiecki, Ignacy, 69

Hudson, William Henry:
  Green Mansions, 297
Hueffer, Catherine (née Brown), 237
Hueffer, Christina, 287
Hueffer, Elsie (née Martindale), 237, 259, 277, 285, 287, 288, 291, 293, 296, 306, 322, 329, 334, 347–349, 375, 465, 551–555, 557, 561, 563, 564, 568, 574, 575, 600
Hueffer, Ford Madox. *See* Ford, Ford Madox
Hueffer, Francis, 237
Hüffer, Franz. *See* Hueffer, Francis
Hugo, Victor, 5, 13, 16, 19, 22, 25, 26, 30, 34, 178, 179, 179n, 189, 502
Hugues, Clovis, 510
Hull, 85
Humań, 120
Humières, Charles Robert d', 312, 338, 346, 460, 565, 568
Huneker, James Gibbons, 351, 380, 512, 568, 576, 579
Hunt, Violet, 348, 375, 575
Huxley, Aldous, 452
Huxley, Thomas Henry, 250, 545
  "Ethics and Evolution," 249
Hyères, 49
Hyne, Charles John Cutliffe Wright, 244, 543
Hynes, Samuel, 543
Hythe (Kent), 234, 250

Ile-Grande, 196, 198, 535
Illdegonde (cutter), 186
Illustrated London News, 232, 234, 253, 393
Ilustrowany Kurier Codzienny, 582
India, 85, 86
Indonesia, 176
Inglis, Brian, 525, 555
Interlaken, 146
International, First, 88
Ireland, 388, 414, 592
Irresistible (tugboat), 106
Irving, Henry B., 414, 422, 440, 586
Isangila, 139, 527
Italy, 319, 403, 421, 448, 473, 486
Ivensen, Fyodr, 19
Ivy Walls, 207, 234
Iwańkowce, 10n
Iwański, August, 504
Iwaszkiewicz, Anna, 581
Iwaszkiewicz, Jarosław, 581
Izvolsky, Alexandr, 406

Jabłkowska, Róża, 503, 600
Jackson, C. Granville, 157, 530
Jackson, Miss, 307
Jacques, William Henry, 156, 530
Jagiellonian Library (Cracow), 256

Mugliston, Dr., 105
Munich, 34
Munro, A., 64
Munro, Neil, 542
Munsey's Magazine, 392, 420
Muntok, 76–78, 98
Mürsch (owner of *La Roseraie*), 180
Mursia, Ugo, 10n, 509, 532

Najder, Zdzisław, 11n, 531, 534, 558, 571
Naples, 63, 306, 308, 312
Napoleon I, 326, 376, 431, 437, 473, 486
Narcissus (clipper), 82, 83, 516
Nash Eveleigh Ltd., 373, 575
Nash Magazine, 576
Nation, The (London), 332, 373, 597
Nation, The (New York), 451, 584
Nelson, Lord Horatio, 316
Neuchâtel, 177
Nevinson, Henry Wood, 586
Newbolt, Henry John, 290, 311–314, 316, 320,
    551, 553, 555, 556, 558–561
Newcastle-upon-Tyne, 74
New Guinea, 107
New Haven, 478
New Orleans, 508
New Review, 203, 205, 211
New South Wales, 113
New Statesman, 444, 485, 585
Newton, John, 66, 67, 78, 91, 513
New York, 246, 384, 465, 475–477, 484
New York Herald, 366, 374, 411
New York Times Saturday Book Review, The, 275,
    485, 554, 585
New Zealand, 157
Nicholas II, (tsar), 251
Niesiecki, Kasper, 499
Nietzsche, Friedrich Wilhelm, 253
Niger, 147
Niven, John, 97
Noble, Edward, 187, 534
Noble, James Ashcroft, 147
Norfolk Hotel, (London), 592
North American Review, 370
Northcliffe, Lord Alfred Charles William, 411, 419,
    429, 461, 590, 597
Northcote, Lady, 597
Northern Newspapers Syndicate, 303
Nouvelle Amsterdam, 521
Nouvelle Revue Française, 372
Nowak-Kiełbikowa, Maria, 592
Nowochwastów, 10, 19, 24, 119, 501
Nowy Targ, 402, 403
Nürnberg (steamer), 113

Observer, The, 390, 423, 444
Ocean Steam Ship Company, 455
Odessa, 24, 63, 70, 120

Oksza-Orzechowski, Tadeusz, 39
Ołdakowska, Maria, 159, 488, 489, 530
Oliphant, Margaret, 214
Olmeijer, Charles William, 99, 520
Olmeijer, Ninette, 99
Oratów, 158, 159
Orda, Napoleon, 10n
Orkneys, 187
Orléans, 458
Ortega y Gasset, José, 472
Orzeszkowa, Eliza, 255–257, 372n, 400
Osborne (lieutenant in H.M.S. *Ready*), 418
Osborne, J. D., 567
Ostend, 267
Oswalds, 445, 446, 449, 452, 454, 455, 457, 459,
    461, 464, 472, 473, 475, 480, 481–484, 487,
    489, 595, 604
Otago (barque), 103–113, 161, 336, 520–523
Otway, Cape, 521
Outlook (London), 229, 562
Outlook (New York), 576
Oxted, 540

Pacific Ocean, 255
Paderewski, Ignacy, 406, 476, 542, 583
Pahang, 229
Pajewski, Janusz, 583, 586, 590
Pakefield, 58
Palavas-sur-Mer, 326
Palermo, 63
Palestine (barque), 73–80, 514, 515
Palffy, Eleanor, 478, 604
Pall Mall Budget, The, 244
Pall Mall Gazette, 270, 372, 373
Pall Mall Magazine, 281, 305, 577
Panov, Valentin, 501
Pantai. *See* Berau
Panteleyev, Longin, 18, 501
Paris, 40, 146, 147, 155, 177, 182, 183, 186–188,
    306, 312, 325, 406, 407, 458, 483, 487
Pascal, Blaise, 223
Pascalis (allegedly a journalist on the *Figaro*), 186
Passy (Paris), 177, 183, 188
Paszkowski, Lech, 521–523
Pater, Walter, 211
Patras, 63
Pawling, Sidney S., 203, 209, 214, 216, 226, 227,
    247, 275, 280, 283, 541, 548, 552
Pécher, Ed., et Cie, 143, 528
Peel, Mrs. C. S.:
    How to Keep House, 277
Penang, 353
Penarth, 82, 86
Penfield, Frederick C., 402, 451
Pent Farm, 234, 236, 236n, 237, 242, 244, 246,
    247, 259, 267, 273, 277, 279, 282, 285, 288–
    290, 295, 299, 300, 306, 311, 322, 326, 327,
    331, 372n, 551

Subject Index*

*All entries in this section are indexed in relation to Joseph Conrad himself.

Illustration Credits

Unless otherwise stated, the originals of photographs are in the author's possession.

Ewa Korzeniowska in 1862. Beinecke Rare Book and Manuscript Library, Yale University, New Haven, Connecticut.

Apollo Korzeniowski in 1862. Beinecke Rare Book and Manuscript Library, Yale University, New Haven, Connecticut.

Parish church in Oratów where Apollo Korzeniowski and Ewa Bobrowska were married, 8 May 1856. Photograph taken about 1975 by Jan Gliński.

Carmelite monastery in Berdyczów. Etching by Napoleon Orda. National Library, Warsaw.

Nowy Świat street in Warsaw about 1860. The Korzeniowskis lived in the tenth house from the right. Photograph by Konrad Brandel. National Library, Warsaw.

A log house in Vologda similar to the one where the Korzeniowskis lived during their exile there. Photograph taken in 1977 by Zdzisław Najder.

A neo-Gothic pavilion in the Lubowidzkis' park at Nowochwastów (allegedly the house where Joseph Conrad was born). Drawing by Napoleon Orda. Photograph by Zbigniew Malinowski. National Museum, Cracow.

Konrad Korzeniowski in 1863. Photograph by Stanisław Kraków. Beinecke Rare Book and Manuscript Library, Yale University, New Haven, Connecticut.

Dedication in verso of photograph no. 8: "To my dear Granny who helped me send pastries to my poor Daddy in prison—grandson, Pole-Catholic, and szlachcic, Konrad." Beinecke Rare Book and Manuscript Library, Yale University, New Haven, Connecticut.

Robert Korzeniowski (?) in typical attire of an 1863 insurgent. William R. Perkins Library, Duke University, Durham, North Carolina.

Stefan Bobrowski and Antoni Syroczyński. Jagiellonian Library, Cracow.

First and last page of Regina Korzeniowska's letter to Konrad Korzeniowski, 26 November 1865. Beinecke Rare Book and Manuscript Library, Yale University, New Haven, Connecticut.

Tadeusz Bobrowski about 1870. Photograph by A. Schubert. Jagiellonian Library, Cracow.

Apollo Korzeniowski's tombstone: "A victim of Muscovite martyrdom." Photograph by Tadeusz Chrzanowski.

Teofila Bobrowska. Photograph by Karol Beyer. William R. Perkins Library, Duke University, Durham, North Carolina.

Konrad Korzeniowski in 1874. Photograph by W. Rzewuski. Beinecke Rare Book and Manuscript Library, Yale University, New Haven, Connecticut.

Circular Quay, Sydney. Ugo Mursia.

Dynevor Road, London. Conrad lodged here, 1880–1886. Photograph taken in 1957 by Zdzisław Najder.

Konrad Korzeniowski in 1883 in Marienbad. Photograph by Otto Bielefeldt. National Library, Warsaw.

Design of the construction of the *Narcissus*. Giuseppe Annovazzi, *50 navi italiane famose*, Milan 1970.

Tanjung Redeb; on the left, the house of William Charles Olmeijer, Conrad's Kaspar Almayer. Photograph taken in 1903 by E. van der Wÿk. Hans van Marle.

Sambaliung on the River Kelai, Borneo. Hans van Marle.

Aniela Zagórska with daughters Aniela and Karola. Photograph by A. Stepanow. William R. Perkins Library, Duke University, Durham, North Carolina.

Marguerite Poradowska. Photograph by A. Barrès. William R. Perkins Library, Duke University, Durham, North Carolina.

Two pages from the second part of Conrad's *Congo Diary*. Houghton Library, Harvard University, Cambridge, Massachusetts.

The *Torrens*. National Maritime Museum, Greenwich, England.

Conrad with five apprentices on the deck of the *Torrens*. Beinecke Rare Book and Manuscript Library, Yale University, New Haven, Connecticut.

First page of Tadeusz Bobrowski's letter to his nephew Konrad Korzeniowski, 9 November 1891. National Library, Warsaw.

Conrad's certificate of discharge from the *Adowa*, his last ship. Beinecke Rare Book and Manuscript Library, Yale University, New Haven, Connecticut.

Emilie Briquel. Mme Françoise Meykiechel.

Conrad's letter to Emilie Briquel. Mme Françoise Meykiechel.

Jessie George in 1896, before her marriage to Joseph Conrad. Borys Conrad.

The house of Mme Le Bail in Ile-Grande, where the Conrads stayed during their honeymoon. Photograph taken in 1973 by Tadeusz Chrzanowski.

The gardens of Le Peyrou in Montpellier. Photograph by Zdzisław Najder.

Arthur Marwood. John Conrad.

Capel House, where the Conrads lived, 1910–1919. Photograph taken in 1957 by Zdzisław Najder.

Joseph Conrad in 1912. Photograph by William Cadby. John Conrad.

Jessie, John, and Joseph Conrad in 1912. Photograph by William Cadby. John Conrad.

Joseph Conrad with his son John. Photograph by William Cadby. John Conrad.

Józef Hieronim Retinger in 1912. Władysław Dobrowolski.

Otolia Retinger, née Zubrzycka. Otolia Retingerowa.

Ellen Glasgow and Joseph Conrad in June 1914. Photograph by F. Warrington Dawson. William R. Perkins Library, Duke University, Durham, North Carolina.

John Conrad (right) and Robin Douglas in 1914. Photograph by F. Warrington Dawson. William R. Perkins Library, Duke University, Durham, North Carolina.

Apollo Korzeniowski's grave. Photograph by Tadeusz Chrzanowski.

Conrad with Aniela Zagórska (daughter) in Zakopane in 1914. National Library, Warsaw.

Borys Conrad in military uniform. Perkins Library, Duke University, Durham, North Carolina.

Jane Anderson. Joan Givner.

From the right: Joseph Conrad, Jessie, Jane Anderson, and John Conrad. John Conrad.

Drawing room at Oswalds. John Conrad.

Conrad with Karola Zagórska at Oswalds in summer 1920. Andrzej Biernacki.

Conrad in 1923. Photograph by T. R. Annan and Sons.

Joseph Conrad's grave. Photograph taken in 1957 by Zdzisław Najder.